1000 *Women for the Nobel Peace Prize 2005*

1000 Frauen für den Friedensnobelpreis 2005

1000 FEMMES POUR LE PRIX NOBEL DE LA PAIX 2005

1000 женщинам – Нобелевская премия мира

ألف إمرأة لجائزة نوبل للسلام لعام ألفين وخمسة

一千婦女得諾貝爾平和獎

1000 *MUJERES Y UN PREMIO NOBEL DE LA PAZ DEL 2005*

1000 பெண்களுக்கு சமாதானத்திற்கான நோபல்பரிசு 2005 இல்

1000 *žena za Nobelovu nagradu za mir 2005*

TUZO LA NOBEL PEACE PRIZE 2005 KWA WAKINAMAMA ELFU MOJA

1000 नारीयों को 2005 में नोबेल शांति पुरस्कार

1000 *MULHERES PARA O PRÉMIO NOBEL DA PAZ 2005*

2005 Nobel Barış Ödülü için 1000 Kadın

۱۰۰۰ زن برای جایزه صلح نوبل ۲۰۰۵

www.1000peacewomen.org

1000 PeaceWomen

Across the Globe

a KONTRAST book

published by the Association
1000 Women for the Nobel Peace Prize 2005

SCALO

Table of Contents

1000 Women for a World Peace Site

Ruth-Gaby Vermot-Mangold

It was a crazy idea, crazy in financial, logistical even in personal terms to strive for the nomination of 1000 women from around the world for the Nobel Peace Prize 2005. Nevertheless we wanted to make it happen. And we have succeeded! The board, the office, the coordinators in the various regions and many committed persons worldwide have found 1000 Peacewoman and nominated them for the Nobel Peace Prize in 2005.

The book on the 1000 Peacewoman is now in your hands. It is rather large and heavy. And that's how it should be! Let it impress you, let it touch you! We invite you to reflect with us, and to act. This volume is intended as a guidebook to a world aligned to human needs, a world that offers everyone hope in a future in which we can all live life to the fullest, with courage and creativity, drive and tenacity, with the capacity not only to survive but to flourish.

Peace cannot be achieved alone. That is why women get together in networks, in groups, in alliances. They see in their daily work that peace is more than the absence of war, violence and armed conflict. Women negotiate between enemy groups; they report on the atrocities of war, and rebuild what has been destroyed. In Africa, they fight against genital mutilation of little girls; in South America, they search for loved ones who have disappeared; in Asia, they denounce poverty and child labor; in Europe, they stand up against sexual exploitation and domestic violence.

Around the world, women combat abuses committed against other women in prisons; they speak out against the abduction of civilians and the criminal trafficking in human beings; they protest tirelessly against political assassinations and all forms of aggression. They condemn violations of human rights and torture. They engage in silent public protests and search for ways to counter the devastating effects of war.

These courageous women act without heed for their own safety. Strong and assertive, they assume responsibility for their village, their region, their country, for other human beings. They are expert peace workers, experienced, knowledgeable and demanding harbingers of hope.

Convinced that the commitment of these women deserves public recognition and should be made visible, we launched the 1000 Peacewoman project in 2003. We did so with much enthusiasm and little money. But what began as a Swiss initiative backed by Swiss Foreign Minister Micheline Calmy-Rey, and by UNESCO Switzerland, quickly gained international support.

Recognition via the Nobel Peace Prize is one of the three pillars of this initiative. The book you are holding, an exhibition and an interactive website will throw more light on the peace work of the women. Scientific research will record and analyze the interfaces of power, where decisions are made concerning war and peace, exploitation and human dignity.

—

A

We must learn from the Peacewoman.

These 1000 women from 150 countries, guided in their work by non-violence, integrity and selflessness, were nominated in a painstaking and scrupulous process. All of them have a long-term commitment to peace work. All have had to contend repeatedly with conflicting parties.

The 1000 women, who were selected from close to 2,000 nominees, symbolize the hundreds of thousands, the millions of women who stand up everyday against violence and destruction and for peace. In January 2005, we presented their names to the Nobel Prize Committee in Oslo, in the belief that, 100 years after Bertha von Suttner, the first woman to be awarded the Nobel Peace Prize in 1905, it is time that more women be honored for their efforts, their courage and their determination in building peace. "Lay down arms" was Bertha's rousing slogan.

In this book, we introduce 1000 women. We have called the 1000th woman "Anonyma", to stand for all the nameless women whose work has been overlooked, and for those endangered women who set things in motion and bring about change but who must remain nameless.

Convinced that mainstream international politics alone does not bring about peace, these women have opted for a new perspective and created new paths. Their commitment is their activity. Let us learn from these women and allow ourselves to be infected by their courage. Let us help them carry on with their work and contribute to human security and peace in the world.

Dr Ruth-Gaby Vermot-Mangold is the president of the Association 1000 Women for the Nobel Peace Prize 2005, a member of the National Council (Swiss Parliament) and of the Council of Europe.

—

A

"I want to learn from the 1000 Peacewomen"

An interview with the Swiss Minister of Foreign Affairs
Micheline Calmy-Rey

Proposing 1000 women for the Nobel Peace Prize is a bold idea. One of the first to welcome the idea was Swiss Foreign Minister Micheline Calmy-Rey. She has supported the idea from the outset. In the following interview, she explains why, and also tells us of her hopes and expectations in connection with the project. Two key points emerge from the interview: she believes that peace is possible and as a politician and member of the government she wants to learn from the 1000 Peacewoman.

What was your first reaction when you heard that 1000 women had been nominated for the Nobel Peace Prize?
I was delighted to hear that the peace activities of women were being given center stage. In the course of my visits abroad I have met many courageous women who deserve this prize. I am convinced that because of their diverse experiences and roles women bring different social and political perspectives to peace processes. Without these perspectives, it would be impossible to conduct successful and sustainable peace policy. The Nobel Prize initiative gives women's potential for peace and security greater visibility.

And what is it that you like about the 1000 Peacewoman project?
I have great respect for the work of the initiators who — with a small team — have built up a worldwide network. This civil society approach reflects my conviction. Peace processes must be broadly based and supported by civil society if they are to be successful in the long term. I regard this project as a persuasive example and model of goal-oriented networking.
The support of my ministry is particularly directed at the idea of net-working. I like that the project is aimed at raising the profile of women's peace potential. That is an aspect that has also been given priority in Swiss peace policy. To give this idea of networking a permanent basis, Switzerland supports the construction of an interactive Internet platform where Peacewoman can meet in virtual form.

How do you evaluate the work done by these 1000 women?
A glance at the biographies of these women shows how strongly their peace activities are rooted in reality and characterized by pragmatic action. This

capacity for overcoming divides and for building bridges is what impresses me about the Peacewoman. In Srebrenica for example, the mothers of the murdered children offered the dove of peace to the mothers of the killers. Specific network building and the initiation of interethnic and interreligious dialogue are further strengths of their work for peace. It was the determination to find a joint solution to the armed conflicts that led women from Sierra Leone, Liberia and Guinea to launch their peace initiatives, which played a major role in bringing the warring parties to the negotiating table. I hope that this Nobel Peace Prize initiative will give these women strength and encouragement to continue their activities for peace, human rights and social justice in their home countries.

The initiators of the 1000 Peacewoman project say that "women feel responsible". Do you feel responsible?
Yes, I do. As a politician and the foreign minister of my country I have a strong sense of responsibility towards the people of my country and those who have put their trust in me.

Many of these women work alone or in small organizations and networks. What can you, as foreign minister, do?
Contributing to the peaceful coexistence of peoples is one of the central goals of Swiss foreign policy. The world is indivisible. The interests of other countries are also our interests. If there is poverty or instability elsewhere, we feel the effects in our own country. The best way to avoid the consequences of a conflict is to prevent it, to ensure that it does not occur. In the framework of our civil peace promotion and promotion of human rights, we deliberately work to a considerable extent with committed and knowledgeable civil society organizations, which we also support financially. Successful peace promotion requires cooperation between state and non-state actors.

What difficulties do women working at government level face?
As in all areas, women in conflict regions are underrepresented in peace processes at the highest political levels. We therefore support all efforts to enable women to actively engage in negotiating processes. It is also crucial that peace processes should be as comprehensive and inclusive as possible, i.e. that civil society should also be involved. This will also promote the inclusion of women's experiences and interests.

Bertha von Suttner, the first woman who won the Nobel Peace Prize, said, "Down with the weapons." That was 100 years ago. Why is it not possible?

It is possible. West Europe was a battlefield for centuries. However no wars have occurred there for the past 60 years. We have a duty, and it is also in our interest, to help ensure that the same happens in other regions of the world. With the "soft power" instruments of civil peace promotion we help to transform conflicts. This means that conflicts are resolved not with weapons but through negotiations.

What is your personal vision of peace?

Living in peace means living in security and free from fear, i.e. without fear of violence and human rights violations, and being able to realize one's potential in a just manner. Peace is a process in which conflicts are increasingly resolved through negotiations and less and less by violence.

What is your commitment to peace policy?

By its credible peace promotion policy, Switzerland contributes to stability and security in crisis areas. This also underlines the great importance that it attaches to partnerly cooperation within the community of states. Peace policy is an ethical duty as well as an important instrument for protecting this country's interests.

The 1000 Peacewoman project aims not only to raise the visibility of peace work by women but also to carry out research on this work. The results of the research will later be submitted to governments. Do you believe that governments can learn from the 1000 women?

Yes, but they must be willing and able to learn. It seems to me that what is important is the willingness of governments to evaluate peace work and, even more important, to implement the lessons learnt.

And what can they learn?

I believe that not only governments but also parliamentarians, especially women parliamentarians, should take a keen interest in this initiative and in women's peace potential. This would serve to strengthen solidarity among women, regardless of party affiliations. It was with this idea in mind that I initiated the "marrainage projects" last year, which over 40 Swiss women parliamentarians have since joined. Over the course of this and next year they will visit women's organizations in Colombia, Bosnia and Herzegovina and Pakistan that my department supports.

Do you believe that governments want to learn from the 1000 women?
I can only speak for myself as an individual government minister. I certainly do wish to learn from the 1000 women.

And can you do anything as an individual minister?
Yes, I can provide financial and moral support. Besides, I would not be in the government if I did not believe that I could make an important contribution within the government.

The mainstream in contemporary politics has not produced global peace. There are over 100 conflicts worldwide. What can be done?
Fortunately, the situation is sometimes better than one might think in the light of media reports.
The Human Security Report that appeared in summer 2005 showed that the number of victims of violent conflicts and human rights violations has decreased considerably in the past ten years, thanks to the end of the East-West conflict and thanks to successful UN peace missions. Visibly our efforts are producing results. These findings make me confident that we are on the right path. But there is still a long way to go!

What are your personal priorities with regard to women's issues?
One of the objectives of Swiss foreign policy is to ensure the well-being of all Swiss men and women. This goal is particularly close to my heart. It is therefore evident for me to strongly advocate the cause of women, not only in Switzerland but throughout the world.
I attach great importance to gender mainstreaming in Swiss development and peace promotion policy. There are no social, cultural or religious factors that can justify the infringement of women's rights.
Together with my women foreign minister colleagues, we created — in the margins of the UN General Assembly in New York in autumn 2003 — an informal network to advocate women's rights. We have met three times since to work out joint concepts for action to deal with violence against women and the problem of trafficking of women.

How was your awareness raised? What has your experience been?
I have had the same experiences as all women living in countries like Switzerland. Difficulties combining family and professional life, difficulties in asserting oneself as a woman in the work place, family responsibilities. Because of this, I understand the importance of the role of women in the fight against poverty and in the resolution of conflicts. The activity of women and the recognition of this activity are vital.

What place does your commitment to peace have in your foreign policy?
Commitment to peace is one of the central pillars of our foreign policy. In the past the Federal Assembly has repeatedly stressed that it attaches the greatest importance to a credible commitment by Switzerland in this field. There are few areas of politics in which such positive results can be achieved with relatively modest means. I will therefore use every possibility at my disposal to raise the status of peace policy in our country. I am also pleased that in my conversations with citizens I have received support for my view that this approach is very much in the interest of our country.

What do you believe in?
In human beings and their capacity to find solutions.

Are you confident about the future?
Yes, otherwise I wouldn't be where I am.

Federal Councillor Micheline Calmy-Rey was born on 8 July 1945. A social democrat, she has been foreign minister in the Swiss government since 2002. She was head of the finance department in the Geneva Cantonal Government for five years. Micheline Calmy-Rey is married. She has two children and three grandchildren.

Christine Loriol is a journalist who lives and works in Switzerland.

"I am not a wall that divides – I am a crack in that wall"

Kamla Bhasin

c

In this adventure called 1000 Women for the Nobel Peace Prize 2005, we are not talking of peace in a narrow sense. We are actually concerned with and are talking about life, about survival, survival of Mother Earth and of all the species including human beings.

Millions of women wish to protect and celebrate life itself and therefore we wish to end all kinds of violence, conflict and war. The present economic, political, religious, military, patriarchal wars are anti-life; we are for life.

We wish to stop this huge wave of violence which is destroying our diversity, our humanity, our interconnectedness; which is poisoning our rivers and seas and lands; which is cutting down our forests, destroying people's livelihoods, knowledge systems, belief systems. We wish to end wars and violence based on insatiable greed which have turned dignified, rooted, caring human beings into paupers, refugees, migrants, selfish, individualistic, terrorists, criminals; violence which is making millions hungry, sick, insecure.

Ours is a holistic, integrative and ecological perspective and vision. We recognize and respect the diversity and the interconnectedness of all phenomena; we realize that people on this planet are more alike than different in our common goals — peace, justice, dignity, a safe future for our children, a healthy planet and healthy environment for all living beings.

As feminists we believe the personal is political; hence for us, peace also means personal transformation, inner peace. For us, peace must begin within each one of us, in our homes, organizations and communities and then move onwards to encompass our countries and the world.

For us the other names of peace are diversity, dialogue, justice, democracy, transparency, human rights, caring, nurturing, love. For us other faces of peace are enough and healthy food, health, education, clean environment. For us peace is creativity, hope and trust.

We know that there are millions of women in different parts of the world working fearlessly and ceaselessly for this holistic vision of peace. This adventure will make the ideas, experiences and struggles of these Peacewoman visible. We will celebrate their work so that planet earth can be saved, our life and our humanity can be protected.

The idea of giving the Nobel Peace Prize to 1000 women (as opposed to one man) is not because 1000 women's work is equal to one man's. For us recognizing 1000 women is symbolic of several ideas like:

Creating peace requires a culture of peace practiced by millions in our daily life.

Women's peace work has not been recognized nor appreciated or celebrated. This project aims to make ordinary women's extraordinary peace work visible and valued and to popularize a holistic definition of peace.

One of our slogans is: "I am not a wall that divides — I am a crack in that wall."

Kamla Bhasin, is the project coordinator for South Asia. A feminist, economist and sociologist, she worked on South Asia for the United Nations for 28 years strengthening civil society organizations and encouraging networking between them on issues related to sustainable livelihoods, gender, human rights, peace etc. She is currently coordinating SANGAT (South Asian Network of Gender Activists and Trainers) working closely with Jagori — Women's Training, Documentation and Resource Centre in New Delhi. She has written many books and songs related to justice, peace, gender equality and development.

Project Diary – the Organizers' Journal

Maren Haartje and Rebecca Vermot

January 2003 — 1000 women for the Nobel Peace Prize 2005. Outside an old hotel high in the Swiss mountains the snow keeps falling. Inside, Maren Haartje types the first concept paper for the "1000 Women for the Nobel Peace Prize 2005" project on her laptop. Now the work can begin but first the idea needs a visual symbol. Various suggestions are tossed back and forth at a multicultural women's meeting. A 1 and three 0's are obvious. One zero is shown as a globe, another as the peace symbol we know from the 1960s, and one zero has a cross beneath it — the astrological symbol for the feminine.

But in parts of Asia, it is said, the peace symbol is associated with US imperialism. The cross is also a Christian symbol and we are told that it is not well-known in the Arab world as the symbol for women. We hesitate to use other symbols such as a dove, the olive branch or a mother and child. But everyone likes the idea of women's profiles, but not just two, and not in black and white or with typical features.

Our graphic artist Jenny Leibundgut makes suggestions. The globe changes into a tilted ellipse featuring the profiles of three women and the 1000 on an orange background. Finally we all agree on the logo to symbolize the 1000 women worldwide. Later, the project title "1000 Women for the Nobel Peace Prize 2005" and a short project description will be translated into 13 languages.

March 2003 — In a tiny office under the roof of the Swiss peace foundation swisspeace, are two computers, two telephones, a bookshelf and empty orange binders. Before us is the concept paper for a global project with three main themes: peace prize, documentation and research. There is no shortage of ideas, but we all know that we Swiss women — the executive committee and office staff — cannot realize such a project by ourselves.

How can we locate, contact and assess "Peacewoman" if they are to come from Turkmenistan, Sri Lanka, Vanuatu, China, Guatemala, Russia, Iceland, Japan and other countries? We know we need help from the different regions. But will we be able to inspire well-connected experts who, from long experience in women's rights, peace and development work, understand the social and political situation in their regions?

We start asking women we know from our own years of peace networking, and find spontaneous support. First we meet with Zainap Gaschaeva from Chechnya. Will she like the project? Yes, she is with us. Then we talk with Vera Chirwa from Malawi during her visit to Bern, and she is also enthusiastic. Margo Okazawa-Rey from the USA is asked in Zurich, and will cooperate. At the same time we start developing a data bank and website, working up a budget and speaking with potential contributors.

—

D

May 2003 — The network of coordinators is growing. We have asked Fadila Memisevic from Sarajevo to support us, and Kamla Bhasin, a pioneering feminist from India, is won over. Sima Samar, a doctor and the first female minister from Afghanistan, and Marina Pikulina from Uzbekistan also accept. The Argentinian journalist Nora Franco agrees enthusiastically to coordinate Latin America, and recommends Clara Charf to be the coordinator for Brazil. We find our first partner for the academic research in Doris Wastl-Walter from Bern University.

July 2003 — The binders in our office are filling up with papers, correspondence with the coordinators and ideas for sponsoring, information on possible peace women and fundraising efforts. The international team keeps growing: Nicci Simmonds from New Zealand is recommended to us, Fatoumata Maiga from Mali, Paulynn Sicam from the Philippines and Cassandra Balchin, who has good contacts in the Maghreb, join the team. We are feeling the responsibility, and how difficult it is to find money for international peace projects. At the same time, there are many examples of solidarity and enthusiasm.

It's hot in Bern. On the roof terrace, we work with Andrea Kofler and Anja Sieber from Bern University on a definition of peace that can be universally and interculturally acceptable. It should be the basis for the first discussion with the, so far, 13 coordinators.

September 2003 — Our first coordinators' meeting has just ended. Concentrated woman power has focused for long days on a common understanding of peace, one that can be accepted by the Brazilian Clara Charf as well as by Cassandra Balchin from England, by Marina Pikulina from Uzbekistan and Kamla Bhasin from India. All 12 women present agree to work on the project in their regions, despite minimal compensation and the unpredictable time commitment involved. But we see that we need more coordinators. Another highlight in September is the visit to the director of the Nobel Institute in Oslo. He finds our project interesting and encourages us to continue.

November 2003 — The timeline is ready and the coordinators launch the project in their own regions, requiring support that only the head office in Switzerland can provide. Often it is hard for the local partners to believe that anyone has really initiated such a crazy project. For four weeks, Rebecca Vermot flies around the world, visiting innumerable organizations, members of parliament and representatives of Swiss embassies or consulates. First stop is Brazil, then El Salvador, where Nora Franco takes on the task of coordinating the project in whole Spanish-speaking Latin America and the

Caribbean. Rebecca meets the co-coordinators in Fiji, Sandy Fong, Nicci Simmonds and Koila Costello-Olsen. She travels to the Philippines to meet Paulynn Sicam and Karen Tanada. Rebecca flies to Hong Kong to win the support of Kin Chi Lau for the project, as her network is strong in China. We are still missing a woman who can help us in the Mekong region. Finally, after careful consideration, Kratae Supawadee in Bangkok agrees to join in. Meanwhile, Maren Haartje travels to Sarajevo to discuss with Fadila Memisevic the steps that need to be taken and possible difficulties.

January 2004 — While Rebecca Vermot supports Fatoumata Maiga with the launching of the project in Mali, preparations for the second coordinators' meeting are underway in Bern. We have to develop a nomination form to be distributed worldwide. It must be simple and understandable, and at the same time comprehensive. Along with biographical information, the work of the potential nominee must be adequately described and confirmed by two references.

The coordination team is now almost complete, as Asha Elkarib from the Sudan, Cecile Mukarubuga from Kenya and Aida Abu Ras from Jordan have joined. Carolina Monteiro has agreed to help Paulynn Sicam and Karen Tanada coordinate the search for nominees in Indonesia.

The research group has expanded as well, with media experts from the University of Klagenfurt coming on board. Regula Küng starts working as assistant in the project coordination office in Bern.

March 2004 — The nomination form that the coordinators prepared at their second meeting is ready, and copies are sent out. We contact networks around the world, and send the forms by e-mail, post and fax. When we receive an e-mail from East Timor, we know that the information has made its way around the world. Dalit women from Nepal want specific details. And soon comes the first proposal. A woman from Burkina Faso is nominated. What excitement!

Meanwhile, Rebecca Vermot speaks in New Delhi at an international feminist conference, and in Uzbekistan to representatives of non-governmental organizations, explaining the idea of 1000 Women for the Nobel Peace Prize 2005 and encouraging them to nominate.

May 2004 — As ever, only small amounts of money are coming in. But the idea of buying a symbolic "peace share" for 1000 Swiss francs has promise. Optimistically, we have 1000 pieces printed. And they "sell" well. Nominations are coming in every day now, to the coordinators and to the little office in Bern. We expand the office with two more shelves and two dozen more binders.

Inquiries accumulate, by phone and e-mail. Because of the global time zones, the day is really 24 hours long. We lobby, make arrangements, raise funds at home and abroad, and present our project to different international organizations. Maren Haartje travels to Germany and Rebecca Vermot goes once again to Africa. In Kenya, Burundi and Sudan, she meets women who have been nominated. With her is a film team from "Offroad Reports", making a documentary about the project. In Malawi, she meets Nomvuyo Skota Dayile, who will from then on, with Vera Chirwa, be responsible for Southern Africa. In Israel, Mirit Balkan, and in Palestine, Faiha Abdulhadi, support the project during the nomination phase.

July 2004 — We have the support of UNIFEM and UNDP, and UNESCO in Switzerland. A wonderful feeling. Meanwhile, in the 14-square-meter office, chaos reigns — nominations are closed. Requests to extend the deadline come in from around the world. The mailbox is overflowing, the fax machine breaks down! What do we do with all the information? It has to be sent to the responsible regional coordinators. But Fatoumata in Bamako has neither fax nor e-mail. Connections in many parts of this world are often difficult.

September 2004 — Once again, there is a coordinators' meeting. The mood is tense. Do we have 1000 good suggestions? More than 2000 nominations have come in, but are they all really good? Do the women fill our strict criteria of non-violence, long-term engagement, integrity and fairness? The data bank is filled and world-wide, regional advisory bodies are evaluating their suggestions and preparing proposals.
Maren Haartje travels to Moscow and meets with Zainap Gashaeva, Fadila Memisevic and Marina Pikulina, to work on the nominations from the related regions of the Russian Federation, and Central Asia, the Balkans, Southeastern and Western Europe. Sandy Fong from Fiji takes over responsibility for Oceania and Anita Mir replaces Cassandra Balchin.

November 2004 — We still don't have 1000 women and some regions are not represented, so the search begins anew, because we all have a goal in sight that we want to achieve. 1000 women for the Nobel Peace Prize 2005, worldwide. They should be honored for representing millions of courageous women peace activists.
And the office has grown. Barbara Mangold has joined the team and we now have around 20 square meters and a fourth desk. The academic research group at the Interdisciplinary Center for Women's and Gender Studies at the University of Bern receives an international research loan for evaluation of the 1000 nominations!

—

D

January 2005 — We have far more than 1000 women who we can nominate, together, for the Nobel Peace Prize. The international project team works hard on the selection. Each and every candidate for nomination is impressive. We prepare the letter for the Norwegian Nobel Prize Committee and do everything we can to convince the Nobel prize jury that to honor 1000 women collectively with the Nobel Peace Prize is unique, because peace can never be created alone, but only in dialogue and cooperation with others. We start to think about the continuation of the project beyond 2005.

March 2005 — More relaxed, we prepare the fourth coordinators' meeting. It won't be about selection, assessment and hard decisions, but about making the 1000 peace women visible. We talk about the book, the exhibition and — above all — the international announcement of the 1000 names, a step eagerly awaited in many quarters. We choose June 29, an unspectacular day, being neither a memorial nor a religious holiday, not a Friday or Sunday, and right before the European summer holiday.
Everyone works on the book. The coordinators commission local journalists and photographers for portraits of women in their region. An international editorial group is put together. A new network of journalists, women and men, is created. Everyone wants to know who the 1000 women are. But the names are still secret.

May 2005 — 1000 confirmation letters and information letters to the non-selected women are sent out. Many women answer, we receive very moving letters. Some are disappointed because they are not among the 1000 women, most are happy to have been considered. Press conferences are organized, and hundreds of photos are sorted for the book and exhibition. Translators and editors work at full speed; not all writers have followed the format guidelines.
The 1000 women and their work are becoming ever more familiar to us. First the nomination, then the text for the book, a photo, a personal letter or phone call. We are overwhelmed and know that we have reached the first goal. We have 1000 women from more than 150 countries who are working impressively and uniquely for peace and a future worth living. We have nominated them for the 2005 Nobel Peace Prize, and are making their peace work known in a book and exhibition.

29 June 2005 — Today the names of the 1000 Peacewoman will be revealed at press conferences worldwide. Around the globe there are more than 40 press conferences, and nominated women participate in almost all of them. The coordinators have very different concepts for this day, but can't be everywhere. In some countries, the authors of the biographies organize media conferences, some Peacewoman organize the meetings themselves. Sandy Fong is the first to make the names public, in Fiji. Then it continues, in Asia, Africa and Europe. And on to Brazil and the USA. Media response is good, and the project is now finally known worldwide.

July 2005 — One of the most hectic periods of the project is over. However press conferences still have to be organized, the book put together and the exhibition planned. Hundreds of journalists and writers have written the text, but parts are still missing: sections of text, statements, information, quotes. The book is the result of an unbelievable effort by the coordinators, but also by all the editors who have read the texts, corrected and revised everything. Without them, we never could have done it. Our three telephones are never still; by now we can give information in many languages. Ever more often we are asked: What happens after 2005? The "1000 Women for the Nobel Peace Prize 2005" project ends on December 31. But it will continue. The executive committee will be more international, the focus will change — but it will go on.

September 2005 — We are preparing for the fifth and last coordinators' meeting, and for October 14th, the day when the Nobel Peace Prize winner for 2005 should be announced. We have decided to celebrate on that day, whether or not the 1000 women are honored with the Nobel Peace Prize. We will open the exhibition on our Peacewoman in Zurich, Switzerland, and celebrate with the coordinators and the many volunteers, contributors, sponsors and supporters of this crazy project, that perhaps will make the world a somewhat kinder and gentler place.

Maren Haartje is project manager of 1000 Women for the Nobel Peace Prize 2005 and an academic expert on feminist policy and education.

Rebecca Vermot is project manager of 1000 Women for the Nobel Peace Prize 2005 and a political scientist and journalist.

—
D

Stumbling Blocks and Stepping Stones on a Unique Journey!

Christine Menz

E

When we set out to make women's contributions to peace in the world visible thousand-fold, our goal was clear, but the path was obscure. New roads had to be explored, new boundaries breached. Our most precious guides were the coordinators from the various regions of the world. Their networks and varied cultural backgrounds helped us to deal with over 2000 nominations and choose 1000 women.

Would the women we found be the "right" ones? What about those we did not find, the forgotten ones?

Finding a common meaning of peace proved to be a great challenge. Together with participating researchers, we arrived at a generic definition based on human security and dignity. Yet we wanted the criteria for nomination to be as measurable, comprehensible and comprehensive as possible. This, in turn, made us aware of the degree to which language is shaped by culture.

What does "exemplary" connote in Fiji? What is the meaning of "transparent" in West Africa? What is the significance of "sustainable" in the Philippines or of "non-violent" in Bosnia or Serbia? These experiences were both stumbling blocks and stepping stones.

Communication was also a major problem. English was and is our working language, although not all the coordinators speak or understand it. The coordinating team used German, English, French, Russian and Spanish. But we were helped by skilled translators, while we learned to listen carefully and do our best to understand. Mutual trust made this approach possible.

Our project did not always meet with a positive response. There were those who tried to manipulate our project or set politically unacceptable conditions. We had to decide whether we would exclude the nominations of women who are active in blatantly violent environments. Not wanting to endanger anyone, we had to weigh the risks. We finally decided that "Anonyma" would represent the brave women who have had to remain nameless for their own safety.

Funding was a major hurdle. Who would be mad enough to spend money on such a visionary, non-mainstream project? The project was far from cheap. Some coordinators had to be provided with basic equipment, their travel expenses had to be covered, and a cost-effective but reliable support infrastructure had to be set up in Switzerland.

For the book, the exhibition, the website, we visited potential sponsors who simply laughed at us or hinted that we were megalomaniacs. We heard excuses of all kinds, even from friendly organizations. And yet we succeeded! Our success was due mainly to the many individuals and groups who laid the project's financial foundation by buying our peace shares and assuming sponsorships. Trust in the power of an idea and unremitting dedication, are probably the only ways to get funding for such a unique global undertaking.

Gradually, our fear of not being able to identify a thousand women for nomination disappeared. By mid-2004, we had received 2000 names from about 150 countries. But we were facing the next difficulty: how could we do justice to all these women who all do excellent work?

Together with the coordinators, we organized advisory boards in the various regions. These boards adopted a transparent process to select the names to be included in the list. As happens in every selection process, there were those nominees who were disappointed, those who asked for clarification, those who understood and those who did not. But until the end, we continued to ask ourselves: have we made the right choices? What is certain is that we reached decisions according to the best of our knowledge and ability, and the information available to us.

Did we make mistakes? Unfortunately, mistakes cannot be completely ruled out in a global project of such scope, implemented within a very strict timeframe.

The announcement of the nominations on 29 June 2005 in press conferences worldwide was the next challenge. In 24 hours, in over 40 press conferences organized by the coordinators, the 1000 Peacewoman and their work were introduced around the globe. The media took a concrete interest in peace issues, and certain governments had to admit that in their country, there are women working for peace. But was the timing correct? Was the announcement made too early? Might it compromise the chance of the Peacewoman to obtain the Nobel Peace Prize? We dared to wager — and won! It was a memorable day of power and hope!

Three years is a very short time. Yet, thanks to the commitment of the many women who worked far beyond the call of duty, thanks to a transcontinental network that gave us strength and confidence, thanks to our curiosity and concern, we overcame all obstacles. Much energy was generated by these consecutive victories! Shared responsibility, mutual trust and esteem — these were the pillars of the project's ultimate success.

Dr Christine Menz is a member of the board of the Association 1000 Women for the Nobel Peace Prize 2005 and a communications specialist.

E

Index by name

Alianza de Mujeres Viequenses	Puerto Rico	612
Alieva Svetlana	Russian Federation	7
Alimbekova Dildora	Uzbekistan	343
Allaghi Farida	Libyan Arab Jamahiriya	492
Allo Alina	Russian Federation	8
Allport Dupont Maire-Bopp	French Polynesia	613
Almeida Vanete	Brazil	344
Alomang Yosepha	Indonesia	493
Alterman Blay Eva	Brazil	709
Álvarez Llave María Luisa	Peru	169
Alves Genoveva Ximenes	Timor-Leste	710
Amanan Dandi Lou Hélène	Côte d'Ivoire	9
Amiro Anita	Sudan	856
Amma Leelakumari	India	818
Anderson Shelley J.	Netherlands	10
Andi Baso Zohra	Indonesia	170
Ando Yuki	Japan	171
Ang-See Teresita	Philippines	857
Angami Neidonuo	India	11
Anglo Siham	Sudan	345
Aniceto Pardo María Beatriz	Colombia	261
Anonyma	International	172
Anwar Zainah	Malaysia	858
Apa Shahjahan	India	173
Ara Nusrat	Pakistan	346
Arafat Insaf	Jordan	614
Arbana Sevim	Albania	12
Arbour Louise	Canada	494
Arns Neumann Zilda	Brazil	615
Arshad Zakia	Pakistan	819
Arulampalam Shanti Christine	Sri Lanka	13
Ashenafi Meaza	Ethiopia	495
Ashrawi Hanan	Occupied Palestinian Territory	916
Ates Seyran	Germany	174
Ato Oywa Rosalba	Uganda	14
Auguste Marie Carmèle Rose-Anne	Haiti	616
Awan Nasreen	Pakistan	711
Ayo Aidari Trust	India	262

Ciciek Farha	Indonesia	186
Cimpaye Marie Rose	Burundi	44
Civikova Jana	Slovakia	727
Clara Mirta Susana	Argentina	627
Clermont Péan Paula	Haiti	863
Coll Torrente Pilar	Peru	506
Coomaraswamy Radhika	Sri Lanka	187
Córdoba Mosquera Luz Perly	Colombia	369
Cornelia Negoita	Romania	628
Cornelius Stella	Australia	728
Coronel Ferrer Miriam	Philippines	45
Corrneck Jean	Zimbabwe	729
Costa Leonardo Nuria	Mexico	370
Cour Ajeet	India	46
Crook Isabel	China	864
Cruz Avisado Adoracion	Philippines	507
Cruz Córdoba Norma Angélica	Guatemala	188
Cruz Rodríguez Esperanza	Nicaragua	47
Curbelo Cora Nelsa Libertad	Ecuador	48
Curbelo Morales María Elena	Uruguay	629

D

D'Almeida Grace Antonia	Benin	508
da Silva Benedita	Brazil	923
da Silva Givânia Maria	Brazil	275
Damba Semjidmaa	Mongolia	276
Daraba Hadja Saran	Guinea	49
Das Hena	Bangladesh	371
Das Nanda Rani	Bangladesh	372
Dawan Chantarahassadee	Thailand	824
de Almeida Teles Maria Amélia	Brazil	509
de Araújo Zenilda Maria	Brazil	277
de Azevedo Santos Maria Stella	Brazil	865
de Carvalho Lenira Maria	Brazil	373
de Godoy Zerbini Therezinha	Brazil	510
de Ishtar Zohl	Australia	278
de Jesus Haller Maria	Angola	924
de Oliveira Araújo Maria José	Brazil	630
de Silva Dulcy	Sri Lanka	189
de Souza Luiza Erundina	Brazil	925
de Souza Ruth	Brazil	866

F Index by name

F Index by name

H

I

J

L

Lanz Anni	Switzerland	546
Latrous Lotti	Côte d'Ivoire	652
Law Blanco Hazel María	Nicaragua	306
Layvanh Phanludeth	Lao People's Dem. Republic	410
Le Thi Quy	Viet Nam	214
Lee Barbara	United States of America	956
Lee Ching Chee	China, Hong Kong SAR	881
Lee Hyun-Sook	Republic of Korea	103
Lei Kun	China, Taiwan	411
Léno Joséphine	Guinea	412
Leontyeva Yevgeniya	Ukraine	753
Lepcha Keepu Tsering	India	307
Leslie Emma	Cambodia	104
Li Chunxia	China	308
Li Guilian	China	413
Li Jiyue	China	653
Li Jun	China	957
Li Tete	China	414
Li Xiaoliang	China	654
Li Xiaoxi	China	831
Li Xuebo	China	958
Liang Jun	China	754
Libera Viezzer Moema	Brazil	755
Lichtenfels Sabine	Portugal	832
Lin Shu Ying	China, Taiwan	833
Linares Meneses Felicitas Estela	Peru	834
Linhares Barsted Leila	Brazil	547
Lini Hilda	Vanuatu	959
Liu Fenglan	China	882
Liu Ngun Fung	China, Hong Kong SAR	215
Liu Zhongxun	China	548
Livne Angelica	Israel	105
Long Sihai	China	216
Los Hilan	Papua New Guinea	549
Lovera López Sara	Mexico	756
Lozanova Valcheva Liliana	Bulgaria	757
Lubich Chiara	Italy	883

M

Ma Qingrong	China	415
Ma Xinlan	China	758

N

F Index by name

Yokoi Kumiko	Japan	702
Yondon Tuul	Mongolia	995
Yoon Geum-Soon	Republic of Korea	481
Yorac Haydee B.	Philippines	608
Yu Fan Ying	China, Taiwan	812
Yu Guixin	China	996
Yudea Henny	Indonesia	703
Yue Daiyun	China	908
Yun Jianli	China	852
Yunusova Toita	Russian Federation	163
Yusupova Rano	Uzbekistan	609

Z

Zabala viuda de Polo María Eugenia	Colombia	164
Zajovic Stanislavka	Serbia and Montenegro	165
Zana Leyla	Turkey	333
Zatz Mayana	Brazil	704
Zhang Guimei	China	813
Zhang Hua	China	814
Zhang Jihui	China	705
Zhang Jinming	China	997
Zhang Luping	China	853
Zhang Shuqin	China	256
Zhang Wenqing	China	706
Zhang Youyun	China	998
Zhao Fenglan	China	482
Zhao Ling	China	909
Zheng Bing	China	483
Zheng Xiaoying	China	910
Zhou Guangren	China	911
Zhu Xiaoxia	China	815
Zhu Yinxiu	China	999
Zia Shehla	Pakistan	1000
Zulminarni Nani	Indonesia	484

Index by countries

China, Taiwan	Lucie Cheng	726
	Sheng Hsin Chou	43
	Shou E. Feng	59
	Chuen Juei "Josephine" Ho	941
	De Fen Ho	532
	Hsiao Chuan Hsia	204
	Lin Ching Hsia	745
	Chin Yu Hsu	83
	Lan Hsiang Hsu	642
	Chiu Hsiang Huang	391
	Mei Ying Huang	297
	Su Mei Kao Chin	303
	Yu Jane Ku	955
	Kun Lei	411
	Shu Ying Lin	833
	Ching Feng Wang	604
	Tsu Chuen Yang	907
	Fan Ying Yu	812
Colombia	María Beatriz Aniceto Pardo	261
	Yolanda Becerra Vega	23
	Ana Teresa Bernal	28
	Norha Patricia Buriticá Céspedes	40
	Nubia Castañeda Bustamante	41
	Virgelina Chará	273
	Luz Perly Córdoba Mosquera	369
	Hilda Liria Domicó Bailarín	282
	Beatriz Elena Rodríguez Rengifo	451
	María Tila Uribe	799
	Rafaela Vos Obeso	804
	María Eugenia Zabala viuda de Polo	164
Cook Islands	Paddy Walker	903
Costa Rica	Elizabeth Odio Benito	566
Côte d'Ivoire	Dandi Lou Hélène Amanan	9
	Lotti Latrous	652
Croatia	Dragica Aleksa	6
	Mirjana Bilopavlovic	32
	Jelka Glumicic	70

F

Fiji	Sharon Bhagwan-Rolls	30
	Jane Keith-Reid	644
	Amelia Rokotuivuna	579
	Suliana Siwatibau	842
Finland	Barbro Sundback	987
France	Solange Fernex	826
	Zarina Khan	878
	Annie Sasco	684
	Cristina Tézenas du Montcel	696
French Polynesia	Maire-Bopp Allport Dupont	613
	Unutea Hirshon	294

G

Georgia	Nino Burjanadze	920
	Tiina Ilsen	947
	Nino Javakhishvili	398
	Tsisana Rapava	577
	Irina Yanovskaya	162
Germany	Lea Ackermann	167
	Seyran Ates	174
	Judith Brand	37
	Maria Christina Färber	62
	Monika Gerstendörfer	199
	Barbara Gladysch	69
	Marianne Grosspietsch	638
	Heide Göttner-Abendroth	739
	Monika Hauser	203
	Cathrin Schauer	237
	Bosiljka Schedlich	145
	Karla Schefter	686
	Karla-Maria Schälike	687
	Sabriye Tenberken	797
	Ruth Weiss	605
Ghana	Kate Adoo Adeku	610
Greece	Daphne Economou	634

J

Jamaica	Marjorie Prentice Saunders	780
Japan	Yuki Ando	171
	Katsuko Nomura	436
	Yukika Sohma	897
	Siin-Do Song	244
	Suzuyo Takazato	247
	Kumiko Yokoi	702
Jordan	Haifa Abu Ghazaleh	335
	Insaf Arafat	614
	Tagreed Hikmat	531
	Laurice Hlass	940

K

Kazakhstan	Dametken Alenova	915
	Lazzat Ishmukhamedova	394
	Rozlana Taukina	989
	Irina Unzhakova	990
Kenya	Dekha Ibrahim Abdi	85
	Wahu Kaara	952
	Musimbi Kanyoro	403
	Veronica Wanjiru Kinyanjui	213
	Florence Muia	665
	Litha Musyimi-Ogana	428
	Rhoda Chepkobus Rotino	229
	Tecla Wanjala	160
Korea (Republic of)	Yu-Jin Jeong	950
	Sook-Im Kim	100
	Hyun-Sook Lee	103
	Maria Chol Soon Rhie	450
	Heisoo Shin	240
	Geum-Soon Yoon	481
Kuwait	Mudi Al-Essa	340
	Nabeela Al-Mulla	817
	Lulwa Al-Qitami	5
Kyrgyzstan	Aziza Abdirasulova	485
	Gulnara Derbisheva	374

	Sheema Kermani	877
	Mehmooda Salim Khan	646
	Parveen Azam Khan	647
	Salma Maqbool	658
	Khawar Mumtaz	218
	Dilshad Murtaza	766
	Kishwar Naheed	886
	Akeela Naz	431
	Akhtar Riazuddin	136
	Majida Rizvi	227
	Hilda Saeed	233
	Zari Sarfaraz	683
	Nafisa Shah	981
	Farida Shaheed	457
	Shehla Zia	1000
Palau	Gabriela Ngirmang	836
Panama	Ediofelina Fuentes González	382
	Marta Matamoros	418
	Alma Montenegro de Fletcher	557
Papua New Guinea	Lorraine Garasu	66
	Helen Hakena	76
	Mary Kini	212
	Hilan Los	549
	Josie Tankunani Sirivi	461
	Freda Talao	248
Paraguay	Maggiorina Balbuena	263
	María del Pilar Callizo López Moreira	502
	Nilda Estigarribia	929
	María Ramona Isabel Noguera Dominguez	564
Peru	María Luisa Álvarez Llave	169
	Carmen Rosa Campos Mendoza	722
	Pilar Coll Torrente	506
	Felicitas Estela Linares Meneses	834
	Angélica Mendoza Almeida	555
	María Cleofé Sumire López	594

Slovenia	Anica Mikus Kos	663
	Svetlana Slapsak	149
Solomon Islands	Kathleen Kapei	210
	Ceciliana Olilaeni	124
	Apollonia Bola Talo	153
Somalia	Zam-zam Abdi	1
	Elmi Asha Hagi Amin	935
South Africa	Jenet B. Dlamini	733
	Lesley Ann Foster	196
	Busisiwe Virginia Hlomuka	744
	Daphne Jansen	208
	Veronica Khosa	648
	Regina Makunga	762
	Mirriam Malala	416
	Nosandla Malindi	417
	Edith Matshikiza	419
	Rolene Miller	664
	Nikiwe Nyamakazi	776
	Lorna Philander	446
	Adelle Potgieter	574
	Cordelia Nozukile Tshaka	698
Spain	Mercedes García Fornieles	524
	Maite Pagazaurtundúa	567
	Montserrat Sampere Martín	455
	Mireia Uranga Arakistain	157
Sri Lanka	Sunila Abeysekera	487
	Shanti Christine Arulampalam	13
	Radhika Coomaraswamy	187
	Dulcy de Silva	189
	Visakha Dharamadasa	52
	A. H.	75
	Saila Ithayaraj	207
	Kumari Jayawardena	209
	Immaculate Josef	93
	Wimalee Karunaretna	97
	Vijayakumary Murugiah	220
	Kumudini Samuel	141

Reconciliation
and Reconstruction

Koila Costello-Olsson

In peace-building, different approaches are needed at different stages of the conflict.

Reconciliation is about transforming relationships. It is a journey that must address the traumas of those who are affected by ensuring the delivery of justice which includes restorative justice. For most people, reconciliation is both a process and a goal.

In this context, reconstruction can include the rebuilding of bodies and souls, communities and nations. It could mean the reconstruction of a person wounded in conflict, the reconstruction of relationships that have been destroyed or frayed, the reconstruction of the environment, or the reconstruction of a nation. The reconstruction of nation states has sometimes led to the creation of truth and reconciliation commissions, which have left the world with many lessons that it can build peace on.

In the Pacific Region, there are traditional mechanisms in place for reconciliation within the various communities without need of going to the courts. Our indigenous processes have elements of restorative justice. In New Zealand, the Maoris have the so-called circle process where all parties involved in a crime or conflict come together with a respected mediator to discuss the needs of the victims, the role and obligations of the offenders, and the communities' needs, obligations and roles.

In Fiji, we have the traditional kava ceremony where someone who has wronged another apologizes and presents a symbolic object called the tabua or whale's tooth. In this ceremony, much value is placed on dialogue. However, the dialogue process needs to be strengthened and modified so that the ceremonies are not hurried and women's and children's views are sought and taken into account.

In Bougainville and the Solomons, the women were instrumental in initiating peace and reconciliation during the time of their crisis. With the support of the churches, especially the Catholic Church, they initiated and pushed the process. However their role in the formal decision-making processes in the community was not officially recognized.

In most of the world, the dominant powers are often oblivious to the plight of women, children and the oppressed. Though some countries have admirable constitutions and have ratified international conventions and covenants, they have not succeeded in dismantling the structural violence that has led to secondary violence such as domestic violence, criminality, substance abuse and suicides.

The 1000 women we have nominated for the Nobel Peace Prize are living evidence of what the famous peace-builder Elise Boulding once said, quoting her husband Kenneth: "What exists is possible."

Every time reconciliation takes place, especially among people who have done their best to hurt each other, we are given a blessed reminder that it is possible for human beings to deal with their differences peaceably.

In the face of many challenges, in spite of the risks involved, the sacrifices they have had to make, the women are out there doing tremendous work sowing the seeds of peace and nurturing them. The joy, love and compassion that has accompanied their work for peace and justice, constitute the loudest message that we need to hear in this century.

We are honored and privileged to make their lifework known to the world. There are many lessons that we can learn from their stories, which should influence the way we feel, think and act in our own lives and work. The stories on wisdom, dedication and experience of these 1000 peacewomen should inspire us, and especially the younger generation, to work for a better, more just and humane world.

Koila Costello-Olsson, coordinator of the Peace Program of ECREA, the Ecumenical Centre for Research, Education and Advocacy, for the last five years holds a M.A. in conflict transformation and peace-building from the Conflict Transformation Program of Eastern Mennonite University, USA. She is a consultant to the 1000 peacewomen project for the Pacific region.

—

H

Zam—zam Abdi

Somali Children Advocacy (SCA)

Zam-zam Abdi (28) completed her primary, secondary and university education in Mogadishu, Somalia. Now she is the coordinator of Somali Children Advocacy (SCA), which is mainly concerned with the rehabilitation of street children and child soldiers, children's rights, and peace building. Zam-zam works untiringly to achieve gender equity. She encourages Somali people to become involved in social work and to participate in the development of their community, regardless of their clan affiliation.

The civil war in the Somali capital Mogadishu had forced its people to leave their homes and seek shelter in other places. The streets were so unsafe that people could not walk around day and night. Houses were mainly occupied by gangs and rapists. Despite these perilous conditions, Zam-zam has managed to mobilize a group of 20 young men who held talks with the fighting militias and have peacefully succeeded in disarming many of the militia members and in reinstating peace and stability in some villages.

The inhabitants of these villages benefited from Zam-zam's initiative and formed a number of peace-restoring groups in order to protect their lives and properties. The peaceful atmosphere in the villages has helped people to go back to work and resume a normal life. These villages are now among the calmest areas of Mogadishu. However, Zam-zam is still encountering constant threats from the insurgent militias, who refuse to disarm. She was forced to move out of her house and to be on the run to save her life. Her office was attacked and all its furniture was looted. However, the threats did not weaken her determination to achieve peace.

Zam-zam's work has inspired many women, journalists and social workers in Somalia. She has pledged to preserve children's rights and to achieve long-term improvements in the community. She takes a firm stand on serious issues such as Female Genital Circumcision (FGC). Thanks to her efforts many women have decided to inhibit this traditional practice in their families following a campaign Zam-zam launched in the local media to raise peoples' awareness of this serious issue. She also supports women journalists against discrimination and defamation by private newspapers and radio stations. She helped to establish a number of associations that are concerned with defending the rights of women journalists.

Men and women in Somalia have benefited from Zam-zam's significant work. She inspired many of them to stand up for peace and justice in their communities. Many women journalists have started forming human rights organizations, despite the challenges they face from local press and radio stations.

Somalia

"I fight to keep the rainbow over Mali, my beautiful, multi-ethnic homeland, and all the while I continue to help these children who one day will be called upon to build our country."

Tahanouma Walet Abeb

Mouvement National des Femmes pour la Sauvegarde de la Paix et de l'Unité Nationale

Born in 1939 in Kidal, this magnificent grandmother served her country well in the Touareg rebellion in the north of Mali between 1990 and 1996. Tahanouma Walet Abeb is the widow of a French colonial administrator and mother of a daughter and son. She has no formal education, but she has learned many things in life that have made her a follower of peace. Many call her "Mother Peace."

Tahounouna Walet Abeb, a Touareg, lived in Bamako for a number of years to help re-establish peace in her country and reconcile hearts and spirits. She committed to peace throughout the rebellion period until its end to convince the different movements to sit and negotiate with the central government to sign for peace. This objective was attained and Walet was there throughout. She is the leader of the National Women's Movement for the Safeguarding of Peace and National Unity. It is a powerful structure that has worked for some time for a peaceful and stable Mali. Walet's strength is that she always understood that development problems are not resolved with weapons, but with understanding peace and the initiation of projects supported by the government and development partners. She and her movement strive to sensitize the nomadic women to understand their citizenship regarding the statute of entire life.

Additionally, her fight in favor of the young, disinherited Malians has been ongoing since the independence of Mali in 1960. In the early 1990s, the determined lady walked into the bases of the rebels with young women to convince them to start a dialogue with the government.

The Touareg Rebellion began in the 1990s by Touareg groups with the aim of achieving autonomy or forming their own nation. Desertification and drought forced the alteration of traditional migration routes, increasing conflict between neighboring groups. Mali effectively fell into a civil war, until, in 1995, moderates on both sides negotiated a peace settlement.

Mali

Amina Afzali

For 23 years Amina Safi Afzali has fought for women's rights, beginning shortly after obtaining her BSc from Kabul University. When the Russians invaded Afghanistan, she fled to Iran and established a multi-purpose educational institution that fights illiteracy, enhances computer skills and teaches English to Afghani refugee girls who dropped out of Iranian schools. From Iran, Amina headed an Afghani delegation to the Fourth Women's Conference in Beijing, China. She set up several female athletic teams participating in the Olympic games. She is a signatory of the Bonn Peace Accord of 2001.

Like many Afghani educated women, Amina Afzali feels that women in Afghanistan are discriminated against. She was therefore motivated to help improve Afghani women's status. Through her activities in Iran and participation in international conferences, Amina Afzali was impressed by the extent of other countries' women's participation in every aspect of life. These experiences, coupled with the tangible benefits that emerged from her activities through the association, have strengthened her commitment and sense of responsibility to work hard towards the welfare of women, especially in Afghanistan, even from her exile. As a signatory of the Bonn Peace Accord, Amina Afzali is very optimistic that in due time the unfortunate situation of women in Afghanistan will improve and a free, just and democratic future will prevail in the country. Although the existing circumstances present numerous hurdles to this vision, they are not insurmountable and, according to her, with persistent and dedicated effort this vision can be realized.

Sowing the seeds of a better future, respect for human and women's rights, and a non-violent society in a country that for the past two decades has been suffering the perversities of war, lawlessness, impunity and drugs, are all part of the unrelenting effort that Amina Afzali is making in Afghanistan.

Afghanistan

Susan Ahmed–Böhme

Iraqi Women's League (IWL)

Born in 1953 in Baghdad, Susan Ahmed is a biologist and a member of the Iraqi Women's League. Due to her covert work on issues of ethnic and religious diversity and her opposition to the former Iraqi president, Saddam Hussein, Susan and her family faced severe persecution in Iraq. Her father was tortured and her sister was murdered. In 1982 she fled to East Germany, where between 1991 and 2003, she campaigned courageously against Saddam Hussein's despotic regime as well as US imperialism. Her campaigns continue to this day. Susan emphasizes, "There is always an alternative to war."

Susan Ahmed is an Iraqi woman who could be dead, just like her sister. On the wall of her apartment in Berlin hangs a picture of her sister, Shatha. The two sisters were members of the Iraqi Women's League, and in the 1970s they fought together covertly against the dictatorial regime of the former Iraqi president, Saddam Hussein. The League, already banned in 1975, was and continues to be one of the few organizations in Iraq that has worked with people of all ethnicities and religious settings. Women from Shiite, Sunni and Christian backgrounds; Arabic, Kurdish, and Turkmen, all teamed up and campaigned for women's rights. In 1980, Shatha was arrested, and her family never heard from her again. Her father was also arrested, tortured and luckily set free after three months. After watching in silence the terrible fate of her sister, no better than that of many Iraqi families, Susan quitted Iraq in 1980 and managed to reach former East Germany in 1982. She found a job with the International Democratic Women's Federation, and then began campaigning for the release of the members of the Iraqi Women's League who were being tortured in Iraqi prisons.

The opposition in Iraq was chiefly ignored in the East and the West settings. Susan says bitterly, "Saddam's military power was built up by the West, and then, from 1991 to 2003, it was destroyed with weapons from the West." Susan strongly opposed the US invasion of Iraq. "There have always been political alternatives to war," she emphasizes. "I cried every day after the Americans invaded Iraq on March 20, 2003," Susan admits. "To me, the occupation was like rape," she exclaimed. Yet, as Saddam's regime was toppled on April 9th, she says she was "indescribably" happy. When the former dictator was arrested, "I sat for hours in front of my TV and laughed and cried; my whole body was shaking," said Susan.

Susan Ahmed is a member of the Iraqi Women's League, which was one of the few organizations in Iraq that ignored ethnic and religious markers. Women from diverse ethnic and sectarian backgrounds teamed up against Saddam's despotic regime, the Gulf wars and the US invasion of Iraq.

Iraq

Lulwa Al-Qitami

The Women Cultural and Social Society (WCSS)

Lulwa Al-Qitami, born 1931 in Kuwait, completed her education in Edinburgh between 1952 and 1960. Illuminated by British women's energetic participation in their society, she returned to Kuwait with a lifelong goal to improve the social, economic, educational status of Kuwaiti women. She co-founded The Women's Cultural and Social Society (WCSS) in 1963 with the aim of gradually changing the local anti-women culture and opening a space for Kuwaiti women's public participation. She placed children's welfare in Kuwait and elsewhere at the center of her consideration.

Inspired by British women's dynamic participation in their society, Lulwa Al-Qitami mobilized a group of Kuwaiti women to found The Women's Cultural and Social Society (WCSS) in 1963 with the aim of gradually changing the local culture that marginalized Kuwaiti women's public participation. Lulwa says, "I worked with my team to mobilize the Kuwaiti society towards change." In order to get closer to the local community, Lulwa and her WCSS members set out on a simple but symbolic task in order to motivate people to get involved in voluntary social work. They set off to sweep the streets of Kuwait city in 1966, visiting many houses and introducing local women to the objectives of the WCSS. Lulwa refered to the arduous economic status of women and the challenges that they would encounter if they decided to go to work, with the issue of looking after young children at the forefreont. The WCSS responded to working mothers' needs by opening its first nursery in 1974.

Lulwa also put a lot of effort into getting Education College students of the University of Kuwait involved in the activities of the WCSS nursery in order to gain experience. In so doing Lulwa has managed to secure fresh annual university graduates to join the work at the WCSS and turn them into potential future volunteers. Lulwa is highly dedicated to alleviating the distress of children with special needs and health problems. In 1987 she was inspired to found Al-Amal ("hope"), a center with qualified psychologists that provides a positive atmosphere for children with cancer as well as follow-up visits from doctors.

Lulwa Al-Qitami refered to the arduous economic status of women in Kuwait. Inspired by British women's participation in their society, Lulwa returned to Kuwait in 1960 with a lifelong goal to improve the circumstances of Kuwaiti women. She founded The Women's Cultural and Social Society (WCSS) in 1963 to end the marginalization of Kuwaiti women's social role.

Kuwait

Dragica Aleksa

Center for Peace, Nonviolence, and Human Rights

Before the war, Dragica Aleksa lived comfortably with her husband and two children on their farm in the village of Berak. The war in 1991 tore mothers and their children from their families, and Dragica and her son were not spared. Her family was reunited in another village later, but after the war, in 1998, Dragica returned to Berak. She joined the Center for Peace, Nonviolence, and Human Rights and took part in its Active Listening project. The result was her collection of "Stories from Berak." Dragica also actively worked to find missing persons and in peace building efforts.

Dragica Aleksa always thought that if there was to be a war, it certainly would not be in her village, Berak. But on 30 September 1991, two men came and told her that she and her son (11) had to leave for a couple of days. Together with all the women and children of Berak they left in organized transports that took them to a village 30 kilometers away. That was the most difficult night of her life. Inside a gymnasium, each woman held a child with one hand and a plastic bag in the other. Dragica was desperate. Her family had been dispersed. What happened to her daughter and husband? Those days were full of fear and uncertainty. From dusk until dawn she sat in the Red Cross headquarters listening to the news. Then the news came: "Berak has fallen." Dragica did not dare to think what that meant. Later, she was informed that her husband had been wounded and taken to a hospital. After his recovery, they wandered about for months until they settled in Suhopolje. The village people understood their suffering and accepted and helped them. At first, Dragica found it hard to accept help. Instead, she wanted to help, but did not know how. She could only donate her blood. It was a great joy whenever she met someone from her own village. They talked about their homes, their friends. They counted the dead, the "missing" and they swore that once they got back, nothing could ever separate them again. Then, Dragica learned to listen. She listened to the old Berak women talk about their lives and the wars they lived through. They taught her that only evil people do evil things, and there are no such things as collective blame, collective sadness, or collective responsibility. She saw how much a few honest and warm words could help. She wrote down the stories in her book "Stories from Berak." The book had two Croatian editions and was later translated into German and English.

The war in 1991 expelled most of the Croatian farmers in Berak to distant villages such as Suhopolje. After the war, the tension between returning Croatians and the Serbs who had stayed in the village during the war was high. Everyone had a story to tell and a person to blame. Peace work was needed badly.

Croatia

Svetlana Alieva

Soyuz zhenshchin repressirovanykh narodov Severnogo Kavkaza (The Union
of Women of Repressed Peoples of the North Caucasus)
Miezhdunarodnaya pravozashchitnaya assambleya (Int. Assembly f. Human Right

Svetlana Alieva (born 1936), a philologist by training, experienced mass ethnic deportation staged by the Communist regime in the USSR (1948). In 1991, she published the book 'The way it was' — uncovering the truth about the nationality-motivated repression in the USSR. Since 1992, she has been engaged in the anti-war movement, cooperating with a range of NGOs in the Caucasus region. Her activities have been aimed at putting an end to the ethnic conflict in North Ossetia (1992) and to the Russian–Chechen wars (1994—1996 / 1999—2001).

Svetlana Alieva was only 12, in 1948, when she was brought to the special headquarters of the Nkvd (later to become the KGB), where she was charged with treason against the motherland and forced to write a 'confession.' She was being repressed simply because her father was an ethnic Karachaev. At that time, the Soviet regime was staging mass repression against this Caucasian nation. The personal tragedy intertwined with the tragedy of the whole people affected her for many years. Because of the stress, experienced during the interrogation sessions, she afterwards suffered from speech neurosis and trembling hands.

After Gorbatchev announced Glasnost in the middle of the 1980s, Svetlana initiated independent research on the nationality-motivated repression in the USSR. This resulted in the book 'The way it was' — this book, published in 1991, is dedicated to the repression conducted against the Caucasian peoples. Her bitter personal memories, as well as many documents of the epoch disclosing the truth about the deportation of entire ethnic groups from their native territories in the USSR, are revealed therein. Probably these biographical elements have shaped her character and her yearning for truth and justice.

When the mass murders and ethnic cleansing of the Ingush population were committed in October and November 1992 in North Ossetia (a Caucasian republic in the Russian Federation), it was only natural for Svetlana to fight to protect the rights of the victims of this conflict. The Russian–Chechen war, which soon followed the events in North Ossetia, led to her founding the NGO Soyuz zhenshchin repressirovanykh narodov Severnogo Kavkaza (The Union of Women of Repressed Peoples of the North Caucasus) and becoming actively engaged in the antiwar movement.

Svetlana Alieva is fighting to put an end to the armed conflict in Chechnya. Remembering the mass deportation of peoples in the Stalin epoch, she uncovers cases of ethnic cleansing in this unstable region which have taken place in the recent past (Russia, North Ossetia, 1992).

Russian Federation

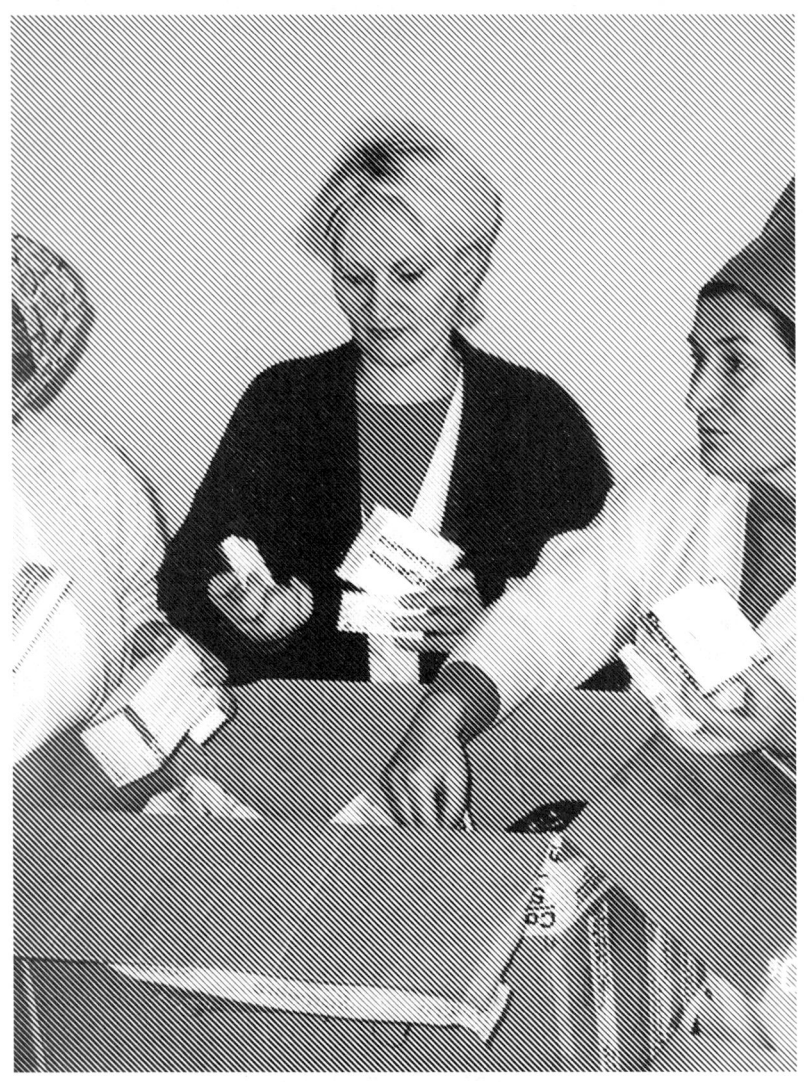

Alina Allo

Lutheran Evangelical Church (LEC)
Catholic Relief Agency Caritas Internationalis (CI)
Soviet Soldatskikh Matieriey (SSM)

Alina Allo (born 1958) spent her childhood years in Grozny in the Caucasus. 40 years ago, her family moved to Omsk, where she studied history and where she now works as a radio- and TV-journalist. She used to report on the repression years (1930s—1950s), drug abuse, and other social problems, until she went to war-torn Chechnya in 1998. She initiated a project: 'White Dove' — an appeal by Russian parents to Chechen parents who have lost their children as soldiers in this war, to forgive each other. She organizes treatment of Chechen children in Omsk and delivery of medicine to refugee camps.

When Alina Allo first traveled to the Caucasus, she had in her bag an appeal from the parents of Russian soldiers who had died in the Russian-Chechen war (1994—96). For the sake of peace between their peoples, the Russian parents had launched this appeal, called 'White Dove,' in which they asked for the forgiveness of the Chechen people for having shed the blood of their children. Later on, they suggested uniting their forces in order to bring the second war (1999—2001) to an end. Of course this was very difficult. In her book, Alina reflects: "More than anything, I was afraid that they would ridicule and reject the White Dove appeal. But they assumed I was a secret service agent and I was actually quite relieved — that was better than being taken for a madwoman … I was deeply shaken by seeing the nightmare of the consequences of this war. I so much wanted to do something about it. I suggested that the fighters take me hostage and exchange me for war prisoners. 'And how much is your country paying you for this?' they asked me, meaning money of course. 'My country is not paying me anything!' I replied. 'So why would we need you here then?' I was very offended by this." Every time Alina Allo travels to Chechnya, she takes the White Dove appeal with her, about which the controversies continue. "It is so difficult to find a space in the hearts of the people! Yet, if we want to stop this war, we need to stop it in our hearts," she says.

One of the happiest days in her life was the day when she was taken to a holy place of the Caucasus, to the tomb of the Muslim Saint Knead, where she met an elderly woman, one of his descendants. "I, a Christian, went down on my knees in front of the tomb of Saint Kheda together with this old Muslim woman, a Chechen, who had survived the genocide and the death of her children. We both cried and prayed for peace there."

Two wars with Russia have ruined Chechnya and killed thousands of people. In her peace efforts, Alina has never been supported by those in power. When she travels to Chechnya — to bring together parents from both sides who have lost children in the war — her safety is never guaranteed.

Russian Federation

"The exclusion of
women in early
crisis talks was a
huge mistake.
It is now up to the
women of Ivory
Coast to correct
that mistake."

Dandi Lou Hélène Amanan

Women in Peacebuilding Network (WIPNET)
Vision et action des femmes africaines contre les guerres (VAFAG)

Hélène Amanan served as a secretary of the permanent mission of the Ivory Coast for the United Nations in New York, was an international official (1992−1999) in charge of coordination of social affairs and protection of refugees for the High Commission for Refugees (UNHCR) in Ivory Coast and in the Democratic Republic of Congo. She was coordinator of the program Women in Peacebuilding Network (WIPNET) of the West Africa Network for Peacebuilding. Since 2004, Madame Dandi has been the French regional adviser (West Africa) of the Network of African Women for Peace.

The reality and consequences of conflicts remain unfair and intolerable situations that Dandi Lou Hélène Amanan does not allow to pass without reacting. As a leader of the NGO Vision and Action of Women Against Wars (VAFAG) she worked on a national and international plan to carry the message to women affected by wars. The goal of her NGO is to involve African women in building peace, prevention and management of conflicts, and to give urgent help to vulnerable people. Since its creation in 1999, VAFAG uses radio, television, newspapers, and public lectures to voice its appeals. The NGO lobbies with the parties involved in inter-Ivorian conflicts to encourage them to reach lasting peace in the Ivory Coast. In order not to be labelled as partisan, VAFAG chose absolute neutrality in dealing with all the parties in the conflict; thus, VAFAG is apolitical and characterized by moral integrity.

Hélène works in difficult conditions with her NGO, but she increases the initiative and work against the war everyday. The political actors attracted by power have very little consideration for the efforts and aims of VAFAG for peace. The people of the NGO often travelled in dangerous conditions at risk to their lives. This was especially true of the many journeys into rebel areas and the area of a former leader in order to promote a positive mood and to persuade the different parties to participate in the democratization process of the Ivory Coast. This last initiative was a success since that former leader ended up listening to them even though he later was killed in unknown conditions.

Madame Dandi Lou saw the consequence of conflicts first in Sierra-Leone, then Liberia, Ivory Coast, the Democratic Republic of Congo, then Darfur and the list continues. In all these conflicts, women were among the first victims.

Côte d'Ivoire

Shelley J. Anderson

International Fellowship of Reconciliation's Women Peacemakers Program
(IFOR WPP)

At the heart of the Women Peacemakers Program (WPP) and Shelley Anderson's approach is dialogue and listening. "We actively ask the women we work with 'What do you need?' and really try to listen," she says. The requests for nonviolence training are increasing every year. Since the WPP began in 1997, they have trained at least 15,000 people.

"As a white western woman — especially at the beginning, when I went to places like Cambodia or Ghana to do a training — I thought I cannot tell people from Sierra Leone and Liberia what nonviolence is. They were right in the middle of a war. What opened my eyes was when I started to talk about what I knew about nonviolence," Shelley Anderson recalls. "People were so hungry for a nonviolent alternative to war. Women came up to me and said, 'This has changed my life. I always felt there was a better way, that there had to be an alternative to what was happening, but I did not know there was a word for it.' They did not know there were books about nonviolence or real studies about Martin Luther King Jr. or Gandhi, that there were theories about it, and that there were actual trainings for nonviolence. I can remember a woman friend who went to Burma to train underground democracy activists. She also felt hesitant, but she just started sharing what she knew. The students asked why they had not been told these things before. They said if they had known maybe the people's uprising in 1988 would not have been so violent. That really opened my mind. People are very hungry. They want and are desperately looking for alternatives. I think that is one reason why the requests for nonviolence training are increasing."

A defining moment for Shelley Anderson was when "two young women from Sierra Leone, both refugees, came up to me and said, 'Learning about nonviolence has changed my life. Now, I know what I am supposed to do, now I know what I can do.' They have gone back to Sierra Leone and they are doing a lot of nonviolence trainings. They are trainers now."

The Women Peacemaker Program (WPP) of the International Fellowship of Reconciliation (IFOR) attempts to bring awareness of gender into all of IFOR's work, to increase the nonviolent empowerment of women, and to promote and support women's peacemaking efforts in their countries and communities.

Netherlands

Neidonuo Angami

Naga Mothers Association (NMA)

Neidonuo Angami (born 1950), one of the founding members and former president of the Naga Mothers Association (NMA), has never known a peaceful life. She realized that the fierce fighting between the Naga underground army and the Indian security forces directly impacts the lives of mothers who lose their children to violence and resort to substance abuse in reaction to the conflict. So, she and other Naga mothers launched the Shed No More Blood campaign, which has proved to be a crucial link in the Naga peace process.

Neidonuo Angami was born at a time when Nagaland was ravaged by combat between the Naga underground army and Indian security forces. She spent her early childhood hiding in the dense jungles. The mother of three girls, Neidonuo is the driving force behind the NMA, which was formed in 1984, and of which she is one of the founding members and former president. In the late 1970s and the early 1980s, social problems in the state — especially alcoholism and drug addiction — had become severe. Neidonuo and a few mothers, while meeting to share their concerns, felt very strongly that mothers suffer the most in conflict situations, and that there ought to be a common platform for them.

Neidonuo's signal contribution is the fillip her activities have given the peace process. She launched the Shed No More Blood campaign, which led to a meeting between various Naga underground groups and the NMA. Neidonuo and her colleagues often virtually inserted themselves between warring factions and risked becoming victims. In the long run, however, these trust-building meetings have helped the government and the underground leaders to keep extending the ceasefire. Another remarkable initiative was the Journey of Conscience, a people-to-people dialogue in 2000. Neidonuo was involved with it from its conception through execution and completion. About 70 Nagas traveled to New Delhi to meet civil society groups, officials, and other concerned people. They felt that colloquy must go beyond negotiating rooms, and that people on both sides must get fully involved in the peace process.

With no professional skills or support, Neidonuo and her colleagues have built up a successful peace initiative. Today, Naga women have a role in the peace process between the state agencies and the nonstate army.

The prolonged and sustained half-century-long Naga political standoff with the Indian government has resulted in killings, displacements, militarization, and economic disparities. The conflict and tension have also led to incredible levels of alcoholism and drug abuse in Nagaland.

India

Sevim Arbana

Useful to Albanian Women (UAW)
Woman Bridge for Peace and Understanding

Sevim Arbana, born 1951, was one of the first activists of the democratic movement in Albania and the founder of the organization Useful to Albanian Women (UAW). She is also a human rights activist who supports groups in need and was a founder of the peace movement, Woman Bridge for Peace and Understanding, in the Balkans.

During the transition period to democracy, Sevim Arbana was one of the first activists of the democratic movement in Albania. In 1993, she founded the NGO Useful to Albanian Women (UAW). Under her leadership, many important projects were initiated that later on would influence Albanian society, including a rehabilitation center for street children, a campaign against trafficking of Albanian girls and women, and the first Women's Club in Albania. A human rights activist, she supports marginalized women, poor and homeless children, and the elderly.

In 1997, she was elected president of the NGO Forum, the first umbrella NGO in the country. As such, she led the movement for peace and development. The building of a greenhouse by a women's NGO was her idea — an idea that brought a great message of peace in time of war. The flowers were donated and given as gifts at concerts and activities as well as to the President of Albania. During the Kosovo war her organization supported 3800 Kosovo Albanians with food, shelter, and other humanitarian aid, and showed that women know how to combine devotion and professionalism, simplicity and sincerity in all their actions. After the end of the Kosovo war, having successfully cooperated with other feminist groups, Sevim Arbana — together with a friend and Women in Black — initiated a "Woman Bridge for Peace and Understanding" between the different ethnic groups in Serbia, Montenegro, Macedonia, Kosovo, and Albania. United and working together the different women groups became closer. They all know and understand that women in the Balkans are in a similar situation: they are violated, they are poor, they were raped and have no voice, and yet, they are tolerant and have many ideas and the passion to fight for changes.

Albania is a country devastated from years of dictatorship and mass poverty. After opening to the world in the 1990s, the old structures, standards, and systems collapsed finally. Corruption, mafia infiltration of the economy and state, and violence are widespread.

Albania

Shanti Christine Arulampalam

Survivors Associated

As executive director of Survivors Associated, which works for the psychosocial healing of people affected by war, Shanti Christine Arulampalam has helped transform many formerly ravaged lives. She and her organization have assisted more than 27,000 people in four districts of northern and eastern Sri Lanka. As a Sinhala working among Tamils, Shanti has often been viewed with suspicion, but has won over her critics with her hard work and transparent approach.

After finishing her studies in business management, Shanti Christine Arulampalam taught English and mathematics in the Maldives for two years. She then returned to Sri Lanka to work as a business manager. In 1967, Shanti, who is a Sinhala, married a Tamil, but the marriage was not happy. She was left to take care of her two boys, and she went to work in a premier export house.

The event that changed Shanti's life was her gratuitous, inexplicable arrest by the police in 1986. Her surname, which was that of her estranged husband, had led to her being misidentified as a Tamil, and she was imprisoned. In jail, Shanti met many Tamil women and heard their stories of human rights abuses. Her influential Sinhala family tracked her down and secured her release, but her experience decided her life's course — to serve people affected by the ethnic conflict. Paradoxically, she felt that her Tamil surname might actually be helpful. From 1987 to 1989, several refugee camps were set up around her home in Colombo's suburbs. She subsequently worked for the Family Rehabilitation Centre, helping those whom the war had devastated. She developed programs of training and services in psychosocial care, working through young educated persons from conflict zones. They were designated "befrienders" and "counselors".

In 1996, she decided to set up her own organization, Survivors Associated, of which she is voluntary executive director. She and her organization have helped more than 27,000 people in four districts of northern and eastern Sri Lanka.

Internal displacement and the aftermath of family members joining State security or the LTTE (Liberation Tigers of Tamil Eelam) have led to noncombatant Sri Lankans experiencing systematic privations. The WHO has identified mental health as the most significant health issue in Sri Lanka.

Rosalba Ato Oywa

People's Voice for Peace (PVP)
Coalition for Peace in Africa (Copa)
Agency for Co-operation and Research in Development (Acord)

Rosalba Oywa, a 52-year-old widow from Gulu District in Northern Uganda, is the founding member and volunteer coordinator of People's Voice for Peace (PVP), a local NGO that assists victims of the war in Northern Uganda. Over a thousand women and men, the most vulnerable victims of the war, have benefited from her work since 1989. A teacher by profession and the mother of three boys and two girls, Rosalba also works at international level and sees it her mission "to turn vulnerable victims into peace agents".

Covered only in rags, the young teacher hastily grabbed her three children and ran one early morning in 1986. Fighting had broken out in Gulu, a rural town in Northern Uganda, between government forces and a rebel movement, in a war that continues until today. "I became destitute, living entirely on charity," Rosalba Oywa recalls. "But my bitter experience was a motivation to change the conflict situation, especially the life of the victims."

In 1988, the British Agency for Co-operation and Research in Development (Acord) employed Rosalba as a social worker. She was involved in peace building initiatives but she felt she needed to do more. The following year she mobilized women in a public demonstration demanding an end to the war, an activity that initiated a network for the peace process.

When concerned journalists documented women's experiences of the armed conflict in Northern Uganda, their stories brought back the memory of Rosalba Oywa's own experience. "This forced me to found People's Voice for Peace (PVP), a local NGO which supports the most vulnerable victims of war, particularly the sexually abused women, land mine victims, the maimed and mutilated." Currently, more than a thousand women and men are being assisted. They meet, share their horrible experiences and thus break the isolation each person suffers. PVP also secures funds for medical checkups and treatment, counseling services and support for income-generating projects. "The aim is to turn vulnerable victims into peace agents," says the courageous mother of five children.

Rosalba Oywa volunteers with PVP and works part-time for the Coalition for Peace in Africa (Copa) and as a freelance consultant for international organizations. "I do what I feel I should be doing," she says firmly with a winning smile.

Since 1986 the Lord's Resistance Army (LRA) has waged war against the Ugandan government. It claims to be fighting for a better life for the Acholi tribe in Northern Uganda. The LRA replenishes its ranks by abducting children. However, both sides of the conflict carry out atrocities.

Uganda

Zuleikhan Bagalova

LAM — Center for Complex Research and Popularization of Chechen Culture

Zuleikhan Bagalova (born 1945) is a leading actress of the Chechen theater. She holds the titles People's Actress of Checheno-Ingushetia and Distinguished Actress of the Russian Federation. For her theatrical achievements, she was awarded the order Symbol of Honor. Zuleikhan already began her social activities in Soviet times. She was three times elected to the Supreme Council of Chechen-Ingushetia. Since 1995, she has been directing the LAM Center which focuses on reviving Chechen culture, providing humanitarian aid, and taking a stand against the war in Chechnya.

The Chechen theater was Zuleikhan's life. And she herself was the main heroine and director of the drama. She has always had many friends and admirers. The war turned her sunny city of Grozny into a pile of rubble, and her audience had either died or been dispersed over the four corners of the world. During the dreadful hours of bombing and artillery fire, she wanted to stay with the living and to live completely differently, to love the whole world, and to cherish every moment. When she went out into the streets, she no longer recognized her city and its people: these were different faces, gray, sullen, and unhappy.

Zuleikhan felt like doing something to change this distressing life, to breathe color and joy into it. She conceived the idea of uniting the forces of many people — writers, students, doctors, and actors — to revive and popularize Chechen culture. The LAM Center was born. The first major projects of the organization were the video film 'Vaynakh Songs' and the book 'Chechnya: The Right of Culture.'

But then a new, even bloodier war broke out. Zuleikhan had to leave for Ingushetia. Her hometown, the theater, old friends — everything was left behind in this dreadful war. In Chechnya, it was dangerous not only to talk about anything in public, not to mention to protest, but also simply to live. In Ingushetia, a new life began for Zuleikhan. And she decided to dedicate it to those people who had stayed in Chechnya, to the refugees, and to the victims of war. The LAM Center continued its activities and took a very determined anti-war stand. The organization was one of the first to publicly announce its anti-war position, support refugees in court, carry out humanitarian activities, and publish an anti-war bulletin. Behind all this stood the well-known actress and peace activist Zuleikhan Bagalova.

Together with like-minded people, Zuleikhan Bagalova has founded the LAM Center, which conducts humanitarian and anti-war activities, and zealously works to revive the national culture of the Chechen people, who have suffered greatly as a result of the Russian-Chechen wars.

Russian Federation

Macaria Barai

Women In Peace-building Network (WIPNET)
Chamber of Commerce of Guinea-Bissau
Citoyens de bonne volonté

A national of Guinea-Bissau, Madame Macaria Barai is very devoted and always available to give people her time. Having studied in Guinea-Bissau and Portugal, today she lives with her mother and her children and has 15 years of experience in fighting for peace on the one hand and on the other hand fighting for the emancipation of Guinea-Bissau women. She is a very pious woman who is widely respected nationally. Her work is highly regarded by the archbishop of Guinea-Bissau and his office.

Madame Macaria understands that one can use religion in an effective way to create a culture of peace. Her religion, therefore, is an instrument of peace. She has not stopped supporting, as a leader of a Catholic religious association, the victims of internal conflicts. Conflicts that paralyzed Guinea-Bissau under its former presidents. She assisted refugees in the conflicts of Casamance (Senegal) that fled Senegal for Guinea-Bissau and she was at the heart of the negotiations and inter-community talks as well as annual meetings between groups from neighboring countries and those of her country with religious leaders. After the military coup against the former president, she became involved with the leaders of the Economic Community of West African States (Cedeao) to convince them to renounce a takeover of power and to install an interim civil president.

Being involved in the management of internal conflicts is not typical in a country of Mandingue traditions where women do not have a decision-making role in the matters of the community. But the reputation of this woman leader and her religion in her country meant that she was accepted by all. Through her, Guinea-Bissau women have mobilized themselves within several peace associations that have worked to establish a dialogue between the civil populations and central power. She worked, at the same time, with people at the borders of Guinea-Bissau and neighboring countries to involve themselves in the resolution of the conflicts of the region. Her immense work serves as model since it is now accepted that a woman may be more credible in management of the important portfolios in Guinea-Bissau.

Madame Macaria Barai stands out in a poor country that has seen mutinies, military coups and the effects of conflicts in Casamance (Senegal).

Guinea-Bissau

Léonie Barakomeza

Twishakira amahoro
Search for Common Ground Burundi

After civil war had broken out in Burundi, Léonie Barakomeza founded — together with former Hutu neighbor Yvonne Ryakiye and other women — the self-help organization Twishakira amahoro, which means "We want peace". The women of the peace organisation have helped in reconstructing war-damaged houses.

Léonie Barakomeza, born in 1946, and her family were driven out of her village of Musaga by marauding Hutus because she was a Tutsi. The ethnic groups entrenched themselves on either side of the Kanyosha river. She and her former Hutu neighbor Yvonne Ryakiye gathered the courage and crossed the river in order to visit each other.

This break of a strong taboo was the first step to a rapprochement of the warring parties. Over time, the Kanyosha river has dug a deep gorge through the fertile hills of Bujumbura. An equally deep rift of fear and hatred hindered the people living on its banks to use the shallow ford near Busoro. Léonie was one of the Tutsis who had been forced to flee across the river when the slaughter began in 1994. The warring parties entrenched themselves on either side of the river, which was considered a natural boundary. But Leonie refused to accept the situation of mounting tension, and she and her former neighbour Yvonne Ryakije dared to cross the river and visit each other. When they remained unharmed, other people followed their example.

"Our men didn't like this," remembers Léonie, "but when they saw that the Hutu women brought us food and that we started to repair our houses together, they accepted our action." Together with Ryakiye and other women, she founded Twishakira amahoro. Thanks to their initiative, the Tutsi and Hutu refugees were able to return to their villages, where the women of the peace organization help them reconstruct their war-damaged houses. Léonie says, "There is still a lot to do. Human rights are not respected in Burundi; people starve or are robbed and murdered." Her vision is that peace will one day prevail in Burundi. Although she knows that this goal is still far from being achieved, she is no longer afraid.

In 1993 civil war broke out in Burundi between the Tutsi and the Hutu ethnic groups, claiming over 200,000 lives. There are still many refugees living in neighboring countries or displaced within the country. Many villages remain destroyed and the fields of Bujumbura are full of landmines.

Burundi

Marguerite Barankitse

Maison Shalom

During the genocide of 1993/94, Marguerite "Maggy" Barankitse saved thousands of children from death or abduction at great personal risk. Her Maison Shalom has become an island of peace in a strife-torn country.

Marguerite Barankitse is dedicated to ending hatred and violence. With the financial help that she secured abroad, she has founded several villages in which Hutu and Tutsi orphans are working together and where they also learn to protect themselves against Aids.

Maggy is laughing and crying at the same time. The students of the YCEE School in Ruyigi organized a welcome celebration in her honor, presenting her with a picture that they painted. Maggy, the most famous alumni and teacher of this school, had just returned from the US, where she received the Four Freedoms Award of the Franklin and Eleanor Roosevelt Institute, together with UN General Secretary Kofi Annan. But she values the painting even more, which depicts her in the middle of many children. "We have stuck together to life during the worst times," is her summary of a situation which can hardly be put in words. She owes her international fame, which was acknowledged by the Children's Nobel Prize and the North-South Award, to a terrible incident. In October 1993 she witnessed the massacre of 72 people. She saved 25 children. She says: "In this night I became father and mother of 25 children abandoned in the middle of a bloody war. They gave me the courage to hang on." At a time when hatred, fear and violence ruled the country, she relentlessly worked for the salvation of Tutsi and Hutu children. With finances from donors, Maggy has built Maison Shalom, a haven of peace and hope, which has saved thousands of lives. Young orphaned Hutus and Tutsis live and work together in Maison Shalom, learning agricultural or trade skills. Maggy says she has renounced marriage in order to dedicate her life to the education of children.

Since 1993, more than 200,000 people have died in the war in Burundi and thousands others have been displaced. Some refugees have returned to their villages. The only chance for lasting peace is the reconciliation of the Hutus and Tutsis.

Burundi

Sushobha Barve

Centre for Dialogue and Reconciliation

For more than two decades, Sushobha Barve (born 1949) has been working tirelessly, often without any organizational support, to create dialogue and reconciliation in conflict-stricken areas. Her philosophy is based on the need for reconciliation, whether it is in Maharashtra, Bihar, Sri Lanka, or Jammu and Kashmir. Sushobha believes that people do not need state agencies to solve their problems.

Sushobha Barve's lifelong work on peace and conflict resolution began with her firsthand experience of communal violence during the 1984 riots. The anti-Sikh riots (which followed the then prime minister Indira Gandhi's assassination by her Sikh bodyguards) sensitized her to the trauma of the victims of violence, and the need to help the so-called dominant group, which inflicted the violence. But her work has not been limited to one region—wherever there is conflict, a need for peace-building and reconciliation, she is there. Sushobha has worked to create dialogue and reconciliation between Hindus and Muslims in the communal-conflagration areas of Maharashtra, like Mumbai, Bhiwandi, and Malegaon. She set up the Mumbai Mohalla Committee Movement Trust in 1992, and mobilized a citizens' police force, which keeps communal irruptions in check. She believes that where citizens take the lead, state agencies do not need to intervene.

Sushobha now spends much of her time in Jammu and Kashmir, where she has set up several innovative women's empowerment and peace initiatives such as peace education training for teachers. She has also set up interregional, intercommunity, and intracommunity dialogue between Hindus and Muslims, and Kashmiris and residents of Jammu.

For Sushobha, a single woman, working in conflict-ridden areas carries its own baggage. Most of her ventures into high-risk areas have been personally driven because organizations are unwilling to take the responsibility that attends such excursions. At the end of the day, though, Sushobha's sensitive and democratic approach to conflict resolution has helped her reach out and build bridges where none were thought possible.

India has a long history of communal violence: postpartition riots in 1947; anti-Sikh riots in 1984; riots after the Babri Masjid demolition by Hindu right-wing stormtroopers in 1992. Jammu and Kashmir is even more complex, being the focus of political maneuvering by India and Pakistan.

India

Cynthia Basinet

Actress, model, and singer Cynthia Basinet understood the power of the internet to connect people when the medium rocketed her song "Santa Baby" around the world. The empowerment and self-determination she experienced prompted her to seek new connections in new ways. In May 2001 she sang for a different audience — refugees living in the western Sahara desert. More than 80 percent women and children, 200,000 refugees are struggling to survive in the southwest corner of Algeria. Their refusal to return home and their fight for self-determination captured the attention of Cynthia Basinet.

Growing up in San Jose, California, Cynthia sang and played the flute and saxophone as a child. Her life has been a succession of journeys. In 1984, she and her infant son left San Francisco and an abusive husband to spend five years in Europe, and there she learned more about world issues. In Paris she learned to speak fluent French, studied cinematography, and became a successful model. Cynthia returned to Los Angeles with an expanded vision and a determination to become socially active.

Her goal in visiting the Saharawis was to help communicate their value to the world. "We are all linked," she said. "The strength and conviction of the Saharawis is something that deserves to be highlighted in the conscience of not only America, but the world. The same issues of power apply to the 85 percent working class that makes up America."

She was moved by the connection she felt to the Saharawis. "I hit this note, and all the women started warbling. You know, that Arabic sound the women make. It was the most healing moment in my life."

Some 200,000 Saharawi nomads were living in refugee camps in Algeria when Spain withdrew from the Western Sahara following the death of military dictator Francisco Franco. Before Cynthia's visit, few outsiders knew of the plight of these Saharawians who were seeking self-determination.

United States of America

Lyubov Baskhanova

Informational Analytical Center
Administration of the Government of the Chechen Republic

Lyubov Baskhanova was born in the suburbs of Grozny. In 1989, she obtained a degree in Psychology from Leningrad University and, in 2002, a degree in Business Administration after studying in Makhachkala. In 2004, she defended her thesis at Rostov State University, receiving a PhD in Sociology. Lyubov has worked as lecturer at Grozny Institutes and University departments, and headed the Informational Analytical Center under the Presidential Administration of Chechnya. Since 2000, she has been working in the Chechen Administration conducting sociological research in the zone of conflict.

Lyubov Baskhanova never ignores the interests of ordinary people. In 2000, Lyubov risked her life by preventing the shooting down of a column of refugees on the Achkha-Martanov section of the road from Rostov (Russia) to Baku (Azerbaijan). Lyubov and her colleagues were conducting a sociological survey, accompanying a group of 120 refugees from Chechnya. There were 85 women and children in the group. The column was stopped by federal forces. Two of the soldiers opened fire at the trucks with the refugees on board, then a machine gun on one of the armored vehicles started shooting at the entire column. When Lyubov saw what was happening, she ran to one of the soldiers and tried to snatch the gun from his hands. The soldiers were so surprised that they immediately stopped fire. This gave just enough time for one of the officers, who was the highest in rank, to realize that the people jumping off the trucks were unarmed. He ordered the firing to cease. However, two of the troops — who had recovered from their surprise and felt extremely angry at Lyubov's unexpected intervention — started beating her up. Later, a criminal lawsuit was filed against her for attacking soldiers and attempting to acquire weapons. Lyubov does not regret her purely impulsive actions, since they were the only means by which the massacre of innocent people could be prevented. Later, in an interview with a local newspaper, Lyubov confessed that it was only on this day that she finally and fully understood what peace activism meant: a constant risk, like walking on a cliff. After this episode, Lyubov continued her sociological research on the territory of Chechnya despite the ongoing hostilities, trying to shape future models for a peaceful settlement to the conflict.

Lyubov Baskhanova organizes aid to refugees and conducts surveys in Chechnya which show the real picture of the conflict and shape a platform for the negotiation process. She works in contact with the authorities, trying to influence their policies and to help the victims of the war.

Russian Federation

Eve's work has benefited women, children and victims of armed conflicts – the entire population of the Great Lakes Region. Women are now more involved in preventing and managing conflicts.

Eve Bazaiba Masudi

Women as Partners for Peace in Africa (Woppa)

Eve Bazaiba Masudi (39) has been active since 1995 in the Democratic Republic of Congo (DRC), working in human rights issues, international negotiation, and recently as a member of Women as Partners for Peace in Africa (Woppa). She advocates non-violence, dialogue, tolerance and humility through training and sensitizing women, to promote citizenship and republican values. She has no institutional support and is often incapacitated in her work.

Eve Bazaiba Masudi works within a global vision of peace, surpassing tribalism. She doubles as a university student and an activist and holds a diploma in international relations. As a Muslim, Eve Bazaiba has struck a balance between Christian and Muslim education.

Her work involves regularly contacting fighting factions in the conflict areas and holding late-night meetings. Her quest for consensus motivates her: an involvement made without any personal gains or expectations. It is remarkable to note that she uses what is available and has no institutional support. She is nationally recognized, yet she lives a modest life believing in peace, dialogue, democracy, cooperation and collaboration, respect of women and children's rights, tolerance, prosperity and development. But she is often challenged in her work by corruption, prejudices, backward customs, and discrimination against women.

Woppa works in eight countries. It aims at reinforcing power and capacity of women in Africa, and particularly in the Great Lakes Region. Eve Bazaida's work has undeniably benefited women, children and victims of armed conflicts, fighting factions and the entire population of the Great Lakes Region. Women are now more involved in preventing and managing conflicts. Numerous organisations similar to Woppa have emerged in the east of the region — thanks to Eve Bazaiba's efforts. Today, the Congolese men and women, specifically those living in the eastern part of the country, understand the importance of the pacific resolution of conflicts and cohabitation, as well as the utility of the interstate good-neighborhood policy.

The DRC is still implementing the peace agreement signed among warlords. Warring factions frustrate human rights activists' work in order to keep their control and power over the local population.

Democratic Republic of the Congo

Yolanda Becerra Vega

Popular Feminine Organization (OFP)

Yolanda Becerra is as old as the civil war that devastates Colombia and has destroyed the life of Barrancabermeja, the oil city, where she was born. It has a strategic position and is the subject of a dispute between the armed forces. From there, Yolanda leads the Popular Feminine Organization, a social and political movement that brings together women who refuse to give their families up to death. They resist, with great courage, to the constant threat of crime and terror brought about by the paramilitary campaigns.

Yolanda Becerra was born in 1959, in Barrancabermeja, Colombia, in the midst of the armed conflict between the guerrilla and military and paramilitary forces. She began as an adolescent with teaching people to read and write in the community parish churches, inspired by the Theology of Liberation. In 1980, she entered the Popular Feminine Organization (OFP), created originally by the Church, for women who plied the sex trade and who had come to the region to entertain the men working in the oil trade. The war transformed the organization into a political and spiritual refuge for mothers who had lost their families in the conflict.

In 1988, she was elected director of the OFP. Year after year she has been mobilizing efforts against the anguish spread by the paramilitary forces: "They came, murdered a woman and inscribed on her body the words 'Mother of a guerrilla.' In 2000, we began with the campaign 'Let's react to fear with love.' We discovered that fear could be transformed into organization, solidarity and resistance, and we discovered that it no longer had the power to paralyze us."

Since then, Yolanda and the activists of the OFP have received death threats and some of its leaders have been murdered. "When we buried them, we felt that we gained the strength to resist." International Peace Brigades support the activity of the OFP and are at Yolanda's side 24 hours a day. "We have been libertarians in the midst of an institutionalization committed to killing. We have been able to be free and to build our lives amidst the anguish and the bullets. When a woman comes to us with her pain, it is as if we have known her for a long time."

Colombia is the scene of an armed conflict: the popular guerrilla forces confronting the national military and paramilitary forces. The warlike tactics used by the government to pacify the region have militarized society and have obliged poor families to give up their children to death.

Colombia

Kiran Bedi

Kiran Bedi (born 1949) is India's best-known woman police officer. In a ferociously male bastion, Kiran, with her firm footing, has been using the police service as a medium for social change. She sees prisons and jails as an opportunity to bring criminals back to society's fold, reversing the dehumanization for which prisons are known. She began meditation classes and education and vocational training programs for prison inmates and put in place an unprecedented democratic panchayat system in prisons.

Kiran Bedi, one of India's best-known female cops, is exemplary for using the much-demonized police service as a vehicle for social change. This was not an easy thing to do. Over the years, Kiran has built a rock-solid reputation for being entirely intolerant of dishonesty and favoritism. While supporting and protecting junior officers from the claw of politics, she ensures their accountability both to herself and to the public. Her approach to people who commit crimes is constructive rather than punitive. Her open-door policy and belief in transparency have helped change the dynamics of official accountability in India.

Kiran envisions prisons as an opportunity to bring criminals back into the societal fold. When she took over as inspector of general prisons in New Delhi in 1993, she began literacy and education programs for prison inmates; she set up a system whereby prisoners could receive vocational training and work to earn wages; she also set up a panchayat system, where inmates could meet every evening with senior officials to sort out their problems. What won her national and international acclaim were the Yogic Vipassana meditation classes for prisoners. But her incorruptible inflexibility took its toll — she was not allowed to last long in any assignment. This vested victimization she took in stride, continuing to live by her own stringent standards.

Kiran and her work have become a benchmark in the nascent imprisonment-and-rehabilitation process in the country. Hers is the voice of the incarcerated and the forgotten in India's gargantuan and Byzantine prison system.

There are 304,893 prisoners in Indian jails, 225,817 of whom are awaiting trial, many of them innocent. Women account for about 3.5 percent of the prison population. Many prisons are still seen as inhuman institutions — they are overcrowded by 31.19 percent — that end up brutalizing their inmates.

India

Medea Benjamin

Global Exchange
Code Pink: Women for Peace

Medea Benjamin, a powerful force in human rights activism, has struggled for justice in Asia, the Americas, and Africa for more than 20 years. Her mission as founding director of Global Exchange has been to make labor and environmental concerns more important than corporate profits. After September 11, she mobilized thousands of women when she cofounded the peace group, Code Pink: Women for Peace. Believing in the power of people-to-people communication to change the course of war, she organized delegations of families to travel to Afghanistan and Iraq.

"How do you know when darkness is over? When you can see the face of your brother or sister in everyone you pass." This saying became real for Medea Benjamin when she saw the light in the face of a six-year-old boy, Mohammed, during one of her post-September 11 visits to Iraq. She and her delegation gave food and medicine to Mohammed, who suffered from leukemia, a disease on the rise in Iraq following years of US bombs that have polluted the soil and water with depleted uranium. "Mohammed, who has every reason to be sad, mistrustful, and angry, has nothing but a smile for the world," Medea writes. "What Mohammed needs is not food or even medicine — he needs to be spared."

By linking ordinary American families with ordinary Iraqis, Medea Benjamin has made it possible for many people to "see the face of their brother and sister," and to tell and retell their stories. In 2002, she went to Afghanistan with four Americans who had lost loved ones in the September 11 attack to meet with Afghanis who had lost relatives during the US bombing of their country. Their extraordinary journey received such international attention that the US government was pressured to discuss civilian causalities and to create a compensation fund for Afghan victims. Closer to home, she mobilized to join a four-month vigil in front of the White House.

Medea believes that issues of fair trade and peace are closely tied, and has used her organization, Global Exchange, to lobby on issues such as sweatshop conditions, the role of big energy companies in California's energy crisis, universal health care, and the necessity of a living wage for all.

After September 11, there was a virulent pro-war climate in the USA. People who criticized US policy were labeled un-American and unpatriotic. Some, like Medea, received death threats and were arrested for antiwar protests. Mistrust of Americans made traveling dangerous.

United States of America

Yusra Berberi

Palestinian Women's Union (PWU)

Born in 1923 in Gaza, Palestine, Yusra Berbari began a successful teaching career. Raised in a scholarly renowned family, she was educated at the Schmidt School in Jerusalem. Yusra speaks three foreign languages beside her Arabic mother tongue and is the first women in the Gaza Strip to hold an accademic degree, a BA in Social Sciences which she received from Cairo University in 1949. She is now the head of the Palestinian Women's Union (PWU) in Gaza.

Yusra Berbari played a crucial role in social, political and educational activities in the Gaza Strip. After graduation, she began a teaching career and later became the headmistress of the only girls' preparatory school in Gaza, where she set up a teacher training program for women, which evolved into an Institute for women teachers. Yusra headed the women's branch of the Gaza Open University, was the only women in the Palestinian delegation to the UN in 1963 and one of the few women members of the Palestinian National Council (PNC) in 1964. Since 1964, she has been the head of the Palestinian Women's Union (PWU) in the Gaza Strip and she helped to found ten illiteracy-fighting centers. Since 1972, Yusra has been a member of the board of directors of the Red Crescent Society, and she has continued to provide assistance to the needy and the families of Palestinian detainees and politically activist prisoners.

An an active participant in non-violent resistance against the Israeli occupation, joining demonstrations and sit-ins and preparing memorandums on national issues, Yusra also participated in the first committee of the new women's movement in 1978. She was tried before an Israeli court on the claim that she organized sewing classes and ran English language teaching sessions, activities that the court ruled to be provocative against the Israeli occupation. The court verdict was to ban her from traveling for a number of years. Yusra is a dedicated and self-motivated person, with a distinguished record of educational and nationalist achievements. At a young age, she launched a fund raising appeal to collect money for the wounded Palestinians, and she worked with the Red Crescent Society during the Second World War. In 1948, she gave aid and shelter to Palestinian refugees. Later, she became a member of the National Rehabilitation Society for the disabled in Gaza.

For nearly six decades, Palestinians have suffered in appalling conditions. In the course of the British Mandate, which began in 1919, in the ensuing Jewish immigration and sale of the Palestinian land between 1936 and 1939, Yusra Berberi became active in politics and women's affairs in Gaza.

Occupied Palestinian Territory

Natalya Berezhnaya

Ravenstvo i mir — ARM (Equality and Peace)
Zhenschiny Moskvy (Women of Moscow)
Women's International League for Peace and Freedom (Wilpf)

Natalya Berezhnaya was born in 1930. Since the 1950s, she has been involved in the areas of peace building, gender equality, and conflict resolution. She has always been active in various Soviet and Russian women's organizations and has worked for the UN. Her recent activism focuses on the elimination of violence against women, on women trafficking and domestic violence, as well as women's contribution to conflict resolution and disarmament. She has a particular interest in bringing about peace in the Caucasus. The success of her efforts is reflected in the numerous awards she has received.

Natalya Berezhnaya was just 12 years old when, during World War II, she was evacuated with her family from Stalingrad to the small town of Krasny Kut. Everyone was suffering from hunger. One day, her mother, a very kind and gentle person, gave a captured German soldier a piece of bread. Some women who witnessed this exclaimed angrily: "They kill our husbands and sons!" Yet they were silenced and shamed when her mother calmly replied: "But they too are somebody's husbands and children."

Memories of childhood often leave lasting traces in people's lives. So, too, in Natalya's life. This experience, amongst others, triggered her activism in women's and peace movements, and today she is a shining star in the women's movement of Russia. She is a historian by training, a philosopher by conviction, a mother, grandmother, and a true friend. Battling on various fronts, Natalya pays special attention to the most pressing problems of domestic violence, women trafficking, and gender inequality. Her lectures in different cities across Russia are usually attended by many, since she is not only an intellectual, but also has a strong sense of humor and has remained youthful and witty. Natalya's memorable words and phrases are frequently quoted, and some have even attained the status of 'classics.' Many people turn to her for advice and to find answers to their questions because they trust her. On the local level, Natalya is not only a committed member of the Women of Moscow, but also regularly takes an active part in the cultural and sport events that are organized by the Central Sport Club Spartak on International Women's Day on 8 March. Despite her global outlook, Natalya is an ardent patriot. She is committed to the humanistic ideals that shaped so much of Russia's history. She is an advocate of negotiations as opposed to violent confrontation.

Natalya Berezhnaya focuses her activities on combating gender discrimination in Russia. She gives lectures, takes part in conferences both in Russia and abroad, and often represents Russia's interests at international events promoting women's rights and peaceful settlement of conflicts.

Russian Federation

Ana Teresa Bernal

Red Nacional de Iniciativas por la Paz y contra la Guerra (Redepaz)

When Ana Teresa Bernal was an adolescent, she distributed food to children living on the streets. As a young woman, she continued her social work and created a movement called Life. Later, as a woman, she founded Redepaz, the National Network of Citizen Initiatives against War. Her personal fight is against war. She dreams of a Colombia at peace. She has been working, day after day, for more than two decades to achieve this. "I believe that this is our country and that we have to defend life."

Ana Teresa Bernal's voice does not cry out in the wilderness. It is not heard in vain. Her voice was noticed for the first time in 1986, when she created a movement called Life. Later on, her voice was heard even more loudly when she founded Redepaz, the National Network of Citizen Initiatives against War. "It was formed in 1993 as the citizens' answer to the president of Colombia at that time, César Gaviria. He proposed what was called an integral war. We said that what the country needed was integral peace."

And Ana Teresa Bernal went more over when, in 1996, Redepaz organized what became known as the Mandato Ciudadano por la Paz (Mandate against Violence). They asked boys and girls from more than a hundred municipalities all over Colombia to choose, from 12 fundamental rights, the one they considered to be the most important. Then, 2.7 million children voted for the right to peace. Their voices were heard all over the country. One year later, Redepaz organized a new vote when more than ten million adult Colombians called for the same thing.

Each year, in Colombia, approximately 30,000 people die. According to the United Nations, more than 1 million inhabitants have been displaced by the war and thousands have been killed or remain missing. The country has been devastated by armed conflict for more than three decades.

Colombia

Zalpa Bersanova

The International Center for Chechen Studies (ICCS)

Zalpa Bersanova was born into the big family of the famous Chechen writer Bersanov. Holder of a PhD in Ethnology, she is renowned for her sociological research on aspects of the Chechen culture. She is the author of several books promoting reconciliation and analyzing the consequences of the Russian-Chechen wars. After a series of meetings at scientific conferences in the USA (2004 and 2005), together with like-minded researchers, she created the International Center for Chechen Studies, which contributes to an unbiased approach for the enhanced understanding of the Chechen issue.

When the Russian-Chechen war broke out, in 1994, Zalpa Bersanova was working on her PhD thesis at Moscow State University (MGU). Shocked by the incoming news, she spent entire days at home watching TV. Grozny was being bombarded by the Russian Air Force, and innocent civilians were dying in their homes and in the streets. She understood that she could not remain idle. First she took part in the protest meetings; then she began to write articles and books about the war. She said to herself that if at least one person read what she wrote and if that person took a stand against the war, it would mean that she had succeeded in making her small contribution to stopping the bloody nightmare.

Together with the other misfortunes the war has wrought, it has also inflicted upon the Chechen people a deep moral trauma. The Russian mass media often try to represent the Chechens as ancestral bandits capable of doing nothing other than stealing, committing murder, and kidnapping.

For several years now, Zalpa has been doing research on the spiritual values of the present-day Chechens. Her findings convincingly prove that the Chechen people have a considerable positive potential even after the inhumane tragedy of war. They still maintain their faith in human compassion and in their traditional ideals. In 1999, Zalpa Bersanova presented her research in a lecture held in the Sakharov Museum (Moscow) and, in 2004 and 2005, she participated in a series of conferences in the USA on the issues of war and peace. It was there that she conceived the idea of consolidating the efforts of all those doing research on the Chechen culture in order to help stop the violence. Together with her fellow researchers, Zalpa founded the International Center for Chechen Studies (ICCS), striving to make the world see the real face of the Chechen people, their history, and rich spiritual culture.

Zalpa Bersanova writes books and does sociological research on the consequences of the Russian-Chechen war. In the framework of the International Center for Chechen Studies (ICCS), founded in 2005, she is trying to find support and to promote peace in the Caucasus.

Russian Federation

Sharon Bhagwan-Rolls

Young Women's Christian Association (YWCA)
National Council of Women (NCW)

Sharon Bhagwan-Rolls (38) gained national prominence in Fiji by organizing, through the National Council of Women, a daily prayer vigil when government leaders were held hostage for 56 days during the 2000 coup. She now produces the monthly e-news bulletin "FemLINKpacific," originally to give voice to women affected by the coup and a quarterly magazine "femTALK 1325" covering women's peace initiatives and post-conflict needs in the region and advocating for UN Security Council Resolution 1325 implementation. She also runs FemTALK 89.2FM, a monthly mobile women's community radio service.

"When I was trying to leave Fiji in August 1987 to attend the YWCA World Council meeting in Phoenix, Arizona, I was detained by police at the airport. Later, a Fijian woman from Namoli Village who was a domestic worker for my parents, apologized to my parents for having inadvertently provided information about my travel plans to a man who had come to drink yagona at her village the night before. The incident illustrated how women's networks can be used. I have come to appreciate the importance of women's networks in early warning systems for conflict prevention. Women are sources of information around peace and security matters. They are often asked for information about other women in their networks and it is important that they develop safe forms of communication with one another. Women have so many women's groups and clubs. We can use our own networks to get word out and to be able to secure ourselves, and to give counseling and support in situations of violence or conflict. I began to think a lot about how women could use their networks to do conflict prevention work, and whether we could use community radio as a conduit for that, for teaching that."

1987, democratic rule in Fiji was interrupted by two military coups, caused by concern over a government perceived as dominated by the Indo-Fijian (Indian) community. After a new constitution in 1990 and free and peaceful elections in 1999 there was another coup led by a hardline Fijian nationalist, in 2000. Democracy was restored towards the end of 2000.

Fiji

Anat Biletzki

The Israeli Information Center for Human Rights in the Occupied Territories (B'Tselem)

Professor Anat Biletzki is a leading human rights activist. She is chairperson of the board of the B'Tselem and has been involved in peace-building projects in Israel for over 25 years. She stands firm in her uncompromising defense of Palestinian human rights and desire to educate the Israeli public to respect human rights. Biletzki's academic and public work is intertwined to mobilize and accompany the constant commitment to these pursuits.

Professor Biletzki was voted chairperson of the board of B'Tselem, the Israeli Information Center for Human Rights in the Occupied Territories, a few months after the start of the current Intifada (Palestinian Uprising). A steep deterioration in human rights was accompanied by a polarization of Israeli and Palestinian societies, increasing support among Israelis for harsh measures against the Palestinians and increasing hostility towards anything relating to human rights. This reality posed — and still poses — a great challenge to B'Tselem and its goal of protecting human rights and generating any sort of commitment to human rights in Israeli societies. The board of B'Tselem views these agendas as crucial for progress in developing a climate conducive to peace.

In this context of furthering any activity that will promote peace, not only via human rights, Biletzki has also been vocal in the academic arena, working with faculties at Tel Aviv University to raise anti-occupation voices on campus. Several years of such work have now brought about a change in students' attitudes, with a new Coalition of Anti-Occupation Student Movements becoming active in these very issues. Since B'Tselem serves as a model for professional human rights research and documentation, other organizations look to it for trustworthy and reliable information. In her educational endeavors the B'Tselem mouthpiece has assisted in furthering human rights awareness in universities in Israel. Several symposia, conferences and workshops have taken place during the past few years, all dealing with human rights and the consequences of the occupation. As chairperson of B'Tselem, Biletzki views herself as representing the organization in all contexts and all circumstances.

Professor Biletzki became chairperson of the board of B'Tselem in 2001, a few months after the start of the Intifada. A steep deterioration in human rights accompanied a polarization of Israeli and Palestinian societies, resulting in harsh measures against the Palestinians.

Israel

Mirjana Bilopavlovic

Delfin
Women's Club Pakrac (WCP)

Mirjana Bilopavlovic began her peace work in 1994, during the war in Croatia. After the war, she worked in the Center for Social Work for refugees and coordinated the activities of the Women's Club in war-torn Pakrac. The Club encouraged women's empowerment through awareness campaigns and community action. Since 2001, she has coordinated the biggest network of women's organizations in Croatia. In 2002, she co-founded Delfin, an organization that provides health care and counseling to women. Throughout these activities, she has actively promoted peace, reconciliation, and tolerance.

Mirjana Bilopavlovic's engagement as an activist, pacifist, and feminist began when a group of young people came to the Volunteer Project Pakrac through the Anti-War Campaign of Croatia in 1994. During the peace training courses, MIRamiDA and MIRamiDA PLUS, Mirjana learned how to live and work in a war-torn town, burdened with nationalistic sentiments. It was difficult to be a member of a NGO in Pakrac at that time, especially a women's NGO. With support of young people from other countries, Mirjana and her colleagues established the Women's Club Pakrac (WCP). She was the coordinator of the club from 1997 to 2002, therefore, responsible for almost everything: organizing the work of the association, writing project proposals, maintaining contacts with potential donors, local authorities, and other associations. This NGO was the first to publicly promote peace, reconciliation, and tolerance.

When the Women's Club Pakrac was established in 1994, its first activity was a community laundromat. It also encouraged women's empowerment through awareness campaigns, public discussions, and community action. Soon the Club joined the Women's Network, the biggest network of women's organizations in Croatia, participating in and co-creating all its major campaigns, especially those related to political empowerment, reproductive health, and gender education. Since 2003, Mirjana is in charge of the SOS hotline for victims of violence, addicts, persons affected by post-trauma stress, displaced persons, and refugees. She is also a co-leader of the Advisory Center for girls, pregnant women, and mothers.

Pakrac was one of the most devastated towns in the recent Croatian war, with more than 70 percent of its houses damaged or destroyed. In 1994, the Anti-War Campaign of Croatia started a Women's Club in Pakrac that encouraged women's empowerment through awareness campaigns and community action.

Croatia

Sonja Biserko

Helsinki Committee for Human Rights in Serbia

In 1994, Sonja Biserko set up the Helsinki Committee for Human Rights in Serbia in the wake of the break-up of former Yugoslavia. War was raging and two million people were on the run in the former country. She organized the third international conference on the International Tribunal and War Crimes Project in Brussels and mobilized a lobby group for the prosecution of war criminals. With the Civic Link from Slovenia, she arranged a training course for lawyers to prepare them to argue their case before the War Crimes Tribunal. She continues to work in defense of human rights in the Balkans.

Sonja Biserko's engagement with the Helsinki Committee for Human Rights in Serbia became a defining moment of her life, at a time of unprecedented political darkness and depression in Serbia and the region. The urgent need for action to uphold basic human dignity in a politically and morally devastated country challenged her then, and continues to do so today. She has dedicated her whole being to meet this challenge. The Helsinki Committee for Human Rights has been the most active, and, for much of the time, one of few institutional bodies for the defense and protection of human rights in Serbia. It has been the voice of truth and sanity in a deeply troubled society, abused by a repressive and militant regime. And it has been the focus of Sonja's life and work since 1994.

The last ten years of Sonja Biserko's life have been the first ten years in the history of the Helsinki Committee for Human Rights in Serbia. She has lived to make the Helsinki Committee live up to its aims, in the interest of the people in Serbia and the region. She is proud of the Helsinki Committee's achievements, of their strong position, role, and respect among refugees, minorities, war crime victims, but also in the wider public in Serbia and abroad. Her activities have given her, both in the successes and disappointments, a new moral and professional strength, and have deepened her commitment and resolve. They have strengthened her in the belief that one can make a difference, that she can make a difference, that indeed one has to try to make a difference, and that indeed she has to make a difference in the lives of her fellow human beings who have been or are still victimized by bad governance and lack of respect for our common basic humanity.

The rise of fanatical nationalism in Serbia under the Milosovic regime led to war, millions of refugees and internally displaced persons, war crimes and human rights abuses. In this darkness, some courageous people and organizations, like the Helsinki Human Rights Committee, lit candles of hope.

Serbia and Montenegro

"In our discriminative societies there are women, including traditional ones, who have become role models because they manage public property in a satisfactory manner."

Venantie Bisimwa Nabintu

Women Network for Justice (Rfdp)

Venantie Bisimwa Nabintu (45) is the executive secretary of Women's Network for Justice and Peace (Rfdp) in the Democratic Republic of the Congo (DRC). Since 1992, Rfdp has fought against all forms of discrimination and violence against women and other vulnerable members of society. She is a human rights activist and she mobilizes women to repel violence.

Venantie Bisimwa affirms that the world was created for men and women and therefore she should not ask anyone permission to live a better life. A married mother of three, Venantie holds a university degree. Her professional experience helps her encourage other women, who in her opinion benefit the society and must therefore be valued. She notes, "In our discriminative societies there are women, including traditional ones, who have become role models because they manage public property in a satisfactory manner." These examples she says impelled her to form two women NGOs. Presently Rfdp supports Congolese women from diverse political and ideological backgrounds in the South Kivu region through networking, in order to safeguard peace and advocate for gender-based interests in the DRC. Through her organization she sensitizes and trains women and men on human rights, peace and gender. She also organizes conferences, presents radio programs with debates, carries out research and writes publications denouncing violence. The moral and material support she receives from her family has sustained her work. She recalls that her parents brought up both male and female children equally. She says there is no need to have an unjust and discriminatory society. She adds that with sustained hope any action, however small, towards building a just society, will give chances to women. That society will already have sown seeds for needed change.

After the infamous Rwandan genocide in 1994, war ravaged the DRC. Women and other vulnerable members of society witnessed many injustices. As a result of this, Women's Network for Justice was formed to assist the victims against all forms of discrimination.

Democratic Republic of the Congo

Svetlana Bocharova

Dobro biez granits (Good without borders)

A journalist by profession, Svetlana Bocharova (born 1941) has been working with NGOs since 1991. In 1996, she became one of the leaders of Dobro biez granits (Good without borders). The organization has initiated 30 different projects to help orphans, children with limited abilities, and children who are victims of armed conflicts. As the artistic director of the Magic Lamp Theater (Moscow), she actively introduces artistic activities as part of rehabilitation programs. She helps carry out informative and educational projects to raise society's awareness of children's problems.

The people who know Svetlana Bocharova personally often say that she is an extraordinary person. When she came to the Magic Lamp Puppet Theater (Moscow), she immediately fell in love with the show and the moving characters. But her main love, her principal concern is children: handicapped children, orphan children, Chechen children who suffered during the war and lost their close relatives. She brought children from Chechnya to Moscow and had them hosted by her friends and acquaintances. She herself put up some Chechen girls as well. She took them to the Magic Lamp Theater. Children remain children — even if they have grown up in the dreadful conditions of war. Boys and girls, who had become adults so early in life, watched the play 'The Princess and the Pea,' adapted from the fairy-tale by Hans-Christian Andersen. They were captivated by the beautiful show of the little delicate puppets, they were charmed by the waltzes and minuets. What did these children feel, coming from the war directly into a fairy-tale? They plunged into the beautiful imaginary world, into this enchantment. Early the next day, just before their departure, everyone gathered for another activity. They went to the shops to buy little pieces of beautiful fabrics, as now they were going to create a fairy-tale themselves: they were going to create a theater back home in Chechnya.

Some time later, Svetlana Bocharova went to a refugee camp in Ingushetia to visit the children. The news of her arrival quickly spread around the little tent city. Children are running towards her, embracing her as if she were a family member. They are shouting, interrupting each other, telling her about their theater, about this tiny slice of a different, better world that they have created amidst the war, the suffering, and the separations.

In 1995, Svetlana Bocharova, together with other Russian human rights activists, created the organization Dobro biez granits (Good without borders), whose main activity is to provide humanitarian and psychological aid to children, including help through artistic activity.

Russian Federation

Boua Chanthou

Partnership for Development in Kampuchea (Padek)

Boua Chanthou (born 1952) left Cambodia to go to school abroad in 1972. When she returned eight years later at the end of the civil war, her country was devastated and deserted. Boua decided to work for its reconstruction. To bring back the community spirit among Cambodians, she encouraged the setting up of a small savings program, vocational skills training and monitoring development aid to ensure that it benefits the grassroots communities. Now Boua heads the Partnership for Development in Kampuchea (Padek), which was established in 1979.

When Boua Chanthou left her country in 1972 to continue her studies abroad, she did not know it would take eight years before she could return. And when she did, she learned that her parents and siblings had not survived the atrocities of the Khmer Rouge. Her return to Cambodia in 1980, "influenced the way I looked at life, "she says. Confused and desperate to find out how her family perished, she traveled all over the country, talking to people to learn about their suffering. Seeing the devastation in the country, she decided to do something to rebuild her motherland. "The suffering of my people that I learned about, taught me many things. After seeing what the Khmer Rouge had done and studying the ideology that they adhere to, I learned to appreciate practical things rather than ideology," says Boua Chanthou, who wrote about the internal war in books she co-authored.

After also doing consultancy work abroad from 1980 to 1995, she returned to Cambodia. Through Partnership for Development in Kampuchea (Padek) and with her educational background in economics, education and multicultural studies, she now helps to bring back the spirit of community by crafting development programs that respond to the needs of the community. As a result, small credit programs have been set up in over 250 villages where community members invest, save and assist each other. Padek focuses on development and democracy, skills training, food distribution and drought relief. After dialogues with farmers, teachers, and parents, Boua helped organize vocational training and training programs in fisheries, veterinary sciences, and health. She hopes that through Padek, people will learn the importance of working together in a transparent and democratic manner.

Cambodia after the Khmer Rouge era was isolated from the international community. In the process of rebuilding the country, it was imperative that development aid and monitoring were put in place in order to ensure transparency and effective management of development.

Cambodia

Judith Brand

Amica e.V.
Iropé e.V.

Coming from a south German home, Judith Brand (born 1969) soon decided that her aim was to make things better for less fortunate people. She got to know the situation of war-traumatized women by working and doing research for her social work diploma in Bosnia. After having received her diploma, Judith started a multi-ethnic center for women and children from different ethnic communities in Kosovo. With the initial help of the NGO Amica e.V. a self-supporting project prospered in the embattled surroundings of Rahovec/Orahovac, Kosovo.

When the war in Croatia and Bosnia started in 1992, Judith Brand got the feeling that she had to do something more than just watching news on TV. She got involved with supporting Bosnian war refugees in collective camps in Croatia and Bosnia during her summer holidays every year. Since then, the social worker keeps on returning to the Balkans: for her internship as part of the studies of social work she supported traumatized women refugees in Tuzla, Bosnia and Herzegovina, for the German NGO Amica (Latin for "friend"). These women were also part of her study research for the diploma on how war changed life circumstances for Bosnian women. After having graduated in 1999, she started working in Kosovo and installed various projects for women and girls regardless of their ethnic belonging. With the help of the organization Amica, a multi-ethnic self-supporting project prospered in the embattled surroundings of Rahovec/Orahovac, Kosovo.

Five years later, when Judith left Rahovec, the local organization Hareja employed 40 women in different positions, such as school support, child care, computer classes, or running a coffee house. These women forgot about old feuds, they stood up even to their own husbands, and went to work.

In the Balkans, although torn by ethnic conflict, war-traumatized Serbian and Kosovan women are learning to work together and rebuild their lives. In Freiburg, Germany, people come together trying to change circumstances for other people from different cultural backgrounds.

Germany

"We are not waiting for you to take up arms for our cause, but at least to hear on the BBC or receive letters of encouragement saying, we recognize ourselves in you."

Mary Brownell

Liberian Women's Initiative (LWI)
Women in Peacebuilding Network (Wipnet)
Mano River Women's Peace Network (Marwopnet)

Mary Brownell, chairperson of LWI and founding member of Marwopnet, was born in Maryland, Liberia, holds a degree from the University of Liberia and studied school administration and supervision in San Francisco. When war broke out in Liberia she transformed women's engagement from humanitarian aid to active peace building and also managed to involve civil society in a process that was pivotal to success. She took risks to become an activist and to raise her voice in a country where not only the interference of women is disapproved of, but also where there is no respect for human life.

Mary Brownell, convinced that women had the right to participate in the peace process, mobilized women, soon founding Liberian Women's Initiative (LWI) to create a neutral force between the warring factions of Liberia. Using all the strategies that could be conceived, LWI pressured leaders to involve women in all political processes. In effect, the creation of LWI marked the point of entry for woman in Liberian politics. In 1994, LWI chose a delegation of six members to force their way into a conference held in Accra, Ghana, despite a refusal to invite them under pretext that they were not directly linked to the parties to the conflict. Nevertheless, their strategic presence at the conference and their interaction with the participants prepared the way for the future participation of women. Mary Brownell and her friends always proved to be influential consultants and their advice was listened to during the process thanks to their determination and constant presence of their voice. The points they strived for — disarmament, free and transparent elections, education and the reunification of the country — were all applied in 1997 under the government directed by a woman. They remain crucial points of the peace process until today. As the conflict resumed, Mary worked through Marwopnet, a joint initiative of women of the region of the River Mano for peace. The influx of refugees to Guinea originating from Liberia and Sierra Leone had became worrying, and the involvement of Marwopnet prevented the explosion of hostilities. Mary Brownell and others acted as a conduit between the three countries and succeeded in bringing three leaders to the negotiating table in 2003 where the final agreement was signed. Thanks to this action, Marwopnet prevented the deterioration of human rights and encouraged the application of Resolution 1325 of the UN Security Council.

It was at the most critical time in the Liberian crisis that Mary Brownell chose to get involved in activism. The instability began in 1989 with the Nimba rebellion which quickly transformed itself in a destructive war that lasted seven years.

Liberia

Anna Bu

Ecumenical Humanitarian Organization (EHO)

Born in 1946 in a concentration camp for ethnic Germans in the aftermath of World War II, Anna Bu grew up in the town of Zrenjanin. In 1993, amidst the sadness and helplessness felt by so many in former Yugoslavia, she joined the Ecumenical Humanitarian Organization (EHO) and worked to provide humanitarian aid to victims of war, refugees, and displaced persons, regardless of religious affiliation or ethnicity. At a time, when the word "peace" could hardly be spoken in Serbia, she joined others in peace activities. EHO continues to help build a civil society devoted to peace and understanding.

The Ecumenical Humanitarian Organization was set up to provide efficient distribution of humanitarian aid to the needy in Vojvodina, via a shared commitment among local churches and international faith-based development agencies. The most visible element of the work has been the distribution of food, medicine, and clothes, but the most important impact on Vojvodina has been the encouragement of civil society. With a unique reputation as a church-based organization concerned about social problems, EHO has used material assistance to teach broader lessons about civic initiatives: It was the first NGO to initiate a project linking young volunteers with the elderly, and it was also the first in Serbia to start an HIV/Aids helpline for confidential information and counseling on a subject otherwise considered taboo in the society. During the NATO bombing of 1999, EHO was the only organization that worked without interruption in a city without bridges, electricity, or water; providing help — as in 1995 — to refugees and displaced alike, regardless of religious affiliation or ethnicity.

Today, Anna looks back at the 12 years she spent working at EHO with boundless gratitude. She has found it a privilege to work with an organization that assists and empowers people, always initiating enough hope to make it through the day despite times of overall despair and deprivation. To her, the EHO served as witness to the fact that there were still people in Serbia who disagreed with official policies: activists initiating peace prayers at a time when the very word "peace" could not be uttered, or people appealing for assistance for Muslim refugees from Bosnia at a time when Muslims were being killed elsewhere. EHO initiated a revival of volunteering as a way out of apathy, and as a means of showing solidarity.

In the early 1990s, amidst fanatical nationalism and growing ethnic hatred, many Serbians in ex-Yugoslavia watched helplessly as war approached. Many others, however, courageously opposed the war and provided humanitarian aid to war victims, regardless of religion or ethnic origin.

Serbia and Montenegro

Norha Patricia Buriticá Céspedes

Colombian Women's Initiative Alliance for Peace (IMP)

In Colombia, human voices have been superimposed by the noise of bullets. The words, which are articulated, are only heard as a monologue uttered by the owners of the weapons. The trade union leader, Patricia Buriticá, is convinced that words should serve for something other than to legitimize the power of the warmongers. She has been putting intensive efforts into the creation of a movement in favour of peace, a movement in which the voices of women are heard.

"I consider that nothing can justify war or any kind of violence. I think that societies can advance without people killing each other. No death is justified," says Patricia Buriticá. This experienced trade union leader, born in Bogota, puts her finger on it, when she claims that, even if the entire Colombian society suffers due to the endemic violence that affects this South American country, when the time comes to search for solutions, one important part of society is excluded: the women.

From the United Workers Confederation (CUT), Patricia began the arduous work of creating a women's trade union movement that would have an impact on the negotiations between the opposing parts of the conflict. At an international conference of pacifist women, she learned about the experience of Central American women that were left outside of the negotiation processes in their countries. The conclusion was civil war. Colombian women learned from this experience and examined their own approach. "We realized then that, when we lacked a unified argument, we were like the tower of Babel. So we began to work with a unified goal and to see ourselves as actors on the political stage in our work for peace." This work was crystallized in a document with the title: Agenda of Women for Peace, and in the creation of the Constituyente Emancipatoria (Emancipating Constitutional Group) of Women for Peace.

"The voices of women must be heard in the peace process. We have so much to say. And men do not hear us," she reflects. "Women are the ones who suffer the greatest hardships of war and, therefore, they are the ones who can make common sense prevail when faced with arbitrariness and the desire for power."

The violence experienced in Colombia dates back to 1948. Far from been solved, the armed conflict drew new groups into the confrontation; the left wing guerrillas, the paramilitary forces and the drug traffickers. Women suffered from violence, but their voices were not taken into account.

Colombia

Nubia Castañeda Bustamante

Women's Pacific Route (Choco)

Surviving in a country as violent as Colombia is an achievement. Indigenous and Afro-Colombian women from the Choco administrative district near the Pacific Ocean suffer violence and exclusion. For that reason, Nubia Castañeda Bustamante has been working hard to integrate the women of Choco into the Women's Pacific Route, an organization in which Colombian women from all over the country participate. Her dream is that women of all ages will not be obliged to undertake heroic feats just to survive. That they will have the right to live a happy life.

When Colombian Nubia Castañeda was only a little girl, she had a decisive experience: "I came home and my mother was crying disconsolately in front of the TV. She was watching a soap opera. The heroine and her man were kissing each other. I was very surprised and asked her what had happened. Still crying, devastated, she answered: 'I have given birth to 14 children, but your father has never ever kissed me on the lips or said that he loves me. At that moment, I made the decision: I should never be a mother. And I promised myself that I would fight to stop other women from suffering like my mother did."

Today, Nubia (39) is fighting to stop the suffering of the population of Choco, due to the hostilities between the guerrillas, the paramilitary and government forces. In 1996, the region was devastated by the left-wing guerrillas and by the paramilitary forces of extreme right-wing ideology. The population was forced to move in order to escape from death. For that reason, Nubia has been working with the women's movement, fighting for their rights and for peace. They realized that they were not alone: The desolation caused by the armed conflict was sensed throughout the country.

On July 25th, 2002, the women of Choco participated in a national demonstration campaigning for the end of the armed confrontations. It was one of the most significant public acts led by the Women's Pacific Route, which was founded, among others, by Nubia. The Pacific Route is currently an amalgamation of 380 women's organizations from all over the county. Nubia coordinates the region of Choco and works with women who were displaced because of the conflict. One of her concerns is to present evidence of the acts of aggression against them and to fight for the opportunity "to choose something better. Because wars do not bring improvement — they just destroy."

Violence in Colombia is experienced in different ways depending on the location of the victims. The administrative district of Choco is bathed by the waters of the Pacific Ocean and borders with Panama. There, Afro-Colombian and indigenous women experience violence as part of their marginalization.

Valentina Cherevatenko

Soyuz zhenshchin Dona (Union of Women of the Don)

Valentina Cherevatenko is a specialized consultant on social and labor issues, and a PhD holder in Political Science. In 1993, in Novocherkassk, together with like-minded people, she founded a regional organization of the NGO Union of Women of the Don (SZD). As President of this organization, she focuses her efforts on peacekeeping activities and reconciliation of the Chechen and Russian peoples. She has organized several seminars dealing with the issues of healing the psychological trauma of the victims of war.

Valentina Cherevatenko often remembers her first three-day seminar — psychological healing of participants in armed conflicts. Among those present were servicemen, who had taken part in the armed conflicts, as well as Chechen and Russian women, who had lost their husbands and sons in the war. Valentina felt a growing tension and hatred among the people in the audience. A confrontation between the Russians and the Chechens seemed inevitable. Gradually, however, the two sides began to understand that, although the tragedies they had experienced were impossible to forget, they had to move on and stop the vicious circle of hatred. Sharing their sorrows with each other, they freed themselves from their pain. In one of the activities during the seminar, each participant had to draw a picture. Valentina especially remembers two drawings. One of them was the drawing of a Chechen woman, a mother of three children. She drew a beautiful birch tree with a broken trunk. Its branches were still alive. Out of the broken trunk, drops of tears and blood were pouring. Near the birch, there were three little girls. The drops symbolized the ebbing life of the mother leaving behind her very blood to sustain the lives of her daughters. The other picture was the drawing made by a Russian officer. He spent a long time choosing his crayons, but when he showed his work, everyone simply saw a white sheet. "How else can one draw a void?" he asked. It was not until the last day of the seminar that everything changed. The people suddenly began to speak to each other. They showed each other photos of their children, spoke about their families; their hatred seemed to have vanished. Valentina still keeps in touch with the participants of this seminar, for it provided proof that forgiveness and reconciliation still remain possible for those filled with mutual hate.

The Russian-Chechen conflict has resulted in mutual hatred between many Russians and Chechens. Valentina strives to counter the official, aggressive propaganda in her efforts to reconcile those who have suffered losses during the war.

Russian Federation

"As common and insignificant as we are, we probably cannot change this world. Yet, we can contribute our heart, no matter how small it is, in the search for a peaceful tomorrow."

Sheng Hsin Chou

National Association for the Promotion of Community Universities (Napcu)

Chou Sheng Hsin (38) is a board member of the National Association for the Promotion of Community Universities (Napcu), and special assistant at the Yung-he Community College. When the Taiwanese government approved an arms purchase in 2004, Chou and a group of concerned friends launched an anti-campaign.

Chou Sheng Hsin promotes alternative education for adults, opposes arms purchases and fights for peace. Since the 90s she has been raising concerns and questions about the conservative, anti-human-rights and oppressive education system in Taiwan. For the past decade, Chou and other groups have been promoting educational reforms — smaller classes for smaller schools — and a 12-year compulsory education program. The government continues to give the same excuses for inaction: no money and no land.

In May 2004, the Taiwanese government approved an arms purchase budget worth over 18 billion US dollars. The amount is to be realized by selling state-owned land, issuing treasury bonds and selling stocks. This decision came as a shock to Chou Sheng Hsin and her friends, who decided to oppose it. On June 19, they kicked off an anti-arms-purchase campaign. Over a thousand people took the streets demanding a referendum for the arms purchase. To date, this demand is active.

Chou also decided to work through community colleges to expand the movement and to encourage people concerned with the future of Taiwan to think critically. She says "The road to democratic development is long. What forces propel us? I think that the answer lies in the most basic common values: respect and care for every life, and a vision of peace. The realization of these values rests not only on education, but also on daily living. As common and insignificant as we are, we probably cannot change this world, not to mention the grand vision of world peace. Yet, we can contribute our heart, no matter how small it is, in the search for a peaceful tomorrow. I hope everyone can grow up in a better environment and truly become themselves."

Over the last decades, the ruling parties in Taiwan have claimed a shortage of funds for education. Yet, an arms purchase budget of over 18 billion US dollars was approved in 2004 with a plan to sell state-owned land, to issue treasury bonds, and to sell stocks.

China, Taiwan

Marie Rose Cimpaye

Habamahoro

Marie Rose Cimpaye, of the Tutsi ethinic group, was born in 1961 in Karuzi, Burundi. She enjoyed the good relations among her neighbors, until they fled for their lives in 1993. That shocked her. She how has to strive to regain the lost social environment. With her friend and neighbor she founded a women's association, Habamahoro, meaning "Let there be peace".

When 1993 her neighbors fled for their lives, Marie Rose Cimpaye decided to act to create a better life for all. She and her friend and neighbor, Colette Ndaruaniye, began to risk their lives trying to reconcile their communities by visiting one another. However, they were tortured, tied up by their respective communities for their initiatives. This did not deter them: Habamahoro brings together women from both Hutu and Tutsi communities.

Paradoxically, Marie Rose admits that the hostility manifested by the people of her own ethnic group, gives her energy to go on. She is also encouraged by the warm welcome she receives from those who are not from her ethnic group.

Her vision of the future is to regain the trust and the good coexistence that their ancestors once knew and lived with. The reality however is one full of fear and lack of confidence among people, which makes life miserable among residents and the displaced people. Moreover, injustice is prevalent because the guilty are not punished for their crimes.

Although Marie Rose did not have an official network, she and Colette Ndaruaniye, together with their 15-member women's group, were trained in Peaceful Conflict Resolution by Accord Burundi.

In 1993 Burundi's first democratically elected president was killed. A war broke out between the Hutu and Tutsi ethnic groups, who had formerly lived peacefully as neighbors. Different warring factions were formed, and the civil population was not spared the violence.

Burundi

Miriam Coronel Ferrer

University of the Philippines (UP)
Philippine Campaign to Ban Landmines (PCBL)
Non-State Actors Working Group (NSAWG)

As co-chair of the Non-State Actors Working Group (NSAWG) of the International Campaign to Ban Landmines (PCBL), Miriam Coronel-Ferrer (born 1959) is a key player in the campaign to urge armed insurgents to stop using landmines in their war against government. A political science professor and multi-tasker who deftly manages several projects at the same time, she maintains that peace work is her priority, something she tries to bring into the classroom and transmit through her work as a peace researcher, writer and editor.

With internal armed conflicts and other challenges to peace in the Philippines, Miriam Coronel-Ferrer's peace work — teaching, organizing, researching, writing and helping civil society groups mediate the peace process — is never done. She has led notable projects on peace, such as committing rebel groups to stop using landmines. At the University of the Philippines' Center for Integrative and Development Studies (UP-CIDS), she coordinates the Peace, Conflict Resolution and Human Rights Program. "There is always a matter to respond to — outbreaks of violence, policy shifts, the usual grind of gathering information, analyzing and understanding developments, leveling off and getting consensus among ourselves as peace advocates and getting our message across to the public and the policymakers on all sides of the conflict," she says of her typical 16-hour workday.

Miriam Coronel-Ferrer has contributed to the literature on conflict and peace studies for the academic community, analyzed the conflict and peace situation for civil society organizations and improved the quality of life of communities living in armed conflict areas where the armed rebel groups have committed not to use landmines. Recently, she initiated the Sulong Comprehensive Agreement on Respect for Human Right and International Humanitarian Law (Sulong CARHRIHL), a civil society initiative promoting the implementation of an agreement signed by the government and communist insurgents. Her academic work and advocacies have strengthened her belief that the path to peace starts at home: "Peace at home is really very important to get the day started right. It frees you to deal with the conflict in the bigger world outside." Miriam has successfully bridged peace research with peace advocacy through her involvement in the academic world, in civil society movements and campaigns.

Peace has been an elusive dream in the Philippines where several long-running insurgencies have perpetuated a cycle of violence that has eaten up the nation's resources, destroyed the social fabric and left much of what they are trying to solve in abject poverty and injustice.

Philippines

Ajeet Cour

Academy of Fine Arts and Literature (Afal)
Foundation of Saarc Writers and Literature (FSWL)
Indian Council for Poverty Alleviation (Icpa)

Ajeet Cour (born 1934), one of the best-known writers in the Punjabi language, believes that the arts and literature can help build bridges across cultures. She set up the Foundation of Saarc Writers and Literature, a unique track II (people-to-people contact) initiative to establish peace on the subcontinent. In pursuing what she calls her "mad dream" with single-minded passion, Ajeet has drawn together writers, artists, politicians, and educationists from all over South Asia to establish a community of like-minded individuals who hope to change people's way of thinking.

Ajeet Cour began her career as a romantic, but soon matured into a realist. Women's issues and peace have always been the overriding concerns in her works. Her columns and writing have established her role as a crusader for women's issues. Known for having pioneered the art of writing novelettes in Punjabi, she has authored 17 books of fiction and two volumes of autobiography.

One of Ajeet's major contributions to connecting people through the arts and literature is the setting up of the Foundation of Saarc Writers and Literature, a unique track II initiative to supplement official efforts to establish peace on the subcontinent. The recent improvement of relations between India and Pakistan is in no small measure attributable to the ambience of understanding and goodwill created by her bringing Saarc literary figures and distinguished journalists together, even when circumstances were adverse. Ajeet also set up the Academy of Fine Arts and Literature, which aims to create an atmosphere of greater understanding through the arts.

Ajeet's work has satisfied a common thirst for freedom of speech, knowledge, creativity, and peaceful initiative. She has also initiated a process of translation of literary works in different languages of the region, believing that this will help the people of South Asia develop a more broad-based and genuine understanding of one another. One day, she dreams, the culture of peace will be the dominant reality.

Ever since the Partition of 1947, India and Pakistan have been bitter, even warring, rivals. Even as the two governments tread unsure ground, the people of both nations have welcomed a slow walk toward peace. Track II diplomacy has helped.

India

"A new world is not built
in one day. We need
an effort from all of us,
every day of our lives."

Esperanza Cruz Rodríguez

Comité de Madres de Héroes y Mártires "Nora Astorga"
(Nora Astorga Commitee of Mothers of Heroes and Martyrs)

Esperanza Cruz (77) was born in Jinotepe, the main city of Carazo, an administrative district of Nicaragua. She has a huge social conscience and has been committed to supporting the more needy populations of the rural areas, since a very young age. During the government of the Popular Sandinist Revolutionary Party (1979-1990) and in the middle of the conflict between the Administration and different counter revolutionary armed groups, Esperanza founded the Nora Astorga Committee of Mothers of Heroes and Martyrs.

November of 1984 was very sad for Esperanza Cruz. One of her sons died, assassinated by a counter revolutionary military force opposed to the government of the Popular Sandinist Revolutionary Party (1979-1990) in Nicaragua. "When I lost my son, I realized that I was not alone, that thousands of other women had also lost their sons. I began to initiate actions that would unify the mothers of Sandinist supporters and the mothers of counter revolutionaries, so that a kind of reconciliation would not be far off."

In 1985, Esperanza founded the Nora Astorga Committee of Mothers of Heroes and Martyrs. Along with the mothers of Sandinist combatants, who had died in the war, she consolidated and expanded the organization until it had 5000 members. How to incorporate the other mothers? Two years later, in the middle of the armed conflict, she convened an assembly. She stated that, in order to obtain peace, it is necessary to reach reconciliation between Nicaraguan brothers and sisters. This statement was first seen with great resistance, but, in the end, all the women burst into tears and understood Esperanza's motivation. She began to prepare the meeting between the mothers of both sides in the war. "Then they had to meet each other face to face; mothers of dead sons from both sides. Everything went differently than what I had thought. There was no conflict, no violence and no accusation. The women in front of us were very humble, repressed, quiet and sad. When the meeting was over, it ended with all of us hugging each other, all of us filled with tears in our eyes. It was something we will not forget for the rest of our lives."

Two decades after those hugs, Esperanza Cruz assures us that "the problems of the people who suffer from the effects of war must constantly energize us and motivate us to strive for peace and justice."

In Nicaragua, during the 1980s, the political forces opposed to the Sandinist Administration were in military conflict with the Army, for ten years. The anti-sandinist forces were known as the Contras, because they were counter revolutionaries. Later on, they were called the Resistance.

Nelsa Libertad Curbelo Cora

Peace for Living Together

Nelsa Curbelo lives in Ecuador since 1970. She has been a key player in the fight for indigenous rights, a pacifist leader for non-violence and a mediator engaged in finding a solution to national and international armed conflicts. In 1999, she founded Peace for Living Together, an organization for capacitating the youth gangs of Guayaquil for an understanding with the government and to interrupt the violence and repression, recreating opportunities for friendship and artistic expression — opportunities which will lead to a better human future.

Nelsa Curbelo was born in Montevideo, Uruguay, into a laboring and atheist family. At age 20, Nelsa decided to be baptized and embarked for France to join a Catholic congregation. In 1970, attracted by the Indigenous-American culture, she went to Ecuador as a missionary. There, she coexisted with the discrimination and military repression suffered by native communities. Her role in investigating and making public, the murders, disappearances and tortures, converted her into a reference in the fight for human rights. As the director of Serpaj, the Servicio Paz y Justicia (Service for Peace and Justice), she assisted as a mediator engaged in finding solutions for armed conflicts inside and outside the country. During the first indigenous uprising, in Ecuador in 1990, she was the link in the dialogue between the government and the indigenous leaders. She was also an observer during the Peace Agreement between the guerrillas and the Guatemalan government, and during the handover of arms by the counter-revolutionary groups to the Sandinista government, in Nicaragua. She went through difficult moments when she detected the infiltration of the Serpaj headquarter, in Peru, by activists of the Sendero Luminoso, which resulted in the closure of the office. In 1994, Nelsa published the book 'Walking with the people' and was nominated Woman of the Year, in Guayaquil. This city was trembling and fearful because of the phenomenon of the gangs. She founded the organization Peace for Living Together. It brought about meetings between the gangs and representatives from the government, the police and the university. Since 1999, the violent energy of the young people has been transformed into other forms of expression such as dance, music, making murals and handicrafts. These are now available in the squares and markets that were previously used as battlefields.

In the Ecuadorian society there are two phenomena: one was inherited from colonial times, excluding the indigenous communities; the other is a leftover from a violent system of private ownership, which forms new generations that are segregated — then, they express their disaffection through gangs.

Ecuador

"I think that minimizing the role of civil society was one of the failures of the peace process in Sierra Leone."

Hadja Saran Daraba

Coordination des ONG Féminines de Guinée (COFEG)
Réseau des femmes du Fleuve Mano pour la paix (REFMAP)

Hadja Saran Daraba, a pharmacist, was the first woman to take advantage of the liberalism established in Guinea in 1984, creating a pharmaceutical office. She is president of COFEG, am organization that oversees about 60 women's NGOs. She was also minister for the promotion of women and children, a function which has provided her with great experience in humanitarian activities and to research and consolidate peace.

Hadja Saran Daraba and the Women Network of the River Mano for Peace (REFMAP) appeared in public in 2001 when the situation in the region of Mano was very dramatic, and when the three governments of Guinea, Liberia, and Sierra Leone refused to meet. The political dialogue, according to Saran Daraba, was completely blocked and people were killed. NGOs working in the field could not move because the army factions were controlled by a criminal economic system that had developed in the region of the river — there was trafficking in drugs, children, women, and weapons. Thus, a sort of parallel economy was installed and certain people had no interest in peace. It was in this situation that the organisation of Saran Daraba became involved, among others, fighting against the raping of women and the forced enrollment of children in armed groups. REFMAP also fought successfully for women to have a place in the different peace negotiations so that their views were taken into account. The leader of REFMAP gave a pertinent analysis to the leaders, of which here some extracts: "You cannot say: 'I do not care if that happens in Sierra Leone or in Liberia because I am Guinean.' Not at all! What happens to your neighbor will soon happen to you, and vice versa. We did not move quickly enough to stop the war in Liberia. Liberia burned, then Sierra Leone and then Guinea itself. We should say: 'Listen, all that must stop.'"

Hadja Saran Daraba is engaged, at the national level, in a vision to reinforce the culture of peace by encouraging the contributions of all social actors (NGOs, media, traditional communicators, women, traditional leadership, religious leaders, etc). The goal is the consolidation of peace and the prevention of conflict in West Africa and poverty in Africa.

Independent from France since 1958, Guinea did not hold democratic elections until 1993. Although the country has so far avoided the civil wars which have engulfed four of its neighbours in recent years, its economy is fragile and diplomats fear the country could become a future flashpoint. Unrest in Sierra Leone also continues to threaten Guinea's stability.

Guinea

Irina Dementieva

On graduating from Leningrad University, Irina Dementieva worked as a journalist with Russian publications. After the suppression of democracy in the Czech Republic (1968), the staff of the 'Zhurnalist' magazine, where she worked as an editor, was dismissed for their pro-democracy stance. Throughout her career as journalist, Irina has unceasingly promoted the ideals of a free press and free access of society to unbiased information. One of the focal points of her activism is humanitarian aid in Chechnya, where she has worked trying to bring home the truth about the war to the Russian people.

Irina Dementieva spent New Year's eve (1995) in the basement of the presidential palace in Grozny. The day before, a group of members of the Russian parliament had arrived in the city accompanied by journalists; Irina was one of them. They were to meet with the Chechen authorities in order to discuss the situation in the Republic. But the Russian assault of the palace began, and the visitors were blocked in the basement of the building. From the windows Irina saw burning tanks and dying soldiers. The Russian troops had been bombing Grozny for almost half a month. There were a lot of innocent civilians dead and wounded. Both the scale of destruction and the number of deaths were the worst that Russia had seen since World War II. It was reported that a hundred Russian tanks and armored vehicles had been burned to ashes.

The war was being waged by politicians and generals who pretended they wanted to save Russia: in the same way that they had saved the Communist Bloc in Berlin (1953), Budapest (1956), and Prague (1968); just as they had saved the Soviet regime in Novocherkassk (1961) and Tbilisi (1989); the way they had saved the USSR in Baku (1990), in Vilnius, and Moscow (1991); and the way they had saved democracy in 1993 in Moscow and, before that, for nine long years in Afghanistan. In the course of all these bloody events, Russian troops were responsible for numerous civilian casualities.

On the morning of 1 January 1995, while still under fire, Irina managed to escape from the presidential palace. Running across the square, she saw the entire sky behind her obscured by the smoke. The Russian troops were burning down Grozny, a city of 400,000 inhabitants. The next day, at a press conference in Moscow, Irina reported what she had witnessed in Grozny, and published the article 'New Year in Grozny' in the 'Novosti' newspaper.

Working as a journalist, Irina Dementieva — often risking not only her career, but her very life — has always fought against human rights violations. Since the beginning of the war in Chechnya (1994), she has been protecting the fundamental rights of local citizens.

Nirmala Deshpande

All-India Harijan Sevak Sangh (AIHSS)
Akhil Bharat Rachanatmak Samaj (ABRS)
National Centre for Rural Development (NCRD)

Nirmala Deshpande (born 1929) is the face of Gandhianism in a world torn apart by strife and communal hatred. A pioneer of peace work, Nirmala has been especially successful in mobilizing women and girls, founding several organizations that function as platforms for people who believe in peace and nonviolence to come together. Also crucial are her numerous Track II initiatives to establish peace with Pakistan at a people-to-people level.

Nirmala Deshpande is the quiet face of Gandhianism in a world bloodied by strife and communal hatred. To the many people whose lives she has touched, Nirmala is known as didi (elder sister). Steadfast in her belief in Gandhianism, Nirmala joined the Bhoodan Yatra in 1952, walking more than 25,000 miles asking for gifts of land to distribute to landless peasants. To enshrine the spirit of the movement, she set up the Akhil Bharat Rachanatmak Samaj, which has thousands of dedicated activists committed to peace and nonviolence.

Nirmala is a pioneer of peace work, especially in terms of mobilizing women and girls to engage in establishing pacifism. Her mass mobilizations in Punjab during the 1980s, and in the conflict-ridden state of Jammu and Kashmir, are indicators. During the 2002 Gujarat riots, Nirmala and some friends formed various forums to fight communalism and help secular forces — the Sanjhi Virasat (a forum of writers and artists); the Adhyatma Jagaran Manch (with Swami Agnivesh and Reverend Valson Thampu, the collective voice of the opressed and the poor in India, to use spirituality to counter the misuse of religion); and the Peoples' Integration Council (to mobilize all sections of society for national integration and communal harmony).

Nirmala has also been active in Track II initiatives to bring peace with Pakistan. She organized the Indo-Pak Amity Meet in Delhi in 1996, and a women's bus for peace from Delhi to Lahore. She also founded the Women's Initiative for Peace in South Asia. Her Indo-Pak Soldiers' Initiative for Peace in India, and its counterpart in Pakistan, is a strangely emotive initiative-those who fought each other in three wars were embracing one another and pledging to work for peace. It is not a sight that can leave any eyes dry on the subcontinent.

During the course of India's struggle for freedom, Gandhi had propagated his unique concept of a "peaceful revolution". He also advocated the participation of women in social and political life. Part of that message has come down the dusty road of history along with his women followers.

India

Visakha Dharamadasa

Association of Parents of Soldiers Missing in Action (APSMA)
Association of War-Affected Women (AWAW)

Visakha Dharamadasa (born 1960) is the driving force behind the Association of Parents of Soldiers Missing in Action, and the Association of War-Affected Women. A woman who has radically transformed herself in response to personal suffering, she has accomplished the unique and path-breaking feat of bringing together mothers from the Tamil-dominated north and the Sinhala-dominated south of the country to ask one question: where are our children?

When Visakha Dharamadasa's 23-year-old second son was classified "missing in action" by the army in 1997, her life changed overnight. She met many people seeking information about their own missing children. In 1998, she became a founder-member of the Association of Parents of Soldiers Missing in Action. This gave Visakha a platform for initiating negotiations with both the military and the Libaration Tigers of Tamil Eelan (LTTE).

Over the years, Visakha, who lives in Kandy in central Sri Lanka, has been an indefatigable organizer of meetings and demonstrations to draw attention to the "disappeared". She has also worked closely with the International Committee of the Red Cross, and international human rights and humanitarian agencies to ensure the protection of prisoners of war. One of the achievements of her organization has been ensuring compulsory identity tags on soldiers. Married to an Indian, Visakha has two other sons apart from the one missing in action, one of whom still serves with the army.

One of Visakha's unique contributions is bringing together women from both sides of the conflict. In the process, she has undergone a remarkable personal transformation. When she began her work, she inevitably perceived the LTTE as "the enemy". But understanding the conflict's root causes brought a radical societal understanding. She also became aware that negotiation and alliance-building was critical to end the war. Thanks to her work, the Sri Lankan military has changed some of its attitudes. It has included humanitarian law and human rights teaching in its military academy curriculum. Visakha has also helped to change LTTE's attitude — it is today ready to meet and discuss matters with representatives of civil society organizations from the "hated" south.

As internecine fighting intensified in the late 1990s in Sri Lanka, hundreds of members of the Sri Lankan security forces and the LTTE were classified as "disappeared" or "missing in action". This meant that their family members never got closure. They live on in hope.

Sri Lanka

Viviana Elisa Díaz Caro

Agrupación de Familiares de Detenidos Desaparecidos (Association of Relatives of Disappeared Political Prisoners)

Since 1976, when her father was kidnapped by the Chilean Armed Forces, Viviana Díaz has never stopped looking for him. Along with the Association of Relatives of Disappeared Political Prisoners, she broke the wall of silence that tried to hide the facts from the world and from Chilean society's conscience. Her constant claims and protests saved uncountable lives from the claws of the Chilean dictatorship. Her fight for justice reached its highest point with the capture of General Pinochet, in London, in 1998.

"On September 11th, 1973, the day of the state coup led by General Augusto Pinochet, my life changed forever. That morning, my father left the house and never came back. I was 22 years old," remembers Viviana Díaz. In 1976, Víctor "El Chino" Díaz, who was sub-secretary of the Communist Party, was living clandestinely far away from his beloved family when he was taken by force from his place of refuge. "From that moment on, a search began that has not yet finished." While asking about the whereabouts of her father, Viviana found other families in the same situation and she joined the Association of Relatives of Disappeared Political Prisoners (Afdd). "Our aim was to find out where they were kept and to save their lives."

"The representatives of the Chilean government denied, both, to the relatives and to the world at large, the existence of 'the tortured and the missing.'" The Afdd began an untiring campaign of protest, during which women chained themselves to the doors of the Ministries, began numerous hunger strikes and even went to the UN. "Although there came a time, when we understood that our loved ones were dead, the constant mobilization allowed us to save other lives and forced the dictatorship to modify its repressive strategy." The dictatorship ended in 1990. Ten years later, General Pinochet was captured in London and extradited to Chile to be judged under a commitment made to the international community. The process is still running, as is the prosecution of 300 others held to be responsible for the exterminations. "In 2001, the army handed over information about 175 of the 1197 prisoners who had disappeared. They stated that my father had been thrown into the sea. What had happened to the others? We know that this information exists. Knowing the truth is the indispensable condition for the rebuilding of dignity and peace for Chile's future."

With the state coup in 1973, the Armed Forces, led by Augusto Pinochet, began a massive campaign to arrest people who then disappeared. Their arrest, torture and murder were systematically denied, in spite of the repeated claims and protests of the families and international indignation.

Chile

Martine Bonny Dikongue

Inser
Internationale Weiterbildung und Entwicklung GmbH (InWent)

Martine Bonny Dikongue from Cameroon was born in 1960. She is an economist and trainer for non-violent conflict resolution. She helps traumatized survivors of the Rwanda genocide to re-learn to trust people. She works with teachers and other professionals in a project financed by the German government and the Protestant Church of Rwanda. She has developed her own approach to trauma work, called the "white dove method".

Martine Bonny Dikongue tells stories to heal traumatized survivors of the Rwanda genocide. The 45-year-old trainer in non-violent conflict resolution defines peace with a story. "One very dark night villagers could not see their surroundings. But they felt that a strange creature was present. The first person said: I touched it and felt something long. A second person said it was something thick. For a third one, something wet. No, said the fourth person, something dry. They could not agree what the creature was. The next day they saw it: an elephant. They had all touched it, but each at a different spot. The story shows us that each sex, ethnic group and minority has their own perspective on issues. If one perspective is excluded, conflict is inevitable. If the people had accepted each other's perceptions, they would have recognized the elephant." Dikongue, a Cameroonian national, spends several months a year in Rwanda helping to restore trust in the world among the traumatized survivors. Her "white dove method" is a combination of cultural techniques grounded in African traditions, including storytelling, theatre, dancing and singing. "There were several genocides in Rwanda before the 1994 genocide, but the memory of the past was repressed and mention of them was taboo. This resulted in a culture of silence and mistrust. It allowed violence to return with a terrible force. I felt we needed a new way of relating with each other, an active and participatory kind of education where children can speak their minds." Slowly and gently, Bonny is able to heal devastated souls. "My dream is to see all people smiling again," she says. "Not because they have to smile, but because it comes from within. Now you see smiling children and laughing people in the streets of Rwanda. It's a beginning. People are starting to live their lives again."

There were almost one million victims of the 1994 Rwanda genocide. It was the latest in a string of genocides. Previous ones had been repressed with silence and taboos. To prevent this from happening again, it is important to work with traumatized survivors and break through their silence.

Rwanda

"I receive so much more from my work than I am able to give back. I live with gratitude that I get to do such transcendent and meaningful work."

Marta Drury

Heart and Hand Fund
Responsible Wealth
Global Fund for Women

Marta Drury, who believes in the power of women to lead sustainable peace-keeping, provides support from her own personal resources to grassroots organizations throughout the world. She tells the stories of women who are making a difference, and created The Resourceful Women Awards, which honor and reward women who work at the frontlines. Marta is an outspoken member of Responsible Wealth, a national network of wealthy Americans who believe it is wrong to give tax breaks to the rich.

When Marta Drury was six years old, her father bought his first truck. In the mornings he was a mailman and in the afternoons he collected garbage. "My parents' bedroom was the office for the first four or five years, as they took a one-truck business to an international conglomerate," Marta recalls. While growing up, Marta worked in the family business and went on to receive a master's degree in special education. But when her daughter arrived, the single-mother did not want to spend her energy teaching, and instead supported herself with a variety of small businesses.

When she was in her 40s, Marta inherited her parents' wealth and plunged into a lifetime of commitment to women's peace organizations. In many cases, her investment has begun a long-term peace-building process. For example, in March 2004, a mob of ethnic Albanians attacked Serbian communities in Kosova, killing 28 people and burning hundreds of homes. An ethnic Albanian activist who was receiving grant money from Heart and Hand Fund helped Serbian victims recover. Not only did the funds allow women and their families to rebuild their homes, the process began healing relationships between individual Serbians and ethnic Albanians. "In my experience," says Marta, "this happens first among women. I feel that most international funders ignore the work of women activists and underestimate its significance, even though it is women activists who rush in to provide emergency humanitarian aid and organize their communities. In the Balkans, it is women who cross borders to support one another in spite of civil wars. After the war, the same women who have worked on the frontlines are usually shut out of the decision-making that affects the reconstruction of the country. At the same time, the men who were holding the guns a few weeks earlier are invited to sit at those same tables."

Marta Drury believes that one of the greatest hurdles to empowering women is institutionalized patriarchy. "I am dismayed at the aggressive stance the US is taking in the name of national security — there seem to be fewer and fewer limits to what our government can do."

United States of America

Annelise Ebbe

Women's International League for Peace and Freedom (WILPF)
Women in Black Denmark
Danish Peace Council

For 40 years, Annelise Ebbe has been actively engaged in peace work and women's rights worldwide and in Denmark. As vice president of the Women's International League for Peace and Freedom (WILPF), president of Danish WILPF, founder of the Danish Women in Black network, president of the Danish Peace Council, and an eager contributor to discussions on the public agenda, her continuous work and personal engagement as a pacifist and feminist has made her a well-respected and outspoken leading figure in the anti-war movement, the women's movement as well as on the public agenda.

Ever since she was a young girl Annelise Ebbe has feared war. Growing up in the aftermath of World War II, in a family linked to the Danish resistance movement, the issues of war, death, and destruction were deeply rooted in her conscience from early on. Stories of imprisonment or death of family members did not escape her attention. Neither did the fear of the cold war and a possible nuclear threat which followed. Throughout her childhood, she was haunted by nightmares of war, even in daytime she would suddenly start crying when horrible images and thoughts of war loomed up in her.

With fear it is all or nothing. Either you embrace it or you fight it. Annelise chose the latter. At 15 years of age, she joined the Danish Campaign against Nuclear Weapons and thereby took her first step into a life-long career as a pacifist, which has gained her major recognition internationally.

In 1996, Annelise visited the former Yugoslavia and found herself passing through her very own childhood nightmare. War had torn the region apart and entire villages were burnt down. She met women who had lost husbands, children, and homes. Annelise was paralyzed by the misery and horror around her, but she also found herself questioning the very meaning of peace work. Does it actually make sense? The local women engaged in peace work she met provided her with the answer: Yes! Across ethnic and religious boundaries these women joined forces in a common striving for peace and nonviolent conflict solutions. For Annelise this experience today stands as one of the major rays of hope and reasons for keeping up the fight for a peaceful future.

Since the end of World War II, women's rights and women's peace organizations in Europe and worldwide have worked at local, national, and international levels against war, nuclear weapons, and for lasting peace.

Denmark

In many, many ways, Sister Elizabeth personifies the words "in the service of God", bringing together two neighboring communities separated by ethnic distrust.

Elizabeth Edattukaran

Salesian Sisters

Sister Elizabeth Edattukaran (born 1938) has worked fearlessly and relentlessly under the most trying circumstances, and at considerable personal risk, to provide healthcare and relief to people affected by conflict and violence in northeast India. She has also been instrumental in setting into motion several conflict resolution initiatives, and in providing livelihood options to women affected by ethnic violence. Her deep faith in god and her humane touch have helped dispel much of the fear and distrust that result from endemic conflicts.

Sister Elizabeth Edattukaran, a nurse by training, works in conflict-ridden northeast India, providing health services and relief to people affected by violence. She played a leadership role in providing basic necessities, healthcare, and trauma counseling to victims who had witnessed the killings of their most loved people. Since 1991, she has been working under very difficult circumstances in the Kokrajhar district of Assam; in 1996, when communal and ethnic violence broke out, she immersed herself completely in providing much-needed medical and emotional support to the broken communities. She has also been instrumental in setting into motion several confidence-building and conflict resolution initiatives. An intercultural peace meeting was organized, with Elizabeth as a key member of the committee. Equally remarkable is her work on enhancing skills and providing livelihood options to women affected by ethnic violence.

Sister Elizabeth has worked relentlessly, fearlessly-and silently-under the most trying circumstances, with the deep belief that providing much-needed support with a humane touch will help build the injured psyches of people affected by violence and discrimination. She has largely managed to dispel the fear and distrust that crept up between two ethnic communities, which have otherwise lived in close proximity, sharing the meager resources of the forests. Her selfless dedication to the most dispossessed groups, her courage in venturing out into highly unsafe areas, and her belief that peace can only be achieved through constructive hands-on work at the grassroots level have had a profound influence on everyone who has had the opportunity to interact with her. In many ways, Sister Elizabeth personifies the words "in the service of God".

Several states in India's northeast have been torn apart by conflict, both internal and with the security forces, leaving their economies in a shambles. The region sorely needs better healthcare facilities, especially reproductive health facilities for women.

India

Fatmire Feka

Kids for Peace

Fatmire Feka (17) is a Muslim Albanian girl from an ethnically divided town. In 1999, she lost a brother and a sister in the war in Kosovo and her family's house was set on fire. Since then, she has organized and led many peace building initiatives and is the driving force of a children's peace movement in Kosovo. In 2002, she started the Kids for Peace movement in her community, which has grown to over 14 multi-ethnic clubs across Kosovo. She has also organized multi-ethnic summer peace camps. She is a member of her town's Council for Peace and Tolerance.

Fatmire was living in a transit camp for internally displaced persons (IDPs) in 1999, after she lost a brother and a sister in the war in Kosovo and her family's house was set on fire. Eleven years old at the time, Fatmire watched how the camp staff members from World Vision were implementing a number of peace-building projects. One day she approached one of the staff and asked, "How can I help you make peace in Kosovo?" Since then, Fatmire has eagerly helped in a number of peace-building projects. Her first effort was in the summer of 2001, when she participated in a series of workshops on Local Capacities for Peace. Her story, poems and her passion for peace were so inspiring that the workshop participants responded with a sincere and emotional pledge to help do what they could in order to bring peace to Kosovo. Fatmire followed that up with a sponsored visit to Toronto, Canada, where she repeated her pleas for peace through poems that she had written. She made presentations to a number of civil society groups, churches, and to the local and national media. In 2002, Fatmire approached World Vision staff asking for help. She had conceived a program where children from various ethnic groups in Kosovo could come together to share their war experiences and learn from each other. She wanted to "make friends with the others." Soon, her idea developed into the Kids for Peace movement. The goal of the program is to positively impact the children of Kosovo by promoting peace and understanding among elementary school children. The program currently has 14 clubs in five towns. In November 2002, Fatmire was selected as an Angel of Hope by World Vision Canada. She was chosen because she "brought hope to others and made a difference in her community."

Ethnic conflict broke out between Albanians, Serbian forces, and Kosovo Serb civilians in the late 1990s, with a massive displacement of the population of Kosovo. The United Nations estimated that nearly 640,000 Albanians fled or were expelled from Kosovo between March 1998 and the end of April 1999.

Serbia and Montenegro

Shou E Feng

After Japan's surrender in 1945, during the purge of left intellectuals in Taiwan, Feng Shou E was sentenced to ten years' imprisonment. But her passion for social justice and peace have not changed, and she has participated in various campaigns against war and colonialism. In 2003, she filed a lawsuit in the Osaka Court against the Japanese Prime Minister's visit to the Yasukuni Shrine in Tokyo.

As a child, Feng Shou E was witness to the abuse and oppression of ordinary folk under the Japanese colonial regime. After 1945, she started to learn Chinese at the Lanyang Women's Middle School, and within two years, she was able to write in Chinese. It was around this time that she became aware of the targeting of left intellectuals by the post-war rightist Nationalist regime. Her Chinese teacher disappeared suddenly from the school. In 1950, her elder brother Feng Chin Hui and she were arrested on the same day. Her brother was executed on the charge of organizing teachers' associations in the school. She was given a sentence of ten years on the charge of joining an insurgent organization.

On release from jail ten years later, Feng Shou E married Chen Ming Chong, also a political prisoner. In 1976, the couple was again arrested. Feng Shou E was released after interrogation, and Chen Ming Chong was almost sentenced to capital punishment, but Feng Shou E lobbied public support and there was also international pressure to which the Nationalist regime conceded. Chen's sentence was changed to 15 years imprisonment.

When her husband was jailed for the second time, Feng Shou E went through the tremendous hardship of bringing up two young daughters alone. However, her passion for social justice have not changed. Long years of imprisonment have taken their toll on her health, but she still participates in various international campaigns against war and colonialism. Feng has also often made common cause with the Taiwanese indigenous peoples in Japan to protest the immense harm inflicted on them by Japanese colonialism.

In 2003, Feng Shou E filed her personal lawsuit in the Osaka Court in Japan against the Japanese Prime Minister Junichiro Koizumi's visit to the Yasukuni Shrine, calling the visit a eulogy to Japan's militaristic war of aggression.

After Japan surrendered in 1945, Taiwan went into a new post-war phase. Soon the rightist Nationalist government began its persecution of leftist intellectuals. Conservative estimates have it that in the White Terror of the 1950s, over 3000 people were executed, and over 8000 were imprisoned.

China, Taiwan

"We have the capacity
to choose against war
and so to give peace
a chance: to want to
do so is a sign of sanity
rather than madness.
The first step is to
understand that there
is a choice."

Diana Francis

Committee for Conflict Transformation Support (CCTS)
International Fellowship of Reconciliation (IFOR)
Campaign for Nuclear Disarmament (CND)

Diana Francis has been working on non-violent conflict resolution, mediation and reconciliation in England and worldwide. She is widely involved in training people in community reconciliation and peace work. Her work has inspired many people to engage in non-violent activism. She has trained women, who have vividly become trainers and peace-workers in their own communities. Diana is the author of two books, both published by Pluto Press: "People, Peace and Power: Conflict Transformation in Action" (2002) and "Rethinking War and Peace" (2004).

For more than 40 years, Diana Francis has been working on non-violent conflict resolution, mediation and reconciliation. She has also been involved in training people in community reconciliation and peace work, and through this work she has mobilized people enormously to engage in non-violent activism. When asked about her vision for the future, Diana replied, "My longings are interpreted more in terms of process than of end points. I endeavor to be part of a process towards a fundamental shift in culture from one that accommodates violence as 'normal' and defines power in terms of control, to one in which care, respect and compassion for each other and for humanity predominate . This will mean learning to build bridges of love and co-operation between people rather than fear and antipathy. My vision is to teach young children that to be tender and caring is not equivalent to being weak. At the same time we, women and men, have to work untiringly with courage and determination to effectuate radical social changes that will help the youth think about their behavior. This will give them the courage, over and over again, to stand up and be counted for their deeds, and will make them able to link analysis with imagination and find happiness in solidarity. 'Non-violence' means living the future in the present, so we just have to get on and do that."

Diana Francis began voluntary peace work during the Cold War. Through her assiduous work she was inspired to create a pioneering approach to non-violence training. She has been advocating respect for people's culture and freedom, and peaceful resolutions for indigenous conflict .

United Kingdom

Erni Friholt

Svenska Kvinnors Vänsterförbund (SKV, Federation of Leftist Swedish Women)
Women's International Democratic Federation
Swedish Women's Council for Development

For 37 years, Erni Friholt has been an activist in peace building and peace education, women's rights and solidarity, both locally and internationally in the Balkans, Bangladesh, India, and Ethiopia. She has been a journalist, speaker, volunteer and project manager, a demonstrator and organizer of an alternative solidarity fair trade café. For many years, she was editor-in-chief of the women's magazine "Vi Mänskor" of the Federation of Leftist Swedish Women and chair of the organization. She has participated in many international women's conferences, peace marches, and peace organizations.

In Erni and Ola's Solidariskt summer café, there are cakes that Erni baked in the wee hours of the morning. A Rosa Luxemburg cake with rum, one with meringue and almonds that she calls Amandla Mandela, a cake with nuts and coffee cream called Mahatma Gandhi's Dream, and the Elin Wägner bread, a homemade rye named for the feminist writer. The small handwritten tags offer guests interesting reading from the biographies of the namesakes.

Since the 1990s, there has also been the Zitzer cake with red currants. How did this come about? During the war between Serbia and Croatia, 200 men from the village in Tresnjevac in the northern Serbian province Vojvodina were called up for military service. Prompted by the village's school principal and the women, those who had been called up decided to refuse to go. They refused to shoot their compatriots simply because power-hungry politicians wanted them to. In the village's pizzeria, The Zitzer, a peace camp was established. The government in Belgrade ordered numerous panzers to encircle the village. The peace camp lasted two months. Afterwards the village declared its independence from Belgrade and called itself "the Zitzer Spiritual Republic that has no territory and is a community of people who want peace." Erni drove there with her husband to learn about the local peace movement and to refute the lies about the alleged violent nature of the Serbs. She was impressed with the spirit of peace that reigned there and supported the population. In autumn 1995, the peace movement on the island of Orust, Sweden, opened a Zitzer consulate. In Tresnjevac in 2001, Erni and Ola, as Zitzer consuls on Orust, received the Pro Urbe Prize, an honor awarded to those who had helped the town in its time of need. Today, the Zitzer Republic no longer exists, but it lives on in Erni's heart. The sign "Consulate of Zitzer" still hangs on their house.

Think globally, act locally: the rich experience of support and solidarity with peoples from Bangladesh, India, Ethiopia, Boliva, Mexico, Zimababwe Tanzania, Vietnam, and the Balkans are the basis for local peace education and a fair trade café on the island of Orust, Sweden.

Sweden

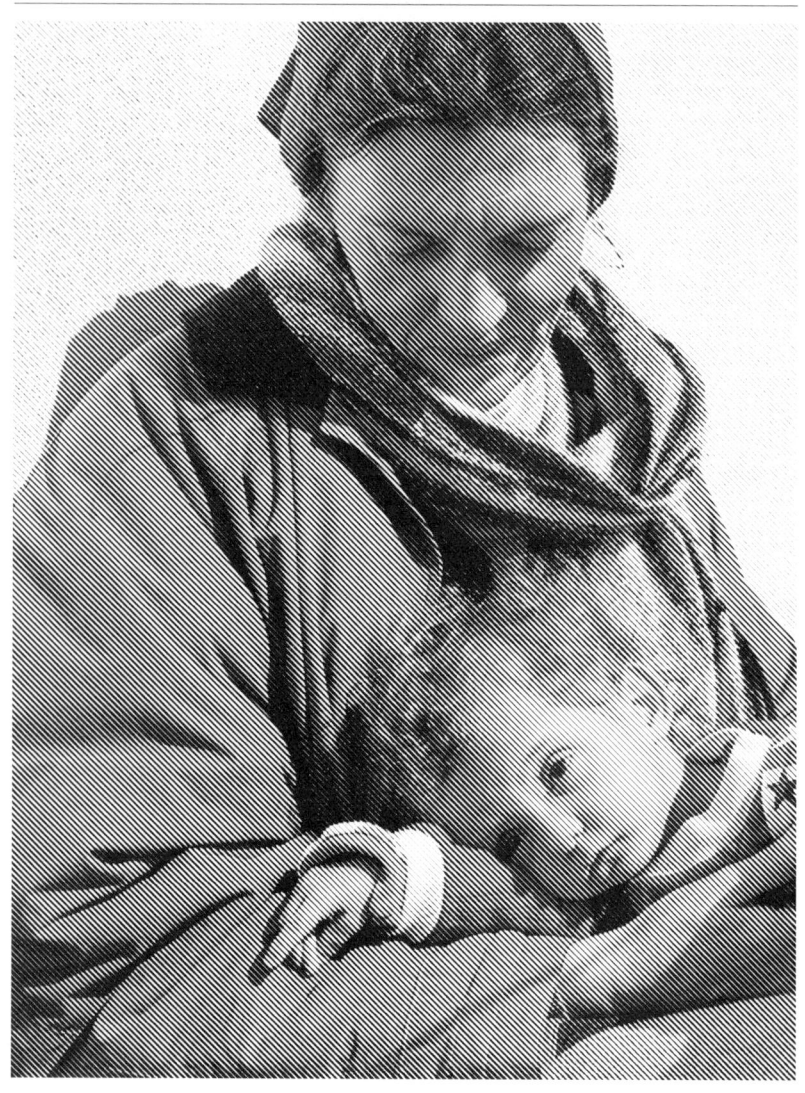

Maria Christina Färber

Caritas International
Spiritual Community

A nurse and therapeutic specialist, Sr Maria Christina Färber (born in 1957) worked with children from broken homes in Germany. In 1999, during the Kosovo War, she moved to the Albanian city of Shkodra, where she helped refugees from Kosovo. After the war she took over Caritas International's psychological and social care of Albanian families involved in blood feuds. With the reconciliation of hostile clans, counseling mothers, and organizing children's therapy sessions, Christina does everything possible to help families step out of the vicious circle of violence, revenge, and death.

Sr Maria Christina Färber enters homes where curtains are drawn over the windows, women wear black, the children's laughter has gone silent, and men sit in front of the television with stony faces. Fear reigns in these homes. "There are too many of them in Albania," she says. In the city of Shkodra with a population of 110,000, more than 500 families live shut up in their own four walls. The reason is the fatal tradition of blood vendetta. "In the name of blood relationships and family honor, vicious circles of murder are set in motion, which escalate more and more," she explains.

As her uncompromising path of nonviolence leads her to the homes of offenders as well as victims, she has won not only friends. From time to time, she also meets with hate. Going as far as death threats. "But with my faith," she says, "I can stick it out." For the prevention of violence, a committee of men was gathered discussing the most urgent needs of the population in village meetings. Eventually, the people of Dobrac started to repair their streets, organize refuse disposal.

For a long time, Sr Maria Christina has experienced her chosen home country of Albania as the place of her calling, as only someone with strong spiritual roots can do. That is also why she entered the Catholic order of the "Spirituelle Weggemeinschaft." Every now and then, she spends a few weeks in the community's Swiss center to draw strength for her life in Dobrac. She is convinced that "without the others, without my religious community, without our Albanian colleagues and everybody who is making one more step towards peace, without so many prayers by so many friends, without so many people constantly helping, without God, I could not achieve anything in this country, nothing at all."

In the remote Albanian mountains the Kanun governs everything. A 600-year-old body of legislation handed down orally, the Kanun was powerful and is once again. According to the Kanun, in cases of murder only shedding the blood of a male from the offender's family can restore justice.

Germany

Patricia Gaffney

Pax Christi British Section (PCBS)
Peace Education Network (PEN)
Catholic Fund for Overseas Development (CAFOD)

Patricia was raised in a hard-working Irish immigrant community in west London, with strong Catholic roots. After training as a schoolteacher, she taught for six years at a Comprehensive in west London. In 1980 she joined the Catholic Fund for Overseas Development (CAFOD) as Schools and Youth Education Officer. Since 1990 she has been the General Secretary of Pax Christi. Through annual monitoring Patricia has played a key role in calling on church institutions to cease investment in arms industries. As a result, no Catholic dioceses or religious orders now have arms investments.

Patricia Gaffney is a central figure in the Christian peace movement in Britain, working diligently and creatively and leading unobtrusively. Through her work she is involved in lobbying and campaigning within church and political networks on peace and security-related issues, offering support and facilitation for church-related groups on Christian peacemaking, as well as coordinating the day-to-day running of Pax Christi in Britain. She recalls one fascinating experience of advocating peace in the world in the following: "Some years back I was involved in a peace exercise, planting a cherry tree outside the Ministry of Defense in London on Hiroshima Day. We wanted a creative enterprise, a lasting memory of the people of Hiroshima. We planted a tree and hung the names of those who had died on its branches. We knelt to pray for the victims of nuclear war. Suddenly a coach pulled up and tourists spilled out. One ran towards us and began crying when she saw what we were doing. She was Japanese, from Hiroshima, and could not believe that people in London were remembering the tragic history of her home. As we tried to calm her I was more worried that she might accidentally be arrested with us. In the end, the tree was the only thing to be arrested on that day. It was excavated brutally from the earth by the police, leaving an ugly hole in its place. We were all a little shaken by the experience, but proud of the effect that our act of solidarity had created. Making connections, crossing barriers of time and place, being human with one another, are to me important elements of peacemaking that cannot really be measured or evaluated. You have to trust others and be open to accept whatever may happen during, and as a consequence of your actions. And this too is what peacemaking is about: finding freedom in doing what is right and creating human security in the process."

Through annual monitoring, Patricia has been the driving force in calling on church institutions to cease investment in the arms industry.

United Kingdom

Elisa Gahapon del Puerto

Christian Children's Fund (CCF)

Elisa Gahapon del Puerto (born 1957), a social worker, has spent more than two decades forging peace and healing the wounds of war in the province of Basilan. Her efforts have led to a continuing dialogue among warring rebel factions such as the Moro National Liberation Front (MNLF), the Moro Islamic Liberation Front (MILF) and the Abu Sayyaf Group. Under the Prelature of Isabela and the Christian Children's Fund (CCF), she implements programs and services to address the people's urgent needs such as health, water supply, housing, literacy, environmental conservation and peace advocacy.

It was early dawn in 2001 when Elisa set out with her driver for Maluso, a municipality 30 kms from Isabela, the capital city of Basilan. On their way, she noticed a body sprawled by the roadside. She asked her driver to stop, they picked up the man and brought him to the hospital, where he was declared dead on arrival from loss of blood. Elisa was to learn later that hiding just behind the bushes where she stopped to pick up the wounded man were some of the men who had earlier ambushed a public utility vehicle, leaving four persons beheaded and mutilated. When she met one of these ambushers later, he told her they could easily have taken her hostage, but they did not because, he said, "You have done a lot for our children."

An island province in Southern Philippines, Basilan has long been enmeshed in a cycle of war and violence, but it is the dreaded kidnap-for-ransom Abu Sayyaf ('Bearer of the Sword') Group that brought global notoriety to the place. Elisa remembers her childhood in Basilan when Muslims and Christians coexisted harmoniously. "It was a few months before Martial Law was declared in 1972 when peace and order deteriorated," she recalls. As a working student serving the Prelature of Basilan, she saw the need to do her part in healing this wounded land. "Who can serve Basilan better than Basileños themselves?" she asks, adding, "The children in Basilan suffer the most from this senseless war and they need all the love and help we can give them."

In Basilan province in southern Philippines, children are easy targets of kidnappers and hostage takers. They also suffer the effects of poverty resulting from such disturbances. The Christian Children's Fund program in Basilan promotes the welfare of children using a holistic approach.

Philippines

"The gap between our longings and aspirations and the way we actually live can be hugely painful and disappointing, especially if our spirituality is unnamed, unrecognized and unloved."

Kathy Galloway

Scottish Churches Council
Church Action on Poverty
Joseph Rowntree Foundation

Kathy Galloway is a distinguished theologian and the leader of the Iona Community who has a long history of academic and community work. Based in Scotland and a single mum with three children, she has been working to enhance spiritual and cultural development for the last twenty years. She is connected with a wide range of local and global organizations, including ecumenical Christian centers and other social justice organizations. She has focused her efforts on issues pertaining to gender equality, poverty, and cross-religious and cross-cultural understanding.

Kathy Galloway is an academic, feminist, theologian, and, a social worker, writer and organizer of workshops on cultural and spiritual values development. She is a recognized consultant to a number of international bodies, such as the World Council of Churches. Kathy has set her goal in life to promote spiritual and cultural understanding. She believes that this goal comes from her strong Christian belief in a "God of action". When writing recently to the members of the Iona Community about the impact of the Tsunami of December 2004, Kathy explained her understanding of God and her relationship with him in the following words: "If I had to choose a description for the God I am in love with, I think it would be this: God is the Life of life. My being in love with the Life of life is mostly expressed in two ways. The first one is a kind of wordless gratitude, appreciation and mindfulness which is what prayer is for me. 'The turn of a leaf in morning sun and the catch in our throat drives us to our knees and into prayer,' as Yvonne Morland said. The other is in my very human and fallible effort to love people, to act justly, to live in the flow of life. Belief in God for me is a practice, not a proposition."

Kathy Galloway leads the Iona Community, that addresses issues of great significance to the lives of people in Scotland and everywhere, from a Christian perspective. She is committed to work with the marginalized members of society and to promote social inclusion of all.

United Kingdom

Lorraine Garasu

Bougainville Inter-Church Women's Forum (BICWF)
Congregation of the Sisters of Nazareth (CSN)

Sister Lorraine of the Congregation of the Sisters of Nazareth in Bougainville, is trained as a community development worker. She has worked as a teacher and social worker and co-founded Bougainville Inter-Church Women's Forum (BICWF) in 1995 during the civil war between Papua New Guinea and Bougainville. Sister Lorraine became a facilitator for the women who were negotiating peace and services for the people with the Bougainville Revolutionary Army. She bravely negotiated life issues such as safety, medical emergencies, and women's livelihoods with all combatant sides.

The civil war (1988–1998) and blockade brought particular hardships to life in Bougainville. Having concern for justice and human rights issues, Sister Lorraine concentrated on working with women throughout "the crisis," bravely negotiating life issues such as safety, medical emergencies, and women's livelihoods with the Papua New Guinea and Bougainville combatant sides. All social services systems broke down, and women did what they could to keep things going. Through literacy training and other courses run by Sister Lorraine, both men and women acquired small business skills to help overcome poverty and received help through the Nazareth Rehabilitation Center for traumatized people she helped establish. As co-founder and main force behind the ecumenical Bougainville Inter-Church Women's Forum (BICWF), she worked at grassroots and political negotiations levels for peace, moving between the different fronts, always helping children, women, the sick and aged of all sides.

In 1996, the BICWF organized the Arawa Peace Forum attended by 700 women; it played a fundamental role in ending the war. Sister Lorraine continues to work with other women of the BICWF, setting up training courses in conflict resolution and literacy, capacity building for women's groups, working on projects for creating incomes on the local level and consolidating peace programs for reconstruction, reconciliation and lasting peaceful development on Bougainville. At all times, she has worked to strengthen the role of Bougainville women in education, work, and political activity.

Sr Lorraine, a catalyst for peace, described life and work during the PNG–Bougainville civil war (1988–1998) and blockade as "life between two guns." Social services and infrastructure completely broke down, thousands died and women suffered from hardship at the hands of all combatant sides.

Papua New Guinea

Fatima Gazieva

Ekho Voiny (Echo of War)
Soyuz Zhenshchin Severnogo Kavkaza (Union of Women of the
Northern Caucasus)

Fatima Gazieva was born 1960 in Kazakhstan. At the beginning of the 1990s, she returned to her historical motherland, Checheno-Ingushetia. Since 1995, Fatima has been taking part in the anti-war movement. Being an active member of the human rights organizations Soyuz Zhenshchin Severnogo Kavkaza (Union of Women of the Northern Caucasus) and Ekho Voiny (Echo of War), she strives to help the people of Chechnya who have become victims of the atrocities of the bloody Russian-Chechen wars. Her activities are getting more and more dangerous under the pressure of the Russian authorities.

On 8 March 1995, Russian and Chechen women started the Peace March intending to walk from Moscow to Grozny. Learning about the March, Fatima went to the village of Sleptsovskaya (Ingushetia) to join in. A column of 500 marchers walked with posters to the Chechen village of Sernovodsk, where they were stopped by the Federals who threatened to use weapons, in the face of which the women appeared to be helpless. Nevertheless, they did not lose heart. The active members of the March created the NGOs Union of Women of the Northern Caucasus (SZSK) and Echo of War.

Of course, Fatima's activities could not remain unnoticed by those who violated human rights. In 2004, Fatima and her husband were kidnapped by armed people wearing masks and brought to a military base of the Federal troops. They realized that they had fallen into the hands of the special services of the Russian Federation. Fatima and her husband were interrogated and threatened. That night on the military base seemed to be endless. Fatima recalled her happy childhood and peaceful Kazakh prairies. "What brought me to this unstable region? Why could I not have stayed where I was, baking cakes and raising my daughters? What else did I need?" These sad thoughts ran through her mind while she stared at the stone ceiling. "Many people in the same situation disappeared forever. I have dealt with so many similar cases myself." When in the morning the door of her cell opened, Fatima was ready for the worst. But a miracle happened and, together with her husband, she was released. "This is the will of God. He has granted me life so that I can help the least privileged victims of war. I have no right to betray them. They are waiting for me. And I will go back to baking cakes when the war is over," Fatima said to herself smiling at the bright autumn sun.

The first war broke out in Chechnya in 1994 and lasted until 1996, the second from 1999 to 2001. Many people of the anti-war movement face constant threats and persecution from the Russian authorities.

Russian Federation

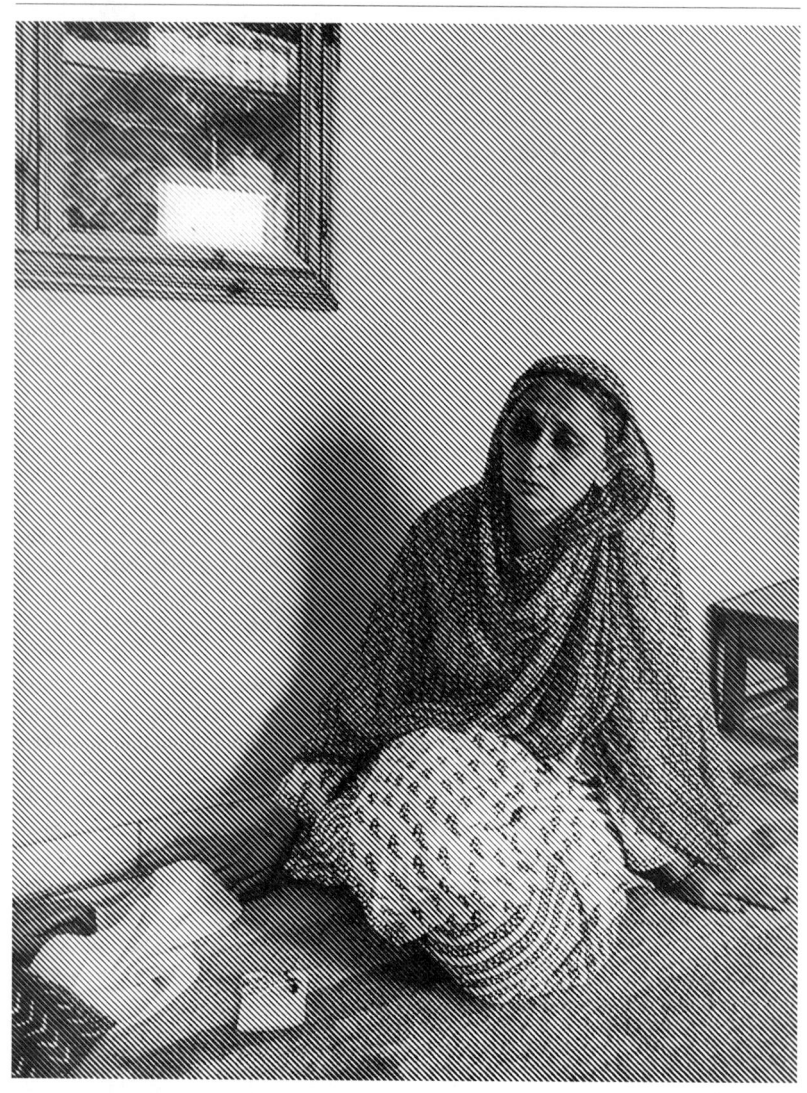

Latifabano Mohammad Yusuf Getali

Al-Fazal Educational and Charitable Trust (Afec)

The very worst situations bring out the very best in some of us: that is what the Gujarat riots of 2002 did to Latifabano Mohammad Yusuf Getali (born 1962). From the uneventful life of a Muslim housewife to a relief and peace activist, she has walked a long mile. Braving the wrath of her conservative community, Latifabano has helped hundreds of Muslim women in the state gain access to relief and legal assistance. She backs this up with capacity-building activities for the women, helping them rebuild their lives.

The largely uneventful life that Latifabano Mohammad Yusuf Getali had expected to lead was severely challenged during the Gujarat carnage following the riots in 2002. And she was at the riot epicenter: Godhra. The atmosphere in the crowded relief camps, where Latifabano became a relief worker, was one of incessant terror and apprehension. Her skill in assisting and supporting women was given due recognition, despite the fact that others doing the same work were legion. When the relief camps eventually shut down, Latifabano started her own organization: the Al-Fazal Educational and Charitable Trust (Afec). Afec has been supporting underprivileged women, building their capabilities through information dissemination, and working tirelessly for peace between the mutually bellicose majority Hindu and minority Muslim communities.

Latifabano's organization was the first Muslim women's organization in Godhra, so she faced the considerable wrath of the conservative Muslim community. But she continued undeterred, and the community gradually turned supportive. In the past couple of years, she has helped many families gain access to relief and legal assistance-in essence, bridging the gap between those working to help the affected and the victims themselves. Her work has also promoted a dialogue between Hindu and Muslim women in Godhra, where seeking peace, under the circumstances, seemed like asking for a miracle. Furthermore, her work has inspired a number of women into examining the rest of their lives with a positive outlook. Latifabano is one of several women who have challenged the stereotype of Muslim women in India.

The 2002 Gujarat communal riots, which much of the media called a "state-sponsored genocide of the minority community", affected over 100,000 families. Thousands lost loved ones, were displaced, and rebuilt their lives from scratch. The conditions at the refugee camps were abysmal.

India

Barbara Gladysch

Mothers for Peace

Barbara Gladysch (born 1940) worked for 36 years as a special needs teacher for children. She has devoted herself to securing a peaceful life for children worldwide. In 1981, she founded Mothers for Peace, as part of the German peace movement. Since then, she has assisted refugees from the Balkan war region, organized holiday programs for children from Chernobyl, and has been active against nuclear weapons and energy. In 1997, she founded Little Star Points, a therapy center for children traumatized by war in Grosny. In 1998, she was awarded the highest German service medal.

In 1996, when Barbara Gladysch traveled to Grosny, the capital of war-torn Chechnya, for the first time, she was moved by the plight of the children. Some had been so badly damaged psychologically that they had stopped speaking, playing, or looking directly at anyone. The special needs teacher who had worked with children with behavioral problems until her retirement, was motivated to set up a therapy center for traumatized children: the Little Star Points. Here, children are encouraged by therapists and educators to talk about their war experiences; it is here that they learn to sing and dance again.

"Children have a right to peace, and we adults have to provide it," says Barbara Gladysch, who founded the Mothers for Peace in Düsseldorf in 1981. She has participated in countless demonstrations and other activities for peace and has traveled frequently to war-torn parts of the world, such as former Yugoslavia. Her sheer joy in life motivates others to support her projects: for example, primary school children from Düsseldorf who raised over 5000 euros for the Little Star Points.

There were a lot of other projects Barbara Gladysch initiated. After the Chernobyl disaster in 1986 she founded the organization Children of Chernobyl, which is involved in environmental issues and fights against nuclear power, and has brought children with radiation sickness to Germany to recuperate. She also worked with war refugees from Bosnia, Serbia, Croatia, and Kosovo, trying to improve the situation of children by providing help with homework and leisure activities. When founding the organization Mothers for Peace, Barbara Gladysch wrote, "We have no enemies. We are 'declaring peace' on all countries. Children all over the world are our children." The pacifist and peacemaker has always been faithful to this motto.

In all crisis-torn areas of the world, women and children suffer from violence. The Mothers for Peace try to help in areas of conflict, working to help children traumatized by war in Chechnya and with refugees from Bosnia, Serbia, or Kosovo, as well as victims of the nuclear disaster in Chernobyl.

Germany

Jelka Glumicic

Center for Peace Studies

When the war broke out in Croatia in 1991, Jelka Glumicic witnessed the suffering of innocent people. Surrounded by fanatical and violent nationalists, she vowed to dedicate her life to peace building. In 1996, Jelka established the Shelter for the Aged in Dunjak, a home which accommodated more than 30 people over a period of three years. She established an international volunteering network, where more than 40 volunteers from Canada, Japan, New Zealand, and other countries came to help. She has also established links with an organization that helpes rebuild ruined homes.

Jelka Glumicic believes in the old saying that "actions speak louder than words." She also believes in leading by example. In 1992, Jelka Glumicic was one of the founders of the Democratic Union, an independent political party in Croatia headed by Branko Horvat who is a world-renowned economist and Nobel prize nominee. The party stood for anti-fascism, human rights, and gender equality. The government viewed the party very unfavorably and party members often received death threats if they persisted in their activities.

In 1996, Jelka established the Shelter for the Aged in Dunjak and an international volunteer network. She also relates with Tools for Reconciliation, another organization which helps rebuild ruined homes. In 1997, she organized a workshop with the help of a Dutch organization that managed to repair over 600 homes devastated by war and assisted in cleaning over 200 water sources. In 1997, Jelka also established a partnership with the United Nations Refugee Agency to help Croatian refugees return home and provide them with legal and psychological support. Over 20,000 refugees benefited from this project. She believes violence harms both the victim and the perpetrator. She has been lobbying and establishing a network of like-minded organizations that are engaged in reconciliation and the prosecution of war crimes in Croatia. Jelka has been working intensively on initiatives that promote education on how to build a democratic and civilized society. In 1998, she initiated a Committee for Women's Rights with a helpline and a shelter for women and children who are victims of violence. This is the second shelter of such kind established in Croatia. Jelka also organized the Committee for Civilian Service to lobby for civilian instead of military service for conscientious objectors.

During the war in Croatia, unspeakable violence was perpetrated on innocent people in the name of nationalism. There was an urgent need for genuine peacemakers.

Croatia

Hildegard Goss-Mayr

International Fellowship of Reconciliation (IFOR)
Service for Peace and Justice (SERPAJ), Brazil

For more than 52 years, Hildegard Goss-Mayr has been teaching nonviolent resistance against injustice and repression as part of the International Fellowship of Reconciliation. She was influential in the 1986 nonviolent People Power Revolution in the Philippines, in the Liberation Theology Movement in Latin America, and the peaceful overthrow of tyranny in Madagascar. The organization Service for Peace and Justice (SERPAJ) that she co-founded, denounced human rights violations during military dictatorships in Brazil, Argentina, and Chile under the most difficult conditions.

Hildegard Goss-Mayr is deeply convinced that each person has a conscience that can be reached. In 1968, she and her late husband, Jean Goss, held a seminar about nonviolence in a local Christian community in Medellín, Colombia, in a mountainside slum with no running water. In the weeks and months afterwards, she relates, the women of the area decided not to put up any longer with the deaths of their children due to the lack of clean water. "So they went down to the town center with their children, to the beautiful plaza with its fountains and clear water, where the wind sweeps over, making little puddles. The first group began to wash their children in a puddle. The rich women, strolling by as usual, scolded them: 'Your children will die if you wash them in the puddles.' That was exactly the reaction they wanted. The women began to speak, explaining their situation until the police came and chased them away. But ten minutes later, a second group arrived. More and more rich women stopped and spoke with them. The police wanted to arrest them, and a policeman hit one woman. But a well-off woman stood between them and said, 'If your wife were in this situation, she would have done the same thing.' That day, a group of poor and rich women was formed. They went to the city administration and were successful." When the Gosses returned six months later, water was already flowing on the mountain. "These women understood the power of nonviolence. They spoke to the conscience of those who were better off, and were ready to take the consequences, whether blows or prison. And that is why they were successful. A school was built, electricity laid. All because of their brave example."

The International Fellowship of Reconciliation was founded in 1919. Today, with a network of peace groups in more than 40 countries, its activities include the training of women peace activists. The spiritually-oriented fellowship has been an ecumenical movement from its beginning.

Austria

"Borders are no obstacle for women. Led by our feelings and instincts, women will cross them. Even when we are women whose very existence contradicts each other, we will talk; we will not shoot."

Terry Greenblatt

Bat Shalom
Kol Ha-Isha
Shani

Terry Greenblatt, formerly director of Bat Shalom, Israel's national women's peace organization, and activist in residence at the Global Fund for Women, has been a women's rights and antioccupation activist in Israel for the past 20 years. She lectures and lobbies internationally on the enforcement of equal rights for all in Israel and Palestine — Jews and Arabs. She cofounded Kol Ha-Isha (The Women's Voice) Center of Jerusalem, Shani (Israeli Women Against the Occupation), and the Community School for Women's Studies and Economic Development.

"I live in Jerusalem and I have spent the past ten months being scared," Terry told an audience. "We are scared as we protest in the streets of Tel Aviv and in Palestinian villages under siege. We have stood huddled in small groups of six or seven, as well as with the over 10,000 women and men in 150 cities and towns around the world. We are harassed and cursed and arrested."

Born in New York, Terry lived in Israel from 1971 to 2003 and has served as executive director of Bat Shalom. Bat Shalom is a grassroots organization of Jewish and Palestinian Israeli women working for peace that is grounded in a just resolution of the Israel–Palestine conflict, respect for human rights, and an equal voice for Jewish and Arab women in Israeli society. Since 1994, Bat Shalom has partnered with the Jerusalem Center for Women, a Palestinian organization in East Jerusalem, on a project called the Jerusalem Link. Working with a coalition of more than 100 women's peace and antioccupation initiatives around the world, the goal of Jerusalem Link is to help bring a sustainable peace to the two nations.

"The world needs the skills that women bring to peacemaking," Terry told the United Nations Security Council in 2002. "It is our role, women on both sides, to speak out loudly against the humanitarian crimes committed in order to permanently subjugate an entire nation. You need us, because if the goal is not simply the absence of war, but the creation of a sustainable peace by fostering fundamental societal changes, we are crucial to everyone's security concerns. You need us, because wars are no longer fought on battlefields. You have brought the war home to us. Women's characteristic life experience gives us the potential for two things: a very special kind of intelligence — social intelligence — and a very special kind of courage — social courage."

As a Jewish peace activist living in Israel, Terry risked her life every day to accomplish her life's work. In the midst of violence, she models her unshakeable faith that peace is possible.

United States of America

Hadja Bainon Guiabar Karon

Federation of United Mindanawan Bangsamoro Women Multi-Purpose Cooperative
Bangsamoro Women's Committee
Moro National Liberation Front (MNLF)

Hadja Bainon Karon (born 1953) is an empowered woman with a vision. Her struggle for the Bangsamoro homeland is as much a struggle for survival as it is for lasting and sustainable peace. She believes that peace in Mindanao can only be achieved through sincere dialogue and the delivery of justice. This means justice for the Moros, the Lumads and the Christians, and a genuine recognition of their right to self-determination. Her guiding philosophy is "Peace is love as Islam is for peace".

Hadja Bainon Guibar Karon is the eldest of nine siblings, all of whom are committed to the Bangsamoro revolution. Five of her brothers were killed in the war of liberation waged by the Moros against the Philippine government. She joined the revolution at 18, married the chief military commander of the Moro National Liberation Front (MNLF), and rose to become chair of the MNLF Women's Committee of the Central Committee. With the signing of the peace accord between the government and the MNLF in 1996, Hadja Bainon joined the Department of Agriculture as division chief and the Southern Philippines Council for Peace and Development as a member of the consultative assembly. She was appointed regional secretary for Social Welfare in 2002. Even after joining the government, she continues to fight for her ideals by empowering women and the youth sector.

In 1997, she founded the Federation of United Mindanawan Bangsamoro Women's Multi-Purpose Cooperative, which operates on the principle of proactive participation of women in peace building and development. The Federation helps coordinate, make linkages and source funds for livelihood and other socio-economic programs, and assists donor agencies in identifying their target groups. It has 120 primary cooperatives within and outside the Autonomous Region of Muslim Mindanao (ARMM). Since 1990, Hadja Bainon has attended trainings and exposure trips in the country and abroad on peace development, social welfare and empowerment. She says that she does not expect any reward for what she has done for her people because she believes that the reward will come from Allah. "For as long as I can help, I will," says Hadja Bainon, a workaholic who sleeps only four hours a day.

After the signing of the peace accord between the Moro National Liberation Front (MNLF) and the Philippine government in 1996, the agenda for development included coordinating services for human and natural calamities and moving local, national and international resources where they are needed.

Bertha Oliva Guiffarro de Nativí

Comité de Familiares de Detenidos–Desaparecidos en Honduras (Cofadeh)

When Bertha was about 20 years old, she fell in love with "the tenderest man in the world." Both were in love with a world they wanted to change. They fought for bread and smiles. One night in 1981, he was kidnapped. He is one of the 184 missing people in the country. Bertha Oliva de Nativí is today the General Coordinator of the Committee of Relatives of Missing Prisoners in Honduras (Cofadeh). This organization was founded by Bertha, along with other women like her, who are searching for their loved ones.

"They entered my home, killed our friend, and beat my husband until he was unconscious. Just before he became unconscious, he said to me: 'They may leave you alive to give birth to our son.'" On that day, in 1981, Bertha Oliva de Nativí was 25 years old. She continued to fight for justice. Without a father and with a mother obliged to hide her real name, the boy was born secretly.

Bertha Oliva de Nativí's husband is one of the 184 missing people in Honduras. That was the information given, some years ago, by the National Committee for Human Rights. Bertha was the driving force behind the creation of this committee, along with her companions in the Committee of Relatives of Missing Prisoners in Honduras (Cofadeh), created by them, in 1982. "Since then, we have planted ourselves in La Merced Park, on the first Friday, of every month. They look at us with contempt and call us the lepers. Slowly, we have demonstrated that those with leprosy in their souls are the ones capable of causing so much hurt." In 1987, Honduras became the first state to be condemned by the Inter-American Court for Human Rights. One year later, a new case, this time concerning disappearances, was presented to the Court by their organization, the Committee of Relatives of Missing Prisoners in Honduras, achieving a similar sentence. They have managed to cause the dissolution of the Department of National Investigations — "the most criminal body in the country" — the repeal of Compulsory Military Service and, in 1992, the liberation of the last political prisoners.

Between 1979 and 1989, the Honduran State imposed the installation of an institutional network, composed of civil, military and paramilitary structures. That repression resulted in almost 200 missing people, 300 political assassinations and 1500 survivors of torture.

Honduras

Working among Tamils in a Sri Lankan war zone, A. H. bridges the faultlines that deeply divide communities in her country.

A. H.

Working in the Sri Lankan war zone in the east, A. H., together with the affected families in this deeply divided community, struggles to overcome fear and respond to crippling life situations that attempt to crush the human spirit. A. H. is constantly engaged and involved with many women whose life journeys are intertwined with hers. She works in quiet intense one-to-one engagements with persons at different levels on many life situations, struggling with fears to increase space, and taking small steps.

In her personal and her professional life, A. H. has bridged ethnic faultlines. A high-school graduate, A. H. grew up in the south in a middle-class family. Today, she is living and working in eastern Sri Lanka, which is a war zone.

For over 20 years, A. H. has been a member of a Citizens' Committee, and has worked with Tamil victims of torture. She currently plays a crucial role in helping families, especially mothers' collectives, organize themselves to resist forced conscription and reconscription of their children by the LTTE (Liberation Tigers of Tamil Eelam).

A deeply spiritual woman, A. H. was horrified by the violence, trauma, and tragedy unleashed by the war, and decided to devote her entire life to working toward peace and reconciliation. She is not funded by any organization, and refuses to accept funding from the many international NGOs that have flocked to Sri Lanka during these past conflict-riven 20 years. She shuns publicity — the courageous and inspirational work she does is neither recognized nor acknowledged nationally. That makes A. H. an extraordinary anomaly on Sri Lanka's humanitarian landscape.

A. H. campaigns tenaciously against ethnic chauvinism, militarism, and structures of inequality, be they gender based, economic, or political. She works among the Tamil population of eastern Sri Lanka, despite not being from this region.

The Citizens' Committee is at the forefront of efforts to defuse tensions between Tamil and Muslim civilians, between Tamil civilians and government forces, and between Tamil civilians and the LTTE.

Sri Lanka

Helen Hakena

Leitana Nehan Women's Development Agency (LNWDA)
Pacific Women Against Violence Network
International Action Network Against Small Arms (IANSA)

Helen Hakena co-founded Leitana Nehan Women's Development Agency (LNWDA) in 1992 and is its executive director. The key area of commitment was to restore peaceful lives for the people of Bougainville during the civil war with Papua New Guinea (1988—1998) over the destructive Panguna copper mine and to achieve gender equality. Women in Bougainville played a key role in bringing the conflict to an end but now in a time of relative peace, their role is overlooked and they have struggled to be involved in key peace negotiations and reconciliation and reconstruction programs for the island.

"One of the moments that I will not forget was going to New York to receive the Millennium Peace Prize Award for Leitana Nehan Women's Development Agency (LNWDA) on 8 March 2001. I was nominated by Unifem to represent the women of the world in presenting a petition to the UN Secretary General. It was signed by 350,000 women leaders from all over the world calling on the United Nations Security Council to include women in peacekeeping missions. The petition also called on governments to include women in decision-making committees. I never dreamt that I would one day be called upon to represent the women of the world.

The reality now in Bougainville (PNG) is that women's rights have been violated and are still being violated by men. The negative experiences that I went through personally gave me the strength to work for peace. What keeps me going is how our women struggle for peace and security in their homes as well as in our country and the appreciation women have for my work and the work of LNWDA. I gain strength from the commitment of LNWDA volunteers in Bougainville's 13 districts to work for a violence-free Bougainville where women's human rights are respected. Women are not passive victims. We contribute actively to peacemaking. Our courage and contributions have made the world a better place to live and work. Imagine what more we could do if we women were enabled to take an equal place at the negotiating table. Thus LNWDA's motto is 'Women weaving Bougainville together.'"

Bougainville's long struggle for autonomy from Papua New Guinea erupted into civil war and a blockade (1990s) over the destruction caused by the huge Australian-owned Panguna copper mine on the island. Women led the opposition to the mine and also the peacebuilding efforts to end the civil war.

Papua New Guinea

Azra Hasanbegovic

Žena Bosnia and Herzegovina (Žena BiH)

Since the beginning of the armed conflict in Mostar in April 1992, Azra Hasanbegovic helped organize small groups that assisted people most badly struck by the war. She initiated the women's association Žena BiH, whose main mission is to struggle for women's right to work. She also established the Agency for Free Legal Aid and Services and an SOS hotline. At the same time, she worked on documentation of the suffering of Mostar and Prozor women and submitted a detailed report to the United Nations Commission on Human Rights.

In September 1993, during the armed conflict, Azra Hasanbegovic was expelled from her apartment and took refuge at a Jew's house. Owing to his efforts and freedom of movement, the two of them were able to bring tons of food to the completely blocked and isolated East Mostar. In February 1994, she was forced to leave Mostar as her life was threatened. Together with a convoy of Jews, with forged documents and a Jewish name, she escaped from Mostar and went to Zagreb. As soon as she arrived in Zagreb, she engaged in the activities of Žena BiH, a women's association established by women refugees from Bosnia and Herzegovina. Although it was considered impossible at that time to conduct peace gatherings, Azra was able to participate in a peace meeting in Vukovar, together with other women from all over the world. After returning to East Mostar, she immediately organized a local association of the Žena BiH whose main mission is to struggle for women's right to work. The association started off with 32 members; after three months, there were 700 and, shortly afterwards, 2000 members, most of them women refugees. Azra also gathered 250 former women prisoners of war and established the Agency for Free Legal Aid and Services as well as the SOS hotline. She mobilized women to supervise these projects. At the same time, she worked on documentation about the suffering of Mostar and Prozor women, prepared a detailed report and submitted it to the United Nations Commission on Human Rights in 1995. She has taken part in numerous peace conferences and conferences organized by women activists in Bosnia and Herzogovina and other countries of Europe, and also in meetings about the former Yugoslavia.

After the war, Mostar, like other cities in Bosnia and Herzogovina, was in chaos. Among the worst victims were women, who needed food, shelter, a source of livelihood, legal assistance, and — most important — their human rights so they could actively participate in the rebuilding of their lives and city.

Bosnia and Herzegovina

Jemma Hasratyan

Armenian Association of Women with University Education
Armenian National Committee of the International Campaign to
Ban Landmines (ICBL)

Jemma Hasratyan's engagement in peace building activities was triggered by the Karabakh conflict. Aware of the need for armed hostilities to stop, she became active in women's dialogue and in a women's association that was one of the first women's NGOs established after Armenia gained independence. Within this framework, Jemma persevered in carrying out a dialogue with Azeri women. This took place during the most difficult years of military hostility, when all and any dialogue-oriented efforts seemed to be unrealistic and even dangerous.

Jemma Hasratyan is the head of the Armenian Association of Women with University Education. Her vision of a peaceful future is based on the ideology of a culture of peace and a dialogue between the civilizations that is realized through peace building projects, publications, research initiatives, and numerous interactions within a peoples' diplomacy framework. At this stage of the conflict in the Nagorno Karabakh region, the consolidation efforts of women's NGOs are directed toward the avoidance of war, dispelling an atmosphere of hostilities, and strengthening peace in the region. Jemma belongs to a category of people, who do not avoid difficult and complicated responsibilities. She has an unflagging optimism, self-confidence, and firmness of purpose. This firmness is a source of her optimism and the motor that gives her energy at the most difficult and trying moments, when many others are losing heart and the responsibilities are enormous. Her ability to attract and engage people is recognized by everybody who has a chance to communicate and work with her. Moreover, she never pursues her own goals but all her goals are directly related to the problems of her people and the people for whom she feels responsible so that they may live in a stable society, in peace, having a firm perspective for their future. That is why she does her best to achieve goals and targets that are oriented exclusively to the welfare of her people and the peoples of the region in which she lives.

A former Soviet Republic, Armenia suffers from a lack of education on human rights. Even with the success of multilateral efforts to terminate warfare in the Nagorno Karabakh region, the conflict has not been solved and there is a real danger of the resumption of military hostilities.

Armenia

Noeleen Heyzer

United Nations Development Fund for Women (Unifem)
Development Alternative for Women for a New Era (Dawn)
Asia Pacific Women in Law and Development

As the executive director of the UN's leading agency to promote women's empowerment and gender equality, Noeleen Heyzer has made a difference in the lives of women throughout the world. Since Noeleen's arrival in 1994, Unifem has expanded its resource base, formed strategic partnerships and grown in visibility and impact. Her leadership helped the organization to identify three central themes: building women's economic capacities and rights, engendering governance and leadership, and promoting the realization of women's human rights, with the elimination of violence against women.

Noeleen Heyzer believes that peace is a mindset and a way of living. She also believes peace is security. Her beliefs inform her vision and her vision gives strength to pioneers of peace. For example, on a recent trip to Rwanda she met with widows of the genocide, many who live with HIV/Aids and care for orphans who also live with the disease. Noeleen noticed that Hutu and Tutsi women had come together to weave baskets. While basket weaving has been a tradition in Rwanda for many years, the partnership of historic enemies allowed the baskets to provide a different purpose. The women told Noeleen that they represented hope and peace, a means to reconcile differences and to heal the wounds of a devastating conflict. Noeleen returned to New York, met with businesswomen, and shared the story. Less than six months later, the baskets were marketed in the United States with the profits going back to Rwandan widows. Today, the baskets have become a national symbol of peace and the second largest export for Rwanda.

A sustainable peace must begin in homes and communities before it can flow out into the world, says Noeleen. "What people tolerate in peacetime determines what they will tolerate in war. We can only start building peace by ending the violence in our homes, our schools and our streets. Violence as a personal and political strategy is no longer compatible with human survival at this stage of our evolution. Sustainable peace hinges on the presence of economic and social systems that put the majority of people and their needs at the center of development, not the greed of the powerful minority."

The nature of war reaches beyond battlefields, into schools and communities. But while women are increasingly victims, they are also the ones who hold communities together during crisis. And it is for this reason, says Noeleen, that women must be brought to positions of power and influence.

United States of America

Joan Hinton

Chinese Academy of Agricultural Mechanization Sciences

Joan Hinton, who was born in 1921, is an American nuclear physicist who worked on the Manhattan Project, the world's first nuclear experiment. Shocked by the destruction of Hiroshima and Nagasaki, she came to China in 1948 to take part in the Communist Revolution. Instead of making weapons that kill, she has applied all her energy to improving agricultural machinery and dairy farming. Now she is an adviser to a state dairy farm in a suburb of Beijing.

As a young woman, nuclear physicist Joan Hinton (Chinese name Han Chun) took part in the Manhattan Project. When the United States dropped two atomic bombs on Japan in 1945, Hinton was totally shocked by the destructive force of nuclear weapons. She then protested the government's use of scientific research, and lobbied in Washington as part of the peace movement. However, she was very disappointed at the widespread belief in the USA's righteous morality and military supremacy. She went to China to join the Communist Revolution in 1948. Labeled as "the Atom Spy that Got Away" in the McCarthy-era media, Hinton claimed that she never worked on nuclear weapons in China. Rather, she helped the Chinese mechanize agriculture. She explained with her unbending social conscience: "I did not want to spend my life killing people, but rather to make people have a better life, not worse." From being a nuclear physicist to a dairy farmer, Hinton described the turning point in her life as a disillusionment with pure science, and a new belief in communism and internationalism. Hinton and her husband, Erwin Engst, dedicated their lives to building the New China. They lived in cave-dwellings in the early years of her stay in China and worked together in different dairy farms. Making use of the limited local resources, Hinton developed farm tools, such as donkey dump carts and a silage combine. She also designed a milking system, farm machinery and even an irrigation system. Reminiscing about her life, Hinton once said, "I have taken part in two of the greatest things of the 20th century — the development of the atom bomb and the Chinese revolution. Who could ask for more?"

From making nuclear bombs to breeding livestock, Hinton demonstrates to us how an organic woman intellectual makes science work for peace and for the people.

In 1945 the United States dropped two bombs on Hiroshima and Nagasaki causing the loss of 150,000 lives. Its attitude of self-righteous morality was disillusioning for many people, and some went away to join the Chinese Revolution, which offered an alternative to capitalism.

China

Anna Hoare

Community of the Sisters of the Love of God
Lagan College

Sister Anna Hoare has been working for peace all her life. Her major achievement was the creation of the first Protestant and Catholic integrated school, Lagan College, in Northern Ireland. Today there are over 50 integrated schools in Northern Ireland, with a total student body of over 12,000. Her work has been a beacon to the communities she has directly served and an exemplum of what is possible in one of the most unstable and violent regions.

By establishing Northern Ireland's first integrated school, Lagan College, Sr Anna Hoare has created a living and sustainable legacy for communal harmony in the region. When, in 1972, she moved to Belfast, it was the early years of 'The Troubles' — the increased violence that began in the late '60s and only came to an end in the '90s. As a result, the prevailing 'ghettoization' of Catholics and Protestants was exacerbated and the British Army was called onto the streets, an act which resulted in yet further hostility and violence.

Sr Anna began her work by arranging holidays in Northern Ireland for children from both confessions. From this developed the idea of an integrated school. Today Lagan College has 1000 students and the total number of students enrolled in Northern Ireland's integrated schools in the region is 12,000. Lagan College's purpose is to break down barriers of 'us' and 'them' between Catholics and Protestants by fostering a climate of reconciliation and understanding. Students from both denominations study together and learn how to coexist peacefully with one another. As more and more alumni emerge from Lagan College and Northern Ireland's other integrated schools, it is hoped that by sharing their experiences with their colleagues, families and friends they can produce a society in which peace and tolerance are not regarded as an aberration, but as the norm.

Sr Anna Hoare began her peace work in Northern Ireland in the early years of 'The Troubles'. "When I first moved to Northern Ireland I saw that people were frustrated. The chasm between Catholic and Protestant came from the political situation. There was a demand for change."

United Kingdom

Benazir Hotaki

Ministry of Information and Culture (MIC)

Born in 1939 in Kabul, Benazir Hotaki attended Malalai School in Kabul. After her graduation from high school, she traveled to Australia where she obtained a BA in Education from the University of Queensland. Upon completion of her degree, she returned to Afghanistan and served as an educator in several schools. She is one of the few women who were able to study abroad. Hotaki was also involved in the reconciliation process between the government and different opposition groups in the years 1985—1986.

Serving in different capacities as an educator, Benazir Hotaki was at the forefront of the women's movement in Afghanistan and has first hand experience of educating many women. She was selected as "teacher of the year" on four occasions. She has also been a prolific writer, publishing numerous articles for the local media. As an advocate of the women's rights movement in Afghanistan, she intends to nominate herself for the upcoming parliamentary election, as a symbolic gesture to encourage women in Afghanistan to participate in political and social activities.

Benazir Hotaki currently chairs the Council of Information and Culture at the Ministry of Information and Culture (MIC) in Kabul. She liaises with women journalists and advises them on different issues concerning women. Drawing from her experiences as a participant in the reconciliation movement in 1986, Benazir is confident that the Afghans will avail themselves of this opportunity. While the emergence of women leaders and the agenda of women's rights are resisted by many voices in the country, she is hopeful that in due time this resistance will be overcome.

Active as an educator for the past four decades in Afghanistan, Benazir Hotaki has overseen the education and training of several generations of young Afghan girls. She puts great emphasis on education.

Afghanistan

Chin Yu Hsu

Gu Jinliang Cultural Foundation

Hsu Chin Yu grew up in Taiwan during the period of the Japanese colonization. In the White Terror period in the 1950s, when many intellectuals, workers and peasants were charged as spies, communist bandits and traitors, she entered a reading club, and took part in the labor movement. Later she was arrested and imprisoned for 15 years, which changed her life.

As a child, Hsu Chin Yu learnt what it meant to be a second-class citizen. In the early years after the liberation of Taiwan in 1947, the nationalist government arrested many civilians. After the February 28 incident, about 10,000 people were arrested or killed.

Hsu Chin Yu entered a reading club and this was a turning point for her. Though she was shy and introverted, she took part in the labor movement organized by the post and telecommunications labor union fighting on the issue of the rights of Taiwanese staff. At the age of 30, in March 1950, she was arrested and involved in the case regarding Taiwan post and telecommunications general office. She was in prison for 15 years. After her release, Hsu was still monitored and harassed and lived under great practical and psychological pressure.

Later she met Gu Jinliang, another victim suffering from the White Terror. They married, and set up a preserved-egg firm in Pingtung despite employment difficulties and obstacles. They persisted in their ideas and aided fellow victims who had been in prison. Their firm turned into a revolutionary cause through which they realized their ideals for labor.

Hsu contributed to the compensation from their White Terror years and founded the Gu Jinliang Cultural Foundation to promote cross-strait youth cultural exchange and literary activities between Taiwan and mainland China.

Taiwan went through the White Terror period in the 1950s. The government arrested many intellectuals, workers and peasants, charging them as spies, communist bandits and traitors. Taiwan society was full of fear and discontent, but many people resisted.

China, Taiwan

Alice Ophelia Hyman Lynch

Black, Indian, Hispanic and Asian Women in Action
Women of Color Network on Domestic Abuse and Sexual Assault
Women's Action for New Directions (Wand)

Alice Ophelia Hyman Lynch (born 1950) is Executive Director of Black, Indian, Hispanic and Asian Women in Action (Biha). She has conducted over 1000 trainings on domestic violence, sexual assault, child abuse, chemical dependency, and HIV/Aids, looking specifically at how these issues impact communities of color. Since 1997, Alice has worked to establish restorative justice programs in her own community and across the nation. Through this process she has helped empower communities to take the lead in solving their problems in ways that promote healing and prevent future harm.

The chairs form a circle in the community center in North Minneapolis. Neighbors have gathered. The focus turns to Marcus, a young man who has just completed a seven-year prison sentence for vehicular manslaughter. Now Marcus has an apartment, a job, and is attending college. Still, he wants to do more to make things right with the family whose loved ones he killed. In this hard time, Marcus is not alone. The circle offers support and is a constant in what has been a chaotic life. He knows that, no matter what, the circle is there for him.

In 1997, while serving on the Minnesota Department of Corrections Restorative Justice Initiative Advisory Council, Alice developed a deep appreciation for the process of restorative justice in which communities, working with criminal justice professionals, take the lead in addressing their own problems. One component of restorative justice is the circle: within the circle people speak from the heart in a shared search for understanding, and together identify steps necessary for healing and preventing future harm. It was such a circle that gave Marcus the support he needed to make a successful transition from prison back into the community.

Alice speaks of the process: "The idea that the community was making decisions for itself on how to handle harm done was something that got my attention immediately because I could see the possibilities. I was interested in providing circles of support to individuals and families, particularly juvenile offenders. Many of the women I worked with had youth in the criminal justice system and I felt that this was a way to give them a new start." Alice integrates her work with restorative justice into a life dedicated to nonviolence and the empowerment of women.

Prisons consume an increasing percentage of tax dollars at the expense of human services. The prison system addresses problems after they occur rather than focusing on prevention, even though prevention is more cost-effective. It is into this costly system that restorative justice offers life-giving possibilities.

United States of America

Dekha Ibrahim Abdi

Coalition for Peace in Africa (Copa)
Responding to Conflict (RTC)

Dekha Ibrahim Abdi, a 40-year-old Kenyan from the Muslim Somali community, is a consultant, practitioner and trainer in peace building and conflict management. She started her peace work about 13 years ago when yet another conflict broke out in her home town of Wajir, in north-eastern Kenya. At the beginning the quest was to find sustainable peace. Today Dekha Abdi looks back on established peace-finding structures and networks. She is a founding member of the regional Coalition of Peace in Africa (Copa) and lead trainer of Responding to Conflict (RTC) in conflict transformation.

Dekha Abdi's peace work began in 1993. A statement by her mother inspired her. "Daughter, when you were a child, I hid with you under the bed. Am I supposed to hide now with your daughter under the same bed? When will all this finally stop?" She was referring to the conflicts between different Somali communities in Wajir District and cross-border conflicts in north-eastern Kenya. The news headlines then were concerned with the large numbers of refugees entering Kenya from Somalia. With other men and women Dekha Abdi discussed how to realize peace and harmony. As more people got involved, the Wajir Peace and Development Committee was formed. The concept of peace and reconciliation was planted in people's minds. The youth also demanded to participate: "We want to be involved. We are today's leaders, not tomorrow's!"

"To combine the wisdom of elders and the energy of the youth is one of our approaches for sustaining peace," Dekha Abdi explains the philosophy of the regional Copa. "The organization wants to raise the profile of peace, using the approach of our African culture and wisdom — solving conflicts through consensus, not violence," says Abdi. Despite the fact that women in Somali communities do not traditionally play a leadership role in the society, Abdi has gained the respect and acknowledgement of the elders for her work in peace building. She currently works part-time as a policy and learning advisor for Copa where she links practical peace work at community level and engagement with policy makers at national and regional level. She is a consultant for various organizations. Her unique personality wins her unusual allies: "It is an honor to have a military leader call and ask me what to do in a particular conflict situation," she says.

The arid north-eastern part of Kenya, populated mostly by pastoral Muslim Somali communities, is a common conflict zone. Water and grazing land for livestock are scarce invaluable resources. Tension intensified when refugees entered the region after the breakup of Somalia in the early 1990s.

Kenya

Eunice Nangueve Inacio

Eunice Nangueve Inacio was born in Angola in 1948 into a religious protestant family. Her background and academic pursuits did not distance Eunice from local people. In 1985, she headed the welfare program in Ministry of Social Affairs, focusing on children and war-displaced people. In 1991, she became the national director for training social workers. Through her efforts today about 600 local peace promoters have been trained and work in 14 provinces. Approximately 120 communities have been supported with local peace initiative grants to provide shelter to thousands affected by war.

When the Civil War resumed after elections failed in 1992, Eunice Inacio became a focal point for running the humanitarian programs for children in Huambo, during the two-year occupation of the province by the Unita rebel army. After the first cease-fire in 1995 she coordinated the National Program for Family Tracing of Separated Children. After the breakdown of the cease-fire and Angola's return to civil war in 2000, Eunice Inacio became the coordinator of the Angolan Peace Building Program (PCP), a national civil society and ecumenical initiative to end the recurring cycles of war.

With strong support from PCP, and Inacio's mediation and consensus building, the Comité Intereclesial para a Paz em Angola (Coiepa), an ecumenical advocate for peace in the country, was founded. This powerful peace movement grew out of an emerging civil society and increasingly articulated popular demands for an end to the war.

Ms Inacio has been actively involved in creating regional linkages and exchanges with Democratic Republic of Congo, Mozambique, Zimbabwe, Zambia, Namibia and South Africa, aimed at strengthening the peace process and peace culture in Angola. Peace movements, including all the principal churches under the leadership of Coiepa and the national NGO Forum have all benefited from Inacio's participation.

"We do not hear about peace-keeping forces. Ms Inacio has managed to bring peacekeeping to the people and challenged them to take responsibilities and protect each other. She is our leader, she knows our context," says one supporter of her work.

Years of mistrust have produced an environment of fear in Angola, in which large numbers of people continue to flee the country. Women and children become destitute. Continued tension and increasing hostilities had left international mediators unable to influence events in the country.

Angola

"When I commenced my work in Sri Lanka, with Quaker Peace & Service, the situation was so fraught that the word 'peace' had a theoretical sense only."

Jennifer Ingram

Peace and Community Action (PCA)

Jennifer Carnelly Ingram's life has been fostered by Quaker values, such as respect for all, unmitigated experience of God, simplicity of living, honesty, pacifism and struggle against injustice. Her father, Eric Baker, was a cofounder of Amnesty International. She has a BA in Education and Community Relations and has been working on peace-building, dialogue and inter-ethnic harmony in the eastern part of Sri Lanka since 1994. Jennifer is the founder and national director of Sri Lankan NGO Peace and Community Action (PCA).

During the course of over a decade of peace-building work in Sri Lanka, Jenny encountered a number of challenges. When she commenced work there the situation was so fraught that even the word "Peace" had a theoretical sense only. Communities were not actively involved in the process of peace-building, a mechanism that they generally conceived to be implemented only at top political levels. Through Quaker Peace & Service (QPS) — though people very often did not know what the abbreviation stood for — Jenny and her energetic team worked to develop capacity at grassroots level to contribute to the national peace process. When the QPS organization changed from being an international NGO to a local NGO there were new challenges awaiting. Local NGOs do not have the same power and as such she came to realize that the organization's former competency, knowledge and value were lingering — even though the same work was still being undertaken and, to some extent, developed. However, the organization was able to surmount these challenges through incessant cooperation with local communities, ensuring that all disputing parties are taken on board. Jenny grew up in a cultural setting where men and women are treated equally. She had to come to terms with the fact that this was not the norm in Sri Lanka. Despite working in a joint capacity with her husband, she had to accept that it was her husband to whom most of the comments and queries were addressed. Furthermore, because of the peculiar Sri Lankan ethos, expatriates from the north are often given a privileged position and their ideas and suggestions are unquestionable. She therefore became aware of the need to avoid falling into the trap of assuming a "big boss" identity. However, she dealt with these peculiarities and has managed to bring harmony to the disputing ethnic communities in the region.

Twenty years of civil war in Sri Lanka made people unaware of non-violent solutions. Jenny's NGO has assisted in boosting the peace-building capacities of local organizations and pooling all potential bodies and individuals in the community to promote the culture of peace and shun violence.

United Kingdom

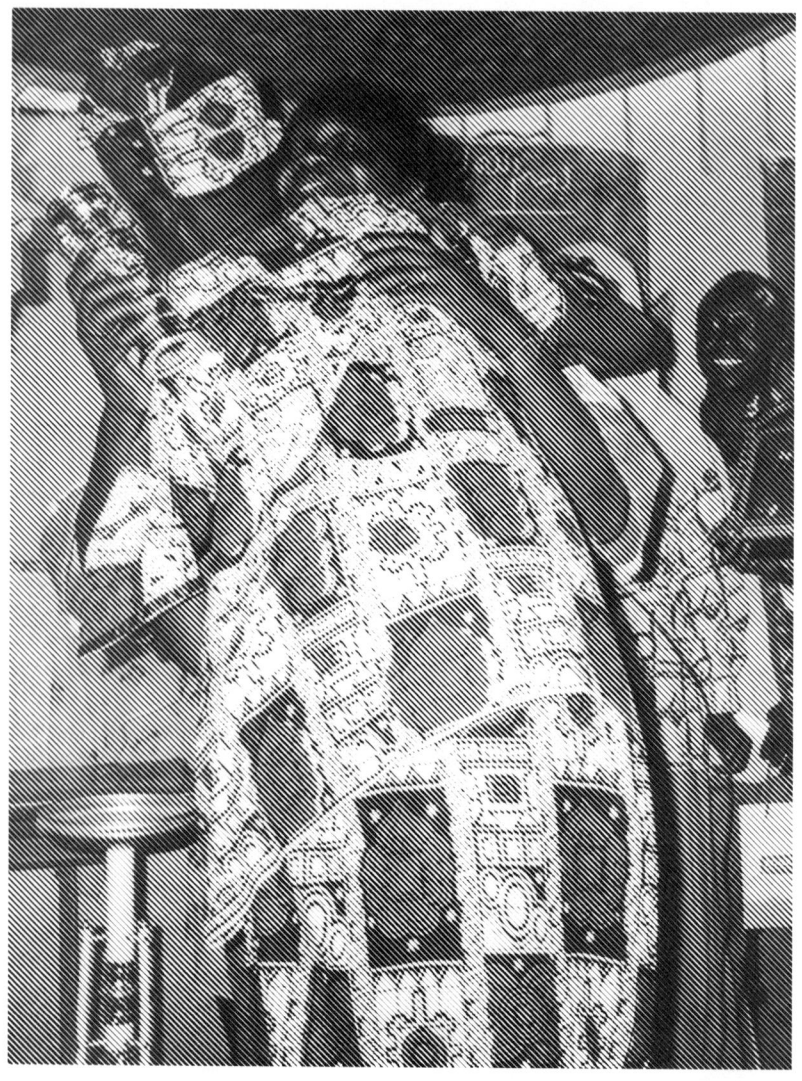

Bruna Iro

Sudanese Women Research & Development (SWRD)
Sudan's Council of Churches (SCC)

Bruna Siricio Iro (46) is a coordinator of the Sudanese Women Research & Development, which was established in 1996. She completed her basic education in Numuli, South Sudan, obtained a Bsc from the Faculty of Economics, Juba University, and in 1992 a Masters in 'Development Planning' from the University of Khartoum. She is affiliated to many social associations and academic institutions working in economic development, such as Education for All (EFA) and United Nations Millennium Development Goal (MDG). Her focus is on peace promotion, education, women's empowerment and fighting HIV/Aids.

By the time Bruna Iro began working in the area of Bahr El Ghazal in Sudan, the civil war in the country was at its peak. Human rights were being appallingly violated, arbitrary arrests were very common and the trafficking and abduction of women and children was extremely widespread. Under such circumstances Bruna was ready to help establish a Committee for the Elimination of Abduction of Women and Children (CEAWC). The impacts on her work of crucial challenges, such as ethnic, cultural and religious diversity, have obstructed her commitment as chairwoman of the Christian Women Justice and Peace Committee emanating from Sudan's Council of Churches (SCC).

Bruna Iro has worked hard to match the programs of the committee with the aims of the national Islamic constitution in the Sudan. She used to run a school that educates both Muslim and Christian children. The outstanding success of the school has raised suspicion about it being a center for missionary activities that seek to convert Muslim children to Christianity. As a result, some parents began to prevent their children from going to the school. But, Bruna quietly met with those parents and successfully resolved the issue through dialogue. Not having regular funding resources to support her projects, she relied on charitable funds, with which she ran the school. Sometimes donations fell short and she had to suspend the services. Among the improvements is the resettlement of Internally Displaced People (IDP) and various activities, such as building new schools, improving healthcare services, raising funds for drinking water projects with the help of local and international bodies, NGOs, Community Based Organizations (CBOs) and churches.

Bruna Iro works courageously under very stressful conditions in Sudan to bring harmony and peace to the whole country. The long-term improvements in social services, resulting from her outstanding efforts, have helped enhance living conditions in the Sudan.

Sudan

Hadizatou Issa Iyayi

Association of Widows and Victims of the Rebellion of Niger (AWVRN)

Born in Diffa in 1957, Hadizatou Issa Iyayi is known in her country for her courage and her consistency in fighting against injustice and the relegation of women to second place in Niger.

Supporters of the AWVRN lost people dear to them — their husbands, their parents or others close to them — during the internal conflicts provoked by the Touareg rebels. It left them in a situation of poverty and total confusion. At the end of the rebellion, these women were afraid and bound to be forgotten by everyone, including Nigerian authorities. This is why Hadizatou initiated this organization. Another reason is that she wanted to mobilize means to allow the widows and victims of the rebellion to take up activities in order to earn their living and not lapse into begging, desolation, and disgrace.

Hadizatou Issa Iyayi and her colleagues know how to work in difficult and very hard conditions with depressed populations in an environment made hostile by the persistence of deforestation and drought. Poverty is increased due to the constraints linked to the threat of the Toubou rebels present in the border triangle of Nigeria — Chad — Niger. These rebels move very easily in the field and constitute a serious threat since they strip the peasants of all their goods. Despite all this, Hadizatou and the others in her association did not lose hope and organized the production of local goods for use in the markets. Hadiza urged people to settle down and to participate fully in development that cannot be obtained without peace. In her understanding, without peace, the construction of the country and the search for stability to build a better future is not possible. With this in mind, the leader of the AWVRN approached the armies. And there were many who agreed to lay down their weapons and to renounce all forms of revenge. Still, she often receives death threats by people who do not understand that peace cannot be obtained without laying down weapons.

Her main work is the creation of the Association of Widows and Victims of the Rebellion of Niger (AWVRN). This structure operates in the Diffa region where she organizes widows and victims of the rebellion to defend their rights and those of their children.

Niger

Myla Jabilles Leguro

Catholic Relief Services (CRS)
Mindanao Peacebuilding Institute (MPI)
Grassroots Peace Learning Center (GPLC)

Myla Jabilles Leguro (born 1968) is the Peace and Reconciliation Program Manager of Catholic Relief Services (CRS) where she works on Muslim-Christian dialogue in war-torn Mindanao. She has been involved in peace and reconciliation projects in areas with histories of violent conflicts like Jolo and Basilan. She organized two major peace-building institutions: the Mindanao Peacebuilding Institute (MPI) and the Grassroots Peace Learning Center (GPLC). Through these institutions, Myla helps create peaceful communities in Mindanao.

Myla Jabilles Leguro has spent most of her professional life building peaceful communities in Mindanao through her involvement with Catholic Relief Services (CRS). She joined CRS in 1991 working on enterprise, agriculture, health, food and education in Mindanao. Then she moved to CRS's Enterprise Development Program where she was instrumental in the creation of two successful Garmeen-type banks. In 1998, she conceived the idea of establishing a peace institute in Mindanao after she studied at the Summer Peacebuilding Institute of a Conflict Transformation Program in Virginia, USA. Myla organized the Mindanao Peacebuilding Institute (MPI) which was formally established in 2001.

The MPI promotes grassroots empowerment and brings together communities for training in peace building. Myla believes that her work is not only limited to grassroots empowerment, advocacy and capacity building, but extends to developing personal relationships with the people to whom she extends help. "[This job is] challenging because you take it to heart," she discloses. Above all, she has kept a sense of balance between her personal issues and her social responsibilities. In another response to the conflict in Mindanao, Myla organized the Grassroots Peace Learning Center (GPLC) in 2003, which takes a multi-track approach to addressing the complexity of the issues on the island. Among the goals of GPLC that Myla is proudest of is the enhancement of women's participation in peace building. She organizes women within communities who will benefit from the livelihood projects that GPLC initiates. Myla believes that the participation of women in peace building will hasten the development of areas identified as "zones of peace" and that peace education is very important in planting the seeds of peace in Mindanao.

In Muslim Mindanao, centuries-old interreligious prejudices at grassroots level among indigenous peoples, Muslims and Christians, who inhabit the conflict-ridden region, need to be disentangled as part of the peace-building process.

Philippines

Asma Jahangir

Human Rights Commission of Pakistan (HRC)

Asma Jahangir (born 1952) is a thorn in the side of Pakistan's powerful. For a quarter-century, this human rights' lawyer has defended the oppressed in Pakistani society, among them political prisoners, bonded laborers, women, and minorities sentenced under unjust laws. She has also played a pivotal role in building institutional structures to provide free legal aid and monitoring human rights in Pakistan. Internationally recognized for her achievements, Jahangir also works with the International Commission of Jurists, and is a senior UN official.

She is the subject of innumerable media interviews and profiles, has won prestigious international awards like the Ramon Magsaysay Award and holds a high-profile UN post. Despite this, Pakistani human rights' lawyer Asma Jahangir remains a fighter for unpopular causes. She still runs into trouble with the Pakistani establishment for raising issues that many ignore.

Asma grew up in the school of hard knocks. She was not yet a lawyer during her first legal battle in 1972: her father, a legislator in the national assembly, had been detained by the then prime minister, Zulgikar Ali Bhutto. Asma filed a constitutional petition in the supreme court challenging his arrest, winning in a year and a half. In 1980, Asma, a law graduate from Punjab University, started Pakistan's first all-woman law firm along with three partners. Pakistan was under martial law and Zia-ul-Haq's regime tried to bring the country under Sharia' diktat. A founder-member of the Women's Action Forum (WAF), Asma earned the nickname "little heroine" for leading a protest march against the laws in 1983. In 1986, Asma set up Pakistan's first free legal aid center, the AGHS Legal Aid Cell. Apart from helping hundreds of oppressed people-minorities, bonded labor, and grassroots women-the AGHS is also highly regarded for its expertise in legal research and its effective lobbying for reforming laws that discriminate against women. The same year, Asma helped set up the Human Rights' Commission of Pakistan, an independent body of lawyers and activists, in which she served as founding secretary general and chairperson.

Since 1998, Asma has also been speaking up for the oppressed in some of the world's worst trouble spots, as the UN's special rapporteur on extrajudicial, summary, or arbitrary executions. Married with three children, she lives in Lahore.

Zia-ul-Haq's regime tried to bring Pakistan under the diktat of Islamic laws. Among the most significant were those that denied women the equal rights they already enjoyed under the constitution, relegating them to second-class citizenship, and those which severely restricted freedom of expression.

Christiane Johnson

Mouvement contre les Armes Légères en Afrique de l'Ouest (MALAO)
Réseau d'Action sur les Armes Légères en Afrique de l'Ouest (RASALAO)
International Action Network Against Small Arms (IANSA)

A doctor and dental surgeon, Christiane Agboton Johnson is an inveterate follower of peace. She is enthusiastic and deeply humane. Born in Benin 50 years ago, she now lives in in Dakar, Senegal, with her three children whose father died some time ago.

Christiane Agboton Johnson, president of Malao said once in a conference: "Indeed, women are often to be found at the origin of initiatives for reconciliation, mediation, and conflict resolution, even if they do not show up at the negotiation table. In peace negotiations as in declarations of war, men are more numerous than women. This is where the link between women as builders of peace and the struggle against small arms becomes evident. These so-called light weapons have killed more than four million people in the last ten years. They have become the instrument of choice in most armed conflicts, and the UN Secretary General has rightly described them as weapons of mass destruction. After wars, they are the tools of banditry, crime, and conjugal violence. Hence, women can no longer limit themselves to repairing the damage caused by conflict, as in humanitarian action, demobilisation, and reintegration. Today, they are obliged to wage an additional battle, the one to eliminate light weapons."

If Christiane had the idea of launching MALAO, it is because she heard countless times the crackling of firearms in Africa due to the trafficking of arms. She is a doctor, but, she is known in Africa and elsewhere as a peace campaigner. With MALAO, she works on all sites of peace in West Africa. The movement is active in the fight against small arms and light weapons, for security, peace, and development, and opted very early on to include gender considerations in the carrying out of its programmes, especially in Casamance, a region in constant insecurity in southern Senegal.

It is difficult to speak about women and small arms in a country where stereotypes about small arms and the clear division of men's and women's roles remain strong, rooted in tradition and culture.

Senegal

Although she has few resources and fewer funds, Immaculate has the gift of hope and confidence to give to people shattered by the conflict – that is all that can help people survive the reality of war.

Immaculate Josef

Holy Cross Sisters

Sister Immaculate Josef (born 1950) is a doctor by training and a sister of the church by choice. She combines these two facets of her life to work with persons displaced by civil strife in Sri Lanka. Immaculate works in difficult conditions that get more strenuous as the conflict escalates, but her persistence and courage and that of her team have helped save the lives of thousands of children. Their work also supports the fragile peace in the region by motivating young people to engage in peace-building efforts.

Sister Immaculate Josef pursued her religious education and her academic career in medicine with equal zeal. From 1996 to 1997, she served at the Mallavi Hospital, Kilinochchi, which served displaced people. This was the beginning of her enduring association with people rendered homeless in their own country by conflict. Since 2003, she has been a province matron of the Holy Cross Sisters, with 85 sisters working under her guidance.

Immaculate works in difficult conditions that get choppier by the day as the conflict vacillates. Transportation is difficult and time-consuming; Immaculate has to put up with humiliating searches at various checkpoints; she has to brave bombings, landmines, and armed attacks; the embargo means a paucity of funds and resources. The most painful part of her work, though, is to be confronted with the destruction of the people's homeland, and the fragmentation of families, with innumerable people scattered in exile across the world. Then, of course, there is the perennial paucity of funds. The medical assistance that the sisters provide, despite these impediments, has helped save the lives of thousands of children. Immaculate also collaborates with various NGOs and church organizations to spread the net of services as wide as possible.

Immaculate's work also supports the extremely fragile peace in the region by motivating young people to engage in peace-building efforts. She has devised a unique way to help children and young people connect with others from a different ethnic background–games. Although she has scarce resources and scarcer funds, Immaculate has the fortune of hope and confidence — it is hope alone that can help anyone get through the desperate reality of the war.

Life in Sri Lanka is a running battle between the Sinhala government forces and the minority Tamil rebels, and the victims are mostly noncombatants. Tens of thousands have died in confrontations and crossfire, many women have been widowed, and children are recruited as cannon fodder.

Sri Lanka

Corazon "Dinky" Juliano-Soliman

Department of Social Welfare and Development (DSWD)
CODE-NGO
Community Organizers Multiversity (CO-Multiversity)

Before joining government in 2001, Corazon "Dinky" Soliman worked for 30 years organizing and training grassroots organizations of peasants and urban poor. Her skills in participatory methods, capacity building and creative approaches to problems have benefited the marginalized, NGOs and the government. Through the CO-Multiversity, Dinky promoted peace education, peace zones, peace negotiations and conflict resolution. Her engagement included advocating for funding mechanisms such as debt swap arrangements, the use of recovered ill-gotten wealth and the coconut levy for agrarian reform.

When Dinky Soliman was a political science student at the University of the Philippines, she felt she was studying theories. "Where are the people?" she asked, and shifted to social work. Dinky credits her parents, both community and church leaders, for her love of service to the people. When she was growing up, people kept coming to their house to ask for help or attend meetings. Other influences were her grandmother, who was with the Red Cross, and an aunt who was a juvenile domestic relations court judge in Manila. Prior to her appointment in 2001 as Secretary of the Department of Social Welfare and Development (DSWD), Dinky was an NGO leader who had worked with the urban poor and peasant organizations.

Unforgettable moments in her life are not dramatic. She remembers a farmer who was so afraid of the mayor that Dinky and her group worked with him for three months and then arranged a meeting with the mayor. After the meeting, the farmer said, "I am so surprised the mayor is human after all. It feels good to know I can talk to him and not die." For Dinky, "That was such a high. That's what we live for — when you see the fruits or signs of development come to life." As DSWD Secretary, she values the dignity of the poor. "We work with the poor and they come to us in their most vulnerable state. The least we can do is to give them service with dignity." Next to the President, the diminutive DSWD Secretary is probably the most covered government official in the media. And Dinky stands out because of a whimsical streak of color in her hair that she says she wears to remind herself not to be too serious. "Quirky, irreverent, colorful — that's who you are," she tells herself. To remind herself of where she came from: "You are there because you fought for an accountable and transparent governance. I must be rooted in that."

When the conflict between farmers and landowners is not resolved, it becomes a seedbed for insurgency, terrorism and drugs. Dinky helps them name the problem and see their own power to transform an unjust situation into one with respect for peace and justice.

Raisa Kadyrova

Foundation for Tolerance International (FTI)

Raisa "Raya" Kadyrova (born 1957) is the president and founder of the Kyrgyz NGO Foundation of Tolerance International (FTI), operating within the cross-border communities of Central Asia. She is a well-known peacemaker who works in the Ferghana Valley. Social, economic, interethnic conflicts, corruption, and crime make this region dangerous. Raya organizes people to help resolve these problems and conflicts.

Raisa "Raya" Kadyrova is the president and founder of the Foundation for Tolerance International (FTI). This organization's mission is to prevent and resolve interethnic conflicts in the cross-border areas of Central Asia, comprised of five post-Soviet Union Republics. The problems the Central Asia region faces today are disputed lands and borders, scarcity of natural resources, especially water and land, militarization and small arms, religious extremism and terrorism, land mines, interethnic conflicts, poverty, and drug trafficking. "Our NGO is one of the few in Central Asia working on problems of interethnic hostilities," Raya says.

As part of her activities, she monitors and evaluates the conflict situation, organizes and facilitates negotiation and mediation processes, conducts trainings and consensus-building activities, and communicates with the divided local populace. Raya works on grassroots, national, and international levels, while cooperating closely with government representatives and members of the Parliament. The activities of her organization are recognized as successful by the people, the government and Parliament. However, the growing number of victims of violent conflicts makes her realize "that our activities must be more effective." Because she is so heavily involved in many activities at the same time and bears the load of implementing activities over the entire Central Asia region, she has not had time to document the processes and results, failures and successes of her activities.

"International donors often ask us, 'What makes FTI successful?' and we cannot always answer that question because we do not have time to sit down and document and analyze what we have achieved. Sometimes it seems to us that we work like a fire brigade, reacting to emerging issues, without being able to slow down and take a breath," Raya says.

Having acquired independence after the disintegration of the USSR, the Kyrgyz Republic found itself to be free, but completely undeveloped and facing a whole range of problems, including economic development, foreign and internal political strategies, poverty, and restoration of its own culture.

Kyrgyzstan

Zahira Kamal

Palestinian Ministry of Women's Affairs (PMWA)
Women's Study Center for Legal and Social Consultation (WSCLSC)
Palestinian Democratic Union (PDU)

Zahira Kamal, born in 1945, is a leading Palestinian activist who has worked towards the welfare of Palestinian woman. She obtained a BSc in Physics from Ain Shams University, Cairo, in 1968. She also received a Diploma in Teaching Methodology from the University of Jordan in 1978. She has taught physics and science for many years at the Women's Teacher Training Center in Ramallah. Currently, she is the Palestinian Authority Minister for Women's Affairs.

Zahira Kamal has played a large part in the modernization of Palestinian society. She strongly believes in the empowerment of Palestinian women through education, and held the post of Director General of the Directorate of the Gender Planning and International Cooperation at the Palestinian National Authority (PNA) from 1995 until 2004. In this capacity, she formed an inter-ministerial coordination committee for the advancement of woman. Zahira is the founder of Palestinian Women's Action, the first grassroots organization dealing with women's empowerment issues, which she chaired from 1978—1991. She is affiliated with many women's NGO's in Palestine, including the Woman's Study Center for Legal and Social Consultation and the Jerusalem Center for Women.

Zahira Kamal has worked as a spokeswoman for the Palestinian Federation of Women's Action (PFWA) in many countries, including Russia and the USA, exposing the Palestinian issue in several conferences. She was a member of the Palestinian Advisory Council to the Middle East Peace Conference in Madrid, Washington and Moscow. Zahira has actively participated in meetings with Israeli peace promotion groups and she is a member of both the Israeli and Palestinian Networking and the Jerusalem Link — two cooperating women centers in East and West Jerusalem. She has written extensively on a number of key issues including women's empowerment, occupation, women's political participation, the peace process and women under administrative detention.

Zahira Kamal was born in Jerusalem and was three years old when the war of 1948 broke out, forcing Palestinians to quit their homes and land. In her life she has witnessed a war in her country, Palestine, every decade.

Occupied Palestinian Territory

Wimalee Karunaretna

Sinhala Tamil Rural Women's Organization (STRWO)
Nuwara Eliya

Poverty and the trauma of war have not stopped Wimalee Karunaretna (born 1961) from making common cause with thousands of poor families in her district, and helping them persevere for a better life. In a country ripped by ethnic conflict, Karunaretna builds hopes for a peaceful future by running preschools where Sinhala and Tamil children play and study together, learn each others' languages, and cut through the prejudices and stereotypes that divide their elders.

Lack of money forced Wimalee Karunaretna, eldest of five children of a farmer, to give up her dreams of going to university. But, today, she is president of a 36,000-person organization in Sri Lanka's poverty-stricken plantation areas.

Growing up poor in a village a mile from Nuwara Eliya town in Sri Lanka's central province, Wimalee secured a place at university, but her family's situation interfered with her education. However, she wrote, particularly on women's socioeconomic issues, and sent her work to the local paper. It was here that she met her husband, a reporter with the paper. The two moved to Trincomalee in the country's eastern province, where three communities — Sinhala, Tamil, and Muslim — live together. Wimalee, a Sinhala, continued to write, and got involved in social work. She joined a local organization, the Rural Women's Association, becoming its president. But, in 1998, the family lost everything to heavy fighting between the Liberation Tigers of Tamil Eelan and the army. They returned to Nuwara Eliya, where Wimalee began her work anew. She formed a women's group in which they pooled their small savings for mutual benefit. Wimalee's main focus was empowering women economically, creating space for them to share their experiences and problems, and providing them with information about their rights. She started a preschool for children from all three communities.

Wimalee, who also started a rural bank, has received awards including the President's Award in 1998 for leadership in community development and peace-building, the Rural Women Organization Award in 2000 for creative work in rural areas, the Sri Lankan NGO Council's Sevajoth Award in 2001 for peace-building, an award by the women's affairs ministry for working with women, and the NGO Samaseva's award for peace-building.

Plantation laborers in Sri Lanka are extremely poorly paid, and education levels in these hilly areas are appalling, compared to the rest of the country. There are not enough teachers, and students have to travel long distances on bad roads to access schooling, where possible.

Sri Lanka

"What gives me energy is the success in the setting-up of peace centers in villages: our principle of non-violence in action."

Gege Katana Bukuru

Solidarity of Activist Women for Human Rights (Sofad)

Gege Katana Bukuru (44) is known as the "Iron Lady" of the Democratic Republic of Congo (DRC) for her courageous activism for women's rights. She has been imprisoned several times and witnessed people being tortured. Gege has been a member of Solidarity of Activist Women for Human Rights (Sofad) for four years. She forms groups of women leaders and organizes campaigns to support women victims of sexual violence. In addition to workshops, training and advocacy campaigns, she has created peace centers in villages which have earned her respect in many provinces.

Despite facing enormous difficulties and the pain of being forsaken by colleagues, Gege Katana will not abandon her people. She is the eldest daughter of a traditional chief, who instilled in her a strong conscience regarding her responsibilities toward her people. Gege believes in God and in His power to help her focus on her work despite her shortcomings. She is gifted in identifying people and circumstances that are resourceful for her activities. Gege expresses herself clearly and simply, earning the respect of even her opponents. Her frail appearance hides the perseverance and strong will that earned her the nickname "Iron Lady". As a member of Sofad, she has formed groups of women leaders and organized campaigns to support victims of sexual violence. Her initiatives have helped 1700 women. She has also conducted workshops, training and advocacy and peace centers in villages. Gege is renowned and emulated in many provinces. Her network comprises many women at the grassroots level. Sofad members are determined to realize peace cells and to structure women's rights activities in order to sensitize more women on their rights. Sofad works in collaboration with other institutions that work for peace, for the protection of human rights and NGOs involved in local and international development. At international level Sofad partners with Amnesty International and others. Gege's vision is for women to enjoy their rights without restrictions, injustice and fear.

Armed rebels are a constant threat to the people in Uvira, South Kivu region of the DRC. They see their authority and reign of terror threatened by peace activists like Gege who mobilize people to stand up for their rights. Peace activists limit the illegitimate power of the rebels.

Democratic Republic of the Congo

Mary Kayitesi Blewitt

Survivors Fund (Surf)

Mary Kayitesi Blewitt was born in 1962 in a refugee camp in Burundi. She is the founder of Survivors Fund (Surf) in London, a non-governmental organization concerned with advocacy, litigation and fundraising to support survivors of the massacre and genocide that took place in Rwanda in 1994. She works through eight Rwandese organizations supporting girls, women and orphans who are heads of households. The organizations provide material support and create opportunities to meet and treat trauma, an essential condition for peaceful co-existence.

The genocide that took place in Rwanda in 1994 shaped the mission and destiny of Mary Kayitesi Blewitt. The turbulence that had driven her parents into the camp came back to haunt her. Most of her family members were butchered. Grief and trauma engulfed the survivors. Few were lucky to give a decent burial to their loved ones.

Being a Tutsi in Rwanda during the 1959 revolution and later in 1994 was considered a curse. Insecurity and fear dominated their lives. At the time of Mary's birth, her parents were in Burundi as refugees. Her father died when she was five. Her mother remarried but her stepfather later died, leaving her to fend for eight children. The family then moved to Uganda. In 1986, Mary went to the UK to study at the School of Oriental and African Studies. Life was beginning to look normal until suddenly in 1994 when the genocide began. A million lives were lost in 100 days, 50 of the victims were those of her immediate family.

Mary's stepfather had been a doctor. From him she learnt the great value of support and providing relief where and when one can. So when the killing stopped, she went to Rwanda to bury her family and try to help. The countless corpses and mass graves were a daily sight. The survivors recounted harrowing tales. She describes the eight months she spent in the country as her most trying time.

Back in the UK, she set up Surf to help the survivors. The funds benefits especially the hundreds of Rwandian survivors in the UK who had no support. Surf also assists survivors in Rwanda through grassroots organizations like Associations des Veuves du Génocide, Solace Ministries, and Ibuka, the survivors' umbrella group. Surf also ensures that the voices of the survivors are heard, that the memories of the genocide are kept alive and that the victims are never forgotten.

Violence in Rwanda has its roots in the country's colonial history. A racial and ethnic ideology divided the population into two, the Hutu majority and the Tutsi minority, and laid the ground for the repeated genocides. In the 1994 genocide one million people died in just a hundred days.

Rwanda

Sook-Im Kim

Peace and Reunification Committee of the Korea Women's Association
Unification and Peace in Korean Women's United Association
Korea Campaign to Ban Landmines

Sook-Im Kim began empowering women to make a difference in Korea in the late 1970s, in what she calls the "dark ages for women's movements". In the face of military dictatorship, a divided country, and an inflated national defense budget, women's voices were silent. Understanding that women's welfare was at stake, Sook-Im pioneered the women's peace movement by organizing the radical group, Korean Association of Christian Women, for whom she and her husband built a church and kindergarten. For 26 years, Sook-Im has modeled leadership in her quest for peace.

The daughter of a wealthy businessman, Sook-Im Kim was always encouraged by her parents to become socially active. But a quiet reader and musician, Sook-Im preferred to keep to herself. She enrolled in Seoul's Women's University to study literature, and there her life took a sharp turn. A jazz pianist and dancer, her performance of a masque dance caught the attention of the military police. Believing it was a form of government resistance, they sent Sook-Im to prison.

Ironically, it was at this point that her true resistance began. She became very ill in prison and an operation on her spine ended her days of dancing. But a new kind of dance was born. Upon her release from prison, she became an activist, fired by her firsthand understanding of an unjust political system.

Working with the Korean Association of Christian Women, Sook-Im developed many national unification, disarmament, and peace campaigns. Understanding that the hardships of the people of Korea were closely linked to the division of their country and the exclusion of women in their own and their country's destiny, Kim wanted to learn more. She studied social welfare policy at graduate school. In the years that followed, she reported on Korean women's organizations at the Beijing World Women's Summit, and chaired many committees to ban landmines, reconcile a divided Korea, and end weapon proliferation. Women who had kept silent during the Vietnam War now spoke out against dispatching Korean troops to Iraq. The emphasis of her work has been on daily peacemaking programs, peace mediation, and policies based on a feminist perspective of diplomacy and security. As coordinator for South-North Women's Interchange, she led an effort to rethink old laws that block the nation's reunification.

A prison experience that inspired her activism also destroyed her health. Sook-Im works tirelessly in a climate of tension. The peace movement in her country is still in its youth, making it difficult for her to build strong networks and a sound infrastructure.

Republic of Korea

Nina Kolybashkina

Department of Social Policy and Social Work, Oxford University
Center for Ethnic and Social Studies
Network of Intercultural Exchange and Interethnic Tolerance

Nina Kolybashkina (born 1958) has worked in the fields of civil society and democratic governance, conflict prevention, and capacity building of non-governmental organizations in different parts of the world. She was a local municipal and community development officer of the United Nations Interim Administration Mission (UNMIK) in Kosovo. She is also experienced in working with minority communities and youth. Nina was a founding member of the Association of Youth Centers. Together with the UN Youth Foundation, she prepared a Young Peace builders' Conference held in Crimea, in 2005.

"In the common enterprise of peace building, my humble role is that of an interpreter," Nina Kolybashkina says. Her career started when she worked as an interpreter for a UN construction project in Simferopol. That job taught her that translation requires not merely shifting between languages, but also finding common points between the systems of thinking of diverse groups. Later, in managing social projects, she realized that providing basic social services was essentially a work of translating the needs of community members into the language of project proposals and policy recommendations. A former project officer of the United Nations (UN) mission in Kosovo, she then worked in the resettlement of people, primarily Crimean Tatars, who were Muslim. The work in the settlements made her aware of the differences in culture and religion, but also of similarities in their social problems. Recently in Kosovo, while establishing a dialogue between Albanian and Serbian civil servants about the common problems in Orahovac∕Rahovec municipality, Nina had a look at the social and economic costs of war and the difficulties of reconciliation. It made it very clear for her that prevention is better than cure. Prevention strategies are especially effective with young people and so the youth became Nina's major focus in Crimea, not only as a UN project officer, but also as an active citizen. She began training and public awareness campaigns in conflict prevention and tolerance education among the youth. Nina was a founding member of the Association of Youth Centers. Together with the UN Youth Foundation, they prepared a Young Peace Builders' Conference to be held in Crimea in 2005. Nina represents the special generation of people born under the Soviet system but given a fresh opportunity to live in a democratic world.

In work with multi-ethnic communities, there is need not only to translate languages but to look at the common points in ways of thinking. The best way to deal with conflicts is to prevent them early on, and that means working with the youth.

Ukraine

"In Central African Republic during the tribal wars, women, the mothers of humanity, stood up like one person, green leaves in their hands to ask the opposing combatants to stop the bloodshed."

Simone Clara Kossianga

Union of Baptist Churches (Ufeb)

Simone Clara Kossianga (49) leads a religious-based organization, the Union of Baptist Churches (Ufeb). She is a secondary school teacher and helps women to assist one another, gain additional training through religious-based seminars, and thus be peace and reconciliation facilitators in Central Africa.

"Being the head of this women network for peace, I am sustained by conviction," says Clara Kossianga. She is well placed to advocate for peace because she has lived through crisis, political disturbances and riots. The search for a long lasting peace has become a daily labor of love. "The courage of the women, their determination enables me to go on fighting to the end," she says.

Living in a country that has known political and military turmoil, Clara Kossianga has had to make a lot of sacrifices to visit local provinces to work with women's groups. With limited funding, visiting remote areas, particularly those more than 1200 km away from the capital, is but a labor of love. She often has to use her own resources to do that. Her salary as a school teacher and additional incomes from odd jobs are what enable her to meet the demands of her children including school fees and to supplement the organization as necessary. She works with more than 10,000 women in the entire country. She encourages women to participate without taking sides in the national reconciliation processes in crisis time, in order to link them to decision making in churches and the society. She also encourages women to improve their ability to manage themselves and others especially the elderly, orphans and pygmies who are dependent on humanitarian support. Now, training is oriented to development and capacity building, including HIV/Aids awareness. She helps them in the fight against HIV/Aids in the family and religious environments. For instance after several seminars on HIV/Aids, women volunteered themselves for testing, and committed to using preventive methods in Christian environment (use of condoms). They realized that with a prevalence level of 15 percent no one was safe in the country.

The Central African Republic, particularly Bangui, has experienced repeated mutinies from 1996. Peace negotiations undertaken by a few groups have not reached any long-lasting peace accord.

Central African Republic

"We have suffered for over half a century. That is too much. We firmly believe it is now time to live together with parents, sisters, brothers, all our families, in a reunited, peaceful Korea."

Hyun-Sook Lee

Women Making Peace; Council of Unification Education
Global Partnership for Prevention of Armed Conflict,
Northeast Asia Region (GPPAC)

Hyun-Sook Lee is the cofounder and former Executive Director of Women Making Peace, an organization established in 1997 with the goal of creating a culture of peace and reunification on the Korean peninsula. She helped open the door between North and South Korea by getting the first humanitarian aid to the North and encouraging the first people-to-people visits. Hyun-Sook is also cofounder of the Korea Women's Hotline, which provides guidance and support to victims of domestic abuse, and which was instrumental in establishing domestic and sexual violence as criminal acts in South Korea.

Hyun-Sook Lee has over 20 years of experience in human rights and peacemaking. One of her earliest efforts was to work with several colleagues at the Korea Christian Academy to initiate a program to raise awareness and eradicate domestic violence in South Korea. The Korea Women's Hotline enabled victims of domestic abuse to receive guidance and support, and it was instrumental in establishing domestic and sexual violence as criminal acts in South Korea. It also served as a catalyst for the progressive women's movement in Korea.

In 1997, Hyun-Sook initiated and later became the executive director of Women Making Peace. Its first project was a Sharing Food-Sharing Love campaign for North Korean women and children that resulted in the sending of 26 tons of milk powder to the North, and which laid the foundations for North and South Korean exchanges known as the Sunshine Policy. Since 2001, she has engaged in negotiation activities between the two Koreas. And in October 2002, Hyun-Sook finally succeeded in organizing the "North and South Korean Women's Reunification Rally for Peace and the Implementation of the June 15th Joint Declaration". For many of the 700 delegates, the opportunity to meet women from the other country in a spirit of peace and tolerance proved to be an extraordinarily emotional experience.

In May 2003, Hyun-Sook organized a coalition of bipartisan Korean elected representatives, NGO leaders, and scholars to go to the USA to speak to members of the US Congress and opinion makers on the impact of US withdrawal from engagement with North Korea. In December 2003, Hyun-Sook received the prestigious National Reconciliation Award from the Korean Council of Reconciliation and Cooperation, made up of NGO leaders and members of parliament.

After World War II, Korea was a society marked by poverty, tension, and militarization due to the political division between the North and South. Overcoming traditional gender biases inherent in Korean society, Hyun-Sook Lee is working to bridge that division and effect social change.

Republic of Korea

Emma Leslie

Action Asia Network

Emma Leslie (born 1971), an Australian actively engaged in peace building and conflict transformation, came to Cambodia in 1997 and helped develop a peace education curriculum for Cambodian high schools and peace training programs. Emma and her colleagues established Action Asia Network, a regional network of peace builders, focused on supporting people living in violent conflict. She also works internationally in conflict transformation through the South Africa-based Action Network and the UK-based organization Responding to Conflict (RTC).

Emma Leslie has contributed to conflict transformation and peace education in Cambodia and plays an important role in peace networking in Asia. She grew up in the country town of Bathurst, Australia, and worked in community development with the Anglican Board of Mission-Australia (ABM), where she helped to establish an exchange program for young people with mission partners throughout the Asia Pacific region. She was also active in a number of ecumenical youth networks and organizations, including the Christian Conference of Asia Youth Committee.

In 1997, she moved to Cambodia where she worked with the Cambodia Campaign to Ban Landmines (CCBL) focusing on conflict issues related to the distribution of land after de-mining. Consequently she became involved in a number of Cambodian organizations, namely the Working Group for Weapon Reduction's Peace Education Project (WGWR), the nationalism and identity research program of the Alliance for Conflict Transformation (ACT) and the Cambodia Peace and Development Center's (CPD) conflict transformation training.

Emma also helped found Action, an international network, and Action Asia, a regional network. With the Action Asia network, she has established relations among peace builders in Cambodia, Burma, Nepal, Sri Lanka, Kyrgyzstan and other parts of the region. With her husband, Emma is building a community and education center in northwestern Cambodia for isolated and rural communities. "Our children need these lessons in problem solving, peace, prejudice, discrimination, cooperation and vision building," Emma reflected at a workshop in a primary school in Kampong Thom province. Currently, Emma is writing a curriculum for community level training on mediation and alternative dispute resolution. She also hopes to operate an action research master's degree course on applied conflict transformation by December 2005.

After going through genocide and internal war, Cambodia is struggling to reconstruct the country. While people continue to be traumatized by the war, violence is still prevalent, and conflicts abound, there is no systematic conflict response curriculum in the country's educational institutions.

Angelica Livne

Bereshit LeShalom Foundation (BLF)
Rainbow Theater in the Upper Galilee (RTiUG)

Angelica Edna Calo Livne is an educator and advocate of peace through arts, among children from different religious and cultural backgrounds. In 2002, Angelica created the Rainbow Theater, in the Upper Galilee of Israel, involving young Jews and Arabs, Christians, Muslims and Druses, who with mime and dance narrate what goes on in the mind of an adolescent living in a country at war. Using their bodies, the actors express their inner thoughts and burning desires to accept people and be accepted as they are. One of Angelica's projects is to help children physically hurt by terrorist attacks.

At the break of the Intifada in 2000, Angelica felt she needed to do something to bring about a change. She could not just stand by and watch the terrible events traumatizing the lives of people in the Middle East and around the world. She was driven by her conscience, a sense of responsibility and an inner feeling to help the children suffering from these tragic times. Angelica lives in a Kibbutz near the border with Lebanon. Only few people believed in the importance of her project in the beginning. She has worked voluntarily for many years, rewarded only by the spark she sees in the eyes of the children and adults who work with her. The costs of her first theatre performance about peace, Bereshit, were financed thanks to her family's savings. More than once the members of her Kibbutz have tried to convince her to give up her projects, stating that they are based on arts and education and so cannot provide concrete influential results. However, she is convinced of the importance of her project.

Angelica Livne has been living in a very small house, filled with papers, books and information about projects from all over the world. She has no car, no office, and no facilities to operate such projects. Yet she writes books and articles on education and operates projects to help children hurt by terrorism. She also gives theatre lessons and runs artistic workshops, and is active in the forum for Jewish and Arabic people. Moreover she travels into vulnerable areas with the theatre and with the wounded children to spread the message of peace. Angelica presents her vision for peace, saying, "I believe that the person who is rich inside, who loves what he has, who is sure of himself and his faith, can love and accept others without reservations! He has no need to predominate, to impose himself and his faith on others."

Angelica Livne is an educator of peace through arts, promoting peace among children from different faiths and cultural backgrounds. In 2002, she was inspired to create the Rainbow Theater, where young Jews, Muslims, Christians and Druses perform.

Israel

Savitri MacCuish

World Peace Flame Foundation
Life Foundation International

Savitri MacCuish, born in Scotland in 1959, lives in the Netherlands as the founder and director of the World Peace Flame Foundation and Life Foundation International. She has pioneered unique detraumatization programs in crisis areas and teaches practical peacemaking techniques in workshops all over the world. In 1999, she was the driving force behind the creation of the eternal World Peace Flame (WPF), lit by peacemakers from five continents. The WPF burns in monuments in cities around the world. In 2004, it brought together ambassadors from every country to sign a statement for peace.

Savitri MacCuish is guided by the motto: "Transform the world by giving people the tools to transform themselves." There is one key event that moved Savitri MacCuish to become the sensitive peacemaker she is today. One day in 1994, she was driving through war-torn Bosnia when she was stopped by some old women dressed in black. One came to Savitri's van, which was loaded with aid materials. "I looked at her, but somehow I could not bear to look in her eyes. She had lost everything. I fumbled for some food to give her. She just stared. Suddenly, it occurred to me, 'What if this were my own mother?' Then I stopped trying to her give things and realized that I could help her simply by being unafraid to look at the pain in her eyes. The old woman reached out and patted my hand."

Savitri longed to find a symbol that could give people the hope and strength to help them heal at a deep level, both as individuals and as societies. And so, in 1999, she was the driving force behind the creation of the World Peace Flame. For the first time in history, seven flames of peace were lit by eminent peacemakers on five continents, flown across the oceans by military and commercial aircrafts, and united into one eternally burning World Peace Flame, representing humanity's highest aspirations for peace. Since then, Savitri's work has extended to people of all backgrounds, with a variety of innovative peace projects involving politicians, business leaders, and Hollywood stars, as well as refugees and victims of violence, and more recently school children. At the heart of Savitri's vision is the belief that each and every one of us is responsible for building peace.

Savitri teaches self-help techniques for healing and empowerment with programs in the crisis areas of Eastern Europe, Africa, and Northern Ireland, as well as throughout North America, Europe, and Australia. It is her dream to unite all people in peace.

Netherlands

"I request people
to unconditionally help
victims of violence
and war. Unforgettable
moments occur when
I successfully mediate
for families and then
see women return
to their matrimonial
homes."

Justine Masika Bihamba

Pole Institute
Synergy des Femmes pour les Victimes des violences Sexuelles (Sfvs)

Justine Masika Bihamba (40) has worked in the Democratic Republic of the Congo (DRC) since 1990 fighting poverty, promoting peace and human rights, promoting rural women, fighting sexual violence and supporting war victims. She organizes workshops within local communities and listening centers, grants rotating credits, and provides psychosocial, medical and legal support for victims of sexual violence. Through her dedicated work people are overjoyed to have obtained justice, gained back their health and independence and experience.

Justine Masika Bihamba fights injustice in the society. This is often attributed to social and structural mindsets that hurt women. During her activities, she encounters conflicts because of rivalry and misunderstanding. To surmount these difficulties, Mrs Masika gets strength from her Christian faith. Her infectious personality encourages her colleagues. She watches in disbelief, when funds, which she desperately needs, are wasted. What also gives her the needed punch when she is tempted to abandon the work, are the constant requests from women and victims, whom she quickly defends. She is motivated by her achievements and the gratitude from those she helps. The collective responsibility of the network provides an opportunity for a greater impact. She manages the social division at Pole Institute, where she coordinates a platform entitled "Women Synergy for Sexual Violence Victims of the North Kivu". She is an active member of diverse networks such as Glideric, Inter-Congolese Dialogue and Reflexion Group, Information and Communication, Women Leaders of North Kivu (Novib), Human Rights Watch, Amnesty International and Alert International, the Belgium Cooperation, Usaid and other humanitarian, political and development actors. She obtained Swiss cooperation funding in 2000 to train counselors and assist victims, who obtained justice, health, independence and their joy back, thanks to her dedication. She hopes to see rural women organized to take their lives and destiny in their own hands, without fear of abuses.

The Global and Inclusive Agreement on Transition in the DRC provided an opportunity to wrongdoers, warlords, rapists and disappointed politicians to commit atrocities. The population continues to sink into abject poverty. Times are hard in DRC, with everyone pursuing selfish interests at the expense of the poor.

Democratic Republic of the Congo

Hatidza Mehmedovic

Srebrenica Mothers

Hatidza Mehmedovic's husband, two sons, and brothers were among those murdered when the United Nations protected city of Srebrenica was attacked by Serbs in 1995. She and other surviving mothers of the Srebrenica massacre encourage and motivate organizations and individuals to help the survivors. She works to establish the truth concerning the fate of the victims and tries to help the returnees to have a better life. While she encourages the reconciliation and cohabitation of Bosnians and Serbs, she knows this can only happen once the war criminals have been arrested and put on trial.

Until the war in Bosnia and Herzegovina began in 1992, Hatidza Mehmedovic peacefully lived with her family in a village near the town of Srebrenica in northeast Bosnia. After Serbian troops had burned down her village, Hatidza fled to Srebrenica with her family where over 40,000 other Bosnian Muslim refugees gathered. Hatidza lived among the desperate refugees, searching for food and comfort. After a three-month siege, the formerly rich mining town run out of electricity and drinking water. Many died from treatable wounds and infections. To prevent famine, the United Nations (UN) commander in Bosnia, Phillipe Morillon, delivered food by parachute. He and a small convoy of UN troops passed the Serbian front and entered Srebrenica to discuss the demilitarization of Srebrenica with Muslim leaders. The next day, Morillon was blockaded by a group of women and children as he prepared to leave Srebrenica. The leader was Hatidza who had become a symbol of resistance. She told the general, "If you can promise to fully secure the town, I will then allow you to leave!" General Morillon said, "You are under protection of the UN now. I will never leave you to suffer." Morillon's initiative led to the declaration of Srebrenica as "a securely protected zone under the UN." Two years later, however, in July 1995, Srebrenica experienced the biggest mass killing in Europe since World War II, committed by Serbian troops under General Ratko Mladic. Together with her husband and sons, Hatidza Mehmedovic attempted to find safety in a nearby UN base along with more than 30,000 other people seeking protection from the Dutch troops. Hatidza and her family spent three days and nights in the open field. On 13 July, following the orders of Mladic, the Serbs began separating men from their women. To this day, Hatidza still does not know the fate of her sons, husband, and other male relatives.

After war broke out in Bosnia and Herzegovina in 1992, thousands of Bosnian Muslims fled to Srebrenica, which was declared a UN protected zone in 1993. In July 1995, however, the Serb army launched a massive offensive and 10,000 unarmed civilians were murdered brutally.

Bosnia and Herzegovina

Ermira Mehmeti

Democratic Union for Integration

Ermira Mehmeti is the spokesperson for the Democratic Union for Integration, which emerged following the 2001 conflict in the country. Its leaders are those who fought for more rights and equal treatment of ethnic Albanians and Macedonians. Ermira is working to bring together the youth of the two major communities that were in conflict. Her message is that peace and democracy are the crucial values that can bring the country into Europe, that diversity makes the country stronger and should be the cornerstone of this young democracy and that reconciliation must be promoted.

Ermira Mehmeti is the symbol of young and emancipated Albanian women living in Macedonia with clear perspectives on their future. She has become the voice of moderation of the young educated generation of ethnic Albanians living in Macedonia. The myth of the uneducated and primitive Albanian community living in the country was broken as she emerged on the political scene.

Ermira is the daughter of a retired lawyer and a social worker working for the Macedonian Red Cross. Her father was a political prisoner in the times of the communist regime in the former Yugoslavia. Her mother has spent her life helping those in need, especially families that need social assistance and children without care. Currently, Ermira is finishing her legal studies at the South East European University in Tetovo, Macedonia. She has committed her time and energy to work in the post-conflict Kosovo as well as contribute to the peace process in Macedonia. In Kosovo, Ermira Mehmeti served as one of the main interpreters for the International War Crimes Tribunal for former Yugoslavia, providing assistance during the drafting of witness statements to be used in the case against Slobodan Milosevic. For over a year, she has been engaged with the European Community Humanitarian Office (Echo) in provision of assistance to the families in post-conflict Kosovo. In 2001, Ermira worked as a reporter for the Associated Press news agency and as the main English-Albanian interpreter during the peace negotiations held in Ohrid, which resulted in the Framework Agreement that put an end to the conflict in Macedonia. In 2002, she was hired by the Democratic Union for Integration to work as the spokesperson for the party, a job that she has been doing ever since.

Macedonia became independent after the breakup of Yugoslavia in the early 1990s. Albanians, who make up a third of the population, had long been subject to discrimination and abuse. In 2001, an armed conflict broke out between ethnic groups and ended with the signing of a peace agreement in August 2001.

TFYR Macedonia

Godelive Miburo

New Life for Reconciliation (VNR)

Sister Godelive Miburo runs two centers for orphans and follows up their integration into foster families. New Life for Reconciliation (VNR) trains on reconciliation and peace, awakening and reinforcing forgiveness and helps the weak, the rejected, battered women and widows through diverse projects. She helps war and Aids orphans to attend school and universities in the country. Her work also targets prisoners. All target groups are taught communication, non-violence and peaceful co-existence between ethnic groups.

Sr Godelive Miburo was born in 1958 to a rural family. The Burundian Catholic nun followed her catechism studies in various institutes in Abidjan and in Fribourg, Switzerland. She has trained in non-violent communication. She worked as primary school teacher and as an animator in a parish/pastoral center, before becoming the assistant in the bishop's office.

In 1997 Sr Godelive began apostolic work with New Life for Reconciliation (Vie Nouvelle pour la Reconciliation, VNR) that was founded by the country's bishop. Sr Godelive is an elder in the women's branch of VNR, which welcomes any person without distinction of race, culture, sex, or religion who wishes to work for reconciliation. It works with several groups: abandoned children and orphans, widows, prisoners, refugees and displaced people, armed groups, poor and impoverished people. They participate in diverse income-generating projects.

With the support of VNR, Sr Godelive opened two centers for orphans and follows up their integration into foster families. She works all around the country, having covered five provinces in eight years.

Sr Godelive opened a novitiate in 2003 to train future workers of the Apostolate. Girls who have been assisted run a nursery school. Her work also targets prisoners whom she visits. All are taught communication, non-violence and peaceful co-existence between ethnic groups. As a result of the work, 3000 children, war and Aids orphans, are taken care of and sent to school and universities in the country.

Bloody conflicts between the Hutus and Tutsis create much misery. Individuals, entire families, even regions live in extreme poverty, without accommodation, clothing, money and medical care.

Burundi

Annapurna Moharana

Kasturba Gandhi Memorial National Trust (KGMNT)
Sarvodaya
Utkal Naagari Lipi Parishad (UNLP)

Annapurna Moharana (born 1917) has been working since she was 13 to carry forward the Gandhian tradition of peaceful protest and refusing to compromise with corruption or oppression. In the past 75-odd years, Annapurna has worked on issues ranging from setting up a tribal residential school for girls, sensitizing dacoits (members of robber bands) to pacifism, and resisting the 1975 emergency, to setting up a nursing training center that recruits and trains young women in maternity services.

Freedom-fighter Annapurna Moharana began active social work as a girl. She worked at the Alaka Ashram at Bari, a small village near Puri, Orissa, to implement Gandhi's vision of village India. She lived with the rural people, sensitizing them about untouchability, illiteracy, and colonial rule. She was, obviously, arrested several times. Her methods throughout, though, were nonviolent. She continues the tradition of padyatras (marches) and peaceful protest. In 1972 to 1973, she marched to the notorious Chambal Valley to ask dacoits to lay down their arms. In 1975, during the emergency, she confronted strong police opposition when she went about raising the consciousness of the people.

Annapurna is saddened that so many of the relief works she begins are mired in bureaucratic corruption — a far cry from the India that she and other freedom-fighters had fought for. An example of this is the tribal residential complex for girls in Rayagod that Annapurna set up: although the institute has been sanctioned funds from central government, the releasing authority is demanding a bribe. Annapurna will not compromise, and so the money remains unutilized.

As an active trustee member of the Kasturba Gandhi National Memorial Trust, which was started by Gandhi in memory of his wife, Annapurna has initiated several innovative projects, among them maternity centers across Orissa to recruit and train young women in maternity services. Age has not slowed Annapurna down, nor diminished her optimism that she can make a difference to a world so different from that of her dreams.

In the early 1930s, Orissa was one of the most backward of Indian states. Education and literacy levels, the status of women, and civil and labor rights were huge problem areas. There was almost no antenatal or postnatal care for pregnant women and young mothers, and women were denied political participation.

India

Biserka Momcinovic

Center for Civil Initiatives (CCI)

In the last 13 years, Biserka Momcinovic, mother and grandmother, former accountant and commercial officer, has worked for the promotion of human rights and has helped hundreds of people reunite with their families. A co-founder and leader of the Center for Civil Initiatives (CCI), she organized public discussions on human rights and offered direct support to victims of human rights abuses. She was coordinator of the Women's Network of Croatia and contributed significantly to its becoming one of the biggest and most respected Croatian NGO networks.

Biserka (Biba) Momcinovic started her involvement in organized work on the protection and promotion of human rights in 1992, when she co-founded the Civil Committee for Human Rights in Zagreb, which later became the Center for Civil Initiatives (CCI). She decided to get involved when her friend, an ethnic Serb, was not able to get help from any institution when she needed it. The Serb woman's friends were her only support in her struggle for survival and for the right to live in her own city while she was jobless. Biba realized that it was time for active engagement. Her instincts told her that innocent people are the ones who suffer most in the high tide of ultra-nationalism. Since 1993, Biba has actively organized round tables and public discussions in and outside Istria, bringing in speakers who advocated a multi-ethnic, multi-cultural, egalitarian society that does not tolerate any form of discrimination. She has always been committed to the promotion of human rights related to conscientious objection, citizenship, apartheid, forced military draft, and migrants. At the same time, she offered direct support to victims of human rights abuses and war, particularly the ethnic Serbs who had been expelled from their homes during the war. She also played an important role in finding and reuniting missing persons after the war.

Since 1995, her interests have widened to include women's rights and gender equality. She was the first coordinator of the Women's Network of Croatia and has contributed significantly to its becoming one of the biggest and most respected Croatian NGO networks. Her day-to-day activities include public discussions that promote awareness and sensitivity to human rights issues and the creation of new non-governmental organizations.

Before the end of the war in Croatia, the military and police undertook several operations that killed many ethnic Serbs, destroyed and plundered their properties, and drove hundreds of them into exile. The remaining ones were subjected to human rights abuses and denied their basic needs.

Croatia

"If there is to be a positive change in society, someone has to sacrifice."

Monowara Begum Monu

Mohila Muktijodha Samiti

Monowara Begum (born 1953), one of the 1971 Bangladesh war of liberation's best-known freedom-fighters, today battles on various beachheads and is active in advocacy work as well. The mutilated postwar economy saw Monowara get down to building the Bangladesh of a collective dream. She has worked for more than three decades, both within the government system and through the Mohila Muktijodha Samiti (women freedom-fighters' cooperative), to make the government system accountable to the greater good.

Monowara was politically active even at school, when Borisal (in south-central Bangladesh) was the epicenter of political activity in then East Pakistan. When political activists and students banded together to form the Borisal Sangram Parishad, Monowara joined the Parishad, and the war for independence from Pakistan, in 1971. She was forced to go underground in the dense Sundarban jungles, where she trained in active combat and fought on different fronts. Simultaneously, Monowara continued spurring on the concept of freedom to people. "To participate in a war against injustice is a holy thing," she says. "Women can fight in the battlefield if they are trained."

The war left Bangladesh's people and economy in a shambles. Monowara worked from within the government system, through the National Social Welfare Board, the National Nutrition Council, the Committee for Protection from Violence against Women and Children, and other organizations. She joined the government cooperative department in 1983, and still works there. She enjoys her work, and believes that good people can do a lot functioning within the system.

Never one to work within the strict mandates of her job, Monowara organized women freedom-fighters and formed Mohila Muktijodha Samiti in the late 1980s. She initiated income-generating activities for women, set up mass education schools, provided health services for the economically disadvantaged, and established, through Mohila Muktijodha Samiti, a school for the disabled. Monowara's work is an affirmation that, in the most adverse of conditions, the much-derided government machinery can still be made to work for the greater good.

Bangladesh's struggle for independence from Pakistan in 1971 was perilous for the politically active. Women, rarely participating in active combat, were involved in important support activities. Monowara's work extended into the postwar shambles, when the disempowered were marginalized.

Bangladesh

Luisa Morgantini

European Parliament
Confederal Group of the European United Left
Women in Black

Luisa Morgantini is a member of the European Parliament. The leftist politician from northern Italy supports people in areas of tension. She makes every effort to see that conflicts are resolved through peaceful dialogue. As a trade unionist she started more than 20 years ago to establish solidarity projects in South American and African countries. Since 1982, she has been working closely with Israeli and Palestinian peace initiatives, above all Women in Black, and has risked her life in peace missions. In Palestinian areas she demonstrated with the people against the Israeli occupation.

The Middle East, Iraq, Afghanistan, former Yugoslavia. Luisa Morgantini makes dangerous trips to crisis areas. She tries to mediate between conflict parties. "Practical solidarity" is what the north Italian calls her missions. "I am not naïve," she says. Negotiations are very difficult. But dialogue is the only way to end war and terror. In the European Parliament and at international conferences she reports about her experiences with sensitivity. At the center of her speeches are the people who have experienced injustice and live with violence daily. Since 1982, Luisa Morgantini has supported peace activists in the Middle East, especially the women's organization Women in Black. Palestinian and Israeli women prove that it is possible to live together.

"Never again war," said her father when she was still a little girl. He was a partisan, fighting against German Nazis and Italian fascists. He did not talk much about his experiences, but Luisa Morgantini could not forget his warning, which gave her energy for her peace work. Already as a young girl she resisted social injustice. In her home town of Villadossola, she was, at age 14, already an active member of the leftist metal workers union (FLM). And later she was the first woman to be elected to the secretariat of the workers' organization in Milan.

The severe earthquake in the southern Italian Irpinia in 1980 interrupted her trade union involvement. For almost a year, she did voluntary reconstruction work in the area affected by the catastrophe. This experience changed her life. She got involved in solidarity projects in South American and African countries. In 1999, Luisa Morgantini ran for European Parliament for the first time as an independent candidate. Currently, she is chairwoman of the Committee on Development and a member of the Delegation for Relations with the Palestinian Legislative Council.

Italian trade unions are very strong. Since the end of the war they have been fighting for greater social justice. Millions of Italians also work as volunteers, at home or abroad, offering relief to people in need.

Italy

Spasenija Moro

Center for Peace, Nonviolence, and Human Rights

When war first broke out in Croatia, Spasenija Moro tried to escape its horrors. She found the strength to return and back in Osijek in 1992, she took the job of a German translator in the Center for Peace. Later, she engaged in projects that provided psychological and social support to the refugees and displaced persons, especially children. From 1992 to 1998, she participated in national and international efforts of reconciliation, peacemaking, and empowerment for traumatized persons and in the peaceful reintegration of Baranja and Eastern Slavonia in 1998.

The announcement of war in Croatia disrupted the peaceful life of Spasenija Moro. An optimist, she believed that war could not really happen in Yugoslavia. The painful confrontation with the state of war, sounds of shells, burning smell, and the destruction and decline of physical and mental systems made her wish to escape. She fled to Germany, but after some months, she found the courage and strength to return to the besieged city of Osijek. There, she came into contact with a group of intellectuals who were conducting a poll among returnees to Osijek. That is how peacemaking took hold in her life; how development started in new conditions with new encounters and learning. The Center for Peace, Nonviolence, and Human Rights in Osijek gathered some ten people willing to learn and get involved in preserving the nucleus of a civil society that appreciates the differences among people. It was an opportunity for people to speak in public about the horrors happening in the war.

Spasenija began as a translator at the Center for Peace. Although the work was exhausting, it regenerated and strengthened her. She tried to learn many new skills and gain knowledge so she could provide support to others when they needed it. And there were many people in Osijek and its surroundings who needed support: refugees, displaced persons, and especially children. In 1994, the refugee community living in Osijek began to meet with the people from Baranja. From 1994 to 1998, Spasenija participated in those meetings through the joint projects of Germany, Hungary, and the Netherlands in "Kuca susreta" (House of Meetings) in Mohacs, Hungary. The goal of the projects was to empower populations to return. In 1998, Baranja and Eastern Slavonia were peacefully reintegrated into the territory of the Republic of Croatia.

Ethnic tensions and war broke out in Croatia in the 1990s, bringing with it death, destruction, and thousands of refugees. In this situation, the Center for Peace, Nonviolence, and Human Rights gathered people to preserve the nucleus of a civil society and work for reconciliation and reconstruction.

Croatia

Daphrose Mukarutamu

Duhozanye
Nzambazamariya Veneranda

Daphrose Mukarutamu, a 57-year-old widow from Rwanda, is the founder of Duhozanye, an association whose objective is to restore hope to widows and orphans. The association closely follows up and defends the rights of rural communities. It promotes economic development, provides shelter to members and helps them grapple loneliness and trauma. Daphrose is also the director of an interethnic cultural group that sensitizes people on peaceful coexistence. She intervenes in conflict resolution at administrative and community level.

Daphrose Mukarutamu is a member of several rural associations and has been elected to local committees. She helps to resolve confilcts at administrative and community level. Duhozanye, located in Save, Rwanda, aims to rehabilitate widows and orphans by closely monitoring their rights and living conditions. Duhozanye means "console each other". The association also defends the rights of rural communities, provides counseling, gives opportunities for dialogue and promotes economic development through income-generating activities.

The focus of Daphrose's work is rural development and the empowerment of women victims of genocide. This is achieved through peace building, support for quick-impact projects and community sensitization on peaceful coexistence through mutual work. A cultural group conveys messages on truth and forgiveness. Daphrose's charisma and her motherly support touch everyone she interacts with. She draws her strength from helping women realize a better world without any discrimination and by encouraging cohesion among members of the association. Daphrose listens to members, encourages dialogue, openness and participation. She leads by example and is transparent in managing collective property. Despite having no prior training in accounting or management, she successfully secured funding for the construction of houses and training workshops for orphans. A victim who was trained by the association and worked as its coordinator was elected mayor and later elected to the National Assembly. With the support of the Programme Régional d'Echanges et de Formation pour le Développement, Duhozanye's future strategies include expanding its membership to include those who advocate against genocide and are involved in sustainable development.

Although the political situation in Rwanda is now more stable, the aftermath of war and genocide are still visible in many regions and in its socio-economy. Most development organizations working there today are involved in reconstruction.

Rwanda

Snjezana Mulic—Busatlija

Dani Magazine Sarajevo
Women's Association Bosancica

For the past 12 years, Snjezana Mulic-Busatlija has been working to promote and protect human rights, exposing herself to innumerable risks in
a militarized environment and a society driven by nationalism and ethnic
division. Through her work as a journalist, she has drawn public attention
at national and international levels to the conditions of people during
and after the war in Bosnia and Herzegovina. She has never renounced the
highest journalistic principles or given in to numerous forms of pressure. Her
courage demonstrated that it is possible to implement the Dayton Peace
Agreement.

Before the ink on the Dayton Peace Agreement was dry, Snjezana Mulic-
Busatlija, a journalist of the magazine "Dani" (The Days) from Sarajevo,
already championed the principles guaranteed by the Agreement: freedom
of movement, return of refugees and displaced persons to their pre-war
homes, reintegration of the disintegrated country. "Armed" with courage,
professionalism, and rarely seen enthusiasm, Snjezana went to Mostar — one
of the most devastated and divided cities in Europe after the fall of the
Berlin wall — in January 1996. Although the town was divided physically into two
parts at that time, she succeeded in visiting both parts and writing about
"one Mostar." She also managed to interview the untouchable "Mayor" of so-
called West Mostar — Mijo Brajkovic. Her article encouraged the Journalists'
Association of Bosnia and Herzegovina to nominate her as Journalist of the
Year in 1996.
Immediately after the war, she took the first bus that traveled to the
Republika Srpska and wrote a story about the people from "the other side."
In so doing, she demonstrated that it was possible to implement the Dayton
Agreement. She was the first journalist from the Federation of Bosnia and
Herzogovina to travel to Pale, the war headquarters of Radovan Karadzic and
the seat of government of the Republika Srpska. There, she was maltreated
and handcuffed for a short time because she dared to come from the "Muslim
part of Bosnia and Herzegovina." In spite of this, she resumed talking to
the people about living together and the return of refugees, the minute her
handcuffs were removed. She monitored the return of refugees to Bosnia
and Herzogovian and wrote about the problems they faced after returning.
Snjezana Mulic-Busatlija's work had a therapeutic effect on still frightened
people from both sides and encouraged them to return to their homes.

After the declaration of independence in 1992, Bosnia and Herzegovina (BiH)
was attacked by Serb forces who did not want to secede from Yugoslavia.
Bosnian people were murdered, imprisoned, or expelled from almost 70% of
the territory. Today, BiH is administratively divided into two entities, the
Federation of Bosnia and Herzegovina and the Republika Srpska.

Bosnia and Herzegovina

Kongosi Onia Mussanzi

Centre Médical Evangélique (CME)
Centre Résolution Conflits (CRC)

Kongosi Onia Mussanzi (52) has spent ten years campaigning and advocating for peace. She co-founded the Centre Résolution Conflits (CRC) in the Democratic Republic of the Congo (DRC), but had to flee to the UK because of death threats. She is involved in conflict resolution, trauma counseling and reconciliation, with NGOs, churches and political leaders, students and women traumatized through rape. As a peacemaker she now works at a global level moving across UK to give talks in collaboration with Tearfund and Amnesty International.

Danger lurked as the conditions worsened. She had to hide in the bushes with her children. Then, troops loyal to Laurent Kabila attacked her hometown of Nyankunde. She was forced to relocate to Bunia but continued to travel to the communities to provide relief food. In 2002, the threats heightened and she fled to England, where she now has refugee status. Clinging on to her dream for peace, thousands of miles away from home, she gives talks in the UK, working with institutions like Action for Conflict Transformation.

Kongosi Mussanzi completed an M.A. in Education Sciences and Psychology and worked as a teacher before heading the Internal Audit section of the Centre Médical Evangélique (CME) in the DRC. In 1993, Kongosi Mussanzi co-founded with her husband the CRC, involved in peace education, conflict resolution, reconciliation and trauma counseling, together with NGOs, churches and political leaders, students, teenagers and women who have been raped.

Kongossi attended an intensive training session provided by Working With Conflict in 2000. She later became the director of CRC while her husband studied in England. She longs for the day she will return home to continue with the peace building process.

The Eastern Province of DRC and the Ituri Province are notorious for human rights violations: horrific violence and looting. The country is slowly recovering and preparing for elections but without much enthusiasm as unruly factions attempt to dominate in the political battle for supremacy.

Democratic Republic of the Congo

"There is an Arabic saying, whose literal translation means: 'Work for your life as though you will live forever and work for your afterlife as if you will die tomorrow'."

Laila Nabih Al-0Namani

Women's Welfare Society (WWS)
Dar El Hekma Private College (HPC)
Al Maha Literary Group (MLG)

Laila Nabih Al-Namani was born in Beirut and now resides and works in Jeddah, Saudi Arabia. For over 40 years she has worked with the Women's Welfare Society (WWS) in Jeddah, the first registered private charity in Saudi Arabia, since its inception in 1963. She concentrated her efforts on the Women's Vocational Training Committee and has been in charge of the Orphanage Committee and in the Treasury of the organization. Her work has significantly helped to provide women and their families with a wide range of services, including social and medical provisions, childcare, and health awareness.

A married mother of four children and grandmother of 12 grandchildren, Laila Al-Namani is a writer and artist in Saudi Arabia. Having completed a Bachelor's Degree in Art, Arabic Literature and Philosophy she is keenly devoted to arts and the written word as cultural expressions. As someone who takes seriously the importance of books, she gains much of her inspiration from the many texts she reads: "I am an avid reader and there are lots of examples of men and women that inspire me, especially the ones that go to war torn countries to help." Her love of reading inspired her to establish a literary group that brings together people within her community to discuss books and other cultural and social subjects. Inspired by the stories of courage and work of so many people across the world, Laila Al-Namani is also motivated by the memory of her late father. "My late father was the most generous, gentle and active peace mediator and person I have ever known. I always think of him and hope he is happy with me and my work."

Laila Al-Namani has translated this motivation into a deep commitment to social and charity organizations in Saudi Arabia, most notably the Women's Welfare Society (WWS). As one of the original members from its inception in 1963, she has worked in numerous capacities in the organization, overseen its expansion, with over 5500 registered families, representing over 35,000 individuals. She humbly says, "in my field of work it is very difficult to talk about personal achievements." Her commitment to the social and charitable organizations has benefited a large number of families and individuals.

Laila Al-Namani is involved with charity organizations in Saudi Arabia, such as Women's Welfare Society (WWS), the oldest in the country, providing a range of services and skills to improve women and family living standards. She has worked with Saudi government officials, developing and implementing welfare policies.

Saudi Arabia

"You are half Hutu and half Tutsi. If you identify yourselves as Hutus, then you must hate me, and if you identify yourself as Tutsi, then it is as if you killed your father a second time."

Jeannine Nahigombeye

Radio Isanganiro

Jeannine Nahigombeye (32) is a journalist. Since 2003, she has been the director of Radio Isanganiro, a national broadcaster. She uses the media for conflict resolution and as a means to get all warring parties involved in peace negotiations in her country. Despite several government bans she has continued using the radio as her weapon against conflict. The radio provides its listeners with information that helps them in their daily lives and keeps politicians and the army accountable for their actions.

Jeannine Nahigombeye is married with one child. She has seven brothers and sisters. Since her Hutu father died in 1972, her mother, who is a Tutsi, raised them to be ethnic-neutral. At the beginning of the 1993 conflict in Burundi, Jeannine's mother warned her and her siblings never to align themselves with any ethnic group. Jeannine has a diploma in french literature from the country's national university. She has been a journalist since 1998. She worked at Studio Ijambo and was a correspondent for Voice of America. Since 2003, she has been the director of Radio Isanganiro based in Bujumbura, the capital. The radio station reaches almost 90 percent of the population. It was created out of the initiative of a group of journalists who elected her as director. The focus of her work is on problems of community development, everyday life issues and issues linked directly to the civil war. Jeannine uses the media to assist in conflict resolution. During the conflict, the station was a means to get all warring parties involved in the peace negotiations. This involved getting the opposition's and rebels' views heard and giving balanced information to the people. She was engaged in this proactive but risky situation despite several bans by the government against her radio station. Through the radio station, Jeannine has often denounced human rights abuses and corruption. Jeannine also broadcasts positive issues going on in Burundi. The radio station provides its listeners with information that helps them in their daily lives and keeps politicians and the army accountable for their actions. For instance, a section of the population now has access to clean drinking water thanks to the radio station's campaign about their plight. In addition, some displaced people were settled after Radio Isanganiro had highlighted their problems.

President Buyoya, who took power in a coup in 1998, has begun dialogue with Hutu rebel groups. Radio stations were forbidden to feature rebels in their broadcasts. Burundi has been at civil war since the assassination of the first democratically elected president, Melchior Ndadaye, in October 1993.

Burundi

Nguyen Thi Binh

Fund for Child Protection
The Vietnam Association for Victims of Agent Orange/Dioxin
Committee in Solidarity with People in Asia and Africa

In Vietnamese students' manuals, Nguyen Thi Binh is known as a "woman diplomatic peace general" for her role as Minister of Foreign Affairs of the Provisionary Revolutionary Government of South Vietnam during the signing of the Paris Agreement in 1973. She was elected Minister of Education and Training, Vice President of the National Committee for the Advancement of Women, and Vice President of the Socialist Republic of Vietnam. Now retired, she is helping uplift victims of the war and other disadvantaged groups such as children and women.

Nguyen Thi Binh was Minister of Foreign Affairs for the Provisionary Revolutionary Government of South Vietnam during the negotiations to end the Vietnam War in Paris in 1973. Her persuasive speeches at the Paris Conference forced the enemy to sign the Paris Agreement with the Democratic Republic of Vietnam (North Vietnam) and the Provisional Revolutionary Government of South Vietnam. The Agreement was a great diplomatic victory for the Vietnamese people. It also showcased the talent and bravery of Nguyen Thi Binh, whose intelligence, dedication and patriotism helped make peace and independence possible for millions of Vietnamese.

During her years at the negotiating table in Paris, she educated her children (then eight and 12 years old) by recording tapes for them. Her father was ill at the time, but because of her work in Paris she could not care for him or see him before he died. Nguyen Thi Binh says, "I cried while signing the Paris Agreement because I thought of my deceased compatriots and comrades who could not know about that important event. It was a great honor in Paris to represent the Vietnamese people and revolutionary soldiers in the direct struggle against invaders and to sign the successful agreement after the Vietnamese people's 18 years of just war. I thought about my family, my husband and children, my relatives, compatriots and comrades, my international friends and overseas Vietnamese. My tears flowed again. That was surely the deepest experience in my diplomatic life." Now retired, Nguyen Thi Binh is president of the Fund for Child Protection, honorary president of The Vietnam Association for Victims of Agent Orange/Dioxin, vice president of the Committee in Solidarity with People in Asia and Africa, and president of the Kovalevskaja Fund for Vietnamese.

During the 18-year Vietnam War thousands of Vietnamese were killed and millions more were separated from their families. Now, in peace time, the country is dealing with nearly four million victims of Agent Orange/Dioxin, many of them women and children.

Viet Nam

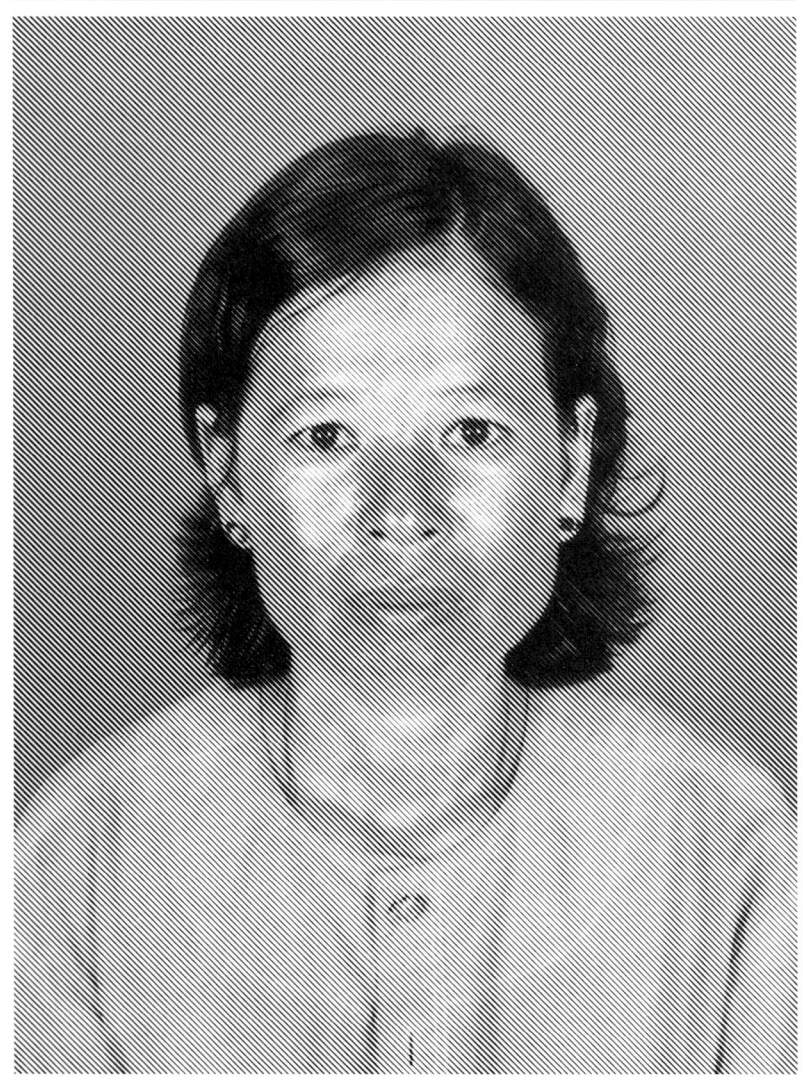

Oddom Van Syvorn

Dhammayietra Center for Peace and Non-violence

Oddom Van Syvorn (born 1962) is a Cambodian woman who has dedicated her life to promoting peace and non-violence through the annual peace walk to war-ravaged areas in Cambodia. She joined the first Dhammayietra, which literally means walking with dharma, in 1992 and has coordinated the pilgrimage since 1999. In her work, she teaches Buddhist precepts to the young, blesses and plants trees to raise awareness about environmental preservation and promotes compassion for people living with HIV/Aids.

Oddom Van Syvorn has walked over 4000 kilometers to almost all regions of Cambodia, passing through jungles and landmine-infested areas covering 70 percent of the country. In these pilgrimages, Oddom brings messages of love and compassion for all human beings and the environment. Her peace walks began in 1992 when she first heard about the Dhammayietra walk for peace, initiated by the Venerable Maha Ghosananda, a revered Cambodian monk. Out of curiosity and amid her own doubts about the prospects for peace in Cambodia, Oddom joined the pilgrimage. Seven years later, she became its coordinator and a faithful believer in its active campaign for peace. "I want to truly understand Buddhist teaching," says Oddom, a former trader who quit her small business to dedicate her life to the peace walk. It has not been an easy walk. She recounts, "People do not give much support, and they do not have confidence in peace." Support from the authorities has been mixed and applications for the walk are sometimes lost in the bureaucratic maze. There is also a shortage of funds and limited media coverage. But Syvorn finds strength in these challenges in the quest for a more peaceful Cambodia.

During the march, Oddom Syvorn teaches meditation, peace, conflict resolution, non-violence, prevention of HIV/Aids and drug abuse to villagers, school children, traditional midwives, prisoners, monks, nuns and lay Buddhists in the temples. She says she has seen the impact of the peace walk in some communities, where there are fewer reports of domestic violence and fighting, problems that are frequent in the villages. Her vision is to carry the message of the Dhammayietra to the youth of the countryside. "I want them to learn to meditate, the type of meditation which brings them the wisdom of the Khmer heart."

After the Khmer Rouge's reign of terror from 1975-1979, people in war-torn Cambodia needed a sense of normalcy. After general elections in 1993, a law was enacted for a special tribunal to try former Khmer Rouge leaders. But the culture of non-peace continues to fester in post-war Cambodia.

Cambodia

"I know what it is like to walk through the bushes with grenades strapped to your waist."

Jolly Grace Okot

Alliance of African Assistance (AAA)

Jolly Grace Okot (36) was born in Pader District in Uganda. She is the country director of Alliance for African Assistance (AAA). Since 2003, she has been involved in sport for peace and community development for children. By respecting and fulfilling children's right to play, Jolly brings an element of normalcy to a community that has been ravaged by war for nearly two decades.

Jolly's first and most terrible brush with the Lord's Resistance Army occurred when she was 18 years old. On the way home from school one day, she and a friend were abducted into rebel ranks. This was both physically and emotionally traumatizing. She was often forced to demand money from neighbors and local merchants while armed with a rifle. She is among the few abductees who have managed to break free. Perhaps it was as a result of her troubled childhood that she started a program to promote the protection of children's rights including their right to play. The AAA program focuses on the individual and emotional needs of children, which are often overlooked. The program allows all children into its playgroups regardless of their sex or background. Over a thousand children now play everyday in Gulu for at least two hours each day. Their laughter brings a smile to the faces of hundreds of on-lookers for whom the harsh reality is suspended for those brief moments. Jolly has gained access to top government officials and ministers. Thanks to her unwavering faith and persistence, she has managed to get a free plot of land to build a children's center. She has risen above the adversity in her life to become a role model to many in her country and beyond. She attributes her rise from shame and trauma to faith, education and her interest in helping others.

The situation in Northern Uganda is turbulent. Children are abducted and forced to join rebel fighters. They are deprived of their childhood, education and often lose their parents. Many organizations work to rehabilitate and bring relief to such vulnerable groups.

Uganda

Ceciliana Olilaeni

Honiara Women for Peace
Conference for Women Religious (CWR)

Sister Ceciliana's education and training as a nurse with the Catholic Sisters of the Church in Solomon Islands opened the door for her to shoulder a very important role in peacebuilding in the country when the "social unrest and ethnic violence" between Malaitans and Guadalcanalese erupted in the late 1990s. She joined concerned women in this patriarchal country in such work, helping to change entrenched attitudes and secure peace.

Sister Ceciliana decided very young to join the Catholic Church Sisters of the Church order in Solomon Islands because she saw their good work, helping the sick in hospital. The Sisterhood enabled her to continue her education, train as a nurse, and become a nurse trainer. Her training in the Natural Family Planning program led to her later work on Family Life and Women in Auki, Malaita. From 1999 onwards, when the country was rocked by the "social unrest and ethnic violence" between Malaitans and Guadalcanalese, Sister Ceciliana shouldered a very important role for peace building. She joined a number of concerned women in Honiara in discussions on how they could make contributions towards peace. Her responsibility was also to do away with ethnic differences within the Sisterhood. These were challenging times and many lessons were learned.

A retreat helped Sisters of the two warring ethnic groups sort out their own differences and look for solutions, encouraging them to observe the principle of equality and peace; their unity became a model for the people. They learned about dedication and commitment to their common cause of peace and well being for all. They saw first hand the suffering of families and visited the militants' camps, mediating with them to secure ceasefires and to be able to distribute food to all sides. Fear was not in the women's vocabulary and time was not a concern: they did what had to be done despite the trauma, arguments with militants and being shot at when distributing and exchanging food. When caught in the crossfire, their presence often secured a ceasefire and saved a village or center from being burned down.

It can be confronting for a male-dominated, largely Christian society like Solomon Islands to see a woman of the church involved in work such as family life, women's rights and peace building (late 1990s). Sister Ceciliana helped to change attitudes and behavior.

Solomon Islands

Zarema Omarova

Ekho Voiny (Echo of War)
Dieti Chiechni (Children of Chechnya)

Victims of Stalin's deportation of the Chechen people to Central Asia, Zarema Omarova (born 1941) and her parents returned to their motherland in 1957. Zarema has worked in different educational establishments in Grozny introducing progressive teaching techniques. She also worked as a secretary at the regional Communist Party committee and for the Deputy Minister of Education of Chechnya. In both these positions, she promoted inter-ethnic peace. An active member of the NGOs Echo of War and Children of Chechnya, she is engaged in peace activities and providing humanitarian aid to Chechnya.

Zarema Omarova, together with her parents, suffered Stalin's deportation of the Chechen people when she was only three years old. As a schoolgirl, the reasons behind the humiliation of the Principal's disparaging label as a special migrant — reserved for people's enemy deportees — were incomprehensible to her, yet awakened protest in her child's soul. When Khrushchev's thaw began in the late 1950s, the Chechens were rehabilitated and allowed to move back to the Caucasus. Zarema spent her student years in Grozny. This was the time of her youth and of her people's revival. Deported Chechens had been accepted neither to technical colleges nor to institutes. Now they had to catch up on the lost opportunities. Zarema understood that a people's prosperity depends on education; so she decided to become a teacher. When the Russian troops invaded Chechnya in 1995, Zarema's peaceful profession (she was vice-principal of the College) did not cease to exist; only now, it required much more courage and self-sacrifice. The classes took place in unheated rooms, with the distant sound of bombs being dropped. It was then that Zarema enrolled in the anti-war humanitarian NGOs Echo of War and Children of Chechnya in order to help people in these most inhumane circumstances. One of the projects that Zarema organized was the trip of a group of Chechen children to Moscow, where they lived with Russian families. There they could recuperate and warm their souls a little with the realization that many people of good will in Russia sympathized with them. Many of Zarema's students are no longer in Chechnya today. Some of them have perished in the war; others have fled the Republic. Her lessons of tolerance, understanding, and compassion have not been in vain, but will always remain in the hearts of those who have known her.

The war has left tens of thousands of Chechens dead and wounded. The impoverished population has been deprived of its fundamental rights. In these conditions, Zarema carries out humanitarian projects in the war-torn country and advocates the cause of peace.

Russian Federation

María Esperanza Ortega

Coordination for Communities and Repopulation
Association of the War Victims of El Salvador

María Esperanza Ortega has been working half her life for human rights. For 12 of those years, she fought against death during the armed conflict that devastated her country, El Salvador. Her task was to organize groups of civilians trapped in the war zones. An untiring leader, her work continues today, in other directions.

María Esperanza's day begins when the last stars are still in the sky, just before dawn. She gets up and makes breakfast for her husband. He has to go to the fields to work, cultivating the land. When he leaves, she takes care of the children and does the housework. "We had eight children, but three of them died in the war. Two died as combatants and one girl died of hunger." The war she speaks about is the one that devastated her country, El Salvador, for more than a decade. But her daily work has hardly begun. Soon, she leaves her housework and begins her other work, the work she does in the community. María Esperanza Ortega has been working for more than 25 years in the Coordination for Communities and Repopulation. She also gives her support to the apostolic team of the Catholic Church and she is a promoter of physiotherapy in the Association of the War Victims of El Salvador (Alges). "The struggle is one of the most important weapons in reaching equality; and solidarity and equality are peace."

With her dark hair tied up in a plait, her dark eyes and her skin tanned by the implacable sun of her country, María Esperanza (51) is an exact reflection of her people. She was born in the El Sitio canton, in the Arcatao municipality, in the administrative district of Chalatenango, in the Northern zone of El Salvador. She has always lived in the countryside and has no intention of leaving it: "I like to see the farmers on their horses, with their sandals and their earthenware jugs filled with water." She is a simple, humble woman with an amazing strength of purpose: "I may not be so strong, but I am full of such a big faith that it makes me keep going." And she moves forward, always forward.

El Salvador suffered from a devastating civil war for more than 12 years. Social inequalities were the main reason why the conflict developed. In spite of the peace agreement — signed in 1992 — those problems are still alive.

El Salvador

Bakhita Osman

Community Based Organizations (CBO)

Bakhita Mohamed (45) is a lecturer in economics. Her major aim is to empower women at all levels in the Sudan, particularly in rural areas. She also works to raise people's awareness of environmental conservation and peaceful coexistence between the multi-ethnic communities. Bakhita is a talented storywriter, whose main theme is the promotion of peace. She believes that writing is a powerful and rich tool to effectuate and sustain peace. She has conducted extensive scientific research and studies, especially on the root causes of women's poverty.

Bakhita works in an area dominated by violence and tribal disputes. The instable national political situation and the domination of one ideology stood as stiff barriers to her work. But she has the determination to tackle these areas in order to achieve her goals. Her catchphrase "together to sustain peace" is her source of strength. Bakhita has faced many difficulties in her work, the greatest of which was the lack of financial support for her social projects. On a personal level, she lives away from her husband, who works abroad and rarely sends her money to subsist her family. She raises two children and has also looked after her two younger brothers since the death of her parents. On a societal level, Bakhita works with exigent communities with no financial support from the government or any other organization. The lack of financial resources is one of the crucial constraints on her, as the local communities are very adverse. Yet, with very humble personal resources she has managed to achieve fantastic successes. The results and impact of her work have influenced the attitude and behavior of local people, who she has inspired to maintain a peaceful community with better conditions. This social mobilization and awareness raising are factual evidence of Bakhita's significant work.

Bakhita has worked hard towards implementing the United Nations Educational, Scientific and Cultural Organization (Unesco) goals, women's empowerment, poverty alleviation, and establishing the culture of peace and coexistence in the Sudan. She has participated in founding the Community Based Organizations (CBO), which sustain peace and development in the community.

Sudan

June Caridad Pagaduan-Lopez

International Rehabilitation Council for Torture Victims (IRCT)
University of the Philippines Center for Gender and Women's Studies
Sexual Violence Research Initiative of the World Health Organization (WHO)

June Pagaduan-Lopez (born 1951) has worked for more than three decades in human rights protection, psychosocial intervention and peace advocacy. As a professor at the University of the Philippines (UP) and a psychiatrist, she has helped human rights abuse victims in the Philippines and in other countries and contributed to the development of a more humane approach to medical practice. During the Martial Law regime, she risked arrest and detention and suffered personal and professional persecution because of her activism. She is currently head of the UP Center for Gender and Women's Studies.

The work of Dr June Pagaduan-Lopez is well known and respected internationally because of her involvement both in the academe and in global networks that share her advocacy. In the medical profession, she is at the forefront of psychosocial trauma management. She got involved in human rights work as a student activist before and during the Martial Law era. After graduating from medical school in 1976 and having finished her residency in psychiatry in 1979, she helped found the Medical Action Group (MAG), a non-government, cause-oriented organization that provided medical and psychosocial support to victims of human rights abuses of the Marcos regime. Her work on torture victims resulted in the establishment of the Philippine Action Against Torture. At the UP Medical School, she worked for the implementation of a ten-hour Human Rights Course for Medical Students, the only one of its kind to be mainstreamed into an undergraduate medical curriculum in the country.

A founding member of the International Rehabilitation Council for Torture Victims (IRCT), she has trained medical practitioners in the detection, management and rehabilitation of torture victims and other survivors of political violence in the Philippines, East Timor, Nepal, India, Pakistan, Indonesia, Burma, Cambodia and Kosovo. In East Timor, she managed a nationwide research project on the psychosocial effects of war trauma in coordination with the United Nations Transition Administration (UNTAET). Back in the Philippines, June Lopez decided to implement the East Timor concept in the war-torn regions of Muslim Mindanao. In 2002, using foreign and local government funds, she started "Balik-Kalipay" (Return to Happiness), a psychosocial intervention project for victims of armed conflict. It now covers 15 villages and has trained 46 teachers and more than 200 youth volunteers.

In current and post-conflict communities, community organization, healing and empowerment can be integrated into reconstruction and rehabilitation efforts. Dr June Lopez has mobilized the academe, government and international institutions and NGOs to help the traumatized sectors in conflict areas.

Philippines

Nighat Shafi Pandit

Human Efforts for Love and Peace Foundation (Help Foundation)

Braving physical danger and other risks, Nighat Shafi Pandit (born 1951) works with rural communities in violence-scarred Jammu and Kashmir. Belonging to a well-known Kashmiri family, Pandit is one of those rare women who stepped out of a comfortable home to address the pain and trauma of people caught up in a 16-year-long conflict. Her organization, the Help Foundation, Jammu and Kashmir, focuses on, among other things, educating orphans, rehabilitating widows, and promoting peace and intercommunal harmony.

Nighat Shafi Pandit stepped out of her home at a time when very few Kashmiri women were responding to the crisis in their midst. In 1997, she was the first woman to start an orphanage for children left homeless by the armed conflict in the Kashmir Valley. Today, the Help Foundation, Jammu and Kashmir, works overtime to provide succor to those worst affected by the conflict. The Help foundation is the only organization that operates effectively in both regions — Jammu and Kashmir — of this deeply divided state. The main activities of the organization are the education and raising of orphans, the rehabilitation of widows, mental health counseling for women and children, and the rehabilitation of physically and visually challenged children. It also works for the promotion of peace and intercommunal harmony: Nighat, a Muslim, works closely with the minority Hindu community — those living in the valley, and those displaced and living in refugee camps in Jammu.

Nighat's "theater of operations" in the Kashmir Valley — the city of Srinagar, and the districts of Badgam, Pulwama, Baramulla, and Kupwara — is prone to militancy and violence. As she has learnt only too well, it is not the scale of violence in the valley as much as its unpredictable nature that poses the greatest danger. What keeps Nighat going is her close affinity with the land and people of the region. She belongs to a well-known family of Kashmir, which played a pioneering role in spreading education in the state — her grandfather was the first registrar of Jammu and Kashmir University. Like every family in Kashmir, hers, too, has been touched by the conflict. Her children (a son and two daughters) had to leave the valley at a time when children most need their parents, because of threats of kidnapping. But Nighat has stuck on.

Jammu and Kashmir is torn not only by continuing warfare between separatist militants and Indian security forces but also divided by a deep chasm between its original inhabitants: the Muslim majority and the Hindu Pandit minority, almost irrevocably dispossessed of ancestral land and home.

India

Rachael Paul

Presbyterian Church of the Sudan (PCOS)

Rachael Nyadak Paul (37) was born in Malakal, Sudan. She was Secretary in the Women's Desk of the Presbyterian Church of the Sudan (PCOS) in Akobo. Through her work in South Sudan with PCOS, she has supported women and the facilitation of their leadership training after the backlash of the civil war. Rachael's major efforts are centered on issues like women's empowerment and networking, migrant work conditions and peace building.

Rachael was raised in a Christian family in South Sudan. Her father worked as a Pastor with the Presbyterian Church of the Sudan (PCOS) Akobo. After receiving her early education in South Sudan she obtained a certificate in Public Administration from Port Harre University, South Africa. In 1996 she volunteered to work in the women's desk of the PCOS. Later, the General Assembly of the PCOS elected her to work officially in that position from 2001 onward.

Rachael is involved in many activities concerning women's empowerment and networking, migrants' and peace building issues. Her achievements in peace promotion are spectacular, as she participated in concluding a peace agreement between North and South Sudan, ending the longest phase of civil war in recent history. Her motivation for peace work comes from her awareness of its significance and from the terrible impacts of war upon her personal life. She lost her husband in the North-South war while she was still young. The only compensation for this, she believes, is to put more effort into peace work so that the Sudanese families can live in peace together. She traveled across the Sudan, particularly in the South, to raise peoples' awareness of the devastation that civil war brings to the Sudanese people. She knows that many women have lost their husbands or their loved ones in the war and always presents her exemplum to show how war can make people's life a misery. As a result she is called "Mother of Widows". Rachael works voluntarily in a vulnerable war zone, facing lots of difficulties.

Rachael Paul sacrified her time and efforts working for peace, expecting no personal gain except a peaceful community for the Sudanese people. She traveled across the Sudan to raise peoples' awareness of the devastation that civil war brings. Therefore, she regularly participates in people-to-people peace promotion, such as reconciliatory clan meetings.

Sudan

Lyudmila Pavlichenko

Kavkazsky Forum
Soyuz Zhenshchin Dona (Union of Women of the Don)

Lyudmila Pavlichenko was born in 1949, in the Rostov Region. Since 1996, she has been actively involved in the activities of the NGO Union of Women of the Don (SZD). She also participated in the projects Women's Rights, Public Social Reception Offices, Dagestan — the Peacekeeping Center, and others. Since 1998, she has been a coordinator of the international organization Kavkazsky Forum (Caucasian Forum), and she has organized a lot of humanitarian projects in Chechnya and the whole of the Caucasian region trying to promote peace and reconciliation.

Summer 1995. Chechnya. Heat, burning sun, stale hot air. Two tents with 43 women on a hunger strike. They are Chechens and Dagestanians. Among them there is one Russian woman — Lyudmila Pavlichenko. They are all protesting against the Russian-Chechen war. The participants of the hunger strike are suffering from high blood pressure and general weakness. From time to time, some of them are taken to the hospital. Lyudmila has not given up yet. Her friend from Dagestan is sitting next to her and is trying to persuade the women to stop starving because, according to the Koran, one can only starve in the name of Allah, not in pursuit of political goals. Russian, Dagestanian, and Chechen women are sitting shoulder to shoulder holding each other's hands like sisters. During these few days, Lyudmila has learned a lot about the way of life, mentality, and customs of the Chechen people. She has become acquainted with a Chechen poet, who is on hunger strike too, despite the fact that he goes around on crutches (he stepped on a land mine while herding a cow). He reads his poems in the Chechen language to her, and Lyudmila translates them into Russian. The poems bring them together. It is the first time that she sees the common prayer — which leaves her spellbound. She watches men dancing in the circle with an air of detachment. During her hunger strike, she has not stayed in bed in her tent, but continues to give consultations and looks after the children. Speaking to many Russian journalists, she tries to tell the truth about the war in Chechnya, but her interviews never appear in the media uncensored.

Since 1994, Chechnya has been engulfed in a bitter war. Shocked by what she saw in Chechnya, Lyudmila fights to stop the armed conflict. Facing pressure and defamation, she is still convinced that she cannot be considered a traitor by making a stand with Chechens and helping to stop the bloodshed.

Russian Federation

Prak Sokhany

Australian Catholic Relief (ACR)

Prak Sokhany (born 1958) has channeled her life and work into peace building and conflict resolution in Cambodia, where people are still traumatized by the wounds of war. For nearly ten years, she and her organization, Australian Catholic Relief (ACR), with its allies in peace work, have trained NGO workers, government officials and entire communities in conflict resolution and peace building. Prak works with the grassroots, designs training programs, facilitating training and networking with numerous institutions.

Prak Sokhany has dedicated her life to making a better, more peaceful world, where people work together to create a civil society and collaborate to solve problems that cause violence. After surviving the Khmer Rouge regime, she has had to deal with the reality of Cambodian society after the war, where people have lost trust in each other and violence continues to wreak havoc on their culture and daily life. In 1998, Prak, a former schoolteacher, formed a volunteer group to train municipal officers in Phnom Penh in conflict resolution. They developed the training curriculum, which focuses on changing participants' own behavior in problem solving and on strategies to make these changes. Prak Sokhany says that even people involved in conflict resolution did not know how to do it properly. "Participants acknowledged that they often made mistakes, that they dominated the conflict resolution process and threatened the parties in conflict if they failed to reach a resolution. Now they have knowledge and skills. They have learned to ask each party in the conflict to speak about their problems and to identify the conflict's root causes."

The volunteer group was transformed into the Alliance for Conflict Transformation (ACT). Along with ACT, Sokhany and ACR have provided training in conflict resolution, peace building and capacity building for NGOs, government officials and communities. The NGO staff that Sokhany and ACT have trained have become trainers themselves and have facilitated the conflict resolution process in the communities where they work. "Perhaps the deep wounds of the war are impossible to erase. Perhaps we can only come to understand it better. Yet, through conflict resolution and peace building, we may evolve out of it into a better world," she says.

After the Khmer Rouge's reign of terror (1975—1979), the wounds of the war continue to affect people's lives. Violence is common, and people have lost trust in each other. Peace training, which focuses on changing participants' own behavior in problem solving, is an urgent need.

Cambodia

Teresita Quintos-Deles

Office of the Presidential Adviser on the Peace Process (OPAPP)
Gaston Z Ortigas Peace Institute
Coalition for Peace (CFP)

Teresita Quintos-Deles (born 1948), has come full circle as adviser to President Gloria Macapagal-Arroyo on the peace process. From 1987 to 2001, Teresita Deles was one of leaders of the peace movement in civil society as chair of the Coalition for Peace (CFP) and executive director of the GZO Peace Institute. She joined government in 2001 as lead convenor of the National Anti-Poverty Commission, addressing social justice issues that bear on peace and development. She was appointed to her current job, overseeing government strategies and programs related to peace building, in 2003.

Teresita Quintos-Deles has been part of every effort by civil society to build peace in the country since 1986. She was convenor and chair of the Coalition for Peace (CFP) founded in 1987, the first citizens' alliance focused on seeking an end to the armed conflict. In 1990, she helped convene the National Peace Conference that forged a broad-based consensus among 17 basic sectors on a national vision and agenda for peace. From 1991 to 2001, she was executive director of the Gaston Z Ortigas Peace Institute, created to provide a permanent support base for citizens' peace initiatives. From 1990 to 1995, the Multi-Sectoral Peace Advocates and the Philippine Independent Peace Advocates pursued dialogues and liaisons for setting up formal peace talks between the government and the two main armed groups, the communists and the Muslim rebels.

Teresita was also a member of the Peace Consortium composed of ten peace institutes, centers and program desks that carried out research into and training for conflict resolution. Joining government in 2001, she was finally in a position to influence policy on the peace process. Her vision of peace is holistic: "A society where there is no armed conflict, when people's basic needs are met, children are in school, people have choices and can make choices, women are respected and have the same rights as men, land is distributed fairly, different cultures have full faith and confidence in their place in this country, access to political power is expanded and devolved so our people of diverse cultures and geographical conditions can govern themselves in a way that is most true for them." Although this may not materialize anytime soon, she says, "Hope is the lifeblood of peace advocacy."

The peace movement in the Philippines started right after the 1986 People Power Revolution when advocates of social change saw the peaceful over-throw of the Marcos dictatorship as an opportunity to end the armed conflicts that prospered during those repressive years.

Philippines

Ana Raffai

Center for Peace Studies
Rand
European Church and Peace Network

Ana Raffai, a Roman Catholic Croatian theologian, has been training and mentoring over 500 peace activists on nonviolence and peace mediation over the last ten years. Together with her husband, she has designed and led various workshops for the Center for Peace Studies. Some of their trainees are now trainers in peace education themselves. She also works with the non-governmental organization (NGO) Rand in peace education for different faith groups. Recently, she has become more involved with NGOs that are active in protest and training for protest.

Ana Raffai encountered the word "peacemaking" back at the beginning of the war in Croatia. Looking back to her years of study, she does not think she demonstrated the expected characteristics of a peacemaker. On her right hand, she has a scar — an evidence of her boldness but also aggressiveness in the battle for her rights: she received it in a fight with her younger brother who was at primary school while she was in her second year studying Germanic and Romance languages. He had taken something from her room and she had chased him around the apartment. When he tried to save his skin by locking himself in the bathroom, she hit the glass in the door and smashed it.

Ana's next encounter with peacemaking was before the war. Her husband, a conscientious objector, said, "I am a pacifist." Later, Ana was glad that he turned his back on weapons because at that time he was important to their small family. In 1990, she gave birth to a daughter, and then in 1991, to a son. It bothered her at that time when the war was bubbling away that there was no space for other priorities. Anyone opposed to current ideas was branded negatively. During this time, a priest found a family with whom her husband could stay, as at that time there was no legal framework for conscientious objection. In 1992, thanks to the priest, Ana took part in the Hildegard Goss-Mayr seminar in Zagreb where they worked on the question of peacemaking, faith, and how to overcome violence. It was not easy. Not until she completed an advanced training course for service in peace in 1995, did she connect with the people and the peace issues and began to think differently, subsequently changing the direction of her life. Towards the end of this course in Germany, organized by a group called Ecumenical Service, she decided to change her first calling as a high school teacher of German to that of peace worker.

With the war and the disintegration of Yugoslavia, Roman Catholic Croatians did not recognize disintegration as something against which to fight but as a way to liberation and of securing the rights of which they had been deprived in Yugoslavia.

Croatia

Elisabeth Reusse-Decrey

Geneva Call

Elisabeth Reusse-Decrey started Geneva Call in 1998 as an independent, humanitarian NGO to complement the work of the Ottawa Treaty to ban landmines. The purpose of Geneva Call is to engage armed non-state actors to respect and to adhere to humanitarian norms, starting with the ban on anti-personnel mines. To date, 27 groups in Africa, the Middle East, and Asia have signed the Deed of Commitment which is registered in the Republic and Canton of Geneva, Switzerland.

Why is a 50-year-old mother of six children (four adopted) climbing up a mountain in Iraqi Kurdistan all by herself to meet rebel leaders? What is the former president of the Geneva Parliament doing in a high security prison in Colombia eating fried grasshoppers with the imprisoned leader of the National Liberation Army (ELN)? In 1995, Elisabeth Reusse-Decrey accepted to replace a friend in the Swiss campaign against mines for two months — and ten years later she is the founder and executive president of Geneva Call. Driven by a sense of revulsion at the injustices in the world and strongly involved in associations dealing with peace and disarmament as an active politician, she has put together a vibrant NGO with dedicated collaborators that reaches throughout the world where landmines are used by non-state actors. Seeing a road demined with safe access for farmers and children drives her to try to come to terms with groups often considered terrorists by government officials. Her strong convictions about safety and physical handicaps, coming from her background as a physiotherapist, allow her to successfully negotiate with armed leaders from the Southern Sudan to the Philippines. Her vision of a mine-free world is not one of perpetual peace, but one in which humanitarian norms are respected and innocent non-combatants allowed the freedom and liberty she enjoyed as a child roaming freely in the forests of her mountains of Valais.

Most armed conflicts today involve armed non-state actors (NSAs) fighting government forces or each other. Many NSAs produce, stockpile, and use mines. Between 2001 and 2003, NSAs reportedly have used land mines in at least 27 countries, causing between 15,000 and 20,000 casualties every year.

Akhtar Riazuddin

Behbud Association of Pakistan (BAP)

Akhtar Riazuddin (born 1928) reaches out to thousands of poor homes in Pakistan through the Behbud Association of Pakistan (BAP), an NGO that she founded in 1968 for community development. A woman of many talents, Akhtar brought significant changes to the status of women in Pakistan when she served as a top-ranking bureaucrat in the federal government. She is also a gifted Urdu writer and has extensively researched the crafts of India and Pakistan.

When Akhtar Riazuddin served as federal secretary (1986 to 1989) in the ministry of women's development, academies were set up to train urban community workers, and women's studies were introduced at universities. Marginalized women were provided with mental homes, jails, shelters, micro-credit schemes, libraries, and rural mobile dispensaries. NGOs were given unprecedented moral and financial support. Akhtar persuaded Pakistan's finance minister to expand the budgets for NGOs and community-based organizations. A maternity hospital was set up in Lahore and other provinces.

Since 1967, Akhtar has worked with the Behbud Association of Pakistan, which she founded to help deprived women and children, especially those in urban slums, secure health services, education, and vocational training. BAP has brought basic health services and the message of family planning to millions of homes. Thousands of others have been provided access to functional literacy, and primary, home, and community-based schools. Women have been given piece-rate work for decent wages, eliminating middlemen, and have been trained as community leaders and elected as local counselors. Pressure groups formed in Rawalpindi and Islamabad have persuaded the administration to provide water, gas, children's parks, land for schools, and low-cost housing. The NGO has helped women negotiate marriage contracts that include giving them the right to initiate divorce.

Akhtar, who started work as a college lecturer in Lahore, was drawn to social work by her mother's example, and was awarded the Sitara I Imtiaz, one of the country's highest civilian awards.

In conservative Pakistan, marginalized women lacked developmental givens like mental homes, jails, shelters, microcredit schemes, libraries, rural mobile dispensaries, recourse to family planning, middlemen-free work, and the right to initiate divorce proceedings.

Hilda Djulaida Rolobessy

Yayasan Pengembangan dan Pemberdayaan Masyarakat (YPPM)

Since the violence in Maluku erupted in 1998, Hilda Rolobessy (born 1972) has been actively involved in providing assistance to Internally Displaced Persons (IDPs). In 1999, she founded Yayasan Pengembangan dan Pemberdayaan Masyarakat (YPPM), the Development and Improvement for Society Association, which provides comprehensive support for IDPs, especially women, and promotes peace and reconciliation among parties involved in conflict. YPPM's impartial and courageous efforts have encouraged communities in conflict to bury the hatchet and gradually reinstate peace in their communities.

Hilda Rolobessy had been living a peaceful life in Ambon, Maluku until 1998 when the poor political economy and social tensions between the Moslem and Christian communities broke out into violent conflict. Thousands of people were killed in the strife and thousands more fled to other areas. Houses, mosques and churches were burned and Moslems and Christians began to live in segregated areas. Hilda and her family were forced to hide in the mountains to escape a mob attack on Moslem communities. Since the conflict erupted, Hilda has been a volunteer working with internally displaced persons in Maluku. Of the many problems she encountered in her work, one of the most critical was security. The situation in Maluku was very tense and it was not safe for humanitarian workers to travel by land or by sea. Mob attacks were staged against communities in areas controlled by opposing sides. Roadblocks were placed everywhere and snipers hid in deserted buildings shooting at everything that moved.

Hilda's work was also hampered by religious prejudice. "It was hard to gain people's trust. The Christians, for example, thought we could not be neutral, simply because we are Moslems," she says. In 1999, Hilda founded Yayasan Pengembangan dan Pemberdayaan Masyarakat (YPPM) that incorporates Christian activists in its peace building activities and promotes peace and reconciliation through advocacy, negotiation, mediation and trauma counseling in the Maluku and North Maluku provinces. "I believe that peace is possible. I dream of a peaceful Maluku, like it was before the conflict, where people lived side by side harmoniously, regardless of their religious differences," she says. Tensions are still high in Maluku. But more people have started to get a better understanding of the nature of the conflict and are trying not to be easily provoked by rumors.

When the violence broke out in Maluku in late 1998, thousands of Moslems and Christians were killed. Houses, churches and mosques were destroyed in vengeful attacks, and survivors were forced to live in segregated areas.

Indonesia

Yvonne Ryakiye

Twishakira amahoro
Search for Common Ground Burundi

Yvonne Ryakiye lives at the foothills of Bujumbura, where many Tutsi families were killed or driven away during the 1993/1994 genocide. Yvonne, a Hutu, started her organization by hiding Tutsi refugees. With the Hutu and the Tutsi entrenched on either side of the Kanyosha River, she took the initiative to re-establish contact with her former Tutsi neighbor Léonie Barakomeza. The two women risked their lives as they crossed the river to visit one another. This began the warming-up of the relations between two hostile ethnic groups.

"As women we have done our best to make the Hutus and Tutsis live together peacefully again, because we do not want to lose our husbands and children," says Yvonne Ryakiye, a Hutu farmer who lives in Busoro village, where the Kanyosha flows through a deep gorge. The river was considered a natural boundary. Recalls Yvonne, "It was like a wall protecting us from being murdered, because nobody dared to cross it." During the 1993/1994 genocide the Tutsis were driven from their homes on one side of the river, while the Hutus fled from the opposite bank of the river to Busoro. In the beginning, Yvonne hid Tutsi refugees in her house, but this became too dangerous. However, she was not willing to accept this situation, and when the tension became unbearable, she arranged for a secret meeting with her former neighbor Léonie Barakomeza, a Tutsi. "The fact that she was willing to risk her life to meet me, strengthened me," says Yvonne today. "Women are the center of the family, that is why we suffer most during times of war and must do anything to end it." Both women decided to break the ban, by crossing the hitherto insurmountable barrier to visit each other. When they remained unharmed, other women followed their example. Yvonne recalls, "The men were relieved to see the friendly encounter between the women, and those who had previously forbidden their wives to meet with other women now allowed it." Thereafter Yvonne and Léonie, with other women, founded the Twishakira amahoro ("We want peace") peace organization. Under the organization, the women jointly cultivate fields, reconstruct houses and assist refugees. Yvonne's assessment of the present situation is, "Although the ethnic conflict has not been forgotten, there is a glimmer of hope for reconciliation and mutual tolerance."

In 1993 civil war broke out in Burundi between Tutsi and the Hutu ethnic groups, claiming over 200,000 lives. The conflict often recurs. Many refugees still live across the borders or were displaced within the country. Whole villages remain destroyed and the fields are still full of landmines.

Burundi

Amma Sakina

For the past ten years Amma Sakina has worked on issues such as raising awareness of and campaigning against violations of women and human rights, and the eradication of all forms of discrimination. She works on grassroots as well as on organizational levels where she concerts efforts of community-based groups and NGOs. She has also worked with people with disabilities. Amma advocates education for all children and has run her own house as a school.

Amma's work was triggered by her observation of the extreme injustice and discrimination against women that has prevailed in Afghanistan for decades. As an active participant in the peaceful resistance movement, she witnessed the incarceration for five years of her own son. In spite of these circumstances, she did not waiver in her commitment to achieving her goal of helping women in Afghanistan. At present, Amma works closely with vulnerable people, such as women, children and disabled groups. She is optimistic about the future of women in Afghanistan, especially after the incorporation of an article that codifies equal rights for men and women in the Afghan constitution. In order to set an example for women to gain self-confidence Amma has nominated herself for the presidential elections, and she has now redoubled her activities in the community-based groups.

The participation of women in every aspect of life forms the cornerstone of her future vision for a peaceful and prosperous Afghanistan. Warlords and armed groups still dominate large parts of Afghanistan, and violence against women is still quite prevalent. However, Amma believes that there is a need for concerted effort in demilitarizing and rehabilitating the men fighting as guerrillas and to raise the population's awareness of respecting women's and human rights. Despite all these hurdles, Amma's objective remains the protection and promotion of human rights in general and women's rights in particular.

In a country devastated by warfare, promotion and protection of human rights and women's rights is the main goal of Amma Sakina's work. In order to effectuate these changes, she conducts workshops and meets with different sections of Afghan society, putting great emphasis on education.

Afghanistan

Colette Samoya Kirura

Bangwe and Dialogue

Colette Samoya Kirura, born 1952, is a pioneer. From her student days she has been politically active; she was one of only two women elected to the Burundi's parliament in 1982. In 1992 she became her country's ambassador to the UN in Geneva. She headed the Union des Femmes Burundaises, and in 1998 she founded the peace organization Bangwe and Dialogue. It unites women of Burundi, Rwanda and the Democratic Republic of Congo, strengthening their power in the reconciliation process and providing education, especially for displaced people.

Colette does not like to mention her ethnic affiliation, because, "It is high time we played down tribal differences, which the colonial powers stressed for their own interest. Tutsis and Hutus lived in peace before and can do it again!" Colette is a pioneer in many ways. She was the first girl from her village to attend a high school and one of the first two women to obtain a Masters Degree (in History and Geography). On graduation she became a college teacher. Politically active even in her student days, she was elected to parliament between 1982 and 1987, one of only two women. From 1992 to 1994 she served as Ambassador to the UN in Geneva, where she dedicated herself to the defense of human rights.

She travelled several times back to her country, often at considerable risk, from 1987 to 1991 when she headed the Union des Femmes Burundaises. In 1998 she founded the Peace Organization Bangwe, which means "Stop fighting!" in Kirundi. It is developed on the women's traditional mediation tasks when men fight. The organization, uniting women from all social and ethnic backgrounds, meets alternatively in one of the three war-stricken countries of the Great Lakes region to establish dialogue and cooperation. It strengthens women's power in the peace process, using cultural tools such as poetry, song, theatre performances and works of art. The organization helps displaced people not only with material assistance, but education for women, young people and children.

Widowed in 1992 and mother of three children, Colette does all this work on a voluntary basis, including the difficult task of securing the funds for the organization. She says, "I cannot stand violence, so I have to do something against it. Even as a child I could not tolerate injustice." This is also the subject of her book, "La Femme au regard triste".

Although the situation has improved in the Great Lakes region since the genocide of 1993/94, Burundi has a precarious peace. Widespread hatred and fear persist. By getting to know each other and by uniting their efforts, women can play an important part in the difficult process of reconciliation.

Burundi

Kumudini Samuel

Women and Media Collective (WMC)
Coalition for Assisting Tsunami-Affected Women (Cataw)

Since the 1980s, Kumudini Samuel (born 1958) has played a key role in the women's movement and the antiwar movement in Sri Lanka. In 2002, she organized a campaign involving international feminists to press for the inclusion of women in a peace process aimed at ending Sri Lanka's two-decade-old civil war. Her campaign led to the appointment of a gender subcommittee to advise the peace process, and she is one of five women nominated by the government to serve on this body.

Kumudini Samuel, who has a Sinhala mother and a Tamil father, has never let mixed-origin issues hold her back. She became involved in activism in the early 1980s, through her engagement with women garment workers in north Colombo, who had gone on strike against the unfair dismissal of some active workers' organizers in their factory. She was a key figure in the women's solidarity movement that evolved around this strike.

Kumudini is a significant figure in the women's movement and the antiwar movement in Sri Lanka. She is an active campaigner for peace and justice for minorities. Despite all the difficulties posed by the shrinking conflict-riven democratic space, Kumudini maintains a strong engagement with women's rights and human rights. The high point of Kumudini's involvement with the antiwar movement was her campaign to include women in the peace process. She initiated the idea of bringing a group of international feminists to Sri Lanka in October 2002 to support a public campaign to pressure the government and the Liberation Tigers of Tamil Eelam. In November 2002, the government appointed a subcommittee on gender issues to advise the parties to the peace process–Kumudini was one of five women nominated by the government to be part of this subcommittee. However, the subcommittee had had only one preliminary meeting, when the peace talks stalled.

Kumudini is one of the coordinators of the Women and Media Collective, a Colombo-based feminist group that promotes women's rights. She is also deeply involved in the Coalition for Assisting Tsunami-Affected Women (Cataw). She combines activism with analytical work, and has written and published papers on the situation of women in the conflict. She is also studying for a masters in women's studies at the University of Colombo.

Although the present process of peace negotiations in Sri Lanka's inter-necine war began in 2001, women have largely been kept out of the dealings between the parties. All that might change now, with a greater recognition of negotiable certainties.

Sri Lanka

Delia Ediltrudes "Duds" Santiago-Locsin

Paghiliusa sa Paghidaet-Negros (PSPN)

Delia Ediltrudes Santiago-Locsin (born 1939), a social worker, is executive director of "Paghiliusa sa Paghidaet" (Unity for Peace)-Negros (PSPN) in Negros Occidental. Her involvement in peace advocacy began in 1988 when she helped evacuees from armed conflict establish peace zones that were off limits to the military and the rebels. She has negotiated peace between groups in conflict, such as the government and the rebels, and the sugar planters and the hacienda workers. She is also involved in the protection of the environment and strengthening the family as the basic unit of society.

Delia Ediltrudes Santiago-Locsin, or "Duds" as she is better known, became involved in peace initiatives when she was chosen by Unicef to lead the rehabilitation work on Children in Situations of Armed Conflict (CSAC) in Negros. Thousands of peasants had to escape the armed conflict between the military and the Communist Party of the Philippines-New People's Army (CPP-NPA). Since then, Duds has been the popular choice to negotiate agreements between groups with adversely opposed interests, such as the peace talks between the government and the CPP-NPA-National Democratic Front (NDF), and the implementation of agrarian reform between landlords and hacienda workers.

Duds is actively involved in media and policy advocacy regarding environmental issues like illegal logging, the building of a geothermal power plant in a national park and large-scale mining. She is also active in the protection of women and children against abuse and violence. She is part of Green Alert, an environmental monitoring group that pointed out the adverse effects of mine tailings from the two big mining firms on the water system of Sipalay town. Both firms — Maricalum and Philex — have been closed. "People should learn to let public officials know that what they are doing is wrong," says Duds. Currently, her peace initiatives have moved to strengthening the family as the basic unit of society. She helped establish Healthy Start with the Bulig Foundation, which promotes the mental, spiritual and physical growth of children by working with high-risk expectant mothers who have a history of drug, alcohol, physical and sexual abuse. Her advocacies have been funded by the Canadian International Development Agency (Cida), the Office of the Presidential Adviser on the Peace Process (OPAPP) and the provincial government.

Peace building is urgent in the province of Negros where wide gaps exist between landowners and the landless, the government's agrarian reform program still has to be fully implemented, there is wanton exploitation of natural resources and an armed insurgency continues to flourish.

Philippines

Julien Florence Mona Saroinsong

Crisis Center SAG SULUTTENG

Julien Florence Mona Saroinsong (born 1958) is a full-time lecturer and researcher at a university in Manado, North Sulawesi, Indonesia and a volunteer at the Crisis Center of Sinode Am church network. In 2001, when thousands of refugees from violent conflicts in Poso, Central Sulawesi and Maluku poured into North Sulawesi, Mona visited refugees and used her networks as a church activist to provide them with assistance. She also trained volunteers and refugees in trauma healing and organized dialogues between conflicting religious communities in Poso and Maluku.

When armed conflict swept through Central Sulawesi and Maluku in 2001, more than 20,000 people were forced to leave their homes and seek refuge in Central and North Sulawesi. Mona Saroinsong established a crisis center from scratch for refugees in North Sulawesi . Using her personal contacts, she was able to access the survivors of the conflict in the heart of Central Sulawesi. "It was very hard to get past the armed civilian guards to go to the Muslim communities, but I managed somehow," she recounts. Being a woman, a Christian and a church activist, Mona had to deal with the suspicions of the Muslim communities. "I learned that after getting food and shelter, the refugees needed people to listen to their stories. So I asked friends who were interested in volunteering and gathered information for those who wanted to help," she says.

After almost a year of working with her colleagues from the church community, Mona met some refugees who saw the importance of storytelling as a tool to help them overcome their trauma and volunteered to collect information and listen to the stories of other refugees. Mona's network grew and she gained enough trust from both the Muslim and Christian communities to initiate reconciliation talks among the survivors. In 2001, the Sinode Am church network appointed her to the executive board of the Crisis Center. She got mixed reactions to her work at the center, with suspicions and accusations growing stronger after each attack following the declaration of a peace pact between conflicting parties.

Today Mona Saroinsong is still teaching and remains actively involved in church community activities. She continues to critically monitor the peace process in Maluku and Poso. She also publishes her reflections on the peace process in the local media and on websites.

From 1999 to 2002, more than 20,000 Muslims and Christians in Central Sulawesi and Maluku fled from the armed conflict that erupted there. Many refugees, who accessed social services outside their religious communities, were forced to abandon their religions under threat from the civilian militia.

Indonesia

Gordana Savin

Red Cross Sombor/Vojvodina

Gordana Savin (born 1955) provides humanitarian assistance to refugees and internally displaced persons through her work with the Red Cross of Sombor and Vojvodina. When war broke out in Kosovo, she led a Red Cross team and, with Nato Kosovo Forces, provided aid to isolated villages. Under extremely difficult conditions, she also organized a reception center for displaced persons. In October 1995, the Municipal Assembly of Sombor awarded Gordana for her extraordinary work.

Gordana Savin's first encounter with the Red Cross Organization was when she was a child. In the summer of 1965, the waters of the river Danube reached a critical level and a decision was made to break the dam and let the water flood hundreds of acres of the plain, in order to save the cities along the course of the Danube from flooding. Her grandparents' farmhouse, where she had been staying, was destroyed, the animals died. Sadness and loss overwhelmed the family. Then, one morning in September, the postman brought a letter from Sombor addressed to her mother. The next day, her mother went to Sombor. When she came back, she started taking out things from the bags: new shoes for each child, clothes and winter jackets, four school bags, notebooks and all that children needed for school. They all were dumbfounded and she simply said: "This is why the Sombor Red Cross invited me. You should remember this and, God forbid, if needed, return the favor." Gordana still remembers.

In 1987, Gordana got a full-time job with the Red Cross, working with youth and health protection. In 1991, she was appointed Secretary of the Red Cross in Sombor, taking over the position on 1 July. In the beginning of August, the war started fully and terribly. There was no time for hesitation, she knew that the "God-forbidden time" her mother had been talking about had come. She led Red Cross teams to Kosovo and, with the Nato Kosovo Force, distributed humanitarian aid to isolated villages, and took out messages from the inhabitants to their relatives. She organized a displaced persons center and, in a matter of days, turned it from a chaotic and unhygienic situation to a clean and well-functioning center.

In October 1995, the Municipal Assembly of Sombor handed to Gordana Savin, leader of the Red Cross in Sombor, the October Award of the City of Sombor, for her extraordinary work.

In 1998, conflict broke out in Kosovo between ethnic Serbs and Albanians resulting in thousands of deaths and hundreds of thousands of refugees and internally displaced persons in desperate need of humanitarian aid.

Serbia and Montenegro

Bosiljka Schedlich

Southeast European Cultural Center Berlin

Bosiljka Schedlich, born in 1948 in what is today Croatia, founded the Southeast European Cultural Center in Berlin in 1991. Since then, some 30,000 war refugees from former Yugoslavia have received care, counseling, and therapy. Bosiljka led therapy groups of people traumatized from the war and soon became an expert on trauma. Meanwhile, many war refugees have returned voluntarily. Bosiljka and her colleagues have recreated their reconciliation projects in former war zones through sponsorships or "storytelling cafés" in which people can speak freely about their war experiences.

The Southeast European Cultural Center in Berlin, founded by Bosiljka Schedlich, runs many projects for traumatized war victims in former Yugoslavia. These include: therapy groups, social counseling, language courses, training programs for youth, children's art groups, sponsorship of people returning to war zones, and schools for Roma children in Bosnia.

When asked about her favorite project, Bosiljka's answer is clear: "the storytelling cafés" in Bosnia which she organized and now number more than 60. The basic idea is that older people from the community and foreign guests can tell the stories of their life in a pleasant coffee house atmosphere. In this way people can acknowledge the suffering in the stories of others without an ethnic context. The report of elderly about World War II and others tell of their experiences in other wars. There was, for instance, someone who had escaped the Algerian war. Or a German couple who had hidden Jews during the Hitler era. In Bjeljina, still one of the strongholds of Serb extremism, a Muslim woman had the courage to speak about her encounter with one of the infamous Serb militia leaders. "She told about the many corpses outside of the hospital," Bosiljka said. "People shot by the militia. It was deathly quiet. An old teacher, whose son had founded the extremist Serb party and for whom this leader was a hero, kept signaling me to interrupt the woman. My colleagues left the room. They thought that now the bombs would fall. When she was finished speaking, I let the teacher speak. He rattled on in a loud voice all the Serb propaganda. When he finished, I thanked him, but said that we would not go into it further. We were only interested in what each individual had experienced, not their ethnic or religious group. That was the worst bomb for him. It really worked. Afterwards, everyone was more relaxed and we sang together."

When war broke out in former Yugoslavia, some 45,000 people fled to the German capital Berlin. In the Southeast European Cultural Center they found protection, counseling, and help. The center restored people's sense of dignity. Today, projects in the former war-torn areas are also run by the center.

Germany

Tatyana Senyushkina

Taurida National University Simferopol
Crimean Branch of the Ukrainian Conflictologist Association

Tatyana Senyushkina has been studying ethnic conflicts and how to anticipate, prevent, and manage them since 1995. She has published a large number
of studies in this field including the "Prevention and Management of Ethnic
Conflicts: State and Administrative Measures." She works with the Crimean
Branch of the Ukrainian Conflictologist Association and a wide network of
people active in this field. She is working for change within ethnically hostile
settings and is promoting interethnic trust within communities. She has
developed training materials on peace building.

Tatyana Senyushkina promotes the culture of peace and interethnic trust in
the conflict regions of Crimea. "The words of Lao Tse — 'if one wants peace,
he should perceive a war,' inspired me in my work," she says. She remembers
another ancient Chinese saying: "Night is followed by day, darkness by light.
So, a war is followed by peace, as naturally as the day follows night."
In the 1990s, Crimean Tatars started returning to Crimea after their
deportation to Central Asia by Stalin in 1944, and the flashes of international
discord between the Tatars and Ukrainians flared up. "Peace seemed fragile,
sliding out from under us," Tatyana remembers. It was then that her research
on ethnic conflicts began. At the start, it was necessary to define what a
conflict was and to learn how to manage it. Soon her work allowed her to explore
this phenomenon more deeply. She began to identify allies and collaborators
within a growing network: teachers, psychologists, scientists, humanitarians
and naturalists, military servicemen, journalists, state officials, students,
representatives of women's and youth organizations, artists — all united —
as Tatyana says "by the goal of making progress through tiny steps to a
peaceful life, to knowing more about different cultures, to understanding
the peoples with whom we live in our neighborhoods, and to trusting them."
Tatyana together with a baker invented a cake — a balloon symbolizing our
planet: "If people do not learn to live in peace, the balloon cannot carry
them further. And, it is very tasty — of chocolate and cream: We gave it to
Crimean Tatar children who were just starting their life in this complicated
world," Tatyana recounts. "Eating it with childlike joy, perhaps they will begin
to understand peace."

In the 1990s, as Crimean Tatars exiled by Stalin in 1944 returned to Crimea
from deportations, the first flashes of violence began. Returning with injured minds and broken souls; many people were afraid of the future.

Ukraine

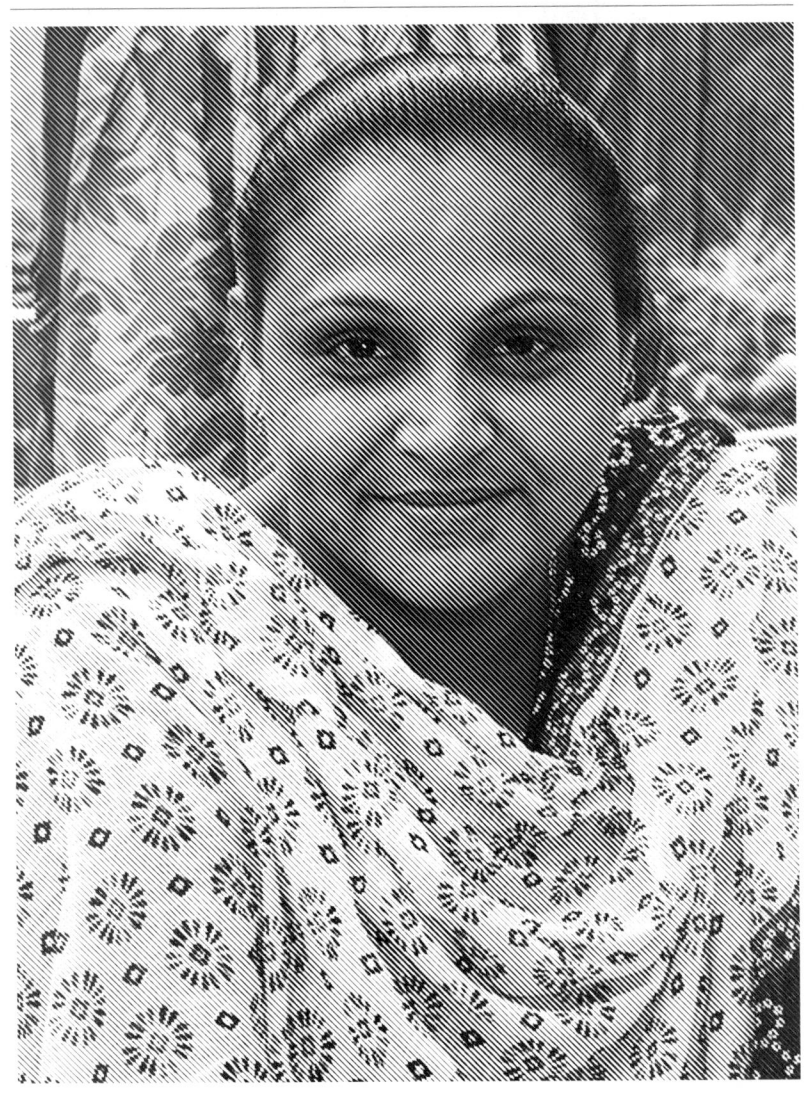

Naseeb Mohammad Shaikh

Aman Samuday

Naseeb Mohammad Shaikh lost 11 members of the family she had married into, and 14 members of her parents' families during the 2002 Gujarat riots. Since then, she has been a prime initiator of peace and communal harmony, leading the fight for rights for the minority communities in and around Gujarat's Kalol region. At last count, she was fighting 37 cases of atrocities, including ones by the police.

Naseeb Mohammad Shaikh is from a well-off Muslim landowning family whose life was torn asunder by the 2002 Gujarat communal riot: 11 members of the family she had married into and 14 members of her parents' families were slaughtered. Her daughter was brutally raped in front of her relatives before being killed. Naseeb, who escaped death, was left with her son and social ostracism, and has since lived in a rehabilitation colony in Kalol. Soon after the event, Naseeb joined the social organization Sewa for six months, during which time she traveled around villages in the vicinity to work with riot-affected women and children. Finding nothing constructive coming out of her efforts, she then joined Aman Samuday, an organization propelling people toward peace and communal harmony.

Moving from village to village, Naseeb spread the message of peace, justice, communal harmony, and a common humanity. Of significance was her campaign against a local Muslim cleric who ran a relief camp: Naseeb mobilized a small army of women to rally against him and demand their rights. She has since then campaigned for the rights of Dalits in nearby villages, and of other minority communities through her peace committee initiative.

At last count, she was fighting 37 cases of atrocities, including ones by the police. She is a regular at forums that discuss injustices relating to the 2002 Godhra conflagration. Naseeb recently participated in an international peace conference in New Delhi, where she spoke on the violation of the human rights of marginalized societies in the villages of Gujarat.

The Gujarat communal riots of 2002, which affected more than 100,000 families, were a shameful turning point in India's secular dispensation. The displaced rebuilt their lives from virtually nothing. The refugee camps were cesspools of terror, anxiety, and exploitation.

India

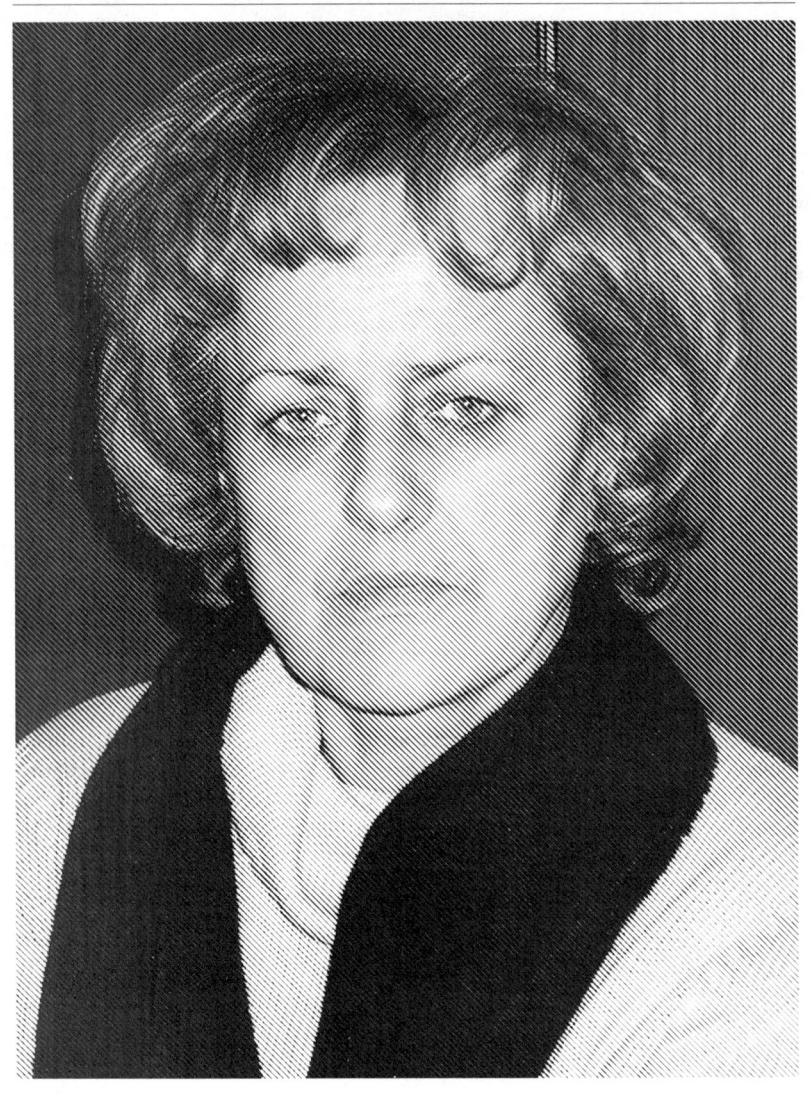

Nusreta Sivac

Srcem do Mira (Through Heart to Peace)

A judge by profession in Prijedor, Nusreta Sivac experienced the worst kind of physical and psychological torture, rape, and imprisonment when she was deported to the Omarska extermination camp in June 1992. Together with other imprisoned men and women, she witnessed countless crimes and executions. In August, she was released and fled to Zagreb. She became active in the Women's Association and its work with refugees from Bosnia and Herzegovina. Nusreta seeks to make known the truth about the war and especially the imprisonment and torture in the concentration camps.

Nusreta Sivac, born in Prijedor in 1951, worked as a judge in Prijedor until 1992. In the end of April 1992, the Serb Democratic Party (SDS), with the help of army and police forces, violently took control of Prijedor. Consequently, Nusreta wasn't allowed to work any longer because of her nationality. The SDS held absolute authority in the town. After its occupation, a large formation of troops came from Serbia and Montenegro and provided full support to the local Serb extremists. The local media, controlled by the SDS, was broadcasting the programs of the instigators whose goal was to ethnically cleanse the city of all non-Serbians. The Serbs set up three concentration camps in Prijedor: Omarska, Keraterm, and Trnopolje, where non-Serbians were taken and murdered in the process of ethnic cleansing. The local military and paramilitary formations, supported by those from Serbia and Montenegro, began the destruction of the villages and surrounding areas where the non-Serbians lived, along with the cleansing of its citizens. Murder of men, women, and children was done on a daily basis. Nusreta was invited to the police station of Prijedor for an informative conversation that never took place. Instead, she was ordered by armed men to get on the bus parked in front of the police building. It was her trip to hell in Omarska. There, she witnessed the everyday systematic and brutal torture and killing of her people. In August, she was released and she then fled to Zagreb, Croatia. There, she became active in the Women's Association of Bosnia and Herzegovina. This organization works with many refugees from the country. Primarily, Nusreta seeks to make the truth about the war crimes that took place in Bosnia and Herzegovina, and especially the imprisonment and torture in the concentration camps, known to the public.

In April 1992, the Serb Democratic Party violently took control of Prijedor and set up three concentration camps. The local Serbs, supported by those from Serbia and Montenegro, began destroying the villages where non-Serbians lived, and imprisoning, expelling, and murdering the non-Serbians.

Bosnia and Herzegovina

Svetlana Slapsak

Ljubljana Graduate School of Humanities
Balkan Women Against War

Svetlana Slapsak has promoted freedom of expression and human rights since the 1960s. She initiated a petition to ban the death penalty in 1983, the first to be published in the Yugoslav media. She also initiated a series of activities to support political detainees. With the growth of aggressive nationalism in the Yugoslav republics in the 1980s, she focused on promoting peace in her country. When the war began, Svetlana fled to Ljubljana. There, she organized a women's peace group and support for war refugees. She continues to work for a culture of peace throughout former Yugoslavia.

When war broke out in Croatia, Svetlana Slapsak organized a peace group for women, "Silence Kills, Let us Speak for Peace," from her exile in Ljubljana. For several months, the group held candlelight vigils, signed petitions, and collected contributions in Ljubljana's central park for all of Yugoslavia's war victims. The group's actions helped create an atmosphere of solidarity for the victims of war and the influx of refugees in 1992. Many refugees found shelter with Svetlana and her husband.

Born to ethnic Serb parents, she has always promoted ideas of multiculturalism. As president of the Writers' Association of Serbia's Committee for the Freedom of Expression, she initiated a series of activities to support political detainees. With the growth of aggressive nationalism in the Yugoslav republics in the 1980s, she focused on promoting peace in her country. In 1988 and 1989, Svetlana extensively traveled throughout Yugoslavia lecturing about the impending war and the possibilities for peace. She organized several initiatives aimed at opposing the threat of war. When the war began, Svetlana fled to Ljubljana. After being refused Slovenian citizenship on the grounds of "national security" twice, she received support from the diplomatic community and was finally granted citizenship. She continued her political activism throughout the war in Yugoslavia, working with victims and promoting peace. She also addressed international organizations and funding bodies, coordinated assistance for people in distress, established a women's support group for information and aid. Svetlana organized intellectuals against nationalism, and persistently criticized the role of nationalist intellectuals, who provided the political elite with a justification for war. As a writer and teacher at the graduate school level, she continues to promote a culture of peace.

Former Yugoslavia was characterized by political repression and silencing of dissent. In the 1980s, aggressive nationalism escalated in the Yugoslav republics and resulted in the outbreak of war in the Balkans.

Slovenia

Miriam Suacito

Nagdilaab Foundation
Inter-religious Dialogue Program of Isabela Prelature

Miriam Suacito (born 1959), fondly known as "Dedet", saw how her home province, Basilan, was transformed from a peaceful place to a war-torn community where people live in abject poverty and constant fear. She put to good use her training as a psychologist by organizing trauma-healing sessions for war widows and orphans and former hostages of the notorious Muslim extremist Abu Sayyaf kidnap-for-ransom group. Miriam undertakes community-based poverty alleviation programs and implements inter-religious dialogue as a way of fostering peace.

Valentine's Day 1999 is etched in Miriam Suacito's mind as the day when the dreaded Muslim extremist Abu Sayyaf group killed six of her fellow catechists from Tumahubong, Basilan province. The catechists were on their way to an "Alay Kapwa" (Offering for Others) seminar in Isabela, the capital, when they were ambushed. Dedet could not believe how such gentle people could meet such a violent and senseless death. Some were felled by gunshots, some mercilessly hacked with "bolos" (local swords). However, despite the atrocities that some Muslims have committed, ostensibly in the name of their faith, Dedet feels only compassion for her Muslim neighbors in Basilan. She has seen how many of them have suffered in the inter-religious conflict spawned needlessly by misunderstanding and government neglect. "Peace," she asserts, "is the dream of every resident of Basilan, Muslim and Christian alike", and she has worked very hard to bring this about.

In 2001, Miriam helped start the Nagdilaab Foundation which has programs on peace and development, human rights, community development, education, research and training, resource development and agricultural production. Nagdilaab's project, "Recycling War Trash for Peace", was chosen for funding by the World Bank in its search for innovative community initiatives in 2004. The project promotes the culture of peace among the youth in Basilan by developing their earning potentials through creative arts and peace-oriented values. In the hands of the youth, war trash like spent bullets and cannon shells are turned into peace symbols — angels, gongs, flowers and doves. The Peace Advocates of Zamboanga (PAZ) gave her the Peace Weaver's Award in 1999 saying: "This one woman's life has been one of witnessing her desire for all peoples to live in dignity, justice, peace and lasting harmony."

Basilan, one of the poorest provinces in the Philippines, earned international notoriety when the Abu Sayyaf Group (ASG) of extremist Muslim rebels made the island their lair for kidnappings and the murder of Christians. There have been reports of human rights abuses during military operations there.

Amneh Kamal Sulaiman

General Union of Palestinian Women (GUPW)

Amneh Sulaiman, originally from Palestine, was born and raised in a Palestinian refugee camp in Beirut, Lebanon in 1951. She graduated from Beirut Arab University (BAU) in 1977 with a BA in English Literature and attended several workshops on rehabilitation, illiteracy, child labor and gender issues. She has worked with the United Nations Relief and Works Agency (UNRWA), became a refugee camp advisor in 1973 and Deputy Chairwoman of the General Union of Palestinian Women (GUPW) in 1981, whose Lebanon branch she headed in 1982. In 1983 she became a member of the Palestinian National Council.

Amneh Sulaiman has suffered immensely as a refugee, and her conditions were no better than those of all Palestinian women in the refugee camps in Lebanon. Despite the siege, hunger and the death of many family members and friends, they were determined to continue work to maintain their households and keep their lives going. Amneh liaises with the refugees to organize social and patriotic work. The residents of the camps feel they are one family, and they work hard as a group, each in their own capacities. Even the elderly women tidy up the dwellings of the members of the Palestinian fighting guerillas, cook food for them and donate blood for the wounded.

The Palestinian refugee camps in Lebanon have always been the resistance nucleus against the Israeli occupation of Palestine. Many voices tried to disband the militia of the camps in order to undermine the Palestinian Liberation Organization (PLO).

Occupied Palestinian Territory

Alma Suljevic

Academy of Fine Arts Sarajevo

Alma Suljevic is a "land mine" artist who lives in Sarajevo, Bosnia and Herzegovina. During and after the war (1992—1995), she worked as a de-miner. A performance artist and sculptor, she uses these war-time experiences as basis for her artistic work. Currently, Alma is a professor at the Academy of Fine Arts in Sarajevo. She has exhibited her work throughout Europe and raises awareness about land mines. She also raises money for de-mining.

Alma Suljevic was born in Kakanj, a little mining town in Central Bosnia, in 1963. She grew up in Sarajevo and has been living there ever since, including the period of aggression. Today, she is a professor at the Academy of Fine Arts in Sarajevo, where she obtained her M.A. in sculpture studies. The professor under whom she graduated was killed by a grenade fired from Serb positions around the besieged city of Sarajevo in June 1992. During the war, Alma Suljevic made a sculpture that symbolized freedom and hope, a sculpture that is not forgotten by citizens of the biggest, most modern concentration camp in the history of humankind — a sculpture made of a tram that was left for 850 days at Skenderija (downtown Sarajevo), scene of the fiercest battles of May 1992. This work of art is, according to Professor Tvrtko Kulenovic, the "apogee of creativity within the besieged Sarajevo." After the war, Alma was working on her sculptures, widely known as "Bleeding Grass," when suddenly a tragedy occurred in Zenica: a family of "returnees" lost all their children. A land mine killed the two sons and one daughter. At this point, Alma actively started getting involved in dealing with the problem of mines and minefields in her environment. A creator without pretending to create miracles in art, she wished that no child would ever be killed again. Drawing and marking maps was the first step, but it did not satisfy her. She wanted to do more and to point out the issue of the fields of death in the very center of town more critically. With "Elektra 98," a video work, her active involvement in removing landmines in her country began. Her art makes people go through the painful stages of awareness: they do not know, they do not want to know, they must see.

Several hundred thousand antipersonnel landmines are still buried around Bosnia and Herzegovina. Hundreds of people have been killed and wounded. Landmine clearance has decreased the number of casualties, but one still cannot walk in the fields and forests without risking one's life and limb.

Bosnia and Herzegovina

Apollonia Bola Talo

Family Support Centre
Guadalcanal Provincial Council of Women
National Peace Council

Apollonia Bola Talo is a grassroots activist from Guadalcanal Province, Solomon Islands. She has worked extensively on advancing women's issues and interests relating to HIV/Aids, income generating enterprises, training, policy development, social justice, and peace. During the late 1990s' social unrest and ethnic tension, Apollonia worked with other committed women to restore peace. Her commitment to working for peace and women's and children's rights has seen her engagement with the Peace Monitoring Council (now known as the National Peace Council).

Appollonia Bola Talo's son says: "I have no enemies. Just like my mother, I believe in peace. Everyone comes to my mother for assistance; whatever it is and what time it is, does not matter. That is how I grew up and that is how I will live my life. My mother is a leader, teacher, and a human rights advocate." He is a mechanic. At the height of the ethnic tension in Solomon Islands, news went around of another murder. Appollonia had to travel a long way to come to town to see for herself if her son was the latest victim. She worked closely with the Franciscan Brothers from Hautambu (West Guadalcanal) and the Patterson House in Honiara for security reasons, to get through the many checkpoints and gunpoints. Fortunately, her son was safe but Appollonia made him return home with her.

During bad times, Appollonia was not only worrying about her own family but the people as a whole: "In a later stage of the tension, when the country was moving into peace and the maintenance of law and order, I played an active role in the collection of arms from militants and those who were illegally in possession of guns around Guadalcanal. I had to travel with men around the island to collect arms from the militants. This may sound easy but in fact it was difficult as it involved a lot of negotiations and convincing to do. Talks and a lot of awareness work had to be organized and done, not only with the militants but with the parents and the general public as a whole, on the importance of the surrender and collection of arms."

Solomon Islands is a male dominated society in which traditional ways of doing things often clash with Western cultural systems. Thus, women involved in Apollonia's kind of work face challenges and opposition. As a pioneer in such work, Apollonia is a role model for future generations

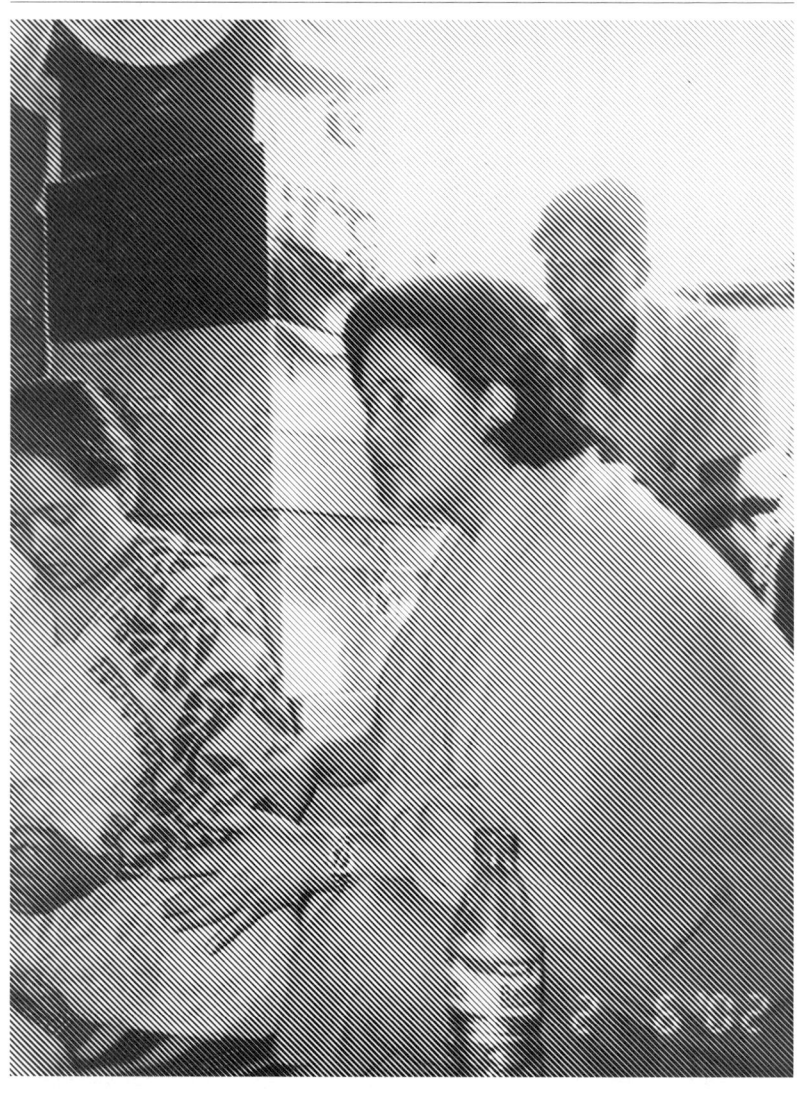

Rita Thapa

Tewa
Nagarik Awaz

For the past 24 years, Rita Thapa (born 1952) has devoted her personal and professional life to founding and supporting institutions working for women's empowerment and for the development of philanthropy and peace-building in Nepal. Through Tewa, established in 1996, she has worked for grassroots women throughout Nepal. Nagarik Awaz (Citizen's Voice), set up in 2001, provides support to thousands of people whose lives have been turned upside down by the Maoist insurgency and the government's overkill retaliation.

As the Maoist insurgency in Nepal gained ground, Rita Thapa knew she could not sit on the sidelines and just watch her fellow countrymen and -women kill each other. So in 2001, she founded Nagarik Awaz to help those affected by the conflict, without taking sides. A cadre of committed peace workers has been created. Transit homes and temporary shelters have been set up for the internally displaced, the injured, and those traumatized by the Maoist and government forces. Thapa's work is often focused on women, widows, and children. She and her team have helped form local communities where conflict-related and everyday issues are openly discussed and strategies evolved to tackle them.

Thapa works with little support from family and friends, but that does not stop her. Born into a conservative family and married according to custom at 18, she completed her education after marriage. Widowed in 1988 and with three children to raise, Thapa became a social activist in a society where widows often have to settle for humble anonymity. She built up her career by working for Oxfam and Unifem in the early to mid-1990s. In 1996, she came up with Tewa, an organization that promotes localized philanthropy for self-reliant development in Nepal, particularly with respect to grassroots women, which has now become a model the world over. It has managed to raise millions of rupees locally to support the efforts of grassroots women through strategies such as walkathons, events, and piggy banks.

Thapa has helped grassroots women build up their self-confidence, encouraging them to network and providing them with training in cooperation, teamwork, fund-raising, and creating peaceful communities. She has traveled to communities and villages in remote areas, on foot when no other transport was available.

During the ten-year face-off between the Maoists and government forces, nearly 15,000 people have died, thousands of people have been displaced, and millions of dollars of public property and infrastructure destroyed. The process of democratization has been severely damaged.

Marion Thuswald

Österreichische Friedensdienste (ÖFD, Austrian Peace Service)
International Fellowship of Reconciliation (IFOR)
Youth Peace Group Danube (YPGD)

Marion Thuswald was born in Austria in 1978. In 1997 and 1998, after completing her training in social education, she worked as a peace service volunteer for ÖFD (Austrian Peace Service) with a youth peace project in the war-torn city of Vukovar in Croatia. Back in Austria, she became a member of the staff and later of the board of the ÖFD. She also was the managing director for some time. She maintains and strengthens contacts she made in Croatia with people needing help, many Roma among others.

After finishing school, Marion Thuswald was sent to Vukovar, the most destroyed city in Croatia, for a year, as a peace volunteer for the Österreichische Friedensdienste (ÖFD, Austrian Peace Service). There, she supported the Youth Peace Group Danube (YPGD), an interethnic youth project founded by local young people. With much tact and teamwork she supported the local people, motivating them to be active themselves. She strengthened their self-confidence while keeping herself in the background. Among her strengths are awareness and pragmatism. She is very down to earth and constantly aware of her privileged position, in which she is allowed to "help." She led play workshops for children in English, and intercultural summer camps in Austria with Serb, Croatian, and Austrian children. Back in Austria, she became a staff member, later a board member of the ÖFD (Austrian Peace Service) in Vienna. Based in Vienna, she visits and coordinates the team in Vukovar every two to three months. In so doing, she has given other young women the courage to participate as well. It is not surprising that a lot of young men are working as peace volunteers in Croatia, as the volunteer year counts as alternative military service for them, and war areas seem to be predestined for men. Yet as active thinkers and helpers women are especially needed in such challenging places. Marion Thuswald builds and strengthens the contacts she was able to make in Croatia with, among others, many Roma. Some of the young people from the YPGD are now working, for example, in other organizations in leading positions or have found work abroad. Marion arranged most of the contacts despite her ambivalence: was it not her responsibility to encourage people to stay? But not at any price, because "… staying must be voluntary, not forced."

The working conditions of the Austrian Peace Service have become harder since the formation of a neo-liberal-conservative government in Austria in 2000. The restrictive policy against immigrants, despite the wealth of the country, has become even tighter since 2000.

Austria

Fatimata Touré

Association des Femmes pour la Paix et le Développement au Nord Mali

Fatimata Touré was born in Gao (the sixth administrative region of Mali) in 1956. She is the leader of the Association of Women for Peace and Development in Northern Mali, an organization that works particularly in the regions of Gao, Tombouctou, and Kidal. She contributed also to the consolidation of peace in the north of Mali and fights against the circulation of weapons in the sixth, seventh, and eighth administrative region of Mali.

Since the explosion of conflict in the north of Mali in the early 1990s, Madame Fatimata Touré, the president of the Association of Women for Peace and Development in Northern Mali, and her comrades worked with the Touareg rebels to persuade them to sit at the negotiating table with the central authorities to discuss a ceasefire. This had the effect that the rebel movements accepted negotiations and, in some places, a ceasefire.

What's more, Madam Touré went through the long process of encouraging communities of the north to participate in the consolidation of peace and to collect weapons held by civilian populations. She was always concerned that intercommunity conflict would affect the northern parts of Mali. Fortunately, her work bore fruit and weapons were collected and burned by authorities in 1996 at the time of the Flame of Peace in Timbuktu. Fatimata Touré is also involved in the process of re-integration of the former fighters of the Touareg movements. 3000 former rebels were absorbed into the Malian army, the French police force, and customs authorities. Those that were not employed were helped to find activities allowing them to re-integrate into civilian life.

The Touareg Rebellion began in the 1990s by Touareg groups with the aim of achieving autonomy or forming their own nation. Desertification and drought forced the alteration of traditional migration routes, increasing conflict between neighboring groups. Mali effectively fell into a civil war, until, in 1995, moderates on both sides negotiated a peace settlement.

Mireia Uranga Arakistain

Gernika Gogoratuz Peace Research Center
Indargi Center

Mireia Uranga, born in Spain in 1966, is a peace educator who believes in dialogue and conflict mediation. She is an adviser at Gernika Gogoratuz Peace Research Center, an independent center that applies new strategies for the development of a culture of peace. Since 2003, Mireia has also been co-director of the Indargi Center (Strength and Light) and collaborates in international projects for the development of education for peace. She is part of the European Education as a member of the Peace Education group.

Mireia Uranga is a vibrant and positive woman whose major goals are peace and harmonious living. Her strategy is dialogue and active commitment in conflict mediation. For Mireia, "a conflict is an inherent part of the human being," and her aim is "to approach all those aspects that make conflict situations negative and destructive and to transform them into peaceful processes, eliminating violence and destructiveness that is often generated." The first step to solve any conflict and walk towards peace begins in "accepting the existence of conflict."

Since 1989, her work at the Gernika Gogoratuz Peace Research Center has been a search for strategies for peace education. The first seed for the center was sown by a member of the German Green Party who requested the German Parliament to create a research center for peace in the Basque country, as a gesture of reconciliation after Guernica's bombardment by the Nazi army in 1937. This proposal was rejected, but the Basque Parliament instead pursued it and unanimously decided to create a peace studies center linked to Guernica's symbol. "The center was born to stimulate a peace culture from the local to a global scale, in a systematic way. Its specific characteristic has been the transformation of conflicts into searching for reconciliation, as the process of reconciliation between Germany and the people of Guernica has shown," notes Mireia. Since its opening 18 years ago, the center has made a discreet but firm effort that has received recognition within the international network of peace studies centers. For eight years, Mireia took part in training activities and experimenting in the field of education. For six years, she has devoted herself to the development of peace education. The work of the Gernika Gogoratuz center has been widely recognized not only in the Basque country, but in the rest of Spain and worldwide.

In 1937, the Nazi Army brutally bombarded the town of Guernica, in the Basque region. The Basque country suffered harsh cultural and political repression under Franco's dictatorship. This created a culture of resistance that still exists. Today, political tension, repression, and terrorism continue.

———
Spain

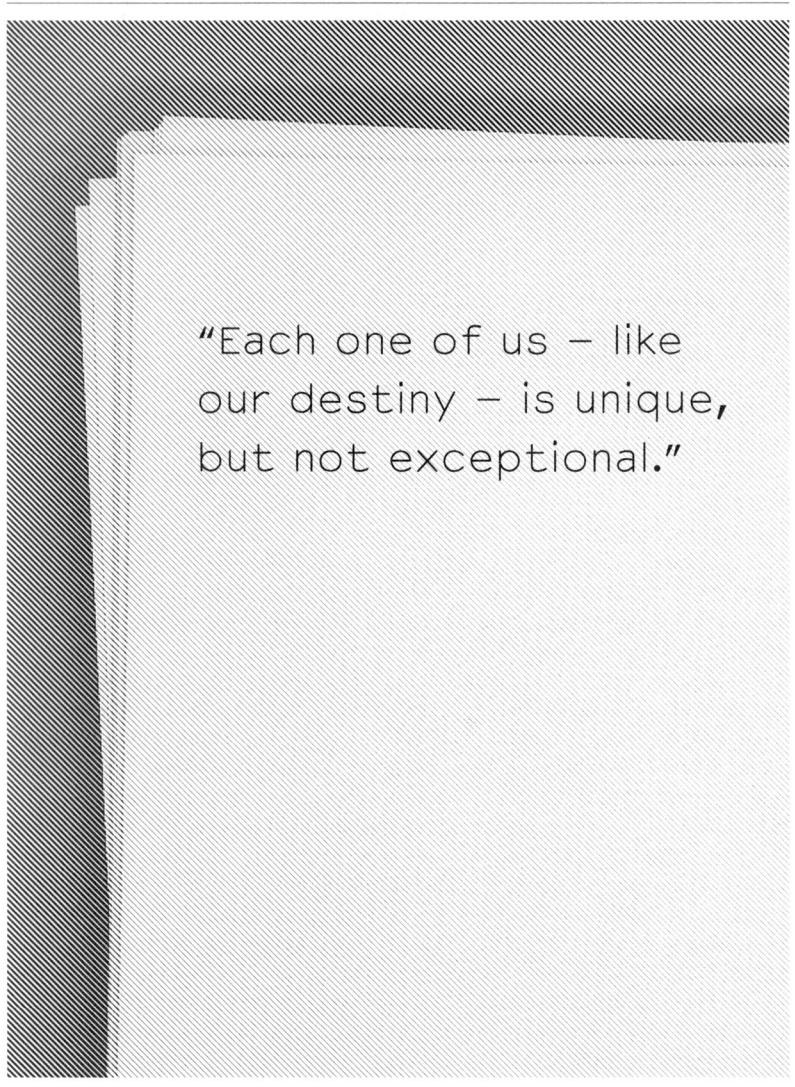

"Each one of us — like our destiny — is unique, but not exceptional."

Vera Vohlidalova

Research Library of Liberec, Building of Peace and Reconciliation
Deutsch-Tschechisches Forum der Frauen, FrauenNetzwerk für Frieden
Reconciliation Project for the Euroregion Neisse-Nysa-Nisa

Knowledge, human rights, and reconciliation are the decisive forces in the life of Vera Vohlidalova. She is "a product of Europe," a witness to our recent warring and turbulent history who has decided to speak out. Even now, Vera is still active in the reconciliation project of the Euroregion Neisse-Nysa-Nisa for living in harmony across borders of the Czech Republic, Poland, and Germany. The Czech-German women's forum "Deutsch-Tschechisches Forum der Frauen," of which she is president and speaker, is part of this project.

Vera Vohlidalova's German mother and Czech father were both active anti-fascists. After the Nazis occupied Czechoslovakia, her parents emigrated to London where Vera was born. After the war they returned to Liberec (formerly Reichenberg) and experienced the expulsion of the Germans.
Vera became a librarian. In the summer of 1968, all hope for political change during the Prague Spring was destroyed abruptly by Warsaw Pact tanks. Vera was among the many who protested. Pregnancy and motherhood saved her from dismissal and prison. Under strict political control and for low wages, she was able to continue working in the information office of the hospital of Liberec. She updated the existing documentation and smuggled in forbidden foreign literature. Until the end of the cold war in 1989, she was a victim of discrimination and persecution because of her political views and because of her family: her half-German origin and her father who was a signatory to the dissident document Charta 77.
"The library is the image and the memory of a society," Vera says. In 1995, a library was built in Liberec on the site of the synagogue the Nazis had destroyed during the Night of Broken Glass. Vera became director and put all her energy into the construction and equipment of this "Building of Peace and Reconciliation." It became a place of information on shared history, a place where democratic values and the reconciliation of formerly antagonistic groups are promoted. More than 2000 people, Czechs and foreigners, visit the library daily. They are interested in material such as cause-and-effect relationships and are open to cross-culture, cross-border support. There is a prayer room for the Jewish minority and a room for all on local Jewish history. Vera has been retired for two years, but she continues to speak of the library, among the most modern in Europe, as "her child."

Throughout the past century, the border regions of the Czech Republic, Poland, and Germany have experienced ethnic conflicts, invasions and the expulsion of peoples. Today, attempts are being made to reconcile formerly antagonistic ethnic groups.

Czech Republic

Xuan Wang

In 1995, Wang Xuan joined the Japanese bacteriological warfare fact-finding mission. After a lawsuit of seven years, the Japanese court for the first time admitted the fact that Japan had used bacteriological weapons on the Chinese people during its invasion of China in Word War II. With her mission Wang Xuan upholds the dignity of victims, lives and the pride of the Chinese nation.

Wang Xuan was born in Shanghai in 1952. In 1987, she obtained a Master's from Shubo University in Japan. In August 1995, a newspaper report on Japan's bacteriological warfare changed the path of her life. Wang became the team leader and general representative of the bacteriological warfare plaintiff team. She gave up her lucrative job and her plans of being a mother.

It was a purely people's lawsuit, without any funding, and most plaintiffs are aged over 70. Yet the team had to deal with investigation, getting evidence, and other complex legal matters with legal implications as well as with the deliberate and organized cover-up and elimination of evidence by the Japanese during and after the war. For the investigation, Wang traveled frequently between China and Japan. In order to find convincing evidence, she went through all kinds of hardships and successfully invited some soldiers of the Japanese 731 Unit to come out as witnesses in the law court. In China, she traveled to over ten provincial cities and interviewed thousands of victims and witnesses. Exhibitions, conferences, and public lectures were held in different parts of the world, to expose the war crimes of Unit 731 and to solicit support from the international community. The plaintiffs submitted 430 legal evidences, and presented 46 persons in court, including 24 plaintiffs, four old soldiers of Unit 731, and 18 scholars and experts.

On 27 August 2002, the Tokyo district court gave a verdict to confirm the Japanese army's bacteriological war crimes in China, but rejected the demand for apology and compensation. Wang says that Chinese victims will carry on the appeal process until the Japanese government concedes these demands. The second appeal will be decided in mid-2005.

Wang Xuan is convinced that the history of suffering has to be respected, and human dignity is inviolable.

The Japanese army conducted bacteriological experiments on humans during its occupation of China in Word War II. Unit 731 was notorious for these experiments. The Japanese government has not admitted to these experiments and refused to apologize or compensate the victims.

China

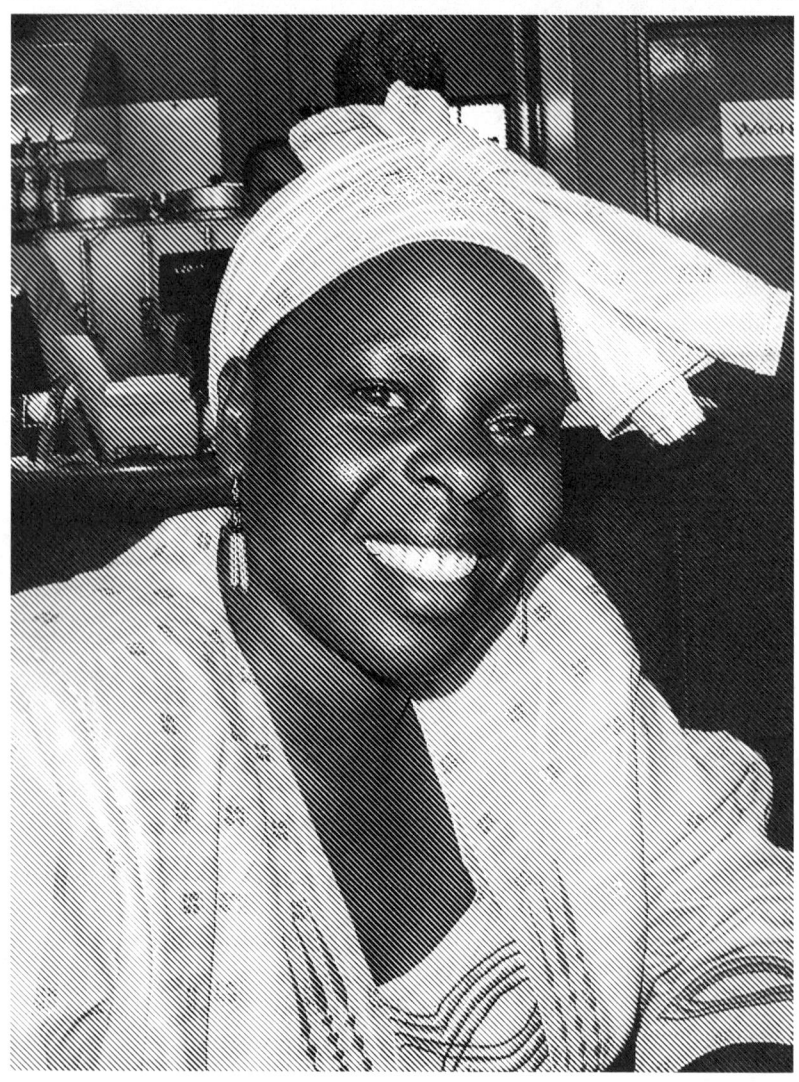

Tecla Wanjala

Japan International Cooperation Agency (Jica)
Peace and Development Network of the NGO Council (PeaceNet)
Coalition for Peace in Africa (Copa)

Tecla Wanjala, a Kenyan 43-year-old mother of four, has dedicated her work to peace building. The trained social worker holds a master's degree in conflict resolution. She started working with refugees in 1991 and later with internally displaced persons in her home district in Western Kenya. She initiated reconciliation meetings between opposing ethnic groups. Today, she works on peace building and post-conflict reconstruction from community to national level. "I don't want my children to suffer the way I saw others suffering," she explains her motivation.

The American University accepted Tecla Wanjala directly for a master's course in conflict resolution, because of her outstanding experience in this field. Ten years earlier, while working as a social worker in camps for refugees and internally displaced persons, Tecla was frustrated by the conditions the people lived in, by their traumatic stories and their desperation. This frustration turned a committed social worker into a peace builder. Tecla comes from a poor community in Western Kenya, which she describes as marginalized. She completed a diploma in social work in 1991 and started to work in a camp for 30,000 Somali refugees. Assigned to teach Kiswahili to children, Tecla became aware of their desperation, especially of single women and mothers who had no maintenance support. In 1992, she joined the Catholic Diocese of her home district, Bungoma, as a relief and rehabilitation coordinator for 40,000 internally displaced persons driven away by the ethnic clashes in Kenya in 1991/92. She got many of them involved in small farming projects to gain a humble income. It was here that Tecla Wanjala found ways to talk to opposing ethnic groups and bring them together to start a reconciliation process. "They are all victims," Tecla Wanjala says. "At one point, they said, 'We realize what we have done to each other. We need to apologize, too.' This is the beginning of reconciliation." From 1996 to 2003, she was the coordinator of PeaceNet. She trained hundreds of peace practitioners, from community to national level, in basic skills in conflict transformation, including lobbying and advocacy. Currently she works on post-conflict reconstruction with the Jica organization and is establishing a trauma-healing program.

The breakdown of Somalia and the politically motivated ethnic clashes in Kenya in 1991/92 saw an influx of refugees into Kenya and displaced many Kenyan citizens. Tensions were high since the refugees presented an economic pressure to the resident communities.

Kenya

Mariam Yandieva

Memorial, Ingush Section

Of Ingush extraction, Mariam Yandieva (born 1953) graduated in Philology and later taught at Grozny University and different Moscow institutes. Since 1992, after the ethnic cleansing in North Ossetia, she has been engaged in human rights activities. She is the author of a dozen articles on issues of human rights protection and history published in Russia, Germany and the UK. She has participated in forums on the issues of the North Caucasus in Europe and the USA. Her works focus on finding ways to peaceful coexistence among the nations in the Caucasus and on the promotion of democracy.

Mariam Yandieva's grandfather was an officer in the Tsarist army who, after escaping from a communist concentration camp (the so-called Gulag), found shelter in Finland and later in Poland. In 1926, in London, he published the book 'An Island Hell' (1926), a documentary testimony to his personal experience in Solovki (one of the major Gulag concentration camps in Northern Russia), and a revelation of the communist terror in the USSR. Needless to say that the book was forbidden on the territory of the USSR. However, Mariam learned about its existence from one of her friends who had been abroad. From then on, she dreamed of once holding it in her hands. In 1988, 62 years after its publication, the book of her grandfather finally reached Russia and the Caucasus. Mariam's brother translated the text into Russian. Today it is studied in schools and universities in Ingushetia, and it has generated many articles of commentary. This book proved a powerful impulse for the restoration of many texts and materials about the history of the Caucasian nations that had been forbidden in Soviet times.

At the beginning of 1990s, a group of like-minded people who wanted to know the truth about the tragic events in the history of the Ingush people in the 20th century, gathered around Mariam. The Communist revolution, wars, deportation, ethnic cleansing and brutal social changes were the main subjects of research for this small group of enthusiasts who, in fact, established the real, true history of the Ingush people, uncovering historical facts that used to be taboo. Their work has enabled people to better understand the political and social processes taking place in present-day Russia and the Caucasus.

Following the ethnic cleansing of the Ingush in North Ossetia (1992), Mariam Yandieva has been actively involved in the defense of human rights regardless of national belonging. She is convinced that the wars in Chechnya are a continuation of the history of communist, ethnic-motivated terror.

Russian Federation

Irina Yanovskaya

Journalists for Human Rights
Caucasus Network on Conflict Resolution

A well-known journalist in South Ossetia, Irina Yanovskaya (43) founded and directs the organization Journalists for Human Rights with the aim of preserving peace. The organization has become an important part of a broader network of conflict resolution groups. Irina focuses her efforts on the area of interethnic conflict resolution. She has made her way into people's hearts, finding ways to unite rather than separate groups, thus, helping to establish peace in South Ossetia.

Irina Yanovskaya is a very modest person and a valiant activist. She has worked in peacemaking and conflict resolution since 1998, when ethnic clashes between Georgian and Ossetian villages began. "[The] absurd death of innocent people who killed each other only because of their different national origin, astonished me completely," Irina says. She could not let go of this idea. In 1998, she started working towards the reconciliation of hostile parties. She has worked with soldiers and military officers, taught children, and hosted different seminars to bring together people of different national origin and help them find points of convergence. Irina explains that a child does not understand that people of different national origin exist, and so the child sees no need to hate. A culture of peace should therefore be cultivated from early childhood, and in fact, Irina works often with children.

As a journalist she works for a program that is devoted to resolving the Georgian-Ossetian conflict. Irina published a special calendar with photographs of children and war. "These are children and women, who suffer from wars most of all," she says. "Children and women who [have] experienced the horror of violence, murder, need to be helped to overcome their trauma." She initiated a special program to help women and children injured by war. Irina also organizes seminars for Ossetian and Georgian women and children, in which they learn to understand one another and to live together in peace. "The most difficult thing for people who have experienced a war is to forgive the death of close people," Irina says, "to stop looking at the people of other national origin as enemies and murderers and to see in them only neighbors." Irina's efforts for peace are helping improve the world around her.

Interethnic conflict between Georgians and Ossetians began in the early 1990s in South Ossetia, resulting in many deaths. Although peacemakers managed to bring hostile parties to an armistice, hatred remains. Peacemaking efforts are now directed to surmounting hostility and developing trust.

Toita Yunusova

Ekho Voiny (Echo of War)

Since 1995 Toita Yunusova (born 1966) has actively participated in the anti-war movement trying to stop the bloodshed in Chechnya. She is a peace activist and a member of the NGO Ekho Voiny (Echo of War). Working on humanitarian projects to help refugees in the Caucasus region and cooperating with Russian NGOs fighting for a peaceful solution to the Chechen problem, Toita has collected photo and video materials which she hopes will become evidence of war crimes and human rights violations in Chechnya.

When in December 1994 the Russian-Chechen war broke out, Toita was visiting her relatives in Volgograd (Russia). On coming back home to Ingushetia, she immediately joined the anti-war movement. She decided that she could not remain idle; she had to act. Her activities were varied — she fed orphaned children, helped Russian mothers find their soldier sons, provided humanitarian aid to refugees, took part in anti-war demonstrations, and organized peace and relief initiatives. She became adept at operating a video camera in order to show the entire world what she herself saw in Chechnya.

She always took along her camera with herself in order to document war episodes, cases of human rights violations, and war crimes. She did what she could, spreading the atrocious truth about the war. In the archives of the anti-war NGO Echo of war, to which Toita belongs, there are more than 200 video cassettes and more than 2000 photographs bearing witness to the horrors of the war in Chechnya. Toita hopes that some day they will become evidence in lawsuits against those who started the bloody war and those who are guilty of killing some 100,000 innocent people in Chechnya.

In conducting her work, Toita has repeatedly risked her life. In November 1999, having escaped from the air raid over Grozny, she came to the village of Alkhan-Yurt. Instead of finding refuge, she found herself in the epicenter of the most atrocious war actions. The Russian troops launched an attack on the village with intensive bombing and artillery fire. Within a few hours, half the village lay in ruins and was reduced to ashes. Dozens of civilians died. Having miraculously escaped death, Toita filmed the events with her video camera. Later the video was passed on to the media so that the whole world could see the carpet bombing of a peaceful Chechen village.

Toita feeds orphaned children, helps Russian mothers find their soldier sons, and organizes both humanitarian aid to refugees and relief initiatives. Often at the risk of life and limb, she films the hostilities with her video camera so that the whole world will learn the truth about the war in Chechnya.

Russian Federation

María Eugenia Zabala viuda de Polo

Enchanted Valley Cooperative
Colombian Women's Initiative for Peace

María Eugenia Zabala takes her strength and hope from the Colombian earth. She is a midwife who opens future horizons with each child she delivers. María Eugenia Zabala is a widow, a displaced woman and the head of her family. She leads a women's cooperative, the Enchanted Valley. She promotes the collective future of the group, a group formed by women who are single parents. She does not back down: she promotes a culture of peace and campaigns for the rights of women who are displaced and the victims of a political war.

She grew up in the care of her grandmother, playing hide and seek. Vowels, notebooks and school did not break the monotony of her rural childhood. In her adolescence, she discovered that the future was only limited by her aspirations. She took the risk: "I made the decision and went away to work. I decided to take care of myself, to be responsible for my actions."

The violence of war began early on December 14th, 1989. It destroyed María Eugenia Zabala's 'nest.' From that moment on, she had to begin the difficult task of surviving: "There was no time for crying for the dead, no time for grief, for mourning, for anything like that." She left the countryside, taking on her new identity as a widow, a displaced person and the head of a family. In the city, the cruel urban environment and the indifference of the human swarm around her sparked off the beginning of her work campaigning, for the rights of the displaced women and victims of the Colombian political war. "In those neighborhoods, I got to know women and families that had fled from their original homes. Seeing people in need, I turned my home into a refuge for all of them. I also raised the flag and began to knock on doors."

María Eugenia Zabala organized, participated in and invented different initiatives to aid the cause of the displaced population. She transmitted her love of nature to the women's group, and they decided to go back to the countryside. In her role as a leadership, she was the first in Colombia to negotiate for plots of land for women and their families, as part of the agrarian reforms. Along with other women, they fulfilled a dream when they built the Enchanted Valley — a cooperative for agricultural and livestock production — where, on the human level, neither daughters nor sons have commerce with the war and whose desire is to achieve "a peace born from justice."

Civil society in Colombia has to withstand attacks from paramilitary groups besides all the problems associated with drug trafficking. In spite of the statements saying that "there is no civil war," a multifaceted conflict does exist and it results in the displacement of many rural families.

Colombia

Stanislavka Zajovic

Women in Black
Women's Peace Network against War

Even before the war, Stanislavka Zajovic was actively involved in the first feminist initiatives in former Yugoslavia. When war broke out, Stanislavka, together with others, founded Women in Black (inspired by the Women in Black of Israel and Palestine). From October 1991 until the war ended, Women in Black organized weekly peace demonstrations in Belgrade and across Serbia and Montenegro: in silence and dressed in black, they condemned the war and crimes committed falsely in the name of the interests of the Serbian nation. Thus, one of their key slogans became and remained: Not in Our Name!

Stanislavka (Stasa) Zajovic, born in former Yugoslavia in 1953, holds a degree in Romance languages from the University of Belgrade and is fluent in Spanish, Italian, and English. A civil rights activist since her student days, she has organized feminist and peace workshops, anti-war demonstrations, campaigns for conscientious objection, and programs in refugee centers, contributing also to publications on feminism, militarism and anti-militarism, nationalism, and fundamentalism. In 1991, she helped establish Women in Black in former Yugoslavia and founded the Women's Peace Network against War.

Stasa's fundamental motives are moral: the responsibility for war and crimes committed "in our name," and solidarity with those in Serbia and around the world for the promotion of nonviolence, peace, and civil society. Her energy comes from those who feel powerless, but transform anger into action; those who strive to show that nonviolent action is the only way to peace; and those who know that a passive attitude is participation in crime, especially crime committed in our name.

Stasa imagines a world without military, without hunger, violence, or structural injustice — a different but possible world. She knows that realizing this requires the long-term participation of millions of women and men, and that the reality of Serbia seems particularly hopeless; characterized by xenophobia, intolerance, and social misery. International solidarity, founded on the principles of peace and justice, gives hope. Stasa uses "spiritual demilitarization" to refer to the kind of transformation that re-establishes disrupted threads through dialogue, to overcome the futile logic of victory for one side over another. Stasa uses this idea to guide her peace politics, her vision of solidarity, and the particular kind of anti-militaristic activity of Women in Black.

In the early 1990s, amidst fanatical nationalism and growing ethnic hatred, many Serbians in ex-Yugoslavia watched helplessly as war approached. Others, however, courageously and openly opposed the war and are working to build a culture of peace today.

Serbia and Montenegro

Women's Rights –

Human Rights

on the Way to

Gender Democracy

Helga Konrad

"It took humankind 2000 years to get but an inkling of the message that all men are equal. And only since a tiny little moment in history — since about three decades — the disaster is dawning on them: namely that all women are equal too!" (Alberto Godensi, Researcher, Fribourg/Switzerland)

Whenever the gender relationship is critically addressed one invariably comes up against violence against women — the worst form of discrimination on grounds of sex. Even if we do not start from the assumption that all men are perpetrators and all women are victims of violence — it is a fact that the widespread violence against women impacts on all men and on all women, and is a yardstick for the level of human dignity in our societies.

Even today women's rights are frequently not recognized as human rights — violations of women's rights are still very often the rule and not the exception, and violence against women is very often taken for granted. Many encroachments on women's rights committed in the private sphere are not even considered human rights violations.

Women around the world have to suffer domestic and sexual as well as structural violence. From countless armed conflicts and wars throughout the world we know that raping women has become part of war strategy and that the bodies of women are instrumentalized by men in the conduct of their hostilities.

It is the dignity and the right of women to physical and mental integrity that are exposed to specific, sexist forms of violation through torture, sexual abuse, rape and not least trafficking in women and girls. This is why the issues of rights, justice and violation of human rights are of utmost and immediate importance to women.

Violence and gender is an old problem to which we need to respond with a new awareness. Developing new democratic gender relations is not an easy task, but it is the precondition for a peaceful world based on justice, fairness and equality. What is at stake is the redistribution of privileges, of roles and positions in society, and of course power and the control of power. A society that tolerates violence is a society of accomplices.

Over the past three decades women and women's organizations have broken the silence, but have had to realize that they have only scratched the surface and that they have only melted down the tip of the iceberg.

The empowerment of women is certainly the key to the prevention of violence.

Empowerment of women means the establishment of equal opportunities between the genders; it means extending choices: choices about if and when to get married, choices about education and employment opportunities, choices about their lives.

Equality and empowerment of women also means power-sharing, it means better access to political leadership, it means economic self-reliance of women, it means redistribution in all spheres of life. Moreover, the so-called second generation of human rights, namely the social and economic rights, are of vital importance to women in all parts of the world. The economic independence of women is crucial, if equality is to be achieved. Women must have access to secure well-paid employment as a key to tackling other problems, such as poverty, exclusion and violence.

Much remains to be done to rid the world of violence against women. The mechanisms of such violence need to be analyzed, international agreements have to be comprehensively implemented, any kind of violence against women needs to be punished. It will be for women to step up pertinent action and the men are called upon to join in.

Substantial progress could be made, if governments were to spend as little as 10 percent of their military expenditure on women including combating violence against women. And they should at least be confronted with the question of why they don't do it (as was suggested by Greetje den Ouden-Dekkers on the occasion of a follow-up conference in Austria to the Fourth Women's World Conference in Beijing).

Dr Helga Konrad, a former Austrian Federal Minister for Women's Issues, was appointed OSCE Special Representative on Combating Trafficking in Human Beings in May 2004. From 2000 to 2004 she chaired the Stability Pact Task Force on Trafficking in Human Beings for South Eastern Europe.

Saeeda Abu Hadia

Abu Hadia Society (AHS)

Saeeda Mohd Badri Abu Hadia (34) was born in Sinkat, Port Sudan, where she completed her early education. In 1995 she obtained an MSc from the College of Management, Ahfad University for Women in Khartoum. Saeeda is now a gender and development analyst in Eastern Sudan, addressing women's issues, particularly combating female genital circumcision among the Beja nomads and in other primitive areas. This work links her to activists on this issue nationally and worldwide. She helps to organize women's groups in the Red Sea area to address their common strategic issues and to participate in decision-making.

The Eastern Part of Sudan, where Saeeda works with the Beja nomads, is an absolutely tribal society. The climate of the Red Sea Hills is arid and dry; the area is also on the front line of the eastern conflict zone. The status of women there is very unfortunate, and they have no participation in society. Female genital circumcision is a very sensitive and challenging issue in the Sudanese traditional communities. The dominant culture and traditions stand against endeavors to change the local people's social habits, which they consider part of their ethos and value systems. When Saeeda embarked on her campaign against female genital excision she faced austere resistance from tribal leaders, who looked at her efforts as a serious threat to their belief systems and cultural identity. She has overcome these challenges with support from her father, mother and other like-minded people who were determined to bring justice and peace to the community. Her work was greatly inspired and impacted by the thoughts of her father, who was always very supportive of her standpoint. He was an unswerving activist in support of girls' education and women's rights, though he himself did not receive a formal education.

Saeeda and her supporting group have managed to vocalize women's exigent issues in decision-making spheres and to launch many campaigns to defend women's rights. She has risked her life many times while getting on with her work, seeking to change people's concepts and attitudes towards women in rural areas.

Saeeda's life-long goal is to achieve social justice for women in the Sudan. With her unrelenting efforts she saved 30% of infant girls from female genital circumcision, despite the severe renitency of the tribal communities.

Sudan

Lea Ackermann

Solidarity with Women in Distress (Solwodi)
Solidarity with Girls in Distress (Solgidi)
Missionary Sisters of Our Lady of Africa

Sister Lea helps women who have been victims of trafficking. She and her colleagues assist them while giving testimony about the perpetrators in court. The association Solidarity with Women in Distress (Solwodi) supports prostitutes who are caught up in prostitution tourism in Kenya. Solwodi provides training to young women and their daughters and helps them build up a life without prostitution. Because of Aids, working with the daughters of prostitutes has become increasingly important. Therefore, the organization Solidarity with Girls in Distress (Solgidi) was established in 2002.

During Sr Lea's visits to Mombasa, people on the streets welcome her by cheering "Sr Lea, Sr Lea!". With her work she made a lasting impression on Kenyan women. When Sr Lea came to Mombasa in the 1980s, she was already concerned about women trafficking. Mombasa was a center of prostitution tourism, and as a military port, it was also one of military prostitution. Sr Lea established Solidarity with Women in Distress (Solwodi) and training facilities for dozens of young prostitutes.

In the mid-1980s, I was able to observe Sr Lea at work. A young prostitute had a German boyfriend and gave birth to his child. Every few months, he came to Mombasa and stayed at his girlfriend's place. He usually gave each of them, woman and child, a t-shirt. He also contributed a little bit to the household while he was there — but overall, it was a cheap vacation for him — until Sr Lea took him to task and told him to make provisions for the woman and his child. She told him to buy a small plot of land for his girlfriend and to register it in her name. And so it happened. The man gave money to Sr Lea, who made sure that the plot was bought. After receiving this start-up financing, the woman built one small house after another and rented out the apartments. She was able to ensure her and her child's future — increasingly without the help of Sr Lea, who still dropped by to see how she was doing. When Sr Lea realized how difficult it was for the daughters of prostitutes to deal with the fact that their mothers supported them through prostitution, she initiated the project Solidarity with Girls in Distress (Solgidi), with groups for mothers and daughters in which both could talk about their feelings. As there are countless Aids victims on the African continent, it is especially important for survivors to reconcile with each other, despite the generation gap.

The Solwodi counseling centers are supported and ran by Catholic nuns. Solwodi assists women victims of trafficking who are brought to the center after raids on brothels during their trials and provides for their safety. In spite of the Catholic background, Solwodi helps people with different religious denominations.

Germany

Nigar Ahmad

Aurat Foundation

Nigar Ahmad (born 1945) has worked tirelessly for nearly 20 years for the political, social, and economic empowerment of Pakistani women, as executive director of the Aurat Publication and Information Service Foundation. Under her stewardship, the Aurat (woman) Foundation has taken up a range of "provocative" causes, from mobilizing women candidates for local government elections to generating debate across the country about the World Trade Organization and the controversial issue of intellectual property rights.

Nigar topped Punjab University in her masters in economics, and went on to study economics at Cambridge University. She was also a Commonwealth scholar. While teaching economics for 16 years as a member of the faculty of Islamabad's Quaid-e-Azam University, Nigar was drawn into the struggle against the antiwomen policies of Zia-ul-Haq's military dictatorship. From 1983 to 1985, she was a member of the Women's Action Forum, the pioneering women's organization formed to protest these developments. Since 1986, Nigar, who lives in Lahore, has been associated with the Aurat Foundation, a civil society organization that works for women's empowerment in tandem with a nationwide network of citizen's groups and civil activists.

Nigar has been politically educating activists to help them participate more effectively in decision-making processes. Her work helped to put women on the electoral agenda during the 1993 and 1997 general elections. She is responsible for organizing networks of citizens' action committees in 70 districts to provide support to women. Nigar has researched the work of women in the informal sector, organizing national conferences for peasant women, and radio programs to inform them on health and agricultural issues. She was a consultant to the United Nations Development Programme (UNDP) in 1991 on the gender impact of a watershed management project in Azad Kashmir. She presented a case study to the Asian Development Bank on a pilot on credit for rural women, and, as a consultant to the United Nations Development Fund For Women, has been involved in a rural credit and gender sensitization training program of UNDP staff. Nigar has also been involved with the National Commission on the Status of Women, and the South Asian Partnership. She was a coauthor for the report on Women's Development Programs for Pakistan's Eighth Five-Year Plan.

The leaders of Pakistan's women's movement, forged in the fire of retrograde martial law, have effortlessly merged the emancipation of the impoverished and the unorganized to the UN's macrodevelopment programs for women.

Pakistan

María Luisa Álvarez Llave

Union of Housewives of Cuzco

María Luisa Álvarez Llave is a Peruvian woman who knows that what she experienced should not be experienced by any other young woman. She was raped when she was nine years old. She worked for shelter and food. From being illiterate, she became literate and bilingual; later on, she became the protagonist in a book published in Peru and republished in Mexico. She was the force behind the nomination of the International Day of Housewives. She is the co-founder of the Union of Cuzco and of the Latin-American Confederation of Housewives. She has a son and a grandson.

María Luisa Álvarez Llave had to rebuild herself. When she was nine, she was raped and violated. She is determined to fight to prevent what she experienced from happening to anyone else. She has been a serf and a slave. She was born in Altohuarca, Espinar, in Cuzco. Her history has been recounted (using another name) in the book 'BASTA — Testimonios' ('Enough! — Testimonies'), from 1982. Her friend Domitila Chungara, the Bolivian activist, presented the book.

In 1971, she and Egidia Laime Jancco founded the Union of Housewives of Cuzco. They demanded a salary, a ten hour work-day, weekly rest and holidays. It is a project that has lasted for more than 33 years. She takes care of women, adolescents and migrant girls, many of them from the Quechua and Aymara indigenous communities. They denounce sexual abuses committed by the employers. María Luisa Álvarez Llave was co-founder of the Latin American and Caribbean Confederation of Housewives (Conlactraho), in Colombia, and participated in the designation of their International Day and the achievement of a law concerning their situation.

She is 58 years old and enjoys her son and grandson. She is sustained by her dreams and the improvements that can be achieved. With dedication and determination, she positions herself so that she is always in the vicinity of the fight for others. That is her life.

In Peru, girls and young immigrants from the mountain areas are given to relatives and friends as housewives. Many are the victims of sexual abuse. The organizations that act in their defense have achieved a number of rights for them.

Peru

Zohra Andi Baso

South Sulawesi Consumer Association
Forum for Women's Issues in South Sulawesi

Zohra Andi Baso (born 1952) is an activist working on empowering women to be aware of their rights so they can defend them. She began as a journalist and a consumer rights activist focusing on women. She has shifting focus onto dealing with violence against women, both in domestic and public spaces, social and political, through an organization she founded, the Forum for Women's Issues in South Sulawesi, her home province. The endless work has kept her from finishing her dissertation for her doctorate degree.

Back in the "era of normalcy" — this is the cynical phrase to describe the 32 years of Suharto's dictatorship when Indonesia seemed to enjoy what they now know to be superficial prosperity — Zohra Andi Baso could see the ugly face of consumerism and its effect on women. "Women are prone to be the victims. They are the ones who consume, and just looking at the advertising, they are also the ones to be manipulated." The partial information given about a product or a government program, and the state's campaign on certain issues such as birth control contraceptives as part of the family planning program, often left women with very few options, if any.

That was when Zohra Andi Baso was still a young, passionate student. This passion has driven her for the past 30 years. Even after the country entered a new era, the so-called Reformasi, that followed Suharto's downfall in 1998, her passion has not waned. Inter-ethnic conflicts as some parts of the nation disintegrate and other violence in society are in Zohra's agenda as she fights to empower women to stand up for their rights. A national figure, Zohra has authored several books, and is head of the Presidium of the National Women's Coalition. "Homework is aplenty. The only thing that is different now (compared to Suharto's era) is that we can discuss things that were once so difficult to discuss. We can have more dialogue, but violence against women keeps taking place both in the domestic and public domains."

Indonesia is still a very patriarchal society. Even among the middle-classes, Indonesian women face challenges coming from several variables — social, political and even cultural. The awareness level of women's rights and issues such as gender equality and justice is still relatively low.

Indonesia

Yuki Ando

Child Abuse Prevention (CAP)
Peace Violence Prevention Training Center

Yuki Ando has combined her artistic talent, compassion for children, and teaching and organizational skills to protect Japan's most vulnerable citizens: its children. She learned about a successful child abuse prevention program called CAP (Child Abuse Prevention), which uses role-play and other activities to teach children of all ages about their fundamental right to live free from emotional and physical violence. She adapted the program for Japan in 1994 and today 160 CAP groups are active throughout the country.

How can children be taught to protect themselves in a country where discussion of sex is taboo? By bringing sex education into the light. By telling stories, drawing pictures, and keeping a sense of humor. Yuki Ando has used her unique talents to make a difference. She had studied child abuse in Canada and understood the extent of the problem. In 1991, she participated in a self-help group of survivors, caseworkers, and scholars in Tokyo. Yuki's interest grew, resulting in the establishment of CAP programs and the Peace Violence Prevention Training Center.

The vision of the Peace Center is to establish a nonviolent society by providing training and workshops on human rights, developing leadership, and communicating support and respect. Children are taught that they have the right to be secure, confident, and free. Role-play allows children and teens to gain skills and to "practice" emotions. Survivors of sexual assault are offered counseling and support, and workshops are also provided for parents and teachers.

In Japan, as in many countries, children have no skills to protect themselves from violation, assault, and abuse. When discussion of sex is taboo, prevention and recovery are difficult. The 160 CAP programs that grew from Yuki Ando's introduction of the program in Japan were unprecedented.

Japan

"Even if they made me
a gift of a better world,
I would refuse it. My
home is with those who
have no rights — women,
children, and men."

Anonyma

Anonyma is her name — she represents all the women we were not able to reach, or whose names we could not publish for fear of jeopardizing their work. Anonyma may belong to a marginalized minority group. She may be a farmer battling for access to land and clean water. She may be a scientist who publicizes abuses, organizes peace watches and faces threats to her life. She makes violence and its mechanisms visible to others. Anonyma is a name synonymous with courage, peaceful action and the future. Whoever she is, and wherever she is, she lives in a world in which working for peace is dangerous.

Anonyma's life stories differ widely. It may be that Anonyma was born in a country that never welcomed her, since she is member of a minority group. There were schools in this country, but they were for others. Educational opportunities were closed to her. There was paid work, but not for her. She had no rights. Her sisters and mother before her had had no rights either. She may have been beaten and exploited. Many years later, having married, born children, endured blows, hunger and aggression, she met women who were caught in the same vicious circle as herself. Often clandestinely, and in fear for their lives, they fought to break out of their terrible isolation, exclusion and disenfranchisement; out of illiteracy and exploitation.

Or maybe Anonyma lives in a country which we shall call X. Her peace work prompted us to ask her and her network to nominate peacewomen. At the time, the political situation in X was extremely volatile and dangerous. A bomb exploded in the neighborhood the day of their first meeting. No one was hurt, but it was clear that there were people who would go to any lengths to keep Anonyma and others from joining an international network and the 1000 peacewomen project. They refused to let themselves be intimidated. They decided not to nominate anyone, so that they could continue with their work.

Then again Anonyma might be a very young woman who rescues children from bombed-out houses. She thinks they should go to school, since children have a right to education, even in times of war. She and the children use various ruses to reach the ruined schoolhouse. The children read and write, they sing softly so as not to be heard by the enemy soldiers. Anonyma is aware of the danger but she is brave, brave for the children and for her shattered country. She gets caught, is raped and tortured. Yet she preservers — children have a right to education.

Anonyma represents all the women who deserved to be included in this book. They live in countries that leave too little space for their hopes, their dignity, and their rights. They could not be nominated because of inadequate communications, or because they must, for security reasons, work under-cover. Although she remains unnamed, she is part of our community.

International

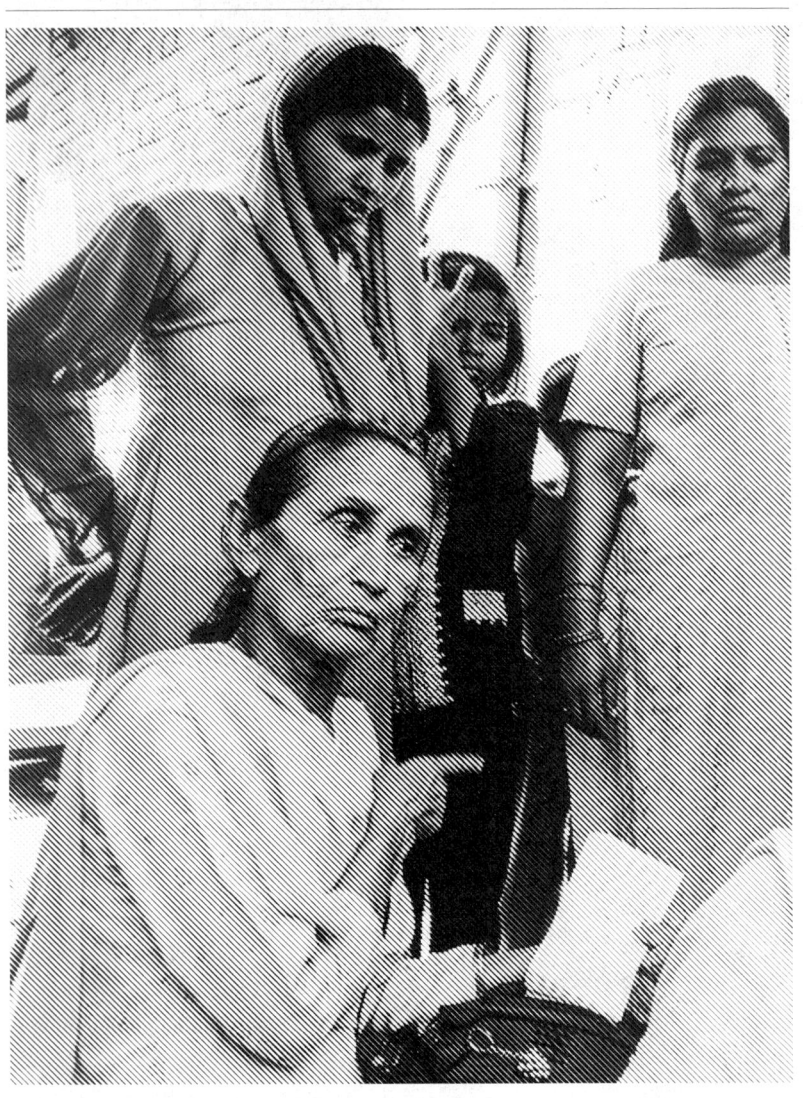

Shahjahan Apa

Shaktishalini

Shahjahan Apa (born 1945) has channeled the trauma over the murder of her daughter to ensure that no other woman should suffer the same fate: dowry death. She set up Shaktishalini to fight dowry and violence against women. The organization offers temporary shelter to affected women, provides them with legal information and counseling, and, most importantly, listens to them, helping them unburden themselves and providing them with an objective viewpoint and legal advice.

Shahjahan Apa's daughter was murdered by Shahjahan's in-laws for dowry. While the trauma of losing her child cut deep, it also ensured that Shahjahan's life has had only one aim since: "I could not get justice. Yet I had faith in Allah's rehmat (mercy), and began working for the society, so that such horrors will never again be repeated."

Shahjahan set up Shaktishalini to fight against dowry and violence against women. She runs three service centers in Delhi's slum areas of Nangloi, Shakur ki Dandy, and Jahangirpuri. She is also involved in disseminating information on dowry, and organizes workshops, street theater, and sustained media campaigns. Furthermore, Shaktishalini runs a temporary shelter for dowry victims, where women are given support, legal information, and counseling. The focus is on encouraging women to be self-reliant. She also conducts workshops for women in slums as well as in schools and colleges — not hesitating to involve men who wish to pitch in — and organizes streetplays to convey the message effectively in areas where literacy levels are low. Shahjahan's arduous struggle has led the authorities and political parties to look at objectively and strengthen the existing antidowry laws and policies.

Shahjahan feels that it is imperative to listen to women and girls in distress. This not only brings understanding, it is also cathartic for them. Her network of listeners takes care of about 400 such cases every year, providing objective viewpoints as well as legal advice. Once women are confident, Shahjahan believes, they can fight their own battles.

Official figures put the annual number of dowry deaths in India at around 5000. Unofficial estimates, however, hover round 25,000. Although India has a stringent antidowry law, enacted in 1961, it oddly criminalizes both husband and wife. The laws have done nothing to halt dowry transactions.

India

Seyran Ates

Seyran Ates, born in Turkey in 1963, works in Berlin as a lawyer opposed to forced marriages and so-called "honor killings." In 1984, working as a law student in a counseling center for Turkish women, she was shot by an assailant. Another woman died on the spot. Despite this painful experience, Seyran Ates did not give up her public support for women's rights. When Berlin was struck by a series of "honor killings" during the winter of 2004/2005, she asked the government to strengthen certain criminal laws. In reaction, a popular Turkish newspaper started a campaign against the "crazy lawyer."

Seyran Ates (42) sits in her office in the center of Berlin and rocks her infant daughter. It is Saturday, and the lawyer of Turkish-Kurdish background would rather be playing with her little daughter than meeting with the press. But she has no time during the week. Seyran Ates is a woman in great demand, always busy giving interviews or speaking at meetings. Media interest in her has increased recently, when Berlin was the scene of five "honor killings" within four months. Five young Turkish women who lived their own lives and did not agree to forced marriages were killed by men from their own families for offending the family's "honor." Seyran Ates tries to help women before it is too late. She represents them in court when they annul their forced marriages or divorce their violent husbands. And she represents them in public politically.

Her public speeches put her at risk. After having been shot and wounded in 1984, she is aware of this danger only too well. Her left arm was paralyzed and still hurts. She needed several years to recover her inner balance. Now, she feels threatened again, as the popular Turkish newspaper "Hürriyet," widely read in Germany, has started a campaign against her. "This lawyer has gone crazy," the paper stated, saying she claimed that all Turks were thugs. Of course, Seyran never said that. She is neither a man-hater nor an Islam-hater. She tries to argue in as careful a manner as possible. But she will not abandon her belief that women have the same rights as men.

Her clients know and appreciate her position. "Many say that I give them courage and strength," Seyran Ates says and beams with joy. "Every woman who leaves my office happy is a success for me. Women's rights are my life's work."

Around two million people in Germany are of Turkish or Kurdish descent. Economic and social discrimination have led them to follow a traditional lifestyle. Many young women have to accept arranged marriages. If they rebel, they run the risk of being killed by men in their own families.

Germany

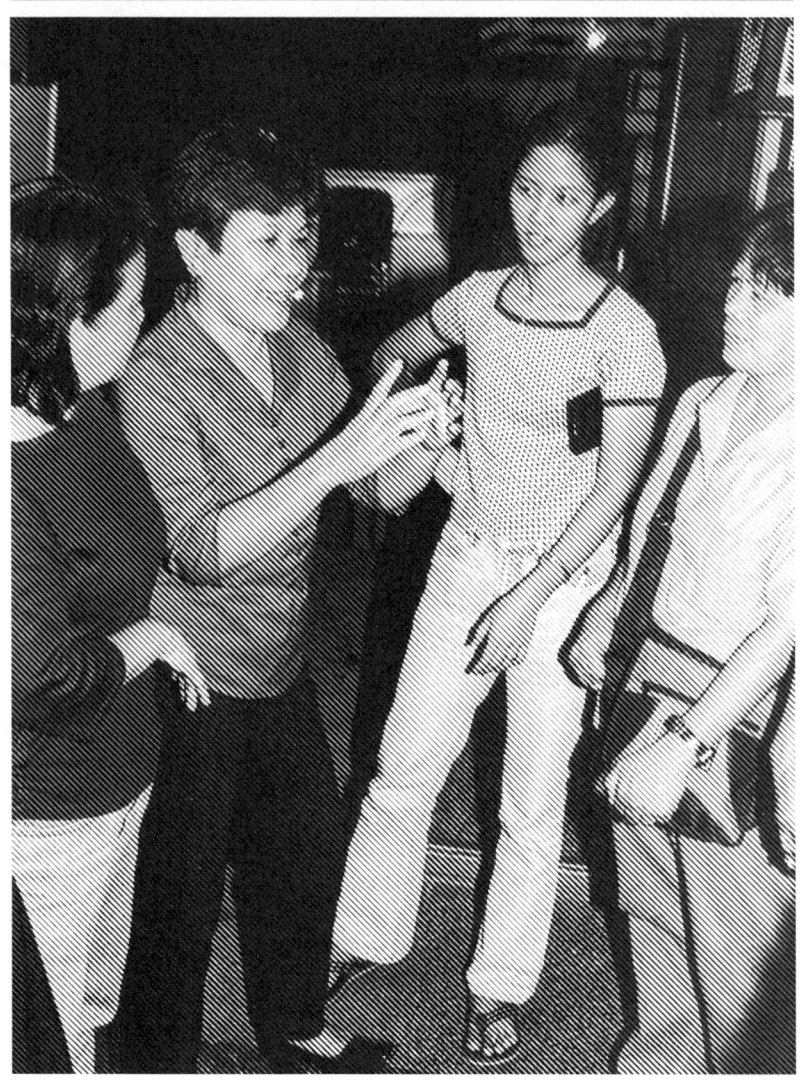

Teresa Banaynal Fernandez

Lihok Filipina Foundation
Commmission for the Urban Poor

Teresa "Tessie" Banaynal Fernandez (born 1953), the executive director of Lihok Filipina Foundation, is the passionate soul of the movement for women's rights and empowerment in Cebu City, a trailblazer in "alternative politics" for its ubiquitous but voiceless urban poor residents. Her tireless advocacy of women's rights has helped change the lives of many women and influenced government institutions, non-government organizations, and universities to take on such "unpopular" issues as domestic violence, gender sensitivity, good governance, environmental protection and human rights.

Tessie Banaynal Fernandez began her advocacy for women's rights, gender sensitivity, and environmental action in her college days and continued during the perilous times of the Marcos dictatorship. She grew up in Lanao province, the second of seven children in a modest home, finished her degree in sociology and history at Xavier University in Cagayan de Oro City and worked on Catholic Church-based programs for the poor and the tribal communities in Mindanao. Joining her husband in Cebu, she continued working, this time for the rights of the urban poor to housing, livelihood and welfare.

Tessie also set up the Lihok Filipina Foundation, which pioneered in women's rights and gender sensitivity. Appointed to head Cebu City's urban poor office, she conducted a survey on domestic violence, which found that six out of ten women in the community were being battered. This led to the formation of "Bantay Banay" (community watch) in 1992, a community-based and multi-stakeholder approach to end domestic violence. Police enforcers, social workers, councilors, lawyers and village chiefs were trained in gender sensitivity and human rights to help them respond to domestic problems. "It was time to realize that domestic violence and gender sensitivity are public concerns because they are commonly felt by women," asserts Tessie. "Barangay" (village) volunteers were trained and a referral system was opened where non-government organizations, government agencies and professionals are tapped to help. Bantay Banay has been replicated in 70 cities and towns all over the country, effectively making the issue of domestic violence not only a public issue but also one of governance. Tessie continues to pursue her other concern, the environment, particularly solid waste management, water conservation and watershed protection.

After 14 years of martial rule, people's organizations and NGOs mistrusted government and vice-versa. Tessie Banaynal Fernandez facilitated their collaboration in the delivery of basic services and in responding to domestic violence, among other concerns.

Philippines

Abha Bhaiya

Jagori
Olakh
Ankur

Abha Bhaiya (born 1948) sees herself as a product of the last wave of the feminist movement of the 1970s. Among the first women in India to take up the issue of single women, putting them on the agenda of the feminist movement, Abha's work is also aimed at assisting rural women to emerge as independent leaders, and creating linkages between work at the grassroots level and the international feminist movement.

Abha Bhaiya had to rebel against her middle-class, conservative Marwari family to carve out an identity for herself. As she grappled with the politics of poverty and powerlessness, Abha started looking at the question of women's oppression and subordination. In 1984, she set up Jagori, a women's resource, documentation, and communications center. Abha is equally concerned with the rights of marginalized communities, especially Dalit and tribal women. Her work is aimed at assisting rural women emerge as independent leaders: she is a founder-member of Nishtha, a Himachal Pradesh-based NGO that works on rural health; she was a member of Frea-India, a documentation-research center in Mumbai; she is a member of Ankur, an educational center for women and children in New Delhi; she is a founder-member of Olakh, a women's resource center in Gujarat; she is also a founder-member of the Mahila Samakhya's (women's collective) national resource group; and she was on the executive committee of the Uttar Pradesh wing of the Mahila Samakhya.

One of the unique features of Abha's work has been the creation of linkages between community and international arenas. She has used the spaces at various levels to design and evolve a strategy for the convergence of many diverse women's groups, exposing the limitations of mainstream discourse. In the process, she has also created a fresh linguistic and spatial idiom for feminist expression. Abha has worked out a striking synthesis between the movement on the ideological plane and the involvement of women in the movement at the practical level.

When Abha Bhaiya began working in the 1970s, single women had little prominence within the feminist movement. Violence against women, leadership among rural women, and women's contribution to India's economy demanded highlighting, and their lives, achievements, and traditional knowledge needed documenting.

India

Rubina Feroze Bhatti

Tangh Wasaib Tanzeem

Rubina Feroze Bhatti (born 1969), who works in two largely rural districts of Pakistan's Punjab province, has been a driving force against domestic violence in her area. Thanks to the work of this young grassroots activist, many women have been speaking out against ill treatment at home, and more such cases have been reported to the police and the press in the previous three years than ever before.

In 1991, while Rubina Feroze Bhatti was a masters student at Bahuddin Zakria University in Multan in southern Punjab, one of her relatives was arrested under Pakistan's infamous blasphemy laws, and given the death sentence. In 1992, Rubina campaigned against the law, writing articles and organizing a procession in Sargodha and Multan. Her relative survived.

Rubina, who is Christian, took up the issue of separate electorates, a form of religious apartheid imposed by the political establishment from 1979 to 2002, which prevented non-Muslims from voting. She galvanized public opinion, writing articles and making speeches. Many people in Sargodha and Khushab districts boycotted the elections to local bodies for 2000 and 2001. From 1996 to 2001, Rubina worked as a lecturer in chemistry at a local women's college, and then founded the Taangh Wasaib Tanzeem (longing for hope), of which she is general secretary.

Violence against women — such as "honor killings" — is key to Rubina's schema. She has trained a women's group to report on violence against women. She visits victims, supporting them with counseling, legal aid, and highlighting issues in the local media. In district Sargodha, the media reported ten cases of acid thrown on women, and 24 cases of honor killings. Rubina then launched a media campaign, along with civil society organizations, to highlight domestic violence. She set up an educational and healthcare facility in a village in Khushab for children slaving in Pakistan's famous carpet-weaving industry. Rubina also focuses on building interfaith and intersect harmony in an area teeming with different faiths — primarily Muslim, but also Christian and Hindu. She has penned scripts for theater productions, developed a peace education manual, and built a sustainable peace education program.

A Punjab women development and social welfare department study released in October 2001 showed that 42 percent of women accepted violence as their fate, while more than 33 percent felt helpless to defend themselves. Only 19 percent protested and four percent took remedial action.

Pakistan

Chaggi Bai Bhil

Association of Strong Women Alone (Aswa)

Chaggi Bai Bhil (born 1958), a single woman and a tribal, left her husband because of his violence, and became part of the women's movement. In 1999, when the Association of Strong Women Alone (Aswa) was formed, Chaggi was an integral part of the process. Today, she is one of the organization's pillars, helping other single women gain access to their property, resist physical, sexual, and mental torture, lobbying the government for widows' rights, and using the law to prevent social stigma and branding of single women.

Chaggi Bai Bhil comes from a small, marginal farming family belonging to the Bhil tribe. A determined woman, Chaggi left her husband when she realized that he was not going to stop beating her. She got a job with a church-affiliated organization, where she worked with women's groups. With this began Chaggi's association with women's groups and the larger women's movement. In 1999, when Aswa was formed, Chaggi was an integral part of the process. Rajasthan has about two million widows and separated women-it is estimated that at least 1.2 million are impoverished. One of the major foci of Aswa is getting widows their legal right to property. Male relatives — often even unrelated men — believe that a woman alone cannot assert her rights and, therefore, seize her land with impunity.

Beside being denied access to property, widows and separated women are also subject to social stigma. Through the use of law (the "defamation" section in the Indian penal code) and community meetings, Aswa, under Chaggi's able guidance, has been able to curtail the practice of abusing single women as "witches". Chaggi is also helping Aswa deal with cases of physical, sexual, and mental atrocities against single women. Furthermore, Aswa and Chaggi have been lobbying the government for increases in pension payments, and for changes in rules and regulations regarding widows' pensions.

In the past 20 years, Chaggi has mobilized and organized thousands of low-income women; she is currently an unusually strong force at the regional and state levels.

While about 9.5 percent of women in Rajasthan are either widowed or sepa-rated, low-income single women, whether divorced, separated, or widowed, are highly marginalized and unwelcome in their natal families. The superstition that widows are responsible for their husband's deaths haunts their lives.

India

Betty Blake

Catholic Women's League (CWL)
Regional Rights Resource Team (RRRT)
Pan Pacific and South East Asia Women's Association (PPSEAWA)

Betty Blake, the only legal rights training veteran in the Kingdom of Tonga, is an intense bundle of energy. The retired primary school teacher turned human rights activist, mother of five grown children, taught for 33 years and studied as a mature student at the University of the South Pacific in Fiji. Her formerly quiet life as teacher and mother in mono-cultural, patriarchal, and hierarchical Tonga was totally transformed when she decided to become a paralegal trainer and human rights counsellor, less than a decade ago.

As Tonga's first Legal Rights Training Officer, President of the powerful Catholic Women's League, and head of the League's pioneering Center for Women and Children, Betty battled with harsh criticism from opinionated, extremely conservative Tongans, with failed clients, red tape and lack of finances and support, but always persevered: "My 33 years in the classroom were nothing compared to the work stresses of the last seven years. But the rewards of seeing peace settle into an abused woman's face, of reconciling a family after conflict, can never be equalled. My husband warned me that the women coming to the center might just be using me, but when, one evening, we heard cries outside our home and my husband finally met one of our clients, bleeding all over and accompanied by crying infants, our house became theirs. My husband became their spokesman and protector. My passion has now become his. Another client I met when she was only 13. She visited our center as a client but also as a burglar! I had stocked my room with food, clothes, and a pillow to make her feel at home there. She broke the law, broke my windows, broke into my room, stole from me, stole from the center — just to find solace for her tired head and feed her hungry body. She is 15 now and in prison for three months. She breaks my heart — I feel for her out there — so young, so lost, so unwanted. I will not have peace until she regains hers."

When three of Tonga's princesses endorsed the work Betty said: "I felt so good, grinning from ear to ear — even with tears streaming at the same time — relishing the moment of having these Princesses, so rare in the histor y of our tiny, rank-conscious Kingdom, pledge their full support for this event, but also for peace … yes, for peace and understanding in our hearts, in our bedrooms, in our offices, in our streets, in our land."

Betty's pioneering paralegal advocacy, counseling and community outreach work takes place in Tonga, the South Pacific's only monarchy. Shame, stigmatization, and family honor battle Christian teachings of love and forgiveness in this patriarchal, class-conscious, tradition-bound society.

Tonga

Charlotte Bunch

Center for Women's Global Leadership
Human Rights Watch
International Council on Human Rights Policy

Charlotte Bunch, founder and executive director of the Center for Women's Global Leadership, has been an activist, author, and organizer in women's and human rights movements for more than three decades. An influential advocate and activist, Charlotte has increased the visibility and importance of women's rights internationally. She has written numerous articles and edited or coedited nine anthologies. Charlotte is a distinguished professor in the Women's and Gender Studies Department at Rutgers University.

Charlotte has been instrumental in shifting the issue of violence against women into the realm of human rights. This new way of viewing violence against women has elevated its prominence and brought greater pressure to bear upon organizations with the resources to address the issue. "For women, this has been empowering as it has moved such violence out of the category of the individual unfortunate occurrence, or 'just life', into something that is political and that society says should not happen in a powerful way by calling it a violation of basic human rights," Charlotte said. "For example, by showing how domestic violence often parallels other forms of violation seen as unacceptable, like torture, or that rape in armed conflict can constitute a war crime, has increased the pressure that these issues be taken onto local, national, and global agendas."

According to Charlotte it is just as important that framing violence against women as a human rights issue empowers women themselves to strengthen their fight against such injustice. "It has encouraged women to pose many of our struggles and issues as questions of 'rights' not just of 'needs' or 'desires'. This involves seeing women as full citizens who have the right to participate in the shaping of all social matters, including in what is understood and treated as fundamental 'human rights'." She said: "This has been part of women seeing themselves not just as victims, but as subjects with rights they can demand, including the right to a life free of violence."

Some view today's increasing religious fundamentalisms as a reaction to feminist successes in asserting women's rights and putting new issues like reproductive rights and violence against women on national and global agendas. This backlash has put women, and especially feminists, on the defensive.

United States of America

Dorothée Cesnabmihlo Aken'ova is well known as a tireless communicator able to open a debate on any difficult or sensitive subject among people who do not like to approach such subjects.

Dorothée Cesnabmihlo Aken'ova

Women's Health Organization of Nigeria (WHON); Intern. Center for Reproductive Health and Sexual Rights (Increse); African Partnership for Sexual and Reproductive Health and the Rights of Women and Girls (Amanitare)

Dorothée Cesnabmihlo Aken'ova was born in Diko, Niger. With a degree in French that she obtained in 1992 from the University of Zaria, she worked for two years with an agency that reinforced the law against drugs. She became interim coordinator of the Women's Health Organization of Nigeria. The Founder and president of the NGO Increse, she is a resource for various organizations such as UNFPA, WHO, Unicef, IPAS, Rainbo, Amanitare, and local NGOs. She is the married mother of two children.

Dorothée Cesnabmihlo Aken'ova's activism began in 1994. Unfortunately for her, this was during a military dictatorship when conditions were not easy for accomplishing her work. In 1997, she left for New York to present a bleak report from the first and second Nigerian conventions on the elimination of all violence against women. It was a report that put the Nigerian government on the spot because of her politics and her stiff report on women's sexual rights and rights over their bodies. She then had a difficult fight in the 12 states of northern Nigeria, challenging the authorities on their interpretation of the law and its discriminatory application. Dorothée also worked in close collaboration with Amnesty International, IWHC, and the Human Rights Commission to put pressure on the Nigerian government to free women sentenced to death by stoning for alleged sexual offences, and at the same time to repeal the law. In addition, she fought for sexual rights, especially those of lesbian and bisexual women. Because of her commitment and her deliberate choice to work in rural areas under Sharia law under where conditions for women are deplorable, she was obliged to separate from her children and leave them in Lagos for their security. Because of her activism, the political career of her older brother was jeopardized when it was discovered she lodged with him.

She uses any opportunity to start a debate — on public transport, in banks, or the hairdressers. Recently, she developed devices such as badges and posters created by her to start conversations because of their power to attract attention. And they raised strong reactions, such as: "How can you expose women intimately in this manner, can't you use a different part of the body to depict women, a hand or something else?" At the same time many asked for information on women's sexuality and women's rights.

Dorothée began her activism when Nigeria was under a military dictatorship. She fought hard against the introduction of Sharia law and the judicial system of the twelve states of northern Nigeria. She exposed herself to attacks and the risk of jail.

Nigeria

Kamala Chandrakirana

The National Commission on Violence Against Women

Kamala Chandrakirana (born 1960) became involved in the women's movement when she joined a volunteer group established to respond to the May 1998 riots. That same year, she became Secretary General of the National Commission on Violence Against Women, set up by the government under pressure from the women's movement. The commission is engaged in policy and legal reform at national level to ensure state responsibility for the elimination of violence against women. Having been Secretary General from 1998-2003, Kamala is currently the Chairperson of the Commission.

In 1998, following the brutal rape of Chinese-Indonesian women during the May riots, a group of women activists met with Indonesian President B.J. Habibie to demand state responsibility for the violence against women that had occurred in a number of cities. Kamala Chandrakirana, who was present at that historic event, recalls: "This meeting was set following the President's statement that saving Indonesia's economy was more important than the fate of the 100 women raped." So she was quite astonished that, "After listening to the testimonies of several of the victims' counselors, the President was convinced that his leadership was needed by women and that he should take a firm stand concerning the violence against women which occurred in the May tragedy by condemning what happened." The women also demanded that an investigation into the violence against women during the riots be part of the mandate of the official investigating team appointed by the President.

Finally, they demanded that the President take proactive measures to respond to all forms of violence against women throughout the country. "The National Commission on Violence Against Women was established for the latter," explains Kamala who was appointed the first Secretary General of the Commission. She recalls the long negotiations between the women and Habibie about the independence of the Commission, its name, position and membership. And the women won the day. In the end, the President compromised. The Commission was established as an independent body with independent membership. As Chairperson of the Commission, Kamala is recognized for her ability to strengthen networks with local groups and increase solidarity among women's rights and human rights activists. She has inspired the new generation of women activists and has become a role model for tireless commitment and dedication.

After the fall of the Suharto regime, investigating teams were set up to look into the government's human rights abuses. Gender-based violence in human rights violations and crimes against humanity were not recognized as violative of the human rights of women even by human rights defenders.

Indonesia

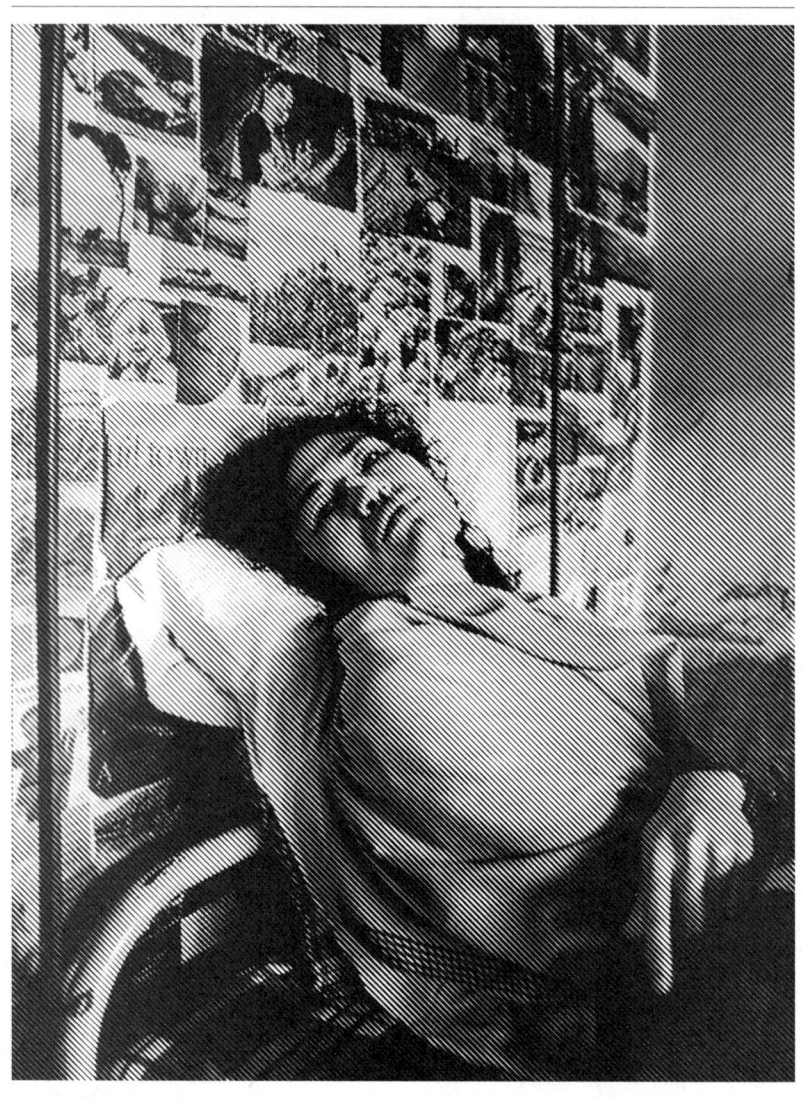

Irom Sharmila Chanu

Irom Sharmila Chanu (born 1972) is the face of the Manipuri protests against the savage Armed Forces Special Powers Act in force in the state, and military excesses and atrocities. In November 2000, Sharmila went on a fast-unto-death, protesting against the killing of 11 civilians in Malom. The government promptly arrested her for attempted suicide. Since that day, she has been in the security ward of a government hospital, force-fed through her nose. Although greatly weakened, Sharmila refuses to break her fast.

Irom Sharmila Chanu lost her father in 1980 and her eldest brother in 1997. When this sensitive women volunteered her services to the Justice Suresh's People's Tribunal of Justice in October 2000, she was witness to the testimony of Mercy Kabui of Lamdam, who had been raped by state forces' personnel in front of her father-in-law. The shock and turmoil of this experience turned her personal tide in November 2000, when she went on a fast-unto-death, protesting against the Malom massacre in Manipur, where Assam Rifles opened fire, killing 11 civilians. Her demand remains that the intemperate Armed Forces Special Powers Act, a virtually extralegal measure in force in Manipur, be repealed. On the third day of her fast, she was arrested on charges of attempted suicide.

Irom's fast, which she steadfastly refuses to break, has brought the issue of human rights' violations into the public domain, sparking off a cloudburst of protests and reactions by human rights organizations. She remains in the security ward of the government hospital in Imphal. Nasogastric tube feeding started in November 2000, and continues, despite her absence of cooperation. She is only 32 years old, but has stopped menstruating, is appallingly weak, and her locomotive capacities have worsened over the years. Her family is distraught and helpless in the face of her determination.

Two women who were inspired to follow Irom's fast-unto-death were persuaded to withdraw, since they have children. Irom continues to fast alone-peacefully resisting, from her bed, the extremely violent reality of Manipur today.

The Armed Forces Special Powers Act, introduced in 1980, is being used indiscriminately in Manipur to deal with the 30-year-long counterinsurgency. Human rights violations and transgressions against women by state security forces are routine. The act analogy is with Gestapo powers.

India

Mingxia Chen

Gender and Law Research Center at the Chinese Academy of Social Sciences

Chen Mingxia is the Director of the Gender and Law Research Center at the Chinese Academy of Social Sciences, and the Board Chair of the Network Against Domestic Violence at the Chinese Law Society. She has helped many victims of violence, has run a pilot scheme on legal implementation, and works on training people to use law. She has evolved democratic management systems in NGOs working on human rights and domestic violence. Her work has been widely appreciated.

Human rights and domestic violence were sensitive issues in China at the time Chen Mingxia (64) started to research these two areas. She has since helped many victims of violence and evolved democratic management systems for NGOs. Chen began researching civil law in 1964, focusing on the human rights of women in 1990. In 1993, under her leadership, a pilot scheme on the implementation of women's law was conducted in Qianxi County, Hebei Province. The scheme gave impetus to work for women in the county; judges, lawyers and the staff of women's federations were given comprehensive training and women's centers were established in villages. Experiences in Qianxi County were shared with the whole of Hebei Province in 1996. Chen's pilot scheme was awarded a Government Innovative Prize. The Local Law on Domestic Violence in Hebei Province was then formulated. The project of protecting women's rights was unique and was subsequently extended to protect human rights as well. In 1998 feminists in Beijing got together to form an NGO to stop violence against women. Chen had influence in the field of law and substantial experience in implementation of women's rights law. She took up the job of chief project coordinator to lead and coordinate the simultaneous implementation of more than ten projects. Her work was rewarded by the achievement of public awareness, judicial intervention and social support. A patient of Systemic Lupus Erythematosus, and devoted to research on women's rights, Chin was unable to take good care of her sick husband.

When Chen started research into human rights for women and fighting against domestic violence, these issues were very sensitive matters in Chinese society; people even denied the existence of such problems. Chen wanted Chinese women to have their rights and gender equality protected by law.

China

"I would like to tell
the women inmates and
the policewomen in
the prisons that we
should be self-confident,
self-respecting, and
hopeful about the
future."

Yue Chen

Chen Yue, a Communist Youth League member, is from the city of Jianyang, Sichuan Province, and now serves as a policewoman in the Women's Prison there. On one occasion she fought against armed robbers and, along with her younger brother, sustained injuries. The public's initial indifference to their plight is what led Chen Yue to understand the importance of human compassion and work as a policewoman with women prisoners.

One day in December 2001, 21-year-old Chen Yue and her 17-year-old brother witnessed a robbery on the street. With no hesitation, they chased after the robbers and fought fearlessly. Their cries for help went unheard and none of the spectators even bothered to call the police. Both brother and sister were critically injured. The incident was widely covered in the media the next day and suddenly baskets of flowers began to arrive in their hotel rooms. For ten days there were endless queues of visitors, including teachers, schoolmates, friends, colleagues and Chengdu citizens who knew them only through the media. From the indifference of the onlookers to the enthusiasm of the public, Chen Yue experienced the two dramatic extremes. Her reaction to the robber was appraised as a "just act" — an impulsive response in a dangerous situation, an act that is not the result of rational consideration. As the head of the prison in which Chen Yue serves said, "I am not sure what would have happened if someone else were involved in this case, but Chen Yue's reaction is nothing new to us." Society's responses to Chen Yue's act reflect the hope and desire for decency and the rejection of indifference. After this incident the Provincial Fund for Just Acts increased from 80,000 yuan to one million yuan.

Chen Yue is now a policewoman in charge of 16 inmates in a women's prison. She considers her job worthwhile if she can help inmates assume new lives and identities in society with confidence. She believes that most inmates have committed crimes for reasons of compassion or finance, and not out of their own free will. Inmates having a better understanding of the laws are better able to protect their rights and themselves.

Violent crimes are on the rise in China after the reforms. With the blatant pursuit of self-interest, social ethics have also changed. Crimes are sometimes committed in cold blood, in broad daylight, and sadly onlookers are often indifferent to what is happening in front of them.

China

Farha Ciciek

Pesantren
Community Development Association (P3M)
Rahima

Farha Ciciek (born 1963), an advocate of women's rights in Islam, is one of Indonesia's leading facilitators and trainers on gender and Islam. She works for Pesantren, an Islamic Boarding School, the Community Development Association (P3M) and Rahima, a women's rights and Islam information and training center. In her 13 years of dedicated work, she has enriched the discourse on women's rights in Islam and contributed to intercultural and inter-religious efforts in peace building and democracy.

"This was an important experience in my life. It was really interesting to see women of different classes and even political ideologies working together for one cause," says Farha Ciciek, speaking of her involvement in the Volunteer Team for Humanity, a support group for rape victims, during the May 1998 riots in Indonesia. It was her first time working in a group where people from different religious, racial, ethnic and social classes, as well as political backgrounds, joined in solidarity for a cause: the Chinese-Indonesian women who were raped. Farha saw that this could not have been possible during the New Order of the Suharto regime, when government segregated people according to race, ethnicity and political background. She recalls how her work with the rape victims affected her emotionally and mentally, having to deal with first-hand, detailed information on what the women went through. "I was not strong enough," she confesses. But through this experience, she learned that women and men have different ways of resolving conflict.

Farha began her career as a researcher, but in the late 1980s, she began working on gender issues in Islam. She is director of Rahima and a founder of the Puan Amal Hayati Foundation, an Islamic women's crisis center. Today, as a leading facilitator and trainer on gender and Islam, she says, violence against women in Pesantren communities is "a substantial problem", especially because discrimination against women is contrary to the Koran, which stresses that Islamic tradition is pluralist and does not discriminate based on gender, race or ethnicity.

In many communities in Indonesia, Islam is practiced in a dogmatic manner. Religious values and the patriarchal culture have affected the way women live their lives. To speak about women's rights in Islam can be considered as opposing the holy religion itself.

Indonesia

Radhika Coomaraswamy

International Centre for Ethnic Studies (ICES)

Sri Lankan lawyer and academic Radhika Coomaraswamy (born 1953) has written and published extensively on issues such as women and conflict, minority rights and governance. Through her work, this brilliant scholar has created new conceptual and theoretical frameworks for understanding women and conflict. As a senior UN official, she has laid down new standards for investigating and analyzing violence against women at all levels.

Radhika Coomaraswamy returned from a brilliant academic career at Yale University and Harvard Law School in the late 1970s to a country that was just entering a conflict based on ethnic discrimination. In the 1980s, Radhika established the International Centre for Ethnic Studies (ICES) in Sri Lanka. This institution has provided a much-needed space for researchers, academics, and activists to mingle and produce pathbreaking work on nationalism, ethnicity, identity politics, and women. The ICES works nationally as well as at the South Asian and international levels. A conference it organized in 2002 focused on issues of women and peace-building set the ball rolling within Sri Lanka for women activists to campaign for the inclusion of women in the peace process.

A founder-member of the Asia Pacific Forum on Women, Law, and Development, Radhika was in 1994 appointed special rapporteur on Violence Against Women by the UN commission on human rights. She served in this capacity for nine years, the maximal term, and created a definitive framework for investigating and analyzing violence against women within the family and the community, and through actions of state and nonstate actors.

In 2003, Radhika was appointed chairperson of Sri Lanka's human rights commission (HRC), whose members are nominated by the president, and given a broad mandate to monitor the implementation of human rights guarantees set out in the constitution and under international law. The HRC has set out to strengthen its regional presence, establishing a special unit to monitor the human rights compliance of state mechanisms set up to work on posttsunami reconstruction and rehabilitation.

The internecine conflict in Sri Lanka has brought out the best in its women- on both sides. There is grassroots resonance in progress, as well as more macro conceptual and theoretical examination of the issue of conflict resolution.

Sri Lanka

Norma Angélica Cruz Córdoba

Sobrevivient (Survivors)
Tierra Viva (Live Land)

Norma Angélica Cruz was a student leader and a Catholic missionary, a mother, political militant and widow. A daughter of the war, she survived not only the armed violence, but also violence within her family. When her life partner abused her daughter, she took legal action against him, which led to his trial and sentence. She founded the organization Sobrevivient (Survivors) that takes care of victims of violence, including women and their families. Norma Angélica Cruz is, in Guatemala, a recognized defender of women's rights.

Norma was born in Guatemala. During her adolescence, she was a student leader and participated in the Ecclesiastical Base Communities, where she became a Catholic missionary. When she was 15 years old, she entered a convent. Two years later, she found that life in a convent was not enough for her, and she opted for political militancy. In December 1996, after 36 years of war, the government of Guatemala and the guerrillas (National Revolutionary Guatemalan Unit) signed the Peace Agreement that put an end to the armed conflict. With the end of the war, aspects of the society — that had been hidden — became perceptible, like violence within families, for example. In 1999, Norma took legal actions against her life partner, for the abuses to which he had subjected her daughter to. The abuser was condemned. Mother and daughter founded the association called Sobrevivient (Survivors). It was created to take care of the victims of domestic violence — the women themselves and the rest of their families.

A diminutive woman with liquid eyes, she thinks that a part of the struggle is decoding pain and going back following its tracks. "Deciding to break the silence is to start traveling along the path. Afterwards, comes the hardest part." Her life is an ode to hope. She dreams of a world that fully values the resources of nature and the beauty of the human being. She dreams of a world without war, where there is no place for the trading of arms, a society without inequalities or discrimination, where opportunities for schools, food, health and work are abundant. "That is the kind of life that I would want for my children. That is the life I fight for."

75% of the population of Guatemala live below the poverty level, 58% live in extreme poverty. Most women are excluded from all the social benefits and from any possibility of obtaining justice. Being a society that suffers from sexism and domestic violence is in the order of the day.

Guatemala

Dulcy de Silva

Mothers and Daughters of Sri Lanka

Cofounder of the Mothers and Daughters of Sri Lanka, Dulcy de Silva (born 1933) is convinced that because women are the most severely affected by conflict, they are also the key to peace efforts. She has founded a dynamic peace movement that has gained in influence and recognition. At 71, an indefatigable Dulcy continues to travel throughout the country, braving personal danger. She is respected by Tamils and Sinhalese alike as an honest negotiator, and talks to people on both sides of the ethnic divide.

Dulcy de Silva has been politically active since her school and university days. After she finished her education, she began teaching, but knew that she needed to involve herself more vigorously with the sociopolitical movements in Sri Lanka. In 1970, she joined the NGO National Peace Movement in Sri Lanka, working with the peace movement for almost two decades before cofounding Mothers and Daughters of Sri Lanka in 1989. Dulcy still codirects this movement, which strives to end the civil war in the country. She also coordinates the World Solidarity Forum Sri Lanka. Mothers and Daughters of Sri Lanka is based on Dulcy's deep conviction that women are the key to all peace efforts, since, as mothers, sisters, daughters, and wives, they are the most traumatically affected by situations of conflict.

Even though a septuagenarian, Dulcy travels throughout the country, talking to people on both sides of the ethnic chasm. She is known in all of Sri Lanka, and respected by Tamils and Sinhalese alike as an honest negotiator. Although conditions are slowly improving, traveling in Sri Lanka remains jeopardous. Bus accidents are not uncommon, and some remote areas have not yet heard of the armistice. For many years now, Dulcy's unwavering standpoint has made her a target of aggression. Her dynamic women's peace movement is spreading the idea among both the informed population and those who cannot read or access television. In a sense, everyone in Sri Lanka is benefiting from her activity, but mainly women and poor farmers. Hers is a new way of thinking.

Sri Lankan political life has been a standoff between the majority Sinhalas and the minority Tamils since 1948. Since internecine conflict erupted in 1983, tens of thousands have died, many in the government-organized genocide of Tamils and Tamil Tigers attrition.

Sri Lanka

Sharda Devi

Action India

Sharda Devi grew up in an orthodox and conservative family, whose displeasure she braved in order to take up a job outside the home to support herself and her family. She is a pillar of strength and commitment and continues every day to fight on behalf of women, with dignity, perseverance, and courage.

Sharda Devi, affectionately known as Sharda Behn, was born in 1936 to an affluent, but very conservative and orthodox family of landlords in Uttar Pradesh. She grew up in a typically feudal environment characterized by enormous differences in the status of men and women. Sharda barely completed elementary school: after finishing the fourth grade she was compelled to leave school to look after her young siblings, learn household work, and prepare herself for marriage. However even as a young child, Sharda did not believe in differences of class or caste. Her family's attitude of caste discrimination irked her and led her to begin thinking about unequal power relations in Indian society.

Marriage brought Sharda to Delhi. The economic condition of her marital home was not good and Sharda often thought about going out to work. However it was only in 1974, after 28 years of constant struggle, that she was able to break the shackles of patriarchy and take up a job to support the family. In 1976, she joined Action India and through her work with the organization, she succeeded in persuading women to take control of their lives and question their subordinate status and roles. It was at this time that she facilitated the formation of Sabla Sanghs in the slum and resettlement colonies in which she worked. She herself faced a lot of hostility, abuse, and threats from men in the communities in which she worked. Undeterred by these obstacles, she continued in her mission. Through Sabla Sanghs and Mahila Panchayats, Sharda has reached nearly 3000 women and their families who have been in situations of crisis. She is actively involved in a campaign to promote a national domestic violence bill which, if passed by parliament, will go a long way toward ensuring the safely of women.

When Sharda Devi joined Action India in the mid 1970s, she did not regard herself as a catalyzing force in her community. At that time she was focused on fighting for her own rights and dignity. Twenty-eight years later, she inspires women around her to wage social change and thus better their own situation.

India

Fatoumata Diakité

Association pour le Progrès et la Défense des Droits de la Femme (APDF)

Fatoumata Diakité (50) was born in Bamako and has fought for the Malian women's movement for many years. She denounces female genital mutilation in Mali and is a defender of the cause of the African woman. Her association runs a law clinic for woman and child victims of social injustice.

Fatoumata Siré Diakité is a major name in the Malian women's movement. Her face is one of the most well-known and visible in the fight for Malian women's rights. She created the Association for the Progress and Defense of the Rights of Women (APDF). This structure very quickly had an effect on the national landscape. The association spent a number of years appealing to decision-makers for the adoption of a law against female circumcision. At the same time, there was a focus on raising women's awareness on their rights. Through the association, Fatoumata Siré Diakité immediately won national confidence. She made it known internationally and, as its president, was invited to many international fora because of her fight for rights in Mali. In her fight, she had to come up against a lack of understanding in certain militant environments. She became the target of Islamists who have fought against her ideas in defense of the rights of women.

Fatoumata had a long career of responsibility within the National Union of the Workers of Mali (UNTM). Awarded a diploma in Bamako, English became her speciality and she was trained at the university of Lancaster, England, and at the International Center of Work Formation (BBIT) in Turin, Italy. Fatoumata Siré lectures on the establishment of women's rights around the world and to the United Nations. She has many responsibilities within the French-speaking world and in the West African coalition against the illegal trade in women and children. She also coordinated the activities of French-speaking women at the Summit of Beijing in 1995.

In Mali, the president of the APDF sponsored and financed the marriage of about 100 couples and materially supported the treatment of the sick children evacuated with cancer to French hospitals.

Mali

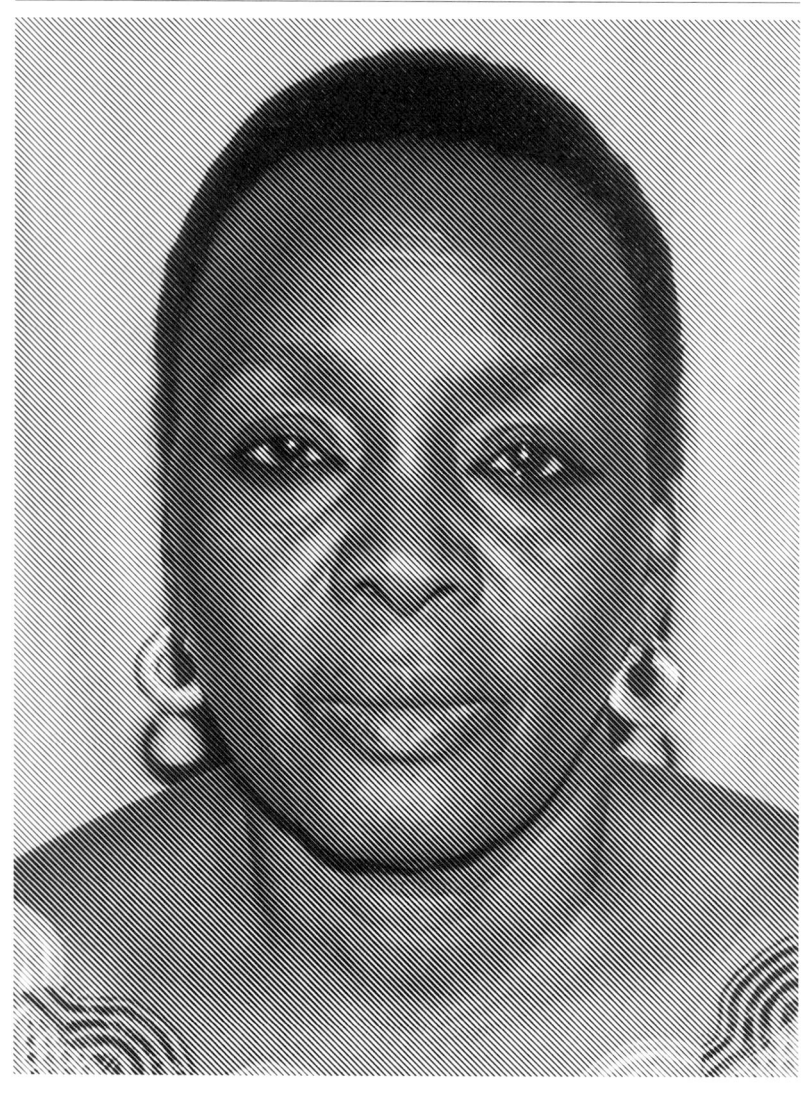

Souna Hadizatou Diallo

Saphta

Souna Hadizatou Diallo (60) was born in Maïné Soroa, lives in Niamey and is the prototype of women's group members. Her area of work is violence against women and the well-being of women.

Souna Hadizatou Diallo has made women's associations and non-governmental organizations one of the important pillars of civil society in Niger. Hadizatou always encouraged Niger families to send their children to school and accord peaceful behavior towards all. She informs, makes aware and supports women on the promotion of their rights. She relies on the NGO Saphta which is particularly dynamic in Niger. She has worked in difficult, sometimes very hard conditions with dispossessed people, she has fought against deforestation and the aridity that affects Niger and accelerates the poverty of rural women. Hadizatou works with women who are confronted by insecurity problems and cannot sell their agricultural and pastoral products in the markets. She is the general secretary of the Network of Women Ministers and Parliamentarians of Niger which aims to promote the rights of women and to oppose violence against them. Intimidation by men and the risk in creating awareness did not discourage her as she knew before that in the fight for the promotion of women's rights nothing is easy, and that the final battle will be won with self-sacrifice. She fights for women's causes with care and without procrastination.

Hadizatou has wide knowledge of the Niger rural environment and women's problems. She never backed away from being engaged in the resolution of conflicts and the restoration of the culture of peace. She has also contributed to training a number of women for the defense of their rights.

Niger

Lily Djenaan

Suara Parangpuan Sulut

As a student, Lily Djenaan (born 1966) was a volunteer at a legal aid organization, but she began her professional life as a journalist for a local newspaper in North Sulawesi, Indonesia. After two years, she joined Kelola Manado, a non-governmental organization dealing with environmental issues. In 1998, she founded Suara Parangpuan Sulut (The Voice of North Sulawesi Women), which works mainly on the issue of violence against women. She also works for Sabuah Parangpuan, a crisis center in North Sulawesi.

Lily Djenaan comes from a family of teachers and social activists. During her student years, she was involved in study clubs and volunteered for an NGO doing legal aid. In 1996, she founded Kelola Manado, an NGO working on environmental issues, providing information on and advocating for the right of coastal communities to their natural resources. She also supported local communities against the unfair appropriation of their lands by a multinational mining company, by warning them about the dangers of hazardous industrial wastes. The mining company was alleged to have caused severe pollution in Buyat Gulf, North Sulawesi in 2004.

The political upheaval in Indonesia in 1998 claimed many women casualties. Lily and her colleagues sought to continue the long history of the women's movement in the area and founded Suara Parangpuan Sulut (The Voice of North Sulawesi Women), the first women's NGO in the region. Lily's work involves raising public awareness of violence against women through the media and policy advocacy. Suara Parangpuan Sulut helps the local government draw up regulations to prevent the trafficking of women and children. Lily's dream is to organize public support for women survivors of violence. With her colleagues at the NGO, she has called for public fundraising, which she calls Dompet Perempuan (Women's Wallet), to build a shelter for battered women called Sabuah Parangpuan (Women's Hut). She maintains that it is only right that the shelter be built using publicly-raised funds and that it is publicly accountable so that the people will have a real sense of responsibility for the care of survivors of violence against women.

The coastal area of North Sulawesi, Indonesia, has one of the most diverse arrays of marine life in the world. The province also has a long history of human trafficking, especially of women and children.

Indonesia

Achta Djibrine Sy

Intermón Oxfam (IO)
Groupe informel de réflexion et de recherche action feminine (GIRAF)
Said-Al-Awine (Women's Union)

Achta Djibrine Sy (born 1962) obtained her first degree in Management and Economics from the University of N'Djaména. She is Intermón Oxfam Representative in Chad and has been advocating women's work to be visible, regardless of their ethnical and religious background. She encourages women to gain self-confidence and to pool their labor to bring about peace in Chad. Thanks to her splendid efforts, women who were very poor some years ago are now self-dependent and are even able to give loans to others.

After the civil war in Chad, a non-democratic regime seized power in the country. Due to the political upheaval at that time, it was difficult to work together in groups — people had lost trust in each other. Women, the weakest section of the community, suffered. But Achta Djibrine Sy succeeded in teaming up women from different social and educational backgrounds and formed the Said-Al-Awine (Women's Union) where they collaborated to help the local community. "I have to capitalize information, think about women's situation and help them in different ways. I wanted Chadian women to be self-dependent and self-confident. My dream was to boast their capabilities in order to achieve their responsibilities and act for peace in the country", Achta explains.

At the beginning she was told that it was not easy to work with underprivileged people, especially urban women who were burdened with a lot of problems. According to Achta, even the group of women with whom she worked did not believe that they could achieve any progress. That is why the only way they could work was within the private sector. These women thought that only women who work in governmental institutions can succeed in their lives. Achta helped them to gain self-esteem and self-confidence. She recalls the day when she accompanied these ladies to sign their recognition paper: "At the entrance to the Ministry office, following local traditional etiquette, they took off their shoes before entering the office. Today, they are more self-confident and they know how to negotiate with the mayor and with development partners. They travel abroad and exchange their views with others." Today, the Women's Union is able to achieve its aims with the auspicious financial contributions of these women, their resources and the loans given to less-fortunate members.

Achta Djibrine Sy began her work in 1987. Until 1990 the political and economic situation in Chad was characterised by repression and corruption. In 1990 Idriss Deby seized power and initiated a multi-party regime. Consequently, many social and political associations were created.

Chad

Frances Iona Erlinger-Ford

Centro de Crisis de Santa Lucía (Saint Lucia Crisis Center)

Her family taught her the love for social attendance and the work in local organizations. She was an excellent student, however, she could not go to university because the few overseas scholarships were for male students. Frances Iona Erlinger-Ford, natural of Saint Lucia, did not understand this. She also did not understand that domestic violence grew unpunished and that the rights of women were not recognized. She recruited, offered conferences, prepared workshops. She was placed in the head of the Saint Lucia Crisis Center.

Frances Iona Erlinger-Ford, born in Saint Lucia, is the third of seven children. When only 15 years old, she obtained the first place in Cambridge's exams, but she was denied a more advanced education by the lack of university facilities in the Caribbean. More than that, she suffered discrimination: Why could the male students study on scholarships abroad, but she could not? The barriers were imposed, and she had to fight. From very early, she worked so that the government of Saint Lucia would respect the UN Convention for the Elimination of all Forms of Violence against Women and Children. She was a member of the Advocacy Committee in the government's Ministry of Social Services that, later, developed into the Ministry of Women's Affairs.

With the help of the Professional and Business Women's Club, of which she was president, and of the National Council for Voluntary Women's Organizations, she founded, in 1988, the Saint Lucia Crisis Center. Her mission: indefatigable work to eliminate all forms of domestic violence and social abuses. But, she went further, she did not stop. She helped to understand that the attention should not only be focused on the woman, but also on the orientation of the family, with the same concern for the men and the children. The government offered them a place in the first three years. With donations, they were able to buy equipment and furniture. The legal help for clients that did not have resources was possible through the Roman Catholic Church. All the personnel, administrative and counseling, offered eight hours of daily services. Today, more than 6000 victims have been helped and, with her indefatigable work, Frances Iona Erlinger-Ford has managed to open other Crisis Centers in the Caribbean.

Until 1995, in Saint Lucia, 'domestic violence' was never used as a technical term. Inside the homes, masculine dominance prevailed as well as their right to concubinage. Incest among members of the family was ignored. There were no shelters for women in danger.

Saint Lucia

"I admire her for her perseverance and her capacity to keep this issue in the mainstream, in a society where too often women fall through the cracks." Anu Pillay, Ashoka Representative

Lesley Ann Foster

Masimanyane Women's Support Centre

Lesley was born and raised in East London, in the Eastern Cape Province of South Africa. She began her career as a salesperson. In 1996, Lesley established the Masimanyane Women's Support Centre; the first organization in the Eastern Cape devoted exclusively to combating violence against women and girls. Through the center Leslie is developing and implementing several services at the grassroots level and leading an initiative to heighten public understanding of the problem.

Lesley Ann Foster began her career as a salesperson and design consultant for a firm in Cape Town. In 1991 she joined the staff of the Daily Bread Charitable Trust in East London. In 1995, Lesley became the personal assistant of the chief executive officer of the Independent Business Enrichment Centre (Ibec). She organized a series of national conferences on micro-enterprise development projects, which exposed her to the problems faced by women trying to establish income-earning projects. This assignment, combined with her personal experience as a victim of sexual and domestic abuse, compelled her to find ways of finding solutions. In February 1996, Lesley established the Masimanyane Women's Support Centre devoted to combating violence against women and girls. Women who decide to get out of abusive relationships and become independent are referred to the local Independent Business Enrichment Centre, a state-funded initiative with offices throughout the country. The women are provided with job skills training and, in some instances, start-up loans for self-employment projects. The Masimanyane Centre has organized a series of workshops on awareness and prevention of sexual abuse for teachers from schools throughout the province. Lesley also hopes to establish a shelter for battered women and their children. She has recently secured funds for this project from the Japanese government. Lesley is also laying plans for a national summit where she intends to propose a "Survivor's Bill of Rights" and to encourage each of the nine provinces to develop its own "No Violence Against Women Action Plan". There are more than 20 women's organizations in rural and urban areas, which provide support services to victims of sexual and domestic abuse in the province.

Some surveys suggest that less than three percent of rape victims in South Africa report the crime to the police, and that in only 15 percent of the cases so reported are the perpetrators actually charged with the offense.

South Africa

"My dream is slowly
becoming reality. At last
rape victims are finding
a way out of shame
and silence. They are
speaking up."

Jeanne M. Gacoreke

Union des Groupements et Association pour la Promotion de la Femme

Jeanne Gacoreke (49) is a teacher in Bujumbura. She helps orphans and widows of war and sexually abused women, fights poverty and reintegrates refugees within the country and those from abroad. She founded the Maison d'écoute, where victims of war and sexual violence receive physical and psychological help and legal advice. Thanks to her, the local radio has presented women's personal stories about rape, thus raising public awareness on their plight. Jeanne is trained in psycho-pedagogy, peaceful conflict resolution and modern communication technology.

Jeanne Gacoreke's children live in exile for fear of victimization. She denounces rapists and restores social justice to the victims of war and rape. To her, silence is not golden, and as a result she is always criticized, and even threatened.

Her village, a poor quarter on the outskirts of Bujumbura, has been destroyed four times in the last ten years. Each time the village has been rebuilt. Twice she had to take a bank loan to rebuild her own house. After the fourth attack, she remained in exile in order to spare her children the sight of dead bodies. She helped the women of the village to rebuild their homes and she eventually returned. One day her 70-year-old neighbor was raped. Jeanne secretly brought her to the hospital, because she was afraid of the military and the rebels. Soon after that, a 12-year-old girl was raped. Again she brought her to the hospital.

International organizations and other women recognized Jeanne's individual assistance and helped her develop a health center for women, where physical and psychological wounds can be healed. There is also a counseling center for the victims of sexual violence to reintegrate them socially, regardless of ethnic background. Jeanne sensitizes and persuades women who are raped to speak up, even on the radio. Today the traditionally shunned topic of rape has been exposed. Her work has made people more aware and sensitive. This she does at her own risk, because rapists bay for revenge.

She is a teacher and also represents a group of organizations which works for the rights of women and children. She heads the Union des Groupements et Association pour la Promotion de la Femme. Jeanne is trained in psycho-pedagogy, peaceful conflict resolution and modern communication technology. She has attended courses on interviewing victims of sexual violence and now helps them to overcome their trauma.

The strife between Hutus and Tutsis lead to armed conflicts in 1972, 1988 and from 1993 onwards. Women were and still are victims of rape and hardly speak about it — because of tradition, fear and shame.

Burundi

"My dream came true. I have managed to set up a social project that incorporates essential community services, such as a school, a library, a community resources center and a health advice center."

Bogaletch Gebre

Kembatti Mentti Gezzimma–Topa (KMG)

Bogaletch Gebre was the first woman from her village to receive higher education. In 1975 she set off to the United States after she won a Fulbright scholarship to study parasitology. Later, she secured another scholarship from the Israeli government to study microbiology and physiology at the Hebrew University in Jerusalem. She was the first Ethiopian woman to teach in the Faculty of Science at Addis Ababa University. She strives to improve the conditions of women in rural areas and give them access to a better life.

Bogaletch Gebre was born in Zato, a small village in Ethiopia. The infrastructure in the region was very poor. There is no electricity, no running drinking water, no road network, and unemployment is at its highest, particularly among the youth. Bogaletch was raised in an area deeply embedded with cultural values, where taboos such as female genital circumcision were dominant. Women had no access to education and health services. The area was so primitive that no birth certificates were issued. Bogaletch strove to raise awareness of HIV/Aids, prevention of female genital circumcision, domestic violence and gender based discrimination. She dedicated her life to working for the enhancement of her community, and she has been involved in effectuating a sustainable change to her country, particularly during the Ethiopian famine in 1984. She believes that misunderstanding of cultural principles and social customs can sometimes make life harder and limit people's social development. In her view, it is the duty of social and political activists to bridge the information gap between the local communities and to help people make informed decisions regarding development. In 1997 Bogaletch returned to her birthplace and helped to found women's integrated community-based organizations, such as Kembatti Mentti Gezzimma-Topa (KMG) or the Kembatti Women Self-Help Center in Ethiopia. This center supports women's right to identify their needs and to take initiatives towards the betterment of their communities. KMG uses transformational methodologies that enhance communities' capacities through dialogue. She has also helped establish multi-purpose social projects, including the Women's Center, a school, a library, a community resources center, and a health advice center. In her work she has confronted many challenges, such as political threat, bureaucracy and lack of modern amenities.

The population of the area, where Bogaletch's organization is active, is very large. Women and young people in Ethiopia are the direct beneficiaries of her contribution, although her activities cover other countries working to protect human rights.

Ethiopia

Monika Gerstendörfer

Lobby für Menschenrechte e. V.

The human rights expert and psychologist Monika Gerstendörfer (47) does invaluable educational work on the dangers of sexual violence in Germany. The co-founder and director of Lobby für Menschenrechte (Lobby for Human Rights Association) has significantly changed attitudes towards violence against women and children. She has done very useful networking among numerous associations, initiatives, criminal police, journalists, and parliamentarians. Born in Wittenberg, she now lives in Baden-Württemberg.

For 15 years the human rights expert Monika Gerstendörfer has done invaluable work in the field of sexual violence education in Germany. She has studied four languages, art history, law and psychology, and has contributed significantly to changes in social attitudes concerning violence against women and children. It is thanks to her fight that rape in marriage is now a criminal offense. She makes a special effort to use a language that adequately reflects the crimes involved. A co-founder and director of Lobby für Menschenrechte (Lobby for Human Rights Association), she counsels victims, does crisis intervention, is an expert witness at hearings at European Union, federal, and state levels, and works with numerous committees and organizations. She makes speeches, leads workshops, writes articles, press releases, and letters of protest. For six years she was employed in IBM Germany's science center. This experience helps her to assess the downside of the internet and oppose torture of children on the internet.

Monika Gerstendörfer has worked on issues of trafficking women, forced prostitution, sex work and the internet for Irmengard Schewe-Gerigk, member of the German parliament. In addition, she has worked on mass rape in war, sexual harassment in the workplace, domestic violence, human rights for sex workers, genital mutilation, discrimination against gays and lesbians, forced prostitution as modern slavery, killing of infant girls, and sexual torture.

Because even experienced professionals are threatened by burnout after intensive involvement with sexual torture and trauma, Monika belongs to a writers' association and writes fairy tales, fables, poems, and stories.

The internet has become a purveyor of sexual violence against women and children. Trafficking in women and children, forced prostitution, sexual harassment at the workplace, domestic violence, and genital mutilation are all too common in Germany and on the wider European scale.

Germany

"They were my university.
Every woman. Every life.
I have learned everything
I know from them."

Angela Gomes

Banchte Shekha

Angela Gomes (born 1952) is founder-director of Banchte Shekha (learning to survive), one of the most respected women's organizations in Bangladesh. Set up on a modest scale in 1981, the organization now accommodates 200 live-in trainees and also serves as a women's shelter. More than 25,000 women in 750 village-based organizations are active members of Banchte Shekha, and more than 200,000 benefit indirectly from its agenda. Angela has been working on the issue of gender rights through social rights education and income generation programs.

Angela was the seventh of four brothers and five sisters. Resisting her parents' attempts to marry her off early, she managed to get herself an education, paying her own way through school with community service. It was even at this precocious age that she knew what to do with her life. "At the age of 13, when I was studying with the nuns, I clearly saw the inequality between the sexes, especially among the poor," she recalls. "I hated the fact that women were abused and humiliated and I wanted to do something for them—particularly widows, divorcees, and single women."

In 1975, after she got her bachelor's degree in economics, history and geography, Angela finally began her work in the villages. She set up Banchte Shekha (learning to survive) in 1981 in a small fashion. Initially, the fact that she was very young, single, childless, and Christian was a massive hurdle. "I would try to talk to the women about their problems and they would say 'Where is the problem?' They had all kinds of problems, but only I was aware of them," she says. With no resources or staff to support her, Angela traversed her villages alone, largely walking, or being boated over the considerable riparian distances. It took time, but with patience and single-minded devotion to her cause, she overcame the odds.

On her personal front, though, Angela is going through a formidably difficult time: she is fighting ovarian cancer and undergoing chemotherapy. This is bound to have slowed her down somewhat, but she continues to travel and be actively involved in the running of Banchte Shekha. Initially confronted by prejudice for her youth, Angela today is Boro Apa (eldest sister) to the people she serves.

Women's rights in Bangladesh — despite legislation such as seat reservation for women in parliament — have a very long way to go. When Angela Gomes began her work, the position of women here was little better than cattle and chattel. In every aspect, their lives were dictated by men.

Bangladesh

Maria Inês Gomes Rodrigues Fontinha

European Federation for the Eradication of Prostitution (FEDIP)
O Ninho

The social scientist Inês Fontinha (born 1943) has been fighting the sexual exploitation of women for over 30 years. In the beginning, she supported Portuguese prostitutes through her work for the non-governmental organization O Ninho (The Nest). Years later, she also started to combat sexual trafficking in children, young and adult women. In 1992, she founded the European Federation for the Eradication of Prostitution (FEDIP), a network in several European countries against this crime.

"Lost women, women who took the easy way," that is how people used to call prostitutes in Madeira Island, where Inês Fontinha was born. "In my generation, those women faced a lot of prejudices. It was a problem nobody talked about. Women were always seen as the guilty ones." In the early 1960s, Inês had just graduated in social science, and was invited by a friend to visit O Ninho. The organization, founded in Portugal in 1967 to support young prostitutes, followed the example and was named after a French organization created in 1936. "My friend was a volunteer, teaching the women to read and write." When she first met the sex workers, Inês realized their "way" was not "easy" at all. "I saw the suffering in their faces. I heard their stories and decided to explore through them that unknown world I had ignored until then." From that moment on, Inês dedicated her life to fight the sexual exploitation of women. She took different positions in O Ninho before becoming its director, her current post. Besides psychological and legal support, the organization provides vocational courses, a house for temporary accommodation of women in danger, and a stand to sell handicrafts made in their own workshops. It also works on sensitivity training, information, and reporting of exploitation of women.

As the years went by, foreign women also started to ask for help at O Ninho. "In Lisbon, the number of young women from Africa, Asia, Latin America, and Eastern Europe has increased. Women come to Europe with the promise of work, but once they are here, they do not have documents, do not speak the language, and so they become prostitutes, slaves." To fight sexual trafficking in children, young and adult women, Inês founded the European Federation for the Eradication of Prostitution (FEDIP) in 1992. She was the president of FEDIP until 1997. Currently, she is part of its secretariat.

The United Nations estimates that every year four million people in the world are victims of human trafficking, mainly women and girls.

Portugal

Anis Haroon

Aurat Foundation

For the past 36 years, Anis Haroon (born 1946) has made a major contribution to raising levels of awareness on women's rights and other social issues through her work as a journalist and social activist. Currently resident director of the Aurat Foundation for the Sindh province, she mainly works out of Karachi, but reaches out to thousands of ordinary people across Pakistan through her articles and radio programs.

Anis Haroon began her career as a political activist early. In 1956, as a ten-year-old student, she participated in a youth demonstration in Karachi against the occupation of the Suez Canal by the USA, the UK, and France. As a young woman, she became active in the students' movement in the mid-1960s against dictator Ayub Khan. Driven by a continuing need to contribute to the debate on social issues in Pakistan, Anis entered journalism in Pakistan in 1970 armed with degrees in law and international relations from Karachi University. She worked as an assistant editor for Akhbar-e-Khawateen, a large-circulation women's magazine. She was also a reporter and feature writer for the daily The Leader. Anis clashed with the newspaper's management over the plans of the martial law regime to hang ousted prime minister Zulfiqar Ali Bhutto. In the 1980s, she decided to work as a freelance print, radio, and television journalist on social issues. She writes on women's issues in Urdu and English newspapers. She is one of the founder-members of the Women's Action Forum (WAF), which was set up to address the antiwomen policies of Zia-ul-Haq's martial law regime.

Anis has been associated with leading women's rights and human rights organizations — the Applied Socioeconomic Research Foundation and Resource Center, the South Asia Partnership, and the Aurat Foundation, which works for women's empowerment in concert with a nationwide network of citizen's groups. In 1995, in the wake of a mini-insurgency in the Sindh's major cities by militants from the Mohajir Qaumi Movement, the State retaliated with unprecedented violence. The WAF brought a group of women together from different political and ethnic backgrounds, pushing for peace. In 2000, Anis compiled a book, Dard Ke Rishtay (which means relations of pain), based on true stories of violence-affected women.

Women journalists in Pakistan are some of South Asia's most fearless scribes today, but it was not always so: it took the dictatorial martial law regimes to put them in the vanguard of the women's movement.

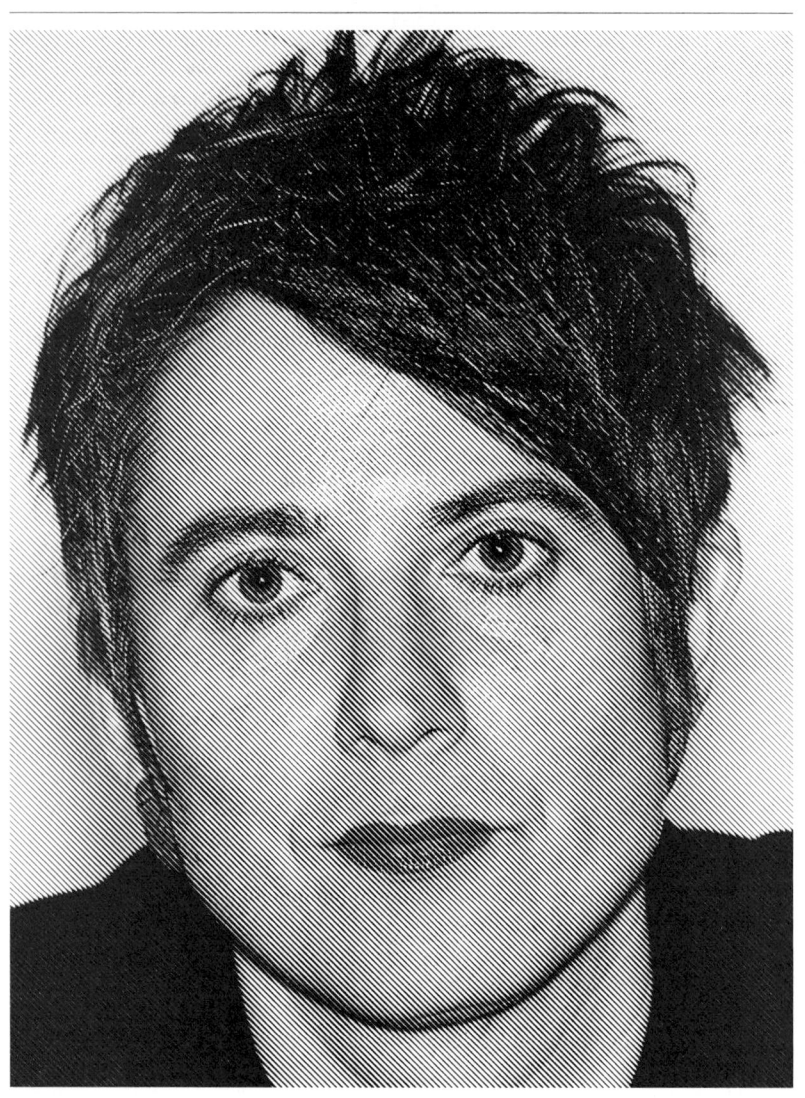

Monika Hauser

Medica Mondiale

Monika Hauser, an Italian citizen, born in 1959 in Switzerland, is a gynecologist and director of the women's aid association Medica Mondiale in Cologne, Germany. In 1992, in the middle of the Bosnian war, she opened a therapy center in the city of Zenica for women victims of rape and war trauma. Now more than 80 Bosnian women doctors, nurses, therapists, and other professionals work there. She also founded projects for victims of sexual violence in Kosovo, Albania, and Afghanistan. Medica Mondiale supports local women's organizations in other countries, including Indonesia, Iraq, and Congo.

A hot wind blew through Kabul. In 2002, Monika Hauser, who had opened a therapy center for women victims of rape in the middle of the Bosnian war and later founded projects in Kosovo and Albania, flew to Afghanistan to care for women and girls traumatized by war. Monika Hauser visited the women's prison in Kabul along with two colleagues from the international women's support organization Medica Mondiale, active in Kabul since early 2002. The prison was dilapidated, the food awful, the prisoners often beaten. Most women were imprisoned for "crimes against morality": refusing to enter forced marriages or leaving violent husbands. Depressed, the doctor left the prison.

In the entrance, she met a prisoner's brother and daughter. The prisoner's son was allowed to visit his mother but the daughter had to stay outside. "Only one person," the guard had ordered, and the prisoner's brother sent in the son. Monika Hauser saw the girl's empty look — panic, doubt, abandonment, and complete hopelessness. The entire misery of Afghan women and children, terrorized by war and male violence, was reflected in these eyes. Monika could not stop herself from crying. "What is wrong with that woman?" asked the guard mystified. When it was explained, he said: "I am not a bad person, let the girl visit her mother."

"This scene reflects how completely arbitrary men can be," Monika Hauser said later. "There is a conspiracy between men in the families, police, judicial system, and in the mosques, putting women at their mercy. Violence is everywhere, but women have never experienced anything else and don't even recognize and name it. They just say 'I feel bad.'"

But there is a ray of light. Since October 2003, ten members of Medica Mondiale are taking care for 150 women in the prisons of Kabul and Herat. They have succeeded in winning the releases of over 90 prisoners.

Sexual violence against women and girls plays a role in all wars. The international women's organization Medica Mondiale organizes therapeutic and medical support for survivors of war and torture through projects in Bosnia, Kosovo, Albania, and Afghanistan.

Germany

Hsiao Chuan Hsia

TransAsia Sisters Association, Taiwan (Tasat)
Associate Professor, Graduate Institute for Social Tansformation Studies,
Shih Hsin University

Hsia Hsiao Chuan, born in 1953, is a sociologist. She is the backstage promoter of the rights of so-called foreign brides. In eight years of work, she noticed the inequitable distribution of wealth, which forces Southeast Asian women to marry foreigners and migrate to faraway shores like Taiwan. She also noticed the similarities in historical migration patterns. Through close contact with these foreign brides, Hsia has extended the scope of her social activism. The situation of these women provides an opportunity to rethink Taiwanese society.

Hsia Hsiao Chuan started to promote alphabetization after her return to Taiwan. She always remembered to "start with their real experiences in daily life, do not take for granted that one has the power to change them." Since its start in 1995, the curriculum of her courses has continued to evolve to take account of changes. The underlying question is "what should be taught? Foreign brides can't even leave their houses because they can't read. I don't want to teach them professional Chinese or make them put pretty signatures in their children's handbooks. I hope to awaken consciousness through language, not adaptation."

To begin with, she invited people's theatre organizers to help women express themselves through body language. Many foreign brides have left aside their housewifely duties and came to take classes not because they want to play, but because they want to learn something useful. They asked Hsia Hsiao Chuan to use examinations so they could improve. Hsia says that these foreign women have adapted to discrimination; they have accepted oppression. Often when they are asked what they feel about something, they say they don't know. And this is why she teaches them, so they can have the confidence to express themselves and a chance to move out of the home. "Education should teach people to have the courage to express themselves, not to ignore one self's feelings and accommodate others." Therefore, she keeps changing the curriculum. They practice dialogue using real-life experiences that indirectly bring out their feelings. She asks them about their personal views in her Chinese language program through pictures and dialogues. Sometimes, she awakens memories of home, their first days in Taiwan and uses newspaper reports about "foreign wives" to initiate group discussions.

Hsia Hsiao Chuan said that at the beginning, nobody cared about their social action, and even ignored their group. In two years' time, government and civil organizations have started to provide assistance. Taiwanese society is starting to rethink itself.

China, Taiwan

Meiqing Hua

Qingdao Public Security Bureau

Hua Meiqing is a policewoman serving at the Pingan Road Police Station of the Sifang Substation of the Qingdao Public Security Bureau. In 1993 she began to work supervising prostitutes; in 2002 she started to take on tasks aimed at tackling domestic violence. She took care of victimized women and created a way in which the police could intervene in domestic violence. She writes extensively on the subject.

Dressed in police uniform, Hua Meiqing is like a rose in a sea of green. She is strong-willed, sensible, and responsible. After leaving school, Hua took up a career in the police force. As a policewoman, she has found her own position in her life; as a woman, she has become aware of her value in the process of helping other women. She has had to face many problems in her work: people tend to misunderstand her work, her unit did not have enough funds, sometimes her emotions have got in the way. Slowly things began to improve as her work progressed. Compared with the progress being made in other countries, in China the campaign against domestic violence has only just started. Many legal areas in this area are inadequate, and conceptual work is lacking. Hua Meiqing feels that there is a long way to go as the number of cases of domestic violence is still very high. She is doing her best to encourage people around her to act against domestic violence. She is a woman who loves letters, and currently she is a member of Qingdao Writers' Association. She always writes articles about police work and tries to get them published so as to publicize their work against domestic violence. She once said, "As a policewoman involved in political work, I should, more than my male colleagues, pay attention to affected women, and try to encourage the male police officers to take on tasks to help these women."

Work against domestic violence is just starting in China, and there are a lot of gaps and inadequacies. There is need to draw the attention of the public and the government to this issue.

China

Shuhua Huang

After Huang Shuhua's daughter Huang Jing died under suspicious circumstances in 2003, she was sorrow-stricken and bedridden. Then, she decided to fight back. Attacked and reviled on the one hand and supported on the other, her battle — which used the Internet — had a major impact on women's rights.

Huang Jing, daughter of Huang Shuhua, was found naked and dead on her bed on February 23, 2003. There were bruises on her lower body and private parts. Huang Shuhua could hardly compose herself from sorrow, and found it difficult to believe the conclusion reached by the public security bureau that Huang Jing had died of heart disease. She suspected that her daughter had died from rape by her boyfriend, who had been with her in the hours before her death. Huang Shuhua asked the public security bureau to conduct an autopsy on her daughter. Three autopsy reports were later issued, but with the same conclusion as before. She was not discouraged. Though facing all kinds of pressures and threats, she traveled to Xiangtan, Changsha, Guangzhou, Beijing and Shanghai to seek legal assistance from experts, scholars and the public. The procuratorate put the boyfriend on trial for charge of rape on December 7, 2004.

The death of Huang Jing has drawn increasing attention to the problem of rape along with the reports in the media and the Internet. Huang Shuhua's courage and perseverance have created awareness towards date rape. This is an important contribution to the protection of women's rights and the improvement on China's judiciary system. After receiving support from many people, Huang Shuhua is now trying to help others. Websites that are specially set up for this case have attracted more than 200,000 hits. Under this pressure, the police office has also established its own website to communicate with the public. The Internet, as a new venue for public opinion, has played an important role.

In a traditional patriarchal society, preferential treatment for the male is the order of the day. The survival and human rights for women do not count. Society cares little about such crimes as sexual assault and date rape.

China

A widow's daughter who is herself a widow, Saila Ithayaraj has made it her life's mission to help others in her situation, battling inbred cultural prejudices.

Saila Ithayaraj

Tharaka Center for Widows

A widow's daughter who is herself a widow, Saila Ithayaraj's life changed when she came into contact in 2002 with an organization called Shantiham, which works for the well-being of people living in Sri Lanka's long-ravaged conflict zones. Rising above her own sorrows, she has herself become an activist in a village with 65 widows, and travels around the country to relate her experiences and bond with others like herself.

Saila Ithayaraj (born 1977) is the eldest of four children of a fisherman, and lives in the war-torn Jaffna province in northern Sri Lanka. Her father was killed at sea during shelling in 1987 by the Indian peacekeeping force which intervened in the Sri Lankan civil war. The tragedy interrupted her education beyond class ten, and she married a cousin in 1994 at the age of 17. Tribulation came visiting a second time when her husband, also a fisherman, was arrested by the Sri Lankan navy in 1996 — his body was found a month and half later. By then, Saila had a daughter. As two women with four younger dependents to feed, she and her mother had a hard life. Depressed and frustrated, Saila confined herself to her house for five years. The problems became worse when the family were displaced by intrastate conflicts. In 2002, Saila's life began to change: an organization called Shantiham, which works for the psychosocial well-being of people in Sri Lanka's conflict zones, began to work with 65 widows in her village. They were formed into a group; Saila became its president.

Saila has now been an activist for over three years, working mainly on the empowerment of widows, and village development through infrastructure and education. Her group, Tharaka, has raised funds to build houses and wells for villagers, not only for the families of widows, but also those of the other underprivileged. It managed to return to school all the children who had dropped out due to the internecine conflict, and arranged private classes at its center for the village students. Saila also networks with women from other parts of Sri Lanka who are in a similar situation.

Knowing how it felt to be ostracized as a widow, Saila has worked hard to raise the self-esteem of the women, changing cultural prejudices about widowhood.

Widespread widowhood, in the tens of thousands, has been the major fallout of the decade-long internecine war in Sri Lanka, and chauvinism against dispossessed women persists despite revolutionary ideals, on the Tamil side, and developmental government proclamations, on the other.

Sri Lanka

01 05 '05

Daphne Jansen

Network on Violence Against Women
Development Education Leadership Teams in Action (Delta)

Daphne Jansen is a project coordinator for the Network on Violence Against Women in Mitchell's Plain, Cape Town. Born in 1956, Daphne has been involved in bringing change for women in her community, focusing on eradicating violence against women. She is also a motivational speaker. Daphne is a graduate of Development Education Leadership Teams in Action (Delta). She obtained a certificate in adult education and a higher diploma in adult education training and development from the University of the Western Cape, South Africa, where she worked as a part-time tutor.

Daphne Jansen has been volunteering her services as an educator in her community for many years. She is a dynamic woman whose action in development issues has won her many awards. Drawing from general community meetings she established the Network on Violence Against Women in 1996.

Daphne spends minimal amount of time with her family causing some marital problems. But she walks tall and says: "We all have our calling in life. This is my calling and I believe that God will not put me in a difficult situation because of my calling."

She has influenced other women to take up the fight to eradicate violence against women. Women who have attended her workshops are encouraged to become members of the organization.

There now are more women coming out of the closet to talk about their personal experiences of domestic violence. And as more women come out, the need to expand support services for them increases.

The Network faces severe funding shortfalls. They would like to have additional services to counseling, which is what the organization currently offers women suffering domestic abuse. Because domestic violence happens all the time to different women, there is need for more and better response to assist women when they call in for help. Currently, one disadvantage at the Network is that sometimes women have to wait for a while before they can get assistance. This does not augur well for those in need of immediate help.

"Because of funding constraints we do not have an office conducive to the organization's work and our training room cannot accommodate all our clients. In fact we need four more such training rooms," says Daphne.

Meanwhile Daphne and some of the members bear all costs related to the running of the Network.

Hundreds of women in South Africa, particularly in Indian, mixed-race and African communities live their lives believing that it is taboo to speak out about domestic violence. But these days women are learning to claim their rightful positions in the society.

South Africa

Kumari Jayawardena

Social Scientists' Association (SSA)

Kumari Jayawardena (born 1931) stands out in Sri Lanka and beyond for her pioneering activism and scholarship on left and feminist issues, and for the large number of human rights activists and scholars that she has supported, inspired and mentored over several decades. She has been an extraordinary leader at the national level of crucial feminist campaigns, particularly for bringing about a politically negotiated settlement to the civil war that has been raging in Sri Lanka for over two decades.

Kumari is the daughter of a reputed Sinhala scholar and politician, and a British radical. She was born in Colombo and attended Ladies College. She married an economist who was once ambassador for Sri Lanka at Brussels. With a doctorate in political science, Kumari has taught at the University of Colombo and the Institute of Social Sciences at The Hague, and also pioneered research and analyses on the feminist movement. This multilinguist has traveled throughout Sri Lanka to raise the consciousness of women, support strikes and rallies, advise women's groups and share her thoughts and ideas.

Kumari is a remarkable left and feminist scholar, and the author of several books and innumerable articles on labor and feminist movements in Sri Lanka. Her book, "Feminism and Nationalism in the Third World", is regarded as a pathbreaking work on feminism in the south in the 1980s. She writes and teaches feminist history with a special focus on antiracism and women, and has been intimately connected with initiatives for women and peace since the mid 1980s. Kumari initiated some of the first teaching and awareness- raising programs on feminism not just in Sri Lanka but throughout the region. She has also cofounded several feminist journals and magazines, many feminist and civil rights organizations, and has supported, pushed and inspired a formidable array of other causes.

Kumari was also the cofounder of one of the country's leading left research organizations, the Social Scientists' Association, set up to create a space for Sri Lankan academics to work and write on social justice. She began her work by focusing on women laborers and socialist activism, and then moved on to issues such as nationalism and gender.

The feminist movement in Sri Lanka is small but vibrant. It embraces women from all sectors-rural/agricultural, urban/factory workers, academics, students, social activists-and from all ethnic and religious communities. This diversity has enabled feminist activism to survive the ethnic conflict.

Sri Lanka

Kathleen Kapei

Church of Melanesia
Save the Children
Family Support Center

Christian faith and love for local communities triggered Sister Kathleen's work for the welfare of women and children, human rights, social justice, and peace in Solomon Islands.

Prior to the social unrest and ethnic conflict in the late 1990s, women and children already faced discrimination relating to recognition, education, health and other social, economic, and cultural factors. The troubles worsened their situation: children could not go to school, women were raped, and general violence against women and children increased. Family survival became an issue in both the urban and the rural areas. The Sisters Household was located in the no-go (war) zone so for Sister Kathleen to work meant she risked being abused and harassed by both warring parties. But it also meant she could influence both sides, too.

One day, because Sister Kathleen and her party had to work in between the two warring parties, both sides called a ceasefire for that day. On another occasion, Sister Kathleen and a member of the Melanesian Brotherhood were camped in between the two warring parties. That day, members of the Malaita Eagle Force signaled to them that they wanted to discuss something. The member of the Melanesian Brotherhood suggested that Sister Kathleen should go and talk because Solomons' women are respected in culture and peacemaking. When Sister Kathleen arrived, the Malaita Eagle Force asked for permission to fight the other party for five minutes. With courage, Sister Kathleen refused permission. Her order was heard and respected during that day. These are only two examples of Sister Kathleen's many involvements and peace building experiences during the troubles.

Solomon Islands is a patriarchal society where age and sex/gender determine status and power and the success of one's work. Sister Kathleen's pioneering involvement in peace building work was thus open to challenge and danger and often questioned.

Nursyahbani Katjasungkana

Koalisi Perempuan Indonesia
Women's Association for Justice (APIK)
Women's Legal Aid of the Indonesian Women's Association for Justice (LBH APIK)

Nursyahbani Katjasungkana (born 1956) is a feminist lawyer and advocate of women's human rights. In 1995, she founded the Women's Association for Justice (APIK) and established the Women's Legal Aid institution in Jakarta, the members of which were initially recruited from among former clients and survivors and trained as paralegals. During the 1998 reformation, along with several other women activists, Nursyahbani founded the Indonesian Women's Coalition for Justice and Democracy, the first mass-based women's organization in the country since 1965, and was elected its first Secretary General.

When Nursyahbani Katjasungkana began her career as a lawyer and director of Jakarta Women's Legal Aid in 1987, the profession was a male dominated field and expressions like "women's rights", "feminism" and "violence against women" were not part of the language. But early on, the young lawyer was aware of the poor legal status of Indonesian women and women's rights. This led her to found the Women's Association for Justice (APIK) and the Women's Legal Aid of the Indonesian Women's Association for Justice (LBH APIK) in 1995. Nursyahbani believes that through what she calls "transformative legal aid", the law can be reformed to serve the interests of women.

Running a legal aid institution for women, Nursyahbani has learned that a client's dependence on her lawyer is not beneficial to a community and that a community needs to develop its own support system. This is why LBH APIK is founded on the fundamental principle of community-based legal aid, where ex-clients and survivors are trained to be paralegals and are in turn expected to transfer their skills and knowledge to the community. Nursyahbani explains: "LBH APIK uses legal cases as an entry point to see how existing laws serve women. If it is found that the law is not responsive (to the needs of women), then we will carry out policy advocacy to change the law." She adds, "We use these cases as a 'radar' to monitor how the system works." As a feminist lawyer, Nursyahbani recognizes the vital role of the community in the process of legal transformation. She envisions an "alternative legal system that is bottom-up" through community empower-ment. In her vision, "legal reform from the perspective of the people" underlies the transformative legal change that will help achieve women's equality.

To look at women specifically as an oppressed group was viewed by most activists as detrimental to the pro-democracy movement in Indonesia in the mid-1980s. It was within this socio-political context that the awareness of women's oppression and feminist consciousness began to grow in Indonesia.

Mary Kini

Kup Women for Peace
Meri Kirap Sapotim
Welfare Dorcas

Constant tribal fighting in her Papua New Guinea (PNG) village prevented Mary Kini from completing her agricultural studies. Instead, she worked with church, community, and women's groups on trainings for rural development projects. In 2000, Mary was the key person to set up Kup Women for Peace, doing the ground work of awareness raising and mobilization of people on the dangers of tribal fights, and organizing the activities developed by Kup Women for Peace as a result of a community commitment to say "No to tribal fights" and general lawlessness in PNG.

Mary Kini campaigns against tribal fights and "pay-back" attacks in Papua New Guinea. An uncle who did not have any girl children adopted her so she is now displaced from her home village in Kup and lives with her family in her uncle's land. All village children were raised to know who their tribe's traditional enemies were, taught how to behave, what to do during ceremonial gatherings and especially during tribal fights. Mary, one of few girls in her region to be sent to school, was in sixth grade when her adoptive father was killed in a tribal fight. Her natural father risked his own life crossing enemy lines to bring his brother's body home. He came home in pieces. Mary never forgot the sight of the pieces being lined up by her father for proper burial. A few years later, her father died in tribal fights and, as years went by, other close relatives were killed in tribal fights. Women from rival tribal groups, even sisters, married into enemy clans and though innocent, they bore the brunt of the sufferings. In 1999, Mary and her very young children had to run for their lives from a new kind of tribal fight: people were now being killed with high powered guns, anything that moved was attacked, and all their property — houses, gardens, trees, were set on fire. In a women's solidarity gathering in 2000, three women involved in the 1999 fight hugged and wept in a display of the pain all the women felt. Mary and a friend were moved to set up Kup Women for Peace. Mary puts such passion into building peace, even walking into the battlefield to stop fighting, unheard of for a Highlands woman, and walking in mountains and valleys in hard weather with no resources, because: "I am a victim of our very bad custom — tribal fights and lawlessness. It must stop. I do not want to see my children run as I have been running in the past 35 years of my life."

In Kup, an area in Kerowagi, Chimbu Province, there's been years and years of tribal fighting. Schools were closed down, government services withdrawn. The three goals of Kup Women for Peace are: Stop tribal fighting and ensure respect for law and order. Protect women's rights and increase women's role in decision-making. Promote sustainable livelihoods.

Papua New Guinea

Veronica Wanjiru Kinyanjui

Kangemi Women Empowerment Center
Kenya Human Rights Commission (Khrc)
Federation of Women Lawyers in Kenya (Fida)

Veronica Wanjiru Kinyanjui (43) is a trained counselor working in Nairobi, the Kenyan capital. Since 2003, she has worked on a voluntary basis as the acting project coordinator of the Kangemi Women Empowerment Center, a community-based organization. Kangemi is a poor, neglected and congested neighborhood in Nairobi with an unidentified number of inhabitants from different ethnic backgrounds. The center, which was founded in 1997, runs programs for health, economic empowerment, human rights, youth and children and community organization.

"Mummy, why do you not look for a real job?" the 19-year-old boy repeatedly asks his mother. Veronica Kinyanjui just laughs about her son's concern. "God will give me a job one day," she replies. For two years now, she has been running the Kangemi Women Empowerment Center in Kangemi without pay. "We do not have funds," she says, then adds, "but I want to do community work." Born into a well-off family in Kangemi, she lives in one of her father's houses and earns a little income from the rent of other houses. As a young woman, she was sexually abused, and only two years ago did she go public about her ordeal in a magazine interview. "I felt relieved after that. I want all abused and battered women in Kangemi to feel this relief too. "Kangemi Women — as Veronica Kinyanjui refers to her Center — runs programs for health, economic empowerment, human rights, youth and children and community organization. Once a week free medical attention is available and free legal advise is offered by a lawyer from the Kenya Human Rights Commission. The center does not only want to empower women. Veronica Kinyanjui estimates that up to 10,000 people in 60 self-help groups are supported — directly and indirectly — by the center. "My happiness is to see this office is open everyday. When I am not in the office I miss it," she reflects. Intervening against drug abuse, rape and family violence is Veronica Kinyanjui's daily concern. "I pray a lot to be able to do this job," says the God-fearing woman. "I think God wants me here." Then the well-composed, almost reserved woman becomes passionate, "I was born an activist. I want to fight for the rights of people."

Approximately ten percent, or three million, of Kenya's population lives in the capital, Nairobi. Most of them live in congested and poor areas with inadequate water and power supply, in poor health care and surrounded by high crime rates. More than half of all Kenyans live below the poverty line.

Kenya

Le Thi Quy

Center for Gender and Development Research, Hanoi University

Le Thi Quy, born in 1950 in Hanoi, is a sociologist and Director of the Center for Gender and Development Research, Hanoi University. After graduating from the History Department of Hanoi University, she earned her PhD in Russia, did pioneering research on issues related to families and women, and she is the first Vietnamese lecturer on gender issues in Vietnam. Government has used her research to develop social policies. She founded "returned women" — groups that have helped 53 women victims of trafficking overcome practical difficulties and integrate into the community.

Researching gender issues, particularly prostitution, domestic violence and women-trafficking, Le Thi Quy realized that these are urgent social problems rooted in poverty and domestic violence, which government and society should look at more realistically. It distresses her that punishment is imposed on prostitutes, while no action is taken against sex-buyers. She has therefore worked to direct the public's attention to the difficulties that these unfortunate women undergo, and to change the public's negative attitude towards them. Her goal is to create a better society, where women do not become victims of prostitution, human-trafficking and domestic violence.

Among her allies in this struggle for the emancipation of women in Vietnam are sociologists and agencies such as the Commission for Social Affairs of the National Assembly of Vietnam, Vietnam Women's Union and the National Committee for the Advancement of Women. The government has since put the results of her research on women and domestic violence in Vietnam into practice. Le Thi Quy has written five books and co-authored 32 others on prostitution, domestic violence and women-trafficking that have attracted the attention of both Vietnamese and foreign readers. She says, "I have worked very hard, but I am happy and satisfied with my job because my work is very useful to many women. As a sociologist, I am happy that my research results have been put into practice."

Prostitution and women-trafficking are urgent social problems in Vietnam, rooted in poverty and domestic violence. The government and society should look at these problems more realistically. Not only punishment of the prostitutes but also action against sex-buyers is important.

Viet Nam

Ngun Fung Liu

Hong Kong Association for the Survivors of Women Abuse (Kwan Fook)

Liu Ngun Fung, born in 1949, is chairlady of the Hong Kong Association for the Survivors of Women Abuse (Kwan Fook), which advocates self/mutual-assistance. Having liberated herself from her husband's violence, Liu provides services to the women in need as a counter to the patriarchal contempt of the female body and autonomy. She demands an improvement of various social policies, including those on welfare, housing and medicine, so as to build a better environment for the abused women and their children.

Kwan Fook was established as an independent NGO in 1997. Its aim is to bring together abused women to help each other so that they can gain support from each other to begin a new life.

The population policy effective on 1 January 2004 bars new immigrants from China from receiving benefits and housing assistance from the government in their first seven years of stay in Hong Kong. This unfavorable policy pushes many abused new immigrants into staying with their abusers.

Liu is trying hard to plead a modification to this sexually/racially discriminatory policy in order to avoid new immigrant women becoming double victims. In 2004, a family tragedy happened in Hong Kong. The involved social worker and sanctuary, and the police shirked their responsibilities; Liu and her teammates did all they could to expose the truth, forcing the police to admit their mistakes and the cover-up. The police paid her back with a warning letter, saying the mourning activities she arranged for the victims were characterized as public procession and hence violated the public order ordinance. But, Liu did not panic; she advised people not to be afraid for she believes social justice will not be deferred by patriarchal or police power. Liu demands an improvement in social policies, including those on welfare, housing and medicine, so as to build a better environment for the abused women and their children, helping them to begin a new life.

Hong Kong is still a male-dominant society and women abuse is common. With tighter government budgets and the family being held up as an ideal, abused women are forced to accept their plight. Without support from the government, the police, society or the family, it is hard to escape the violence.

China, Hong Kong SAR

Sihai Long

Long Sihai works in the Bureau of Justice in Yunnan province. Her work on advocacy of legal rights led her to set up a support center for women and children of ethnic minorities — particularly those who are abducted or suffering from Aids in southwest China. Long Sihai also organizes touring programs aimed at working to prevent abduction. These involve not only the support center, but also the Bureau of Justice, education departments, the Office of Legal Advocacy, provincial television stations, and arts troupes of the Dai national minority.

Long Sihai has long been working for the advocacy of legal rights. During her extensive work experience and social participation, she noticed that women and children from ethnic minorities in remote areas were always disadvantaged in terms of resources. This is not only the case in traditional societies, but also in modern ones. After she graduated in 1983, Long Sihai was assigned to work in the Bureau of Justice. She chose to follow in her parents' footsteps when she took up law as a profession. Her career direction, however, took a different turn because of the suicide of her younger sister, and there was a shift in emphasis towards public education to foster individual rights and protection.

In 1998 there was a case of a girl from the minority Dai community being raped by her step-father over a five-year period. Neighbors and relatives of the victim, including her mother and grandparents, were aware of what was happening, but no one had filed a report. This was one of the reasons that led to Long to establish a support center to provide such substantial services as legal consultation, and professional assistance in areas of psychology, social service and health. Given the increasing numbers of cases of abduction of ethnic minority women and children, the center became very important and the programs it ran very popular. The center is currently working with the local Bulang community to set up a support unit. A review of collaborative efforts between various departments has also been undertaken.

In southwest China, especially among the national minorities, the abduction of women for trafficking and the incidence of them contracting Aids is widespread. It is therefore necessary to coordinate various departments to provide support services, and in particular, to implement preventive measures.

China

Hadayai Majeed

Baitul Salaam Network, Inc.

Hadayai Majeed's vision is both simple and huge: give Muslim women the tools to change their climate by changing themselves. A member of a religion that is focused on service, Hadayai was called to reach out to her sisters, and in 1997 she founded Baitul Salaam Network, Inc. to help victims of domestic abuse. The goal of the network is to end silence about domestic violence and to help abused Muslim women and children with shelter, food, and clothing. The organization also teaches strategies for self-sufficiency: how to be confident in speech, mannerisms, and body language.

Hadayai Majeed's marriage was one of neglect and denigration. But when she sought intervention, counsel, encouragement, and financial assistance from Muslim families and friends, she was told she was at fault. The policy of the community's one shelter was to tell abused women to be quiet and to "move on". Instead, Hadayai saw a need and she moved to fill it. Although her mother was a social worker, Hadayai had avoided following in her footsteps, observing its personal demands. But in 1997, she responded to the call of her faith and founded Baitul Salaam. The vision of Baitul Salaam is to provide a community in which women are self-empowered through their spiritual beliefs and which respects the rights and liberties of every person.

Baitul Salaam Network operates at local, state, and national levels: requests for help are frequent. Locally, the network focuses on providing shelter as well as training in prevention and intervention. Information about the program is widely disseminated on bulletin boards in mosques, Islamic centers, and on the Internet. Hadayai is a frequent presenter at her mosque in Atlanta and at national conferences and women's gatherings. She is a recognized resource concerning abused and neglected Muslim women and children for social workers, mental health professionals, and abuse victims' advocates throughout the state of Georgia.

Hadayai has been challenged by lack of cooperation from some Muslim leaders, who interpret her work as "rebellious". Nevertheless, her group has succeeded in making domestic violence awareness a focus of national conferences, and some local leaders now give khutbahs (Friday prayer lectures) to raise awareness about the issue. The network and its leaders have received formal recognition from several Muslim organizations and from the state of Georgia.

Any association with feminism is alienating in Muslim cultural circles and Hadayai's group lost funding and cofounders because of a perceived affiliation. Sisters who feared loss of status among men would not embrace the cause and in some cases were used as pawns to fight against the effort.

United States of America

Khawar Mumtaz

Shirkat Gah Women's Resource Center

The work of activist and writer Khawar Mumtaz (born 1945) over more than two decades has helped to place women's rights on the agenda of government, political parties, and religious parties in Pakistan. The 33 percent reservation of seats for women in local government, and in provincial and national parliaments, was achieved through the collective action of Khawar and other women activists. Her visible activism continues to inspire many others to fight for women's rights.

Khawar Mumtaz raised her voice against injustice and discrimination, even though it meant giving up her job as a university lecturer. When the university questioned her involvement in street protests against Pakistan's military regime in the 1980s, she quit. Civil society in Pakistan has been enriched by her decision: Khawar coauthored the definitive book on Pakistani women's struggle for their rights, becoming one of the country's most prominent activists.

This great-niece of Ismat Chughtai, a leading Indian writer and feminist, became involved with the left movement in Pakistan in the 1970s. In the 1980s, she joined other Pakistani women in their struggle against the antiwomen laws of the military regime. She was arrested at a rally against the proposed Law of Evidence in 1983. Giving up her job the same year, Khawar spent two years writing Women in Pakistan: Two Steps Forward, One Step Back? with her friend, the sociologist und women's rights activist, Farida Shaheed. The book documents the path of the Muslim women's movement from the 20th century fin de siecle to contemporary times, and received the Prime Minister's Award in 1989.

Khawar joined the Shirkat Gah Women's Resource Center in 1985, later becoming a fulltime coordinator. She worked without pay for years to establish the organization and consolidate its financial base. Over the previous decade, Khawar has increasingly focused on reproductive rights, health, poverty and environmental issues, especially those relating to women. She is respected in Pakistan as someone whose working style is inclusive and interactive. Khawar is a team player. As coordinator of the NGO forum, which has more than 2500 members, she has been a model of participatory decision-making. Thanks to her leadership, this forum, comprised of diverse interest groups and members, has remained cohesive and relevant.

Civil society in Pakistan, traditionally zealously male-centric, is active today with a modicum of gender equity because of the likes of Khawar Mumtaz. In the 1980s, she joined other Pakistani women in their struggle against the antiwomen laws of the military regime.

Pakistan

Anne Firth Murray

Global Fund for Women

In 1987, Anne Firth Murray saw a need and had an idea. The world needed an organization that would link caring donors with activist women around the world, dedicated to ensuring human rights for women. Her driving belief was that when women were empowered to address violence and injustice at a local level there would be an international impact. Today, the Global Fund for Women has become the largest foundation in the world focused exclusively on women and girls, granting more than $35 million to approximately 2500 women's groups in 180 countries.

Eighteen years ago, the inspiration for Anne's idea came when she was in Nigeria, evaluating some donors' work with family planning clinics. When three women told her they would like to talk with her about an idea, she met with them late into the night. The women were looking for a small grant to fund an organization that would help street-women address the issue of violence and women's access to paid employment. Thus began Anne's idea of a global fund that would foster indigenous philanthropy by awarding grants to women's rights organizations, which in turn would provide small grants to local women's groups. In the process, the women would develop skills in grant making, reach new groups, and cultivate local traditions of giving.

Anne, a consulting professor in human biology at Stanford University, has made developing the Global Fund for Women her life's work. She has pushed the boundaries of traditional grant making by giving resources to women's groups that would not ordinarily qualify for attention from traditional foundations that have their own agendas. Funding has empowered groups that seek to eliminate the trafficking and slavery of women and girls, advance health and sexual and reproductive rights, expand civic and political participation, ensure economic and environmental justice, increase access to education, advance peace, and end gender-based violence. What began as Anne's vision to get money into the hands of women so that their voices would be heard and their choices respected has grown into a movement that has strengthened marginalized groups and increased their influence on the larger society.

Anne: "Being born a woman is a health hazard." Sex-selective abortion and female infanticide persist; girls suffer more malnutrition than boys; 50,000 women die each year from childbirth and pregnancy-related illnesses; and more than 30 percent of women suffer violence from an intimate partner.

United States of America

Vijayakumary Murugiah

Suriya

Vijayakumary Murugiah has witnessed and endured a series of violent acts since she was a child. But rather than being consumed by her own trauma, or running away from violence to seek a separate peace, Vijayakumary has devoted herself to helping women victims of violence. She has been doing this for over a decade, at considerable risk to her own life. But the frustrations of her work have not defeated her — she constantly pushes against the boundaries of what can be done to stop the rampant violence against women.

One of seven children of a paddy laborer, Vijayakumary Murugiah grew up in the village Varani, 19 miles from Jaffna town in Sri Lanka's conflict-torn Northern Province. As a child, she saw harsh poverty and endured her father's violent alcoholism. This class X dropout's life changed in 1989 when she decided to join Poorani, a safehouse and vocational training group for women. It exposed her to a group of women bent on changing women's status. Unfortunately, political pressure forced Poorani to close down in 1991.

Some Poorani women and feminists from Sri Lanka's south and east formed Suriya in Colombo; in 1992, Vijayakumary joined them, working for displaced women and families from the east and the north. In 1994, when the displaced from the east returned to Batticaloa, Suriya relocated, and so did Vijayakumary a year later. From 1999, she focused on violence against women, dealing with cases of rape — including gang rape — by the military, religious fundamentalists and civilians, and incest, harassment and domestic violence. Collecting and documenting data, Vijayakumary interviews women, counsels and mobilizes them, and provides them with support and information about their rights. She organizes social campaigns, works for advocacy with the relevant officials, and initiates legal actions — 600 so far. District officials and NGOs today recognize that domestic violence and other forms of violation of women's rights are a serious problem. Police are quicker to take action as more women come forward to protest the violations.

A Tamil from Sri Lanka's embattled north, Vijayakumary lives with discrimination. She encountered problems when she moved to the south and the east, was arrested twice by the Sri Lankan army, and put in detention for 12 days in Colombo and a day in Batticaloa. But the intimidation has not worked.

Sri Lanka's north and east have been ravaged by 20 years of internecine combat. Violence against women has worsened with displacement, disap-pear-ances and death, and due to the omnipotent military. Domestic violence, incest, and rape by government forces, armed groups and civilians are rampant.

Sri Lanka

"The methodology of active public education, with a deep understanding and respect for Shona and Ndebele cultures, has benefited the program."

Netsai Mushonga

Fellowship of Reconciliation Zimbabwe (For/z)

Netsai Mushonga was born in 1969 in Bindura, Zimbabwe. She is a media coordinator of Women's Coalition and a member of the International Committee of International Fellowship. In 1995, Netsai worked as a social worker for Danhiko, an NGO providing education and job training for young people with disabilities. In 1996, Netsai joined the Fellowship of Reconciliation in Zimbabwe, and in 1997 she started the women peacemakers program of For/z. She secured funding to raise awareness within churches on the need to confront gender violence.

Netsai was born in rural Zimbabwe, the fourth in a family of eight children. She graduated from the University of Zimbabwe with BA in sociology. After she had started the women peacemakers program of For/z in 1997, she secured funding to raise awareness within churches on the need to confront gender violence. Beginning in 2000, she volunteered as an election monitor and supervisor, despite the risk of physical violence and political intimidation. She joined the Women's Coalition in 2003 and developed a program to respond to politically motivated sexual violence against women and girls in Zimbabwe. With her good organization skills she run a regional consultation conference of African women in conflict situations. She has organized and conducted many training workshops in Zimbabwe and within and outside Africa focusing on gender and violence.

Her fearless speaking out about the deteriorating political conditions and lack of security for women in Zimbabwe has inspired others. Victims of sexual violence have benefited from her work in concrete ways. The Danhiko project has an emergency shelter to accommodate women victims of violence. Its programs include counseling, economic and emotional support.

Netsai says, "I have benefited more from the work I do than the women I have come across, because they have taught me survival skills in dignity." This is a modest statement typical of her.

The hopes for a free and self-reliant Zimbabwe have been dashed. The political situation has deteriorated rapidly since independence. Politically motivated sexual violence is increasing. The economic situation has deteriorated too, resulting in food and petrol shortages and long waits in queues.

Zimbabwe

Oung Chanthol

Cambodian Women's Crisis Center (CWCC)

Oung Chanthol (born 1967), was cofounder of the Cambodian Women's Crisis Center (CWCC) in 1997 and is its current executive director. The CWCC has helped over 55,600 female victims of violence, rape and trafficking in its drop-in centers and shelters. It provides legal counseling, victims' reintegration, community awareness programs, and raises general public awareness through a media campaign. The center receives financial support from the German government and international NGOs.

With her educational and social background, Oung Chanthol could have chosen to work with any government agency or international organization. But she chose to help the many Cambodian women who are victims of trafficking, domestic violence and sexual abuse. With her colleagues in NGOs, Chanthol cofounded CWCC, but did not realize that the task ahead would be so arduous. Within a week, they were overloaded with cases that needed urgent attention. "We intended to provide a shelter for about 20 women per day. In just one week, it was full. From word of mouth, hundreds of women came," recalls Chanthol. "We could not just turn these women away." With 71 full-time staff and over 300 village volunteers, the CWCC provides integrated intervention services to the victims. These services include monitoring gender-based violence and rescuing victims, provision of shelter to victims, counseling, empowering women through skills training, scholarships to prevent trafficking, legal assistance, and reintegration of victims into the community.

An average of 1800 seek the services of the center every year. "The suffering of women encourages us to work. There are many cases and we felt that something needed to be done to help the injured women," she declares. Chanthol assisted the United Nations Center for Human Rights in Cambodia where she monitored the freedom of the press, labor rights and land rights, investigating and preparing reports on abuses by the state. She also helped establish dialogue between government, human rights organizations, journalist associations, labor unions and employer associations. Chanthol received the Ramon Magsaysay Award for emergent leadership in 2000 and the Japan Human Rights award in 2001.

After decades of internal war, the culture of violence persists in war-torn Cambodia. Domestic violence is prevalent, rape cases are rampant, and ever-larger numbers of women and children have been reported as being trafficked into the sex industry and other forms of forced labor.

"I look with pride
at the Afghan women's
participation in the
Presidential elections.
This is an indication that
our decades-long
efforts have not been
brought to naught."

Suraya Parlika

Democratic Women's Organization (DWO)
All Afghan Women Union (AAWU)

Suraya Parlika was born in Kamari Village of Bagrami District in 1944 to an educated family. She completed her secondary education in 1962 at Zarghona High School. In 1963, Suraya was full of fervor for academic education, and in 1966 she obtained a BSc from the Faculty of Economics, Kabul University. In 1973, she went to Kiev, the Republic of Ukraine, to pursue her postgraduate studies, and in 1977 she obtained her Masters Degree in Economics and Bilateral Relationship. Suraya Parlika returned to Afghanistan and secured a teaching post in the Foreign Relations Department at Kabul University.

Witnessing the injustice and the degraded status of women in Afghan society, Suraya Parlika was inspired to motivate a group of dedicated women and found the Democratic Women's Organization (DWO). Along with the DWO members, Parlika started to mobilize women to take part in the parliamentary election. She also took an active role against a proposal of some of the parliament members who wanted to ban girls and women from traveling abroad to receive education.

At present, Parlika's network extends nationwide and she acts as president of the All Afghan Women Union (AAWU). This organization represents women of all sectors. The relative stability and women's involvement in social work in Afghanistan, make her optimistic about the future of women. She looks with pride and joy at the incorporation of an article that codifies the equal rights of men and women in the Afghan Constitution. Parlika is also delighted by the participation of Afghan women in the Presidential elections, a step that for a long time she has encouraged women to take.

Suraya Parlika is very active in advocating human rights and women's rights as well as education and vocational training for women. Empowering women is a life-long goal that she has been dedicated to for decades.

Afghanistan

Mary Soledad Perpiñan

Third World Movement Against the Exploitation of Women (TW-MAE-W)
Asia Pacific Peace Research Association (Appra)
International Peace Research Association (Ipra)

Sister Mary Soledad Perpiñan (born 1937) is a Good Shepherd nun who has worked for the rights of abused women and children, Aids victims, exploited laborers, indigenous peoples and other marginalized groups for more than 30 years. Working mainly with exploited and abused women and children in urban communities, she founded the Third World Movement Against the Exploitation of Women (TW-MAE-W) on December 10, 1980. After 25 years, TW-MAE-W has seven drop-in centers and four growth homes nationwide, helping abused women and children reconstruct their lives to become springs of hope in society.

Mary Soledad Perpiñan is a Good Shepherd Sister by vocation, an educator and writer by profession and a social activist by conviction. For over three decades, she has worked on trafficking and violence against women (providing direct services for affected women and children), women and peace, gender and development, ecofeminism and spirituality. A graduate of Journalism and Humanities, Sister Sol has undertaken commissioned research for the United Nations (UN) and has presented papers in international fora, putting forward the Third World feminist perspective on peace, development, environment, equality and spirituality.

Mary Soledad Perpiñan has edited several publications, including the Philippine Report for the UN Fourth World Conference on Women, has served as an expert for UN bodies on women's issues, and participated in most of the major UN world conferences in the 1980s and 1990s. Sister Sol's most visible initiative is the Third World Movement Against the Exploitation of Women (TW-MAE-W), an NGO that takes care of exploited and abused women and children in urban communities in the Philippines. In 1987, she started TW-MAE-W direct services with drop-in centers in areas known for sex tourism, military and ship prostitution, "development" prostitution, street prostitution, and slum prostitution. Between 1990 and 2002, TW-MAE-W established renewal and training centers, hostels for growth home graduates involved in alternative jobs, and a home for HIV positive women and children suffering from Aids. Apart from being President and CEO of TW-MAE-W, Sister Sol is Secretary General of the Asia-Pacific Peace Research Association (Appra) and a Council Member of the International Peace Research Association (Ipra). In 2000, Sister Sol was one of the women activists of the 20th century cited in the "Roll of Honor" of the United Nations General Assembly.

Abused women and children, persons with Aids and their families, exploited laborers and indigenous peoples need advocates to speak up and work for their rights. Sister Sol uses her knowledge and skills in writing, research, alliance and capacity building to help the marginalized.

Philippines

Maria Manuela Perreira

Fokupers

At age 18, Maria Manuela Perreira decided not to flee with her family to Portugal because she felt her life and commitment lay in East Timor. Since then, she has unwaveringly committed to the principles of equity, justice, and peace in a country that has experienced decades of oppression, conflict, and destruction. In a new era of independence and reconstruction, Maria Manuela shows outstanding vision and compassion as the director of a women's organization that works tirelessly for the social, economic, and political rights of women against a backdrop of patriarchy and immense poverty.

The second eldest of 11 children, Maria Manuela Perreira decided not to go with her family to Portugal in 1986 when they were fleeing from life in Indonesian-occupied East Timor. She felt her life and responsibility lay in Timor. She returned to Timor after studies in Yogyakarta and worked as a trainer at Bia Hula NGO, training communities in water and sanitation. She enjoyed the work principles of community consultation and providing communities with the means to help themselves.

Maria Manuela has always been opposed to the strictures of Timorese cultural and traditional expectations, particularly regarding women's status, relationships and the acceptable paths for women to take in life. In 1998, she began working as a volunteer at Fokupers, the newly established women's organization, and spent much time in the women's shelters, talking to female victims of domestic violence and becoming a proxy counselor to them.

In 1999, much of Fokupers' work was destroyed and Maria became part of the team rebuilding the organization. She took on the roles of treasurer and office manager. A year later, Maria was elected as the new director of Fokupers and remains until now a respected mentor and leader to staff and clients alike. Her work has inspired the NGO community in East Timor, and the Action Men against Violence (AMKV), and facilitated men's acceptance of gender equality in society. Her work has also gained support for pending domestic violence legislation, strengthened the role of women in the community, and has introduced a model of women's shelters (Uma Feto) that the new government can adopt. Maria Manuela is passionate about empowering women at the grassroots level so that they have the skills and confidence to be actively engaged in the development of their own villages and instigate sustainable social change.

When Manuela began to work on women's issues in East Timor, the country was under Indonesian occupation. Women faced multiple discrimination — from Timorese patriarchy, from the Indonesian administration, from occupying forces. Changing this status quo is a challenge for independent Timor-Leste.

Timor-Leste

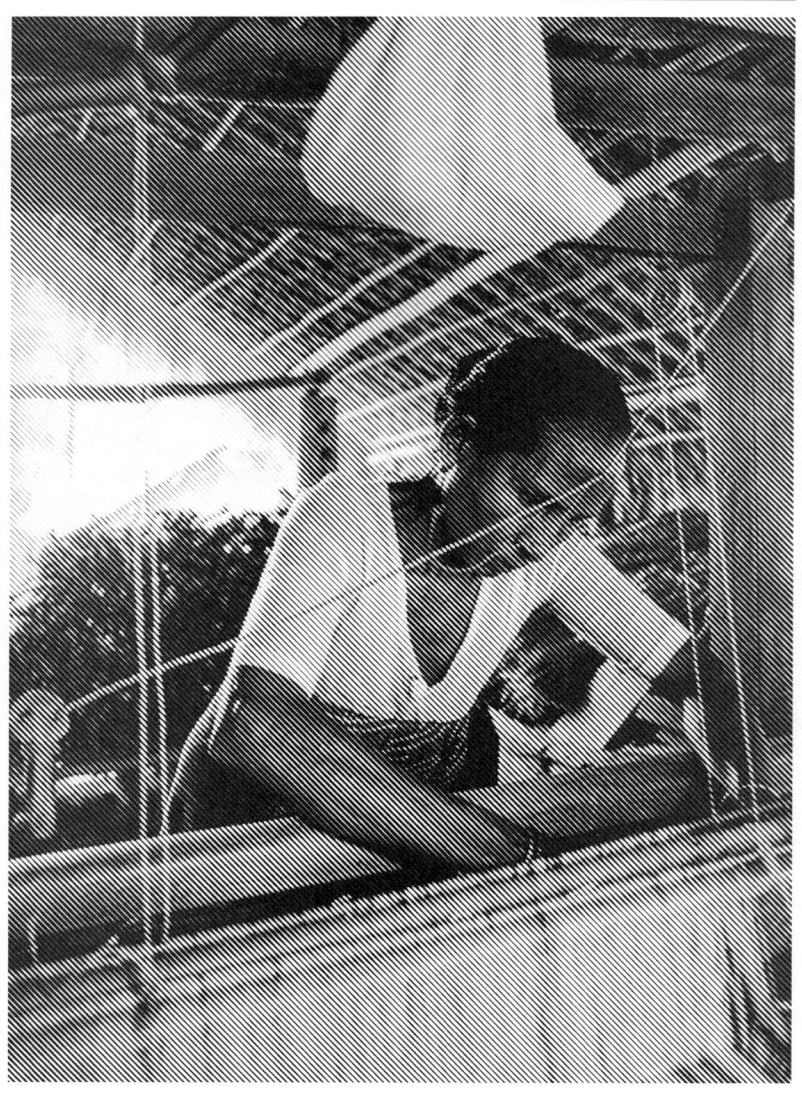

Biro Bala Rava

Borjhara Tobarani Mahila Samata Sangha

The story of Biro Bala Rava (born 1959) reads like an inspirational, if medieval, battle between good and evil: Biro lives in a remote, backward village in Assam, where she has been fighting to save women condemned to death as "witches". She then moved on to other equally vitiating issues that affect the lives of those around her, showing exceptional courage in the face of personal danger and isolation by family and community, and perseverance in fighting against the custom that demonizes women. And she is winning.

The first foray of Biro Bala Rava into working with her community's women was her confrontation with the custom of identifying dainy (witches), trying them in the patriarchal panchayat (village council), and sentencing them to death. She campaigned strongly against the dainy system-citing the incident where an ojha (exorcist) had declared that her mentally disturbed son would die because he was married to a fairy-in close collaboration with the Assam Mahila Samata Society. The fight was long and hard, but eventually she managed to convince more and more women that they were victims of vested-interest superstition. In 2001, the community took a collective decision not to torture or kill women "witches". This process also led to her working with other women in her village to confront problems such as alcohol and environmental issues-even, for instance, that they needed to construct a hut in which to conduct the activities of the women's group: Borjhara Tobarani Mahila Samata Sangha. Today, liquor is history, and for each tree felled, a hard-nosed fine is levied. Biro also motivated the community about the advantages of education.

Biro's perseverance has inspired neighboring villages as well, where the women have also formed sanghas (congregations). There has been a considerable drop in the number of dainy deaths in the area. Many neighboring villages have stopped selling country liquor. They also protest against police or army atrocities, and come forward to participate in community development works.

Biro is an extraordinary woman-fighting medieval battles with modern weaponry, an inspiration to others more literate than herself.

The new millennium has seen an increase in hunting "witches" in India. Black magic has little to do with it-inheritance and superstition do. The victims are often women from Dalit or tribal communities: killing them is a tradition-sanctioned way of stripping them of property and ideology.

India

Majida Rizvi

National Commission for the Status of Women in Pakistan

Majida Rizvi (born 1937) has the unique honor of having been the first woman to serve as a judge in a high court in Pakistan. A tireless campaigner for women's legal rights for the past three-and-a-half decades, Majida is a role model for young women lawyers. In her current position as chairperson of the National Commission for the Status of Women in Pakistan, she has worked hard to educate politicians, other opinion-makers, and the public about the urgent need to reform a slew of laws that discriminate against women.

When Majida Rizvi's family finally relented, the law and political science graduate from Karachi became a lawyer in the 1960s, a time when women lawyers were rare. Majida remembered the day a client was openly skeptical. "What will this girl do?" he asked one of her seniors. When the client's case was brought to court, the senior lawyer was busy, so Majida handled it — and won. The client apologized. Such experiences helped make Majida a campaigner for gender equality. Appointed a judge of the Sindh High Court in 1994, she delivered landmark judgments that upheld the rights of women against discriminatory state practices, which were in contravention of the Constitution. As chairperson since March 2002 of the National Commission for the Status of Women in Pakistan, a government organization, Majida has traveled throughout the country collecting data on laws that discriminate against women. She has also held seminars and workshops to dialogue with different groups on the subject.

Majida's contention is that Islam confers rights on women that are denied to them by laws currently in force in Pakistan. Her greatest achievement has been to help bring the debate on these issues to the forefront of national life. Parliament has placed them on its agenda, and the president and prime minister have been obliged to ask for further study and research.

Majida has sometimes clashed with the religious establishment, which has stood against the repeal of laws like the Hudood Ordinance introduced in the name of Islam by the 1980s martial law regime. Religious groups opposed to Majida's arguments have been doing their own "negative research" on this subject. Even though her security has sometimes been under threat, it has left her unfazed.

Pakistan's long history of intractable patriarchy has enshrined laws that discriminate against women, such as the Law of Evidence, which makes evidence given by four women equivalent to that given by a single man, and the 1980s Hudood Ordinance.

Pakistan

Irene Rodriguez

Minka alter Latina
Infoladen Kasama
Women's Information Center (FIZ)

Irene Rodriguez was born into a large poor family in Argentina. Her life was filled with rape, brute force, pain, and misery. With only three years of school, Irene soon became a victim of prostitution and slave trade. With unbelievable toughness she managed to survive, to actually free herself, and legalize her existence in Switzerland. She is now a source of power for those who are in the hands of prostitution and slave trade, a tireless fighter for those who are willing to get out. Irene Rodriguez fights for the basic rights of illegal migrants, a voice for those who have none.

Irene Rodriguez never gets tired of opening up new possibilities of a better life to illegal women in Switzerland. She has set up her own radio program to reach as many listeners as possible. She participates in demonstrations against every abuse of basic human rights. Every voice that reaches her finds understanding, shelter, and practical help. Irene is the guardian angel for battered souls. She knows what it is like. She has been there herself. Battered and abused in body and soul as a child, a victim of prostitution and slave trade, escaping more than once only to become ensnared another time, she finally managed to escape and free herself.

Now, she works to free other women victims of violence and forced prostitution and to help illegal domestic workers. She shares her experience with others not so fortunate and helps them solve their problems even if it puts herself back into dangerous situations. Indefatigable, Irene travels through Europe to arrange escapes, rescues, salvation for women in desperate situations. The basic problem is always the same: illegal status, no knowledge of personal rights, no self-esteem, and no light at the end of the tunnel. Quite a few can look back today owing their new freedom to Irene's intervention. She herself is one example of women's efficiency: finally legal in Switzerland, finally with a voice, working as journalist in a radio station in a program for Latinas, finally free to make her own decisions. She now dedicates her life to those who seek her presence, sometimes just to talk about their problems but more often to beg for help. Each second of her life is dedicated to the fight against violence against women, to better the situation of illegal housemaids, to bring an end to the women slave trade.

Each year, millions of individuals, mostly women and children, are tricked, sold, coerced or otherwise forced into situations of exploitation from which they cannot escape. They are commodities in a multi-billion dollar global industry dominated by highly organized criminal groups.

Switzerland

"Alternatives to FGM should not break traditions. If somebody came and said that the tradition needs to be stopped, it would not work. Our goal is to continue the tradition without mutilation."

Rhoda Chepkobus Rotino

World Vision

Rhoda Rotino (42) is a trained teacher from West Pokot in Kenya. She is currently engaged as an area development program leader by World Vision Kenya in her home district. For years she has campaigned against female genital mutilation (FGM) and early marriage of girls. She insists on the rights of girls to go to school. Based on her own experience, she has helped introduce an alternative right of passage to adulthood for girls. She works tirelessly on training and awareness creation against FGM among the Pokot community.

She has been roundly condemned and criticized as a traitor of the community. However, her passion and determination to fight for the rights of women and girls still burns. In an area where female genital mutilation (FGM) is rampant and considered a right of passage for all girls, it takes more than courage to stand up against it. That is the step Rhoda Rotino has taken in Pokot District in Kenya.

FGM and early marriages violate the rights of girls and keeps them out of school. Many die as a result of the circumcision or later while giving birth because their bodies are not mature to have children. Rhoda's engagement and her fight for the women and girls started as a volunteer in her own community where she rescued girls from FGM. Although FGM is illegal in Kenya, it continues to be carried out by many communities. "As one of the few girls in my community to be educated, I was enlightened and informed about my rights," says the mother of two boys and three girls.

Thanks to her efforts, more than a thousand girls have gone through alternative rights of passage. Rhoda says these rights instead "circumcise" the mind to adulthood and the girls can continue with education. More than ten circumcisers have been assisted to find alternative sources of income. Thousands of people in the area have received information on FGM and the awareness is increasing.

FGM is practiced in at least 28 countries in Africa. An estimated two million girls annually fall victim to the harmful tradition. Genital cutting, ongoing because of poverty and illiteracy, is entrenched in Kenya where in some communities about 50 percent of the women are mutilated.

Kenya

Alzira Rufino

Casa de Cultura da Mulher Negra (CCMN)

Alzira Rufino (1950) is the founder and director of the House of Culture of the Afro-Brazilian Woman (CCMN), which has its headquarters in the city of Santos, in the State of São Paulo. Her life and her social work are references for the feminists and for the Afro-Brazilian female organizations. In 1992, she received the title of 'Honorable Citizen of the city of Santos.'

Alzira Rufino was born in a tenement. Besides economic poverty, she lived with domestic violence. Her feminism was also born inside her house: "My father and my brother wanted to boss me around. Negative!" Alzira got her will to fight from her mother. "She taught me that there is no point in complaining; you have to get out there and fight."

Alzira fought and studied. She graduated in nursing. For being an Afro-Brazilian woman, she opened up different paths: to make domestic violence socially visible and to raise Afro-Brazilian women's self-esteem. "In 1990, when we created the House of Culture of the Afro-Brazilian Woman, there was resistance regarding the name. The oppositionists asked: 'Why Afro-Brazilian women?'" She had the answer on the tip of her heart: Afro-Brazilian women need to become visible and to assert themselves. Many people took long to understand. "Some white men came after the Afro-Brazilian girls looking for prostitutes. Some white women came to look for cleaners." After 15 years, the House is a reference in the area of assistance to victims of domestic violence, providing psychological and judicial support. It is also a reference in the fight against racism. The House also elaborates the rescue of African culture, in every detail: the furniture, the cuisine, the colors, the editing of the 'Eparrei Magazine,' the mentioning of the orixás (Gods of the Candomblé, a religion brought to Brazil by the Africans captured by the slave trade). Alzira is a multifaceted figure: Ialorixá (religious status in the Candomblé), communicator, political articulator and a claimant with a sharp tongue.

Alzira mixes determination with poetry — "because the world is in need of another way to say things."

Domestic violence against women is a widespread epidemic that does not choose social class, race or educational status. It is a well-known fact that the eradication of it depends on a number of factors: judicial, psychological, cultural and interpersonal.

Brazil

Byubyusara Ryskulova

Psychological Crisis Center for Women and Families "Sezim"

Byubyusara Ryskulova (born 1947) is a human rights activist dedicated to preventing domestic abuse and protecting those who have been victimized. She founded the first domestic violence prevention center in Kyrgyzstan. This organization is committed to assisting and rehabilitating abused women, providing protection for victims, researching the roots of violence within the Kyrgyz society, and the education of rights. Byubyusara gives hope to many people. She carries out her mission against violence through peaceful measures including seminars, campaigns, advocacy, protests, and education.

Byubyusara Ryskulova's activities began as part of a grassroots movement focused on women's rights and the development of a more democratic and civil society in the Republic. In 1998, Byubyusara founded the first organization in the area dedicated to combating domestic abuse and the dehumanizing practice of trafficking in human beings. This organization assists victimized women and their families through rehabilitation and the provision of legal, social, and economic protection. A director of the Psychological Crisis Center for Women and Families "Sezim" in Bishkek, Byubyusara is on the front lines in the fight against all forms of domestic violence. In conjunction with other NGOs, she coordinates an effort geared toward helping Central Asian refugees. The "Refugees: Victims of Violence, including Slave Trade" project provides protection for refugees who are citizens of Kyrgyzstan, Uzbekistan, and Kazakhstan. This international mission works to meet the needs of some of the most vulnerable citizens of Central Asia, protecting them from human rights abuses and working toward the development of a free society. According to her colleagues, Byubyusara works for the people. The name Byubyusara Ryskulova is synonymous with help and support. "She has saved many people from the plight of slave trading," they say. Byubyusara has successfully established a presence in the social and political spheres of Kyrgyzstan and participates in democratic and judicial elections in the area. While her scope has grown considerably over the years from charity work to establishing an NGO to encouraging the development of a free society, her mission remains the same: to provide real help to the people who need it.

Human rights abuses are rampant in the Kyrgyz Republic. The mistreatment of women and their families is a common affliction. This demands the sustained attention and action of those who can carry out the difficult task of establishing basic human rights and fighting for the dignity of all.

Kyrgyzstan

Zazi Sadou

Algerian Assembly of Democratic Women (AADW)
Women Living under Muslim Laws (WLUML)

Over the last decade Zazi Sadou has been actively advocating women's rights in a highly vulnerable environment. She has been sentenced to death by Algerian religious extremists for probing the question of how and why hundreds of Algerian girls were raped by Islamist militants. Sadou is a spokeswoman and founding member of The Algerian Assembly of Democratic Women (AADW). Created in 1993, the Assembly is dedicated to combating human rights violations and to advance women's legal status.

Exposing her vision of peace in the world, Zazi Sadou says, "Peace must become the focal issue in all international relations talks. It has become clear that we need to re-consider the significance of peace in our lives and to advocate social justice. To get to that point, it is essential to bolster and help women worldwide, especially those in the South, to rise to their duties. We have to strive for women to be represented in governments and decision-making spheres so that their needs are vocalized in official platforms. In Algeria, for instance, it is difficult to envisage the state accepting equal treatment of men and women. The future of our world depends equally on women and men. In Algeria women's participation in every sphere of private and public life is of paramount importance, where the long-entrenched fundamentalist regime is violating women's rights as citizens." Zazi emphasizes the influential role that women undertake in society. She adds, "A woman's life is replete with painstaking commitments. She has work duties outside the home, as well as domestic and social duties within the family. And if she is involved in political activities, the situation becomes even more exacerbated; for in a conservative society the realm of expressing public opinion is strictly male-dominated. Women who publicly vocalize their political views are invariably underrespected, for this indicates that they have no family or male guardian to control their behavior. There are many factors which bar women from full participation in public life. Primarily these include the unfounded long-established traditional customs and value systems in society. It is with this reality that we have to contend and against which we have to continue to fight in order to change the established order."

Since its independence from the French occupation in 1962, Algeria has been ruled by the military National Liberation Front (NLF). This fundamentalist regime set out to crack down on gender equality. Zazi rose up against the fundamentalists, putting women's issues on top of her political agenda.

Algeria

Hilda Saeed

Shirkat Gah Women's Resource Center

Hilda Saeed (born 1936) battled discrimination in her own life: as a Christian married to a Muslim in Muslim-majority Pakistan she faced all-round hostility. That firsthand experience of insular discrimination contributed to her decision, later in life, to become a tireless campaigner for the rights of women, as well as for minority rights and interfaith dialogue and harmony.

Hilda Saeed had an early introduction to the turbulent politics of the Indian subcontinent when she witnessed, as a child, the sectarian riots that erupted in Karachi when India was partitioned and Pakistan was born. She began her professional career with an 18-year-long stint as a teacher of university undergraduates, and as a medical researcher and forensic serologist, after which she moved into journalism, editing a health journal for several years. It was during this latter period that she became a women's rights activist, joining the Shirkat Gah Women's Resource Center in 1978, and becoming a member of the Shirkat Collective, a position she still holds today.

Hilda entered activism at a time when the political climate was hostile to activists. Human rights were severely compromised under Zia-ul-Haq's military dictatorship. Women activists ran great personal risks, marching when congregations of more than four people were banned. Hilda became a founder-member of the Women's Action Forum. She helped take to court several cases that related to unjust accusations against women and members of minority communities. As a result, her family life suffered — but today, her only child, a daughter, is also an active feminist.

Hilda's outstanding contribution has been in raising awareness about women's reproductive and sexual health rights through her work as a media practitioner, and by participating in dialogues with both community members and government officials. From these efforts emerged the Pakistan Reproductive Health Network, of which she is a founder-member. This organization has raised issues related to sexual rights that are unpalatable to many Pakistanis. Hilda has also been an outspoken critic of discrimination against minorities, opposing, for example, the separate electorates' scheme that has denied minorities the same voting rights as Muslims.

Women and minorities struggle for air in Pakistani law, which does not guarantee women the same rights as men, nor minorities the same rights as its Muslim citizens. Although the 1973 constitution promised equality, it has undergone so many amendments that the original intent has been lost.

Samsidar

National Commission on Violence Against Women

Samsidar (born 1965) was trained as an agricultural engineer specializing in plant diseases. On assignment at a people's coffee plantation development project in Central Aceh in 1991, she saw that the farmers did not have the means to process their own crops. So she organized credit unions with the village women. She has since become involved in women's issues, such as violence against women, reconciliation initiatives and trauma healing. Samsidar is Secretary General of Indonesia's National Commission on Violence Against Women.

It has not been a small leap for Samsidar, an agricultural engineer trained in plant diseases who organized credit unions for women in Aceh, who has ended up running the affairs of the National Commission on Violence Against Women as its Secretary General. From being a small collective scale enterprise, the credit unions evolved into a space for women to share experiences and discuss issues regarding their families and communities. It also enabled women from different villages to interact. Facing pressure from local authorities, Samsidar established a network of volunteers to found a legal body for the credit unions. She also helped organize an Aceh Farmer Society Union.

By the end of the 1990s, despite the national government's decision to end Aceh's status as a Military Operation Region, the armed conflict intensified in Central Aceh. Samsidar worked with several women's organizations to document cases of violence against women: In 1995, she founded the Aceh Gender Transformation Working Group and she also served as chairperson of the Executive Board of Flower Aceh, a women's organization focused on violence against women. In 1998, she founded the Aceh Women Volunteer for Humanity to support women survivors of the armed conflict and in 2000, Samsidar and her colleagues organized the Aceh Women's Congress which produced a resolution demanding that the Indonesian government put an end to the violence in Aceh and bring the perpetrators before the courts. Samsidar travels around the country to facilitate meetings and training seminars on women's rights and to document human rights violations at local and national levels. She has been appointed by the National Commission as Special Rapporteur on Women's Human Rights in Aceh.

Aceh in Indonesia has rich oil and gas reserves. Unfair sharing of revenues from these resources between the national and the local government has triggered nationalist sentiments in the area. During the Suharto regime, Aceh was declared a Military Operation Region, claiming many Acehnese lives.

Indonesia

"Women should have their own space. I think there should be a women's political party; that's my long-time dream."

Saraswathi

Tamil Nadu Women's Forum
Tamil Refugees Rehabilitation Association
Tamil Nadu Dalit Women's Network

Saraswathi (born 1944) has fearlessly challenged atrocities by the state on women, Dalits, and society's other marginalized. She has encouraged and performed many inter-caste and widow marriages, and has played a significant role in building and strengthening women's movements and human rights activism in Tamil Nadu. Her opposition to the draconian Terrorism and Disruptive Activities (Prevention) Act, her support of the peace mission to Sri Lanka, and her campaign against capital punishment are particularly notable.

Saraswathi saw her mother suffering from the repressive customs and rituals that haunt widowhood. Even that young, she knew she would fight the oppressive social systems that made the life of many women a living hell. Saraswathi challenges atrocities by the state on women, Dalits, and the marginalized through fearless and vibrant oratorical and writing skills. Apart from encouraging and performing many inter-caste and widow remarriages, for 35 years, she has also been organizing and addressing press meetings, interfacing with government machineries, speaking at public meetings and other campaigns, and integrating social concerns with teaching. None of this has come without personal danger. When she addressed a public meeting to condemn state atrocities on Dalits in Tamil Nadu, she lost both her job as head of department of a government women's college, and her pension. She has also been arrested several times while staging peaceful demonstrations against repressive laws and state-sponsored violence.

Saraswathi played a significant role in building and strengthening women's movements and human rights activism in Tamil Nadu: the iron-fisted Terrorism and Disruptive Activities (Prevention) Act was withdrawn, the peace mission to Sri Lanka was strengthened, and her campaign against capital punishment helped save 26 lives. She is an inspiration to many, especially her students, many of whom have dedicated their lives to the fight for justice. "Women should have their own space," she says. "I think there should be a women's political party; that's my long-time dream."

Widows in much of India are forced to undergo dehumanizing rituals such as tonsuring and meager meals. While widow remarriage is a government mandate, it remains uncommon. Women are denied land rights, girls' education is not a priority, and domestic violence is a social disease.

India

María del Carmen Sarthes

Catholics for the Right to Decide

She has been weaving for 23 years. Her name is María del Carmen Sarthes. She comes from Argentina. With this traditionally female activity, she weaves hope, fighting for the rights of women, children and adolescents. She supports raped and maltreated women, gives workshops and seminars about sexual and reproductive health and against violence. She marches, teaches, accompanies and continues weaving. She has a husband, four sons and female companions. She teaches them how to weave and how to value and love themselves.

While hundreds of young members of the Argentinean Army died frozen during the The Falklands War (the Malvinas War), María del Carmen Sarthes wove overcoats, in red, green, pink and violet. Each hank of thread was part of the struggle: "During the dictatorship (1976—1983), we lived with fear, but when the military forced the Falklands War upon us, we regained our strength and campaigned for it to end." The war finished in 1982, but it was only the beginning of Carmen's fight. With her woven scarves, she could wrap up and protect many violated women.

She began to teach catechism in the Catholic Church of Virrey de Pino, in the province of Buenos Aires, where she was born. Later on, she came into contact with the Theology of Liberation, which changed her vision: "I saw the situation of many maltreated women. I felt bad because I could not find a solution within the Church." Theology of Liberation is a Christian theological movement, which arose in South America. It was based on the fight against oppression and exploitation of the human being.

After, she joined other women, also related to the Church, in their work against violence. It was the year 1996, and there were six women. The name of the group was Awakening, and they awoke to several truths: that women did not decide on their reproductive lives, that they had no access to sexual health, that they were solely responsible for their families, that they reared the children and did not have any time for themselves. And this was violence. Between 1996 and 2005, she gave around 30 workshops and seminars. Today, at age 55, María del Carmen Sarthes is a member of Catholics for the Right to Decide (CDD). She continues with her weaving, and each time she has her needles and wool, she thinks "women learn to weave, but they also have to learn about their rights as women."

The dictatorial regime (1976—1983) was responsible for more than 30,000 disappearances and many murders. In 1998, the Argentinean peso was devalued. Foreign debt and unemployment are a type of violence directed against the country. 76% of women are victims of violence.

Argentina

Cathrin Schauer

Karo e.V.

In the last 15 years, the number of prostitutes along the border between Germany and the Czech Republic has increased dramatically, and so have the brutality and the miserable situation of these women and children. Cathrin Schauer, nurse and social worker, gives advice, health care, and human care to more than a thousand of these women and children, most of whom are victims of trafficking. She and her co-worker are the only ones assisting them. For this work Cathrin founded the organization Karo whose public funding has run out, so it is now fully dependent on private donors.

On an approximately 250 km-long stretch along the border between Germany and the Czech Republic, a new scene of prostitution established over the last 15 years. The number of prostitutes and clients has increased dramatically, and so have the brutality, hierarchical systems of the gangs, and the miserable situation of the women and children. Virtually without exception, the clients come from Germany. Among the more than thousand prostitutes are women, girls, and an increasing number of children coming from the Czech Republic, Eastern Europe and some from Asia. This is the work place of Cathrin Schauer. A nurse and social worker, she visits every place in the biggest red light district of Europe once a week, the street walkers and the brothels. She brings them condoms, advice, and a glimpse of normality. "Every day I meet women who were never really asked how they feel. Just to listen to them, to embrace them, to listen to the problems of their desperate lives brings help."

But this is only a part of her work. Over the years, she has helped 168 women to get out of prostitution. She has opened a consultation center in the city of Cheb, in the Czech Republic, named after her friend Marita P., who died of Aids. Cathrin wrote a book about the situation and started campaigns to raise public awareness. She and her co-worker are all the help the prostitutes can get in the region. Funds have run out; thus, the organization Karo e.V., which Cathrin founded, is financed only by private contributions. "I wish the politicians who are responsible for the distribution of funding would accompany us just for 24 hours. Nobody can imagine how these women and children have to live. It is no marginal problem. The scale and misery of prostitution in this region indicate a fundamental problem at the core of the whole society. Germany must take responsibility."

Along the border between Germany and the Czech Republic, the number of prostitutes and their clients has increased dramatically in the last 15 years, and so have the brutality, gangs, and the miserable situation of the women and children. Virtually without exception, the clients come from Germany.

Germany

Through her years
of working with women
victims of violence,
Beena began to make
the larger connection
between conflict in
the public sphere and
violence in the private
domain.

Beena Sebastian

Cultural Academy for Peace (CAP)
International Fellowship of Reconciliation (IFR)

Beena Sebastian's life and work illustrate how an ordinary woman with no special qualification can change the lives of many people around her. Among her most creative efforts are gender sensitivity training for police and lawyers and instituting an annual award for public officials who have done the most to prevent violence against women. These efforts have helped break the silence surrounding sexual violence in Kerala. She has also set up a shelter for abused women, providing them with both protection and a friend to accompany them to the police and the courts.

Beena Sebastian (born 1959) has been working toward the empowerment of the poor and marginalized formally and informally since she was a child. It was in the 1990s, though, that she began working in an organized manner toward the issue that most deeply concerns her, the welfare of disempowered women. In the early 1990s, she began classes in life skills for slum women and girls, many of them immigrants from Tamil Nadu, who came to Kerala seeking work. As part of this effort, she also began a successful income generation project, teaching women the nontraditional skill of making motorcycle batteries. Beena founded an NGO, the Cultural Academy for Peace (CAP), which runs a shelter for abused women and their children, provides legal counseling and accompanies women to the police and court.

Beena's approach to her work is creative and sensitive. Her gender sensitivity training for police and lawyers, aimed at improving legal services and police protection for women, is a case in point. Another of her major successes has been bringing into the open the issue of sexual violence-an issue that no one was willing to speak about in Kerala. Even parents would hide evidence of their daughters' trauma in order to protect their daughters' "reputation". Beena has instituted an annual public award for public officials who have done the most to prevent violence against women, which has helped break the silence surrounding sexual violence, and led to improved services for rape and domestic-abuse survivors.

Rape, pornography, scandals, sexual abuse, harassment, dowry and domestic violence make Kerala-India's most literate state-a bad place for women. In a study by an international center for research on women, 30 percent of the women complained of physical torture, and 69 percent of psychological torture.

India

Marjana Senjak

Medica — Women's Therapy Center Zenica

In August 1992, Marjana Senjak established the Center for Psychological Help in Zenica. She initiated cooperation among her professional colleagues and began working at collective refugee centers. She and her colleagues established a SOS hotline for people with war traumas, also for soldiers. In 1993, Marjana co-founded the Medica Zenica Center for treatment of women survivors of rape and people suffering from war trauma. Over the last few years, the center has been expanded to include survivors of domestic violence and incest.

Marjana Senjak utilizes a wide range of psychological theories and techniques, including general psychological concepts, transactional analysis, psychodrama, gestalt, and body-oriented healing in her work. She also uses her knowledge of alcoholism and addiction in work with youth and family counseling. Since the beginning of her work at the Women's Therapy Center, Marjana established psychotherapy groups for women survivors of war rape. Together with her colleagues she innovated three different psychotherapy approaches for group treatment of war rape survivors. The first approach is based on general psychotherapy concepts; the second is an adaptation of Ellen Bass and Laura Davis' approach to incest survivors in their book "The Courage to Heal." The third approach is based on an adaptation of the therapy process in Judith Lewis Herman's "Trauma and Recovery."

In her organizational and management work she uses a community-based approach with a decentralized decision-making structure. A true leader, Marjana has all the abilities great leaders possess. She is inspiring, supportive of others' leadership qualities, able to share her vision, encourages the active involvement of others in teamwork and manages to bring out the best in everyone. She uses a client-oriented approach with deep respect for the needs, characteristics, and culture of each person. She provides unconditional acceptance of each human being — whether it be in her psychotherapeutic, educational, organizational, or community work. Marjana also has taken on promoting and defending the human rights of war rape survivors. She works on peace building, conflict resolution, and reconciliation in Bosnia and Herzegovina, Croatia, and Kosovo. She believes in the therapeutic and healing effect of truthful human engagement and its contribution to the recovery of individuals and communities.

In the 1990s, the city of Zenica was a war-torn place besieged with victims of the war. Among the most unfortunate were women who were raped, mentally and physically tortured and still had to bear responsibility for their children. Psychological help and spiritual healing were needed badly.

Bosnia and Herzegovina

Heisoo Shin

Korean Council for the Women Drafted for Military Sexual Slavery by Japan
Korea Women's Hot Line
Asia Pacific Forum on Women, Law & Development

Heisoo Shin has been a leader in bringing the issues of sexual slavery and other women's human rights abuses to the forefront of the international justice agenda. She served for seven years as president of Hotline for Women in Need, created to receive information from women forced to serve as sexual slaves by the Japanese military in World War II. She is a leading member of the United Nations Commission on Human Rights, and is vice-chair of the Commission on the Elimination of All Forms of Discrimination Against Women.

Heisoo's role in the Commission on the Elimination of All Forms of Discrimination Against Women is central in an effort to monitor the world's conditions for women. Formed in 1982, the commission is comprised of 23 experts on women's issues from around the world. At meetings held twice annually, the commission reviews data and makes recommendations for services or legislation that will protect women against personal and institutional violence.

Heisoo, one of the world's leading experts on the sexual slavery of Korean women by the Japanese military, served for 11 years on a national committee created to help these so-called "comfort women". A visiting professor at Kyunghee University since 2001, she uses her considerable expertise to educate, monitor, and demand change. In her various roles, her goals are full disclosure of the truth about the Japanese military's role in sexual slavery, acknowledgment of the crime, punishment of the criminals, and legal reparation for their victims.

When she began her work, Korea had just joined the United Nations. Through the work of Heisoo and her colleagues, legal judgments for wartime perpetrators of crimes against women is expected from the United Nations Commission on Human Rights. Heisoo's international activities resulted in representatives from many countries also declaring the violation of their women by Japanese military.

It is estimated that approximately 200,000 women were enslaved during World War II. Most have died or cannot bring themselves to speak of their past. To date, the Japanese government has not acknowledged this war crime.

Republic of Korea

Indrani Sinha

Sanlaap

When a study on sexually abused children took Indrani Sinha (born 1950) to the brothel areas of Kolkata, the lives of the women there shook her to the core. From then on, she and Sanlaap (sanlaap means dialogue), the organization she set up, have been working to eliminate stigma, and to integrate women in prostitution and their children into mainstream society. While the setting up of safe homes and motivating government agencies have been significant victories, Indrani's greatest triumph is the fulfilling lives that the women in and from Sanlaap's shelter homes now lead.

Indrani Sinha began her career teaching, but soon realized that her interest lay in the development sector. A study she was conducting on sexually abused girls took her to Kolkata's infamous brothel areas and the suburbs, where she met hundreds of women and girls. Their stories about being tricked into prostitution, their afflicted health conditions, and the torture they endured shook Indrani up. In 1987, she started Sanlaap, an antitrafficking human rights center that focuses on mainstreaming rescued women and girls. Their economic rehabilitation includes vocational education, skill training, and collaboration with the corporate sector for jobs, volunteers, programs, and mainstream occupations. The Sanlaap shelter homes also house HIV+ girls, many of whom are not accommodated in state-run homes.

Indrani's key strategy is collaboration. Already, Sanlaap has won considerable, even high-profile, victories against the system: the team's dedication has gradually shoveled away apathy in the judiciary, police, the youth of the red-light areas, and the administration. A government officer says, "We are interdependent. Sanlaap is solving many problems that government departments are unable to solve." The Sanlaap team, and Indrani herself, though, continue to face considerable personal jeopardy from the powerful prostitution mafia: the nexus of politicians, police, and traffickers is particularly malignant. The divide within the NGO sector on the issue of prostitution legalization has also taken its toll on Sanlaap. But Indrani is relatively content: the more than 600 girls who have come to the Sanlaap homes since 1989 lead productive and comfortable lives.

In the 1980s, trafficking in women and prostitution were taboo topics. Women in prostitution were harassed by a nexus of officials and pimps, and an insensitive judiciary. The stigma attached to sex work was so extreme that these women could not even send their children to school.

India

Sister Cecilia

Forum Peduli Perempuan Atambua (FPPA)
Sisters of the Holy Spirit (SSPS)

Sister Cecilia (born 1958) is a courageous nun who hails from Bali. Since conflict broke out on Timor Island in 1999, she has been working tirelessly to help women refugees in West Timor. She offers free counselling for women seeking shelter in refugee camps, which can be hostile to women. She founded the Forum Peduli Perempuan Atambua (FPPA), a Women's Concern Forum in the refugee town Atambua. Sister Cecilia is also a critical commentator on local policies concerning refugees.

During a field visit to Atapupu near the border between East and West Timor, Sister Cecilia saw hundreds of East Timorese refugees scattered in the woods. Many of them were in a poor condition, very sick and traumatized. In 1999, she sought permission from the head of her order to move to Atambua town in Belu district where she devoted her life to helping the refugees. "I felt that our assistance was nothing compared to that given by the UN High Commission on Refugees and other international agencies, so I attended counselling training," she relates. She decided to help traumatized women refugees, especially victims of domestic violence in the camps. Cecilia visited one camp after another, listening to heartbreaking stories of survivors and helping them to stand on their own feet.

Initially, her work did not have any support. "Even the head of my order never provided me with any resources to help me continue my work, although we survived anyway." Sister Cecilia started with a staff of two; now she has six women working in the office. In 2000, she joined the West Timor Humanitarian Team, founded by the Eastern Indonesia Women's Health Network (JKPIT), whose work is focused on documenting and investigating violence against women in West Timor camps. Cecilia's involvement with the JKPIT network helped her sharpen her perspective on women's rights issues in conflict areas. The network funded trauma counseling training for trainers in a program to help Atambua women. The network is sponsored by Pikul, which is a Kupang-based group supported by Oxfam Autralia that offers support to West Timor local NGOs. After this training, the group founded the Forum Peduli Perempuan Atambua (FPPA). "Every year, violence against women in Atambua continues to increase," observes Cecilia. "But people now know where to go. Women come from all sub-districts of Atambua."

In September 1999, some 280,000 people fled East Timor to safety in several towns of West Timor. In the town of Atambua, (with a population of 70,000), refugees are sheltered in 41 camps. Women refugees live in a harsh and hostile environment in many poorly maintained camps.

Indonesia

Andrea Smith

Incite! Women of Color Against Violence

Andrea Smith combines intellectual study, professional skill, and personal passion to shed light on violence against women of color in the USA. The violence comes from many corners of society, including family members, immigration officials, police, and employers. Andrea began her advocacy work as a rape crisis counselor with Chicago Women of All Red Nations. She cofounded Incite! Women of Color Against Violence, a national organization that uses direct action, dialogue, and grassroots organizing to end violence against women of color. Andrea teaches at the University of Michigan.

Andrea Smith, who is a Western Band Cherokee, tells the story of a woman from her community: "A young native woman was gang raped by prominent members of an urban Indian community where I lived. When she sought justice, the community blamed her and told her she was dividing the community by airing its 'dirty laundry'. At the same time, she had difficulty getting help from the mainstream antiviolence movement. In fact, the year before I began working in sexual assault services in that city, only one native woman had received services at a rape crisis center. The primary reason native women give for not going outside the community for help was that it was like appealing to a 'foreign government' for assistance."

Indeed, it is often government officials who perpetrate violence, says Andrea. "The challenge women of color face is to combat both personal and state violence." Andrea has done this by organizing, speaking, and writing. She was the Women of Color Caucus chair of the National Coalition Against Sexual Assault and coordinated the first Color of Violence national conference held in 2000 at the University of California, Santa Cruz. This important gathering brought together activists and scholars who discussed relationships between racism, colonialism, homophobia, and gender violence in the lives and histories of women of color. When a second national conference was held in 2002, Andrea served on the conference planning committee.

Andrea has received numerous honors and awards for her academic excellence teaching native American and women's studies courses. She holds a bachelor of arts from Harvard University in the comparative study of religion, a master of divinity from the Union Theological Institute and a PhD from the University of California, Santa Cruz, in the history of consciousness.

In the USA, many resources exist to address violence against women, but native women, and other women of color, often find it difficult to seek help from mainstream organizations.

United States of America

"Siin-Do Song's actions
make us realize that
the impunity of crimes of
violence against women
in war should be ended."

Yuko Sugiyama

Siin-Do Song

VAWW-NET Japan

Telling the story of her experience as a sex slave, Siin-Do Song (born 1923) is paving the way for thousands of women to pursue justice. Siin-Do was one of the "comfort women" to the Japanese military during World War II. Following the war, Siin-Do faced harsh racial and ethnic discrimination as a Korean living in Japan. Using her own name in a culture that forbids talking of such things, Siin-Do filed a lawsuit against the Japanese government asking for an apology and compensation. Her quest for justice is a protest against both sexual violence during the war and racism after it.

The tragedy of Siin-Do's victimization began when she was a young girl growing up in Korea at a time when her country was under Japanese rule. At age 16, she ran away from an arranged marriage on the day of her wedding, and was approached by a Korean woman who told her she could make money if she went to the battlefield of "her nation" (Japan). Siin-Do was taken to China, which had just been invaded by the Japanese. There, she was forced to serve for years as a "comfort woman" in a "comfort station", which meant servicing hundreds of soldiers who would wait in line for their few minutes of rape. When Japan surrendered in 1945, Siin-Do fled China, leaving behind children who were born in a brothel.

Supported by various human rights groups, in 1993, Siin-Do filed a lawsuit against the government in the Tokyo District Court. In 1994, she testified at a public hearing of the Asian Tribunal on Women's Human Rights in Tokyo, organized by the Asian Women Human Rights Council and the Women's Human Rights Committee of Japan. The "military comfort women" issue was recognized as a violation of women's human rights. However, in 2003, the Japanese supreme court dismissed her case.

An elderly Korean living in Japan, Siin-Do has few social rights — she cannot vote, nor is she entitled to a pension. Although her case has been dismissed, her commitment to public speaking has resulted in widespread awareness of the issue and the empowerment of other survivors of sexual violence. The formation of VAWW-NET Japan, an NGO founded in 1997 to fight for government redress for "comfort women", was inspired by Siin-Do's work. VAWW-NET Japan was responsible for the Women's International War Crimes Tribunal for Sexual Slavery by Japan's Military (2000), which found Emperor Hirohito guilty of war crimes and state responsibilties during World War II.

The citizens of Japan tend to be ignorant of many of the crimes perpetrated by their government during the War. Accordingly, they dismiss and slander someone who speaks out publicly. The time it has taken Sinn-Do to wage her battle has exhausted financial resources.

Japan

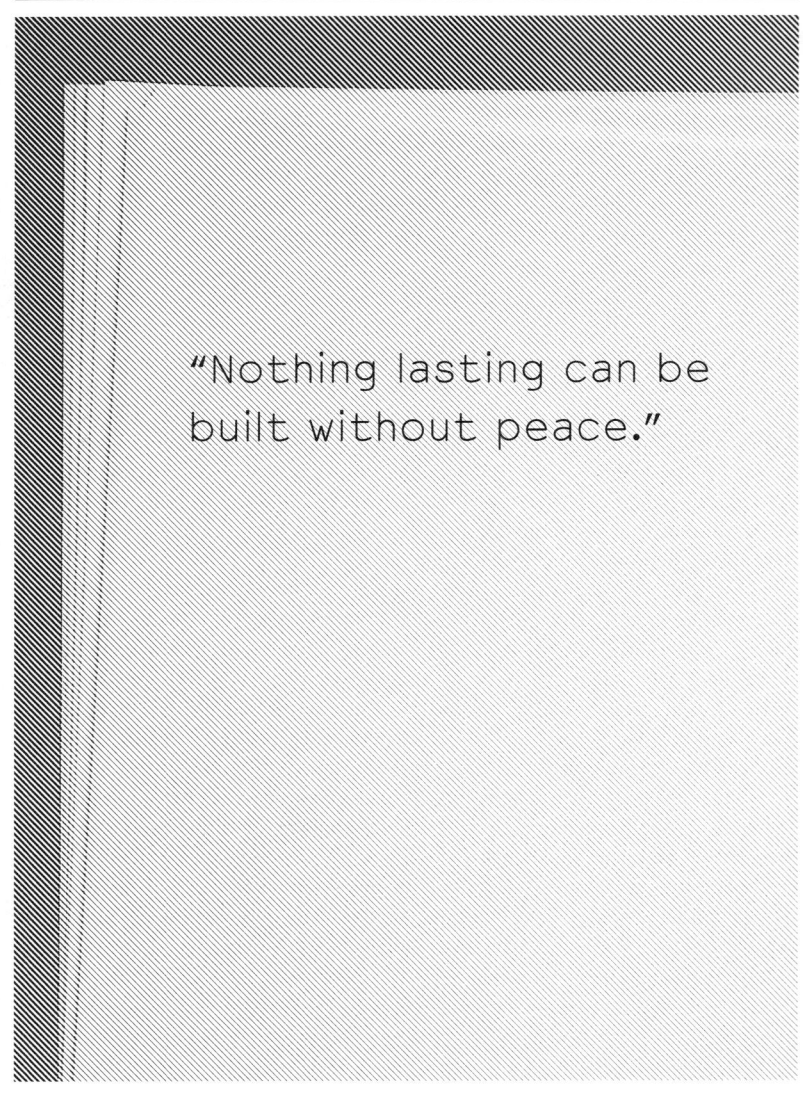

"Nothing lasting can be built without peace."

Amsatou Sow Sidibé

Réseau Africain pour la Promotion de la Femme Travailleuse (Rafet)

Amsatou Sow Sidibé (52) has a doctorate in law and political science from the Université Paris II. She is a full professor and holds the Chair of Private Law at the Université Cheikh Anta Diop (UCAD) in Dakar; she also heads the university's Institute for Human Rights and Peace. She is the president of Rafet, the African Network for the Promotion of Working Women, and has published numerous works and papers on human rights. Very early on, she produced programs on women's rights on national radio as a direct form of awareness-raising among women.

Amsatou Sow Sidibé is a committed and tireless activist, fighting on all battlefields where human life and dignity are threatened. A volume would not suffice to list her academic accomplishments and her activities against violence and the exploitation of women, against poverty, injustice, and political lawlessness. Her impressive curriculum vitae reflects her intellectual prowess. But there are things which cannot be expressed in a curriculum vitae, yet reveal a person's personality. Rafet, the African Network for the Promotion of Working Women, over which Amsatou Sow Sidibé presides, is one such thing. The highly symbolic meaning of this acronym — which designates a women's organization — could not have escaped Amsatou Sow Sidibé. In Wolof (most widely-spoken language in Senegal), rafet means "beautiful." It also refers to any action, gesture, or word which shows moral nobility, greatness of soul, and control. In other words, the cardinal virtues without which peace cannot thrive. In the word "rafet" we see the graceful and proud figures of women who sacrifice themselves daily for the good of the societies they live in. Since the dawn of time, they have learned to hold their tongues and obey. And yet, in spite of their difficult status and the natural or man-made scourges they are subject to, they are so beautiful, so strong. That seems to be the message of Amsatou Sow Sidibé. "Life continues because we are upright. We have resisted so that our children may live, to maintain the structure of the family, to spread the good word, to educate, to heal. Now the time has come to marshal our physical, moral, cultural, and spiritual resources, for a better life without discrimination, in spite of the obstacles the world puts in the way of human dignity. Let us truly comprehend that we can change the world."

Rafet is an organization that helps women like Amsatou to earn and save money and to gain access to social services. Most of these workers are not well educated, and struggle to be recognized by Senegalese society as the head of their household.

Senegal

Hilaria Supa Huamán

Foundational Line Ample Movement of Women
House of Awakening

She loves life in spite of everything. Conceived as the result of a rape, she herself was raped at the age of 14. Her name is Hilaria Supa Huamán. She is 47 years old and self-educated. She has lived in Lima, the capital of Peru. She now lives in Huallaccocha, in Cuzco. She campaigns for agriculture and for the women of the countryside. For more than 20 years, she has been dedicated to organizing women and preserving the ancient wisdom and culture of the Andes. For the last six years, she has also been working in search of justice for women who were forcefully sterilized.

Hilaria Supa Huamán faced discrimination and abandonment. She claims attention to the needs of the rural areas, celebrates the harvest, applies her ancestral wisdom and acts as a facilitator and mediator. For over 20 years, she has been dedicating herself to organizing women collectively. She lives in Huallacocha, Anta, in Cuzco. Along with others, she contributed to the creation of women's committees and, in 1991, to the creation of the Women's Federation of Anta. They worked on literacy programs. She learned the first letters; she was a self-taught person.

In 1995, she traveled to the Conference of Women in Beijing. At that meeting, the Peruvian government offered to implement a family planning program. However, then it was transformed into the forced sterilization of poor and indigenous women. In 2001, Hilaria and 12 female companions from the countryside went to Lima to denounce those abuses. Nowadays, she is a member of the Foundational Line Ample Movement of Women, that leads the Campaign For Truth, Justice and Compensation on the forced sterilizations. The investigations have been reinstated and hope has been revived. Lilia Lazo, a popular Peruvian leader, says: "Hilaria has already surpassed herself. She has the wisdom to know where to go and what to say. She speaks with a Minister or member of Parliament without losing her own identity."

Hilaria Supa Huamán wrote the book 'Thread of my life' and has inaugurated the House of Awakening, a place for the teaching of indigenous history and customs, a place where people can come to thank the Pachamama (Mother Earth) and ask her for the strength to continue the fight for truth, justice and peace.

Indigenous women in Peru are the most affected by poverty and illiteracy. The government of Alberto Fujimori implemented a policy of forced sterilization against them. Their human rights were violated. Investigations have been reinstated, and hope for justice has been revived.

Peru

Suzuyo Takazato

Okinawa Women Act Against Military Violence
East Asia–US–Puerto Rico Women's Network against Militarism

Suzuyo Takazato (born 1940) is a long-time feminist peace activist who has analyzed the interplay between sexism and militarism from the experiences of women in Okinawa. Her work has inspired global feminist peace movements for structural understanding of violence against women. Suzuyo helped create Okinawa's first rape crisis center to provide hotline and face-to-face counseling to victims of sexual violence, and in 1995, Suzuyo's activism led to a large-scale protest by people of Okinawa against US military bases.

In the early 1980s, while Suzuyo was working closely with female victims of sexual violence and women working in the sex industry, she encountered many barriers to protecting them and ensuring their basic human rights. Realizing that the efforts of social workers alone were not enough to change institutions, she decided to run for Naha city assembly. She won, and served four terms, focusing on such areas as the rights of women, children, and people with disabilities, demilitarization, environmental safety, and food safety.

In 1995, she attended the 4th World Conference of Women held in China. She was the president of the Okinawa delegation, and organized a workshop entitled "Military: Structural Violence and Women." There, she and other delegates explained their gender analysis of violence against women by the US military stationed in Okinawa. Upon their return to Okinawa, the delegates learned of yet another occurrence of sexual assault by US soldiers against a minor. Suzuyo was a driving force behind the protest to express the women's deep anger, deciding "enough is enough". She and other feminists organized sit-ins, demanding that the Japanese government take effective measures to stop the violence by US soldiers. The reluctant response of the Japanese government, combined with the US military's nominal apologies, incited the women to strengthen their movement. As a result, in November 1995, Okinawa Women Act Against Military Violence (OWAAMV) was established to connect the various women's networks that had been working on women's rights and peace issues.

Since then, OWAAMV women have worked to define sexual violence against women by US soldiers as both a peace and a security issue. They began compiling a chronology of sexual crimes committed by US soldiers since 1945. New information is added periodically, and the chronology is now in its 7th edition.

World War II ended in 1945 and US occupation of Japan continued until 1952 but Okinawa remained occupied for another 27 years. Sexual assaults, rapes, and murders of Okinawan women and children by US servicemen have been documented for long after the island reverted to Japanese control.

Japan

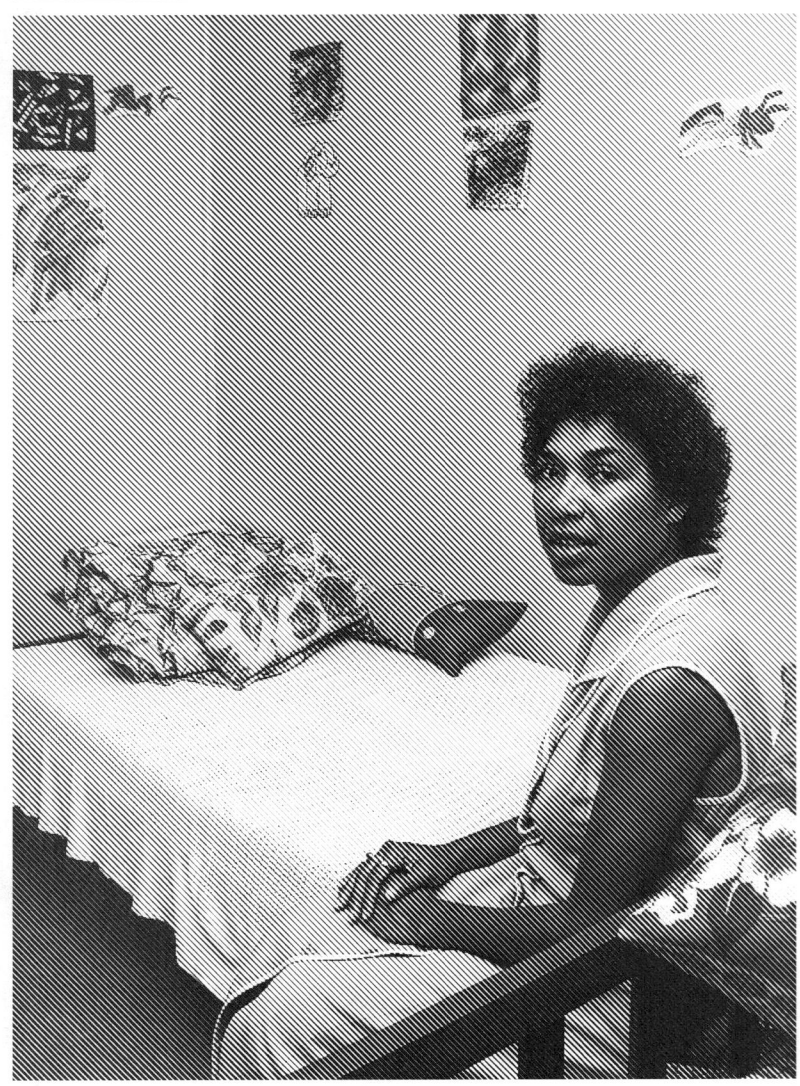

Freda Talao

Individual and Community Rights Advocacy Forum (ICRAF)
Business and Professional Women International (BPWI)
Papua New Guinea Conservation Trust

Lawyer Freda Talao (40) is senior program officer for AusAID working mainly in the Law and Justice sector. She is also chair person of ICRAF, a human rights NGO in Papua New Guinea. She was executive director of the Family and Sexual Violence Action Committee. Over the years, she has worked extensively through government and the NGO sector on human rights, the environment, violence against women, and legislative reform issues such as family law reform and juvenile justice protocols. She was involved in peace building processes after Bougainville's civil war.

"Going back to Bougainville as a 'red skin' after the 12-year civil war against the Papua New Guinea (PNG) Government, I represented the enemy. The steely eyes of the Bougainville 'black skins' cut through your soul; you do not know if you should continue or not. They do not trust you; they have no emotions left. Such was my experience when I started working on post-war Bougainville. Any minute a stray bullet could have landed on me. I always prayed quietly, 'Lord, do not let that stray bullet hit me.' Fear, anxiety, overwhelmed me. But then, as we celebrated the conclusion of a conflict resolution workshop that my organization had conducted in one of the strong rebel areas, a 'No Go Zone,' the people sang and praised God; their faith was the source of strength for them throughout the crisis. They had not lost their faith in God. I wept. I sobbed uncontrollably. I was a total disaster by the time I had to give my speech. All I did was weep and say sorry to them: sorry for all that had happened to them. Five, ten minutes went by; the cloud over my head lifted, the anxiety and fear left me. I could sense release, relief, and, most of all, acceptance. My tears were not alone. I looked around. Not a dry eye in sight. Even the peace monitors were wiping their eyes. It was the most moving moment, one I will never forget. Being a woman, a mother, my emotions had spoken the truth for me, said things that a thousand words could never say. As I celebrated afterwards in a dance with all the little girls hanging onto me, I knew peace, hope, reconciliation, were in sight. God gave me the privilege of being a bridge between the black skins of Bougainville and the red skins of PNG. Now, Bougainville is like home to me: no more fear, no more anxiety, absolutely beautiful!"

Bougainville's long struggle for autonomy from Papua New Guinea erupted into civil war and a blockade (1990s) over the destruction caused by the huge Australian-owned Panguna copper mine on the island. Women led the opposition to the mine and also the peacebuilding efforts to end the civil war.

Papua New Guinea

"Protecting the individual person and working for the society as a whole is a token of success."

Genoveva Tisheva

Bulgarian Gender Research Foundation

Genoveva Tisheva (born 1957) currently is the managing director of the Bulgarian Gender Research Foundation. She has extensive experience in the fields of civil law, women's human rights, gender equality, and socio-economic rights of women. She is working on issues of violence against women and trafficking in women. Genoveva is involved in the creation of a legal basis for combating violence. She initiated the drafting of a law on protection against domestic violence and successfully lobbied for its passage. The law was adopted by parliament on 16 March 2004.

Genoveva Tisheva was born in Sofia in 1957. As a child she had the opportunity to live in Rome, Italy, for about four years and later she studied in a French school in Addis Ababa, Ethiopia. Since an early age she has been used to an international and multicultural environment. A lawyer with an M.A. in law from Sofia University, she specialized in international human rights law in Strasbourg, France, and in international comparative law in Strasbourg and Trier, Germany. In 2004, she took a special course on development, law, and social justice in The Hague, Netherlands.

Genoveva Tisheva developed high sensitivity to the problems of women and in-depth knowledge about the situation of violence against women and discrimination based on sex. In 1995, she developed partnerships with two new NGOs on violence against women in Bulgaria, Animus and Nadia. She helped provide psychological support to victims through these organizations and worked on legal regulations and policy on violence against women. In order to promote the new legal basis in the field of domestic violence, Genoveva established relations with lawyers sensitive to the issue and started working with them on a voluntary basis on a draft law for protection against domestic violence. In less than one year the draft was prepared by this group of lawyers. At the end of 2001, Genoveva found journalists who promoted her idea through the media by interviewing parliamentarians. Genoveva started a successful lobbying campaign with the members of parliament from the party in power for the adoption of the law. The draft law was reviewed by the Ministry of Justice and introduced in parliament in April 2003 with a big press conference. The law was adopted by parliament on 16 March 2004 .

Until the beginning of the 1990s, Bulgaria had a strong communist regime and almost no civil society. As a transition country, Bulgaria is trying to build a civil society, and attempts are being made to work on issues of gender equality and socio-economic rights of women.

Bulgaria

"The majority of women feminists in our society are aware of the repression against them and reject it silently. But very few of them take the initiative to change the situation."

Aida Touma-Suliman

Women Against Violence (WAV)

13 years ago in Nazareth, Aida Touma-Suliman — a Palestinian with Israeli citizenship — and six other women founded Women Against Violence (WAV), an organization that advocates Palestinian women's rights. In 1993, WAV founded the first shelters and crisis centers for battered women in the Arab world. The group also established a halfway house for women trying to rebuild their lives after leaving abusive husbands. Touma has been active in the international arena defending the rights of Palestinian society and Palestinian women, as well as promoting Israeli-Palestinian peace.

In 1992, when Women Against Violence (WAV) was established, the issue of gender-based violence was a total taboo that no one among the Palestinian community wanted to deal with. The society did not want to reveal the problem and it was not acceptable to bring the issue into the public arena or persuade women to seek refuge outside their families. Only very few women had visions of analyzing society's perceptions of the role of women. Among these women is Aida Touma Suliman. She says, "We were feminists: psychologists, social workers and lawyers. We faced many situations where we were either witnessing violence, or our clients were victims of violence. And what shocked us was that everyone accepted this. It happened, it was normal, and nobody wanted to speak about it. That drove us from the beginning. We decided we had to act."

In her work Touma faces the opposition of the most conservative and religious forces in the community. She has become famous for dealing with the most difficult cases of gender-based violence and is sometimes the target of violent anger, directed by men whose wives and daughters are using the discourse and services of the WAV. Leading the lobbying and advocacy activities for justice and against the Israeli government's discrimination of Palestinian women led to Touma's nonacceptance by the decision makers in the various governmental agencies. Touma indicates, "The fact that we are part of the Palestinian people also makes it difficult for us, because whenever we as women want to talk about our problems, the public discourse is, 'It is not the time to deal with these issues. We have more important things.' But this is not an excuse at all for ignoring women's rights."

In 1992, when WAV was established, the issue of gender-based violence was a total taboo within the Palestinian community. The major change that has resulted from WAV and Touma's activities is that this was condemned in Palestinian society.

Israel

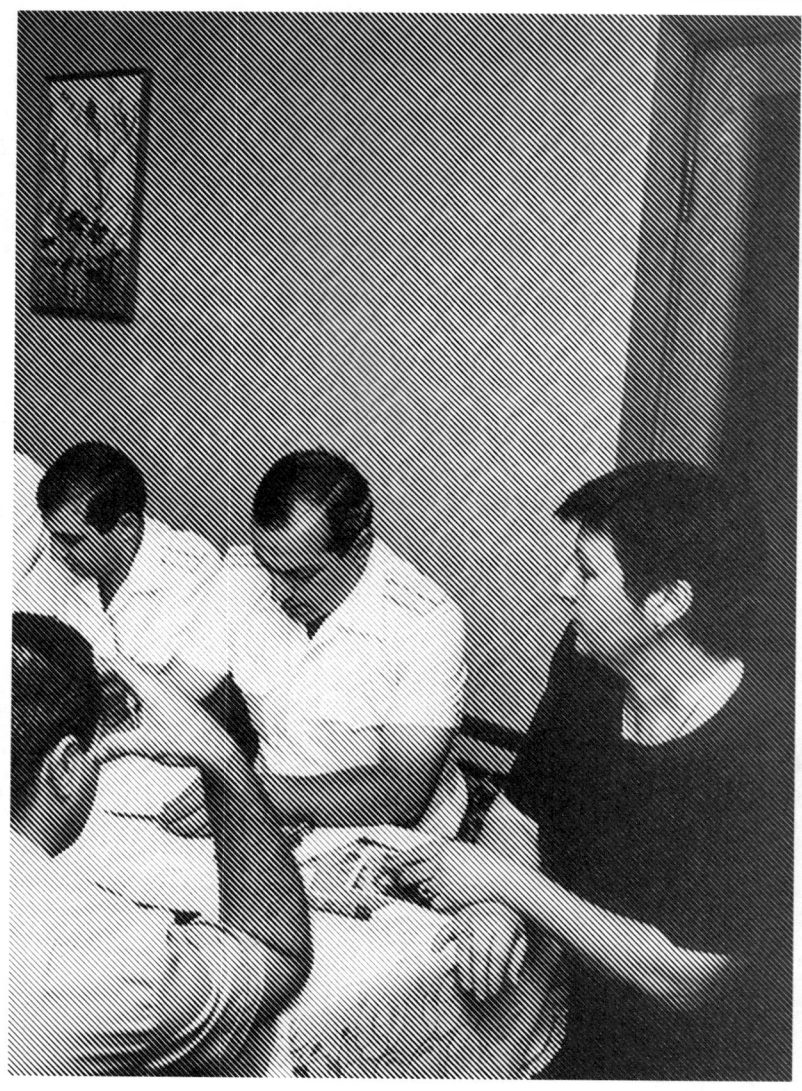

Susanna Vardanyan

Women's Rights Center (WRC)
Astra, Central and Eastern European Women's Network for Sexual and
Reproductive Health and Rights

Susanna Vardanyan (born 1951) is an obstetrician-gynecologist by profession: she graduated from the Yerevan Medical Institute and has worked at the Institute for Family Planning and Reproductive Health in the city of Yerevan for over 25 years. She is also the founder of one of the first women's organizations in Armenia, and a leader of the women's movement in the country. She works for the prevention of violence against women and provides support to victims.

Susanna Vardanyan is the founder of not only the first women's organization, but of the first NGO in Armenia. Led by Susanna, the Women's Rights Center (WRC) focuses on "Breaking the Silence About Violence Against Women." Its core goals are the prevention of violence against women and children, the defense of their rights, and the development and support of systems to counter persecution and violence against them. Their telephone hotline for women was the first such service for victims of violence in the entire country, and their Crisis Center and Women's Support Group (WSG) unite women suffering from domestic violence, offering therapy and talks where women share experiences, learning to find their own solutions to their situations. In seven years, the Center has been contacted for help by over 9166 women: 5321 were given psychological help, 3840 were given legal advice, and 86 were defended in court. WRC also works against the trafficking and trade of women, and is a member of Astra, the Central and Eastern European Women's Network for Sexual and Reproductive Health and Rights. Astra, of which Susanna is a founder, too, is lobbying for safe abortions and better access to information on safe sex, abortion, contraception, Aids, and sexually transmitted diseases.

Susanna participated in the United Nations Fourth World Conference on Women in Beijing, China, as well as in the NGO Forum in New York, and in 2002 was recognized for her work by the Minnesota Advocates for Human Rights. Through Susanna and her team, the problem of violence against women has been acknowledged in Armenia. She has great plans for the future, working hardest on issuing a law on domestic violence, and the establishment of a state infrastructure: "When the law is accepted and the infrastructure works, I will be confident of real help for women."

In Armenia, rigid national traditions exist, forcing women to play secondary roles. Disrespect and domestic violence towards women have become a national problem, and thousands of women fight for equal rights and for active participation in the public, political, and economic life.

Armenia

Galuh Wandita

Commission for Reception, Truth and Reconciliation (CAVR)

Galuh Wandita (born 1966) is an activist working for human rights in conflict areas. She frames her work with a gender perspective irrespective of whether it deals with industry/corporate-triggered conflict in Kalimantan or Papua or atrocities following the referendum in East Timor prior to the birth of the new nation. With her professional contribution spanning more than a dozen years, Galuh has established herself in the forefront of the feminist movement. Her work has not only changed the lives of the people she works for, but also the way human rights are applied, promoted and protected.

Galuh Wandita was in East Timor during the referendum in 1999 where she witnessed terrible human rights violations on an unthinkable scale. "That is when I saw the worst and the best of human beings," she says. "That is probably what made me stay for another five years — to heal my own trauma by pro-actively working with the people in the process of reconciliation." At the Commission for Reception, Truth and Reconciliation (CAVR), Galuh Wandita carries out a mandate to record the human rights violations that took place in East Timor from 1974 to 1999, helping to document confessions and public hearings, lending support to the victims, rehabilitating them and facilitating reconciliation between those who committed lesser crimes — such as burning, looting and minor assaults — and the communities they victimized.

Galuh has been working on the impact of human rights violations on women for more than a dozen years. She worked for an NGO in the US dealing with reproductive health and HIV/Aids. In Indonesia, in 1989, she worked in the field of women and development, joining Oxfam Great Britain, which was starting to move from a welfare-based approach to a rights-based approach to development. Moving to East Nusa Tenggara, one of the poorest provinces in Indonesia, she got in touch with individuals and groups working with factory workers, urban slum dwellers and poor rural communities in the faraway eastern islands. Later, as Oxfam Australia's Country Representative in Indonesia, she developed a program to support local groups run by indigenous community leaders fighting for survival in conflict areas in the eastern islands, including West Papua, Kalimantan, East and West Timor.

After 24 years of colonization, East Timor gained its independence in 1999. But it went through a phase of violence committed by the Indonesian military and its militias, in which women suffered rape, sexual slavery and other traumas that left them with unwanted children and deep psychological scars.

Indonesia

Xingjuan Wang

Red Maple Women's Consultation and Service Center

Wang Xingjuan became a reporter at 20. She has been particularly concerned with the scale of problems — many of them new — that women are facing during the process of China's reform and opening-up. She founded an organization, the Red Maple Women's Consultation and Service Center, which launched the first of many hotlines for women. Retired since 1998, Wang continues to work for women.

Since she became a reporter for the Xihua Daily, Wang Xingjuan had been dealing with words. In 1951 she worked for China Youth as one of the first youth reporters. From 1974 she worked at the Beijing Publishing Company. When she retired, she could have chosen a writing career, but she was concerned that the process of reform was creating new problems for women, and she wanted to do something for them. She founded the Women's Research Institute, which was affiliated to the School of Management Science and later renamed The Red Maple Women's Consultation and Service Center. Red Maple began without an office in a one-story house that leaked rain in the summer and was windy in the winter, and was furnished with second-hand desks and chairs. "Tell us your worries, we will do our best to help" is the motto of Red Maple, which in September 1992 opened the first hotline for women in China. A year later, the women experts hotline and a second hotline for women were opened. In January 1998 a new hotline was opened for elderly women, and in March 2004 a hotline for victims of domestic violence. These hotlines have played an important role in relieving the psychological pressure on women, improving their self-confidence and self-strengthening, and enhancing their mental health. Red Maple has recruited and trained many volunteers, most of whom are highly qualified intellectual women. "Loving people, loving lives, loving society," is how Red Maple describes its spirit.

China's social and economic reform process has created new problems for women. Many feel they can stand on their own feet only with support, but others are trying to deal with reform in different ways. Only a few manage to be independent in the competitive environment created by the reform process.

China

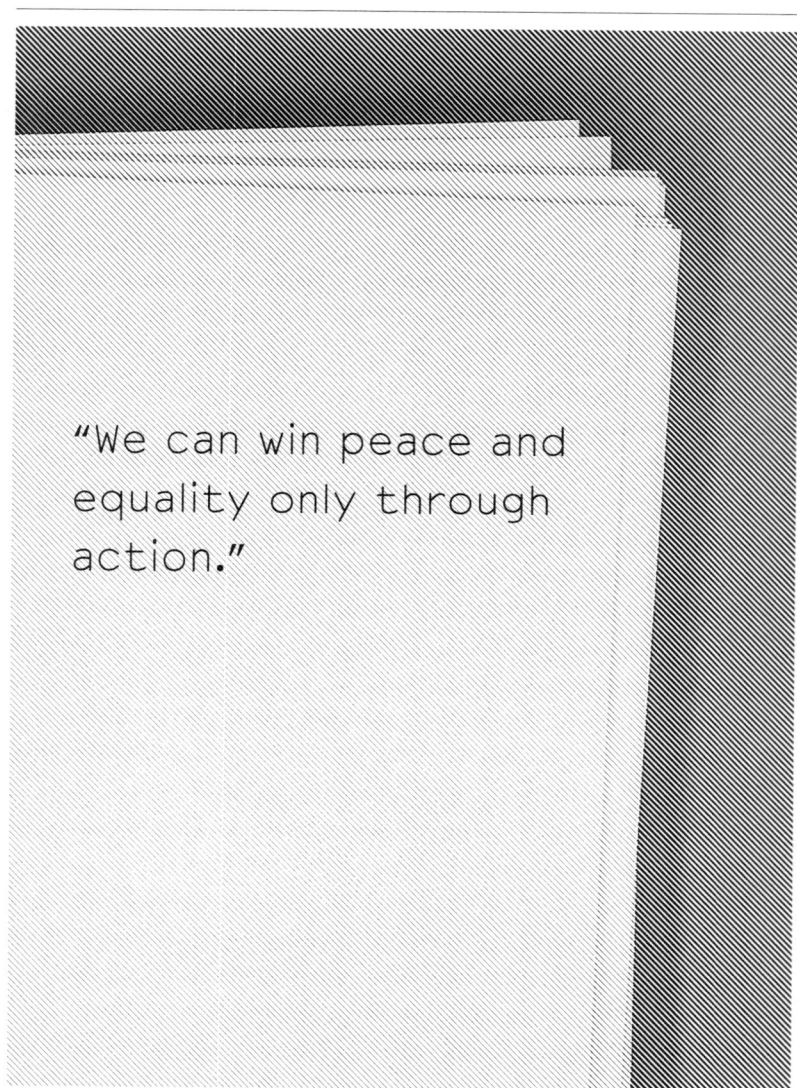

"We can win peace and equality only through action."

Meirong Wu

Women's Federation of Hebei Province

Wu Meirong (48) is a defender of women's rights. She takes every opportunity to conduct trainings and spread the message of law, while at the same time setting up various kinds of institutions to tackle the problems. Her work has helped to change the usual perception of domestic violence as a private, family affair in indictments and verdicts in court, and has also helped courts to take into consideration cases of women who practice violence to counter the violence they are exposed to.

Wu Meirong was born in a remote village in Hebei Province. When she was young, her studies were repeatedly interrupted because her family was poor and because of discrimination towards women. She finished high school with support from her teachers. She also faced discrimination when she entered the job market. Thus, when she joined the Women's Federation in 1985, she was determined to try her best to defend women's rights. With the cooperation of her colleagues, in four years' time, Wu Meirong successfully lobbied the people's representatives of Hebei Province to draft the "Regulations on Preventing and Deterring Domestic Violence in Hebei Province", which was the first regulation against domestic violence in China, and the best implemented so far at a provincial level.

Based on international practice, the women's federation cooperated with different units in the establishment of 185 women's legal support centers, 1988 township women's legal claim stations, eight domestic violence injury evaluation centers, and 21 shelter stations. Wu Meirong used her writing skills to help produce material on domestic violence, to publish articles on the subject and to present detailed reports of typical cases. She initiated a signature campaign entitled "starting from me, resist domestic violence" which had a strong impact. Among the 85,000 signatories, 69,000 were men.

Learning from some typical cases, she managed to persuade the court to take a new perspective in indictments and verdicts on women who practice violence to counter the violence inflicted on them. Wu has made many personal sacrifices in her work. Once when she was involved in a property case, the head of a civil court took revenge on her and caused her to lose over 100,000 yuan. But Wu Meirong managed to get through the difficult times. She knew that she needed to face many obstacles on the road to peace.

Though women have aquired new spaces for development due to reform measures, they are also confronted with new problems and challenges. In particular, domestic violence and the violation of their labor and land rights are major obstacles to women's development.

China

Yusan Yeblo

Yayasan Angganeta
The Eastern Indonesian Women Health Network (JKPIT)
Kelompok Kerja Wanita (KKW)

Yusan Yeblo (born 1951) is a dedicated social worker from Jayapura, Papua. Her enthusiasm and perseverance in helping Papuan women to have a better life has taken her through an exhausting three-decade journey. She has travelled throughout the islands and lived in remote villages setting up a vast network. Her decades as a social activist have been humbling, she says, but they have also enlivened her spirit and heightened her conviction that a change for a better Papua is possible. Yusan has been a commissioner of the National Commission on Anti-Violence against Women since 1999.

Yusan Yeblo began her social work in the early 1970s, at a Catholic mission near the border of Papua New Guinea. "When I first started my work, Papuan women had no rights at all. We lived in an 'uncle-dominated' world, when our uncles could stop us from realizing our dreams. They could stop us from working, from having hopes and they also decided to whom and when we got married," she says. Yusan worked in the remote areas, helping village women improve their skills. "We trained them to sew, to cook, to become nutrition workers or health workers." She also worked with farmers on the distribution of their cash crops to the capital town.

In the 1980s, Yusan relocated to Jayapura, where she engaged women activists in discussions on the role of women and social activism, with particular focus on the dowry issue and the position of women in their culture. She joined Yayasan Pengembangan Masyarakat Desa (YPMD), an NGO based in Jayapura. Later, she founded Kelompok Kerja Wanita (KKW) or Women Work Group, to help give a voice to women on issues that relate to their own welfare. Yusan considers her work with the women to be apolitical but she recalls: "It was hard at the beginning, there were suspicions, because we were non-government. We started with our own resources, no money at all." One of the most senior social workers in the women's network in Papua, Yusan supports the other Papuan NGOs, especially those working on women's rights and violence against women. The outspoken Yusan speaks up at the annual meetings of the traditional council Dewan Adat where she challenges the way Papuan men perceive women and discusses roles women can play in development.

Papua, formerly known as Irian Jaya, was under martial law from the 1960s to the 1990s due to an active separatist insurgency in the province. During those difficult years, the women suffered the most, as victims of rape and other degrading treatment.

Indonesia

Shuqin Zhang

Beijing Sun Village Special Children Aid Center

Zhang Shuqin is director of the Beijing Sun Village Special Children Aid Center. Since 1994 she has set up five villages for unattended minors whose parents are serving prison sentences. She has also helped many people that have been released from prison, despite money constraints and a lack of enabling government policies.

Zhang Shuqin was a reporter for a newspaper produced specially for prisoners in Shaanxi Province in China. In her spare time she also produced literary, film and TV works on prisoners and prisons. In the course of visiting virtually all the prisons in Shaanxi Province, she became increasingly concerned about juvenile delinquents in juvenile halls and female prisoners in women's prisons. Many children of prisoners became delinquents only because they were left unattended. Many female prisoners became insane because their children were left unattended.

As a policewoman, journalist, and writer, Zhang could not sit quietly in her cozy office, and she decided to help the imprisoned mothers and their children. She was keen to set up a shelter for the children who she believed should not be held responsible for their parents' mistakes. She went from place to place on her bicycle in her quest for help, and between 1996 and 2004 she managed to set up five children's villages to take care of the unattended children. She has also built a transit house for women released from prison.

She has so far helped more than 600 unattended children and more than 180 women released from prison. She is called "Grandma Zhang" in the children's villages and was nicknamed "Leader of Beggar Gang" by the public. She knows that her fate is now tied up with the children's villages and the unattended children. "The measures of success are not power, wealth, or status, but the meaning and value of life," Zhang often says. She defines her life's work as changing the fate of the vulnerable groups.

When the state imprisons people, it seldom has strategies or service organizations that can cope with the children of prisoners, and the neglect they face often turns them into juvenile delinquents. This is what happened in Shaanxi Province where Zhang Shuqin began work.

China

The Struggle for Survival: Minorities and Indigenous Peoples

Leonardo Boff

The Indian communities are, almost all of them, survivors of centuries of extermination perpetrated by the western imperialist and colonizer culture. As a result of this, Indians have become minorities in their own lands.

But they have shown that they cannot be exterminated. They are everywhere, still growing in numbers, rebuilding their culture, rescuing their traditions and invigorating their religion. Because of the predominant bias against them — that they are not truly human beings — the Indians have waged an uphill struggle for survival. Just as it happened in Brazil, their lands have been invaded and many Indians have been killed.

Fortunately many humanitarian organizations and religious groups have been helping the cause of the Indians and have supported their claims. In all these struggles for resistance and liberation, the women have been present and active. Together with the men, they have fought hard to survive and to retain their lands. However, their greatest struggle is how to interact with the dominant modern culture. The Indian communities cannot be isolated or treated like a natural holy place. There has to be an interchange of cultures and knowledge, from their own identity, so they can develop and benefit from the modern world.

The most difficult issue is the deep inequality in the relationship between the Indian communities and the modern world. It is like David and Goliath, with Goliath, the dominant culture, showing itself as implacable, unable to open its mind to learn from the wisdom that the Indian cultures can impart, specially their knowledge concerning the environment, community life and a sense of the spiritual.

Many women have made use of this dialogue, studying and helping to keep alive the identity in their communities, while incorporating what could make their lives better. As an Indian chief from the Krenac Community in Brazil said: "I want a truck in my community, not just to increase our production, but also to be less tired, and to have some more free time to enjoy living together and hold our parties."

The Indians are true environmentalists. They have learned how to manage their lands without demeaning the environment. Many people imagine that the Amazon is a savage and uncultured land. In truth, there are hundreds of nations living there that protect the forest. The Indians manage 12 percent of the forest, promoting "resource lands" where they cultivate fruit and vegetable species in limited areas for use of the community and for others who may be in need.

The Yanomami Indians utilize 78 percent of the tree species in their land, and know 100 different species of cassava (the so-called potato of the tropics), their main aliment, while the rest of the world knows only 12.

The Indians say that the land is their mother, because it produces everything they need. They therefore treat it with reverence and respect. An animal is never killed or a tree chopped down without reason, but to meet a human need. And when they have to do these things, the Indians conduct rituals where they seek permission, in order not to break the link of friendship between man and nature.

Such values should motivate us to preserve the natural heritage that we have received and in our irresponsibility, have misappropriated. The Indians (men and women) can be, in my view, our masters. If we adopt the attitudes and values that the Indians live by, the Pacha Mama and the Big Land Mother will be saved.

Leonardo Boff, a recipient of the Right Livelihood Award in 2001, is one of the pioneers of liberation theology. Silenced by the Vatican in 1985 because of his criticism of the Catholic Church in his book "The Church, Charisma and Power", he remains active as a lay priest working among poor communities through the comunidades de base or "Basic Christian Communities".

J

María Eugenia Aguilar Castro

Rescate Ancestral Indígena Salvadoreño (RAIS)

María Eugenia Aguilar was introduced to the ancestral world through an indigenous nanny who spoke the Quiché language. After spending time with notable Indigenous Americans, she began to identify herself fully with the indigenous world. She is the founder of Kal Tunal (The House of the Sun) and of the Salvadorian Institute for Indigenous Ancestral Rescue (Rais). Their aim is to investigate and to make visible indigenous customs and values, helping them to take their place in popular national culture.

María Eugenia Aguilar (born in 1948) was greatly influenced by several accidental meetings she had with notable Indigenous Americans. There was no way out of it. An indigenous nanny had inclined her sense of hearing towards the sweet sound of the birds. Some years later, a Mexican Nahua speaker and bonesetter awakened in her the will to recover the earth where she lived her childhood. She soon learned the Náhuatl in Nahuizalco (indigenous region in the West of El Salvador). An indigenous Guatemalan changed her life forever, naming her "Tzunún Ja," which means 'sparrow,' the one who carries the message. When the Venezuelan Domingo Díaz Port founded the Association of Solar Indigenous America (Mais) — an international organization located in Mexico — María Eugenia joined it, giving seminars and workshops on culture and language. Later, she attended the encounter called 'Song for the earth' — organized by the Navajo Indigenous Americans from Arizona. The year after, she acted as coordinator for the event known as 'In Lakech' (You are my other ego), in El Salvador. In 1992, she founded the Centre for Cultural Training and Human Development, Escuela de Tejedores Kal Tunal o Casa Del Sol (The House of the Sun), and, in 1994, the Salvadorian Institute for Indigenous Ancestral Rescue (Rais), of which she is still the director. She is the author of the book 'Women's empowerment through their ancestral wisdom,' and has compiled the first indigenous profile of El Salvador.

María Eugenia Aguilar, the Mayan priestess, maintains that "a peaceful world will be possible when elderly people are involved with young people, so that traditional cultures will not be forgotten and destroyed. The current concept of sustainability shall be understood as the sustainability of life itself. That is why part of my work is to validate memory, wisdom, knowledge and the art of the communities."

The Spanish conquest devastated indigenous culture. Native lands have been expropriated, reducing the men to day workers. A peasant uprising, in 1932, was put down by the government with vast murders. To survive, the indigenous communities made themselves invisible inside Salvadoran society.

El Salvador

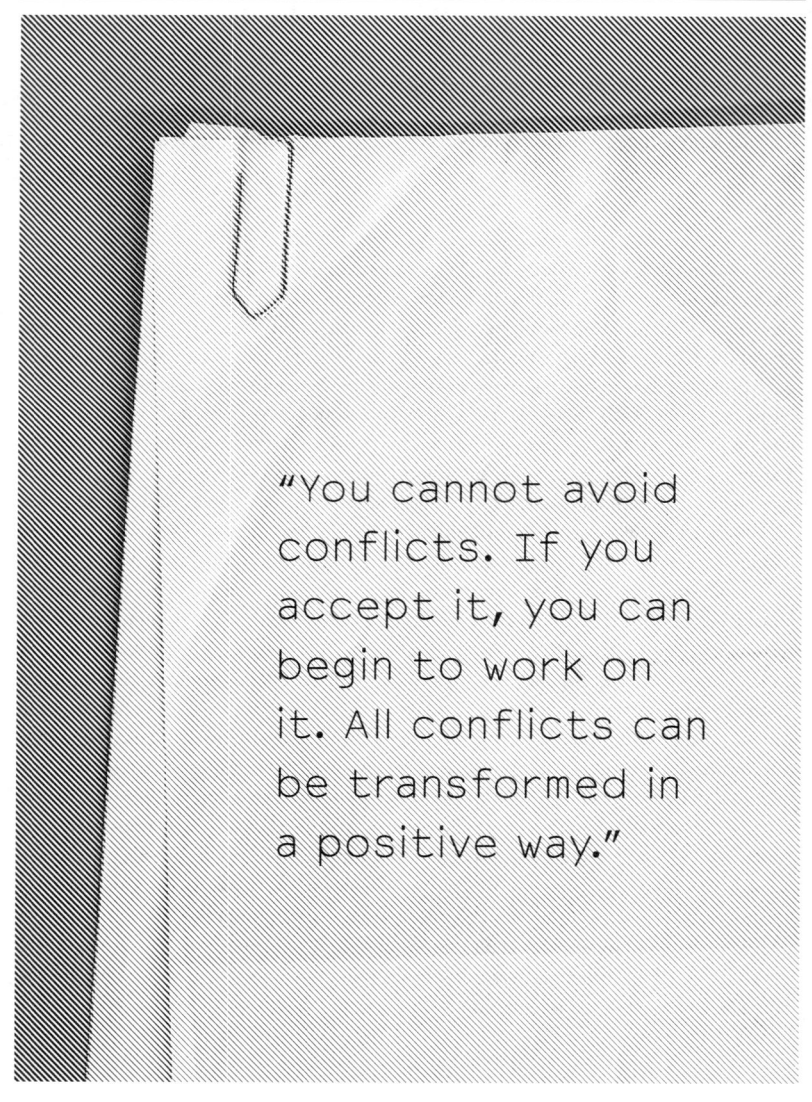

"You cannot avoid conflicts. If you accept it, you can begin to work on it. All conflicts can be transformed in a positive way."

Sylvia Aguilera Garcia

Action for Conflict Transformation

Sylvia Aguilera Garcia was born in Mexico City, in 1974. She belongs to a large family. She was the only girl and the oldest granddaughter. She has worked for peace since her college years, when she began to question the lack of order in the world. These thoughts motivated her to work for the defense of human rights of the indigenous people, women and political prisoners.

She is only 31 years old and has already been director of a non-governmental organization, which was recognized in Mexico for its work on human rights. Sylvia Aguilera Garcia is a young Mexican. "I am the second of five children, the only girl. I grew up in an extended family, Catholic, where women have had a very important role, specially my maternal grandmother and my mother." She has been involved in situations that were ground-breaking in her country, for example the case of general Gallardo. In 1993, he made public the violations of human rights perpetrated by military forces that included torture and the disappearance of prisoners. He was accused of slander against the Military Forces, and condemned to 28 years in jail; after 8 years, he was liberated thanks to international pressure. Sylvia Aguilera Garcia has also been involved in the defense of the Tzotziles indigenous women raped by the Mexican military and the follow up to the assassinations of the women of Ciudad Juárez. A social movement has been formed against what is known as the 'feminicide' in Ciudad Juárez. Those are part of her experience as a worker for human rights, and later on as a director of the Mexican Commission for the Promotion and Defense of Human Rights.

"I had the opportunity to participate in the coordination of the Civil Mission for Peace, a network of organizations that wanted not only to intercede in the Chiapas conflict, but was also interested in taking part in the wider process of promoting the ethical and cultural values of non violence in the country." That is her preoccupation and her main goal: to transform conflicts involved in all human situations, into sources of positive learning. "In the international network Action for Conflict Transformation, I have found a place where it has been possible to crystallize the idea: think globally, act locally."

Human rights are violated in the Mexican Republic in spite of the country wide official talks. The existence of an increasing percentage of poor people demonstrates this fact. Desperation and tiredness mobilizes people to organize and defend themselves with whatever means they have at hand.

Mexico

Parveena Ahangar

Association of Parents of Disappeared Persons (APDP)

Parveena Ahangar (born approximately 1957) is an extraordinary woman who has risen above personal trauma to rally against injustice. The mother of a son who "disappeared", she formed the Association of Parents of Disappeared Persons (APDP) to fight this pernicious form of human rights' abuse. Thanks to the APDP's efforts, the government has finally acknowledged that almost 4000 people have vanished in custody, and has promised to bring this practice to an end.

Parveena Ahangar is an ordinary housewife from a lower–middle–class family whose young son "disappeared" after being abducted by three army officers from outside his house when he had just returned from school. Parveena brazenly demanded information on his whereabouts, and later formed an association of parents whose children had become victims of "enforced disappearances". The APDP is tenacious in demanding information on disappearances during the 16 years of conflict in Jammu and Kashmir. The organization, which brings together nearly 450 such families, finally forced the government to acknowledge that almost 4000 people have disappeared, although its numbers are disputed by civil society groups.

Parveena relies on advocacy, visiting the relatives of the disappeared, helping them work out strategies for action and peaceful forms of agitation. She also provides counseling to traumatized women by holding regular meetings with them. She formed the APDP in 1994, when disappearances were peaking, and the existence of such a watchdog body was chancy. Parveena persuaded the families of the disappeared, mostly uneducated people, to persist in demanding information. Her actions were timely, since the rate of enforced disappearances in Kashmir grew exponentially after the 1989 outbreak of armed conflict in the valley. Parveena's work was fraught with risks. At a demonstration in Srinagar in 1998, the security forces shot dead a prominent woman APDP member on the spot.

Parveena still has no information about her son's fate. She is not reconciled to his loss, demanding accountability through her movement and the courts.

Many students, civilians, political activists, and militants have "disappeared" in custody during the 16 years of armed separatist struggle in Kashmir – 3931 people, by the government's (disputed) estimates. The true statistics could be closer to 8000 to 10,000.

India

Hero Ahmad

Kurdistan Save the Children (KSC)
Khak Press and Media Centre (KPMC)
Ibrahim Ahmad Foundation (IAF)

Hero Ahmad comes from a high-profile family, as her father was a leading political activist, who was imprisoned in Abu Ghraib during her infancy. Her work has mainly focused on the Suleimaniya district of Kurdistan, Iraq. She is the founder and director of Kurdistan Save the Children (KSC), Khak Press and Media Centre (KPMC) and KURDSAT Satellite TV. KSC's main objective is to ensure a better future for children, focusing on the economic and social spheres of family, health, education and housing.

Much of Hero Ahmad's peace activities have been through Kurdistan Save the Children, which she worked hard to found and which she now presides, focusing on the betterment of conditions for Iraqi children and families. Among Hero's recent projects is the full refurbishment of 50 kindergartens in the district of Suleimaniya. She has also opened a Youth Activity Center in Khanaqeen and the Children's Rehabilitation Centre (CRC) for street children in Baghdad, now accommodating an average of 100 children.

However, funding the charitable projects in Iraq in the last 15 years was a real challenge to the KSC, because of the UN Sanctions. With the auspicious sponsorship of the KSC, approximately 10,000 undernourished children are now leading a normal life and are able to attend school regularly. Around 5000 children have benefited from the centers and special schools of the KSC. In total there are 26 centers for street children, orphans and those with special needs or learning difficulties.

Hero also became a member of the Kurdish Parliament, which was established in 2001. Since then she has devoted her time to children, widows and displaced persons, as well as to art. She has organized a number of artistic events, such as "The World We Want" art exhibition, in association with the University of Victoria, Canada, and also supports the work of young musicians, writers, poets and painters. Moreover she has transformed many of the former government's intelligence buildings, which were used for torture, into museums and has worked on the restoration of archaeological sites in Iraq. For the genocide widows she has established various income-generating projects, such as local handicraft workshops. Her work has inspired the setting up of similar centers and schools in other parts of Iraq since the collapse of Saddam's regime, particularly in the South of Iraq.

Much of Hero's peace activities have been through Kurdistan Save the Children (KSC), which she worked hard to found and which she now presides. She focuses on the betterment of conditions for Iraqi children and families.

María Beatriz Aniceto Pardo

Asociación de Cabildos NASA CHXACHXA
Colombian Women's Pacific Path

María Beatriz Aniceto Pardo (40) is an indigenous woman. She lives where she was born, in the Cauca Valley, in Colombia. When she was a little girl, she was employed as a domestic worker. When she became a woman, she was already committed to fighting for justice for her own ethnic group, the Nasa. Today, she fights against the compulsory conscription of young indigenous men by the armed forces and the guerrillas, and also for respect for their territory, their autonomy and their vision of the world, centered in their love of the earth and nature.

María Beatriz Aniceto Pardo is a 'cuetandera' maker: this is a backpack made of sheep's wool and cabuya thread. The cabuya is a tiny plant that grows in the heights of Cauca. The cuetanderas are woven by hand, by the Nasa women. María Beatriz is a Nasa woman, born in the Colombian region of Cauca. A cuetandera "is like a woman's womb; growing like the child inside, the womb widens in order to provide enough space for all those who want to come inside it," she explains.

In Colombia, there are 86 indigenous territories, where eight ethnic groups survive, although, "we are near the end." When María Beatriz Aniceto Pardo was a child, she lived in her 'resguardo' — as the indigenous community is called. Later on, she had to work as a domestic worker and had to withstand abuse. The 'cuetandera' got wider and María Beatriz even found time to study. She successfully completed her secondary studies and returned to Cauca, determined to not allow anyone to disrespect the women of her ethnic group. She joined the Cabildos Nasa Chxachxa, a political organization for preserving the ancestral heritage of the indigenous people. From the years 1998 to 2000, she was the first woman to govern her 'cabildo,' in Avirama. She had to face challenges: the Revolutionary Colombian Armed Forces and the Army for National Liberation — both guerrilla organizations — that came into the 'resguardos' to conscript young Nasa boys by force. First there was the encroachment, then Nasan opposition and then dialog.

María Beatriz is still dedicated to the fight for her ethnic group. In 2004, she led an extremely well attended march (70,000 people) that went through a part of Colombia asking for the end of the war and for respect for the indigenous 'resguardos.' The 'cuetandera' widens: It has enough space for peace.

Since the 1960s, Colombia has been going through a civil war. In the 1970s and 1980s, the guerilla groups killed the leaders of the indigenous population and conscripted the young men against their will. The indigenous communities struggle for respect for their position and their way of life.

Colombia

Munni Hembrom, Agnes Murmu, and Agatha Baskey have shown true grit and resourcefulness by setting up an organization that empowers women of the Santhal tribe, to which they belong.

Ayo Aidari Trust

Munni Hembrom, (born 1969), Agnes Murmu (born 1962), and Agatha Baskey (born 1975) are trailblazers. They have shown courage and resourcefulness by setting up an organization that mobilizes women of the Santhal tribe, to which they belong. Their Ayo Aidari (women's rights) Trust works for the empowerment of women through women's organizations, fights for women's rights — such as property rights — and targets retrograde practices like witch-hunting, forced marriage, and bigamy among Santhals. It promotes sustainable agriculture, tree-planting, and forest and environmental protection.

Munni Hembrom, Agnes Murmu, and Agatha Baskey live and work in the Dumka district of Jharkhand state and together run the Ayo Aidari Trust. The organization mobilizes Santhal women, acting to enforce their rights. The trust works for the empowerment of women through women's organizations, fights for women's rights — such as property rights — and targets retrograde practices like witch-hunting, forced marriage, and bigamy among the Santhals. It promotes sustainable agriculture, tree-planting, forest protection, and protection of the environment by the community. It has set up mothers' committees to promote the education of children and helps establish primary health services at the village level. It also enhances the capacity of Santhal women to liaise with the government to initiate development programs in their areas.

The activities of the Ayo Aidari Trust are funded with contributions from encouraging individuals. They have also built institutional collaborations with agencies like the Sir Dorabji Tata Trust, Mumbai, and the Pratichi (India) Trust, Shantiniketan. Ayo Aidari works with more than 5000 Santhal women. The trust's involvement in the lives of the villagers has brought visible changes. Women now participate in meetings and make decisions. Savings groups have been set up. While moneylenders still hover around, their role is diminishing. Debts have been reduced, and the freed land is being cultivated. The tribals now sell their products in the regular market. Women also have a better understanding of health issues, and pay for medical treatment with the savings they generate.

Munni, Agnes, and Agatha started their work in five villages-now, they are in 40. They are continuously invited by other villages to work in them, and it is not hard to see why.

Santhals are the largest adivasi (tribal) group in India, with more than ten million living in the east of the country. While Santhal women play productive roles, both customary practices and codified law provide few rights to them, particularly rights assuring ownership and control over property.

India

Maggiorina Balbuena

National Coordination of Organizations of Female Peasants and Indigenous Women

"Maggi" — Maggiorina Balbuena (54) — was born and raised in the countryside where the green color of the foliage is mixed with the yellow color of the maize. She was the oldest daughter, and took care of her nine brothers and sisters as if they were a precious treasure. She learned to cultivate and to love the earth. She suffered from the extreme poverty that enveloped all the peasant farmers. Her awareness and determination to fight came from her background.

Maggiorina Balbuena is a tiny woman with a great commitment to the fierce struggle to reverse the situation endured by the Paraguayan rural population. She was convinced that the rich lived in the cities and the poor in the countryside, and decided to search for a formula that could give relief to the rural workers. At age 21, she entered the Agrarian Catholic Youth, a movement inside the Paraguayan Catholic Church that existed since the period of the Dictatorship. They attempted to create rural communities based on cooperative effort. Due to her militancy in this organization, she was imprisoned. She became a so-called dangerous person. She remembers how they described her: "She is a chattering communist who taught too many things to peasants" — a communist that was already a militant member of the Agrarian Peasant Leagues.

In 1975, due to the bloody governmental repression unleashed against activists from her organization, she exiled herself in Brazil. She returned clandestinely in 1977, and helped to found the Paraguayan Peasant Movement in 1980. Five years later, she created the Coordination of Peasant Women that, in 1999, led to the foundation of the National Coordination of the Organizations of Female Peasants and Indigenous Women. Maggiorina Balbuena says, "My immediate goal is to encourage concrete actions from the State that will help rural and indigenous women to improve their life conditions. When I see that women have the basic things they deserve as human beings, I will then feel that I have done something."

The Paraguayan women of the rural regions of the country agreed that "there is not much difference between the suffering of the peasant women and the indigenous women." Shortly afterwards, in 1999, they founded the National Coordination of Organizations of Female Peasants and Indigenous Women.

Paraguay

Faith Bandler

Aboriginal–Australian Fellowship; Women's Electoral Lobby (WEL)
Federal Council for the Advancement of Aboriginals and Torres Strait
Islanders (FCAATSI)

Even as a child, Faith Bandler (86) showed the many qualities that blossomed in her later life. The abuse and exclusion she experienced as an indigenous schoolgirl in white Australia left a lasting impression on her, but she still exudes a serenity that belies her extraordinary energy for the cause of justice for indigenous peoples, for women, and for the peace movement. Indigenous Australians and Pacific Islanders have been the direct beneficiaries of her crusade. Her work for abolition of war and elimination of poverty has been of international significance, earning her several major awards.

Growing up as an indigenous person in Australia and knowing of the horror and destruction of World War II made Faith Bandler dedicate her life to the cause of indigenous peoples, peace, and abolition of war. "For a black person, living in a white society, the discrimination is there since birth. Blacks were always being treated as third class citizens and women were at a disadvantage in many ways. I always had a great sense of justice and felt a strong urge to rectify these problems. This is the driving force that gives me energy and keeps me going in my fight for human rights and peace." Confronted with racism at all levels — institutional, social, and personal — Faith says there were always difficulties in the struggle. Her vision of a peaceful future is the total absence of war and elimination of poverty. "We should remember that we have maintained relatively constant world peace since World War II. We, as people, have to be vigilant and keep governments vigilant. We have to condemn people who think war is a solution and encourage verbal communication." Even today, Faith participates in peace marches. She was there when Sydneysiders walked the streets to stop the Australian government from joining the Coalition of the Willing in the invasion of Iraq in 2003. With two lovely granddaughters to improve the world for, she hopes for nothing more than total abolition of war. "When we take war out, we take hatred out and encourage communication, leading to a peaceful world," says Faith, whose vision for the future is a world where the poor have the opportunity to be educated, have good housing, reliable communications and all those human rights many people take for granted. She has utmost conviction that, "We can change anything. Nothing is set in concrete. We can have a peaceful world."

The Australian Constitution originally did not permit indigenous people to be counted in the census, thereby denying their right to vote. The successful 1967 referendum put an end to this inequity and encouraged the government to make laws for the benefit of indigenous Australians.

Australia

Domitila Barrios de Chungara

Mobile School Project

'Let me speak' is the name of her famous book. Moema Viezzer is the co-author. It has been the object of numerous translations and editions. In it, Domitila Chungara (born in 1937), a Bolivian indigenous, speaks. Daughter and wife of miners, she survived a massacre and the denunciation she made conducted her to imprisonment. She has been put in jail and tortured numerous times. She had seven children, but lost four of them because of this violence. Later, along with other women, she began a hunger strike that gathered support and brought down Hugo Bánzer, the Bolivian dictator.

"In the richest mines live the poorest people. When the urine reaches the ground it has already turned to ice. Only people with the capacity to work have the right to housing and food. If a worker is killed or incapacitated as a result of an accident, his family will be left homeless." The woman who tells us these things is one of the indigenous people of Bolivia, Domitila Chungara. Both daughter and wife of miners, she lived in between tin and silver mining areas of the high plateau. She was General Secretary of the Syndicate of Housewives. She suffered repressions, but never lost "that hope we always have that one day things will change."

The miners organized themselves. The government of René Barrientos (1966—69) was afraid. They sent planes on the night of San Juan. "We were dancing and celebrating and the bullets being fired got mixed up with the fireworks of San Juan. The soldiers murdered men, women and children without pity." Domitila was captured. She was pregnant. Because of the torture, her baby died. Time went on, and another dictator arose, Hugo Bánzer (1971—78). Then, the unbelievable happened: Domitila, along with four other women, went to the Capital and began a hunger strike. Soon, thousands joined them and the dictator fell. Injustices continued. Domitila went abroad and denounced the wrong doings from there. They forbade her from returning. With the help of a teacher, she wrote the book 'Let me speak.' In the 1980s, she lived, in exile, in Sweden. A sister of hers continued her fight in Bolivia. She was murdered. Domitila returned and created her Mobile School Project. With it, she went to remote villages. She talked about her hopes for a better world. "My people have given me my strength. They never give up."

Politically, Bolivia has a history of instability. Dictator Hugo Bánzer, who governed the country between 1971 and 1978, came to power after 186 coups. His was the 187th in 146 years. Bolivia, a country of large tin and silver mines, has an enormous indigenous population living in misery.

Bolivia

Joênia Batista de Carvalho

Conselho Indígena de Roraima (CIR)

Joênia Batista de Carvalho (1974) is part of the Wapicharas, an indigenous ethnic group. She was born in Roraima, a Brazilian state, where indigenous rights still face great resistance to be recognized. She was the first indigenous in the country to become a lawyer. She works at the Indigenous Council of Roraima and is mainly focused on indigenous territorial rights. She seeks for justice for victims of violations: death threats, persecutions, torture and racial discrimination.

Until she was seven years old, Wapichara Joênia Batista de Carvalho lived in many indigenous villages. "My father used to move a lot because he believed a spirit was following him." One day, her mother got sick of that and decided to settle down. She moved to Boa Vista, capital of Roraima, and enrolled her kids in school. Joênia learned how to read and to use mathematical operations. She also learned how to defend herself. "People used to bother me because I am an indigenous. I would talk back and my mother would tell me to be quiet, but I never lost my pride."
She got into the Roraima Federal University Law School in fifth place. "Most students — whose parents were judges, district attorneys, politicians — asked what I was doing there." In a state where indigenous people are extremely discriminated, Joênia has not only graduated, but has also made people hear her. Nowadays, she is a national role model recognized by public powers and indigenous people, who were not used to female leaderships up until then.
Joênia Batista de Carvalho is the only lawyer at the Indigenous Council of Roraima (CIR), and she provides assistance to 238 communities from all over the state. Her main challenge is to obtain full legal recognition of the indigenous land Raposa do Sol, home of 15,000 people. Currently, it is one of the country's major conflict areas between indigenous people and invaders — gold miners, ranchers, rice growers. "A lot of indigenous people have been killed there." Joênia (31) faces "constant prejudice, discrimination and death threats." She does not feel intimidated: she is a mediator between indigenous people and government authorities. She gives countless lectures in Brazil and abroad about her people's situation. She also participates in courses for indigenous leaderships.

The indigenous area Raposa do Sol is located in Northwestern Roraima and has 1.67 million hectares. In 1998, it was legally recognized as the permanent territory of five indigenous groups, by former Minister of Justice, Renan Calheiros. Since then, they await for the President's ratification.

Brazil

"I believe that one day women's leadership among our indigenous elders will be recognized. We just need to work very hard to convince our elders and to raise our women's awareness and education."

Aleta Ba'un

Lembaga Masyarakat Adat
Women Voice Center Sanggar Suara Perempuan (SSP)

Aleta Ba'un (born 1966) is a West Timorese community organizer who defends the rights of indigenous peoples. She has helped found many local NGOs, including the Women Voice Center Sanggar Suara Perempuan (SSP) and the Eastern Indonesia Women's Health Network (JKPIT). Her leadership has been an inspiration to other activists, especially to other indigenous women.

Aleta Ba'un, a West Timorese indigenous woman, says, "Indigenous people are always left behind. We have to struggle to maintain our way of life." Aleta was born to a family of farmers in the remote village of Lelobatan in West Timor. She graduated from high school and, unable to pursue her studies because of poverty, she found work in the city as a housemaid. In 1993, she met some activists from the Haumeni Foundation, an NGO based in Soe City. Aleta recalls, "I experienced first-hand village organizing and raising awareness in the community, especially in regard to women's economic empowerment and health issues for the poor." Initially, she worked as a community organizer; being an indigenous person, she did not have trouble integrating with the people. Later, Aleta worked with Sanggar Suara Perempuan (SSP), an NGO that documents women's health problems, women's issues and the violations of women's rights. SSP trains village women and advocates for regulations in support of women and their health rights, and introduces local women to a rights perspective, especially the right to health services and law enforcement.

Aleta also worked on indigenous rights, founding the Alliance of Indigenous People in Kupang with some colleagues. In 1999, she engaged in a three-year battle against an investor, who tried to mine marble from an area considered by the indigenous people as a sacred heritage from their ancestors. The case drew national and international attention for months. Also known as "Mama Leta", Aleta is currently working to establish an Indigenous Peoples Council in 21 villages stretching from Soe City to Lelobatan village.

West Timor is a multi-ethnic society rich in natural resources. The indigenous peoples' claim that the area is sacred means that it cannot be exploited without the consent of the tribal leaders. The entry of mining investors has therefore angered the indigenous groups.

Indonesia

"I look at the world
through the prism
of social work. That's
who I am, that's
who I'll always be."

Akua Benjamin

Congress of Black Women of Canada—Toronto Chapter
Coalition of Visible Minority Women
National Organization of Immigrant and Visible Minority Women

Akua Benjamin is a noted activist, lobbyist, grassroots organizer, educator, and advocate for peace in Canada. A native of Trinidad, Benjamin has dedicated her life to fighting for the civil rights of marginalized populations, especially immigrant women and other women of color. Her intervention and advocacy have contributed to bringing to public attention the increasing need for changes to the social, economic, political, and cultural structures and systems that keep women and their families marginalized and suffering discrimination.

Akua's work has impacted the lives of many women through her active community involvement, sometimes at great sacrifice to her personal life. While gladly devoting a large measure of her time to her role as an activist and social-change agent, Akua also headed a single-parent household. Her responsibilities included raising a son, juggling full-time jobs as social worker, human rights worker, community organizer, and faculty member, as well as pursuing postsecondary studies. Throughout all of these full-time responsibilities, she undertook her community work on a voluntary basis, giving considerable time, energy, and often finances to these organizations.

Her activism comes with other costs as well. She has come under attack by the media, and several newspaper articles have attempted to delegitimize and marginalize her efforts at drawing attention to racism and injustice.

Akua says her career in social work grew from lifelong interests in community development and the promotion of human rights. As a social work educator, she has taught courses on community practice, group work, antioppression, ethnic diversity and social issues, intercultural communication, and families in the Caribbean. Her research interests and community work are in the areas of antiracism, crime, feminism, equity, antioppression, human rights, and other related social-justice issues. She has worked extensively with coalitions that focus on meaningful social, economic, and political change, and is currently a member of the management team on a project examining the impact of racism, violence, and health issues on African Canadians and their families.

In a patriarchal society, the rights and liberties of women have long been marginalized. Especially vulnerable are immigrant and minority women facing racism, sexism, and poverty. Many have been victimized by political and justice systems, the very institutions created to ensure equality for all.

Canada

Macedonia Blas

Fot'zi Ñañhö A.C.

Macedonia Blas is a Ñañhú (Mexican indigenous ethnic group) woman whose first child died when she was only 18 years old. She did not know how to take care of a little baby and, in her community, there were no doctors and there was no money. Later on, she had 11 more children. Nowadays, she is not only a mother; she is an organizer, a trainer and a defender of Mexican indigenous women.

To fight against the indigenous practices and customs that subjugate women, especially the customs related to sexuality, is a difficult task. That is one of the missions of Macedonia Blas, a Ñañhú (Mexican indigenous ethnic group; the Spanish name is Otomí; they live mainly in the states of Hidalgo and Querétaro) woman who pursues her struggle in her own community, in Mexico and in many other parts of the world. "I would have liked to begin to learn when I was young, but I could not. Now, no one can stop me. Little by little, things change."

Macedonia's community was reforested by the women who formed her group. They have different projects like farming mushrooms or holding workshops on human rights. "We have to learn about the rights of women. Only in this way can we achieve peace in our world. Today, we indigenous women live with a lot of violence, but our grandmothers suffered even more. People do not look on us in the way they should because we are indigenous. And for that reason we have to know our rights and learn." This racism is very alive in Mexico. It expresses itself in the lack of response when women make official denunciations of their violent husbands. It is evident in the migrations up to the North (the USA). It is evident in their customs and traditions. "We owe it to the girls to talk to them about their bodies, to explain about menstruation, and the bodily changes that take place as they mature. We also need jobs for our young girls. More and more of them jump to 'the other side' — where they find even more suffering. This is very bad."

Of all the things she has learned, the thing she likes best is to speak in front of an audience. "I felt so ashamed that I thought I was not capable of it, that I thought people would mock me. Now I talk about everything I know and even about what I do not know."

Like other Mexican women, indigenous women suffer discrimination and gender violence. The patriarchal system treats them harshly. More than other women, they are excluded, attacked, and silenced by traditions and customs. Little by little, they are taking charge of their words and destinies.

Mexico

Ute Bock

Ute Bock worked professionally for many years as a social worker and educator. In the early 1990s, she started to take care of teenage immigrants. She also took in underage refugees from countries at war, who came to Austria on their own looking for asylum. Ute Bock was the last hope for many teenage immigrants for whom nobody else cared. Her small project has grown into a community of 50 apartments where over 200 people find a home. She has also provided a legal address and legal aid for more than 1000 immigrants so that they can pursue their asylum procedures.

A note on the door, written with highlighter, announces: "This way to Mama Bock." Two dozen Africans are squeezed into the tiny storefront quarters on Zollergasse in Vienna. Some are at computers surfing the Internet while others are sitting around shooting the breeze. "Mama Bock" is an address for them, a place where they hope to find refuge, shelter, or where they have already been given help. Ute Bock was a social worker even before such a word had been coined. In those days, they were called something like "tutor." Nearly a hundred homeless people seeking asylum, by far most from Africa, have been given shelter in apartments that Ute Bock has rented at her own personal expense. The majority of those seeking asylum in Austria receive neither room nor board, nor medical care from the state, not to mention work permits. Ute Bock, a spirited retiree, has rented apartments for them. Each and every month, she pays on average 10,000 euros for rent, gas, and electricity. Not that Ute Bock ever wanted to become what she is now! "Mama Africa" is what TV-broadcasters call her. "Grande Dame of the Outcasts" is one of the other names the media uses. She often is not so kindly received when, for instance, she is riding the streetcar, for it is not very seldom that she hears herself being cursed at as "Niggermama" by some of her fellow Viennese. And that for someone who cannot stand reggae! But now she hears African rhythm on and on in the little storefront headquarters. She jests, "You are upping the penalty!" when a group of young Africans join in and chant along to Bob Marley's "Get Up! Stand Up!" African cuisine? "Never tried it." She has also missed some other things: "I never got around to starting a family." No, but what she does have are about a thousand men who call her "Mama."

Austria is a country that does not provide immigrants who are asylum seekers with sufficient housing and other services, such as health care. Today, there is increasing distrust, suspicion, and discrimination of immigrants.

Austria

"Our struggle is hard and full of sorrow. But there are instances that give so much power and hope. These moments let us stand up again after having fallen down."

Pervin Buldan

Center of Support and Solidarity for the Family Members of Forcibly Disappeared People (Yakay-der)

Pervin Buldan's political life began when her husband was murdered on 3 June 1994. This killing alerted her to the dirty war waged in Turkey. She first joined the Saturday Mothers, the relatives of those who had disappeared. She then worked at Mag-der, an association to assist these relatives, which was subsequently closed by the state. In spite of many difficulties, Yakay-der, the Center of Support and Solidarity for the Family Members of Forcibly Disappeared People was founded in 2002, and Pervin became president. She is also the mother of two children.

"Turkey needs peace. In spite of all the sorrow and aggression, the people have never abandoned the struggle for peace. People in this country have suffered so much pain, shed so much blood. Villages were destroyed, people were driven away from their homes, their earth. Children lost their fathers. Women fighting for peace and unity were attacked. Being a human capable of loving and feeling was forbidden. Despite all this, we do not want anyone else to experience this misery. The only thing that gives us energy and allows us to carry on is our struggle and yearning for peace. We believe that this country needs love. It needs to have unity. It has to be free from enmity and killings between siblings. This was taught to us by our common life and history. Our history teaches us to live together in peace. To live in a democratic Turkey is everybody's dream. We need to realize this yearning. A democratic Turkey that has resolved the Kurdish question; a country where everyone can express oneself without restraint, where murders by unidentified murderers are solved and the perpetrators brought to justice — that is our common yearning.

Our struggle is hard and full of sorrow. But there are instances I cannot describe, that give so much power and hope. These moments let us stand up again, after having fallen down. The fire of hope in the eyes of mothers, as we sent the dossiers of all murder cases with unidentified murderers in Turkey to the European Court for Human Rights, released fire in our hearts. As do the women and children, who applauded us and welcomed us as we took the donation of 6000 items of clothing to the village of Kirkkoyun in Diyarbakir. These are moments that show us that our struggle is not for nothing. And they give us the power to continue."

An ethnic minority in Turkey, Kurds have retained their own customs, language, and identity. Together with Kurds in Iraq and Iran, they have always aspired for an independent state of Kurdistan. Turkey strongly opposes secession and sometimes uses unlawful ways to control the Kurds.

Turkey

Linda Burnham

Third World Women's Alliance
Alliance Against Women's Oppression
Women of Color Resource Center

Linda Burnham has been an organizer and a human rights activist for her entire life. In 1990, she founded the Women of Color Resource Center, which organizes and trains women of color to work on social justice issues. In 1995, Linda led a delegation to the UN World Conference on Women in Beijing and a delegation in 1999 to the UN World Conference Against Racism in Durban, South Africa. She has worked locally and nationally with coalitions that oppose war, as well as groups that protect civil liberties and immigrant rights.

Originally from Brooklyn, New York, Linda comes from a family of social activists. Her father was a student leader at the City College in New York and became the organizational leader of the Southern Negro Youth Congress and founding editor of the Harlem-based newspaper Freedom. Linda's mother has been active in housing and community issues in Brooklyn for more than 50 years.

As a teenager, Linda began organizing communities of color in New York City to support the Ban the Bomb protest and to oppose the Vietnam War. She attended Reed College in Oregon and was a founding member of the Third World Women's Alliance and the Alliance Against Women's Oppression — both major forces for social change in the 1970s. She has written extensively on the topics of women's rights and African American politics. As the first editor of Race File (a publication that compiles and analyzes articles highlighting key trends in communities of color), and an editor of Crossroads and Colorlines, she promotes progressive dialogue on issues of race, class, gender, and their intersections. She founded the Women of Color Resource Center to address the roles that race, gender, class, and their intersections play in women's social justice and economic well-being. Center programs such as Women's Education in the Global Economy and the Women's Literacy Collaborative develop organizational and strategic planning skills and provide technical assistance. Linda also works on projects that monitor trends affecting social welfare policies in the USA.

Linda has written many newsletter, magazine, and journal articles, essays, and reports, including "Women's Education in the Global Economy", "Women, Raise Your Voices", "The Wellspring of Black Feminist Theory", "Racism in US Welfare Policy", and "Sexual Domination in Uniform: An American Value", an analysis of Abu Ghraib prison atrocities.

Linda's uniqueness is that she is a builder — she brings women together. Her leadership style is crucial in today's United States where politicians and right-wing groups seek to "divide and conquer".

United States of America

Virgelina Chará

Cooperativa Multiactiva Interétnica Nuevo Horizonte Limitada (Inter-ethnical Multi-active Cooperative)

Virgelina Chará is an African Colombian, born half a century ago in the Valle del Cauca, in Colombia. She has been threatened with death five times and cannot remember how many times she has been displaced from her home. She has been arrested, kidnapped, beaten and persecuted. She has seven children, three grandchildren and she never rests "because of my desire to live and to live with under dignified conditions."

"They have threatened me with death," says Virgelina Chará when talking about her life, which has lasted for half a century, punctuated by displacements and persecutions. She has been threatened with death, five times during the last 20 years.

She was the first of four children born in Cauca, in Colombia. She was Afro-Colombian and poor, raised by her mother and grandmother: "I worked from the age of six helping my family." From ages 12 to 18, she worked as a maid in Calí. She managed to go to school in the evenings and graduated from the primary level at age 24. She returned to Cauca, where she worked with miners and peasants who had been forced to sell their lands: "When you are helping people in the community, you realize what is going on." And what was going on was that she was threatened with death. She escaped with her five children and began a journey of living underground and fleeing persecution. She joined the revolutionary Movement 19th of April until the peace agreement was signed in 1990. The Movement 19th of April, known as M-19, was a Colombian insurgent group that used guerrilla tactics and was demobilized in 1990 with the signing of the peace agreement. Many of her companions have been massacred and tortured and Virgelina Chará's children, who now number seven, have been threatened.

In 2002, she arrived in Bogota, as always escaping from death. There she works as a legal adviser to the Cooperativa Multiactiva Interétnica Nuevo Horizonte Limitada (Inter-ethnical Multi-active Cooperative), a cooperative that fights for human rights and gives training courses in maintenance and nutrition. She says that she is on a list the government has of people that may be killed, but that does not stop her from taking risks. "It is because of my desire to live under dignified conditions."

Since the 1960s, Colombia has been living through an internal war involving the army, guerrilla groups and paramilitary groups. The civilian population, which has suffered deaths and displacement, has had to flee from the conflict. In Bogota, there are around one million displaced women.

Colombia

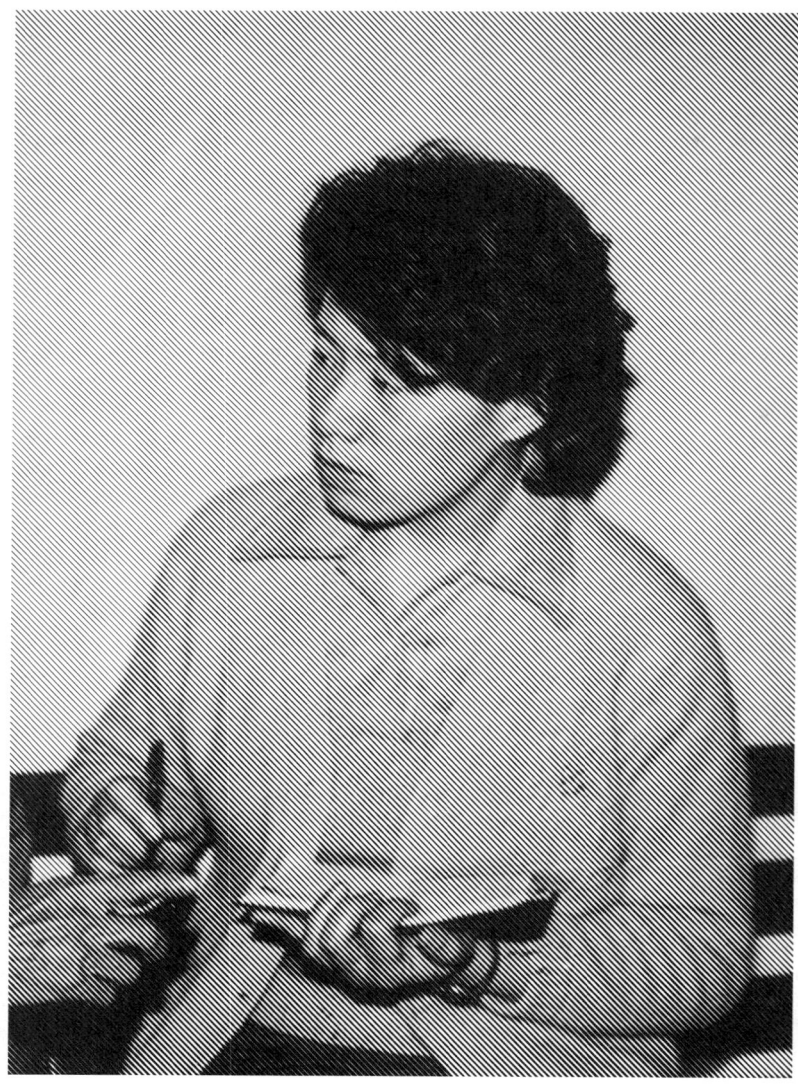

Daofu Chen

Economic Daily
China Association of Female Entrepreneurs
Capital Association of Women Reporters

Chen Daofu is editor of Economic Daily, director of the China Association of Female Entrepreneurs, and director of the Capital Association of Women Reporters. She has been working as a journalist for 20 years and has persisted in maintaining professional ethics, that is, the principle of taking on-the-spot interviews to obtain information. She always pays attention to vulnerable sectors of the population such as peasants and national minorities. She is also concerned about China's situation since the reform and opening-up, such as the quality of its entrepreneurs.

Chen Daofu worked in a minority area in Northeast China as an urban youth. She found many extended families living in humble shanties when she was reporting from Harbin in Heilongjiang Province in 1992. The shanties were congested, with piles of waste lying around. To prevent fire, an ever-present threat, the residents did not light coal stoves on windy days. She drew this to the attention of the authorities and the shanties were soon removed, and more than 100 households then had their poor living conditions greatly improved.

Illness did not deter Chen from making on-the-spot investigations in Henan and Xinjiang Provinces in 2003. She published several articles in Economic Daily based on these investigations. She recommended new methods and feasible modes for the orderly export of labor services, as well as incomed increase for surplus labor, especially for rural women in poorer areas. Chen's reports on the Mosuo people, a national minority in Yunnan Province who remain matriarchal, and live at an altitude of nearly 5000 meters, are well regarded. She was the first journalist from Beijing that the Mosuo people met. Together with her friends Chen founded the China Association of Female Entrepreneurs at the end of the 1980s. She then looked at the positive achievements of female entrepreneurs, as well as taking a critical look at the quality and ethics of their endeavors. To enhance the quality of entrepreneurs, she added a column "Famous Entrepreneurs Talk about Entrepreneurs" to the magazine Chinese Entrepreneurs.

The economy has developed rapidly in China since the start of the reform process in 1980. However, vulnerable sectors of the population, such as peasants and national minorities, are in a relatively disadvantageous position. Commercial enterprises have also developed rapidly but the quality of entrepreneurs needs considerable improvement.

China

Givânia Maria da Silva

Comissão Nacional de Articulação das Comunidades Negras Rurais
Quilombolas (National Coordination of Quilombos Communities)

Givânia Maria da Silva (1966) is threatened to be killed. The fear of losing her life so early, in a country that had already killed Chico Mendes, Dorothy Stang and many other leaders, does not discourage her. She fights for the retake and legalization of the Quilombos — secular rural communities secretly organized by former slaves — and against racism. She is an educator and is on her second political terms as town councilor in Salgueiro, countryside of Pernambuco.

Six Afro-Brazilian women, running away from the slavery, arrived at the hinterland of Pernambuco. The group grew and gave origin to the quilombo called Conceição das Crioulas. 200 years later, Givânia Maria da Silva was born, first woman from her community to receive a university diploma — she graduated in Arts and in Portuguese Literature — and to occupy a political post.

She attended school up to the fourth grade of elementary school at Conceição das Crioulas. After, she enrolled herself in a weekend course for laic teachers. She gave lessons to the community. At the end of the 1980s, she wrote with her students a project about the history of Conceição das Crioulas. "It was when we found out that we were a Quilombo." In 1992, she and some friends organized, in association with the Unified Afro-Brazilian Movement, the first meeting of Afro-Brazilians of the hinterland. In 1995, they helped to organize in Brasilia the first meeting between Quilombola representatives from the entire country. In the year 2000, it was created the National Coordination of Quilombos Communities (Conaq), of which she is one of the coordinators. On that same year, Conceição das Crioulas received the title of proprietorship.

Messages like "we will fill her mouth with bullets" do not intimidate her. She was elected town councilor (2000), and she was re-elected in 2004. Conceição das Crioulas, where around 3000 people live currently, has a school that teaches from grade five to grade eight, water tanks, family health programs. But the region still suffers with the lack of water in the drought period; there is no land for many families and no jobs for the youngsters. "The government needs not only to give back lands to the Afro-Brazilians, but also to provide a life with dignity."

The total area of Conceição das Crioulas is around 20,000 hectares, but 70% are still in the hands of the latifundium owners. The number of Quilombola communities in the entire country is approximately 4000. Only 800 of them are recognized and 29 received the title of land proprietorship.

Brazil

Semjidmaa Damba

Mongolian Union of Vulnerable Group Business Women

Born in 1943 to a nomadic Buryat family in Mongolia, Semjidmaa Damba was an enthusiastic student who chose to become a telecommunications engineer. Her diploma work at the Odessa Institute (former Soviet Union) in 1967 helped to considerably improve local automatic telephone stations in Mongolia. Semjidmaa taught telecommunications and information technology for many years, but stopped when she lost her working capacity because of disability. Her spirit, however, remained strong and soon she started, alongside other women, the Mongolian Union of Vulnerable Group Business Women.

Semjidmaa began to read before she joined school. As a pre-school girl she could often be found talking to her neighbors, trying to teach them to read and write. A promising career in telecommunications engineering, with her diploma work helping to improve local automatic telephone stations in Mongolia, was cut short by illness and disability. But rather than despair, Semjidmaa took advantage of the opening up of democratic spaces in the 1990s and, along with a group of other women, formed the Mongolian Union of Vulnerable Group Business Women of which she is now the president. Semjidmaa estimates that at present, Mongolia has more than 40,000 disabled former workers, while the total number of disabled persons of all ages may touch 120,000. Conditions of economic collapse, political turmoil, massive unemployment and poverty as well as indifference on the part of the State, pose particular problems for this group. The Mongolian Union of Vulnerable Group Business Women has grown quickly and now has a considerable number of contributors and volunteers. It runs six clubs and has three local branches, with each of the clubs specializing in a particular area, for example Parkinson's disease, traditional Mongolian medicine or on developing gifted children from vulnerable groups. The Union also offers training in different areas for thousands of disabled and unemployed women, as well as adolescents and adults from low-income families. Semjidmaa's new plans include working on preventing desertification, and on the government program Green Wall. A priority here is to involve disabled citizens as a workforce in large-scale cultivation projects such as that in the Kherulen river basin and in this way to expand the scale of her work.

Economic collapse in Mongolia had particularly negative consequences for disabled women. Thousands lost their jobs and found themselves socially isolated. New market economy jobs were available only for women under 25. However, women's NGOs continue to play a crucial role in fighting to change this.

Mongolia

Zenilda Maria de Araújo

Considered to be the mother of the Xukuru of Ororubá, an indigenous tribe, Zenilda Maria de Araújo (1950) stimulated the rescue of the culture and territory of this ethic group from Pernambuco. Until 1998, alongside her husband — an Indigenous Chief — she showed the indigenous their rights and created leaderships. On that year, he was assassinated. Zenilda was threatened, but she continued ahead of the land retakes and of the appreciation of the rituals and costumes of the Xucurus.

"Welcome your son, my mother nature! He will not be buried; he will be planted, so other warriors will be born." In May 1998, by the sound of the maracás (indigenous rattles), Zenilda Maria de Araújo buried her murdered husband. "The farmers killed him to frighten us, to stop our fight. On the contrary, this made the Xucurus more united." One of Zenilda's sons was acclaimed the new Indigenous Chief. The threats were now directed at the mother and at her son.

For about five years, she only left the indigenous village accompanied and when she was invited to participate in indigenous meetings in other Brazilian states. Her daily activity is going from village to village on mount Ororubu, in the city of Pesqueiro, countryside of Pernambuco, where 9000 Xucurus live divided throughout 24 villages. She speaks with families; she is present in the monthly meetings between health agents, professors and leaderships.

Thanks to Zenilda's, her husband's and the Pajé's (a witch doctor and priest in indigenous tribes) initiative and persistence, the Xucurus retook part of their land and became an organized community. In the 1980s, the three of them initiated a mobilization against prejudice and for the rescue of their people's culture and territory. The first retake happened in November 1990, in the village of Pedra D'água. "The farmers and the occupiers were deforesting our territory, covering it all with pasture for cattle. Our children would die of starvation. Today, they grow healthy because their parents have land to plant and a place to raise cattle that will provide milk." Another great conquest for the little Xucurus was the indigenous schools installed in the villages, with bilingual teaching and ethnic valorization. "The fight for our rights is still long and rough. But the seed that was planted by my husband bloomed."

According to the Social-Environmental Institute, the land of the Xucurus corresponds to 26,980 hectares, in the city of Pesqueiro, located 219 kilometers from Recife, capital of Pernambuco. Therefore, a large portion of this territory is still occupied by farmers, mostly cattlemen.

Brazil

Zohl de Ishtar

Nuclear Free and Independent Pacific Movement (NFIP)
Greenham Common Women's Peace Camp
Lesbian movement

An Irish-Australian lesbian, Zohl de Ishtar works with indigenous women in indigenous-led and initiated projects at community and international levels. She has campaigned on abolition of nuclear weapons and militarism, eradication of colonialism, promotion of inalienable sovereign rights of all peoples, protection of cultural integrity, and ending discrimination in any form, including that based on sexuality.

Zohl de Ishtar has long been encouraging white people to unlearn and undo their negative cultural behaviors towards indigenous peoples. Her sense of urgency was stirred afresh while working with the women elders of Wirrimanu (aka Balgo) in Western Australia's Great Sandy Desert. From 1999 to 2001, she lived with and assisted the women elders of this remote Aboriginal community to establish the Kapululangu Women's Law and Culture Centre, one of Australia's most vibrant cultural revitalization projects. As Zohl worked with these women elders who were leading custodians and teachers of cultural knowledge for their peoples she realized how concerned they were for their peoples, and for their future generations.

Historically, white Australian society has eliminated and restricted opportunities for indigenous Aboriginal elders to pass on their cultural knowledge to future generations. "Indigenous lives are still being torn apart by intrusive white cultural practices, which operate on the hidden assumption of white supremacy," says Zohl. "Even the most well-meaning white people have little understanding of their complicity in these flawed cultural traits". The knowledge that white people must unlearn their prejudices and dismantle their structural racism before they can become true allies of indigenous peoples in the struggle for justice inspires Zohl to continue her commitment to raise awareness of the impacts of cultural colonialism.

Historically, encroaching white Australian society has eliminated and restricted opportunities for indigenous Aboriginal elders to pass on their cultural knowledge to future generations. As a result, Aboriginal cultural archives have been severely depleted and indigenous identities and self-esteem undermined.

Australia

America Devi

Lok Shakti Sangathan (LSS)

America Devi, from the Mushar community in Dalit Bihar's heartland, started her journey in activism as part of the Lok Shakti Sangathan. Becoming part of their campaign was only the first step, as America later took on the Bihar government — first, a state minister who had taken over a village pond belonging to the Dalits, and then the government, which had denied the Dalits employment. She won both fights, and even forced a re-examination of government policy.

America Devi spent the best part of her childhood and youth as a bonded agricultural laborer, first at her parents' house and then at her husband's. She came into her own only around the time the Lok Shakti Sangathan (LSS), a people's organization working among Bihar's downtrodden, came to her village calling out to women to join their campaign for a better life. America had her first brush with education after joining the LSS; she learnt to read and write, and her work involved introducing women from her own village and neighboring villages to the LSS process. America also contributed by creating a Gramkosh (fund for village development).

Her first involvement with activism came when she fought for the rights of her villagers in connection with a village pond belonging to the Dalits, which had been illegally taken over by a state minister. She led the protests against the minister and his cronies along with the rest of the women in the community, even as the men held back for fear of a backlash. Some years later, the Dalits were allowed to reclaim possession of the pond.

The Mushars are employed through a government policy when there is any big government project that needs laborers. In 2002, the Bihar government began repair work on a particular river embankment: even as the Mushars waited to be informed about work, things started going wrong. The government replaced the men with machines, and the Mushars were left in suspended anticipation. But the series of protests America initiated forced the government to re-examine its policy, and 150,000 Mushars finally got the employment they needed.

The Mushars in Bihar are among the most neglected of Dalit communities, with their condition further worsened by the nonimplementation of policies aimed at their betterment. Entire generations waste away as bonded laborers working for rich landowners to repay ancient, unending debts.

India

Mahashweta Devi

Budhan

Mahashweta Devi (born 1926) is one of India's best-known writers and activists: each persona deeply informs the other. She was greatly influenced by the People's Theater Movement of the 1940s. This blend of creativity and political activism influenced the course of Mahashweta's life: her work with the rights and empowerment of tribal and marginal groups — their right to forest resources, cultural and environmental rights, and governance — is path-breaking. So is her documentation of their struggles in her critically acclaimed works of both fiction and nonfiction.

Mahashweta Devi was born in Dhaka in East Bengal (Bangladesh) into a family of poets, writers, and artists: her father, Manish Ghatak, was a well-known poet; his brother, Ritwik Ghatak, a legendary filmmaker; her mother, Dharitri Devi, a writer and activist. After her family moved to West Bengal, Mahashweta studied at Rabindranath Tagore's Visva Bharati University at Shantiniketan. Here, she came into contact with the People's Theater Movement, which aspired to take sociopolitical theater to rural Bengal in the 1940s. This blend of political activism and creativity, combined with Mahashweta's familial, ideological, and artistic leverage, give her the edge she is famous for. In 1965, Mahashweta visited Palamau, a remote, impoverished district in Bihar. She calls Palamau a "mirror of tribal India". As she walked the terrain, she witnessed firsthand the impact of debt bondage and the embedded agricultural slavery system. Since the 1970s, she has interposed herself directly in helping the indigenous peoples lodge grievances, set aside rivalries, and move toward development. In 1979, she received the Sahitya Akademi Award for her novel "Aranyer Adhikar" ("The Right to the Forest"), based on the life of tribal revolutionary Birsa Munda. In 1995, she won the Jnanpith Award, India's highest literary award, and the Ramon Magsasay Award in 1997. She donated the prize money to tribal communities. The profile of the Magsasay Award says, "Devi's searing stories and novels not only give voice to India's forgotten tribals but also stress the profound subordination of women in Indian society."

Mahashweta is editorial advisor for Budhan, a newsletter of the Denotified and Nomadic Tribes Action Group. She sums up in her simple, evocative, and compelling words: "Language is a weapon, it's not for shaving your armpits."

Even among the peripheral tribals is a further marginalized group — the denotified tribal groups that had once been historically miscalled "criminal". The denotification has had no impact on the official or social attitudes to these groups. Righting this wrong is Mahashweta's domain.

India

Tiliya Devi

Samajik Shaikshnik Vikas Kendra (SSVK)

A Mushar (Dalit community) woman, Tiliya Devi fought opposition from all quarters — including within her home — to bring about a better life for her downtrodden community. Along the way, she succeeded in rallying together hordes of women in search of a better life, and took on the might of the upper-caste Yadavs who had encroached upon agricultural land belonging to the Mushars. After contesting the Panchayat (village council) elections, Tiliya has, since 2001, also been working as a Panchayat Samity (village council group) member.

Tiliya Devi (born 1963), from the Mushar community in the Dalit heartland in Bihar, grew up as most Mushar girls do: slaving as a bonded laborer. She was married off at 14, and continued being a bonded laborer — at her husband's house. The lives of the Mushar women took a turn for the better when the Lok Shakti Sangathan (LSS) came to their villages, promising them training in developmental work, and improved living conditions. Tiliya joined the campaign despite opposition from her husband. The Mushars were all farmers, but because of the lack of land in their settlements, they were forced to be "bonded" with big landlords. Tiliya discovered a 156 — acre plot of land in her village belonging to the Dalits which upper-caste Yadav landlords had encroached on. Initiating a series of protest rallies, Tiliya spread the word for the imperative to reclaim the land that was rightfully theirs. The men refused outright, although the women stood beside Tiliya. There was such outrage that Tiliya's husband evicted her from the house. The reason: fear of a backlash from the upper-castes. And the upper-castes, obviously, vented their fury, attacking the Mushar men, women, even children. They looted the Mushars' cattle, and torched their houses.

But Tiliya was not about to give up, and neither were the rest of the Mushars. Supported by the LSS, Tiliya led a protest and charted out their demands. The agitation finally bore fruit in 2004, when the land was legally handed over to the Mushars. In 2001, Tiliya contested the Panchayat elections and was appointed member to the Panchayat Samity. Her victory came almost undisputed. No justice could have been sweeter.

Bihar's Mushars are among the most neglected of Dalit communities: the upper-castes rob them of their meager possessions, and mire them in inheritable debt, forcing the Mushars to spend their lives as bonded laborers.

India

Hilda Liria Domicó Bailarín

Multiethnic Organization of Antioquia

"It was very sad to see my people suffering from hunger, when in the forest we had everything," says Hilda Domicó (30), a displaced Colombian. She was born into the Embera-Katio ethnic group. Her father, her brother and her uncle, all of them community leaders, were massacred by the guerrillas in the 1990s. She works for the recovery of her ethnic group's identity and for other peasant, afro-descendent and indigenous communities. She has suffered death threats. She has not yet been able to return to her territory, the forest.

Hilda Domicó was born into the Embera-Katio ethnic group, 30 years ago, in Urabá, Colombia, in the administrative district of Antioquia. At age six, she was sent to study with other children, white children. She could not understand anything because she did not speak any Spanish. "It is very difficult to meet another world," she says. Today, she teaches her native language, Embera-Katio, at the University of Antioquia.

She inherited the fight for her community from her father, an indigenous leader assassinated in 1997 by the Colombian Revolutionary Armed Forces. Her brother, uncle and other community leaders were also murdered. Hilda was threatened with death. It was a year of massacres and displacements. The survivors left the forest and went to villages in the urban area: "It was very sad to see my people suffering from hunger, when in the forest we had everything," she remembers. The young and the elderly died. They still cannot return to their territory because the guerrillas and the army have occupied it.

"Our people will be happy only if we live in the forest; we cannot live in villages or urban places; for us that is not life," says Hilda. She is not only the president of the Multiethnic Organization of Antioquia, she has also joined a project called Puppets against Bullets, with which she travels to villages where peasants, indigenous and black people have suffered persecution and displacement. The displaced people, as a form of therapy, make the puppets and act out situations, providing them with dialog. It helps people to face the traumas. In the meantime, the children dance the 'cumbia': "Mom, I cannot stand it," they say. No, no one can stand the war.

Colombia has 86 indigenous territories where eight ethnic groups survive. Since the 1960s, the country has been suffering from an internal war. The Armed Forces and the Revolutionary Forces conscripted young boys from the indigenous communities. A number of ethnic groups have been displaced.

Colombia

Procópia dos Santos Rosa

Procópia dos Santos Rosa (1933) is leader of the Calunga's Quilombo. At first, 'quilombos' were places where runaway slaves used to found secret and free communities. Procópia can not read or write, but she knows everything about the grammar of life.

To get to the Calunga's Quilombo, in Brazil's countryside, you have to cross streams and balance yourself on the edge of mountains. It is like going back in time: the rediscovery of a subsistence economy. Procópia dos Santos Rosa has been a midwife her whole life. "When you help in the birth of a child, he or she grows up calling you mom. I go out and hear: 'Bless me, mother Procópia.'" They are the Calunga people of Monte Alegre, a region in the State of Goiás. They are about 1500 people whose ancestors, running away from the violence of slavery, established the community two centuries ago. Nowadays — even though they have rights such as land titles, recognized by the Constitution — they suffer with threats of invasion.

Procópia dos Santos Rosa is a natural leader. She does not belong to any associations. For decades, she has been fighting. Along with her friend (who has already passed away), she used to take a canoe and row up and down the river. They would go talk to the mayor, to the governor, to the minister or the president in their offices. They managed to get a school and teachers. "My children and I are illiterate; however, my grandchildren can read and write." An Afro-Brazilian woman who knows how to stop Caucasian people's greed: that is how she was able to stop the building of a dam, on the Paraná River, which would flood the Calunga's land. "They have offered me a house in the city and a piece of land with orange trees. I said no to all that! I want to stay in my ancestor's land, and I fight for it, so my great-grandchildren's kids can stay in it." At age 63, Procópia's current battle is for a health center.

Brazil has around 800 communities remaining from the Quilombos. As a result of the geographical isolation and racism, those communities are extremely poor and have just recently been noticed.

Brazil

"No one can relieve your itchy back like the scratch of your fingers. – Don't accept the role of the victim. Take active measures to change things for the better. Use your strength!"

Nabila Espanioly

Advocacy Center for Arab Citizens in Israel (Mossawa)
The Feminist Center in Haifa (FCiH)
Jewish–Arabic Women for Peace (JAWfP)

Nabila Espanioly, an active Palestinian feminist and clinical psychologist, was born to a Catholic family in Nazareth in 1955. For more than three decades, Espanioly has energetically campaigned to protect the civil rights of the Palestinian minority in Israel, to promote peace between Israel and Palestine on the basis of the two-state solution and to establish equal rights for women. In 2003, she shared the international Aachen Peace Prize with the Jewish-Israeli historian and peace activist Reuven Moskowitz, in recognition of her efforts to promote peace in the Middle East.

Since the '80s, Nabila Espanioly has been politically active, not just as a Palestinian but as a feminist. She says, "Female Palestinians in Israel are subjected to three kinds of discrimination: as members of the Palestinian minority, as women in Israel and as women in conservative Palestinian society." Today, she works alongside Jewish and Palestinian women to combat violence against women and to promote equal labor rights. Together with the international organization "Women in Black" (WiB) and the Israeli-Palestinian "Coalition of Women for Just Peace" (CWfJP), Espanioly coordinates campaigns against the Israeli occupation of the West Bank and the Gaza Strip, and organizes aid convoys for the areas cut off from the outside world.

For Nabila Espanioly, peace policy, the promotion of women and children's education are indispensable. She says, "The Palestinian population in Israel does not have equal rights and is exposed to a growing discrimination in all spheres of life. Especially Palestinian women come last in Israel when it comes to job opportunities. Since the expulsion in 1948 and the expropriations in subsequent years, the traditional jobs in agriculture no longer exist. Since the landless Palestinian men are now predominantly employed as unskilled workers in low-income jobs, it is essential that women also seek employment. Yet, nursery places are also lacking. While 95.4 percent of the Jewish children go to nursery, such places are only available for 36 percent of the Palestinian children. The children's books and toys issued by the Israeli Ministry of Education are based on Jewish living conditions and do not take into account the language and cultural heritage of the Palestinians." For Espanioly the strengthening of a Palestinian identity is therefore an absolutely essential foundation of a multi-cultural society in Israel.

Nabila Espanioly is a campaigner for the civil rights of the Palestinian minority in Israel, for peace between Israel and Palestine and for equal rights for women in general and for Palestinian women in particular. She acts to promote peace and advocate human rights in the Middle East.

Israel

Albertina García Argueta

National Organization of Native Lencas of Honduras

This girl from Honduras made great efforts to study. She was the daughter of poor peasants, born in 1962 in a small village that only had a primary school. Despite this, she managed to achieve her degree and took some university level courses. Her achievements were exceptional, but her economic limitations stopped her studies. Albertina García Argueta returned to her home and found that she had been dispossessed. So she created a training center, started a support network for battered women, managed assistance to micro enterprises and promoted the Lenca culture.

Her parents, Lenca indigenous of Honduras, lived in a small, humble village. There was no secondary school, and Albertina García Argueta longed to study. She convinced her parents, as young as she was, to let her go to school in the nearby city of Marcala, in the department of La Paz. She was a leader of the youth ministry and a first aid volunteer. She graduated with distinction; however, thereafter she had to work to survive. She went to Tegucigalpa, the capital of Honduras, and registered in the Pedagogical University. Neither her intelligence, nor her good grades, nor her leadership allowed her to finish her studies. She needed money to finish, and money was something she did not have. Albertina García Argueta returned to Marcala without having fulfilled her aspirations, but she returned with another view of the world. The strange routes of destiny have brought her to realize that her personal accomplishments should be for the benefit of her people.

Today, Albertina García Argueta (43) feels proud. She has succeeded in organizing an indigenous association that has become the engine of the community, promoting the pride of the indigenous group and affirming its culture. She has succeeded in securing economic benefits for indigenous organizations from inside the country and abroad. She has created a support network for battered women. She has initiated improvements in health and nutrition, and she continues working.

During the 20th century, the Lenca communities in the mountains were forgotten, left behind. The progress of Honduras was centered on the 'banana coast,' which generated wealth for North American companies. A powerful local oligarchy was not formed like it was in neighboring countries.

Honduras

Alexandra Gater

Anglican Church of Queensland
Murri Magistrate Court

Reverend Alexandra Hazel Gater (59), a prominent member of the Aboriginal and Torres Strait Island community in Brisbane, is an Anglican priest and chaplain at the Brisbane Women's and Sir David Longland Correctional Centers. An elder in the Murri Magistrate Court, she advocates tirelessly in the justice system for humane treatment of incarcerated indigenous people. For over a decade, she has represented Brisbane on the National Torres Strait Islander Anglican Council, fighting to raise awareness of issues such as racism, the Stolen Generation, and the need for reconciliation.

Growing up on Cherbourg Aboriginal Mission in rural Queensland, Alexandra (Alex) Gater attended church regularly. When the priest failed to turn up one Sunday, she decided to lead the service herself. "I was just 12 years old," she laughs. "I thought, obviously God's got plans for me!" More than 40 years later, "Aunty Alex" returned as an Anglican priest, the first Aboriginal woman in Queensland to be ordained, and baptized 12 of her own community. It was a moment of joy for the human rights advocate and proved that a young Aboriginal woman could rise above a background of severe poverty, limited education, and racial intolerance (that blights the lives of so many indigenous Australians) to live the life of her dreams. Few would aspire to such a life, or have the stamina to deal with it. Alex works as a chaplain at two women's prisons and does emergency visits to eight more. In one day, she might provide counseling for a prisoner contemplating suicide at one prison then comfort the grieving family of a suicide victim at another. Her anger at the ready incarceration of indigenous youths for minor offences and the disproportionate number of Aboriginals in Australian prisons (at one percent of the population, Aboriginals are jailed at 18 times the rate of non-indigenous Australians) made Alex challenge the mindsets of church groups, national bodies, and the government itself. "I have a right to be angry when I see how God's people have been oppressed," she declares. She was recently appointed to the Crime and Misconduct Committee, investigating allegations of unfair treatment of indigenous people by the police and other agencies. Alex's energy for realizing her dream of improved lives for Aboriginals is unwavering: "We were all created in God's image, all of us. It is time Aboriginal people were acknowledged and accepted."

Despite a campaign and a Royal Commission, Australian Aboriginal imprisonment rates and deaths in custody remain high. Many Aboriginal prisoners are descended from the Stolen Generation, Aboriginal children forcibly removed from their families and "assimilated" into white society (1910–1970).

Australia

Dewe Gorode

Government of New Caledonia
Parti de Libération Kanak (PALIKA)
Nuclear Free and Independent Pacific movement (NFIP)

Poet, teacher, politician — Déwé Gorodé is a leading independence activist in the French Pacific territory of Kanaky/New Caledonia. For over 30 years, Déwé has contributed to peace building and self-determination: as an author and poet; as a teacher and member of the Kanak popular schools movement; and as a leader of the Kanak independence movement Front de Libération Nationale Kanak et Socialiste (FLNKS). Jailed by the French authorities in the 1970s, she is the vice president of the government of New Caledonia today.

"My political awakening came in 1969, when I was 20. Then we young people were talking about our heritage as Kanaks, the indigenous Melanesian people of New Caledonia, colonized by France since 1853. The week before I left for university in France was filled with moments that sparked my understanding of colonialism and set me on my future path of political action to work for my people as writer, teacher, and Kanak independence activist. My cousin had just returned from military service in France. He invited me to a political meeting about our land, our future, organized by a pioneering Kanak university graduate, deeply influenced by the student and worker uprisings of May 1968. On the way, we passed a large house in the Vallée des Colons. My cousin asked: "Whose house is that?" I answered: "It belongs to those who live there, of course." My cousin: "But whose land is it on?" And I realized that it was the land of our people. My cousin: "That is why we are going to the meeting!" The room was full of men, with the Kanak graduate at the front wearing the symbolic red scarf of his Foulard Rouges movement. I was the only woman. I felt I should leave. But an old man offered me a seat. So I listened to their talk of colonialism, the land, pride in our Melanesian culture and heritage, of the need for action. I was to travel to Montpellier with a friend, but he and that Kanak graduate were arrested after a brawl between Kanaks and Caldoche (French settlers). I did not want to go alone, but that same week a taxi driver and a French doctor both told me that Kanaks must be trained to run their own country. So I went. Student life was in turmoil after May 1968: every Marxist group — communist, Trotskyist, gauchiste — was handing out leaflets; there were protests, debates, strikes. It was a time of anti-colonialism, though French people knew nothing of my islands."

The indigenous Kanaks of the French Pacific colony of New Caledonia are a minority in their own land. Since the 1970s, independence activists have campaigned to reassert Kanak culture, language and identity, and now support reconciliation with the descendants of settlers and immigrants.

New Caledonia

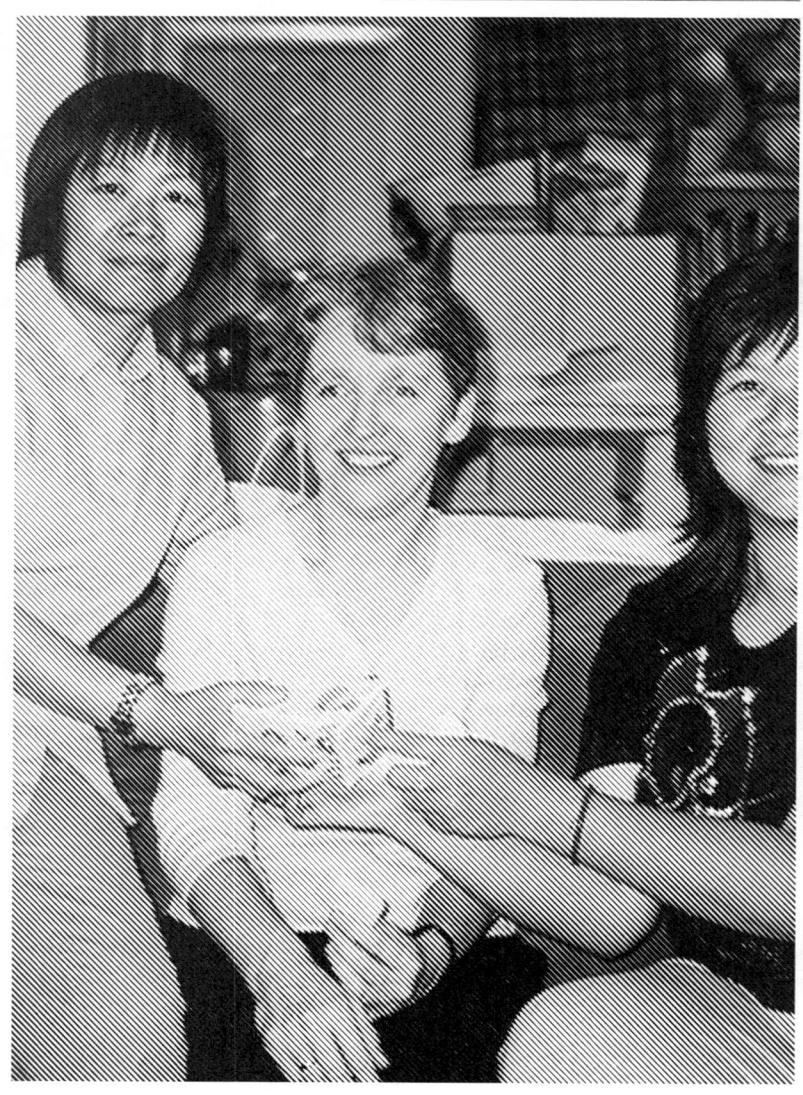

Elizabeth Ann Gray

Action for Reach out

Elizabeth Ann Gray (53) is a Columban Sister from Scotland. She is one of the founding members of Action for Reach out, the first NGO that provides support and services to sex workers in Hong Kong. As a foreigner, Ann not only has to overcome the language barrier, but also other social and cultural boundaries in working frontline with these women, who are being looked upon as outcasts and considered immoral. Over the past 13 years, Ann has serviced and empowered this stigmatized and marginalized group, fostering their self-esteem, and promoting and protecting their basic human rights.

It is the belief that every woman should be treated fairly that has driven the missionary sisters of St. Columban to start the project on sex workers in Hong Kong in the early 90s. Sister Elizabeth Ann Gray (53) was charged with this responsibility and laid solid groundwork for Action for Reach out, the first sex workers' organization in the territory with the ultimate goal of helping sex workers to form their own support group. "Ever since arriving in Hong Kong, I had wanted to work with this group of women. I saw they were the outcasts of a society in which it was acceptable for a man to go to a prostitute but not for a woman to be a prostitute. They are looked on as the lowest of the low," Sister Gray wrote in the article "On the Streets of Hong Kong". To facilitate her working in Hong Kong, she studied Cantonese for two years and has now been working with Action for Reach out for the last 13 years. Sister Gray and her colleagues experience embarrassment, rejection and many difficulties in their work. Sister Gray also faces criticism and disapproval from within the Church, where commercial sex workers are considered sinners who should repent. But Sister Gray stays on with patience, courage and persistence, and most importantly with a non-judgmental attitude that builds on acceptance and inclusiveness. To-day many sex workers have rebuilt their self-esteem. Many more are aware of their legal rights, and approach Reach out and other organizations for assistance as needed. "These women live at the margin of society. In trying to accompany them in their struggle, I too have experienced being pushed onto the margins of Hong Kong society as I come face to face with the refusal of officials at various levels to address their problems. To my surprise and deep gratitude, this has developed in me a strong sense of the need for solidarity among women," Sister Gray says.

Sex work is not illegal in Hong Kong. But the laws related to it make it difficult for sex workers to work in a safe and healthy environment with respect and dignity. They are often treated unfairly and denied their basic human rights. Worse still, they are often targets of police abuse and harassment.

China, Hong Kong SAR

"All guerrillas, soldiers, and prisoners are my children. I shall be there for all of them. I will continue to struggle for peace so that they do not die."

Müyesser Günes

Peace Mothers

In response to years of oppression by the Turkish state, the death of two sons, and the shattering of her family, Müyesser Güneş, a Kurd living in Turkey, founded Peace Mothers, an organization encouraging peace and equality between Turks and Kurds. It also provides an international voice for solidarity among women, specifically mothers, whose families have been the victims of oppression by political regimes. Müyesser is a tireless advocate for human rights and promotes the need for peace between Kurds and Turks to foreign governments and to other mothers' groups throughout the world.

Until 1990, Müyesser Güneş spent most of her life as a typical Kurdish village woman: early marriage, birth of her children, care for ailing parents, farming. But then, after suffering harassment, her oldest son left school to join the guerrilla forces, while her husband moved to Istanbul to find work. Müyesser was subject to nearly daily persecution in her home by the military special forces looking for her son. When her younger son was taken by the police and interrogated, something inside her changed. As a mother, she felt she had to act. She set about informing herself about the Kurdish issue in Turkey and started mobilizing and educating the older people in her village. After her husband and other sons were taken by police, she could no longer bear the uncertainty and abuse. She started Peace Mothers, a group of mothers to bring about peace for the sake of the children. The mothers met professors, journalists, authors, politicians, the press, and actors. They described their suffering from the loss of their children who had joined the guerrillas or were taken by police. They told them that Kurds and Turks are brothers and sisters; that they needed to help put an end to the struggle between them. They traveled with their message throughout the country, garnering the support of the German, French, Italian, Dutch, and Greek embassies. As Peace Mothers toured the country, thousands filled the narrow roads with flowers in their hands. They freed white pigeons, sang songs, and danced. They brought their message of peace to the Basque region in Spain, to the Mothers of the Plaza de Mayo in Argentina, to the Kurdish Women's Peace Office in Germany and to women in France, Ireland, and Palestine. Sadly, Müyesser's two sons were killed in their struggle for Kurdish human rights, causing her tremendous pain. But today, she continues her work for the sake of peace.

The Kurds constitute over 20% of the Turkish population. Any expression by Kurds of unique ethnic identity has been harshly repressed. The Turkish government has consistently thwarted attempts by the Kurds to organize politically. This was often accompanied by massive human rights abuses by the Turkish army, recorded by various human rights organizations.

Turkey

Zenaida Brigida Hamada-Pawid

Cordillera People's Alliance
Cordillera Ancestral Domain Partners for Peace and Development (CADPPD)

Zenaida Brigida Hamada-Pawid (born 1942), has been a peace advocate since 1987. Her presentation of the perspectives of the indigenous peoples of the Cordillera was vital in the passage of the Indigenous People's Rights Act (IPRA), the most important tool for their self-determination. She helped conceptualize peace zones, defined as communities in conflict areas that resist militarization by any armed group. She represented the indigenous peoples sector in the government's peace negotiations with the Cordillera People's Liberation Army (CPLA) and the Communist Party of the Philippines (CPP).

Zenaida Brigida Hamada-Pawid, better known among peace advocates as "Manang Briggs" (elder sister Briggs), believes that peace work is an everyday thing and that anyone who takes away the source of unpeace is a peacemaker. Her father was a lawyer who fought passionately for the rights of indigenous peoples and her mother was a social worker. "A mother who picks up a crying baby is a peacemaker," Zenaida says. "Peacemakers are like a field of wildflowers; the job cannot be done by one alone," she says. While the list of her advocacy achievements over the last 18 years may be long, she insists that the credit belongs to many people. She not only refused to divulge her citations and awards, she also asked for them not to be highlighted. "The work of peace making is simply doing what has to be done at that moment," she says. "Everybody is a peacemaker. As a woman, your first role is as a peacemaker." She adds, "Peacemaking is never done because the roots of unrest are not really resolved. We just keep picking up the pieces after the war, and the face of war is always changing."

Zenaida's peace advocacy combines her gentle side as a woman with her firm convictions, making her a passionate voice for 'the other side' in the government panels in its peace negotiations with the Cordillera People's Liberation Army (CPLA) and the Communist Party of the Philippines (CPP). A tireless advocate, on any given day Manang Briggs has meetings set up, either on ancestral claim issues or peace concerns. She is known for her strong convictions, articulated in a clear unwavering voice, and her excellent insights that have helped in the formulation of government policies. Her clarity stems from her being an Ibaloy woman with an ability to articulate the memories in the hearts of her people. "We are all advocates of indigenous peoples' rights in the family," she says.

The Ibaloy, the original settlers of Benguet Province, were stripped of their ancestral domain at the turn of the century by the American colonizers. To this day, the conflicts over land are unresolved, with the Ibaloy losing their land to mining claims, dams, real estate and golf courses.

Philippines

Aileen Clarke Hernandez

California Women's Agenda

Aileen Clarke Hernandez (born 1926) has worked tirelessly for labor rights, women's rights, and civil rights for US people of color for over 50 years, and sees these issues as ultimately interconnected. Her life of service includes public appointments and innumerable projects at local, state, and national levels. A committed feminist, she was the second national president of the National Organization for Women, and is currently chair of the California Women's Agenda, a coalition of 600 local women's organizations.

Born in Brooklyn, New York, Aileen attended Howard University, a traditionally black institution in Washington, DC. She earned a bachelor of arts in political science and sociology while also picketing and demonstrating against racism in the nation's capital, a segregated city. Aileen experienced sexism at Howard, and comments, "As a black woman I have had no choice but to be involved in both struggles." After graduation, she became an organizer for the International Lady Garment Workers Union. Later she was the only woman on the original five-member US Equal Employment Opportunity Commission, appointed by president Johnson in 1965 and charged with investigating discrimination in employment. Aileen threw herself into this work with characteristic energy, integrity, and enthusiasm, but resigned in 1967, frustrated with the caution and slow progress in the agency's work.

A committed feminist, Aileen was a founding member of the National Women's Political Caucus and the second national president of the National Organization for Women. She currently chairs the California Women's Agenda, a network that seeks to implement the Beijing Plan of Action and to make connections among women leaders internationally.

As a participant in three major movements (for worker's rights, civil rights, and women's rights) Aileen has seen significant change in her long activist life although, since the 1990s, these changes have been under attack. Aileen has served on innumerable committees and boards, and participated in even more projects. Her insistence that racism and sexism are interrelated is both a gift and a lesson to contemporary organizers and activists. For over 50 years she has worked tirelessly at local, national, and UN levels, yet she remains remarkably modest, approachable, and open to challenges, always "ahead of the curve".

Through demonstrations, strikes, lawsuits, and grassroots organizing, the activism of the 20th century achieved significant gains, but generated backlash and resistance.

United States of America

Guadalupe Hernández Dimas

Uarhi (Woman)

A lake and an indigenous community are her historical references. She is the only daughter of two women: her mother and grandmother. She is unique in a man's world. Guadalupe Hernández Dimas is known as "Nana Lu" — an honorary name given to her in recognition of her work for the P'urhepecha people (indigenous people located in the State of Michoacán, in the West of Mexico, its cities are built in the brooks of the big lake Pátzcuaro, Guadalupe's birth place).

"Language is an element of culture. It is so valuable because it contains the richness of your way of looking at the world. It allows you to understand the world. If you lose it, you lose a window to the world." With this conviction, Guadalupe Hernández Dimas put together, along with the Institute of Anthropology of the Autonomous National University of Mexico, the first grammar book, Janhaskapani, in the P'urhepecha language.

"One day, my grandmother told me, 'You are soon going to be a woman and you must be very careful in this life; you must walk safely. You must know where you are going in life and you must ask for other women's support.'" Brought up by women, in a community with a non-occidental view of life, Guadalupe tries to get women to continue caring for this way of looking at the world. For that reason, they have founded the women's organization Uarhi (Woman). With this organization they have initiated various collective projects for indigenous women. They have meetings, demonstrations and workshops for reflection. They produce publications and make official protests and complaints.

"Nana Lu", as she is called (a deserving name among her people), has also been interested in maintaining the presence of indigenous women in the national and international communication medias. She designed the first critical news program for Michoacán television in P'urhepecha and she takes part in the publication of bulletins and newspapers in her language, as well as in the radio news updates. She is a member of the Academy of the P'urhepecha language. And she is also a poet.

The indigenous women of Mexico suffer from class, gender and racial discrimination. They are the most oppressed among the oppressed. Organized, alone, sometimes even rejected by their own people, they have decided to leave the way of life that restricts and imprisons them, and they have decided to go out into the world.

Mexico

"As long as I have
the support of
my people, I shall
never surrender."

Candelaria Hernández Gabriel

Asociación para la Promoción y el Desarrollo de la Comunidad (Ceiba)
Asociación de Mujeres Mam para el Desarrollo (Asomamd)

A Guatemalan woman, of Maya-Mam origins, Candelaria is a displaced person (internal and external refugees, mostly indigenous, who had to flee their homes and communities due to the indiscriminate bombardments carried out by the Armed Forces), a community leader and mother of five children. Self-taught, she learned to read and write — driven by the desire to improve herself. Candelaria Hernández Gabriel, known as "La Cande," weaves, cooks, cleans and talks about justice, human rights and freedom. She is a woman of the people, a humble woman. She speaks freely and smiles openly.

Candelaria Hernández Gabriel was born in 1968, in Ixconlaj, a village in the Guatemalan mountain range of Colotenango. As a small girl, she followed the footsteps of her parents going, like most of the families in the region, from ranch to ranch throughout the district of Huehuetenango, earning their salaries as itinerant workers who gathered the harvest of others.

Woman of Peace (Xüj Té Zálabil), she grew up in The Democracy — the ironical name given to this municipality — from which she would later have to flee. School made her very happy, but it lasted only two months: "The army burnt down the school and I had to abandon my studies." Like every woman in the village, she learned how to do housework and how to work the land. In 1980, along with her family, she was forced to flee because of the incursions of the army and the massacres that they had been carrying out in the nearby villages. "In the beginning they forcefully conscripted men. Later on, the threats, rapes and murders of the women began." In 1984, "La Cande" abandoned the village and went to the mountains with a bundle of her dreams and hopes.

Woman of stone and fire, she returned five years later and joined the Committee for Peasant's Unity (CUC), in their fight for human rights. Along with other mothers and widows, she opposed the compulsory conscription imposed by the Guatemalan army. In 1996, the war ended as a result of an agreement between the government and the guerrillas (National Guatemalan Revolutionary Unit). It allowed Candelaria to dream, but her dream did not last long. "It is a shame, but we still need to take action to improve the situation of women and to fight, so that the agreements become a reality." She is a promoter of human rights, of the cause of women and of indigenous people. She wants what her ancestors wanted: "For no one to be left behind."

Guatemala's history is associated with severe violations of human rights. The Commission of Historic Elucidation of Guatemala, which was created with the support of the United Nations, concluded that the actions of the security forces against the Mayan population is akin to genocide.

Guatemala

Unutea Hirshon

Tavini Huiraatira no Te Ao Maohi (serve the Polynesian people)
Women's International League for Peace and Freedom (WILPF)
Nuclear Free and Independent Pacific movement (NFIP)

Tahitian activist Unutea Hirshon campaigns for a nuclear-free and independent French Polynesia and for peace in the wider Pacific. Unutea's work covers many spheres: as a member of the independence party Tavini Huiraatira no Te Ao Maohi, supporting those affected by French nuclear testing with the Tahitian branch of WILPF, networking across the region with the Nuclear-Free and Independent Pacific movement, documenting her colonized people's cultural heritage through dance, music, and tattooing, and serving as an elected member of the local Assembly since 2001.

A campaigner for a nuclear-free and independent Pacific, Tahitian activist Unutea (Tea) Hirshon is inspired by those who have gone before, and by young people who take action today. In 1966 — the year France detonated its first nuclear weapon at Moruroa Atoll in French Polynesia — Tea met the ageing Polynesian independence leader Pouvanaa a Oopa, in Paris. A charismatic figure, Pouvanaa was exiled from Tahiti in the late 1950s, an act that disrupted French Polynesia's burgeoning independence struggle as France was setting up its nuclear testing program in its colony. For the young Tea, the meeting was inspirational, linking the struggles of the past with the promise of the future: "I was 20 when a friend in Paris brought me to visit him. Tahitians visiting France would pay Pouvanaa a visit, while he was under house arrest there: he was already a legend. I was really moved to see him, but I said little. He was an imposing man — not the type you could have a chit-chat conversation with. But just being in the same room and feeling his presence was impressive." For Tea, this link with past struggles inspired her to work for peace and self-determination: "When I was young, I overheard conversations in my home about Pouvanaa. My French stepfather would speak about him as a crazy man, one who would speak about the Bible when he held political meetings. Of course, a French mind would consider that totally strange! But it impressed me as a ten-year-old girl, so when I actually met him, I remembered right away what was said about him." Today, Tea is herself an elder in the independence movement of French Polynesia and a role model for young activists, describing herself as "godmother" of Generation Taui, a movement of young people campaigning for self-determination in the French Pacific colony.

French Polynesia was the site of French nuclear testing at Moruroa and Fangataufa atolls from 1966 to 1996. Maohi activists are campaigning for independence, a nuclear-free Pacific, and support for islanders living with the radioactive legacy of 193 atmospheric and underground nuclear tests.

French Polynesia

Daniela Hivesova-Silanova

Jekhetane (Together)

Since Daniela Hivesova-Silanova discovered the Roma community for the first time over 22 years ago, she has worked continually for the bettering of Romany life in Slovakia, and for the fight against discrimination and violence against them, speaking out where otherwise they would not be heard. Not only has she challenged and enabled many Roma to find confidence and pride in their talents, but she has made these talents visible to the public as well — through a journal, a theater, her writing, and her poetry.

A poet and thespian graduate from Bratislava, Daniela Hivesova-Silanova met her destiny by chance: while working in an electronics factory in the Slovak city of Presov, she noticed "workers with darker skin than mine and beautiful women sweeping the floors." Daniela often chatted with the Roma workers and was touched by their singing: "I wanted to show them how gifted and outstanding they were — and I wanted to show the "Gadze" (the non-Roma), who Roma really were."

So began a lifelong, passionate mission. In 1991, Daniela co-founded the journal "Romano nevo l'il" (New Romany Journal) of which she is the deputy editor, as well as the first and only Romany theater, Romathan (which stands for Romanesthan, the country of Roma people), in Slovakia. In 1993, with a group of 15 people, Roma and non-Roma intellectuals from Bratislava, Presov, and Kosice, Daniela founded the organization Jekhetane (Together) to unite all citizens of the Slovak Republic to increase Romany pride, confidence, and identity, inform the public about the Romany community, and act against prejudice and stereotyped thinking of the Roma minority. Daniela is also a co-founder of a unique art school in Kosice, where she teaches Slovak, theater, and Romany culture and history to Roma and non-Roma teenagers. Through her articles, books, lectures, poetry, plays, and through her fundraising efforts, Daniela has worked continuously over 22 years for the bettering of Romany life in Slovakia.

With an estimated 400,000 Roma, the Romany population forms the second largest minority group in Slovakia. They tend to suffer disproportionately from higher rates of poverty, unemployment, and illiteracy. After a long history of injustice and discrimination, equalization for Roma finally was accepted by the Slovak government in 1991.

Slovakia

Marjorie "Maggie" Hodgson

National Day of Healing and Reconciliation
Healing Our Spirit Worldwide

The cornerstone of Marjorie "Maggie" Hodgson's accomplishments as a leader of international networks to fight aboriginal substance abuse is her belief that success must be celebrated and that success is contagious. Marjorie has created two successful national and international networks and has facilitated the worldwide sharing of knowledge between indigenous communities. She also facilitates healing between victims and perpetrators of past government policies that allowed personnel working at mandated residential schools to abuse their aboriginal students.

The youngest of six children, Maggie Hodgson was born in British Columbia, Canada, to an aboriginal woman who had survived one of the residential schools the Canadian government forced upon the aboriginals as part of an assimilation policy. The widespread physical and sexual abuse of more than 12,000 aboriginals in the schools led to ongoing cycles of mistreatment, emotional devastation, and substance abuse. Maggie's home was no exception. Her parents were alcoholic and poor; Maggie married at 17 and was a mother of two by age 18. As an activist in poverty law, she was plunged into a lifetime of work when she spurred the investigation of the abuse of 26 aboriginal foster children. As director of an aboriginal training institute, she began researching and developing methods of education, intervention, and healing, which for the next 34 years would transform communities worldwide. Cofounder of the National Day of Healing and Reconciliation, as well as Healing Our Spirit Worldwide, Maggie believes that individuals, families, and communities that have lived with tragedies have a thirst to celebrate even the smallest successes. The success of her own movements is testimony to her beliefs. She developed the world's first National Addictions Awareness Week, which began with no funds and 25 aboriginal communities; in three years it had grown to 1500 communities with 700,000 participants. She conducts healing workshops across Canada with both perpetrators and victims and is working on a process to settle cases outside court for the 13,000 aboriginals who are suing the government for physical and sexual abuse. She is co-chair of a working caucus that advocates for policy changes and which has convinced the government to allocate USD 74 million for counseling services for residential school survivors and USD 10 million for commemoration activities.

As a teenager Maggie was raped by a businessman. When her mother reported the rape, the officer said, "What do you expect? You are an alcoholic and an Indian." At 59, Marjorie is frail; she has suffered a heart attack and four strokes. But she continues her work of healing.

Canada

Mei Ying Huang

Kahabu Cultural Organization

Huang Mei Ying (54), an anthropologist and part-time instructor at the history department of Chinan University, has long worked for aborigine rights. In 1998 she worked with the Kahabu, a tribe not yet formally acknowledged by the Taiwanese government. Her group helped locals to build alliances and promote the protection of the underprivileged.

"To strengthen your roots you must take into account the local culture. The Kahabu for instance, have not been considered while formulating cultural policies; they have been neglected, their history and their rights have been overlooked." This is how long-term social activist Huang Mei Ying justified her work in a village in 1998, when the Kahabu tribe was not yet officially acknowledged.

On September 20th, 1999, Huang Mei Ying was at a preliminary meeting of the Kahabu Cultural Organization; after that, she and people from the tribe went back to her office to continue discussions. Suddenly, at 1:47 am, the ground started to quake with a force of 7.3 on the Richter scale. The whole Pu-li area was devastated; the place she lived in was also shattered. In these chaotic circumstances, Huang decided to stay on and help rebuild the village, uniting the grassroots people. She founded a reconstruction station and collected funds, inviting professionals to rebuild and improve the cultural habitat. Using anthropological methodology and practice, she helped to revive traditions lost over fifty years ago and awaken a community consciousness. She taught communities to organize themselves into intertribal groups to be legitimately represented in a just system. She further helped expand the alliances.

Huang Mei-ying says: "I was too deeply involved in the community, never had time to write or time for myself. People came and went in the station and I could barely sleep. Sometimes I had to hide and would fall asleep on a chair. That stage is now over. In the reconstruction of the Kahabu tribe, the focus is now on training the younger generation."

In the 90s, social movements were gradually absorbed into the political realm. Identities started to diverge within Taiwan; politicians competed for power and ignored cultural diversity.There were vast differences in policies, economy and distribution of resources between urban and rural communities.

China, Taiwan

Nilza Iraci

Geledés — Instituto da Mulher Negra

Nilza Iraci (1950) is part of the Afro-Brazilian Women Feminist Movement, communicator and political articulator. Tireless, she works behind the scenes and on stage at the meetings of women and UN social conferences. Her role: to guarantee that the subject of racism is present in documents and in public policies. She has a daughter, and she defines herself as an obstacle jumper.

Nilza Iraci lived a tough childhood: she had an aggressive mother, a missing father and was extremely poor. She was a maid from ages nine to 13. When she was 14, she worked in a factory. But the girl made of her doubts a door to the world. Nilza Iraci rewrote her destiny. After her work in the factory, she attended school. "I wanted to learn, learn, and learn." She approximated herself to the studentile movement, without feeling that she belonged there. In the most repressive moment of the military dictatorship, she dove into left-wing militancy. She was arrested in 1972. Again, she did not feel like she belonged. "My fellow militants were revolutionary in their speech, but sexist in their daily life." The sensation of finally belonging happened in her meeting with the feminist movement. Nilza realized her mission inside the feminism: to include the specific problems of the Afro-Brazilians to increase awareness of racial discrimination. She also joined the Afro-Brazilian movement and discovered her second challenge: to include the matters of women in the agenda of anti-racist fights. "I would go back and forth in these two spaces. I insisted for the feminists to include Afro-Brazilian women. I insisted for the Afro-Brazilian women to accept feminism."

Nilza Iraci is responsible for the communication project of Geledés — the largest female Afro-Brazilian NGO. Politically, she believes in the union of flags. Class, Gender and Race are of a unique effort: to reduce inequalities. Her work was recognized by Latin-American women to such a degree that she represented them in the evaluation meeting of the 10 years of the Women's World Conference (Beijing +10). National born articulator, she goes from meeting to meeting, from conference to conference introducing her message. "All my energy is used to transform the reality."

In Brazil, the Afro-Brazilian movement was born to question centuries of privileges conferred to the Caucasian population. These privileges are translated in opportunities, income and valorization. Inside the movement, the Afro-Brazilian organizations of women are active and audacious.

———

Brazil

Krishnammal Jagannaathan

Land for Tillers Freedom (Lafti)

Freedom-fighter and Dalit activist Krishnammal Jagannaathan is often referred to as India's Joan of Arc. Krishnammal believes in a participatory approach, motivating people to change their own lives. In 1981, she cofounded Land for Tillers Freedom (Lafti) to facilitate the distribution of land to landless peasants. Lafti takes bank loans to buy land; the peasants pay the organization back over time. She has also mobilized women on many issues, including wages, land, housing, and sexual harassment, and encouraged many of them to better their own lives.

Krishnammal Jagannaathan was born in 1926 into a Dalit family in Tamil Nadu. Her earliest memories are of caste segregation, and of the dehumanized existence led by her mother and other women in her community. In class V, she realized "that being a peasant woman was hard enough, but to be a Harijan woman was harder still." An important turning point in her life was the news that 44 Dalit women and children had been burnt alive in a village in Thanjavur district, Tamil Nadu, in 1969. Based on the resistance to this incident, Krishnammal built up a women's movement there and expanded the struggle beyond wage issues to the appropriation of land and houses. "I have always considered this incident as a call from God to take up greater challenges," she says.

In 1981, Krishnammal cofounded Lafti to facilitate distribution of land to the landless. Over the years, Lafti has purchased more than 10,000 acres with bank loans, and distributed them to as many families, making sure that the land is usually registered in the name of the woman. This "mother of the landless" — or, as she is better known, India's Joan of Arc — also met with many absentee landowners, and "convinced" several of them to sell their land to Lafti and relocate out of the area.

Krishnammal started another revolutionary project in 2003 in Nagapattinam district — the construction of weatherproof houses in a Dalit colony. Using the participatory approach that has been her signature method to goad the beneficiaries to action, Krishnammal asked, "Even 56 years after Independence, why should you live in huts?" Krishnammal's work has encouraged thousands of women to act toward bettering their own lives.

A landless Dalit woman is thrice disadvantaged: as a Dalit, a woman, and because of her class. Six decades after independence, Dalits continue to suffer from caste stigma. A truly egalitarian India escapes them — from the denial of their rights as citizens to caste identity-based attacks.

India

Chekkottu Kariyan Janu

Adivasi Gothra Mahasabha

Chekkottu Kariyan Janu (born 1970) is the unquestioned leader of the indigenous peoples in Kerala. Formally uneducated, what she has nevertheless done is put the problems of Adivasis (tribals) on the world map. The movements she has led — most notably the Thrissileri struggle in her Wayanad district to regain the burial grounds of the tribals, and the Muthanga forest struggle which exposed the antitribal and ultraviolent nature of the state government — are the stuff of legend.

Chekkottu Kariyan Janu is barely literate and unaffiliated with any political party. Born into the Adiya (slave) tribe, one of the most downtrodden indigenous communities in the state, Janu started working, as domestic help, when she was only seven years old. As she grew up, Janu found herself increasingly troubled by the myriad aspects of the tribal communities' situation in Kerala. Then, she began speaking her mind out. The Adivasis identified with what she was saying — soon, her voice was their voice. In 1992, she was selected chairperson of the South Zone Adivasi Forum, an organization that coordinates the land struggles of south India's indigenous peoples. She has since represented India at international conferences, meetings, and protest demonstrations, entirely understanding the need to interconnect her people's struggle with similar concerns the world over.

One of the first land struggles she led, in the 1980s, was for the right of the Adivasis to their burial land in Thrissileri in her Wayanad district. When a nontribal landowner summoned the police to harass and arrest the Adivasis, the women marched to the police station armed with pickaxes and shovels, had their men released, and reclaimed their land.

Chekkottu's engagement in the Adivasis' struggle for land rights in the Muthanga forest established the viability of the tribal way of life and demonstrated the brutality of the government machinery. The danger of protests remains lethal: about 30 people disappeared after the police fired on them in February 2003. Children were incarcerated and women raped and tortured. Chekkottu called it a "war with racial overtones". The government machinery is not the only adversary Janu has to face: mafia lords and political parties alike view her as a threat. But she continues with her work, pretty much undaunted and unchangeable.

Before Chekkottu Kariyan Janu changed the dynamics of discussions on indigenous communities, Kerala's Adivasis were among the most marginalized in the state. Deprived of access to land, resources, and the right to their way of life, they were forced to integrate into the "mainstream" at the lowest levels.

India

Meihua Jin

Wunan Mosque, Wuzhong city, Ningxia Hui Autonomous Region

Born in 1964, Jin Meihua belongs to the first generation of registered female imams in China's Ningxia Muslim Autonomous Region. Negotiating with the patriarchal tradition, Jin was determined to learn to read and write Arabic at the age of 32. Now she teaches around 50 female students at the Wunan Mosque, Wuzhong City. Through her interpretations of the Koran are from a gender perspective, Jin not only addresses women's literacy, but also creates an unusual woman's space in Chinese Muslim society.

Jin Meihua was able to study only up to primary school level because her family was too poor to support her through high school, despite her good performance. Disappointed, she questioned such injustice and it was this spirit of questioning that became the driving force for her to become a learner and a teacher. Negotiating with the patriarchal tradition, Jin was determined to learn to read and write Arabic, and did so when she turned 32. She was inspired by the sermons of a 60-year-old male imam. With his help she made an effort to learn the Arabic Koran. In 2001 she managed to qualify and got a license to practice from the Ningxia Islamic Association. The examination covered the Koran, Muslim law, and traditional sayings of Muhammad. Jin was overjoyed when she got the result. Jin belongs to the first generation of registered female imams in the Ningxia Muslim Autonomous Region. Now she teaches passages from the Koran, and practices religious rituals for women in the Wunan Mosque, Wuzhong City. Her sermons have earned her a fine reputation. "Women should have the same rights as men. I teach the Koran to illiterate women, and I hope they will keep an open mind, and learn to think," she explains her mission of education through the Koran. In the process of self-learning, Jin negotiates with the patriarchal prejudices and she has fought to earn a right to social mobility. Her story well illustrates the mission of education: to transform the self and the world at the same time. Through her interpretations of the Koran from a gender perspective, Jin not only addresses women's literacy, but also creates an unusual woman's space in Muslim society.

The Ningxia Autonomous Region in northwest China, where one-third of the Muslim minority lives, has 5000 registered imams, only 30 of whom are women. Jin Meihua is one of the eight female imams in Wuzhong City. Female imams are unusual in most Muslim societies.

China

Szilvia S. Kállai

Radio C, Roma radio station, Budapest
Roma Mediacenter, Budapest

Szilvia S. Kállai is a journalist and editor for the Roma radio station Radio C and the Roma Mediacenter in Budapest. Radio C broadcasts to about 60,000 people in Budapest and surroundings, while the Roma Mediacenter compiles material for the Hungarian media and abroad. Szilvia especially deals with women's issues and problems in the Roma community and runs her own Roma women's program. Szilvia encourages young Roma to take up this work, emphasizing that the main responsibility for work that contributes to Roma interests remains on Roma shoulders.

Szilvia S. Kállai was born in 1969 to a Roma father and a non-Roma mother. Because of her family background, Szilvia always had to face questions concerning the Roma minority. After graduating from university in 1998, she joined the Roma Mediacenter, where she still works as a journalist and editor today. In 2001, Szilvia also started working for Radio C, Budapest's Roma radio station broadcasting to about 60,000 people. Both at Radio C and the Roma Mediacenter, Szilvia mainly deals with the situation of women, children, and social politics, as well as education, public health, employment, and economics. She combines these themes to show how the situation of women is inseparable from questions of family, work, and health. An example of the effect of her work: one of her reports about the unfair treatment of Roma patients in the hospital of Eger gave rise to an examination of the hospital's practices, as well as that of other hospitals.

As a mother of two, Szilvia is also very engaged in the field of child protection. She has criticized the Hungarian educational system, showing how Roma children are not given equal treatment with non-Roma children in school admissions and that many who do not have learning disabilities often get placed in special schools. Szilvia also criticizes the legal framework, which provides only marginal protection against discrimination, and she has taken a stand for changes in this field.

Her radio program is interactive most of the time, but sometimes interviews are recorded before the show. Szilvia's goal is to deal with problems and real life situations affecting women in a way that leads to solutions.

The Roma community in Hungary has long suffered discrimination that continues to threaten and impede progress in employment, standards of living, education, and the status of women. The Roma Mediacenter and the Roma C radio station in Budapest are addressing these problems.

Hungary

Su Mei Kao Chin

Legislative Yuan (Taiwan's parliament)

Kao Chin Su Mei (40) is a legislator who fights for the rights of aboriginals of Taiwan and Lanyu Islands. Kao Chin has reactivated aborigines' rights movements, silent for years. In 2004, Kao Chin consolidated the effort of aboriginal representatives in the Legislative Yuan to pass the Basic Law for Aboriginals.

Kao Chin Su Mei was a famous performing artist with a promising career until five years ago when she found out that she had liver cancer. One month after she had surgery, the great earthquake of 1999 hit Taiwan. Kao Chin's attitude towards life was transformed. Together with other charity relief forces, she visited the aboriginal villages and started her new career, fighting for their rights. In 2002, Kao Chin was elected legislator in Taiwan's parliament. Many were skeptical about this career change. She knew of their doubts and decided to prove them wrong through action. She worked hard, found good aides, visited every village and recorded their lives using the footage as evidence for her debates at the Legislative Yuan.

In May 2002, Kao Chin demanded an official apology from the minister of economy for a nuclear waste disposal project in the Lanyu Islands, where the Tao tribe resides. TV cameras showed a relentless Kao Chin Su Mei, dramatically in contrast to the former artist. This changed the way people viewed her. On 26 October 2002, Kao Chin initiated a social movement for the revival of traditions, opposing the Magau National Park. This not only prevented the approval of the program, but also reactivated aboriginal movements in Taiwan. "You cannot gain your dignity without action. You can only defend yourself against the violence of the government by demonstrating the integrity of your power. A movement does not mean bloodshed. You can only touch people's hearts by showing how persistent you are", says Kao Chin.

Aboriginals in Taiwan constitute two percent of the population. They are underprivileged politically, economically, socially and culturally. Their lands were stolen, their rights denied, their cultural heritage overlooked and their social status downgraded. They are also the most socially unprotected.

China, Taiwan

"Don't become
too narrow. Live fully.
Meet all kinds of
people. You'll learn
something from
everyone. Follow what
you feel in your
heart."

Yuri Kochiyama

Organization for Afro-American Unity
National Committee for the Defense of Political Prisoners
Asian Americans for Action

A daughter of Japanese immigrants, Yuri Kochiyama (born 1921) grew up in California. Following the bombing of Pearl Harbor, her life changed dramatically in 1942 when people of Japanese ancestry in the USA were sent to internment camps. After World War II, she joined movements for civil rights and black liberation in New York City; she opposed US imperialism and supported radical grassroots organizations and political prisoners. She has spoken out for racial justice and human rights for over 40 years.

Yuri Kochiyama was among the 120,000 people forced into internment camps after the bombing of Pearl Harbor. This traumatic experience was the beginning of Yuri's political awakening, and her subsequent work for social and economic justice. To counter the deprivations of camp life, Yuri led an organization for young women and volunteered for various community programs. After leaving the camp, she saw the oppression of African Americans in the segregated south when she worked with the Aloha United Service Organization for Japanese American soldiers. She married in 1946, moved to New York City with her husband and had six children. They lived in low-income housing in Harlem, surrounded by black and Latino families. Yuri became involved in the Organization for Afro-American Unity founded by Malcolm X. With her husband and three older children, she attended its Liberation School to learn about black history, thought, and culture. She was present in the Audubon Ballroom in 1965 when Malcolm X was shot. A famous Life magazine photo shows her cradling his head in her lap. With her children, Yuri attended countless protests and demonstrations. She supported the Black Panthers, Young Lords, and other radical activists. She participated in Asian Americans for Action, the Asian Coalition Against the Vietnam War, the Japanese American Redress and Reparations Movement, and the New York Justice for Vincent Chin Coalition, among many others.

Yuri Kochiyama has worked unstintingly for over 40 years for racial justice and human rights, making alliances between diverse communities, especially communities of color. Despite her age and frailty she continues to speak out, urging Japanese Americans to oppose US government harassment of Arabs, Arab Americans, and South Asians, also labeled as a "national security risk".

US policies and institutions have long exploited racial differences to divide people. Immigration policies fluctuate with economic growth or perceived threats to national security. After the bombing of Pearl Harbor, people of Japanese ancestry were labeled "aliens" and held in internment camps.

United States of America

Kupa Piti Kungka Tjuta

Irati Wanti
Senior Aboriginal Women's Council of Coober Pedy

Half a century ago, members of Kupa Piti Kungka Tjuta survived atomic testing in the South Australian desert. In 1998, the Australian government proposed a national nuclear waste dump for their homelands. The Kungkas — Aboriginal Women Elders looking after country and culture — spearheaded an inspiring and unique campaign called Irati Wanti (The Poison — Leave it!). Overcoming significant barriers, they joined forces with diverse groups across the country to eventually stop the multi-million dollar project in 2004.

Coober Pedy is an isolated opal mining town in outback South Australia. Since 1998, it hosted an extraordinary frontline campaign to protect precious underground water reserves from a proposed national radioactive waste dump.

The federal government pushed an image of the desert as an empty place devoid of life, with no use to the economy except as a dumping ground for poisonous waste. But the government and the nuclear industry did not expect the groundswell of resistance, especially from the Kupa Piti Kungka Tjuta — a group of Aboriginal culture women in their late sixties and seventies. With the help of a nun and a fax machine, their sustained battle against the dump was launched immediately after they heard of the proposal. Their statement of opposition slowly circulated around Australia: "We are Aboriginal women. We know the country. The poison the government is talking about will poison the land." The Kungkas recounted their nightmarish experiences as survivors of atomic testing in the 1950s as proof of their first hand knowledge of the Irati (poison). Their message struck a chord with urban communities and the Irati Wanti (The poison — Leave it!) campaign was born. Enlisting and mentoring young non-indigenous environmentalists, the Kungkas bravely traversed the continent, spoke to numerous media, held big meetings, attended hearings, and built a website — all to educate and inspire the wider community of the vital need to protect their beautiful desert country. All of this took place while the Kungkas fulfilled important duties as Elders in their community. The tactics worked: they spearheaded a successful national campaign. With a federal election looming, the government abandoned its multi-million dollar proposal in July 2004.

In 1953, an atomic bomb was detonated in the South Australia desert, homelands of Aboriginal people, without warning. Nuclear fallout was responsible for a massive increase in radiation-related illness and genetic birth defects in communities. In 1998, the government planned a nuclear waste dump in the area. The Kungkas have been campaigning against this for years.

Australia

Hazel María Law Blanco

Yatama
Prinsu Association
Civil Coordination of Bilwi

Hazel María Law Blanco was born in the municipality of Waspán, in the Autonomous Region of The Northern Atlantic, Nicaragua. Since she was 16 years old, she has fought against racial discrimination. She is a defender of human rights for the indigenous communities and a promoter of equality between men and women. As a member of the National Parliament, in 1990, she achieved the passing of the Autonomy Law, which recognizes the historical rights of the indigenous people and communities to the Atlantic Coast of Nicaragua.

"As a native, I was excluded from education, and, as woman, I was limited to doing the housework." Hazel María Law Blanco, Mískita, born in the municipality of Waspán, in the Autonomous Region of The Northern Atlantic, which borders with Honduras, decided to challenge the established order. She studied hard. She completed her secondary studies and, in 1980, received a degree in Education (with mention in Spanish and Literature) in the National Autonomous University of Nicaragua. In 1993, she obtained a degree in Law. "Hearing teachers say that the Mískitos were ignorant, has always had an impact on me. But, when I worked as a teacher, I was able to observe the students' response. The ignorants were the teachers that did not teach using the right method."

Her organizational work began in the 1970s, fighting for the legalization of the lands of the indigenous communities and also for education to be offered in the native language of the Atlantic Region. With the triumph of the Sandinist Popular Revolution in 1979, she had the opportunity to make her dream come true: in 1980, a literacy crusade for indigenous languages took place in the Nicaraguan Caribbean region. This historic event was also a personal success for Hazel. "We began to teach a group of ladies from Waspán to read and write."

In 1990, as a member of the National Parliament, Hazel achieved the passing of the Autonomy Law, which recognized the historical rights of the indigenous people and communities of the Atlantic Coast of Nicaragua.

The Atlantic Coast of Nicaragua is characterized by a huge natural richness and the extreme poverty of its inhabitants. Its territory has 70% of the forest reserve and 70% of the fishing production of Nicaragua. Of its 500,000 inhabitants, 250,000 are indigenous or Afro-descendents.

Keepu Tsering Lepcha, teacher and retired civil servant, has devoted herself to the survival of her rapidly diminishing Lepcha community, particularly educating the girls of this tiny tribe.

Keepu Tsering Lepcha

Human Development Foundation of Sikkim (HDFS)

Keepu Tsering Lepcha (born 1942) has devoted her life to the uplift of her Lepcha community, indigenous to the Himalayan region of Sikkim. A teacher and retired civil servant, she helps educate members, especially the girls, of this diminishing tribe, which today numbers around 30,000. With the help of European donors, she has founded an NGO, the Human Development Foundation of Sikkim (HDFS), which has been working since 1997 with underprivileged families.

Keepu Tsering Lepcha was driven by the need to help her Lepcha community, whose members have found it hard to keep pace with an increasingly competitive society. Her father was a government official whose job took him to the remote areas of Sikkim, so she grew up hearing her father talk about the need to do something for the community. She fulfilled her father's desire through her careers as teacher, government official and, eventually, social activist. After postgraduate studies, Keepu became a teacher at the Enchey Senior Secondary School in Gangtok, Sikkim's capital. The government school had mainly been established to help refugee Tibetan children. Later, Keepu was deputed to work with the state government's education department as assistant director. In 1994, she was inducted into the state civil service, promoted to the rank of joint secretary, and posted outside the education department. Over 28 years, she served as project director in the Rural Development Agency, dealing with projects for people living below the poverty line. She retired from government service in 2000. Starting 1989, Keepu embarked as a mentor for her community's children, with Lepcha children living with her in her six-roomed home, Lepcha Cottage. Her work is focused on girls, women, orphans, the elderly and the neglected.

Keepu also works through an NGO, the Human Development Foundation of Sikkim, of which she is chairperson. It was started in 1997, with help from Swiss and other donors; its major aim is to cater to the needs of underprivileged children in Sikkim mainly through education. Keepu's work has led to significant improvements in children's healthcare and basic education. It is the Lepcha tribe that counts.

Lepchas are Sikkim's indigenous inhabitants, who now number less than 30,000. The statistical decline is blamed on low literacy rates, high infant mortality and high liquor consumption. Despite many government schemes addressed to them, most Lepchas still live below the poverty line.

India

Chunxia Li

Li Chunxia is a disabled worker from Xian, Shaanxi Province of China. She has been paraplegic since childhood. With the enthusiastic help of the others and her independent character, she had managed to complete schooling and to take up different jobs. Her life is exemplary for being able to raise her daughter — now a post-graduate student — on her own with a meager living and all kinds of hardships. Her independence is a living model to her daughter and to society.

Li Chunxia suffered from paraplegia at a very young age. Refusing to be marginalized by being out of school, she wrote to the newspapers to draw public attention to her plight and managed to complete her schooling. Subsequently, she worked in a factory from where she was dismissed with a labor insurance compensation because the new manager did not like to see her wheelchair at the entrance of the sales department where she worked. When her daughter was only 18 months old, she and her blind husband divorced. A few years later, her father's death left Li Chunxia on her own, with the responsibility of her daughter. Seeking a better education environment for her, Li Chunxia moved several times to different places, some with very poor living conditions, surviving on a meager allowance of only 164 yuan a month from the factory. In times of illness, they could not afford to see a doctor and just bought some medicines. Whenever they could not pay the tuition fee, the daughter had to study at home. Here, mother and daughter read famous works together and discussed stories, plots, characters, and themes. "I have never experienced love in my life, that's why I want to let my child know how true love is like." Whenever the daughter encountered problems in her studies, Li Chunxia stepped in to help. "Mum and I are just like peers," she says. She had striven to work hard and performed very well in school. In 1999, she succeeded in entering the Shaanxi Normal University. Now she is a post-graduate student working for her master's degree. Though disabled people are entitled to social support at a minimal level, Li Chunxia's story tells us that they have to be strong-minded and active to get through studying, working and even family life. Li Chunxia's self-determination and optimism in face of adversity have inspired many.

The rapid transformation of urban society requires new social welfare systems and relief mechanisms to cope with change. The emphasis on profit means that sympathy and love are diminishing. Care and concern for the disabled also lags far behind, forcing them to seek their own means of survival.

China

Nicolasa Machaca Alejandro

Tomás Katari Polytechnic Institute
Juana Azurduy Center
Small Milk Producers Association

She was born a peasant and indigenous woman (1952). She tended the sheep and cows and cultivated potatoes and broad beans. She learned to read late. She was a reading promoter. She established Mother's Clubs where women could be trained. She unified the efforts of different organizations working to support the communities. She was arrested, tortured and was obliged to flee the country. She became a paramedic and returned to help the poor of Bolivia. She is Nicolasa Machaca.

She was an indigenous shepherdess of Bolivia. At age 15, she went to a meeting of the Mother's Club. She was not yet a mother, but they taught her to read. It was 1970. One year later, she became a reading promoter. Then she became the president of the Club. When they needed a venue, she found the plot and they built on it. They put up their looms and they studied. She was called to other places to organize Mother's Clubs. She received training in different crafts and taught others what she learned. At age 18, she was the leader of 12 communities. When she was 20, she was a representative of her province. As a handicrafts promoter, she traveled throughout the country and heard about the trade unions. But why was it such a scattered effort? And why were there no women in the trade unions? Her questions gave origin to the Single Trade Union Federation of Workers from Oruro.

Identified as an activist, she was arrested and tortured. She was hurled from a light aircraft. Some farmers found her. A political leader helped her to flee the country. Her contacts said only a few words: "Go to that place and someone will pick you up." In Peru, a doctor told her that it was necessary to amputate one of her feet and maybe the other one too. They took her to Cuba, where they managed to save both. She returned to Bolivia to continue learning, to increase her knowledge, to coordinate more efforts. People do not always pay attention to her because she is a woman, and indigenous. But she is stubborn — or enlightened.

In Bolivia's mountains, there are scattered indigenous communities that are generally isolated, outside the centers of civilization. The country has had various military governments. Historically, the revolts of hungry peasants have been brutally repressed.

Bolivia

Concita Maia

Movimento Articulado de Mulheres da Amazônia (Mama)

Educator Concita Maia (1951) is the founder and president of the Articulated Movement of Women from the Amazon (Mama), a feminist and environmental NGO that unites and strengthens women from the Legal Amazon, a region formed by nine states and with an area of five million square kilometers. There are 117 indigenous, Afro-Brazilian and Caucasian groups with whom Concita discusses themes such as female health, education, violence, environment and income generation.

Forbidden by her Caucasian mother of talking about her origins, Concita Maia silently held on to the history of her paternal grandmother. She was an indigenous who was hunted down and marked, on her arm, with the letters FC, which are the initials of the man who stole her freedom. Her grandmother was given as a present to another man with whom she had many children, including Concita's father. "My mom denied my indigenous background. It did not matter. It runs in my blood." Popular education was the means that Concita found to take women like her grandmother away from invisibility. "Women who live in the depths of the forest and who are not even a part of the population data of the Brazilian Institute of Geography and Statistics." In the 1980s, as a graduate and postgraduate in pedagogy, Concita moved to a tribe located along the border with Peru, where she implanted Acre's first indigenous school. One year later, when she returned to the capital, Rio Branco, she widened the militancy for the fight for the rights of women from the Amazon. They work as agriculturists, gatherers of serum for the fabrication of rubber, breakers of the babaçu coconut (to extract an essence used to make soaps and oils), fisherwomen, sexual professionals and midwives, surviving in inhospitable places of difficult access. In 1997, Concita Maia founded the Articulated Movement of Women from the Amazon (Mama). In the presidency of this movement, she articulates, informs and capacitates women's groups, aiming to strengthen them and to put them in conditions to seek social justice and gender equality. The movement also supports around 200 midwives in the state's countryside. She helps in the elaboration of the annual activity planning; she administers qualifying courses and fights for this profession to be recognized and legalized.

Concita Maia participated in the creation of the Movement of Women from Acre, the Network of Men and Women of Acre, the Association of Traditional Midwives from the city of Marechal Thaumaturgo, the Group of Indigenous Women from Acre and from the South of the Amazon, and the Feminist Youth Movement.

Brazil

Paula Makabory

Elsham

Paula Makabory (born 1970) is one of many women activists in Papua who were inspired by the 1998 student movement to pay close attention to human rights issues in Indonesia's easternmost province. She worked for the human rights NGO, Elsham, documenting human rights violations in Timika in the late 1990s. She is currently involved with a network of civil society groups run mostly by indigenous peoples working for participatory development.

Paula's human rights work began in 1997 shortly after graduating from the Cendrawasih University's faculty of English literature in Jayapura. She says she has been interested in social issues since her college years. When an offer came to work for a respected human rights organization, the Jayapura-based Elsham, she accepted immediately. Paula was assigned to Timika where a riot had just broken out in the mining town of Tembagapura and gross human rights violations had allegedly occurred. Assigned to document the violations, she met with the families of victims, working enthusiastically although she was risking her life. Her social activism in Timika brought her closer to many other social issues besides human rights.

In the past few years, Paula has worked on women's issues like domestic violence, which is rampant in the male-dominated Papuan culture. Collaborating closely with a network of NGOs involved in the same issue, she counsels victims of violence so they can again stand on their own. She also conducts regular discussions where women participate and discuss various problems they face and ways to resolve them. Paula believes that these discussion groups and sharing sessions help instil confidence in the women. A colleague describes Paula as a hard worker, adding: "She has established strong networks both overseas and here in Papua."

In Timika, where Freeport McMoran, the world's biggest gold mining company, operates, the marginalization of indigenous peoples has led to poverty and environmental degradation. Indigenous women caught in the socio-political situation and a paternalistic culture, bear the brunt of the suffering.

Indonesia

Ruth Manorama

National Alliance of Women
National Federation of Dalit Women
Women's Voice

Ruth Manorama (born 1952) grew up seeing her parents engaged in active social work. She has been consistently associated with a range of issues — the rights of slum dwellers, domestic workers, unorganized labor and Dalits', and the empowerment of marginalized women. She sees the interconnectedness between these issues, and the common cause that marginalized people share the world over. Her work crosses the borders between grassroots movements, mass mobilization, and international movements.

Ruth Manorama began working with the urban poor — particularly slum dwellers — women workers, and domestic workers. The result was the birth of Women's Voice, and the registration of the Bangalore Gruhakarmikara Sangha (domestic workers' union). In 1988, a meeting of NGO leaders on NGO interventions provided the impetus for Ruth and like-minded people to set up initiatives, including Women in Development, one of the country's premier gender and development training institutions. Ruth has also contributed enormously to mainstreaming Dalit issues, especially those of Dalit women. She realized that large, mass-based organizations were necessary to handle issues related to societal structures that affected vast areas. Thus was born the National Federation of Dalit Women. She was also closely associated with the mobilization of Dalits for the World Conference Against Racism in Durban, which put the issue on the international map.

Ruth's contribution also runs to breaking the upper-class, upper-caste image of India's women's movement. Her work on coordinating the south India chapter of the preparations for the Fourth UN World Conference on Women in Beijing in 1995 had a signal role to play in this. After returning to India, the advisory group decided that ten regional members of the task force would come together as the National Alliance of Women, with Ruth as president.

"Whenever I feel discouraged or tired, one look at the dedication of the poor women to their families and society is enough to move me," says Ruth. "I have tremendous confidence in the capacity of the poor to transform not only their own lives, but also to build a just, humane, and democratic society."

India's 160 million Dalits are marginalized: no legislation protects unorganized workers, 93 percent of the labor force; women are victims of domestic and social violence; and Karnataka's slum dwellers are arbitrarily evicted, and lack basic amenities and protective legislation.

India

"My only wish is that peace and freedom shall prevail in our homeland, in particular among women."

Nang Charm Tong

Shan Women's Action Network (SWAN)

Charm Tong was born in 1981 in southern Shan State, Burma. When she was young, her family moved to the Thai border. After completing the ninth grade in Chiang Mai, she joined the Shan Herald Agency for News as an intern and worked with various human rights organizations. In 1999, with her colleagues in Chiang Mai, she formed the Shan Women's Action Network (SWAN). As a member of the Advocacy Team of SWAN, her responsibilities include fact finding, training, campaigning and advocacy on human rights and democracy in Burma.

Born in a time of conflict when her homeland was ravaged by war waged by the Burmese government for total control of Shan State, Charm Tong has many painful memories that are hard to forget. As the conflict intensified and education opportunities for her and her siblings as well as their safety were jeopardized, her parents decided to send them away to Thailand. As a result, the family broke up. Charm Tong stayed with one of her younger siblings, the rest were spread out to survive by themselves.

Charm settled in Thai territory, Wiang Haeng district, Chiang Mai, where, under the care of a Catholic sister at an orphanage, Charm Tong learned English while she pursued her normal education. On March 28, 1999, she and fellow human rights advocates formed the Shan Women's Action Network (SWAN). A few months later, Charm Tong went to Geneva to present cases of rape of women and girls by the Burmese army, stories of Shan villages set on fire and villagers who were forced to provide slave labor for the Burmese Army.

SWAN has grown into an influential community-based organization, providing education for Shan refugee children and health information for refugee women. It assists women who have been raped, promotes opportunities for women and provides capacity building for refugees so that they can assert their rights. Charm and her colleagues in SWAN place great importance on assisting children who have fled from wars inside Burma. Because the Thai government has failed to recognize the refugee status of Shan people who have fled Burma, they are not eligible for humanitarian assistance. It was only recently that a temporary shelter for a small group of Shan refugees was set up near Ban Piang Luang, after intense lobbying by SWAN and other organizations.

From 1996 until today, the Burmese army has attacked more than 2000 Shan villages, affecting more than 400,000 people in central Shan State, Burma. Many have fled into Thailand. The attacks continue unabated.

Burma

Nasae Yapa

Lahu Hill Tribe Network

Nasae Yapa (born 1966) is a Lahu hill tribe farmer and village headwoman who has advocated the protection of the rights of the hill tribes since 1990. In the process, she has been intimidated and imprisoned by the authorities. She has remained steadfast to the cause, however, conveying to local officials that they cannot take the hill tribes for granted.

Nasae Yapa of the Lahu Hill Tribe Network is an active member of the network of Seven Tribal Groups of Thailand. She has been trained on laws concerning women and serves as a volunteer for a project campaigning against the flesh trade and promoting the rights and dignity of indigenous peoples.

When the government launched its 'War on drugs' in 2001, she assisted the local police by providing information on drug smugglers. But the authorities, who earned points from the national government on the basis of the number of arrests they made, took advantage of her and other villagers. Uniformed officers entered their homes and planted metamphetamine tablets when the owners were not looking. Then, they forced the villagers to plead guilty before the courts or face longer prison terms. Since most villagers do not have land titles or even Thai citizenship, it is almost impossible for them to get bail. Many villagers, including Nasae Yapa's younger brother, were arrested on similar charges of drug possession. When she spoke up for the villagers who were being abused, she was charged with obstructing the work of the officers. Although many villagers testified on her behalf and insisted that she did not physically harm an officer, she was charged with harming officers and helping drug traffickers escape the law and was sentenced to a six-month prison term.

After her release, Nasae Yapa vowed to continue the fight against corruption and abuse of power. "Now I am not afraid of the officers. In the beginning, it was quite difficult to convince the others in the community, because they believed the officers were always right. But since the people witnessed direct abuse, they are now willing to stand up and fight."

The Thai government's war on drugs put pressure on the police to arrest as many people as they could for possession of narcotics. However, instead of getting the real culprits, many of whom are politically influential, the authorities target innocent villagers.

Thailand

Medha Patkar

Narmada Bachao Andolan (NBA)
National Alliance of People's Movements (NAPM)

Medha Patkar (born 1954) has been the force behind the Narmada Bachao Andolan (NBA), a massive grassroots mobilization of people against the construction of a series of dams across the Narmada river. For two decades, Medha has led the people in a struggle to win recognition for the rights of indigenous communities to their natural resources, and to establish the need for a sustainable model of development. While the Narmada question remains unresolved, Medha and her colleagues have managed to prominently pin the issue of big dams on the world map.

Medha Patkar is the face of the NBA, arguably one of the largest people's struggles worldwide. The World Bank-financed Sardar Sarovar and other big dam projects were coming up on the Narmada river about the time Medha began working in the tribal areas of Gujarat, Maharashtra, and Madhya Pradesh. In 1985, she organized the peasants and tribals of the three states to fight for information about the Narmada Valley Development Project. The NBA stressed the government's failure to involve the local communities in decisions that affect their lives and livelihoods. As Medha and the NBA continued their work, and emerged as one of the strongest voices against this manner of insensate "development", even the World Bank was forced to undertake an unprecedented review of the Sardar Sarovar dam. The World Bank completed its review in 1991, concluding that the project had been ill-conceived.

Medha's work did not begin and end with just the protest against unplanned and unsystematic development: she worked with villagers to develop alternative sources of energy and water. Education is another area she focused on: the Reva Jeevanshala, which the NBA set up, is a network of nine residential schools in the villages across the Narmada belt in Maharashtra, Madhya Pradesh, and Gujarat.

A veteran of several fasts (including a 22-day fast in 1991 which nearly killed her), monsoon satyagrahas, marches, and rallies, Medha is almost single-handedly responsible for bringing the concerns of the tribals from the Narmada valley into the living rooms of the urban elite.

The Narmada Valley Development Project, India's single largest river development scheme, will displace about 1.5 million people, ruin biodiversity by inundating thousands of acres, and degrade agricultural soils by continuous irrigation and salinization, making the soil biomorphically toxic.

India

Pinee Moonkaew

Pakakayaw tribe

Pinee Moonkaew (born 1961) is a Karen woman who proudly calls her tribe "Pakakayaw", which literally means "we are human beings". At 44, she has transformed from an ordinary woman to one who fights for her people's right to their land. She is one of the leading voices demanding the participation of ethnic people in natural resource management — in particular the watersheds. In spite of a logging ban and other regulations, Thailand has been suffering from rampant deforestation.

In the past ten years, the ethnic people of the Wang River Basin have been demanding their right to their land. They have walked from their high mountain to Bangkok to tell the residents of the capital city stories about how the ethnic people live with nature. Their protests are aimed at reaching an agreement with the state to allow tribal people to have a say in the management of the watershed. In these protests, women always stand in the frontline, side by side with the male leadership, to demand justice. For ten years, Pinee Moonkaew has traveled from her highland home to other parts of the country to bring her people's message that the tribal people have a right to manage their natural resources. She wants to correct the notion among urban residents that the tribal people are destroying the watershed. She wants the urban residents to understand that the ethnic people cannot be held liable for deforestation because, although many of them rely on nature, they do not simply take away from nature, but replenish what they use to keep the ecological balance.

Pinee Moonkaew's life changed when the government, claiming to uphold national forest reserve laws, announced that people living in the forests must leave their homes. In response, 50,000 people, many of them ethnic people, signed a draft of the Community Forest Act and proposed it for consideration by the Parliament. The struggle has motivated Pinee Moonkaew, an ordinary woman, to come to the forefront and demand justice for ethnic women. "The problems affect all of us, men and women alike," she says. "The Pakakayaw hold that their struggles will not succeed if women are not included, as they believe the paddy rice fields belong to men, but the farmland belongs to women. As such we have to fight together."

Thailand has been suffering from rampant deforestation, affecting the environment immensely. But all the laws and regulations drawn up by the government cannot solve this problem due to a lack of public awareness of the importance of forests and nature.

Thailand

Noelí Pocaterra

Network of Wayuu Indigenous Women
Permanent Commission for Indigenous People in the National Assembly
of the Bolivarian Republic of Venezuela

She is an indigenous woman, a Wayuu woman. She is militant, socially and politically, and has committed herself, for over 40 years, to the defense of the human, political and territorial rights of her country's native people. The discrimination and exclusion experienced by her people motivated her to fight tirelessly, in a number of different ways, for the inclusion, in 1999, of the indigenous people's rights in the Constitution of the Bolivarian Republic of Venezuela.

Noelí Pocaterra was born in Mocoomatira, in 1936, in the Venezuelan Guajira. In 1956, she was the first Venezuelan indigenous woman to graduate as a social worker. She has a long history of social and political militancy dedicated to the promotion of culture and to the defense of justice, freedom and rights for the indigenous communities and their people. She is a founder member of the National Indigenous Council of Venezuela (Conive), which served her as platform during the process when the new constitution of the Bolivarian Republic of Venezuela was being drawn up, in 1999. She was the co-writer of the section about Indigenous People's Rights, where, for the first time in the country, those rights were explicitly recognized.

As a member of the National Assembly, she has been the driving force behind the discussion and approval of several laws in favor of the native communities, such as the ones concerning the demarcation of their habitat and land, providing them with guarantees and others about education and use of their language. There are also laws regarding their identification as citizens.

"I feel so pleased when I look at what our struggle has achieved. I feel happy. Before I joined the constituent process, when we came to Caracas to talk with the deputies, some of our men were not allowed to enter because they were not wearing jackets or ties. Nowadays, my work in the Assembly puts me in contact with resources and power. But I am aware that this is transitory, so we have a lot to do and no time to waste."

Until the end of the last century, the culture, languages and rights of the indigenous communities were not recognized in the Venezuelan Constitution. For the first time, in 1999, they were incorporated into the Constitution as a part of the process promoted by President Hugo Chávez.

Venezuela

Eliane Potiguara

Rede de Comunicação Indígena (Network of Indigenous Communication)
Rede de Escritores Indígenas (Network of Indigenous Writers)

Eliane Potiguara (1950) was born in an indigenous ghetto in Rio, formed by indigenous people from Paraíba, a poor state in the Northeast of Brazil. Eliane is the founder of Brazil's first indigenous organization, the Grumin (Woman and Indigenous Education Group), which has now been transformed into the Network of Indigenous Communication. As a writer, Eliane also articulates a group of indigenous authors that fight for the preservation of their culture.

Eliane Potiguara's memories of her childhood are of a life marked by poverty and exclusion. Raised in an indigenous ghetto near one of the city's prostitution areas, her family reached the point where they had to live on the streets. Her grandmother used to sell bananas at the entrance of the school where Eliane studied. The inspiration for her efforts to defend indigenous women comes from the drive and the interest in literature of the women who raised her. "We live a historical violence; my grandmother left her tribe after being molested at age 12," she says. Throughout her trajectory of fighting on behalf of indigenous women, she also suffered violence, humiliation and sexual abuse. She is the mother of three daughters and grandmother of two grandsons. She still struggles to support her family. Licensed in education, she was very young when she started to teach in the poor community where she lived. As a writer, she remembers being responsible for letters that her grandmother used to send her family that stayed in Paraíba. From this grandmother, Eliane inherited the interest in indigenous traditions. For this purpose, she is a part of the Network of Indigenous Writers and she is an advisor at the Brazilian Indigenous Institute of Intellectual Property (Inbrapi). In 2004, this institute promoted, in Rio, the first meeting of indigenous authors.

One of Eliane's main achievements was accomplished in 1991, when she organized the National Meeting of Indigenous Women, in Rio de Janeiro. More than 200 representatives of different communities attended the meeting. On that same year, in Geneva, she was part of the work group that rewrote the Universal Declaration of Indigenous Rights. "All my strength was determined in my childhood, when I learned, with my grandmother, the value of the indigenous people," she says.

The Grumin association, founded by Eliane, was the creator of Brazil's first indigenous newspaper, which was published internationally to divulge the cause of indigenous women. The newspaper played a fundamental role in the integration of the tribes that still survive throughout Brazil.

Brazil

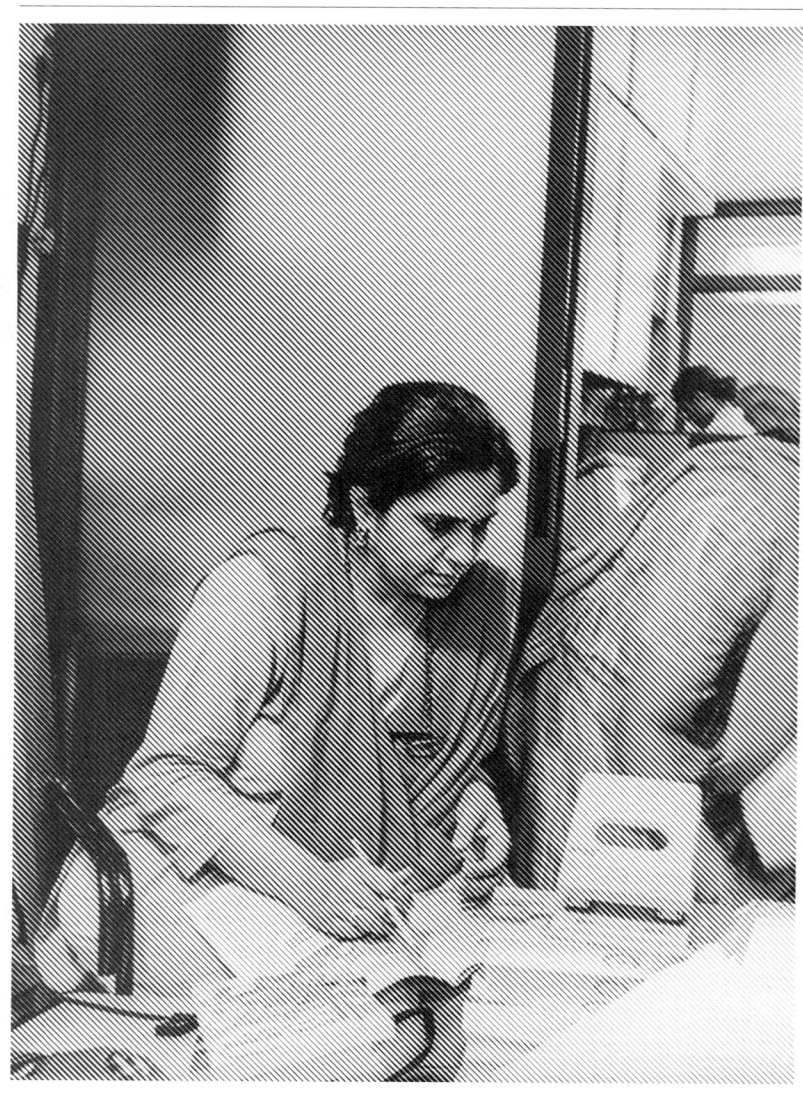

Teesta Setalvad

Communalism Combat

Teesta Setalvad is an activist for communal harmony who has made headlines in India for her valiant efforts to bring to justice those responsible for brutal crimes against women in the Gujarat pogrom in 2002. For more than a decade, Setalvad has worked tirelessly to put the spotlight on human rights' violations in communal situations through her research work, and by organizing interventions such as citizens' inquiries, meetings, and other forms of advocacy, and legal intervention.

Teesta Setalvad began to focus on communal issues when India was in the grip of deep religious conflicts and tensions. The country's cultural plurality was being questioned and threatened by resurgent religious fundamentalism. Teesta, originally a mainstream journalist, decided to respond to the challenge by publishing Communalism Combat, a publication that stood for tolerance and communal amity, and intervened in various ways during communal irruptions.

Engagement with these issues came naturally to Teesta. Her father is a legal luminary, an expert in jurisprudence, and an authority on constitutional law; her husband is also a journalist and activist working for communal harmony.

Teesta works on conflict amelioration, communal harmony and tolerance, and human rights issues in conflict situations. She also analyzes mechanisms that endanger peace, and documents both violations of human rights and communitarian peacemaking efforts. Furthermore, she negotiates on communal issues, organizes interventions such as citizens' inquiries, meetings, and other forms of advocacy, and seeks legal redress for human rights' abuses. These aspects of her work coalesced after the communal killings in Gujarat in 2002. Teesta's role in trying to nail the guilty earned her widespread respect. She exposed atrocities that had been suppressed and supported victims muted by choice or force. This was particularly evident in the case of Zahira Sheikh, witness in the Best Bakery case, one of the most horrific incidents of communal murder.

Gujarat 2002 was a turning point in India's much-vaunted "secular" history, with religious fanatics turning into remorseless hatchetmen for politically vested interests in the state administration, particularly right-wing do-minators of the nation's honor.

India

Chhing Lamu Sherpa

Plan Nepal
Mountain Spirit

For the past two decades, Chhing Lamu Sherpa (born 1960) has played a pivotal role in empowering women and extremely marginalized groups in eastern Nepal. As an educated professional woman working to improve the lives of poor and deprived mountain communities, she is a role model for other members of Nepal's Sherpa community, an ethnic minority living off the rural mountainous areas, often as expedition guides.

Chhing Lamu Sherpa faced ridicule when she started to go to school — she was an "old" 17 years of age. Family problems had prevented her from attending school earlier. But, putting in a lot of hard work, she obtained her school-leaving certificate at 23.

The determination that took Chhing to her first village school in Phinjoling village in the Udaipur district of eastern Nepal also helped her make a success of her life. Not only was this farmer's daughter the first girl in her village to complete high school, she also went to college, earning a graduate diploma in Rural Extension and Women from Reading University (UK). She started out in 1982 as a junior instructor in a government-run women's training center, training women workers, and advising housewives on managing their kitchen gardens. Five years later, she worked with Action Aid Nepal (AAN) as senior community organizer and gender development coordinator for five years. Chhing left AAN to join the Makalu-Barun National Park and Conservation Project, wanting to learn about environment and conservation issues. She organized local women in conservation and development.

In 1994, the young men of the area, especially Sherpas, motivated her to form Mountain Spirit, an organization for the uplift of the young. She helped mobilize about 2000 community members and 75 youths to work as trainers, of whom 20 have become national-level trainers. Seven years later, Chhing transferred Mountain Spirit's leadership to the youth she had enlisted. Since 2004, she has been employed by Plan Nepal, a nonpolitical and nongovernmental child-centered community development organization, as a district program manager. Initially criticized for traveling with male colleagues, she has today been honored by organizations like the Nepal Sherpa Association for her contribution to the social sector.

The Sherpas, one of Nepal's subsistence communities, are paradoxically known the world over for their mountain guide skills. While the rare few have migrated abroad, the majority still depend on agriculture and livestock-rearing for their livelihood.

Nepal

Barbara Smith

Albany's Stand for Peace Antiracism Committee
Coalition for Accountable Police and Government
Justice for Diallo Committee

Barbara Smith is an author, activist, and independent scholar who has played a groundbreaking role in opening up a national dialogue about the intersections of race, class, sexuality, and gender. She was among the first to define an African American women's literary tradition and to build black women's studies and black feminism in the United States. She has been politically active in many movements for social justice since the 1960s. Currently, her focus is on neighborhood and community organizing, especially regarding youth issues, in the poor black community where she resides.

From the time she was in high school and became involved in Cleveland's civil rights struggle, Barbara Smith has been an untiring political activist, doing both direct-action work and writing to bring about social change. Smith has worked to end sterilization abuse, to insure reproductive freedom and quality health care for all women, to end apartheid in South Africa, to stop US-funded warfare against indigenous people of Central and South America, to challenge police brutality, to eradicate violence against women, and to challenge homophobia and heterosexism.

One of her earliest causes established the first publishing house run by women of color and committed to publishing work by diverse women of color, Kitchen Table: Women of Color Press. Because she has dedicated herself to causes, she has always lived in precarious financial circumstances. Further, as an outspoken and courageous black lesbian feminist, Barbara's physical safety has always been at issue; most recently her home was vandalized when she spoke out about police and political corruption in Albany, New York, where she has lived since 1984.

As a leader in articulating all political, economic, and social issues as inherently black women's issues, Barbara has forever changed progressive political discourse. As a founder of Kitchen Table, she brought the writing of women of color into print and to public attention. She established an entire academic discourse — black feminist criticism — that has had a profound effect on scholars and students. Further, black women's studies is an acknowledged discipline because of her work as an editor of the groundbreaking collection of work in black women's studies ("All the Women Are White, All the Blacks Are Men, But Some of Us Are Brave: Black Women's Studies", 1982).

When Barbara Smith began her life's work, the civil rights act had only recently been passed, and overt discrimination against people of color and women of all races was still the norm. More recently, single-issue politics keeps marginalized people from working together for social change.

United States of America

Nasra Souelem

Polisario Front (PF)
National Union of Saharawi Women (NUSW)

Nasra Mahmoud Souelem has been working as a nursery teacher in the camps in Western Sahara for 29 years. She has suffered great afflictions in her life; perhaps the most harrowing of which was losing her husband in the war four years after their marriage. In the Saharan camps, to where her family had to move, she began her training as a nursery teacher. Despite the gradual improvement of the conditions in the camps, the situation there often remains bleak. In this climate, Nasra's work to provide education for children is an investment in a more promising future.

Nasra Mahmoud Souelem was born as a slave girl in Agmar in Western Sahara. In 1976, fighting broke out between the occupying Moroccan armed forces and the Saharan insurgents. Nasra and her family were forced to quit their homes and move to live in the Saharan camps. When the Saharan traditions abolished slavery and Nasra became free, she learnt to read and write and had the right to choose her own husband — two remarkable milestones in her life. After the early death of her husband in the fighting, Nasra pledged her personal life to bringing up her only child, and to serving her people in the camps, whom she now considers as her entire family. Nasra was trained as a nursery teacher and has given care and education to a generation of Saharan children.

The Saharan issue is waiting for a political solution from the international community. As such, people in the refugee camps continue to depend greatly on international aid supplies. But people like Nasra, who have borne great pain with fortitude, took many initiatives to transform the camps into productive self-dependant communities. Nasra's work may not have a global or even a reputable national outreach. However, her efforts to improve the quality of life of her people for the last 29 years, providing a sense of normalcy in such an afflicted situation, are heroic.

Nasra Souelem has dedicated herself to raising people's awareness of the significance of education. Her working agenda focuses grassroots efforts on establishing a sustainable developmental infrastructure through the education of children in the refugee camps in the Western Sahara.

Western Sahara

Doreen Spence

Canadian Indigenous Women's Resource Institute (Ciwri)
Plains Indian Cultural Survival School Society
Alberta Civil Liberties Association

Doreen Spence has dedicated the majority of her life to volunteering in native and nonnative communities with a consistent emphasis on aboriginal issues and concerns. Her work in the field of human rights and the protection of fundamental freedoms for her people is unsurpassed. She is active in many organizations, including the Alberta Civil Liberties Association and the Committee Against Racism. Doreen is founder and serves as the executive director of the Canadian Indigenous Women's Resource Institute.

Like many effective activists, Doreen works tirelessly to advocate for the rights of those she serves. She communicates her vision through the usual means — passionate speeches, face-to-face negotiations, grassroots community building, among other vehicles. But unlike other activists, Doreen shares with her audiences a unique set of cultural activities that underscore the fight to which she has dedicated her life — uplifting and empowering indigenous people, especially women. It is not uncommon for Doreen to incorporate in her presentations songs, dances, chants, traditional knowledge, medicinal healing, and storytelling by indigenous women themselves. And she encourages her audience to leave their seats and participate. One participant, initially unfamiliar with the culture, was amazed by its impact on her during an event led by Doreen: "I joined in, ate dried chokecherries, danced the round dance, made and wore my own parfleche (pouch), participated in the smudge (medicinal healing) ceremony, drum-danced as the Inuit do, throat sang, and performed a Greenlandic mask dance."

Doreen says: "My soul has been touched by women's stories of racism, exclusion, prostitution, and death. I have laughed with the comics, cried with the truth tellers, and I hope to continue my journey, joining with native women and building our future together."

The plight of the indigenous people for whom Doreen advocates is dire. According to Doreen, they are the least educated, least employed, and lowest paid in the workforce. Babies die at a rate three times higher than others and teenagers kill themselves six times more often.

Canada

Kama Steliga

Lillooet Friendship Centre

Kama Steliga, born 1967 in Kenniwick, Washington State, USA, came to Canada when she was ten. She is the executive director and driving force behind The Lillooet Friendship Centre Society, an Aboriginal organization that supports individual, family, and community empowerment through culturally sensitive programs and services. Her work at Lillooet Friendship Centre has led to her advising and assisting similar operations at a provincial level.

Kama Steliga always speaks her mind and has become quite vocal in her opposition to established authorities who downplay social problems in her home town of Lillooett. For example, government officials have denied Lillooett funding for the homeless because it has a population of less than 5000. According to officials, such a small town cannot have a problem with homelessness. "Tell that to the people living under the bridge outside town," says Kama.

She believes communities need a healthy mix of self-reliance and support from outside sources. Especially disappointing to her are recent cuts in the latter. "I really believe in the liberal motto 'Communities taking care of communities'," she says. "But the cuts took away our ability to do that. They were too deep, too broad, too fast, and without enough forethought. There just didn't seem to be any kind of humane strategy to deal with social health."

The lack of resources especially touches Kama when she sees the direct effect on individuals. She notes that the population relying on Lillooet's food bank for meals has swelled to 300 people a month, about ten percent of the town's population. In this small rural Canadian town devasted by a poor economy, government cutbacks, and racial tension, Kama Steliga has provided much-needed leadership and inspiration. She has organized a community to action while instilling in its citizens tolerance, compassion, and understanding for those of differing ethnicities, those suffering the seen and unseen wounds of trauma, and those suffering from HIV/Aids. "I welcome the opportunity to empower communities and to be a part of a movement that encourages diversity and acceptance. I wanted to work here because I love the emphases on community, family, and individuals," she says.

Lillooet is a small community divided largely between settlers and the descendants of indigenous peoples, which is suffering from an economic downturn in the forestry industry. A series of racial conflicts has also contributed to a general deterioration in the area's quality of life.

Canada

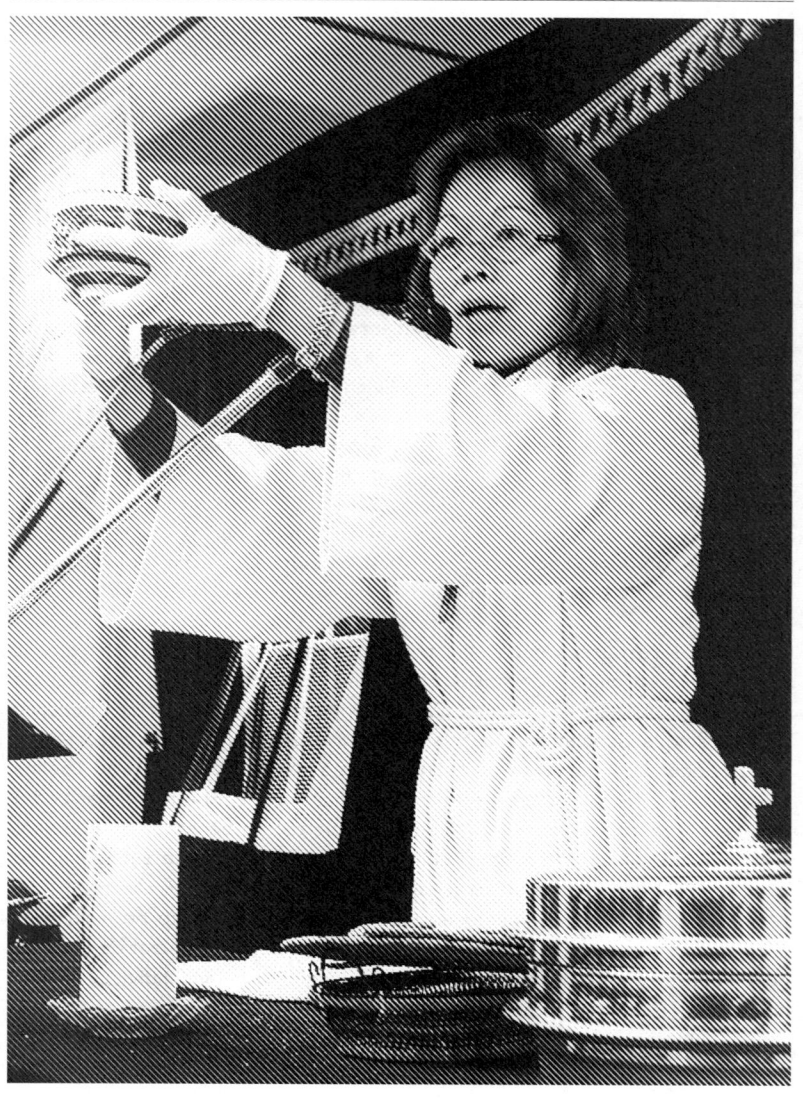

Shuk Man "Selina" Sun

Hong Kong Blessed Minority Christian Fellowship (Hkbmcf)

A Hong Kong native, Shuk Man "Selina" Sun (43) was ordained pastor by the Hong Kong Blessed Minority Christian Fellowship (Hkbmcf), a Christian group for sexual minorities. Selina serves as the pastor of the Hkbmcf and actively promotes dialogue and understanding between church organizations and communities. She stands firm on the side of this group and helps rebuild their self-esteem and confidence. In the past few years, membership of the Hkbmcf has steadily increased and sexual minorities are coming to be accepted by the church and society.

Hkbmcf was formed in 1992 and is the only one of its kind in Hong Kong. It all began when Selina Sun was invited to help train members of the Hkbmcf on caring work in 2002. The first Hkbmcf event she participated in was its tenth anniversary gathering. And she was deeply impressed because Hkbmcf as a group without a pastor and with members whose sexuality is denied by the mainstream Church has survived the storms over the past decade. She participated in the small group activities and meetings, and was soon accepted like a member of the family. They shared with her their struggle and bewilderment in their religion. They poured out to Selina their joys and worries in their love relationships.

"All in all, we begin by living and playing together. I am myself. It is very similar to the situation when I see how Christ lives in the ones who talk to him. His wisdom is alive in the daily living. He is the Way and the Truth," Selina recalls her early experience with Hkbmcf. "Because of denial and disapproval by their family, the Church and the society, sexual minorities live under tremendous pressure and are tormented with fear and worries. They lock up these feelings and bury them deep down inside to protect themselves," Selina says. Joining Hkbmcf in 2003, Selina works on church ministration, pastoral counseling, spiritual direction and religious education with fellow Christians in Hkbmcf. She walks together with these brothers and sisters out of their impasse. To change the external environment, Selina has put a lot of effort onto public education, contributing to church publications and other printed media, doing interviews, organizing workshops and seminars in universities, religious organizations and sexual minorities groups.

The church considers homosexuals criminals and denies them access or forces them to repent. Hong Kong offers no legal protection for the human rights of sexual minorities. Its society is still biased against them despite the efforts of some groups to raise awareness and call for legal reforms.

China, Hong Kong SAR

Stella Tamang

Milijuli Nepal
Bikalpa Gyan Tatha Bikas Kendra Ashram (BGTBKA)

Stella Tamang (born 1948) is a member of the minority indigenous Lama community and, to boot, a Buddhist woman in the world's only Hindu kingdom. Her situation has shaped her life and her values, making her a determined advocate for the rights of women, indigenous peoples, and religious minorities. The name of her organization, Milijuli Nepal, means "together", and that is her message indeed: that diverse groups in society can work together for their respective rights, with mutual toleration, without violence.

Stella Tamang was always dismayed by the lowly status of women in Nepali society. She was equally moved by the plight of indigenous groups like her own Lama community (and the Tamang community she married into), which lacked access to education and jobs and were far from the power structure. As a Buddhist in the world's only Hindu kingdom, she also felt compelled to work for greater mutual respect for diverse religious traditions. Stella founded Bhrikuti School in 1975, when she was a student, with five local children. Today, it is a secondary school with about 900 students. Later, she started Milijuli Nepal to work for justice and peace. In 1995, she founded the Bikalpa Gyan Tatha Bikas Kendra Ashram, an alternative learning center, for indigenous girls and women.

Through Milijuli, Stella encourages Buddhist monks and youth to spread a pacifist message. In her struggle for equal rights for women, her message has been: "We will protect ourselves not by defeating anyone but by transforming men." The BGTBKA has educated more than 100 girls, who come from the central and western hills and the mountain regions; many belong to marginalized communities. Not only do these learning centers empower and educate women, making them employable, they also help reduce the rampant sex trade in women.

Stella has been following and participating within the UN system, in international processes relating to indigenous peoples. She also tries to unite indigenous women who face political marginalization, displacement from their ancestral domains, lands, and territories, cultural genocide, and Hindu religious hegemony. She wants the issues to become part of the larger Nepali women's movements.

Nepal recognizes 59 ethnic groups — 42 percent of the population — as indigenous nationalities, whose population sizes range between 164 and 1.6 million. These groups are marginalized, with abysmal literacy, child and bonded labor, and women in the sex trade. The Tamang have 1.5 million members.

Nepal

"I honor the path each person is on. I believe that all of our prayer paths lead to the Great Mystery, or Spirit, or God."

Mary Thunder

Church of the Blue Star
Thunder Ranch

Rev. Mother Mary Elizabeth Thunder, founder of Thunder Ranch and the Blue Star Church in West Point, Texas, is known worldwide for her teachings on the power of women to achieve peace. She is also known for her own power to unite people of many faiths and cultures. Thunder has played key roles at various Wolf Songs, international gatherings of indigenous peace elders. She was invited by the Dalai Lama to speak about peace and women at the Spiritual United Nations, an international gathering of spiritual representatives, and is developing a survey about women's roles in world religions.

Born 1944 on "D-Day", the beginning of the deliverance of Europe in World War II, Mary Elizabeth Thunder believes her birth date is significant: she was meant to lead people to peace. The path she has taken is one of learning, service, and enlightenment. Part Native American, Irish, and adopted Lakota, Thunder left a background of abandonment, abuse, and family neglect to graduate from Warren Central High School in Indianapolis and to attend Indiana University. She worked as secretary to the Board of Public Safety for the City of Indianapolis and served as liaison with the Human Rights Board, working with Martin Luther King, Dick Gregory, and others. She was subsequently awarded Seven Keys to the City and two Governor State Awards.

In 1981, a heart attack changed her course. She describes an "afterlife experience" that prompted her to work as a drug and alcohol specialist for an Indian center in Texas. Her year as a drug counselor would help shape future models of service, healing, and spirituality. She resigned her position as a drug counselor and began her life on the road as an itinerant teacher. For the next seven years she lived in her van and taught, often using the sundance, a Native American prayer ritual, to minister to others.

Thunder's ongoing quest for vision led her to a breakthrough understanding of a new way to heal addiction by merging Native American ceremonial traditions, modern addiction counseling, and the 12-Step Program. In 1989, she was led by a vision and the advice of her elders to found Thunder Ranch and the Church of the Blue Star. There, thousands of people have been taught a better way to live, to overcome addiction and abuse, and to live in peace and service.

As a woman of mixed race, Thunder faced opposition in a patriarchal society that valued "full blooded" members. She renounced her home and her belongings at a time when homeless persons were considered society's most powerless.

United States of America

Tran Thi Lanh

Towards Ethnic Women (TEW)
Center for Human Ecology Study of Highlands (CHESH)
Center for Indigenous Knowledge Research and Development (CIRD)

Watersheds play a vital role in the destiny of a nation. The 53 indigenous communities living in the watershed near the marginal borders of Vietnam are the only groups protecting the forest resources. Supporting sustainable livelihoods for these communities means increasing their awareness of building harmonious lifestyles by their own efforts and based on their own rights to natural resources. Tran Thi Lanh is a unique Vietnamese woman intellectual who has dedicated her life to caring for the vulnerable indigenous women and children who live in the watershed of the Mekong region.

Over the last 14 years, Tran Thi Lanh and 180 colleagues in the three NGOs Towards Ethnic Women (TEW), Center for Human Ecology Study of Highlands (CHESH) and Center for Indigenous Knowledge Research and Development (CIRD) have helped 61,799 women and children regain their self-confidence by making them aware of the need to improve their lives by controlling their natural resources. The certification of the rights to land use for female owners was first implemented by Towards Ethnic Women (TEW) for Sinh Mun women in 1997. The government of Vietnam finally recognized women's role in natural resources management and included it in the revised Law on Lands in 2003. Because of Tran's work, 12,401 indigenous women have been officially recognized in land use rights certificates and over 35,000 hectares of forestlands have been allocated to 8,000 households. Tran has worked with networks of indigenous women to find ways of creating space for their right to existence, identifying strategies to decentralize the right to natural resources and ecological diversity, and maintaining traditional cultural values while respecting their distinct social, natural, cultural, political, and ethical features.

With thousands of farmers, Tran continues to study the impact and consequences of centralizing natural resources and to come up with economic, social, and political solutions that protect individual rights while preserving cultural values. "Respecting and listening to our natural resources will prevent catastrophes. Solidarity and non-discrimination will nurture a world of peace," she says. The work done by Tran and affiliated NGOs since 1989 has been vital to the development goals of the government of Vietnam for sustainable development. They are even more vital to the long-term survival of 53 indigenous communities in the watershed areas.

In the centralized power structure in Vietnam the indigenous communities have not been included and recognized in the decision-making processes. This centralization has broken up social harmony and threatened individual liberties, causing internal conflict and unsustainable development.

Viet Nam

Rosalina Tuyuc Velásquez

Coordinadora Nacional de Viudas de Guatemala (Conavigua)

Rosalina Tuyuc Velásquez (49) belongs to the Maya-Kaqchikel ethnic group. Orphan, wife, mother and widow, displaced and persecuted. She fights so that the Guatemalan State will admit its responsibility for the arrest, disappearance and death of thousands of Guatemalan people. She tries to overcome her terror and embraces life. She demands justice, dreams of peace, respect towards women, the well being of the indigenous people.

Rosalina Tuyuc Velásquez is a Guatemalan indigenous woman who belongs to the Maya-Kaqchikel ethnic group. She is from a family of agriculturists. She is Catholic with the spirituality of her Mayan people. This woman, short in stature, carries within her the memories of the armed forces of her country committing atrocities against the indigenous people. "When I was removed from my land, when I became a widow and an orphan, I began to see the pain and suffering of the people. I was not the only one in that situation. Hundreds of thousands of families shared it. Mothers and widows joined forces searching for a solution for the conflict. We wanted to defend our children from compulsory military service, to confront the menace of the Civil Self-Defense patrols (similar to the death squadrons)."
There is something terrible in all wars, "the indifference towards the most weak, towards the ones who cannot speak, towards pain and suffering." And it is precisely this indifference that pushes Rosalina Tuyuc Velásquez into militancy. "I feel happy to belong to an organization like the National Coordination of Widows of Guatemala (Conavigua) and to work for the people, for the indigenous people, even if I continue to feel afraid." But she goes on. And she dreams "of that day when the demands of the indigenous people will be understood: the demand for respect for life, the right to their own culture, the right to be different."

During 36 years of war in Guatemala, more than 42,000 people were victims of arrests, compulsory disappearances, torture and murder. According to the Commission for Historical Clarification, the army is responsible for 93% of those events.

Guatemala

Lyudmila Varfolomeeva

Fond zashchity konstitutsyonnykh prav koriennykh narodov Rossii (Fund for
the Protection of the Constitutional Rights of Indigenous Peoples of Russia)
Baikalsky regionalny soyuz zhenshchin Angara

Lyudmila Varfolomeeva (born 1957) grew up near Lake Baikal. She graduated from the Medical University in Irkutsk and later obtained a degree in Business Administration. She has worked at the Russian Academy of Sciences and participated in the Russian-American Project for Sustainable Development of Lake Baikal. Today, as vice-president of the fund dealing with the protection of the constitutional rights of indigenous peoples of Russia and an activist in the Regional Union of Women Angara, she promotes the protection of the cultural heritage and the safeguard of the environment in Russia.

In 1992 on Olkhon Island (Lake Baikal), the newly revived ritual of an All-Buryat shamanistic tailagan (a communal sacrifice, usually performed by a shaman) took place. Lyudmila Varfolomeeva was invited as guest of honor. "You belong to a special family. You have a special role in life. The spirits of your ancestors say that you are destined to fulfill a very important mission — to help your native land. Do not be surprised by anything and do not be afraid of anything — there is a long road ahead of you." This is what the shamans and elders of Olkhon told her. These words have motivated Lyudmila in different situations. At the beginning, she lacked funds and the support of the authorities. She even faced a certain resistance, but impossible things became possible, and the unreal became reality. It seemed as if heavenly powers were helping her in her activities and projects. She has never wavered from her commitment to protect Lake Baikal and to revive and preserve the old indigenous traditions of the Baikal region.

Today it can easily be said that on the shores of Lake Baikal, the world's deepest and cleanest lake which became part of the UNESCO World Heritage in 1996, extraordinary events have not ceased to occur. It was Lyudmila who once proposed and worked out the master plan for the now popular Baikal Economic and Baikal Women's Fora. She organized and participated in the sacred Erdyn Games festival whose historical roots stretch back into antiquity and which is nowadays celebrated on Olkhon Island. Lyudmila strives to raise the awareness of Russian society and the world about the necessity to protect local indigenous cultures of this region which, both geographically and spiritually, has always played an important role as a bridge and a meeting point between Eastern and Western traditions.

Lyudmila Varfolomeeva helps the indigenous peoples of Russia to keep their traditions and customs alive. Despite the lack of support and financial backing, she has succeeded in laying the foundations for the future, sustainable development of her native Baikal region.

Russian Federation

Lucía Willis Paau

Foundation of the Mayan Woman of the North (Funmmayan)

She is a Guatemalan woman, the worthy heiress of two great ancestral cultures: the Maya Q'eqchi (direct descendents of the Mayans) and the Garífuna (descendents of former African slaves). During her life, Lucía Willis Paau (46) has played many roles: nurse's aide, researcher, social worker, mother, and defender of human rights. From her mother, she learned to fight. She has faced poverty, discrimination and marginalization, but she never forgets her origins. Lucía has an unbreakable fighting spirit. She weaves her life with threads of work and hope.

Lucía Willis Paau was born in 1959, in the city of Cobán, the capital of Alta Verapaz, Guatemala. After her father died, she worked like so many other child laborers, learning to weave the products that were later sold in the market. Even though her mother was illiterate, she was wise. She urged her daughter to study. Lucía was discriminated against because of the color of her skin and the way she dressed, which reflected her ethnic origins. She learned to pick coffee, beans and other crops. She remembers these times as some of the happiest times of her life. She has been a cook, a typist, and a nurse's aide. After many sacrifices and due to her persistence, she finished her studies.

From 1980 to 1997, Lucía Willis Paau co-founded many indigenous women's organizations. During 1998 and 1999, she worked as a researcher in Mayas-Pocomchíes women's political participation projects and in mental health with the victims of the armed confrontation (1960-1996). In addition, she has been the negotiator in conflicts over agrarian issues and family problems over pension payments. In the last few years, her efforts have been directed towards the empowerment of women.

As a woman of firm principles and with the determination to fight against all adversities, for her, peace is synonymous with "coexisting in harmony and freedom, without violence, without social, economic or political injustice." She dreams about a world of opportunities for women. The injustices upset her, yet she smiles at life. A woman of faith: strict, strong, tenacious, and reflective. Currently she is battling against cancer. She wants to live to dream, to fight, and to contribute to the consolidation of peace.

In Guatemala, indigenous women confront the effects of racism, discrimination and sexism. In order to overcome ongoing abuse, they organize and participate, building their self-esteem, empowering women, promoting human rights and constructing their identities.

Guatemala

Maninha Xukuru

Articulação dos Povos e Organizações Indígenas do Nordeste,
Minas Gerais e Espírito Santo (APOINME)

During the first days of 2005, an indigenous baby died of malnutrition. Less than a month later, in another indigenous settlement, a little girl was unable to reach age four. She also had nothing to eat. In two decades, Maninha Xukuru (born 1966) has challenged latifundiary land owners, politicians, unlawful land possessors and citizens in general. Her battle: to win back the land of her people, the Xukuru-Kariri. Her goal: to ensure the effectiveness of indigenous rights.

Whether under the sweltering summer sun or the long winter rains, this girl would not give up. Maninha Xukuru who, at the time was ten years old, would face barefoot the seven kilometers dirt road from her settlement to the town school, in Palmeira dos Índios, Alagoas. When she turned 18, she left the settlement. She moved to Recife, capital of Pernambuco, where she got a scholarship from Funai (National Indigenous Foundation) to study at a preparatory course to get into university. "Five months later, I was invited to leave. Funai had only paid for the first two months." She got a job as a sales clerk, but her salary was not enough. "It was a terrible shock. I had never lived outside of the settlement. I could no longer be a Xukuru-Kariri, nor be a person from the city."

In 1989, when Maninha Xukuru was still living in Recife, she participated in her first public act beside indigenous leaders, demanding public hospital. "It was when I realized who I was." She returned to the settlement and found her people fighting against each other over tiny pieces of land. She started to organize meetings. Currently, there are 1300 Xukuru-Kariris living in six settlements, located in about 1000 hectares. "Our fight will be long; we have the right to 15,000 hectares."

Some conquests that her people achieved were the construction of health centers and a school. She began meeting with other ethnic leaders and also participating in forums in other states. In 1994, she took part in the foundation of APOINME (Articulation of the Indigenous People), of which she is one of the coordinators. She does not give up, even facing death threats. "I was born in a family of warriors. Our fight runs in our blood."

The total extension of the lands reserved for the indigenous people is correspondent to 12.3 percent of Brazil's national territory. It is estimated that around 200 million Reais (ca. 75 million USD) are necessary to legalize the situation of the indigenous lands already demarked all over the country.

Brazil

Leyla Zana

Democratic Party (DEP)
Demokratik Toplum Hareketi (DTH)

Since 1980, Leyla Zana has been active in gaining recognition of the social, political, and cultural rights of Kurdish populations and for a peaceful resolution of the Kurdish conflict. She was a Representative of the Democratic Party in the Turkish Parliament (1991–1994), a political prisoner (1994–2004), and since 2004 a co-initiator of DTH, a new movement for democratic society. She has become a symbol of the struggle for human rights, democracy, and peace. Her courage has sensitized European public opinion about the problems of the Kurds and inspired numerous women to become active.

Once there was a small girl who was not allowed to speak or to learn, who was not allowed to go out without covering her hair, and who had many questions: Why did boys but not girls go to school? Why did men not go to hell but women did when they went around freely? The girl loved the meadows, the mountains, the landscape, and its freedom. Here and there, she rebelled and refused to wear a headscarf, but at barely 14, she had to bow to her family and marry the man chosen for her, a man 20 years her senior. When she was 16 — and pregnant — she learned of her husband's arrest and torture. In her land, villages were burned and people were massacred. She found herself alone with her two small children. She was forced to stand on her own and move on. A life of suffering that strengthened her.

Ten years later a young woman wearing a headband of red, yellow, and green — the colors of her people — spoke before tens of thousands of people at an election gathering. Men cheered her on. This woman was elected and spoke out. In Parliament she was shouted down by the old men because she spoke a few words in a language that had been banned and called for fraternity. She was arrested and still was not silenced: She wrote letters about her longing for peace and freedom, for spring, when "within a few days, the landscape is covered with flowers… . Then sometimes I am as free as a bird in the mountains of Kurdistan." She wanted to convey this message to Kurdish women — and to all women: "Speak up! Begin to speak! Express yourselves in a way that is appropriate for you! So no one can say to us: 'Keep quiet, woman!'" Many women are no longer silent; their solidarity is great and gives strength and support. After ten years in prison, Leyla Zana is free and continues to fight for peace and freedom.

The Kurds, a large and distinct ethnic minority, constitute over 20 percent of the Turkish population. Any expression by the Kurds of unique ethnic identity has been harshly repressed. In Turkey, no political speeches can be made in the Kurdish language. The Turkish government has consistently thwarted attempts by the Kurds to organize politically.

Turkey

Economic Rights

and Livelihood

Lau Kin Chi

K

Global figures on poverty are shocking and show little sign of declining. The deaths of 30,000 children every day from starvation or preventable disease no longer make news. There seems to be a widespread acceptance of this crude reality as if this were the fitting fate of the poor in developing countries that have uncontrolled population growth. If this seemingly innocent "common sense" has for so long made things tolerable, it is high time we questioned such a position, for even as the world is becoming more developed, it is also becoming increasingly polarized, with growing numbers of people being subjected to worsening poverty and ecological devastation. Consequently, as the conditions of life become much harsher, and this harshness finds its way into the interstices of daily life, so does insecurity. Even the rich are not immune to this, despite the fact that they have the means to screen themselves off from the violence that haunts the daily lives of those who lack practically any means of social mobility.

It is necessary for us to go beyond the public face of poverty to trace the processes by which hundreds of millions of people have been thrust into conditions that deprive them of a decent, sustainable livelihood — displacement, loss of land, contamination of water resources, degeneration of artisan skills, an abysmal, exploitative labor market, the swelling of the ranks of the unemployed, the destruction of kinship or community support networks. This may allow us to better understand that "modernization" and "development" are not all they are trumped up to be. Not only have they not delivered on their many promises, but they are also often the very forces that destroy the conditions of subsistence for large sectors of people. Megaprojects like dams or nuclear plants; battles over energy and resources, which often form the roots of larger wars and conflicts; the modern projects of nation-building privileging majoritarian identities and denying cultural and ethnic diversities; the growing emphasis on commodi-fication and capitalization at the cost of human relationships and communities; the replacement of decency and reciprocity by greed and indifference as the prevailing values … These are problems that now seem so serious that many see them as signaling the loss of hope, sometimes even presaging the apocalyptic downfall of humanity.

Yet, despite this often very real doomsday scenario, there is hope. It bears remembering that the world today is not ruled only by capital, greed, or egoism. Many of the dispossessed, the disenfranchised have refused to be victims waiting for meager humanitarian aid parcels to drop from the air. Silent, determined, persevering, invisible, their chosen path is arduous as they endeavor to rebuild from the fragments, to restore conditions for self-reliance, to delink from globalizing forces, to persist in their peripheral efforts, in the twilight, in the oblivion of "progress". They are convinced that indigenous wisdoms, values and lifestyles cannot be wiped out just because they are seen as "primitive", that the world can be other than the dismal one of corruption and crime. Their message to the world of neon lights and casino economies is unambiguous: that unless there is a major change in the current path of so-called development and modernization, it is not only the poor who will suffer, but also the rich and powerful who will go down as the economic bubble bursts.

Alternative ways of livelihood, in which human beings live with restraint and humility with other human beings, with other living species, with nature, can be found among indigenous, rural and marginal communities. For such communities, livelihood is not merely a matter of earning money, accumulating capital, or consuming commodities; the human being is not only an economic being, but is instead a cultural and social being. The moving and inspirational stories of the women in the following pages show the many such alternatives being lived out every day, in different contexts and under different constraints. They show how thousands of peacewomen are working for sustained peace. They remind us of alternative practices and ways of thinking, seeing, relating to one another, and relating to nature. The appropriation of science and technology in modern development is made possible by the language of progress, efficiency and calculated rationality. Such language, and indeed the many cultural processes that are harnessed to this project, work towards liberating greed by equipping it with powerful means of control and destruction for the appropriation of resources and energies from nature and from human beings. The stories below show us the importance of different cultural processes for the cultivation of different mentalities other than those of arrogance and greed. They show us that, without mental transformation, without paying attention to an "ecology of mind", no political processes can resolve the question of violence and attain the balance necessary for human beings to exist in peace and harmony. It is in this spirit that we honor, with these stories, the minimal demand of economic rights for sustainable livelihoods.

Dr Lau Kin Chi teaches comparative literature, critical pedagogy, global culture, local governance, and negotiating violence at the Department of Cultural Studies, Lingnan University, Hong Kong. She is a member of the editorial board of the Cultural and Social Studies and Asian Exchange, a founding member of the China Social Services and Development Research Center.

Aida Abdalla Ahmed

Small-Scale Enterprise Society (SSES)
Sudanese Family Planning Society (SFPS)

Aida Ahmed (40) is the coordinator of outlying rural women's developments in conflict-based underprivileged areas in the Sudan. She is an active member of several community-serving societies, such as the SOS Sahel-UK, the Small-Scale Enterprise Society (SSES) and the Sudanese Family Planning Society (SFPS). She works hard towards financing small projects and marketing processes for rural people. Her main goal is particularly to support rural women to become self-dependent by reducing poverty impacts upon their lives and introducing alternative options for income and sustainable development.

Since April 2002 Aida has been working on capacity-building of rural women with emphasis on pastoralists. She is working in an absolutely traditional and tribal-based society. Over 90% of the women there are illiterate. The living conditions are challengingly critical, where poverty and limited sources are very obvious and health care is very poor. Young women face crucial problems, such as early marriage and young maternity as well as circumcision. With a determination to improve the conditions of the underprivileged women, Aida set out to work hard on a life-long mission, often relying on her mother — who strongly believes in Aida's mission — to look after her children. Aida created many methods to boost women's work capacity through mass media, airing edifying programs on the state-run radio and TV, presenting video shows and holding discussion groups. She fights for rural women's right to education and representation as well as to express a positive viewpoint to solve local conflicts.

Aida has worked hard for women's right to education and representation. She has been significantly supportive of gender participation in social work and has developed a strategy of empowering women to become independent in her region.

Sudan

Haifa Abu Ghazaleh

United Nations Development Fund for Women (Unifem)
Jordanian Ministry of Education
General Federation of Jordanian Women (GFJW)

For over 30 years Haifa Abu Ghazaleh has worked with governmental ministries, NGOs and UN bodies, striving to integrate women's economic, political, social and cultural rights into development planning. Through her work as Regional Program Director (RPD) at Unifem, she has developed programs and projects in the Arab world, supporting issues such as peace, domestic violence, women's rights and political participation. She invested this opportunity to create a common agenda for gender equality amongst the UN members and government agencies.

With obligations and commitments across the Arab region and indeed the entire world, Haifa Abu Ghazaleh manages to maintain her passionate energy to work on women's issues. As she says, "As an advocate of human rights and gender equality, women's situation in my region is the reason and motivation for my continuous work to stop their daily suffering from poverty, illiteracy, deteriorated health conditions and limited participation in economic, social and political activities." Her commitment to the individual and collective security of women is what motivated her to work for peace, which she sees as intimately tied to human security issues: "Upholding people's fundamental freedoms, protecting them from severe threats and building on their own strengths and aspirations is the path towards achieving peace." In her view peace is subject to the attainment of human, social, economic and political security. It is this idea — the achievement of each person's human security — that motivates her to work towards peace and a better life for all those around her. Her vision of a peaceful future is one in which all peoples — men and women — are protected. And this can happen once the exclusion of women within society is addressed, and the obstacles that prevent women from achieving their goals and expressing their needs are removed.

One of these obstacles is the major economic insecurity women and children face. Haifa Abu Ghazaleh believes that combating this insecurity is a major challenge to her vision. Her experiences have taught her that the fulfilment of her vision is nothing short of an uphill battle. Despite the setbacks, struggles and obstacles, she remains committed as ever to her vision of the future: "I continue to work towards peace because I believe that it is my mission and I have to continue this work until I feel that one day it is fulfilled."

Haifa Abu Ghazaleh is currently Regional Program Director (RPD) for the Arab World with the United Nations Development Fund for Women (Unifem). She also works to apply the Beijing Declaration and Platform for Action, UN Millennium Development Goals as well as International Human Rights Legal legislation with various other organizations with which she is affiliated.

Jordan

Safaa Adam

Community Development Association (CDA)
Oxfam-UK
Friedrich Ebert Foundation

Safaa El Agib Adam was born in 1960 in El Geneina, West Darfur. After graduating from the Faculty of Economics, University of Khartoum, she joined the Save the Children Fund (SCF) UK for one year, working on relief operations in Darfur and relief coordination in Port Sudan. She is affiliated with many organizations, as a volunteer and as a private consultant. Her chief aim is to support underprivileged women to become productive and self-dependent workers. She helps them to build up better careers by enrolling them in various training and consultation sessions. Safaa is also a peace activist.

The growing number of women hawkers in the streets of Khartoum, especially food and tea peddlers, has raised Safaa Adam's concerns about the social and economic conditions of these women. When the government of Sudan, called "the Salvation Regime", came to power after a coup in June 1989, all NGOs, civil society organizations and political parties were suspended and their activities were banned. Emergency public order laws were enforced, which hindered women's participation in social work. Safaa, together with other women activists, challenged these austere conditions by constellating women in working groups, defying the tight security measures and helping unfortunate women.

Safaa has participated extensively in public debates on women's rights and has contributed to regional and international conferences in Africa, Europe and the USA. She is also a member of many active networks working on peace building, conflict resolution, human rights and environment protection, and she is the founder of the Community Development Association (CDA), an organization concerned with women's economic and social empowerment, especially in Khartoum and Darfur regions.

Safaa collaborates relentlessly with peace activists, lawyers, women's groups and politicians, lobbying for a peaceful solution to the conflict in Darfur through dialogue and negotiation. However, she is underpinning the critical impact of the Darfur conflict on women, with special emphasis on sexual violence and rape. In the course of this work, Safaa and her family members are frequently interrogated by the Sudanese Bureau of Intelligence. However, she has unfailing stamina and courage to pursue her mission, providing the motive and example for the younger generation to follow her steps.

Safaa Adam's work mainly seeks to change the conditions of unprivileged women so that they can have a better social and economic life. She is diligently involved in peace endeavors in vulnerable areas of armed conflict, where women are facing continuous threat of armed conflict, sexual violence and insecurity.

Sudan

Krishna Ahooja-Patel

Women's International League for Peace and Freedom (WILPF)

Krishna Ahooja-Patel's training in law prepared her for a 25-year-long career with the United Nations, where she worked in various capacities around the world-with the International Labor Organization, the UN Institute of Research and Training for the Advancement of Women, and the Women's World Summit. As president of the Women's International League for Peace and Freedom (WILPF), Krishna brings decades of experience to take forward the many WILPF agendas for peace education, women's rights, disarmament, and strengthening the UN.

Influenced very early in her life by Gandhian ideals, Krishna (born 1929) has been a tireless advocate of peace, social justice, and women's empowerment. Her education and training in law prepared her for a 25-year-long career with the UN, where she worked in various capacities around the world, for example with the International Labor Organization (ILO), the UN Institute of Research and Training for the Advancement of Women (Instraw) and the Women's World Summit. In 1995, she traveled with a "peace train" organized by the WILPF to the UN Women's Conference in Beijing. It was Krishna who came up with the startling and now-famous UN statistic about women: "Women are half of the world's population, do two-thirds of the work, get one-tenth of the income, and are owners of one percent of the property."

An important area for the WILPF and for Krishna, personally, since 2000 has been to have the UN Security Council's Resolution 1325 translated into as many languages as possible, in order to spread it worldwide to ensure concerted pressure on the Security Council for its implementation. The resolution reaffirms the important role of women in prevention and resolution of conflicts, and in peace-building processes.

Krishna's involvement with feminist issues and peace initiatives has placed her at the forefront of national and international movements, where she has contributed as an ideologue as well as an action-initiator.

Women are integral to the prevention and resolution of conflicts, and in the peace-building process. For them to play a key role, their voices have to be heard, their rights protected, and their participation strengthened-the UN Security Council's Resolution 1325 could propel the cause along.

India

Nafeesa Al Deek

Kafr Ne'meh Women Society (KNWS)

Born in Kafr Ne'meh near Ramallah in 1940, Nafeesa Al Deek is a women's rights activist and social reformist. Left by her husband, she has dedicated her life to raising her children: two sons and a daughter. Her strong charisma has given her courage and unrelenting determination to fight for women's rights. She was the first woman to found community-serving projects in Palestine, such as sewing workshops, that have assisted hundreds of women in her village to generate work skills and have better careers.

Nafeesa Al Deek was a young girl when she was married to her cousin through arranged marriage. He subsequently migrated to Brazil and left her for good with her three young children. Despite these difficult circumstances, she has successfully raised her kids and they now occupy very respected positions in society. Nafeesa began her voluntary social work, one year after the Israeli occupation of the West Bank, by establishing a women's association in her village with a grant from a German association, in order to help many Palestinian women survive during this hard time. Despite the fact that she was totally devastated by her husband's departure, she believes that "If my husband had been there, I would never have been able to achieve so many things in life. I am proud of what I have done and will do." Nafeesa helped in the reconstruction of the village girls' school by raising funds through the association she formed. She has always advocated girls' education as the fundamental step towards forming their identity and facilitating an independent prosperous future.

The 1967 war and the Israeli occupation of the West Bank and Gaza Strip brought suffering to hundreds of thousands of Palestinians. Decades have since elapsed, but the Palestinian Women's Movement has assumed a clear role in invigorating the new generations and preparing them for the future.

Occupied Palestinian Territory

Lubna Al Qasimi

Tejari.com
UAE Ministry of Economy & Planning (UAEMEP)
Dubai Chamber of Commerce & Industry (DCCI)

Sheikha Lubna Al Qasimi obtained a BS from California State University of Chico, and a MBA from the American University of Sharjah. She was the CEO of Tejari.com, one of the giant successful business-to-business marketplaces in the U.R.E. Sheikha Lubna Al Qasimi became the first woman minister of the UAE. She has a global reputation and a well-connected network both at home and abroad. She lectures in universities worldwide, putting her emphasis on equal rights of gender. Sheikha Lubna is a role model to young women in the UAE with an inspiring charisma for young girls.

High profile, striking, observant, knowledgeable … and many other attributes you hear from the people who meet Sheikha Lubna Al Qasimi and describe her personality. She is proud of her femininity and her Arab identity. In a state of shock after the events of September 11th, Sheikha Lubna expressed her feelings saying, "All of a sudden my religion (Islam) was stained with violence, and its followers are considered criminals and terrorists, suffering from prejudice everywhere as a result." The internationally recognized businesswoman has utilized her high profile to fight for peace for all people in the world. She seizes every opportunity to combine business with visits to universities where she gives lectures. Speaking about the memories of her early education and how her personality has set up a model for many young women in the Arab world, Sheikha Lubna Al Qasimi says, "My blooming career and diligence have inspired many young women to change for the better. Sometimes young women lose self-confidence when struck by difficulties in life and feel down. To those women I always say: "Nothing is impossible as long as you have a genuine will. Keep your spirits high and do not give up! Life has many hazards, but no pain no gain! Do not let your fears take away your dreams!"

Sheikha Lubna sees herself as an agent of change. Her self-motivated character has impacted the youth in her country, both women and men. She is proud of herself. You can tell how proud she is from the pictures she has in her office of all the celebrities she met worldwide and the medals and prizes she won, which decorate the entrance of Tejari.com, the company she has brought success to. Sheikha Lubna is determined to fight gender discrimination. "What matters is the personality of people, not their gender. This is the battle that I am determined to win," says Sheikha Lubna.

Sheikha Lubna is determined to assist in building up a prosperous society that does not admit gender discrimination, nationality, or superficial appraisal factors. She is longing for the day when gender does not matter, and she does her best to have her message heard by more and more people.

Mudi Al-Essa

Arab Child House Society (ACHS)
Kuwait Society for the Handicapped (KSH)

Mudi Al-Essa, born in the 1920s, was nine years old when she used to assist her father in giving aid to unfortunate people he used to sponsor. She also remembers her mother sending her to donate some garments to unfortunate women and children in the community. When she was 28 she volunteered to work with the Jordanian Arab Child House Society (ACHS) from Kuwait. Mudi also worked hard towards establishing a society for assisting the handicapped people in Kuwait, the Kuwait Society for the Handicapped (KSH).

Mudi Al-Essa received traditional schooling in Kuwait. From the age of nine she used to help her father to support the needy people in her community. In her teens, Mudi and her mother learned the seamstress trade, and they very often donated some of their garments to the less-privileged women and children of the community. Some years later, Mudi volunteered to work with the Jordanian Arab Child House Society (ACHS) from Kuwait, successfully raising 13,000 Kuwaiti Dinars in 1948 for Jordanian homeless children. The success of helping an expatriate woman patient in Kuwait in 1962 inspired Mudi to establish a society for assisting the handicapped people in Kuwait, the Kuwait Society for the Handicapped (KSH).

However, her work was a personal initiative, contingent upon generous donations and still unofficial. In 1971 the Kuwaiti official authority licensed KSH to formally operate in Kuwait. Now, KSH offers permanent full board accommodation as well as medical, social and psychological care to hundreds of unfortunate people in Kuwait. Also, it provides children with daycare between 7am and 2pm to help working parents, and arranges home visits by trained nurses for handicapped people who are confined to their houses so that they can receive medical care. In the late 1980s, Mudi established an orphanage in Hanan, a village in east Sudan, to assist the displaced children who had fled to Sudan because of the civil war between Ethiopia and Eritrea. She has also co-sponsored similar children's projects in Jordan, Lebanon, India and Pakistan. Mudi, who is now in her late 80s, attends her office every working day from 9am to 1:30pm. She emphasizes, "The teachings of my great religion, Islam, encourage me to help all people, especially those with special needs. Bringing happiness and peace to the handicapped and their families motivates me to continue work with KSH members."

Mudi Al-Essa is committed to helping the poor and handicapped, a habit that her parents ingrained in her from childhood by involving her in their charitable activities. Her energetic, charitable activities helped thousands of disabled children, women and men in Kuwait and in many other countries.

Kuwait

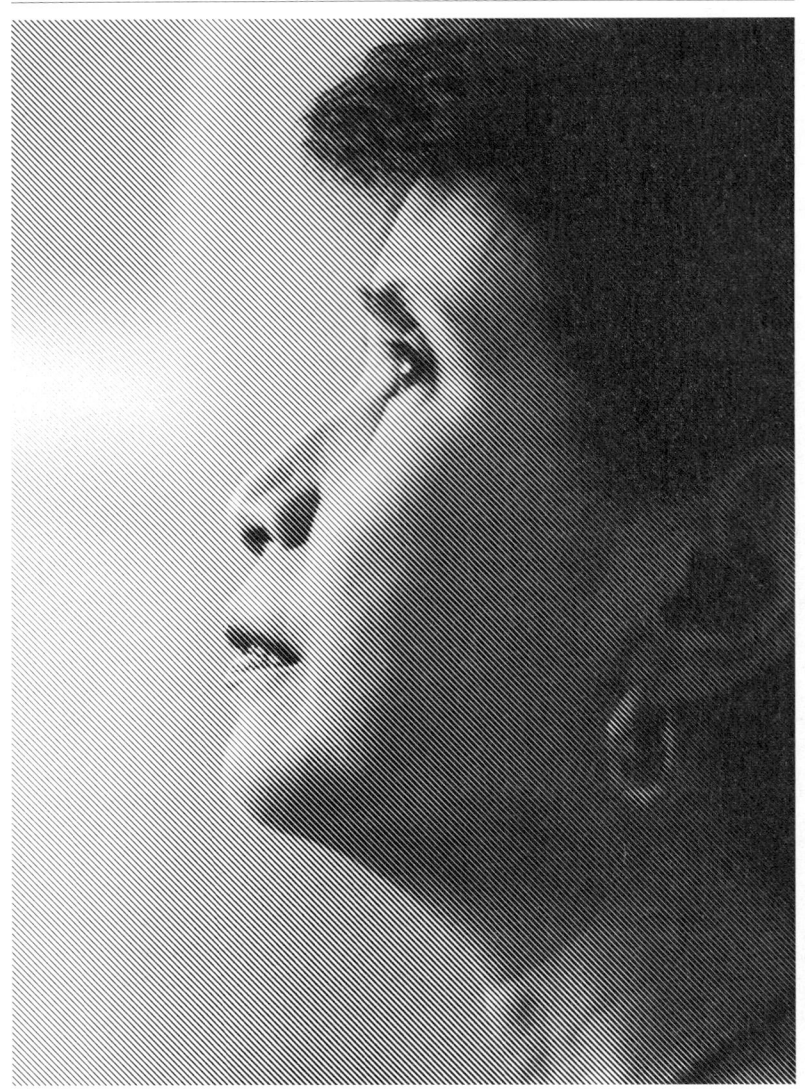

Mary Lou Alcid

Kanlungan Center Foundation
Migrant Forum in Asia (MFA)

Mary Lou Alcid's name is synonymous to the cause of migrants' rights. She has blazed trails advocating migrant rights and welfare, especially of migrant women who are the most abused. Through her NGO, Kanlungan Center Foundation, of which she has been executive director since 1995, and in alliance with others, Mary Lou (born 1955) has lobbied government to protect Overseas Filipino Workers (OFW), helped in community organizing, provided feminist counseling for women migrant workers and put up support structures to empower OFWs and their families.

"Peace," says Mary Lou Alcid, a social worker who has advocated for the welfare of Overseas Filipino Workers (OFW) for close to two decades, "is not just the absence of conflict, structural violence, social injustice and all forms of discrimination. There should be respect for human rights and diversity, with mechanisms for people to resolve various levels of conflict. There must be no injustice in society, even in the smallest unit like the family, from the micro to the macro. Peace cannot be attained while there is injustice, a wide gap between rich and poor." As a professor of social work at the University of the Philippines, Alcid inculcates this culture of peace in her students. As Executive Director of Kanlungan Center Foundation and Executive Chair of Migrant Forum in Asia (MFA), Mary Lou applies this concept of peace to migrants as well. "Peace work connected to migration is to keep pressing government to address fundamental economic problems. For the past 40 years the government has been dependent on labor export. Instead of improving the economy, they even encourage us to go abroad."
In Mary Lou Alcid's work, the key word is "integrative" which means (using the Kanlungan framework on international labor migration) levels of intervention are identified: from individual to family to community to the barangay/municipal level up to the national and international levels. Strategies — singly or in combination — are utilized to achieve identified objectives: case management with community organizing, advocacy and development of the local economy. From her broad and diverse experience in migration, from working with rural communities to NGO management and advocacy on an international level, Mary Lou has learned to appreciate individual persons, espouse change on various levels and organize and link up with similar organizations to pursue a common agenda.

What was meant as a temporary measure to ease unemployment in the Philippines by sending workers abroad 40 years ago has become an unstoppable Diaspora. Today, some eight million Filipinos work overseas, many of whom live and work in harsh conditions, their basic rights curtailed.

Amal Alh'jooj

Arab-Jewish Center for Equality, Empowerment and Cooperation (AJEEC)
National Council of Arab Women in Israel (NCAWiI)
Negev Forum of Bedouin Arab Women's Organizations (NFBAWOs)

Amal Elsana Alh'jooj has dedicated her life to improving the living conditions of her people, the Bedouin Arab community of the Negev. Over the past 15 years she has developed strategies of community work that operate on community and political levels, aiding thousands of Bedouin women and children in Israel. Since October 2000, Amal has served as the director of the Arab-Jewish Center for Equality, Empowerment and Cooperation (AJEEC), a division of the Negev Institute for Strategies of Peace and Development. Amal is an outspoken advocate of Arab-Jewish cooperation and coexistence.

Amal Elsana Alh'jooj has an invigorating vision of social work and society welfare that, she believes, drastically changes the community perception of women's role. She recounts, "I remember once speaking with my father, who tried to explain to me that engaging in revolutions only creates anger and disorder in society, and ultimately gets you nowhere. However, I believe my generation thinks differently. We won't allow ourselves to be led to the gallows. We have to get rid of the defeated past of our parents' generation. I took upon myself the task of changing for the better, within my time and age, as much as I can for the welfare of my people, and for women in particular. I owe it to my children and to the generations to come."

Amal was born in the temporary Bedouin settlement of Tel Arad near the Dead Sea as the fifth daughter of a traditional family. When she was three years old, the Israeli government finally allowed her tribe to return to its lands in the village of Laqiya, from which it had been expelled, and it was there that she grew up. From the age of five onwards, she helped to subsist her family by tending sheep herds, getting up at 6 a.m. to herd the sheep before school and continuing after her return home in the afternoon. Amal is a staunch advocate of peaceful resolutions. She initiated the Arab Jewish Center for Equality, Empowerment and Cooperation (AJEEC), dedicated to achieving equality in all aspects of life, empowerment of the Palestinian-Israeli community in Israel and cooperation between the Jewish and Arab populations, out of a deep conviction that only by working together can both peoples survive. Amal has been actively involved in initiating and operating joint Palestinian-Israeli projects and training courses in Palestine and in Israel — which continue, despite extremely difficult circumstances.

Approximately 140,000 Bedouin live in the Southern Negev region: about half in seven towns established since the late '60s and the rest in 45 unrecognized villages. This population is the poorest in the country and suffers from significant inequality in economic, social, educational and cultural terms.

Israel

Dildora Alimbekova

Association of Business Women of Uzbekistan

Dildora Alimbekova (born 1954) is chairperson of the Association of Business Women, helping women to increase their employment and living standards and improve their role in society through the promotion of small entrepreneurship for women. In Uzbekistan, the transition to the market economy is a heavy burden on the people from the socially vulnerable layers of the population — women, children, older persons, and people with disabilities. Dildora's organization has created 70,000 jobs, 12,000 women passed courses on starting small businesses, and 10,000 unemployed women were employed.

Dildora Alimbekova is the chairperson of the Association of Business Women of Uzbekistan, founded in 1991. Aware of the difficult economic situation of women in Uzbekistan, she decided to share her knowledge and experience with other women to assist them in solving their economic and social problems. In the difficult transition period in Uzbekistan, Dildora devoted her energy and knowledge to the people. "It is important for me to live without wars, revolutions, or dictatorial regimes that separate people from their native land. It is important for all people not to fear for themselves and their children, to live in their native country, favorite city, in their own family, to choose their own work, to be able to think and speak freely," she says. Over a 14-year period, her organization has created 70,000 new jobs. 12,000 women passed training courses on entrepreneurship and 10,000 unemployed women acquired a new profession.

After the tragic events of 1999, when young extremists organized terrorist actions in Tashkent, Dildora has been giving great attention to the education of young people. She says: "We cannot confine ourselves to taking care of own welfare. I became more convinced of this after that black day of 16 February 1999, when a series of explosions took place in Tashkent. My daughter's classmate was hurrying to his office with a joyful piece of news — his son was born, when a terrorist bomb broke off his life. Later, I examined the pictures of the terrorists — young men who were contemporaries of those killed. I decided to do my best for our children, who are our future, so that they will not be plunged into the abyss of evil." It has not been easy. Dildora has had to surmount hindrances and misunderstandings. There were moments of disappointment and pain. However, the main support for Dildora are the grateful eyes of the people she manages to help.

After the fall of the Soviet Union, the transition to the market economy in Uzbekistan has been difficult for people from socially vulnerable layers of the population — women, children, older persons, and the disabled. Traditional views of the role of women in society have re-emerged.

Vanete Almeida

Rede Latino-Americana e do Caribe das Mulheres Trabalhadoras Rurais
(The Network of Latin American and Caribbean Rural Women)

In the 1980s, Vanete Almeida (1943) began participating in rural workers' unions from the central hinterland of Pernambuco State. As the only woman in a place dominated by men, she broke the sexism barrier and stimulated the mobilization of women in rural areas. Now, there are 800 groups of women in the Northeast. Those women, who used to be quiet, are now directing unions, coordinating meetings and demanding labor rights, health, education and the preservation of the environment.

When Vanete Almeida began the task of making female agriculturists more aware of their rights, they were disrespected, isolated and invisible to society. She used to be the only woman in the union meetings, and so she decided to go look for female partners at their homes. Then, Vanete started to organize workshops. "We used to talk about everything: how to not waste beans or corn, how to take care of chickens, hygiene, health, their children's education and their affectionate and sexual problems."

Vanete's battle began in the 1970s when she joined a Catholic volunteer group involved in political education. "In the plantation fields, I used to see women working really hard from sunrise till sunset. Most of them did not even have identification documents." In 1980, Vanete started working as a counselor for the Federation of Agriculturists from Pernambuco State. In 1982, the third year of a very long drought, she was ahead of a group that demanded that the Federal Government include women in the emergency fronts-up until then the program only gave jobs to men. Two years later, they organized the First Meeting of Rural Women from the Central Hinterland Area. Now, there are 800 groups of agriculturists in the Northeast. Among other rights, they conquered the right to be the legally recognized land owners — before, only men had the right to own land. They conquered also the right to retirement and to continue receiving their salary during maternity-leave.

Now, Vanete Almeida coordinates the Network of Latin American and Caribbean Rural Women, articulating groups from 25 countries. When she is in Brazil, she continues to do what gives her the most pleasure in life: meeting with female agriculturists from her region. "As long as there are people without land and women without an active power of speech, I will be there."

The Network of Latin American and Caribbean Rural Women, which is coordinated by Vanete Almeida, was funded in 1990. It has the goal to strengthen and articulate groups, organizations and movements from several countries.

Brazil

Siham Anglo

Nuba Mountains' Women for Peace (NMWP)

Siham Daoud (born 1961) is an activist in community development and peace building. In 1994 she initiated a project in Omdurman Town called "Zagalona Women's Sewing and Tie-Dye". The project supports displaced Nubian women, women from other tribes, and their families in the Zagalona area. Thanks to Siham's efforts, 180 women have now completed their training and are able to subsist their families. The illiteracy fighting classes that Siham runs have helped many women in the Sudan to read and write. Siham actively participated in the Nuba Mountains' Women for Peace (NMWP) in 1998.

In 1987 Siham took the initiative of assisting the displaced women in the Sudan. She established a training center that generates women's labor skills in many work areas. She began the work from her own house, which put a lot of pressure on her family. Her children at that time were still young and her husband was tied to a job outside the capital Khartoum. So, she had to arrange with a friend or family member to baby-sit the children every time she needed to go to work. Over the years Siham faced severe financial difficulties. In order to keep the project running she sometimes had to pay outstanding balances from her own pocket or from the donations that came from volunteers. Despite these burdens — family and financial constraints — Siham insists on continuing her work and supporting unfortunate women.

The project received a big boost in 1994, through the aid of an American donor who visited the Zagalona Women's Sewing and Tie-Dye group in 1993 and donated ten sewing machines. The machines were shipped from Nairobi, through the Rhama Organization, to the Sudan; it took nine months to clear customs in the airport. The shipment of the machines alerted the Sudanese intelligence department, which was suspicious of Siham's connections to foreign people. The machines were tracked down and Siham was interrogated about the source of the machines, the project and who she was working with. When the project grew big and Siham's house became too small to accommodate the center's activities, she started looking for a suitable place to build a purpose-built center. She spotted a piece of land near her house and launched an appeal to raise funds to buy it. A group of churchwomen from Great Britain promptly responded to the appeal and transfered the required funds. The project now has 38 machines, 16 in the main center and the rest in other places in Khartoum.

Thanks to Siham's efforts, 180 displaced women from the Nuba and other tribes in the Sudan can now work and subsist their families. Many of those who attended her evening beginners classes have become literate. She is also working hard on peace building and justice for all Sudanese people.

Sudan

Nusrat Ara

Women's Development Organization

Nusrat Ara (born 1954), who hails from the North Western Frontier Province, took charge of her life, first by educating herself after marriage and then by launching an organization for women's development in her hometown, Mardan. Her pioneering work at the district and community levels for more than two decades has helped women empower themselves in a gravely conservative society, without losing their traditional moorings.

Nusrat Ara overcame stiff resistance to complete a master's program and a course in homeopathy. Fortunately, with her father's support, she finished school and joined college. Her husband, a cousin, supported her desire to work for the welfare and social development of women. Nusrat saw women experiencing domestic violence and other forms of oppression. She focused on helping them generate income. With no infrastructure, she launched her Women's Development Organization in 1995, organizing committed social activists who had few resources, but extended their work in 2000 with funding from the South Asia Partnership, Pakistan.

Nusrat has focused on the socioeconomic development of women, their political empowerment, gender development, combating violence against women, and child labor. She set up skills training and literacy centers for them, along with awareness-building and mobilization programs. Women were taught sewing, knitting, and embroidery, and many went on to earn their own living. Nusrat has targeted reprobate customs such as Karo-Kari (honor killings), and swarah, which leads to women being married off to men to settle disputes. She also worked to end the custom of women being married off to much older men for a "bride price". Nusrat motivated women to fight local elections. Although there are 33 percent seats earmarked for them, women are discouraged from participating in the political process. So, Nusrat contested, and won: she is now a member of the district council.

Women have learnt to exercise their rights without losing their traditional moorings. Although the region remains puritanical, much greater tolerance for Nusrat's work has seeped in. It is reason enough for her children to follow in her footsteps.

The fiercely independent North West Frontier Province has long been a hotbed of militant orthodoxy — despite the pacifist influence of its late philosopher — guide, the Frontier Gandhi-and women have been at the re-ceiving end.

Pakistan

Runa Banerjee

Self-Employed Women's Association (Sewa)–Lucknow

Runa Banerjee (born 1950) set up the Self-Employed Women's Association (Sewa) in Lucknow in 1984 after she realized that self-employment was the only real answer to the plight of women chikankari (traditional embroidery of Uttar Pradesh) artisans. Her work has since reached out to more than 10,000 women; another 8000 women have been trained in the intricate craft of chikankari. Not only are many previously desperately poor women now living comfortably on their earnings, it has also revived the ancient and comatose craft of chikankari.

Runa Banerjee's involvement with chikankari handicraft artists began with a Unicef-supported study on the lives of artisans in India. Discovering that the chikankari craft in Lucknow was highly exploitative, especially for women and children, she decided to remain and work for them. Her interaction with the women convinced her that self-reliance was the only real solution to the privations. So, in 1984, she set up the Sewa in Lucknow, setting about obtaining training in the craft and then extending the expertise to other women. Runa, who works in Lucknow and ten other districts of Uttar Pradesh, focuses on the social and economic empowerment of deprived and exploited women. Over the years, Runa's work has reached out directly to over 10,000 women. About 8000 women have been trained in the difficult craft of chikankari, which is today a nationwide fashion rage and has spawned thousands of imitations. Chikankari had gone into sharp decline after independence, but Sewa's efforts revived it. Now many previously very poor women are able to live from their earnings.

Initially, there was such dogged resistance from their families that a number of the women were physically assaulted when they joined Sewa. Contractors, business houses, and middlepersons saw Sewa activities in Lucknow as a trade threat.

Runa, who has been consistently devoted to the cause of secularism, harmony, sisterhood, and peace, has also undertaken some interstate interventions in this context, most recently in Gujarat, where the victims of the 2002 pogrom are being rehabilitated under her guidance.

When Runa Banerjee began her work in 1984, chikankari exploited its women artisans. Beside poor working conditions, and the fact that most chikan work was done by women from Muslim families, the craft itself had become monotonous, lacking variety in production and designs.

India

Nasreen Bano

Self-Employed Women's Association (Sewa)-Lucknow

Nasreen Bano (born 1978) has been working as a community mobilizer and trainer at the Self-Employed Women's Association (Sewa) in Lucknow for more than a decade. While she exhorts women to find economic independence and security, Nasreen also directs them to train more women in their art—the resurgent chikankari, the traditional embroidery of Uttar Pradesh that Sewa has lately brought back to the limelight.

Nasreen Bano's mother enquired about opportunities at the Sewa after her husband died. Nasreen, then eight, tagged along when her mother joined Sewa. Nasreen, therefore, practically grew up in Sewa, training, as the years went by, in chikankari. Then, she took on the role as a trainer and mobilizer. Today, she heads a team of 2500 women artisans. Nasreen's mobilizing technique includes not only encouraging women to find economic independence and security, but also training more women.

Nasreen has been working on these issues for more than ten years. During this period, she has trained and provided self-employment to more than 500 women artisans. The average monthly income of each woman artisan has grown from 1000 to 1200 rupees.

Hailing from a conservative Muslim family, Nasreen had to fight many prejudices to retain her status as an economically independent woman. Her mother, though, has been extremely open and supportive. Today, Nasreen's work has inspired hundreds of women artisans in Uttar Pradesh. Soft-spoken and gentle, Nasreen is a pillar of strength for many girls whose education she supports in every way she can. Her youth apart, her skills in chikankari are superlative and comprehensive — from sourcing raw materials to marketing the finished product. Her outstanding quality is her eagerness to share her skills with other women. Nasreen's world does not stop at herself.

Chikankari was dying before the Sewa stepped in with a cooperative structure. Today, chikankari is a fashion statement. Sewa's idea was to provide self-employment to marginalized women artisans.

India

Marie Bapu Bidibundu

Promotion de la Femme Rurale (Profer)

Marie Bapu Bidibundu from the Democratic Republic of Congo (DRC) works with an NGO, Promotion de la Femme Rurale (Profer), in promoting and defending rural women's socio-cultural and economic rights. Since 1978 she has raised awareness through writing, to awaken consciences. She works in harsh conditions to insure that people receive training without discrimination in various fields: health, literacy, access to resources and education in local languages. This has improved people's status, work conditions and ability to defend and promote their rights against political and police harassment.

Marie Bapu Bidibundu is a jurist, an activist in human rights, a peace agent and a member of parliament. Marie insures that women and girls are trained in health and agricultural production, to fight hunger and poverty. She assists women to express themselves against violence and to fight repressive customs that hamper peace in their families and society. Rural women are now respected, listened to, and emulate and train men in their rural settings. They defend their rights, avoid revenge and peacefully resolve conflicts that arise in their areas. Moreover, during the peace negotiating process, women were also encouraged to participate in political negotiations aimed at stopping the war. These efforts were and are aimed at reunifying and reconciling the country's warring factions to ultimately organize elections. She also participated in the Inter Congolese Dialogue, negotiations aimed to bring peace in DRC, she mobilized resources to peacefully negotiate during the ousting of Kasai people from the Shaba region in the 1990s crisis. This defused the hatred and revenge among the people.
Her work is emulated by other women who are now involved in the research for peace and well being, in appropriating equity to men and women and other basic human rights.

The DRC is in strife led by militias and warlords who have signed a peace agreement, which they find difficult to implement. The country's natural resources are the cause of the regional crisis.

Democratic Republic of the Congo

Aminata Touré Barry

Association Malienne pour la Sauvegarde du Bien-être Familial (AMASBIF)
Coalitions des Alternatives Dette et Développement (CAD-Mali)

Aminata Touré Barry was born in 1955. She is from Goundam, a region of Timbuktu, Mali. She is the president of the Malian Association for the Safeguard of Family Welfare (AMASBIF) and the African Coalition on Debt and Development (CAD-Mali). Since 1977, she has been an Inspector of the Treasury. Before that, she gained qualification from the Central School for Industry, Commerce, and Administration in Bamako specializing in budgeting.

Madame Barry is a versatile person who is very interested in all aspects of development. This is fortunate as she is involved in issues as diverse as the reforestation and rehabilitation of dunes, the civic education of women, and the participation of women in public life. Her non-governmental organization AMASBIF promotes and contributes to the well-being of the family from the perspective of sustainable development and stability for Mali. She is also the president of the Coalition on Debt and Development (CAD-Mali) whose objective is to pursue the cancellation of the country's debt and to oppose the politics that keep the communities in a position of extreme poverty.

Madame Aminata Touré Barry has a rich administrative background that gave her experience with many situations that she could later draw on. Eventually, she became involved in fighting issues of poverty and of indebtedness with which she was familiar. She also has a rich union history with the National Union of the Workers of Mali. She was well-trained in the economics of human rights and in English. Madam Aminata Touré Barry has participated in about 30 seminars on various issues: violence against women, the fight against poverty, African debt, and sustainable human development.

Aminata Touré Barry is a powerful activist distinguished by her fight for social and economic justice and a just and united world. She never ceases campaigning to cancel foreign debt by analysing international politics and contributing to the Heavily Indebted Poor Countries Initiative.

Mali

From despair to
hope, Rafiza has
traveled far.
She now wants to
devote her time
to making that
journey easier for
other women.

Rafiza Begum

Thana Federation
Narikuli Women's Group

From a timid wife whose husband abandoned her to a Union Parishad leader, Rafiza Begum (born around 1965) has traveled a long, bumpy road. When she contacted the NGO Proshika and its women's microcredit group, she could hardly imagine that one day she would be looking well beyond her own life toward improving the lot of all women in her village. Nor did she think that she would inspire scores of village women to break social, religious, and cultural barriers and move toward empowerment.

The tireless and fiery Rafiza Begum was once a retiring housewife in a Bangladeshi village, wondering how she would pull her life together after her husband abandoned her. "I had no education, no training," she says. "My father and mother were also very poor. But they supported me. They gave me shelter."

In 1982, wondering what to do next, she heard about the development and support programs of Proshika, one of Bangladesh's largest NGOs, and contacted it. She undertook income-generating projects with a loan from Proshika, becoming active in a Proshika-facilitated microcredit women's group. For 22 years, she has been working to build awareness among the impoverished, particularly women, on child marriage, dowry, repression of women, and the need to maintain local law and order. Rafiza has also been encouraging women to engage in income-generating activities such as poultry farming and tree plantation. Proshika provides loans to members of the women's group to get them going. Her work has inspired scores of village women to break a panoply of barriers and edge toward empowerment. A prominent woman leader in the area, Rafiza has been elected to the Union Parishad three times.

Despite the support, Rafiza has had to brave enormous opposition. Her engagement with "sensitive" issues has created unprecedented turmoil in the village, and she has been threatend by local religious leaders and power cliques. But, undeterred, Rafiza wants to devote her time to making her journey easier for other women.

In Rafiza's society, women did not move around freely and alone, or become income generators. A woman abandoned by her husband is expected to live by stricter moral codes. Religious clerics resort to moral posturing and threats to control the lives of women in the village.

Bangladesh

Beatriz Benzano Seré

Dawn of New Paris Group — Women for a Dignified Life

As a Dominican nun, Beatriz Benzano knew the suffering of the marginalized populations of Montevideo, Buenos Aires and Santiago. She left her order and joined the legendary Tupamaros movement, until she was captured, tortured and confined to prison for four years. She returned to Uruguay, from her exile in France, to organize the group Dawn of New Paris — Women for a Dignified Life, helping people living on the streets and families whose lives had been destroyed by unemployment. She particularly dedicated her work to the aid and defense of abandoned women.

Motivated by the idea that it is not possible to be happy without other people, at the age of 21, Beatriz Benzano entered the Dominican Order, where she had received her education. As a nun, she shared the life of poor families in the shanty towns of her native Montevideo and in the poor neighborhoods of Buenos Aires. Trying to understand the causes of the marginalization they suffered, she moved to Chile to do political, economic and social studies with Paulo Freire. After her return, she decided to leave the religious order for the militancy in the Tupamaros movement for national liberation. In 1972, she was captured, tortured and, without any trial, confined to Punta de Rieles Prison. She remained there, along with other political female prisoners, for four years. On her liberation, Beatriz Benzano had to seek exile in France. From there, she collaborated with the dissemination of information about her people's fight and the fight of the other Latin-American populations who were struggling to break the power of dictatorships. Along with a group of internationalists, she joined a solidarity brigade with the triumphant victors of the revolution in Nicaragua.

After the democratic liberalization in Uruguay, she returned from exile to create the Dawn of New Paris Group — Women for a Dignified Life, a NGO that organizes construction cooperatives and work projects, which encourage the creation of small businesses in addition to organizing nurseries for the care of children. Beatriz gives special attention to lonely women and young girls excluded from the educational system. She is particularly concerned with the defense of reproductive rights and the struggle to decriminalize abortion. The path is uncertain, but there is a fountain of hope bringing better conditions for individuals and collective change.

Since the 1950s, South American economies have revealed a decline in productivity that the world of free trade imposed. The reality was that military dictatorships crushed the liberation movements and concentrated the riches in a small section of the population. Uruguay is part of this reality.

Uruguay

Radha Bhatt

Kasturba National Memorial Trust (KNMT)

From protesting against the raw deal uneducated women in the Uttaranchal Himalayas are handed out to becoming one of the best known social and political activists in the country — that has been Radha Bhatt's journey over the past 70-odd years. Along the way, she has tackled alcoholism among men in Uttaranchal, the empowerment of women, the Chipko (tree-hugging) movement, open mining on the fragile Uttaranchal highlands, and has been part of the nationwide protest against big dams.

Life in the mountains around the foothills of the Himalayas in Uttaranchal is tough. When Radha Bhatt was born 70-odd years ago, the condition of women in the region was abysmal. Education was out of the question and, for married women, alcoholism among men was a constant vice that needed to be negotiated. Although born into a repressive social milieu, Radha was made of different stuff, and refused to agree when her parents wanted to marry her off at 16. She also chose to associate herself with Lakshmi Ashram, a local organization working for the uplift of women in the region. On the one hand, Radha had her own constructive and progressive ideas, on the other, she had the organization's Gandhian principles to help her along. She changed the mindsets of the women she came in contact with, educating, enlightening, and empowering them. And her work did not end just with the women; girl-children, grown-up men — everyone came under her influence.

But Radha's life was not restricted to the foothills of the Himalayas, or to rural women. She was actively involved in organizing more than seven women's protests against the sale and consumption of liquor. She has also been one of the most important faces of the Chipko movement aimed at saving the Himalayan forests. Her efforts, along with those of many others, helped prevent landslides in more than 50 villages of the region. Radha's outstanding work led to her receiving the Indira Priyadarshini Environment Award. She has also focused her attention on open mining on the fragile highlands in the Uttaranchal Himalayas, as well as the protests against big dams. Furthermore, Radha is involved with the Kasturba National Memorial Trust, an organization mainly concerned with training rural women for voluntary services.

Life in the Himalayan foothills is tough and male alcoholism is rampant, disrupting social and familial harmony and setting back local economies. These isolated regions often do not have schools or adequate medical facilities. Deforestation and open mining take their toll.

India

Pushpa Bhave

Social Gratitude Fund (SGF)

For five decades now, Pushpa Bhave (born 1939) has been part of a series of struggles, starting with the movement aimed at lending voice to the Maharashtrian working class. She has fought for the empowerment of Dalit women, the cause of women head-loaders and sweepers, women beedi (tobacco rolled in leaves to make cigarettes) workers, and of the temple prostitute system. She has been at the forefront of several political struggles, and is campaigning to introduce a bill in parliament to prevent the "dedication" of children to religious sects.

Even when she was a student, Pushpa Bhave was aware of the issues she wanted to work with later. She got in touch with leftist theater artistes, and joined the Samyukta Maharashtra movement in 1956, which aimed to lend voice to the aspirations of peasants and the working class. Pushpa later joined the Dalits' cause, working for the empowerment and education of rural women, and gradually came to participate in the Dalit Panther Movement. She was even jailed for her commitment to the Dalit struggle. Pushpa moved to organizing the Hamal and Mapadi (head-loaders and sweepers) workers' movement, leading the struggles of the women beedi workers of Nippani, and the devadasi system (ritualized prostitution). During the emergency in 1975, she sheltered many underground political workers, gradually becoming an important member of the underground opposition. She has also worked against the rabidly right-wing Shiv Sena government in Maharashtra-during the 1992 communal riots that followed the demolition of the Babri Masjid, she belligerently challenged the Shiv Sena.

Pushpa is a trustee of the Social Gratitude Fund (SGF), which supports activists who do not wish to take funds from international agencies. She is currently campaigning to introduce a bill in parliament to prevent the "dedication" of children to religious sects. Only an adult, she feels, should have that choice, and parents cannot have the right to decide so drastically on behalf of their children.

Despite independence, the condition of Dalit women in India is a mess, as is that of other working-class women. Some of the most desperately wounded were the Hamal and Mapadi workers, women beedi workers, and devadasis.

India

Ebadon Bibi

Landless Organization of Hosenpur

Ebadon Bibi (born 1945), once a daily-wage laborer, is now a spirited activist fighting for the rights of landless people like herself. Bold and innovative, Ebadon is a natural motivator. She is credited with popularizing the Rokeya Day celebrations on the birthday of Rokeya Sakhawat Hossain (renowned educationist and philosopher), which remain a clarion call to defeat fundamentalist and regressive forces. Her work has brought about a sea-change in the lives and attitudes of the landless people in her village and its surrounding areas.

Ebadon Bibi lived her youth in drudgery, working for a pittance to feed her family, and married off at age 11. Then she came into contact with Nijera Kori (which means doing it ourselves). She heard the Nijera Kori activists who visited her village, and was deeply impressed by the idea that she and other landless people could refashion a better life by organizing themselves. So, she was the first person in her village, Sekhahati Gram, to welcome the activists and show them around. Sekhahati, in Dogra, one of Bangladesh's poorest districts, was conservative: it was atypical of women to take such an active role in village matters. But Ebadon worked patiently to mobilize the women, forming women's groups, inspiring the groups' members to take up issues that affected their lives and livelihood.

From the very beginning, Ebadon's activities with the landless were rooted in steely ideological conviction. Under her leadership, the group has been celebrating Rokeya Day on December 9, organizing mass gatherings and cultural events, even influencing other organizations to join in. Rokeya Sakhawat Hossain, a renowned educationist and philosopher, was born in the village where Ebadon now lives. For her, the celebrations are a vehicle for challenging fundamentalist forces and the prejudices that disempower women.

Ebadon believes that if women are to take control of and change their lives, they need to unite. She has inspired women to break with the antipathies and illiberalities that reined them in, and she has been active in the education of both girls and boys.

Bangladesh, one of the world's most congested nations, has 85 percent of its population living in rural areas, with about 60 percent landless or nearly so. They are all terrorized by fundamentalists, particularly the women. This is the environment that Ebadon works in tirelessly.

Bangladesh

Maryam Bibi

Khwendo Kor

Radical feminists call her a conformist and extreme religious-political groups think she promotes western agendas. But Maryam Bibi (born 1950) deals with this dilemma just as she has handled all other challenges in her remarkable life — with courage, humor, and optimism. The founder of Khwendo Kor, an NGO that works for women's development through education, healthcare, and microcredit in Pakistan's Federally Administered Tribal Areas, has a genius for turning foes into friends with her inclusive and evolutionary approach.

Born in Pakistan's Federally Administered Tribal Areas (Fata), Maryam Bibi was married young to her cousin, a schizophrenic unable to work. It took Maryam 17 years of negotiation and consultation to get permission to work outside the home. In 1987, she joined an NGO, the All Pakistan Women's Association. Two years later, she embarked on a four-year stint with a German agency for a technical support project. Six years after she began working, Bibi started her own NGO, Khwendo Kor (which means in Pushto, sister's home), for women and children's development through education, healthcare, and microcredit. Khwendo Kor has expanded from a staff of four to 129, with four regional offices in some of Pakistan's remotest areas, difficult to access and hostile to the concept of female emancipation and empowerment. Yet, today there are 7000 girls studying in villages across the region.

For Maryam, "collaboration" and "consensus" are key words to her inclusive approach. In the tribal areas, Khwendo Kor formed a committee of the main stakeholders (civil society, government, religious leaders) to advise and support it in all important matters, including the selection of villages, teachers, and developmental schemes. There is now a demand for its services even in villages that were once hostile. At the district level, Maryam collaborates with local government departments to help people gain better access to public services, actively seeking the involvement of the establishment by handing over the girls' schools it sets up to the government; it also mobilizes communities to participate in government health campaigns.

Khwendo Kor is the only women's NGO in the arch-conservative north-west frontier province that has a decentralized management structure with independent regional offices run by predominantly local female staff.

Sixty percent of the population of Pakistan's Federally Administered Tribal Areas (Fata) live below the UN poverty line, and the literacy rate for females ranges between zero to three percent. Much of the tribal belt is hostile to the slightest idea of female emancipation.

Carmen Bigler

Women United Together in Marshall Islands (WUTMI)

Carmen Bigler has worn many hats in her long career. She was the first Marshallese woman to obtain a degree and the first woman to join the Congress of Micronesia during an era when men dominated the political arena. She is an advocate for women's issues and a firm believer in the preservation of culture, helping to develop the nation's only cultural-historical museum, library, and archive. The outcome was a significant revival of interest in cultural activity by many young mothers and youths. Currently, Carmen is the president of Women United Together in Marshall Islands.

Carmen Bigler is no stranger to hardship. The common household saying for her family was "No work, no food!" Her father was killed by the Japanese during World War II, and in those difficult times for the family Carmen learned values such as sharing, equality, and caring for others. During her college years abroad, her Hawaiian college friends were always telling her how lucky she was to still speak her own vernacular language. Thus, Carmen learned to appreciate her own culture and gradually developed her passion for preserving it. Armed with an anthropology degree, she returned to the Marshalls and worked on various community projects. It was not until a Peace Corps volunteer friend of hers drowned while snorkeling that an opportunity for cultural revival presented itself to Carmen. Handicrafts were sent to the volunteer's parents and in return, money was sent back to her. Carmen used the funds to establish a historical/cultural museum. The first of its kind in the country, the museum went on to start its own radio program, the Alele Program, that was aired weekly. Through this program, women for the first time were given a voice and were heard throughout the nation. Topics such as women's roles and responsibilities, and issues and concerns they faced in their daily lives were discussed.

The Marshall Islands suffered Japanese invasion in World War II and US nuclear testing in its territory after the war. To this day, the Marshallese live with the terrible aftermath of the war, the tests, and United States political and cultural colonization.

Marshall Islands

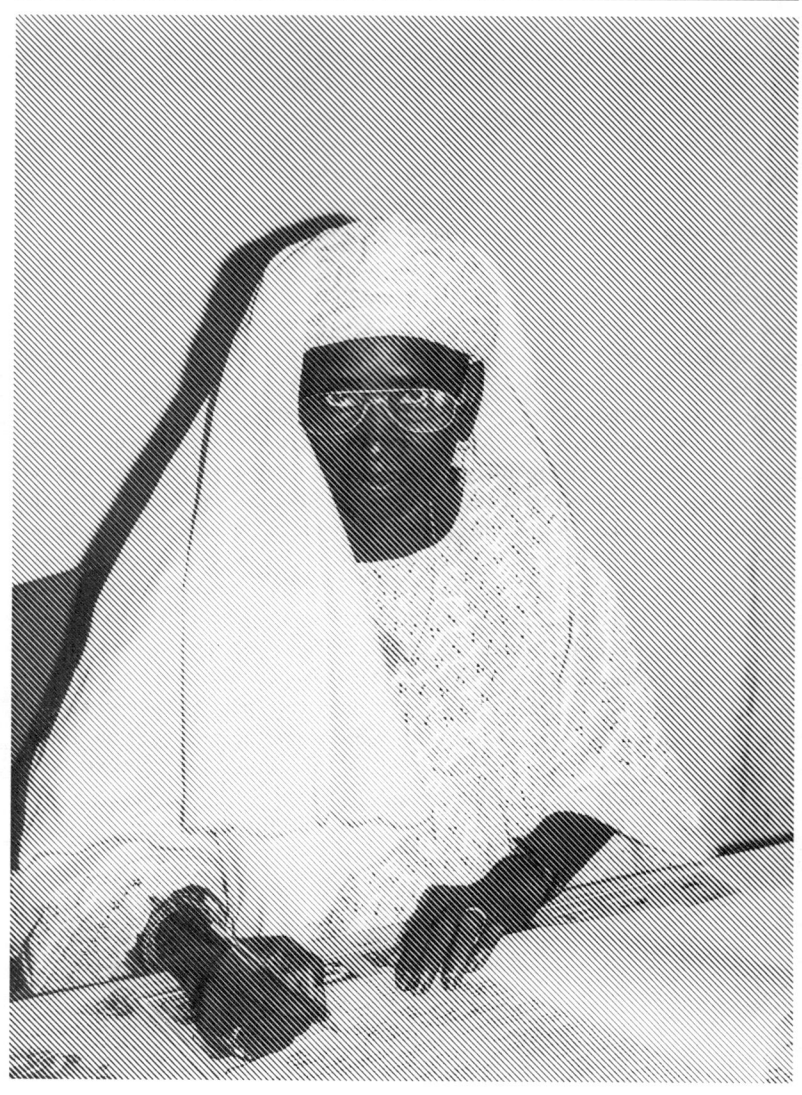

Sirandou Bocoum

Association for the Protection of Children and Domestic Workers

Sirandou Bocoum (born 1945) is a teacher and believes women need to continue the fight to realize the recommendations of the 1995 Beijing Summit. She also understands the importance of making women aware of the implications of decisions on local development in the Djenné area. Her activities support the fight against illegal trade in children and awareness raising on women's rights.

Madam Sirandou, having reflected a great deal on the position of children and domestic workers in Djenné, could not help but mobilize women for their emancipation. She understood very quickly the need to take the initiative to protect and send children to school, girls in particular. Today, Sirandou Bocoum is the leader of the Association for the Protection of Children and Domestic Workers. She chose the Djenné area to fight for women's rights because she saw an area that was poorly serviced by the national women's associations which concentrated their efforts in the capital, Bamako. Djenné is a very religious city which does not support the work of Sirandou and her colleagues. At first, she had many problems defending her opinions in an environment dominated by men. But she was not discouraged even though she came to realize that her fight was a solitary one at the start, but not in vain. Sirandou Bocoum made the effort and took a lot of risks to improve women's position in Djenné aiming at the creation of other women's organizations. Today, she is highly appreciated by the women of the area who see in her an important person at the head of the local women's movement. She is one of those rare women of the region who embrace both the women's community and political life, being second assistant mayor of the city hall in Djenné, a post that allows her to be involved in local decisions concerning the life of the urban community of Djenné.

This courageous lady works in very difficult conditions that require a lot of physical and financial effort. The issues are poorly understood in Djenné because of cultural and religious beliefs. Djenné is a city where traditions are strong.

Mali

Seiko Bodios Ohashi

Japan Committee for Negros Campaign (JCNC)

Seiko Bodios Ohashi (born 1960) is the liaison officer of the Japan Committee for Negros Campaign (JCNC) that facilitates people-to-people trading of agricultural products by farmers' cooperatives in Negros province in the Philippines to consumer groups in Japan. JCNC gets funding from donations of various Japanese consumer groups who want to help Negros farmers become economically independent. People-to-people trading is an alternative scheme that allows farmer producers to directly market their goods to consumers, thus doing away with middlemen.

Seiko Ohashi first came to Negros Island in June 1991. When the airplane she was on approached the island, she could see the vast green fields from the sky. "I wondered why there was so much hunger when there was this wide 'green pasture'," she recalls.

The "tiempos muertes" or dead season had begun, the period between the planting and harvesting of sugarcane when there is hardly any work at the hacienda and the "sacadas" (migrant agricultural workers) become heavily indebted to their landlords for their families' daily needs. By the time the harvest season comes, their earnings are hardly enough to pay their debts. "I spent several nights in the house of a sacada in La Castellana (about two hours from Bacolod City). I thought I knew enough about the Philippines and its people from my previous visits, but this experience gave me a very different view of their reality."

The sacadas gladly shared their food with her, even if they did not have enough. They gave her the most comfortable space in the house to sleep in. "I told them, 'Sorry to disturb you, but can I stay a few more days to learn about your life?' They said, 'Do not say sorry. We are very proud to have you in our house. We thought only hacenderos could have guests. We are happy that even if our house is small, we also have a foreign visitor. We are no longer second or third class citizens'." Seiko finally appreciated the situation of sugar workers behind the façade of the "green pasture" she saw from an airplane in the sky. Through the Japan Committee for Negros Campaign (JCNC), Seiko helps rehabilitate the socio-economic life of sugar workers by promoting independent agriculture and encouraging them to break away from their feudal relations with landlords who have enslaved them for decades.

Scores of evacuees fled the hinterlands to avoid the conflict between the military and the rebel New People's Army (NPA). The military was out to crush the rebellion sparked by grave social injustice in the Philippines, of which Negros Island is a glaring symbol.

Philippines

"I do not waste
time, ever. I did not
waste even an
hour in my whole
student life for any
boyfriend. I did
not even get married.
I believe in hard
work and sacrifice."

Asha Lata Baidya

Surjamukhi Sangstha (SMS)

Asha Lata Baidya (born 1956) is one of Bangladesh's best-known freedom-fighters. She joined the freedom struggle of 1971 against Pakistan when she was only 15 years old and went on to lead the women's guerrilla corps. After she completed her studies — suspended until her country won independence — she set up the Surjamukhi Sangstha (SMS). SMS has been working on issues ranging from setting up cooperatives and helping with loans to women's empowerment, education, and environmental issues. More than 200,000 families have benefited from Asha Lata's 34 years of tireless activism.

Asha Lata Baidya joined the struggle for freedom from Pakistan when she was still 15 and at middle school. "My father told them that he had no son," she says. "His daughter, meaning me, would join them (the freedom-fighters). I was very excited." Asha learnt how to operate firearms and was trained in guerrilla combat. She led several operations as commander of the women guerrillas, the Mohila Muktijodha Dal. Only after Bangladesh had won its independence in January 1972 did Asha Lata resume her education, going on to complete her Bachelors and Masters in Bengali literature. In college, she set up small women's cooperatives. Capitalizing on this experience, she formed the SMS soon after she completed her Masters. Today, Surjamukhi works in 42 upazilas in 17 districts, and about 200,000 families have benefited from their input.

Asha has been working for 34 years now, organizing people at the grassroots level and aiding them to attain economic solvency. Surjamukhi has helped people set up cooperatives and small businesses. Asha Lata combines her business acumen with advocacy and awareness raising on subjects including human rights, gender issues, the environment, primary health, and HIV/Aids. She has also conducted programs on community-based disaster preparedness and nonformal education, simultaneously working to strengthen local government initiatives for women's empowerment. Asha fiercely promotes literacy and enrolls children in schools. "I do not waste time, ever," says Asha Lata. "I did not waste even an hour in my whole student life for any boyfriend. I did not even get married. I believe in hard work and sacrifice. I am hopeful that things will change for the better. 'Asha' means hope, you see!"

Women guerrillas erased the myth that women could not engage in active combat with their male counterparts. But, with the country's economy wrecked, the benefits of liberation escaped women, agricultural workers, laborers, and other marginalized classes. Literacy and education levels were dismal.

Bangladesh

"Sometimes I feel
I want to give up, but
when someone comes
along and needs help,
I cannot say 'no'."

Bridget Lew

Humanitarian Organization for Migration Economics (Home)

Bridget Lew (Bridget Tan Teck Sim) was born in 1948. She is an expert in human resources and employment law and helped to set up the Commission for Migrants and Itinerant People (CMI), under the auspices of the Catholic Church in 1998. She left CMI in 2004 to establish the Humanitarian Organization for Migration Economics (Home) which helps semi-skilled foreign workers, refugees and tourists passing through Singapore. Home also provides administrative assistance and shelter to migrants. It was recently recognized as a charity and an NGO by the government.

Bridget Lew admits that she has a radical style of doing things that those in power sometimes find uncomfortable. "Employers come and bang on the table. Some have threatened to sue me," she says, speaking from her sparsely furnished office at the Humanitarian Organization for Migration Economics (Home). "People do not like an assertive woman." Using her own savings, Lew set up Home in September 2004 to help foreign workers in Singapore. Since then, the organization has won government approval to receive a grant of S$ 100,000 from the National Volunteer and Philanthropy Center (NVPC). Lew and ten part-time employees provide administrative and legal assistance to workers who are in conflict with their employers or who face abuse in their jobs. Home also runs two shelters — one with accommodation for 12 men, the other for 20 women.

Singapore is host to some 500,000 skilled and semi-skilled holders of work permits, about 150,000 of whom are domestic workers. Bridget says, "Some of them are really powerless and voiceless. When they call me, I respond personally." She receives calls throughout the day and often in the middle of the night. One morning, as she is talking to a visitor in Home, her mobile phone rings. It is clear the caller is in trouble. "Do not cry," Lew says. "Listen to me. My name is Bridget. If your employer does not pay you, she is doing something wrong. Where are you? Go to (a restaurant) and I will get some girls to bring you to our shelter." The caller says she can leave only at night, and Lew arranges to get her to safety. Lew, who is married and has two grown children, says her work "eats up all my family time, my social time" and that her family often wishes she would do something else. "Sometimes I feel I want to give up, but when someone comes along and needs help, I cannot say 'no'," she says.

Singapore is host to some 500,000 skilled and semi-skilled holders of work permits, about 150,000 of whom are domestic workers. The latter, all women, are particularly vulnerable to unscrupulous employers.

Bui Thi Dung

3T Group of Hop Thanh commune

Bui Thi Dung (born 1959) was trafficked to China in 1991, but fled back to her homeland in 1992. She heads a "returned women" group — also called 3T Group (which stands for voluntary, self-reliant and confident) — established in 1997, a project of the Institute of Youth Studies and the Research Center for Gender and Development to help victims of trafficking integrate into the community. Ignoring other people's contempt, Dung and her group borrowed money to start a business. They are now well-off and help the authorities educate young girls on how to avoid the traps laid by traffickers.

Bui Thi Dung is a shining example to the members of the Hop Thanh commune in Cao Loc district, Lang Son province, of how disadvantaged women can return to society and make a good living. Sold to prostitution in China and returning empty-handed and in disgrace, Dung, a small, brave woman who refused to give in to her fate, managed to escape from poverty and assist others like herself to regain their happiness and self-respect.

It was very difficult for her to come home to Vietnam where she was disdained by her relatives and the rest of her community for having been a prostitute. But she persisted for the sake of her husband and children, to whom she is deeply dedicated. She joined a group of "returned women" organized by Hanoi University, where she was able to help herself and other former prostitutes to overcome their difficulties and integrate into the community. By sharing their knowledge of the tricks used by traffickers and the traps they lay for their victims, her group was able to change the community's negative attitudes towards former prostitutes.

Bui Thi Dung led the way for the other women in her group by encouraging them to borrow money to start their own businesses. Borrowing one million Dong, she bought a couple of pigs for fattening. After selling the first two, she bought more pigs until the business grew. Dung and her family are now well-off. An industrious, tender and responsible woman, Bui Thi Dung wants to make a better world for everybody, particularly women like herself who, she says, deserve sympathy and assistance from the community.

To help trafficked women in post-war Vietnam reintegrate into the community, the Vietnam Institute of Youth Studies and the Research Center for Gender and Development created the "returned women" groups. These groups try to change the negative attitudes towards former prostitutes.

Viet Nam

Maïmouna Coulibaly Camara

Coordination des Associations et ONG Feminines du Mali (CAFO)
Centre Aoua Keita

This grand lady with her engaging style has had a brilliant teaching career in which the main concern always was to contribute to the preparation of younger generations to confront life better. Maïmouna Coulibaly Camara was the first general director of the Center Aoua Keita in Ouolofobougou, in the district of Bamako. The center is specializing in the professional development of female school graduates.

Maïmouna Coulibaly Camara managed the Center Aoua Keita since its creation in 1996 until 2005 with flawless determination and courage. Teaching being her profession, she was and is a person who is ready to honestly serve her country. She was the hope of female graduates, intending for them a better future that assures them professional independence.

Born in Gao (200 kilometers from Bamako), Maïmouna Coulibaly Camara is a secondary school teacher. She has already formed many national bodies exercising various trades: accounting, inspector of customs, management secretary, and administration editor. This calm lady is very attentive to all that happens around her and knows how to welcome people and keep her center alive. In 1996, when the Commissioner for the Promotion of Women proposed her as director of the Center Aoua Keita, very few people paid attention. It was an unknown Madame Coulibaly, ambitious to be useful to her country and orientate her efforts towards the socio-professional improvement of girls that had not had the opportunity to complete their studies. For those in danger of marginalization and prostitution, she wanted to provide assistance, for instance in teaching them sewing or training them for jobs in the hotel business. This suggestion soon was welcomed by young women and their parents.

Many girls leaving school early jostle to get into the Center Aoua Keita and apply for the many different courses initiated by Maïmouna Coulibaly Camara. Thanks to this structure, girls who had lost all hope of success, learn a trade and today are integrated in professional life.

Mali

Nora Castañeda

Bank of the Woman (Banmujer)

Nora Castañeda is an economist committed to her work with the Venezuelan people. She has been fighting for the rights of women, both from inside the academic world and out in the community. She was the driving force behind the creation of the Coordination of Women's Non-Governmental Organizations and the Center for Women's Studies. She has supported the reform of several laws and the incorporation of gender issues into the constitution. She is the President of the Women's Bank, which gives poor women the means to have a better future.

She was born into a humble family, in Caracas, in 1942. Her mother, who was of a peasant origin, was a "father and a mother at the same time." From her mother, Nora Castañeda inherited her love of studying and honorable work. "La profa" — as her fellows call her — came from a generation greatly influenced by the happenings in France in 1968. In the 1970s, she was one of those mobilizing to strive for the necessary social and political changes in her country. Already involved in organizations with other women within the left-wing political movement, they began to think about the situation of their own lives. That was the birth of the Venezuelan Feminist Movement.

She graduated as an economist and, for 33 years, worked as a professor at the Central University of Venezuela, where she was head of the Faculty. Besides her work within the academic world, she worked outside in the community and was the driving force behind the creation of the Coordination of Women's Non-Governmental Organizations and of the Center for Women's Studies. She also supported the reform of several laws and the incorporation of gender issues into the constitution. Due to her long history of work within the female movement, she was elected as president of the Bank of the Women (Banmujer), under the current administration of President Hugo Chávez. With this post, Nora Castañeda plans to give needy Venezuelan women the possibility of improving their quality of life. "We do not want women to be poor and in debt. We do not want them to be managing on the poverty line." The project's aim is to build an economic model with gender equality.

The 1960s was a time characterized by the formation and consolidation of social and political movements. The current situation in Venezuela is centered on the search for a new economic model, with equality and solidarity.

Venezuela

Yuzhen Chang

Changji Store in Tangshan

From her modest beginnings selling soybeans Chang Yuzhen went on to become a successful businesswoman. She now puts the bulk of her wealth into helping others. Coming from a family of soldiers, she knows well their hardships and has set up a veterans' home, a veterans' welfare settlement, a soldiers' resort village and an orphans' village in the old Liberated Areas. She also set up an exhibition hall for patriotism education, an ecological garden for the protection of the environment, and has donated money to disaster-affected areas.

From selling soybeans, wheat, seedcakes and soybean milk, Chang Yuzhen gradually developed her own store, and now she runs the Changji Shopping Mall with six sub-stores, covering 21,000 square meters and with 60 million yuan of fixed assets. It is difficult to imagine the problems she confronted. But when she became wealthy, she decided it was important to repay society, and devoted her life to welfare undertakings. After the severe earthquake in Tangshan, Chang invested 240,000 yuan in 1991 in the place to set up two wholesale markets in textile goods, and gave them to the local bureau for industry and commerce. In order to revive Pingju, a local opera of China, she invested 1.6 million yuan to construct an opera building. She endowed this free to the Tangshang Pingju troupe. To help the old veterans who had contributed to New China, from 1995 to 1996, she spent 7.6 million yuan to establish a veterans' home, a veterans' welfare settlement, a soldiers' resort village and an orphans' village in the old Liberated Areas. She particularly wanted veteran soldiers without children to enjoy their last days in a good environment. To promote an awareness of patriotism among the new generation, she spent over 400,000 yuan to set up a patriotism exhibition hall. She is also concerned about the ecological environment, and has put in 1.5 million yuan for an ecological garden and ecological exhibitions, which people can visit free of charge. She has also given donations to poor students and to disaster-inflicted areas. Virtually all her income goes to the common wealth undertaking, which has won her much praise from the public.

The reform and opening policy has brought about more opportunities to many people. Yet, most people go after their own profits and comfortable life. Very few people are willing to spend their money in common good work.

China

Yuying Chen

Chen Yuying was seriously injured in a factory fire in 1993. Ten years later, she set up a Handicapped Service Station in Zhongxian County of Chongqing City. This station focuses on migrant workers, victims of industrial hazards, and the handicapped, and provides knowledge assistance, as well as physical and moral support. It has helped many handicapped people regain their confidence in life, and to find work.

Chen Yuying is from Zhongxian County in Chongqing City. At the beginning of the 1990s, when she was only 15 and had not even finished junior high school, she went to the Shenzhen Special Economic Zone and worked in the Zhili Toy Plant, supporting her brother's desire to go to university. There, a big factory fire changed her life: 75 percent of her body was covered with third degree burns. She was unable to work. She also lost over 80 co-workers in the fire. However, within one year, with the support of her relatives and friends, Chen regained her wish to live.

Despite the emotional trauma she had to face, she took up the fight for the welfare of migrant workers from rural areas and against the factory. She also wished to do something for those who had cared for her. Thus the Self-support Service Station became a new start in life for Chen, as well as for her fellow workers and handicapped friends.

Chen was kind to her handicapped friends. A woman, Yanzi, was a dwarf and a hunchback, and felt terrible about her physical appearance. Chen spent a great deal of time with her and won her confidence. Gradually, Yanzi was able to confront the outside world and start her own business, and soon she met someone and fell in love.

Yanzi is only one of the many people Chen has supported. On June 18, 2002, Chen set up a sign for a handicapped service station at her home, with two hotlines. She runs this service station on a voluntary basis and is happy that she has a chance to repay society.

Since the 1980s, China has seen much industrial development. But the problems of industrial safety and workers' rights are becoming increasingly serious. Workers have fought hard to get state legislation and implementation of laws safeguarding workers, particularly migrants from the country.

China

Wei Cheng

Jinyita Village, Daning County, Shanxi Province, China

Cheng Wei (54) left her comfortable job and home and moved to a remote village in Shanxi Province, China. She put all her efforts — and her own funds — into developing the economy and culture of the area, focusing on road building, electricity and water supplies, schools, and the purchase of trees and seeds.

Cheng Wei was 18 years old when she joined the production team in Fensi County, Shanxi Province in 1968. After graduating in chemistry from Qinghua University, she wanted to work in Fensi County. In late 1978 she was transferred to a secondary school in Beijing as a chemistry teacher. Since 1997 she has been working, at her own expense, on poverty alleviation in Jinyita Village, Yuchun Township, Daning County of Shanxi Province. In the past eight years she has had over ten kilometers of roads built, enabling the villagers to export their agricultural by-products and thus increase their incomes. She has also built a new school for over 50 students. Kerosene lamps have been phased out with the connection of electricity. She has also motivated the government to construct teletransmission towers, thus solving the communication problem of local farmers in an area covering several dozen square kilometers. The improved communication network has boosted the sales coordination of agricultural by-products. Animal husbandry has also benefited from this communication network since veterinary aid is now available. New technology has been introduced to irrigate fields and to help dig wells to provide for the water needs of people and animals. She has also supplied farmers with good quality seeds, trees and sheep. New forestry and animal husbandry procedures have in turn greatly improved the habitat and ecology.

After eight years of Cheng's efforts, it is time for tourism development, for which the infrastructure has been laid. Invitations for investments in the tourism development of Erlong Mountain is underway — which will be a continuation of the village's poverty alleviation program.

Cheng's committed initiative has contributed to a greener environment, a better ecology and a higher standard of living for the people.

On Cheng's arrival at the village, there was no drinking water or electricity, and no road, but more than 20 school dropouts. About 90 percent of the village land was wasteland. There was no industry, not even a brick kiln. Poverty, misunderstandings and rumors created difficulties.

China

Purevsuren Choijamts

Purevsuren Choijamts, born in 1957, is a hydro-geologist who graduated from the Mongolian Technical University. In 2002 she founded the Nature and Women Center to work on ecological education and awareness. Purevsuren's nationwide project to bring in ecologically clean household fuel is considered very important both ecologically and economically. Purevsuren is an efficient organizer and promoter of small-business development in the poor Gobi areas, and has worked in collaboration with the World Bank for the benefit of herder families.

Born in the Khangai forest-steppe region, Purevsuren began by being very fearful of camels when she came to the Gobi desert region as a volunteer. But then she produced a pasture management map of the South Gobi aimak, which both local state administrations and livestock-breeding households use. She has reorganised the water management scheme in Gobi and other dry-climate regions within the framework of her Water-21 project. Being practically oriented, Purevsuren secured funds from Holland to repair wells in the South Gobi area and other dry-climate regions. There are more than 190,000 nomadic herder households in Mongolia, 86 percent of whom are economically poor, possessing less than 200 animals. With rapidly deteriorating forest cover, their situation is even more precarious. Purevsuren's training activities and organizational skills have helped these communities set up small business units producing and marketing different goods, many with the help of World Bank microloans. She has also helped to revive age-old local traditions of silver craftsmanship. The Nature and Women Center founded by Purevsuren works to improve ecological education and for the implementation of ecologically clean technologies. Purevsuren's new technology of pressed-coal fuel for rural and urban everyday household needs can also help to reduce air pollution in urban areas. "The State has virtually ceased to reach out to rural communities here. NGOs work hard, but they often face problems. Once a local head of administration said he would attend my training if only I paid him to do so." She feels the government only makes declarations on paper. In such circumstances Purevsuren's step of having persuaded ecology students to plant 3000 bushes in the national protection Bogdo-Uul area is doubly significant.

The emphasis on economic accumulation has meant that the natural environment in Mongolia is deteriorating faster than ever before. NGOs are trying to prevent this. The government has only made declarations on paper although its Green Wall program may mean some change.

Luz Perly Córdoba Mosquera

National Federation Union of Unitarian Farming
Arauca's Peasants Association

She lights up in the Colombian night; she is like a constantly erupting volcano: Luz Perly Córdoba Mosquera is a mother, peasant, student, trade union worker and a fighter for life. Committed to the core to the fight against the injustices suffered by her people, she is an international representative for her country. She never rests. She leads, organizes and manages collective efforts that work towards the fulfillment of a dignified life.

"I could not stand it anymore / Doing nothing / before my people's night, / I could not stand it anymore / And declared myself to be a fighter for life, / Renewing the hope / That they want to snatch from us." (Fragment of a poem by Kenny Rodríguez)

"My father taught me my first letters and, when the time came for me to go to school, he proved his love for me. There was no school in my village and because of that my father decided that we had to move to another village. We left our plot of land and moved away. He was not able to be a peasant anymore and became a factory worker again." Luz Perly Córdoba Mosquera is a woman of rural and indigenous origins. Her fight began when she was an adolescent campaigning for the rights of the Colombian rural workers. "What disconcerted me was that, in spite of the exploitation of petroleum in our region, we received no benefits, only more taxes to pay." This woman is a mother, a student, a trade union activist, a peasant, an ex-political prisoner, who has worked for the promotion and defense of integral human rights. She has developed community projects, given aid to political prisoners and she works untiringly for the organization of the peasant sector. This work has made her the target of State intolerance or victimization to the extent of needing protective measures from the OAS (Organization of the American States), Inter-American Commission on Human Rights. For her exceptional work, she was granted the Danish Peace Price, in 2004, as she was also granted a three month stay in prison. "As in other cases, the government treats those who fight for social change with prosecution in the courts." In spite of the political persecution and the humiliations she has suffered, she has not given up her ideal: to see peace and social justice in Colombia.

Social injustice marks the life of the Colombian people. In the face of any type of popular organization, the institutionalized violence practiced by the government of president Álvaro Uribe Vélez, with its policy for 'democratic security,' worsens. The violation of human rights is permanent.

Colombia

Nuria Costa Leonardo

National Network of Rural Women

When Nuria Costa Leonardo was 13 years old, she helped in her father's publishing house. She learned to work hard, to value her independence and to be firm in her judgments. With the richness of her background, she went to the mountains at the age of 19 and lived in rural Mexican communities for the next 20 years. She made close contact with the women of the countryside. She has been fighting by their side, day after day, since then.

Her father was a Catalan exile, her mother a Guatemalan woman. She was born in the spirit of the 1960s. At age 19, she abandoned her studies of Economy and decided to live in the Oaxaca jungle, in the South of the country, along with other companions from the Mexican National Autonomous University. She stayed there for nine years. During that time she had a son. She experienced the military repression and founded a school for superior studies, a combination of work, solidarity and conviction towards the indigenous communities. This was her formal schooling, and the schooling for the many others that, later on, became popular leaders.

She stayed for another nine years in the North of the country, in Durango, where she made her first contact with the women who would become the center of her activities. For more than 30 years, she has been working to achieve justice for the rural areas. "People must turn back to the countryside; it is the only way to attain an appreciation of life. Our society looks down on women as well as on the rural areas. We urgently need to retrieve dignity for them and for the rural people."

Today she lives in Mexico City, traveling continuously across the country, holding workshops and having meetings with women from the National Network of Rural Women. She developed the proposal of a social bank, with and for women. "Our idea has nothing to do with the credit perversion that happened in other places. For us, it is a means, not a goal. The main thing is that women should organize and mobilize themselves. They should solve their problems together and have a happy life."

The Mexican countryside is rife with poverty, injustice, inequalities, racism and repression. Women live in the hardest conditions. "Their self-esteem is damaged, but, at the same time, the female peasants have a great desire for knowledge and a lot of initiative."

Mexico

Hena Das

Bangla Mohila Parishad

When Hena Das (born 1924) was barely 13, she joined the struggle for independence against then-undivided India's British rulers. That was the beginning of a lifelong struggle against every form of injustice. Although best known for her pioneering work in the field of gender justice, she has also been deeply involved with the communist party, farmers' rights, teachers' rights, and labor rights. At a time when stepping out of the home was virtually prohibited to women, Hena was enunciating women's empowerment and the rights of women.

Hena Das was born into a well-known and well-off zamindar (landlord) family in Sylhet, Bangladesh. Despite some opposition from her mother, she completed her bachelors, her bachelor of education and her masters with no great difficulty. Hena, politically active through school and college, was only 13 when she joined the anti-British-rule movement in the Indian subcontinent. In 1942, she joined the communist party of East Pakistan, and became involved in farmers' and trade union movements. Given the political mise-en-scene, she had to work underground, but her resistance led to the abolition of the agricultural slavery system and the zamindari system.

Hena's deep involvement with human rights and dignity is reflected in her range of involvement: she worked for the Language Movement in 1952, designed to get Bangla recognized as a state language in Bangladesh's fledgling struggle for independence from Pakistan. In 1960, she moved to Dhaka where, as a high school assistant teacher, she became deeply engaged with the teacher's movement. A decade later, she formed the Bangladesh Mohila Parishad with other like-minded women.

As one of the pioneers of the Bangladesh women's movement, Hena has been working on awareness-building and empowerment of women for more than 60 years, founding many movements for women's rights. She remains the driving force behind Bangla Monila Parishad, the largest women's human rights organization in the country. Intensely focused and continuing to work at the grassroots, her greatest gift is her abiding faith in the ability of people to better themselves and the world around them. "I have been fighting all my life," she says. "This society is not the society I dreamt of. We have won some battles. But there is much we have yet to achieve."

The independence struggles — first against the British, and then against Pakistan — were fraught with peril for the politically active such as Hena. Bangladesh was a feudal society, where agricultural slavery and conservatism were rampant, and women had no access to spaces outside the home.

Nanda Rani Das

Jharabarsha Women's Landless Organization

Nanda Rani Das (born 1960) is much of many things — women's rights activist, mobilizer of the landless, an ideal of courage and integrity. For more than 24 years, ignoring her own hand-to-mouth existence, she has been organizing landless people to regroup for their rights. Fighting corruption in its every den, she was the first to bring up the issue of land rights for minority community women at the local level.

Nanda Rani Das was the only child of a low-caste but landed Hindu family. When she was barely ten years old, some relatives married her off to a 37-year-old, once-married compulsive gambler. In 1982, the couple moved to Jharabarsha, where Nanda serendipitously met an activist from the NGO Nijera Kori (which means doing it ourselves), and became involved in community welfare activities. Over time, she became increasingly concerned with, and vocal about, women's status in the village, the underbelly of superstition, and religious fanaticism. She organized a mass movement against corruption by some government officials, a movement that proved to be the watershed of her mobilization of the landless to fight for their rights.

One of the most crucial elements of her work centers round her concern for the hereditary property entitlements of women from the minority community. National debates on the issue are ongoing, but Nanda was the first to take it up at the local level. As it spread rapidly through landless people's organizations, it became a nationwide focal issue.

For the past 24 years, Nanda's work has been the focus of her life. She has had to bear the brunt of reactionary fundamentalist forces and the influential land-grabbers in her village, who managed to usurp the land on which she was living. She has received several death threats and has had false cases filed against her. Meanwhile, she and her family are scraping by. In every sense, Nanda is more than the sum of her substantial achievements, a symbol of the best in all of us.

Corruption, dowry, child marriage, and denial of land rights to women persist in Bangladesh. With the landless existing on the margins of society, their livelihoods and rights at the mercy of resurgent fundamentalist forces and land sharks, an equitable constitution means little.

Bangladesh

Lenira Maria de Carvalho

Sindicato dos Empregados Domésticos da Região Metropolitanado Recife

Lenira Maria de Carvalho (1932), in her childhood, had to take care of children instead of playing with dolls. Just like her mother, she faced a working day of 12 hours in exchange for food and a place to sleep. She did not put with that situation. Along with other young women, she took on the task of increasing awareness in the districts of Recife. In 1988, she founded a Union that provides judicial support to 50 maids per day.

For over 50 years, Lenira Maria de Carvalho has pursued ideals to conquer rights for domestic workers. Lenira was born in a sugar-cane plantation farm inside Alagoas. Her mother worked in the big house, the farm owner's house. Without a father and with no house to call her own, she shared a bed with her mother and sister and she ate left-over food. "My mother worked her whole life and never saw any money." Lenira moved to Recife, when she was 14, to work as a maid for her mother's boss' son. She managed to enroll in a night school run by nuns, where she concluded elementary school. Her awakening to militancy occurred when she was 24 years old and attended meetings at the Juventude Católica Operária (JCO) — a group of young catholic manual workers.

As a missionary in the JCO, Lenira helped organize state and regional meetings. In 1964, with the military coup, came the repression. She was taken into prison. After, she continued mobilizing maids. In the 1970s, she founded the category's association. She traveled to other states and met many leaders to make sure that their rights would be recognized in the 1988 Brazilian Constitution. "We got the right to vacation, to receive prior warning before getting fired, to be paid a 13th salary at the end of each year and to continue getting paid during maternity leave.

Lenira and her partners inaugurated the Domestic Worker's Union in Recife, which sees about 7000 people a year. She was elected president of the Union. She also wrote a textbook called 'The Social Value of Domestic Work.' Now, 72 years old, she is tireless. Currently, she fights to be able to give domestic workers the right to their own house and to a fair retirement.

According to data from the Brazilian Institute of Geography and Statistics (Igbe), there are more than five million domestic workers in Brazil, most of them are women. Only in Recife, there are 109,000 professionals, 101,000 are women and 8000 are men.

Brazil

Gulnara Derbisheva

Insan-Leylek
Babushka Adoption Fund

Gulnara Derbisheva (born 1968) is a human rights activist who lives in one of the poorest regions of Kyrgyzstan. She is committed to helping the unemployed, destitute and elderly people of rural Kyrgyzstan through her work with two funds that serve as lifelines for many. Gulnara is active in local government and community affairs, and reaches out to the media to bring attention to the problems of her region. She is also a tireless advocate for the removal of landmines along the border territories. More than 100 civilians have been killed by these deadly mines, including friends and colleagues.

Over the last ten years, Gulnara Derbisheva has been on a mission to bring peace and opportunity to the rural poor of her native country of Kyrgyzstan. She is involved with two funds designed to overcome poverty, educate, and protect the rights and interests of the people of the Kyrgyz Republic who live on the brink of extreme poverty. As executive director of Insan-Leylek, an NGO focusing on the rural poor, unemployed women, youth, and teachers in the area, she is an educator and human rights activist, working each day for the creation of a civil society in the region. Realizing a desperate need to reach out to the elderly men and women of the area, Gulnara was instrumental in bringing the Babushka Adoption fund to Batken. This NGO offers social support and aid through a program which finds sponsors to "adopt" elderly "babushkas" (grannies) and "dedushkas" (grandpas) living in extreme poverty.

Gulnara is also a passionate advocate dedicated to the removal of the dangerous landmines still buried along the border territories. These mines are the result of mine-laying by Uzbek soldiers in 1999 and 2000 after 300 militants tried to seize the Ferghana Valley. In one mine-affected area, there are two or three mine explosions every month. Gulnara has lost ten colleagues along the Uzbek-Kyrgyz border due to the blasts of these deadly weapons. With the help of local authorities, government representatives, local farmers, citizens, and the world community, she successfully is bringing attention to this dangerous problem plaguing her country. "There were real difficulties, when local authorities exerted pressure on me during the monitoring of the elections, threatening physical violence," Gulnara recalls. "When I walked along the mined fields with the employees of the frontier posts, without knowing where the mines were buried. That was difficult."

In the Batken region of the Kyrgyz Republic, the unemployment rate is 66 percent, and 88 percent of the population lives below the poverty level. Many of the unemployed young people in the area are vulnerable to the influence of Islamic extremist propaganda and often join Islamic militant organizations.

Kyrgyzstan

Mama Koité Doumbia

Union Nationale des Travailleurs du Mali (UNTM)
Femnet, The African Women's Development and Communication Network

Mama Koité Doumbia, born in Thiès, Senegal, in 1950, holds a higher diploma in youth training. She is particularly well-known for her long support of union causes and her determination to find ways to re-inforce the capacities of national women's NGOs in the area of training, speaking, communication, and leadership. She is married and has five children. And she says: "My dream is to fight against social injustice, especially when it is directed against women."

Madame Mama Koité Doumbia is known both nationally and internationally. She is the president of Femnet, the African Women's Development and Communication Network. Her election was due to her long experience in teaching and as a union leader in Mali. Mama Koité knew how to persuade African women because of her union experiences. Since her election as a president she has mobilized Malian women to familiarize themselves with the objectives of the network and to make concrete suggestions. This was not in vain if you look at the results she obtained.

Mama Koité is a member of the National Union of Education and Culture of Mali (SNEC) affiliated to the central Union of the Workers of Mali (UNTM). For about 20 years, she has fought for human rights in Mali and in Africa. The tireless woman with many family responsibilities and a modest income fights vehemently against social injustice and violence and supports peace. The defense of workers' and women's rights is part of her cause.

Mama Koité negotiates, creates awareness, informs, and educates in her everyday work. Her primary concern is to find ways to promote the well-being of both the Malian and African community. On the whole, she fights for a better world without violence.

Galina Drebezova

Grazhdansky soyuz antibankrotnykh menedzherov (Gsam)
Byelorusskaya Assotsyatsya zhenshchin-yuristov (Bazy)

Galina Drebezova (born 1950) has worked as a lawyer for many years. In 1995 she headed the local branch of the Association of Women Lawyers in Brest, and was later to be elected its national chairwoman. She leads a major movement to protect the human rights of Byelorussian citizens. It was Galina who uncovered the rigged results of the referendum on the amendments to the Constitution (1996). Heading the Civil Union of Anti-Bankruptcy Managers (Bazy), she has earned the reputation of an excellent crisis manager. She is a deputy of the parliament.

In Galina Drebezova's office, there is a map garnished with little flags like those depicting actions on a battlefield. They indicate some 500 Byelorussian cities, remote villages and towns which Galina, together with her fellow lawyers, has visited in the past ten years. She travels on her own initiative, in her own car, to provide legal assistance to the citizens of her country, to hold lectures, and to initiate discussions on the most topical problems in present-day Belarus. She helps senior citizens complete all the paperwork necessary to receive their pensions. She provides consultations to simple citizens on state-benefit issues, on employment contracts, and on a wide range of everyday problems. This benevolent work, compensated for only by personal satisfaction, is of extremely vital importance in Belarus where a large portion of the population is poorly informed on the legal procedures to be taken in defending their political and economic rights.
Together with the rights of individuals, Galina is also active in the field of crisis management, helping out Byelorussian enterprises and their workers.
A very beautiful woman, Galina Drebezova radiates warmth and a magnetic attraction that draws people to her and cheers them up. In return, they give her their support. Galina has been elected to parliament, where she keeps on protecting people's rights, making her contribution to the building of civil society in Belarus, the country which is often called the last dictatorship in Europe.

Galina leads a huge effort in the field of human rights, helping youth, women, senior citizens, and disabled persons to defend their rights. She has been persecuted by the Byelorussian authorities for uncovering the rigged results of the referendum on the amendments to the Constitution (1996).

Belarus

Duiji

Duiji (born 1942) has single-handedly changed the face of an entire village. She mobilized her community against caste-based oppression and injustice. Her efforts have led to a drastic reduction in atrocities against the Kol community. Caste-based sexual violence is practically nonexistent in her village now, and the tribals are no longer afraid of approaching the police and courts for redress. The literacy rates have shot up and the women participate more actively in community affairs.

Duiji, an illiterate Kol tribal from Uttar Pradesh, saw such terrifying excesses of poverty and oppression in her childhood and youth that even today the pain is starkly etched on her face. No matter how hard and long they worked, they could not afford a square meal a day. Duiji gradually began to protest against extremely low payments for backbreaking work. She spoke to fellow laborers. After a prolonged face-off between the laborers and landowners, the latter agreed to pay the workers five kilos of food grain. In 1998, Duiji finally found an anchor in the Mahila Samakhya. Her association with the organization opened her eyes to many issues of rights and the law, and to the tremendous exploitation under which her community labored. She began to speak to the Kols in the village, and her efforts have led to a drastic reduction in atrocities against the community. These adivasis (indigenous people) are no longer scared of approaching police stations and the courts to demand their rights. Sexual violence by the upper-castes against Kol women is practically nonexistent in the village. Duiji has arranged for handpumps, and the women received a 15-day training course on how to repair them. Furthermore, most children now attend school.

The community's economic situation is also much improved. Duiji stays updated on various welfare schemes for the old and the handicapped, and helps people access welfare schemes that the government periodically announces. She has also come to understand the Byzantine laws of the land, and various government programs. She processes this information, and uses it to raise awareness among the tribal people.

There is something awe-inspiring in an illiterate tribal woman, struggling to survive, yet almost single-handedly changing the face of an entire village.

Agricultural laborers in India are an unorganized group, illiterate, unaware of their rights, and paid a pittance for backbreaking work. The laborers are usually from the "lower" castes or tribals like Duiji, who are twice repressed: on the basis of their class and their caste identities.

India

Bilquis Edhi

Bilquis Edhi Foundation Trust
Abdul Sattar Edhi Foundation
International Relief Foundation

Bilquis Edhi (born 1947) is synonymous in Pakistan with patience, farsighted-ness, compassion, and integrity. Through the Bilquis Edhi Foundation Trust, which Bilquis set up with her husband, she has established 17 homes for children and women, where more than 4000 children and 250 women live. She provides the women with legal assistance and counseling, and the children with career options and training.

The family of Bilquis Edhi moved to Pakistan after the subcontinent's par-tition. Following matriculation, Bilquis trained as a nurse, and joined a nursing school set up by Abdul Sattar Edhi, who was deeply concerned about the state of reproductive health in Pakistan. Here, Bilquis and Abdul decided to marry. Since 1966, they have been working together in their humanitarian assistance projects.

Bilquis works primarily with women and children, for whom she has established 17 homes so far, including homes for children and women, an adoption center, a shelter for victims of violence, a home for the elderly, a home for mentally challenged children, and maternity and nursing care homes. Bilquis, in fact, places empty cradles outside each Edhi center, so that people can leave their unwanted children there instead of stoning them to death or dumping them on rubbish heaps, as is the practice. Bilquis also personally oversees the adoption process to ensure the greatest care in placing babies, and a smooth transition. She reaches out with a compassion born of experience to women who have been abused. Bilquis gives them counseling and legal assistance. She also encourages the children in her charge to obtain training and adopt careers so that they can be independent.

It was a given fact that her work would bring Bilquis powerful enemies, who have threatened to kill her and the women who seek shelter in the Trust's homes. The Pakistani people, however, repose enormous faith in the Edhi Trusts, and liberal donations pour in from ordinary people-money, food, clothing, and medicines. They know that the money will be honestly used to the best possible public benefit.

Women comprise 48 percent of Pakistan's population. The country has a high fertility rate (four births per woman). Maternal mortality is 350 to 500 per 100,000 births; infant mortality is 123 per 1000 live births. Female literacy rates are about 42 percent, and are even lower in rural areas.

Qionghua Fan

Fangguang Village, Xujia Town, Peng'an County, Sichuan Province

Fan Qionghua (40) is the first female party secretary in Fangguang Village, Xujia Town, Peng'an County, Sichuan Province. The village is a poverty-stricken place where fights within families frequently occur. While arbitrating a family dispute, Fan persuaded a young couple to find jobs in the city. Since then she has shouldered the responsibility of taking care of the children of such families and is known as "Mother Fan."

In Fangguang Village, which has a population of more than 600, the arable land per capita is only a little over 50,000 square meters. The villagers lived in very poor conditions. In order to alleviate poverty, Fan Qionghua encouraged young adults to leave the village and seek work elsewhere. Parents then entrusted their children to Fan and left. Since 1998 she has taken care of 36 children aged from 10 to 18.

It has not been easy. Once a girl caught a fever and Fan carried her eight kilometers to the hospital in heavy rain. She was so tired when she arrived at the hospital that she fainted. One set of parents have not been heard of since they left. Fan has spent more than 6000 yuan on their two children. She keeps the children in school, feeds them and keeps them warm, and never asks for any material reward for her work.

Her love for the children she has raised has been compensated in a spiritual way — 17 of her children were admitted to junior middle school, 12 to senior high school, and five to colleges. Fan Qionghua, known as "Mother Fan" in the village, says, "The biggest compensation for me is to see the children entering colleges and achieving great things." Mother Fan has successfully improved the living conditions in this poor village.

Fangguang Village is a mountainous area with lots of rocks and slopes. The villagers are very poor. To relieve their poverty, many parents have their daughters married far away. Young adults go out to look for jobs, leaving many children unattended.

China

Kulsoom Farman

Aga Khan Rural Support Program (AKRSP)

When Kulsoom Farman (born 1957) started working for women's development in her native Baltisan — a mountainous and desperately poor region of Pakistan — a fatwa was issued by a religious leader asking people not to cooperate with her. Today, Kulsoom is a role model for women in this intensely patriarchal society. She has played a vital part in bringing women out of their homes for education and employment, for the betterment of their own lives and that of the community.

When Kulsoom Farman took up a job with the Aga Khan Rural Support Program (AKRSP) in 1986, she became the first woman in Baltistan to be formally employed in a full-time job by an NGO. Her job — to promote the empowerment of her region's women — was by no means easy, since women were the most deprived members of a community surviving through subsistence farming. When Kulsoom began her work, the women did not have the confidence to speak freely, let alone work outside the home. Kulsoom initially met with stiff resistance from both men and women. Over time, she networked with politicians, religious leaders, community leaders, and the women. As a local, she understood the reality, and devised a pragmatic program for women's development. She focused on promoting health and hygiene, and helped women run small businesses, and form their own organizations, nudging them toward literacy and vocational training.

Today, more than 6000 women have been trained in agricultural work and livestock and poultry rearing, and have participated in forestry, adult literacy, and vocational training programs. Almost 2000 women have participated in conferences, learning about life beyond Baltistan. Kulsoom has facilitated the formation of 476 women's organizations with more than 12,000 members. Recently, on a new assignment as a poverty coordinator, she helped more than 500 impoverished households take part in mainstream development activities.

Traveling to far-flung parts of Baltistan, usually in the company of male colleagues, Kulsoom has become a role model for women in the region. Parents are less inclined to prevent their daughters from seeking education. Within a short time of her starting out, other women began working with NGOs and government organizations. Today, some women are even willing to contest elections.

Baltistan, situated between the Indus and its tributaries, is one of Pakistan's financially feeblest regions. The per capita income is 14,000 rupees; 70 percent of its population are subsistence farmers, whose access to modern farming technology is denied by scare resources and topography.

Pakistan

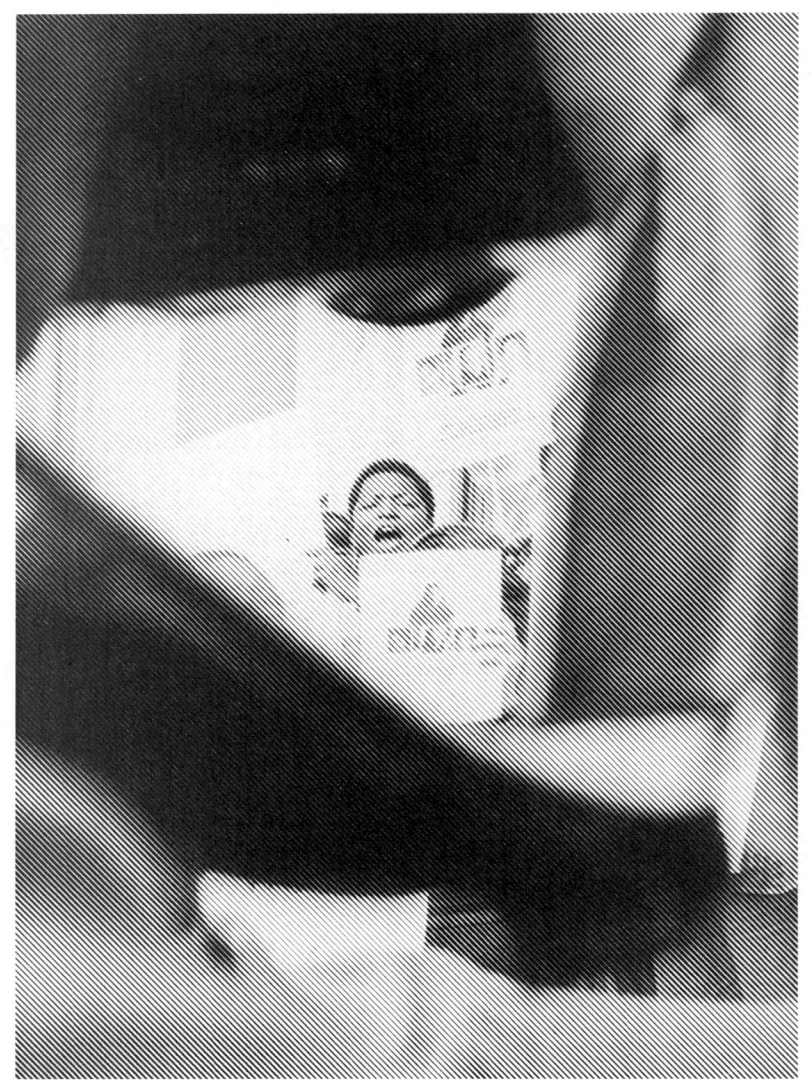

Juana Ferrer

Vía Campesina
Rural Women's National Confederation

Juana Ferrer (born in 1965) is a woman, and that, in itself, is a weight to carry and a reason to have to fight. That was enough reason for this Dominican woman to have to work from the age of 14 for land, for equality between men and women, for equality of resources and rights. She is an 'active' activist: she is an ecologist, a feminist and a fighter against violence, oppression and despoilment.

There is a woman who walks. She walks between the zinc roofs and the coffee of the poor earth. She is ebony: It is as if she was carved from an ebony tree to fight for her race, to fight for the land, to fight for women. There is a woman who fights. There is a Juana Ferrer. As the Afro-descendent woman that she is — and "la Negrita," as she is called — she wears her color with pride. Juana Ferrer sings and works. She has a husband, three children and the height of one and a half meters. She fights for the poor, for the peasants, for women, for the victims of violence, and for her race and color. Since she was 14 years old, she has walked through the Dominican Republic informing peasants and women about their rights. She was born 40 years ago, in Niza, 39 kilometres from Santo Domingo, the capital of the country. In her village, houses are made of zinc and wood and people work in agriculture. When people have neither rights nor opportunities to work the land, they have to organize themselves. Juana has organized herself. Since 1980, she has been a member of the National Peasant Confederation of Women of the Dominican Republic. Since 1992, she has been the general coordinator, in her country, of Vía Campesina (an international movement that, since 1992, has coordinated peasant organizations).

Once she went on a motorcycle, along with another companion, to a rural region. When they arrived, the police were waiting for them. "We had to turn back, to run, run and run in the midst of a hail of bullets." They escaped, jumping from a ravine.

The shots did not stop her. Her conviction has been, and still is today, strong. "Being a woman from a poor peasant family gives me the political and moral commitment to fight for the rights of our people, to fight for freedom and equality." Juana, "la Negrita," is still walking. The sun tests her, but it is hers.

The rural population of the Dominican Republic represents almost half of the total population. Agriculture is the main source of work and livelihood, but harvests have suffered losses from 30% up to 50%, and the people do not always own the land they work on.

Dominican Republic

Ediofelina Fuentes González

United Carrizalan Women

In 1962, when Ediofelina Fuentes González was 12 years old, she co-founded the organization United Carrizalan Women, for Panamanian peasant women from Carrizal. They raised funds with which to pay lawyers to defend people that had been imprisoned for land occupation. At age 17, she finished her primary education. She became a peasant woman "who ironed and sewed," and created a sewing workshop for the community. So that her fellow women could have an opportunity to study, she created a day care for their children. Thanks to her work, the community has drinking water, a school and latrines.

Ediofelina Fuentes González, known as Ilia, has separated parents. She was only one and a half years old when she was left to depend on her grandparents, who had limited resources. She became a rural worker at age 12, and, then, in 1962, she co-founded the organization United Carrizal Women. They raised funds with which to pay lawyers to defend people who, driven by misery and accused of being communists, were imprisoned for land occupation. Ediofelina created a community workshop where the women of her community could learn to sew — using sewing machines that she had obtained from Unicef. As there were so few doctors, she learned to apply injections. At age 15, she began primary school and created a day care so that other women could also have the opportunity to study. She got married two years later, on the same year that she finished school. She received her diploma while she held her first-born child in her arms. Thanks to her efforts, the Carrizal community got fresh drinking water, latrines and a school. She helped to build the school, making adobe blocks, carrying water from the river, and bringing sand from the beach. She also founded the House of Handcrafts, where women worked with natural elements. Due to this activity, the women of the community were able to improve their economy. Ilia had three children. The boy died as a young adult in an accident. Ilia fought to give a good education to her daughters. Both are teachers, the younger one is a University student. For her people, Ilia, the girl who was abandoned to the winds of fate, has been like a shining star of hope.

Since the beginning of the 20th century, Panama has been modernized around the zone of the inter-oceanic channel, leaving rural regions such as the administrative district of Veraguas, totally relegated to oblivion.

Panama

Raimunda Gomes da Silva

Conselho Nacional dos Seringueiros (CNS)

Raimunda Gomes da Silva (1944), 'dona Raimunda do Coco' (lady Raimunda of the Coconut), is respected for her leadership in the fight for the rights of female peasants and environment protection. Presently, she coordinates the Secretariat of the Rural Extractivist Woman, which gives courses about gender on politics and income-generating activities. Raimunda emphasizes the importance of babaçu (type of coconut) extractivism. She has been facing large landowners since the 1980s, when she began community work in Tocantins countryside.

Abandoned by her husband, with six young children to care for, Raimunda Gomes da Silva had survived working hard on another people's land, in the countryside of Maranhão, where she was born. On Sundays, a day of rest, she tried to find comfort in community meetings of the Pastoral of the Land, a progressist wing of the Catholic Church. There, she realized that many female peasants were discriminated at home and at work. "I used to see the suffering of poor and illiterate women: single and married women, their sons and daughters, kids abandoned by their father." Her spirit of leadership, that would make her known allover Brazil, was awakening.

In 1979, she moved to Sete Barracas, in the North of Tocantins, where her brother had some land. 52 families lived there, threatened by squatters. Supported by the Pastoral of the Land, Raimunda founded the Union of Rural Workers. In spite of the distance between the communities, she gathered 552 members. "In 1985, we were evicted from our land by police officials. We had no food or place to live." With the Union's help they were able to recover the land. However, the conflict escalated. One year later, catholic priest Josimo Tavares, an important ally of the rural workers, was murdered. Raimunda traveled to many cities to denounce the crime. She went back home as a well known figure allover the country. Even facing threats, she kept on fighting. In 1988, she participated in the creation of the Peasant Federation of Tocantins. She gathered women and founded, in 1992, an association of coconut breakers aiming to improve the productivity of the extractivism and handicraft. In 1995, Raimunda became the coordinator of the Secretariat of the Rural Extractivist Woman, which gives assistance to about 8000 women from eight Amazonic States.

In Brazil, about 16,000 women survive selling babaçu coconuts. The palm trees grow in the Amazon Forest and in the same semi-arid land of the Northeast. The entire fruit is used: the coconut is used to make hammocks, carpets, handicraft, the straw is used to cover houses.

Brazil

Lidia Grafova

Forum pieriesielienchieskikh organizatsyi (FPO)

Lidia Grafova, a Moscow journalist, has been active in providing help to forced migrants since the ethnic conflict in Azerbaijan triggered a wave of refugees. She heads the NGO Forum pieriesielienchieskikh organizatsyi (Forum of Migrants' Organizations), cooperating with a wide range of international organizations in the same field. She also directs the news agency Migratsiya, which advocates for migrants' rights by informing the public. She often travels to Chechen refugee camps in the Caucasus and regularly visits Beslan to provide psychological assistance to the victims of terrorism.

In 1990, when the first waves of Armenian refugees — forced to leave Baku (Azerbaijan) after the ethnic clashes — arrived in Moscow, Lidia Grafova successively published articles trying to attract the attention of the authorities to this humanitarian problem. The situation of these homeless people with neither the means to earn a living nor prospects for the future, was constantly growing ever more tragic. Meanwhile, the Soviet government was both grossly inept and absolutely incapable of coping with the refugee problem. Continuing to write about the refugees in the press seemed pointless, yet Lidia could not forget the suffering of these people. So she launched the NGO Grazhdanskaya pomoshch (Civic Aid), the first NGO in Russia whose goal was to help refugees. The NGO closely cooperates with the Russian Red Cross, Caritas Moscow, and other humanitarian organizations. In 1996, the NGO Forum pieriesielienchieskikh organizatsyi (Forum of Migrants' Organizations) was created as an umbrella for more than 200 migrants' associations in 43 regions of Russia. Lidia has headed the Forum since its very beginning. Because of her passionate efforts to help the refugees in Russia, Lidia's friends often refer to her as the Refugees' Mamma.

In 2000, Lidia set up the news agency Migratsiya to provide wide news coverage on all aspects of migration and refugee issues. In the course of the past 15 years, she has published some 400 articles in Russian and foreign newspapers defending the cause of migrants. Lidia's tireless work as an organizer of humanitarian aid projects, coupled with her journalistic activities, has greatly contributed to raising awareness of migration issues in Russian society and to the shaping of Russia's migration policy in a compassionate manner.

Lidia Grafova fights to protect the rights of refugees and migrants all over the Russian Federation. She travels to the Caucasus region organizing humanitarian aid to people who were forced out of their homes and who have suffered from political and ethnic armed conflicts.

Russian Federation

Jagan Suba Gurung

As a single woman seeking higher education and working for the improvement of women's lives, Jagan Suba Gurung stands out in her Gurung community village. Her involvement in women's empowerment and community development has made her an icon for societal alteration in a largely conservative social setting.

In 1990, when Jagan Suba Gurung began working with her community's women, they would not step out of their homes in the evening and at night to attend her adult literacy classes. It was an uphill task for her to launch such revolutionary programs in Ghndruk, a Gurung village located in the Annapurna Conservation Area, a protected area rich in environmental and cultural diversity.

Much, though, has changed over the decade. Jagan's work, which involves appraisals, home visits, organizing meetings, and adult literacy classes, has made a difference. Women are able to make crucial decisions about their lives; children's health and education have improved; mothers are aware of the value of nutritious food, reproductive health issues, and ambient hygiene. Organic farming and the filtering of water to make it potable have entered their lives.

Jagan herself runs a guesthouse together with her sister and sister-in-law. She has done her intermediate course in economics from an institution affiliated to Nepal's Tribhuvan University, and is doing a Bachelors degree in hotel management from Pokhara University. She has also been invited to give talks and presentations abroad.

It took a long time for the male elite in her community to recognize her achievements. Her outspokenness, confidence, and tendency to question conflict issues have not endeared her to the Maoists either.

Nepal's conservative Gurung community is surrounded by dogmatic Maoist ideologues who have little concern for those who question the rationale for constant conflict. Development, including women and children's health and education, has taken a consequent beating.

Nepal

Roma Pauline Guy

San Francisco State University
Women's and Girls Network
California Women's Agenda

Roma Pauline Guy, a social justice activist and policy leader in public health, women's rights, poverty, and homelessness, has worked all her adult life to improve conditions for women. She helped found the San Francisco Women's Building, and developed community-based institutions including a battered women's shelter and a family resource center. Coauthor of "Historical Perspectives on Homelessness, The Police and the Homeless", she has helped to redefine housing as a public health issue and has developed an innovative curriculum at San Francisco State University.

Roma is the eldest child of a rural Franco-American working-class family of eight children living on the US/Canadian border. She was educated in public schools and universities (University of Maine, Orono, Maine; Wayne State University, Detroit, Michigan) and worked for nine years in the West African countries of Ivory Coast, Togo, Niger, and Mali.

Beginning in middle school, Roma learned what it takes to transform an idea into collective action. Whether it was organizing peers into softball and basketball school yard games, creating a history club, or leading antiwar groups, Roma began early to develop skills that would help her bridge the racial, ethnic, and socioeconomic divides that often plague US women's rights efforts.

In 1995, Roma and several longtime women's and human rights leaders formed the California Women's Agenda, where she advocates for universal culturally and linguistically competent healthcare and reproductive rights. Roma focuses on the socioeconomic justice relationships of wealth and poverty: land use/taxation and community building/democracy. She protests wars of occupation and the consequences of displacement resulting in homelessness, criminalizing immigrant populations, and worldwide sexual slavery. She advocates for human rights priorities in electoral politics, especially universal healthcare, equality and safety in public education, and affordable housing. She has consistently challenged racism and class privilege within the women's movement and has struggled to make the movement inclusive and part of a broadening human rights agenda. In higher education at San Francisco State University, she has developed innovative curricula that link values, skills, and public accountability.

Working on the frontlines, Roma's position is often a precarious one. Despite slanderous attacks, physical assault, low income, and social marginalization, she has embraced a life that benefits her community and her world.

United States of America

Fatma Hamisi Misango

Songea District Council
Songea Legal Aid Program (Soplu)

Fatma Hamisi Misango was born in 1961 in the poor and neglected Songea District in south western Tanzania. She is a district counsellor and coordinator of a legal aid program in the district. She is engaged in governance issues, legal aid to women and children, particularly those orphaned by HIV/Aids, income generation and political participation. As a result of her work, women's participation in the civil society in Songea has increased, and they have started their own initiatives to help widows of HIV/Aids.

Fatma Misango is a coordinator of Songea Legal Aid Program. Educated to secondary school level, she has built formal and informal networks. She belongs to the Sahiba Sisters Foundation, a network of Muslim women engaged in development. Other affiliations are the Tanzania Gender Network, the Intermediary Gender Network and Songea Counsellors and Women in Enterprise. "She values mass support and has made extensive networks with religious and community leaders and local government officials," says a colleague who knows her well.

Songea District is one of the least developed areas in Tanzania, but its location on the borders to Malawi and Zambia offers countless opportunities for women and youth in cross-border trading, agriculture and development linkages. As a result of Fatma Misango's work, the participation of women in the civil society has increased. The women have begun initiatives to help widows of HIV/Aids and a legal aid scheme. "Fatma knows how to involve others in development activities," says the colleague. "She has been instrumental in networking seven community groups and promotes the inclusion of more women in training."

Fatma Misango addresses culture and religion issues, often contradicting religious leaders who feel that she wants to question religious authorities. Perhaps her greatest challenge is motivating women in believing they can improve their lives. They face many problems as a result of oppressive laws and customs, as well as discrimination and hunger. She wants to make a difference in women's lives; to better their lives. This is her driving force.

Songea District, the south western part of Tanzania, is one of the poorest regions of the country. Its location makes it invisible in national development priorities. There is low investment and minimal presence of international donors in the region.

United Republic of Tanzania

"I know that securing women's rights in Afghanistan will be a long process. But I am confident that with diligent collaborative efforts of dedicated men and women we can overcome all challenges."

Palwasha Hassan

Afghan Women's Education Center (AWEC)
Afghan Women's Network (AWN)
UN Assistance Mission to Afghanistan's Gender Network (UNAMAGN)

Palwasha Hassan, born in 1969 in Kabul, Afghanistan, obtained a BSc in the Science Program from a government-run college in Islamabad, Pakistan. She is the founder of the Afghan Women's Education Center, a well-established Afghan women's organization. She is also a cofounder of the Afghan Women's Network. As the representative of Rights & Democracy in Afghanistan, Palwasha Hassan is the first Afghan woman to head an NGO in Afghanistan since the establishment of the new interim government in 2001.

Palwasha Hassan has been part of the nucleus of a growing women's movement in Afghanistan. The challenges and improvements relating to the expansion of the Afghan Women's Network are very hard to articulate in tangible terms. These challenges are often subtle, evolving processes that gradually encourage a strengthened relationship across many ethnic, religious, and cultural boundaries. Long-term improvements as a direct result of her work are reflected in the many grassroots women's organizations and projects that received funds to survive, thanks to her efforts. The beneficiaries of Palwasha Hassan's works are destitute Afghan women and their families who are either unemployed, funded by grants from her organization or impoverished students and community members. She supports a large number of local NGOs in Afghanistan. Among these are organizations promoting the rights of women, gender equality and the empowerment of women. They also include human rights organizations that focus on an agenda of women's human rights, newly established organizations with projects directed towards the advancement of women's financial conditions in partnership with, or under the umbrella of, an existing, established organization and initiatives aimed at linking and networking activities.

Palwasha Hassan's main area and context of work is the empowerment of potential women leaders, human rights and women's rights in Afghanistan. She is dedicated to helping destitute Afghan women and their families, who are either unemployed or impoverished students and community members.

Afghanistan

Rosa María Herrera de Hernandez

Salud para Guayana (Health for Guayana)

She has been a worker since her adolescence and she, herself, has experienced exploitation. A youth activist and promoter of human rights, Rosa María Herrera was born in Mexico, and now she works with and for women from poor Venezuelan communities: they support preventive health projects, create groups for developing ways of improving their quality of life and work for the right to a dignified life.

She was born in 1945, in Zacatecas, Mexico. She was the second daughter of ten brothers and sisters. Her father was an agriculturist and her mother a seamstress. "I grew up in a solid family, where there was a lot of respect and parents whose example was vital." She had basic education but the family resources were not enough for her to continue her schooling. Her father lost his job. In 1962, she and her sister went to Mexico City. The day after they arrived, they were both hired to work in a dress factory. "I have been a worker since my adolescence and have experienced exploitation for myself: ten working hours a day, 56 hours per week, for a miserable salary. I lived with many other girls and boys that were experiencing the same reality and I knew that I belonged to the working class."

A militant since 1965, she was nominated as national coordinator of the organization Young Working Catholics (JOC). In 1970, three years later, she was elected coordinator for Latin America. "I always say that the JOC was my school and that the experience there made me a committed person for the rest of my life."

Love took her to Venezuela. In 1975, she married a militant worker and adopted his nationality. She began to work for women's rights in the Feminine Popular Circles in the Community Education and in Health for Guayana (Sapagua). In Sapagua she worked promoting health, for the improvement of women's quality of life and for the exercise of their rights. "There are fewer opportunities for women. They are trapped by the burden of looking after the family and that narrows their vision and makes them less likely to look towards other areas for their personal development. Poverty is a problem that particularly affects women. "Each day I am more and more convinced that we have to work hard so that the face of poverty will not be the one of woman."

Like the rest of Latin America, the reality of the situation in Venezuela is that wealth is distributed in such a way that there is a deep gulf between rich and poor. People die of hunger. The Venezuelan revolutionary process provides a good possibility of confronting social injustice.

Venezuela

Jianjun Hong

Women's Federation, Chifeng City, Inner Mongolia

Hong Jianjun, deputy president of Chifeng City Women's Federation in Inner Mongolia since 1998, has worked hard to help the women in this disaster-ridden region to fight poverty and improve their income. Apart from skills training to enable the women to find jobs outside, she also helped them with building women's groups and networks.

Hong Jianjun demonstrates strong gender consciousness in her work, fighting for the women's rights and those of other minority groups. She also uses various means to increase the self-confidence of women so that they can improve their lives by mutual support. Hong has a spirit of total devotion to her work, no matter how difficult it is. Responsible, consistent, and unafraid of taking risks, she encourages women farmers and pastoralists to work outside Inner Mongolia, where people are relatively conservative. There is continuous criticism, discouragement and pressure from people, including her colleagues, but she disregards all opposing opinions and pressures, and gradually people have become more open to this new phenomenon. More than 24,000 women have been introduced to outside work by the Women's Federation. Hong regularly goes to the pastoral areas to visit the families living there. She talks with the women and the officials, listening carefully to the women, the aged, the disabled and other minority groups, aiming to solve their problems. She is aware that women should raise their own consciousness and she leads them to work together voluntarily. This is her creative idea and work model to "build up a cooperative network and organization" among the women pastors and farmers. As of now, there are already 4146 women cooperative groups, 3330 group networks and 12 women mutual help groups being formed in the city. The number of women participating in these groups is around 86,000, and a total of 340,000 people have benefited. However, because of her dedication to work, Hong has little left to take care of her 80-year-old mother and her young daughter. She herself tends to fall ill.

Chifeng of Inner Mongolia is one of the 18 poorest regions of China with an adverse natural environment and a low living standard. People are conservative; it is difficult for them to adapt to new ideas, and working with them is even more difficult.

China

Chiu Hsiang Huang

Huang Chiu Hsiang was born in a tea farmers' family in the deep mountains of Hsin Chu County. Since 1987, she has been a key trade union leader and is a founding member of the Workers Party and the Labor Party. She has excellent communication and networking skills. She is committed to fighting gender discrimination, sexual harassment and violations of women workers' rights in factories and within trade unions, and opposing legal amendments to reduce protection of women workers.

Huang Chiu Hsiang was born in 1960. After she graduated from secondary school, she joined the artificial fiber factory of Taiwan's famous corporation, the Far East Textile Factory, situated in Hsinpu Township. There, she started shift duty work on production of artificial silk. From 1987 to 1989, she led the workers' movement in the post-White Terror period, particularly the Far East Factory Trade Union's strikes, and was deeply engaged in the autonomous workers' movements.

Founding member of the Workers Party and the Labor Party, and after 1989, as standing committee member, she was de facto leader of the entire Far East Factory Trade Union. She had also served as board member of the Taiwan Artificial Fiber Trade Union Federation. Huang is now board chair of the Women Workers Rights Promotion Association, deputy convener of the Labor Party Central Monitoring Committee, and advisor of Industrial Workers General Trade Union of Hsinchu County. She is good at conceptual communication and education, and in over a decade, has supported the autonomous development of many trade unions. She has also assisted networking among autonomous trade unions. Numerous trade union cadres and general members have been influenced by her and have joined the movement. Due to her long-term involvement in the trade union movement, she has been discriminated against and oppressed by the management, but she has persisted on this path.

Huang has been the most outstanding women workers' representative of the Taiwan autonomous movement after the lifting of the martial law.

In 1987, Taiwan lifted martial law. Workers' movements started in 1988 helping to develop class-consciousness, such as the strikes of the Far East Artificial Fiber Trade Union, the Taiwan Automobile Factory, the Miao-Li Transport Trade Union, and the Asian Cement Factory struggle.

China, Taiwan

Maya John Ingty

Diocesan Board for Participatory Development
Interdenominational Christian Women's Forum
Northeast Christian Council Women's Assembly

Maya John Ingty (born 1932) plays a unique role in the northeast, bringing together powerful Christian and secular organizations to work for peace. She is strongly driven by her conviction that working for social justice issues should not be determined by caste, creed, or religious persuasions. She also mobilizes the youth and women-through group discussions, skill-building, and alternative ideas for sustainable development for women-toward education and employment as a means of drawing people away from the pervasive culture of the gun.

Maya John Ingty, the first woman from the Karbi tribe to complete a masters degree, has been involved in social activities from her college days. Her appointment as an upper-level bureaucrat left her unsatisfied: she needed to be engaged with grassroots activities. In 1958, she quit her government job and joined the Union Christian College, where she mobilized a group of women and formed a women's association which conducted health programs, and started a primary school in the village.

Maya, who has been involved with people who work in conflict situations, is well-known in the region, and is often sought out for counseling. Her genuine warmth and outgoing personality make it easy for her to connect with people. She is also a respected member of the church, but that does not stop her from critiquing the church's regressive positions. Maya has been instrumental in pushing for greater commitment to social issues by the church, and involvement with other secular and non-Christian peace organizations. As secretary of the Diocesan Board for Participatory Development, she has undertaken programs to help young people develop self-employment skills, which she believes will lead them away from the gun culture. Maya has also been active in ecological and conservation programs. It was through her initiative that vermicomposting training was imparted in Tinsukia (Upper Assam) as part of an ecofriendly waste control program. Since then, many young people, trained in this process, have taken up organic farming.

With no skillset, and often without the support of a forum, Maya has been working single-mindedly with the marginalized in the villages since 1956.

For 30-odd years, several states in the Indian northeast have been torn by internal and state conflict. It has left the economy and society in a shambles-an astronomically high school and college dropout rate, and young widows left to fend for themselves and their young.

Sakhibakhon Irgasheva

Business Women's Association (BWA)
Mekhr
Open Society Institute

Sakhibakhon Irgasheva (born 1948) has headed the Kokand branch of the Business Women's Association (BWA) since 1994, which provides training, advice, and support to women in developing small and medium enterprises. From 1991 to 1994, she was chairperson of Nodira, an NGO working for the protection of mothers and children. She is vice chairperson of Mekhr, a women's forum in the Ferghana region. Sakhibakhon has played a significant role in supporting the establishment of over 60 NGOs in the Kokand area, in raising civic awareness and building civil society.

Sakhibakhon Irgasheva decided early on to devote her life to the protection of women's rights. Since 1991, she has headed the Kokand branch of the Business Women's Association (BWA), one of the first NGOs in the newly-established Republic of Uzbekistan. At that time, the idea of an NGO was received with hostility because the government viewed "non-governmental" as "anti-governmental." Since 1991, Sakhiba has managed to establish many NGOs in Kokand, a small city in the Ferghana Valley with a population of about 200,000. Currently, there are over 60 NGOs in the area, 30 of which are run by women. This is particularly noteworthy in a region like the Ferghana Valley in which Islamic traditionalism is severe and women are expected to be passive, subordinate, obliging, and obedient to men.

As an Open Society Institute National Board Member, Sakhibakhon has contributed greatly to the development of the general strategy of the women's movement in Uzbekistan. She personally assists women leaders in working out their NGO's strategies and the implementation of their projects. The BWA of Kokand focuses on six priorities: women's issues, civil society and local community, public health, youth, and environment. Since its establishment, the BWA has worked in close collaboration with a number of international donor organizations and implemented over ten large projects. The most significant impact of the BWA's activity is the organization, establishment, and development of NGOs run by and for women, such as the women's centers Kamolon, Mohlar Oyim, Family and Child, Adolat, and the Children's Puppet Theater Semurg. The creation of Mekhr, a women's forum in Ferghana Valley, was one of the significant steps in strengthening the status of rural women in society, releasing them from the feudal home-fortresses.

In Uzbekistan, 28 percent of the population lives in poverty. Chronic underemployment and a discouraging entrepreneurial business climate have resulted in unfavorable socio-economic conditions. Major health and education needs are not being met and environmental issues are plaguing the country.

Uzbekistan

Lazzat Ishmukhamedova

Ishenim Regional Partnership Network
Moldir Women's Association (MWA)

Lazzat Ishmukhamedova founded the Association of Single Mothers in 1993. In 1998, the association adapted an Indian model for poverty reduction, a self-help group concept. In 2001, the organization was renamed Moldir Women's Association (MWA). It has implemented 23 social projects with 10,000 people, including the Moldir Micro-Credit Organization. It also assists the establishment of other self-help federations in rural areas.

The founder of the Association of Single Mothers, Lazzat Ishmukhamedova is first of all a teacher at heart. She worked for several years teaching in a vocational school. Then, in the early 1990s, single mothers, widows, and divorced women with children were the most affected by the sudden unemployment after the collapse of the Soviet Union. In 1993, Lazzat lost her job. She resented the fact that educated women were not in demand. However, her son's birth that same year gave her inexhaustible energy, strength, inspiration, and renewal. It encouraged her to give birth to another baby: the Association of Single Mothers. The organization's mission was to support vulnerable families, give them hope in their social standing and to promote gender equality. In 1998, the association adapted an Indian model for poverty reduction, a self-help group concept. In 2001, the organization was renamed Moldir Women's Association (MWA). Today, the association is known inside and outside Kazakhstan. It provides support to NGOs in rural areas through training and sharing its experience in implementing the self-help concept. MWA unites thousands of poor families and helps them resolve their problems. So far, it has implemented 23 social projects with 10,000 beneficiaries and provided some financial assistance. Lazzat and the Association have received several awards for their work. She says, "I am filled with joy, satisfaction, and pride by everything the association has done: a support center for children from poor families, the Moldir Micro-Credit Organization, and the establishment of other self-help federations with the help of MWA."

Kazakhstan is one of the poorest countries in the world. The difficult economic situation is especially hard on women. In rural districts, Muslim traditions are usually so strong that single and divorced women have many limitations.

Kazakhstan

Janaki

Mahila Samakhya
Women's self-help group

Janaki (born 1954) is a symbol of power and possibilities for the women in her village. When she started, it was unusual for a woman to engage in developmental work, and she had to face bellicose opposition from her family. Janaki, though, is a determined, remarkably fearless woman: she continued with her mobilization of women, eventually forming a village self-help group. The work done by the group has helped establish its credibility and, today, most disputes in the village are settled in the group's women's court.

For Janaki, a chance encounter with the NGO Mahila Samakhya opened out a whole new world of perceptions. The concepts of women's rights and social development excited and moved the illiterate young woman. Janaki's husband, a physically abusive man, was strongly opposed to her work. Over time, Janaki gathered the courage to resist him, not only preventing him from abusing her, but also exhorting all other women in the village to resist physical violence by their husbands.

Janaki initially began work as a Sakhi (friend). She went on to set up a women's village self-help group. The good work that Janaki and her group have done has established their credentials: most disputes in the area now arrive at the self-help group's women's court for resolution. Although Janaki is a member of the Mahila Samakhya's women's court, she still believes in direct intervention and immediate action along with her women colleagues. Whether it is an issue of grabbing a Dalit's or a woman's land, they ensure that justice is delivered precisely and immediately.

Janaki is a determined, remarkably fearless woman, single-minded in her pursuit of justice, and incapable of intimidation by the many powerful people-including police officials-with whom she has clashed over the years. Police functionaries tend to take bribes and harass women in the self-help group. None of this fazed Janaki. She has proven that the capacity for social change is not linked to educational or other qualifications: to the women in her village, she is a symbol of power and possibilities.

When Janaki began working, it was unusual for women to engage in developmental work and awareness-raising activities. Today, most disputes in her region of influence are settled in the self-help group's women's court.

India

Alkaben Jani

Kutch Mahila Vikas Sangathan (KMVS)

Alkaben Jani's work in the Kutch area of Gujarat is informed by her intimate knowledge of the oppressive social fabric of the region. For the past 15 years, she has been extensively organizing, mobilizing, and training rural women, focusing on capacity-building and leadership training. The result of these efforts is the emergence of a strong and motivated team of 12,712 leaders at the community level, who are leading other women in the area to surface and take the reins both in their homes and outside.

Alkaben Jani (born 1964) is a single woman who has had to struggle against family expectations and pressures to pursue her convictions and work with women less privileged than herself. Alkaben's work in the Kutch district of Gujarat, where she has lived since birth, is informed by her intimate knowledge of the area. She works in a region that has one of the highest rates of women driven to suicide by oppressive patriarchal practices, where one in 20 women faces severely debilitating conditions such as a prolapsed uterus, and where women face the major brunt of the near-perennial drought conditions and scarce water resources.

For the past 15 years, Alkaben has contributed extensively to organizing, mobilizing, and training rural women in poverty alleviation. She has inspired them to transcend social pressures and move toward transforming themselves and their environment. Today, the Kutch Mahila Vikas Sangathan (KMVS) — one of the first grassroots rural women's collectives in India — comprises 12,000 women, and much of the credit goes to Alkaben's sustaining leadership and commitment.

Alkaben's focus is on the capacity-building of rural women through training, and the identification of women who can lead and manage the community. She creates spaces for women to express themselves, and encourages a process of self-reflection, so that they analyze their situation in a larger political and socioeconomic context.

When she looks back, Alkaben has no regrets that she stood up to her family and society, and lived by her commitment to work with the poor.

Gujarat's Kutch area has one of the highest rates of women driven to suicide by oppressive patriarchal practices. One in 20 women faces debilitations such as prolapsed uteruses. They also suffer the brunt of the constant drought conditions and scant water resources.

India

Byats-Khandaa Jargal

Mongolian Women Farmers' Association (Mwfa)

Byats-Khandaa Jargal, an agronomist and a farmer, was born in a Nomadic herder family. A gold medallist in her academic work, she now heads the Mongolian Women Farmers' Association founded by her in 1999 and devoted to supporting livelihoods of the poor. In 2003 she was awarded the International Prize for Women's Creativity in Rural Life by the Women's World Summit Foundation. Byats-Khandaa is known as one of the most socially oriented, realistic and practical leaders in the women's movement in Mongolia.

Byats-Khandaa would often go round to people's homes and offer advice on farming. At one place, she found the garden overgrown with wild grass and suggested that the owners cut the grass so the vegetables underneath could grow. The next day when she returned, she found all the vegetables had been dug up and the grass left intact! Despite such confusions, she has made a success of her small-farming concept, and for the poor it has also proved a good business. With permission from the local administration she set up a successful six-hectare community garden in 1999 that operates on a rotational basis, with each family being given a plot of land for one year. Its purpose is to provide practical horticultural training so that the poor have a fighting chance of surviving in conditions of mass unemployment and poverty. Many do well and also become trainers themselves. One of the initiators of the Green Revolution in the post-socialist Mongolia, Byats-Khandaa at first lacked funds and had to rent out her two-room flat in the city center. She put the money gained into a project supporting low-income households. She has for many years run a soup kitchen that serves 30 to 150 poor children and women every day. In return, they are asked to attend training in handicrafts in the same kitchen. Byats-Khandaa works closely with the Mongolian Women Farmers' Association (Mwfa). The Mwfa constructed a new spacious and well equipped training center that aims at transforming the Bayankhoshuu gher-dwelling (felt tents) area into a prosperous oasis of small horticulture, pig and chicken farming adapted to the peri-urban social and natural environment. The Center develops techniques of organic vegetable growing and is already capable of marketing its produce in the city areas.

Byats-Khandaa's work has been widely appreciated.

Government poverty elimination programs in Mongolia during the last 15 years have generally been failures. Corruption is one reason. Poverty has increased and the gap between rich and poor has widened. NGOs like the Mwfa are working hard to change this.

Mongolia

"If I do not work, who will? I have the necessary skills and I should be using them to accomplish the work I do for peace and women's rights."

Nino Javakhishvili

Georgian Women's Council
Georgian Association of Women in Business
Women's Non-Governmental Organization Coalition

A renowned scientist in medical biology, Nino Javakhishvili is a devoted activist for peace and women's rights. She currently is the president of the Georgian Women's Council and focuses on drawing attention to the plight of marginalized women. She provides a voice for those oppressed by unjust political, economic and social environments. She believes that women are the future of potential human capital and she is committed to using her skills to help alleviate poverty.

Dr Javakhishvili is an accomplished scientist and researcher in medical biology. In addition to her academic work, she is a devoted activist for peace and women's rights. For more than 50 years, she has made tremendous contributions to advance women's role in society, believing that peace is sustainable only when people are actively involved in achieving it. She works closely with thousands of individuals from the public and private sectors including government officials and executives to teach the basic tenets of economic development, civil society, democracy, leadership, transparency, and advocacy. She believes these elements are intertwined with the promise of peace. Nino helps to develop women leaders at NGOs and for high political offices, where currently very few women hold top positions. In her work to shed light on marginalized women, she provides a voice for those who cannot be heard and for those oppressed by unjust political and economic structures. For her, economic self-sufficiency, education, and the ability to provide for one's family are the keys to improving one's life and for advancing the next generation. She has traveled extensively to present her medical research and advocate the need for self-sufficiency. She goes beyond her message to actively help build self-esteem in individuals as they work to build their communities and strengthen the political processes. Across ethnic, cultural, and social lines Nino Javakhishvili has worked diligently with integrity and full commitment to promote a better place in society for women and to ensure peace.

Georgia is plagued by ongoing political and economic struggles, organized crime, and high unemployment. This environment has upset the lives of women, children, and the elderly. The help of dedicated NGOs will have a significant impact on their progress as Georgia works to build its civil society.

Georgia

Khushi Kabir

Nijera Kori

Khushi Kabir (born 1948) embodies the very spirit of the socioeconomic empowerment of women, peace, and democracy in Bangladesh. For more than 30 years, she has been involved with working-class rural communities on issues ranging from people's control over their own resources, challenging antipeople policies and programs, secularism, and human rights. She has been integral to the forging of strong national coalitions of civil society groups, and the creation and sustenance of global networks and coalitions for human rights, gender equality, and democracy.

When Khushi Kabir was finishing her graduation in fine arts from Dhaka University, Bangladesh was going through tremendous turmoil. The country had just won its independence from Pakistan in January 1972 after being struck by a megacyclone two years before. Deeply affected by the crisis, Khushi began work with the Bangladesh Rural Advancement Committee, becoming among the first middle-class, educated and jeans-clad women to join an NGO or work in the remote rural areas.

In 1980, Khushi joined Nijera Kori (which means doing it ourselves). The organization, which started in a small way in 1974, today works in 38 thanas (administrative units) and 1126 villages in Bangladesh, organizing 175,000 landless women and men in their socioeconomic struggles; it facilitates better access to rural services and available resources by building self-reliance and improved production through mobilization and collective action. Khushi's work with Nijera Kori has been instrumental in giving it a new direction and dynamism. "It is the people themselves who have resisted this invasion into their communities and their lives," she says. "We came to strengthen the movement, add voice, and support it."

Khushi had understood fairly early the need to build common platforms for similar-agenda civil society groups. She played an important role in augmenting the Association of Development Agencies in Bangladesh into a potent network of NGOs. Khushi also built and sustained global networks and coalitions and other peoples' movements for human rights, justice, gender equality, and democracy. Over the long haul, Khushi has braved criticism, threats, and attacks for, and on, her political stance and work among the dispossessed. But it has not dented her appetite for goal convergence across the NGO board.

Bangladesh had emerged from a brutalizing war that left the rural areas suffering badly from a broken national economy. The marginalized communities — particularly women — were neither empowered nor organized and had no access to resources or information before NGOs such as Nijera Kori stepped in.

Bangladesh

"It is not just in
Bangladesh, everywhere
in the world inhumanity
and fundamentalism
are major forces now!
If we are to make
a good future, more
people need to
be more proactive."

Rokeya Kabir

Bangladesh Nari Progati Sangha

Rokeya Kabir (born 1952) was one of the first activists in Bangladesh to forge the crucial link between grassroots women and the national and international women's movements. To materialize this global interconnection of grassroots movements, she and other women's activists set up the Bangladesh Nari Progati Sangha in 1986. For 25 years now, she has been working on women's rights and minorities issues, incurring the wrath of the country's fundamentalist forces. Undeterred, she wades on — downsizing her operations and functioning with practically no funding.

Rokeya Kabir was among the vanguard in Bangladesh to bridge the grassroots-global gap between women's movements. Working on women's issues in various capacities and with different organizations for over a decade, she set up the Bangladesh Nari Progati Sangha (women's progress organization) in 1986, along with some like-minded people. "My involvement in working with people at the grassroots level in the rural and urban settings, especially with women, provided me with both insights and the opportunity to understand the problems in depth," she says. "I felt a dire need to build up a link between grassroots women and the national and international women's movements."

For more than a quarter century, women's human rights and engaging minority rights issues through media, advocacy, campaigns, and awareness generation have been Rokeya's priorities. She has also contributed to policy issues, especially reforms in education policy and inheritance law, increased parliamentary representation for women with a provision for direct elections, and devolution of power to the local government, with women's effective participation. But choppiness seems to have tagged her for the past couple of decades. She and the Bangladesh Nari Progati Sangha have been victimized by the present government, which has religious fundamentalist parties sharing power. "They have filed false cases against me," she says. "My organization has not been able to receive any funds for the past three years. At present, I am sustaining the Sangha by sizing it down and mobilizing voluntary efforts." She continues: "It is not just in Bangladesh, everywhere in the world inhumanity and fundamentalism are major forces now! But I am optimistic. If we are to make a good future, more people need to be more proactive."

Although women fought along with men in the 1971 Bangladesh liberation war, after the struggle, they were denied their due share of freedom's benefits. And with the burgeoning of fundamentalism since the mid-1980s, minority rights have also been seriously neglected.

Bangladesh

"Old age should not hinder women from helping to build their country, rather it should be seen as an asset because of all the experience that comes with it."

Aïssata Kane

Association pour la Protection de l'Environnement en Mauritanie (APEM)
Association Mauritanienne pour la Protection de l'Enfant et de la Femme
Association Internationale des Femmes Francophones (AIFF)

Aïssata Kane currently is considered as the mother of Mauritanian women because of her great wisdom and common sense and her open spirit that fuels her mission to help women leave obscurity to meet the virtues of the modern world: liberty, gender equality, respect for women's rights, and for the right for young girls to enroll at school. Aïssata Kane is a consultant on women and development and spends her time working on respect for women's rights, the involvement of women in development, research into ways and means for sustainable development.

Aïssata Kane was one of the first three Mauritanian girls to be admitted to secondary school. She very quickly caught the social and political activism bug that saw her become the head of the Mauritanian Women's Council in 1970. Aïssata is, within the human rights network, specifically involved in the rights of women and children. More than that, she is in reality a national and international reference point. Thanks to her experience as an emancipated woman who is not dominated by traditional rules, the Mauritanian woman has come a long way to assert her social promotion. The Mauritanian women's movement has pressured the government for projects to be initiated for women. For example, because of the actions of women of this Muslim Republic of Africa, the difference in the education rate between girls and boys has been reduced considerably. Aïssata Kane is also known as a political activist involved in the construction of Mauritania. She never accepted a secondary role in matters of her country. She held the post of Minister for the Protection of the Family and Social Affairs from 1975 to 1977 and was, thus, the first woman minister in Mauritania. After the state military coup, she committed herself to community life with the Conference on African Women. This allowed her to establish important international relations in the African women's movement. Aïssata Kane (67) still does not feel tired and wants to go further. In her understanding, the fight does not end until the many steps have been taken for equality between men and women to be attained in all development areas of Mauritania.

The granddaughter of Elimane Mame Diack Kane is also the founder of AIFF, the International Association of French-speaking Women which resides in Nouakchott, Mauritania's capital city. This structure has developed several projects on Francophone women's rights.

Mauritania

Vasanth Kannabiran

National Alliance for Women (NAW)

For over 30 years, Vasanth Kannabiran (born 1939) has been closely involved with questions of armed militancy, civil liberties, and the meaning of peace for women in her native state of Andhra Pradesh. She is among the first women in the country to move into feminist activism through the Stree Shakti Sangathana. Ten years ago, she set up a radical women's collective in Andhra Pradesh called Asmita, which brings diverse groups of women into networks addressing issues spanning conflict, peace, survival, women's rights, and secularism.

As a child, Vasanth Kannabiran was taught to question and assert herself, and it is a habit that has stayed. Born into a family of first-generation communist leaders in Andhra Pradesh, Vasanth secured a masters in English literature from the Central Institute of English and Foreign Languages in Hyderabad, the state capital, and went on to teach English at a woman's college from 1961 to 1985.

Vasanth, a lawyer and leading civil and democratic rights activist, has worked alongside her husband since the mid-1970s for the rights of political dissidents. When she began work on human rights, the emergency had just been declared, and all civil liberties stood suspended. Vasanth sheltered underground activists. She also became a member of one of the earliest women's collectives in India, Stree Shakti Sangathana, and eventually moved from college teaching to development work. Ten years ago, she set up a radical women's collective in Andhra Pradesh called Asmita, which brings diverse groups of women into networks that address issues spanning conflict, peace, survival, women's rights, and secularism. Vasanth is also a founder-member of Hyderabad Ekta, the first anticommunal front in Hyderabad, which began its work amid deepening communal polarization. She has played an invaluable role in initiating, sustaining, and supporting campaigns for a democratic order by offering her services, shelter, critiques, resources, advocacy efforts, and creative energies. What is unique about her is her capacity to train leaders and build alliances. She has been able to straddle the local and the international, addressing questions of inequality, discrimination, and diversity in every sphere of her work.

The Telangana region is one of the most developmentally backward in Andhra Pradesh, and is prone to sectarian Hindu-Muslim tension. The region is also the state's most politically vibrant and has witnessed a major communist armed struggle and struggle for secessionism.

India

Musimbi Kanyoro

World Young Women's Christian Association (Ywca)

Since 1998, Musimbi Kanyoro (53) has been chief executive officer of the World Young Women's Christian Association (Ywca). World Ywca reaches more than 25 million women and girls in 122 countries. It promotes leadership development of women of all ages. Musimbi holds a PhD in linguistics and a doctor of ministry. Dr Kanyoro is the first woman from the South to head the largest and oldest women's ecumenical organization.

As the chief executive officer of the World Ywca, Musimbi Kanyoro has influenced the 150-year-old NGO to focus on the promotion of leadership for young women and to campaign against HIV and Aids. "I know I am walking a thin rope," says the dynamic CEO when asked if advocating the use of condoms does not clash with traditional church doctrines. "But what is more important than saving lives? Women must be empowered to make their own, informed decisions." The lives of women, especially in Africa, are her major concern, having been influenced by her parents, who were health workers. Volunteering at a shelter for abused women, she became aware of women's rights, culminating in the 1985 UN Women's Conference in Nairobi. "I began a whole new education," she remembers, "realizing that cultural traditions both nourish and imprison us, and that we must sift out the bad habits and only keep what makes us grow."

Born in rural Kenya, Musimbi and her nine siblings received a good education, supported by their parents, who considered this the best inheritance for their children. After the village primary school, she went to a girls-only secondary school, which she says "gave us the assurance that girls can do any subject and become whatever they want." After her undergraduate degree at the University of Nairobi, she obtained a PhD in linguistics at the University of Texas and later a doctor of ministry. After working on language research and training of Bible translators, she was active for ten years in the Lutheran World Federation. Musimbi has published 11 books and many articles on feminist theology, development and women's leadership.

After three decades of working with women, she knows: "We are all connected. Our life conditions may differ, but our problems are similar, and we must learn from each other."

The empowerment of women and girls is in an era of globalization, poverty and unequal trade relations, economic injustices and the violation of women's rights in the domestic and public sphere.

Kenya

Yasmin Karim

Aga Khan Rural Support Program (AKRSP)

Yasmin Karim — born 1962 in Hunza Karimabad, Northern Areas of Pakistan — is an energetic pioneer in women's development in the remote Northern Areas and Chitral. She is an inspiration to the women of this rugged, mountainous, and desperately poor region. Yasmin has traveled from village to village to motivate women to set up their own organizations, and acquire vocational and professional skills that have transformed their lives. She formed 600 such organizations, covering about 80 percent of the households in the area under her charge.

Yasmin Karim's personal journey has been an extraordinary one. After a makeshift schooling that ended in grade three, Yasmin, daughter of a widow, managed to secure a scholarship to study at a boarding school for girls, hundreds of miles away in the port city of Karachi. She went on to obtain a bachelors degree, and then a masters in gender and development from the University of Sussex in the UK.

While transforming her own life, Yasmin has helped other women in her region transform theirs. She has spent two decades with the Aga Khan Rural Support Program (AKRSP) formulating and implementing community development programs that emphasize women's social and economic empowerment. Her work has contributed to the formation of nearly 1500 women's organizations-600 of them largely due to her efforts-and the involvement of about 50,000 women in these programs. Yasmin has been an outstanding coordinator of grassroots networks, making a significant contribution to the setting up of cottage industries like weaving fabrics and carpets, and has been an effective member of the AKRSP's core and regional policymaking groups. She has also developed modules on entrepreneurship development for women.

Like other women working among fiercely patriarchal tribal communities, Yasmin has had to battle prejudice and hostility. Once, a gun was placed on her back by the men of a village on the orders of a cleric who wished no discussion on discrimination against women. But the threats did not work. Perhaps she was inspired by her own parents: her father was the first law graduate in Hunza in the late 1960s; her mother defied tradition to work as a nurse in order to provide for her family after the death of her husband.

The Northern Areas and Chitral, a poor mountainous region of Pakistan, is a hotbed of orthodoxy in which most of the population live in small, scattered riparian settlements and are primarily engaged in subsistence agriculture. Women remain disempowered second-class citizens, if that.

Pakistan

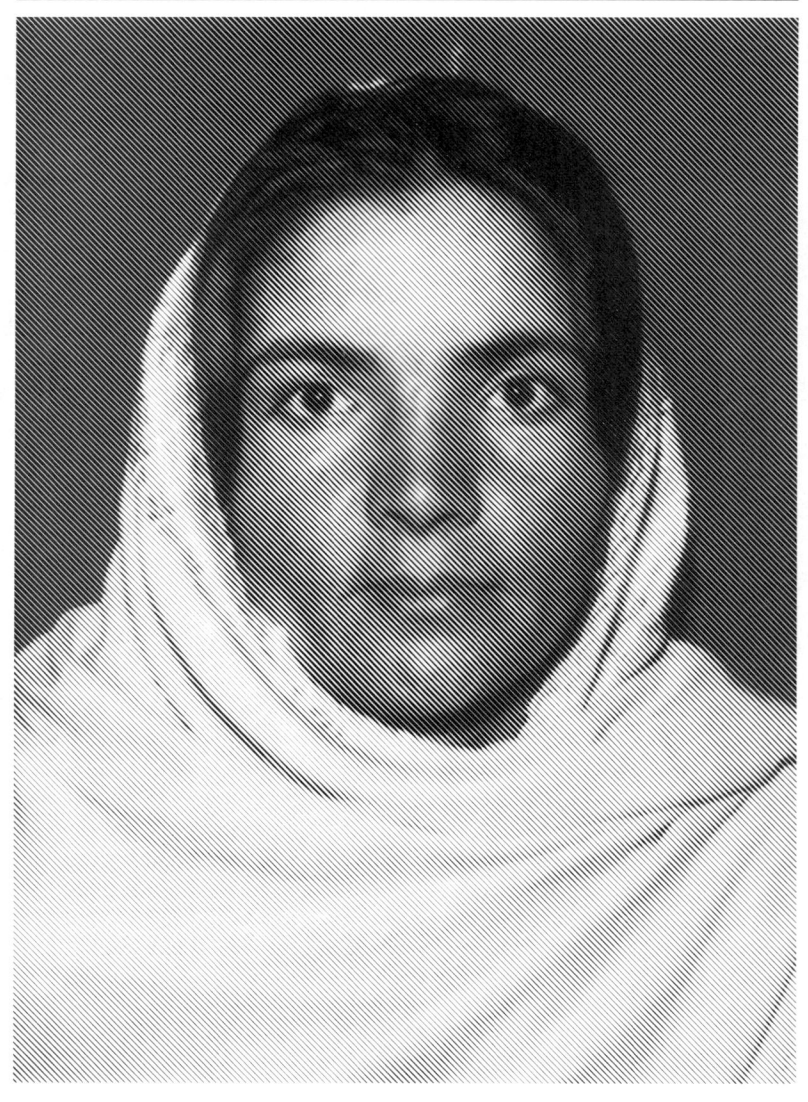

Lawangina Khan

Swedish Committee for Afghanistan (SCA)

Lawangina Khan was born in 1977 in Paktika province, Afghanistan, but she completed her early schooling in Islamabad, Pakistan. She has received training as a community health worker and as an educator. She has also attended several workshops on human rights and women's rights and has represented women in the emergency Loya Jirga. Lawangina has worked diligently with many NGOs as well as the Provincial Reconstruction Teams (PRT) and received several commendations for her services. She has stood firmly in her defense of the rights of women and children.

Lawangina Khan is dedicated to the improvement of women's conditions in Afghanistan, and to this end she has traveled extensively to different parts of her home province Paktika as an educator in order to raise women's awareness of their rights and role in society. She has also been involved in providing counseling to the families of Zirok district and helps them to resolve their problems. In addition, she has been actively involved in the peace building initiatives in Paktika province.

Paktika, like Paktia, is one of the most conservative provinces across Afghanistan; a fact that further highlights the importance of Lawangina Khan's activities and the immensity of the barriers that she has overcome. Therefore, she deserves much appreciation and encouragement for her work. After losing her husband, she continued to work as a health educator with an NGO. Lawangina has been instrumental not only in encouraging women to participate in the daily activities in their communities, but also in recruiting the efforts of national and international organizations in the reconstruction processes of her province.

Being active in one of the most conservative communities in the nation, the main area of Lawangina Khan's work is the education of people, especially women and girls. She works to raise women's awareness of their rights in society.

Afghanistan

Rahela Khatun

Noai Landless Women Organization
Deluti Landless Union Committee

Rahela Khatun was born in 1965 into a large, impoverished family in Noai village, Khulna district. Rising above her poverty and desertion by both father and husband, she mobilizes support against the powerful shrimp aquaculture lobbies that are depriving people of their livelihoods. Despite attempts to introduce shrimp farming by both the government and farmers, her village and adjacent ones continue to be shrimp-free zones.

Rahela Khatun was born in 1965 into a family of eight brothers and two sisters in Noai village, Khulna district. After her father married a second time and abandoned the family, she, her siblings, and her mother worked as manual labor or joined the fishing industry. Rahela, who had neither the time nor the opportunity to go to school, was married off against her will when she was 15 years old.

Since 1980, after a meeting with an activist who spoke to her village about landless people's rights, and the environmental dangers and livelihood robbery of shrimp farming, Rahela has been working against commercial shrimp aquaculture and related human rights' violations in her village and neighboring communities.

Despite her husband's evident displeasure, Rahela continues her engagement, essentially mobilizing people. In the course of their work, Rahela and her colleagues face intimidation — torture, killing, and terrorizing by the hired goons of shrimp farmers. Riding out several attempts by both government and farmers to introduce shrimp farming, her village and neighboring ones remain shrimp-free zones, even as shrimp culture is literally sweeping the entire area like a commercial epidemic.

The shrimp farming industry seriously harms the environment. When mangroves are cleared and saltwater is pumped into shrimp ponds, the soil is destroyed, as are paddy fields, wells, and vegetable plots. Traditional fishing communities are wrecked, often being forced to migrate.

Bangladesh

Sufia Khatun

Landless Organization of Atabarpur
Regional Committee of the Landless

A silent victim of domestic violence until 1984, Sufia Khatun's life changed dramatically after she met with activists from the NGO Nijera Kori (which means doing it ourselves) who told her about human rights and the need for collective action to assert those rights. Mobilizing women, she set up a women's group first in her own, then in neighboring villages, where organizations of landless people formed a regional committee. Her mobilization has led to a reduction in domestic violence in the area, and the weakening of fundamentalist forces.

Sufia Khatun (born 1967), married at the age of 14, silently bore marital violence until, in 1984, activists from Nijera Kori changed the course of her life. They spoke rousingly about fighting against injustices, the rights of the landless, and the importance of collectively raising voices on issues affecting their lives and livelihood.

Sufia related directly to the fact that women and men earned unequal wages; she saw the prevalence of domestic violence, dowry, and child marriages, and that women were prohibited from approaching the village courts. She also realized that when she spoke alone, she spoke to deaf ears. Sufia then started mobilizing people, establishing a women's group in her village. Under her leadership, the organizations of landless people formed a regional committee, which hears out issues of human rights' violations, and organizes protests and discussions. One of the effects was a steep drop in domestic violence in the area. Sufia began questioning the vaunted microcredit programs that caused farmers to sink deeper into debt, and chemical-based agriculture that reduced land fertility. She promoted indigenous methods of cultivation, which has led to higher crop returns.

Sufia has also struggled to weaken the fundamentalist forces and the ubiquitous fatwa (legal pronouncement) culture, retorting to the various fatwas issued against her with demonstrations, mass gatherings, and memoranda. This has led to the administration investigating and declaring the rampant pronouncement of fatwas illegal. This young, illiterate woman, who had braved almost incapacitating personal odds, is today a pillar of strength to once lost causes.

Bangladesh has 1763 people packed into each square mile, about 85 percent of them in rural areas. Over 60 percent of the population is landless or nearly so. The microcredit system has weakened them further, with women, almost entirely unorganized, bearing the brunt.

Bangladesh

"Women spreading bridges of peace, solidarity and fraternity contributes to reaching the supreme values of justice."

Hazel Magdalene King

Hazel's School of Arts and Crafts

She raised her two children alone and took care of her mother while enduring her husband's abuses. When she was laid off from a restaurant in Bridgetown, Barbados, she understood that her hands could work miracles. Hazel Magdalene King lifted up a flag: self-employment for self-sufficiency. She invited other women, taught them how to make cake icing and handicraft. She underwent radical breast cancer surgery, but she did not stop. She has never stopped. Hazel inspires other women in the Service for the Support for Cancer.

Hazel Magdalene King was born in Barbados, in 1939. For many years, she was victim of abuse in her marriage, until she gained courage and ended the relationship. In 1988, she was laid off from a restaurant in Bridgetown. She was alone in front to her two children when she looked at her hands and thought: "It's time to use my skills of cake icing and handicraft to make a living."

She understood that the best thing would be to share these experiences with other women who, as her, did not have help. Soon her desire became reality. In 1988, she founded, in the kitchen of her own house, Hazel's School of Arts and Crafts. In the following year, her small home was not big enough for all her students. She wanted to become self-sufficient and she achieved it; she trained many women so that they could also become self-sufficient. But there was another love in Hazel's life: the Church. She is a member of the African Methodist Episcopal Church. She has had several responsibilities at a local level, including the distribution of food and clothes to needy people. She is President of the missionary department and, three years ago, she took on the challenge of developing missionary work in Haiti.

She was diagnosed with breast cancer in 1995. The radical surgery was applied in the same year. She uses her experience to inspire and encourage other women in the Service for Support for Cancer.

During the 1980s, the economic situation of Barbados was unstable. Many companies laid off their personnel. Insecurity reigned, mainly for the more needy sectors. Most people depended on the government's help. Women began to realize that there was the possibility of self-employment.

Barbados

Kommaly Chanthavong

Kommaly Chantavong (born 1950) is a farmer's daughter from the mountains of eastern Laos. When her village was bombed by the Americans in 1961, she fled to Vientiane. In 1976, she founded a cooperative for the production of silk, which she still heads. The cooperative teaches mostly women traditional skills in raising silkworms, making natural dyes and weaving traditional patterns. The successful marketing of the products provides a fair and steady income to several hundred families that used to be very poor.

Kommaly was 11 years old when her village was destroyed by US bombers attacking the Ho Chi Minh Trail. She walked for a month to Vientiane, the capital, bringing with her silk weaving skills that her family had handed down over generations. "I learned to weave from my mother, when I was six years old and I loved it," she recollects. Kommaly studied nursing, but then she found her life's goal: "I met many desperately poor families displaced from rural areas without any marketable skills," she remembers, "so I started to teach the women how to weave silk." In 1976, she founded a cooperative with ten members; now there are over 3000. Kommaly runs it like a mother: energetically, efficiently and warm-heartedly.

In a model farm which she manages with her equally dedicated husband, Kommaly offers free courses on the production of high quality textiles: from raising silkworms (the most difficult part), to growing mulberry trees for their fodder, to spinning the ultra-fine threads, to preparing natural dyes, to weaving traditional patterns. The results are available in a shop that Kommaly set up in Vientiane and which guarantees the silk producers fair and steady earnings. "Our greatest challenge is to compete against cheaper low-quality imports," she says. One of her daughters helps with the marketing in Australia, another in the US. "Our goal is to strengthen the position of women by giving them a dependable income and thus improving the chances of their children," says Kommaly with a gentle but radiant smile.

Ten years of war forced many Laotian farmers to flee to the capital, where they lived in poverty, unable to return to their lands which were dotted with landmines. Traditional silk weaving is one of the skills taught to Laotian women to help them earn a steady income for their families.

Lao People's Democratic Republic

Layvanh Phanludeth

Laos Women's Union

Layvanh Phanludeth was born in 1962 in Pak-ngum, Nakhon Luang, Vientiane. After junior high school, she went into farming, got married and had four children, like other Laotian women. Layvanh has worked to improve the status of women in the community. Joining the Laos Women's Union in 1993, she got involved in social work and community development, which made her see the important roles of women in society. She organized the women in Ban Na Koong into a savings group for emergencies and income generating activities.

After Layvanh Phanludeth joined the Laos Women's Union in 1993, she became active in social issues. In 1998, she was elected chairperson of the Union in her village, after which she became village chief from 1998 to 2000. "The Women's Union works on the most immediate issues, namely, developing ourselves, our families and our society," says Layvanh of her work. In her village of Ban Na Koong, Women's Union members meet every three months to discuss issues concerning family and community development; the roles, rights and duties of women and the promotion of equal rights for women and men. Layvanh's first project was to persuade her neighbors to set up a savings group where members could tap into a common fund during emergencies or for investing in income generating activities, without having to borrow money from loan sharks. For her commitment and devotion to the work, the members elected her chairperson of the Ban Na Koong Savings Group.

Layvanh has introduced many innovations, setting an inspiring example for the community. She was the first to try integrated farming and production of bio-fertilizer for non-chemical farming. Layvanh's inputs have been very relevant to her farming community, which must survive in an increasingly developmental system. She has helped the villagers realize the importance of self-reliance and organization. At the same time, she has helped push Lao women, who, by tradition, stick to their role as homemakers, to be more aware of the situation and to get involved in the life of the community and the country. "Though we are women, we tolerate no oppression. We want women's rights. This is the underlying philosophy of my work. The role of women must be accepted in society. They should be encouraged to work for development side by side with men," declares Layvanh.

Laos counts equality of its citizens as a primary goal. A key policy for the country is therefore the promotion of the role of women. The Laos Women's Union was organized to carry out this mission. Lao women from 18 to 55 years of age are eligible to be members of the Union.

Lao People's Democratic Republic

Kun Lei

Collevtive of Sex Workers and Supporters (Coswas)

Lei Kun (a pseudonym) began her transformative journey from sex worker to sex worker activist in 1997, when the Taipei City government decided to abolish licensed prostitution and declared its more than 120 licensed prostitutes illegal. She has transformed sex work into social movement activism.

At 64, Lei Kun is no longer a sex worker. She decided to fight for the collective survival of sex workers, demanding that they be given the right to live and work in peace and with dignity.

As a girl, Lei Kun was undervalued and not given an education. She then had a bad marriage ending in divorce. Without family resources or an education, a single mother with two children, she finally turned to sex work. Lei Kun had already planned to retire after paying the mortgage on her home. But when she saw how the new policy affected some of her sex worker colleagues in Taipei, driving many to hunger and suicide, she decided to fight and join her co-workers in their struggle.

Through seeing her own development as a process of empowerment, she came to understand the kinds of structural injustices that kept the poor and the marginal downtrodden and stigmatized. The Taipei licensed prostitutes' struggle brought about a two-year respite before sex work was finally made legal again. Afterwards, she suffered from breast cancer. But no sooner had she recovered from the operation that she was back in action.

On April 30, 1999, the Collective of Sex Workers and Supporters (Coswas) was founded with the collaboration of the existing Datong Area Licensed Prostitutes Cooperative, two women's labor groups and other supporters of the licensed prostitutes' movement. Lei Kun actively took part in the organization and quickly took on a leadership role as a sex worker activist. Her work and energy has been an inspiration for Taiwan's sex workers, as well as for other social movements and activists.

Taiwan society has a very moralistic and controlling attitude toward sex and women's sexuality. Both government and many citizens are hypocritical and uncaring toward sex workers, who are subjected to all kinds of control and punishment.

China, Taiwan

"Improving the lives of women in countries with high illiteracy rates also means improving the lives of the entire community."

Joséphine Léno

Economic and Social Council of Guinea

Joséphine Léno (her surname is both written Léno and Lenaud) is a well-known personality in the trade union world of her country and, today, is vice-president of the Economic and Social Council of Guinea. It is an institution that enforces and oversees a consultation process aimed at improving people's social and economic conditions. Joséphine fights for the economic and social well being of this West African country, after a long trade union and teaching career.

Madame is an experienced unionist. In her current functions, but especially in her fight to get more girls in schools, Josephine Léno is confronted by the reluctance of parents and some traditional leaders who exercise strong influence over students. This unschooling of girls for the aim of early marriages brings with it equally difficult problems in the fight against illiteracy among women. Thanks to her action, change is observable in Kissidougou (a prefecture 592 kilometers to the north of Conakry, the capital of Guinea) in the area of education, but also in the trade union environment, where she continues to serve as a mediator between the state and the trade unions during a crisis. By virtue of her current office, Joséphine is at the centre of all questions linked to improvements in people's socio-economic conditions. Her work also benefits people living in rural areas and workers who accept her mediatory role in social conflicts.

As a teacher and mother of three children, of which two are alive, Madame Guilano, born Joséphine Léno, headed the powerful National Union of Teachers of Guinea for several years under a president Ahmed Sékou Touré, whose reign was based on a one-party system renowned for its massive violations of human rights. With the death of Touré in April 1984, she became a member of the International Union of Teachers. For a period of four years, she was member of the Transitional Council of National Recovery (CTRN) that served as legislative body until legislative elections in June 1995. Named Minister of Labour and Social Affairs, she contributed to the containment of social turmoil in the working world, while engaging in dialog with those in charge of the various unions at the time.

Avowed patriot, Guilao Josephine Léno worked with organisations to promote union rights, but especially to establish a process of dialogue between the unions and the state. She is actively engaged in the fight to reduce illiteracy in her country, especially among women.

Guinea

Guilian Li

Guizhou Agricultural Science Institute

Li Guilian of Huayin City, Shanxi Province, graduated from the Department of Gardening, Agricultural University, Guizhou Province in 1964, specializing in fruit and vegetables. She is vice dean at Guizhou Provincial Agricultural Science Institute and has been engaged in researching and promoting vegetable-growing technoloies for 40 years. Farmers in over 20 counties and cities of the province now grow vegetables all year round, resulting in better incomes, the development of agricultural plastic sheeting, chemical fertilizer, pesticide, vegetable seeds, restaurants, hotels and transportation.

In 1979 China was still at the first stage of reform. Luodian County was in a remote and underdeveloped mountainous area. The people did not plant many crops, mainly just hot peppers and soybeans. Rice was planted only once a year. Thus economic development was slow and the peasants had low incomes. That year Li Guilian brought her vegetable technologies to Luodian. She traveled from village to village in the mountains, training peasants to grow out-of-season vegetables, and to spread the technology further, particularly to the younger generation. Li wanted to change a natural advantage into an economic advantage through scientific means, so that peasant incomes would increase. Growing out-of-season vegetables is now the main produce of low-temperature areas such as Luodian, Guanling, Zhenning, and Wangmo, improving farmers' incomes. It also increases possibilities for a livestock breeding industry. The rearing of pigs can provide natural fertilizer for growing vegetables, creating a fine and sustainable agricultural cycle.

In 1996 Li suggested an innovative and scientific means of using the cool climate of summer and autumn in high-altitude areas of Guizhou to develop summer and autumn out-of-season non-toxic vegetables. Now Li is almost 60. But, as before, she goes without her holidays and frequently lives in the villages of Dafang, Weining and Longli, imparting her knowlege of cultivation technologies. Her long dedication to such work has made her a friend and teacher to many a peasant. In 1987, when she was hospitalized, four peasants and four children from Luodian visited her in hospital. This was an especially memorable scene in her life. Overall, Li Guilian has dedicated her life to peasants, agriculture, and the villages with courage and creativity, and has achieved great things despite all the difficulties.

Luodian County is a remote and under-developed mountainous area, a "national poor county." Minorities constitute 64 percent of a population that is mostly illiterate or semi-literate. The agricultural foundation in Guizhou is weak and in need of technological support, and peasants' incomes are correspondingly low.

China

Tete Li

Li Tete, a strong-willed woman, possesses the courage and wisdom of the first-generation leaders of the People's Republic of China (PRC). Her conviction that the revolution is not complete if there is still poverty, has let her to commit herself to poverty alleviation in China, helping people in poor districts and especially the rural regions. Her contributions here have been widely recognized and appreciated by government and ordinary people.

Li Tete was born in France. Her father was a proletarian revolutionary and former vice-premier in the State Council. Her mother was a pioneer of China's modern women's movement, and former vice-chairperson of the standing committee of the National People's Congress, and the former president of the All China Women's Federation. In 1960s and 1970s, Li visited the nuclear experiment base in West China, passing Inner Mongolia, Shaanxi, and Gansu provinces on her way. Along the railway, nothing existed except yellow soil. The houses of peasants had only some worn-out quilts and broken tile jars. The villagers were all in shabby clothes and had little to eat. Li was very sad to see this. She said, "I do not think our revolution is thorough enough. Socialism should guarantee basic living conditions." And "I am the offspring of revolutionaries, and we are obliged to accomplish the cause that our predecessors left us. Poverty alleviation is the best way for us to continue with the revolution." For these 14 years, she has visited dozens of provincial districts in the country. She changed the poverty alleviation method from "blood-transfusion" into "blood-forming", that is, to encourage people in poor areas to get rid of poverty by using their own strengths. She suggests that intellectual training and education should be the most important for poverty alleviation, thus emphasizing the training of teachers and establishing a remote education network, so as to foster various skills. Li has devoted all her heart to poverty alleviation. She has managed to get donations and subsidies of 16 million yuan, freeing tens of thousands of people from poverty.

Many of China's poverty-trapped areas lie in difficult terrain, and are not easily accessible. With primitive modes of production and little education, these regions are backward, and their ability to resist natural disasters is much reduced. Poverty persists in several such areas.

China

Qingrong Ma

Xingfu Village Women's Association

Ma Qingrong initiated the Xingfu Village Women's Association of the Longyu Township. During the last 20 years she has worked at a grassroots level in the countryside, helping countless poor villagers. The Women's Association she organized has voluntarily done a lot to improve the status of women in the village and the township and inspired them with confidence and hope. Under her influence, many women have made changes in their lives, their families, and in the society.

Ma Qingrong was born in 1943 in the Gaocao Township, Xichang City, Sichuan Province. She is a member of the Muslim community and believes in Islam. She was married in the Xingfu Village, Yulong township, when she was 18. Since then she has never left the place. Ma has had a difficult life; she is sympathetic and is concerned about the poor. She has spent the past 20 years helping people; whatever the matter she tries to help. In Xingfu Village women were maltreated, sometimes beaten or abused by their husbands. Ma would speak out and stand up for the women, telling them they were not subordinate to men.She offered support to women who were abused and helpless.

The Xingfu Village Women's Association, which she organized together with a few of these women, aimed to mediate in family disputes, to prevent further violent acts against women, and to provide help for the victims of violence. In one incident, a villager who used to belittle his wife, and even beat and abuse his daughter frequently, again used violence to settle a trivial family dispute. Ma came to stop him and, with the help of other members of the Women's Association, educated him about the principles of family harmony. Being reprimanded by so many people for the first time, the man unwillingly became silent. But the incident had a profound demonstration effect on those women who endured humiliation without complaint. Some men started to change their attitude. More women joined the Association, strengthening its efforts for women's rights. The sound of quarrelling gradually died out, and the village became more peaceful and harmonious. The efforts made by Ma Qingrong have been understood and supported by the villagers. Under her influence, all the villagers, especially women, changed themselves, their families, and the society.

In villages around the Xichang County, Sichuan Province, women's status is low and many of them suffer from family violence. It is common to see women being beaten or abused by their husbands.

China

Mirriam Malala

Mam'u Mirriam Malala was born in 1936 in the Eastern Cape, South Africa. Mam'u Malala founded the Zanoxolo Junior Secondary School in 1978 in Sinyonwani. It catered for children who had to travel long distances, as there was no school nearby. In the 80s and 90s she founded a crèche and started HIV/Aids and women projects. Mam'u Malala has been an inspiration in the community for her strong will to achieve.

The villages in the heart of Transkei are very remote. They are barren and difficult to cultivate. Bad weather such as drought and snow or heavy rain kills the animals and crops. Sinyonwani is one of the barren villages left by the colonialist when they took over all the fertile land. It was left to be the home of Africans. Poverty is rampant. The majority of the men are forced to become mine workers.

Mirriam Malala has lived in the area since her childhood and wished to change its destiny. She founded a secondary school, Zanoxolo Junior Secondary School in 1978. From 1982, it has also been used for adult education classes. She saw the need for a crèche, which she opened in 1987. The department of education in the Transkei has used it since 1996 for early childhood development programs. Unemployment is a big problem in Transkei. "Our people are trained to be jobseekers rather than job creators," she says. When many men returned after being retrenched from the mines, tension in the homes resulted in more problems. Women needed empowerment.

The main obstacle was that most of the rural women are illiterate. As a remedy, Mam'u Malala, along with other 12 women, started an income-generating project in 1997. Women took on different activities based on what they could do best. Some went into bread baking for schools through a government-feeding scheme for the underprivileged children; some took on sewing projects, while others started vegetable projects. These projects have been of great help to the Aids project called Siyakhathala, "we care". Since then, the women's self-esteem has improved.

The villages in the heart of Transkei are very remote. Sinyonwani is a barren village abandoned to Africans by the colonialists. Poverty, hunger, inability to access social and economic resources are prevalent in the area. Women's empowerment is the key to improvement of life.

Nosandla Malindi

Development Education Leadership Teams in Action (Delta)

Nosandla Malindi was born in 1960. She has diplomas in business counseling and democratic development. Nosandla is trainer and coordinator of Development Education Leadership Teams in Action (Delta) in Libode, an organization that empowers women from grassroots communities to participate and hold leadership positions in decision-making in South Africa. Nosandla imparts skills, and models self-confidence and self-esteem to the women.

Working with local women was an uphill task at first. Most of them were fussy about cultural values and norms. They were illiterate but knowledgeable. Nosandla Malindi had to localize and add creativity to the training programs so that the women could be convinced to attend workshops through her organization, Delta. The program has three levels. Each phase runs over a year. The gender empowerment and leadership training is their flagship program.

Gender empowerment aims at assisting the women with their initiatives by training them on how to start a project, write a constitution and funding proposals. They also learn project management, conflict resolution, teamwork and leadership skills, relevant to their particular project. The women get referrals to relevant service providers for technical assistance. Delta also helps the women understand their role in community development and to see themselves as the main beneficiaries of the development programs.

Delta started in 1992 as a project of the Catholic Welfare Development (CWD). In 1995 it became independent from CWD. Delta has been empowering women in the urban and rural areas in the Western Cape. Nosandla has been a learner and staff from the time of its inception.

The NGO has been the only one able to stand the rural challenges in the area of Libode. The organization is a vital link in creating and reviving several women groups in the area. Nosandla is a living example of what she teaches and the women are confident in her abilities.

The Eastern Cape is one of the four poorest provinces in South Africa. Insecurity, poverty, ill health and hunger are escalating. Programs like Delta assist women to take control of the environment for their own benefit.

Marta Matamoros

Union of Tailors and Similars of Panama
Panamanian Women's Alliance
National Center of Workers of Panama

A pioneer of the trade union movement and in the struggle for women's rights in her native Panama, Marta Matamoros has turned her solitary life of self-sacrifice into a gift for other people. She has fought many battles, suffered persecution and imprisonment, but, thanks to her, women workers in Panama now enjoy maternity rights. Loved and admired, she lives in an elderly home in what used to be a US military base in the Canal Zone.

Marta Matamoros, a young Panamanian girl, born in 1909, started to work in El Bazar Francés, a company that made clothes for the Canal troops, for government employees and for members of the diplomatic corps. "The conditions were unhealthy and humiliating for the women who worked there. There was very little space, the heat was suffocating and everything was controlled, even when we went to the bathroom. The wages were terribly low." She joined the trade union, and they managed to get the company to pay the workers the Panama Day holiday. Soon afterwards, she was fired, but by then she had discovered that her destiny was in the defense of human rights. "In the factory I witnessed the fatigue of the pregnant women. They worked right up till the last day and left directly to give birth. Many lost their jobs." Marta launched a draft bill for paid maternity leave, and the National Assembly approved it. The employers did their best to evade the law by laying off women they suspected of being pregnant. Marta's next fight was to get the women to be reinstated.

She participated in the struggle to decolonize the Panama Canal. She played a leading role in the movement to establish a minimum wage and a substantial reduction in the rent for housing for people in need. She was imprisoned several times, but her family's support and her achievements gave her strength. "In 1972, we fought for a maternity law by which no woman could be fired during the first year after giving birth." It was another success story.

Now, loved and admired, she lives off her pension in an elderly retirement home.

In 1914, the USA inaugurated the Panama Canal; the zone was declared an American protectorate. The wealth created by the Canal did not reach the majority of the population. President Omar Torrijos (1968–1981) negotiated for the Canal to become Panamanian again, at the end of the 20th century.

Edith Matshikiza

Community water initiative

Edith Mathsikiza was born in 1943 in the rural Transkei, South Africa. She and her late husband were blessed with four children. After completing school, Edith joined the Transkei Girl Guide Project as an instructor to teach girls life skills. She decided early to dedicate her life to the betterment of her community. Edith developed a water scheme that has improved the health of the community and engaged them in managing their own water resources. Her involvement also resulted in the building of roads and other infrastructures. She has also been instrumental in reducing unemployment.

Edith is committed to instilling a sense of patriotism in young girls. As a Girl Guide instructor, she is committed to doing her best "to God and my country". She has traveled across Transkei and witnessed the suffering of her people. She decided early in her life that she was going to dedicate her life to the betterment of her community. She has done this with grace and passion. She has been instrumental in reducing unemployment by introducing poultry farming, business skills and trade to the unemployed local women, as part of a poverty alleviation program. The businesses are wholly community-owned and all profit made goes towards improving the lives of the community. In Edith's village people fetched water from a river that was also used by the local tuberculosis (TB) center as a drainage passage. This often resulted in the spread of TB and other related infections and diseases. Edith together with some other concerned members of her community initiated a community water scheme. The main objective of this project was to supply the community with clean running water and also to provide skills so that the community could operate the scheme and do minor repairs whenever necessary. The project is community-based with only financial assistance from the government. Through the water scheme Edith has managed to improve the health of the community and engage them in managing their own water resources. Her involvement has also resulted in the creation of roads and other infrastructures. This she has done without any promise of rewards or glory.

During the rainy seasons the rural settlements of the Transkei witness numerous cholera cases due to unclean water and contaminated water supplies.

South Africa

Vina Mazumdar

Centre for Women's Development Studies (CWDS)

Vina Mazumdar (born 1927) is called "the grandmother of women's studies in South Asia". Her transformation from an activist academic to a grassroots intervention worker began with a project that took her across the country. Her distress at the condition of women migrant laborers was the impetus for an experiment on the use of wastelands to provide sustenance for rural women. The project, widely emulated, changed the lives of the women. Vina's mix of academic enquiry, dialoguing with policy-planners, and engaging with grassroots initiatives, is a whole new way of looking at women's issues.

Vina Mazumdar is a social scientist by training, a women's activist and feminist by instinct and choice, a "troublemaker" by her own confession, and a "recorder and chronicler of the Indian Women's Movement". Trained as a social scientist, Vina naturally moved into the academy. It was her appointment as member-secretary of the Committee on the Status of Women in India that radically altered the direction of her life and work. A report that she was working on took her across the country. The large-scale marginalization, poverty, and invisibility of India's laboring women — "the hidden and unacknowledged majority" — moved her deeply.

In 1981, with some like-minded people, she founded the autonomous Centre for Women's Development Studies to carry on the task of fighting for women's rights. She has since been working with peasant women in two districts of West Bengal. The partnership began as an experiment in mobilizing women's groups around wasteland development and livelihood issues. Realizing that the biggest challenge was to create productive work in the women's own villages, Vina organized a group of assetless women from Bankura district, West Bengal, managing to obtain eight acres of wasteland. It took three years of hard labor to demonstrate — against all odds, local and official hurdles — that wasteland can be regenerated to provide sustenance. It was the women's organization, Vina says self-deprecatingly, that demonstrated "a great political dynamism, and they themselves became the agents of change". Vina has followed no models, no conventions, or markers in her long career. Her mix of academic enquiry, dialoguing with policy-planners, and engaging with grassroots initiatives of rural women is her creation alone.

When many women migrant workers return to their villages, they find debris. The annual migratory process means high infant mortality, indebtedness, and sexual exploitation. The biggest challenge is to create productive work in the villages.

India

"My daily life is made up
of meetings with people
from all walks of life, who,
each in their own way,
enrich my experience with
something new. To all of
them I am so indebted."

Fawzia Talout Meknassi

Presse Marocaine
International Forum for Women
Arab Women's Council

Fawzia Talout Meknassi is an economics and management graduate of the University Hassan II, Casablanca, and has trained at the International Press Institute (IPI) in Paris and the Global Leadership Programme, Manhattanville College, Purchase/NY. A gifted journalist and the Director General of the Presse Marocaine, a leading Moroccan press agency, she is not only a correspondent for the Al-Ahram Press group in Cairo, but also a university teacher for communication, marketing, advertising and journalism.

Fawzia Talout Meknassi's achievements include the establishment of the Salon for Mediterranean Women in 1997 and the International Forum for Women in 1999. Already in 1995 she was selected by the French magazine "Marie Claire" as one of a hundred women who have contributed to the advancement of the world. Fawzia has also opened a multimedia communication center for young people, in order to bridge the gap in information technology between the North and the South. She is Executive Director of the International Forum for Women and a key figure of the United Nations International Research and Training Institute for the Advancement of Women (INSTRAW). Talking about herself and her work Fawzia says, "My daily life is made up of meetings with people from all walks of life, who, each in their own way, enrich my experience with something new. To all of them I am so indebted. And if I were to name them individually, this would take me ages to do! I have very little to say about myself. The word 'I' barely exists in my vocabulary! To be a journalist, I believe, is to be part of society. For me, knowing the world leads to pluralism, respect of others' opinions and tolerance. Life comprises both good and evil, peace and fear. But one should not be afraid of confrontation. Journalists are solitary, yet they still belong to all humanity. The world turns, and situations present themselves: women's rights, the future of the planet, the reduction of poverty, technological advancement ... and the journalist must keep pace!"

Fawzia Talout Meknassi indicates that the fundamental impediment to women's socio-economic development in Morocco is the cultural setting. Women's productivity is under-valued in the public and private sectors. In order for women to progress, a radical change in the ethos is needed.

Morocco

Netsanet Mengistu

Progynist
Meklit Microcreditbank

Netsanet Mengistu has a BA in Management and Administration. She is the founder of Progynist, an Ethiopian women's empowerment NGO, and Meklit, a pioneering local microcredit bank. Netsanet focuses on gender discrimination. She is committed to building up and enhancing the infrastructure in the underprivileged areas in Ethiopia. As an active member in the Ethiopian opposition for many years, Netsanet mobilizes women to strive for social development and the establishment of community projects in healthcare, education and legal consultation for marginalized Ethiopian citizens.

Netsanet Mengistu was born in 1951 in Assosa near the Ethiopian-Sudanese border, far from the privileged Amharic center of Addis Ababa. At the age of 25, with a BA in Management and Administration, she gained a unique experience working underground in the opposition party for ten years to bring justice and development to Ethiopian society. However, she was later arrested and imprisoned for six years. After her release, she assumed various positions in government offices and in several international NGOs. She was inspired to found a local NGO in 1997 to fight injustice against women in her country. She says, "I am committed to helping Ethiopian women to become full participants in society: to participate in achieving political, economic and social welfare in their country."

Netsanet has successfully networked groups of women from all political levels, social backgrounds and religious — based organizations. She says, "We have to be able to gain the trust and respect of those in power as well as the people around us, without compromising our fundamental principles." Starting out from one small room in the marginalized quarter Kifle Ketema, in Addis Ababa, Netsanet made visits and carried out interviews to mobilize the community with its existing social organizations and local authorities to set up basic social, educational and health services for the destitute people. 8000 urban and 4000 rural school dropouts, single mothers without income, illiterate and HIV patients have so far found support in diverse ways to generate their income and maintain their standard of living. Netsanet also organizes alternative basic education classes, provides support to impoverished children to continue their education and offers tutorial classes for girls to enhance their chances of getting to university.

Netsanet is committed to helping Ethiopian women become full participants in society's political and economic development. She believes that such an aim should not be "a temporary solution or a springboard to something else".

Ethiopia

Viloyat Mirzoyeva

Women in Development Bureau (WID)
Gender and Development

Viloyat Mirzoyeva (born 1952) heads the Women in Development Bureau and the NGO Gender and Development, both of which promote equal rights for women in society. She trains leaders of governmental and non-governmental women's organizations. As a result of her work, hundreds of women are successfully working in various areas of society. She has helped Tajik women create NGOs that aim to solve gender problems in Tajikistan.

Head of the Women and Development Bureau (WID) and director of the association Gender and Development, Viloyat Mirzoyeva helps Tajik women find their place in political, economic, and social life through training and educational programs. "As a consequence of the civil war in Tajikistan, many men left the country to earn money. All difficulties lay on women's shoulders. The desire to help women ensure their economic independence and the survival of their families, made me and my team make the first step forward," Viloyat says. The WID Bureau and the Gender and Development organization have united their efforts in carrying out activities with one aim: increasing national awareness and women's development in society. Both organizations envisage women's involvement in the process of the social and cultural advancement of society, along with gender equality in all spheres of society, including political life.

Initially, the WID Bureau worked through projects and programs that developed a credit scheme for widows who had lost their husbands during the war and their homes in the Vakhdat district, a locus of conflict in the country until 2001. Meetings with the women in each of the 28 settlements became the starting point of fruitful work. A learning center for 100 girls was established, where girls from remote districts of Tajikistan could study and learn leadership skills. The WID Bureau has promoted the emergence of civil society organizations and encouraged NGOs to work together to solve women's problems. In the end, women's organizations of Tajikistan have raised the country's awareness of the need to achieve equality of women and their involvement in all spheres of public life.

Although Tajikistan has made great progress since gaining independence and ending civil war, it is still struggling to transform the former Soviet system into an open and democratic society. Poverty remains the greatest concern with 64% of the population living below the national poverty line.

Mogullamma, finally
self-mobile in her
motorized wheelchair,
has become a
resource center,
training disability
activists in
social mobilization
and community
organization.

Mogullamma

Disabled, with no strength in her legs since childhood, Mogullamma has been a crusader for the rights of disabled people. She started with an NGO working with disabled people, eventually becoming a psychotherapist. Mogullamma is today involved mainly with the facilitation of life skills among disabled women, and providing them with legal literacy on public works department rights. The Andhra Pradesh government has adopted her concept of a "neighborhood center" for people with disabilities.

When she was just one year old, a local doctor misdiagnosed a minor health problem, and the treatment left Mogullamma-a child from the Munnuru Kaapu caste in Andhra Pradesh-with polio. Primarily because of her family's determination, she got an education, and landed a job as a bookkeeper with a local organization. But it was after joining an NGO working with the disabled that she really came into her own. Mogullamma has rehabilitated people with different disabilities, and persuaded public works departments (PWDs) to set up groups to give disabled people vocational training. Some of her work also involves dealing with the particular problems facing different people-many children have benefited from Mogullamma's initiatives to get them corrective surgeries. In August 2001, she underwent an operation on both her legs, after which she moved into a wheelchair, finally self-mobile. In 2003, she was given a motorized tricycle, which is what she now uses.

Mogullamma is involved mainly with community mobilization, motivation, and facilitation of life skills among disabled women, and in providing them with legal literacy on their PWD rights. She has also taken on the social responsibility of building awareness about issues of health, education, and livelihoods. Mogullama has set up 11 PWD groups across six villages, all of which are now self-sustainable. She has also been able to leverage resources and entitlements from the state government for healthcare, education, livelihood, mobility access, and social inclusion. Most important, her concept of the "neighborhood center" has been adopted by the Andhra Pradesh government under the disability component of the Velegu Project, aided by the World Bank through supplemental executive retirement plans.

India remains a grossly disabled-unfriendly country by most yardsticks. Among the ignored areas are social inclusion for the disabled, an understanding of their mental health, and the issue of their livelihoods.

India

"If only women united,
we would be able to
stop talking about
injustices and human
rights violations."

Azza Mint Moma

Born in Atar, in the mountainous region of Adrar, Azza Mint Moma (39) is well-known in her country for her struggle to liberate Mauritanian women. She claims the right of women to liberty and to freedom of choice in their life, especially in their choice of husband.

Azza Mint Moma's struggle is centered in the mountainous region of the Adrar within a very religious community that is closed to external influence and rigid in the face of world change. Madame Azza Mint Moma was lucky enough to go to school; this was believed to be a big adventure and a great risk. Her mother, who was divorced from her father, removed her from her traditional family environment and placed her in a school against the will of the paternal family. After brilliant primary and secondary school studies, Azza specialised in computer science in Morocco. She returned to Mauritania with her diploma and attempted to re-integrate herself into her family environment, but her reputation for an open-minded spirit and progress preceded her and she faced serious difficulties and a lack of understanding. Azza faced resistance from traditionalist elements who saw her as a western woman trying to introduce a behavior that is foreign to them. Azza decided to take up a courageous fight against the closed minds and religious and social intolerance that, according to her, are the sources of many conflicts and injustices. This is why she claims the right of women to liberty and to freedom of choice in their life, especially in their choice of husband. While claiming these rights, she tirelessly campaigns for human rights that take into account tradition, religion, and progress for women. To accomplish her fight, Azza Mint has shown great courage and tremendous perseverance in denouncing harmful and unfair practices towards Mauritanian women, who make up the majority of society. She also denounces injustice towards former slaves and marginalized people.

Azza Mint Moma was saddened by conditions to which women, coming from dogmatic environments, were subjected. She reacted by arranging meetings and speaking in various forums. She fought with determination to have meetings open to both women and men.

Mauritania

Elsie Monge

Ecumenical Commission of Human Rights
Ecuadorian Front for Human Rights

She entered the missionary community of Maryknoll and worked with people who had gone astray. She denounced a murder during a radio transmission in Panama and was forced to leave the country. Back in Ecuador, her native country, Elsie Monge collaborated with agricultural cooperatives of afro-descendent peasants. Later, she started working with the Ecumenical Commission of Human Rights, which she has directed since 1986. She is helping refugees, denouncing crimes and other abuses. Eternally young, Elsie Monge (72) continues to lead the Commission.

From a young age, Elsie Monge worked with her grandmother, who was the founder of the Red Cross of Ecuador. Later, she studied in the United States and graduated in education. During her studies, she learned about the Catholic missionary group at Maryknoll, which she later joined. She worked throughout Latin America as a missionary with people who have strayed from the Catholic Church's teachings. She worked at a Catholic radio station in Panama and was "invited to leave" the country after denouncing the murder of a clergyman during a radio program. So she returned to Ecuador. She worked in a community of afro-descendent peasants. At that time, the peasants held the land and confronted the powerful landowners. She participated in the formation of the Federation of Agricultural Workers. During one confrontation, one of the peasants was killed and others were hurt. In the hospital, they were denied treatment because one of the nurses belonged to the family of the landowner involved in the conflict. Elsie came with the Ecumenical Commission of Human Rights and changed mindsets. The peasants received land and an irrigation channel.

In 1981, Elsie began her service with the Commission. She supported political refugees of Chile, Uruguay and El Salvador. Shortly after, she was called on to face the dictatorship of Leon Febres Cordero, in Ecuador. She gave legal and humanitarian assistance to political prisoners, and she denounced the disappearances carried out by state security. She has been threatened. The police fabricated an incriminating video to discredit her. She pushed for the creation of a Provincial Commission for Human Rights, which later became the Ecuadorian Front for Human Rights, an organization which she heads. Elsie Monge, the rich girl who decided to dedicate her life to the poor, declares: "The worse attack on human rights is poverty."

The Catholic missionary congregation of Maryknoll was founded in 1911. The four sisters assassinated in El Salvador by right-wing forces came from this congregation. Leaders of the Presbyterian, Lutheran, and Catholic Churches founded the Ecumenical Commission of Human Rights of Ecuador, in 1978.

Ecuador

Asipa Musayeva

Independent Association of Disabled Women

Asipa Musayeva (born 1947) is the president of the Independent Association of Disabled Women of the Kyrgyz Republic. Over the past 15 years, she has accomplished a great deal for the organization and for disabled people, protecting their rights and advocating for them on a national level. She has successfully lobbied for laws to increase opportunities for disabled people to work and participate in society. Asipa conducts seminars, training courses for leaders, particularly from rural areas, on the importance of civil and economic rights for people with disabilities.

Asipa Musayeva began her activity in 1989 addressing economic and social problems of the disabled. She is disabled herself and carries out her work walking on crutches. Asipa is acutely aware of difficulties faced by people with disabilities. Fighting society's discrimination against the disabled has become Asipa's main objective. A strong and determined woman, she never gives up. For many of her compatriots who have experienced complicated, limiting physical situations, Asipa gives hope and provides an example of courage and optimism. She believes that the disabled are not a burden on society, but equal members of it, enjoying full rights together with other citizens, including the right to work. Asipa's organization is the first cooperative body for disabled people in her country.

Asipa realized that she would not achieve much working alone, so she decided to unite disabled people in an organization to fight for their rights in a joint effort. As it was previously prohibited for the disabled to work in Kyrgyzstan, she wanted to achieve the right to work. Under the former policy, people with disabilities would receive a meager allowance and had to stay home, idle. People approach her with their problems, and Asipa never refuses them help. She teaches people to remain determined, fight unjust circumstances, believe in their future, and embrace life.

She works in cooperation with the government to gain recognition of her organization's direct benefit to thousands of Kyrgyz citizens with disabilities. She lobbies for laws protecting the civil and social rights of disabled women of Kyrgyzstan. "At present in Kyrgyzstan, people with disabilities are not included in the process of designing laws affecting them," Asipa says. Therefore, many laws intended to protect the interests of the disabled often do not do so.

Disabled people's rights had previously been ignored in Kyrgyz society, their problems being overlooked in the media and by the State. Following the disintegration of the Soviet Union, non-governmental organizations began to be formed, some of them focusing on the rights of people with disabilities.

Kyrgyzstan

Litha Musyimi-Ogana

New Partnership for Africa's Development (Nepad)

Litha Musyimi-Ogana, a 45-year-old Kenyan mother of three, is currently the gender advisor of New Partnership for Africa's Development (Nepad) in South Africa. Previously, she worked as the regional director of the African Centre for Empowerment, Gender and Advocacy (Acega) based in Nairobi, Kenya. In that capacity, she successfully organized the women peace train from Kampala (Uganda) to Johannesburg (South Africa) to the World Summit for Sustainable Development in 2002.

The peace torch traversed the continent on the women peace train. Women handed it over to other women six times from Kampala to Johannesburg. In between, ceremonies took place in transit towns across Africa. Litha Musyimi-Ogana took her smallest child along. The initiative, whose theme was "You cannot have sustainable development without peace in Africa," was a success. More than 10,000 participants benefited from the train's journey in different ways. Since women bear the major burden of war and conflict in Africa, they saw the World Summit as a good opportunity to campaign for the end of wars. They used the peace train and the peace torch to pass this message to the people on the continent and the rest of the world. Litha was identified as the perfect candidate to take care of the advocacy project.

In her 20 years as an activist and lobbyist, she has organized and participated in peaceful street demonstrations, drafted, endorsed and circulated petitions and criticized the government on gender discriminative policies and practices. She has been involved in influencing policy decisions at global, regional and national levels.

Litha Musyimi-Ogana holds a bachelor of commerce degree and an MA of economics degree, both from the University of Nairobi. She has recently become the gender advisor for the Nepad in South Africa. Litha has published two books, one on lobbying and one on monitoring United Nations commitments at national level.

Women in Africa bear the major burden of war and conflict; they saw the World Summit as a good opportunity to campaign for the end of wars. They used the peace train and the peace torch to pass this message to the people on the continent and to the rest of the world.

Kenya

Najat M'jid

Mother and Child Clinic
BAYTI Association

Najat M'jid is a paediatrician and director of Mother and Child Clinic, Casablanca. She is the head and founder of the association BAYTI, the first Moroccan tailored institution for street children's rehabilitation and reintegration that works directly with children. The institution's programs squarely address problems such as child labor, violation of the law, child maltreatment — including sexual abuse — and child trafficking. In 2000 Dr Najat M'jid was nominated for the "Chevalier de la Legion d'Honneur" (Knight of the Legion of Honor) in France for her work on Human Rights.

The driving force for the protection of children's rights in Morocco, Najat M'jid has lobbied for effectuating legislative reforms in the country, which denounce violations of children's rights. Najat has assumed her grassroots work through a number of foundations concerned with children's welfare, at both national and international levels. She is a consultant for The United Nations Children's Fund (Unicef) and the State Secretariat for Childhood, NGOs, and she is the regional focal point for the Middle East and North Africa (MENA), analyzing and evaluating issues regarding child sexual abuse, health, education, poverty and family rejection.

Najat has worked untiringly towards the adoption of national rehabilitative plans for vulnerable children and the foundation of state-run agencies to deal with children's problems. Her lobby has effectively assisted in improving the living conditions of minors in detention and in saving street children from sexual exploitation, about which she has vocalized concerns in the MENA region. Najat has made great strides forward in the creation of a network of Arab NGOs working for childhood welfare. With the sponsorship of the World Bank and European Union (EU), she has also participated in a number of international conferences on the rights of children and other connected issues in Stockholm, Yokohama, New York and also for example in Madrid at the International Summit on Democracy, Terrorism and Security. The rehabilitative plans that Najat M'jid has set up have been adopted in Tunisia, France, Cambodia, Spain, Jordan, Yemen, Senegal and Mali.

Najat M'jid has been the driving force for the advocacy of children's rights in Morocco over the last sixteen years. She has participated in effectuating legislative reforms, denouncing violations of children's rights and raising awareness of children's severe vulnerability.

Morocco

Nalini speaks with awe about the stamina and dexterity of the women who process and sell fish. She speaks with rage about the processes that undermine their very livelihoods.

Nalini Nayak

Self-Employed Women's Association (Sewa)
Program for Community Organization (PCO)
Coastal Women's Association (CWA)

Before Nalini Nayak (born 1946) stepped in, small fishworkers were among the most unorganized groups in Kerala. She has since helped them set up cooperatives and organize themselves into a registered trade union. She founded the Kerala chapter of the Self-Employed Women's Association (Sewa) and helped set up the Program for Community Organization. Nalini's holistic view of development has helped Kerala's fishworker community emerge into a vocal, aware group that can protect its own interests.

Nalini Nayak set off from Bangalore to Kerala to work with virtually the most unorganized group in the state-the small fishworkers. With the help of friends, she organized a series of marketing and credit cooperatives among the fishworkers, and helped them set up a registered trade union that has very effectively put forward the interests of fishworkers to the authorities. Nalini also founded the Kerala chapter of the Sewa at Thiruvananthapuram, which helps women from the fishing communities find alternative jobs. These movements have also strengthened the voice of the fishworker community, which today has access to special vehicles, at least in some areas, as opposed to the complete denial of public transport to fishworkers in the past.

In Kerala, Nalini also helped set up the Program for Community Organization (PCO), which works with men, women, and young people to focus them on better management of fishery resources, better education, health, sanitation, transportation, and housing. Through the PCO, women traders and vendors have been able to confront exploitative taxes and harassment at the markets. While she is intensely involved with the rights and interests of fishworkers, Nalini sees the need to balance their interests with that of their ecosystem. That is, in the end, the source of their sustenance. She has been particularly vocal about the need to protect and regenerate the coastal ecosystem, and to protest against the industrialization of the coastal shrimp culture.

Nalini has learnt to admire the skill and courage of the fishworkers who brave the seas in tiny boats. She speaks with awe about the stamina and dexterity of the women who process and sell fish. She speaks with rage about the processes that undermine their very livelihoods.

In the late 1960s, a period of euphoria over the industrial model of technological fishery development, small fishing communities and their ways were condemned as backward and inefficient. By the 1970s, it had become evident that technology was overkilling the fish resource.

India

Akeela Naz

Anjuman Muzareen-Punjab

The daughter of farmers, Akeela Naz (born 1976) was the first woman to join Anjuman Muzareen-Punjab, a movement of landless tenants in Punjab, Pakistan's largest province, and she has been at the forefront of their struggle for ownership rights to the lands they have cultivated for generations. She has motivated many women to join this million-strong movement, of which she is now general secretary.

A high school graduate from a farming family who could not continue with her education for lack of money, Akeela Naz has secured far more than a college education through her involvement with Anjuman Muzareen-Punjab. As one of the leaders of this movement to secure the rights of tenant farmers, Akeela has weathered false accusations, attacks by rangers and the police, the enmity of landlords, and the disapproval of maulvis (clergies).

The movement, which has spread over ten districts of Punjab, was born in 1988 when tenant farmers decided to challenge government departments that controlled the lands they had been cultivating for four generations. The farmers argued, on the basis of revenue records, that the departments did not own these lands. The movement spread rapidly in the 1990s, and mobilized one million tenant farmers under the slogan "ownership or death". Akeela joined the Anjuman-e-Mazarin in May 2000. She wanted women at the movement's vanguard because she knew that women had no role in decision-making, and that even if the farmers got their land back, the women might not be able to exercise control. Today, women farmers are at the heart of this struggle, and refuse to be intimidated by the landholders' aggression. For her work, Akeela, who lives in Khanewal district in Punjab, was elected general secretary of Anjuman Muzareen-Punjab.

Akeela is an excellent public speaker and writer, and an efficient organizer. She has worked on other causes such as equal rights for minorities, bonded labor, child labor, and domestic violence. She is chairperson of the Minority Rights Commission of Khanewal, and an executive member of the Minority Rights Commission of Pakistan.

Of Pakistan's 196.63 million acres, only 52.21 million are available for cultivation. About four million landless farmers work as tenant farmers, earning only a 30 percent share of the production. Those fighting for their rights confront feudal landowners and government rangers.

Pakistan

Pélagie Nduwayo—Ndikuriyo

Solidarité pour Aider les Sinisterés Burundais (Sasb)

Pélagie Nduwayo-Ndikuriyo works with women, students, girls and the disabled. She supports disadvantaged people in different ways with the aim of reducing poverty. She offers sewing courses for women and girls, provides seeds to ensure the survival of families, and pays for children to receive an education. She works with people of different ethnic groups.

In a refugee camp, she once met a woman who owned nothing except a paigne, the brightly colored piece of cloth that is commonly worn in Africa, wrapped around the waist. The woman had her menstruation and was crouched in a corner. Without a change of clothes or another piece of cloth, she was messed up and could not move from that spot.

Uprooted from her relatively sheltered life as a Tutsi and wife of a former Burundi prime minister, Pélagie Nduwayo began to support individual women in the camp by distributing clothes, food and sometimes also money. This was at first merely a drop in the ocean, but eventually picked momentum. The women organized themselves into a group as they realized that this help might one day cease. So they asked Pélagie Nduwayo to assist them to become self-reliant.

Younger women make sweet fried pastries for sale at the markets and on the streets of Bujumbura, and widows weave cloth in their own workshop. Orphans go to school, through the assistance of Solidarité pour Aider les Sinisterés Burundais (Sasb), which pays their fees. Girls now sew and organize fashion shows in the organization's foyer. Meetings are also held at the organization's office with donors, to discuss the positive outcomes of Pélagie's work. She insures that people get a meal and has adopted a boy from the rural area and cares for him as if he was her own son. The people honor her in song and pray for the continued success of her work. The students' spokesman, who was adopted and is still under her care since the war, sums up the aspirations of all: "Nous sommes qui nous sommes grâce à elle." Meaning, "We are who we are, thanks to her."

The conflict between the Tutsi minority and the Hutu majority in Burundi left many women widowed and children orphaned, reducing many families to poverty. The country, which is very fertile, has been mined and deforested. It is very difficult to recover from the varied losses.

Burundi

Elizabeth Neuenschwander

Elizabeth Neuenschwander has spent almost 50 years of her life working abroad. She became a dressmaker and left Emmental, a remote Swiss region, at age 19. Since the late 1950s, she has worked in developing countries for different organizations: with Tibetan refugees in Nepal and India, as a nutrition advisor in Biafra and Nigeria. Those were only a few stations on her way from a dressmaker to a project manager. Since 1986, she has worked in Quetta, Pakistan, where she founded self-help projects for Afghan refugees. In 2001, the Canton of Berne gave her the renowned Trudi-Schlatter Award.

Elizabeth Neuenschwander (76) takes pictures of every bridge she sees. "Bridges lead over abysses, they are connections between two different shores," she explains. She was born in 1929 in Schangnau, Switzerland, and left her village early. It was the narrowness of the remote Emmental that made her leave plus her deep interest in foreign cultures. She went to Denmark for further education. From there her path went further — step by step. Gradually, the dressmaker from Schangnau turned into a project manager for several international organizations such as Unicef and the Red Cross, working in African and Asian developing countries. Since 1986, she has been running her own private projects in Pakistan. Overall, her objective has remained the same: help people to help themselves.

She travels to Pakistan twice a year, stays there for a few weeks supervising her projects in Quetta near the Afghan border, comes back to Switzerland giving presentations, showing pictures and selling blouses and shawls that "her" women sew and embroider in Pakistan. With the aid of her projects, she wants to give women more self-confidence and self-esteem in an Islamic country where honor killings still are a part of daily life. "This is my small contribution to a better world. A world where everybody knows his and her values is a better world," Elizabeth Neuenschwander explains and goes on traveling between Switzerland and Pakistan: twice a year she crosses the bridge that she has built between two countries and two worlds.

In Quetta, Pakistan, near the Afghan border, hundreds of Afghan women have found shelter in refugee camps. They desperately need to find ways to make an income and ensure their own survival and that of their families.

Switzerland

Nguyen Thi Hoe

Kova Traffic Paint Company

Nguyen Thi Hoe, a Professor-Doctor and the General Director of Kova Traffic Paint Company, was born in 1946 to a poor family. She had to overcome many obstacles to become successful in science and business, which are considered men's fields. Her subjects for scientific research are practical and make a high economic and social contribution without pollution.

According to Nguyen Thi Hoe, an aspiring woman scientist can overcome obstacles to her advancement with strong determination and a profound love for science. "I was told, 'Scientific research is not for women, especially for a 20-year-old with three children'. Instead of buckling under their prejudice, I became determined to prove them wrong." It was wartime and the university was in an evacuated area with no equipment or materials. She was always hungry because she had to share the little food she had with her children. To earn money for her studies, she raised pigs. Her hard work paid off when she graduated with high marks and was chosen to be a lecturer at the Hanoi Polytechnic University (HPU). She studied waterproofing materials, a practical choice in Vietnam, a tropical country with lots of rain and humidity that can wreak havoc on buildings, and she developed a substance that resulted in a tenfold increase in water resistance. Nguyen Thi Hoe also figured out how to blend it into house paint.

By 1993, at the age of 46, Hoe had authored 20 scientific research projects on the study of color and highly ground materials. Named director of research at Ho Chi Minh Polytechnic University, she developed a manufacturing process that could turn cheap local substances into usable materials that retailed at half the price of imported materials. She received the Kovalevskaja Award for "women with scientific research projects that serve their country's life and society" from an NGO and the San Francisco State University. She organized the Kova Paint Company that produces quality but inexpensive and non-polluting products. To help young women with a passion for science pursue their dream, Nguyen Thi Hoe established the Kova Awards in 2002, which provides scholarships to women who have achieved excellence in science and community activities.

In a developing country like Vietnam, doing scientific research with practical applications and high economic and social value is the best way to advance in life.

Nirmala

Mahila Samakhya

When Nirmala (born 1959) began work with women at the village level, she had to find ways to dodge her family so that she could attend school. Today, Nirmala is a strong campaigner for women's rights, and an active member of women's courts. A seasoned arbitrator, Nirmala is adept at sorting out issues amicably, steering both parties away from the police court rigmarole. She has also brought about a revolution in the way midwives operate in the region: they display a high level of professionalism and attention to hygiene.

When Nirmala began her association with the NGO Mahila Samakhya, things were not easy — her husband and in-laws strongly opposed her going out to work. Nirmala, though, attends cluster meetings regularly, laughing off her family's jibes and threats. Well-known at the village and block level as a strong campaigner for women's rights, she is an active member of the women's courts and has a knack for tackling tricky situations amicably. She is particularly alert to discrimination against women, invariably standing up for women's rights.

As is the mark of a true leader, Nirmala's attempt is always to sort out all issues amicably, through mutual consent. She attempts to solve every dispute that arises at the village self-help group's women's court. This ensures that neither party gets stuck in the police court rigmarole, wasting both time and money. However, in cases where either party is uncooperative, she does not hesitate to involve the police and the judiciary.

Nirmala has also trained to be a midwife, which helps her in matters of women's health, hygiene, and childcare. She is largely responsible for the high level of professionalism and attention to hygiene — especially in cutting and tying the umbilical cord — which midwives in the region today display. This attention to basics has also helped bring to the forefront the issues of women and reproductive health. At the village-level meetings of the women's group, Nirmala is at the forefront, calling for a change in antiwomen practices. From struggling to work outside the home to becoming the pivot of awareness generation on women's issues in her area of work, Nirmala's footing is sure and nimble.

Midwifery is an ancient practice in rural India, but it is hobbled by arcane convention and, sometimes, outright quackery. Only lately has it shown signs of a more modern, hygienic outlook, brought about by women's awareness.

India

Katsuko Nomura

Livelihood Cooperative Association
Women's Occupational Association
Laborers' Families' Organization

Katsuko Nomura, called the pioneer of Japan's NGO movement, has helped to ensure social justice for Japan's citizens for more than half a century. She began her work by lobbying for a consumer cooperative law, which was passed in 1948. She went on to establish a Livelihood Cooperative Association, laying the groundwork for the development of co-ops, and founded the Women's Occupational Association and the Laborers' Families' Organization. She established the Information Center for Public Citizens and worked there until 1998, when she retired at age 87.

From her youth, Katsuko Nomura was appalled by the poverty she saw in the Nishijin neighborhood in Kyoto, Japan. Her family supplied tools to weavers, who lived in destitution as they created beautiful kimonos for the wealthy. Katsuko's family, moderately well-off and liberal, encouraged her to attend university, which was exceptional for Japanese girls in the 1930s. Katsuko took advantage of the opportunity and enrolled at Doshisha University, where she studied ethics and social work. In 1944, when people were evacuating to other areas of Japan during the aerial attacks by the US military, Katsuko went to Kokyo to work for the Eto Consumers' Cooperative. Her passion to change the lives of people living in poverty began to bear fruit in 1948, when she lobbied for a consumer cooperative law, giving consumers more rights. Nomura went on to establish organizations that developed cooperatives, trained and educated women, and changed the inhumane conditions of mine workers.

The goal of her most recent organization, the Information Center for Public Citizens, is to facilitate the exchange of information about citizens' movements among Japan and other nations, especially countries in Asia.

Katsuko Nomura began her work at a time when Japanese society was very stratified and the gender gap was unbridgeable. Japan's widespread poverty and famine affected the country's lower classes and most vulnerable members.

Japan

Christine Ntahe

Search for Common Ground Burundi

Christine Ntahe was born in 1949 and is regarded as "mother" of street children in Burundi. For 30 years she worked as a journalist and manager with Radio Télévision Nationale de Burundi (RTNB). She became famous for her Saturday children's program. During the crisis years, which begun in 1994, her program frequently addressed the themes of peace and coexistence between the Hutus and Tutsis. Today, she works for Search for Common Ground at the Women's Peace Center and for Studio Ijambo. In 2000 the youth of Bujumbura named her "Citizen of Peace" and "Best Mother of the Country".

Every Saturday for the last 30 years Christine Ntahe has given children a voice through her radio program "Tuganirizibibondo" (dialogue with children). In 1994 when the civil war was raging, the program attracted attention in neighboring Tanzania, the Democratic Republic of Congo and Rwanda. She spoke to children about peace and the reality of Tutsis and Hutus living together. Children took part by calling in, writing or by visiting the studio. At that time many war orphans lived on the streets where they were often victims of beating or discrimination. She began to involve street children in the programs, so that they could speak out. Although it took a long time before these children could trust Christine, she recalls that some did become involved and would say on the air, "Stop! We are just like other children and we did not choose to live on the streets." Today, she is their "mother" and her door is open to them every Sunday. She gives the children food, lets them have a bath and wash their clothes. She talks to the children about the importance of school, Aids prevention, their rights, solidarity and mutual support. As she talks, Christine Ntahe holds 12-year-old Adam in her arms. Adam is an orphan, who begs on the streets of Bujumbura for food and clothes. Sometimes the little money he gets is only enough for some bread or an avocado and not clothes. So he wears a dirty, flea-ridden T-shirt and sleeps next to a petrol station. She has not yet been able to persuade Adam to live with a family and attend school. To date, Christine Ntahe has rescued a dozen children from the streets, paid for their school and healthcare costs and given them love. Sometimes she goes into debt providing for the children. She has no network to support her children's program.

In Burundi there are frequent conflicts between the Hutu majority and the Tutsi elite. In 1994, more than 200,000 people lost their lives. Since then many orphaned children have lived either in refugee camps or on the streets.

"The universal protection of fundamental needs of both men and women and the enforcement of human dignity – this is my motto."

Teclaire Ntomp

Community Based self help Association

Teclaire Ntomp (67) has contributed to the well-being of fellow Cameroonians by providing training on sanitation, education, agriculture and nutrition. Her projects base on simple, indigenous techniques that provide income to self-help groups. Teclaire Ntomp's efforts have helped develop food products that are now marketed and consumed nationally and internationally.

Teclaire Ntomp learned as a pastor's daughter about the value of respecting and sharing with others in order to create true social harmony. A teacher by profession, she lived in different regions where she dealt with different people. She discovered that poverty and ignorance transforms people into egoists, partisans and creates low self-esteem. She thus ended her teaching career to focus on changing people's living conditions by promoting their local potentials. To achieve that she uses an organized work process that integrates solidarity and mutual assistance.

Acceptance by the target community and encouraged by others to succeed, gives energy to Teclaire Ntomp, whose husband and children also support and encourage her. As a result, village populations have mobilized over the past 13 years through the association set up by Ntomp Teclaire, the Community Based self help Association; and the American NGO African Action on Aids collaborated with her to publish "Fighting Hunger with Cassava: A Gift of 22 Recipes from the Rural Women of Bogso".

It has not always been easy. Teclaire often faces traditional customs that do not favor modern development. A peaceful future will be realized when women are educated and become financially and materially independent to subsequently improve education and health standards. Inadequate resources create all sorts of conflicts in societies. Hence, she keeps her motto: the universal protection of fundamental needs of both men and women and the enforcement of human dignity.

Life in Cameroon is harsh for ordinary citizens. The social and economic setting does not always facilitate the exploitation of local resources that could help alleviate poverty in some regions. Several organizations are remedying the situation with local and international networks.

Cameroon

Ny Luangkhot

Ny Luangkhot was born in Nongbon village Chaichettha district, Vientiane in 1953. She has a master's degree in economics from the University of Kiev and another in Sociology from the Sociology Institute of Moscow State University. She worked for the Ministry of Commerce and Industry, and was an interpreter for high-ranking officers. She lectured on Marxism to senior members of the Communist Party and worked for NGOs. Currently a consultant on development issues, she trains local workers in community development project evaluation for local and international organizations.

Ny Luangkhot was one of 19 children of a poor family — only eight children survived. As the eldest sister of the remaining offspring, she had to take on great responsibilities. After school, she collected vegetables and fresh water crabs and fish from rice fields to sell and so earn income for her family. She took her education seriously and completed her elementary education with high grades. After high school, she applied for a scholarship to study abroad. Having passed the test, she was sponsored by the party to study in the Soviet Union (USSR). After completing her studies, she returned to the Lao People's Democratic Republic (Lao PDR) and worked for three years at the Ministry of Commerce and Industry. She was promoted to a high-ranking position, translating for the central Politburo. In 1985, the Party sent her to the Sociology Institute of Moscow State University for her second master's degree in sociology. Upon her return in 1989, she worked as an interpreter and lectured on Marxism to senior party members.

As Laos opened up, a number of international NGOs came in and Ny Luangkhot resigned from government to work with NGOs for a couple of years. Working as a freelance consultant on community development, focusing on human development, she operates mostly in far-flung rural areas with the least facilities. Many times, she has had to lead her team up the mountains during the rainy season when travel is most difficult. Ny Luangkhot is part of an early group of local Lao who promote public participation and community empowerment. Her concepts and approach have led to changes in community development work in her country. She has inspired many development motivators who have worked with her through the years.

When Laos, which stayed in isolation for a long time during the Cold War period, decided to open up to the world, foreigners poured into the country as tourists, investors, diplomats and international NGO workers. The latter have helped create a vibrant movement of social development workers there.

Lao People's Democratic Republic

Creuza Maria Oliveira

Federação Nacional das Trabalhadoras Domésticas (President of the National Federation of Domestic Workers)

Creuza Maria Oliveira (1957) became a domestic worker at age ten. Her first payment, which was worthless, came at 15. As thousands of Brazilian children, she increased the child labor statistics. As not many of them were able to do, she changed her life. President of the National Federation of Domestic Workers (Fenatrad), she is currently a national role model in the fight for the rights of her working class, for racial equality and for the elimination of child domestic labor.

In Brazil, half a million kids and teenagers between 5 and 18 years old are domestic workers. They have to leave their toys and books behind, in order to support themselves. Creuza Maria Oliveira is the portrait of something that still happens all over Brazil. At age ten, she exchanged her childhood for never-ending working hours. "A lot of girls leave school, move out of their families' house, and lose touch with children of their age and social class. As they grow up, their only role model is their employer."
Creuza used to live in the countryside in the hinterland of Bahia. There was not enough food for everyone. Her mother sent her to the city. She used to cook, clean and do the laundry seven days a week. This lonely life lasted until she was 26, when she found out, through a radio show, that domestic workers were meeting to discuss their rights. In 1985, along with her colleagues, she created an association. They joined leaderships from other states and managed to include domestic worker's rights in the new 1988 Brazilian Constitution. She founded the Union of Domestic Workers of Bahia and she also founded the National Federation of Domestic Workers (Fenatrad), presided by her.
Creuza attends meetings throughout the country and abroad. She has regained her self-esteem and always has a beautiful smile on her face. She is the reason for eight million Brazilian domestic workers to be proud. She uses her history to fight against child domestic labor. She tries to increase the awareness of politicians and society regarding the situation and gives classes to young domestic workers. She teaches them their rights as citizens. And, on top of all that, she tells them to love themselves as Afro-Brazilian women and competent professionals.

According to a research called Pnad (2001), 2.2 million Brazilian children and teenagers, between ages 5 and 14, work in different positions. This number goes as high as 5.5 million, between the ages of 5 and 17; one million of them do not study and 49% do not receive payment.

Brazil

Fatima Osman

Sudanese Women General Union (SWGU)

Fatima Abdel Rahim (69) did not receive a formal education. In 1960 she started a farming business in the private sector in the village El Gadar, Northern Sudan. Her farms annually yield heavy crops of dates, groundnuts and sorghum. She recruits a large number of laborers in her business and has a pragmatic approach to social development. The main issues she focuses on, according to her social reform views, are poverty reduction and an improvement of the living conditions of the unfortunate people in Sudan. Fatima is a member of the Sudanese Women General Union (SWGU).

Fatima did not receive a formal education, as she lived in a small tribal village in the far North of Sudan. When her husband died and left her a heavy burden of five children to raise, she was forced to work and subsist her kids. At the same time she has been inspired to create an idea about how to improve the economical conditions of her village. When she began working in 1960, Fatima had no financial resources. But due to the trust that local people have put in her, she managed to borrow some money and run a small business with it. Her business grew progressively till she could buy a five-acre farm with palm trees. At the beginning she depended on traditional manual farming methods. Then, when her income improved she bought some machinery, such as tractors, to help her cultivate the land. In addition to dates, she began to grow pasture for animal fodder, some of which she sells, the rest she keeps for the goats and sheep she raises.

The high productivity of her land has won Fatima a reputation as a farmer. She not only produces a heavy crop of dates, groundnuts and sorghum annually, but has also provided job opportunities for a lot of women and men in the village. Through creating a large number of jobs, she believes that she has taken some steps forward towards improving the living conditions of the people in her village. Fatima is therefore applauded as a successful model for women, as a breadwinner in a society that is still male dominated and despises women's role in becoming financially self-dependent. She has set an exemplum to other women, which inspires them to have confidence in their capacities and has proved that deprivation from formal education should not prevent people from taking up their chances in life and from participating in the improvement and welfare of society.

Fatima began her business in the Sudan from scratch. Now her work helps to improve the economic conditions of many families in the Sudan, especially the villagers. The heavy crop of her farms provides Northern Sudan with essential food, such as dates and groundnuts.

Sudan

Dora Ignacia Paiva da Silva

Housing Cooperative of La Tablada

Dora Paiva has worked on many different projects; constructing houses, making rag dolls, planting trees and organizing weaving workshops to make artisan products by hand and on the loom using rustic wool. For decades, she has been working on activities to aid social development. Her work has been unified by one aim: to teach her people to have hope.

"I planted seedlings and, today, I can see how big the plants are." Dora Paiva is now 73 years old and has seen many things grow during her lifetime. When she came to the neighborhood of La Tablada, in the administrative district of Salto, in the countryside of Uruguay, she found a place inhabited by people filled with a great fear. They were on the point of being evicted from their homes. They were living in extremely poor shacks, which they had lifted to provide themselves with shelter, in order to survive. Dora organized them and they fought their first fight together: to stay in their homes. "We were able to prove that their plots of land could not be expropriated." Later on, they fought and won their second battle, the battle for solidarity: "We managed to get the bishop to pay three architects to draw up plans, and we began to build solid houses. Everyone helped to build everyone else's house. All the arms became one." And Dora Paiva saw in La Tablada how the people's dignity grew as their houses took shape.

From 1964 until 1976, Dora took her social work to the rural areas. Later, when she returned to Montevideo, she put all her determination into projects for the creation of work opportunities: "We promoted textile works. We made dolls from maize leaves. We made a variety of utilitarian and decorative artisan products. We wove by hand and on the loom with rustic wool." But above all, Dora Paiva saw how something very special grew in her people: hope.

Poverty in Uruguay, like in the rest of Latin America, is a constant fact of life. The lack of conditions for a dignified life, the lack of work opportunities and the impossibility of having access to health and education are very present.

Uruguay

Binda Pandey

General Federation of Nepalese Trade Unions (Gefont)
International Federation of Chemical, Energy, Mines and General Workers'
Unions (Icem)

Binda Pandey (born 1966) has been involved in Nepal's trade union movement for the past 15 years as an activist and educator. She is a leader of the iron and chemical workers' unions, and the driving force behind most publications brought out by Gefont, one of the largest confederations of Nepalese trade unions. Responsible for many women joining trade unions and fighting for their rights, she currently plays an active role in the movement for the restoration of democracy in Nepal.

Binda was born into a rural farming family in Nuwakot, a hill district. Growing up in a conservative milieu, she charted her own path by acquiring a Masters in science and gender development, and then by going unionist. Her choices encouraged other young women to join the movement. During the 1990 pro-democracy movement, Binda played a critical coordinating role.

Binda is at the forefront of the fight to restore democracy to Nepal. This firebrand trade union leader was arrested and released three times in 2004 alone for campaigning for democracy. Since February 2005, she has been on a government watchlist, and is prohibited from leaving Kathmandu valley. Binda is a leader of major iron and chemical workers' unions in Nepal. Since May 2004, she has been deputy secretary general of Gefont, a confederation of Nepali trade unions. She was a central secretariat member and chief of its department of education from 2001 to 2004, and secretary of its department of foreign affairs from 1997 to 2000. From 1993 to 2000, she was secretary of its central women workers' department. Binda, who is close to the international trade union movement, is presidium member of the International Federation of Chemical, Energy, Mines and General Workers' Unions (Icem). It is a forum she uses to condemn emphatically the crackdown on pro-democracy activists in Nepal.

From 1994 to 1997, Binda worked as program coordinator for the Committee for Asian Women-Regional Labor, a Hong-Kong-based NGO, and was an executive committee member from 1997 to 2000. She also served on the Nepal government's National Women's Commission from March 2001 to 2003.

The major labor issues that drive Binda and her compatriots are unionization, implementation of labor law, gender equality in the workplace, social security, and the effectiveness of labor administration. Since the monarchic emergency of February 2005, trade unions have been eviscerated.

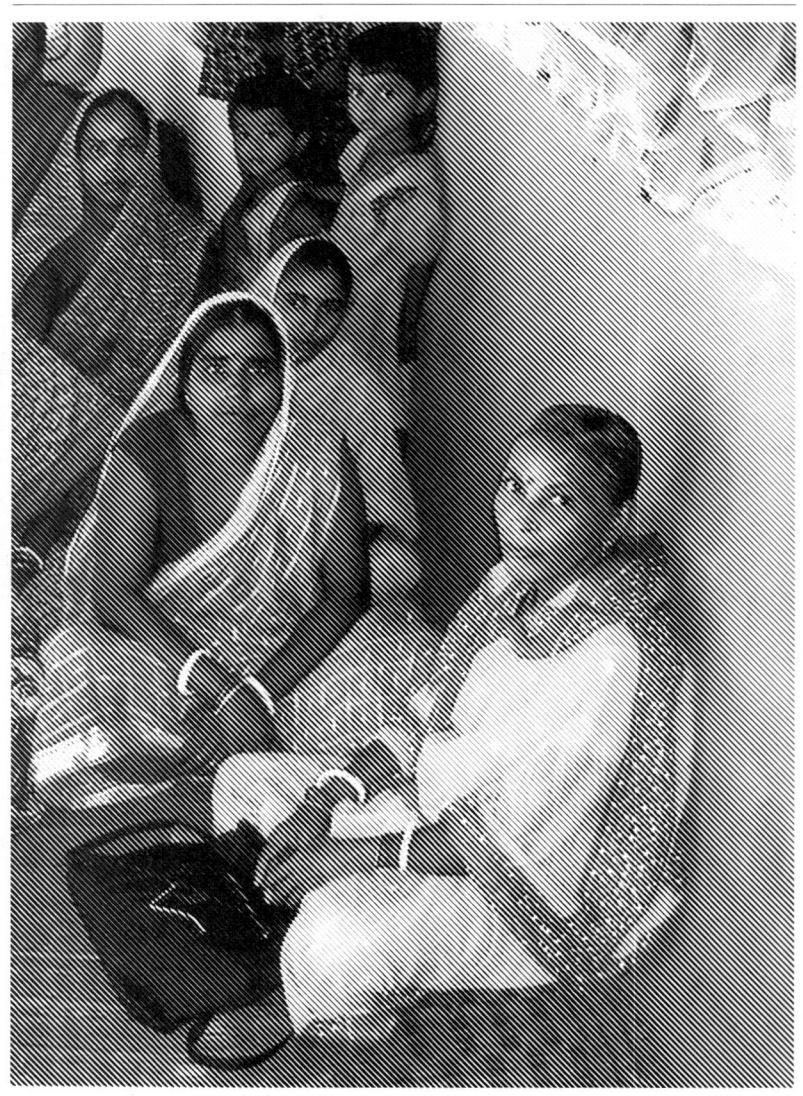

Nilu Rani Patra

Mahila Samiti

Nilu Rani Patra (born 1954), a peasant woman with little formal education, has been working for over two decades toward the empowerment of women and fishworkers' rights. She was also instrumental in organizing a mass protest against the setting up in her district of a missile base, which evicted more than 100,000 people from 132 villages.

Nilu's involvement with women's and fishworkers' rights began with an encounter with the Institute for Motivating Self-Employment (Imse). When its activists spoke of the environmental and social impact of shrimp monoculture, Nilu knew that she had seen this fallout in her own daily experience. She participated in an in-depth action research program organized by the Imse to gain deeper knowledge on the issue, armed with which she initiated an intensive dialogue with the women in her village. This process was a catalyst for the mass movement organized by Mahila Samitis (women's groups) spread across 100 villages, which grew to become a vibrant women's empowerment movement. But the big commercial interests behind the shrimp farms are not easily cowed: while Nilu continues her work, she has been attacked, harassed, and tortured by the police-goon nexus that buttresses the shrimp mafia.

Nilu also played a commendable role in organizing the common people, in general, and women, in particular, against the wanton imposition of a missile base by the central government in the Bhograi-Baliapal block in the district of Balasore, an exercise that evicted more than 100,000 people from 132 villages. The police assaulted her several times during her involvement with this movement, but Nilu stood firm.

The conversion of agricultural land and land under salt production to shrimp farms has become such common practice that shrimp monoculture has uprooted thousands of peasants and fishworkers from their homes and deprived them a livelihood. Brackish water is killing ecologically fragile areas.

India

Maglin Peter

Sramasakthi
National Fishworkers Forum (NFF)
Kerala Swathanthra Malsyathozhilali Federation (KSMF)

Maglin Peter (born 1970) has been deeply involved with issues faced by women fish vendors. She has managed to organize the strength of the fish vendors and elicit from them a creative and organized response against discrimination and violence. Maglin, who hails from the same community, understands the importance of connecting these movements with larger women's movements, environmental groups, trade unions, and human rights forums.

Maglin Peter has been actively involved with the fishworkers' movement in the state for close to two decades now, with her focus on women in the community. Maglin initiated, and continues to manage, the women's self-help group Sramasakthi. She is also involved with networks of women's groups like Sthree Vedi and the Self-Employed Women's Association. Maglin is also the program manager for Neeraksha, a women's cultural forum. She is intricately involved with issues faced by the women fish vendors, such as excess tax collection, excess loading charges, street vending and harassment, sexual harassment, working conditions in the prawn-peeling sheds, harbor access by the women vendors, goondaism, family-related issues, and off-season welfare. Also important is alternate employment generation for women displaced in the fisheries sector due to resource depletion.

Maglin has, over the years, organized the strength of the fish vendors, and elicited a creative and collective response to discrimination and violence. The transportation facilities that are now available to fish vendors are proof of this assertion of identity and dignity. The fishworkers also have access to women's self-help groups and microcredit facilities.

For over a decade, Maglin has been organizing small groups in the villages and getting them to network. She also realizes the importance of interlinking these groups with the larger women's movements, environmental groups, trade unions, and human rights forums. Maglin has managed to do so much so young despite being burdened thrice over: by being from the fishing community, by being a woman from that community, and by being in a third world nation where fishing is considered menial.

Fishworker women traditionally face discrimination in the markets and public transport systems. Market contractors bully them and collect exorbitant taxes. They have little access to hygienic conditions or welfare schemes like pension, credit, savings groups, and transportation facilities.

India

Lorna Philander

Mamre Farmers' Organisation

Lorna Philander (45), a mother of three, grew up as a street child in the Western Cape. As she matured she started realizing that a person can start building on their dreams. She rose above her personal predicament and now works to improve the lives of many helpless. She is involved in women's rights issues and matters affecting children and delinquents.

Lorna started out on the hard side of life. She was poor, homeless and alone. She had to learn at an early age how to fend for herself. She lived in the harsh and unforgiving streets of the Western Cape. As a girl she was prone to abuse and exploitation from the male street children and the gangs that engage in illicit trades of drugs and prostitution. Lorna is a living testimony to the strength of the human spirit and the will to change one's life completely. Her life has been full of hardships including an abusive marriage and the death of three of her six children. She married young and divorced early. As a child, Lorna had always dreamt of taking all her friends from the streets into a safe haven. So she got involved in community projects. She established a soup kitchen. She got involved in women's rights issues and matters affecting children and delinquents. She has faced many dangers from various gangs that accuse her of intrusion. She is an active member of an organization that promotes urban farming. Lorna is a member of the Blaauwberg Early Learning Association, an organization that is dedicated to improving the lives of underprivileged children. She is the chairperson of the Mamre Farmers' Organisation, which is dedicated to reviving farming in urban areas. One of the missions of this organization is to empower women in farming and farm management.

The South African government's program of land restitution has given previously landless people an opportunity to uplift themselves through farming. Through the Mamre Farmers' Organisation, Lorna equips women with farming skills and teaches them how to make their enterprises sustainable and profitable.

South Africa

Itsmania Erohyna Pineda Platero

Xibalbá: Arte y Cultura

Honduras is a country broken by the chronic inequality that has excluded young people from the centers of economic and cultural opportunity, forcing them to survive on the margins of society, with the violence and inscrutability of the gangs. With the foundation, in 1989, of Xibalbá, Itsmania Pineda created a space and an opportunity where young people have the chance to change their lives and channel their artistic energies into different socially beneficial projects. With these activities they are able to discover new identities, based on admiration and respect from the community.

During her childhood in Comayagüela, on the periphery of Tegucigalpa, Itsmania Pineda was part of the expansion of the youth organizations that are recognized all over Central America by the name of maras. Those brotherhoods were originated in the United States as a reaction to the violence related to inter-ethnic and economic factors that created conflicts inside the immigrant community. With the deportation of their leaders and members, the gangs were reproduced in their native territories.

In 1989, along with a group of artists and community activists, inspired on the Mayan idea of the labyrinth-like essence of the human spirit, Itsmania founded the Xibalbá Art and Culture. Honduran youth, despised and excluded because of their way of dressing and their gang symbols, found, in Xibalbá, a place to develop their creative and cooperative potential, participating, for example, in a series of concerts and art marathons. Since then, they were able to express themselves, showing their sensibilities, and responding in benefit to social needs. The repercussions of those manifestations helped to melt the masks of public prejudice and gave the young people from Xibalbá a prestige that travels far beyond the Honduran national borders.

In her book 'Why I joined the gangs,' Itsmania — officially named by the Honduran courts as the only expert and adviser in the interpretation of tattoos — approached the dynamics of the youth gangs from a panoramic vision, which she gained due to her privileged experience. The book acted as immediate stimuli for the international mechanisms of solidarity and is considered of inestimable value to the field of social science. "If the youth can function together to give a violent response to situations, they can act together in order to respond with their art."

Since the end of the 1980s, young people, deported by the Unites States, found in their native countries the same situation of economic exclusion and police persecution that they encountered in the USA. In self-defense, they reproduced the gangs that they formed as a means of survival.

Honduras

In 2004, the governor praised Shinobu as "distinguished CWC president and chiefly woman's leader." She accepted for "all the women who contributed energy, time, and passion to the CWC."

Shinobu Mailo Poll

Chuuk Women's Council (CWC)
FSM Women's Association Network
Chuuk Government Women's Affairs

Shinobu Mailo Poll, a veteran public servant with over 38 years in management and nursing posts, retired from the health field in 1996. She became president of the Chuuk Women's Council (CWC), a women's umbrella organization in 1997. Her continued presidency has improved CWC's public profile and its leadership role in gender empowerment in the state and nation, manifested locally in CWC's Small Micro-enterprise Development program, Handicraft Shop and Market Stall and regionally in projects like Pacific Diabetes Today and Pacific Regional HIV/Aids.

"I have always known I have a greater social responsibility to help the needy," says Shinobu Mailo Poll, a health professional and traditional women's leader in Chuuk. Such sentiments led to her career at Chuuk State Hospital, retiring as chief nurse in 1996. Her greatest contribution to the health field was the establishment of high quality nursing procedures and standards. She retired early because she had "lived her dream" but realized there was a limit to her powers to effect change. As president of Chuuk Women's Council (CWC), she realized she was "better off than most women of my state," so she started the Small Micro-Enterprise Development (SMED) program to intensify her commitment to Chuuk women and people: "One day at the hospital, I met a very sick woman. She was given a prescription and left. Later, I saw her, alone and miserable, at a clinic. She said she could not pay for her medicine. My heart broke for her: I paid for her medicine and sent her home. I swore then that CWC would do whatever it takes to help women like her. Thus our SMED program was born. It trains unemployed women and at-risk youth in handicraft-making, lei-making, sewing and such. The little they earn from selling their products helps with basic needs. I hope to expand CWC but we need more secure funding: we raise funds now from handicrafts, food sales, user fees from the market stalls. My vision for women is self-reliance and empowerment through the expansion of SMED, a women's center, getting women into decision-making roles. I hope our good track record for running community initiatives like the diabetes and HIV/Aids projects attracts the donor support we need. Meanwhile, our SMED experience is encouraging and we will carry on with our own meagre resources."

Shinobu Poll is president of Chuuk Women's Council, the women's umbrella organization tasked with gender empowerment through leadership development, health promotion, income generation, and poverty alleviation. She provides advice and policy-making aid to the Women's Affairs Office.

Lalao Flaurence Randriamampionona

Coalition of Women Associations (DRV)
Fiantso
Taratra

For the last ten years, Lalao Flaurence Randriamampionona (64), an anthropologist and sociologist, has been actively involved in diverse development activities involving women, children and the most impoverished in Madagascar. Lalao delegates some of her duties to her team members in the organizations she leads or is a member of. She advocates teamwork and participatory approaches from members of her team and the local population, who are the prime beneficiaries of the development projects she has initiated. She considers them a source of untapped knowledge.

Lalao Flaurence Randriamampionona lives in Antananarivo, Madagascar. She is married, has one child and one grandchild. From 1995 to 1999, she was among the few specialists that provided training on gender to different organizations in Madagascar. Through DRV, a coalition of women associations, she is involved in activities in four major areas: the empowerment of women, promoting the country's cultural heritage, access to resources and governance. Since 1996 she has worked with different NGOs primarily in poverty eradication. In 2001, she represented Madagascar at the African Forum on Poverty Reduction Strategies organized by the World Bank and others, and was elected speaker for 34 countries at the forum. These NGOs examine the development and implementation of fair economic systems, access to resources and safeguard of the environment and ecology. The organizations under her leadership, namely DRV, Taratra and Fiantso, have become reference points at national and international forums.

Lalao's other work includes the promotion of good governance and the strengthening of civil society at a national and international level; participation in the national committee on the fight against corruption, and the promotion of her cultural heritage through popular and traditional Malagasy music. She advocates for teamwork and participatory approaches from members of her team and the local population, who are prime beneficiaries of the development projects and a source of untapped knowledge. Lalao works under hard conditions, as some sites she travels to are only accessible on foot. Even though her days are busy, she manages to cope because she has a supportive family.

Since the 1970's Madagascar has undergone decades of political crisis, and a catastrophic earthquake has devastated the country. Many of the impoverished regions, which have potential, have either not been exploited or invested in.

Madagascar

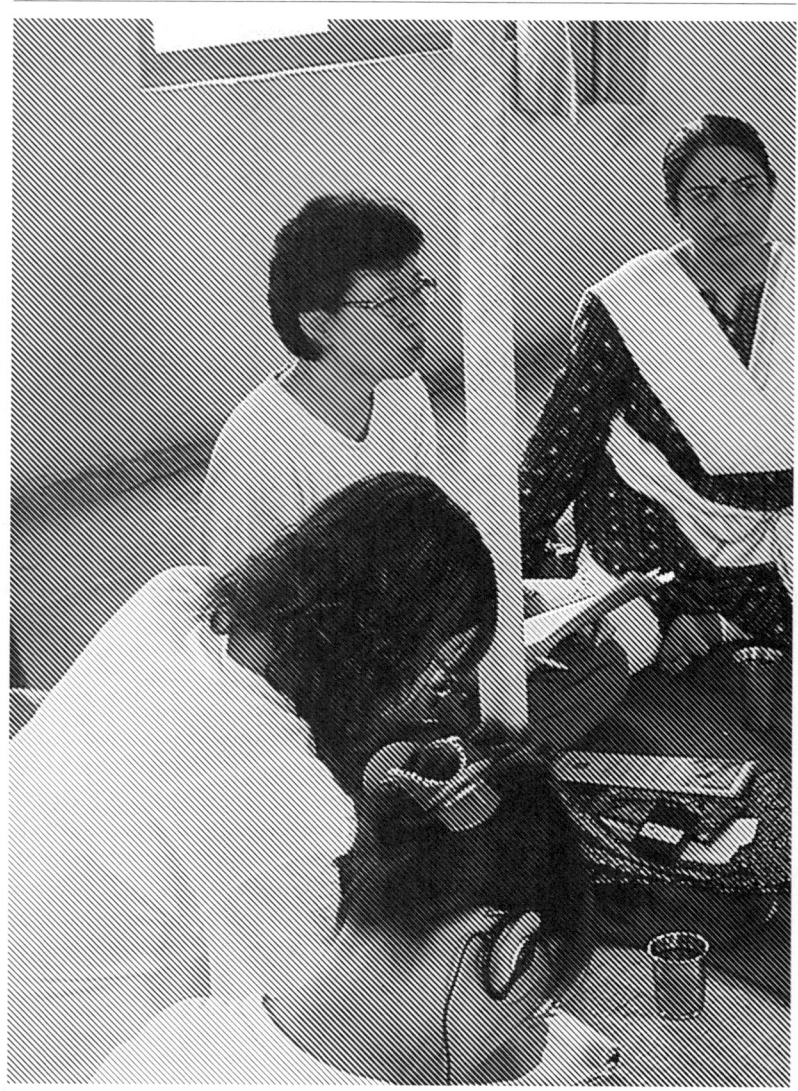

Maria Chol Soon Rhie

Committee for Asian Women (CAW)
Korean Women Workers Associations United (KWWAU)
Action Center for Women's Unemployment

Maria Chol Soon Rhie has dedicated her life to social work ever since graduating from high school in the early 1970s. She spent the next 15 years as a grassroots organizer, educator, and advocate for women's and human rights, eventually earning a university degree in social work. Since then she has led several workers' organizations and has founded two others: the Women's Unemployment Center and the Women's Trade Union. She also serves on the executive committee of the Committee for Asian Women. Her dedication has earned her the respect of workers all over the world.

Early in her life Maria spent two years working in a factory where she learned firsthand about the challenges facing women workers in Korea. After she became friends with her coworkers, Maria helped them form a small social group where they talked over many of the issues confronting Korean society. As membership grew, the group expanded its focus and developed into an organization that successfully advocated for improved working conditions for women.

Maria became further involved in workers' rights after the 1997 economic crisis in Korea. Although women were one of the groups most affected by the crisis, public attention focused only on the problems of unemployed men. To help the women and to draw attention to their situation, Maria started an unemployment center for women.

Maria's commitment to women workers has had far-reaching effects. She inspired women to become leaders in the Korean labor movement, encouraged women who were in night school to become activists, and helped to raise awareness among the general public of women's issues. While she was chairperson of the Korean Women Workers Associations United (KWWAU), the organization grew dramatically and became a strong advocate for social and legal change. KWWAU received a special award from the government in 1999 for its role in working toward gender equality in Korean society. Maria also began a women's trade union, and more recently, a training organization.

Moreover, her activities have not been confined to Korea. After spending 15 years as an organizer in Korea, she began working with the Committee for Asian Women (CAW) and serves on its executive committee. The CAW seeks to support activities of grassroots women's groups, to mobilize women workers' movements in Asian countries, and to promote international solidarity among women workers.

In the 1970s when Maria began her work, Korea was ruled by a dictatorship. The government suppressed the labor movement, regarding it as a hindrance to industrial development. Today, women workers routinely face gender discrimination in the workplace in Korea and other Asian countries.

Republic of Korea

Beatriz Elena Rodríguez Rengifo

Asociación de Mujeres Productoras de Cárnicos (Association of Women Butchers/Meatpackers of Caquetá — Asomupcar)

Beatriz Rodríguez was born in Dosquebradas, Risaralda, Colombia. She was a 'sex worker' in a bar called California. Through a municipal civil servant, a client of that bar, she got to know the mayoress, Lucrecia Murcia, who supported her in the development of programs to bring upon improvements for her and her work mates. So Beatriz, along with her companions, formed a micro-company of meatpackers/butchers and other projects to benefit women in their position and allow them to be economically self-sufficient.

After Beatriz Rodríguez' first sexual relations with her boyfriend, her mother took her to a brothel. After working as a prostitute for many years, she met the mayoress, Lucrecia Murcia, through a municipal civil servant who was a client of the bar where she worked. As a result, the mayor's office created a program called Resocialization of vulnerable groups. Part of its role was to inform sex workers about their rights. There were people against it and the women were threatened, kidnapped and even murdered by illegal armed groups. They were accused of collaborating with the government and of spreading the HIV virus.

Beatriz and the other women fought against those accusations, proving that they were false. They managed to get training courses sponsored by the mayor's office. Thanks to that they formed a micro-company of meatpackers/butchers. In spite of the social discrimination they have suffered, a number of institutions have supported them. Amongst them are the University of the Amazon that helped them with training courses and consultancy, and the Canadian Fund for Local Initiatives in Colombia that supported them economically. They grew bigger and were able to implement several other projects for women, such as the Villa Lucrecia housing project, or training courses and workshops on gender perspective with the collaboration of the Ecumenical Network of Women for Peace.

Colombia is going through a time of social conflict that has caused a huge portion of the population to be 'displaced.' Prostitution is a common phenomenon in this society where women are reduced to a subordinate and marginal role, without opportunities to improve themselves.

Colombia

Aruna Roy

Mazdoor Kisan Shakti Sangathan (MKSS)

Through struggles for the right to minimum wages and employment, Aruna Roy (born 1946) united the people of central Rajasthan under the Mazdoor Kisan Shakti Sangathan (MKSS). In 1994, the MKSS began the Right to Information movement. What started as a local intervention against corruption now stands as a national movement that has won freedom of information laws in ten states and at the center. The way in which Aruna bridged the interests of the middle class and the impoverished is remarkable.

Aruna Roy left a lucrative career in the civil services to join the Social Work and Research Centre (SWRC) in Tilonia village in Rajasthan in 1975. At the SWRC, she set about replacing the top-down approach to development and facilitated the evolution of the concepts of group action and rural women's leadership.

In 1986, she moved to central Rajasthan to work with workers and peasants. Through the struggles for minimum wages and employment in a chronically drought-affected area, the people came together on one platform — the MKSS. In 1994, the MKSS initiated the Right to Information movement through a series of public hearings, which it also used very effectively to expose corruption. Central Rajasthan is today edging toward a corruption-free Panchayati Raj zone, for the corrupt are scared of public humiliation. This "model" is now being used to bring accountability to most government schemes in the social sector. In 2003, the Right to Information was also connected to the process of elections, with the support of MKSS and the National Campaign for People's Right to Information.

In 2000, Aruna's work was acknowledged by the Ramon Magsaysay Foundation. She is now involved in advocating with the government that an employment guarantee act be formulated nationally, to give the dispossessed a level chance at obtaining livelihood options. The most unique feature of Aruna's leadership is her ability to connect macro and micro issues to build a continuum of struggle. The manner in which she bridged the interests of the middle class and the impoverished on the issue of the right to information is remarkable. It is the simplicity that counts: that the collective exercise of a right can force the establishment to acquiesce.

The Indian constitution did not enshrine the right to information. Withholding information, as governments do, weakens struggles. In areas such as arid Rajasthan, peoples' demand for a right to livelihood, wages, and employment is hobbled by not knowing how much money went where.

India

María Esther Ruiz Ortega

The New Hope Women's Association

María Esther Ruiz, a feminist from rural Honduras, had to act as mother for her brothers and sisters since 1961, when she was 11. She was educated by a religious order called the Pasionistas. She transferred her knowledge to other women in the groups that she created. She was attacked by religious traditionalists and even by the government. She understood that if peasant women were to improve their situation, they needed not only education, but also independence. For that reason, the New Hope Women's Association promotes economic projects.

"My father was a rural teacher and my mother a housewife. My father became an alcoholic; I experienced domestic violence during my childhood. He mistreated my mother, both physically and psychologically. I could not stand it, so — when I was only four years old — I took my little dress and went away to my grandmother's and my aunt's house. And I think that was the beginning. That marked my life."

The one speaking is María Esther Ruiz, a feminist from rural Honduras. Her mother thought she was mentally retarded because she was so silent, but her father registered her at school when she was nine years old. Shortly afterwards, he was murdered for being an active member of the Liberal Party. Two years later, her mother began a new relationship, and María Esther had to take care of her grandmother and her three brothers and sisters. Her aunt was already dead. She worked in a tobacco factory and, on Sundays, she washed clothes and took her brothers and sister to mass. The priests, who belonged to the Pasionista order, were impressed by that girl and gave her a religious and social education, even sending her on training courses in other countries. From that moment on, María Esther began writing down her ideas, to organizing women's groups for the creation of a new consciousness to defend the rights of the peasant women, to fight against sexism and subservience. But that new consciousness generated clashes with the more traditional priests. One of them, with the support of governmental representatives, got rid of these women and expelled them from the parish church. They regarded María Esther as a communist trying to snatch men's power.

She founded, in 1998, along with 200 other women, the New Hope Women's Association. It facilitates access to education and to economic activities that allow women to act independently and to be treated with dignity.

During the Cold War, the Church in Latin America was divided between those who wanted to contribute to social change and those who were opposed to it. In Honduras, authoritarian governments consider everything that they do not understand to be subversive, using repression to combat it.

Honduras

Meghiben Samariya

Ujjas Mahila Sangathan (UMS)

Meghiben Samariya (born 1966) has successfully combated the stigma associated with her status as a divorcee. For the past ten years, she has been working to strengthen women's grassroots collectives and women's involvement in the socioeconomic arena in her village and district. Her work with legal aid has been crucial to women's lives in the area. Most innovative of all her efforts, though, is the printing of a newsletter for neoliterates, encouraging them to express themselves in print and thus making a public space available to women.

Meghiben Samariya is divorced and lives with her parents in the conservative Bhuj district of Gujarat, where her marital status could have been the source of considerable social stigma. However, with her keen mind and instinctive grasp of situations, she has built herself into a force to reckon with.

Meghiben has been associated with the women's collective Kutch Mahila Vikas Sangathan (KMVS) for the past ten years, working to build the capacities of grassroots women's collectives. Initially, the KMVS helped the team form the collectives, but the collective in Meghiben's Mundra taluka has become a registered community-based organization, the Ujjas Mahila Sangathan (UMS). As a senior member of the UMS, Meghiben guides the organization in further developing its collective potency. It works to eliminate domestic violence by creating a social movement of men and women, and by developing multiple mechanisms for community and sociolegal redress. Meghiben lays stress on the commitment of the UMS to focus on and develop the economic security of women and the community at large by promoting female self-enterprise. Meghiben has also learnt screen printing from the core members of the KMVS team, and is now printing a newsletter for neoliterates, encouraging them to express themselves in print, thus making a public space available to women. She also helped to develop the legal aid clinic in her area, and now focuses on issues of social justice and human rights. Dealing mostly with domestic violence, divorce, and sexual violence cases, she is now part of the team working on problems that may arise due to the industrialization of the coastal area of Mundra.

Looking to the future, Meghiben says, "I would also like to see women control the resources they generate, resulting in the complete socioeconomic empowerment of rural women."

The Kutch area in Gujarat has one of the highest female suicide rates provoked by patriarchal practices. One in 20 women faces debilitations such as prolapsed uteruses. Women there also bear the brunt of near-perennial drought conditions and scarce water resources.

India

Montserrat Sampere Martín

San Fermín Project Association

Montserrat Sampere Martín (36) works for equality at the San Fermín Project Association, initiated in 1991 by the neighborhood association in San Fermín, a Madrid suburb. The town is faced with serious social problems. The Association has taken over responsibility for local and social development projects on employment, prevention of drug abuse, and social rehabilitation, revitalizing these projects and giving them a new dimension. Montserrat coordinates a project for the women of the neighborhood to promote equal opportunities for them.

The granddaughter of an exiled Republican political activist, Montserrat Sampere Martín was born and raised in San Fermín. From an early age, she rebelled against injustice and was frustrated by the reality in which she lived: "My first memories are participating with my parents in demonstrations and on highways protesting about the lack of safe housing and public services in our neighborhood." After her studies at the University of Madrid, Montserrat completed a post-graduate degree in education, motivated by a desire to become more involved in addressing her neighborhood's problems. An energetic woman with an active social conscience, she is ready to confront the injustice and oppression in her surroundings. "Justice begins locally, in the actual environment where you live. If all people creating local environments were coming out of other safe environments, the world would be a more human place," she explains with hope. She started working at the San Fermín Project Association in 1997 and later developed the gender program. This project for the women of the neighborhood provides a wide range of services from employment and legal advice to seminars on the prevention of domestic violence and courses on new technologies.

San Fermín is located in southern Madrid, enclosed between the highways surrounding the city. The population of 15,000 co-exists with Roma settlements and is plagued by strikes, school failures, illiteracy, problems of integration, and drug addiction.

Spain

"People are very greedy:
they could manage if
they learnt to share."

Sara

Refugee Council
Save the Children's Fund

Sara is a 18-year-old exile in the UK and works to transform her cruel experience of losing her parents and being raped into a positive example for her child. Soon after she arrived in 2003, she was alone and ashamed of her pregnancy. She joined the Mother and Baby Club at St. George Hospital. Today she advocates for the Refugee Council and uses her writing talent to tell her life story. She thus increases public understanding about asylum seekers and teenage mothers and counteracts prejudices against them. Her name is incomplete for security reasons.

She had all a young girl could desire: a lovely family, friends and the opportunity to attend school. All that was shuttered when soldiers attacked her home, brutally murdered her mother and father, tortured and raped her, leaving her for dead. At a tender age of 16 Sara had experienced the bitter side of the world.

Her father was suspected to be supplying arms and logistical information to rebels fighting the government of Uganda. Following her parents' murder, her life was also in danger because government officials thought she had useful information concerning the arms trade and their movement.

A doctor at a hospital came to her rescue. He encouraged her to eat and drink to become strong and promised to help her escape from her attackers. He was true to his word.

An agent left the young girl at a foreign airport in the foreign country. She was pregnant and sick and had to make her way to the Refugee Council in Brixton to ask for help. Sara had lost everything: family, friends, culture and school life. Overnight she had changed from a child to an adult, with a new life to consider. But the girl did not allow herself to be bogged down by the bitterness of what had happened. She decided that her unborn would be her hope and her new family. Sara uses the traumatic experience to encourage others; she is involved in advocacy for refugees and asylum seekers, offers her services to the Refugee Council and to the Save the Children's Fund. And she has allowed her story to be used to explain why people seek asylum. This Ugandan girl is extremely forgiving and compassionate: Despite her horrific experience in her home country, Uganda, she wrote to Gordon Brown, Chancellor to the Treasury, on how to help Uganda achieve the Millennium Development Goals. This young mother of a daughter is known to the persons in charge of the project.

Northern Uganda is a very volatile area due to persistent conflict. Most affected are women and girls, who are often raped. As a result there are numerous teenage mothers who have to abandon their childhood and take on the role of mothers.

Uganda

Farida Shaheed

Shirkat Gah Women's Resource Centre
Women Living under Muslim Laws (WLUML)

One of Pakistan's foremost women activists, Farida Shaheed leads the Women, Law, and Status program at the Shirkat Gah Women's Resource Centre. Farida was one of the first in Pakistan to promote the need for 33 percent reserved seats for women in direct elections, a measure that has been implemented at the district and other levels. Since 1986, she has been part of the core of the international network, Women Living under Muslim Laws (WLUML), and has helped many women whose rights and / or lives are endangered by discriminatory laws.

One of Farida Shaheed's happiest memories is the reaction of men from Pakistan's conservative North West Frontier Province to a legal awareness session on women's family rights. They urged Farida and her colleagues from Shirkat Gah, a collective that works for women's empowerment, to conduct a similar session for women posthaste. Over the past three decades, Farida's life has been enlivened by such moments. At other times, particularly in the 1980s, she has been monitored and questioned by intelligence agencies. Shaheed was then a member of the Women's Action Forum (WAF), mandated to resist the retrogressive policies and laws introduced in the name of Islam by Zia-ul-Haq (1977 to 1988). Farida and her colleagues have faced pressure from hostile local elites, and threatened with death (although skilful strategizing allowed them to operate even when other groups had to stop working). Her greatest success, she feels, has been that more women now know of their marital rights and can negotiate more spaces and rights, step out of abusive matrimony, register their marriages, and insert rights within the marriage contract.

Since 1986, Farida has been part of the plinth of Women Living under Muslim Laws (WLUML), an international network that provides information, solidarity, and support to women whose lives are shaped, conditioned, or governed by laws and customs ostensibly derived from Islam. Farida has personally helped two women leave Pakistan to circumvent death threats by well-connected families.

Shaheed and Khawar Mumtaz wrote "Women in Pakistan: Two Steps Forward, One Step Back?", which documents the Muslim women's movement from the turn of the 20th century to today. It received the Prime Minister's Award in 1989. Shaheed, who is in her early 50s, lives in Lahore with her educationist and journalist husband.

The Shirkat Gah Women's Resource Center (SG), established in 1975, is a nonhierarchical collective that works toward women's empowerment for social justice and vice versa. It focuses on law and status, and women and sustainable development, including reproductive rights.

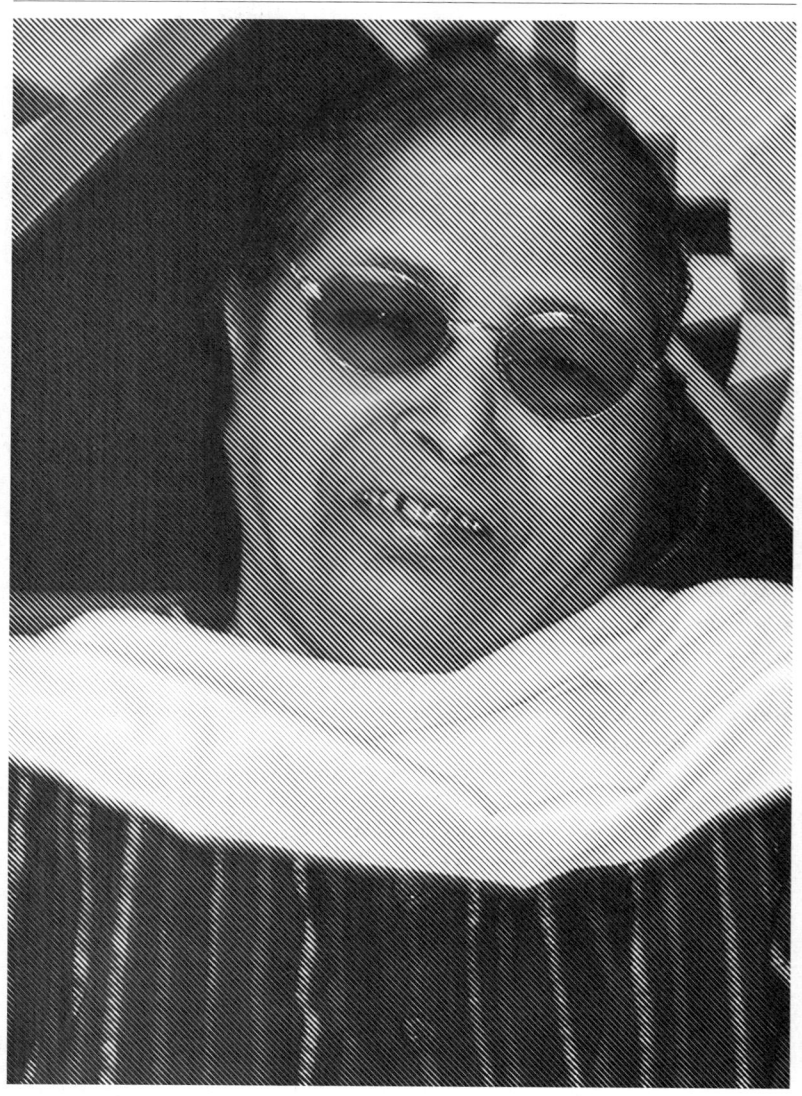

Roshanben M Shaikh

Mahila Patchwork Cooperative Society (MPCS)

Roshanben M Shaikh (born 1950) showed rare courage by marrying again after her husband died, leaving her with two little daughters — and then walking out of the unhappy second marriage. When the Sabarmati river floods washed away her hut — along with those of hundreds of others — Roshanben was at the forefront of the rehabilitation work, brokering peace between communities, and working toward the economic independence of women, which she continues to do to this day.

In 1973, the Sabarmati floods destroyed the houses of over 3000 families — including Roshanben's little hut. People were out on the streets with whatever little they could save. A number of nongovernmental agencies came out to set up relief and rehabilitation camps for the flood affected, and an NGO introduced Roshanben to the National Institute of Design (NID). The NID was looking for hands to train in patchwork design, and the NGO was in charge of the project planning and implementation. Roshanben fit in immediately, learning faster than most others. Not just that, she soon became a trainer for more women. She eventually trained over 100 women, and was part of a group of about 100 women who formed a cooperative called the Mahila Patchwork Cooperative Society (MPCS) in 1978.

The government was simultaneously carrying out resettlement work, and Roshanben played a big role in mobilizing the whole community, as well as in brokering peace between communities when the government handed out alternate sites for resettlement and friction threatened the calm.

For the past 28 years, Roshanben has been striving in the area of economic independence for women. Her place of work has been Juhapura, and it has even seen her being elected to the Makarba Village Panchayat (village council). The MPCS remains solidly with her, and her inherent leadership ability has helped her mobilize massive numbers into following her train.

The Sabarmati River floods of 1973 washed away the houses of hundreds of families: the imperative was to look for livelihoods, and support the authorities in their rehabilitation work. But the economic independence of women was hampered by their lack of education.

India

Ginny Shrivastava

Astha
Association of Strong Women Alone (Aswa)
Budget Analysis Rajasthan Center (Barc)

Ginny Shrivastava (born 1943), a Canadian by birth, has been working with women in Rajasthan since 1970. The main driving force behind the Association of Strong Women Alone, a registered society of low-income single women, Ginny has focused on building the leadership capabilities of grassroots women. Also actively involved with tribal groups, Ginny mobilized them to pressure the government to give them minimum wages for collecting tendu patta (tobacco leaves), and helped them form a Tendu Patta Cooperative.

The Canadian Ginny arrived in Udaipur in 1970 after marrying an Indian. Her doctoral thesis was on nonformal education programs for women in Indian villages. She studied the social change and leadership patterns through her thesis work. In 1986, Seva Mandir (an NGO working on rural and tribal development in and around Udaipur) abruptly terminated her services without notice: the organization was getting nervous about her increasing clashes with the local authorities. Ginny and some friends formed Astha, also based in Udaipur, focusing on awareness generation through training programs, action, and reflection.

One of Ginny's most crucial contributions is her work with low-income widows and separated women. In India, social restrictions on widows force them to live in subhuman conditions. Ginny and her team mobilized widows in many districts of Rajasthan. Today, there is the state-level Association of Strong Women Alone (Ekal Nari Shakti Sangathan-Aswa), a registered society. Aswa is a splendid example of the success of Ginny's efforts in building the leadership capabilities of women at the grassroots level. It was built entirely by grassroots women, and they handle their organizational responsibilities very effectively. Ginny is also actively involved with tribal groups. Her most successful effort was in mobilizing tribals to put pressure on the government to give minimum wages for collecting tobacco leaves, and, more recently, helping them form a Tendu Patta Cooperative to tender bids for tobacco leaf collection.

Ginny works to build people's movements around issues of social justice, livelihoods, environmental issues, women's rights, and human rights. Her forte is her great faith in the ability of the people to better their own lives.

Its castles and color apart, Rajasthan has a feudal history. Marginalization is based on caste and class. Literacy levels are low, and women's empowerment is not a familiar concept. Widowed, separated, or divorced women have a particularly nasty time.

India

Dembélé Mariam Sidibé

Muso Danbé Center

Born in Kayes in 1965, Madame Dembélé Mariam Sidibé is the director of the Muso Danbé Center situated in the heart of the capital of Kayes, the first administrative region of Mali. Dembélé Mariam Sidibé is married and the mother of six children. She has always had a desire to help those less fortunate than her. Early on, she saw the need to provide trade skills to orphaned and handicapped girls because of the difficulties they face in Malian society.

Madame Dembélé Mariam Sidibé is the founder and director of Muso Danbé, a life-skills center for orphaned and handicapped young girls in Kayes, Mali. Muso Danbé means women's dignity in Bambara, the predominate local language of Mali. Mariam has always had a desire to help those less fortunate than her. Mariam knew that without marriage or some other means of providing for themselves, these handicapped girls would be forced onto the street as beggars or prostitutes. Although Mali is a poor country, some trades can bring in good money, such as cloth dyeing, tailoring, and cooking. Mariam, a consummate cook and creative artist, started her center in 1998 and soon began to teach these girls how to cook, design and sew clothing, make soap and learn French. The center produces beautiful, high-quality cloth ranging from rich bazin, to colorful batik to traditional mud cloth and indigo. The organisation over which she presides is highly recognized in public because of the interest that it represents for the women of the Kayes region. Mariam is full of appreciation for the people and their performance at her center. She has accumulated a lot of knowledge on women's activities that she wants to pass on to other interested women who want to do something to increase their economic independence. She never ceases telling her trainees that one is never too old for training, especially when it will generate income.

One of the roles a Malian woman must play is to be a wife and mother. Since family and community traditions are passed down from mother to daughter, orphaned girls often lack critical domestic skills. Handicapped girls are considered less desirable for marriage.

Mali

Josie Tankunani Sirivi

Bougainville Women for Peace and Freedom (BWPF)

Hunted by the Papua New Guinea Defense Force as bait to capture her husband, Josie Sirivi took to the jungle during the Bougainville crisis. She saw women and children suffering and organized local women to earn income and assist other families in need. She lobbied and obtained relief supplies from NGO agencies to distribute through women's groups. She founded and was the first president of Bougainville Women for Peace and Freedom and led a women's team to conduct a peace awareness campaign. She was a key negotiator representing women in the peace process that started in October 1997.

Young, pregnant, and married to a Bougainville Revolutionary Army general with a 200,000 kina (PNG currency) dead-or-alive price on his head, Josie Sirivi and her husband were forced to take refuge from the Papua New Guinea Defense Force in the Bougainville jungle during the 1990s civil war. There she witnessed the loss of life and suffering of many mothers and children, and decided to do everything she could to help. She initiated and organized a women's group to earn a little income to help under-resourced families in the villages. She supported women in setting up schools in the bush community during the war, and in reopening former schools upon return to villages after the war. She was the founding president of the Bougainville Women for Peace and Freedom (BWPF) organization which not only survived the initial reason for its existence (i.e. as a forum for women during the peace talks and a mechanism for the appointment of women by women as negotiators to peace talks) but became a grassroots indigenous organization that founded several community initiatives that continue to operate today. She led a women's team to conduct a campaign of visits to Bougainville communities to explain the peace process, especially to outlying community groups. These peace campaign meetings were instrumental in breaking down communication barriers so people were correctly informed about the peace process at every stage of the negotiation process. Josie represented women at negotiation tables since 1997. Currently, she is setting up an Open Learning Center for people of all ages who have been deprived of an education due to the protracted length of the war and blockade. Together with her husband, Josie is trying to develop a Bougainville cash-crop economy and they have several self-help community projects to maintain with local village communities.

Bougainville's long struggle for autonomy from Papua New Guinea erupted in the 1990s civil war and blockade over the destruction caused by the huge Australian-owned Panguna copper mine on the island. Josie's work began because her people were being killed and denied basic rights and freedoms.

Candi Smucker

Ten Thousand Villages

Candi Smucker believes the workers of the world deserve to earn a sustaining wage. And she knows that there are many shoppers who want to purchase goods that benefit the people who created them. Her first belief is grounded in humanitarianism; the second comes from solid experience. Her success as a retail manager for bookstores and fair trade gift stores prompted her to begin working with Ten Thousand Villages, a job creation program for third world artisans. She spearheaded the creation of five stores, authored a training manual, and trained 150 Ten Thousand Villages storeowners.

Candi Smucker knows what sells. Beginning as a clerk at a Christian bookstore in Seattle, she rose to general manager and then moved to Chicago to manage the headquarters bookstore for Scripture Press. She joined a Christian bookstore franchise group as vice-president of operations and opened 17 stores. When she managed Cross Cultural Crafts, a fair trade gift store in the Chicago area, it grew from a small-scale, start-up shop to two successful stores.

In the Ten Thousand Villages project, Candi found a cause that would take full advantage of her business acumen. For the past 15 years, she has invested her energy in creating and managing stores and training storeowners and volunteers. The stores do business with workers who create their products in good conditions, cooperate with local villages, do not use child labor in substitution for school attendance, and receive a fair wage for their work. The Ten Thousand Villages stores are making a difference, and Candi joined in the chorus of voices telling stories of success. She visited with artist groups in Guatemala, Bangladesh, India, Ecuador, Peru, Bolivia, Chile, and Nepal, learning that the stores make the difference between one and two meals a day. In some cases, income from the stores made schooling and medical services possible. Villages were able to establish schools and health care clinics, pave streets, and provide recreation for young people.

After opening four schools in other communities, Candi opened her own store, and now manages Baksheesh, a fair trade store in Sonoma, California. Since opening in May of 1997, the store has grown to over $500,000 in annual sales. Baksheesh opened a second store in Healdsburg, California, in 1993.

Fair trade helps small-scale producers — artistans, farmers, textile workers — become financially independent by providing markets for their goods. In contrast to many large-scale wholesalers, fair trade organizations do not exploit people or the environment.

United States of America

"I wish to see communities of the underprivileged people have the opportunity to mobilize power as a group, to develop themselves as part of the ongoing social development."

Somsook Boonyabancha

Community Organizations Development Institute (CODI)

Somsook Boonyabancha (born 1952) obtained a Master's Degree in Housing and Urbanization from the School of Architecture of the Royal Danish Academy of Fine Arts in Copenhagen, Denmark. Returning to Thailand, she worked in the state-run National Housing Authority of Thailand. For 27 years she has contributed actively to the development of Thailand's social infrastructure. As director of the Community Organizations Development Institute (CODI), a public organization funded by government, her main role is to strengthen the capacity of communities for self-reliance and development.

Somsook Boonyabancha believes that the problems of slum communities can only be resolved if the marginalized urban poor are able to live on their own land, and this can happen only if they are actively involved in the decision-making with regard to policies that shape their future. Since CODI is funded by the state, Somsook's most important task is to generate better understanding between other state organizations and the people affected by their decisions. Somsook is determined to push for more recognition of the rights and decisions of the grassroots population. She strongly believes that the people should have a say in the policies that affect their lives, and that state organizations should not assume that they have the right to make decisions for the people.

Somsook has also been actively involved in linking different national and international community groups to enable them to exchange information and experiences, so that they gain more confidence as they move towards self-reliance and development. "While the overall picture may show that the problems are not that bad, in reality it is much more complicated," she says. The inequalities of the social system leave one-third of the country's population without basic requirements that provide security, such as housing and job opportunities. In attempting to reduce poverty in the country, CODI, which is both a development fund and a government public institution, has been channeling funds directly to Thailand's poorest communities and has been working closely with NGOs and public foundations in generating community-driven welfare programs.

Pollution, lack of infrastructure, breakdown of the Thai society, and increasing numbers of urban poor, lie underneath the surface of what looks like the economic prosperity of Bangkok. The problems of the slum communities can only be resolved if the marginalized urban poor are actively involved in the decision-making.

Omana T K

Rural Agency for Social and Technological Advancement

When she was 18 years old, Omana T K (born 1959) ran away from home to work in an NGO in Rajasthan. Returning to Kerala eight years later, she sold off all her assets to set up the Rural Agency for Social and Technological Advancement in 1989. That was the start of a veritable revolution in the villages of the backward Wayanad district; today, it has several women's self-help groups and sees active participation by women in village-level activities. She also established a highly successful rainwater-harvesting movement.

Omana T K left home to follow her dream of associating with developmental activism. She heard about and was fascinated by the Social Welfare and Research Center's work in Tilonia, Rajasthan. After working in Tilonia for eight years, she and her husband returned to Kerala, settling down in the impoverished Wayanad district. Omana sold all her assets to found the Rural Agency for Social and Technological Advancement in 1989. It took patience and perseverance to win over the trust of the women in the district and to set up small self-help groups. Today, the groups' combined membership is in the thousands: they have become a veritable movement in Wayanad's villages. Piggybacking on financial empowerment was social participation by women.

Of equal importance is Omana's work on the conservation of natural resources such as soil, water, and biodiversity through community-based action programs and the implementation of rainwater-harvesting technologies. She informed 50,000 people in 30 villages about water conservation through puppet shows and street plays. Today, the rainwater-harvesting structures ensure that potable water is available during dry summers. The district's population have formed community-based water use and conservation-monitoring committees. Omana has also popularized the idea of a village-level seed exchange program to protect and propagate indigenous seed varieties. Most important, more than 20,000 impoverished families, tribal groups with poor educational opportunities, and Muslim women have been included in the development process.

Omana's life is inspirational: a woman from a rural agricultural background who stood convention on its head, changing the lives of thousands of rural men and women.

Wayanad district in Kerala is listed as among India's 90 poorest districts. When Omana T K went to work there, women were domestically secluded, walked long distances to fetch potable water during the dry summers, and the men eyed her activities with suspicion.

India

Shen Tan

Chinese Academy of Social Sciences (Cass)

Tan Shen was born in 1951. She worked in county government and in a factory before becoming a journalist. Years of working with peasants helped her identify with ordinary people. Since 1993 Tan has been active as a committed, socially aware and responsible intellectual. Engaged in academic research and social activities concerned with rural-urban migration, she provides decision-makers with information and constructive suggestions for social transformation. She is currently with the Chinese Academy of Social Sciences (Cass).

Tan Shen was born in Guangxi Province. In 1968 she moved to the countryside in Shanxi Province after finishing junior high school education in Beijing. She recalls: "Thirty years ago, as one of millions of educated youths leaving for the countryside, I lived in the rural areas for several years. Those years of living on the land molded my everlasting 'popular mentality', i.e., what I am most deeply concerned and impressed with is the ordinary people's status and changes. This is because the harmony and stability of society do not hinge on a handful of the privileged, but rather, the majority at the bottom layer of society."

In 1986, Tan began work as a researcher at the Institute of Sociology at Cass. Since 1993 she has worked on specific issues of rural women workers in Beijing, Sichuan Province, Hunan Province and Guangdong Province.

Tan provides decision-makers at central or local government level with constructive suggestions about rural-urban migration. She directs public attention to the marginal group of rural migrants through seminars, conferences and publications. Her works have inspired a number of students, particularly postgraduates, to be committed, socially concerned and re-sponsible scholars. Tan is always careful to represent others with care and respect: "I have a deep respect for rural women workers who have to negotiate difficult conditions. Their toughness and determination are not only the foundation of this old country's everlasting spirit, but also the great driving force of social transformation." As an organic intellectual, Tan also makes use of her scholarly research for social transformation.

Since China has speeded up its modernization policy there has been a ceaseless wave of rural people going to the coastal cities to work. Rural migrants mainly do low-paid, dangerous and dirty work, and they do not have any legal rights or social benefits. Among them, women are a particularly vulnerable group.

China

Elizabeth Teixeira

Elizabeth Teixeira (1925) is a national symbol in the fight for the right to have land. When she was young, she faced prejudice from her father, a small landowner, and she ran away from home to marry a black and poor man. As an adult, mother of 11 children, she took over her husband's battle when he was murdered by powerful landowners. "My life is protesting against misery, lack of health and education, and the abandonment of the rural population."

When Elizabeth Teixeira found her husband fallen on the road, in 1962, with the dry soil of the hinterland mixed with his blood, she held his hand and said: "I will continue your fight." She took over the presidency of the Peasant League in the State of Paraíba, which was founded by her husband in 1958. She started to receive threats. Her ten year old son promised to avenge his father's death, in the future. He was shot in the head and was left with permanent health problems. Policemen once again surrounded the house, this time searching for Elizabeth Teixeira. When she returned from prison, she found her oldest daughter, who, at the time, was 17 years old, dead. "She drank poison."

She was not discouraged. The League became the largest in the Northeast. In 1964, with the beginning of the military regime, she returned to prison. Six months later, she was freed, but she had to run away leaving her children with her father and brothers. With her, she took a son, who was rejected by her family for being physically similar to her dead husband. They traveled to another state, where they lived with fake identifications. After 16 years, she had not received any news regarding her other nine children. She only saw them again in 1981, with the amnesty. One of her sons founded the João Pedro Teixeira Association in 1987 with his mother's support. But Elizabeth's oldest son did not accept a new peasant leader in the family. He killed his brother. She kept on participating in meetings. Today, Elizabeth Teixeira is 80 years old and lives on a small retirement pension. "I do not have any regrets. My fight will not be over until every rural worker has his or her own piece of land."

The Peasant Leagues were the first organs for the defense of rural workers. Within them began the fight for better conditions of life and the construction of a peasant identity. Years later, these experiences led to various movements related to this category.

Brazil

Hakkuben Theba

Saiyerejo Sangathan

Hakkuben Theba was born in 1966 into a poor farming family from the highly conservative Theba community in Gujarat. Her journey, from a destitute widow to a community leader and a trainer of leaders, was arduous. In the past 15 years, this woman has inspired more than 3000 women to become active members of a women's collective. Gradually, Hakkuben and her colleagues have changed the nature of the village through women's empowerment, generating alternative sources of income during drought, and ecological regeneration.

Hakkuben Theba hails from the small but conservative Theba community in Dador, Gujarat. Married early and widowed, Hakkuben had never known economic security. In 1998, she came into contact with the women's collective Kutch Mahila Vikas Sangathan (KMVS), and joined them. She began by working on the education of adolescent girls, which also gave her the opportunity to learn how to read and write, the first person in her family to do so.

Defying social norms and pressures, Hakkuben engaged with the training of grassroots collectives that the KMVS was organizing. These collectives of rural women have now taken the shape of a community-based organization, the Saiyere Jo Sangathan. Her natural intelligence, leadership skills, and deftness in organizing the village group gained her the respect of the men and village elders. In the 15 years that Hakkuben has been working, she has inspired more than 3000 women within her geographical domain. The Sangathan, which she leads, works toward making women members and their families' assets truly productive. It also works toward developing traditional livelihoods of the community as sustainable sources of income, especially in times of drought. She has delivered significant empowerment to the women through natural resource management, concentrating on the recharging of wells and other water resources.

Hakkuben's methodology is simple: the Gandhian principle of nonviolence, taking on the oppressor first, and then creating confidence within the existing environment for change. In the process, she has formed a team of women leaders and inspired young girls in the area. "I would like to create a platform for the next generation of women so that they can learn from our experience and their life becomes easier," she says.

The Theba are a small, conservative Muslim community in Gujarat. A proud people, they do not practice dowry, and domestic violence is practically nonexistent. But they also disapprove of women working outside the home. Literacy levels are very low in Dador, Hakkuben's domain.

India

"If we care enough
to take the risk of being
human, together we
can change the world."

Kip Tiernan

Rosie's Place
Boston Food Bank
Poor People's United Fund

At a time when society believed that women's place was in the home, Kip Tiernan reached out to those women who had no home. In 1974, she founded Rosie's Place, the United States' first drop-in, emergency shelter for women. Kip has been at the center of the fight for economic and social justice for nearly three decades, advocating and lobbying for affordable and accessible housing, health care, education, jobs, civil rights, and peace. She currently serves as codirector of the Poor People's United Fund, which she founded.

Born in West Haven, Connecticut, Kip lost both her parents by the time she was 11 and was raised by her grandmother. Always unconventional, she took flying lessons at age 16 and began her interest in jazz. She arrived in Boston in her early 20s and began a successful career in advertising. An active Catholic, Kip's parish work took her to St Philip's Warwick House, which was involved in civil rights and antiwar movements. In 1967, she was asked to help coordinate a press conference at St Philip's and soon after joined the team ministry because "poor people need advertising too". Her work took her into housing projects, mental institutions, jails, and hospitals, and she learnt about the effects of deinstitutionalization and the lack of a coherent public policy to address the needs of the poor and homeless.

Kip has a far-reaching legacy of caring for society's most vulnerable. She understood that to most of the public, homeless women were invisible. While society intoned that women's place was in the home, many women were sleeping in cars, moving from one friend's house to another's, and selling their bodies for shelter. Kip's vision prompted the evolution of Rosie's Place from simply a shelter to an institution that offered solutions. The organization scrutinizes all sources of funding and accepts no government funds. Kip founded the Boston Food Bank and cofounded the Boston Women's Fund, Health Care for the Homeless, and Community Works. In 1980 she cofounded the Poor People's United Fund, a "spare change" funding source for grassroots community groups involved in homelessness, hunger, and access to justice, where she currently serves as codirector.

In 1990, Kip established the Ethical Policy Institute. She teaches at the University of Massachusetts, and is a popular lecturer at schools and churches.

When Kip began her work, homeless women were invisible. While society intoned that women's place was in the home, many were sleeping in cars, living with friends, and selling their bodies for shelter.

United States of America

"I have learned that we will only attain a good quality of life when health becomes a given, and when women in my country become aware of the role they can play in political decision-making."

Cissouma Korotoumou Traoré

Coopération Multifonctionnelle des Femmes de Sikasso (CMFS)
Association de Solidarité des Femmes Minianka

Cissouma Korotoumou Traoré (63) presides over the Association of Solidarity of Minianka Women (an ethnic group of Sikasso), an organization that is also open to all the other ethnic groups in the defense of the interests of women of Sikasso. Characterized by having courage when necessary, Madame Cissouma spent all her professional career in the circle of social affairs. She was member of the regional office of the National Union of Women of Mali under the second republic and president of the multifunctional co-operation of the women of Sikasso (CMFS).

Madam Cissouma Korotoumou Traoré is a Bambara woman married to a Minianka. It is through her husband that she discovered the Minianka world. Her marriage forces Mali people to see that different ethnic groups can live in harmony and in perfect integration. She is not a bureaucrat cut off from her world as she likes direct contact with people. She regularly holds meetings, advising couples and families for a better understanding of the complexity of human relations. She has the tact to work with the body of the community in a conservative society marked by the misunderstanding of the role of women confined to the home. She advises authorities, technical structures, and the general population on how to attain the material and financial means in order to undertake development activities. She knows that, culturally, it is necessary to be honest, transparent, and organized to win the confidence of people. It was necessary also to be courageous and to not become despondent.

Her work benefits the whole Sikasso community; for it has reinforced social cohesion. The dispossessed, women and children regained their rights by the actions of Korotoumou Traoré. Nevertheless, there are many constraints in getting women to mobilize themselves and participate in development activities. Finding funds to finance certain initiatives is often not easy. Korotoumou has also had to come to terms with social work that completely monopolizes family life. She is the mother of six children and has a diploma in social aid which she obtained in 1963.

Madame Cissouma has invested a lot of her time in mediation activities and education for the re-inforcement of social cohesion. She worked in the areas of solidarity and social development for 32 years (1963—1995).

Mali

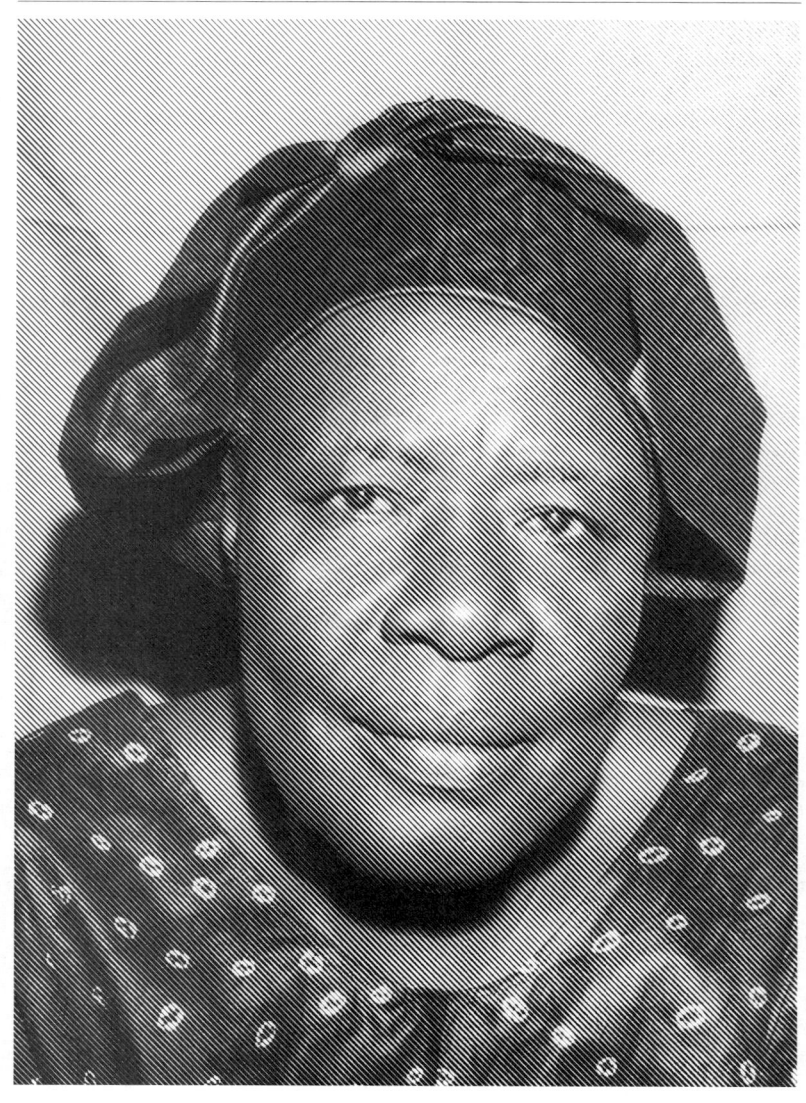

N'Diaye Korotoumou Traoré

Association Malienne pour la Promotion Sociale des Aveugles (AMPSA)

N'Diaye Korotoumou Traoré was born in the town of Toba (area of Bougouni) in 1943. She is the incarnation of a priest woman that concentrates all her energy towards serving her community without any reward. She is a simple woman who understands that Malian women more than ever need support to achieve real equality with men. N'Diaye is married and is the mother of eight children.

N'Diaye Korotoumou Traoré has put her energies into social affairs to help the women of Sikasso. She was a member of the former National Union of the Women of Mali (UNFM) under the second republic. She obtained her social assistance diploma in 1962. She obtained her primary studies certificate in 1955. She had three terms of service in the social health service before retraining to adapt to the frequent change in work methods in the service. By 1957, she was named auxiliary chief of the local social service, then made interim director of the social service. Between 1974 and 1982, she was a member of the Regional Office of the Women of Sikasso. She was a representative from 1982 to the fall of the second republic in 1991. Altogether, she had three mandates of three years each to the cycle of the second republic. This allowed her to be involved in matters of legislature. Madame N'Diaye was secretary to the multi-functional co-operation, then she was in charge of the women's co-operative for consumption and production created by the government in 1985. She was a trainer in the functional literacy service. She serves as member of the piloting office of the Malian Association for the Social Promotion of the Blind Persons (AMPSA) and, finally, as a technical agent of the social service from 1962 to 1994. This brilliant socio-professional journey allowed Korotoumou Traoré to be effective in several areas of development. In the framework of health and education she brought her assistance to families for social well-being. The nutrition of children and pregnant women are the areas in which Madame N'Diaye has fought. She did not stop campaigning for her compatriots to become literate in order to better manage family resources. She put her energies in ensuring that mothers had the knowledge and techniques to assure children's growth and normal development.

N'Diaye Traoré counsels on screening for contagious diseases and the demonstration of child systems. She has created awareness among young girls regarding their position in society in the region of Sikasso. She has the art and technique necessary to pass medical counsel to illiterate women.

Mali

"Breakthroughs are possible only if we can gather the courage to risk stepping outside our colonized worldviews."

Maria Varela

Rural Resources Group

Maria Varela (born 1940) is an economist, photographer, visionary, and organizer extraordinaire. Now based in Albuquerque, she first worked with the Student Nonviolent Coordinating Committee (SNCC), a cutting-edge civil rights organization. In 1968 she moved to northern New Mexico, a poor rural region. She has cofounded, advised, and inspired transformative projects that link economic, cultural, and environmental justice and sustainability. Best known is Ganados Del Valle, a cooperative of sheepherders, weavers, and craftspeople that has revitalized the economy of the Chama valley.

Maria Varela is the oldest of five daughters. Her mother is Irish American, and her father — a chemical engineer — emigrated to the USA from Mexico. After graduating from college she worked for the Student Nonviolent Coordinating Committee (SNCC), a cutting-edge civil rights organization. In 1968 she moved to northern New Mexico to work with families in rural communities who had lived there for generations under collective land grants from Spain and then Mexico, before this region became part of the USA.

Over time, families had subdivided the land and many farms were no longer economically viable. For 150 years, ranchers, environmentalists, and state officials had taken over upland areas traditionally used for summer grazing. Out-migration, especially of young people, was very high. Inspired by the civil rights activism in southern states, New Mexico land grant activists turned to civil disobedience in the late 1960s to protest the appropriation of land by incomers.

Maria cofounded, advised, and inspired Ganados Del Valle (livestock of the valley), a cooperative of sheepherders, weavers, and craftspeople that links economic, cultural, and environmental justice and sustainability. This organization, based in Los Ojos, New Mexico, has revitalized the economy of the Chama valley, based on the breeding of Churro sheep, a near extinct breed well suited to the area. As Ganados members have increased their flocks they have come into conflict with ranchers, environmentalists, and state officials who now own or manage the uplands for cattle grazing or wildlife preservation. Maria has been a key figure in trying to change public policy and the thinking of these groups in support of local sheepherders. A dedicated organizer and committed collaborator, Maria believes in grass-roots change through the empowerment of ordinary people.

Generations of Hispano families lived in what is now New Mexico under land grants from Spain and Mexico. The US border was redrawn in 1848, after the US-Mexican War. Areas traditionally used for summer grazing were taken over by ranchers, corporate interests, and the US forest service.

United States of America

Breaking the silence, Malika Virdi believes, is the starting point of any struggle – and she has broken many silences in her fight for women's rights.

Malika Virdi

Maati
Uttarakhand Mahila Manch (UMM)

Starting with work in relief camps of women victims of the 1984 anti-Sikh riots, Malika Virdi (born 1958) has concerned herself with a series of issues connected to women's rights. She has worked on nonformal education, health issues, violence against women — particularly against dowry-related murders of young brides in North India — on campaigns to amend the rape law, and crisis intervention work. Malika has also entered the Panchayati Raj system for self-governance, and is currently working on issues concerning rural mountain women.

Things changed for Malika Virdi after the 1984 Sikh massacres, when she realized that she was part of a minority community. As part of her first steps toward what she would do for the rest of her life, Malika worked in the relief camps, and recorded the testimonies of women victims of the riots. Around the time, Asiad Village in Delhi was under construction, and migrant labor built their own settlements in various places. When Malika got an offer from the NGO Ankur to associate herself with nonformal education and health issues for women, she promptly took it up. She started with a crusade against all forms of violence against women, particularly against the growing incidence of dowry-related murders of young brides in North India. She was part of a long street theater campaign in Delhi from 1979 to 1984, both on the issue of dowry and to amend the Rape Law.

From 1987 onward, Malika has worked with a series of organizations: first, the Rajasthan Women's Development Program, aimed at tackling women's health; then, she ran a campaign against the program launched by the government in the wake of the 1988 famine, when women were forced to get themselves sterilized; after that, she formed an autonomous women's collective — Mahila Samooh — in Ajmer, which did crisis intervention work and worked as a women's support group.

Since 1994, Mahila has been associated with the Uttarakhand Mahila Manch UMM), a state-level women's network that was at the forefront of the struggle for a separate state, and campaigns against the liquor mafia in the region. In Sarmoli, where she lives, Malika has entered the Panchayati Raj system for self-governance. And through the local rural women's collective, Maati, she is committed to working on issues concerning rural mountain women.

Across North India, the condition of women has historically been worse than in most other parts of India. Basic rights, including education and dignity, are often denied, earning a livelihood is out of the question, and domestic and other violence are an everyday experience.

India

Dianmin Wang

Society for the Elderly in Wanglao Village

Wang Dianmin has been actively engaged in promoting the rights of her fellow villagers. She mobilizes villagers to learn government policies, laws and regulations, so that they are better equipped to protect their rights. She has also set up cultural performance groups and a society for the elderly to enrich people's cultural life and to raise their organizing abilities.

Wang Dianmin was born to a poor peasant family 48 years ago in Anhui Province. When her husband died in 1993, leaving behind an elderly mother and three small children, she became the sole breadwinner of the family. In 1995, Dianmin started to serve as the chairperson of the village women's group. Being witness to the corruption of government officials at the grassroots level, she started to organize villagers to learn government policies to safeguard their lawful rights. In 1999, she was forced to resign because she led a group of villagers to appeal to the central government for intervention in incidents of rights abuse. Agricultural tax reform in Anhui Province took place a few years ago, and relations between farmers and the government have eased after this. The Society for Rights Protection has now shifted its focus to village reconstruction through culture and music. Dianmin worked to help set up the Village Cultural Performance Group and the Society for the Elderly.

Being a widow and a woman alone, Dianmin faced considerable criticism and innuendo in her work but she said, "We should prove that we are able, and live not only for ourselves but also for others. People will understand who we are when the Society for the Elderly turns out to be a success. I am a woman, and I am as good as my male counterparts." This was proved true in the summer of 2004 when The Society for the Elderly elected Dianmin as chair in an open election.

By end of 2004, Dianmin had set up a farmers' cooperative, with the aim of improving the livelihood of villagers.

Before agricultural tax reform, relations between farmers and government officials were tense. Also, with many young people leaving for the city, only elderly people remained in the villages. However, some villages have become active in appealing to the government for intervention in their issues.

China

Hualian Wang

Luxia Wanli Women's Mutual Aid Credit Union (Lwcu)

Wang Hualian (37) is from Jiangxi Province. Since 1994, she has organized rural women in alternative practices through the Luxia Wanli Women's Mutual Aid Credit Union (Lwcu), the first all-woman credit union in China. One of the few women in the village who finished junior high school, Wang works on rural women's education and health, organic farming, alternative trade and community building and represents the peasant community in various fora.

Wang Hualian initially planned to go to the city to work, but gave up the idea and stayed on in her village to work for Lwcu, the first all-woman credit union in China. "The members trust me a lot, and they have elected me several times to be the executive member of the managing committee. I cannot let them down and I cannot deny this responsibility." Her husband and children fully support her decision. Wang enjoys popularity mainly because of her intelligence, competence and honesty. She is one of the few women in the village who finished junior high school. She learnt accounting through the work of Lwcu. Since 1994, Wang has devoted her efforts to Lwcu's collective projects on women's education and health, organic farming, alternative trade and community development. For example, doing an organic lily bulb alternative trade, building a three-story activity center, running a kindergarten, conducting evening literacy and skill classes, and assisting the local health units to arrange gynecological checkups and treatment for the village women. Her contributions to rural society have resulted in Wang being elected as a peasant representative at different levels of various institutions. Since 2001, Wang has been the representative of Yichun District on the People's Congress. She always speaks out about peasants' problems. In her capacity as an Lwcu representative, Wang exchanges experiences with farmers of different countries such as India, Vietnam, Nepal and the Philippines. After various exposure trips, she has introduced alternative ideas of farmers from other countries to her village. This has generated discussions in the rural community on a developmental path that takes women and ecology into consideration.

China's dominant development path has resulted in young peasants flooding to the city to work, and in a still wider gap between the rich and the poor. Patriarchies have also been strengthened.

China

Wilaiwan Saetia

Confederation of Laborers

Wilaiwan Saetia (born 1956) was only a teenager when she began working in a textile factory in Bangkok. Now she is president of Thailand's Women Worker's Unity Group (WWUG), a network of Thai female trade union leaders. She has been actively involved in campaigning for the safety and welfare of factory workers, particularly women, since 1986.

Wilaiwan Saetia did not think she would become a labor activist even though, since her early days as a factory worker, she had witnessed discrimination and deprivation of rights of laborers. In 1992, however, she and her friends were provoked to stand up for their rights, and tried to set up a labor union. Even though that move was suppressed, Wilaiwan Saetia and her colleagues continued their fight until they were able to establish a network for the rights of women workers employed in the textile industry. Wilaiwan says that the rights of the workers are basic human rights, and that social problems will continue to exist if the rights of the workers are not recognized.

One major achievement of her group was the approval by parliament of the 1990 Social Security Act, which improved welfare for women with children. Wilaiwan was among 18 workers and students who went on hunger strike in 1989 to pressure parliament to approve the Act. The 90-day paid maternity leave for all working women which took effect in 1993, was also the result of earnest campaigns and demands pressed by Wilaiwan Saetia and her group. They also contributed to changes in labor legislation such as the Labor Protection Act, the Unemployment Insurance Act and others. The Kader doll factory fire on May 10, 1993 which took 188 lives and injured 469 employees led Wilaiwan and her group to press for increased safety standards in the working environment of laborers. Recently, Wilaiwan raised a number of other unresolved labor problems, such as issues concerning environmental health and occupational health. Wilaiwan says safety measures in factories and in workplaces should be made top priority.

Thai society is centered on the interests of entrepreneurs whose performance indicate the level of economic growth, and not on the workers whose labor makes the economic growth possible. The campaign for the recognition of the rights of laborers still has a long way to go.

Thailand

Women Workers' Cooperative

The Women Workers' Cooperative (WWC) was established in the 1990s when Hong Kong industries were moved north to mainland China. The WWC opens up a new space that is based on mutual support and cooperation: women workers have the opportunity to rediscover and reactivate themselves through cultural and economic involvement.

Early members of the WWC were all women workers who were forced to change profession after working in factories for many years. Women workers of other professions and homemakers joined in later. Not only has the WWC improved the living conditions of its members, it also enables them to live an "alternative life and relationship." They share responsibilities, learn and grow together. Members have equal access to the resources and revenue generated. Democratic decision-making is practiced. Within the WWC, significant emphasis is put on social and cultural participation.

Over the past 11 years, the businesses the WWC undertook included Chinese typesetting and data entry, and a survey on low-income families. In recent years, to address the need of Shum Shui Po, a low-income district, the WWC operates a community recycling shop and engages in collecting and reselling second-hand goods. It also operates the UnionMart that sells daily food and necessities. They have been able to create full-time and part-time positions for themselves and other members.

The WWC is not only a workplace; it is also a place where women workers learn to be self-governed and to make decisions. Their experience has proven that cooperatives work. This has inspired more and more people from other social sectors to work for the reconstruction of low-income communities in Hong Kong. Women workers have been active in various social actions and they rediscover and reactivate themselves in related cultural involvement. The WWC's social and cultural participation has broken down the barriers among various disadvantaged groups, paving the way for a future in which the vulnerable can be more unified and mutually supportive.

Economic restructuring forced many Hong Kong industries to move to China in the last twenty years. The workers were in their mid-30s in the early 1990s and they faced enormous hardships in getting jobs. Unemployment is a serious problem, especially for women. People at the grassroots suffer the most.

China, Hong Kong SAR

Women's Group of the Assembly of the Poor

Assembly of the Poor (AOP)

The Assembly of the Poor (AOP) is a grassroots people's movement consisting of seven social networks including the rural poor, farmers, urban poor, workers, indigenous peoples and NGOs. It is widely supported by community organizations, non-governmental organizations, academics and the general public. It collaborates on regional and international levels with networks on issues such as globalization, human rights, women, indigenous peoples, the environment and the protection of biodiversity.

Women are active participants in every sector of the Assembly of the Poor, which include the Network of the People Affected by Dam Construction, the Network of the People Affected by Unsafe and Unhealthy Working Conditions, the Slum People's Network, the Network of the People Affected by the Forest Management Policy, the Network of the People Affected by the Land Management Policy, the Network of Local Fishery, and the Network of Alternative Agriculture.

The women play a unique role in the Assembly, providing support for logistics and taking on the leadership in coordination, negotiation, and various other activities. A key activity of the assembly is poverty reduction, because it strongly believes that poverty can be alleviated with the participation of all sectors, particularly the marginalized groups. The Assembly of the Poor has played a major role in peacefully pressing the government to focus more attention on the problems and plight of the poor. It has made the government include issues concerned with poverty reduction in a number of its key policies.

In Thailand, fighting for the rights of the poor and vulnerable means having to face intimidation from people with vested interests such as politicians and state officials. The Assembly of the Poor (AOP) pursues its advocacy for the poor and powerless peacefully.

Thailand

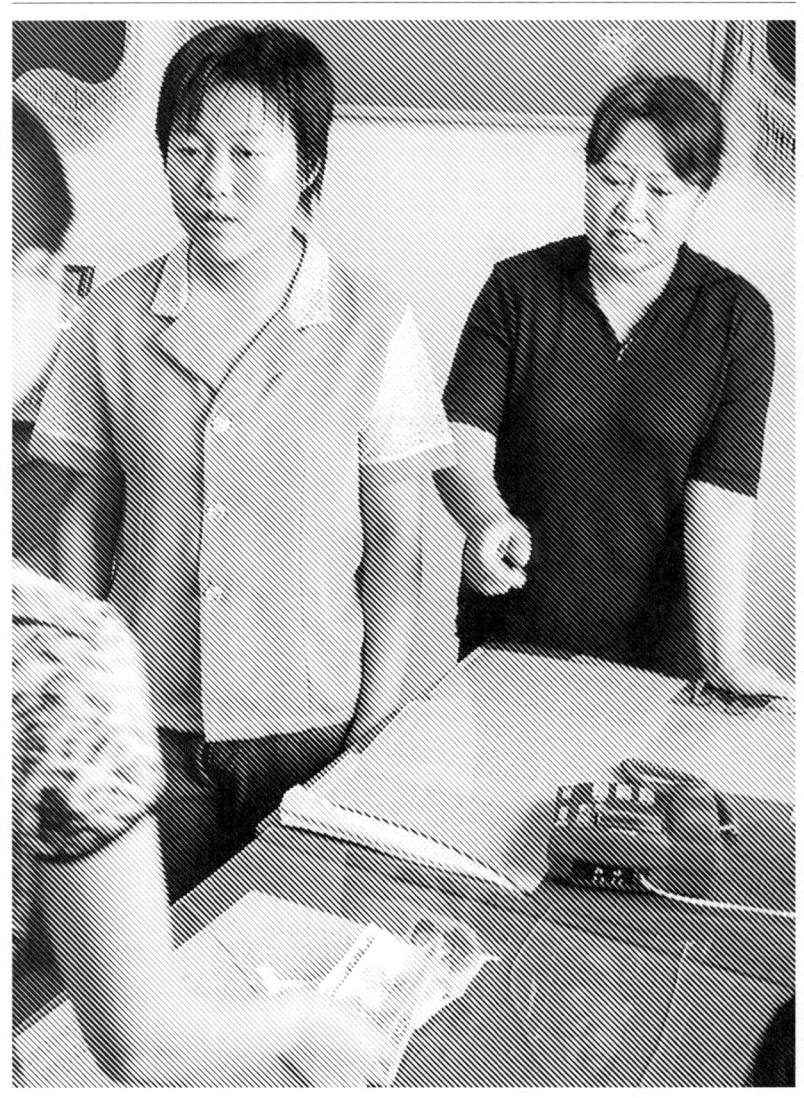

Jiuhua Wu

Women's Federation, Wandu County

Wu Jiuhua is chairperson of the Women's Federation in Wangdu County, Hebei Province. She founded the "Help the Poor Children Fund" to help alleviate poverty among young girls. She has also established more than 30 training bases to train women to change their lives of poverty.

In 1999, when Wu Jiuhua was appointed head of Zhao Zhuang Village, the villages's wheat crops were threatened by the appearance of a new kind of worm. Wu's investigations had revealed the problem and she was quickly able to help control the worm, thereby ensuring a good harvest. The villagers gratefully called Wu "the life-saving village head." When Wu became the chairperson of the Women's Federation in Wangdu County in 2002, she established "Help the Poor Children Fund" to enable poor young girls to finish their education. She convinced entrepreneurs and government officials to donate USD 240,000 to this fund. She has invited experts to give talks to women to improve their level of scientific knowledge and to help change their living standards. She liaised with specialists from the Department of Agriculture to carry out the activities under the "one helps two; one heads ten" program and organized 92 visits for women representatives to agricultural development centers, private enterprises and hi-tech institutes. She cooperated with related departments to organize more than 140 training courses on various techniques, to establish 30 women's bases, and to develop 18 technological advanced and prosperous villages. As a result, conditions improved for over 11,500 village women. She also set up liaison units and women's re-employment centers in every village, which has contributed to the improvement of living standards of poor village women. She set up the "Women's Rights Organization" to protect women's rights, and organized activities such as "I contribute to protect women's rights" and the "March 8th women's rights week." Besides offering training courses on legal knowledge, Wu also started a TV program that dealt with the legal problems faced by women in the process of protecting their rights.

People in most rural areas in China have a relatively low level of education in technology. Children are thus deprived of their right to education. People also lack legal knowledge and thus many women's rights are not protected. There is no government department to take care of these needs.

China

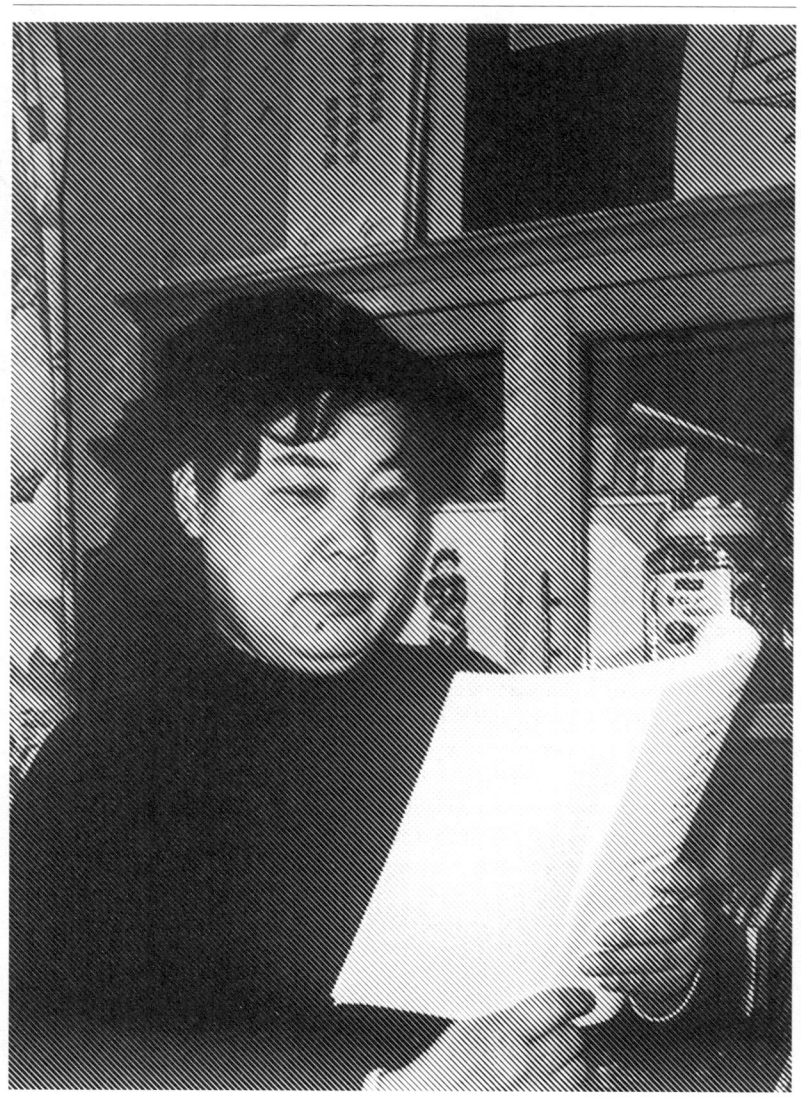

Jiying Xu

Zhonglinluyuan (Beijing) Tea Flowers Research Center

Xu Jiying is director of the Zhonglinluyuan (Beijing) Tea Flowers Research Center. She has devoted more than 20 years to the study of the uses of tea flowers, thus changing this once ignored part of tea trees into an important asset to mankind. Without charging any fees, she has devised and conducted training courses for over 10,000 tea planters from all over China.

In the winter of 1949 various kinds of beautiful tree flowers were blossoming in the tea gardens in the hilly areas of Anhui Province, China. At that time, one child from a Xu family that had grown tea there for generations died. The sad father, accompanied by neighbors, went out for a walk. The biggest blossoming tea tree caught their attention. When they got closer they found that beneath the tree a baby girl covered with torn clothes was almost dead. They regarded this girl as an angel sent by God to the Xu family to compensate their loss. The little girl grew up in this tea garden and has not been separated from tea since then.

The girl's name was Xu Jiying. She is known to be a person crazy about tea and is the first person to do research and development on tea flowers. Her aim was to make them loved and used by adults. Xu finally realized her childhood dream when she was admitted by Anhui Agricultural University to study in the Department of Tea. She learned from the experts and professors, absorbing everything. In the Zhonglinluyuan (Beijing) Tea Flowers Research Center, she is responsible for the development of technology in tea. In addition to her daily work, she spends all of her leisure time studying tea flowers. In the past 20 years, she has invested more than 26 million yuan in her tea tree flower research work and she is devoted to her work. Many call her a workaholic, a maniac or a tea lover. But she does not care.

Tea originated in China, and China has been a major producer of tea. There are tea gardens in 19 provinces/cities with a total area of 18.75 million acres, 80 million tea planters and some 50 million people engaged in tea sales. Altogether, 10 percent of the Chinese population works in the tea production industry.

China

"I am just an ordinary person doing ordinary things."

E Yang

Beacon Cooperative

Yang E encouraged the people of Beacon Village to set up an art troupe and a rural folk dance team. Besides establishing the village cooperative and helping women to apply for microcredits, she has also organized women to participate in planting over 10,000 trees in the village. Yang has helped to change the villagers' preference for boy children and has brought cultural and economic developments to the village.

Yang E moved to Beacon Village, Urad Middle Banner, Ba Yan Lake City, an underdeveloped area in Inner Mongolia, when she got married after graduating from secondary school. Working as officer of the village women's federation, she was responsible for family planning and birth control and she was unhappy with the status and quality of life of the village women. After much thought, Yang decided to set up an art troupe and motivated women and other villagers to participate in it. The women's cultural life was enriched by the activities of the troupe; they also benefited intellectually and many began to rethink their preference for boy children. They gradually gave up taking risks to have children outside the state plan and accepted the idea that fewer births mean a better and wealthier life.

The confidence inspired Yang to set up a cooperative in the village, particularly as it was the time of rural reform in China. Yet the task was not easy, and she came under pressure also from her family who felt neglected. But she bore all this because she had a vision to work for women. She spent two years working to set up microcredit projects for women, and led a program to plant 10,000 trees under the forest plantation program of the March 8 Project. The Beacon Village cooperative, the first of its kind in Inner Mongolia, was founded in July 2004 as a result of her efforts that have also made a significant difference to economic and social life in the village.

Social and cultural activities are lacking in many villages in Inner Mongolia but they are a powerful medium to get across messages for social change, and to inspire people to work for better life conditions in a cooperative way.

China

Geum-Soon Yoon

Reunification Solidarity
Korea Women Farmers Association (KWFA)
Viacampasina

One of the founders of the Korea Women Farmers Association (KWFA), Geum-Soon Yoon has helped to place women and farmers in the forefront of her country's reunification movement. Educated as an environmental engineer, Geum-Soon worked within the farmers' movement to improve the lives of the poor farmers. As vice-president of KWFA, she was instrumental in making the historic first reunification conference between North and South Korean farmers a success. Geum-Soon is a sharp critic of globalization policies that negatively affect farmers' rights and the environment.

One of six children, Geum-Soon was born into a family that had been farming for many generations. To finish her education, when she was in the 6th grade she left her parents to live with her sister in Seoul. With her sister's support, she eventually received a degree in Environmental Engineering. In the early 1980s, Geum-Soon worked to organize and educate young farmers and also began a childcare center for farmers' children.

Geum-Soon married in 1990, moved to Sung-ju, and has worked there as a farmer ever since. In Sung-ju she opened and managed another childcare service. She and her husband have fraternal twins and together they organically cultivate rice, pepper, and cabbage. She has continued her leadership and advocacy for farmers' rights. Having served as policy chair, secretary general, and vice-president of the Korea Women Farmers Association (KWFA), she now serves as its president.

Geum-Soon's work in agriculture, reunification, and international farmers' solidarity continues to make an impact. By conceiving a self-reliant woman farmers movement, she helped to create an ideological and theoretical foundation and vision for some of Korea's least powerful citizens, its women farmers. She is a vigilant watchdog of national and international agricultural policies, protesting against strategies that sacrifice the agricultural sector to rampant industrialization. The day care system that she created in Choong-ju and Sung-ju has spread to other farming villages. And success in the reunification process of North and South Korea has helped women farmers understand that they can be active agents for social change.

Persistent and consistent, Geum-Soon has been a pioneer in a society that historically did not value or give representation to women or farmers. She also swims upstream in her unification work, given the strong anti-North Korea ideology stemming from the division of Korea.

Republic of Korea

Fenglan Zhao

Association for the Elderly

During the collectivization era in China, Zhao Fenglan, director of the Women's Federation in her village and village party secretary, led the 2000 people of Dalizhunag toward self-reliance. Later, during the period of economic reform, she found creative and effective ways to solve community problems. She raised funds to build a school for village children, organized a women's cultural troupe and established an association for the elderly. Her dedication has facilitated collaboration, harmony and progress in the village.

Located in the Yellow River flood zone, Lankao County of Henan Province has abominable natural conditions. During the collectivization era, Zhao Fenglan made the village among the most successful in the county in agricultural infrastructure development, foresting, grain production and industrial income. During economic reform, the village collective economy was in deficit and the village primary school became run down. Zhao persuaded her son, the manager of an enterprise, to collect funds. He raised 500,000 yuan from his friends and colleagues and with the support of the township government, a safe school building was built. In 2002, Zhao Fenglan organised the Dalixi Cultural Troupe. Not only has the troupe brought joy and enrichment to the lives of older people in the village, but it also has become well known throughout the region and formes the backbone of rural cultural rejuvenation. The troupe has been extensively covered by the Kaifeng Television Station, Lankao Television Station and several magazines. In 2003, Zhao founded the Dalixi Elderly Recreational Centre with three temple shrines for the elderly and established the first association for them in 2004. The mission of the association is "the elderly shall be cared for, the elderly shall be happy, the elderly shall be relevant". The association has had a positive impact on culture and recreation, conflict resolution, respect for the young and elderly, supporting those in need, and the creation of local handicrafts and literature. Zhao has worked hard to improve the lives of children, women and the elderly and has made a remarkable difference to rural development.

During collectivization in China, despite abominable natural conditions, villages had to support the industrial development of the cities. After economic reforms, rural resources continue to be drained to cities, villagers lack cultural nourishment and their well-being is not satisfactory.

China

Bing Zheng

Zaizi Village Peasants' Association

Zheng Bing has been engaged in technical training for peasants, and the establishment of a women's association and a peasants' association. She encourages peasants to improve their cultural life and living standards, learn about state policies and regulations and new concepts of rural reconstruction.

Zheng Bing (38) started a peasants' association that gave technical training aimed at both enhancing production and studying state policies and regulations. She created many new concepts in rural reconstruction to improve the lives of peasants in Zhaizi Village, Yongji City, Shanxi Province.

In 1997 she invited experts from Xi'an to give lectures on agricultural science for peasants. She persuaded one woman in each village to come, and then asked them to persuade another five women they knew. In 1998, despite her family's objection, she resigned her teaching post and set up a women's federation, organizing women to sing and dance, have various competitions and learn new activities. She subscribed to Rural Women magazine for women to practice Putonghua, one of the eight major dialect groups of China, and organized debates on topics such as whether it was better to have a son or a daughter, to be a housewife or to develop your potential. Later the association expanded to 35 villages with a membership exceeding 3000, with five divisions, namely, cattle rearing, fish farming, reed division, women's division, and the sci-tech service chain center.

In 2004 the state issued the No. 1 Document relating to agricultural policies. Zheng arranged for peasants to study the document every week so as to enhance their knowledge of state policies and come up with creative concepts. In April 2004, she organized women for handicraft production. In October she organized 82 families to set up a shareholding company to promote projects for environmental protection in the village.

For two years the village committee elected her the head of the village, but she refused. She thought it would take up too much of the time she spent running the peasants' association. She says: "In my childhood, my parents taught me to exert all efforts for whatever things I do."

Zhaizi Village, Shanxi Province, is located in the valley of the Yellow River and has a long history. Most peasants earn a living by planting reeds on the riverbank. In the past, peasants either played mahjong or visited each other in their spare time. They did not have adequate food and clothing.

China

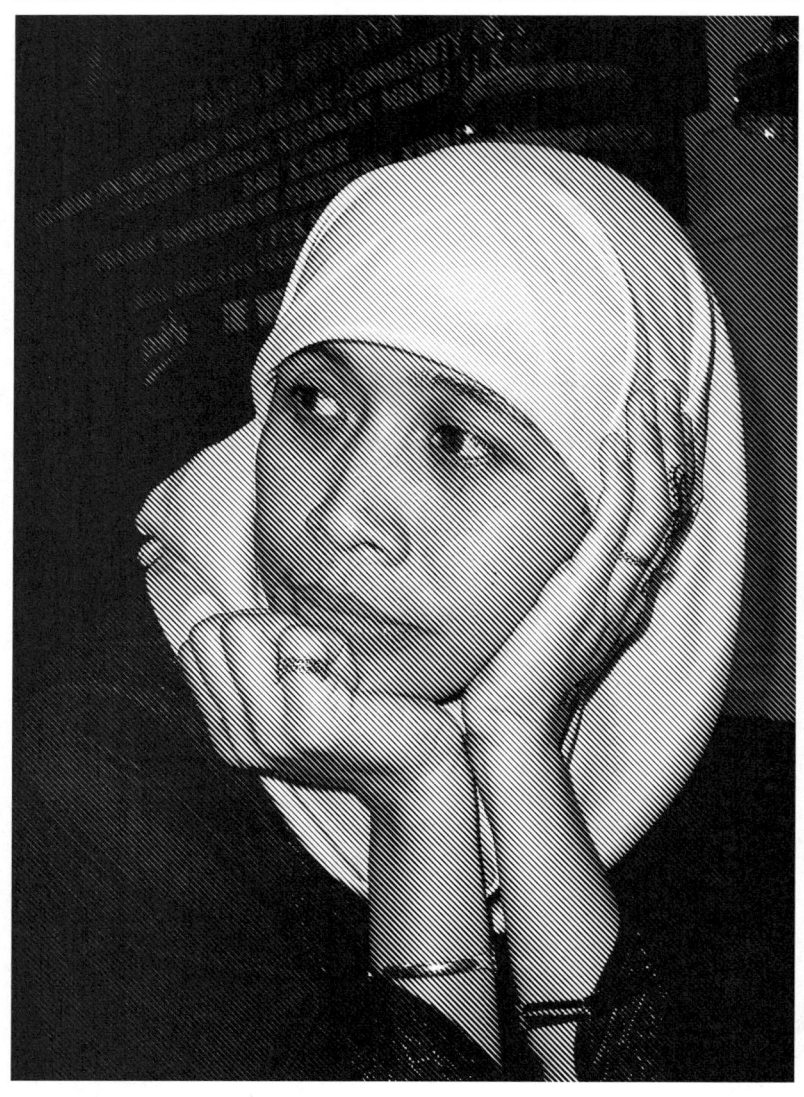

Nani Zulminarni

Program Pemberdayaan Perempuan Kepala Keluarga (Pekka)

Nani Zulminarni (born 1962), a gender and development specialist, has been working on women's issues in Indonesia since 1987. In 2001, she initiated Program Pemberdayaan Perempuan Kepala Keluarga (Pekka), the Female Household Heads Empowerment Program, to instil confidence in women so that they can better deal with gender discrimination in society. At present, there are approximately 6000 female heads of families in over 200 villages in eight provinces who are members of Pekka.

Nani Zulminarni has been fighting gender discrimination for 18 years. In the past few years, she has concentrated on empowering poor female household heads, especially widows and single mothers. She is particularly concerned about the discrimination women face in spite of the central roles they play in the family, especially in the absence of the men. A divorcee and mother of three teenagers, she herself is the sole breadwinner in the family. "I have personally experienced discriminatory treatment, harassment and scorn because of my status as a divorcee," Nani says. But she considers herself luckier than many other women, being educated and more knowledgeable of her rights and fair treatment for women like herself. An economically independent and proud single mother, she wants every single mother and female breadwinner to share such confidence and independence.

In 2001, she initiated the Program Pemberdayaan Perempuan Kepala Keluarga (Pekka), a comprehensive program to economically and politically empower marginalized women breadwinners. "It is the first program in Indonesia that focuses on poor women who have been marginalized because of their marital status," she explains. Pekka works with more than 6000 female household heads in 200 villages in Aceh, Southeast Sulawesi, North Maluku, West Kalimantan, West Java, Central Java, West Nusa Tenggara and East Nusa Tenggara. It facilitates women's economic activities, helps them organize and build networks, raises their awareness of women's rights and gender equality and provides them with training on leadership and practical life skills. Nani says that many widows and single mothers have begun to show the courage to declare their marital status loudly and proudly. "They can now show that their world without husbands can also be beautiful and dynamic."

There are over six million female household heads in Indonesia, about half of whom are illiterate and very poor. Female household heads frequently face discrimination. As widows or single parents, female household heads endure serious social and cultural stigmas.

Indonesia

Justice

and Peace

Walter Kälin

L

Can there be peace without justice? More often than not, the answer in post-conflict situations is yes. When I visited Indonesia some years ago to provide advice on how best to frame a law allowing the prosecution and sentencing of those responsible for the atrocities committed by the Indonesian military and its allies in East Timor before it became independent, even non-governmental human rights organizations told me that restoring harmony would be more important than bringing those responsible to justice.

In the present conflict in Nepal between Maoists and the Royal army, both sides believe that punishing perpetrators of war crimes and crimes against humanity within their own ranks would weaken morale and undermine their ability to win the struggle.

In Bosnia-Herzegovina, the idea was promoted some time ago that reconciliation would be possible if Serb and Bosnian mothers who had lost their sons could grieve together. But this did not work because the women whose loved ones had perished in concentration camps or during campaigns of ethnic cleansing and genocide could not sympathize with the mothers of aggressors who were killed in combat. In Serbia, a large part of the population considers the war crime trials in The Hague not as an instrument to find the truth, but to humiliate the Serbian people once more.

In Sudan and Uganda, there are those who say that the investigations by the International Criminal Court are a serious obstacle to ending the conflict, for one cannot convince those in positions of responsibility to extend the hand of peace to each other if they expect to be sent to The Hague for trial on the day after signing a peace agreement.

Countries and societies use different ways to avoid the need to address past atrocities. Sometimes, there is outright denial — either by not speaking about what has happened, or by seeing oneself merely as a victim and blaming everything on the enemy. In other cases, the truth may be admitted but a culture of impunity makes it impossible to bring those responsible for war crimes and crimes against humanity to account. The culture of impunity is legalized where, in the name of reconciliation, a general amnesty is declared by the government or the parliament. In most cases, the perpetrators remain in positions of power, and traumatized victims have to confront them in their daily lives.

While these strategies have often worked to stabilize fragile peace agreements, they are not in line with the demands of international human rights guarantees. It is acknowledged by all international human rights monitoring bodies that cases of killings, torture or disappearances must be investigated by the competent national authorities and the perpetrators prosecuted. The matter of prosecution must not be left to the discretion of the authorities; it is a matter of entitlement for the victims.

An even more important reason for providing justice to the victims is the fact that, as the American author William Faulkner said in his "Requiem for a Nun", "The past is never dead. It's not even past".

As historical experience has shown, peace without justice is often not sustainable. It is merely a way to freeze a conflict or, at best, to obtain a period of tranquility, which is still volatile. However, such situations bear in themselves the seeds of new atrocities. In order to achieve real peace, justice must both be done, and be seen to be done. But what does this mean?

Truth, accountability and reconciliation are the key elements here: first, the truth must be established. This can be achieved in different ways ranging from fostering open public debate where investigative journalists, academics and artists can shed light upon what has happened, to official commissions of inquiry, truth commissions or even criminal investigations. Second, those who are most responsible for atrocities must be held accountable, whether by offering them the possibility to sincerely repent (as was done in the context of the South African Truth Commission) or by bringing them to justice.

In principle, those responsible for war crimes and crimes against humanity must always be punished. Of course, such judicial proceedings must not be reduced to justice being meted out by the victors but must address crimes committed by all sides.

While it is important to insist that real peace cannot be achieved without doing justice to the victims, one has to be realistic regarding the best strategy to reach this goal. The choice of method and timing may depend on the nature of the conflict in question, the history and cultural context of the country concerned or the dynamics of the peace process. But such considerations should only influence the answer to "how", never to "if" justice can be brought to the survivors of war crimes and crimes against humanity and the families of those who were killed or remain missing because of such atrocities.

Walter Kälin, Dr jur., Professor of constitutional and international public law at the University of Bern/Switzerland; member of the UN Human Rights Committee and Representative of the UN Secretary General. This contribution expresses my personal opinion only.

—

L

Aziza Abdirasulova

Kylym Shamy
Guild of Prisoners of Conscience

Aziza Abdirasulova (born 1958) is a well-known human rights activist who works on behalf of the citizens of the Republic of Kyrgyzstan. She is an advocate for prisoners' rights and the right to assemble peacefully. Her activity is directed towards the fight against injustice and inequality by means of nonviolent conflict resolution. She works for the sake of justice without a personal or political agenda, and her action is based upon tolerance and transparency. She has worked with a diverse range of people in her country and has earned their trust and respect.

Aziza Abdirasulova is a leader of the human rights organization Kylym Shamy (Torch of the Century). She worked as an independent observer during the parliamentary elections of 2000 and noted the gross infringements of voters' rights. After an arrest and two-day imprisonment for this advocacy, she officially began her work in the human rights sphere. She realized that no one's rights were protected from the arbitrary whims of the police and that she would not be able to combat this injustice on her own.

She established the human rights organization Guild of Prisoners of Conscience, in April 2000, and was elected to head this organization. The political prisoners she supported included a popular politician who was arrested on the order of the Kyrgyz President, who feared him as a rival in the elections, and parliamentary deputies who were critical of the President. In September 2000, seven opposition figures were sentenced to 16 and 17 years imprisonment and confiscation of their property. They had been charged with planning to assassinate the Kyrgyz President. During the court hearings, they pleaded innocent and told the court of having been tortured to extract confessions. The court refused to consider their claims. Aziza was present at the court sessions on behalf of the Guild of Prisoners of Conscience and witnessed the infringement of the rights of the accused. This injustice was acknowledged by international human rights organizations, activists, and politicians.

Aziza Abdirasulova led a protest picket demanding their release. The picket lasted for 40 days despite threats from the police, arrest of the protesters, and offers of money to cease protesting. In November 2000, the Bishkek Court reduced the terms of the sentence to six to seven years. A week later, all the accused except one were released on orders of the Kyrgyz President.

Kyrgyzstan is a newly independent country. In the struggle for political power, authorities often arrest their opponents. Corruption and poverty are serious problems. After the parliamentary elections in the spring 2005, a sudden revolution overthrew President Askar Akayev and his government, who in popular opinion had become increasingly corrupt and authoritarian.

Kyrgyzstan

Issam Abdul-Hadi

General Union of Palestinian Women (GUPW)

Issam Abdul-Hadi was born in Nablus in 1928. She attended the first Palestinian National Council (PNC), which formed the General Union of Palestinian Women (GUPW) in 1965. In 1969, Israeli authorities imprisoned Issam and deported her to Amman when she called for a sit-in and hunger strike at the gates of the Church of the Holy Sepulcher in Jerusalem to protest against Israel's killing of women in Gaza. From Amman Issam continued her struggle against the Israeli occupation as a Palestinian Liberation Organization (PLO) member and founded the Save Jerusalem Committee in Amman.

Issam Abdul-Hadi was married at the age of nineteen. She has four children — two boys and two girls — and twelve grandchildren, all of whom, in their own individual way, are immersed in the legacy of a distinguished woman, caring mother and kindhearted grandmother. The awarding panel of the Ibn Rushd Prize for Freedom of Thought aptly described Issam as a "political activist" and "realist feminist" when she won the prize in 2000 . Press coverage of the event extolled her as an individual with "clever remarks, eloquent speeches, rational thinking and a refined sense of humor that captivates and fascinates the audience."

Educated in the city of Nablus and later at the Ramallah Friends School, Issam Abdul-Hadi developed a solid personality: lovable, kind, independent, assertive and eloquently capable of expressing herself in both Arabic and English. These qualities, among others, have earned Issam regional and international recognition. Her strength and courage have won her the respect of all Palestinian factions. She is highly accredited for her full potential of pooling efforts together for a common aim — the end of the belligerent Israeli occupation of Palestine and the support of women's rights throughout the world. Most significantly, she has been a source of inspiration to Palestinian and Arab women who are struggling with the definition of their newly emerging identity as Arab (Muslim or Christian) women in a contemporary, conflict-ridden and constantly changing globalized world.

In July 1965 the General Union of Palestinian Women (GUPW) was established in Jerusalem and Issam Abdul-Hadi was elected as President, a position she has held until now. Imprisonment by the Israeli occupation forces in April 1969 and subsequent deportation to Jordan did not deter her from defending Palestinian rights.

Occupied Palestinian Territory

Sunila Abeysekera

INFORM

Sunila Abeysekera (born 1952) has been a formative voice in the women's movement in Sri Lanka and in South Asia, as well as in international movements for women's human rights. She is a pioneer in human rights documentation, and started her organization, INFORM, in 1989, to collect information about human rights' abuses at a time when repression and terror in the country was at an all-time high.

In 1987, Sunila Abeysekera left Sri Lanka after receiving death threats and witnessing the assassination of a colleague. She lived in The Netherlands for six months, but returned, and is today a single mother of six children, and a women's rights and human rights activist who has lived and worked in Sri Lanka for the past 30 years. Her special focus is on civilians living in war-affected areas, women's rights, and sexual and reproductive rights, including the rights of communities such as sex workers, people living with HIV/Aids, and lesbian, gay and transgender persons.

In 1989, Sunila helped establish INFORM, which documented human rights' abuses at a time when repression and terror in Sri Lanka were peaking. By bringing it before the international community, she played a critical role in seeking redress for human rights' abuses. Since the late 1970s, she has been a key member of civil society groups working for a negotiated solution to the conflict.

Sunila's most effective contribution to women's rights and human rights is through her work at bridging the divide between these two areas. She prepares short and easy-to-understand pamphlets in Sinhala. She has worked with women's groups and social activists on ways to introduce basic concepts of nonviolent ways of conflict resolution, focusing on a feminist perspective on the issues of militarization, conflict, conflict transformation and peace-building. Her experience in bringing together communities of women has been drawn upon by women activists in Gujarat, the Indian Northeast, Uganda and Timor Leste.

Sunila believes that her biggest challenge has been to combine single parenting with her activism. Her comment on receiving the UN Human Rights Prize from Kofi Annan was, "At last my children will see that what I do is recognized as worthwhile!"

Human rights in Sri Lanka emerged as a major issue in the 1970s, as successive governments responded to youth militancy in the south and north with repressive legislation, arbitrary arrest and detention, torture and curbs on the freedom of expression, including censorship.

Sri Lanka

Fatimakhon Ahmedova

Center for Democratic Transformations (CDT)

Fatimakhon Ahmedova received a B.S. in sociology and linguistics and an M.S. in international human rights law. She completed courses in humanities and English language for professionals at the Aga Khan Foundation. Originally from Khojand, a small city in Tajikistan, Fatimakhon now often visits numerous countries for international conferences and seminars. She fights corruption and bribery often at risk to her own life and career. She is also a teacher and works for the Center for Democratic Transformations in Tajikistan.

Fatimakhon Ahmedova is a researcher on human rights violations, ethnic minorities, prisoners, ethnic conflicts, and corruption. Her dedication to the pursuit of human rights has led her to meet with the security services in Tajikistan several times, feeling on each occasion that her own safety had been compromised. Fortunately, nobody dared to challenge her as she has always been open about her work and has an obviously untainted reputation.

Currently working part-time at the Khojand State University in Tajikistan, teaching linguistics and humanities, Fatimakhon also works for the Center for Democratic Transformations. People from all walks of life, especially the impoverished, former women detainees, students, and even children, all lacking resources to pay for legal advice, come to her office seeking assistance. On one occasion, after visiting a local orphanage and a home for elderly people, she decided to organize a permanent committee for making holiday gifts for the elderly, and worked towards organizing two housing facilities for disabled persons and two orphanages. Her students say that if they become teachers they would like to be like Fatimakhon — honest, fair, and always smiling. Many young girls see her as a role model due to the outstanding contribution she continues to make. "Corruption, bribes, unemployment, terribly low salaries, and uneducated leaders within the educational system, are all factors we have to deal with everyday. Due to my family and my mother in particular, I was able to finish my education, find interesting jobs and see the world with open eyes. Not everyone is so fortunate," she says.

The economic situation in Tajikistan is dire and has been worsened by civil war. Muslim and secular groups vie for political influence while domestic violence and women's rights are major social issues. Women in Tajikistan were perhaps the most adversely affected by the collapse of the Soviet Union.

Tajikistan

Sheikha Lulwa Al-Khalifa

The Mother and Child's Welfare Society (MCWS)
The Hope Institute for Handicapped Children
Information Center for Women and Children

Sheikha Lulwa Al-Khalifa (born 1928) has been a wholehearted aficionado of broadening voluntary activities since her youth. The charitable organizations that she has helped to found serve underprivileged families and disabled children. They train and teach unfortunate women new skills so they can become economically productive and self-dependent. With a few Bahraini women she initiated The Mother and Child's Welfare Society (MCWS) in 1960. The event marked the beginning of her organized voluntary participation in local communities of Bahrain and nearby regions.

Bahrain in the 1940s and the 1950s was a very pro-male, conservative society. Sheikha Lulwa Al-Khalifa recalls, "Married women's roles in Bahrain were restrictedly perceived as those of bearing and raising children and looking after the house. They were not expected to participate in public, social and economic activities." Sheikha Lulwa felt that women's development and economic and social status were truly paralyzed by such cultural restrictions, and her mother's narratives of Egyptian women's participation in charity in the 1940s had a tremendous impact on her motivation. "If women in Egypt can publicly advocate the noble cause of aiding less privileged women and children, so can we in Bahrain," she pointed out.

So, Sheikha Lulwa began to work for the socio-cultural development of women and children in Bahrain. In the 1950s, she volunteered to launch a local hospital campaign to visit new mothers in their homes. During this stage of her life she witnessed the dire economical conditions of those disenfranchised women and children. After a decade of informal charity work she decided with a few women from Bahrain to collectively establish The Mother and Child's Welfare Society (MCWS) in 1960. Sheikha Lulwa knew from the beginning that the mission to bring peace and security to the lives of these marginalized and less privileged female members of society meant that she had to convince both women and men of the need to change. Since then, thousands of women and children have benefited from MCWS. After a decade of dedicated informal charity work and intense face-to-face exposure to local community, the public felt the benefit of the personal sacrifices Lulwa has made in order to serve them.

Sheikha Lulwa felt that women's development and economic and social status were truly paralyzed by cultural restrictions on women's social participation. Therefore, she was motivated to work for the socio-cultural development of women and children in Bahrain.

Amneh Al-Rimawi

Palestinian Labor Union (PLU)

Amneh Abdul-Jaber Al-Rimawi was born in 1957 in Beit-Rima, a village near Ramallah. In 1977, she joined the Palestinian Labor Union (PLU) to improve working conditions of men and women through negotiation and mediation. She is working around the clock towards achieving equal rights for Palestinian women, particularly focusing on wage parity, and she managed to establish a center for addressing labor-related issues in Ramallah. She is currently a member of the Labor Union's national secretariat and she heads the women's division of the Union.

Amneh Al-Rimawi grew up in a family of twelve children with an independent and strong personality, always defending the rights of her sisters: She still recounts her fight to persuade her father to allow one of her sisters to join the nursing college. In 1983 Amneh was married to an agricultural engineer and member of the Palestinian Labor Union (PLU). While studying, she embarked on voluntary social activities side by side with men, and also became the only female member of "Dababis", a Palestinian drama group. Since 1977, she has been involved in PLU activities, defending Palestinian women's equal access to employment and advocating the improvement of working conditions. In 1978, she was officially elected as a member of the Union in Ramallah, and from 1985 to 1994 she was its vice-president. Amneh is currently a member of the Labor Union's national secretariat, heading the women's division.

Over many years, she has been pressurizing for wage parity between men and women and has helped to establish a center for labor studies in Ramallah.

From 1985 to 1988, Amneh was placed under house arrest by the Israeli Authorities. Then, she was imprisoned for two years from 1991 to 1993. Despite these adversities, she obtained a diploma in Commerce and Business Administration. She also started a degree at the Beirut Arab University (BAU), but was unable to complete it because the Israeli Authorities prevented her from traveling abroad for fifteen years from 1982 to 1997. However, she was later able to join the International Union Training Center in Turin, Italy, where she was awarded three honorary diplomas in women's empowerment, management of social security funds and union establishments. Amneh Al-Rimawi has participated in several international conferences and seminars on unionism and gender.

Since the occupation of Palestine, Amneh Al-Rimawi has been advocating women's social, economic and educational rights. As a Unionist, she organized strikes to support women's labor rights and to combat the victimization of women in Palestinian society and under the belligerent Israeli occupation.

Occupied Palestinian Territory

Lyudmila Alekseeva

Moskovskaya Helsinskaya gruppa (MHG)
Vsierossiysky grazhdansky kongress (All-Russian Civil Congress)

Lyudmila Alekseeva (born 1927) worked as a researcher at the Academy of Sciences of the USSR. As early as the 1950s, she participated in dissident activities. She helped the cause of political prisoners in the 1960s. In 1976, she became part of the human rights organization Moscow Helsinki Group (MHG). As a result of her activities, she was forced to emigrate to the US in 1977. In 1993, she returned to Russia where, as the head of the MHG, she helps to provide legal and human rights aid to citizens through a network of 'legal clinics.'

Lyudmila Alekseeva and her colleagues have created a network of 'legal clinics' throughout Russia to promote and protect citizens' human rights. Even though the overwhelming majority of complaints relate to violations of socio-economic — rather than civil or political — rights, there are still a good many complaints about civil rights violations as well. Furthermore, new problems have emerged that did not exist in Soviet times, such as the problems faced by refugees and displaced persons. So Lyudmila and other activists have a lot of work to do providing legal help to the citizens of the Russian Federation and educating them on their rights and freedoms.

The path to a law-based, democratic Russia is still long and difficult. However, never before in its centuries-long history has Russia been moving more rapidly towards this goal than over the last decade. Lyudmila says that none of the Soviet-era human rights activists ever believed that, during their lifetime, the Soviet Constitution would be replaced by one which stated the main purpose of the state as being to guarantee and defend human rights. Now such a constitution exists. Lyudmila believes that her country will make its way from the present lawlessness to a genuine rule-of-law state in a relatively short period, much faster than the Western countries needed to achieve democracy. She believes this not because Russia is in some way special, but simply because Russia started out on its journey later than other countries. Lyudmila uses the following analogy: when the first cross-country skier sets out into deep snow, the going is slow as he cuts a new path. The second skier moves faster, and the third simply flies over the trail that the others have made. Lyudmila hopes that Russia will become that third skier.

The communist regime in the USSR harshly restricted personal freedom and human rights. Lyudmila Alekseeva hopes to change the situation in Russia by providing legal consultations to its citizens in the framework of 'legal clinics' created in many regions of the country.

Russian Federation

Farida Allaghi

Arab Gulf Program for United Nations Development Organizations (AGFUND)

In 1980 Dr Farida Allaghi received her PhD in Sociology, 'Planning and Development', from Colorado State University, USA. Her challenging stands in human development and human rights have finally led her to live in exile for the past 25 years in Lebanon, Egypt and Saudi Arabia. She has held many influential positions, such as director of the Women and Children Division of the Arab Gulf Program for United Nations Development Organizations (AGFUND) in Saudi Arabia, general coordinator for the Arab NGOs Committee, and general coordinator of the Arab Council for Children and Development.

Dr Farida Allaghi's early life had a significant impact upon her visions of life and humanity. The open-mindedness of her parents has tremendously impacted her character and ingrained in her love and tolerance for all, irrespective of religion or social strata. She expresses her upbringing and early life experience in the following words: "The inspirational seeds of tolerance and love that my parents implanted in me have matured and impacted me in diverse ways. My father, although a staunch conservative Muslim, sent me to church-based school in Tripoli to receive my early education, and he has ever since been a source of support and empowerment to me through my life. My mother, a compassionate and motivating woman, was the driving force of my educational excellence. Despite her illiteracy, she always pushed me to attain the highest marks in my classes, and at the same time she taught me the significance of giving assistance and care to all."

Dr Allaghi has challenging stands in human rights and development, forcing her finally to live in exile for 25 years. She was the source of inspiration of founding several regional NGOs and networks, aimed at augmenting and protecting the rights of women and children in the Arab world and abroad.

Libyan Arab Jamahiriya

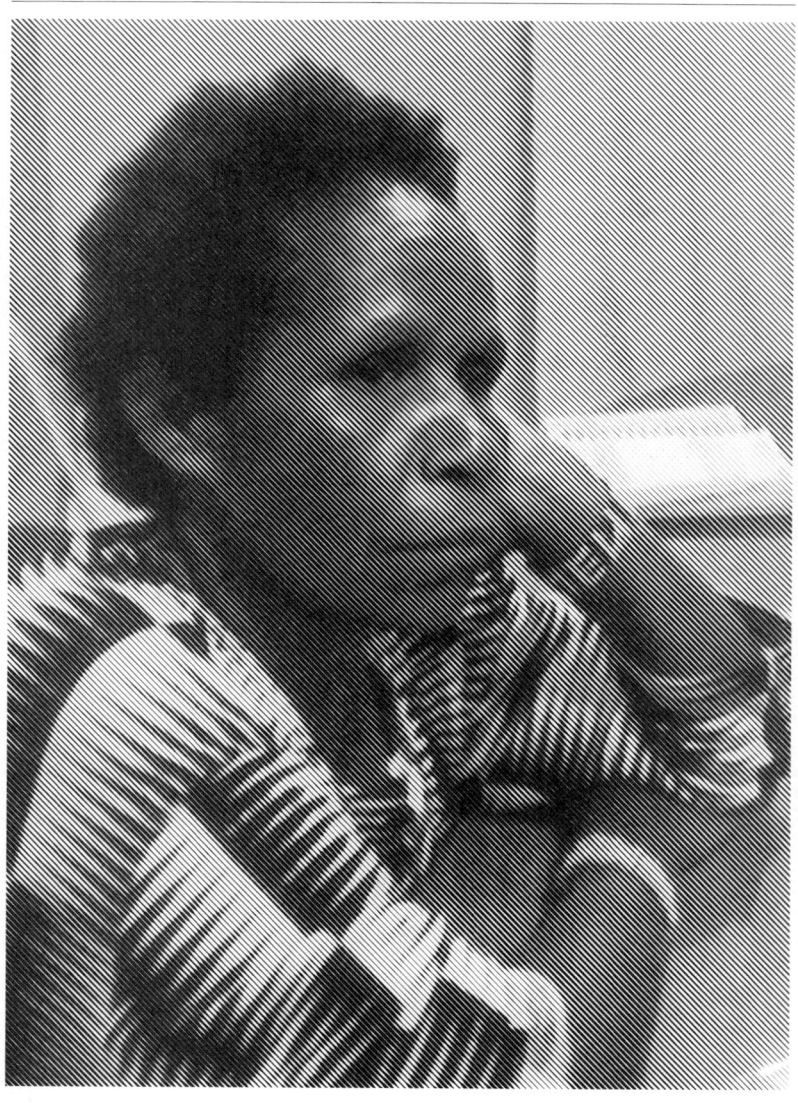

Yosepha Alomang

Yahamak

Yosepha Alomang (born 1950) is a true human rights defender who fights for the right of indigenous peoples to reclaim the titles of their land in Timika from Freeport McMoRan Copper & Gold Inc., a multinational mining company. Human rights violations are rampant in Timika and Yosepha has been detained several times for protesting either against the mining company or the military that backs it up. She chairs the Mama Yosepha Center, which provides counseling to women and empowers women's groups.

There were four women in Papua with good hearts who wanted to make a difference in the lives of the women in Papua. One of them was Yosepha Alomang: "Many of our women were suffering from domestic violence and were marginalized from the public sphere. We wanted to do something." During the military occupation of Papua, Yosepha recalls, "Many women were raped and families lost their loved ones." For voicing her protest, she was jailed several times. "Once I was detained for a month in a container van by the military. General Sutrisno released me when he visited Papua for a mission. I just cannot sit still seeing oppression against my family." And she has kept her resolve. Yosepha does not regard what she is doing for her tribe in Timika as political work. She would rather talk about freedom, and she has been fighting for that freedom for more than a decade.

In 1994, she served as the spokesperson for the Amungme tribespeople during the first major negotiations between Freeport McMoRan Copper & Gold Inc., the multinational mining company in Timika, and the local people. On behalf of her people, she filed a lawsuit against the company in a US court damanding that Freeport close its operations in Timika. But Yosepha could not win, even in a provincial court. Nevertheless she has many dreams for Papuan women. "We have to gather our strength, work together. By working together we could face anything. We also have to learn and understand and make peace with other people outside Papua. We do not want Papuan women to be threatened, killed or excluded."

Timika, West Papua is the site of the world's biggest gold mine, owned and operated by Freeport McMoRan Copper & Gold Inc. since the 1960s. With its rich natural resources, there has been no end to conflict in the region where the indigenous peoples are exploited by state and non-state actors.

Indonesia

Louise Arbour

Office of the United Nations High Commissioner for Human Rights (OHCHR)
Supreme Court of Canada

Louise Arbour is best known as a chief prosecutor for tribunals into the genocide in Rwanda and human rights abuses in Yugoslavia. She earned an international reputation for courage and tenacity and gained the respect of UN Secretary General Kofi Annan and human rights groups worldwide. Louise served as a justice on the supreme court of Canada for five years, leaving in 2004 to become the new UN High Commissioner for Human Rights. She replaced Sergio Vieira de Mello, killed in the bombing of the UN headquarters in Baghdad in 2003.

Louise garnered her current position as UN High Commissioner for Human Rights partly because of her accomplishments in the criminal justice system in Canada. She takes pride in the impressive reputation that the supreme court of Canada has internationally. In 2000, Canada's justice system was ranked second best in the world, behind only Denmark, by the prestigious Davos Institute in Switzerland. "Foreign jurisdictions have looked to our Court on a variety of issues, notably assisted suicide, restrictions on political statements by civil servants, and campaign spending rules," Louise said. In particular, she notes that Canada has taken a leading position in the creation of the International Criminal Court (ICC). As she sees it, such an international criminal justice body can play a leading role in transforming the concept of peacekeeping. "Such a transformation is a very natural one, since criminal law, at the domestic level, is the preferred system for maintaining and restoring peace," she said. "In fact, it is a substitute for the use of force or armed intervention, an approach that all too often seems to be the only option available internationally, albeit the least attractive one."
Louise envisions that military intervention — usually exercised under the guise of keeping the peace — is always governed by law and subject to civil and criminal liability. Those intervening militarily in international conflicts must be held accountable for their actions, she maintains. And she recognizes that Canada can help make the vision of international criminal accountability a reality. "The fundamental principles that make Canada's criminal law legitimate and effective are exportable, and they cannot be conveyed merely by advocating ideas at diplomatic meetings. They must be promoted by commitment to the issue and actual presence on the ground."

Louise was called upon to seek justice in the aftermath of some of the most extensive human tragedies of our time, atrocities committed in Kosovo and Rwanda. The International Criminal Tribunals, over which Louise presided, were compared to the Nuremberg trials.

Canada

"My goal is to eradicate all forms of discrimination against women and to ensure equal opportunities for women in education, employment and public spheres."

Meaza Ashenafi

Ethiopian Women Lawyers Association (EWLA)
Ethiopian Constitution Commission of the Interim Government (ECCIG)

Meaza Ashenafi, born in 1965, was a high court judge in Ethiopia between 1989 and 1992. In 1993 she became a legal advisor to the Ethiopian Constitution Commission. In 1995, she participated in founding the Ethiopian Women Lawyers Association (EWLA) and became its executive directress. Through her work as a lawyer she represented thousands of women clients in courts. She is dedicated to vocalizing the needs of misfortunate women under the social and economic structures. She utilizes her extensive legal background to lobby for the amendment of the constitutional laws against women in Ethiopia.

Ethiopia is the largest country in the Horn of Africa in terms of population and second largest in terms of size. The infrastructure is extremely poor, particularly in rural areas. Ethiopian society remains highly patriarchal against women's participation in most spheres and in obvious violation of the provisions of the national constitution. From government oppression to outright violence, civil society organizations face extreme challenges in their work. Furthermore, the economic situation does not lend itself to women's civil participation. Women in Ethiopia do not play a significant role in the economy and have limited access to its benefits.

As a protest, Meaza is dedicated to achieving social justice and equality for Ethiopian women. Her contribution is centered on the promotion and protection of their political and social rights, as she directs attention to the cultural and attitudinal problems related to gender in a conservative society. As a member of the Ethiopian Women Lawyers Association (EWLA) Meaza sent a proposal to the House of Peoples Representatives and Regional Councils (HPRRC) requesting the amendment of certain laws in the constitution in light of the UN proclaimed human rights. Meaza's prioritized mission is the empowerment of women and the lifting of injustice that the laws have caused. Opposed to the discrimination against women in the 1960s Family Law, she led a campaign that eventually resulted in its modification in 2000. She participated in drafting the Ethiopian Constitution, which now gives women a broad range of political, social, legal and economic rights.

Meaza Ashenafi's outstanding efforts have helped to form an equitable society in Ethiopia. The country now benefits from the contribution of thousands of women, who have been empowered as full participants in society by the social and structural changes in the last ten years .

Ethiopia

Ogul Nabat Babayeva

Hemayat
National Center of Trade Unions of Turkmenistan

Ogul Nabat Babayeva (born 1949) founded the organization Hemayat (protector). It mission is the protection of women's rights in Turkmenistan. The organization offers legal education for women and children and socially aggrieved layers of the population, as well as other services related to issues of labor, family, and civil rights. Ogul Nabat has always given special attention to victims of family violence, trafficking of women, and to women's reproductive health.

A lawyer, Ogul Nabat Babayeva helps realize the hopes for happiness of hundreds of thousands of Turkmen women. She was born to a large Turkmen family. "I am a typical Turkmen woman," she says. "I had everything: home, parents, school, and marriage. Because of my natural aptitude, I chose the profession of law. Since childhood, I could defend myself and I did not let anybody offend my friends." For many years, Ogul has fought for the protection of workers' rights. She works for the department of labor rights in the National Trade Union Organization of Turkmenistan.

"A real revolution took place in my mind during the conference devoted to women's rights in Tashkent, in 2000. Suddenly, I understood clearly that I am a victim of violence, too. Everything that was said by the women, who had suffered from domestic violence, I had felt and experienced once," she said. "But both at that time and even now, our country does not recognize these victims of violence, as there is no legal definition or law on domestic violence." The problem of domestic violence is just as urgent in Turkmenistan as it is in many other countries. "It is difficult to stay indifferent when you know that hundreds of thousands of your fellows experience privation," she adds.

She feels joy when she sees the success of her efforts to spread knowledge, to help relieve the lives of people, especially of women, because it is very hard for women in traditional families. And this joy gives her energy to proceed with her work. Ogul's working day never ends at 6:00 p.m. Women come not just to her office, but to her home. Sometimes, they even find her without knowing her precise address. They arrive in the region and ask someone where Ogul lives. As she is a well-known public person, people always show others the way to her place.

In 2003, in Turkmenistan a new law on NGOs came into force criminalizing the activities of unregistered NGOs. At the same time, it was extremely difficult for organizations to become registered. The law was annulled in 2004, but it remains nearly impossible for independent groups to operate.

Turkmenistan

Ellen Barry

Legal Services for Prisoners with Children (LSPC)
Critical Resistance

Ellen Barry is a prison rights activist, lawyer, and organizer who speaks out about the crucial issues facing women in US jails and prisons. Ellen founded Legal Services for Prisoners with Children (LSPC) and is a central figure in the Critical Resistance prison abolition movement. She has devoted much of her life to challenging the rapidly expanding prison system in the USA; with more than two million prisoners, it is the largest in the world. She has exposed the darkest prison abuses and has helped bring about significant, hard-won improvements to the California state prison system.

Ellen, who grew up in Somerville, Massachusetts, was one of ten children. Her father worked on an assembly line and "hated every day that he had to work," Ellen remembers. "I have always felt that loving your work is a privilege and not something that everyone does." Several of her brothers ran afoul of the law and she saw firsthand the effects of abusive police officers on street youth. She also has a number of brothers and sisters in recovery from addictions.

Her introduction to what would become her life's work began in the mid-1970s, when she received a fellowship to attend New York University Law School. Her mentor was a pioneer in the area of women prisoners' rights, and together they visited the women's prison in Bedford Hills, New York, where they conducted a class for prisoners and worked on individual cases.

As founder and director of LSPC, Ellen led the first national conference to focus on women in prison in the mid-1980s. Made up of approximately 50 percent former prisoners, LSPC uses litigation, advocacy, community organizing, and individual work with families and prisoners. Through litigation, Ellen and her staff have forced communities to end abusive practices of women and their children and to use more progressive rehabilitation methods. For example, in the 1980s, she sued California's department of corrections for not using a residential treatment program called the Community Prisoner Mother-Infant Care Program. Before the suit, three women at a time were referred to the program; after the suit, beds for 100 women and 100 children were filled. In 1998, Ellen received the prestigious MacArthur Award for her groundbreaking work.

When Ellen began working in California in 1978, there were approximately 1000 people in the women's state prison. There are now more than 16,000 women in the state system. California spends more public funds for building and maintaining prisons than on its education system.

Letizia Battaglia

Mezzocielo

Letizia Battaglia, Sicilian, born in 1935, is a photographer. With her camera she captures Sicilian life: the cruel violence of the Cosa Nostra and the deep pain of Mafia victims. With her photographs, she breaks the "omertà", the silence that surrounds the Cosa Nostra. Although she has received death threats, she keeps taking pictures. From 1991 to 2001, as head of the environmental department, she tried to improve living conditions for the inhabitants of Palermo. With women from the anti-Mafia organization Mezzocielo (Half the Sky), she fights against inhumanity and injustice.

Letizia Battaglia (70) does not have her own camera anymore. A friend has lent her one. Thieves broke into her house in the historic part of Palermo, for the third time. They took everything they could carry: her photographic equipment, her portable computer and many memories. Who were these criminals? Mafiosi? Letizia Battaglia shrugs her shoulders. "I am still alive," she says. The Mafia threatened to murder the photographer. She does not want to talk about it, "better not." She continues to take photos.

Letizia Battaglia has been making Mafia crimes public with her camera since 1975. Letizia Battaglia tells about Sicilian life in black and white. Violence and poverty, desperation and hope. "I wanted the world to know how much we suffer," she says. She was a photo-journalist for the daily newspaper "L'Ora di Palermo" during the decades when the Mafia killed four to five people every day in the streets of the Sicilian metropolis: judges, district attorneys, policemen, politicians, journalists. She was 40 when she started taking photographs, out of financial need following the separation from her husband. She has three daughters.

"I am a person who resists," she says. She joined the anti-Mafia movement under the former mayor of Palermo, Leoluca Orlando. She co-founded the women's organization Mezzocielo (Half the Sky), which also publishes a newspaper, and she initiated theater projects with mental patients. In 1991, she entered politics. She headed the environmental department of Palermo. Letizia Battaglia rebelled against injustice and violence with her camera. The Mafia, she says, has become invisible, but it is stronger than ever. It does not need to shoot anyone anymore, because it is all powerful: "What can I, a 70-year-old, do against that?"

Italy is dominated by a large north-south gap, with high unemployment in the south. In Sicily, the Mafia profits from the poverty. For 20 euros adolescents can be hired as drug dealers. The Italian government has never succeeded in destroying the Cosa Nostra. Today, it is stronger than ever.

Italy

Janja Bec

Janja Bec was born in the multicultural environment of Vojvodina. She started working as an engineer, but continued studying and obtained a Ph.D. in sociology at Zagreb University. She left Yugoslavia in 1992 and lived in Germany. A Serb, she wanted to help the Muslim victims of the conflict in Bosnia and Herzegovina (1992—1995) and, thus, started campaigns in support of children and victims of the war. She assisted Bosnian refugees in Slovenia. Committed to helping women recover from war traumas and preserving the memories, she started writing books on the basis of her experience.

A Bosnian woman who met Janja Bec at the Refugee Center in Maribor, Slovenia, in December 1995, was surprised: Janja was a Serb and she was listening to Muslim victims of "ethnic cleansing" in Bosnia and Herzegovina! The Bosnian woman came from a village near Kotor Varos. In the spring of 1992, Serbs slaughtered her son and father-in-law, and her mother and sister were burnt alive in a mosque. She asked Janja if Serbs knew and felt sorry for it. Janja answered that it was taboo to talk about it in Serbia, but she was working to break that "conspiracy of silence."

In 1997, Janja published "The Shattering of the Soul." It contained ten stories of Bosnian women and it was the first book by a Serbian author that acknowledged the genocide against Muslims in Bosnia and Herzegovina. She discussed it in conferences, schools, and universities. The feedback she got from survivors and students gave her energy and motivation to go on. In Serbia, she taught for the first time after 15 years in 2004, in Novi Sad and Kragujevac. At the end of a lecture in Novi Sad, a girl expressed a widespread point of view: "Yes, but everyone did that." It is a sentence that sums up a long process of relativization. Another girl was sensible enough to add a significant part, "Yes, everybody committed war crimes, but this was genocide." The trials of the International Tribunal in The Hague have already confirmed the massacre of about 8000 Bosnian Muslims in the "United Nations safe" area of Srebrenica in July 1995. The girl who spoke first tried to react: "But …" The other girl immediately interrupted her, "There is no 'but' after genocide." Janja thought she could answer that Bosnian woman she met in Maribor at last, "Yes, there are people who feel sorry for you."

After Bosnia and Herzegovina declared independence in 1992, it was attacked by Serb forces who did not want to secede from Yugoslavia. Bosnian Muslims were murdered, imprisoned, or expelled from almost 70 percent of the territory. In July 1995, Serbs attacked Srebrenica and massacred 8000 Bosnian men.

Serbia and Montenegro

Rashida Bee

Rashida Bee is a leading personality in the global campaign to secure justice for the survivors of the 1984 Union Carbide Gas Tragedy in Bhopal, the biggest industrial disaster in history. Rashida took her fight with Union Carbide Company and its giant partner, Dow Chemicals, to the streets of New York. Dow Chemicals is battling a series of cases that Rashida and other protestors filed against it. Rashida received the Goldman Environmental Prize in 2004 for internationally center-staging the Bhopal disaster.

Since December 1984, the Union Carbide Company (UCC) methyl isocyanate gas leak has progressively killed more than 30,000 people in Bhopal, the worst and most shameful industrial disaster in history. Among many others, 48-year-old Rashida Bee, a providential survivor, has been a leading personality in the global campaign to get justice for the survivors, direct and indirect.

Rashida, an uneducated beedi (tobacco)-packer from Bhopal, started her career in activism not quite volitionally when she fought for better labor conditions and wages for women at her factory. In 1989, after the protest reached the prime minister's residence in New Delhi, all the demands were met. Rashida then took the initiative to use the union's sudden self-confidence to seek recompense from UCC. In 1999, she and other activists and disaster victims filed a class action lawsuit against UCC in New York. Rashida then frontlined a series of protest marches, rallies, petitions, and fasts, including a 19-day marathon hunger sit-in in New York in 2002. The following year, Rashida and others confronted Dow Chemicals officials in Mumbai and The Netherlands with "samples" of toxic waste. This resulted in a tour of more than ten American cities, an impassioned siege of a Dow Chemicals shareholders' meeting in Michigan, and culminated in a 12-day hunger strike and rally on New York's Wall Street. American college and university students organized nationwide rallies; thousands joined protests in the United Kingdom, China, Spain, Thailand, and Canada.

Although it is more than two decades since the world's biggest industrial disaster, which has progressively and agonizingly killed more than 30,000 people in Bhopal, the survivors have not yet received all of Union Carbide's shameful USD 470 million compensation payout. Generations have died, and will die.

India

"We have to work
together for
a better world."

Viviane Bikuba Cibalonza

Action for Law Education (AED)
Centre d'Assistance Medico-Juridique (Camej)

Viviane Bikuba (36) is a lawyer and founder of Action for Law Education (AED) and Center for Medical-Judicial Assistance (Camej). She defends and promotes human rights in the Democratic Republic of Congo and the Great Lakes Region. Since 1994, she has conducted workshops, seminars and radio programs to promote women's rights and assist victims of sexual violence.

Viviane Bikuba lost her father early in her life. This led to her family's victimization. The family members had to live with injustice and discrimination, and their rights were violated. Her family only survived because of her mother's courage and the legendary African solidarity. Grown up she studied law and became the first female lawyer from South Kivu taking on a role model for her countrymen and women. She was trained and got involved in human rights in order to fight injustice. She decided to advocate for peace as a primary condition to eradicate injustice in the Great Lakes Region. Viviane benefited from training on peaceful conflict resolution organized by the UN Human Rights Office and the Belgium government. Movements led by Mahatma Gandhi, Martin Luther King and Nelson Mandela, who believed in passive resistance and realized their dreams, have motivated her. She is also motivated by the results she gets for being the voice of the voiceless. In collaboration with other women organizations, Viviane provides legal counsel and mediation to expose and train women on human rights. Her work has awakened the consciences of illiterate women who now fight for their rights. Despite the realities of human rights violations she wants everyone to "work together for a better world".

After the infamous Rwandan genocide in 1994, war ravaged the Democratic Republic of Congo, and many injustices were witnessed on social, judicial, political and international levels. Military factions sometimes dictated their law to the local population in the South Kivu region.

Democratic Republic of the Congo

María del Pilar Callizo López Moreira

Transparency International Paraguay

María del Pilar Callizo López Moreira — "Pili" — comes from a very traditional family from Paraguay. She had a happy childhood, without any kind of deprivation or needs. This situation, however, did not prevent her from feeling the need to contribute to the construction of a better country, championing the cause of women and encouraging them to take on a leading role.

"When I was 14 years old, I wondered why the State radio station cut off the transmission of a beautiful poem by Elvio Romero (political oppositionist of the military regime of General Alfredo Stroessner) that I had recited with such emotion at a festival at school. It was then that I began to acquire the belief that the most valuable possession of humankind is freedom." María del Pilar Callizo, Paraguayan, pinpoints for us the time when she began to search for ways to contribute towards the establishment of a constitutional State, with the participation of women.

She is a lawyer specialized in arbitration and mediation. In 1986, she joined a group of women that founded, in Asunción, the capital of the country, one of the first organizations to fight for the improvement of the position of women in Paraguay. She examined the legal basis that made the role of women in her country almost invisible. "These were times of a cruel dictatorship and it was not easy to talk about gender, when we could not even speak about human rights." The meetings were clandestine. "We knew that we were under continuous surveillance. In our phone calls, we used nicknames and diminutives. Some documents about legal revisions were kept under conditions of extreme secrecy. Those times before democracy were especially hard."

With the end of the dictatorship, in 1989, talking openly about human rights became more acceptable, but other evils arose, like corruption, for example. Pilar faced a new challenge: to encourage accountability and transparency in public administration, to encourage the participation of citizens and to promote actions to diminish impunity. "I dream of a renewed country with ethical and democratic values, with a culture of solidarity and respect for diversity," she says.

During the Paraguayan dictatorship, public demonstrations were forbidden and the people that dared to participate were victims of repression, imprisonment, torture and, in the majority of cases, they went on to swell the lists of the missing or murdered people.

Paraguay

Mandy Carter

Southerners On New Ground (Song)
National Call to Resist
National Black Gay and Lesbian Leadership Forum

Mandy Carter has formed connections among a range of issues: opposition to war and violence, support for social and economic justice for people of color, and equal rights for women, lesbians, gays, bisexual, and transgender people. She works in grassroots campaigns and national coalitions, especially focused on the religious right's antigay organizing in black communities. She is a brilliant coalition builder, highly respected by people from diverse backgrounds. Her work has been essential to the inclusion of gay/lesbian issues as social justice issues in the United States.

Born in upstate New York in 1948, Mandy Carter was raised in foster homes and a state-run children's home. In 1967 she trained at the Institute for the Study of Nonviolence and in 1968 participated in the historic Poor People's Campaign, a huge gathering on the Mall in Washington, DC, organized by the Southern Christian Leadership Conference. She began working for peace and justice with the Quaker-based American Friends Service Committee and pacifist-based War Resisters League. She attributes her nonviolent philosophy and commitment to the nonviolent direct action to these organizations.

A key focus of Mandy's work is to monitor the radical right in communities of color, paying particular attention to the divisive tactic of antigay organizing in black communities and the black church. As someone who straddles several movements, Mandy is respected by people from diverse backgrounds and is a brilliant coalition builder.

As an "out" black lesbian social justice activist, Mandy's work has been an essential contribution to the acceptance and inclusion of gay and lesbian issues as social justice issues in the United States. She exemplifies a model of "bridge building" between the lesbigaytrans movement and communities of color. Mandy has held many staff positions in progressive organizations and campaigns at local and national levels. In 1993, she cofounded Southerners On New Ground to build a movement across the South for progressive social change by developing models for organizing that connect race, class, culture, gender, and sexual identity.

Since the 1950s, movements for civil rights, women's liberation, and gay/lesbian rights have fought discrimination in the USA. In response, well-funded right-wing movements have organized to oppose gains made in these areas. Evangelical churches are key participants in this conservative activism.

United States of America

Journalist and publisher Anju Chhetri has played a pivotal role in making the Nepali media useful, responsible, and accountable in its approach to women's issues.

Anju Chhetri

Asmita Women's Publishing House (AWPH)

Anju Chhetri (born 1961) has been an energetic campaigner for women's human rights through the Asmita Women's Publishing House (AWPH), which she helped found. Through AWPH, the foremost feminist organization in Nepal, and her writings in the mainstream media, Anju has been a pioneer in raising nascent feminist issues in Nepal.

Anju Chhetri and her friends launched a women's magazine, Asmita, in 1988 and set up a feminist media outlet, when nobody was writing about women's issues in the Nepali media. Scholars, intellectuals, and policymakers had no access to women's thoughts, concerns, and ideas. As editor, Anju identified issues, and researched and wrote thought-provoking articles even in the mainstream newspapers and magazines. Equal property rights for women, the right to abortion, sexuality, violence against women, and women's right to health are among the issues that have been brought to the forefront of Nepali life. Their efforts led to a national civil code that replaced archaic laws prohibiting women ancestral property and the right to abortion.

Always prolific, Anju has also been writing about political affairs, high corruption, government policies, development projects, the Maoist people's war, ceasefires, and peace talks. From August 2001 to September 2003, she wrote 86 pieces for her weekly column in Kantipur, the country's largest daily.

Nepal is not journalist friendly. When Asmita was launched, the autocratic Panchayat (village council) system was in force and the mass media were largely state controlled. Anju and her colleagues were spared scrutiny because a women's magazine was considered relatively harmless. They used the opportunity to espouse democracy, and women's inarguable role in regaining their basic rights. While using the media to promote the cause of women's rights, Anju does not demur from also using it to criticize the women's movement and make it accountable to the public.

Three political forces are vying for power in Nepal: the monarchy, democratic parties, and the Maoists. In the beginning of 2005, King Gyanendra declared a state of emergency, suspending most democratic rights, and impacting the work of women activists, to limit their activities to urban centers.

Tamara Chikunova

Mothers Against the Death Penalty and Torture
World Coalition Against the Death Penalty

Born in 1948, Tamara Chikunova heads Mothers Against the Death Penalty and Torture. Her appeals to the public, government, and the international community and open confrontations with persistent violence have had a major impact in Uzbekistan, where the death penalty is widely used and torture is regularly administered. She is an active member of the World Coalition Against the Death Penalty, which she helped establish in May 2002.

Tamara Chikunova's son (28) was sentenced to death in Uzbekistan in 1999 and executed in 2000. She founded Mothers Against the Death Penalty and Torture in 2000. In her view, "The death penalty is a deficiency of humanity in the foundations of society and the state … (It) bears in itself not only the possibility of a mistake, but breaks the most important inalienable right of each person — the right to life."

A single, retired woman without means, Tamara struggles tirelessly to enter into dialogue with the State on the abolishment of the death penalty in Uzbekistan. The government impedes Tamara's efforts to establish a dialogue and to garner support. "Opportunities for action in the territory of Uzbekistan are very small. State newspapers are silent about our initiatives." Undaunted, she works in cooperation with many major human rights organizations, the United Nations, and an international network of sympathizers.

Because of her efforts, people illegally sentenced to death now have hope to return to their families. In many cases, the death penalty has been commuted to a prison term; unjust accusations have been retracted; and the unjustly accused have been released.

Despite her immense personal loss, she responds to the pain of others: "People (who) have survived the death sentence are serving time in prisons, and those sitting in cells for the condemned call me 'Mother.' For me they are children, children whose lives need to be protected. I hope that we can do that and that not only the State of Uzbekistan will eliminate the death penalty, but that this disgraceful punishment will be eliminated all over the world."

In Uzbekistan, the death penalty and all related matters are state secrets. Those sentenced to death and their families are not told the date of execution; they are not allowed to meet one last time; the body of the executed is not released for burial, nor is the family informed of the burial place.

Uzbekistan

Pilar Coll Torrente

La Coordinadora de Derechos Humanos (Cnddhh)
The Bartolomé House Center

Pilar Coll Torrente is inspired by her own life: by the impact of the Spanish Civil War and by her residence in Peru. She traveled from Spain to work as a volunteer in Peru and has remained in the country for 38 years, half of her entire life. In her new country, she has created the Social Service School and the Human Rights Service. She has given form and strength to the National Coordination for Human Rights (Cnddhh). Today, she brings hope and faith to women in prison. She is interested, above all, in justice. Pilar herself feels that she is very Peruvian.

Pilar Coll Torrente was born in Fonz, a village in rural Spain. Her childhood and youth were marked by the Spanish Civil War, during which her father was killed. She is the only survivor of seven brothers and sisters. She arrived in Peru in 1967. She was the director of the Social Service School, in Trujillo, and she taught religion to poor girls. During that time, she was influenced by the Theology of Liberation. In Lima, she worked for the Episcopal Commission for Social Action (Ceas), and she worked in the poor neighborhood of El Agustino. In 1987, she took on the responsibility of Executive Secretary of the National Coordination for Human Rights (Cnddhh). "I have always had to make things from scratch, as in the Social Service School, the Episcopal Commission for Social Action and, later on, with the National Coordination for Human Rights."

These were very violent times. Subversive groups like the Sendero Luminoso and the Revolutionary Movement Tupac Amaru (Mrta) spread death and pain throughout every region of Peru. Pilar Coll Torrente helped many people escape into exile. Because of that, she suffered abuses by the Peruvian military. However, that did not stop her. The National Coordination for Human Rights pressed the Organization of American States (OAS) into examining the dictatorship lead by Alberto Fujimori, which began in 1992. The Peruvian Commission for Truth and Reconciliation states that, "the victims of 20 years of violations of human rights in Peru are mainly poor and indigenous people." Pilar says, "If we want peace and justice we must give those people back their names and their words." She made public the terrible conditions in the women's prison of Santa Mónica and managed to achieve certain improvements. There is a dedication to her that says: "We have received enough heat from your hands so as not to lose our way in the darkness."

The Peruvian Commission for Truth and Reconciliation found that the victims of 20 years of violations of human rights, almost 70,000 people, were mainly poor and indigenous. Giving them back their names and their words is a necessary condition for peace and justice.

Peru

Adoracion Cruz Avisado

Avisado Advocacy, Consultant, Counseling, and Training Services Center
Womenet
National Commission on the Role of Filipino Women

Adoracion C. Avisado (born 1952), a feminist lawyer from Davao City, is an active campaigner for the rights of women against spousal abuse and other reforms in the Philippine judicial system. Appointed trial court judge in 1999, she earned a reputation for her speedy disposition of cases. An activist feminist even within the judiciary, she helped empower court stenographers, who are mostly women, to fight sexual harassment by their superiors. She resigned in 2004, after five years as a judge, and returned to civil society where she continues to advocate for judicial reform.

Gender equality and a sense of fairness were values instilled in Adoracion Avisado by her father, a businessman. Working briefly as clerk of court during the martial law years, she saw how the military threatened the independence of the judiciary by coercing its judges to rule against political activists. She saw the sufferings of women activists who were raped while in detention. As a private law practitioner, Adoracion handled prominent cases involving violence against women. She helped in the conviction of two rapists after traumatic court battles that nearly caused the women accusers to give up, and she trained police personnel in gender sensitivity. Working in an NGO which she formed, she monitored cases of rape, incest and violence against women, and prodded the police to act on such cases quickly. Later, as judge of the lone special drugs court, seeing how delays in court action affected poor litigants, she resolved cases speedily by working double time, conducting full-blown trials, thus earning the respect of the Philippine High Court, which cited her in 2001 for her speedy action on cases. Even as a judge, she remained a feminist activist. She found letter writing an effective means of directing the attention of her fellow judges and her superiors in the High Court to important issues, and helped a court stenographer file a sexual harassment case against a judge. But the High Court did not form a committee on decorum and investigation until a year later, and the local lawyer moved to have the case dismissed. Disappointed by the outcome of the case, she resigned as a judge and is now back in civil society where she speaks from experience and not merely in slogans when she advocates for transformative justice. She remains optimistic, however, that the judiciary can be reformed.

Corruption, fraternal ties and abuse of power are some of the issues that confront women seeking justice for spousal violence in Philippine courts. Delays and inefficiency in the prosecution and resolution of cases have often discouraged the public from relying on the courts for justice.

Grace Antonia D'Almeida

Association des Femmes Juristes du Bénin (AFJB)
Network of the Women Ministers and Parliamentarians

A lawyer, Grace Antonia D'Almeida (1951—2005) was divorced and the mother of three children. She enjoyed her work and excelled at everything she did. She, indeed, was a great fighter in the women's movement in Africa and world-wide. She passed away in early 2005.

Grace Antonia D'Almeida founded the Association of Women Lawyers of Benin (AFJB) and presided over it since 1990. The association aims to defend women's rights nationally, regionally and internationally. The AFJB was quick to take on the task of making important appeals for women's rights both in Benin and in countries south of the Sahara. Grace initiated the opening of the Legal Aid Center in Benin and in the sub-region and the extension of these centers by the creation of the network of centers and legal clinics. Madame Grace Antonia D'Almeida was aware that the fight to obtain legal status for woman was difficult because of the reluctance of a large section of the male population. The AFJB ensured that the training of paralegals was a true initiative in Benin.

The main preoccupation of Madame D'Almeida extended therefore to women's rights in general and to democracy. Her association works with the participation of members and donors. Madame D'Almeida fought for the creation of the association between 1988 and 1989. Nevertheless, the Marxist-Leninist government of that era adamantly refused and asked Madame D'Almeida to return in the organization of revolutionary women. This did not appeal to her so, in the spirit of a democratic revival, she created her association in 1990. The Association of Women Lawyers of Benin was one of the first associations to begin asking questions about the legal status of Benin women, contained in the customary law of Dahomey of 19 March, 1931, which gave women no rights. This battle only ended in 2004 when the code on the family and people was adopted by the National Assembly.

Madame Antonia contributed to giving an example to women in campaigns who quickly understood that women can be educated and have the same abilities as men, and thus, have the same rights. These things are the basis of the reduction of forced marriages in Benin.

Benin

Maria Amélia de Almeida Teles

União de Mulheres de São Paulo (Union of Women of São Paulo)

Maria Amélia de Almeida Teles (1945) is a human rights activist. During her whole life she has been fighting against the many facets of violence: from the State, gender-based or of any other kind. For 11 years, she has been coordinating the Popular Legal Prosecutors Course.

"Police, police!" Since she was a child, Maria Amélia knew that police meant danger. Her father, a syndicalist, used to organize meetings at home to discuss labor rights. He would ask his daughter to watch out and warn him if the police came near. "I knew those meetings were a form of fighting to improve our lives."

Her sense of citizenship grew in the midst of a battle. She lived clandestinely and under torture due to the military coup in 1964, which sentenced Brazil to a dictatorship of over 20 years. "Amelinha" — as everyone calls her — was arrested along with her partner, sister and kids. The leader of the torturers warned: "Hell is here, you have gone to hell!" She endured the horrors of physical torture and the pain of not knowing whether or not her children were alive. It was also in prison, living with other arrested women, that "Amelinha" found out that no democracy can be successful without the effective participation of women. She came out from behind bars and kept on fighting for the end of the dictatorship and to foment the feminist fight against all kinds of authoritarianism. She founded, in 1981, the Union of Women of São Paulo, a place devoted to combating violence against women.

Currently, Maria Amélia de Almeida Teles coordinates the Popular Legal Prosecutors Course in the state of São Paulo that aims to qualify women to be capable of finding justice in a world full of injustices. Thanks to the popular prosecutors, in 1996, the Brazilian Supreme Federal Court revoked a decree that forbade women from going into its building wearing pants. They have also managed to take two cases of murdered women, whose killers had not been punished, to the OAS (Organization of the American States), Inter-American Court of Human Rights.

The Popular Prosecutors Course has qualified, in São Paulo, about 2000 women. They are also multipliers and founders of popular organizations. Brazil is a country full of laws. The great challenge is to bring them from paper to real life.

Brazil

Therezinha de Godoy Zerbini

Instituto Aberto de Redenção das Águas (Iara)

Therezinha Zerbini (1928) is known as "Mrs. Amnesty." As a lawyer, she founded, organized and diffused the Feminist Movement for the Amnesty, to open the door for the return of democracy. Therezinha got to know the political obstacles, and she never lost the capacity to be frustrated with the authoritarianism.

When she was 17 years old, she was diagnosed with tuberculosis. At that time, this disease frightened everyone. To be cured, people were confined in sanatoriums. Therezinha went to one of them. The doctor prohibited her from taking shower. She did not obey his orders.

Her second great outrage came in 1964. Her husband, a general, had his political rights taken away because he did not agree with the military coup that introduced the dictatorship. The army commanded Brazil for more than 20 years. People were arrested, tortured and killed. Therezinha Zerbini, at the time 42 years old and mother of two sons, was also arrested. It was in prison that she had the idea to organize a women movement for the amnesty. "The seed was planted there. But the political situation was so tough that we waited until 1975 to start the movement."

At that moment, there were no parties nor syndicates nor free press in Brazil. "Therefore, we organized the women that knew how to speak from their hearts. Those who speak from the heart do not make mistakes." Therezinha Zerbini mobilized amnesty nucleus allover the country. Convoked public acts, gave lectures, claimed national peace. Her house received political figures being persecuted: "They were hungry, they ate. They needed to sleep, they slept." In 1979 came the victory. The amnesty law was signed and opened the doors for the reconstruction of democracy. Today, with 77 years of age, Therezinha is still active. She founded and is the president of an organization that protects water resources, the Open Institute of Redemption of Water. For her, the fight for democracy and for the well being of the environment is only one. "One who defends life and human rights also works for the integrity of the ecosystem."

With the amnesty law, in 1979, the exiled came back to Brazil. Political prisoners left prisons. The amnesty was the beginning of the end of the military regime, deflagrated by the coup of 1964. Brazilian democracy was consolidated with the Constitution of 1988.

Brazil

Violeta Vanesa Delgado Sarmiento

Women's Network against Violence

Violeta Delgado Sarmiento works in Nicaragua for women's rights. She campaigns to strengthen the political role of women in Nicaragua and to make their presence in the political scene more visible. "We have achieved the passing of the Law to Prevent and Sanction Violence against Women; the implementation of a project to offer aid to mistreated women and, above all, there has been a major social recognition of the gravity of this problem in our country."

"Women in my family have always been engaged in the search for justice. One day I said to myself: I cannot be left behind. How can I join the people that denounce violence and injustice if I am only 11 years old?!" Her father was, and still is, very conservative in thought. In Nicaragua, at that time, nobody in his family was permitted to participate in activities considered then to be just a little better than terrorism. In the 1980s, during the Sandinist Popular Revolution, Violeta Vanesa Delgado Sarmiento started her path down the road towards her search for justice and social equality. "I decided to challenge everything around me and took the first steps by participating in the National Literacy Crusade," she says. And from that moment on, nobody could stop her. She went on to participate in the activities planned by the juvenile section of the Sandinist Youth Organization, mainly taking part in activities related to the harvesting of coffee, cotton and the campaign for better health. But it was in 1993 that she really began to comprehend the problems that women faced. With others companions she founded the Commission for Young Women and after that decided to participate in the preparations for the Fourth World Conference for Women. In 1994, she was appointed as Executive Secretary of the organization Women's Network against Violence. She was only 24 years old!

"Two fundamental things have marked my life: the first was when I supported the denunciation process presented by Zoilamérica Narváez, when she testified that she had been raped by her stepfather, Daniel Ortega, who, at that time, was President of the Republic. The second significant event was when I defended the right of a young girl to interrupt her unwanted pregnancy result of rape. For me, the right to life is a matter of honor."

In Nicaragua, a country of five million inhabitants, 80% of the people live in extreme poverty. Domestic violence increases every year. Official figures show that 54 women were killed by their partners or ex-partners in 2004.

Nicaragua

Jeanne Devos

Welfare Trust for Women and Child Domestic Workers
National Domestic Workers' Movement (NDWM)
Misereor

Sister Jeanne Devos (born 1935) has dedicated her life to the rights of children in India since 1965. In 1985, she founded the network National Domestic Workers' Movement (NDWM) in Mumbai. Today she is co-coordinator of this growing movement against slavery of women and children in 18 Indian states. As a deputy of the Bishops Conference of India to the United Nations and Unicef conferences, she fights against child labor, child trafficking, child prostitution, and child soldiers. On her initiative, the NDWM has also done relief work in the areas of India hit by the tsunami of December 2004.

Jeanne Devos, born in Belgium in 1935, is a sister of the Roman Catholic Congregation ICM. She has dedicated her life to the human rights of children in Mumbai, India, since 1965. "I have always been interested in human rights and the dignity of every person. I felt that my actions should empower the most vulnerable and discriminated. For this reason I opted for domestic workers — be it women or children — because they had no voice, no rights, which is my understanding of slavery. What got me working was the inhuman situation of those women and children. It touched and hurt me as a woman. The urgency started after meeting a 13-year-old girl who was raped, pregnant, and had aborted — without understanding what had happened to her," Jeanne Devos recalls.

"In 1985, I founded the network National Domestic Workers' Movement in Bombay to break slavery. Today this movement in India works in 18 states and 28 languages. The strategies are personal contact and breaking isolation; organizing domestic workers in groups to build solidarity; crisis intervention; legal aid; providing educational opportunities; campaign against trafficking; and public awareness. We believe that individual and group empowerment is the main objective of the movement. We work from a human rights and child rights approach. The main obstacles the network faces are the privacy of private homes — invisibility of domestic workers, power of money in a system that wants cheap labor, and traditional myths that hide slavery. We get our strength from the resilience and collective power of domestic workers and team work. It is my vision of a peaceful future to get domestic workers out of slavery into human dignity and justice."

Although India has many employment codes — outlawing child labor, exploitation of children, and bonded labor — slavery persists. With roughly one billion inhabitants, India may have as many as 15 million people enslaved. Many of these are children working as domestics or in production.

Belgium

"Being able to help others is a great opportunity and a duty toward the most disempowered among us. I dedicate the Nobel Peace Prize 2005 to the victims of all forms of violence the world over."

Fatoumata Dembélé Diarra

Observatoire des Droits de l'Enfant et de la Femme (ODEF)
Fédération Internationale des Femmes des carrières Juridiques (FIFCJ)

Fatoumata Dembélé Diarra (50) was at the heart of the Malian Democratic Movement that opposed the monolithic and dictatorial system of General Moussa Traoré in 1991. At the time of the Sovereign National Lecture of Mali in 1991, Madame Diarra Fatoumata was an expert member of the group of people who contributed to the compilation of fundamental texts of a democratic Mali. She was elected Judge of the International Criminal Court in 2003.

Fatoumata Dembélé Diarra is the founding president of the Office on Relief for Impoverished Women and Children and Observation of the Rights of Children and Women (ODEF). Through these two structures, she has supported hundreds of women and of children in distress. She is at ease in her work since she is a magistrate and knows all the intricacies of Malian justice. Her legal office has given many women free legal assistance to defend their rights. Madame Diarra was vice president of the International Federation of Women in Legal Careers (FIFCJ) from 1994 to 1997. She has also been vice president of the Federation of African Lawyers since March 1995 and has attended several courses on the legal position of women and children in Mali and in Africa. She has published many articles, for example "Rights and Exclusion," "Legal Assistance," "Circumcision and Positive Malian Rights," and "Violence against Women and the Obstacles to the Malian Women Exercising their Rights." Madame Diarra was a member of the national commission on trafficking in children and international adoption, a commission that has done much to protect Malian children against the networks of organized crimes that, ultimately, sell them to the coffee and cocoa plantations in Ivory Coast.

Fatoumata Dembélé Diarra is an enemy of criminals. She is the president of the Special Court of the Children in charge of stopping inhumane practices against women and children.

Mali

Maria Berenice Dias

Court of Appeals of the State of Rio Grande do Sul

Maria Berenice Dias (1947) is a judge of the Court of Appeals, in the State of Rio Grande do Sul. Her specialty is the area of family law. Mother of three children, she was the first female judge in that state. Berenice is nationally known for being a defender of women's rights, including their sexual and reproductive rights, such as legal abortion, sexual orientation and the recognition of rape as a hedonic crime. Fearless and clear-headed, she not only defends, but also embraces the causes of excluded people.

Although she was born into a family of lawyers, she was not meant for that career. After all, "I was raised being told that women just have to work to pay for their pins, that is, a young woman should be, at most, an elementary school teacher." However, Berenice Dias challenged conservatism and built wings — made of intelligence and persistence — so she could fly high. That's how she became the first woman to occupy the post of a judge in the State of Rio Grande do Sul, in 1973. "It was really hard; lawyers openly intended to stop women from becoming judges. They wanted me to fail at all costs." They failed and, in the bargain, started working with an outspoken and wise judge. "I faced gender discrimination at the judicial branch, so I became a true defender of all discriminated people." This Judge spent her life fighting for a fair justice, able to understand the differences and being free of prejudice. "Many judges punish women when they do not submit themselves to the prevailing standards, which are the role of a caring mother and a submissive wife. But, women should have their own lives and decisions."
In 1996, Maria Berenice Dias was the first woman to become a judge in the Court of Appeals in her home state. She works in a difficult area: family law. "We only see love coming to an end." But, she also sees new family models, and Berenice supports them. "If there is affection, there is a family." Based on that, she defends the idea that homosexual and heterosexual couples should have the same rights. Berenice's strength seems to be never ending. She is involved in several non-governmental organizations and embraces many causes, as long as they fight for a better world with better people.

Maria Berenice Dias is responsible for taking actions like JusMulher (voluntary legal and psychological support to women in need), the Lar project, the Disque-Violência help-line. She states that domestic violence is the most common crime in Brazil.

Brazil

Mariani Dimaranan

Task Force Detainees of the Philippines (TFDP)
Franciscan Sisters of the Immaculate Conception (SFIC)

Sister Mariani Dimaranan (born 1925) is a feisty Franciscan nun who chaired Task Force Detainees of the Philippines (TFDP), an organization set up by the major religious superiors in the Philippines to document the human rights abuses against political prisoners under military custody, for 22 years. Until a stroke severely damaged her faculties, Sr Mariani visited more than 100 detention camps all over the country, bringing supplies and comfort to prisoners and working for their release, and exposed the human rights situation in the country in forums and meetings abroad.

Under Sister Mariani's leadership, the Task Force Detainees of the Philippines (TFDP) sought legal and medical attention for political detainees even as it assisted their families to find alternative livelihoods. Through clandestine TFDP publications abroad, Sr Mariani exposed thousands of cases of torture, disappearances and summary executions that belie government propaganda about a "smiling martial law." Despite threats to their personal safety and the difficulties of their work, TFDP workers managed to prove that torture was "routine, systematic and widespread" under martial law. From September 1972 to February 1986, when Marcos was ousted in the popular People Power Revolution, the group was able to document 5531 cases of torture, 2537 cases of summary execution, 783 cases of involuntary disappearance and 92,607 cases of "public order violation" arrests, mainly of people joining street rallies and protests.

Even after the ouster of authoritarian President Ferdinand Marcos, the TFDP has continued its mission to uphold human rights, noting that abuses by the police and military persist in the Philippines to this day. "The struggle is not yet finished," Sr Mariani said shortly before a stroke confined her to her sick bed. "The situation is getting more complicated regionally and globally. I can see the transgression of human rights going on and being repeated in the poverty of our people. The human rights struggle should be more intense. Everyone should remain committed." From her sick bed, Sr Mariani continues to inspire people to advocate for human rights, the definition of which the TFDP has expanded to include "food and freedom, jobs and justice."

When President Ferdinand Marcos declared martial law in the Philippines in 1972, the military arrested the political opposition en masse. But because the local media was heavily censored, cases of torture, involuntary disappearances and extra-judicial killings were kept under a tight lid.

Philippines

Margaret Dongo

Margaret Dongo was born in 1962. She grew up in Harare, Zimbabwe. She fought alongside men, to bring an end to colonial rule. After the war, she was troubled that the government neglected former combatants, especially women. She formed a war veterans association to cater for the needs of ex-fighters and helped them receive compensation from the government. In parliament she advocated for inclusion of women in decision-making positions. She fought against corruption and abuse of public funds and resources and exposed the atrocities committed by Zimbabwe's ministers.

Margaret Dongo was concerned with the plight of female ex-fighters, who had been neglected by the government, and their need for rehabilitation. The negative effects of Esap, a national economic recovery program, took its toll on the common people, especially women. Many girls were out of school and many women and children died of disease when Esap introduced school and hospital fees. Margaret spoke against Esap and dissuaded the government from implementing it.

She advocated for the inclusion of women in decision-making positions in the public sphere. She spoke against gender-based violence in Harare when single parents were harassed by the police and jailed in 1985. Margaret strongly opposed corruption and did research on government financial administration. Her list is known as a tool that exposed corruption in land redistribution in Zimbabwe.

Politics, for Margaret, is a way to gain power for the people and to bring peace and justice, to liberate the people, especially the marginalized, such as women and children. Margaret remains vocal, fighting for women's rights by opposing the government.

Zimbabwe is a country with a history of a very strong colonial patriarchy. When the new government came into power they adopted the same colonial masculine models of oppressions.

Margaret never gave up despite all the difficulties. As a result of her work, a number of changes have occurred for the women. The education of girl children and women has improved. In the past pregnant girls or women were expelled from school or college, but can now get back to school or college. Many women stand for parliamentary elections, following Margaret as a role model and inspiration. Margaret Dongo mentored the members of parliament Priscilla Misihairambwi and Trudy Stevenson.

Many girls were out of school and many women and children died of disease when the national economic recovery program Esap was introduced. Margaret dissuaded the government from implementing Esap, especially the levy of school and hospital fees.

Zimbabwe

Kate Donnelly

War Resisters League (WRL)

Kate Donnelly has spent 30 years participating in movements for social change. The focus of her work is teaching about nonviolence, and includes teaching conflict resolution skills, training people to participate in nonviolent direct action, and campaigning against war toys. Her belief in the intelligence and compassion of young people and the efficacy of local, grassroots struggles for social change are the core of her life and work.

In 1979, Kate Donnelly participated in the groundbreaking conference, Women and Life on Earth, after the near meltdown of the Three Mile Island nuclear power plant. This gathering was a landmark in the development of ecofeminism in the USA. It generated a major women's protest — the first Women's Pentagon Action — and the Unity Statement that developed from that action has become a classic of its time. Kate participated in this action and made a film about the experience. In fact, it may be the only film resource in existence that captured the event.

Kate has been active in the War Resisters League (WRL) for more than 20 years. Through WRL, she initiated a campaign against war toys, and edited The Handbook for Nonviolent Action. She is part of the New England Nonviolence Trainers Network and has organized youth peace camps for children and teenagers. Kate has taught nonviolent conflict resolution in local schools for many years. As a result, many students, including both of her sons, have become high school peer mediators, teaching nonviolent conflict resolution skills to other students.

In 1975, Kate and her partner founded Donnelly/Colt, a family business to produce materials for consciousness raising and fundraising. The couple wanted to incorporate their progressive politics with their love of graphics. The business has supported them and their three children, and is one of the oldest suppliers of "peace merchandise" in the country. Most of their products are union made. The business is at the hub of many interlocking social movements: against war, racism, sexual harassment, corporate globalization, the war on students and the poor; and in favor of Aids research, justice around the world, and talks not troops. In 2001, WRL recognized Kate Donnelly and her husband at its National Awards Dinner.

In 1979, there was a near meltdown at the Three Mile Island nuclear power plant. In 1980, Ronald Reagan was elected president and soon the USA was deep in increased military spending, development of cruise missiles, intervention in Central America, as well as increasing environmental pollution.

United States of America

"I just could not look at
myself in the mirror if
I didn't renounce violence
and devote myself to
peace, love, justice, and
nurturing."

Muriel Helena Duckworth

Canadian Council for International Cooperation
Voice for Women Canada
Canadian Research Institute for the Advancement of Women

Muriel Helena Duckworth is an extraordinary activist whose work for peace, social reform, and educational development has spanned almost 90 years. One of Canada's most distinguished feminists and pacifists, she was a founding member of the Voice of Women (Nova Scotia) and served as national president from 1967 to 1971. She has founded many Canada-wide and province-wide organizations, has worked at the United Nations and has gone on a number of international peace missions.

Muriel admits that much of the inspiration for her own independent thinking and take-action personality came from her unconventional, progressive mother. During a time when women were expected to be silent and subservient, Muriel's mother was neither. "I remember a lot of arguments in the family because my mother had her point of view and it was always taken for granted that she would have," Muriel recalled. "I suppose I've become like that." Unwilling to be dependent on others, her mother always earned money by turning the farmhouse into a summer boarding house. "Then she opened what she called a tearoom — it was a really attractive little place and we all worked there in the summers."

Although academic achievement was important to Muriel's parents, neither of them had much education. The town in which she grew up did not have a library. "We didn't have many books but for the ones we had, my mother took the china out of the china cabinet and put the books in there and made a little book plate and had a little library." Her mother communicated her opinions through letters to the editor of the local paper, much to the chagrin of the community. "That really got her into trouble!" Muriel said. Probably most significant was her mother's active involvement with the Women's Christian Temperance Union (WCTU). At the time, Muriel was greatly amused by her mother's participation in what seemed like a conservative organization. "After I became involved in the women's movement they began giving credit to the WCTU for what they had done," Muriel said. "It changed my thinking and I felt very stupid that I hadn't seen it before. The WCTU was among the groups that had worked for votes for women, and temperance was an important social issue. Women were very angry about how women and children were suffering while men were getting drunk."

In the 20th century, war has been a ubiquitous cause of death and destruction globally. As Muriel said, "I don't think people recognize that war is the greatest destroyer of human life, the greatest polluter, the greatest creator of refugees, the greatest cause of starvation and illness."

Canada

Ayse believes peace
is possible only through
struggle. She hopes
to find a future where
women are not oppressed
and exploited, and she
hopes to find equality,
freedom, and justice in
that future.

Ayse Düzkan

Women's Foundation for Culture and Communication
Pazartesi (Monday newspaper)

Ayse Düzkan, born in 1959, is one of the first feminist activists and writers in Turkey and has been active in various campaigns for women's rights: in the peace struggle after 1990, as a journalist on war crimes and women's issues among the Kurds, with the Women's International League for Peace and Freedom (WILPF) on the Peace Train from Helsinki to Beijing, and the Peace Tent in the NGO Forum in 1995. She has been in and written about post-war Bosnia and Albania, as well as the Women in Black in Serbia and the Balkans. And she has also been active against the war in Iraq.

Ayse Düzkan has written many articles and stories about war victims and women subjected to sexual violence. One of them, a Kurdish woman who was raped by police officers, on applying to the European Court of Human Rights (ECHR) was admitted immediately. Ayse recalls how this woman came to Diyarbakir from the village she lived in, and how they met secretly in an office, communicating via a Kurdish-Turkish translator. Ayse also interviewed many women who lost sons and relatives in the war, and on a trip to Bosnia in 1998, she was moved by the fact that these stories were so common. In 1995, she met the Women in Black of Serbia and interviewed them, writing about their work all over the world.

Ayse's work on achieving fair and just peace between Turks and Kurds has been important, as she is of Turkish background. For her articles and speeches, she had to appear before the court many times . During one trial, appearing in court with her lawyer (who is also Turkish), the judge commented that despite both of them being of Kurdish background one of them was a writer and the other a lawyer, and that this only showed that there was no oppression against Kurds in Turkey. When Ayse and her lawyer reminded the judge that they were, in fact, not Kurdish, he said, "In that case, what are you both doing here?"

Ayse affirms that a woman living in the so-called "Third World" has more risks of being killed in a war than a man living in the so-called "First World," and that peace is a crucially important women's issue. As a member of the dominant national group, she believes she has to support any struggle against injustice on a national or ethnic level in Turkey. She considers herself a part of the peace movement in the Middle East.

A new wave of feminism arose in Turkey in the 1980s. The Turkish feminist movement has taken up many issues including: women's rights as human rights, work, peace, and justice for all members of the community.

Irene Fernandez

Tenaganita (Women's Force)
Voice of the Malaysian People (Suaram)
Asia Pacific Forum on Women Law and Development (APWLD)

Dr Irene Fernandez (born 1946) is a teacher who turned to human rights activism to make a difference in people's lives. Irene saves lives and protects the rights of thousands of migrant workers in Malaysia by providing legal representation, giving them protection from harassment, unjust arrest and persecution, and giving them assistance to return home. In 1991, Irene founded Tenaganita, which champions the rights of migrant workers, the protection of women from HIV/Aids and other related issues.

Irene Fernandez underwent trial that lasted 13 years for publishing a report on the situation of migrant workers in Malaysian detention camps. Her report showed the unsanitary conditions, frequent deaths from beatings, lack of medical care, sexual abuse and corruption rife in Malaysia's immigration detention camps. The revelations severely embarrassed the government and brought changes to camp conditions. But Irene incurred the wrath of the authorities. In October 2003, she was sentenced to one year in prison. She is on bail pending hearing of her appeal. It is unclear at what point the government plans to enforce her sentence. Meanwhile, her right to travel is severely restricted. Over the course of her trial, she appeared in court 310 times and in 2004, she was barred from running in the parliamentary elections.

"I am a mother like all Malaysians who want to believe that our children are growing up in a fair and just society. A society that treats migrant workers as human beings and with dignity," Irene says. "Those in power, however, use the tools of public government to hound activists and paint them as troublemakers, anti-government, anti-development, foreign-influenced. I deny all that. We are just pro-people." Irene worked to empower depressed communities in rubber plantations and squatter settlements. She joined the Consumer Association of Penang in 1976 and campaigned for women's rights, fought multinational companies selling infant formula, formed consumer clubs and organized farmers and workers to protect and defend the environment. She is a founding member of the human rights group Voice of the Malaysian People (Suaram) and the Asia Pacific Forum on Women Law and Development (APWLD). Irene is a member of the Supreme Council of the National Justice Party, an opposition political party formed in 1999.

Hundreds of thousands of undocumented migrant workers from Malaysia's poorer neighbors are regularly arrested, thrown in jail and whipped. Their only crime — working without valid permits. Exploited and regularly hunted, the reward for their labor is jail and the whip.

Malaysia

Pung Chhiv Kek Galabru

Cambodian League for the Promotion and Defense of Human Rights (Licadho)

Kek Galabru (born 1942) is one of Cambodia's foremost defenders of human rights. After studying medicine in France and practicing it while following her diplomat husband to various posts abroad, she became instrumental in achieving political peace in her country. In 1992, she founded the Cambodian League for the Promotion and Defense of Human Rights (Licadho), which she heads at great personal risk. Licadho educates the people on their democratic rights and provides defense in court for victims of torture, domestic violence and police attacks.

Kek Galabru looks like a queen, slim and erect in her long blue silk dress. In fact, her parents, both teachers and later government ministers, were friends of the royal family. This enabled her to play a key role in opening negotiations between Cambodia's Prime Minster, Hun Sen, and opposition leader, Prince Sihanouk, which led to the Paris Peace Accords of 1991. But Dr Kek Galabru is mainly dedicated to grassroots work. The Cambodian League for the Promotion and Defense of Human Rights (Licadho), which she founded in 1992 and continues to direct, has offices in half of Cambodia's provinces, with 1000 collaborators, mostly volunteers.

Its first self-given task is to educate people to vote freely, disregarding the threats of the ruling party. One of its main activities is to represent victims of domestic or police violence — mainly women, children, opposition leaders, teachers, social workers and members of NGOs — in court, where it has won about a third of its cases. It also fights the massive illegal logging condoned by the corrupt government and the army. Above all, it teaches people their rights through classes, comic books, TV and radio programs and theater productions. As Kek says, "The mere fact of our presence makes a difference." And she keeps fighting in spite of serious threats against her person and a brutal attack on one of her two daughters engaged in the same causes. Her definition of courage is, "To do something for the people in spite of the intimidation." No wonder the taxi-driver had no problem finding her modest office in Phnom Penh: Everybody in Cambodia knows Licadho.

Cambodian society is a victim of the brutal past of the Khmer and the oppressive present of a one-party government. This had led to widespread human rights violations, including the domestic abuse of women and children and police violence against opposition leaders, that often remains unpunished.

Cambodia

Svetlana Gannushkina

Komitet Grazhdanskaya pomoshch (Civil Assistance Committee)

Svetlana Gannushkina (born 1942) has been engaged in peace activism since the beginning of the Karabakh conflict (1988), helping to free hundreds of Azerbaijani and Armenian prisoners of war. She is one of the founders of the Komitet Grazhdanskaya pomoshch (Civil Assistance Committee). She has contributed to the creation of Memorial, an NGO and human rights network in the Russian Federation, and of the Migration and Law Network. Svetlana was a member of the Governmental Commission on Migration Policy and is now a member of the Presidential Council on Human Rights.

By the winter of 2002, the Chechen refugee camps had become the evidence of the real state of affairs in Chechnya, and so the Russian authorities decided to close them. They applied various means: threats, refusal of humanitarian aid, and cutting off gas and electricity supply. Nevertheless, people did not want to return to Chechnya, to the hell of the war. In November 2002, the camp Iman in the village of Aki-Yurt (Ingushetia) was dismantled. The refugees were forced to leave the camp. However, Svetlana Gannushkina immediately arrived in Ingushetia and, despite the resistance of the authorities, managed to make the event public. The documents about the forced displacement of the refugees were handed over to the President of Russia at his meeting with the members of the Presidential Commission on Human Rights. Three members of the Commission — Ella Pamfilova, Lyudmila Alekseeva, and Svetlana Gannushkina — headed for Ingushetia and Chechnya. They had little time. Within two days, they had to visit several refugee camps to see everything with their own eyes. Yet, some people from the local authorities, who accompanied them, did their best to prevent human rights activists from communicating with refugees. On 27 December 2002, the peace advocates were invited to the government building of the Chechen Republic for dinner. They refused the invitation, ate a snack, and set out on their way. Forty minutes later, after the group left the building, it was destroyed. A truck loaded with explosives had managed to pass all the security posts. Dozens of people died.

The refugees were not forced to move that winter. Svetlana Gannushkina still goes regularly to Ingushetia and Chechnya, where the Komitet Grazhdanskaya pomoshch and Human Rights Center Memorial organize humanitarian and human rights programs.

In the Caucasus, Russian authorities persecute refugees and migrants. Svetlana, together with her organization, the Komitet Grazhdanskaya pomoshch, do what they can to support and protect the victims of armed conflict.

Ana Lucina García Maldonado

Federación Latinoamericana de Abogadas–Fedla (Latin American Federation of Lawyers)

She was born into a conservative family in Venezuela. Her roots are deeply linked to Andean geography. She is a diplomat by vocation and a lawyer by profession. Ana Lucina García (61) managed to unify her two passions, and with them, she was the driving force behind the legal changes that resulted in the overcoming of gender inequalities in her country. Her practice as a lawyer, besides her work as a parliamentarian and diplomat, demonstrates her continuous commitment to the feminist cause. Through this work, she contributes to the building of a real peace.

Ana Lucina García was born and raised within a conservative family. In 1966, she made an academic option and studied Law at the Andrés Bello Catholic University, in Caracas, the capital city of her country, Venezuela. She was a good student, with "the concepts and values of a perfect lawyer." But, after her graduation, she went into the real world full of imperfections. These were the first years of the fight of women for their rights as human beings. And Ana Lucina was there, in the middle of that fight.

In 1968, she was invited to a meeting of colleagues from the Venezuelan Professional Lawyers' Association and the truth hit her with a shock. She learned, for the first time, of the reality that subjugated Venezuelan women. "I had not seen this situation during my studies; I had no consciousness of the existence of the laws that discriminated against women. I had no consciousness that the law discriminated against me!" And then, along with a group of female lawyers, she began to study the principles contained in the law. She discovered that the principle of equality masked the oppression of women. As soon as 1973, Lucina joined the group of "crazy women" that wanted to change the world. 1975 was declared by the UN as The International Year of Women. Lucina was present at the session where the declaration was made. Afterwards, she began to take direct action: law initiatives; correspondence; lobbying members of parliament; and years and years of legal fights for the improvement of the law, for the repeal of one law, for the approval of another. Today, Ana Lucina García's name is part of the history of the fight of Venezuelan women for their rights.

In the 1960s, Venezuela was marked by the rise of professional women's consciousness of the fact that the law discriminated against them — and against all women. The first organizations for the defense of their rights sprang forth from the female lawyers' public discussion of the problem.

Venezuela

Mercedes García Fornieles

Association of Progressive Women (AMP), El Ejido

Since the 1980s, Mercedes García Fornieles has been working for sustainable development, peace, and the promotion of respect between the local population and migrants working in intensive agriculture in the region of Almeria, Spain. She is the president of the Association of Progressive Women of El Ejido, a NGO that provides assistance to exploited migrant workers. Living in extremely poor conditions between the greenhouses, these migrants are also victims of racism. Mercedes and her organization have also been victims of persistent racist attacks because of their work.

When Mercedes García Fornieles was young she learned that the problem of inequality between sexes could not be separated from the need to struggle for social progress. And this has always been at the center of her life. By supporting migrant workers Mercedes has become the victim of constant attacks and intimidation from the racist mayor, the municipal police, and many of her neighbors who consider her — coming from one of the oldest families in town — a traitor. Mercedes does not let herself be intimidated by malicious posters and pamphlets on walls and distributed in bars that are targeted at her. She continues her path, knowing that her social work is needed. Thanks to her inner strength she has never hesitated to work as a volunteer for the most marginalized people in Almeria. These are the migrant workers in the vast expanses of greenhouses and in the vegetable packing warehouses who only earn scorn, suffer humiliating working conditions, are refused access to bars and public places, and who live between the greenhouses in old huts and plastic shacks without running water.

Mercedes is receiving several journalists and a German television station today. Rather than speaking to them she simply takes them to the greenhouses, to the plastic and cardboard shacks, so that the media becomes aware of the horror of living in the open air, in the street, of not having a proper meal, or of being ill in the midst of abandoned plastic. Today, other volunteers of the Association of Progressive Women are presenting urgent documents to the local government. Others are accompanying a sick migrant without documents to the hospital, and a little later, in their office, Spanish class begins.

It grieves Mercedes that authorities do not fulfil their obligations and that social workers create such obstacles to prevent her from carrying out her commitment to social justice.

The area of Almeria, Spain, used to be very poor, but has become rich thanks to the intensive production of vegetables on 32,000 hectares of greenhouses which relies on the brutal exploitation of migrant workers. There is widespread racism and almost an apartheid attitude towards migrants.

Spain

Margarida Genevois

Rede Brasileira de Educação em Direitos Humanos (Brazilian Network for Human Rights Education)

Human rights are, for Margarida Genevois (1923), just like air. The lack of them is suffocating. During the brutal military regime in Brazil, she hid political prisoners, helped several of them go into exile, informed international organizations of the arbitrary actions. After democracy was restored, she kept denouncing injustices. She has worked for the Justice and Peace Commission of the Archdiocese of São Paulo, for 25 years. Presently, she is part of a national project on human rights education.

Electric shocks, drowning, "Pau de Arara" (suspension by the knees and arms from a metal bar): barbaric torture methods of the military regime prisons. Methods which Margarida Genevois heard of in the 1970s, when the Catholic Church opened its doors to persecuted people, at the time when she started working for the Justice and Peace Commission of the Archdiocese of São Paulo. One of her tasks was to welcome desperate people coming from the whole country. They were victims in search of a hiding place and a way to leave the country. "A lot of them used to be ashamed of talking about their experiences, due to the horribleness and cruelty."

That world was unknown to the sociologist Margarida until then. She married a successful businessman and moved to Campinas, in the countryside of São Paulo. There, she introduced daycares, a child welfare center and a mother's club for the workers. In 1967, back in São Paulo, she created Veritas — a center for political education for middle-class women. Five years later, after accepting an invitation of Cardinal Paulo Evaristo Arns to be part of the newly created Justice and Peace Commission, she began the never-ending fight for human rights. She faced death threats, faced politicians. She crossed borders to support dictatorship victims in Argentina, Chile and Uruguay.

Brazil is, once again, a democratic country, and Margarida Genevois is still present wherever human rights are disrespected. She has led campaigns against the National Security Law, against the death penalty and for the Amnesty. Gentle, but strong, she still believes human beings can change. In 1994, she participated in the creation of the Brazilian Network for Human Rights Education. "We give courses to instigate reflection, constructive criticism and tolerance towards differences."

According to information from the book 'Brasil: Nunca Mais' (Brazil: Never More), based on 695 lawsuits, 38.9% of politically suppressed people were 25 years old or younger. 88% of the accused were male and 12% female. The ones involved in the resistance came mostly from the middle class.

Brazil

Eulalia González Orozco

Organization of the American States (OAS)

She is Nicaraguan and not yet 40 years old. Mother of eight children, she was beaten by her partner. At that time, she lived in a rural community where domestic violence was a daily feature in social interaction and coexisted among the gunshots of the military groups. But not anymore. For a few years now, people have learned to understand each other. It was Eulalia González Orozco who helped them, when, after a period of training, she became a Rural Judicial Facilitator in her community.

"I told myself: sexual violence and the mistreatment of women are going to end. The crimes and the abuses are going to stop. I am going to capacitate myself, whatever it takes, so I can help my community to be different." Eulalia González Orozco is a peasant who lives in Caño Negro, in the municipality of Rancho Grande, in the province of Matagalpa, Nicaragua. Caño Negro is the community that she wanted to change. But for what reason? "It was the 1990s, after the war. There were still many armed military groups killing people. Many conflicts over land tenancy were generated. Families lived with feelings of resentment, with the desire for revenge. Violence was everywhere. I was enraged. Where could we get help when there were neither courts nor police?" She tried to fight for the things that did not exist. The people admired her and chose her as a voluntary Rural Judicial Worker. She accepted the challenge. She began her studies in 1999. Through OAS, the Organization of the American States, she started to study in order to collaborate in the administration of justice in her community area. The most important thing she learned was that a different kind of life was possible, "with respect between all people." She taught that to the people. She practiced it daily, even with a man who, out of spite, burnt her house. She could have moved from her house; she could have given up her new task; but she did not. She went on with her mission. Five years later, Caño Negro was a different place: "No one from our community is imprisoned, there are no conflicts over land tenancy, women are not beaten and many of the shops that sell alcohol are being closed down. Oh! And, as humble as the old one, with the support of contributions, we have built a new house."

When in 1990 the Sandinist Front for National Liberation lost the elections, Nicaragua entered a post-war period. Some military groups were demobilized while others lifted up their arms again. Armed violence in the rural areas continued, increasing the domestic violence.

Nicaragua

Jianmei Guo

Center for Women's Law Studies and Legal Services of Peking University

Guo Jianmei was born in 1961, and has been engaged in the protection of women's rights, and related research. In 1995 she initiated the establishment of the Center for Women's Law Studies and Legal Services of Peking University. This center provides free legal aid, and endeavors to develop the protection of the rights of women in need in China. It has contributed greatly to the progress made by lawyers and NGO's working for civil rights.

Guo Jianmei aims at promoting the endeavors of civil rights lawyers and setting up influential NGO's in China. She committed herself to the protection of women's rights immediately after graduating from university. From 1989 to 1993, Guo worked full time on the drafting of the "Law for Protection of Women's Rights and Interests." She did much research work and wrote related articles of up to 400,000 characters. She also co-published the book "A Guide to the Law for the Protection of Women's Rights and Interests." From 1993 to 1995, Guo cooperated with the Institute of Law, Chinese Academy of Social Sciences to implement the project "A Study on the Existing Problems in Implementing Women's Law in China and its Counter measures." They did extensive investigation of, and research into, the protection of women's rights and interests, and a substantial report was written. In 1995 Guo attended the Fourth International Forum for Women Lawyers. After this she started the Center for Women's Law Studies and Legal Services at the Law School of Peking University. Since resigning her post as assistant editor of the "China Lawyers" journal in 1996, Guo has been working in the Center providing legal aid for women. While representing the poor, Guo once raised the query: "If laws cannot protect poor and helpless persons like my litigant, why should we lawyers exist?"

Guo provides a free legal service to poor people, aiming particularly at protecting the legal rights of poor women. She helps them to solve their problems from a new perspective, guaranteeing their legal rights in the social, political and economic arena. She also arouses women's awareness of their rights and available means of acquiring legal knowledge. Such measures are aimed at eliminating poverty, both spiritual and cultural. This is also the way to enhance women's personal development and fulfillment.

China's legal environment is in need of immense improvement and there is much prejudice against the rights and interests of women. Thus it is imperative to provide professional services for women in terms of knowledge provision, consciousness raising and legal advice.

China

Nandita Haksar

Supreme Court of India

In her three decades as a feminist and human rights lawyer, Nandita Haksar (born 1955) has contributed immensely to the development of a rights-based perspective on complex political issues. Her work in exposing human rights violations by Indian security forces in the northeast, and her efforts to bring to the fore the underground Naga movement were pioneering. Nandita has managed to win for political dissidents not judicial pity but a change in the courts' view of human rights. She was also instrumental in bridging the gap between the feminist and the human rights movements in India.

Nandita Haksar, deeply influenced by the feminist movement of the 1970s, realized the need for a feminist lawyer and set about acquiring a degree in law at a time when there were no feminist lawyers — there were not even that many women lawyers. Her main focus as a lawyer has been on human rights' violations committed by the Indian security forces in the northeast. Nandita took up the question of the people's right to self-determination within India. She coedited the Nagaland Files, which brought to the fore the underground Naga movement for the first time. Nandita's involvement with the issue has been consistent and flexible; at the same time she works with various human rights organizations, has been a defense witness in the Indo-Naga peace process, and worked as secretary of the People's Union for Democratic Rights in 1987.

Nandita also realized that the Naxalites and their ideology were completely misunderstood. Even courts justified the torture of Naxalites. What Nandita wanted from the courts was not judicial pity but a change in its view of human rights. The challenge was to include the Naga insurgents in the negotiations to resolve issues, and to move away from the paradigm that views them as a law-and-order problem alone. Nandita has also been working on refugee law — political refugees, in particular — at the international level.

Since her work involved taking on powerful political adversaries, Nandita was under constant surveillance, her telephone conversations were intercepted, and there remains, even today, a threat to her life. She also had to face army raids because she exposed military atrocities in the northeast. The struggle was well worth it, for Nandita's work has contributed immensely to the development of a feminist and rights-based perspective on complex political issues.

Northeast India has been dealing with insurgency since the 1950s. The government sent in its security forces, protected by the Armed Forces Special Powers Act, which grants them almost unlimited powers in the region, resulting in innumerable instances of human rights' violations.

India

Shabnam Hashmi

Act Now for Harmony and Democracy (Anhad)

Shabnam Hashmi (born 1957) has worked for more than 20 years to combat communalism in India. She was associated with the creation and running of Sahmat, formed by artists and intellectuals in memory of her activist brother, who was murdered while performing a street play in 1989. After the Gujarat carnage, she understood the need for an outfit to systematically counter fascist propaganda, and the NGO Act Now for Harmony and Democracy (Anhad) was born in March 2003. Working voluntarily and without fees and with limited funds, Shabnam has emerged as a single-person pressure group.

For more than two decades, Shabnam Hashmi has worked on a voluntary, no-fee basis on a range of issues — disaster management, women's literacy, environmental issues, children's education, violence against women, adoption, Dalits' rights, and the development of a scientific temper, with a focus on peace and communal harmony. The creative energy that she embodies was unleashed when her theater artiste brother was murdered while performing in the street. The anguish was channeled to create Sahmat, an organization of many of India's prominent artists and intellectuals. For 15 years, she remained the motivating force behind the activities, ideas, and projects collectively generated by this community.

In March 2003, a year after the Gujarat carnage, along with some other intellectuals and activists, Shabnam formed Anhad. The propaganda by fascist outfits had invaded the streets, and Anhad was set up "to wage this battle of the minds". The organization's main objective was to prepare a secular nationwide cadre, and to equip working social and political activists, grassroots workers, students, and youth to counter the ideology of hatred.

Down the years, Shabnam has been through her share of ups and downs. Both as a child and as an adult, her parents' life choices and, later, her own did not ensure financial stability. Her persistent and strident criticism of the communalization of politics has won her many adversaries. She has also been physically attacked several times. Through it all, Shabnam has emerged as a single-person pressure group.

India has had a history of communal conflicts — incited by fascist forces — beginning with the postpartition riots in 1947. The 1984 anti-Sikh pogrom, the 1992 Mumbai riots, and the 2002 Gujarat carnage were three of the largest-scale riots. There have been countless other, smaller rhubarbs.

María Julia Hernández Chavarría

Legal Tutelage of the Archbishops of San Salvador

She was good with a camera since her childhood. As a young girl, she wanted to be a member of a religious order, but gave it up to study and to teach philosophy. She is an untiring traveler and reader, directing her profound compassion and sense of justice towards the defense of human rights in El Salvador, where impunity prevails. María Julia Hernández, honest, sensitive and stable as a rock, works persistently to discover and reveal the truth, to build peace upon justice, and to expand the work of recovering Historical Memory.

"Please help me," asked the archbishop of San Salvador, Monsignor Oscar Arnulfo Romero (he was murdered in 1980), to a group of university students in the end of the 1970s. María Julia Hernández (born 1939) was struck powerfully by these words in a public mass for priest Rutilio Grande (a priest murdered by paramilitary forces, in 1977) and immediately volunteered to help with the labor of the prelate. "Then, I realized that was the opportunity I had been looking for, since I was a girl. It summed up everything for me."

A few years before, when she lived in the United States, she began to understand the complex social problems of the Latin America people. She felt that they needed her help. María Julia Hernández decided to give up her religious vocation. "That was not my path," she says. Back in El Salvador, she studied philosophy at the Centro American University. After that she went on to work as a professor in the Law School of the El Salvador University. In the 1980s, she worked in collaboration with Monsignor Romero, convincing him to publish his homilies (speeches denouncing the abuses suffered by the people, through the hands of the state), arguing that it was his people who demanded it. She went to his personal archive of records, transcribed and edited them. Since 1982, when she accepted the post as Director of the Legal Tutelage of the Archbishops of San Salvador, which she still occupies, her motto was: "God is my rock." She has sacrificed her family, health (in 1994, she went through open-heart surgery). She has never ceased to demand peace and full human dignity, in spite of the constant death threats she has received due to her fight against impunity. Her most recent success was obtaining a judicial sentence, from the International Commission for Human Rights, against one of the people responsible for Monsignor Romero's murder.

The amnesty of 1993 prevented the judgment of the crimes committed against humanity during the Salvadorian war (1980—1992). The peace process is based on impunity. There is no right to the truth, no right to justice for the victims. The only alternative is going to International Courts.

El Salvador

Tagreed Hikmat

United Nations Children's Fund (Unicef)
General Federation of Jordanian Women (GFJW)
Arab Women Organization (AWO)

Tagreed Hikmat, born in 1945, has worked for 20 years at national and international levels advocating human rights and combating domestic violence against children and women. A graduate of Damascus University in 1972, Tagreed eventually became the first female judge in Jordan, in an entirely male-dominated profession. She is the first Arab woman Judge for the United Nations International Criminal Tribunal, currently working on the case of Rwanda. She has worked towards enshrining the rights of children and women in the Jordanian legal system and improving their living conditions.

As a lawyer and then a judge, Tagreed Hikmat has been confronted with a number of struggles and obstacles in her life and career. The first struggle that she recalls was her position as the first female judge in Jordan. Owing to some biased voices in her country with regard to a woman serving as a judge — particularly in a criminal court — she faced fierce opposition towards her appointment to the post. Having proved her aptitude within her society and the country's legal community she has set an avid example as a groundbreaker for so many women in her profession who have come after her. As a lawyer she struggled for 15 years until finally being appointed as a judge. Since then, there have been over 20 female judges appointed in Jordan.

Tagreed also considers her appointment to the UN International Criminal Tribunal as a major challenge. Out of 18 judges elected from around the world to serve on the Tribunal, she received one of the highest scores of votes from the UN member States. Her work now focused on the application of international law, Tagreed considers her upcoming struggle to be the strengthening of the International Criminal Court to combat the continuation of war and violence. Throughout her work, both nationally and internationally, Tagreed has continued to draw her spiritual strength from her personal relationship with God. She also draws a great deal of emotional support from her family and friends, who remain very important to her throughout her activities. In the future, Tagreed hopes to work towards promoting peace in the Middle East, more specifically in Palestine and Israel, because as she says, "Peace is the only solution to all problems, disputes, conflicts and war in the region."

Since June 2003 Tagreed Hikmat has been a judge in the United Nations International Criminal Tribunal for War Crimes in Rwanda. She is participating in the application of international humanitarian and criminal law and the Geneva Conventions to the war crimes in Rwanda in the 1990s.

De Fen Ho

Department of Law, National Taiwan University

Ho De Fen is one of the founders of the Taiwan Association for Human Rights and member of the Taiwan Media Watch Foundation. She participated in the Wild Lilies student movement and has since been active in the Taiwanese human rights movements. She has been promoting democratization since the days of the martial law.

Ho De Fen is a professor of law at the National Taiwan University. With the courage of a responsible scholar, she has devoted herself to political reform in Taiwan: "If we are still capable, especially if we are working for constitutional rights, democratization and human rights, then we should use our capabilities to promote the values of human rights so Taiwan can break out of the ice age."

In 1999 she initiated the Taiwan Association for Human Rights together with human rights groups and other scholars. She believes civic groups can play an important role in the process of democratization. They act as watchdogs and push for improvements in government functioning. With the assistance of other scholars and journalists, she formed the Taiwan Media Watch Foundation, to perform precisely this function. As a teacher and expert in law, she has fought for constitutional amendments in order to legalize teachers' rights to form unions and to make election laws adequate for workers and farmers. She also assisted groups in need, like the students' movement protesting after the assassination attempt on president Chen Shui-bian in March 2004.

In 20 years of struggle in social movements she has never spoken of retirement. She says "If we don't face any storms and challenges in our lives, then we will get used to pre-established concepts. We have felt the power and honesty of not giving in to authoritarian regimes."

Taiwan's martial-law era came to an end in the 80s, but after several decades of political repression, society is still conservative and lacks human rights awareness.

China, Taiwan

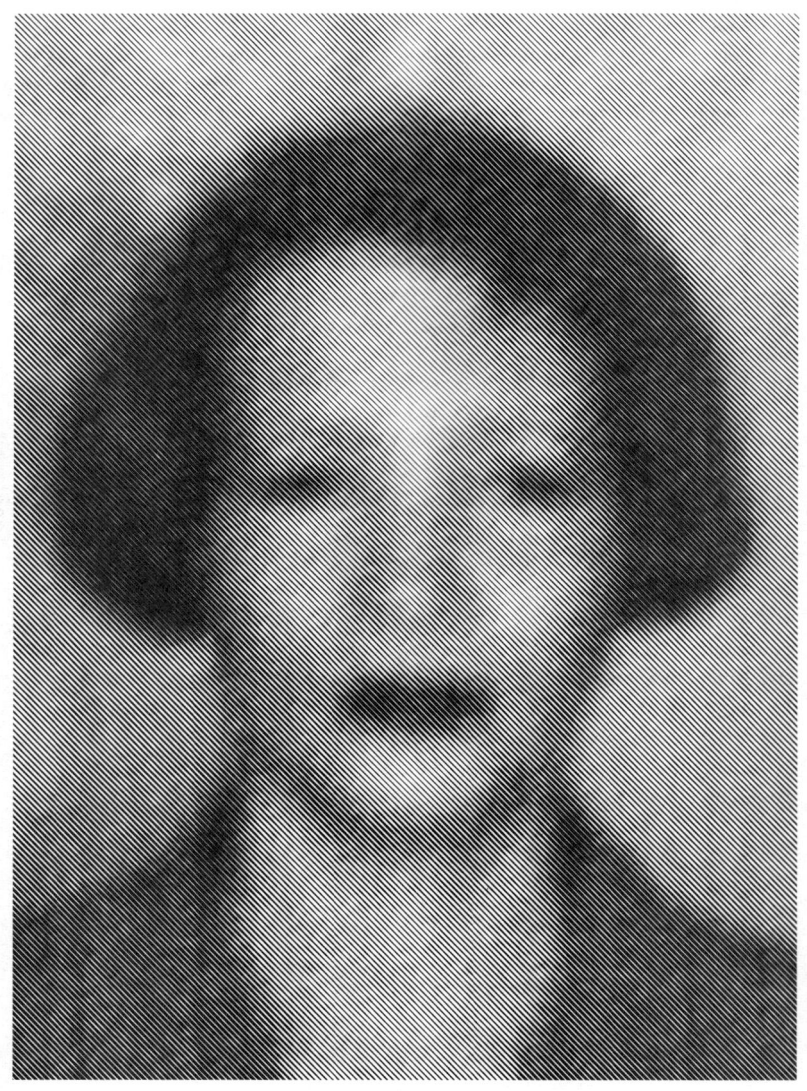

Raqiya Humeidan

Advisory Committee to the Ministry of Human Rights (ACMHR)
Yemen Advocates Union (YAU)
Arab Association for Supporting Women and Juvenile Issues (AASWJI)

Raqiya Humeidan was the first woman in Yemen and the Arab Gulf region to become a lawyer. Born in 1947 in Aden, she graduated with a BA in Law from the University of London in 1971, and the following year obtained a Masters in Law, from the London School of Economics and Political Science (LSEPS). She is currently a private barrister and is also a renowned legal consultant and advisor for the World Bank.

Raqiya Humeidan comes from a middle class family; her mother died when she was still a youngster. Married in 1973, she has one son and two daughters: an engineer, a law graduate and an accountant respectively. Raqiya has 31 years of professional experience in legal consultancy. She worked for seven years as a civil servant and for 24 years as a Supreme Court Attorney. She is a member of the Advisory Committee to the Ministry of Human Rights (ACMHR) in Yemen and has played a key role in monitoring human rights violations.

Raqiya actively participated in the International Visitor Program of the United States Information Agency (USIA) on "The Rule of Law" in 1993. She was also involved in a program on the US Court System sponsored by the National Center for State Courts in August 1999. Raqiya has conducted many studies on various national and international legal issues and has revised drafts of legislation and governmental resolutions. As an intelligent barrister, she has concluded commercial contracts with international companies on behalf of corporations and has provided legal advice to national and international bodies and persons. She was deputized as an expert to talk about the Yemeni Law before the British High Court in London and at an international arbitration tribunal in Northern Ireland.

Raqiya speaks two foreign languages and is a member of several local and regional unions and organizations, including the Yemen Advocates Union (YAU), the Arab Advocates Association, the Yemeni Center for Conciliation and Arbitration and the Arab Association for Supporting Women and Juvenile Issues (AASWJI).

Before unification with the north, the economic, cultural and security conditions in southern Yemen were conducive to the promotion of women's issues. These circumstances greatly impacted and assisted Raqiya Humeidan's work and activities in social and political life from the 1970s to the 1990s.

Rosario Ibarra de Piedra

Comité Eureka

She made herself. Through strong acts and words she refined her personality, accompanied by others like her. With the reins of her life in her hands, Rosario Ibarra, obstinate for justice, built her history and writes about it in letters destined to a missing son. 78 years of life dedicated to activism against impunity, this Mexican woman dreams of a world without nations, nor exploration or persecution.

"A peaceful world is the one where a woman like me should not be famous for being the mother of a missing person. A struggle like this should not even exist." But this struggle does exist, and Rosario Ibarra, along with many other women and men, has pledged never to abandon it. Her name is respected throughout Mexico for her unwavering loyalty to the cause of justice. "No, I do not get tired. How can we get tired? It is not just any simple thing they have taken away from us. They took away a son, a husband, a sister. These bonds are never broken. Our minimum demand is for the maximum, and the maximum is the minimum. A son or a brother is not negotiable. You can negotiate about a salary or a piece of land, but not about a human life — a human life born from our womb or bound to us by blood, by affection or by affinity and convictions."

From an enormous photo, Rosario Ibarras son, 21 years old at the time, missing for 30 years, smiles at his mother. They arrested him in 1975. She is still looking for him, just as she works together with other women to search for other missing sons and daughters. Seven hunger strikes and hundreds of other actions are part of the personal and collective history of the Eureka Committee, as is their success story: 148 missing people have been found. "I believe that we are going to achieve peace because there are many good people on this planet. We should globalize the good and the faith into people who fight for freedom. To see that frontiers are erased, and to see that there are no differences of race or class — that there is only one Human Race and that we are all citizens of the world."

The human rights situation in Mexico is grave. Murders — like the one of the lawyer Digna Ochoa, young Pável Gonzalez, hundreds of women in Juárez City — remain unpunished. The members of indigenous and peasant communities continue to suffer political persecution, as do ecologists and students.

Mexico

Indira Jaising

Lawyer's Collective

Once fighting to establish herself on an equal footing with her male colleagues, Indira Jaising's legal work and her dedication to the cause of the marginalized is today the stuff of legend — her cases include Olga Tellis (pavement-dwellers' rights), the Bhopal Gas Leak (that the government cannot represent the victims to their exclusion), Mary Roy (inheritance for women), Gita Hariharan (mother's right to guardianship of the child), and many others. With each victory, Indira holds the Indian constitution to its covenant-justice for all.

Indira Jaising grew up in a conservative Sindhi household. Defying the future her parents envisioned for her — marriage alone — Indira struck out on her own path: she became a lawyer, in an almost all-male fraternity, both at the bar and bench. While her colleagues and judges refused to take her seriously at first, she stood firm: she knew exactly why she had joined the bar.

In 1982, Indira fought and won the landmark Olga Tellis case, which stopped the authorities from evicting pavement-dwellers from their lean-tos and scrapboard shelters to beautify the city. When she took up the case, the very notion that pavement-dwellers had rights was unheard of. The law books and reports of the 1950s and 1960s show that only the rich used the courts to claim what they considered their inarguable rights: not a single laborer complained that minimum wages were not paid; not a bonded laborer sought freedom; not a woman sought freedom from violence.

Besides Olga Tellis, Indira has repeatedly created Indian legal history, each time winning a substantial victory for society's marginalized: among many others the Bhopal Gas Leak Case (where she was the first person to challenge the government's self-determined right to represent the victims, to the exclusion of the victims) and the Tehri Dam Case (to protect those who lost their lands to submergence). Indira has also fought long and hard against corruption in the judiciary. She is representing in the supreme court of India the victims of the 2002 Gujarat genocide. Both her methodology and her goal are straightforward: to hold law to the promise delivered in the preamble to the constitution of India — justice for all.

Indira Jaising began her career when women in the legal profession were objects of male and judicial patronizing. In the 1950s and 1960s, the only people who had access to the courts were industrialists complaining of tax structures or princes complaining of being deprived of their privy purses.

India

Hina Jilani

AGHS Legal Aid Cell

Hina Jilani (born 1953) has set standards for protecting human rights in Pakistan, especially the rights of women. For over two-and-a-half decades, this dedicated lawyer has fought discriminatory laws that have turned women into second-class citizens in their own country. She has also set standards for her own profession by providing free legal aid to hundreds of clients, and by setting up a shelter for women fleeing violence and abuse.

Hina Jilani started practicing law in 1979, when Pakistan was under martial law, with no sign of democracy on the horizon. The regime used obscurantist interpretations of Islamic law to deny women the equal rights they enjoyed under the constitution. It was the worst of times, but also in a sense, the best: fighting unjust laws became Hina's mission. She took up case after case concerning the violation of women's right to security, and the deprivation of liberty under unjust and discriminatory laws. In many cases, she obtained favorable judgments from the courts: for instance, on a woman's right to marry a man of her own choice, and without the consent of a guardian. These are cited as precedents in courtrooms across the country by lawyers fighting to redress wrongs against women.

Hina's work for women victims of violence led to the setting up of the first women's shelter in the private sector. Indeed, it was the first in the country to be governed by the principle of recognizing its residents as adults who had a right to choose how they wished to live. Hina and her sister, Asma Jahangir, also a human rights lawyer, set up the AGHS Legal Aid Cell in 1986, the first free legal aid center in Pakistan.

Hina's work has benefited other oppressed people. Her work for bonded labor led to an act abolishing it in 1992. Her fight for the rights of children, especially the protection of child laborers engaged in hazardous work, prompted the government to come up with an act regulating the employment of children. In the course of her work, Hina has been threatened time and again. Once, a client was shot dead in front of her eyes; another time, gunmen entered her house and threatened members of her family while she was away. The threats put pressure on her to migrate, but she refused, and continues to live and work in Lahore.

Zia-ul-Haq's regime was one of the most retrograde in Pakistan's history, trying to impose the diktat of archaic Islamic laws that denied women their constitutional rights, and relegated them to second-class citizenship. The courts became an only recourse, and lawyers began to fight tough.

Elsa Patria Jiménez Flores

El closet de Sor Juana

As a girl, she wanted to be a sailor. Her mother did not contradict her and bought her trousers. Her father had long awaited for a daughter and the opportunity to call her by a much-loved name: Patria — fatherland. She has a large family by blood and another one by choice. She is tribal, lesbian and the spiritual daughter of Chavela Vargas — a famous international singer, known for her love songs for women.

Elsa Patria Jiménez Flores began her work in support of lesbians publicly acting in their favor, at a time when they were still persecuted by the authorities. It was the beginning of the gay and lesbian movement in Mexico that has been a paradigm in Latin America and the Caribbean. "My father was political and had a romantic image of a woman with a flag in the clouds. She represented the native land. He wanted to give one of his daughters the patriotic name of Patria. My mother said, 'That is not a name.' However, the name became mine, but my mother negotiated a compound name: I became Elsa Patria Jiménez Flores."

She was born near the Mexican desert and grew up in the streets of Mexico City. She discovered early on that she was a lesbian, but thought, "This is not possible," until she met the activists. From the age of 19, it has been her mission to work in support of women, helping to found one of the first lesbian groups in Mexico and affiliating it with the feminist movement. "My activism was a way of life. Although I was a little late in encountering lesbian organizations, I knew that it was my life."

In 1997, Elsa Patria was made a member of the Parliament. While there, she managed to develop a number of solutions for the problems of women in prison and missing children. She also worked for women's rights, and gay and lesbian rights. When her mandate ended, she directed her work towards denouncing and fighting against the assassinations of the women in Ciudad Juárez, in the North of Mexico. A place sadly known, for over 10 years, for the continuous and increasing assassination and rape of hundreds of poor women — "feminicide".

In Mexico, the human rights of the Lesbian, Gay, Bisexual, Transgender and Transsexual (Lgbtt) community are precarious. The capital has a legislation that punishes discrimination, but there are numerous hate actions against those with sexual differences. Nevertheless, the Mexican Lgbtt movement is one of the best organized movements in the region.

Mexico

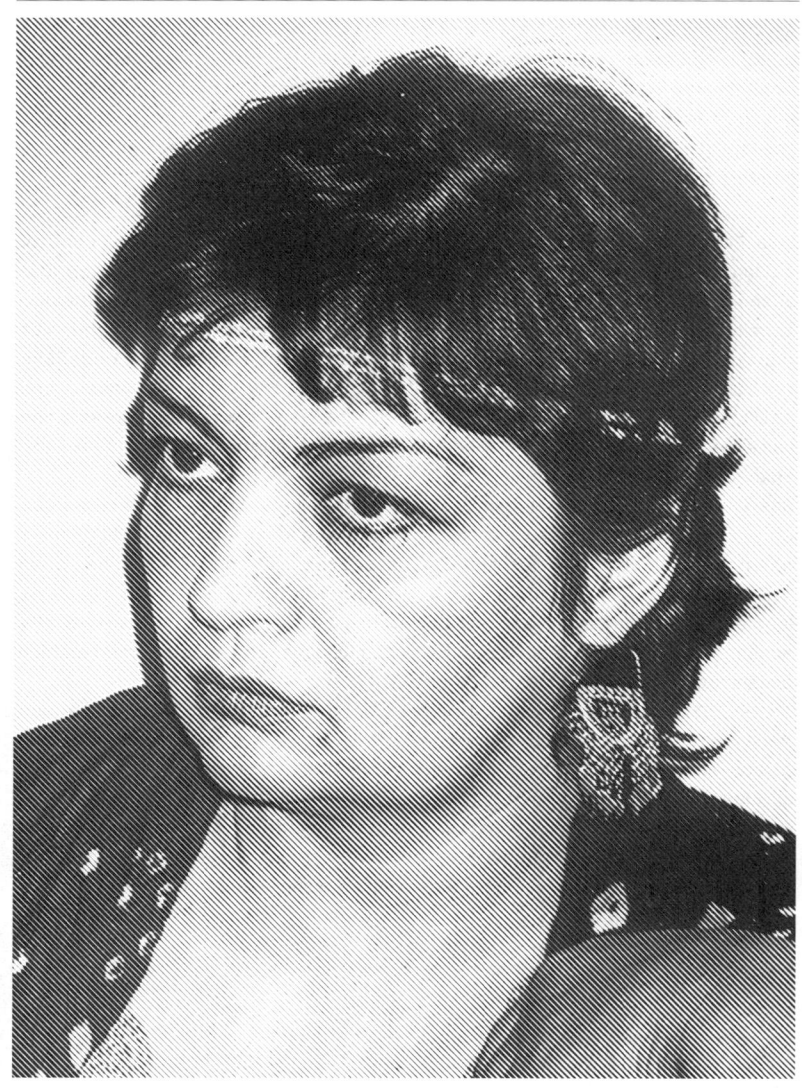

Gavkhar Juraeva

Migration and Law
Loik

An art historian and area studies expert by education, and an editor, writer of documentary and feature films, and political mediator by profession, Gavkhar Juraeva is devoted to serving the truth — and with it, those who suffer and need her help. In the post-Soviet period, when a bloody civil war broke out in her country, she served as a mediator and sought to protect those who suffered at the margins — on both sides of the conflict. She was forced to leave her country in 1992. Gavkhar continues her fight from Russia, her adopted home. She is a writer, editor, and critic.

Gavkhar Juraeva works to protect the rights of and to direct humanitarian help to the most vulnerable parts of society in Tajikistan. During the civil war, she carried out peacemaking activities and sought to protect the rights of those who suffered at the margins of society. In 1992, a seeming resolution to the political conflict only brought a new era of wide-scale repression and ethnic conflict to Tajikistan. Members of her family were victims of various acts of violence, and their homes were destroyed. Gavkhar was forced to leave her country.

Today, she continues her fight from Russia, her adopted home. Among her vulnerable "clients" are victims of violence, fabricated criminal charges, public humiliation, robbery, or passport confiscation. Gavkhar also supports laborers whose employers refuse to pay them. To resolve legal and human rights situations, she directly confronts the often very aggressive employers in their workplaces and has even confronted criminal syndicates. Gavkhar Juraeva is a defender of the law, an ardent worker for justice, and a peacemaker. She considers her legal, humanitarian, and peacemaking activities to be her moral duty. She has founded and/or led numerous public-service organizations, including Tajikistan, a regional public fund for the support of refugees and migrants, and Migration and Law, an international legal center.

The fall of the Soviet Union prompted a bloody civil war in Tajikistan. Thousands died, and many others fled the violence and the resulting economic crisis. A large number of Tajik refugees are still displaced in various former Soviet countries.

Tajikistan

Salima Kadyrova

Center for Human Rights Initiatives of Samarkand

Salima Kadyrova (71) is a lawyer at the Center for Human Rights Initiatives of Samarkand, Uzbekistan. She has been working for the protection of human rights of citizens for the last 24 years and has been a practicing lawyer for the last 40 years. She also works at the Public Legal Consulting Office. Salima is one of few lawyers who defends the human and civil rights of the leaders of the Uzbek opposition. She is a highly respected figure in the human rights movement both within Uzbekistan and abroad.

Salima Kadyrova was born in Bukhara province, Uzbekistan, in 1933. In 1959, she graduated from the Faculty of Law of Tashkent State University. She is now the deputy director of the Center for Human Rights Initiatives. She not only defends citizens' interests, but also highlights legislative shortcomings and contradictions. Salima appeals to the President's administration, to the Uzbek Parliament, the Supreme Court, the Constitutional Court, and the General Prosecutors about every infringement of the law she is made aware of. She does not discriminate when it comes to defending those who come to her for help. She also goes to districts and villages to give legal consultations.

Since 1999, the police have targeted and arrested many young people and religious leaders. On one such occasion, Salima defended seven religious leaders from Ishtehan District in the Syrdaryo Province and won their release. She is also one of the few lawyers who have defended a leader of the Uzbek opposition, Mohamad Solikh. She has devoted her professional career to the fight against injustice in her country by endeavoring to protect the helpless. Her credo is simple: "The law must defend the true rights of the people without being sold or bought by those concerned."

Salima Kadyrova, through her tireless and ceaseless efforts, has proved her honesty in the face of her contemporaries and has shown that she is a real defender of human rights, liberties, and freedom. The struggle against corruption and injustice has been long and arduous, but Salima has not shied away from her moral obligations to the people who come to her for help. Salima dares to criticize the shortcomings in Uzbek legislation and is determined to have laws rewritten and improved. She is not deterred by the possible consequences that she might suffer because of her work.

Uzbekistan's legal defense system is still weak. Human rights defenders face a great challenge in protecting people from injustice and infringements of Uzbek law.

Uzbekistan

Marilee Karl

Isis International

Marilee Karl (born 1941) has devoted her life to the causes of social justice, civil and human rights, equitable development and women's empowerment. She co-founded Isis International in 1974, an organization linking women from South to North and from East to West. Through networking, communication, and capacity building activities for over 30 years, Isis has supported and inspired tens of thousands of activist women and groups around the world, whose work ranges from grassroots empowerment and community action, to conflict resolution and women's rights advocacy at the international level.

Rome 1974: a small international group of women met around a kitchen table and thought about the newly emerging wave of women's rights groups around the world. "We were part of it and we were in contact with many new groups in the South and the North, organizing and mobilizing themselves and other women to overcome discrimination, violence, and lack of opportunity, working in creative ways to empower women to build a more just world," Marilee says. How could these groups be strengthened? "We needed to break our isolation, link up and communicate with each other," she recalls. And so Isis, an information and communication network of women, was born in 1974, co-founded by Marilee Karl. It was named after Isis, the Egyptian goddess of creativity and wisdom. "When we started, we dreamt of a network of women and women's groups and organizations around the world, sharing ideas, experiences, strategies and action, and building solidarity," says Marilee.
In the early years the dream threatened to burst for lack of money. But with a lot of enthusiasm, the work of committed women, and an overwhelming response from women's groups around the world, Isis grew and played an important part in the emergence and blossoming of the global women's movement from the 1970s up until today. And it still does. From two tiny offices in Rome and Geneva, Isis developed into three sister organizations: Isis International in Manila, Philippines; Isis-Wicce in Kampala, Uganda; and Isis International in Santiago, Chile. Marilee led Isis International, as part of a team, until 1994. After two decades, she passed the leadership on to younger women from the South. As a honorary chairperson, Marilee continues to play an active role in Isis International, Manila, as well as in other women's rights, feminist, and development networks and organizations.

Opportunities and channels for direct communication and networking are necessary to break the isolation of women working for peace and justice around the world and to provide support and solidarity in difficult struggles. This was the case three decades ago. It still is today.

Italy

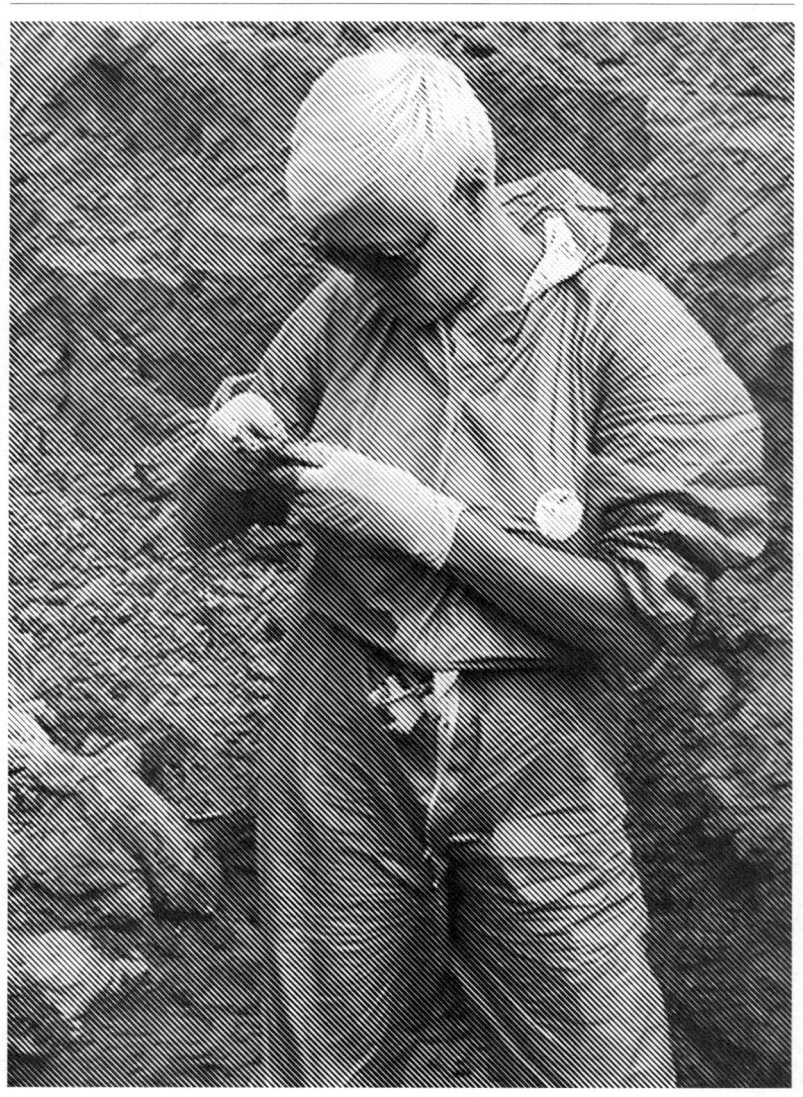

Eva-Elvira Klonowski

International Criminal Tribunal for Former Yugoslavia (ICTY)
International Commission on Missing Persons (ICMP)

Dr Eva-Elvira Klonowski immigrated to Iceland in 1981, after the declaration of martial law in her native Poland. A leading professional in the field of forensic anthropology, she was part of the first forensics team assembled by the International Criminal Tribunal for former Yugoslavia to exhume and identify the remains from mass graves. Since 2001, Dr Klonowski has worked for the International Commission on Missing Persons (ICMP), an intergovernmental organization addressing the issue of persons missing as a result of the conflicts in the Balkan region.

In December 1981, when Eva-Elvira Klonowski, her husband and their young daughter were on vacation abroad, the Polish government, led by General Jaruzelski, declared martial law. Polish borders were closed and all communication with the outside world was prohibited. The young family became "accidental" refugees, finally landing in Iceland in 1982.

Through her work at the department of forensic medicine in Reykjavik, Eva-Elvira specialized in the emerging field of forensic anthropology. A turning point in Eva's career came in the summer of 1996: the first four mass graves had been discovered in the village of Kalesija in the former Yugoslavia. The International Criminal Tribunal for former Yugoslavia (ICTY) asked Eva-Elvira to join a forensics project to exhume and identify the remains of bodies found in the mass graves. She and her team worked in difficult conditions, putting up with the ever-present stench of rotting bodies as they worked in a bombed-out clothing factory which had been converted into a makeshift morgue. At the request of the International Commission on Missing Persons (ICMP), Eva-Elvira delivered a report she had prepared on the current state of existing forensic facilities in Bosnia and Herzegovina in the summer of 1996. After returning to Iceland in 1997, she then volunteered for the Bosnian State Commission for Tracing Missing Persons until 2000. In October 2000, she played a critical role in helping many families identify their missing loved ones, finally allowing the grieving families to bury their relatives properly.

During the Balkan wars, Serb forces were responsible for the massacre and burial of thousands of civilians in mass graves. After the war, efforts have been made to identify the bodies of those who disappeared during the war, both for their families and for evidence at the International Criminal Tribunal.

Iceland

Tatyana Kotlyar

Za prava cheloveka (For Human Rights)

Tatyana Kotlyar was born in 1951. In the USSR, her family was persecuted for anti-Soviet activities, and Tatyana, a mathematician with a postgraduate degree, was reduced to sweeping streets. When Perestroika began, she helped found one of the first democratic NGOs in Russia. In 1995, Tatyana became coordinator of the Obninsk Regional Human Rights Group. She provides legal support to citizens whose social and human rights have been violated. For more than ten years, she has been sitting in local representative bodies. At present, she is a deputy of the Kaluga Regional Legislative Assembly.

In 1999, Tatyana Kotlyar decided to present herself for the Russian State Duma election. A very popular human rights advocate in Obninsk, she was used to winning local and regional elections. But this time the situation was different. Apart from Obninsk, there were also rural areas where the electorate habitually voted communist. The election campaign required enormous strength and funds. As an independent candidate, Tatyana had no substantial financial backing. Moreover, she was often short of time, busy helping to defend people's rights in court. Yet she could not help, but she could respond to appeals like the following: "Our daughter was walking along the street and, at an abrupt turn, a driver lost control of his car, hit her, and left the scene of the crime. Our daughter has become an invalid for the rest of her life. The police found the car the same day and learned that the driver was the regional judge. When we started to protest, they suggested that we just forget it ever happened, as if it had been a bad dream." Countless such appeals have been addressed to this human rights advocate. The election campaign was emotionally very hard for Tatyana. Three weeks before the vote, her son was taken to court and accused of draft evasion. Tatyana had to appeal for a retrial. Sometimes she had to spend the night in a bus — her only means of transport — to meet with her voters in other parts of the region. Her telephone did not work, and she had difficulty in scheduling her meetings. Of course, it was impossible to win the election under such conditions. Then she suffered a grievous loss: her only son tragically died when her house was destroyed by fire. Nevertheless, her courage will have helped her to survive. Today, Tatyana is a deputy of the Kaluga Regional Legislative Assembly, a politician, and a well-known human rights advocate.

Tatyana Kotlyar has been a defender of human rights since Soviet times — when she was persecuted by the authorities. Her activism is still needed today as she continues her combat against economic, political, and other human rights violations in Russia.

Russian Federation

Saskia Kouwenberg

Saskia Kouwenberg has spent 25 years — half her life — as an activist. Everything from indigenous people's land rights, to national independence, to anti-nuclear and anti-war work has been the focus of her campaigning. Although not affiliated to one group, she has worked alongside Amnesty International, the United Nations, and Moluccan and East Timorese organizations, in all kinds of ways. From mediating in conflict resolution classes to trespassing on military bases, Saskia will try any method to achieve her goal of a better, safer, fairer world.

Saskia Kouwenberg grew up in an agricultural area of North Brabant in the Netherlands, near the Belgian border. Political awareness was non-existent in her village of Zundert, so as a teenager she never imagined the future that lay before her. "I was not somebody who said on her twelfth birthday, 'I want to be a peace activist when I grow up.'"

All that changed when she travelled around the world at the age of 19. She followed the hippie trail through India and Afghanistan, where her travels brought her into contact with something unknown in cozy, middle-class Netherlands: poverty. It shocked her. She had never seen it before. And her eyes were opened to other things unimaginable back home in the Netherlands. She met and learned from inspirational people and began to understand that the world is made up of many points of view. This understanding is perhaps the prime mover behind everything she does. "I met people with totally different views on life. That was a very big surprise to me," she recalls. "Different people with totally different opinions can be right. That is maybe what I use most throughout my work."

Through travelling she realized that the world was her problem now, that there was no such thing as "foreign": "From then on, I felt like a world citizen." And you can see from the way that she darts about, taking sides with people who are being treated unfairly, no matter where in the world they may be, that she means it when she says: "Responsibility does not end at borders."

As a "citizen of the world," working alone and with numerous political organizations both in her home country and all over the world, Saskia Kouwenberg's work ranges from anti-war and anti-nuclear protests, to indigenous people's land rights, national independence movements, and conflict resolution.

Netherlands

"Basically, I defend the rights and interests of citizens in the courts by being their representative. I highlight these injustices through the media. People need my work, therefore I keep going."

Zoya Kovalenko

International Society for Human Rights (ISHR)
Union of Ukrainian Journalists

Zoya Kovalenko (54) is the head of the Center for Legal Defense in the Poltava region of Ukraine. Zoya has brought forward proposals on how to improve Ukraine's legal and legislative system to the Ministry of Justice and the Supreme Court. She promotes and encourages a cleaning up of the local court system and strives to increase awareness of the Ukrainian legal system, especially among poor farming communities which otherwise remain uninformed of their rights.

Zoya Dmitriyevna Kovalenko felt there was no other course to take in life. Frustrated by the ill-treatment and injustices meted out to the uninformed and uninitiated among her community, she decided to take things into her own hands. She started out by helping individuals in clear-cut legal cases, but at the beginning of the 1990s, she started offering legal advice and support to collective farmers who were being severely infringed upon. Along with a small group of dedicated supporters, Zoya held meetings in different rural districts, advising those who needed help and encouraging locals to deselect unfit leaders. As a result of her work, the Center for Legal Defense was born. In 1999, she started to develop a district network of legal defense groups. Currently, there are six of them. Zoya has participated in and cooperated with many public organizations, world forums, seminars, and training courses, all dedicated to the dissemination of rights awareness. As a champion of human rights, Zoya has not shirked responsibility in publicly denouncing court mistakes and procedural infringements. As a result of such public denouncements, Poltava's regional military commissar along with the region's military department chief and the military's garrison commandant were all removed from their posts. Zoya's dream is that, one day, Ukrainian people will be able to take their place among other developed and democratic nations in the world, proudly demonstrating their potential and ability.

In this transition period from an authoritarian regime to a democracy, many legal and human rights abuses continue. The courts and legal systems need improvement. Many people are unaware of their rights as citizens.

Ukraine

Krystyna Kurczab-Redlich

Krystyna Kurczab-Redlich is a journalist. Despite the official ban, she regularly visited Chechnya between 1997 and 2004 and made four documentaries: "Chechnya — Death Rattle," "Chechnya — Murder with International Consent," "SOS for Chechnya," and "Chechens after Beslan," exposing the Russian human rights abuses in Chechnya. Her book "Pandrioshka" was published in 2000. After 14 years in Russia, she was not able to get new accreditation and her phone was bugged. She returned to Poland and continues to write about human rights abuses in Russia and to help Chechen refugees.

Playing the idiot or bursting into tears at Russian checkpoints was almost always helpful. Not, however, when the soldiers were women. In 2002, after five years of visits to Chechnya as a freelance journalist, Krystyna Kurczab-Redlich was asked to leave her car at a military checkpoint. "I wrote about it afterwards as if it happened to someone else. I did not want to frighten my family," she says. After she was searched roughly, a woman soldier took her to a huge tent with a hole in the ground stinking of chloride. In the hole filled with water up to the neck stood Chechens. They were dying. The soldier asked the journalist: "Do you want to be there? You will be soon." Krystyna does not like to talk about it. She simply explains that she was going to Chechnya without permission from the Russian authorities because officially journalists could go there only in organized groups with a guide. So she was hiding her hair under a scarf, sitting in the corner of a cab, keeping the tapes with documentaries in her underwear. She bribed greedy soldiers when she had to. She filmed corpses, young people without arms, legs. She talked with people who underwent the most horrible torture, with women who dug through piles of corpses to find their dead brothers or husbands. She met hundreds of mothers who lost their children. "I realized that the saying 'if not me, then who?' fits me perfectly. If I do not go there, if I do not write about it, who will?" In 2004, Chechens started to look at her with hatred: "You do not help us. Just make money on us," they said. "I, then, bought a ring in Dagestan. I said to myself: I will take it off only after my actions have resulted in something concrete. My aim is to make those guilty of crimes in Chechnya undergo a trial similiar to the one of Milosevic. It is where they belong. And I will probably die with that ring. (silent) Maybe not."

Chechens have been the victims of human rights abuses by the Russian military. Journalists are only allowed to visit Chechnya with permission from the Russian authorities and only in organized groups. Still, journalists have managed to go to Chechnya without permission and document the abuses.

Poland

Anni Lanz

Solidarity Network of the Region of Basel
Frauenrat für Aussenpolitik (Women's Council for Foreign Policy)

Anni Lanz has fought for the rights and dignity of refugees for 20 years. The sociologist (59) lobbies on the political level, helps organize public events, and offers direct help by accompanying people during their visits to officials. She writes their applications and, if necessary, even takes them home with her. After years of sparing no effort the Swiss asylum law recognized the need to take into account "reasons specific to women." In 2004, Anni Lanz was awarded a honorary doctoral degree for her work by the faculty of law of the University of Basel.

Anni Lanz lives and works in Basel. She began in the women's movement and later, in her work with refugees was able to combine both themes. "When I joined the asylum movement in 1986, I faced a dilemma. Women were not an issue in the asylum movement and, in the women's movement, immigrants and refugees were not an issue." She found the bridge in working closely with women refugees and immigrants. As part of her studies in sociology she was a participatory observer working as a waitress. Later, she founded an independent restaurant with like-minded people. There, she got to know Turkish and Kurdish women, and established a self-help project with them. Afterwards, she worked for many years as a political secretary for the organization Solidarité sans frontières (Solidarity without Borders). Anni Lanz has been to the asylum and immigration authorities countless times, with hundreds of people, has filed complaints, made applications, challenged laws — and has also won. Each time, it also was about broadening the interpretation of rules.

After years of struggle, the following sentence was added to the Swiss asylum law: "Reasons of flight specific to women are to be taken into account." There used to be more success; today, there is terribly little tolerance. The biggest problem for refugees in Switzerland is the narrow definition of who is a refugee. For those who are really in danger, Switzerland has become too big a risk.

Anni Lanz has always worked on two levels: on the political level as a lobbyist and street activist, and doing the basic work of accompanying refugees. "That was very important to me, because accompanying people and having direct contact with refugees gives the political work credibility."

Swiss asylum law takes into account reasons specific to women. It also uses the "special victim" argument: asylum seekers must have experienced abuse beyond "local standards." Thus, the more systematically human rights are abused in a country, the less this abuse is grounds for granting asylum.

Switzerland

Leila Linhares Barsted

Cidadania, Estudo, Pesquisa, Informação e Ação (Citizenship, Study, Research, Information and Action)

Leila Linhares Barsted (1945) was studying law when she started her left-wing political militancy. She defended political prisoners that were victims of the military dictatorship in the country. In 1975, she participated in the foundation of Ceres Group, pioneer in the new Brazilian feminism and responsible for the activation of the movement in many Brazilian states. In 1990, she founded the Cepia, a non-governmental organization that acts in the area of women rights.

Raised in a family with three brothers and three sisters, it was the different treatment given by her parents to the boys and the girls that made Leila Linhares realize that men and women were not exactly the same. Leila's involvement with feminism came as an answer to the questions that her political militancy did not solve. "In the battles against the dictatorship, the subject of gender did not appear," she remembers. Many years later, in the first international women's conference, promoted by the UN, it was the subject of violence that touched Leila.

"The relationship between men and women is still marked by violence. Women are victims exclusively because they are women, especially in the cases of sexual violence and in conjugal relationships," she says. Leila is part of the group that helped create the first state councils for the defense in the beginning of the 1980s, when the country started to breathe the airs of re-democratization. Today, she is part of a group of lawyers that elaborates a new proposal of punishment in case of domestic violence. The Brazilian law in vigor foresees soft penalties for male aggressors.

Leila participates in the State Commission of Women's Security, created to monitor and to pressure the government in actions such as the maintenance of shelters for women victims of violence, health care centers and specialized police precincts. At Cepia (Citizenship, Study, Research, Information and Action), her agenda has another fundamental item: the fight to legalize abortion. As the director of the NGO, Leila acts in the Journeys for the Right for Legal and Secure Abortion. She was born in Rio, is a mother of three children and grandmother of a girl. She taught her granddaughter to say a sentence that she considers fundamental: "Men and women have same rights."

The Family Planning Law (1996) recognizes women's rights to contraception and gives them autonomy to decide about sterilization. When this law went into force, around 27% of Brazilian women in reproductive age were sterilized. Leila was one of the women that worked on writing this law.

Brazil

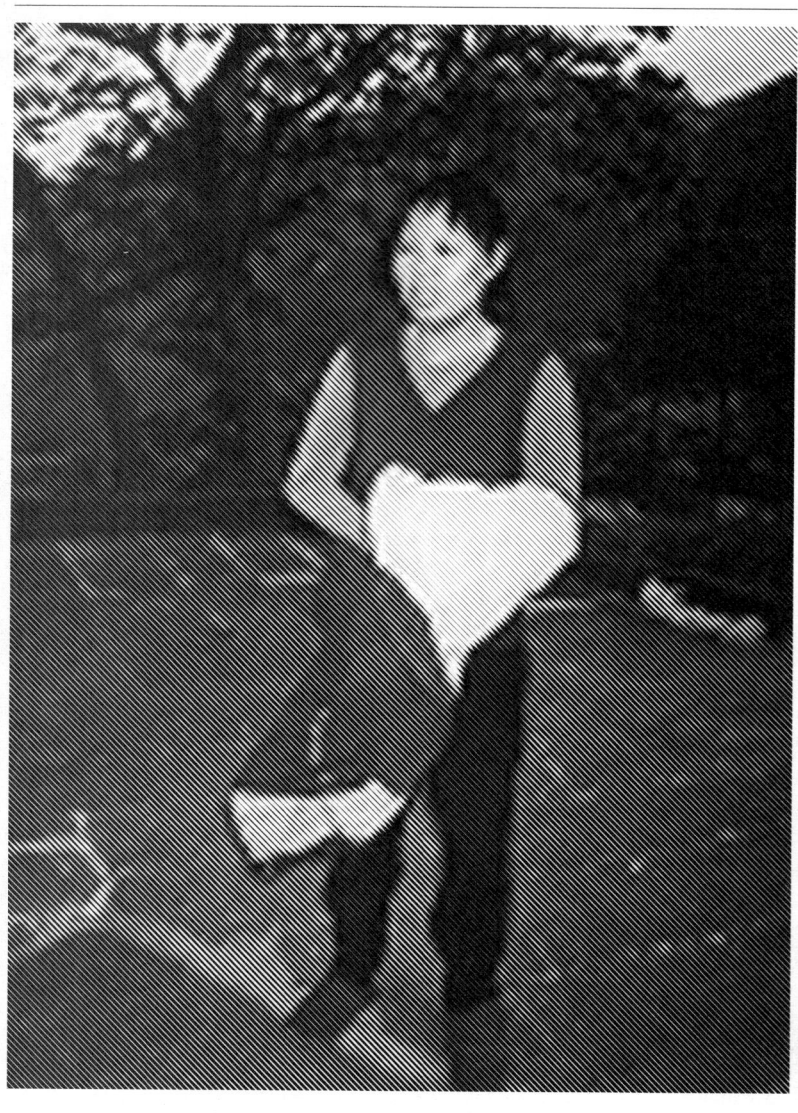

Zhongxun Liu

Born in 1971, Liu Zhongxun grew up in a village beside the Yangtze river. She fights to protect her rights and dignity as a citizen. She resists the unreasonable rules and regulations made by local governments, and brings the local cadres who tyrannize peasants to court. She has no fear of threats, and with law and perseverance, she wins trials. She speaks from a sense of justice for the villagers, and does her best to disseminate knowledge about laws.

Brought up in a village beside the Yangtze river, Liu Zhongxun has learnt the hard way to protect her rights and dignity as a citizen, and to uphold justice. She now spends time talking to the villagers about the importance of law in a system dominated by the will of those in authority.

Liu Zhongxun and her child lived in her parents' home, where she was abused by the village head who intercepted her mail and slapped unreasonable penalties on her. Liu argued with the authorities, but was illegally detained. The township Party secretary was a bully, and he announced publicly, "Nobody, except Party General Secretary Jiang Zemin and Premier Li Peng, can ever have control over me!" But Liu Zhongxun refused to be cowed down.

Using law, she appealed to the higher authorities for help, and asked for administrative reconsideration. She won a partial victory. Liu's family suffered a big loss when the village blasted stones to construct a road. Her three houses were damaged and six pigs died. Instead of proper compensation, Liu Zhongxun got into a lawsuit that lasted several years, and she was treated unfairly. Regardless of the threats, Liu learnt and made use of laws, and persisted till she won the lawsuit.

Because of her activities against abusive local cadres, Liu has had to face retaliation. As defense, she chose to study law. In 2002, a villager named Luo was severely injured by a blast, which was a retaliatory act of the village Party secretary. But no one seemed to be concerned. Liu voluntarily helped Luo to file a lawsuit. By collecting evidence, appealing to different higher authorities for help, they finally won the lawsuit in October 2004. Luo was compensated. Liu's work in the village extends far beyond herself, she represents the efforts of vulnerable sectors to pursue a life of equality and dignity, in a moment of reform and progress in China.

Though there are central government policies and national laws that are in the interest of the peasants and vulnerable groups, they are often not implemented, and peasants suffer from heavy levies of taxes and fines. The law can help to ensure that peasants' rights are protected.

China

"Lady of patience
for PNG women ...
At home, at work, and
in politics, Oh
Lady Los, thank you
for fighting for
our rights in Papua
New Guinea." Eda Walong (2002)

Hilan Los

Individual and Community Rights Advocacy Forum (ICRAF)
Family and Sexual Violence Action Committee
People Against Child Exploitation (PACE)

Hilan Los' work on individual and community rights has resulted in general awareness raising on human rights in Papua New Guinea (PNG), a pool of legal rights trainers being made available in some provinces, some parts of PNG family law being changed, sex workers becoming more aware of their legal and human rights after being abused by clients and law enforcement authorities, and Safe Houses for victims of violence being set up.

"Sometimes I think I am acting like a police detective in my line of work for Individual and Community Rights Advocacy Forum (ICRAF). It is like I am on call all the time. It is a risky job. I get verbal abuse but I have not been physically attacked yet. We try hard not to endanger the lives of our clients and take a low profile approach to our work so that husbands and perpetrators of violence do not connect us directly with the victims of abuse, mostly women and children who seek refuge in our Refuge Center or our unpublicized Safe House.

A young girl sought refuge with us because her relatives in a squatter settlement were fighting over her custody. They told me to mind my own business but I told them the girl was under 18, which meant there were government regulations protecting her rights as a person. Government welfare people then solved this matter of custody and adoption. A husband placed his wife under house arrest after beating her to near death. We had a phone call from a neighbor. We were very cautious and organized to pick her up with the neighbor's help. We cared for her at the Safe House while she sought medical attention and counseling. The longest client we had in the Safe House was a policeman's wife who stayed for one whole year.

There are women out there who are in pain and living in misery. Giving my extra time to assist them helps in a small way and ICRAF as an organization having a mandate to assist is a tool to providing them that needed and important service."

The Individual and Community Rights Advocacy Forum was set up to deal with human rights issues in Papua New Guinea through provision of legal services on human rights and environmental issues, and carry out awareness and educational campaigns to monitor human rights abuses and environmental destruction.

Papua New Guinea

Olga del Valle Márquez de Arédez

Missing Persons of the Department of Ledesma

Olga Márquez was born in Tucumán, a province of Northern Argentina. She married and lived with her husband in Jujuy, a neighboring province. Then, he "was disappeared," by the repressive forces of the Argentinean military dictatorship (1976–1983). Olga organized the resistance movement in Jujuy. Along with the Mothers of the Plaza de Mayo, she was in the vanguard of the fight for truth and justice, which was essential for bringing down the dictators.

In Argentina, the word "mothers" has a powerful symbolic value. The Mothers are the women who, with a raging demand for truth and justice for the missing members of their families, organized a resistance movement against the dictatorship that was terrifying the country (1976–1983). Olga Márquez is one of the Mothers. Her husband is one of the ones who "disappeared."

Olga was born and went to school in Tucumán, a province located in Northwest Argentina. There, she fell in love with a doctor. After their marriage, they moved to Ledesma, in Jujuy, a province that borders Tucumán. This is a region of sugarcane plantations — bitter sugar for the workers who were extremely poor and humiliated. The doctor took care of them and their children. Olga was always at his side. The political situation in the country got worse. One night, in 1976, the lights of the village of Ledesma were extinguished. Olga's husband and hundreds of workers and neighbors were beaten, tortured and imprisoned. After one year, he was liberated for a very brief period. Shortly afterwards he disappeared forever. Olga searched for him in vain. She began, in solitude, the grand march to the main square of Ledesma. But shortly afterwards, she was no longer alone. Hundreds of white handkerchiefs and banners were raised in the plaza: "For our loved ones to appear alive and punishment for the guilty." That was the beginning of the organization Mothers of Jujuy.

Olga continued even through her long illness, a cancer that advanced through her body. In March 2005, she passed away. Her ashes were scattered in front of the Calilegua hills, the place where, as they later discovered, the remains of her husband had been left. The great march goes on. Justice has not yet been reached.

The military coup in Argentina resulted in assassinations, imprisonment, torture and exile. The official amount of missing people is estimated at 30,000. In the Northern province of Jujuy, the owners of the industrial sugarcane plant of Ledesma collaborated in the repression against its workers.

Argentina

Ruchama Marton

Physicians for Human Rights-Israel (PHR-Israel)

Ruchama Marton is a psychiatrist, a psychotherapist and a peace and human rights activist. She is the founder and president of Physicians for Human Rights-Israel (PHR-Israel), a non-profit health and human rights NGO, established in 1988 and based on cooperation between Israeli and Palestinian health professionals and human rights activists. She has been leading the peace movement in Israel, struggling unrelentingly against the Israeli violations of the Palestinians' human rights. In four decades she has also been involved in feminist activities, fighting for a just social order in Israel.

In December 1987, at the outbreak of the First Intifada, Dr Ruchama Marton mobilized a group of Israeli physicians to meet with Palestinians in order to fathom the real conditions of the Palestinians in the Occupied Territories and to build a bridge of peace between the Israelis and the Palestinians. During those days contact with Palestinian Liberation Organization (PLO) members was banned by Israeli law. Ruchama Marton has risked her life both by meeting with Palestinians and by entering the Occupied Territories at the time of the Intifada and exposing herself to Palestinian shooting. Her visit disclosed facts to her that she would not have been able to discover if she hadn't been there. The Israeli army reacted to the Palestinian uprising with an unprecedented level of human rights violations. Collective punishments and brutal actions were perpetrated against the Palestinian population. The Israeli public was being misled and misinformed by its leaders and the media regarding these actions.

Ruchama Marton and her associates drove to the Shifa Governmental Hospital in Gaza. There they saw casualties with multiple fractures of the arms and legs and men unconscious due to clubbing on the head. The hospital reeked of overflowing toilets, bandages stained with blood and puss, and damp and moldy walls; images that do not exist in Israeli hospitals. This visit was the catalyst for the formation of Physicians for Human Rights-Israel (PHR-Israel). For 21 years since 1967, Israel had obstructed the development of the Palestinian civil infrastructure. The Palestinians were therefore dependent on Israel for livelihood, health care and medical treatment. On their way home, Marton's group documented the factual evidence they had seen at first hand. A few months later these rumpled notes came to be the founding basis and ideological ground for the establishment of PHR-Israel.

In 1988, Dr Ruchama Marton founded Physicians for Human Rights-Israel (PHR-Israel), a leading human rights organization that boosts mutual respect and cooperation between Israelis and Palestinians. As its current president, Ruchama Marton works to end the Israeli occupation of Palestine and promote peace.

Israel

Rela Mazali

New Profile Movement for the Civilization of Israeli Society (NPMfCIS)

Rela Mazali, an Israeli writer and feminist activist, is one of the founders of New Profile, an activist group that promotes peace among young Israelis. An outspoken critic of Israeli militarism, Rela has worked for many years to end torture and other human rights violations by Israeli authorities. Since 1980 she has been working at national and international levels on antimilitarism and feminism, especially with regard to the Israel-Palestine conflict. Her strong emphasis on the role of women working towards a demilitarized society is an inspiration to all who work with her.

Rela Mazali is a peace activist, who is networked to some effective peace building groups inside Israel. She is very committed to bringing about peace and tolerance between the Israelis and the Palestinians through mutual understanding and respect. She says, "For the past seven years, I have conducted part of my struggle against militarization with and through a feminist group. We focused on women's position within the context of Israeli militarization, after which we founded New Profile, a feminist antimilitarist group, working to de-militarize the society in Israel. While a number of serious, committed organizations do very important work 'across the lines' to counteract the hatred between Jews and Palestinians, our orientation is 'inwards'. We aim to change the society in which many of us were born and raised, and to readapt the culture that we all share. Our basic tenet is that the existing culture is actively fostering apartheid and inflaming enmity, not simply defending itself against outside aggression. We see this as a result of the deeply rooted mindsets that in turn blind the majority of Israelis from seeing this simple fact. And so we work to raise consciousness regarding this vicious cycle."

The main channels through which Rela Mazali works to counteract it include challenging the militarization of Israeli education, creating public opportunities for discussing and learning about militarization in Israel, and supporting young people, men and women, who refuse to enlist. There is a growing movement of draft resistance in Israel today, and New Profile is providing the young people who are part of it with information as well as moral and emotional support. Mazali says, "most draft resisters start out very isolated, and we put them in touch with each other so they can develop a consciousness of being part of a group."

Rela Mazali is an outspoken critic of Israeli militarism and has been working for many years to end torture and to combat human rights violations by Israeli authorities. She works at national and international levels on antimilitarism and feminism, especially with respect to the Israel-Palestine conflict.

Israel

Nilda Medina-Diaz

Committee for the Rescue and Development of Vieques
Restoration Advisory Board
Military Toxics Project

Nilda Medina-Diaz has dedicated her life to the demilitarization of Vieques. This tiny Puerto Rican island was used by the US Navy for military exercises and weapons training and testing for 63 years. Largely through the work of the Committee for the Rescue and Development of Vieques, cofounded by Nilda, the USA closed its bases in 2003. In addition to coordinating the movement's civil disobedience organizational center, Nilda continues to play a crucial role in the postnavy struggle to ensure that her community is informed and involved in their homeland's environmental cleanup.

Born 1950 in Vega Alta, Puerto Rico, Nilda is the youngest of five children. As a student at the University of Puerto Rico, she began organizing for labor rights and was regional coordinator for the Puerto Rican Socialist Party during the 1970s. Armed with a certificate to teach science — and fierce determination — she moved to Vieques in 1980.

In December 2000, Nilda and other members of the Committee for the Rescue and Development of Vieques placed themselves in front of huge navy tractors to block yet another military action. Riot police arriving at the scene were well equipped with dogs, pepper spray, and handcuffs. But when a large group of community members joined the protesters, the police withdrew. Scenes such as these were common in the battles Nilda fought with and for the citizens of Vieques. Leading the struggle for "the four Ds" (demilitarization, decontamination, devolution, and development), members of the Committee often put themselves in harm's way.

Her work has not ended with the withdrawal of the US military. As a member of the Restoration Advisory Board, she reviews and reports on the military cleanup. She organizes community forums, independent expert evaluation of the progress of the cleanup, activities for teen mothers, and leadership opportunities for the local youth organization. She helps to resolve transportation issues for families with loved ones in hospital or in prison. and arranges legal representation for Viequenses who have been arrested by the US Fish and Wildlife Service for using ex-military lands for community functions. She is a coordinator of "Radio Vieques", a weekly radio program and a vital service for a community that has no newspaper. To help similar communities dealing with problems left by military bases, Nilda serves on the Board of the Military Toxics Project.

Many problems remain in Vieques. The land has not been returned to the people of Puerto Rico; rather, it has been transferred to the US Fish and Wildlife Service, in order to assess environmental damage. So far, the USA has allocated only a small portion of the money needed for the cleanup.

Puerto Rico

Guadalupe Mejía Delgado

Comité de Familiares de Víctimas de las Violaciones de Derechos Humanos de El Salvador Marianella Garcia Villas (Codefam)

She is a woman of the countryside, affable and sensible. Who could guess that behind her serene appearance there is a personal history of pain and loss? Defender of human rights for 22 years, her courage and determination have allowed her to open the doors of prisons and military barracks, achieving freedom for people who were opposed to the regime, during the Salvadoran Civil War (1980–1992). Thirteen years after the signing of the peace agreement, she still works for justice and truth, asking, "Where are the missing people?" She is Guadalupe Mejía, an untiring seeker of peace.

Guadalupe Mejía is a rural woman, born and raised in the canton of La Ceiba, in the municipality of Las Vueltas, in the administrative district of Chalatenango, in the North of El Salvador. She married, when she was barely 17 years old. With her husband, she found love, and their nine sons and daughters were born as a product of that love. Her husband was a farmer, politically and socially aware, who taught her a way of life that she would never abandon: to defend life in the midst of a poor and repressed society. When he was murdered in 1977, Guadalupe continued the fight that he had begun.

Frail and unsophisticated as she was, from that moment on, life was uncertain for herself and her children. In 1980, the civil war began and the repression grew more intense each day. In 1983, she moved to the city of San Salvador to direct the Marianella Garcia Villas Committee of Relatives of Victims of Human Rights Violations in El Salvador (Codefam), which was born two years before that. She went to prisons and military barracks with only a basic knowledge of the penal code. Nevertheless, she managed to rescue nearly 1500 people from the claws of the security forces who had always been skillful in making the people opposed to the regime disappear. The war ended in 1992. Nowadays, she still works for the Marianella Garcia Villas Committee of Relatives of Victims of Human Rights Violations in El Salvador. Now, as she did 22 years ago, she denounces the State and accuses it of hiding behind the veil of an amnesty law to evade answering the question that the families of the missing ones always ask: "Where are they?"

At age 60, she continues her work with a smile. "Peace will only be a reality on the day the truth is known, when violence has ended, and there is bread for everyone."

Between 1980 and 1992, El Salvador went through a civil war during which the security forces, the military and paramilitary forces, protected by the State, captured and made disappear nearly 7000 people. An amnesty law left those crimes unpunished and impeded justice.

El Salvador

Angélica Mendoza Almeida

Asociación Nacional de Familiares de Secuestrados,
Detenidos y Desaparecidos del Perú (Anfasep)

Angélica Mendoza Almeida is a native of Ayacucho, Peru. She has been looking for her son Arquímedes for the past 22 years. He was kidnapped by the military during a dark and bloody period in Peru's history. Through her fight for the disappeared, she formed an organization called Anfasep. Former president Alberto Fujimori accused her of being a terrorist. She had to live clandestinely for some time. She has traveled around the world denouncing what happened. Today, 77 years old, her greatest fear is to die not knowing Arquímedes' whereabouts.

Angélica Mendoza Almeida is a Quechua-speaking woman, born in Ayacucho, Peru. She has happy memories from her childhood: beautiful houses and tranquil landscapes. When she was 18, as is the custom, her mother arranged her marriage. Her husband was a teacher in the village. He was ten years older than she was. They had ten children, including Arquímedes, but Angélica has not seen him during the past 22 years, because he was kidnapped by the military. Ayacucho became a place besieged by the regular army and by the Sendero Luminoso. Arquímedes was 19 when he was taken against his will, in 1983. She looked for him at the military barracks. A piece of paper, written in his own handwriting, sent from the military barracks in Cabito, gave her hope: "Mother, I am here in the barracks, my case is becoming more complicated; please persist in asking about me at the barracks every day." After that, she never heard from him again.

Meeting other mothers, all of them experiencing the same situation, led her to found the National Association of the Relatives of Kidnapped, Imprisoned and Missing People of Peru (Anfasep). This organization has been, and still is, demanding answers about the whereabouts of the disappeared. In 1992, Former President Alberto Fujimori accused her of being a terrorist. She was persecuted because of it. She lived clandestinely, but she was captured two years later. She was liberated because they could never prove that she had committed any crime. When the Commission for Truth was installed in 2001, Angélica was there to give her testimony. She continues to look for her son knowing that she is not alone and that her fight is not a private one. She knows that truth and justice are necessary in order to achieve peace.

Since 1980, the Sendero Luminoso, as well as the Peruvian Army, have turned Ayacucho into a war zone. In 2001, the Commission for Truth investigated 20 years of violence in the country. During this period, 69,000 people were murdered or disappeared.

Peru

Ana Montenegro

Ana Montenegro (1915) has been a communist militant since her youth. She was part of the creation of many female organizations. With the military coup of 1964, she went into exile with her two small children. After 15 years, she came back to her country to continue her battle. As a lawyer, she helped, for free, women suffering with domestic violence. Journalist, writer and a poet, she is an unmistakable reference in the recent history of Brazilian social struggles.

1945 was not just any year. It celebrated the end of the Second World War and of one more Brazilian dictatorship, of Getúlio Vargas' government. It was an interesting year: against fascisms and massacres, in favor of freedom and human rights. It was also the year when Ana Montenegro affiliated herself to the Brazilian Communist Party. Ana wrote for the party's newspapers and magazines. She also wrote for the radio and for diaries of the great press, about health, salaries, education. She was part of the foundation and the daily life of women and social organizations. She is a lawyer convinced that the people are the great master. Today, at age 90, she advises young lawyers "to be sensitive to popular needs."

In 1964, with the tanks on the streets and the military truculence on its way, Ana left for a long exile. But she did not stop. Ana walked around Mexico, Cuba, Chile, Palestine, Eastern Germany. The distance allowed her to improve her thoughts on Brazil. The fight against racism and for women became primary to her. With the amnesty in 1979, Ana came back to do what she has always done: popular mobilization and agitation. She supported "invasions" of neighborhoods of the outskirts of the city of Salvador. She fought alongside underprivileged residents of the Historical Center of Pelourinho, when the region was dominated by real estate speculation.

The participation of women in political parties has not yet been rightfully recognized. Along with Ana Montenegro, hundreds of women have occupied and still occupy important positions in the parties. They deserve larger visibility.

Brazil

Alma Montenegro de Fletcher

Attorney for the Administration

When Alma Montenegro de Fletcher was 11 years old, she taught her first pupil: her mother. She studied for a Law degree because she wanted justice for everyone. Before she accepted the post as Tutelary Judge of Minors, she learned everything the Faculty of Law did not teach her during her studies. She studied even more when she was nominated as Attorney for the Administration. After the USA's invasion in 1989, she became involved with the National Commission for Reconciliation.

"The pot was huge: The milk, oats and 'guinea' boiled inside it. That was the food for the day: My father's wages were poor and our family was big. There were 12 children." When Alma Montenegro was 11 years old, she studied to be a teacher. "Then, I discovered a secret. My mother was illiterate. 'Come on, I will teach you,' I said, but she resisted. I insisted until I caught her interest saying: 'You will see how nice it is to learn to write your own name.' Today, being 70 years old, I can tell you that my mother was my first pupil."

"I always wanted justice for all people and, therefore, I began to study Law. Later on, I realized that justice does not always take the same path as the Law, but I still graduated in 1961." She worked as Tutelary Judge of Minors. Since 1995, she has worked as Attorney for the Administration.

"Never forget December 20th, 1989" is written on a wall in the capital city. That was the date of the American invasion of the country. When the National Commission for Reconciliation was formed, Alma joined it. "The final report recommended clarification of the amount of people who had died and that the Americans should leave." They finally left in June, 1990. "There has not yet been any justice for the people who died."

"Are you sure?" asked the instructor for the third time. The young man kept asking the same question because he did not know the life history of Alma Montenegro, the 60 year old woman who stood in front of him. "Yes!" she answered impatiently. "Then, you have to run, run fast and hold on very tight," said the instructor. "I ran very fast until I had no ground under my feet and then I was flying! Do you know how much I had wanted to fly? Justice will also arrive, even if we are the last ones to receive it."

In 1943, what is now the institution of the Attorney of the Administration was created. Since the beginning, it was weak, without any organic body to guide it. The building where it was housed was known as "the mousetrap." It had more than enough darkness and was short of ventilation.

Panama

Hilda Marina Morales Trujillo

A woman of contrasts. Brave in confronting struggles. Sympathetic. Wise. Serene, as she meditates on what to do. Of solid principles and strong roots. An Ambassador of Conscience. Gentle like the breeze. Persistent. Disapproving of exaggeration. A life full of obstacles in the search for justice. 61 years of hard work against the current tide. Hilda Marina Morales Trujillo, Guatemalan, dreams of a world with equal opportunities for women and men.

A skilled coordinator and negotiator in her search for fairness. She fights with the law in her hands. Lawyer, mother, woman of high ideals, defender of human rights, deep, incorruptible. For Hilda Marina Morales Trujillo (61), peace is a daily task. "Women began to construct peace through continuous dialogue. It can be reached through development and will be achieved, not when it is merely the letter of the law, but when women and men actually have the same opportunities." She dreams of a world where problems are solved through dialogue, where "women can walk safely on the streets, without the fear of being robbed, raped or murdered," where public policies "will include provisions for young people, where women will be supported with more employment opportunities, with access to justice, training, the right to learn to write and read, and the right to have an education."
Her murdered brother, all the "missing" university students and a friend from her adolescence, who was tortured: all of them still live inside her.
Her words come slowly. "Violence is the responsibility of the State. It is necessary to pursue the campaign so that no more women will be murdered. We must have the courage to denunciate. We must bring life to the ideal of justice."

Sexual crimes committed against women in Guatemala are liable to be forgiven, or resolved by negotiation. The women, raped and abused, are coerced into marrying their attackers in order to avoid judicial procedures. The aggressors can therefore be freed from culpability and charges.

Guatemala

Anne-Marie Mukwayanzo Mpundu

Fondation des femmes chrétiennes et démocrates pour le développement (Fcdd)

Anne-Marie Mukwayanzo Mpundu (48) fights destructive values that enslave women in the Democratic Republic of the Congo (DRC). She chairs the Christian Women Organisation for Democracy and Development (Fcdd). She uses a personal approach, local languages to provide information on human rights and justice protection. She actively participates in preventing violence and discrimination and educates on peace and reconciliation in the community.

Anne-Marie Mukwayanzo Mpundu holds a degree in international relations. She has also attended training on conflict management and human rights, specializing in women's rights and on gender and sustainable development. Fcdd, formed 14 years ago, fights against destructive values, promoting the economic and political rehabilitation of women in the DRC, and building the capacity for self-sufficiency. Anne-Marie is a mother of six children and an activist who for the better part of 22 years has argued that women, the illiterate majority, live in ignorance of their fundamental rights, withstanding difficult conditions that hamper their ability to be informed and improve their lives. The women lack empowerment and social peace. Her conviction is that improving womens' status in society is possible, first by women themselves and then through the judicial system. As part of an extended network, she campaigns for WomenAction and works against violence against women and educates on peace culture. She coordinates Recic, a civic education organisation. Her energy comes from her faith in God whom, she believes, created men and women, all equal in rights and dignity. It also comes from other women, adhering to the fight and showing that unity is power; and it comes from women who have benefited from her struggle to awaken their conscience, now independently managing their own association.

The DRC is rising out of an eight-year war. Warlords now share power but the fighting continues. In some regions women are still raped and exploited. The socio-economic situation is worsening. Reconciliation among fighting factions and even among the people has not been fruitful.

Democratic Republic of the Congo

Asiyat Murtazalieva

Memorial

Asiyat Murtazalieva (born 1955) earned a degree in Philology. She has worked as a journalist in many Chechen and Moscow newspapers. Asiyat launched the creation of the Chechen cultural clubs Harmony and Treasure of the Nation to contribute to healing the wounds of the war. She works at the Institute of Human Culture; she is also coordinator of the all-Russian contest Personality of 20th Century Russian History. Her recent cooperation with the Russian NGO Memorial focuses on uncovering violations of human rights in Chechnya and war crimes perpetrated against civilians.

For Asiyat Murtazalieva, journalism is a way to help people. Once, Asiyat wrote a revealing article in the newspaper "Respublika" about the local influential leader of a criminal group. When the article was published, he threatened to sue her, knowing that he could easily bribe the local judges. The directors of the newspaper decided to back down and to publish an apology. But Asiyat did not allow the apology to be published and insisted that the matter be brought to court, hoping for a fair trial despite everything else. The trial lasted for almost a year. The judges at the court of first instance, bribed by the plaintiff, sided with the latter and found Asiyat guilty. But rather than give up, she filed an appeal against the verdict with the Supreme Court of the Chechen Republic. The result was the same. Although her colleagues advised her to resign herself to this outcome, her search for justice took her to Moscow, as she understood that the local judicial system was corrupt to the core. The criminal leader, sensing the woman's unbending spirit, decided to stop all the legal proceedings.

When the Russian-Chechen war began (1994), the subject of war crimes against innocent civilians became vitally important to Asiyat's work. She wrote about the victims of carpet bombings, about the inhuman tortures, and executions without trial. The dream of this journalist is to re-launch her cultural club's publication "Harmony." The magazine used to come out before the Russian-Chechen war, but its publication was stopped because of the armed conflict. Asiyat hopes that the magazine, dedicated to the cultural values of the Chechen people, will promote a better understanding of the Chechen problem in Russia which, in turn, could start healing the wounds of the war.

Asiyat Murtazalieva, working as a journalist and in cooperation with the Russian NGO Memorial, writes about the violation of human rights in Chechnya and about war crimes against civilians. Her energy and commitment give people hope for justice in this war-scarred country.

Russian Federation

Chinchuluun Naidandorj

Women Lawyers' Association
Mongolian Women's Fund (Mones)

As a child, Chinchuluun Naidandorj dreamt of following in her painter-sculptor father's footsteps. Later, she graduated in law from the Mongolian National University and now holds perhaps the most vital women NGO position in Mongolia as head of the Mongolian Women's Fund (Mones) initiated by her in 2000. Previously she had succeeded in making the Women Lawyers' Association, of which she was executive director, a powerful organization. She is founder of the Human Rights & Development Centre (1998), a leading civil society organisation in Mongolia.

After Chinchuluun Naidandorj, at that time 18 years old, had failed her university entrance exams in 1975, her mother found her a technical job in the archives of the former ministry of public security. Three years of work taught her discipline and self-control. In 1979 she became a student of jurisprudence at the then Mongolian State University. Graduating from there with a lawyer's diploma, she was appointed a judge in a rural area. Today Chinchuluun occupies one of the most important positions in Mongolia as the director of Mones. Purevsuren D., program coordinator of the fund, is proud of Chinculuun's efforts. "The fund awarded grants to 28 projects out of 54 applications in 2004. The total of 2004 grants equals almost 21 million tugriks." By now more than 30,000 persons and 87 projects have received financial support from the fund. In an interview Chinchuluun said: "To live in an honorable, responsible way, and try to change what disturbs me, beginning with what I definitely can do, this is my aim." This is proven by her actions. Chinchuluun has also been in the forefront of the campaign to ratify and join the International Criminal Court. In recent years she has been team leader in 12 major projects financed by international organizations. Of particular importance was, among others, the project on documentation of human rights violations in Mongolia. She is also a leading expert in human and women's rights and was the first to start nationwide juridical consultations for women. She initiated and led a series of campaigns for taking legislative measures against family violence, which after seven years culminated in the adoption of a law on domestic violence by the Mongolian Parliament.

Fundraising within Mongolia with its poor economy is a challenging task. While pop groups and rock singers can get funds, others find it difficult. This is why the setting up of the Mongolian Women's Fund was such a bold initiative.

New Territories Female Indigenous Residents' Committee

Hong Kong Federation of Women's Centres

Formed in October 1993, the New Territories Female Indigenous Residents' Committee (Ntfirc) was active in the 1994 campaign to abolish the discriminatory ordinance on women's rights to inherit property in the New Territories. Along with other groups, they encouraged their sisters to fight for their rights, using peaceful means, like signing petitions and singing songs, to lobby for public support. The success of the campaign has not only guaranteed their civic rights, it has also contributed to the women's and civil society movements.

In 1994, the Ntfirc held peaceful negotiations with the government, legislators and conservative, powerful men of the New Territories to campaign for the abolition of the discriminatory part of the New Territories ordinance, that ruled out the rights of women to inherit land and property. For this Ntfirc members were victimized and labeled traitors. A village head, for example, refused to sign the papers that Tang Ying, an Ntfirc member, needed to have access to her mother's grave site. Since she had no rights as a daughter to bury her mother back in the village, Tang had to beg the village head to do so. She was threatened with violence because she criticized the old disciminatory customs against women. Under the auspices of Ntfirc women came together to demand their rights. They included women like the 73-year-old Tang Yuen Tai, who joined the campaign because she did not want the next generation to be victimized by this customary rule of inheritance. There was much opposition, sometimes threats, and even violence from their fellow males. To counter this the indigenous women organized a signature campaign in forty walled villages to secure support from the indigenous community. In order to create public attention, they organized demonstrations, seminars and exhibitions, and wrote traditional songs and dramas in the Hakka dialect that spoke of how indigenous women suffered under the discriminatory custom. The women's perseverance and fighting spirit was the main reason for the success of the campaign, which later included favorable legislative changes and the consolidation of different social forces, particularly the participating women's organizations.

Indigenous women from the New Territories were not permitted to inherit land and property after the death of their fathers or other ancestors, according to the old customs inherited from China's Qing dynasty and the New Territories ordinance inherited from colonial Hong Kong.

China, Hong Kong SAR

Mame Bassine Niang

Mame Bassine Niang was born in Tambacounda in eastern Senegal. She (53) is Minister and High Commissioner for Human Rights and the Promotion of Peace to the Presidency of the Republic of Senegal. She began managing Unesco clubs in high schools and colleges, absorbing the ideals of peace and tolerance, and the principles of civic life. For example, in the Lycée John F. Kennedy in Dakar, she headed a project for girl students aimed at spreading civic virtues and solidarity through theater and poetry.

"A certain event influenced me greatly when I was a little girl. I once overheard one of my father's councilors trying to convince him to put an end to my studies at secondary level. He argued that this was necessary to avoid the possibility of my being intellectually superior to my brothers, a situation that might upset the rights of succession and the traditional order. This profoundly wounded the little girl I was at the time."

Mame Bassine Niang, who would some day become one of the most brilliant legal specialists of her generation, also almost suffered a dreadful fate. Among the many ethnic groups living at her father's court, there were some who practiced female circumcision. As a young woman moved by friendship and compassion, Mame Bassine thought it was her duty to share this ordeal with her friends. She was kept from doing so only by the vigilance and energetic intervention of members of the household. This experience was the origin of her ferocious battle against female genital mutilation.

Her life story makes one think that the term "pioneer" was part of her destiny from the start. She was the first woman Laureate of French-language Bar Associations, the first woman to be admitted to the Bar Association of Senegal and the first woman among the founders of the first League of Human Rights in West Africa (ONDH). She was the first African woman member of the International Office and the Executive Council of the International Federation of Human Rights (FIDH) which is based in Paris, and the Founding and Honorary President of the International Union of Human Rights (UIDH), which has its seat in Ouagadougou. Moreover, she was the first Senegalese woman Minister High Commissioner for Human Rights and Peace Promotion.

Mame Bassine Niang, underlines the commitment of Senegal in the crusade against poverty. This commitment has been materialized by the adoption of the Poverty Reduction Strategic Paper that serves as a compass for all interventions of the State of Senegal in this domain.

Senegal

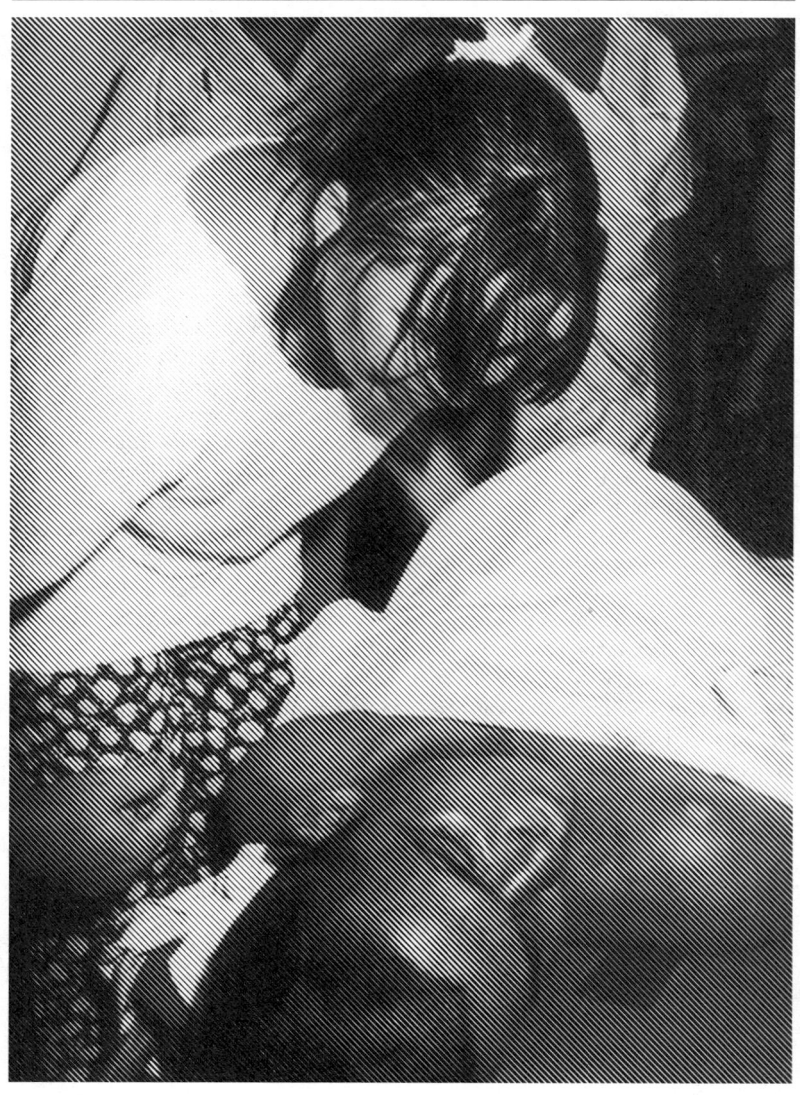

María Ramona Isabel Noguera Dominguez

Association of Relatives of Victims of Mandatory Military Service

Life smiled on María Ramona Noguera, a seamstress, like many others, until one day, in 1996, when her first-born was given back to her, dead (photo). He was delivered to her by his commanders from the unit of the Paraguayan Armed Forces where he was carrying out his mandatory military service. Natural death, they said. It was a lie. The cause of death was torture. From that moment on, she swore that if it was up to her, no mother would shed tears for the death of a son in a military unit ever again.

María Ramona Noguera, whose profession is dressmaking, has become an institution inside the Military Units where young Paraguayans carry out their military service. "Ña María" — as she is known — went through the painful experience of losing a son in doubtful circumstances inside the Armed Forces. From that moment on, she started to fight for other soldiers. She promised that they would never be victims of violence within a military enclosure. "My life was going on calmly and normally, like anyone else's. I had three other children and, in spite of my position as head of a household, my profession allowed us to live without difficulty. But something changed when one morning I got a phone call from the Major of the Military Unit where my son was carrying out his mandatory military service. He told me that on that morning, they had found my son dead in his bed."
From that moment on, María planted herself in front of the military authorities to denounce the doubtful circumstances of the death of her first born child. She also brought his case to the public's attention. She took his body so that a scientific autopsy could be performed. The result was that he had died due to torture. "My son's death marked the beginning of this journey, this campaign." Along with a small group of mothers, she founded the Association of Relatives of Victims of Mandatory Military Service to support young conscripts, in order to prevent maltreatment and death inside the Armed Forces.

In the barracks of the Paraguayan Armed Forces, young boys carrying out their military service are victims of violence. Many are delivered to their families, dead or victims of maltreatment. In 1996, a group of mothers formed the Association of Relatives of Victims of Mandatory Military Service.

Paraguay

"Every time I set
free political prisoners
and they left the
prison to be reunited
with their families,
it moved me deeply.
Especially as I, myself,
have also been a
political prisoner."

Vilma Núñez de Escorcia

Nicaraguan Center for Human Rights
International Federation for Human Rights
Worldwide Organization against Torture

It was the experience of seeing her father imprisoned during the dictatorship of Anastasio Somoza that led Vilma Núñez de Escorcia to become a lawyer for oppositionist politicians, even though, this meant that, later on, she herself would be arrested. As people have looked down on her for being born outside wedlock, she defends everybody who suffers discrimination.

Vilma Núñez de Escorcia started as a lawyer defending political opponents of the Somoza dictatorship in 1965, and had the great satisfaction of liberating most of them, even though she was also imprisoned, as her father had been before. The nights she remembers from her childhood, when the National Guard would go round to the house looking for her father, finally taking him away; the injustices she perceived even when she was still too young to understand them — all led her to choose her career while she was still in her teens. "I did not want anybody else to have to go through what I had suffered. I put myself in the place of the people being pursued and discriminated against, and I opted to take on their defense." She has been fighting for the cause of human rights, for more than 45 years. She has mediated political conflicts, freed hostages and popular freedom fighters, and she has also taken on the defense of those same people who had arrested and tortured her.

Vilma Núñez de Escorcia is President of the Nicaraguan Centre for Human Rights, which she founded in 1990. She was also President of the Central American Commission for Human Rights, from 1990 to 1994; she integrated the Board of Directors of the Worldwide Organization against Torture, from 1992 to 2000; and has been vice-president of the International Federation for Human Rights since then. She has gained innumerous national and international recognitions. She herself only captured one man, 41 years ago. "He is my husband, my admirer and my supporting strength." She has a daughter, a son, four grandchildren, and one truth: "The tears of satisfaction that people shed, when we make an injustice right, are the energy that drives me."

After 1936, Anastasio Somoza imposed decades of dictatorship in Nicaragua. In 1979, a revolutionary government arrived, remaining in power until 1990. Since then, there has been a series of conservative administrations, violating individual guarantees.

Nicaragua

Elizabeth Odio Benito

International Criminal Court in The Hague (ICC)

Elizabeth Odio Benito is vice-president of the International Criminal Court in the Dutch city of The Hague. The Costa Rican law professor was one of the few female judges of the UN court in the former Yugoslavia, where she made a decisive contribution so that war crimes against women, especially rape and other forms of sexual violence, would no longer be treated as small affairs. Thanks to her commitment and that of other women, the Criminal Court's statutes now include forms of sexual violence, rape, sexual slavery, forced prostitution, and others as war crimes and crimes against humanity.

Elizabeth Odio Benito is a former law professor, former secretary of justice of Costa Rica, former judge of the UN court on former Yugoslavia. Since 2003 she has been vice president of the International Criminal Court in The Hague. "My dream is to achieve peace and justice for all and equality for women," she says in her office. "When many people pull in the same direction, you are no longer alone." That is true for her as well as for the presence of women in international legal history. When judges for the ICC were to be elected, international jurists from the NGO Women's Caucus for Gender Justice made sure that the ICC member states put forward enough female candidates. Without this campaign, the world's highest court would have been a men's club. However, now seven of the 18 judges are women. Nevertheless, the election of Elizabeth Odio Benito was not free of obstacles. Her country's head of state was unwilling to support her candidacy, perhaps due to a personal desire for revenge. However, Mireya Moscoso, then president of Panama, jumped in and recommended the candidate along with numerous Latin American women's organizations.

She was supported in part because she had always supported women. As judge of the UN court in former Yugoslavia, she discovered that a Bosnian Serb was not going to be accused of sexual violence despite compelling evidence — he was later sentenced to 20 years in prison for the torture and death of Muslim women and men. Elizabeth Odio Benito undertook an unusual step. "Do not forget the women!" she said publicly to head prosecutor Richard Goldstone, and this was broadcasted worldwide by CNN and other means of media. "As a judge you should not really do something like that," she laughed. "That is the job of the public prosecutor, but I did it anyway." And it worked.

For the first time in the history of humankind, it is possible for potential war criminals to be deterred by the threat of punishment from the International Criminal Court. Women hope that the epidemic of sexual violence, which is part of practically all wars, can finally be stopped.

Costa Rica

Maite Pagazaurtundúa

Basta Ya
Foundation for Victims of Terrorism (FVT)
Socialist Party

Maite Pagazaurtundúa is a Basque philologist and politician. She has been a socialist member of the Basque Parliament and is now a local councilor at Urnieta (Guipuzcoa). In 2000, she was one of the founders of Basta Ya, (Enough is Enough!), a social movement that leads civic opposition to both ETA's separatist terrorism and radical nationalism in the Basque Country. She is also Vice President of the Foundation for Victims of Terrorism (FVT), herself being a victim of terrorism since her brother was killed by ETA.

In the mid-1980s, university student Maite Pagazaurtundúa committed herself to peacefully fight ETA's violence and to build a better future for the Basque Country. She joined the Socialist Party and soon started a political career that led her to be a member of the Basque Parliament and local councilor in Urnieta (Guipuzcoa).

In 1998, the Lizarra Agreement radicalized the governing nationalists, followed by a 14-month long truce by ETA. "An atmosphere of corrupted values," in Maite's opinion, that was rooted in "the idea that only Basque nationalists are Basques, an idea that is at the heart of identity fanaticism." When ETA became active again, non-nationalist Basques felt marginalized and unprotected by regional institutions. Hundreds of them were threatened with death, as Maite Pagazaurtundúa is still today. In 2000, she was one of the founders of Basta Ya, a civic group that aims to peacefully end terrorism. "One of Basta Ya's main achievements is a deeper and more correct analysis of Basque separatist terrorism," she points out. "We have underlined the need to stop being silent about violence." Basta Ya's actions progressively achieved more success. Many Basques started to assemble on the streets and protest against ETA. But in the meantime, some of Maite's friends were killed by armed groups, as was her brother in February 2003. A shock that strengthened her commitment: "I saw clearly that fighting for freedom and the democratic front were the most important things," she says. Maite Pagazaurtundúa has become one of Basta Ya's leaders, acting at a regional, national, and international level. Now she hopes to see the end of terrorism, but also a "moral regeneration" of her fellow citizens and the deradicalization of all Basque nationalism, that she blames for having deepened the social conflict in her homeland.

The armed organization ETA (Basque Country and Freedom) started its violent upheaval to achieve Basque independence from Spain in 1959. Since then, and despite the fact that Basques were given wide autonomy in 1979, ETA has killed hundreds of people, and forced some 200,000 into exile.

Spain

Landon Pearson

Children Learning for Living
Canadian Council on Children and Youth
Canadian Coalition for the Rights of Children

Landon Pearson (born 1930) has been actively involved with children and issues associated with young people for more than 40 years. A Canadian parliamentarian, Landon works for the protection and promotion of children's rights, primarily in national and international contexts. She was instrumental in driving Canada's foreign policy on child labor, war-affected children, and the commercial sexual exploitation of children. In addition to numerous articles on child development and policy questions, she wrote "Children of Glasnost: Growing up Soviet".

Landon had a happy, middle-class childhood. She recalls the only mention of the dismal plight of other children around the world coming from her grandmother. Sometimes, when Landon refused to eat her dinner, her grandmother would admonish, "Remember the starving Armenians!" Landon, in retrospect, realizes that this first glimpse into the lives of less fortunate children did not have much of an impact on her. "My childhood imagination could not grasp that these were children just like me. All I knew was that they were creatures I should feel sorry for. The vocabulary of the time did not include the human rights of children. So I never thought of children in that context." Later in life, that perspective changed.

As the wife of diplomat Geoffrey Pearson, Landon and her family traveled from Canada to France, then to Mexico, then to India, and finally to the Soviet Union. For the first time, observing life's conditions through the eyes of her own children, she gained firsthand insight into the needs of children. "Then the starving children my grandmother told me to pity (but never taught me how to help) became young persons whose rights to survival and protection had been trampled upon, young persons with whom I could now identify and with whom I could work in partnership so that together we could find solutions to their problems." In the USSR, she visited almost every republic to conduct research on all aspects of Soviet children's lives and development. It would be the beginning of her lifelong dedication to advocating for human rights on behalf of children.

From the extermination camps of Europe to the famines of Biafra and the killing grounds of Rwanda, the 20th century wrote some of the most grim chapters in the history of children's suffering.

Canada

Martha Pelloni

The Santa Teresa Foundation

Martha Pelloni is an Argentinian nun who has dedicated her life to sowing tiny seeds. She leaves them in the souls of the people she fights for and of the people she has taught to fight. She knows that from these seeds, trees will grow and that these trees will bear fruit. She has many times moved enormous mountains with her faith — for example, when she suffered from cancer or when she challenged the impunity with which a little girl was raped and murdered in the province of Catamarca. Her fight, daily and untiring, has not stopped for two decades.

Very early in the mornings, before she puts on her habit, nun Martha Pelloni opens the window in her room. When she was a child, her father told her: "You have to open the window and see the light of the day." And that is what she does: she sees the first rays of daylight striking the city. "I think that every morning is a resurrection," Martha often says. She practices what she preaches: she is herself the resurrection of the message of the love of Jesus. Day after day, Martha Pelloni lights a candle in the shadow.

She became well-known in her native Argentina because of the case of a young girl raped and murdered in the Argentinian province of Catamarca, in 1990. The murderers were related to the governor of the province. The authorities, therefore, failed to prosecute. Martha did not accept this impunity. She wanted justice. She organized people, going on the first demonstration with the victim's friends and classmates; they went on, marching along the streets of the province. Then, the fathers and mothers of the children joined them. Later on, they won the support of the people of different communities until the entire population took to the streets with Martha Pelloni. "Up to 30,000 participated in the marches that took place, week after week, for months." And justice prevailed.

Since then, Martha Pelloni has not stopped marching. The light of her candle is still burning.

Argentinian people from the poorest backgrounds are likely to suffer from continuous abuse from, for example, those who organize childhood prostitution or the illegal sale of human organs. The State institutions are corrupt, this prevents the judicial process from being used against such crimes.

Argentina

Sueli Pereira Pini

Juizado Especial Central Cível e Criminal da Comarca de Macapá

Sueli Pereira Pini (born 1960) is a judge of law and coordinator of the Juizado Especial Central Cível e Criminal da Comarca de Macapá (Special Civil Court of Macapá), the capital of Amapá. Her work is of great relevance since it helps guarantee universal access to justice. She is ahead of innovative projects. Among them is the "itinerant justice" — a project that helps citizens in public squares, in extremely poor neighborhoods, in places hidden in the forest. She also develops the Preventive Justice at School Program.

Sueli Pereira Pini's philosophy is very clear: "Justice is there to be made." But how can this service be rendered in settlements spread throughout the forest? Well, if the people cannot go to justice, justice will come to them. The road that leads the court with the judge inside of it is the river. Torrential and fanciful, the Amazon River navigates the boat that makes stops in every settlement. The Ribeirinhos (people who live near the river) line up and wait for their turn to talk to Judge Sueli. She listens to everyone who comes to the fluvial courtroom. They want to solve conflicts or they want to have access to their basic rights as citizens, for example, to get their birth certificates.

Sueli does not only work in the boat. She also works in the miserable districts of Macapá. She demands infrastructural improvements from the mayor. She writes official letters claiming for everything that is of their right. "In order to pay the salary of public servants, the State takes away food from the mouths of many people. We have the obligation to do our work and to do it well." For Sueli Pereira Pini, a true judicial reform has to begin with the judges' attitude: "More important than giving a verdict is seeking a negotiation between the parties involved. More important than analyzing the paper work of the case is listening to the people."

Mother of six children, she jumps out of bed very early and goes to work. She argues that inclusion is the most efficient way to minimize violence. She believes that justice needs essentially to be preventive. Sueli and her team go to classrooms. They talk about the judiciary's role, about the importance of human rights, and especially about the efficiency of dialogue in the resolution of conflicts.

The state of Amapá, in the north of Brazil, has the biggest forest reserve in the world. Its population, of less than 600,000 inhabitants, is spread throughout more than 142,000 square kilometers. People face isolation and employment problems, and also the lack of infrastructure and social equipments.

Brazil

Silvia Pimentel

Comitê Latino-americano e do Caribe para a Defesa dos Direitos da Mulher
(National Section of the Latin American and Caribbean Committee for the
Defense of Women's Rights)

For 30 years, Silvia Pimentel (1940) has been fighting social and legal inequalities against women. Holding a degree in law, she faces controversial issues such as domestic violence, trafficking of girls and women, homosexuality and abortion. With feminist Florisa Verucci, she drew up the New Women's Civil Statute, which was incorporated into the new Brazilian Civil Code, in 2002. She became, in 2005, the vice-president of the highest legal instance in the defense of women's rights, the UN Cedaw Committee.

One of Silvia Pimentel's oldest memories is from 1945. Her neighbors, in a wealthy neighborhood of São Paulo, were Jewish-German, and she witnessed the arrival, from Europe, of the couple's daughter and three grandchildren. War survivors; scarred by Nazism. "The youngest child was blindfolded. She had gone blind. Since then, I have always been very aware of human suffering." She became a great human rights defender. As a law graduate, she refused to accept the Civil Code in force at the time. "The legal inequality between men and women was huge. One of the articles, for instance, used to allow men to annul the marriage if he could prove within ten days that the woman was not a virgin."

In search for a fairer sense of justice, she got involved with the feminist movement, which was rising in the 1970s. She helped found the Feminist National Front, a pioneer Brazilian feminist NGO. In partnership with Florisa Verucci, she drew up the New Women's Civil Statute, a proposal to change to Civil Code that was handed to the National Congress by 50 women from the entire country, in 1981. "Our suggestions — which eliminated every inequality — were transformed into bills in the National Congress. Indeed, most of them were included in the new Civil Code of 2002."

Professor of Philosophy of Law for over 20 years and author of many books, Silvia took part in the formation of two major international networks: the International Women's Rights Action Watch (Iwraw), in 1986, and the Latin American and Caribbean Committee for the Defense of Women's Rights (Cladem), in 1987. Currently, she coordinates Cladem/Brazil that is in charge of important projects alongside networks, women's organizations and governmental organizations for human rights. In January, she was elected, in a plenary session composed of 177 countries, vice-president of the Cedaw Committee.

The Cedaw Committee was created to observe the fulfillment of UN Convention regarding the Elimination of all Forms of Discrimination Against Women (1979). Women from the whole world — once political and legal options are exhausted in their countries — can send a petition denouncing their State.

Brazil

Anna Politkovskaya

Anna Politkovskaya (born 1958) is a reputed Russian journalist. In 1999, Anna started working for the "Novaya Gazeta" newspaper as a special correspondent in the Northern Caucasus. She is the author of several books on the war in Chechnya. Anna advocates for the human rights of Chechen refugees and those who have suffered because of the war. She also investigates cases of corruption among high-ranking military in Chechnya. For her journalistic achievements combined with an active anti-war stand, she has received numerous Russian and international awards.

In 2002, at the height of the second Chechen war, Anna Politkovskaya, working as a special correspondent in the zone of conflict, set off by helicopter, together with a few Russian officers, for the military base of the Federal troops in Khankala. On board, they were transporting the body of a Russian soldier killed in a recent skirmish with Chechen fighters. Spotting his ID, Anna learned that he was a young fellow from the Chelyabinsk region, born in the same year — and even in the same month — as her daughter. She clearly realized that any of her daughter's classmates could have been lying there in his place. The young soldier's body lay in the aisle, and it seemed to her grossly inhuman that nobody noticed it, grieved, or expressed the least emotion. During the whole flight, Anna wept silently over the premature death of this young man whom she had never known. The officers, hardened by the war, only mocked her tears. They were returning from the most dangerous Vedensky region of Chechnya, and Anna knew that an assignment there was usually a means of punishing officers who were guilty of beating their soldiers or killing civilians.

Not only personal tragedies and deaths have left their scars on Anna. The most horrible thing she saw in Chechnya was exhumation of the mass graves occasionally found by the local population. No criminal or forensic investigation has ever been conducted into these mass killings, so that the commonly accepted rule calls for the presence of independent observers when the graves are exhumed. Local Chechen women, hoping to find their husbands and children among the piles of bodies, have repeatedly asked Anna to come and be a witness. She has never refused them, knowing fully well that no excuse would ever be able to appease her conscience. Anna has always felt a strong personal responsibility for her country and its people.

Exercising her profession as journalist by informing society about the Russian-Chechen war, Anna Politkovskaya writes articles and books not only disclosing cases of human rights violations of Chechen civilians, but also documenting the widespread corruption among high-ranking Russian officers.

Russian Federation

Ella-Maria Polyakova

Soldatskiye Matieri Sankt-Pietierburga (Soldiers' Mothers of St. Petersburg)

Ella-Maria Polyakova (born 1941) graduated from the Leningrad Institute of Communication and worked as an engineer and researcher. She is active in the field of human rights. In 1991, she was one of the Russian activists who went to Vilnius and Riga to support democracy. In autumn 1991, she created the NGO Soldatskiye Matieri Sankt-Pietierburga (Soldiers' Mothers of St. Petersburg), which uncovers violations of soldiers' human rights. She participates in conferences in Russia and abroad, speaking on human rights issues and advocating peace.

In March 2004 in St. Petersburg, newly arrived recruits were beaten up by higher-ranking soldiers. The conscripts wanted to go into the army and to see the world. They were proud to soon become part of the navy in the big city of Kaliningrad. But reality turned out to be different from their dreams. The first night they spent in the barracks, they were humiliated and beaten by older soldiers from nine o'clock in the morning to five o'clock in the afternoon. It seemed as if during that night there were no officers on the base. In the morning, the sadists promised their victims they would continue the torture. So the young soldiers had no other choice but to escape. They headed straight to the Military Prosecutor's Office in St. Petersburg. Unfortunately, their story fell on deaf ears. Undeterred, the recruits turned to the human rights organization Soldatskiye Matieri Sankt-Pietierburga (Soldiers' Mothers of St. Petersburg). They were welcomed by the vice-president of the NGO, Ella-Maria Polyakova. She called for ambulances, and the doctors attended to the bruises and contusions of the soldiers. After that, Ella-Maria went to the judicial authorities. She also invited TV, newspaper, and radio journalists. The story was made public. It now became impossible for the officers to cover up the affair. Their attempt to accuse the kids of having beaten themselves up in order to have a reason to leave their military unit failed.

Last year, around 200 soldiers solicited assistance from this human rights organization. "Slave psychology is the main problem," says Ella-Maria Polyakova. "The parents do not know how to negotiate with officials on equal footing. Ignorant of their rights as citizens, they raise children who only know how to be afraid. We teach them to overcome their fear and exercise their rights as dignified human beings."

Efforts to protect young soldiers' rights come up against the resistance of army officials. Uncovering cases of human rights abuse in the army, Ella-Maria Polyakova and her organization are constantly threatened by the authorities and accused of rendering assistance to those who discredit the army.

Russian Federation

Adelle Potgieter

South African Police Services (Saps)
Restoration of Human Abilities (Roha)
Help Our People Excel Foundation (H.O.P.E. Foundation)

Adelle Potgieter (35) graduated from the University of Port Elizabeth in 1991 with a BA degree, majoring in political science and public administration. Born into a conservative Afrikaaner family, she was subjected to family violence as a child. In 1994 Adelle joined the South African Police Service (Saps) and pioneered peaceful conflict resolution in place of covert methods. She also established a rehabilitation center, and founded the Help Our People Excel Foundation (H.O.P.E. Foundation) to aid underdeveloped communities.

Soon after joining the South African Police Service, Adelle Potgieter helped diffuse violence between the police and gangs in Port Elizabeth. In October 1996 she was transferred to Internal Security where she researched the causes of violent community conflict. During fieldwork she diffused, resolved and mediated various violent conflicts in remote rural communities in the Transkei.

As a police officer, Adelle suffered from post-traumatic stress disorder. Her experience with this illness led her to found the Restoration of Human Abilities (Roha) association, a registered non-profit organization that provides rehabilitation services to psychiatric patients. Since 2001 more than two thousand psychiatric, Aids/HIV and drug/alcohol patients have received free art- and craft-based therapy in state hospitals through Roha's intervention. Adelle pioneered this approach to conflict management for the police service.

Mediation and conflict resolution are not the only issues Adelle is passionate about. She is involved in poverty alleviation programs, social equality for women and the disabled and mental health awareness.

In 2002 she founded the H.O.P.E. Foundation to aid underdeveloped communities with educational and job creation projects. H.O.P.E. works among indigenous African tribes, the Mpondo, Mpondomise, Bomvana and Sotho. These communities have high rates of unemployment, low levels of education, and high rates of HIV/Aids and violent crime. Currently the foundation is building a preschool.

In 2002 Adelle also assisted rural communities with entrepreneur and education programs. Most of her work is voluntary and places a financial burden on her and her family. For her public service she was inducted into the royal clan of the Tembu tribe in the Transkei, a huge honor for a white person and a woman.

Adelle works among poor indigenous communities: the Mpondo, Mpondomise, Bomvana and Sotho. These communities have high rates of unemployment, low levels of education, and high rates of HIV/Aids and violent crime.

South Africa

Alina Radu

International Association for Women in Radio and Television (IAWRT)
Moldovan Association of Independent TV Journalists
Network of Investigative Reporters from South Eastern Europe

Alina Radu is an award-winning investigative journalist and the director of the independent investigative newspaper Ziarul de Garda (The Guard newspaper). Through her research and reporting, she has been instrumental in bringing to light trafficking in human beings and organs, which is becoming a major problem in the Republic of Moldova. She has also assisted women victims of trafficking and pays great attention to the rights of women and children in her reports. She has gathered documentation on trafficking for the Council of Europe.

"Corruption, bad economic conditions, and poverty are the main causes for the rise in trafficking in human beings and organs in the Republic of Moldova," Alina Radu says. In spite of threats from criminals who demand that she stop her investigations, Alina Radu goes ahead. "I am trying to help the victims. They have nobody to tell them where danger lies. We journalists, can investigate and find the roots of danger for poor victims of networks of traffickers in children, women, and organs," she says. Alina carried out research about Moldovan women who were victims of trafficking and abused by peacekeeping soldiers in the Balkans. Those women fled from the traffickers and wanted to start life anew, but some of them were in great danger of being trafficked again. Through her articles, Alina has raised awareness of society about this problem and the need for solving it. She also investigated illegal adoptions of babies and trafficking of organs from Moldova to Turkey, Georgia, Estonia, and Germany. "Sometimes we have to face double obstacles — from governments and illegal networks," Alina explains. "We usually get assistance from our NGOs, international organizations, and our citizens."
Alina is a staunch upholder of independence, freedom of speech, and a free press. "After the communists came to government, we lost our freedoms. Freedom of speech and mass media are still limited," says Alina. This does not stop Alina from speaking out.

The Republic of Moldova has been free of major armed conflict since its independence. But there is widespread poverty and unemployment causing massive migration, trafficking in people, and human rights abuses. In the 2001 and 2005 elections, the communist party won and appointed a communist president, Vladmir Voronin.

Republic of Moldova

Dewi Rana Amir

YBH Bantaya

Dewi Rana Amir (born 1973) is a trained legal advisor from Central Sulawesi, Indonesia. She chairs the legal aid organization, YBH Bantaya, in Palu, the capital of Central Sulawesi. YBH Bantaya promotes the right of indigenous communities to manage and benefit from their land and natural resources and encourages local communities to critically examine the government's forestry and agricultural policies. It also helps local people defend their lands or negotiates on their behalf in instances of unfair land appropriation by the government or corporations.

Dewi Rana Amir has been working with farmers and traditional communities in the Indonesian Central Sulawesi province since 1998, helping them settle land disputes with the state and private entities. For decades, thousands of hectares of cultivated land and ancestral forests in the region have been forcibly taken over by either state or non-state actors, who have converted them into large plantations, transmigration areas, national conservation parks or industrial sites. Most of the farmers whose lands were taken ended up working as wage laborers for the companies that took over their land. Traditional communities have lost the land passed down by their ancestors for many generations.

"The poverty of indigenous peoples that I have seen has planted in me the principle that justice must be fought for," Dewi says. YBH Bantaya focuses on areas where agrarian disputes occur, such as in the regencies of Donggala, Poso and Banggai in Central Sulawesi and the Mamuju Utara regency in West Sulawesi. It has assisted in organizing indigenous peoples' protests against the government or corporations that have unfairly taken over their land and has worked to empower local civil society through civil rights education. For instance, YBH Bantaya has involved farmers and community members in paralegal activities and encouraged them to regularly discuss issues related to agriculture and human rights. Local activists and community leaders are trained in important agrarian issues and policies so that they can give advice to their own communities. "By this we hope that the awareness of people at grassroots level of their rights to manage and benefit from the natural resources in their areas will grow," Dewi explains.

Central Sulawesi, a resource-rich region, has been mired in disputes over resource management. Local communities, claiming to own those recources, have pitted against either the state or corporations that have seized control of the resources.

Indonesia

Tsisana Rapava

Association for Protection of the Rights of the Refugees from Abkhazia (APRRA)

Tsisana Rapava, born in 1940, is an economist and a remarkable public figure of Georgia. She works on the problems of refugees from Abkhazia (Autonomous Republic of Georgia), South Ossetia (Shida Kartli region of Georgia), and the Chechen Republic. She herself is a refugee from Abkhazia. A well-known public person, Tsisana actively participated in the movement for the restoration of the independence of the state of Georgia. She was a cofounder of the International Association "Caucasus: Ethnic Relations, Human Rights, Geopolitics."

Tsisana Rapava is an active defender of the human rights of refugees, like herself, from Abkhazia. As chairperson of the Association for Protection of the Rights of the Refugees from Abkhazia (APRRA), she is active in many humanitarian activities. She is also well known as a defender of vulnerable families, particularly those who had to leave their homes as a result of the geopolitical crisis.

Since early 1994, Tsisana has been actively engaged in the political arena. Tsisana has supported the rights of the detained political prisoners who were supporters of the human rights leader and first president of independent Georgia, Zviad K. Gamsakhurdia, who was arrested after the illegal military coup d'etat in December/January of 1991/92. Tsisana actively fought against mass violation of human rights and basic freedoms under the Shevardnadze regime. Because of her opposition, she was repeatedly detained and subjected to persecution. From 1987 to 1997, Tsisana was a member of the International Society for Human Rights (ISHR-SGFM) and a member of the governing board of its Georgian national branch.

Despite all the difficulties and obstacles, Tsisana never gave up her political views and principles. She is fighting for the people's liberties and freedom, for their freedom of choice of their own way of life. Since the end of 1998, Tsisana has participated actively in the International Association "Caucasus: Ethnic Relations, Human Rights, Geopolitics," where she is a member of the governing board. She has participated in a number of international conferences and congresses on the protection of human rights all over the world. She actively supported the International Georgian Rose Revolution that ended Shevardnadze's dictatorial regime.

The political conflict and crooked political games of 1994 brought misery to the people of the Abkhazian-Georgian region. The territorial integrity of Georgia was violated and ethnic cleansing of Georgian people took place. Over 250,000 ethnic Georgians were driven away from their lands.

Alicia Amalia Rodríguez Illescas

Beijing Committee

Alicia Amalia Rodríguez Illescas (57): mother, diplomat, doctor in political science, professor, feminist, promoter of laws, and defender of the human rights of women. She has built her life on wisdom, uprightness and devotion. She dedicates her life to engineering a better future. Along with other women, she rebels, makes proposals and takes decisions.

The fundamental goal of her work is to concretize the institutionalization of women's rights in Guatemala. "If we manage to incorporate them into the State and society's thinking, we will have done the most complicated job, the one of longest duration." She is a woman with soaring ambitions for change. She dreams of "the creation of human beings who are capable of teaching, of investigating, of developing, with a different scientific focus. We have to change the patriarchal view of things in all sectors. The challenge is to make the structure permeable, to change history, science and academic thought."

Alicia Amalia Rodríguez Illescas, diplomat, professor, investigator, promoter of laws, feminist, transforms whatever she touches with her alchemy. She lost her father when she was two years old. With her mother, she learned to fight, not to surrender herself. Rigorous and multifaceted, for her, peace is a state of internal and external harmony. "It can be reached with justice, with access to and equality of opportunities for all humankind to grow up and develop." Bold and reflective, she thinks that "development, peace and justice are synonyms." She introduced an area for women's and young people's studies in the Latin American Faculty of Social Sciences (Flasco), and she is also the coordinator of the Beijing Committee in Guatemala. She has been fighting, with all her strength, for the last 30 years, for a more equal order. Aware of the stumbling blocks in her way, she does not delay and looks forward. "A peaceful woman is a woman who develops, gives her opinion, participates, deliberates, leads. She is capable of evolving along with the social whole, with the country and with peace in world."

Guatemala: patriarchal society, excluding and discriminating, with anti-democratic and repressive leaders. There is an absence of official policies and State development plans that include rights for women. "Feminicide" is committed with impunity.

Guatemala

Amelia Rokotuivuna

Young Women's Christian Association (YWCA)
Fiji Labor Party
World Council of Churches (WCC)

Amelia Rokotuivuna has been a feminist activist for peace and justice all her life. As head of the Fiji YWCA in the 1970s, she was the key spokesperson for NGOs on political, social, and economic justice issues, and a leader of the anti-nuclear movement. She co-organized a demonstration in Fiji against Chilean General Pinochet's visit in the early 1980s, led a youth protest march after the first Fiji military coup in 1987, and worked with the Citizens' Constitutional Forum in the 1990s to secure popular agreement on a new democratic Fiji constitution. She died in May 2005 at the age of 63.

"One of our major achievements in the struggle against French nuclear testing in the Pacific was forcing Air France (UTA) out of Fiji. It resulted from such a very good combination of efforts: by trade unions, by university students, and by the anti-nuclear Pacific movement. Protests by members of the Nuclear-Free and Independent Pacific movement were almost daily events. For several years, every Saturday somebody was out on the streets leafletting. And the University of the South Pacific Students' Association was almost always marching or protesting, either on the streets or outside the UTA offices. The trade unions were seeking the withdrawal of Air France from Fiji. The Prime Minister summoned me and a colleague to his office. We had asked to see him because the leader of the Airline Workers Union, had said they intended to boycott Air France. I had told the leader to go ahead and that we would go and see the Prime Minister, to get a sense of how he would react to this action. The Prime Minister told us he would say nothing — which is of course what he did. He did not say anything; he did not interfere. I read that he wanted the French to stop testing their nuclear bombs in our Pacific and that he was quite happy with what we were doing. He would do his diplomatic thing but he evidently felt the French should decolonize. It was soon after this that the Prime Minister established the South Pacific Forum, the inter-governmental organization for independent states in the Pacific to be able to address issues like French nuclear testing and decolonization."

The regional and national contexts of Amelia's social justice activism were colonialism in the Pacific, the abuse of island colonies through nuclear missile testing, and the struggle in Fiji against political extremism and racism.

Ana Maria Romero de Campero

Unite Bolivia Foundation

A prestigious journalist, Bolivian Ana Maria de Campero (1943) was a Public Defender, from 1998 to 2003. With her, this position was born. Her goal was to defend the human rights of prisoners, coke growers, prostitutes, children, homosexuals and sick people without resources. She has not lost her determination. Today, from the Unite Bolivia Foundation, over which she presides, she promotes non-violent management and dialogue.

In 1998, a new position was introduced in Bolivia: Public Defender. It was headed by a woman of high rank, the distinguished journalist Ana Maria de Campero. Her work as a journalist smoothed the path for her. She fought many battles during her time as Public Defender. In the combat against the cultivators of cocaine, the army and the police burned and ransacked the houses of the coke growers and also destroyed legal crops. The Public Defender protested. In the fight against crime, the government cannot, itself, engage in illegal activities. The medical attention in the jails is deplorable. "They are deprived not only of their freedom, but of everything," she says. She succeeded in getting the National Health Fund to offer dialysis to those who suffer from kidney problems. She traveled to Spain to bring back stolen Bolivian children. She intervened against the mistreatment of prostitutes. She fought against the discrimination of homosexuals. Her time as Public Defender ended in 2003, but her confrontations with the powerful ones did not. In 2003, 80 strikers were killed and 400 were hurt. She started a hunger strike to show solidarity towards the strikers. The demonstrations grew, and the Armed Forces were going to shoot. She talked. The Commander of the Armed Forces intervened and said that the military service would not shoot defenseless civilians. After this announcement, President Gonzalo Sanchez de Lozada submitted his resignation.

When Ana Maria de Campero left the post of Defender, somebody said to her: "They had a reason for not to reappointing you. What you did, you did too well." It does not matter that they did not reappoint her for the position. She continues anyways. From the Foundation Unite Bolivia, over which she presides, Ana Maria de Campero promotes non-violent management and dialogue.

The 20th century ends. Bolivia enters the path of democracy after a series of dictatorships. From those repressive and corrupt military governments, the country has inherited economic, cultural and racial inequalities — as well as impressive impunity rates.

Bolivia

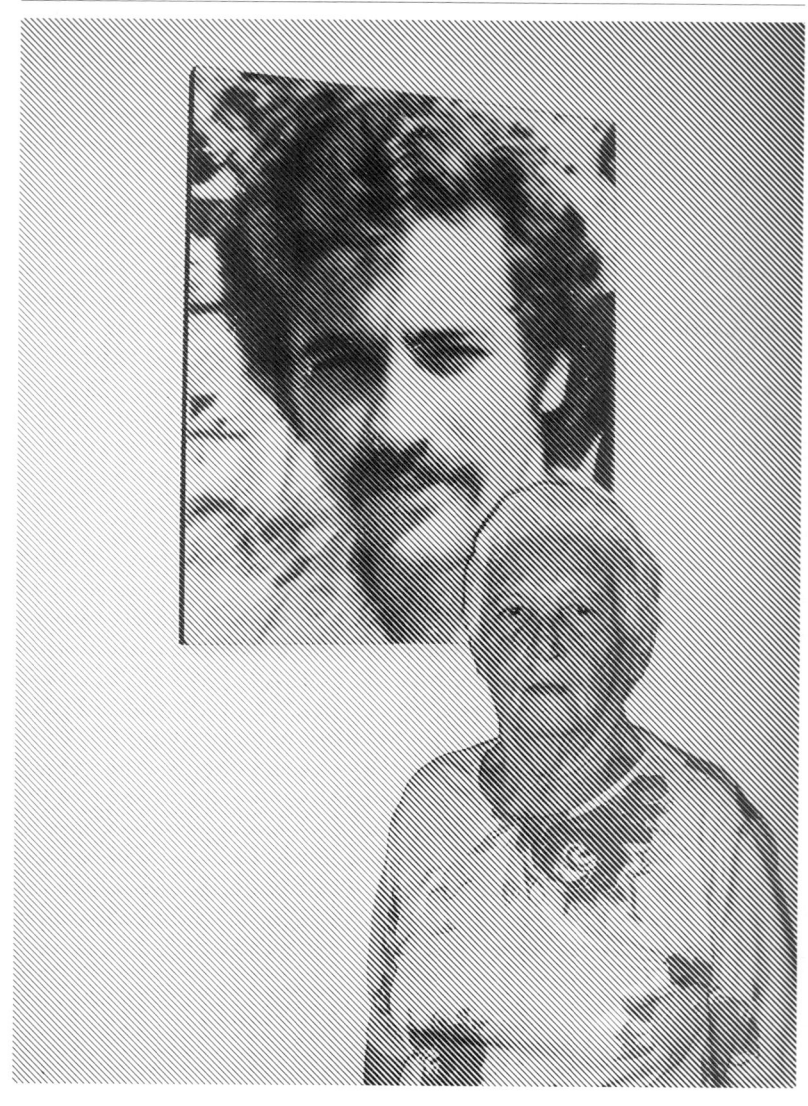

Elzita Santa Cruz Oliveira

"Where is my son?" The question that Elzita Santa Cruz Oliveira (born 1913) asked was never answered. During the 1970s, when Brazil was frightened and terrified, Elzita, a housewife, faced the military forces in the search for the fifth of her ten children. She has written hundreds of letters to politicians, to national and international organizations for human rights. Elzita has gathered mothers who shared her pain. She symbolizes all Brazilian mothers whose children were victims of the military regime's oppression.

"Old Zita! Old Zita!" When Elzita Santa Cruz Oliveira (92) gathers her family, she still feels like she can hear her son — who disappeared in 1974. "He used to call me Old Zita."

The fifth of her ten children, student and militant of the Popular Action — a revolutionary organization of the left-wing Catholic movement — left home in an afternoon during the celebration of carnival in Rio, to meet a friend. He never came back. It makes Elzita sad to remember the past. She goes back to the beginning of the 1970s. That is when the daughter of a sugar plantation owner, a rich girl raised to marry, had her peaceful life as a housewife in Olinda, Pernambuco, shook up by the dictatorship's cruelty. In 1971, her first born daughter was arrested in Rio. Elzita spent three months going from barrack to barrack. "When they allowed me to see her, she had bruises on her body and her nails were blue. She was being tortured." Her daughter was kept in prison for one year. Another one of her sons had to leave his fourth year of law school and exile himself in Europe for one year. Three years later, Elzita Santa Cruz Oliveira was back to the barracks, this time looking for her missing son. It was worthless, so she started writing letters and petitions to politicians, to military officers, to the church, to national and international organizations. She has gathered and encouraged other mothers — most of them frightened — to sign petitions. Elzita has helped found the Movement for Amnesty in Pernambuco and, later on, the Labor Party of that same state. She has gone to Argentina to support the Mothers of May Square. "I have never been scared. I would go inside a fire for a child."

The beginning of the 1970s was one of the most violent periods of the Brazilian military regime. The academic world lost several intellectuals, forced to leave the country. Student organizations were shut down. Students were arrested, tortured, and murdered.

———

Brazil

Shereen Sazawar

Journalist Association of Afghanistan (JAA)
Women's Council in Mazar-e-Sharif
Independent Writers Association (IWA)

Shereen Maira Sazawar, born in Afghanistan, is a talented journalist. She writes regularly in the local newspapers on issues concerning women and human rights. She is an active member of the Women's Council in Mazar-e-Sharif. For the past three decades Shereen has been active through the media and has also penned numerous poems in Dari and Uzbeki. She has recently written an article in a local newspaper about the grievous condition of women and the degrading attitude of the warlords towards them, thus risking her life and attracting accusations of blasphemy by the religious extremists.

Witnessing the inhumane treatment and degrading attitude of warlords and religious extremists towards women in Afghanistan, Shereen Sazawar was motivated to speak out and raise grave concerns about the rights of women in this underdeveloped country. The recent changes in favor of a relatively peaceful situation and a new democratic arena have reinvigorated her commitment to mobilize women to stand up for a better future for themselves and for their children. In one of her latest articles, Shereen has drawn attention to the warlords' brutal crimes against women and the impunity for warlords. This stand has instigated harsh criticism from the extremists who issued a "fatwa" (religious edict) labeling her an apostate and demanding her execution. However, all this harassment did not deter her from continuing her fight to end violence and abusive behavior towards women, despite the vulnerable life in a country like Afghanistan.

Shereen Sazawar is dedicated to the advocacy, promotion and protection of human rights, and specifically women's rights. Though her activities have put her life at risk in many ways, she remains firm in fighting to achieve her goal.

Afghanistan

Irma Schwager

Born in 1920 to politically active Jewish parents in Vienna, Irma Schwager fled to Belgium in 1938 and then to France. Detained in a camp, she escaped and joined the resistance movement. This experience led her to peace work. And the way that women are affected by wars made her an advocate for the independence of women and against structural violence. After Austria's liberation from fascism, she returned and became involved in the International Democratic Women's Federation. She is an advocate for the implementation of the goals of the United Nations Conference on women and for disarmament.

Irma Schwager is listening to the radio speech of the winner of the Nobel Prize for Literature, Elfriede Jelinek. She wants to hear exactly what Elfriede has to say. That is Irma: always interested, committed, informed, and alert, following the events of the times, present as well as the past.

Born in 1920 to Jewish parents, she experienced pogroms in Vienna, when Jews were picked up. When the first transports to the concentration camp Dachau took place in 1938, Irma fled the country. Her parents, who were small merchants, stayed in Vienna and died during the Holocaust, as did two of her brothers. Irma stayed in Belgium illegally joining a group of political emigrants. She learned that "you are not only a victim, you not only can resist, you have to." With the German invasion in May 1940, the situation became dangerous for Irma. She fled to France, was detained in a camp, but escaped with the help of the French resistance movement. With this, her daily political routine in the Resistance began. Austrians made up a group of their own. In 1943, Irma gave birth to her daughter and experienced the solidarity of her French comrades: "I would have been able to clothe six children." She continued her resistance work and transported leaflets in the baby carriage. "That was wonderfully unsuspicious," but perilous.

After Austria's liberation from fascism, she became involved in the International Democratic Women's Federation. She became an advocate for the equality of women, development and peace, the implementation of the goals of the United Nations Conference on Women, and worked for disarmament. As a contemporary witness, she teaches the younger generation to say "No" early enough and to resist injustice. "It looks as if you put yourself in danger when you are active. But that is not the case. You learn to meet the dangers, you experience solidarity."

The early context of Irma Schwager's work was the resistance movement in Nazi-occupied Europe. After liberation from fascism, it has been in movements against concealment of the fascist past and for disarmament, peace, and women's equality and development at national and international levels.

Austria

Haya Shalom

Women in Black Movement (WiB)
Coalition of Women for Just Peace (CWfJP)
International Gay and Lesbians Human Rights Commission (IGLHRC)

Haya Shalom is a feminist and human rights activist. As a lesbian, she is one of the leading forces in promoting women's solidarity for peace and women's rights. Shalom is one of the first women who joined and assisted Women in Black, protesting for more than 16 years against the Israeli occupation of Gaza and the West Bank. This peaceful protestation has expanded beyond the causes of the Palestinian issue to influence women all over the world. Despite the slow and gradual change she has made, Haya is optimistic about the future.

Haya Shalom states that she was given the opportunity to meet some of the most significant people in her life. One of them is Hania, a Palestinian colleague and life-long friend from Ramalla. Shalom speaks warmly of this relationship, which in Israeli and Palestinian reality exists against all odds. They cannot meet very often due to the difficulties of passing the military checkpoints, but nevertheless their friendship remains strong. Their total acceptance of each other is especially magnified due to the fact that Shalom has been a leader in advancing lesbian rights, which is taboo within traditional Palestinian discourse. Admitting at the age of 35 that she is a lesbian triggered an outburst in Shalom's activities and had a substantial effect on her life. For her, this was a renascent birth. It opened to her a new world which included initiating and supporting feminist activities, fighting for women's rights, advancing issues concerning human rights, and striving for a just peace.

Shalom's vision for a peaceful future is based on the initiation of a radical change that will crumble the definitions of the patriarchal society. To date, pacifist and human rights activists, such as Women in Black, are considered traitors in parts of Israeli society. During their demonstrations people tend to reprimand them, curse, yell and spit on them, often accompanying such gestures by sexist remarks (especially by men). At times, the hatred even becomes violent. The networks empowering her are the organizations she is affiliated with: Women in Black, The Coalition of Women for Just Peace, The International Gay and Lesbians Human Rights Commission and International Women's and Lesbian Rights Organizations amongst others. In addition, the human relationships that she has formed with other colleagues involved in her mission are her main source of power and hope.

Shalom is one of the first women who joined and assisted the Women in Black Movement. For more than 16 years she has been protesting against the Israeli occupation of Gaza and the West Bank. She has supported women's solidarity activities for peace between Israelis and Palestinians.

Israel

Xiuyun Shang

People's Court of Haidian District, Beijing

Shang Xiuyun (62) is a communist party member and Deputy Presiding Judge of the second court in the People's Court of Haidian District, Beijing. Known as "Mother Judge", she has transformed a large number of juvenile delinquents, encouraging them to study and take part in ordinary activities.

Shang Xiuyun is deputy presiding judge of the second court in the People's Court of Haidian District, Beijing, in charge of juvenile delinquent cases. Shang remembers the case of a quiet and gentle looking girl who, because of peer influence, became a thief. She could hardly believe that this pretty, quiet child, much the same age as her own daughter, was a hardened thief. She felt a responsibility towards her and had several meetings with the girl and her father, encouraging the family to give the girl their support and encouragement.

In September 1987, Haidian District had an increasing number of young offenders and decided to set up special juvenile courts so as to have greater flexibility in enforcing the law, meting out punishment and implementing preventive measures. Shang was one of the first judges appointed in these courts. Despite an initial lack of experience and a lack of understanding from the public, Shang pushed ahead with a strong sense of responsibility. In these years, she seldom stopped working. Whatever the weather, she would be in her office long after office hours. She would often work on the bus home and though well-meaning colleagues would try to dissuade her, she would respond with a smile of gratitude, saying quietly, "I am used to this." In this way, "Mother Judge" gave her love to the juvenile delinquents. She is convinced that all criminals can be transformed.

Not one of the 710 cases (1300 defendants) presided by her over the last 17 years has been ordered for retrial. Twelve of 'her children' have managed to go to key state universities such as Tsinghua and Peking.

An increase in the number of young offenders in Beijing's Haidian District led to the setting up of special juvenile courts in 1987. This enabled greater flexibility in law enforcement, punishment and prevention, combining these measures with care and positive support from the family and society.

China

"We condemn acts of terrorism irrespectively of whether they are committed by groups of bandits or by the Russian military."

From the appeal of Chechen peace advocates to the world community.

Maya Shovkhalova

Iberia
Yaltinskaya initsyativa za mir v Chechnie (Yimc)

Having suffered Stalin's deportation of the Chechen people to Central Asia, Maya Shovkhalova (born 1936) returned to Grozny in 1958. She graduated from the Tbilisi Music Conservatory. In the 1990s, she was a member of the Commission on Rehabilitation of Victims of the 1944–1956 Repressions in Chechnya. Since the beginning of the Russian-Chechen armed conflict, Maya has been engaged in anti-war activism, cooperating with international as well as Russian NGOs. She is also head of the NGO Iberia which focuses on the issues of demining and banning of land mines.

In February 1944, during the Soviet-staged deportation of the Chechen and Ingush peoples to Central Asia, a horrible tragedy occurred: 700 inhabitants of Khaibakh, a Chechen village high in the mountains, were burned alive in a local club building by a Soviet punitive detachment. It was not until the 1990s that this barbarous act was investigated. Maya Shovkhalova played an important role in the work of the Khaibakh Investigation Commission which publicized this and other crimes against humanity perpetrated by Stalin.

The nascent democratic changes in the Soviet Union, coupled with the committed work of human rights activists in revealing the atrocities of the communist regime, gave hope that such tragedies would never be repeated. But the developments leading up to the Russian-Chechen conflict proved these hopes to be an illusion. During the first military campaign, Maya helped care for the wounded, and took part in negotiations between Chechen President Dudaev's representatives and the Russian mothers who called for an end to the savage war and their sons' return home. The efforts of these peace advocates, however, were doomed to failure.

Maya has nonetheless succeeded in making her contribution to informing the world community about the genocide of her people during the two Russian-Chechen wars waged between 1994 and 2004. She unceasingly continues her numerous and diverse human rights advocacy activities, cooperating with both all-Russian and international NGOs. Thanks to her and her colleagues' work, a great number of people all over the world have learned about the real state of affairs in Chechnya, about the everyday violations of the most fundamental human rights, and about the incidents of mass slaughter of the civilian population which are still being concealed by the authorities.

Under the constant threat of persecution by the Russian military, Maya Shovkhalova combines her efforts to inform the world community of the truth with respect to human rights in Chechnya, with her efforts calling for land mines to be banned.

Russian Federation

Indira Shreshtha

Strii Shakti

Indira Shreshtha has spent 25 years working on all aspects of gender, sustainable development, and peace issues in Nepal. Founder and head of Strii Shakti (women's power), which works in Nepal's conflict-affected districts, and participant in a national network on gender and peace, Indira is a consultant, trainer, planner, and analyst who has challenged patriarchal and upper-class biases in official development programs supported by multinational and bilateral donors. Her landmark study on women in jails put the spotlight on how women suffer as a result of illiberality in the legal system.

The face-off between the government and the Maoist insurgents has been both a challenge and an opportunity for Indira Shreshtha and her band of dedicated workers. Her NGO, Shtrii Shakti, founded in 1991, is focused on people in rural Nepal who are struggling to meet basic needs for food, clothing, and shelter in the midst of coping with the conflict's fallout. Indira's organization has identified and trained social "mobilizers" from 12 village development committees in three maximally insurgency-affected areas. Indira has also spearheaded initiatives to spread the message of peace, collecting signatures in May 2002 from women of diverse backgrounds as a symbol of women's pacifist solidarity. Strii Shakti also plants trees and conducts annual peace walks around Swayambhunath to mark International Peace Day every 6 August.

Furthermore, Indira has taken up issues such as violence against girls and women, and was part of a four-woman team that researched the status of women in Nepal in the 1980s, bringing out ten volumes on the subject. Along with a coworker, she undertook an analysis of official development programs supported by multinational and bilateral donors. Analyzing them from a feminist perspective, they challenged the patriarchal and upper-class biases inherent in the programs.

The well-educated daughter of a middle-class family, Indira was drawn toward development work as soon as she completed her education. She joined the United Nations Development Programme (UNDP) after finishing her studies in Kathmandu and the University of Wales. As one of the first women in Nepal to head an NGO, her work has led to the mainstreaming of gender concerns.

The Maoists began their insurgency in 1996. In 2001, the army rolled in, intensifying the violence. Women are often forced to support one side, only to be punished by the other. Thousands have been trapped in the turmoil, and the nation is being forced to rethink its social and power structures.

Kavita Srivastava believes that village women, coming together, can articulate their problems and find solutions. More than a million village women have proven her belief to be true.

Kavita Srivastava

People's Union for Civil Liberties

For two decades Kavita Srivastava, who was born in 1962, has been promoting, collectively with other social groups, nonviolent ways of ensuring justice to survivors of atrocities committed due to gender, class, caste, religious group or nationality. Her accomplishments include work with the women's movement in Rajasthan, which has initiated laws against widow burning and national guidelines against violence against women. She also succeeded in taking the "Right to Food" issue to the Supreme Court in 2001. She is the national secretary of the Union for Civil Liberties.

Kavita Srivastava is a full-time human rights activist working to protect people's democratic and constitutional rights and to work towards justice in instances of violations of people's rights. The most prominent social injustice and violence committed against people by the state is widespread hunger amidst people and the denial of food and employment to the poor. There exists the paradoxical situation of drought and the breakdown of food distribution systems and surplus food grains in government warehouses.

In 2001 Kavita took the "Right to Food" issue to the Supreme Court. This became the most significant food litigation in democratic India. The court has passed significant decrees relating to deaths from hunger, children's nutrition, social security for the vulnerable, the public distribution system, and the system of redressing grievances.

Kavita started working in 1984, bringing village women together to draw up platforms at the village level for collective articulation of their problems, analysis and the search for solutions. This pioneering work was carried out by a very large collective under the name of the Women's Development Program. More than a million women became involved in creatively denouncing their problems, whether they related to the payment of minimum wages, or domestic violence, or rape, or widow burning. The new central law against the glorification of widow burning and the Supreme Court Guidelines for the Prevention of Sexual Harassment at the Workplace were both initiated by the Rajasthan women's movement.

Since 1994 Kavita has been promoting the formation of citizens' collectives to protect the civil liberties and democratic rights of every citizen. She is also part of a larger effort of bringing about nuclear disarmament and peace in South Asia, and campaigning for mine clearance.

Among the worst social injustice in India is widespread hunger. Other forms of violence include domestic violence, which even today has social legitimacy, hate crimes committed by the dominant caste and religious groups on other castes and religious minorities, and state violation of civil liberties.

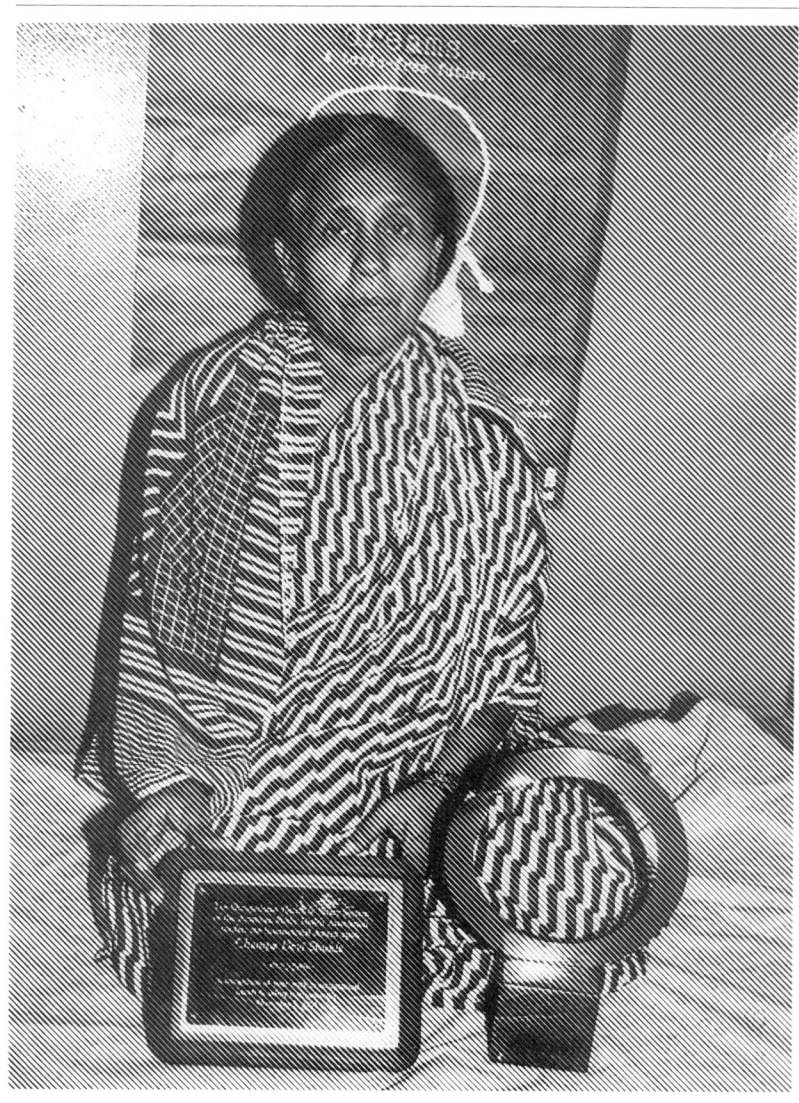

Champa Devi Shukla

Champa Devi Shukla has been a leading figure in the international campaign seeking justice for the survivors of the 1984 Union Carbide Gas Tragedy in Bhopal. Starting with protests and rallies in India, Champa took her fight against Union Carbide Company (UCC) and its partner, Dow Chemicals, to the streets of New York and other American cities. Dow Chemicals is today fighting a series of cases filed by Champa and other protesters. Champa was awarded the 2004 Goldman Environmental Prize for bringing the Bhopal disaster to the international center stage.

It has been over two decades since the Union Carbide gas leak killed more than 30,000 people in Bhopal, the worst industrial disaster in history. In 52-year-old Champa Devi Shukla, the survivors found hope. For 19 years now, she has been leading the international campaign seeking justice for them.

Champa was married to a government employee who was killed by cancer in 1997. Two of Champa's sons also died due to health problems as a result of the methyl isocyanate gas leak. Three other children are still alive, but none lead a normal life. Champa started her career in activism by fighting for better labor conditions and wages for women at the factory where she worked. In 1989, all her demands were met. She then leveraged the union's new-found power to seek justice from UCC. In 1999, she joined activists and disaster victims in a class action lawsuit filed against UCC in New York. Down the years, she has led a series of protest marches, rallies, petitions, and fasts, including a 19-day hunger strike demo in New York in 2002.

In 2003, Champa and others confronted officials of Dow Chemicals — which merged with UCC and has since insisted that it played no role in the disaster — in Mumbai and The Netherlands with samples of toxic waste. Champa's initiative led to a protest tour of more than ten American cities, which culminated in a protest at a Dow shareholders' meeting in Michigan, and a rally on Wall Street. Champa was awarded the 2004 Goldman Environmental Prize, recognition of her efforts in bringing the Bhopal disaster onto the international stage.

In 1984, the Union Carbide factory gas leak killed more than 30,000 people in Bhopal — the biggest industrial disaster in history. And although a series of promises have been made to the survivors, little has happened. Generations are dead, and subsequent generations will suffer from health crises.

India

"I just want to see a civil society that works in Indonesia, where people are aware of their rights and are capable of defending themselves whenever their rights are violated."

Ade Rostina Sitompul

Suara Hak Azasi Manusia

Ade Rostina Sitompul (born 1938) has defended Indonesians who are victims of state-inflicted violence, from political prisoners and their families in 1965 to East Timorese in the late 1990s. She has advocated the cause of prisoners' rights through various NGOs she co-founded. In 2002, after a critical review of her own work over the last three decades, she concluded that she may not have succeeded in assisting political prisoners and their families by making them dependent, and therefore decided to change her methods. Ade now focuses on empowering people to stand up for their rights.

Since 1965, in the aftermath of a massacre that wiped out a million Indonesians and resulted in hundreds of thousands of political prisoners being sent to jail or forced into exile without trial, Ade Rostina Sitompul has been helping victims of state violence. During the 32-year Suharto dictatorship, she faced threats from the authorities for her sustained advocacy against state violence — including the injustice towards political prisoners and their families in the late 1960s, the 1991 Sta Cruz massacre and other violent incidents in East Timor, the violent response to the 1998 riots that finally brought Suharto down and cases of land conflict.

Ade co-founded various organizations such as Kontras (which dealt with the missing political activists during the Suharto regime), Yayasan HAK (the legal consultation in East Timor), Suara Ibu Peduli (an organization that helps urban women improve their welfare), the Trauma Center for children in post-referendum East Timor and Suara Hak Azasi Manusia (Voice of Human Rights) which trains and equips the marginalized to be aware of their civil rights and thus be able to defend themselves in the face of violations by the state or others.

In 2002, after critically reviewing her work over more than three decades in the field, Ade decided to change her methods significantly. She explains, "I was criticized that I tended to take center stage, and many people I represented were not truly aware of the real causes of the repression they were subject to. Now, I just want to stay on the periphery, help them through training and education, and let them deal with the authorities in the course of defending their own rights." In 2005, she was at hand helping the victims of the December 26, 2004 tsunami in Aceh.

Indonesia's modern history is tainted with state-inflicted violence. While a significant number of human rights violations from the Suharto dictatorship remain unpunished, the post-1998 era has had its own share of abuses against citizens.

Indonesia

Marianne Spiller Hadorn

Associação Brasileira de Amparo à Infância (Abai)
Fundação Educacional Meninos e Meninas de Rua
Fazenda da Esperança

When she was a child, Marianne Spiller Hadorn (born 1940) would prick up her ears when her parents talked about poverty and social injustice. As a result of conversations with liberation theologians like Abbé Pierre and Dom Helder Camara, the teacher and psychiatrist and her husband moved to Brazil in 1972, adopted three children, and in 1979 founded Abai. Today, Abai has a day-care center, homes for "social orphans," and training centers. It conducts prevention programs and holds courses for peasant farmers, provides help for alcohol and drug dependency, and runs a community center.

Marianne Spiller Hadorn's eyes light up when she talks about Abai: "In 1983, children came to us who were not looked after, and no one wanted them. We took them in. That was the beginning of our social orphanages. It was a new idea in that area to take in children who had been abandoned by their families and to care for them and live with them in surrogate family groups. The social orphanages were an alternative to the huge institutions that treated children like numbers." As her approach showed positive results, it has often been copied by the state since that time. Her work with endangered children started in 1979 aiming to prevent them from turning into street children. Now, the children from that time help the children of today. Since their parents are often alcoholics, Marianne decided to open a therapy unit for alcohol and drug addicts. Today, 30 men from this unit work in the project's restaurant or with the children, and in so doing, learn how to interact in society again. Brazilian staff members teach children and young adults such skills as carpentry, baking or sewing, and provide help with schoolwork. "Every person is important," says Marianne. "Everyone is needed and everyone helps." By planting vegetables, for example, Abai tries to be self-sufficient in food for the 130 meals it provides each day in the day center. The aim is to be proactive rather than dependent. And Abai gives economic solidarity: it supports sister projects in the region and across the border in Argentina. In this way, inspiration can be shared, synergies exploited, and ideas developed jointly, for "another world is possible." And in Marianne Spiller Hadorn's world no handbag needs to be guarded. Hers is always open, her friends say, be it in Rio de Janeiro or Zurich, for she says that people should be able to have whatever she has.

Every day, street children in Brazil die in fights among themselves or with the police. They have fled family violence and are often forced to prostitute themselves on the streets, or they are enslaved, or they die. They know that their lives are very short, that they have no future.

Switzerland

Sudanese Women Empowerment for Peace Program

Sudanese Women Empowerment for Peace Program (Suwepp)

The Sudanese Women Empowerment for Peace Program (Suwepp), established in 1997, is a national network that focuses on peace building through bridging the gap between North and South in Sudan. It operates nine working groups, five of which are in Khartoum and four in the south, based in Nairobi, Kenya. The groups support peace negotiations and spread the culture of peace in the Sudanese community. Despite the inauspicious political climate, the Suwepp's achievements have paved the way for peace initiatives. Its work is highly appreciated by Sudanese and international partners.

In 1997, in response to exacerbated petitions from the Sudanese women, the Government of the Netherlands took the initiative to support the Sudanese women's ongoing peacemaking efforts. The aim of the initiative was to effectuate the culture of peace and to promote the non-violent forms of conflict in the country. It also worked on persuading the Sudanese people, especially women, to participate in the peace process.

The war in the Sudan has put constraints on people, especially on women's involvement in social work. During wartime, because of male labor migration, women were forced to be self-dependent and to take over men's responsibilities in subsisting their families. The Sudanese Women's Empowerment for Peace Program (Suwepp) reflects the role of women in the peace process. It also puts the Sudanese civil war and the way in which it has affected the Sudanese women on the agenda of both national and international forums and conferences. In so doing, it vocalizes the needs of the Sudanese women and the burdens that the war has brought to their lives.

The Suwepp consists of nine groups, five in Khartoum and four in the south — in Nairobi, Kenya. The five groups in the north are: the National Committee, (representing the government), Southern Women for Peace, the Civil Society Network, the Nuba Women for Peace and the National Democratic Alliance (NDA), that represents the opposition. The four groups in the south are: the Sudanese People's Liberation Movement (SPLM), the Sudanese People's Liberation Movement-United Group (SPLM-UG), the Sudanese People's Development Front Women Group (SPDFWG), and the Non-Partisan Group (NPG). Each group runs different activities in addition to joint activities, such as training sessions, workshops and joint-meetings between the northern and southern groups, which are held periodically every six months.

When the Sudanese Women Empowerment for Peace Program (Suwepp) commenced work in the Sudan, the country had already been torn apart by the civil war that caused chaos and distrust. Because of the continuously changing socio-political climate in Sudan, the Sudanese women have to adapt their strategies according to the changing needs.

Sudan

Elmira Suleymanova

European Ombudsman Institution
International Ombudsman Institution
Azerbaijan Women and Development Center (ADWC)

Elmira Suleymanova (born 1937) is a multi-awarded chemist who has not only distinguished herself in science but in public service as well. Elected by the Azerbaijan Parliament as Human Rights Commissioner in 2002, she has implemented programs that protect and improve the status of women and the elderly, displaced youth, the poor, and victims of violence. She also established the Azerbaijan Women and Development Center (ADWC), the only women's organization in the country in consultative status with the United Nations.

Elmira Suleymanova is one of the leaders of the women's movement in Azerbaijan. Since 1990, she has actively participated in the women's movement for human rights and gender equality on national and international levels. In 1994, she established the Azerbaijan Women and Development Center, the only women's NGO in the country with consultative status with the United Nations (UN). Elmira has initiated and implemented projects for refugees and internally displaced persons (IDPs) in collaboration with the Ministries of Health and Education, UN bodies and international NGOs. The projects covered the Rehabilitation Centers for refugee/IDP children, increasing access to family planning and reproductive health through community-based services and training programs in refugee and IDP communities. Elmira also conducted research on the improvement of the status of women and children, IDPs, elderly people, and youth in the transition period, whose living conditions were aggravated by the combination of poverty and violence. The first Social Resource Center (2001) for elderly people was her creation. She has also organized training, information, and education programs, workshops and conferences for women and children in close collaboration with several UN Agency country offices.

Elmira heads the Gender Department, an NGO forum of over 100 NGOs. In 2002, she was elected to the post of Human Rights Commissioner by the Parliament of Azerbaijan. She has collaborated with ombudspersons from all over the world and was recognized as member of the European Ombudsman Institution. She is well known as an advocate for social justice in a young country that is facing many tasks in the areas of equality of men and women, political liberty of women, and social support to poor families under conditions of transition.

When the USSR collapsed, Armenian forces occupied 20 percent of Azerbaijan, and about one million civilians left their homeland. Their 15-year-long exile in refugee camps around the country brought immense suffering. Over 100,000 children were born in these refugee centers.

María Cleofé Sumire López

Andean Women's Association (AMA)

María Cleofé Sumire López (54) was born in Cuzco, Peru. She followed the path of her father, who was arrested several times because of his fight for land on behalf of the peasants. She lived through the aggression of the Sendero Luminoso and the military. She also experienced exile. María Cleofé created the Andean Women's Association (AMA). She graduated as a lawyer in order to fight more effectively for women's rights.

María Cleofé Sumire López was born in Cuzco, where the Apus hills meet the sky and take care of the land's heart. In the heights of those hills, where she nurtures the dreams of many people, she fell in love and had two children. Her father was an indigenous leader. He was arrested several times after making land claims for the peasants. María Cleofé has experienced very difficult times. She has faced violence, threats and exile. Determined and with a desire to fulfill her aspirations, she entered university and, in 2003, after 20 years, she graduated as a lawyer — so she could be better prepared for the fight for women's rights, for the fight for her people.

Long before, in the 1960s, when in Cuzco the peasant movement made massive land claims, she had to leave the country because of the aggression of Sendero Luminoso, and she suffered discrimination and racism. She created the Andean Women's Association (AMA) through a network of committees and mothers clubs. She held training courses for women, encouraging them to feel recognized as citizens in their own right. "I feel impotent, because I cannot change this world; I feel pain, because of the injustice in my country. Everything that happened in the past has marked me, has affected me and made me stronger and more able to move forward." For María Cleofé, peace is justice.

In Peru, the fight for land has meant death and sacrifice. The country has suffered violence from terrorist groups and the military. Racism and discrimination are endemic in society. Andean Women confront this situation by organizing and educating themselves.

Peru

Sumitra

Milori Women's Group (MLG)
Mahila Samakhya

Sumitra (born 1949) comes from a scheduled caste family and has received no formal education. But she is at the center of a social upheaval in her village. In 1996, braving disapproval and hostility, she set up the self-help Milori Women's Group. The group runs women's courts in the village, making dispute resolution quick, inexpensive, and mutually consensual. The fallout of the popularity of the women's courts has been a drastic reduction in violence against women, and the consolidation of women's power.

The turning point in Sumitra's life was her association with the NGO Mahila Samakhya in 1991, with which she worked for five years. In 1996, inspired by her understanding of women's rights, she formed the Milori Women's Group. The idea of women forming a group was initially received negatively. It was also a tough decision for a frail, uneducated woman from a scheduled caste background to step outside her home and work on development issues. Thanks to her perseverance, though, women from all 60 villages in Nagal block today participate in the group's activities. One of the most important of this group's activities is the women's courts that deal with problems within families, violence against women, and disputes relating to land and family affairs. Sumitra's method of functioning is to listen to both parties and solve the problems through mutual agreement. If either party fails to honor the court's decision, the group calls in the cops — a surefire kick in the pants. The lower cost and quick resolution — and the fact that decisions are arrived at through mutual consent — have helped make these courts universally acceptable. The group has succeeded in drastically reducing violence against women by ensuring very thorough punishment for the per-petrators.
People from all sections in these villages have benefited from Sumitra's work. Now, the next generation, her daughters-in-law, have also joined her. Sumitra has found the one way to avoid the protracted trap of the Indian legal system — consensus and mutuality, with the cops as a final recourse.

Dispute resolution has traditionally been the condominium of male village elders. That a woman from a scheduled caste background can make headway, let alone find mutually consensual ways to settle disputes out of court, is an amazing development.

India

Mutabar Tadjibayeva

Human Rights Society of Uzbekistan (Hrsu)
Organization for the Defense of Rights and Freedoms of Uzbek Journalists
Committee for Freedom of Speech and Expression

Mutabar Tadjibayeva (born 1962) is the head of the legal defense organization and editor of Ut Yuraklar (Fiery Heart) in Ferghana Valley. She founded the organization in 2000 in order to represent and fight for the rights of rural citizens, supporting them in their struggle for justice and organizing nonviolent protests and resistance against illegal State activity. Mutabar considers her primary mission in life to raise awareness of human rights among her fellow citizens.

Officially, Mutabar Tadjibayeva's organization has defended the rights of up to 49,000 people; unofficially, the number is far bigger. The purpose of the organization is twofold: defending human rights and raising awareness of rights among citizens. In December 2002, an attempt was made to arrest Mutabar because of a letter she had written to the official powers about her intention to organize a demonstration to highlight human rights abuses. The civil protest was to coincide with the Day of the Constitution of the Republic, on 8 December, and was to be held just outside of the Uzbek Parliament. On 4 December, she received a letter from the prosecutor's office in Ferghana, stating that her organization was unregistered and that she could be prosecuted for her activities. A militia squad was dispatched to her home to take her into custody. Avoiding arrest, Mutabar went into hiding in Durmon village. The militia, aware that she had sought sanctuary in Durmon, surrounded the village and carried out house-to-house searches in order to try and find her. The villagers were intimidated and threatened to be arrested, should a "foreign agent," as Mutabar was titled, be found in any of their homes. The Service for National Safety (SNS) carried out the search.

Although Mutabar's work is dogged by this type of state intimidation, she still believes that people are capable of influencing their governments and even capable of preventing wars. "People with poor legal awareness cannot resist the initiatives of their governments to begin wars, that is why they suffer. Under conditions of war, there is no place for human rights. People deprived of legal knowledge turn into puppets in the hands of their own governments and therefore encourage abuse of the rights of others, even against their fellow citizens."

Uzbekistan's transition to democracy has been difficult. The old Soviet system has left its mark on local authorities. The Constitution is widely ignored, rights and freedoms are abused and corruption is rampant.

Uzbekistan

"Literacy is important
to the people's struggles
but resilience is key
for any nation to survive."

Marie Lisette Talate

Chagos Refugees Group

Marie Lisette Talate was born on Diego Garcia Island in 1941. She lived on that island for 30 years with her husband and children. In 1972 they were forcefully removed to Mauritius by British forces. Through her efforts together with other human rights activists the removals were nullified in November 2000 by a British high court — only to be legalized once more four years later.

Diego Garcia is the main island of the Chagos Archipelago in the Indian Ocean. The 65 islands, part of the United Kingdom, are beautiful and said to be one of the last paradises on earth. The people of the islands are Chagossians, descendents of a leper colony and of former African slaves. Unfortunately, in 1972 the whole Archipelago had to be given up and the inhabitants were forcefully removed from the modesty of their homes to Mauritius. Their removal was not for the improvement of their livelihood but rather to pave the way for an air and navy base on Diego Garcia. Their removal was not discussed with them. Their livestock, as well as pets such as dogs, were rounded up and gassed. They were not given time to collect, organize and pack their belongings. There were no plans made for decent accommodation on their arrival on Mauritius.

Marie Lisette Talate, like most refugees, lived in a shack made of rusty tin sheets. Approximately 14 people lived in a two-room house. Together with other Chagossians, Marie Lisette established and led the Chagos Refugees Group to fight the injustice that had rendered their population homeless and destitute. She worked hard in support of Islanders' court cases at different levels.

What makes her work unique is the fact that she cannot write but has led notable demonstrations and campaigns. The most effective and visible demonstrations she organized were held outside the British High Commission on the streets of Port-Louis between 1973 and 2000. On one occasion Marie Lisette led a protest that camped outside the High Commission for two weeks. These campaigns were frightening because the protesters would go hungry for days. "It was difficult enough for Chagossians to survive, but going on hunger strike when already hungry was dangerous and a health hazard."

Diego Garcia is the main island of the Chagos Archipelago in the Indian Ocean. Under colonial rule, traditional life was destroyed by forced removals. Most Chagossians are illiterate and poor. They suffer from low self-esteem and their skills need to be developed.

Thicha na Nakhon

Ban Kanchanapisek Youth Training Center
Women's Constitution Network (WCN)
Sahatai Foundation

Thicha na Nakhon (born 1952) is an active campaigner and advocate of the rights of children, youth and women. She is the director of Ban Kanchanapisek Youth Training Center, a detention facility run by the Ministry of Justice, for children facing criminal charges. Her most recent activity involves raising awareness of the problems of women and children in the tsunami-affected areas, and providing direct assistance in the form of psychosocial care to enable them to recover from the trauma and displacement .

With her keen understanding of psychology, Thicha na Nakhon was able to bring many innovative ideas into the government's services for children and youth. She introduced entertainment activities for children confined to hospitals in order to help them feel better while they are away from their homes and families. This project has helped immensely in the psychological and physical healing of the children. At the Pak Kret Welfare Center, Thicha na Nakhon introduced a system that focuses on the benefit and comfort of the children, instead of the staff at the welfare home. For the youth, she introduced a project to promote the development of the personality of youngsters placed in temporary homes. For children living in welfare homes facing charges of narcotics abuse, she initiated a systematic program to build their self-confidence by enabling them to return to their communities without shame. Thicha na Nakhon has been involved in campaigns to bring about more recognition of the role of women in society. She endorsed the Women's Constitution Network (WCN) which empowers women to participate in politics and political reform.

"Our society is male-dominated. Many laws we have to abide by today were written by men and therefore overlook some issues faced by women," she says, citing Article 276 of Criminal Law, which permits men to rape their own wives. In her campaign for the amendment of this article, she was criticized by those who believe that she was provoking problems within the family institution, instead of realizing that she was protecting women from violence and rape at the hands of their own husbands. After giving 27 years to social welfare, Thicha na Nakhon feels that a lot more needs to be done to bring about justice and social equality between men and women.

The majority of laws in Thai society are written by men and are therefore not sensitive to issues which may lead to discrimination against or abuse of the rights of women. Article 276 of Thailand's Criminal Law is a clear example.

Thailand

Teresa Columba Ulloa Ziaurriz

Popular Defenders, A.C.

Teresa was named after her grandmother. Her daughter was named after her mother. Three key women in her life: the first two give her strength, and the little girl gives her happiness for fighting. When she was 20 years old, she was elected Secretary General of a trade-union. Her father felt let down: "So much effort for this," he said. Teresa Ulloa would never leave "this." Since then, she has defended poor women and children in Mexican courts, on the streets and in the community. "There are a lot of them, we cannot stop," she affirms.

"I have worn my knees out walking around this country, and I have been through a lot of hard times, economically." Teresa Ulloa has walked all over the Republic of Mexico to meet with other women, sharing her belief that life should not be lived in fear, demanding the authorities to fulfill their obligations, and teaching people about legal mechanisms and instruments designed to eliminate gender-violence. "I remember a meeting in Guerrero, in the southwestern part of the country. I had to pass through seven military checkpoints and, at every one of them, they wanted to take my materials away from me. We met with the women surrounded by army tanks. Paradoxically, I spoke to them about their right to live without violence. The courage that they showed gave me courage, too."

Now, 54 years old and leaning on her walking stick, she says: "Peace resides in the possibility of a life in which there is no violence of any kind. A life like that is only possible through dialogue and justice, within nations and between them. A future of peace will come about when the inequality between men and women disappears. This starts in everyday life, and it has to go on every day." A trade-unionist, she joined the feminist movement, and from there has fought legal battles to defend thousands of mistreated women and girls. She has freed innocent women from jail, and she has put male aggressors behind bars. "I also found things of vital importance for myself, and, now, life has given me the blessed gift of a late maternity. My daughter gives meaning to my fight and to my whole existence. The little girls in the world are the ones who most need my continued struggle." For the past five years, she has dedicated herself exclusively to fighting against the sexual exploitation of children in Latin America and the Caribbean.

Poverty and male chauvinism in Mexico turn women and young girls into prostitution and subordination.Obliged to live under inhuman conditions, women have to bear the full brunt of injustice. A man can buy a virgin girl for 50 Mexican pesos (about USD 4.50) in a poor tourist area.

Mexico

Jo Vallentine

People for Nuclear Disarmament (PND)
Anti-Nuclear Alliance of Western Australia (ANAWA)
Alternatives to Violence (AVP)

Jo Vallentine is a Quaker, peace activist, and social justice advocate who made history in 1984 when she was elected to the Australian Senate as the world's first single-issue peace politician. She has worked tirelessly for more than three decades at grassroots, national, and international levels, via People for Nuclear Disarmament, the Anti-Nuclear Alliance of Western Australia, the Alternatives to Violence Project, the Greens (WA), and Abolition 2000 (UN) to put these issues onto the political agenda. She has two daughters.

Jo Vallentine has become the public face of political peace activism in Australia. She is much admired in her local, regional, and national communities, and is known especially for her persistence and tenacity. Her work is characterized by a commitment to non-violence; by a commitment to "holy obedience" to the call of direct action lobbying; and by a commitment to community outreach via education in non-violent conflict resolution processes. She has been arrested five times during non-violent direct action protests. She is an optimist, and was inspired by the events of 14/15 February 2003, when 30 million people around the world took to the streets to protest against the imminent invasion of Iraq by the United States. She has great faith in people power. Jo is in awe of the natural world and deeply respectful of the wisdom of other beings. She is driven by a responsibility to act on behalf of two voiceless groups: the other-than-human, and future beings. She envisions a future where, with a positive shift of consciousness, humans will be able to manifest spontaneous right actions through reflection on our past and present interactions with the natural world and all living things. In such a future humans will have evolved to the point where they can act like a flock of geese in flight — moving intuitively, harmoniously and in perfect formation towards a positively imagined future time and place. Jo is sustained by her Quaker faith, by the love and support of her fellow travellers — family, activists, communities — and by a daily ritual expressing gratitude to life and love.

Jo Vallentine does peace activism and social justice advocacy locally (in prisons, grassroots organizations, Quaker meetings), nationally (in Parliament, at demonstrations), and internationally (at protest sites, at the UN). This exposes her to personal risk and potential violence.

Australia

Victoria Marina Velásquez de Avilés

Supreme Court of Justice

She "was born" in the University of El Salvador as a Doctorate in Law (1974). She gave birth to five children. She defended the rights of the workers as the vice-minister of the Ministry of Labor and as a labor law judge. She defended the rights of children and occupied the office of Judge Advocate General for the Defense of the Human Rights, created in 1992. She faced the State to defend the people. She was threatened. She resisted. Now, she is a magistrate of the Supreme Court of Justice.

An innate sense of justice and social sensitivity led her to study law. Married since her first year of university, she kept putting her studies on hold to give birth five times. In a sense she was born twice in the university: the first time with a Doctorate in Law in 1974; the second time with a degree in Political Sciences in 1988. She is Victoria Marina de Avilés, Salvadoran.

Victoria Velásquez — the Avilés would come later — was born in 1943. A dedicated student since her childhood, she is known as the defender of so-called lost causes. According to her father and some of her teachers, she started a degree in social work. But things changed and she ended up studying law. "The Protection of Salaries" was the title of her doctorate thesis at the University of El Salvador, and it lead to the first job of her professional career — she became the vice minister of the Ministry of Labor (1979). During her time as vice-minister, she influenced the minimum period for maternity leave to be increased to 90 days. Soon afterwards, she was a labor law judge (until 1983).

The Office of the Judge Advocate General for the Defense of the Human Rights was created after the Peace Treaties of 1992. She was assigned to the child rights department and, soon thereafter, the director of the Institution (1995). She faced the State to defend the people. She knew of threats — of the signs and the denouncements, of the uncomfortableness of government officials who publicly challenged her. She resisted. Although she was loved by the general public, the political class rejected her and she was not reappointed. She holds, as a reminder, the memory of what a street boy said, with a voice tight with emotion, to the police when he was caught inhaling drugs: "Call my friend, the Advocate." Now she is a magistrate of the Supreme Court of Justice.

The abuse of power by civil servants, the lack of respect to the law and to the constitution, and the rejection of the changes needed to construct a more just society are all constants in El Salvador. This reality demands a more critical scrutiny by the citizens.

El Salvador

"We should preserve in adults the confident and joyful attitude of small children."

Patricia Verdugo Aguirre

Patricia Verdugo is a Chilean journalist and writer. She has oriented her work towards human rights, covering the period before, during and after the military government (1973–1990), and to the promotion of democracy. Since 1979, she has written more than ten books concerning what happened during the dictatorship in Chile. She has received a number of awards: in 1997, in Chile, the National Journalism Prize; in 1993, in the United States, the María Moors Cabot Prize; and in 2000, the Latin American Studies Association recognized her work.

Journalist and writer, she is the daughter of an executed politician and sister of a member of the military. Patricia Verdugo Aguirre, opponent of the military regime set up in Chile from 1973 to 1990, joined the thousands of people who denounced the violations of human rights in her country and who were actively working for the return of democracy. In 1977, she became the co-founder of the magazine "Hoy" (Today), a publication that, along with other written media, maintained an independent and critical position in face of the dictatorship.

Her father's murder prompted her to join the protest movement of many women who were searching for truth and justice. In 1983, she co-founded the Women's Movement for Life, which — along with other women's groups — protested against general Augusto Pinochet and his military regime. Her books, based on rigorous journalistic studies, are crucial, not only for the preservation of historical memory and to promote the human rights, but also for judicial trials. One of them, "Los Zarpazos del Puma" (The Claw Marks of the Puma) (1985), served as a basis for the investigation of the Caravan of Death, which involved the imprisonment of top intelligence chiefs.

Besides the books named above, she also wrote: Una herida abierta (1979), André de La Victoria (1984), Quemados Vivos (Burnt Alive) (1986), Operación Siglo XX (Operation XX Century) (1990), Tiempos de días claros (Times of Clear Days) (1990), Interferencia Secreta (Secret Interference) (1997), Bucarest 187 (2001), Allende: cómo la Casa Blanca provocó su muerte (Allende: how the White House provoked his death) (2003), De la Tortura (no) se habla, (About torture, (no) one talks) (2005), among other books.

On September 11th, 1973, a state coup led by general Pinochet brought down the administration of the United Popular Party. On this day, Salvador Allende, President of Chile, died, as thousands of other people did during the following years. In 1990, the country returned to democracy.

Chile

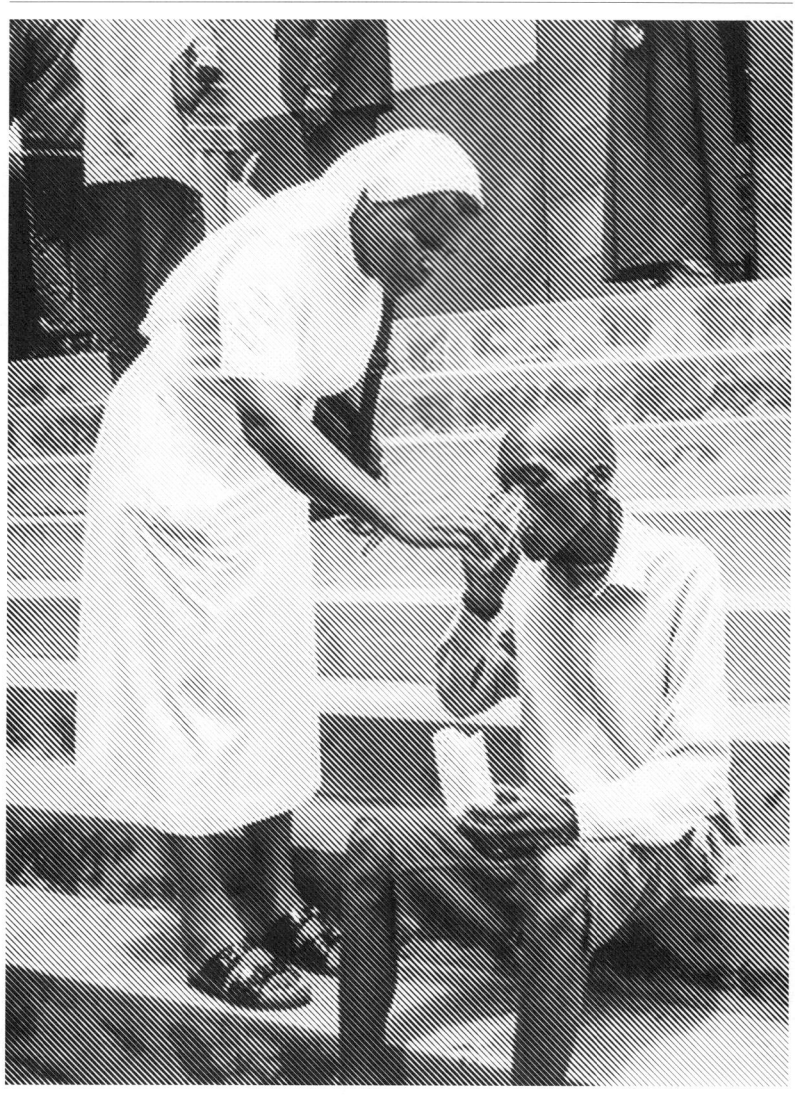

Hedwig Vinyou

Action by Christians for the Abolition of Torture (ACAT)

Sister Hedwig Vinyou was born in 1955, in Mbiim Djottin, North-Western Province of Cameroon. From 1962 to 1968, she attended St. Peter's School, Mbiim. In 1973, she entered the Franciscan Congregation, committing her life to religion and service. She now lives in Bamenda, West of Cameroon, and has worked for many years among prisoners and fought for their rights. Since 1998, she has decongested the Bamenda Central Prison by negotiating and obtained the release of some 2000 prisoners who, for a long time, had been awaiting trial for minor offences.

Undeterred by limited resources, Sister Hedwig is spurred on by her dedication, love and determination. Consequently, the Bamenda Central Prison now has probably the best general sanitation system in the country. She concentrates on the improvement of conditions in the prison, especially in health and sanitation. She also brings the prisoners medicine and extra food, disinfects the rooms and fights for their cases to be heard. She also tries to temper the natural brutality of the guards.

Although she has committed her life to her religion, her care and sympathy has erased religious and tribal borders. Sister Hedwig goes to the prison as a Catholic but treats all the inmates like her brothers. She provides all the necessary materials and assistance for everyone to worship in their own religion. "I don't go there to convert; I go there to show my sympathy, for each prisoner to feel that out there, there is somebody who does not judge them, who cares about them."

She has a vision of a peaceful future if, in spite of poverty, people are able to raise awareness and promote cooperation.

Sister Hedwig underwent extensive professional training between 1977 and 1994 in social development, teaching, scripture and life, and counseling.

Since 1975 she has worked as a pastoral and social worker. She has successfully worked for the improvement of prison conditions at the Bamenda Central Prison. She coordinated renovation of the Bamenda Central Prison, giving the best general sanitation system in Cameroon. She systematically decongested the prison by negotiating the release of more then 2000 inmates, who had been forgotten as they awaited trial for minor offences. As a result, the procedure to grant bail while awaiting trial has been relaxed in the Bamenda Central Prison.

A prisoner's life in Cameroon is very harsh. The toilet facilities, where available, are overstretched. The Aids epidemic prevalent in the country is rife in prisons. Tuberculosis, dysentery and malnutrition are the commonplace.

Cameroon

Ching Feng Wang

Taipei Women's Rescue Foundation

Since 1996, Wang Ching Feng has proactively helped Taiwanese "comfort women", who were forced to perform sexual services within Japanese camps during World War II. She crisscrossed Taiwan with Taipei Women's Rescue Foundation social workers and interviewed over 60 "comfort women". She travelled to Japan, South Korea, North Korea, Chinese Mailand, the USA and Europe to gain support and seek compensation and formal apologies from the Japanese government.

Wang Ching Feng, a lawyer by profession, a legislator and vice-presidential candidate in 1996, remembers when she started demanding apologies. She went to Tokyo with two of the "grannies" to the International Hearing for the Compensation of Wartime Atrocities. Korean and Mainland Chinese elderly "comfort women" were outspoken, while their Taiwanese counterparts tried to hide their identity. They gave their testimonies behind a screen. Thereafter, with Wang's effort, they finally dressed up and stopped seeking protection from a screen; they faced the audience and spoke out: "The Japanese are the ones to be ashamed, not us." Wang was deeply moved by their new-found courage and said: "Japan used its military, administrative and financial power to humiliate women from occupied areas. This was a government-sponsored action, therefore the Japanese government must apologize and compensate its victims. Wartime crimes are legal violations, not just ethical ones."

Wang has spent several million Taiwan dollars of her own money to support the work. In 13 years, her efforts on the issue of "comfort women" coupled with those of the Foundation have yielded results. The government agreed to give a monthly subsidy to the elderly women. Through the years, she has selflessly worked for the Foundation. "Life is too short, we should try to do something meaningful with it. If we can help others, that is already an achievement, a rewarding one," she says.

In 1991, Korean women's groups initiated a process in Japanese courts accusing the Japanese government of forcing women in occupied Asian countries to perform sexual services during Word War II. Two months later, Japanese historians acknowledged that Taiwanese women were also among the sex slaves.

China, Taiwan

Ruth Weiss

An exemplary biography of the 20th century: Ruth Weiss is born into a Jewish family in Germany in 1924. In 1936, she arrives in South Africa with her family and experiences the development of apartheid. She defies the system with her typewriter, quietly but with determination, in South Africa, Zimbabwe, Zambia, and Europe. She does research, reports, forms friendships, participates in projects to overcome racism. Her strongest quality: she listens. Listening is the basis for understanding, understanding paves the way to reconciliation — a model for peace that can be applied globally.

Ruth Weiss was a witness of her time. As a schoolgirl she experienced the destructive force of anti-Semitism and persecution. In 1936, she left Germany with her family and emigrated to South Africa. The South African writer Nadine Gordimer wrote: "Ruth Weiss found herself in a country where the mark of the victim is not the yellow star but the black skin. Being white, she could have been content, in South Africa, with being accepted for full citizenship denied blacks." She had exchanged one unjust system for another: in 1948, racism was legalized in South Africa through the introduction of apartheid.

Ruth Weiss became an economic journalist and worked in the whole of southern Africa and temporarily in Europe. She soon became an accepted authority in her field. She reported the situation in southern Africa without compromise and soon ran into difficulties with the authorities. She was justifiably suspected of making common cause with the oppressed blacks. While working in Zimbabwe (formerly Southern Rhodesia) from 1966 to 1968, she was declared persona non grata, subsequently refused re-entry to South Africa and blacklisted by the Portuguese in Mozambique. She then went on with her quiet work over decades, becoming "a shrewd and greatly trusted interpreter of African thought, aims, and strategies, and a friend of many black leaders and — perhaps more important — ordinary people." (Gordimer)

Beginning in 1988, Ruth Weiss worked at the Harare-based Zimbabwe Institute for Southern Africa, which enabled members of liberation movements to meet white South Africans secretly, to prepare the way for a peaceful end to apartheid. Though she returned subsequently to Europe, Africa remained in her heart. She has published numerous books on a wide range of issues. Her motto is "circles which close." Her struggle for equality is a struggle for peace.

Southern Africa in the last century was a place of colonialism, apartheid, and struggles for liberation. Conflict resolution played an important role in bringing about the peaceful end of apartheid in South Africa.

Germany

Jo Wilding

Circus2Iraq (C2I)

Originally motivated by political demonstrations, Jo set off to the Middle East to advocate peace and justice in Palestine, Israel and Iraq, sometimes risking her life in these vulnerable areas. She has constructed a cyber website where she writes extensively about people who are physically and mentally traumatized as a result of of armed violence. She also took a small circus, in which she herself plays a clown, to Iraq in an effort to bring laughter and healing to the traumatized people, especially the children. Now Jo is receiving legal training to become a human rights lawyer.

One of the most haunting things Jo has done was to bring a circus to Iraq. A few circuses were deployed to politically troubled areas, in the Balkans and East Timor, only after the bloodshed there was ended. There have also been clowns deployed to Nepal, Mongolia and India performing for street children and refugees, but what makes Jo's work unforgettable is that she moved a circus with its full troupe to an area where fighting is still at its zenith. Not only did Jo take the circus to Iraq, but also she has participated in its shows as a clown. The circus group did not just perform for the people, they also "taught" the children how to perform some acrobatics. Jo was enormously affected by the awful condition of hundreds of thousands of Iraqi children. They had been severely traumatized by the eight-year Iraq-Iran war, 13 years of privation during the UN sanctions following the Iraqi Invasion of Kuwait, and outright frustration and terror during the US-led war against Iraq with even more shortages of basic needs of life and suffering. "I met children who had not smiled in over a year," she wrote. The words of one old man, as he stood earnestly observing his grandchildren watching the performance of the circus troupe, say it all: "I never thought I would see the day when my grandchildren would laugh again. Thank you for returning them to the real world." Words cannot describe the smiles that Jo has brought to these traumatized people. No wonder they have great memories of her. In the midst of their terrifying experiences, she has managed to bring joy and breathe hope back into their lives for a better future.

Beside the circus Jo set up networks between medical students in Baghdad and Newcastle in 2003 to rebuild the Iraqi labs and libraries that had been wrecked by 13 years of sanctions. She also launched campaigns to buy CD-ROMs, computer equipment and books to help rebuild Iraqi medical education.

United Kingdom

Women in Black

Women in Black (WIB) is a world-wide network of political activist women committed to peace and justice advocacy. They are actively opposed to injustice, war, militarism and other forms of violence. The WIB-women, often dressed in black, stand in a public place in silent, non-violent vigils at regular times and intervals, carrying placards and handing out leaflets about peace promotion. In 2001 WIB was awarded the Millennium Peace Prize for Women by the United Nations Development Fund for Women.

In January 1988, one month after the first Palestinian Intifada broke out, a small group of Israeli and Palestinian women stood once a week, at the same time and at the same location — a major traffic intersection in Israel. They were dressed in black and holding a black sign in the shape of a hand with the motto "Stop the Occupation" written in white. "It was a simple form of protest that women could do easily," recalls one of the participants. "We could bring our children, there was no chanting or marching, and the medium was the message. Within months vigils sprang up throughout Israel."
Women in Black (WIB) developed as a response to the logic of war. Women who contributed to create WIB refused to raise children for war, to ignore war crimes committed in their name, to support illegal military occupation, to continue their normal lives while other people were deprived of their basic human rights and of their dignity. The dissociation of the movement from political affiliation and the choice of non-violent strategies are the key markers of its success. The strategy of non-violence, in particular, gave the movement great moral strength and persuasiveness.

Women in Black (WIB) adopts a feminist understanding that male violence against women in domestic life and in war are related. WIB believes that women experience a continuum of gendered violence, generated and sustained in masculine cultures. WIB is an attempt to resist violence through non-violent actions.

International

Haydee B. Yorac

Presidential Commission on Good Government (PCGG)

Her reputation as a tough, uncompromising and brilliant human rights lawyer made Haydee Yorac (born 1941) the obvious choice for the most challenging government posts in the post-Martial Law era. Driven by the desire to help the country, she took on the challenge of cleaning up the Commission on Elections (Comelec), heading the National Unification Commission (NUC), and recovering the sagging reputation of the Presidential Commission on Good Government (PCGG). Haydee Yorac is easily one of the most eminent and credible leaders in the Philippines today.

"Fiat justitia ruat coelum" (let justice be done though the heavens fall) — this maxim has guided Haydee Yorac throughout her professional career. And it has served the Filipino people well. A brilliant law professor, she was appointed to the Commission on Elections (Comelec), first as a member then as chair from 1989 to 1991. At the time, the Comelec had very low credibility among the electorate, but Haydee cleaned up its act so that even warlords followed the election gun ban. In 1992, she was appointed to head the National Unification Commission (NUC) tasked with consulting all sectors of society to discover the roots of the insurgency and make recommendations on how to achieve a just and lasting peace. After traveling throughout the country, the NUC recommended six integrated paths to peace that the government should take. In 2001, she was appointed to head the Presidential Commission on Good Government (PCGG) tasked with recovering the ill-gotten wealth of the former dictator and his cronies. Fifteen years after it was created, the PCGG had accomplished little and was on the verge of being abolished. Haydee Yorac mobilized the staff to secure the records of the cases, which were in a mess. She hired the chief librarian of the law library of the state university to organize the litigation records, and invited young, idealistic lawyers who were willing work part-time for less than USD 500 a month. Under her direction, the PCGG recovered USD 683 million (Php38 billion) from the Marcos Swiss accounts, and the Supreme Court issued three major decisions confirming the public nature of the coconut levy funds and assets, effectively returning to 3.4 million coconut farmers ownership of levies they were forced to pay on their produce during the martial law years.

Fifteen years after the fall of the dictator, the Philippine government had not recovered the ill-gotten wealth Marcos and his cronies kept in Swiss banks. Cases were not moving in the courts, and the records were in a mess. And government lawyers were no match for the shrewd Marcos legal team.

"I give new knowledge to people, and I hope it will help them to defend human rights."

Rano Yusupova

Human Rights Clinic

Rano Yusupova (born in 1960) received her law degree from Tashkent State University and worked as a lawyer for over 15 years, and for the past ten years as a barrister. Rano is well regarded as one of Uzbekistan's leading human rights advocates — an experience which has been put to great use in the creation of a Human Rights Clinic. Rano has used her extensive knowledge of human rights to train local judges, barristers, and lawyers in over 40 intensive trainings which cover subjects from juvenile justice to domestic implementation of international legal standards.

A lawyer from Tashkent, Rano Yusupova works in the Human Rights Clinic providing legal assistance and counseling to the elderly, students, and the economically disadvantaged. Through her work with the Human Rights Clinic, Rano has trained more than 100 people, in addition to counseling and defending the rights of hundreds. Rano's students — human rights advocates, lawyers, and barristers — have praised her training skills and seminars: "The legal, theoretical, and practical materials are invaluable. We learned about international standards in the field of human rights, international mechanisms for defending human rights and about the United Nations system." Rano's colleagues have noted that "… the development of the clinic over the last year often put heavy time demands on Rano. Rano always acted and responded to these demands in a professional and responsible manner, oftentimes going extra steps in assessing the situation and making suggestions for improvements."

Rano has a wide range of experience, dealing with the international and national NGOs and government officials; an experience which has given her the ability to interact with and represent entities at top level negotiations and conferences. Her colleagues say, "… she is an asset in the Human Rights Clinic due to her extensive practical and theoretical knowledge of international and domestic human rights law and her professionalism."

Uzbekistan's transition to democracy has been difficult. The old Soviet system has left its mark on local authorities. The Constitution is widely ignored, and rights and freedoms are abused. There is great need for women with the strength and courage to defend human rights and build civil society.

Uzbekistan

Stopping the Hidden War Against Women: Women, Health and Peace

Sima Samar

M

Access to health care is a basic human right. Providing health care to the people is part of the basic social services to which everyone should have access. Without good health care for the people, especially for women, human security and peace are not possible. Health does not mean that you simply can walk. Health means that you should have access to health care, good food, and a healthy environment to live in. If the women are not healthy in society, the family will not be healthy, the nation will not be healthy, and, finally, the world will not be healthy for humanity.

Not having an active war in the country is not the only measure of security. In countries where there is no access to health care, people do not feel secure. We see in every report that maternal and child mortality and morbidity — which is a hidden war against the lives of half of the world human body — are high in such countries.

Women are the primary victims when health care facilities are not adequate. If the mother is not healthy, the child will not be born healthy. With a sickly population, every kind of crime is possible in the society.

Afghanistan is an example of how health for women and peace, sickness and war, are very closely connected. One of the reasons why we had such a long- lasting and violent war in Afghanistan is that people were not healthy in this country. The infrastructure for basic social services, social justice, education, and health care had been destroyed and, as a result, poverty played a big role in the conflict.

Poverty is not a good environment for peace and human security to flourish. The terrorism and fundamentalism, that continue to fester in Afghanistan and have caused a lot of problems for the world, are caused by poverty.

An important part of health care for women is reproductive health care, including family planning, and control of their bodies. Yet, for women, this human right to health is often ignored, restricted or denied because of war, culture, misuse of religion and decision makers who do not put a priority on women's rights or women's lives.

For example, if a woman has ten to 12 children, how she can keep her good health? How can she study or work to get her family out of poverty? How can she have time to take part in political activities and decision making about her daily life?

If women cannot participate in decision making, all the decisions are made by men, resulting in male-oriented ideas. If this exclusion of women from decision making is not remedied, male domination in the home, society, and the country will continue and women will never be empowered.

Another example of the hidden war against women is HIV/Aids. Because of their body structure and their position in society, women are more vulnerable to the virus. There are countries where there is no active war or conflict, but thousands of women and children are dying of HIV/Aids. The majority of the victims of HIV/Aids are women.

We cannot say that countries have peace and security when so many women are dying every day of preventable causes such as HIV/Aids, pregnancy, and domestic violence. Women are the majority of the world's population. Women must be healthy if we want the global human body to be healthy and peaceful.

Dr Sima Samar, a medical doctor, is the chair of the Afghan Independent Human Rights Commission (AIHRC). She was the first deputy prime minister and minister for women's affairs in Afghanistan and director of the Shuhada Organization which supports 12 clinics and four hospitals for women and children, and 60 schools in Afghanistan and Pakistan.

—

M

Good human
relations, that
are a very
important aspect
of the African
culture, have
made Kate
one of the
most distinguished
in her field
of operation.

Kate Adoo Adeku

Peace Now

Professor Kate Adoo Adeku (60) is a courageous lady who grew up in a small farming community. She not only teaches but is also active in different non-governmental organizations such as Population and Development (PAD), the Institute of Adult Education at the University of Ghana, and the Society for Women Against Aids in Africa (SWAA), a pan-African organization doing research on HIV/Aids, gender and violence, orphans and vulnerable children.

Since she was 12 year old, Kate Adoo Adeku took several actions with the intention of changing the situation of her sisters in rural and urban communities for a better quality of life. She has trained trainers for the national literacy programme in the ten regions of Ghana and has coordinated a basic education program for communities. This means that women and men, who received training in reading and writing as well as in managing finances, are now less vulnerable to poverty. Because of this her name resonates in many communities and women say that thanks to Kate Adeku they feel more confident. Her training for adults crosses all sections of society — from workers in the informal sector to doctors.

Her work at the Institute of Adult Education has influenced other institutions in the sub-region. This is especially the case with her distance learning courses on HIV/Aids prevention which has raised interest as far as South Africa.

When HIV/Aids was first identified in Ghana in 1986, the national rate of infection was 1.5%. Today it is 3.6%. More than 52,961 HIV/Aids cases have now been reported which represents 30% of all cases as most people go to traditional centres, prayer camps or do not report their illness.

Ghana

Jowara Al-Angari

Mecca Society for Development and Social Services (MSDSS)
Women's Welfare Society (WWS)
World Organizations for Muslims and Families (WOMF)

Jowara Al-Angari received her BA in Anthropology from the American University of Beirut (AUB) and is a mother of three. Since 1976 she has worked tirelessly on social issues in Saudi Arabia, notably family planning and women's and human rights. She has been involved in community cancer programs, supporting cancer patients and raising cancer awareness within national communities. Her work has promoted the expansion of health and family services to rural Saudi families, where state services are undersupplied and there is great demand for family planning advice and employment training for women.

Almost 14 years ago a well-known religion scholar in Saudi Arabia attacked and maligned the Women's Welfare Society, to which Jowara Al-Angari is so deeply committed. This attack, which was delivered at a public lecture, severely hindered the progress of the organization that she had established in Saudi society. Most damaging, however, was that donations to the organization decreased, and much of the trust it had built up over the years in Saudi society became jeopardized. In response to this, Jowara Al-Angari contacted the scholar and asked him to visit one of the beneficiaries of the Women's Welfare Society: a Center for Disabled Children. After visiting the center he issued a personal apology to her and to the Welfare Society, noting what a positive effect its work has on Saudi society. Since then, this scholar has been an active donor to the Society and has continuously encouraged others to do the same.

This and many other obstacles have plagued Jowara Al-Angari's work over the last 35 years. She has remained steadfast, however, and committed to a world free of violence and social injustice. Her community work extends beyond the Welfare Society into many areas of social concern, particularly cancer patients and the disabled. Her work has touched the lives of many, especially those in the communities to which she has committed so much time and effort. When asked about her work in relation to abuse, she said, "Let us say that all different levels of society benefit — the poor, the sick, orphans, blue-collar workers and intellectuals alike — either through the social welfare programs, my writings or my lectures. With respect to human rights, there are no class distinctions in terms of abuse." Through her work at grassroots level, she has demonstrated that the world can be changed for the better.

Jowara Al-Angari is affiliated with a number of social welfare organizations working with communities stricken with cancer and disabilities. A staunch supporter of women's rights and social equity, she strives to ensure the fulfillment of social, economic and political rights.

Saudi Arabia

"Divine God! I give you thanks for giving me the strength to recognize what my true path was, to my family for believing in me, and to the Vieques Women's Alliance for empowerment." Zaida Torres

Alianza de Mujeres Viequenses

In May 1999, a group of women from Vieques, Puerto Rico, joined for a common cause: to end the American military's occupation of their homeland for military testing. Under the leadership of Judith Conde, the women formed the Alianza de Mujeres Viequenses (AMV) and added their voices to a chorus that resulted in the end of the occupation. After the Navy's departure, the AMV continued to mobilize women from diverse backgrounds to work for the well-being of the island's families and future generations.

Just a month before the women of Vieques' April meeting, one of their countrymen had been accidentally killed by the USA when a test bomb missed its target. And so the women met to discuss the effects the military was having on them as mothers, aunts, and grandmothers. They knew, for example, that cancer rates on their island were higher than on the main island. In fact, the women's alliance had begun with jornadas, which held screenings for breast cancer and free clinical exams.

The AMV women began tying white ribbons to military gates, and the symbol of peace spread throughout the island. In December 1999, they helped to establish the Peace and Justice Camp outside the military gates as an alternative to the more strident demands of their male counterparts. The camp resembled their homes; there they cooked, prayed, and celebrated family activities. In 2000, the group developed a women's cancer support group that established links with local and national providers of cancer healthcare and education. A year later, they developed a health program for the entire community, resulting in services for more than 3000 residents. For the first time in more than 20 years, women were able to deliver babies in their hometown following the reestablishment of the health center. With the support of groups from the main island of Puerto Rico, in 2001 they opened the doors to Casa Alianza, where community services are administered for all Viequenses. They launched a sex education camp for young Vieques women with the goals of reducing teen pregnancy, promoting self-esteem, preventing abusive relationships, and developing leadership skills.

Today, as a result of the work of the Alliance, politics on Vieques is no longer just for men. Alianza's members are frequently asked to join community panels and commissions.

For 65 years, the US navy used Vieques for military training and testing, including routine bombing from the air and sea, and munitions storage and disposal. The Navy's presence provoked tensions, injustice, insensitivity, economic disadvantage, and destroyed much of the natural environment.

Puerto Rico

Maire-Bopp Allport Dupont

Pacific Islands Aids Foundation (PIAF)
Women's International Leage for Peace and Freedom (WILPF)
Nuclear Free and Independent Pacific movement (NFIP)

Colonization, nuclear testing, and the Aids pandemic have broken the peace and paradise of the Pacific islands. From Tahiti, Maire-Bopp Allport — anti-nuclear activist and Aids campaigner — is the founder of the Pacific Islands Aids Foundation (PIAF), supporting islanders living with HIV/Aids. As a journalist, Maire helped put Aids on the Pacific agenda when she courageously spoke of her HIV-positive status at a regional media conference. A member of the Nuclear Free and Independent Pacific movement, Maire campaigns for peace and human security in French Polynesia and the Pacific.

2002: the closing ceremony of the World Aids Conference in Barcelona. Bill Clinton is to introduce Nelson Mandela. Maire-Bopp Allport, a young Tahitian woman, steps out to introduce the former US President. She is one of many Pacific Islanders living with HIV/Aids — a woman with the courage to break taboos to discuss the epidemic afflicting the Pacific and the world. Before the Barcelona audience, Maire stresses that HIV/Aids is a security issue: "The United States voted a military budget of 393 billion US dollars in 2001. But I wish for peace, because in the world now, and in my country, violence is so big that it stops us from giving this message of awareness to stop the spread of HIV/Aids."

Born in Tahiti, Maire was diagnosed in 1998 while studying at the University of the South Pacific in Fiji. Within months, one of the first Pacific islanders to go public, she declared her HIV status at the regional Pacific Islands News Association conference. In pin-drop quiet, her colleagues listened to her moving speech on the challenges of living with the disease. Journalists are rarely lost for words, but all were struck dumb by her bravery and boldness. When colleagues asked if they could use her name, she replied: "Of course. That is why I am here." Today, Maire is chief executive officer of the Pacific Islands Aids Foundation (PIAF), supporting islanders living with HIV/Aids. She believes people living with the virus must take the lead in challenging the stigma associated with Aids. Now based in Cook Islands, Maire travels the Pacific to speak to young people, parents, policy makers, and priests about the Aids pandemic, and how to act to bring security to their lives. As an anti-nuclear activist and journalist, she continues to work with her Maohi people, who suffered 30 years of French nuclear testing.

The HIV/Aids pandemic has spread to the Pacific. Islanders living with HIV/Aids have broken the silence and created community and government programs for prevention, care, and support. They demand money for health, not warfare; they want resources for education, not militarization of the Pacific.

French Polynesia

Insaf Arafat

World Health Organization (WHO)
United Nations Children's Fund (Unicef)
United Nations Women Guild of Jordan (UNWGJ)

As a trained medical doctor and an international expert on child health and family planning, Insaf Arafat has over 30 years experience in promoting health care for mothers and children throughout the Middle East. She has also helped the displaced survivors of wars and disabled land mine victims, and has participated in international conferences on the role of health professionals in fighting violence against women. Her work and contributions have been undertaken through various UN organizations.

As Team Leader of a World Health Organization (WHO) project working on maternal and child health under unstable conditions in Somalia and Congo, Dr Arafat risked her life to ensure the successful completion of the program. At one point, she says, "We were lost in the jungle for many hours, but fortunately we were rescued by the rest of the team." Despite the scare, she has remained steadfast in her commitment to bettering the health and living conditions of women and children in these locations and throughout the world. Her commitment to health issues is matched only by her commitment to peace and stability in the world.

For all her work in the last 30 years, Insaf Arafat still draws her strength from her own experiences as a displaced Arab woman. "I was studying in London in the year 1967, the June war broke out and my town Nablus in Palestine was occupied. I have not been able to return home ever since." Unable to return to her hometown, Insaf Arafat has committed herself to working with refugees, not only on health issues, but also on conflict resolution. As a young physician she began her work helping women and children in war-stricken areas of the world, particularly in Africa where civil wars and difficult political situations often made her peace work strenuous and life-threatening. Now, 30 years later, she is still working towards peace but in a different manner. She concentrates her peace efforts on helping charity institutions concerned with assisting the disabled, land mine survivors and refugees. Insaf Arafat is committed to a peaceful future through working for a new culture of peace in the region. This includes working with organizations committed to peace and to the betterment of peoples everywhere.

Insaf Arafat is a medical doctor, obstetrician and gynecologist. She is currently working on maternal and child health and family planning issues for various United Nations agencies, such as Unicef and the WHO. She is also Vice President of the United Nations Women Guild of Jordan (UNWGJ).

Jordan

Zilda Arns Neumann

Pastoral da Criança (Pastoral of the Child)

Zilda Arns Neumann (born 1943) is a pediatric and sanitary doctor. Founder and national coordinator of Pastoral of the Child, an ecumenical organism of the National Conference of Bishops of Brazil (BNCB). She is also the president of the Intersectorial Commission of Indigenous Health. Recently, she took on the coordination of the elderly. Mother of five children, she is a collector of national and international prizes, granted in recognition to her work in Pastoral of the Child.

Zilda Arns Neumann was born in a small community in the state of Santa Catarina, in the South of Brazil. Forquilinha was so small that everyone knew each other. It was in her childhood that Zilda Arns had the inspiration for her future: "My mom studied homemade medicine in German books. She saw people and knew who needed to go to the hospital and who could be treated at home." Another characteristic of the family was discipline. "We had to wake up very early to milk the cow." According to her, this discipline was providential: "I have no difficulties waking up very early and facing 15 hours of work." In Zilda's day there is always work to be done. She coordinates a true factory of solidary information. Pastoral da Criança (Pastoral of the Child), created in 1983, is present in 36,258 communities, spread throughout more than 3757 Brazilian cities. The basis of work is the volunteer. This philosophy is not to give the bread, but to multiply the information.
Information can be the difference between life and death, to children between one day and six years old. Pregnant and poor mothers are oriented in matters of nutrition, nursing, food preparation, the correct use of drinking water, the preparation of homemade saline solution, basic hygiene. To monitor the progress, there is the Weighing Day — also known as the Day of the Celebration of Life. Weekly, the children are weighed while mothers and grandmothers exchange information and knowledge. In more than 20 years of working with the Pastoral, Zilda affirms that "the women are very creative and they have tremendous force." Zilda is a catholic woman. She believes that hope, along with solidarity, is the antidote against poverty. "God did not create injustices. They were created by humanity." Conclusion: society needs to solve its inequities.

The Pastoral of the Child works with more than 242,000 volunteers, which are mostly women. It reaches 1.3 million poor families. Its actions have impact on the reduction of child mortality. The work is so efficient that it has been used as an example for other countries.

Brazil

Marie Carmèle Rose-Anne Auguste

Clinic for Women of Kafou Fèy

Marie Carmèle Rose-Anne Auguste is a nanny, social worker and activist for human rights from Haiti. In 1991, during the state military coup that attempted to re-establish Jean-Claude Duvalier as life president (a post inherited from his father), soldiers burst into the hospital where she worked, shooting. Rose-Anne risked her life saving the wounded.

"I firmly believe that the overwhelming majority of women need to fight with determination against social inequalities," states Marie Carmèle Rose-Anne Auguste in her autobiographical notes. During the state military coup of 1991, soldiers burst into the hospital where she worked. Rose-Anne risked her life saving the wounded. One year later, she founded the Clinic for Women of Kafou Fèy, one of the poorest neighborhoods in Port-au-Prince, the capital city of Haiti. She was able to count on the support of Partners in Health, an American association that is concerned with the access to health care of poor communities. Since then, the clinic receives around 200 visits from women every day. It looks after children and elderly people as well. That increases the total daily average to 1000 patients. Rose-Anne also offers professional help to women who have been raped and maltreated. In 1994, she received the Reebok Prize for Human Rights. Former American President, Jimmy Carter, called her work "inspired." Rose-Anne is also known as a composer and singer. She often sings to the ill, as part of their therapy.

With more than 200 years of independence, Haiti is the oldest republic with an African-American population in the world. In contrast to those glorious facts, we find poverty (with the lowest social index of the American continent) and constant political instability.

Haiti

"What I find of most satisfaction is when I see victims becoming advocates for change."

Mary V. Balikungeri

Rwanda Women's Community Development Network Kigali (RWN)

Mary V. Balikungeri (51) is the executive director of Rwanda Women's Community Development Network (RWN). The NGO assists widows, victims of sexual violence, people infected with HIV/Aids and orphans. It provides a forum for networking, mobilization, sensitization, training, counseling and material assistance. Thanks to its efforts, more than a thousand women and orphans have rebuilt their lives. The NGO has also helped to build medical clinics, living quarters and training centers.

Mary V. Balikungeri from Rwanda is concerned with the plight of people, especially women affected by war and conflict, in order to rehabilitate them in the community. "Growing up as a refugee in unstable conditions, I was able to experience at first hand the suffering of people affected by the upheavals of war," Mary V. Balikungeri says, hence the creation of Polyclinics of Hope, equipped with a sanitary center, trauma service and counseling. Mary has been active in this work since 1995 when she was involved in the post-war reconstruction of Rwanda.

Mary faces difficulty in acquiring material and financial support for RWN. However, many have benefited from Mary's work. Many suffering from HIV/Aids have received medication for opportunistic diseases. RWN has constructed 150 houses for 750 beneficiaries in Rukara, a medical clinic and a primary school for their children. Some assisted in the rehabilitation of shelter for 50 families and rape victims of the 1994 genocide in Kigali Cty. Some beneficiaries learned trades like tailoring and now earn revenues from their products. RWN has microfinanced women's associations and groups fostering orphans in five prefectures.

Rwanda is under reconstruction and still burdened with issues from the 1994 genocide. Many associations and organisations are involved in the work of rehabilitation to foster development. The President and the First Lady are among the motivators in realizing concrete visions.

Rwanda

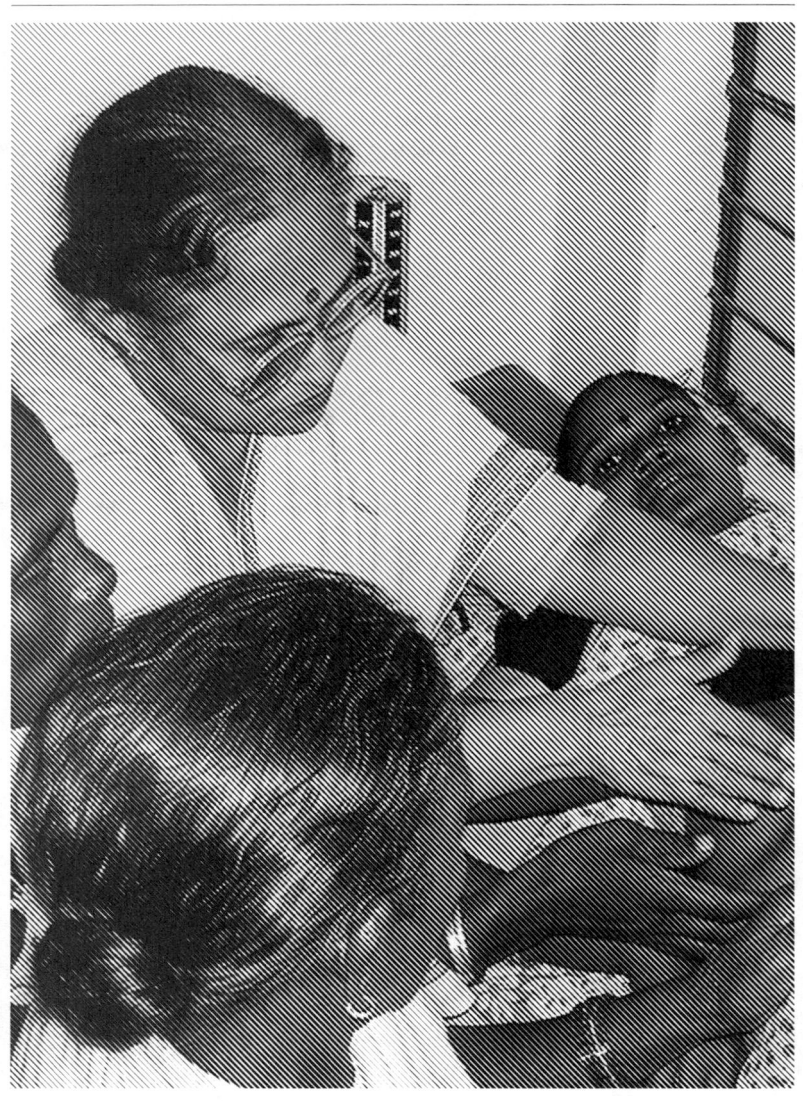

Rani Bang

Society for Education, Action and Research in Community Health (Search)

Rani Bang's work in the Gadchiroli district of Maharashtra has changed the face of the tribal pockets in the area. Where healthcare was once nonexistent, there are now a friendly hospital, experienced healthworkers, and trained traditional birth attendants. Rani also worked actively towards reviving traditional medicine, realizing that community mobilization combined with the optimum use of existing facilities is the only way to solve the crises in the interior areas, largely overlooked by policy and planners alike.

Rani Bang comes from a family with a strong commitment to medical and public service. In the early 1980s, she and her husband did not have to think too hard on their decision to work in the internal tribal pockets of Maharashtra. They set up the Society for Education, Action and Research in Community Health (Search) to provide community healthcare to the people in Gadchiroli district, an almost entirely tribal district. It has abysmally low literacy levels and practically no infrastructural facilities. Healthcare was a distant dream. The Bangs have built a friendly tribal hospital, and have trained village healthworkers and traditional birth attendants in 50 villages to manage reproductive and child health problems. Rani works on healthcare delivery and community medicine, with special emphasis on sexually transmitted diseases and HIV/Aids. The distinguishing feature of her work in the area is her responsiveness to what the people of the area identify as priority areas of concern. She uses rigorous research to understand the needs of the people, and then uses community-based solutions to solve these problems.

The result of Rani's two decades of work is that the region today has improved healthcare facilities and has undertaken pioneering work in community medicine. The most heartening feature of this effort is the revival of traditional medicine. It is Rani's endeavor to also utilize, and improve upon, existing government medical facilities through community mobilization and awareness. Due to Search's efforts, the mortality rate for infants up to five years has dropped from 120 out of 1000 in 1995 to 30 out of 1000 in 1998.

Rani has devoted her entire life to this cause, challenging government officials and the powerful people in the region in the course of her work.

Gadchiroli, the southeastern corner of Maharashtra, is almost entirely rural and has a large tribal population, only 22 percent literacy, meager transportation, and practically no industry. Before Rani and her husband set up facilities in Gadchiroli, it had almost no healthcare.

India

"If you do something in life, you should do it properly and do your best to earn the highest marks; otherwise you should not do it at all."

Rosa Bataeva

Fond komitieta doktorov Garantia (Doctors' Committee Fund Guarantee) Mezhdunarodny komitiet dietiey Chechni (International Committee for the Children of Chechnya); Yaltinskaya initsyativa za mir v Chechnie.

Rosa Bataeva was born in Grozny. She graduated from Medical School and earned a PhD in Medical Science. During the war years in Chechnya, she was the Head of Admissions at Hospital No. 9 in Grozny. From 2000 to 2004, she was medical adviser to the Deputy of the Chechen Republic to the Russian State Duma. Actively cooperating with a range of NGOs in the Russian Federation, she has coordinated a number of humanitarian and medical aid programs in the North Caucasus.

In the summer of 1999, Grozny was scene to air raids, bombings, and an endless flow of wounded people. In one of the reception rooms at Hospital No. 9, a young woman is sitting, swaying from side to side, her face expressionless. She is in a state of shock, all covered with blood. She has just lost almost her entire family. Her husband and her little son have been killed. There is a girl on the operating table — her daughter. Doctors have been fighting for her life for several hours, and nobody knows whether or not she will survive. The woman is sitting speechless and gazing into space. She cannot comprehend what has happened. She will understand and realize her unbearable loss only after she recovers her senses. She needs to change her clothes and, at least, drink some water. Rosa Bataeva gives this woman her own blouse and skirt, tries to remain close to her and not leave her alone. Although there were huge numbers of wounded people, both adults and little children, in the hospital admissions department run by Rosa, it is only this woman that she now remembers distinctly. There will be many wounded and dead people to follow. Later, they will run out of medicine and bandages. And so, Rosa will decide to seek help. Together with her brother, she will go to Naltchik, to the office of the Red Cross. Rosa finally arrived in Naltchik with her appeal for help. At once, trucks loaded with medicines, bandages and a generator were sent to the hospital, thus saving hundreds of lives. Rosa remembers tears in the eyes of the ex-pat Red Cross Coordinator for the Chechen Republic. Chain-smoking, he listened to her story in silence. Rosa will never forget his tears, his compassion and understanding. She needed them so badly at that intolerably difficult moment.

Working in a Grozny hospital during the Russian-Chechen war (1994—96), Rosa Bataeva realized that she had to do what she could to stop the bloodshed. Rosa is trying to help her people and to attract the attention of the world to the atrocities in Chechnya.

Russian Federation

"I will focus on building a democratic culture where everyone can contribute to national development. Education and an improved economic situation will create better lives for everyone."

Florentine Bodo Ramambasoa

Women National Council
Association For The Well Being Of The Family And The Health Of The Mother (Fisa)

Florentine Ramambasoa, a 66-year-old widow from Antananarivo, Madagascar, has worked as a member of various organizations since 1967. She recently became the national coordinator of DRV, a coalition of women associations which focuses on the rehabilitation of women, human rights, women's rights, gender, ecumenism, and reproductive health. Florentine directly contacts beneficiaries, mediates and uses participatory management in her work. She also lobbies decision makers to raise awareness and funds. Colleagues who work in family planning associations around Africa emulate her.

Since 1967 Florentine Ramambasoa, 66, from Antananarivo, Madagascar, has worked as a member of various organizations concerned with women's rehabilitation, gender, and human rights, specifically women's rights, ecumenism and reproductive health. She recently became the national coordinator of DRV, the umbrella body for women's associations in Madagascar. Florentine was awarded the International Planned Parenthood Federation Merit Certificate in recognition of her notable service to the family planning cause in Africa. She is a founder member of the Association For The Well Being Of The Family And The Health Of The Mother (Fisa). In the last three decades the socio-economic and political situation in Madagascar has gradually deteriorated, raising poverty levels, creating tension and conflict. To address these issues, several NGOs, under DRV, focus on sensitizing leaders and the general public on the need to promote peace and justice. This motivated other NGOs to regroup under a common platform to raise public awareness on the environment, globalization and gender, and ensure that coordinated political and strategic development is realized. Mrs Ramambasoa's work ethic involves direct contact with beneficiaries, with whom she espouses a participatory approach. She believes in their direct involvement in project planning and implementation. In addition, she vigorously lobbies decision makers in order to raise awareness and funds. Colleagues who manage family planning associations around Africa emulate her approach. Her success is largely due to her family and her relations with the state and international funding organizations such as Usaid, Cooperation Française, Foundation Friedrich Ebert Stiftung and other partners. She has embarked on an ecumenical project, which seeks to promote better understanding between religious denominations.

The last thirty years, including major crises in 1972, 1991 and 2001, has led to the gradual worsening of the socio-economic and political situation in Madagascar. This is manifested in rising levels of poverty and by the tension and conflict at all levels — religious, ethnic, social, and family.

Madagascar

Boualaphet Chounthavong

Village Focus International (VFI)

Boualaphet Chounthavong was born in 1967 in Salawan province, southern Laos, at the height of the Vietnam War. Her father was a teacher who was promoted after the war to a high-ranking post in the Ministry of Education. Her mother was a member of the Laos Women Union. Studying on a government scholarship, Boualaphet obtained her degree in medicine from the National University of Medicine in Laos in 1993. But instead of opening a high profile medical practice in the capital, she opted to work in public health in the rural areas.

Boualaphet is one of the few Lao women to graduate from a state school of medicine. But she has not used this to her own advantage. Instead of working in a hospital in Vientiane, she chose to return to her home province, Salawan, to work as a staff member for the World Education Project, an NGO. "I want to help cure people to make use of my education. Helping them get better would make me happy. When I was asked by this organization if I would like to do public health work, I decided to give it a try for at least three months, after which I could decide to leave if I did not like it. But the more I worked, the more I liked it. It is one of the ways to help heal people."

Her first assignment was to train the villagers to work with the health care team. She was based in a remote area inhabited by five indigenous groups. Using different dialects, but sharing some cultural beliefs, the peoples are among the poorest tribal groups in the province. Realizing that certain health problems in the area arise from traditional beliefs, instead of concentrating purely on health work, Boualaphet initiated projects to help tackle their root causes. She oversees two projects: firstly the Village-based Education in Southern Laos (VESL), which includes health, education, food, security initiatives, school building construction and informal education, development of learning centers at district level and the provision of clean water for drinking and other uses; secondly the Community-Based Natural Resource Management (CBNRM), which maps the community, identifies and plans land use and develops products from the forests. From her initial plan to work for three months, Boualaphet has now been on the job for more than a decade. In 2000, she set up Village Focus International (VFI), working in more than 70 villages in remote areas from the banks of Mekong River to the border of Vietnam.

In the 1990s, Laos opened itself to the world after years of isolation, and foreign NGOs were allowed to enter and work in the country. Recovering from the war, Laos's economy was weak and fundamental public health services and basic infrastructure did not reach rural communities. VFI is committed to strengthening the capacity of marginalized rural communities.

Lao People's Democratic Republic

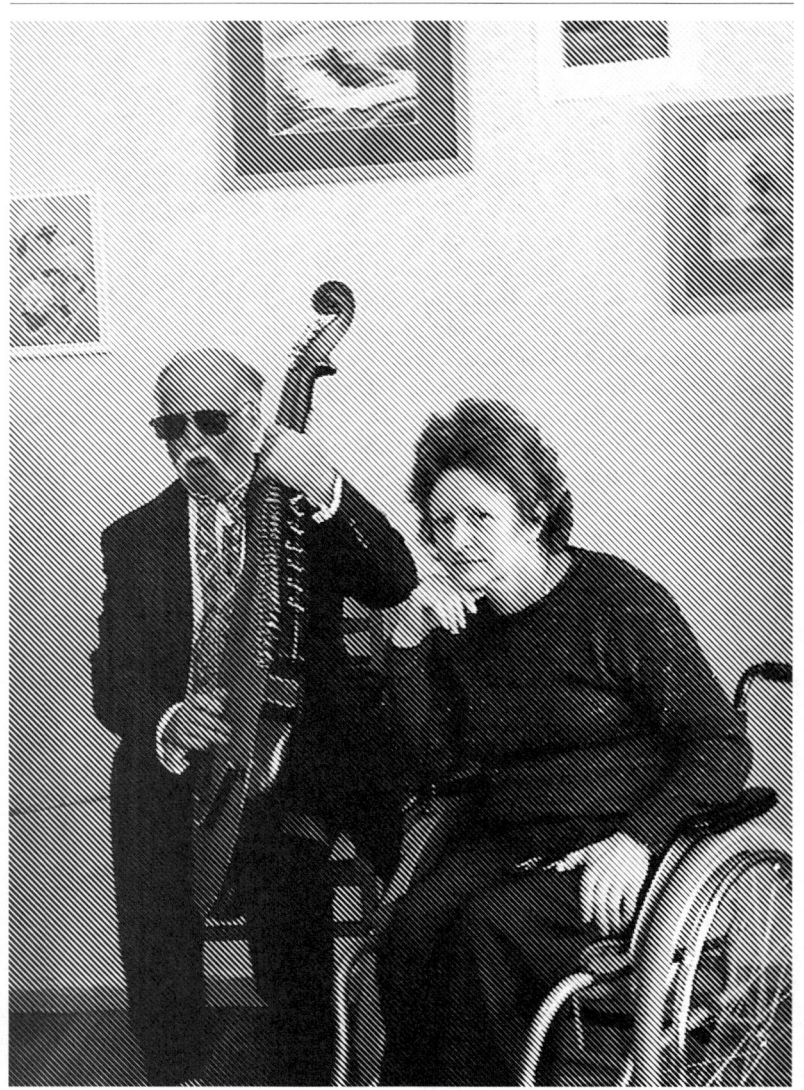

Lyubomira Boychishin

Information and Rehabilitation Center for Disabled Women "Lyubomira"
Union of Ukrainian Women
People's Rukh of Ukraine

Lyubomira Boychishin (born 1952) established the Information and Rehabilitation Center for Disabled Women "Lyubomira." She herself is disabled and in a wheelchair. Since 1998, the center has carried out projects with organizations for disabled women in Ukraine. It is financed by non-governmental donors. As a result of this work, an information network was founded to link organizations for disabled women across Ukraine. Lyubomira is actively raising awareness of society about the problems of women with disabilities and supporting them to become active members of society.

Lyubomira was born in Lvov, Ukraine. A professional civil engineer, she has used a wheelchair since 1990. Since 1989, she has been an active member of the Union of Ukrainian Women and the People's Rukh of Ukraine. The idea of creating a center for disabled women came to Lyubomira's mind after her participation at the NGO Forum at the World Conference on Women in Beijing in 1995 where she met with 200 women in wheelchairs from all over the world, who are all living full lives. In 1997, she established the Information and Rehabilitation Center for Disabled Women "Lyubomira," and since 1998 she has been the editor-in-chief of a magazine for disabled people with the same name. Since 1998, the Lyubomira Center has implemented seven projects, supported by funds from international donors.

The trainings and seminars organized by the Lyubomira Center have enabled many women with disabilities to become active as full citizens of their country. This success gives Lyubomira energy and strength to continue her work. The Lyubomira Center developed an information network linking organizations of disabled women in the cities of Kiev, Lvov, Zhytomyr, and Sevastopol through a project supported by the Canadian-Ukrainian Gender Fund. "Our organization sees its peaceful future in the light of the agreement on cooperation, signed by the President of Ukraine," she says. As a non-profit organization, the Lyubomira Center constantly has to find sources of financing. Not everybody in society understands the problems of people with disabilities. Many people just ignore them. "Our goals are to raise awareness and attention to our problems," Lyubomira says. For this she receives support from international organizations and plays an active role in several non-governmental and governmental organizations in Ukraine.

In Ukraine, the rights of disabled persons are violated. In spite of social support from the government, disabled persons do not have opportunities for employment or for becoming self-sufficient. They are not covered by medical insurance and usually live in poverty.

Ukraine

Irene Chaluluka

Sub-Saharan Family Enrichment program (Safe)
Children Promotion Organisation

Irene Chaluluka is a field coordinator for the Sub-Saharan Africa Family Enrichment program (Safe). For eleven years, Irene has been involved in implementing "Why Wait?", a life skills and HIV/Aids educational program in Malawi. Through "Why Wait?" Irene has successfully promoted abstinence among the youth. She has trained thousands of trainers on the initiative. Irene has also helped to export "Why Wait?" to Uganda, Kenya and Nigeria. Her major challenge in promoting the initiative is inadequate funding. She has personally endured the HIV/Aids affliction.

Irene stood in her hotel room with shedding tears. The images she had seen in an Ugandan video hours before would not escape her mind. She had seen enough of people suffering of Aids. She could not take it anymore. She had to do something.

The Ugandan video was just too appalling. It was the story of a village whose entire adult population had died of Aids. Not a single adult remained. One of the oldest surviving children was eleven. She had assumed parental responsibilities from feeding her siblings to providing security.

The video had evoked emotions within her to try to make a difference.

Two years later, Irene's ex-husband was diagnosed with HIV. Her marriage had crumbled nine years earlier because of his infidelity. Irene nursed her ex-husband in her house. He died on August 9, 1998.

Irene's oldest daughter fell ill. She was HIV positive. On her deathbed, Irene's daughter challenged her mother to fight Aids among the youth.

Irene has focused on HIV/Aids prevention in schools, through life skills training, character development and abstinence. "Why Wait?" has gained popularity among the youth in Malawi and beyond. Kenya, Nigeria and Uganda show interest in the program.

By the end of 2005, "Why Wait?" is expected to be part of the school curriculum in Uganda — a curriculum Irene helped to develop in many ways. A single mother of four boys and two girls, Irene also sits on the board of several youth organizations throughout Malawi.

Her greatest dream is to see "Why Wait?" in every African country.

At the end of 2003, thirty percent of Malawi's population were living with HIV/Aids, with women accounting for more than half. Malawi is ranked as one of the poorest countries in the world. HIV/Aids has added a delicate facet.

Malawi

"There is no other time that I feel on the top of the world then when a childless couple conceives after years of trying."

Felister Chinthunzi

Fasu Consultancy and Maternal Life International (Famli)

Felister Chinthunzi (50) is a trainer of trainers in natural family planning, reproductive health and HIV/Aids with Famli — a community-based non-governmental organization in Lilongwe. She heads the training service, sensitizing women on sexual abstinence before marriage and fidelity to avoid HIV infection. She is currently organising a community orphan care center for over 60 children.

On her vocation, Felister Chinthunzi explains that the liberation of women begins in their sexual life as equal partners with men. "Women must first be respected as mothers, either future or present because they are the bearers of the next generation." At Famli, she advances this by training and raising awareness on fertility issues — "the meaning of sexuality and its place in our total lives," she says. "Sex is not a play thing but God's gift for propagation of the human family, which bonds married couples in love."
Felister Chinthunzi, a mother of four, is convinced that fertility awareness makes people aware of sexual exploitation, dangers of rape, abuse and forced or early marriages, and educates the youth to abstain until marriage. Through family planning, couples make informed choices on conception and preparing for a family. "There has to be an open discussion."
With the formation of Tikhale Moyo Groups (Let's Live), she initiated discussions on traditional customs and practices, which are likely to spread HIV at the village level. "They discuss how some customs can be practiced without putting people at risk of HIV infection. High risk traditions include polygamy, extramarital sexual relations, marital rape, widow and widower inheritance, scarification, circumcision and forced sex for girls coming of age."
Famli's director, Father Richard Cremins, describes Felister: "She has developed a model for family life and reproductive health which can be replicated in every part of Malawi. Her lessons empower women and are passed on from mother to daughter. She is working not for the present, but for future generations."

Malawi has a major unmet need for safe, affordable contraception. According to the 2000 Demographic Health Survey, the total fertility rate is 6.6 children per woman, with only 26 percent of women using modern contraceptive methods and 63 percent giving birth before the age of 20.

Rose Chiwambo

Church Action Relief Development (Card)

Rose Chiwambo (77) was born in Kafukule in Mzimba District. She is the first Malawian woman to hold a cabinet post. She was appointed Deputy Minister of Community and Social Development in 1963 after winning the Mzimba South seat. She began mobilizing Malawian women in 1952 into a political force. She fled the country in 1964 following a cabinet crisis. She stayed in exile for 30 years, until her return in 1993 at the advent of multi-party politics. She is now settled in Mzuzu doing charity work, concentrating on HIV/Aids prevention.

One day in 1951, Rose Chiwambo, a housewife living in the colonial capital of Zomba, was heading home from the market, when she noticed a group of well-known chiefs gathered at the community hall. She approached one chief to inquire on the matter, who firmly replied, "This is not for women." That evening she raised the issue with her husband. His reply, "It's up to you."
"I started going from house to house to get support from the women and soon formed the Nyasaland African Women's League."
The colonial government was trying to influence the chiefs to endorse the federation of Northern Rhodesia (Zambia), South Rhodesia (Zimbabwe) and Nyasaland (Malawi). The plan received resistance from the people of Nyasaland and led to the formation of Nyasaland African Congress. Rose Chiwambo's husband was a leading activist.
Today, the former politician dedicates all her energy and time towards charity work, fighting the HIV/Aids pandemic. She became the first woman cabinet member, when Malawi attained independence in 1964. But her political career was short-lived, after the cabinet crisis in 1968. She went into a 30-year exile with her husband.
In the whole country of Malawi, HIV/Aids has brought havoc in communities, leaving behind thousands of destitute orphans, widows, widowers and old people. Unfortunately, the family's breadwinner is usually the victim.
"It's pathetic, especially here in Mzuzu where traditional practices worsen the irresponsible 'city life'," says Rose Chiwambo. "People need information on the impact of HIV and Aids. Behavioral change must be seriously addressed because closing down the dozens of 'rest houses' is not a solution."
"Alongside promiscuity, there are traditional practices including circumcision, polygamy, ear-piercing and tattooing, widow inheritance and forced marriages that must be tackled."

Malawian is ranked one of the poorest countries in the world. Thousands of Malawians die every day, leaving behind destitute orphans, widows, widowers and the aged. The HIV/Aids scourge has crippled this country and left thousands more in a state of desperation.

Sona Chuli-Kuli

National Union of Journalists
Turkmen Association of Journalists "Shamchyrag"
Patients Rights Association "Arkadag"

Sona Chuli-Kuli is a journalist with more than 20 years of experience. Chuli-Kuli is her pseudonym. She cannot use her real name, because it would be too dangerous for her. She works in the field of conflict resolution and in her articles she addresses critical problems in her country. She founded the Patients Rights Association "Arkadag", a NGO which has provided services to thousands of women all over the country in the areas of reproductive health, domestic violence, prevention of drug abuse, women's human rights, and advocacy.

Sona Chuli-Kuli is a well-known journalist in Turkmenistan. She lives and works under a pseudonym. She has a very determined character and opposes injustice in all its forms. In 2002, she participated in the seminar on Journalism and Democracy in Kalmar, Sweden, against the wishes of the editor of "Neutral Turkmenistan," the daily newspaper she wrote for at that time. She was dismissed for this reason. However, such opposition made her more determined and she began to write for foreign news agencies and regained her professional confidence. Sona is unable to name her employer as it is too dangerous, but she confirms that she writes about the true state of things in her country.

In January 1998, she founded the NGO Patients Rights Association "Arkadag" which she affiliated to another non-governmental organization, the Turkmen Association of Journalists "Shamchyrag." During the eight years it has existed, thousands of women all over the country have benefited from the services of Arkadag in the areas of reproductive health, domestic violence, drug prevention, women's human rights, and advocacy. Supported by advisers, members of the organization carried out seminars, training lessons, and defended many people whose rights had been infringed. Arkadag promotes peace building, both outside and within the family. Domestic violence and the trafficking of women exist in the country, but these are not perceived as such. Statistics show that more than half of the female population suffers from domestic violence. So Sona decided to defend these women. She works with women, victims of domestic violence, and children from these families. Sona believes that civil society in Turkmenistan is in an early stage, but she is determined that it will succeed, especially now that the international community is giving its support.

Turkmenistan is a closed country. To be a member of an NGO is a great risk. Although the 2003 law criminalizing activities of unregistered NGOs was annulled in November 2004, it remains nearly impossible for independent civil society groups to operate.

Turkmenistan

Mirta Susana Clara

Municipal Government of Buenos Aires
Lanas National University

After six years in prison, Mirta Clara, her daughter and son, and the rest of society, slowly, began to become familiar with each other again. Her husband had been killed by the Argentinean military regime (1976—1983). Through her professional specialty, psychology, she tries to construct inclusive policies to help the people excluded by society. Some of them have been affected directly or indirectly by genocide, others have been excluded by unemployment and its consequences, the greatest of which is poverty.

"I am hereby writing to you in order to question the procedure and resolution by which a member of the military forces, accused of participating in the death convoy, which executed 22 young people on December 13th, 1976, is allowed to continue occupying his post as military attaché in Italy. This is of great concern to me." That was the beginning of the letter sent in October 2003 to the Argentinean Chancellor. The letter was signed by Mirta Clara.

In a deserted place in Chaco, a province in the North, Mirta and her husband, militants of the Montoneros guerrilla group, were arrested and imprisoned, separately, in October 1975. In prison, she gave birth to a son. Their daughter, almost one year old, was rescued by relatives. Mirta's husband was one of the 22 people assassinated. Mirta recovered her freedom in November 1983. It was not easy for the three of them to recognize each other. Mirta Susana Clara had been awarded a degree in Psychology, in 1970, and once she was free, she combined her professional work with her fight for human rights. "We are a team of specialists in mental health dependent on the Public Health System. We meet around 10,000 families each month." Past and present: "With our companions in Switzerland and Spain, we are working to build a place for ex-political prisoners. It will be a place to recover the historical memory of what has happened."

"A letter puts an end to impunity," was the headline on the front page of the newspaper 'El Diario de la Región — The Journal of Resistance,' in Resistencia, the capital of the province of Chaco, on October 11th, 2003. It went on saying: "Yesterday, President Kirchner ordered the military attaché in Italy to return to Argentina." Today, this person is imprisoned in the same place where Mirta's husband was tortured.

It was cold in Buenos Aires. Those women embraced each other. Two laws that obstruct the prosecution of the ones responsible for the assassinations and disappearances in Argentina (1976—1983) were finally repealed. It was June 14th, 2005. Memories did not feel the cold that day.

Argentina

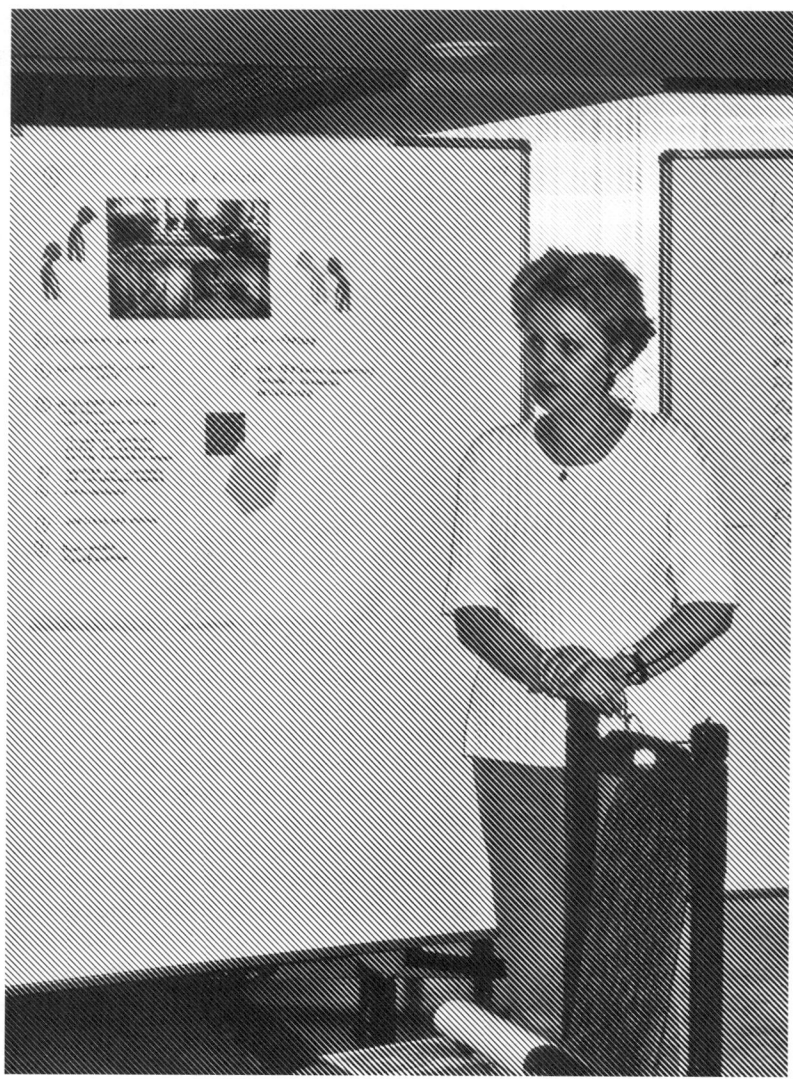

Negoita Cornelia

Pro Homini

Negoita Cornelia works in Braila, a town located in southeast Romania. She has dedicated her life to children in orphanages and psychiatric hospitals. In 1997, she founded Pro Homini, a charitable foundation helping orphans, large families, and senior citizens. Why did she choose this challenging path, rather than developing a profitable business after 1989 and the fall of the Ceausescu regime and the transition to a market economy? The answer is that, for her, people are more important than money. She derives enormous satisfaction knowing her contributions have changed people's lives.

Negoita Cornelia's interest in charitable work began 15 years ago on her first visit to an orphanage. She personally witnessed the children's suffering and the experience inspired her to work with an orphanage hospital with physically disabled children. She followed the children's progress as they grew, encouraging them as they learned a trade and helped find them jobs. In 1997, Negoita founded Pro Homini with a group of like-minded women to help orphans and single mothers responsible for their large families. They provide donations of food and medicine and award scholarships for children in need. Every Saturday, students from 10 to 14 years of age come to the Pro Homini house for courses in computer science, cooking, sewing, and arts and crafts, practical skills they can use in their daily lives. With donations secured from a Dutch foundation, Negoita set out to build a day center for senior citizens. The elderly come to talk, receive hot meals and medical check-ups, and take part in excursions around the country. In 1996, Negoita Cornelia started organizing charity parties. Twice a year, local business leaders take part in the parties and sponsor them financially.
Pro Homini has been awarded the Diploma of Excellence for its achievements. Negoita is fulfilled by her work of improving the lives of children and the elderly. She is one of the first in her town to have created the conditions for building confidence, regaining hope, and improving people's destiny. To promote women's issues, she organized a series of lectures and debates to celebrate International Women's Day on 8 March. Negoita has strived to attract the interest of good-hearted, helpful women to volunteer with charities. Through her own example, perseverance, and hard work, she has successfully developed a network of women who share her values.

After the fall of the Ceausescu regime in 1989, it was revealed that there were more than 150,000 children in Romanian orphanages, most of them malnourished, without health care, and in a state of neglect. Ceausescu left a legacy of poverty, malfunctioning social services, and a weak civil society.

Romania

María Elena Curbelo Morales

The Health Team of Las Láminas y Las Piedras

María Elena Curbelo Morales was born in Montevideo, Uruguay, in 1945. She works as a pediatric doctor in the very poorest of communities treating cases of child malnutrition and doing educational activities with mothers of large families, many of whom are single mothers or have husbands who are absent because of their work. María Elena lives in one of those communities sharing their deprivations, although she herself suffers from a severe motor disability and a number of chronic illnesses.

María Elena Curbelo Morales was born in a humble home in Montevideo, Uruguay. She was born with 'spina-bifida', and she experienced pain and disability from a young age. She underwent a number of surgical operations, but she still continued with her schooling and was able to complete her primary and secondary education — and also win a grant to help finance her medical studies. "Why did I choose medicine? Six years old, I was waiting for my legs to be operated on for the seventh time. I used to lie in the hospital. Each time the door opened, I wondered if they were coming to bring me food, give me an injection or take me to the operating room. It made me mad. At that moment, I made the decision to study medicine and to always explain to children what was going to happen next."

In the 1960s and 1970s, as a member of Tupamaros, the National Liberation Movement, she was involved in political struggles and trade union fights. In 1972, the repressive forces of the Uruguayan army captured her. María Elena remained in prison for years suffering torture. After the liberation, she went into exile, in Sweden and Nicaragua. With tenacity and strong willpower, she learned to walk again and eventually graduated as a pediatric doctor. She returned to Uruguay, and became a mother of two children. Nowadays, her militancy and profession are combined. She uses them to work for the common good in the marginal communities of Montevideo. She focuses on child malnutrition. She lives in Bella Unión, in the administrative district of Salto. She works with disabled children, adolescents and a horse — she works with equine therapy. María Elena shares a project with the parents of her patients: the creation of a rehabilitation center for the children. They can already tell us about the plot of land — where it will be built — and about the name they have chosen: our dream.

After experiencing a dictatorship that persecuted, tortured and massacred thousands of people, Uruguay is reasserting its democratic spirit. The country has a high rate of schooling, but there are still regions with a population that lives in very precarious conditions.

Uruguay

Maria José de Oliveira Araújo

Programa de Assistência Integral à Saúde da Mulher (Paism)
Coletivo Feminista Sexualidade e Saúde

Doctor Maria José de Oliveira Araújo (born 1949) is the coordinator of the Women's Health Division of the Brazilian Ministry of Health. On the front of national politics, she puts into practice the ideals that guide her career: sexual and reproductive rights and humane and respectful care for women during their entire life, from puberty to menopause. Prior to coordinating this program, she supported the creation of major organizations, publications and political actions.

In medical school, the student Maria José de Oliveira Araújo left a class after seeing a woman, on a bed for gynecological examination, ready to be collectively examined by over ten students. Remembering this episode, over three decades later, she says: "The way hospitals treated women really revolted me. I have been a feminist since I was born and just realized it later on." She found herself in the late 1970s, during a postgraduate program on women's and infant's health in France, when she got involved in the feminist movement. She came back to Brazil, in 1980, full of energy. She helped create, in the same year, the Women's House of Grajaú, one of the first health centers in a poor neighborhood in São Paulo. Three years later, she went to Switzerland, where she studied natural and preventive gynecology. Back in Brazil, she founded along with a group of activists the Coletivo Feminista Sexualidade e Saúde, the Feminist Collective of Health and Sexuality, which is still a national example to be followed in human care for women. In 1989 and 2001, when São Paulo elected left-wing mayors, she headed the women's health area. She introduced a service for legal abortion (in case of rape and life risk for the mother) in Brazilian public hospitals. Currently, there are 42 clinics that perform abortions legally. Her house was invaded, and she received death threats. Maria José de Oliveira Araújo also created many centers to help women and teenagers, victims of sexual violence. Intending to spread those victories, she participated in the foundation of the National Feminist Network for Health and Sexual and Reproductive Rights. Since 2003, she works for the Brazilian Ministry of Health, where she still bravely fights as she used to do in her youth.

Founded in 1984, the Feminist Collective of Health and Sexuality provides assistance to around 200 women per month in its model health center. It also helps the development of new technologies, promotes courses, debates, lectures, training programs and the production of articles, manuals and books.

———
Brazil

Durga Devi

Sarva Shakti Sangam
Social Uplift Through Rural Action (Sutra)

Durga Devi (born 1956) always wanted to do something socially productive. Despite her husband's protests, in 1979 she contacted and joined the Social Work and Research Centre. Since then, she has not looked back: she has formed women's groups in her district and was instrumental in forming a coalition of women's groups under the banner, Sarva Shakti Sangam, a watchgroup over atrocities against women.

Even as a young girl, Durga Devi knew that she wanted to do something socially productive, as her mother had done as part of the women's group in her village in Himachal Pradesh. Although married off at the age of 15, Durga kept prospecting for a productive job. In 1979, she found an opening at the Social Work and Research Center in Solan district. It was unusual for a woman to work outside the home — her husband was incensed. In 1983, she convinced the women of Solan district to form a group to discuss their problems. Durga found that smoke from chulhas (a cooking furnace the shape of a bucket) was a major health hazard for the women. She looked for and found a solution — the smokeless chulha — and then got the training in its use. As she got to know the women better, she realized that male alcoholism was a major problem confronting them. So, they organized a protest against local liquor sales, through which she learnt the importance of keeping the women united and calm in the face of threats. The success of this agitation was crucial: women in the neighboring villages now understood the potential of coordinated protests.

Durga and her colleagues in the women's groups have formed a union of women's groups, the Sarva Shakti Sangam, which today raises its considerable voice against any form of injustice against women. "Often I have to face threats and harassment, but I am not scared," says Durga. "I work with truth in my mind, and it is this truth that gets justice for the innocent."

It has been a long way for Durga from that struggling step out of her home to being so involved that finding time for her domestic tasks is difficult. But part of the payoff has been that even her once recalcitrant husband has made an enormous effort to understand her work and adjust to her new life.

When Durga Devi began work, it was entirely unusual for women to work outside the home. Since women's health was not a priority, women worked in damaging environments that no one protested against. Alcoholism, female infanticide, and feticide are even today serious problems in the district.

India

Sukha "Doctor"

Nari Sanjeevani Kendra (NSK)

A training course on the use of traditional medicines changed not only the life of a trolley laborer's wife, Sukha (born 1944), but also that of her entire village. The village, which had practically no medical facilities and assigned very low priority to reproductive health, is today under "Sukha Doctor's" care. Adept at finding and processing herbs and administering them in the right doses, Sukha's cures for reproductive health problems, fever, stomach ailments, and several other common ailments is almost legendary in the area.

Ten years ago, when the people of village Sinkathiya in Varanasi elected Sukha to attend a Mahila Samakhya (women's empowerment) training course on traditional medicines, little did they imagine that she would be Sukha Doctor to them very soon. Sukha was then known only as trolley laborer Ramkishen's wife. Today, she tends to the health of men, women, and children in her area. Although all she can do by way of writing is sign her signature, she can knowledgeably reel off the complicated names of hundreds of medicinal herbs. She is adept at finding and processing these herbs, and then administering them in the right doses to the hundreds of poor and unwell people in her village, and the adjoining villages as well. Sukha's cures for reproductive health problems, fever, stomach ailments, and several other common maladies are almost legendary in the area.

Everyone in the region — her colleagues in the herbal medical center Nari Sanjeevani Kendra (NSK), the villagers she tends to, and even doctors in the area's government hospital — refers to her by the honorific Sukha Doctor. Her medicines are easy to access, cheap, and available in plenty. The demand for Sukha Doctor's medicines has risen so much now that it has become impossible for the NSK to operate only at the two centers it has.

Looking back, Sukha has trouble believing how far she's come. She had to brave initial resentment from the village's power-players, who were unhappy that a poor, scheduled caste woman should be practicing medicine. She also had trouble establishing her credentials as a doctor in her own right: people had little faith in traditional medicines, and they would often approach her for a remedy too late.

Sukha (which means dry) entirely belies her name. This youthful sexagenarian woman can charm the very illness out of people.

In many villages in India, medical facilities are practically nonexistent, the hospitals too far and too costly. Traditional medicinal practices have long been an alternative, but they are being pushed out by more modern invasive therapies, their origins and essence lost.

India

Albertina Duarte Takiuti

Projeto de Apoio à Mulher e ao Adolescente — Secretaria do Estado de Saúde de São Paulo
Centro da Mulher Brasileira

Albertina Duarte Takiuti (1946) is known as one of the best gynecologists in the country. She participated actively in the implementation of Paism (Program for Integral Assistance to Female Health) and of the Program for Integral Assistance to Adolescents. Her work has the goal to transform health assistance into a right of all citizens.

Albertina Duarte Takiuti was not even ten years old when her parents left Portugal and moved to Brazil. Her parents wanted their children to escape from the Salazar dictatorship and from the war in the African colonies. A cousin of Albertina lost an eye in Angola. He told Albertina that the worst part was the other eye that saw everything. In Brazil, she would discover other wars: the military dictatorship (1964—1988), childhood mortality, domestic violence and the difficult access to quality health assistance. She participated in the student movement and was almost extradited. She was scared for her children's safety. In the hospital where she worked, she illegally helped patients who had been exiled from neighboring countries that were also under dictatorship, and she helped also Brazilian women who were being persecuted. "One day, cops came looking for a patient and I hid her in the bathroom." With the return of democracy, she played a main role in the creation of public health policies, especially for women and teenagers. She set up programs to include the Quilombolas (descendents of fugitive slaves), indigenous people and the Sem Terra (no land — movement that pressures for land reform).

Today, she coordinates an integral health assistance program for adolescents, and she has very clear ideas of how to help girls protect themselves from Aids and early pregnancy. "A teenage pregnancy is not only precocious in age, but also in the relationship that the girl has with her partner and in her commitment to a project for her life." Albertina is also a part of the Brazilian Woman's Center, an organization that has world peace as one of its main concerns. She affirms that we need to engender actions of solidarity towards women living in areas of armed conflict. "We have to know what is going on and help them."

Every year, more than a million Brazilian teenagers get pregnant. Most of them do not have financial nor psychological conditions to raise their children. This mission is passed on to the grandmothers. Teenage mothers also face difficulties carrying on their studies and entering the job market.

Brazil

Daphne Economou

Cerebral Palsy Greece
International Cerebral Palsy Society (ICPS)

Daphne Economou has worked to improve the lives of people with cerebral palsy in Greece, to increase public awareness and eliminate physical, social, and legal barriers. With her leadership, commitment and love, she is the inspiring heart and soul of Cerebral Palsy Greece and has pioneered a wide range of essential services. As chairperson of the International Cerebral Palsy Society, she is a voice for peace and social justice worldwide. She received the Gold Cross of the Order of Bienfaisance from the President of Greece in 2001.

Born and raised in India and England, Daphne Economou is the president of Cerebral Palsy Greece, an organization she founded with her husband to promote awareness of childhood disability issues in 1972. It is a very personal issue: her son was diagnosed with the disease and she was determined to improve the services for cerebral palsy patients in Greece. "I recognized the degree of prejudice and ignorance toward disabled children. But I saw the enormous potential in these children and knew that we needed to promote their skills and contributions," she explains. Sadly, Daphne lost her 17-year old son to cerebral palsy: "After this devastating loss, I nearly gave up, but I owed it to him to continue my work to offer brave and wonderful children like him a place in the sun." Because of Daphne's work and strong resolve, the organization is one of Greece's most prestigious. She spends considerable time guaranteeing that its operations run smoothly, but her main purpose is to ensure a harmonious atmosphere for the children and their families. She is also closely involved with the International Cerebral Palsy Society (ICPS) and holds the position of the chairman of the Executive Board. She has traveled for her work extensively, published numerous articles, and spoken at many international conferences on childhood disability. She has met with the European Commission and the Council of Europe. Daphne believes that disability is a universal issue without any borders: "We should recognize that the great work in the welfare field has been accomplished because someone refused, as Bob Dylan sings, 'to turn his head and pretend that he just does not see.'" Daphne believes prejudice, fear, and unawareness are major obstacles to overcoming stereotypes surrounding people with disabilities.

Children with cerebral palsy and other disabilities suffer from prejudice, lack of access to health services and care, and lack of acceptance by the larger community worldwide.

Greece

Yaojie Gao

Doctor Gao Yaojie has made Aids prevention her life's work. She has revealed the severity of Aids infection through medical sources, using her own money to print more than 770,000 pamphlets on preventing and treating Aids, and distributing these to Aids-stricken areas for free. She has also sponsored Aids patients and orphans with a sum totaling one million yuan.

Gao Yaojie, aged 78, is a retired gynecologist and professor of the Henan College of Chinese Traditional Medicine. She is known as "the first person in Chinese civil society for Aids prevention". After 1996, when Gao uncovered cases of HIV infection through blood transfusion, she visited over 100 villages, and interviewed thousands of HIV-positive people and Aids patients. She revealed the severity of Aids infection through medical channels. She began by using her own pension in the campaign against Aids, and soon set up a major resource center in Henan Province for treating and preventing Aids. Gao was alarmed to learn of the sale of infected blood. "Our blood in the blood bank is not safe! Others must also be infected. As a doctor, medical professor and people's representative, I am obliged to tell people to act and prevent Aids." She started to edit and print Aids prevention materials. She has published books including "Preventing and Treating Aids and Venereal Diseases (VD)", "Ten Thousand Letters: What I Witnessed about the Lives of Aids and VD Patients", and "Survey of Aids in China". These she distributed to Aids-stricken areas for free. Every year, she gives 30 to 70 lectures on health knowledge. Since 1996, Aids has featured in her lectures, and she has distributed materials on preventing it.

Gao has faced many challenges from officials, her family and society. She was threatened for exposing the dangers of fake doctors, fake medicines and Aids. With her tireless efforts, she has uncovered cases of Aids infection from selling blood in Henan Province, and exposed the misery and suffering of Aids orphans ensuring that the public has some understanding of the discrimination they face. Her work has inspired many people in China and overseas.

In 2003, China had about 840,000 HIV-positive people including 80,000 Aids patients, 80 percent in the countryside. When Gao first exposed Aids, it was largely unknown, and the government reluctant to reveal its relationship with the sale of blood. Gao faced many pressures to prevent her from speaking.

China

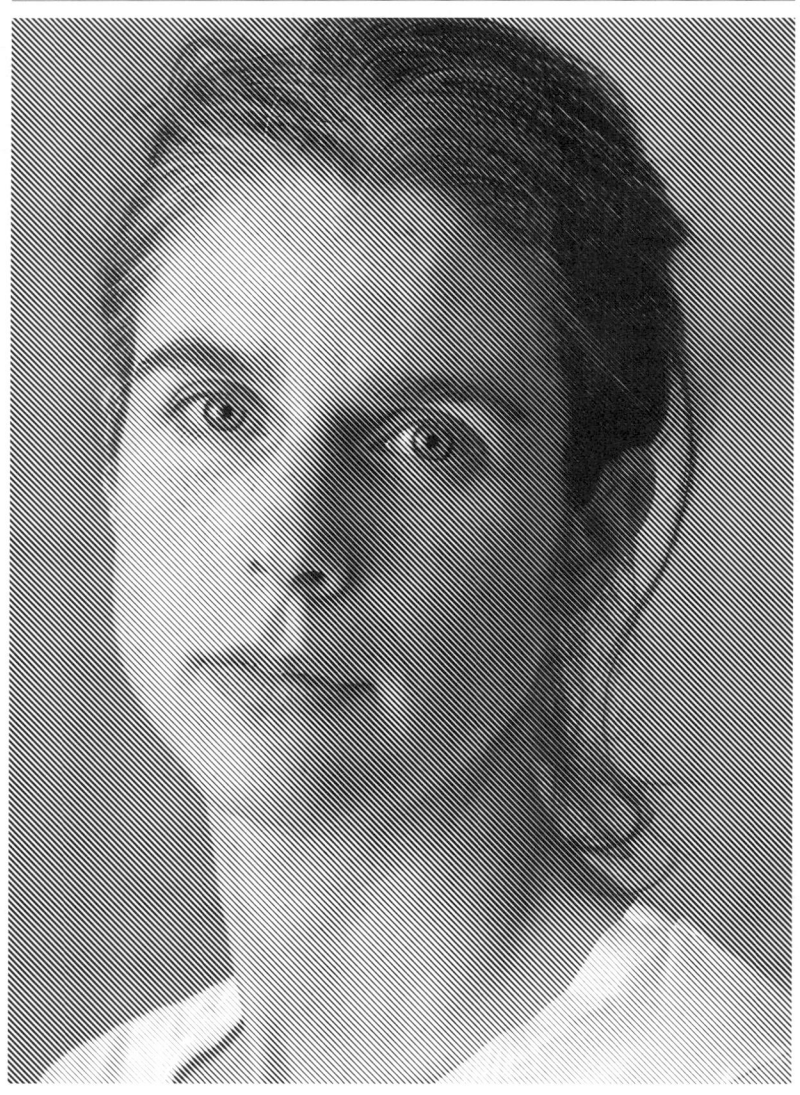

Rebecca Gomperts

Women on Waves

Rebecca Gomperts works with local women's groups to prevent unsafe abortions and empower women to exercise their human rights to physical and mental autonomy. In 1999, Rebecca Gomperts founded the organization, Women on Waves, which operates a mobile abortion clinic on a ship. Despite threats and protests from anti-abortion groups and governments, it has sailed to various countries where abortions are illegal. While in harbor, the ship provides contraceptives, information, and counseling. After sailing into in-ternational waters, early medical abortions are provided safely in the clinic.

A sailor's worst fear is to run into stormy waters. But Rebecca Gomperts' life, both on and off ships, has been marked by her fearlessness in the face of these storms. In her fight to defend women's most basic human rights, she has taken on governments, the media, and anti-abortion groups, regardless of the threats and obstacles they put in her way.

The turning point in Rebecca's life came in her late twenties. A medical doctor, she embarked on a life-changing stint of working aboard a Greenpeace ship around South America: "In Latin America, I listened to appalling stories about the desperate measures women take when they cannot have abortions legally. They are dying because they are being denied the right to decide about their bodies and whether and when they want to have children." The more research she did, the more resolute she became to help prevent women from dying every six minutes as a result of an unsafe, illegal abortion. It took a huge leap of imagination for Rebecca to hatch her extraordinary idea of offering safe, legal abortions aboard a ship in international waters. Like most brilliant schemes, it was shot down in flames by those who first heard it and it triggered fierce debates around the world. "I suddenly realized that ideas are dangerous. Anti-abortion groups were sending threats and I was very scared. But this injustice was crawling under my skin and would not let go." Six years on, Rebecca's ship has sailed out to three countries where abortions are illegal, despite every possible attempt to stop her. Each trip has profoundly influenced the way abortion is discussed and has empowered local women's organizations to get the issue on their country's political agenda. "The ship will never be able to help all the women who need it. But we can inform them and we have greatly influenced the way abortion is perceived. And this is just the beginning."

According to the World Health Organization, a woman dies every six minutes as a result of an unsafe abortion. Induced abortions are one of the most common medical interventions in the world: out of around 46 million abortions performed annually, 20 million are illegal and unsafe.

Netherlands

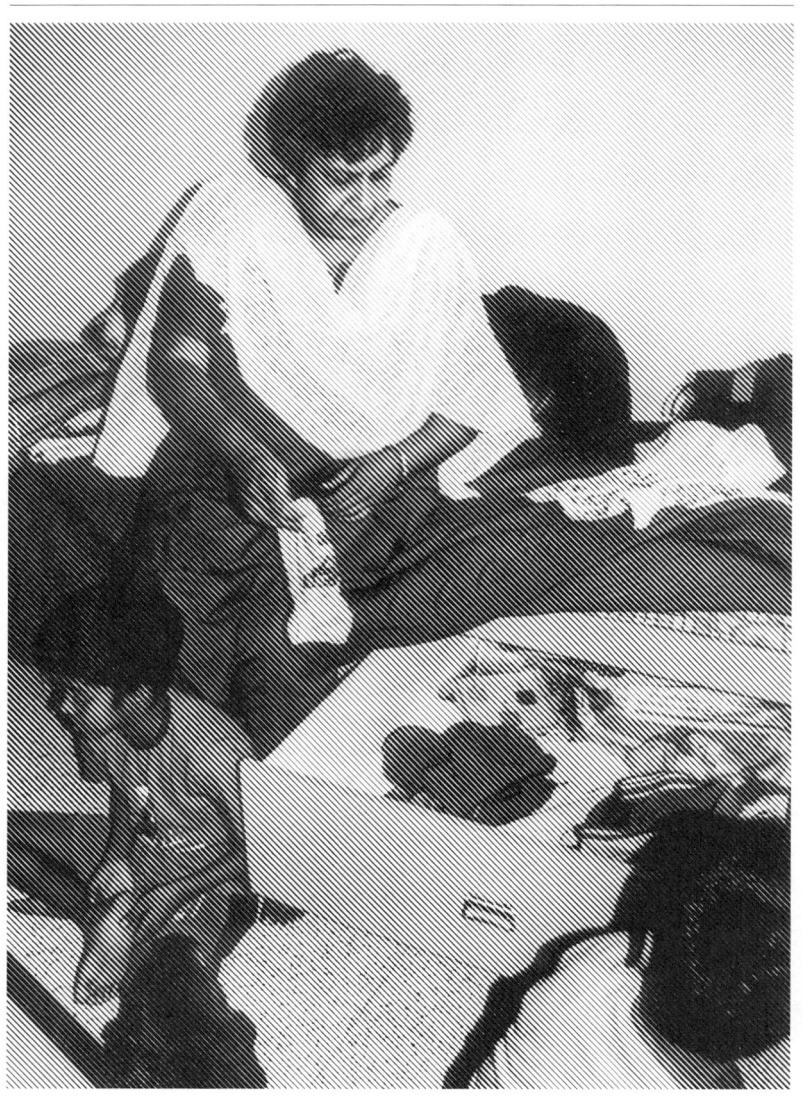

Anjali Gopalan

Naz Foundation (India) Trust

Anjali Gopalan's work on HIV/Aids issues over the past two decades has changed the way India's policymakers address these issues. When the Naz Foundation (India) Trust, which Anjali established in 1995, first began work, there was remarkable resistance to even acknowledging that HIV was a problem. However, through the sustained lobbying of groups working on education, health and women's empowerment, Anjali has not only educated and trained them to incorporate HIV issues in ongoing programs, but also challenged the laws and norms that marginalize women and sexual minorities.

Anjali Gopalan (born 1957) lived and worked in New York for about a decade before returning to India to work on HIV/Aids and issues of marginalization. In 1995, she established the Naz Foundation (India) Trust, an HIV/Aids service organization working on prevention and care. Anjali believes that raising consciousness on these issues facilitates empowered decision-making. When the Naz Foundation began, it confronted a wall of stubborn resistance to the simple acknowledgment that HIV was a problem. But with the sustained lobbying of groups working on education, health and women's empowerment, Anjali and the Naz Foundation persuaded them to incorporate HIV issues into their ongoing programs.

Anjali has been working with HIV+ and affected persons for nearly two decades. Disturbingly often, this involves confronting hostile structures and challenging regressive and oppressive laws and norms. Her work with the MSM (men who have sex with men) community, for instance, is hobbled by an archaic law established in 1860 (section 377 of the Indian penal code) that criminalizes sex between men. She has also had to deal with intimidation and personal imperilment, including an instance where the brother of a gay man lodged a police case against her and threatened to kill her.

After years of unrelenting advocacy and action, both government and society have begun to acknowledge the importance of the work that Anjali has initiated: issues such as access to care and treatment of HIV+ persons — instead of prevention messages alone — are finally being addressed. In fact, the supreme court recently issued notice to the government on a special leave petition filed by the Naz Foundation seeking to legalize homosexuality and to strike down a statute that makes "unnatural sex" a criminal offence. "This work has to be a lifelong commitment," says Anjali.

Although not "officially" a high-prevalence zone, India has a galloping HIV problem, aggravated by population density, topography, official apathy and social taboos. The situation has been amended somewhat in the past 20 years, with the government admitting to a problem and seeking to address it.

India

Marianne Grosspietsch

Shanti Sewa Griha
Shanti Leprahilfe Dortmund e.V

In 1992, Marianne Grosspietsch founded Shanti Sewa Griha, a nursing facility for leprosy patients in Katmandu. Today, Marianne also gives shelter to the poor, the disabled, and the persecuted. More than 1200 persons receive medical care. There are kindergartens, schools, workshops, and agricultural production. Shanti is led by locals, two women and six men. Marianne is the inspiring force for everyone. She returns to Germany quite often to generate essential donations for the project. The extensive social integration of her patients is another main aspect of Marianne's work.

The scene: a very formal assembly in the ceremonial hall of the Congress of Nepal. Marianne Grosspietsch is to receive a prize for her social commitment. Such ceremonies are even more formal in Nepal than in the old days of English monarchy! Three speeches are given and there is a hint of incense. The German Ambassador walks up to the podium and states that there is a lot of praising going on. "I would like to tell you about a bad habit of the honorable …" he begins. — Silence, confusion. The Ambassador enjoys this moment — and continues: "She cannot say no to anybody!" And that is true.

Marianne hardly ever manages to turn away a helpless person who makes it to Shanti and begs for shelter: An orphan is brought, a newborn who has been lying on the roadside for two days. On another day, Marianne Grosspietsch sees a young man inching along on his hands; polio turned his legs into scrawniest bones. She invites him to ride with her in her car. Three girls, maybe ten years old, had to serve as child slaves for wealthy people. They ran away and now ask for a hideout, but first of all need to be fed and cared for. There are cases like these every single day, and Shanti already seems to be bursting with help seekers.

A small commission has to decide whether somebody can be accepted at Shanti or not. But every child, every woman, every old man can stay for a few days "on probation." It is a system that works. Those accepted to stay can choose the work they want to do in the workshops. Everybody has a chance to feel needed and to earn a small living, however disabled they are. Inventing new products for the workshops is one of Marianne's favorite occupations. But she likes it even better to care for children and the elderly.

Nepal is enduring civil war, as Maoists are spreading terror, conquering vast parts of the country, and ruling with brutality. The capital Katmandu is cut off from the hinterland, and often a forced general strike brings all life to a halt. Poverty, fear, and devastation are growing day by day.

Germany

Lair Guerra de Macedo

Lair Guerra de Macedo (1943), infectologist and university professor, architected the National STD/Aids Program of the Brazilian Ministry of Health. In 1986, she began "the work of her life" with only a tiny office and one secretary. She faced the resistance of the State's and the Pharmaceutical Industry's bureaucracy, until a car accident shattered this warrior's sword. Today, with severe consequences, Lair is thinking of writing a book about "the heroic years of the fight against Aids."

In 1986, Aids was collecting lives. It had unpleasant names such as: modern cancer, gay plague, disease of the drug abusers and promiscuous. The Brazilian Government vacillated in the fight against this pandemic. The World Bank was pessimistic; it estimated that Aids would infect Brazilians at a rhythm of 35% a year. But then, Lair Guerra stepped in. Born in the state of Piauí, mother of five children, this infectologist took on the challenge of organizing a governmental response to the disease. "In the beginning we did not have any money or equipments. We lacked people prepared for the job." She crossed the country to attract the attention of and to qualify health agents. She promoted partnerships with NGOs dedicated to the prevention of HIV and to the defense of people living with HIV/Aids. She insisted that blood banks be inspected. She participated in the great outcry for the generalization of health rights that had its high point with the Constitution of 1988. This document states that "health is the right of all citizens. It is the State's obligation to provide it." After that, she worked tirelessly to universally provide the treatment of Aids. Currently, the State, among other actions, distributes the anti-retroviral medication. The country has around 364,000 people infected with the virus. To Lair Guerra de Macedo, science exists to promote quality of life.

In 1996, while leaving a lecture, a bus drove straight into the car she was in. Having suffered cranial traumatism, she spent two months in a coma. She was left with many severe consequences. But she was still alive. In spite of the difficulties, she gives lectures when she is invited to do so and intends to write a book regarding her experience in the National STD/Aids Program.

The Brazilian National STD/Aids Program was created by Lair Guerra de Macedo and is an instance of the Ministry of Health. The Program formulates policies, guidelines and strategies of prevention and treatment of STDs and Aids. The Program has become an international reference on the subject.

Brazil

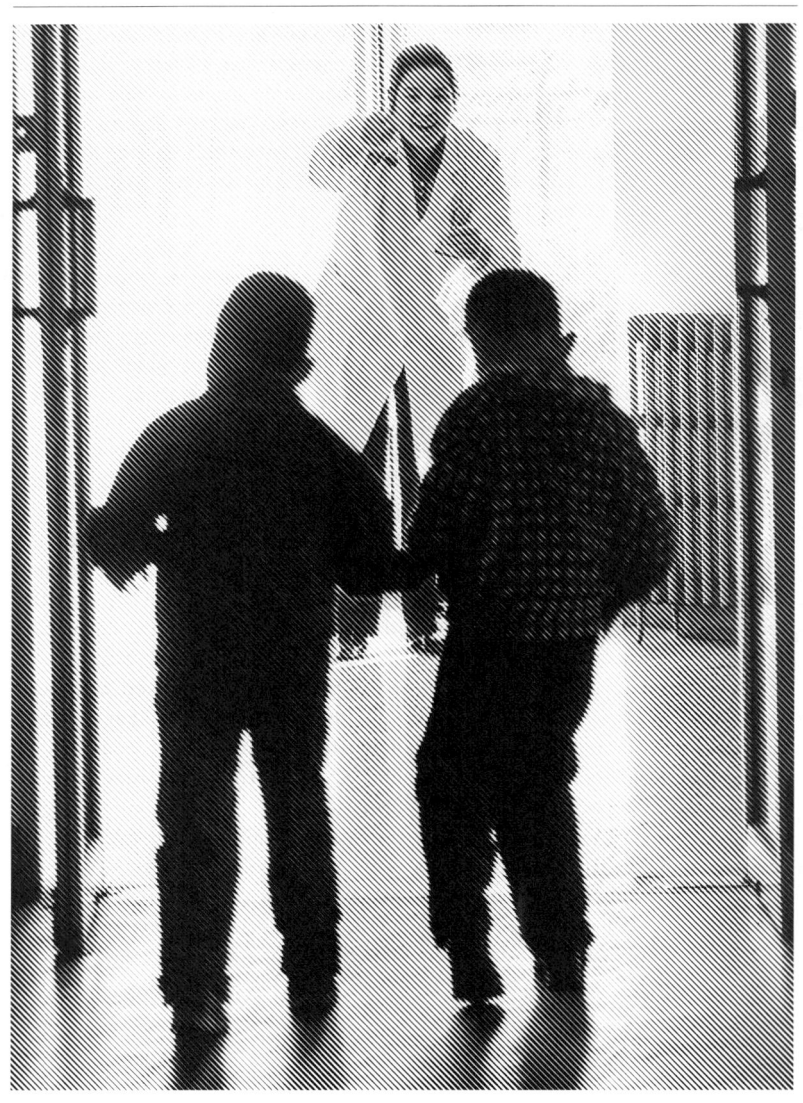

Xinzhi Guo

Guo Xinzhi (46) is the chief medical officer and director of the Shanxi Poliomyelitis Rehabilitation Hospital, and a State Council subsidized specialist and pioneer in the recovery, prevention and study of poliomyelitis and senile dementia. Through various tests, Guo has achieved many breakthroughs in the treatment of these diseases using a combination of Chinese and Western medicine.

Guo Xinzhi has developed treatments for poliomyelitis and senile dementia by means of various tests, including continuous testing of the impact of acupuncture and medicine on her own body, for example important acupoints such as fengfu and yamen. Guo often contacted abandoned children with poliomyelitis. She could not accept such tragedies and felt a strong sense of responsibility for overcoming the disease. After 20 years intensive research and exploration, she found over ten new effective acupoint areas in the head, eye, neck, hands, waist, and belly, and so introducing new rehabilitation theory and experience to the treatment of these diseases. This represents a great leap forward in medicine as poliomyelitis and senile dementia were previously considered incurable.

Despite her extraordinary achievements, Guo is indifferent to fame. She gave the medicine formula freely to the provincial research institute rather than selling it to a pharmaceutical factory in Henan Province that had offered a price of 100,000 yuan. She declined many good offers to give lectures or practice medicine in Europe and America. Moreover, she has donated tens of thousand of yuan that she had received in bonuses from the government in recognition of her scientific research contribution to social welfare agencies. She has said that her roots are in Shanxi Province and her career in China. It is Guo's oath and goal in life to help resolve the problems faced by the Party, the government, and by patients and their families, in order to improve the lives of Chinese people and the general well-being of the human species.

Modern Western medicine cannot cure poliomyelitis and senile dementia. Such patients' lives and daily activities are severely affected. Guo Xinzhi and other doctors trained in Western and Chinese medicine wish to do research in this area by combining the advantages of both approaches.

China

Patricia Henderson

Miriam Centre Child Abuse Research and Treatment Trust

Patricia Henderson works to heal the lives of abused children and their families. An outspoken social worker and mother of six, she is driven by the belief that the deepest desire of children is for safe nurture by their own people; and a determination that families and communities should own and address the issues preventing this. Her pioneering work over 30 years has helped to change the way New Zealand hears the voices of young victims and deals with abuse and violence.

Patricia "Patsy" Henderson is director and co-founder of the Miriam Center Child Abuse Research and Treatment Trust, in the northern New Zealand city of Whangarei. The outspoken social worker has raised six children and has never been afraid to challenge the way the authorities deal with abuse cases. As far back as the 1970s, she was calling for therapists to work with the sex offenders and entire families where abuse had occurred — not simply to "rescue" the child by removing it. Patsy is often called on to provide evidence in court as an expert witness in abuse cases. She says the hardest thing about her job is being called a liar in court — by lawyers defending men who have been sexually abusing children: men who have earlier wept in her office as they confessed their guilt. "To have a lawyer raise an eyebrow at a jury, and suggest you are lying is personally battering. Especially, when the next day, the same lawyer will refer another abused child to me for help. To them it is just part of the legal game. But for a child, not being believed is the worst thing in the world. I say to offenders: 'You hold this child's life in the palm of your hand. You can own up to what you have done and save her, and redeem yourself. Prison can even be therapeutic.'" Some men, says Patsy, accept the challenge and do their time without a court battle. In such cases, she says, healing for the child and her family, and eventually the abuser, becomes possible. The pioneering New Zealand social worker was awarded a Churchill fellowship in 1998 to research child abuse and the law in the United Kingdom. In 2003, she received an award from Auckland's University of Technology as a distinguished social practitioner, committed to just practice.

Patricia Henderson works on child abuse in the wider Northland region of New Zealand, where the first people, Maori, are nearly half the population. Recent changes in economic polices have wrought havoc on jobs and inter-generational family support structures. Incomes are some of the lowest in New Zealand.

New Zealand

Lan Hsiang Hsu

Wild Lily Farm ("Dawan" Farm)

While farming in Hsinchu county, Hsu Lan Hsiang found herself in the middle of terrible pollution from a biochemical plant. Together with local villagers, they had the plant close down. Later, they stopped the construction of a golf course. Through organic farming techniques and education, she helps farmers understand the importance of water and the environment. "Only when we get rid of all the pollutants, and people stop endangering the environment, will the earth be saved."

Born in a farmer's family in 1954, Hsu Lan Hsiang keeps afresh the memories of the villages, ponds and wetlands of her past. In 1971, Hsu left rural life and started to work in a factory. After realizing she could not live her life with pollution and injustice, Hsu moved to Hsinchu County to take up farming, hoping to bring back the sweet memories. To her surprise, she found herself in the middle of pollution from a biochemical plant and serious environmental destruction from a golf course project. In order to rebuild the natural environment, Hsu decided to launch the chapter on environmental protection in her life.

In 1992, Hsu united villagers to force the closure of the biochemical plant. She then launched a project to boycott the golf course and successfully prevented its completion. The Housemakers Union and Foundation and other environmental protection organizations backed her. This is the only successful example of environmental activism that stopped a golf course in the development phase in Taiwan.

After leading several environmental protection campaigns, Hsu Lan Hsiang returned to the mountains and thought of ways to promote the protection of water resources and the environment. Hsu understood well what difficulties farmers faced, and how Taiwanese politicians had compromised to WTO liberalization. In 1995, Hsu started to run organic fermentation experiments to produce vinegar in Hsinchu's mountainous areas. With her understanding of the natural environment and with her search for clean water, air and soil, she founded the Wild Lily Farm ("Dawan" Farm) in Taitung's Tulan in 2002. Hsu Lan-hsiang's organic vinegar has drawn public attention to the close ties between health and environment; she helps farmers gain confidence in organic methods and join the ranks of environment protectors.

Years of industrial development have contaminated Taiwan's water sources and land. Past policies relegated agriculture behind industrial development. Recently, import of agricultural products under the WTO framework has caused serious impact on farms. People have migrated and farms are languishing.

China, Taiwan

Malalai Joya

Hamoon Health Center

Malalai Joya (25) was born in Farah. She had her early schooling in Iran and Pakistan. After the Bonn Peace Accord of 2001 and the toppling of the Taliban regime, she returned to her hometown and started to work as a social worker and women's rights activist. She has helped to establish the Hamoon Health Center to provide free medical treatment and medicines for children and unwaged women. She advocates women's rights and human rights issues through meetings and the distribution of leaflets. She has also worked with the disabled, providing wheelchairs and prosthesis.

Malalai Joya was motivated to finish her education and work as a health educator in the refugee camps in Pakistan. Her father, who had lost a leg in the war, was a member of the resistance against the Russian Occupation of Afghanistan. Malalai was fervently dedicated to becoming an advocate of women's rights after witnessing the despotic and degrading attitude of the mujahideen and the Taliban towards the role of women.

So, Malalai's starting point was to educate women and girls by conducting adult literacy courses for women and girls. Her vision of a peaceful country is to disarm the militia groups and to end the cultivation and trade of opium poppy in the country. A secure and peaceful society, Malalai believes, will lead to the recognition and respect for women and human rights. She is active at grassroots as well as province level, has established an orphanage that provides shelter to children who have lost their parents in the war, and she has founded several adult literacy and computer science courses for women and youths in order to develop their work capacity and keep them up-to-date with information technology. Malalai Joya was chosen as the women's representative to the Constitutional Committee Loya Jirga. At this assembly, she voiced her opposition to the participation of the warlords in the formation of the Constitution. Her challenging speech provoked the wrath of the extremists with the result that she had to be escorted by security guards during the Loya Jirga. Malalai Joya, along with other women delegates, has been loyal to defending women's rights in the new Constitution of Afghanistan.

Experiencing dislocation and the chaos of war personally, the main focus of Malalai Joya's activities is women's rights advocacy in particular and human rights in general. She is working hard to mobilize women in Afghanistan and motivate them to stand up for their rights.

Afghanistan

Jane Keith-Reid

Aids Task Force of Fiji (ATFF)

Jane Keith-Reid (60) founded the Aids Task Force of Fiji in 1993. She pioneered a peer education program to reach vulnerable groups, extended peer education training to eight other Pacific countries, set up a drop-in clinic for vulnerable young people and those living with HIV/Aids, and directed regional research into the closeted issue of "non-gay" men having sex with men. Her work saves lives, prevents new HIV infections, and gives comfort and hope to many. With the Pacific Islands Aids Foundation, she campaigns for free anti-retroviral therapy for HIV-positive Pacific people.

Jane Keith-Reid of Aids Task Force Fiji (ATFF) has worked voluntarily for years to help Pacific people learn of the dangers of HIV/Aids. Despite threat to herself, her work has significantly improved if not actually saved the lives of many by ensuring that people living with HIV have access to treatment, care, and social support. Aids was only just making inroads into the Pacific when Jane foresaw its fatal impact and realized the need to establish prevention and awareness programs. Later, she set up social support and treatment programs. In 1997, through ATFF, Jane initiated peer education training in eight Pacific countries to build NGO capacity in the region for peer education and community education trainings. In 2000, ATFF established a drop-in community clinic in Suva to serve vulnerable young people, commercial sex workers, men who have sex with men, and people living with HIV/Aids. The clinic and ATFF under Jane's guidance directed vital research in Fiji, Samoa, and Vanuatu on sexual behavior of "non-gay" men who have sex with men, to provide information for program design in those countries. Most recently, Jane has been the principal advocate on anti-retroviral combination (ARV) drug therapy for HIV positive people in Fiji and the Pacific and succeeded in securing funding for treatment programs through the Global Fund for Aids, Tuberculosis, and Malaria. As a result of her groundbreaking work in the Pacific, Fiji will soon be the first country in the Pacific to begin free treatment for HIV positive people.

Jane Keith-Reid founded the Aids Task Force of Fiji (1993) in direct response to the growing problem of HIV/Aids in the Pacific. She set up education and prevention work to counter denial and ignorance, stop a major epidemic, and protect those living with HIV/Aids from bigotry, blame, and abuse.

"Il faut toujours
avoir du cœur pour les
autres — one must
always have a heart
for others."

Marie Béatrice Kenfack Tolevi

Organisation for Health, Food Security and Development (Ofsad)

Marie Béatrice Kenfack Tolevi, a Cameroonian, founded a NGO in 1992 that focuses on reproductive health, food and nutrition, human rights and equity. The Center listens and counsels the youth and teenagers. It also has a clinic for adults to seek reproductive health advice. Marie Béatrice reaches the community through educators.

Marie Béatrice Kenfack (54), realizing the misery of the populations living around her, decided to open the Organisation for Health, Food Security and Development (Ofsad). She sustains a polygamous household of 10 children with meager revenue from her work and numerous other activities. She has worked as a midwife for 29 years. The United Nations Population Fund trained her on gender, development and management process, projects and program coordination, youth reproductive health as well as clinical family planning. She reaches the community through educators. Unfortunately, the economic crisis that inspired the need for her services also hampers her from realizing her objectives. This is also compounded by other socio-cultural considerations and financial problems. She is convinced that helping others is her destiny, given the persistent poverty. She derives joy and encouragement in providing services to improve people's lives. Tolevi does not operate on a formal network, but collaborates with any person or organization sharing her vision to help others. Several women have followed her example by launching other human development programs, such as schools and agricultural enterprises to alleviate poverty. She has hope, despite the wars, group or individual egoism and catastrophes that plague her work. "In any individual exists a fiber of humanity that never dies; it survives wars, egoism and catastrophes," she says. Peace is apparently threatened everywhere. Many people do not have access to health and nutrition and freedom of expression, and human rights are violated. The hope is in expecting change.

The socio-economic situation in the country is rough for the ordinary people. Development is generally centered in the capital. Rural areas lack information and large-scale development activities.

Cameroon

At 91, and after a life as a diplomat's wife, Mehmooda Salim Khan has been a committed social worker for the past six decades, working today with tuberculosis patients.

Mehmooda Salim Khan

Red Crescent Society in Pakistan
SOS Children's Villages

Few people in their 90s are fortunate enough to lead as active and socially engaged a life as Mehmooda Salim Khan, who retains her unflagging interest in the causes that have dominated her life for the past six decades, especially the care of people suffering from tuberculosis. Starting out as the wife of a civil servant, Mehmooda embarked on a remarkable career as a social worker and politician after her husband's death, even though this was a period of great difficulty for her and her family.

One of the rare women of her generation to have received a university education, Mehmooda Salim Khan (born 1913) went to school in the Indian town of Aligarh. She studied at the elite Aligarh Muslim Girl's College, and graduated from Queen Mary College, Lahore. Her marriage to Abdul Salim Khan, at 21, took her to Pakistan's remote North West Frontier Province (NWFP), where he was posted, and later catapulted her into a very different life, as she accompanied her husband for nine years on diplomatic postings in Colombo, San Francisco, Tokyo, New York, and London.

Mehmooda's life changed when her husband died in London in 1957. She moved with her three children to Abbotabad in the NWFP, where she lives today. She not only looked after her own children, but took up a range of issues that included the care of tuberculosis patients in this rugged and archconservative region of Pakistan.

Today, Mehmooda runs a tuberculosis clinic in Abbotabad as well as rehabilitation centers for tuberculosis patients and other poor people of the area, where they are taught how to cut and sew garments and weave carpets. She has also worked with refugees, helping them overcome their trauma at the horrors of conflict, and lead normal lives. She has been actively involved with the work of family planning organizations, the activities of the Red Crescent Society in Pakistan, and has helped young orphans in the region through her work with the SOS Children's Villages. Apart from social work, Mehmooda also served for three years as a functionary in the government of East Pakistan (now Bangladesh), first as education minister and then as minister for health.

The North West Frontier Province in Pakistan is rugged, archconservative, and backward in terms of public health. Whoever works there does so at tremendous personal cost, yet with immense personal satisfaction.

Pakistan

Parveen Azam Khan

Dost Welfare Foundation

In Urdu, the word dost means friend. Parveen Azam Khan (born 1938), founder and head of the Dost Welfare Foundation, has been a true friend and a savior to some of the most marginalized people in Pakistani society: drug users, women and juvenile prisoners, refugees, and street-children. Thanks to her work, thousands of drug users in the North West Frontier Province have been rescued from hopeless lives as mendicants, prisoners, or wastrels. She has also managed to push through changes in the way the justice system treats vulnerable prisoners.

Parveen Azam Khan, who spent 35 years working for Pakistan's health services, knew how bad the country's drug abuse situation was. Upon retirement in 1998, she set up an NGO, the Dost Welfare Foundation, in her hometown, Peshawar. She gathered a small core team of voluntary workers and trained them. The following year, Parveen set up a 70-bed treatment and rehabilitation center on donated land. This center provides a range of services under one roof to thousands of clients. Her next goal was to develop an outreach program and establish a treatment continuum between the outreach program and the center. Today, three mobile teams meet about 250 drug users every day, counseling and educating them and providing first aid and social support. They encourage the drug users to visit Dost's drop-in centers: 100 to 150 people daily visit three such centers for counseling, therapy, treatment, a hot meal, a bath and to change their clothes. Every drug user in the area has access to free or affordable treatment and rehabilitation.

Working with prisoners and Afghan refugees in camps in the North West Frontier Province became an extension of Parveen's work, since drug abuse problems are endemic in both settings. "Therapeutic communities" have been established in two prisons in Peshawar and Haripur, which provide prisoners with primary healthcare, counseling, education, vocational-skills training, help in contacting family members, and free legal aid. Parveen has also developed a network of local, regional, national, and international partners, with whom she shares experiences and the latest strategies. Since January 1999, Dost has been running programs in collaboration with Penal Reform International, Unicef, and the provincial government to educate prisoners, police, lawyers, and civil society.

The 1979 Hadd Ordinance cauterized poppy cultivation and opium production until the mid-1980s, when profits ramped up production. Cannabis is processed in the Orakzai and Kurram agencies. Neighboring Afghanistan, the world's largest opium producer, has a porous border with Pakistan.

Pakistan

"Share your knowledge, it is another way of achieving immortality."

Veronica Khosa

Tateni Home Care Services

Veronica Khosa was brought up by her grandmother and aunt in a small rural village of Kwazulu Natal, South Africa. A generous community member educated her. These gestures shaped the way Veronica would work with and treat people for the rest of her life. She chose to study nursing because it provided the immediate means to pay back the community member who had financed her education. Veronica set up the Tateni Home Care Services to provide counseling and support services, and home-based care to HIV/Aids patients.

Families in South Africa tend to lock up HIV/Aids patients in their houses. They are shunned by the community and often dismissed from their working places. The pain and the agony they undergo makes some of them die sooner than if they were given appropriate care.

Veronica Khosa works now as a professional nurse in Pretoria. She formed the Tateni Home Care Services whose main objective is to provide counseling and support services, home-based care to the patients and enhance the community's capacity to provide care and support to the affected and infected. Her ideas are already gaining international attention. She was invited to participate in a conference on aging people in the community. The World Health Organization chose her project to provide a case study on mobilizing family and community care for and by the people with HIV/Aids. The provincial government has adopted Veronica's model and implemented it in all the districts of Gauteng. As a result of her lobbying efforts, the Department of Health has also introduced palliative treatment in its training curriculum for nurses and doctors.

South Africa has one of the highest HIV/Aids infection rates in the world. Most people lack information about the disease and hence hide ill relatives at home. Due to rejection and stress, patients develop full-blown Aids earlier than usual. People also attach superstitious beliefs to the disease.

South Africa

Henriette Carvalho Kouyate

Madame Henriette Carvalho Kouyate was born in Dakar, Senegal, in 1931. She has spent most of her professional career in the area of health, raising awareness on the problems of female genital mutilation.

In 1975, Henriette Carvalho Kouyate was the first Malian woman to get her doctorate in medicine. Before this, she had worked as a midwife after getting a diploma in this specialty in Montpellier, France, in 1953. Henriette distinguished herself in the treatment of sterile women and victims of female genital mutilation so that they have normal fertility and a happy life in the African context. She has fought a great deal for the protection of women, children, and for reproductive control. Henriette also contributed to the struggle in Mali against female genital mutilation and ensured that national opinion came to understand that female genital mutilation is a public health problem for women everywhere. More and more Malian men and women understand today that this ancestral practice cannot be justified anymore due to its negative effects on maternal health.

Henriette Carvalho Kouyate is also a writer and has published a book on female genital mutilation and sexually transmitted diseases. She is, thus, a pioneer in female health and in the well-being of women and children in Mali. After her retirement, she became a counselor to the young in an area that has marked all her professional life as a doctor and writer. Having spent many years in French exile, today Henriette (74) says that she has had a wonderful life as a doctor in the Malian capital. She keeps her memories of the contribution she has made as first wise woman of Mali.

Henriette Carvalho Kouyate introduced family planning to Mali and Senegal, a method that has had positive effects on the quality of life of many Malian families compared to situations in which many births expose children and mothers to all kinds of diseases and which make the economic life of families precarious.

Mali

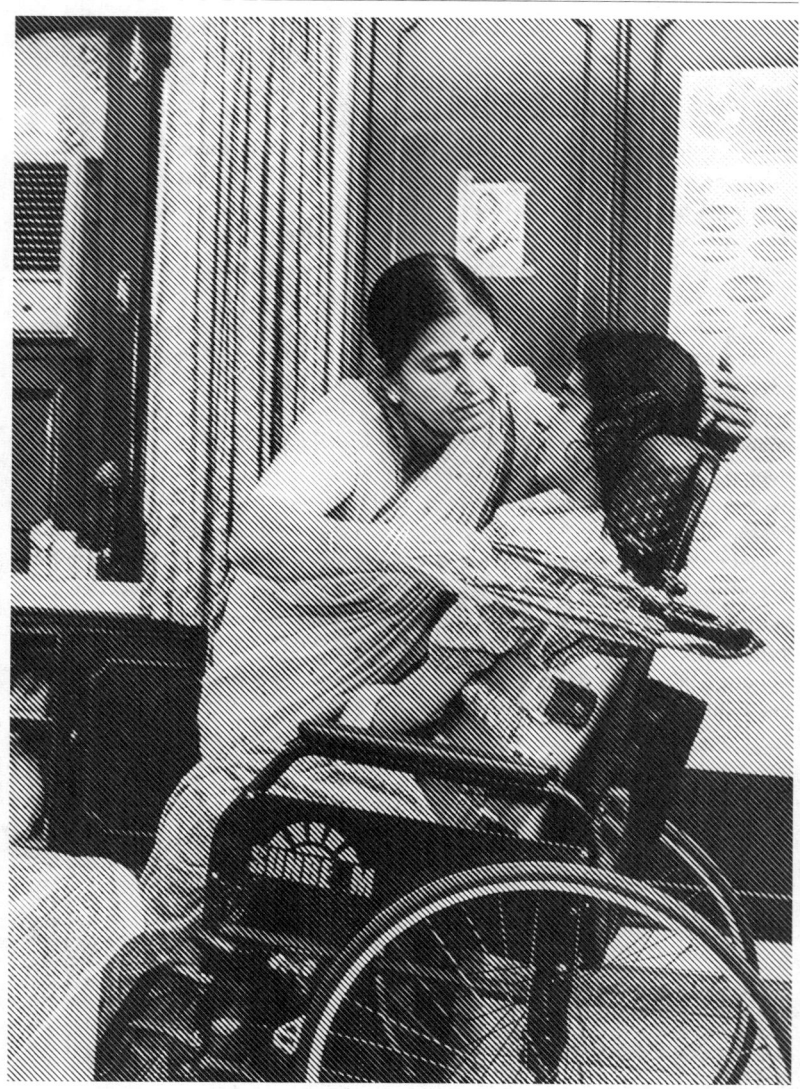

Krishna Kumar

Handicapped Children's Parents Association (HCPA)
Udaan

Krishna Kumar (born 1944) has two daughters with cerebral palsy and understands the anxieties of parents with disabled children. In 1987, she formed the Handicapped Children's Parents Association (HCPA), which now has a home for disabled persons, the only one in India accessible to individuals with severe or multiple disabilities. Krishna's zeal, mettle, and calm are sources of strength for the many who come into contact with her.

Krishna Kumar was staggered when her two daughters were diagnosed with cerebral palsy. She initially found it almost impossible to cope with caring for them, handling household activities, continuing with her teaching career, and coping with her husband's family blame for having borne two children with disabilities. She had to stand up to her in-laws to provide her children with education and requisite training.

Realizing that the parents of other disabled children must be sharing her trauma, in 1987 she formed the HCPA with seven other similarly affected parents. Krishna is the foot soldier of the organization, a position within it being singularly unimportant. She actively organized meetings and raised funds for its activities. Today, the HCPA has a home for disabled persons who have no caregivers: Sneh Kunj is the only one of its kind in India, providing a space for people with multiple and severe disabilities. Krishna was also instrumental in setting up Udaan (flight), a school for disabled children, of which she is a trustee-member.

Krishna's motivation and passion involves her in those areas that compel immediate attention: she helps with the education of children from the weaker sections of society, provides counseling in legal matters, bails out family emergencies, and even facilitates the transfer of parents with disabled children to places with better facilities for their children. Her maturity, calm, acceptance, and courage in the face of a unique responsibility are a source of great fortitude for the many that come into contact with her.

India is a mire of insensitivity to disability: even basic rights — civil rights, access to information, education, and employment, easy entry to buildings and public transport, access to election booths — are wanting. Estimates peg India's disability rate at 2.13 percent of the population.

India

Gynecologist Tsering Lahdol has been an extremely effective agent for social change in Ladakh, thanks to her humane approach and her ability to relate to people.

Tsering Lahdol

Sonam Nurboo Memorial Hospital (SNMH)

Gynecologist Tsering Lahdol lives and works in the mountainous region of Ladakh. When she started her work, healthcare facilities in the region were extremely basic. Today, thanks in no small part to her contribution, healthcare services, in general, and women's reproductive healthcare, in particular, have improved significantly in Ladakh. She has also been a very effective agent for social change in Ladakh, thanks to her humane approach and her ability to relate to people.

Tsering Lahdol has served Ladakh for almost three decades through her work at the Sonam Nurboo Memorial Hospital (SNMH) in Leh. A native, she went to school in Leh, Ladakh's capital. Later, this farmer's daughter went to the state capital, Srinagar, to study at the Srinagar Medical College, specializing in gynecology.

Tsering, a very competent gynecologist, is much more than a doctor. Her work gave her the opportunity to learn about familial and social relationships and practices in Ladakh, and their impact on women and children. She made use of this knowledge to provide counseling services, and sensitize people and spread awareness about gender issues. She is an indispensable resource person for all meetings, seminars, workshops, and policy discussions on Ladakhi society. An extremely humane approach and the ability to relate to people are her ways to change people's attitudes. Thanks to her contribution, healthcare services and women's reproductive health have improved significantly. She has highlighted issues in the region's development debate, in particular, women's health, adolescence, and reproductive roles, which have become matters for reflection in Ladakhi society. As a gynecologist, Tsering remains a symbol of service, dedication, commitment, and compassion. Her concern for women's problems is a quality rare in this roughhouse region.

Ladakh is a tourist destination, but it is an unforgiving moonscape that keeps development very effectively at bay. Women, as usual, were at impoverishment's receiving end, their health a matter of providence — until Tsering Lahdol happened by.

India

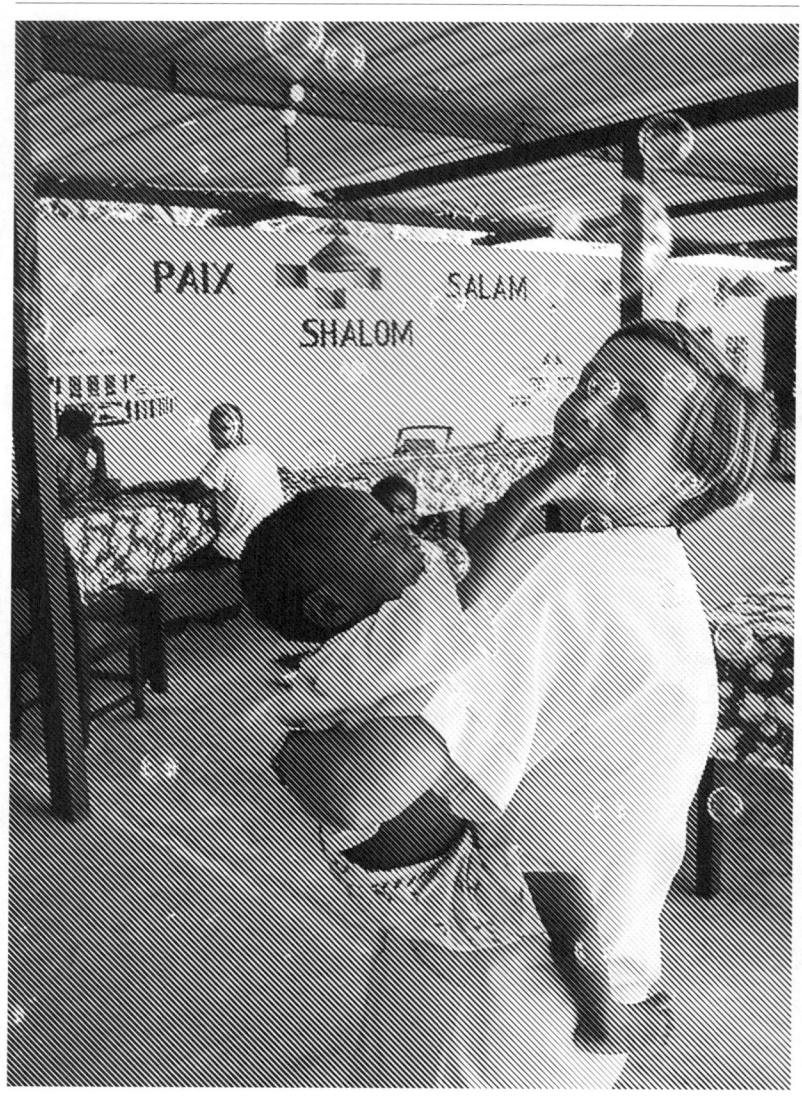

Lotti Latrous

Fondation Lotti Latrous

Lotti Latrous was born in 1953. She has lived in Saudi Arabia, Nigeria and Abidjan, the economic capital of Côte d'Ivoire, where she did volunteer work at the local Mother Theresa Hospital. The contrast between the miseries she witnessed in Abidjan and her privileged life inspired her to found an outpatient clinic in Adjouffou, a slum in Abidjan. In 2002 she opened a hospice for Aids patients. Her next project is to open an orphanage for children whose parents have died of Aids. Her family lives in Cairo and Switzerland.

Lotti recalls, "It was in Abidjan in 2002. I was sitting in my car, when I felt irritated by a sickly smell, like that of a rotting animal. I got out of the car to find out where the irritating smell was emanating from and found a man lying in a hole near the street, wrapped in a garbage bag. He was totally dehydrated. Although ants were crawling out of his ears and mouth, he was still breathing. When he finally looked at me I asked him how long he had been lying there, and he answered that he did not know. As I left to get help, he whispered, 'I am Monsieur René.' People in the slum knew that René had been lying there for at least ten days and they had occasionally brought him food and water. With the slum dwellers' help, we took René to an outpatient clinic, where he stayed for a week. All this inspired me to set up a hospital for dying Aids victims."

Lotti grew up in Zurich, where she met and married Aziz Latrous from Tunisia. They have three children, aged 25, 24 and 16. She moved to Abidjan where her husband worked as a director at Nestlé and lived a privileged life. The misery she witnessed in Abidjan motivated her to build an outpatient clinic in the slums with the full support of her husband. It had just been opened in 1999, when her husband was transferred to Cairo. Lotti would not abandon her work and made a deal with her family — she would alternate between spending two months in Cairo and one in Abidjan. As this did not prove feasible in the long run, her husband asked her to stay with her family, but only if she wanted to, because he feared that her love would turn into hatred. Thereafter, Lotti settled down in Adjouffou — a decision, which despite greatly affecting her marriage and family did not break either. The Latrouses visit each other regularly. Meanwhile Lotti is working on a new project, building a home for mothers and children.

According to the latest UN Aids Report three million people died of Aids in 2003. Of these, 2.2 million died in Sub-Saharan Africa where only ten percent of the world population lives.

Côte d'Ivoire

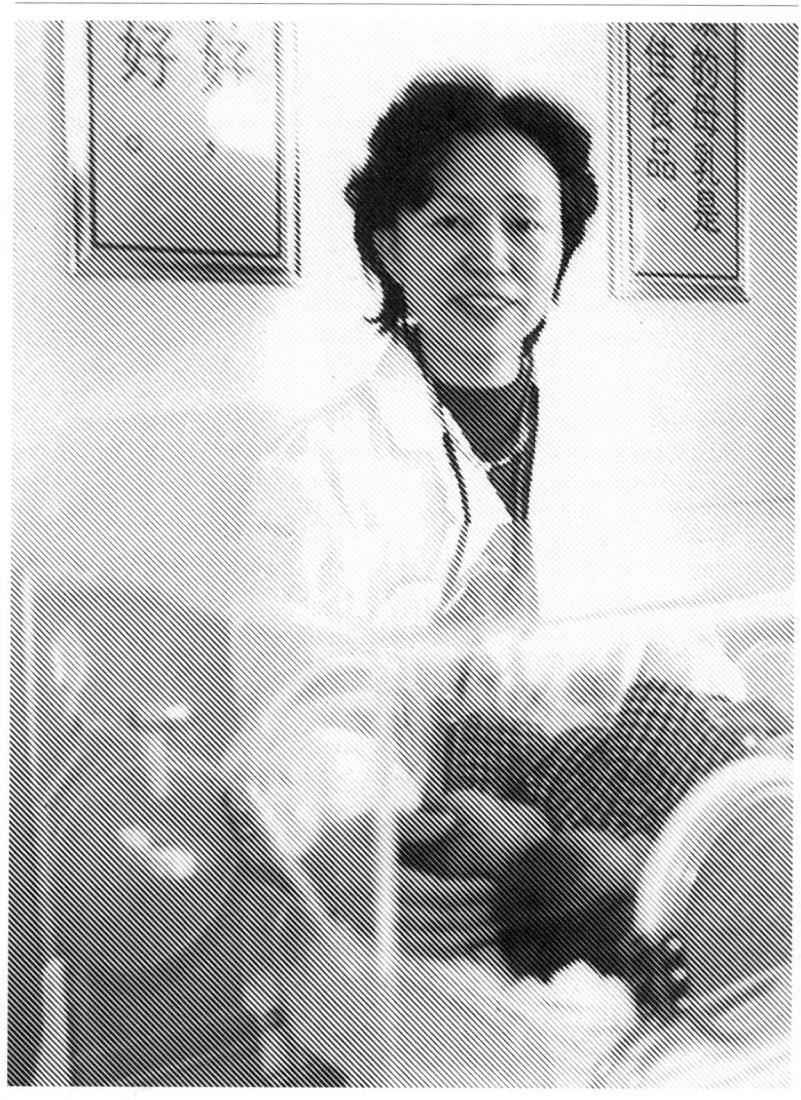

Jiyue Li

Maternity and Child Care Center, Yongning County,
Ningxia Hui Autonomous Region

Li Jiyue has worked in maternity and childcare for 22 years, traveling to the homes of poor peasants in the mountainous area of Ningxia Hui Autonomous Region. By popularizing maternity and childcare knowledge, training health personnel, and performing health checks, she has contributed to the improvement of the quality of life and health levels of women and children in the countryside and they have become her friends. She is loved and respected by the locals.

In 1983 Li Jiyue, who had just graduated as a Maternity and Child Care major from Ningxia Health School, was faced not only with the extreme poverty of the remote mountainous area of Ningxia Hui Autonomous Region, but also the challenge of traditional ideas and practices, and poor natural living conditions. The two colleagues who went with her to a village in the area left the same day. However, Li has retained her position for 22 years.

She has popularized maternity and childcare knowledge, training health care personnel, and performing regular health checks for women and children. Her work has contributed to enhancing the quality of life and health levels of women and children in the countryside. Traveling long distances to the peasants' homes, working with them, making friends with the women, and getting to know their thoughts has stood her in good stead. She is loved and respected by the locals.

After 20 years' of effort, conditions such as prolapse of reproductive organs, urinary fistula, and fecal fistula are now rare, and so she has shifted her focus to improving the quality of life of women, preventing and curing common and frequently-occurring diseases, and conducting a general survey for cancer. The health levels of local women and children have since improved greatly. During this time Li has progressed from being an ordinary health worker to being head of the bureau, as well as a member of the Chinese People's Political Consultative Conference National Committee of Yongning County and Yinchuan City.

No matter how her identity has changed, or how tired or difficult it is, as long as she sees that the mothers and the children are safe and sound, she is happy. Her persistence and her love for maternity and childcare work have ensured the continuity of endeavors in this area. And this has earned her the praise that she is "dearer than our relatives."

Economic and health conditions in the remote mountainous area of Ningxia Hui Autonomous Region are very poor. Traditional beliefs sometimes exacerbate this, as is evident from the high death rates of infants and pregnant women due to indigenous and unsafe delivery methods.

China

Xiaoliang Li

Yunnan Medical University

Li Xiaoliang is Associate Professor of Preventive Medicine at Junming Medical College, and a specialist at the Yunnan Health and Development Research Center. From 1989 she has been giving extensive training on the prevention and control of Aids. Not only has she worked on training materials for teachers, she has also developed peer training for young people, and aroused much public concern on issues of health and sexuality. Such work represents is a breakthrough in a society where sex and Aids are taboo subjects.

In 1989 there were many HIV carriers in Yunnan Province. Li Xiaoliang realized the importance of focusing on the prevention of Aids, improving the public's knowledge, and giving special attention to youth sex education. Most people at that time were either afraid of Aids or too embarrassed to talk about it. Teachers too were afraid to talk to students about the use of condoms. Li and her colleagues did some research, had discussions with teachers, and did a survey in the school. They found out that most students were not unfamiliar with the condom. This gave them the impetus to break through the "forbidden zone" in Yunnan's middle schools and start sex education, setting a good precedent for their future work. Li also organized performances in schools on the subject of drugs and Aids. These were directed and enacted by the students themselves, attracted many parents, and served as a good public education program.

"Little Duck," a young student, was Li's working partner when she implemented "peer education" to prevent Aids in some middle schools in Kunming. He acted as the master of ceremonies when the United Nations Children's Fund came to visit the school, showing the visitors how young Chinese were determined to avoid drugs and Aids. He set a good example to others by embracing HIV carriers in the village.

Li was encouraged by the younger generation who had taken it upon themselves to spread knowledge about Aids. Li has always had original ideas; her practical experience in the field enables her to propose feasible recommendations and working methods, from both macro and micro perspectives.

Yunnan Province was among the first to have Aids patients, mainly in the remote areas. The people were unaware its dangers, considering Aids to be merely a "foreigners' problem." Even teachers held this view and, to make matters worse, they were too embarrassed to talk about Aids and sex in the (middle) schools.

China

Jane Roberts and Lois Abraham

34 Million Friends of UNFPA (United Nations Population Fund)

34 Million Friends of UNFPA got its start in July 2002 with the coincidental, almost simultaneous, inspiration of two women, Jane Roberts and Lois Abraham. Both were outraged by the US decision to withhold from the United Nations Population Fund USD 34 million in congressionally appropriated funds, and each was determined to do something about it. 34 Million Friends has become a grassroots movement supported by 100,000 individuals who have contributed more than USD 2 million and demonstrated widespread commitment to UNFPA's work to improve the health and well-being of people around the world.

Jane Roberts, a teacher and tennis coach from Redlands, California, and Lois Abraham, a lawyer from Taos, New Mexico, had never met. But their independent inspirations to appeal to fellow Americans to donate the money their government was withholding brought them together. More than 100,000 people were as outraged as Jane and Lois by the following story. The USA made a commitment of USD 34 million to the United Nations Population Fund in the 2002 budget, with Congress approving the funds and President Bush signing the bill containing the appropriation. The fund provides family planning and reproductive health services to some of the world's most impoverished and underserved women in 142 countries. The US government reneged on the 2002 commitment and withheld funding in 2003 and 2004, for a total of USD 95 million. The reason given for refusing to release the USD 34 million is that the Fund provides aid to Chinese government agencies that force women to have abortions. Despite a state department investigation that found no substantiation for the allegation, the administration stuck by its decision to withhold funds.

Jane and Lois wrote to fellow Americans, telling them of the consequences of a USD 34 million budget shortfall to the UNFPA: two million unwanted pregnancies per year, nearly 800,000 abortions, 4700 maternal deaths, and 77,000 infant and child deaths. Their initiative took flight in August and by the following May contributions had exceeded one million dollars. Contributions continue to pour in from men and women from every state in the union. The story has sparked widespread media interest and has spurred the launching of a sister campaign, Friends in the European Union, in Brussels.

While US leaders politicize women's family planning and reproductive health services, 100,000 Americans, led by two women, have demonstrated their understanding that women's health services are a humanitarian issue, though heavily politicized.

United States of America

Nicole Magloire

Graduate of the Puerto Príncipe Medical Faculty in Haiti, Doctor Nicole Magloire has dedicated her life to women's health. In the 1960s, she was committed to the opposition against the dictatorship of Duvalier. Since then, she has been involved in the fight for women's sexual and reproductive rights and, aside that, for the support of women victims of domestic and political violence.

After having completed her studies in a very traditional environment, the time came for Nicole to decide on a professional specialty. Her nature, along with her interest in politics and social problems, prompted her choice. "My professional vocation was born thanks to a combination of circumstances that led me from a vague wish to be socially useful to a commitment to Haiti, through the practice of medicine and the participation in the fight for democracy." Her first professional practice put her into contact with peasant women, who are known for not only carrying the country on their heads (in their baskets full of produce for sale), but also for carrying a large part of the national economy on their shoulders. "I discovered my vocation to be a gynecologist during my social service in a remote region of Haiti. That was where I really discovered my country and where I saw that I could be useful in the field of women's health."

Since that time, all of Nicole's activities have been organized around this fundamental concern for securing a healthy life for women. Besides her practice as a gynecologist, she has been a permanent adviser on women's health for many Haitian organizations working to promote and defend women's rights. After the state military coup of 1991, she took care of the women victims of political violence. Meanwhile, she also continued her educational work, writing didactic materials and working on a number of different projects. "Nowadays, I work in a private clinic, in the Ministry of Women's Condition and Women's Rights and also with women's organizations. In the present moment, my particular field of action is in the fight for the support of women victims of domestic and political violence."

In Haiti, more than half of all families are lead by single women. The fertility rate for each woman is about five children. In the year 2000, only 15% of Haitian women declared that they use a modern contraceptive method. Half of them confessed to having had an abortion, even though it is illegal.

Aishat Magomedova

Liga zashchity matieri i rebionka (LZMR)

Aishat Magomedova (born 1948) graduated from the Medical Institute of Dagestan in 1968. In 1994, she left her position as department director at the republic's hospital and dedicated herself completely to civic activities. With the support of the local authorities and the Soros Foundation, she created a free hospital and a rehabilitation center for women and children within the framework of the NGO League for the Protection of Mother and Child (LZMR), which she founded in 1993. She is the author of several books dealing with the consequences of violence and war in the Caucasus region.

Children are the innocent victims of the machinations of political manipulators, the strategies of generals, and the insinuations of political technocrats. Vulnerable and defenseless, they are first in line to suffer from the aberrations of history.

It is impossible to know what the destiny of the 12-year-old Amina would have been, had some good people not shown her the way to Dagestan, to the organization where Aishat Magomedova works. Amina did not smile, did not talk, she had lost all taste for life. Even the psychology of an adult would have broken down because of the things the child had gone through. Amina was 12 years old when the Russian-Chechen war (1994—1999) killed all her relatives — her mother, father, and uncle. When the remains of her relatives were brought back home, the girl saw a horrible sight: the severed heads of those most dear to her. After that, she blacked out. When she came to, she never smiled or talked again. She ran away from Chechnya, ran away from the horror, but she could never run away from the terrible memories. Eventually, she found refuge in Dagestan with the NGO Liga zashchity matieri i rebionka, the League for the Protection of Mother and Child (LZMR). For a long time, Amina could not get used to people smiling and talking a lot. During the four years she spent at the League, she took part in a psychological healing program. The doctors and the psychologists did their best to bring the girl back to life; they gave her all their tenderness and care. Aishat Magomedova put the girl up at her place and became her second mother. It took years for Amina to learn anew to smile and to enjoy life, but Aishat's efforts yielded their results, and the girl gradually got over her deep psychological shock.

Unemployment among women in Dagestan has reached 85%. The basic social needs — medical aid and education — have become practically unavailable for a big part of the population. Aishat Magomedova is trying to protect the rights of the most vulnerable segments of society: women and children.

Russian Federation

Salma Maqbool

Pakistan Foundation Fighting Blindness

For most people, a physical affliction is a devastating setback, but for Salma Maqbool (born 1945) it served as an inspiration. After being diagnosed with a serious eye disease in her late 20s, she decided to devote her life to the cause of the disabled multitude in Pakistan and beyond. Her efforts over nearly three decades have inspired the disabled in her country to combat prejudice and fight for their rights, and have helped sensitize society to their situation and special needs.

In 1974, Salma Maqbool was working at a military hospital when she was diagnosed with retinitis pigmentosa, a genetic eye disease. Giving up her job, she traveled to Boston, London, Moscow, and India in search of a cure for an affliction that would lead to blindness, but doctors told her that the cure was several decades away. Salma used her visits to contact other people with retinitis pigmentosa as well as government and nongovernment institutions caring for the blind. In 1977, a meeting with Fatima Shah, also blind, proved to be a turning point. Fatima encouraged Salma to start a local branch of the Pakistan Association for the Blind in Rawalpindi. It was here that Salma married Maqbool Ahmed, a blind army retiree, in 1978.

Salma, based in Islamabad, has built up self-help organizations for the disabled at provincial, national, and international levels. She is associated with the Pakistan Blind Association, the World Blind Union, and Disabled Peoples International. Women with disabilities in Pakistan are multiply handicapped, facing also gender discrimination and, often, poverty. Salma established a rehabilitation program for disabled women and girls. A center that she helped set up in Rawalpindi, which offers free pick-ups and drop-offs, instruction, Braille education, and audiocassettes, has educated more than 300 girls since 1990. One of its graduates, Rabia Kalsoom, has attained a masters in education, the first women to do so, from Allama Iqbal Open University, Islamabad.

Apart from leveraging the media to raise awareness of the disabled, Salma has helped educational institutions develop suitable curricula and provide facilities for disabled students. An institution she has worked for now offers four options to disabled students sitting for exams: a scribe, recordings on cassettes, computers, and verbal responses.

More than 600 million people in the world are living with some form of disability, about two-thirds in developing countries like Pakistan. Many are destitute and without the support structures and benefits that would enable them to lead normal lives.

Cynthia Maung

Mae Tao Clinic

Cynthia Maung (born 1959), a trained doctor from Karen State in Burma, fled to Thailand in 1988 and set up the Mae Tao Clinic. Every year the clinic saves the lives of thousands of refugees and migrant workers. It supports remote field clinics in Burma serving internally displaced persons and sponsors women's organizations and health education. It trains medics to provide health care throughout the Thai–Burma border. Dr Maung has set up an orphanage, and supports schools and boarding houses. The Mae Tao clinic receives financial support from NGOs and grants from foreign governments.

Cynthia Maung spent seven nights crawling through the jungle to escape civil war in Burma. In 1988 the military junta shot thousands of students calling for democracy. "Everything felt so volatile and dangerous," Cynthia recalls. "And I felt there was not much I could do to help as a young doctor inside Burma." When she arrived in Mae Sot, just over the Thai border, Cynthia was shocked by the number of Burmese pouring into the refugee camps. Many were wounded and traumatized, and hundreds were dying of malaria. "There was a desperate need for emergency healthcare and humanitarian assistance," she says. With the help of foreign relief workers and village leaders, Cynthia started a makeshift clinic in an old barn with a tin roof. Her tools: a medical textbook and a rice cooker for sterilizing instruments. She and her team worked day and night to save the lives of thousands of refugees. "At the start, I only planned to stay three months. But more sick and wounded arrived every day and there was so much to do." Over the past 16 years, Dr Cynthia, as she is known locally, has transformed the Mae Tao Clinic into a multi-speciality medical center that logs more than 58,000 patient visits a year. Over 200 staff and trainees provide everything from care for HIV-positive mothers to rehabilitation for amputees. The clinic supports schools and orphanages and is also a refuge for abused women. "We are always overcrowded, or face a shortage of food or water and electricity," she explains. "And patient numbers keep rising as more flee Burma. But I love what I do." Despite repeated death threats, Dr Cynthia has worked tirelessly to set up field clinics inside Burma. Her staff also trains refugees to become health workers. "We need to fight death and treat disease, but also to empower our people and educate children so that our communities can grow strong."

Thousands of pro-democracy students in Burma fled to Thailand following a violent crackdown by the military junta in 1988. There were no medical facilities at the refugee camps. Ever larger numbers of people continue to flee to escape civil war, human rights abuses and poverty.

Burma

Valentina Merkulova

Kurorty Moskovskoy oblasti
Moscow International Business Association (Miba)
Rossiyskaya Akadiemiya Biznesa i Priedprinimatelstva (Rabp)

Valentina Merkulova is an economist and a top-notch professional in the field of resort management and rehabilitation of children. She has received a number of awards for her excellence in this domain. Since 1999 she has headed the Association of Sanatoria and Resorts "Kurorty Moskovskoy oblasti". As a reputed specialist, she conducts an active dialogue with the government and the State Duma on issues of children's health care. Since 2001 Valentina has been participating in a national program aimed at the medical and social rehabilitation of handicapped children.

Valentina Merkulova has been working for many years in sanatoria specialized in rendering medical and psychological assistance to handicapped children. Time and again she has witnessed definite improvement in gravely ill children that have been provided with medical and rehabilitation therapy. Valentina remembers a case in which a child who had not uttered a word in three years because of a major psychological trauma, started speaking again thanks to the doctors' therapy. She remembers the child's grateful eyes and the happiness of the mother.

From her professional experience as a resort manager, it had always been clear to Valentina that the lack of government support and appropriate legislation were impeding the effectiveness of the rehab system. She therefore set herself the goal of ensuring that there would be an adequate legal basis in place to protect the right of handicapped children to sanatorium treatment. She addressed various governmental and legislative bodies, and spoke to influential people vested with power. The first to respond was the government of Moscow. The personal support of the Mayor of Moscow made it possible to secure financing for the "Program of Handicapped Children's Rehabilitation." This initiative was subsequently supported by the authorities in many other regions across Russia. Her constant dialogue with State Duma committees and the Russian government finally yielded its fruits. The Federal Law on Children's Rights was adopted. Furthermore, amendments to federal legislation now guarantee the funding of sanatorium therapy for handicapped children.

Despite this success, Valentina has not abandoned the cause of children's health care. Her short-term plans are now to include orphans into the program of sanatorium treatment and provide them with an effective and financially backed program of social rehabilitation.

Valentina Merkulova's work with the authorities has contributed to improving children's health care in Russia. Within the framework of the association headed by Valentina, about 20,000 children are able to profit annually from rehabilitation therapy in modernized sanatoria throughout the country.

Russian Federation

Neema Mgana

African Regional Youth Initiative (Aryi)
International Council for Global Initiatives

Neema Mgana (29) is a young African activist who promotes social and political change. As an undergraduate student, she co-founded an Aids organization to serve children affected with HIV/Aids in Tanzania. In 2002 she founded the African Regional Youth Initiative (Aryi), an organization that mobilizes youth and community-based organizations all over Africa on social and economic issues. She is also the Co-Executive Director of the International Council for Global Initiatives.

Neema describes her parents as exemplary role models: "They would tell me when I was young that educating girls was the landmark for social and economic development." While doing her internship in a large hospital in Tanzania, Neema Mgana became aware of acute pain and sorrow. She recalls the moment that prompted her to action: "I realized that we are all responsible for alleviating such pain". She researched and decided that she could do something. In December 2002 she founded the Aryi: "Aryi works with entire communities. The majority of the people leading activities and programs within the organization are under 30 years; this is really energizing," she points out. Aryi addresses HIV/Aids in a comprehensive way: it works on issues around youth, girls and women, and on community development programs. "There was no platform, no vehicle for young people and those at the community level to work and voice our opinions and concerns in a united manner. That is the overall goal of Aryi," she explains.

In 2005, together with a colleague, Neema started to develop a second organization: the International Council for Global Initiatives. "We want to scale up successful models from the community and regional levels, like Aryi, and bring them to the global arena and support cross-regional learning and exchanges. In my opinion it is this cross-cultural collaboration that has lacked in development work."

Neema holds a diploma in health sciences, certificates in international peace studies and humanitarian assistance, a BSc degree in health informatics and a master's degree in international health.

Sub-Saharan Africa is the region worst affected by HIV/Aids, where two-thirds of the world's HIV-positive people live. Close to 60 percent of all adults living with the virus are women. Despite improvements, only one percent of those infected receive antiretroviral drugs.

United Republic of Tanzania

"I decided that one of
the most important
ways I could contribute
to healthier children
and families was to empower
women to bring children
into the world under
circumstances of their
own choosing."

Kate Michelman

Naral Pro-Choice America

In 2005, Kate Michelman announced that she was stepping down as president of Naral Pro-Choice America in order to help elect a pro-choice president of the USA. Under her leadership, Naral has become the nation's premier reproductive rights group. Kate's more than 20 years of advocacy have led to legalization of abortion and access to birth control information and devices. As she educates women about their bodies, Kate also awakens in them their right to autonomy and their right to live in a peaceful world, inspiring countless young women to join the struggle worldwide for women's rights.

Kate's empathy comes from personal understanding. In 1970, she was abandoned by her husband and left alone to care for her three young daughters. Shortly after her husband left, she discovered she was pregnant. Raised in a Catholic family, her decision to abort was a lonely one, and made at a time when abortion was illegal except when a mother's health or life were at stake. Even though the law interpreted the exception broadly, it required Kate to appear before an all-male hospital review panel to obtain permission for the abortion on the grounds that she was unstable and incapable of raising another child. The board granted her request, provided that her ex-husband also agreed. As she waited to get permission for the abortion, she carried with her the name and phone number of an illegal abortionist. Because her ex-husband gave his consent, the abortion was performed legally. "For me, the seeds of activism were planted in my own searing, humiliating experience with a pre-Roe abortion," she remembers.

In speeches, Kate is likely to ask her audience three central questions: First, "Under what circumstances do we bring children into the world, and who makes the decision?" Second, "Should children be born by choice or under the heavy hand of government compulsion?" And third, "Should women be equal, contributing partners in society, or should they be held captive to their reproductive function for the entirety of their childbearing years? In short, who decides? Women or government?"

Kate's influence has been well cited. In 1998, Vanity Fair named her one of America's 200 most influential women and a year earlier named Naral as one of the most influential special-interest groups in Washington D.C. In 1994, Fortune Magazine named Naral one of the top ten advocacy groups in America.

Today's laws reflect nearly 400 state restrictions on a woman's right to choose, imposed by governors and state legislatures. Kate works in an environment in which the current president has become the only one in the nation's history to make abortion a federal crime.

United States of America

Anica Mikus Kos

Foundation "Together," Regional Center for the
Psychosocial Well-Being of Children

Dr Mikus Kos, pediatrician and child psychologist, has provided assistance to refugee children from conflict zones in Croatia, Bosnia and Herzegovina, Macedonia, Kosovo, Ingushetia, Georgia, and Iraq. When refugees from the Balkan conflict came to Slovenia, she helped thousands of children and their parents. Since these children were not accepted in Slovenian schools, Dr Mikus Kos helped organize refugee teachers to run schools for them. Thanks to her belief in the capacities of refugees, thousands of children have finished school and received psychosocial assistance.

Born in Yugoslavia in 1935, Anica Mikus Kos, as a child, was a witness to the terrible events of World War II: bombings, killings, and violence. These experiences also provided her with a basis for optimism: in the face of the brutality of war, people responded with positive actions. She discovered the capacity of human resiliency and the ability of people to cope with traumatic experiences. Her professional activities with war-affected children are based on her experiences as a child during the war. A central tenet of Dr Mikus Kos' work is that while suffering and painful memories are unavoidable outcomes of the experience of war, surviving war should not be treated the same way as other psychological disturbances. She strongly advocates the view that, in spite of suffering and painful memories, most children will not be permanently psychologically disturbed because of their war experiences and losses. A pediatrician and child psychologist herself, she argues that statements by mental health professionals, who condemn children who have gone through war to be psychologically harmed for the rest of their lives, contribute to learned helplessness and a self-fulfilling prophecy of long-lasting psychological problems. She believes that children can be empowered to overcome their trauma and lead fulfilling lives. Dr Mikus Kos' experience as a child during war time has taught her the importance of kindness and compassion in a child's environment. The main goal of her programs is to provide children with positive experiences that will counteract the negative experiences of war by activating and empowering children's social networks. She believes that the role of teachers, volunteers, and primary health care workers that come in contact with children and their parents are central in providing children with exposure to positive human relationships.

Beginning in the early 1990s, conflicts in the Balkans and in parts of the former Soviet Union have resulted in tens of thousands of refugees, including refugee children in need of psychological care, schooling, and support to overcome their trauma.

Slovenia

Rolene Miller

Mosaic Training Services and Healing Centre

Rolene Miller, born in 1938, is a qualified social worker from the University of Cape Town, South Africa. For five years, she worked as a teacher specializing in remedial teaching. She started the Mosaic Training Services and Healing Centre in 1993, a non-profit organiztion for abused women. The focus of the organization was to extend reproductive health services, HIV/Aids awareness, legal rights and food security. Rolene is recognized for her efforts in empowering women to take control of their lives and to bring about peace in their homes and in their communities.

When Rolene Miller began working with gender-based violence in disadvantaged communities, she realized the importance of providing innovative services that were unique to the environment. She knew that she was moving into an unfamiliar territory and had lessons to learn from the community workers who had both knowledge and experience.

She started the Mosaic Training Services and Healing Centre in 1993. In 1994, she teamed up with a psychologist and developed a one-year full-time training program to train grassroots women on community and social work skills. "I had a large learning curve," she confirms. From 1999 to 2002, she trained approximately 100 women to become lay counselors. They needed skills to help victims of abuse to apply for protection orders in domestic violence sections of the magistrates' courts. She educated all her trainees in life skills, human rights and legal rights, according to the Domestic Violence Act of 1998. Many cultural issues were addressed in the training sessions. These included patriarchy within the society. The trained lay counselors had to use their experiences and newly acquired skill to first heal themselves in order to help other clients.

South African women's organisations estimate that perhaps as many as one in every three South African women has been raped and one in six South African women is in an abusive domestic relationship.

South Africa

"I believe every single life is worth living. If we can help even one out of the two million, then I think for me that will be a great achievement."

Florence Muia

Upendo Village

Sister Florence Muia, 45 years old, is the fifth of nine children. She was born and bred in Machakos District, Eastern Kenya, and has been an Assumption Sister of Nairobi (ASN) for 28 years. Sister Florence ministers mainly to women and children affected by HIV/Aids at Upendo Village in Naivasha, Kenya. As a visionary, she dreamed of a safe haven for women and children affected by the disease. Upendo, the Kiswahili word for love, is such a sanctuary. She devotes her energy, commitment and skills to the success of this ecumenical project.

Approximately 2.2 million Kenyans are living with the HIV/Aids virus. Sister Florence has chosen to work with the Kenyan community to build bridges of hope and healing for people affected by the pandemic. She is primarily concerned with the pandemic in the rural area of Naivasha. Kenya is a poor country, and rural areas are acutely affected by poverty.

Sister Florence was keenly aware that international support was necessary for an outreach program to become self-sufficient and independent. She also wanted the beneficiaries to have ownership of the program. With financial support and mentoring from the Wheaton Franciscans, she learnt the techniques necessary for working with charitable boards and non-profit organisations. This included learning how to provide required information in order to solicit assistance in addressing the struggles of the poor. She visited a number of programs in Chicago that had relevance to Upendo Village. These included a local HIV/Aids organisation, a domestic-violence shelter and a comprehensive agency that serves a variety of needs of persons who are poor. From these visits Sister Florence gained insights about policies, regulations and job descriptions that would help her in establishing her own non-profit organization. She has also become involved in national and international HIV/Aids organisations and met people from the National Catholic Aids Network, who challenged her and helped her refine her dream. She is skilled in political advocacy and has visited elected officials to promote help for the HIV/Aids pandemic.

Kenya is one of the countries most affected by HIV/Aids. Poverty, which triggers risky behavior, is widespread in rural areas. Naivasha is situated on a truckers' route, encouraging prostitution. Trends indicate that the annual number of Aids deaths has risen to about 150,000 per year.

Kenya

"I have done my part.
If I die today, I believe
I have left a legacy
that can be carried on
to greater heights."

Helen Munthali

Tovwirane HIV/Aids Organisation

Helen Munthali is the executive director of Tovwirane HIV/Aids Organisation, based in Mzimba in the northern part of Malawi. She was born in 1946 in Nazala Village near the country's commercial city of Blantyre to a Malawian mother and an Indian father. Tovwirane ("Let's help each other") was launched in 1993. Since then it has assisted thousands of people infected and affected by HIV/Aids. It offers orphan care, counseling of people living with HIV/Aids and their caretakers through outreach campaigns and community-based projects.

Helen's life reads like the script of a best-selling novel. Soon after she was born, her father left her mother. She was later rejected by her stepfather because she was colored, and raised by her grandmother.

After obtaining her Cambridge School Certificate at the age of 18, she succumbed to family pressure to get married. She raised her 11 children single-handedly after her husband's death in 1986. Then, her brother-in-law attempted to evict her from her matrimonial home and inherit the property. She had gained resilience at an early age. "I refused and worked tirelessly to bring up my children. Today they are respected personalities working in top government positions and international organizations," she says proudly.

She formed the Mzimba Anti-Aids Support in 1993. "I watched helplessly as my close friends died. I had to do something." The organization later changed its name to Tovwirane HIV/Aids Organisation.

Helen has dealt with suspicion, stigma and discrimination including from churches, as she pursued the Tovwirane mission.

To date, Tovwirane has assisted over 5000 volunteers in home-based care, 560 people living with HIV/Aids and over 7000 orphans. Through its outreach campaign, Tovwirane has initiated over 20 community projects to support the poor and established a resource center with over 10,000 books and resource material with an average readership of about 800 per month. Tovwirane is recognized as a model in sub-Saharan Africa.

Malawi is ranked as one of the poorest countries in the world. More than half its population lives below the poverty line. Aids has worsened the situation. Thousands of Malawians are dying of HIV/Aids across the country leaving behind destitute orphans, widows, widowers and the aged.

Malawi

Zulpa Musostova

Miezhdunarodnaya gumanitarnaya initsyativa (MGI)

Zulpa Musostova was born in 1944. After finishing a medical training college, Zulpa worked for 18 months in the high mountain Shatoevsky region of Chechnya. Later she studied for six years at the Donetsk Medical Institute. On graduating, she worked as a doctor in the same Shatoevsky region. She practiced in many cities of the USSR, including Moscow and Leningrad. As a highly qualified neurologist, she now works in Grozny, helping the people of Chechnya who are in desperate need of medical care. She also organizes humanitarian projects to help the victims of the Russian-Chechen war.

In the destroyed city of Grozny, there is a quiet street with old houses that have suffered from Russian air raids, a street with people of different nationalities who did not have the chance to run away from the war to other regions of Russia. These are the lonely, the elderly, and the sick. Zulpa has become their advocate. She provides them with medical attention, along with moral and material support.

Zulpa is a doctor, a top-notch professional, and an excellent diagnostician — one of the best in neuropathology. The war has changed the routine pace of life. Zulpa could have moved to some other city and worked under conditions of peace and stability, yet she has stayed here, at Polyclinic no.2. The city is deserted; there are ruins everywhere; transportation does not work; there is no electricity or water. Zulpa passes through this desolation daily on her way to work. The polyclinic is badly damaged. There is no door to her office, and instead of glass windows just a sheet of polyethylene; no cabinets for medicines, only chairs for the doctor and the patient. The war has not only harmed the physical well-being of the people, but has damaged their psychological state as well. Anxiety, fear, the horrors experienced, the death of loved ones, and the loss of belongings — all these factors explain why the number of Zulpa's patients has skyrocketed.

She does her best to help them, learning to cure diseases not common in peaceful times. She attends seminars, reads voraciously, and learns from her own experience. All this helps her to treat her patients as successfully as possible in conditions where medical equipment is desperately lacking. Thanks to Zulpa Musostova, hundreds of people have received qualified medical help both in and outside the city of Grozny.

In the aftermath of the war, thousands of people in Chechnya are in great need of psychological rehabilitation, help, and treatment. Doctor Zulpa Musostova, despite the lack of modern equipment, provides highly-qualified medical care and humanitarian aid to the people of Chechnya.

Russian Federation

Over the years, Shyamala has created space to make discussions on HIV/Aids possible, and brought about a whole slew of government policy changes.

Shyamala Natarajan

South India Aids Action Program (Siaap)

When Shyamala Natarajan (born 1963) started working on HIV/Aids and related issues 16 years ago, stigma surrounded the disease. Over the years, Shyamala has been working with sex workers and sexual minorities, such as men having sex with men and eunuchs. Her work aims at the capacity-building of community-based organizations. She has also lobbied the government and brought about many changes in policy, such as one against the detention of people testing HIV+, and against mandatory testing.

Shyamala Natarajan had to fight opposition from her family to set up the South India Aids Action Program. She is actively involved with organizing sex workers, and believes strongly in community-based (as opposed to forced governmental) rehabilitation. Over the years, she has created space to make discussions on HIV/Aids possible. Lobbying the government on this issue, she has brought about many changes in government policy. To list a few: In 1990, the government of Tamil Nadu framed a policy against detention of people testing HIV+; in 1992, the government of India also adopted this policy. In 1994, the health and family welfare department, government of India, adopted a policy to improve condom quality. In 1996, the National Aids Control Organization (Naco) adopted a policy against mandatory testing for HIV. In 1995, the Government of Tamil Nadu adopted a policy to include HIV+ persons in decision-making. Later, the Naco also accepted this principle. In 1996, the Tamil Nadu Panchayat Unions adopted a policy to support the rights of women in sex work. In 2000, the Naco adopted a policy to provide counseling services for reproductive health in government hospitals. In 2003, the Naco adopted a policy to train and place counselors drawn from communities of people marginalized on the basis of sexuality, gender, and HIV.

In the early 1990s, although India had begun waking up to the HIV/Aids threat, strong stigma surrounding the disease stymied implementation of policies. Although the stigma and discrimination remain, work by activists has helped dispel, to some degree, the misconceptions.

India

Barbara Nath Wiser

Nishtha Rural Health, Education, and Environment Center India
Aktion Regen Austria

Born in Austria, Barbara Wiser passed her medical exam in 1977 and travelled to India. There "Dr Barbara" met her husband Baba Krishan Nath. She decided to open a hospital in northern India, specialized in homeopathy and acupuncture. Soon local help was found to run the facility with her. Dr Barbara has dedicated her life and her medical experience to those in India who are not able to pay. She organizes regular health awareness workshops to ensure that people know important facts about their bodies and how to prevent diseases, helps families and tries to improve the situation of the young.

"This is the century of women." Dr Barbara Nath Wiser strongly believes that this Indian prophecy will come true. She opened up her Krishan Nath Baba Memorial Charitable Trust Health Clinic in Sidhbari in 1989. The clinic is dedicated to the memory of her late husband Krishan Nath Baba, who was a respected spiritual personality in the area. He died shortly after they returned to India with two children. Before, he had accompanied her to Austria where she took up an internship in Vienna, and he had looked after the first born. That enabled her to gain a great deal of general medical experience and to study homeopathy and acupuncture.

Dr Barbara built the temple her husband had asked her for at the place he had chosen as the perfect one. It is the center of the village now, a place where people meet. Men and women, no matter of what religious denomination. She likes to see Hindus close to Christians as she believes that all religions serve the same purpose. She would also like to see more happy young people. And she misses the voice of her singing husband, when he met with men and sang and danced with them to keep up traditions. It would make a difference today too, an alternative to alcoholism for which the young and restless fall. It is easy: no work, boredom, alcohol, drunkenness, no work.

Dr Barbara has her priorities: the health of the 5000 inhabitants is still poor, the working situation harsh, the drinking water contaminated. There is clean water at the clinic. But there is more to do. Since 1998, her Nishtha Center Project has been bringing women and some men together for seminars, awareness workshops, and disease prevention. The people of Sidhbari and those who visit from the area of Kangra Valley learn how to plan their families. To work out family crises. And they see that there indeed are perspectives in life. A woman's movement, the path to peace.

The village of Sidhbari, about ten kilometers west of Dharamsala in northern India, has a view onto the Himalaya Mountains. It also has many health problems caused by contaminated drinking water and harsh working conditions. Infectious and degenerative diseases, tuberculosis, and hepatitis are common.

Austria

Ala Nemerenco

University Clinic for Primary Health Care

Ala Nemerenco is the director of the Clinic for Primary Health Care of the State Medical and Pharmaceutical University of Moldova. In only two short years since its opening, the center has become a model for the entire country and has set a new standard for offering health services at the highest international levels, for instructing medical students and residents, and for supporting family medicine practices throughout the country.

In her current capacity as director of the Primary Health Care Clinic, Ala Nemerenco is responsible for overseeing day-to-day management of the clinic and implementation of new pilot project initiatives including instruction of medical students and medical professionals in family medicine, and the creation of community outreach initiatives. A doctor on the front lines of the war on diseases, she is closer to people's pain and suffering than anyone else. To become a doctor it takes more than simply choosing a career, it has to be a lifelong passion. Ala is one of those doctors who have followed the call of their hearts in order to practice medicine. By being next to her patients throughout the years, Ala has had the opportunity to witness the cruel effects on people's lives of a society and an economy in full transition. She has done everything she could to make a difference, and somewhere in between realized that the inherited medical system of the ex-Soviet Union required many changes and adjustments.

Ala Nemerenco's biggest impact has been the creation of the University Clinic for Primary Health Care: a true oasis in the medical system of Moldova, where today well-trained doctors are ready to win the war against pain and suffering. The doctors are aided by high-technology equipment and armed with the two most effective weapons of all: smiles and compassion. The University Clinic has developed projects for young people, pregnant women, small children, high-risk patients, and more. The clinic's director has so many plans for the future that these could last others for a lifetime. Ala has always believed that positive change is possible, and is currently pursuing that dream. There is only one problem: there is so much more that needs to be done!

The Republic of Moldova is fortunate to have been free of major armed conflicts since its independence. However, there are thousands in this country who are victims of poverty, disease, drugs, violence in society and at home, violation of basic human rights, and discrimination every day.

Republic of Moldova

Nguyen Thi Ngoc Phuong

Tu Du Obstetric Hospital
Ho Chi Minh City Association of Agent Orange Victims

Nguyen Thi Ngoc Phuong (born 1944) is director of Tu Du Obstetric Hospital, the largest obstetric hospital in Vietnam. She gained a bachelor's degree in 1970 and a post-graduate degree in obstetrics and gynaecology in 1974. Conferred the title of Medical Professor by the French President in 1994, she is on the Advisory Board on Women's Health in Asia, and the Asia Pacific Initiative on Reproductive Endocrinology (Aspire). She chairs the Vietnam-US Friendship Association in Ho Chi Minh City and is on the executive board of the HCMC Association of Agent Orange Victims.

Nguyen Thi Ngoc Phuong's marriage ended when she refused to leave her war-torn country to settle in France with her husband after the war ended in Vietnam. Instead, she stayed on, devoting her talents to her patients and to transforming the Tu Du Obstetric Hospital into the leading obstetric center in North Vietnam where modern technologies have been successfully applied in scientific researches. The success of its in-vitro fertilization program has made it the largest fertility center in Southeast Asia with a success rate as high as in developed countries. The hospital is run by women, and 70 percent of its doctors and personnel have PhDs in healthcare.

Nguyen Thi Ngoc Phuong has trained many talents, including her daughter, who has also become famous in Vietnam. She has trained over 100 ethnic midwives and provided them with financial support and vehicles for travel to remote mountainous areas, where they perform deliveries for poor people, helping them avoid health risks while giving birth. Despite her age, she brings ultrasound equipment, microscopes, medicines and noodles to mountainous areas, where she gives medical examinations to residents and carries out research on diseases and the status of the victims of the toxic chemical Agent Orange. As a physician for 30 years, she has seen many cases of birth defects, equivalent to 1.5 percent of the total number of births, resulting from Agent Orange. Whether she is in the operation room, lecturing in universities in Vietnam, France or the US, or doing research in the mountainous areas of the country, she reflects what she told her husband when she refused to go with him to France after the war: "The country is still poor, we had better stay. We did not make any contribution during the war, now we have to make some to relieve the people's suffering."

When the war ended, many Vietnamese emigrated to other countries. Nguyen Thi Ngoc Phuong's husband, a doctor, who was studying in a foreign country, returned home to take his wife with him. But seeing how her people suffered from the effects of Agent Orange used during the war, she opted to stay and help.

Viet Nam

Chris Norwood

Health People

Chris Norwood (born 1946) founded Health People, which is located in the South Bronx, New York, and is the largest peer health education and disease prevention organization in the USA. Starting in 1990 as a women's Aids prevention program, the organization now provides 3000 people a year in the sickest, poorest area of New York, with men's, family, and teen HIV programs. It also provides successful asthma, diabetes, and smoking prevention programs, all built by training low-income people affected by chronic disease to become educators and leaders.

"My heart screamed, 'Not the baby, too!' Her mother, named Marty, was a wonderful volunteer who later became staff. She had Aids — not easy to accept, but I really did not think I could stand to know the child and watch her die — which she did a few years later. Within a year, her mother died too, leaving a memory and appreciation that, more than ten years later, remains completely part of me. Marty was extraordinary. She had contracted Aids as a teenager when her own mother had put her on the street to earn money for the mother's drugs. Then the mother killed herself while Marty was in jail. Of all the impressive ways that I have seen people extend themselves, I think that Marty's is the most generous: even while facing her own and her child's deaths, Marty arranged for a special mass to be said for the repose of her mother.

During the times when I'm exhausted and frantic and depressed, I try to keep in mind all the people who have helped us fulfill our mission: the man who spent years in prison — having shot a policeman — who somehow turned himself into the most gentle and inspiring person and helped many kids look to the future. There is our senior coordinator, who started as a client, and was appointed by our governor as the only HIV+ woman on the state Aids Advisory Council. There are the diabetes peers, some of whom who could barely walk when they started their training, and are now out all over educating the community. And, of course, there are the teens, faithfully coming in to be mentors for younger kids even when some of them are virtually homeless themselves.

Again and again, our belief that the community can take positive control of its health — and that people harshly rejected by society can not only go forward, but are outstanding at helping others — is confirmed."

The South Bronx is so overwhelmed by chronic disease that it shreds the social fabric. The key issue is showing people they can develop skills to take control of their own health; then health becomes a transforming issue, a means to move from hopelessness to a focus on building.

United States of America

Christina Nsekela

Family Planning Association of Tanzania (Umati)
Tanzania Association of Non-Governmental Organisations (Tango)
Promotion of Rural Initiatives and Development Enterprises Tanzania (Pride)

Christina Nsekela is the pioneering and now retired Chief Executive Director of Umati, the family planning association of Tanzania. When she started working with communities in the 1960's, family planning was a taboo. Christina Nsekela initiated programs that have destigmatized family planning. Many agencies have adopted her initiatives, such as the teaching of family life education in schools by the Government of Tanzania. In retirement, the mother of two remains an active member of Umati and works with small and medium enterprise organizations in her rural home.

In the poor countryside of south western Tanzania, where Christina Nsekela was born in the late 1930s, many babies and small children died before reaching five years and women gave birth at home at the risk of dying during childbirth. Medical care, as well as safe and clean water, was not within easy reach. Christina Nsekela was concerned about the misery and could not forget it as she grew older. She moved to the capital, Dar es Salaam, to work as a teacher and social worker, for the Girl Guides Association of Tanzania. In 1969, she learned about the Family Planning Association of Tanzania (Fpat) and started to volunteer twice a week after her own office hours. "I appreciated the relevance of the programs in addressing some of the socioeconomic needs of our people. The experience triggered my interest and opened my eyes, so I willingly accepted the post Umati offered me," she recalls. Umati is the better-known Kiswahili acronym for Fpat, namely Chama cha Uzazi na Malezi bora Tanzania. As the first employee and CEO of Umati in September 1969, she became the pioneer of the family planning revolution in Tanzania and East Africa. Her determination, endurance and hard work have destigmatized family planning, saved thousands of lives and steered the Tanzanian government to integrate family life education in the schools' curriculum. Even after her retirement in 1994, the widow and mother of two sons remains an active member of Umati and works with small and medium enterprise organizations in her rural home.

Until gaining independence in 1961, Tanzania was known as Tanganyika. In the 1950s and 1960s, the British colonial power introduced family planning. Suspicion was high about the alien concept and its promoters. The society was strongly opposed to family planning.

United Republic of Tanzania

"We have a lot of work ahead of us. For many generations."

Fátima Oliveira

Rede Nacional Feminista de Saúde e Direitos Reprodutivos (National Feminist Network for Health and Sexual and Reproductive Rights)

Fátima Oliveira (1953) runs Brazil's largest feminist health network, the National Feminist Network for Health and Sexual and Reproductive Rights. Besides practicing medicine, she has published books and articles regarding bioethics, Afro-Brazilian women's health, transgenic (GMOs) and feminism. She is able to articulate scientific knowledge with political pragmatism.

She has five children and two grandchildren. She works as a doctor in a public hospital. She runs a feminist network of 200 organizations. She has a weekly column in an important newspaper. She sends e-mails non-stop and always keeps her cellular phone on. Fátima Oliveira was born in a very poor city in the Northeast of Brazil, where infantile mortality occurs daily. "It shocked me to see so many little angels being buried, to see those little blue coffins. So, I decided to become a doctor." She faced a tough path to get from rural school to medicine school. Her social work started when she joined the Catholic Working-Class Youth. She used to help prostitutes get medicine, clothes and school for their children. "I consider myself a feminist doctor and an anti-racist."

Brazil has the largest black population outside of Africa; half of Brazilian women are black. Research shows that they have a higher incidence of diseases such as sickle cell anemia, uterine fibroids, hypertension, and diabetes, and that these diseases develop differently during black women's pregnancies. "We also have much less access to prenatal care and contraception than white women do."

Fátima Oliveira tries to popularize the concepts of bioethics and biosecurity, which mean nothing more than a complete respect for life. Her goal is to de-mystify the doctors' power and to build a more democratic science in which citizens can take part in the decision making. Fátima Oliveira defends women's rights 24 hours a day. She is currently focused on disqualifying abortion as a crime and guaranteeing quality health services for all Brazilians. "We live in an age where many rights are written down on paper. The difficulty is the access to them. There is still much left to do, for the Afro-Brazilian and poor women, to attain their rights."

In Brazil, abortion is also a matter of public health. Women, who are financially capable, have abortions in a safe manner. But most women have abortions in a very dangerous manner. Due to insecure abortions, the number of deaths of women is very high.

Brazil

Chantal Marie Rachelle Ouédraogo

Association Femmes 2000 (AF 2000)

Chantal Marie Rachelle Ouédraogo (35) is married and the mother of two girls. She is head of the Association Femmes 2000 (Women's Association 2000) fighting HIV/Aids and tuberculosis and taking care of persons living with HIV. She was decorated by the Burkina Faso government for service to the nation on 11 December 2003. She was given the Knight of the Order for Merit medal.

Chantal Marie Rachelle Ouédraogo studied to receive her secondary school level I certificate before settling into professional life with the intention of being of service to those around her. A mother of two, she is well-known for her courage and willingness to help rural women of her country to get involved in development activities, to promote their rights. She is the founder and president of an association of women called Association Femmes 2000. Its objective is to empower women by strengthening local goods such as peanut butter, soumbala (spice), or homemade soap. The association also aims at sensibilizing against desertification. Chantal serves as commercial agent in a service specializing in the mobilization of public savings to meet the social and economical needs of its members.

From 1990 to 1992, she worked as social and cultural field officer for a non-governmental organization in Burkina Faso in the area of community health. From 1992 to 1994, she was director of a business on Performance and Various Services (EPSD). From 1994 to 1996, she founded and chaired the association of rural and semi-urban women of Burkina. From 1996 to 2003, she found herself at the head of a health insurance company in Burkina.

Chantal Marie Rachelle Ouédraogo is a very religious woman characterized by a Christian faith that imposes on her the duty to serve others in the hope of contributing to the progress of humanity.

In Burkina Faso, development is closely related to the fight against desertification. More than half of the national territory is already affected in a significant way by this disaster which is progressing.

Burkina Faso

"The first day, when I was going to office, people from the whole locality came around to watch me go to office in my wheelchair, it was very awkward and I felt terrible."

Mohua Paul

Center for the Rehabilitation of the Paralyzed (CRP)

Mohua Paul (born 1961) was only 12 years old when she was afflicted with lower limb paralysis. A chance visit to the Center for the Rehabilitation of the Paralyzed (CRP) gave her life a new direction. Among Mohua's many contributions to the growth of the CRP is the Women's Center, which provides shelter to women with disabilities who have no home; it also has a program that trains mothers to provide basic treatment to their children with disabilities.

At age 12, Mohua Paul was afflicted by transverse myelitis, which left her with lower-limb paralysis. It also left her educationally stranded because the school was unwilling to handle the extra responsibility of a child with disabilities: she only went in to take her exams. Then, in 1976, during a trip to Dhaka for follow-up treatment, she went to the CRP. Mohua decided to continue her studies at Dhaka, completing her secondary school examination in 1988. She had, meanwhile, begun working at the CRP, starting out in 1982 as a receptionist-cum-secretary and rising to take over as assistant director in 2002. Mohua has long believed that persons with disabilities who work alone face odds that seem insurmountable: however, with an organization and a team of people to back them, life becomes less daunting. "CRP and I were growing together, learning a lot together," she says.

An efficient program implementer and excellent manager, Mohua has built a skilled team in the CRP. The CRP's Women's Center — a place for women with disabilities who have nowhere to go — is her brainchild, rising out of her observation that if the mother of a child with disability is trained to provide basic treatment and comfort to her child, it helps them both cope better. The CRP has inspired other organizations — of which there is a network of 150 in Bangladesh today — to work on issues relating to the rights of persons with disabilities, with Mohua driving the "gender quotient" in these discussions. Mohua's personal philosophy: if one really wants to do something, one can overcome all obstacles to turn that dream into reality.

The disputable government estimate of persons with disabilities is 0.47 percent of the population. Rights for the disabled-civil rights, access to information, education, employment, easy entry to buildings and public transport, and access to election booths-are lacking.

Bangladesh

Paw Lu Lu

Baan Plod-Phai

Paw Lu Lu was born in 1948 in Tongu, Burma. Although she only finished primary school, a friend trained her as a nurse when she went to live in Karen state. She fled to the Thai border when the repression in Burma worsened and has since been taking care of patients in the Sangklaburi district of Kanchanaburi province. She runs the Baan Plod-Phai (Safe-House) founded by the National Women's Council and supported by The Church of Christ and NGOs that work on the Thai-Myanmar border.

Even as a child, Paw Lu Lu wanted to be a nurse, but her family was very poor and Burma was in turmoil. Her family escaped from the violence into Karen state, where she was trained by a friend to be a nurse. After three years, when the Karen minority was brutally repressed by the government, she moved to Thailand, settling in a refugee center in Mae-Sot District, Tak Province. But when the junta burned down all ethnic minority group's houses in Thailand and Burma, she moved to Sangklaburi, walking through the jungle to escape.

Paw opened a grocery store that also sold medicines, and with her knowledge of nursing, she took care of the patients in the village. When the National Women's Council opened Baan Plod-Phai in Sangklaburi, they hired Paw Lu Lu to run it. She took in freed prisoners, the mentally ill, HIV/Aids patients, the elderly, homeless and unwanted and migrants. In the beginning, Paw took care of the patients herself, but eventually, her staff grew. Some villagers help her train well patients in livelihood skills. For patients who have gotten well but do not want to go home, she has jobs like weaving, seeding and farming, making the Baan Plod-Phai look more like a family home than a hospital. Paw runs three schools next to the border for the children of refugees. She says, "I would like to terminate the state of war everywhere and build harmony and dignity for all of us. War has created many problems. It brings immorality and poverty. The war must end and everybody should live in dignity."

Repression by the military junta brought thousands of Burmese refugees to the Thai border. Housed in makeshift centers, but unrecognized as refugees by the Thai government, the expatriates live in poverty with no access to the right to food, shelter, health care and education.

Burma

Murari Prameela

Mercy Integrated Rural Health Care Ministries

A nurse and multipurpose healthworker who leads a team of seven in her native Guntur district in Andhra Pradesh, Murari Prameela is a friend and a carer for the sick and the dying. She targets sick people abandoned by their families. On average, she helps about 300 patients a month, among them Aids/HIV sufferers, and patients with leprosy, tuberculosis, high blood pressure, and heart trouble. Murari and her team also help polio-stricken children, street-children, sick beggars, and impoverished pregnant women who have little support and no access to healthcare.

A lesson on Mother Teresa in her 8th-grade reader inspired Murari Prameela to follow in her footsteps. There was much to be done, since most people in Andhra Pradesh were extremely poor, and 70 percent of the population lived in villages, working mostly as agricultural laborers with scant access to medicare. Aids was a major problem, with Guntur the worst-affected district in Andhra Pradesh, itself one of the worst-affected Indian states.

Murari, now a nurse, works in an organization called Mercy Integrated Rural Health Care Ministries. Her husband is its director; she heads a team of seven caregivers. Murari's concerns are victims of HIV/Aids and others forsaken by their families and friends. As a multipurpose healthworker, she stands out for the level of her commitment, visiting ailing street-people repeatedly, undeterred by signs of civic and personal neglect. By helping HIV/Aids sufferers living on the streets to get medical care, she has enabled them to live in relative comfort for years. As a result of her efforts, the police, business families, and others in society have been sensitized to the situation of the poor and the abandoned dying.

Murari, a devout Christian, has been married since 1993 and has two children. Since her husband shares her vision, they work constructively together.

According to disputed government records, HIV/Aids victims form 3.5 percent of the population of Guntur in Andhra Pradesh, but a survey by social organizations suggests 14.5 percent. The many tribals in the area are extremely poor, illiterate, and prone to ill health and disease.

India

"My son is my university. I have learnt a lot from my son. I had to innovate many things for my child. I want to replicate those things, mainly some treatment devices, among the village people."

Masuda Banu Ratna

Sustainable Centre for the Disabled (SCD)

Masuda Banu Ratna has been able to channel her personal anguish toward building a better society where disabled persons such as her son can claim their due as productive, stigma-free members of society. To this end, she established the Sustainable Centre for the Disabled, which trains local people in providing physiotherapy to the disabled, enabling economically deprived children to access treatment. The SCD also has a school and orphanage for girls with disabilities, perhaps society's most vulnerable section.

Masuda Banu Ratna was born in 1954 in Kaltabazar, Dhaka. She comes from a liberal, well-off family, and early years were comfortable. Masuda married at 19, and has two sons. The birth of her second child, who has cerebral palsy and autism, was the turning point in her life: her in-laws, her relatives, and people in her social circles found it offensive that she had borne a disabled child. The arduousness that she faced made clear to her that the disabled are among the most disempowered of people. Bringing up her son, she understood the problems, the sentiments, and the potential of disabled children. Braving social opposition and economic hardship, Masuda set up the Sustainable Centre for the Disabled. Through unremitting advocacy and awareness-building, she has been able to make others see that the disabled should not be treated as a societal burden. She speaks consistently about the need to help disabled people improve their social skills. Masuda has also established a school and an orphanage for girls with disabilities. Female children from poor or landless families are unbelievably vulnerable. Masuda believes that to minimize vulnerability, education and a safe home are indispensable. The SCD has also set up an alternative healthcare and physiotherapy center, training village people, mostly poor mothers, in the use of child therapy.

"My son is my university," says Masuda. "I had to innovate many things for my child. I want to replicate those things, mainly some treatment devices, among the village people who have no opportunity to see costly doctors for their disabled children." It is Masuda's ability to channel her personal anguish toward building a better society that is an inspiration.

When Masuda Banu Ratna's son was born, disability rights were unheard of. There was social stigma attached to being disabled, even to bearing a disabled child. Treatment options were limited to the fabulously rich. Masuda changed all that-permanently.

Bangladesh

Katrin Rohde

Managré Nooma (What is good is never in vain)

Born 1948 in Hamburg, Germany, Katrin Rohde is recognized in the "country of the upright men" (Burkina Faso) for the foundation of an orphanage for boys in 1996, for girls in 1998, for a home for streetboys and for the foundation of an infirmary for people in need in 1997, for establishing a home for young HIV-infected mothers in 2002, and for producing short-films on the subject of unwed teenage mothers and trafficking of children.

Katrin Rohde did her primary studies and an apprenticeship as a librarian in Hamburg. In 1972, she started a bookstore, in 1982, a second one. Between 1988 and 1999, she constructed three public schools in Burkina Faso. In 1994, she decided to settle in Ouagadougou, the capital of Burkina Faso, to put into action what she had learned: What is good is never in vain!

She sold her bookshop, car, and motorcycles — everything she had — and went off, all alone, to live with eight streetboys in Ouagadougou. After one year, she built her first orphanage and took in 50 boys, then 50 girls. Katrin Rohde, who has a passion to work for others, created a public infirmary that cares for about 150 patients a day, giving medicine away for free to beggars and widows with many children, paying for operations and amputations. She distributes wheelchairs — that are made in the streetboys' welding shop — to the handicapped. She houses 35 streetboys and 20 teenage mothers with their 13 babies, most of them with HIV. All "her" children go to school; again, she pays the school fees for about 500 children out of her projects.

In addition to this, she makes educational films on family planning, combatting HIV/Aids, dealing with abandoned children, and the phenomenon of street children. These films are shown on national TV. Last year, Katrin Rohde also began to organize a mobile cinema that educates and creates awareness on behaviour in the face of HIV/Aids and ways of using contraceptives. This cinemobile visits villages "way out in the bush." Right now, she is opening a new school for farming and agriculture for 100 boys, a social project that keeps young men from living on the streets. Katrin Rohde has also written a book in German and Dutch on her experiences. All her projects are funded by personal donations and private funding. Katrin Rohde never loses confidence in her children.

Burkina Faso is a source, transit, and destination country for child trafficking. Boys are trafficked for exploitation as agricultural laborers, domestics, metalworkers, wood workers, and miners. Girls are trafficked for exploitation as domestic servants, beggars, and prostitutes.

Burkina Faso

"I started my career with a dream — that I will work for the people and bring about a change in society. I still believe that change is possible. I work hard for that change."

Sandhya Roy

Gonoshasthya Kendra

Sandhya Roy (born 1954) was only 17 when she left home to help soldiers wounded in the 1971 Bangladesh war. The end of the war found Sandhya far too immersed in her work to return home. Instead, she joined Gonoshasthya Kendra (which means people's health center — GK), an NGO working to establish a people-centered health system. For more than 30 years now, she has been challenging gender stereotypes, fighting fundamentalists who wish to keep her down, and working toward her dream of a holistic health system.

Sandhya Roy was a young women when the 1971 Bangladesh war for liberation from Pakistan began. In response to a call from some doctors, she left home and school at age 17 to join rescue and treatment operations. The end of the war left Sandhya with the realization that she was way too deep in her work to return home or complete her studies. In 1972, a group of doctors set up GK. Impressed by GK's vision of a people-centered health system, Sandhya decided to pitch in. It was implicit to the GK team that trained paramedics were needed to get healthcare to the people. Sandhya was part of the first batch to receive paramedical training. Her work with GK has been pathbreaking in several ways: she came up with the idea that women should train to be drivers and operate broilers-both jobs that would challenge prevalent gender stereotypes. Her work is also driven by her conviction that the impoverished and the disempowered can be agents of change, and not merely passive recipients of aid.

While the decision on what kind of work she wished to do came easily to Sandhya, living the life she chose did not. In addition to almost mandatory threats and violence, Sandhya has also had to brave people's prejudices against a single woman in a nontraditional profession. She says, "After independence, I started my career with a dream — that I will work for the people and bring about a change in society. I still believe that change is possible. I work hard for that change."

When Sandhya began her work, Bangladesh was in political pandemonium. Years of colonial rule, followed by Pakistan's neglect, had left it with little infra-structure, low human development indices, and poor healthcare. There was also little notion of gender rights.

Bangladesh

Lakshmi Sahgal

All India Democratic Women's Association (Aidwa)

Lakshmi Sahgal (born 1914), better known as "captain" Lakshmi — she was, in fact, a colonel in Subhas Chandra Bose's Indian National Army — offers a legendary personal history. As a medical practitioner, Lakshmi has always used her skills to serve the poorest of the poor. As an activist, she was involved in the creation of one of India's largest women's groups, the All Indian Democratic Women's Association. As a political activist, she stood up to the erstwhile right-wing government's presidential candidate even when all the odds were pitted against her.

Lakshmi Sahgal met Subhas Chandra Bose in Singapore, where he invited her to lead the women's regiment of the Indian National Army in 1942. A doughty fighter, Lakshmi was captured in 1946, by which time she had attained near-mythical status in the popular imagination. After her release, she married a colonel and Indian National Army colleague. Lakshmi worked alongside refugees for many years. She also established a wide network among the poorer settlements in Kanpur, where her service and compassion for the disempowered is the stuff of legends.

In 1981, her commitment to social change and the women's movement was channeled through her involvement with the All Indian Democratic Women's Association. Her activism notwithstanding, Lakshmi has never neglected her medical practice. The people of Kanpur also remember her staunch defense of Sikh families during the 1984 anti-Sikh pogrom that followed former prime minister Indira Gandhi's assassination by her own Sikh bodyguards. Lakshmi was out on the streets, barricading her clinic against any violence.

Lakshmi's efforts to fight caste-based discrimination and to counter communal and divisive agendas, especially in the wake of the state-sponsored genocide in Gujarat in 2002, were remarkable. It was in this context that she agreed to her nomination as a presidential candidate the same year. The left, in the aftermath of the Gujarat riots, felt the need to register a strong protest against the ruling right-wing National Democratic Alliance and decided to oppose the government's presidential candidate, A.P.J. Abdul Kalam, known as the "father of the Indian nuclear bomb". Lakshmi did not win; no one had expected her to. But the point was made, in neon-not everyone in India was willing to stand by and watch the communal forces work their will in the country.

India's post-Independence milieu was enslaved to residual imperialism and feudal principalities-enough fodder for the revolutionaries brought up on the ideology of unshackling the country from colonialism. This was the beginning of developmental activism.

Zari Sarfaraz challenged the regime of military dictator Zia-ul-Haq in the mid-1980s by preparing a report on the status of Pakistani women that was fearless, progressive, and independent.

Zari Sarfaraz

Pakistan Tuberculosis Association (PTA)

Zari Sarfaraz (born 1923) has been in public service ever since her country was born in 1947. Starting out by working for the relief and rehabilitation of refugees who had poured into the new nation from undivided India, Sarfaraz went on to become a politician and parliamentarian with the Muslim League party, and to work for tuberculosis patients in her native North Western Frontier Province. This multifaceted woman also runs industries such as sugar mills and ceramic factories in the region.

Zari Sarfaraz is remembered for her report on Pakistani women during Zia-ul-Haq's regime. Appointed chairperson of a commission on the status of women (1983 to 1985), Zari prepared a report that was fearless, independent, and progressive. The regime so hated her comments that the report remained classified until 1989, a year after Zia's assassination.

Belonging to the Pakhtoon tribe, and growing up in the extremely conservative North Western Frontier Province (NWFP), Zari's actions marked her out as a determined woman. Only in her mid-20s when undivided India was partitioned, she worked day and night to provide emergency relief and rehabilitation to refugees pouring into the newly created Pakistan. Already associated with the Muslim League, the party that spearheaded the creation of Pakistan, she embarked on a career as an active politician. In 1952, she won a seat in the NWFP provincial assembly, one of the rare women to do so. At the end of her four-year term, Zari was elected a member of the national assembly for another four-year term. In the 1960s, working with NGOs in NWFP, she became involved in the care and rehabilitation of tuberculosis patients. For 14 years, she served as the chairperson of the Pakistan Tuberculosis Association, and headed the NWFP Tuberculosis Association. This multifaceted woman's involvements include the care of orphans through the SOS Children's Villages, wildlife conservation, the care of the mentally handicapped, and running a charity hospital in her district. Zari is a life member of the Pakistan Red Crescent Society, NWFP. She is involved with the family planning association, and has served on the governing bodies of universities.

An octogenarian today, Zari is chairperson of the Premier Sugar Mills and Distillery Co in Mardan, her place of birth, where she is based.

Public health and politics remain two of Pakistan's greatest concerns — tuberculosis is widespread, and it will take political will to tackle what seems to be only a medical issue, but is, instead, a humanitarian one.

Annie Sasco

International Agency for Research on Cancer (IARC)

Dr Annie Sasco (born 1951) is a French medical doctor and renowned epidemiologist. Public Health was a vocation she chose in childhood. After medical school and public health training (two Masters degrees and a Doctorate in public health and epidemiology from Harvard), Annie pursued her research on tobacco and several cancers, which has been crucial in establishing links between smoking and breast cancer. Although her work has earned her enemies in the tobacco industry and criticism on diverse fronts, she perseveres.

Annie Sasco grew up in a traditional Basque family where she began her struggle demonstrating that women may be "at least as good as men though they do not receive equal recognition in many parts of the world, including France." At the age of four, she knew she wanted to be a doctor. By the time she was twelve, her sights were set: she would work with the World Health Organization. Annie's aim was to help the greatest number of people possible, all over the world, which she has indeed achieved, though at considerable personal costs. "(Not going into clinical practice) was a difficult choice as I missed out on rewards coming from satisfied patients. I still do. Statistics do not have that warm feeling."

She is a co-founder of a Fair Trade café in France, and remains active in the school community, having recently supervised an extensive research program on adolescents and smoking. She strongly identifies with women's issues, especially as her research, centered on breast cancer, requires sensitivity to women's concerns. The facts motivating Annie are straightforward: ten million new cancer cases each year. Annie's tactic is to make information clear, and bring science home to government organizations and a wide public. She has no fear of transgressing borders, those between science and clinical work, or between the general population and information. As she puts it, she is a kind of translator. But she treads that fine line with difficulty: fellow scientists criticize her for being too close to activists, while activists rebuke her for being too traditional and not close enough to their projects!

Information, or conveying knowledge about epidemiology is the means of translating science into prevention. There is a clear need for Annie's work in both China and on the African continent, where cigarette sales are on the increase.

There are ten million new cancer cases annually, with 4.7 million women and 5.3 million men diagnosed each year. One million new breast cancer cases are diagnosed annually worldwide, with an estimated 370,000 deaths. Breast cancer has now surpassed cervical cancer in the developing world.

France

Parmaben Sava

Pachcham Mahila Vikas Sangathan (PMVS)

Parmaben Sava is a traditional birth attendant who became a leader within her community by educating women on reproductive health issues and rights. A Dalit by birth, she has concentrated her energies in the Kutch area, changing the lives of the women with whom she has interacted, and the generations she has helped bring into the world. At last count, 2496 women had adopted Parmaben as a role model and, over 1000 deliveries later, she is still going strong.

Having given birth to four daughters, Parmaben obviously knew the difficulties a pregnant woman faces and the pathetic situation when giving birth in the region in which she lived. There were birth attendants in the villages, but the services were insufficient, and that motivated her to help other women in giving birth. She learnt from experience and training programs, and these set her on the path to revolutionizing women's health during pregnancy and childbirth.

The 57-year-old mainly lives and works in the villages of Banni Pachcham in Bhuj; her greatest success lies in introducing conventional and innovative approaches in the area of women's health in relation to childbirth. At the last count, 2496 women had adopted Parmaben as a role model, inspired by her ability, zeal, and courage.

Parmaben did not restrict herself to the region to which she belonged. In fact, she has traveled up to 250 miles from Bhuj to work, because that is how far word about her has spread. Receiving requests for help from far-off places is not new to her, and she has, more often than not, attended all calls. Over 1000 deliveries later, Parmaben is still bustling away.

Six decades after Independence, Dalits in India continue to suffer from caste stigma. Confronting denial of rights and caste-based attacks, it is not easy for a Dalit woman to work on reproductive health issues — upper-caste people are unwilling to accept the leadership of someone from a lower caste.

India

Karla Schefter

Chak-e-Wardak-Hospital
Committee for the Promotion of Medical and
Humanitarian Aid to Afghanistan

"Over every mountain there is a path." Is there a better way to describe Karla Schefter's humanitarian work in Afghanistan than to quote this Afghan proverb? She faced countless "mountains," and still managed to find a path over every one. With her unusual courage, enormous stamina, and seemingly inexhaustible perseverance as well as great personal sacrifice, she created her lifework, the Chak-e-Wardak-Hospital in Afghanistan. For the past 15 years, she has managed this hospital, which has provided thousands of people, especially women and children, with desperately needed medical care.

The story begins with Karla Schefter working in Afghanistan as a surgical nurse in a team from Germany some 20 years ago. The misery she saw left her no peace. After returning to Germany, she devised a plan to open a hospital in the country's rural area. With untiring persistence, she collected donations for the project, personally took the money to Afghanistan, and began to build a medical unit in the western Wardak province. From these modest beginnings and after many setbacks, a hospital emerged that cares for some 4200 patients every month, 70 percent of them women and children. Often accompanied by their relatives, people come from far away to seek medical care, and all are given accommodation. In return, the relatives are asked to offer some form of help, whether working in the kitchen or the gardens or assisting in keeping the facilities clean.

The hospital's doctors and nurses deliver babies, treat internal diseases, perform surgery, organize vaccine campaigns, and provide dental and optical services. Teams of physicians travel to Wardak to offer temporary help by conducting examinations or performing surgery. Another focus of the work is training local personnel, especially women, as nurses, traditional birth attendants, and physiotherapists. Upon completion of their education, these people either stay in the hospital or work with other organizations, such as the World Health Organization.

Karla Schefter's commitment to helping the needy in Afghanistan's mountainous areas is recognized and respected in Afghanistan and worldwide, and she has received several honors for this work. No setback — whether it be fighting in the vicinity of her hospital, difficulties with supplies, illness, or personal persecution — could halt this admirable woman from pursuing her goal to secure humane medical care in a remote region of this country still rife with suffering.

Troubled by war and civil unrest for many years, Afghanistan is characterized by extreme poverty and lack of basic necessities and health care, especially in its rugged mountainous areas.

Germany

Karla-Maria Schälike

Children's Center Nadjeschda

When the Children's Center "Nadjeschda" (hope) began to work with abandoned children in 1989, hardly anyone in Kyrgyzstan knew what future these children would face. In the village where the children were to be cared for, feelings of fear, hate, and aggression arose. It was difficult to find people to help. However, it eventually became possible to improve the health of these children and help them become part of society. The Kyrgyz public was made aware that these children are human beings who can be helped. A journalist dubbed the Children's Center Nadjeschda "Island of Brotherly Love."

The founder of the Children's Center Nadjeschda, Karla Maria Schälike explains how it came to be: "When our son Gert-Michael died, I was overwhelmed by inner pain and despair. I cannot find the words to describe it. Then, I remembered a little disabled boy, who was born next to Gert-Michael. The doctors wanted to force the mother to sign a document to give up her child. Even worse is that many mothers give these newborn, disabled children into the hands of the state of their own accord.

After I had found out where these rejected, disabled children were brought, it all went very quickly. At first, my husband and I began adopting babies who had been given away because they were ill. I was able to nurse them myself for a number of years. In our apartment, I began to take care of little groups of neglected or homeless children. I realized the deep pain and sense of loss these little beings were experiencing and applied repeatedly to the appropriate ministry for permission to open a children's center. However, since I might "infect" the children because of my capitalistic background, my request was always refused. After Perestroika the previously capitalistic and dangerous Karla-Maria in the eyes of the Soviet authorities suddenly became a normal member of the Soviet Children's Protection League. And finally, I was able to turn my hope into reality: I opened a center for children who were outcasts, who had no place in the hearts of people, no place in their families or schools. As I had so much hope for opening the hearts of people to these children, I named the Center "Nadjeschda" in Russian and "Ümüt" in Kyrgyz (hope). Today, this ray of hope shines over the snow-topped mountains of Kyrgyzstan and reflects back to us out of the hearts of many good people, even in far-off Europe. For this we are eternally grateful."

Since 1989, the Children's Center Nadjeschda has been working with abandoned children. After years of patient work, the Kyrgyz public is becoming aware that these children are human beings and can be helped. Many of these children have been able to find their way into society and to better health.

Germany

Yashoda Sharma

Social Uplift Through Rural Action (Sutra)

Yashoda Sharma (born 1950) is a trailblazer. By stepping out of her conservative Brahmin home to take up a range of social causes, from installing smokeless stoves in village kitchens to campaigning against alcoholism and domestic violence, she has transformed her own life and is helping change others'. A woman who never went to school, and weathered considerable unhappiness in her personal life, has become a role model for other women in a traditional rural community in Himachal Pradesh.

A young girl in Himachal Pradesh is abducted. Her father goes to the police to lodge a report. The police illegally charge him 500 rupies. When a social worker hears about this, she mobilizes local women's groups and launches an agitation against the police. The women block the national highway, and demand that the erring officials be suspended. The police are forced to return the money; the station house officer is suspended. The girl is tracked down in another district.

The social worker in question, Yashoda Sharma, is a farmer's unschooled daughter and daily wage-earner's wife. Yet, she has led one struggle after another in her traditional rural community. Yashoda has helped women combat domestic violence, demanded justice for rape victims, advised women on legal issues in open courts organized by the district administration, and forced liquor shops to close their shutters.

Sharma has not only changed the lives of other women, but her own as well. Trapped for years in an unhappy marriage, she has won over her husband and built a secure home and life for her children. The turning point came when, living away from her husband with her parents, she trained as a smokeless chullah (stove) mason. Becoming an expert in her job, the smokeless chullah experience led to a full-time job in 1987 as a fieldworker with Sutra (Social Uplift Through Rural Action), the voluntary agency that had facilitated the training. Yashoda revitalized women's groups set up by district officials, began working on the legal rights of women, and persuaded Sutra to start a legal aid program.

Yashoda was nominated to attend the International Conference on Women in Beijing, where she spoke on the status of women in India's hill areas. It has been an amazing journey for a woman whose life could so easily have become another litany of frustration and misery.

Himachal Pradesh has made rapid progress in gender equality, compared to many other states. However, it does not have a coherent policy for women, and women have not secured deserved rewards. Many districts with high gender equality indicators also have a worrying juvenile sex ratio status.

India

Orsoo Shijee

World Vision Mongolia

Born in 1956, Orsoo Shijee is a well-known expert in pediatrics and pre-school education, who has worked for many years in children's clinics and research institutions. In 1997 she joined World Vision Mongolia as coordinator and team leader. She is a key figure in the implementation of programs covering some 15,000 people to support the livelihood of the urban population in the poorest area of Ulaanbataar. She is also author of two widely acknowledged books.

Every year Mongolian Radio makes regular broadcasts of Orsoo's Chart for Child Growth Monitoring and Development, which is used by parents all over the country. As a World Vision activist, Orsoo's policy is concentrated, first of all, on the fate of children in the poor urban areas. She pays particular attention to the promotion of talented children in low-income families and organizes training courses to prepare children of pre-school age for different national competitions. Many of them have won prizes and medals. The children's team representing Bayan-khoshuu won first place at the World Vision Mongolia Stars art festival three years in a row. The Bayan-khoshuu area is the poorest in the Mongolian capital and lies at a distance of 15 kilometers from the city center. Currently she is involved in raising funds for building a local child and youth playground stadium.

In 1997 Orsoo left her research position in the Maternity and Childhood Research Institute and applied to volunteer for World Vision Mongolia. She was offered work with the Early Childhood Care and Development project. Orsoo studied for some time in New Zealand to be certified as a professional early-childhood educator. Soon, she organized a childhood care center in the Tolgoit-gher dwelling zone (felt tents) and issued several handbooks on the topic. In her work to improve the health of children, Orsoo organizes short-term training courses called "Integrated management of childhood illness" for doctors and other medical professionals. In 2004 alone 4320 people attended. Orsoo's activities also focus on the education of disadvantaged and retarded children.

Mongolia's transition to a market economy has resulted in considerable social differentiation and has had many other negative effects. Children in low-income families are extremely vulnerable. However, NGOs are working hard to improve the situation using community resources and international assistance.

Mongolia

Kishwar Ahmed Shirali

Human Effort for Love and Peace Foundation (Help-Foundation)
Atma Swastha Kendra (ASK)

Kishwar Ahmed Shirali (born 1937) was set on the road to becoming an activist as she grew up: she moved toward the mental health of women when teaching at universities in the USA and, later, in India. Along with her involvement in several organizations, Kishwar has done most of her work in the villages of Himachal Pradesh and Kashmir, where she lives among disturbed and distressed women and children, raising their self-esteem through literacy and a host of unique programs.

Kishwar Ahmed Shirali was born into a middle-class, traditional Muslim family. While growing up, the communal riots she witnessed, and the feeling of in-security about her Muslim background, led her to suppress her Muslim identity and move toward a secular one — she married a Hindu Brahmin, with whom she had two sons and a daughter before their separation.

Kishwar became a feminist psychotherapist and activist. After completing her doctorate in 1980, she taught in universities in India and the USA. During these years, she also wrote extensively on women's mental health, and spoke on these issues at various conferences. She decided to move to a village near Shimla in Himachal Pradesh soon afterward, to live with disturbed and distressed women and children. She set up the NGO Atma Swastha Kendra (ASK) in 1984. What was unique was that until 1993, she would live with, and provide therapy to a single woman and her child at a time. From this work followed outreach programs in local villages, raising women's self-esteem through literacy programs, combined with efforts to break down caste differences. Kishwar's work in Kashmir and Himachal Pradesh followed this singular track. She has since been involved with the Voluntary Health Association of India, Human Effort for Love and Peace in Srinagar, and Nishtha, the organization she set up in Himachal Pradesh which works on women's concerns in the area.

Kishwar has also promoted a unique approach to psychotherapy in India, involving not just a feminist questioning of patriarchal constructs, but also using Buddhism, Sufism, and other local traditions as a resource for Indian psychotherapy and approaches to mental health. She has spent her life caring for women and children who are victims of neglect, stress, violence, and oppression, attempting to improve their well-being through studied therapeutic compassion.

In the Himalayan foothills of Jammu and Kashmir and Himachal Pradesh, women's mental health is totally neglected. Socialization means that women are unable to discuss their psychological problems, which are a result of their social and familial roles.

India

Sinuan

Rural Development Project

Sinuan does not know exactly when she was born. In 2005, she estimates that she is around 40 years old. Born in Huay Ung, on the Burmese border, her parents moved to Laos when she was young. Her family moved often to find good land to till, so Sinuan had no chance to go to school. Sinuan works as a field officer for the Rural Development Project which operates in the mountainous northern area of Laos, responding to the needs of the tribal communities who live there. The project is supported by the German International Technical Development Agency.

Sinuan is her Laotian name; Sinuan's indigenous name in Akha is Eusue. She was an ordinary tribal woman of Akha who earned her living through farming and abided by traditional beliefs until 1994, when an epidemic broke out in her village. "In three months, 48 people passed away and many others got so sick that they could no longer work and they had nothing to eat. I heard about the Rural Development Project which was operating in Muang Singha, so I proposed to the City Council that we seek help from them," Sinuan recalls. Impressed by her enthusiasm, the project staff persuaded her to join them. She agreed after some hesitation and against the wishes of her husband.

Her first assignment was to interpret into Akhan for the project staff, a skill she acquired while she learned to speak and write in Lao. Besides language, she has picked up many skills in the course of her work. She does participatory research, provides information on primary health care for the villagers, gives health tips and even helps with child delivery. Of 52 villages covered by the project, Sinuan is in charge of 12, mostly Akhan indigenous people living in mountainous areas where there are no public utilities and no schools, and health facilities provide only basic health care. Sinuan walks from her makeshift office to adjacent villages where she tends to the needs of nearly 3000 people who live in abject poverty. Working with people from outside her tribe has made her reflect on her own traditions, many of which impede progress and make the Akha lag behind other tribes. Sinuan also feels strongly about male-domination in her culture.

The population of Laos is composed of many tribes. The Akha dwell mostly in the highlands. It is believed that in the northern mountain range of Laos, the Akha are the poorest and least developed of the tribes, since many of their traditional beliefs go against changing their way of life.

Lao People's Democratic Republic

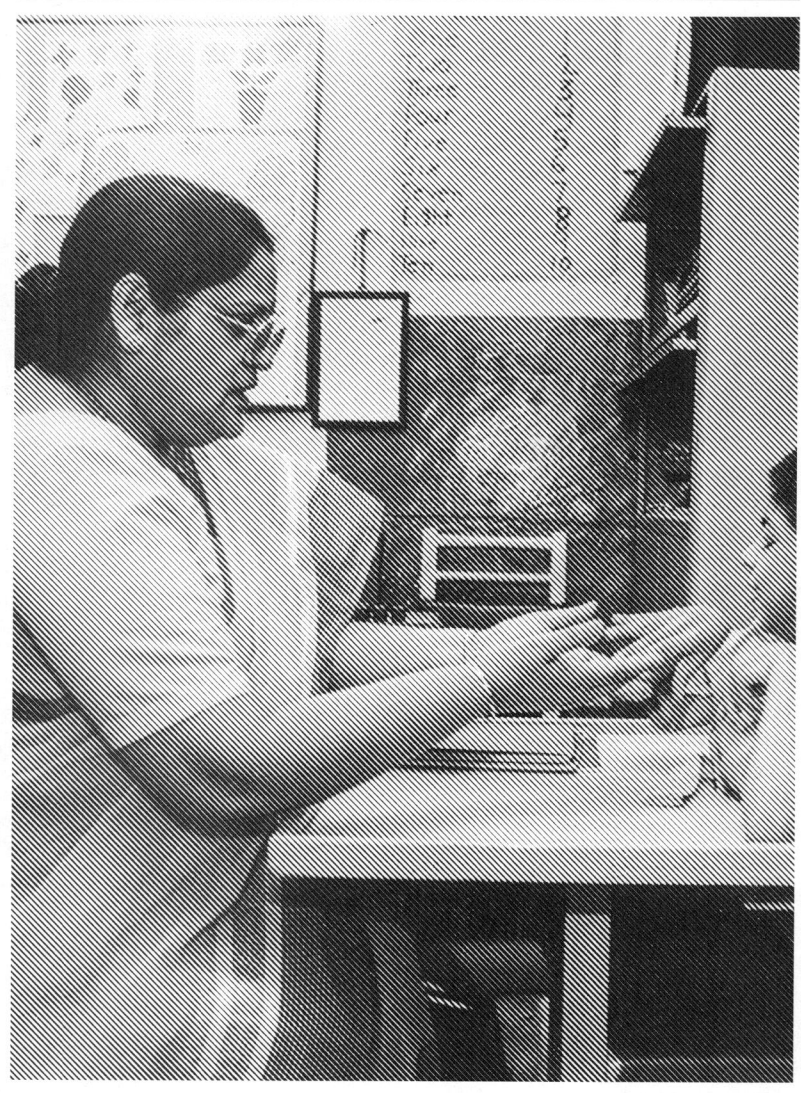

Maninder "Meenu" Sodhi

Umang

Maninder "Meenu" Sodhi (born 1951) has channeled the anguish and the wisdom that comes from being the mother of a child with disability to reach out and help others like herself. Umang, which she set up in 1998, has been providing support services to these children and their parents. Umang has now started a school for disabled children, aimed at integration into the activities of a mainstream school. For Meenu, every day is an opportunity to make a change that will help a person with disabilities–whether it is building a ramp at the local provisions store, or sensitizing railway officials.

Meenu was shattered when her bright and vivacious son was diagnosed with an incurable spinal cerebral degenerative disorder, which affected his mobility, and then his speech. The empathy and support she received from the Action for Ability Development and Inclusion (Aadi) team, whom she had contacted for home management sessions with her son, helped her accept that the best course for him would be therapy and alternative education.

In 1998, Aadi asked to start services for people with disabilities in East Delhi, which had no such facility. "You think your pain is the biggest, then you look around and see others with bigger pain than yours; you forget your pain and start helping others," says Meenu. She began by establishing in 1998 a parental group called Uday, which is now known as Umang, a registered body that caters to the varied needs of people with disability in East Delhi. In November 1999, Umang also started a school for children with disabilities within the premises of the DAV Public School, nursery wing, Dayanand Vihar. In collaboration with the school authorities, the Umang's students are now integrated in various school activities.

For Meenu, sensitizing means highlighting the insensitivity that people with disabilities and their caregivers face in society. She has made a difference — convincing temple and gurudwara (place of worship for the Sikhs) authorities about the need to provide facilities for people with disabilities, and shopping centers and the local provisions store to build a ramp. Meenu's world has grown: it is a world in which there are many people like her son, and she wants to do justice by them all.

Even with disability figures pegged at 2.13 percent of the population, India continues to be insensitive to disability rights. Basic rights — civil rights, access to information, education, employment, easy entry to buildings and public transport, access to election booths — are absent.

India

Olga Sokolova

Shans dlia nadiezhdy (A Chance for Hope)

In 1991 Olga Sokolova (born 1948) was diagnosed with cancer, a fact which radically changed her life. Olga earned a PhD in Psychology, working out a therapeutic method of rehabilitation for cancer patients. In directing the regional organization Shans dlia nadiezhdy (A Chance for Hope), dealing with the problems of those living with terminal illnesses, she conducts 40 seminar groups in many regions of Russia for sick people and members of their families. In 2002, she was awarded the Achievement Prize of the Open Society Institute for her contribution to health care in Russia.

Olga Sokolova was living a quiet life, happy with her family and the project team at the institute where she was a valued colleague. Her work was in total harmony with her expectations, when she was diagnosed with cancer. The illness turned her entire life upside down. When a diagnosis sounds like a death sentence, the inevitable thought follows: why me? And Olga began her long search for an answer, a search for means to defeat fear, to live and enjoy life. She worked out her own diet, her own system of exercise, and she reflected upon the life of her soul. The conclusion that cancer was rooted in anguish and trauma forced deep into the subconscious, led her to psychology and to religion. It is easy to write about it now, when the happy ending is a given. But how difficult it was not to break down, when Olga could not see what the future would bring: her demise or a triumph.

She decided to help not only herself, but other sick people as well. She went to the hospital and worked with the patients. She discussed her ideas with those willing to listen, and she supported those who were losing hope. Then she brought in priests who, in the very wards, baptized and confessed those who so wished. Olga decided to become a medical doctor and began to study despite her advanced age when, according to the generally accepted opinion, all that is left is to wait for retirement. In the course of research activities, Olga gathered a large quantity of material on the psychology of oncology. At first, it was hard to win the recognition of experienced doctors, but now they applaud her after her lectures. Olga, as before, directs exercise groups for cancer patients every Friday. Today, her method of healing is held in high esteem. The free and voluntary sessions have already helped to save the lives of many people, and they helped to provide many others with a chance for hope.

Olga Sokolova conducts 40 seminar groups in many regions of Russia, providing psychological help to cancer patients and members of their families. Her therapeutic approach has saved the lives of many people and given hope to many more.

Russian Federation

Somboon Srikhamdokkhae

The Council of Work and Environment Related Patients' Network of Thailand (Wept)

Somboon Srikhamdokkhae (born 1959) was the first person in Thailand to bring the issue of occupational health and safety to public attention. In 1992, she became a victim of poor environment in the workplace when she acquired bizzinosis, a disease caused by inhaling cotton dust from working in a textile factory. In 1994, she established The Council of Work and Environment Related Patients' Network of Thailand (Wept), a coalition of persons who have fallen ill from work-related illnesses and injuries.

Somboon Srikhamdokkhae walked into a textile factory for the first time on May 10, 1976. Her very first assignment was to go to the factory's spirit house and make a vow to be honest and hard working and abide by the rules. She recalls, "Nothing was said about the dangers workers might have to face." Sometime before completing ten years of service at the factory, Somboon discovered she had to choose between staying alive or continuing to work there. In 1992, she got bizzinosis, an irreversible respiratory disease associated with inhalation of cotton, flax, or hemp dust. Somboon took unpaid sick leave, resting at home for a while, then trying her hand at a couple of odd jobs.

Five months later, Somboon regained her strength sufficiently to return to the factory and fight for her rights and those of her co-workers. Thus, the Council of Work and Environment Related Patients' Network of Thailand was born. Wept operates entirely through the efforts of volunteer members. Somboon has recruited more than 1000 volunteers from different sectors of the economy who almost all share the common problem of having work-related illnesses or injuries. Wept is focused on educational campaigns for appropriate measures be undertaken to prevent work-related diseases and on the promotion of the rights of victims of unhealthy work environments. "Finally", Somboon says, "we hope that our fellow workers, friends and the general public will take measures to protect us all from falling prey to the industrialization development and investment system. And we expect that our fellow workers will change the question frequently posed to us: 'Why do we have to organize ourselves into groups?' and jointly pose the following question to the present government : 'Why is the government inviting lots of foreign investors to Thailand? Why does the government have to be so greedy?'".

With the government's heavy emphasis on industrialization, work-related illnesses have become common in Thailand's industrial sector. The Thailand Office of Labor Compensation Fund reports that 863 workers died from industrial accidents and in 1994 4549 suffered severe injuries.

Thailand

Esthi Susanti Hudiono

Yayasan Hotline Surabaya

Esthi Hudiono, from Surabaya, East Java, is a relentless campaigner on the issue of HIV/Aids. With her NGO, the Yayasan Hotline Surabaya, she has worked to raise public awareness of HIV/Aids issues, providing counseling for those infected, and campaigning for 15 years for comprehensive strategies for its prevention and cure. In 2004, she succeeded in lobbying the local government to endorse the law on HIV/Aids prevention and cure. East Java is Indonesia's first province to have such a law.

Initially, Esthi Hudiono's interest in HIV/Aids issues was provoked by the severe lack of effective intervention programs to prevent or cure the disease. Even the popular condom-use campaign failed to slow down its spread. Esthi and her NGO, the Yayasan Hotline Surabaya, work with sex workers and marginalized women, providing them with outreach services and drop-in health clinics in brothel areas. They also initiate empowerment programs through training, peer education and counseling and advocacy for sex workers and poor women in Surabaya. Surabaya, Indonesia's second biggest city, is infamous for its sex industry, with at least 20,000 women prostitutes working in its five biggest "authorized" brothels. Esthi says that due to poverty and lack of education, marginalized women are at risk of being trafficked and forced into prostitution. "Traditional values, which compel women to submit to their men, mean that even 'well-behaved' women are exposed to HIV/Aids if their husbands are practicing high risk sexual behavior," she adds.

People with HIV/Aids also benefit from counseling and advocacy: "These people face discrimination. Society shuns them, considering HIV/Aids not as a disease, but as a punishment for disobeying laws and religious values. This forces people with HIV/Aids to live in denial to avoid embarrassment," she says. Esthi lobbied relentlessly for government to come up with regulations that support efforts towards prevention and cure. Her work bore fruit when the East Java provincial government passed a law in late 2004 on HIV/Aids prevention and cure, the first of its kind in Indonesia, which requires people with high-risk sexual behavior to wear condoms and receive harm-reduction injections.

Among the six provinces in Indonesia, East Java has the highest number of HIV/Aids cases. Its capital city, Surabaya, is infamous for its sex industry, which employs sex workers from the locality and from other provinces. Most cases of HIV/Aids in Surabaya are related to high-risk sexual activities.

Indonesia

Cristina Tézenas du Montcel

L' Envol pour les enfants européens

Born in 1943, Cristina Tézenas du Montcel studied Russian at the Ecole des Langues Orientales in Paris and comparative European law in Brussels. Since 1968, she pursued a career in politics in the Cultural Department of the French Foreign Ministry. From 1987 to 1990, she was director of external communication for Radio France Internationale. She is president of Envol, a medical recreational facility which organizes vacations for seriously ill children. Since 1997, this center, unique in Europe, has hosted almost 4000 children suffering from cancer, leukemia, and other critical conditions.

Envol was created in September 1994 at the initiative of Cristina's late husband. The medical facility has hosted more than 4000 children since its inauguration in 1997. These children, aged seven to 17, come from approximately 100 hospitals in France and Europe for a short stay, usually 12 days. They suffer from over 130 diseases such as cancer, leukemia, blood diseases and rare or "orphan" illnesses. The goal of Envol is to offer the children some joy of living and give them the strength they need to cope with their condition when they go back home or to the hospital. Serious illness in a child is like a war — it may last over several battles, all of which have to be won. The children themselves are like little warriors; they refuse to succumb to their negative emotions, try not to hurt people's feelings, and smile. They say: "At Envol, I become a child again, whereas in the hospital I am a patient." "Obviously, in such a situation, feelings and heartfelt reactions are more important than intellectual capacities; they light our path. The world must not abandon its sick children," Cristina says.
Envol gives every child the opportunity to recover vital energy by practicing sports or other activities it was barred from for medical reasons, and rediscover the simple pleasure of being like other children — gardener or fisherman, rider or actor, poet or photographer, swimmer or singer, clown or musician, a farmer at the mini-farm, or a hiker through the forest and by the lake, and regain confidence and a measure of happiness. Envol is a response to children's critical illnesses, an attempt to give them hope and some peace.

The objective of Envol is to help seriously ill children to regain hope in the future, enjoyment in living, and provide them with the willpower and strength to combat their illness once back in their family or hospital environment.

France

Nada Thabet

Village of Hope (VoH)
Presbyterian Evangelical Church (PEC)

Nada Thabet is married and has two sons (24 and 26), one of whom has severe learning difficulties. She works in advocacy for the rights of people with learning difficulties through a network of 22 societies and NGOs working in the field. She has called for health insurance, a pension from birth and the issuing of identity cards. Her work raises awareness of societal prejudices and legal inequities in order to improve conditions for people with learning difficulties in Egypt.

"On March 2nd 1980 God gave me my son Maged. After about three months I began to question this gift. I felt he was different, his senses did not seem to function." Thus began Nada Alfy Thabet's painful journey for medical treatment inside Egypt and abroad. Maged was not improving in the slightest, with no hope that he could be a normal child. He suffered from atrophy of the brain cells, particularly those governing vision. Why was Maged not born like other normal kids? Questions tumbled through Nada's mind, followed by silence, anger, bitterness and resentment. "I continued like this until Maged was two-and-a-half years old, by which time I had completely lost all hope," says Nada. She adds, "The strange thing is that this depression led me closer to God, and I felt I needed Him more than ever. I prayed constantly." She recalls, "As I was asking for God's support and His Mercy, my tears brimming over, I saw that Maged was moving, and his eyes were actually seeing the things around him for the first time. I could not believe it." Maged started learning new skills — some were even difficult for 'normal' people.

Everything went well until he was 16, when he started facing different kinds of problems, such as an identity card and military service. Although Maged's problem has improved greatly, still Nada was thinking about other people like him. "I set up a place and called it the 'Village of Hope'. It was established in December 2000, and by October 2001 it was nurturing six children with special needs," says Nada. The Village has a center for technical training, a bakery, carpentry, and agriculture to make it financially independent. From the experience of the Village of Hope sprang the idea of establishing a network of 22 societies working in the same field, to defend the rights of people with learning difficulties.

Nada Alfy Thabet works in advocacy, striving for the rights of people with learning difficulties through a network of societies and NGOs working in the field. Beside the foundation of the Village of Hope (VoH) she has called for health insurance, a pension from birth and the issuing of identity cards.

"God did not give
us a spirit of timidity,
but a spirit of
power, of love and
of self-discipline.
It is that discipline
that I use not
only as a nurse but
as God's child."

Cordelia Nozukile Tshaka

Makukhanye Health Promotion

Cordelia Tshaka was born 1951 in Eastern Cape, South Africa. She holds a diploma in public health nursing and is a registered nurse and midwife. She worked in hospitals before working in community health clinics. Throughout the 1980s running NGOs was difficult but Cordelia and her colleagues persevered. They worked during the violent Crossroads Uprising; relief came in the early 1990s when South Africa held democratic elections. In the late 1990s Cordelia participated in forming Zanempilo, an amalgamation of health NGOs, and initiated Makukhanye, an HIV/Aids program in the Western Cape.

Cordelia Tshaka is involved in a community advocacy initiative to bring health to local communities and change people's attitudes towards HIV/Aids patients. She trains community health workers (Chws) in basic nursing. Cordelia works with Chws in the Makukhanye HIV/Aids program. Since the health services cannot handle all HIV/Aids cases, programs like the Makukhanye Health Promotion Project fill this gap. Women concerned by the inadequate assistance provided by formal health service providers initiated such programs. The South African Christian Leadership Assembly and Zanempilo are health NGOs in which active community participation is integral. They use the World Health Organization's campaign "Health For All" to address the needs of the communities. Chws are elected by the communities as health agents to serve the areas closest to them. They are trained in home nursing and care of minor ailments. Care giving includes washing, feeding and counseling patients who are unable to go to a hospice or have returned home. Chws are also trained in record keeping, report writing and networking.
Cordelia's experience in community-based health care and the community's faith in her work are responsible for the continued success of these programs.

HIV/Aids has a devastating effect in poor communities in South Africa, especially where the majority are black. HIV/Aids education is necessary as families have misunderstood HIV/Aids. Patients lack money for medication and they do not share their pain with nurses, who have little time to counsel them.

South Africa

Erzsebet Turos

Psychiatric Hospital Borsa

Erzsebet Turos has worked as a general practitioner in a psychiatric hospital in Borsa in Cluj county, Romania, for several years. When Dr Turos arrived, the hospital was pure horror and passive euthanasia was repeatedly taking place. Dr Turos is highly appreciated by the 230 patients for her care and help. She has instituted occupational therapy and social activities where before there were none. Since December 2002, she has been cooperating with the German association Beclean e.V, which was founded by the staff of a psychiatric hospital in southern Germany to provide help to Romania.

Erzsebet Turos has been working in the psychiatric hospital in Borsa for the past nine years. When she started to work, there were 215 chronic psychiatric patients with different diagnoses: schizophrenia, alcoholism, epilepsy, and dementia. For these patients there were only two doctors: a psychiatrist who is also the general director of the hospital and another general physician, a woman who left the hospital shortly after Dr Turos arrived. Since then, no other physician has come to work in Borsa.

The hospital is in an old castle, which belonged to a family of barons before the communist era. It is the only chronic psychiatric hospital in Cluj county. The situation of the building was terrible when Dr Turos arrived and still is today. Although it needs to be renovated completely both inside and out, this is not permitted as it is an historical monument. There are several large unhealthy rooms with many beds (15 to 20 in a room), without their own bathrooms. This forces the patients to live together, without privacy, resulting in daily arguments. "When I started to work here, I was touched by the situation of Borsa: disastrous rooms and a bad smell. However, I felt sympathy for the patients, so I focused on what I had to do. Even today, it is very difficult to work in these conditions," Dr Turos says.

Borsa is a small village, and like most Romanian villages, it has a very poor infrastructure. There is no functioning water system. And it is 100 percent dependent on rain water. In these conditions, it is very difficult to maintain hygiene. Scabies and lice are common. Borsa is also very isolated, in every sense of the word. The distance to Cluj-Napoca, the closest city, is only 45 km, but there is only a secondary county road, which is in very bad condition. "All these issues together," Dr Turos says, "are the reason why no new doctors come to work in Borsa."

Most psychiatric patients in Romania have had to endure unbelievably bad conditions. Severe cuts to already poor state funding resulted in cold, damp, and filthy conditions for the most vulnerable in Romanian society.

Lázara Lizette Vila Espina

Proyecto Palomas

For over ten years, Lizette Vila has dedicated herself to working for peace and respect for diversity in society. In Havana, she created a project called Proyecto Palomas (Project Doves) with the goal to bring about changes in people's life styles and promote respect for human diversity, in order to encourage a culture of peace.

Lizette Vila was born in El Cerro, a poor neighborhood of Havana, within a family that supported her artistic education. She studied and became a musical adviser. She makes documentaries, films, television shows and videos. In her audiovisual work, she addresses themes linked to marginality, to discrimination and human suffering in all its forms. She has amassed a vast professional experience and has been awarded more than 50 prizes in her own country and abroad. She has directed numerous documentaries of a humanistic character and others to promote preventative health measures. Lizette comments on her vocation as follows: "The motivation for my work comes from the emotions created in me by human suffering, by marginality, economic difficulties and the many different forms of violence and inequality in society that have allowed me to, day by day, accumulate experiences that have shaped my approach towards life."

Lizette is the creator of the Proyecto Palomas (a non-profit social and cultural organization) with the goal to bring about changes in people's life styles and promote respect for human diversity, in order to encourage a culture of peace. The project generates cultural meetings known as peace encounters, where people can interact and interchange ideas and feelings that will help to promote the harmony, which will lead to sustainable human development. This Cuban documentary maker has managed to combine her particular sensitivity to human suffering with a rich artistic background, putting both into the service of people who are very vulnerable in our society: children, adolescents and young people suffering from cancer, genetic diseases and physical or mental disabilities, women and transvestites with HIV or Aids, elderly people and women who are alcoholics or obese.

In Cuba, Learning and the Arts tend to follow traditional paths and they remain centered around schools, conservatories and theaters. People that are 'different,' such as the disabled, the elderly, addicts and others, have difficulty finding a place in those circles.

Cuba

Wong Ting Hway

Medecins Sans Frontieres (MSF)
International Committee of the Red Cross (ICRC)
Hospice Care Association

Wong Ting Hway (born 1973) has been carrying out humanitarian work since she was a medical student. In 2001, she joined Medecins Sans Frontieres (MSF) and was sent to Angola, where she worked to save people from starvation. In 2002, she became the first Singaporean doctor to work full-time with the International Committee of the Red Cross (ICRC), which posted her to Nepal. Now back in Singapore to complete her training in surgery, Wong is a volunteer with the Hospice Care Association, devoted to the care of the terminally ill in their own homes.

If Dr Wong Ting Hway came to your bedside in a hospital, wearing a white jacket and stethoscope, you would probably think she was trying to impersonate a doctor. The slim, attractive 32-year-old practitioner looks as if she has just graduated from college. But looks are deceiving. Wong has been a doctor for six years and in that time she has managed to accomplish much in the humanitarian field. In 2001, she joined MFS and was sent to Kuito, Angola, where she worked for six months in a "therapeutic feeding center" treating patients who were at risk of dying from starvation. These patients were victims of the 30-year civil war that had decimated the country and split families apart. Each day at the center in Kuito, Wong tried to bring children and adults back from the brink; some survived, some did not. "Every day, I saw death," Wong has written of her experiences. "I saw it in the feeding center, I saw it in the hospital whenever I was on duty there, I saw it in the empty beds the next morning when I came to work and a child who had been critically ill the day before was no longer there."

As Wong Ting Hway worked, bombs sometimes went off around the center, causing her and other staff members to jump. But she learned to regain her equilibrium. "When you are out there, your baseline for being happy or sad changes," she says matter-of-factly. "Happiness can come from the slightest improvement in one of your patients." After Angola, Wong returned to safe and quiet Singapore before applying to work with the ICRC, which posted her to Nepal in 2003. There she examined the impact of conflict on the country's health services and gave support to those in the medical field. Now back in Singapore, Wong is completing her training as a surgeon, a qualification she believes is necessary to continue her humanitarian work.

With an ever-present number of war zones in the world, health workers are constantly in demand, but not all are willing to risk their lives on foreign soil. When doctors volunteer their skills in conflict situations, they can help to save some of the unfortunate civilians caught in the crossfire.

"Sing the love,
love the song

I want to fight
with dreams
in my soul, with you

Sing the love,
love the song,

I want to fight
with dreams
in my soul."

Kumiko Yokoi

Kumiko Yokoi uses the power of music to spread messages of peace, dignity, and hope. Millions of people of all ages in Ireland, Sri Lanka, Nicaragua, Vietnam, and the United States have been inspired by the singer's performances; profits from her concerts and CDs have benefited children, particularly those with disabilities. She is also known as a fighter for worker's rights in her home country, Japan.

When Kumiko Yokoi saw the pain and suffering of children — second- and third-generation victims of Agent Orange (a herbicide developed for military use) — at a rehabilitation center in Vietnam, her heart broke. "The village is a holy place," she said. "It has experienced peace and the cruelty of war." As she has been doing since 1973, she dedicated her 2004 concert to help the children.

The concert was her fourth in Vietnam. She first performed there in 1973 when she sang "Stop! Tank" for northern soldiers during the Vietnam War. She is especially moved by children and families whose health has been devastated by environmental catastrophes. In 1985 she sang in Nicaragua, and in 2001 she donated the income from sales of a CD to children in Afghanistan.

Inspired by Irish songs that arose from the civil rights movement, she has translated Irish ballads into Japanese. Her own songs, such as "Sing the Love, Long the Song" and "Same Sky, Same Children", send the universal message that all children should live in peace in a future that is bright.

Kumiko received a singing degree from the National Music University, sang in a chorus, and became a soloist in 1969. Her popularity in Japan comes without the commercialization that normally accompanies success.

Vietnam has about 1.2 million children with disabilities, 150,000 of whom are Agent Orange victims. Kumiko's concerts and recordings benefit these children and others from around the world who are victims of the world's wars.

Japan

Henny Yudea

Heath Study Institute (Lessan)

Henny Yudea (born 1968) is a health rights activist. Her main interest is developing traditional medicines, which she believes is an answer to the health problems of poor people. Herbal medicines can be made from ingredients which are mostly cheap and easily accessible to many. She works with hundreds of farmers, including women, encouraging them to plant herbs, and educates them in ways to develop medicines and secure a better future that stems from better health.

"I started my work in the late 1980s when villages surrounding Yogyakarta were going through hard times and the economic situation was not good. The government was so repressive that people could not express their opinions and views as citizens," Henny Yudea recalls. As a young activist, she wanted to help people cope with their bitter situation and enjoy better lives. She joined Lessan, or the Health Study Institute, in 1990 as a field worker. "At that time, when a man was sick, he had to go find some cure. When he came back healthy, he no longer had anything left." The situation prompted Henny and her friends to look for ways to provide cheap health services. "We witnessed unfair conditions, but we also saw a local capacity which was still untapped. Traditional medicines became our preference, because ingredients were easily available, and using these to cure people carries a minimal risk of side effects. And these medicines have been used for a long time by our ancestors."

Henny and her colleagues have worked in the area of traditional medicine for 15 years, conducting research and development on herbal medicines, opening health posts where people learn to heal themselves using ingredients found in their surroundings. Henny also helps women farmers organize themselves and she says working as an activist these days is not as difficult as it was in the 1980s. "However, people are still suspicious of NGOs. We are often accused of selling people's poverty," she says. "But the spirit and determination of the people we are working with really keep us going. Their wisdom in living truly gives us a good lesson in life." Her hope for her country is that "Indonesia can be a peaceful nation with its diversity and with space for women to play an active part."

In the early 1990s, in Yogyakarta, many remote villages did not get financial support from the government to develop their health infrastructure. Health care was expensive. Promoting traditional medicines was a way to help people get affordable medicines.

Indonesia

Mayana Zatz

Centro de Estudos do Genoma Humano, Universidade de São Paulo
Associação Brasileira de Distrofia Muscular (Abdim)

Mayana Zatz (1947) is an international reference in the study of human genetics. With around 200 scientific essays published in international magazines, she founded the Brazilian Association of Muscular Dystrophy that helps children, young people and their family members. She is an active voice in the National Congress where she has played an important role in the process of authorizing the research on embrionary cells and where she fights for the legalization of abortions in case of non-rehabilitative genetic diseases.

An internationally well-known biologist, Mayana Zatz was a young university student when she made this decision: "To acquire scientific knowledge to improve people's health and quality of life." The wish of being useful arose when she met, during a research on genetic diseases, a woman — mother of eight children, seven of them with mental or physical deficiencies.

This scientist was born in Israel, moved to Brazil and — in search for knowledge — she went to the United States, where she got a postgraduate degree in Genetic Medicine at the University of California (Ucla). She specialized in muscular dystrophy — a hereditary and irreversible disease that causes the progressive degeneration of the skeletal musculature. When she returned, in 1981, Mayana founded the Brazilian Association of Muscular Dystrophy (Abdim) that is sited inside the University of São Paulo. Considered as the largest center of investigation of genetic problems, Abdim makes diagnoses, gives genetic counseling, orientation for the families and offers children and teenagers the most modern equipments for treatments, physical therapy and hydrotherapy sessions, recreational activities and psychological support. Mayana also coordinates the Center of Studies of the Human Genome. She and her team located six genes linked to dystrophy, an important factor for the future discovery of the cure for this disease. They developed genetic tests for the precocious diagnosis of at least 50 illnesses. During the last three years, the biologist faced a tough challenge: convincing politicians and religious figures of the importance of the research involving embrionary cells, in order to attain the legal approval of this type of research. Successful, she celebrates: "What I most want now is to work with these embrionary cells and try to discover a treatment for the dystrophies."

Genetic diseases reach five million Brazilians; around 80,000 are affected by neuromuscular diseases. Data from the Brazilian Institute of Statistics and Geography (Igbe) indicates that 20% of the deaths of babies happen as a consequence of factors related to genes.

Brazil

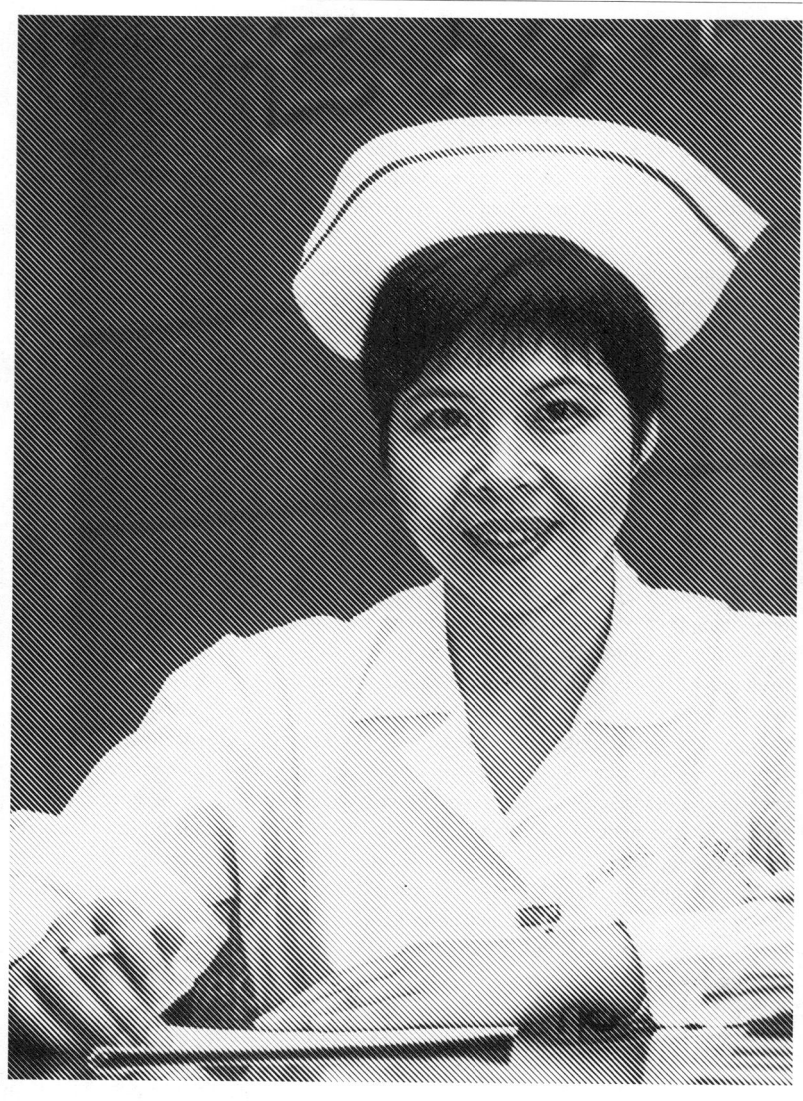

Jihui Zhang

No. 1 People's Hospital in Guangzhou City

Zhang Jihui is a head nurse in the general ward of the No. 1 Hospital in Guangzhou City. During the outbreak of Severe Acute Respiratory Syndrome (Sars) in China in 2003, she accepted the assignment to work in the temporary Sars ward without hesitation. She worked 12 to 16 hours per day for 83 days without adequate supplies of oxygen and water. She served patients selflessly with love and courage. Her efforts have deeply impressed each of her patients, who come to understand what an "angel in white" really means.

In spring 2003 China witnessed the outbreak of the contagious epidemic disease Sars and the situation in Guangdong Province was one of the worst since this was where the first Sars case occurred. As a nurse with 20 years' experience in No. 1 People's Hospital, Zhang Jihui was appointed one of the head nurses in the Sars ward. She took good care of the patients, trying to familiarize herself with the subject of epidemic diseases, while immediately warming to her work under these special circumstances. She carried out antisepsis and isolation work, resulting in a zero record of cross con-tamination among patients in the ward. Furthermore, none of the medical personnel was affected.

Her selfless and courageous actions influenced other nurses who gradually overcome their fears. The doctors and nurses called her "the pillar in the ward." Being overburdened by work for a long period, Zhang came down with a fever but took medicine secretly and continued to work. She worked in the Sars ward for nearly three months.

She says, "What I thought about most was how to keep myself going without fear. Seeing my colleagues fall ill one after another, I thought of finding the most effective way to rescue them as soon as possible. I kept records 24 hours a day, every week. At that time I worked over 16 hours a day, which gave me swollen feet and an aching back. I longed to sleep." Zhang always kept a pen and paper with her to record the events that occurred in the ward. Later these stories were published as a book called "Diaries of the Head Nurse," which became a valuable piece of documentation in the battle against Sars. Zhang said: "it was this 'masking spring' which pushed me from being an ordinary nurse to the forefront of society. The honor should go to all the courageous medical personnel."

In 2003 Sars broke out in China. Due to inadequate knowledge about the disease and its gravity, China missed out on the right moment to control it. When people realized the severity of Sars there was panic.

Wenqing Zhang

Zhang Wenqing works in Taiyuan Central Hospital. In 2003 she volunteered to work in the Severe Acute Respiratory Syndrome (Sars) wards, staying there for two months. In April 2004 she was promoted to head nurse of the gastroenterology department. Her nursing service to over 3,000 people, spanning more than 17 years, has won her love and respect.

Zhang Wenqing was born into an ordinary family in Taiyuan City, Shanxi Province. She liked to study and help others, and each year she was awarded the title of Excellent Student. The hardships and the lack of medicines in the villages that she witnessed in her childhood were deeply imprinted on her mind. She was determined to become a nurse.

In 1985, 15-year-old Zhang Wenqing enrolled in medical school in Taiyuan to study nursing, psychology, and ethics. After graduation she worked in the medical department of Taiyuan Central Hospital. Later she studied to gain an undergraduate diploma. In 2003, entrusting her 3-year-old daughter and 95-year-old father to her mother-in-law, Zhang worked in the Sars wards. The working conditions were almost unbearable, but Zhang and her team managed to achieve a zero infection rate of medical personnel.

In April 2004, due to her excellent work, Zhang Wenqing was promoted to head nurse of the gastroenterology department. The department received an award for being a model department and for excellence in ward management. The average stay of patients in the hospital was shortened by four days, with an eight percent reduction in average expenses. Because of its humanitarian and scientific care, many patients come to be treated here, and have contributed to the 28 percent increase in the department's earnings. Over the last 17 years, more than 3000 people have received the careful nursing offered by Zhang Wenqing. Her work is imbued with humanity and care, reaching out especially to patients suffering from terminal illnesses, the old, and the widowed. Her careful nursing gives them comfort before they leave the world. She says, "Like Florence Nightingale I am determined to devote my life to the medical cause."

Medical personnel faced serious challenges in the spring of 2003. Taiyuan Central Hospital accommodated 90 Sars patients, confirmed and suspected, causing widespread terror. Zhang Wenqing entrusted her 3-year-old daughter to her mother-in-law and volunteered to work in the Sars wards for 2 months.

China

A Thousand Ways to Educate for a Global Culture of Peace

Noa Zanolli Davenport

"There is no way to peace. Peace is the way," Gandhi said. The thousand women show us a thousand ways and many more for educating for a culture of peace. Each of the women is a model for peace, a teacher who creates peace simply by her actions and her words.

Each of the women, in her part of the world, in her environment, in her own unique way, has made her inestimable contribution towards the creation of a more harmonious, inclusive, just, and secure world. These women have, by their integrity, ingenuity and a sense of immediacy, made a difference to millions.

Of the 1000 women, more than 100 have been nominated for making education and educating for peace their life's work, demonstrating superb leadership in the task of expanding the minds and consciousness of children, youth and adults.

They do this essentially in three ways: They change economic conditions by empowering people and communities; they write and teach about peace, in their political work or as academics; or they educate the public on conflict resolution skills.

Some have chosen education as the primary vehicle to change undignified human conditions non-violently and create new opportunities to improve lives. Their achievements are proof that it is possible to change the world without resorting to violence, through education, no matter how adverse and deplorable the circumstances may be.

Other nominees are propelled by a spiritual conviction when they research, write, speak about and teach the art and science of peacemaking.

Driven by a sense of urgency, these women understand that education for peace is a long-term endeavor, a continuing, never-ending process that requires utmost dedication and endurance.

What have these women done specifically? How have they done it? What are the contents of their teaching, and what does their work mean for all of us?

The women are eradicating illiteracy and emancipating girls and women in remote villages in Malawi and in India; creating practical education programs in conflict resolution for the workplace, schools, universities and communities in Australia; spreading peace-focused curricula in the Philippines; founding universities in Bangladesh; educating about human rights and women's rights as an academic or politician in countries where patriarchal structures are still ingrained in cultural traditions; using the radio to educate millions of marginalized people in remote areas in Brazil; establishing a school for blind children in Tibet; changing public policy to ensure more equity and self-government in India; enhancing women's education in Saudi Arabia; teaching peace studies in the United States or across the globe.

Whatever their work may be, these women are spreading the message that broad knowledge and a fundamental understanding of the world beyond one's immediate experience is a fundamental condition for peace.

Their work is based on a hope that — in Deepak Chopra's words — "unmasks denial, inspires an end to apathy, faces up to conflict, brings an end to silent suffering, changes the situation of victims, and brings about realization."

This is precisely what these peace educators do: they unmask, they inspire, they educate to resolve conflicts, they transform minds and shift perspectives, and they empower people to take charge of their own destiny.

Though more than 100 women have been nominated for their specific achievements in education, all the 1000 nominated women are, in their own ways, educators. By their example, they are all teachers and guides. They educate for a culture of peace because their work has meaning that reaches far beyond the immediate contexts of their individual engagements.

They teach us, over and over again, that each person makes a difference. They show us that peace can be created deliberately, anywhere, in one's self, in families, the environment, in communities, in schools, among faiths groups, in organizations and among nations. They demonstrate that one need not resort to violence to achieve one's ends. They appreciate the interdependence of all living beings. They demonstrate that participating in a community means being part of and feeling responsible for the community and the planet, for all generations present and still to come. And, they advocate and educate by the power of their vision of an inclusive global society in which every person participates as an equal.

And, above all, they teach us how to repair the world.

Dr Noa Zanolli Davenport is coach of the project team. An educator, cultural anthropologist and mediator, she does practical and consulting work in international development and teaching/training in conflict resolution in Europe, the USA and in Africa.

—

N

"Supporting girls'
education and the
improvement of
living conditions for
the people in Kedalu
are my life-long
mission that I
am dedicated to."

Amna Abd El Rahman Abd El Rasoul

Women's Section in the Higher Committee for Kedalu Development (WSHCKD)
Peace and Development Center (PDC)
Kedalu Development Corporation (KDC)

Amna Abd El Rahman, (29) is one of very few university graduates in the region of Kedalu and Head of the Women's Section in the Higher Committee for Kedalu Development (WSHCKD). As an active member of the Peace and Development Center (PDC) and the Kedalu Development Corporation (KDC) she is affiliated with both governmental and non-governmental organizations. Amna's major achievements are on issues concerning women's and children's rights and education as an essential right. She strives to reshape the community's biased attitudes and concepts regarding women's participation in society.

The Kedalu area is one of the most underdeveloped areas in the Sudan and suffers from the absence of government's and NGOs' basic community services. There is no access to telephones, road network and marketing facilities. In addition the area is insecure due to the outbreak of civil war in the late 1990s. For more than eight years, Amna has been working with both women's and men's groups to mobilize her community. She has organized many training programs for environment development, management and community planning. Her main aim was to make education an essential right for girls in the area, which was very difficult due to local social and economic constraints. Nowadays the percentage of girls' enrolment in basic education has significantly increased.

Amna's exemplum as a university graduate encourages more families to send their children to school. Visitors to the Kedalu area can clearly observe a fundamental shift in local people's conceptions of women's role and significant participation in different development activities. Throughout her work in Kedalu, Amna has faced many challenges, most exigent of which was the high rate of illiteracy, particularly among women, ubiquitous poverty due to the low incomes of people in the area and the outbreak of the civil war, which lead to massive displacement of Kedalu citizens. This new situation forced Amna and the women in Kedalu to depend on their own resources and they became a successful example for all women, not only in the Kedalu area, but also for all women's groups in Blue Nile State.

Thanks to Amna's efforts, the percentage of girls' enrolment in basic education has significantly increased in the Sudan. The attitude of local people towards women's role in society has changed. Women are now energetically participating in community development activities.

Sudan

Ghada Al—Jabi

The General Union of Syrian Women (GUSW)
The Arab Net for Literacy and Adult Education (ANLAE)
The International Council for Adult Education (ICAE)

Ghada Al-Jabi, born in Syria in 1938, was the Minister of Labor and Social Affairs. She began her social work at the age of 16. Her strong belief in voluntary work prompted her to continue work for 40 years on very demanding issues, such as illiteracy, in coordination with the Syrian Ministry of Culture and the Syrian Women's Union. Thanks to her splendid efforts, the rates of illiteracy in Syria dropped from 53% in 1970 to 14% in 2000. Her work covers local, regional and international issues, and her accomplishments are highly acclaimed in the Middle East, especially in the Arab World.

Ghada Al-Jabi was motivated to become involved in social work by her patriotic dedication to the development and welfare of her homeland and nation, focusing her efforts on the empowerment of the less-privileged members of society. Since 1959, she has devoted herself to eradicating illiteracy through her work with the Ministry of Culture and her voluntary work as head of the Syrian Women's Union. When the Syrian Literacy Act came into force in 1972, Ghada Al-Jabi was appointed as Director of the Department for Illiteracy Eradication at the Ministry of Culture. Thanks to her invigorating ideas and indefatigable efforts, the department launched a number of projects targeting unskilled laborers, especially uneducated women in rural areas. The remarkable successes that her projects have achieved in Syria earned her the respect and approbation of many regional and international organizations.

In 1990 the United Nations Educational, Scientific and Cultural Organization (Unesco) published an article about her significant energetic social projects in its periodical, and she was awarded the title of the Unesco's Honorary Ambassador to the Syrian Arab Republic in recognition of her contribution to the International Decade of Education for All. As a regular participant in international conferences, Ghada Al-Jabi's papers address issues concerning freedom of opinion and independence, which she considers as the most fundamental rights of all nations.

The rate of illiteracy in Syria was very high in the 1970s and up to the early 1990s, particularly among women in rural areas. The cooperation between the government and civil society organizations has succeeded in tackling this problem and lowering this rate.

Syrian Arab Republic

Eva Alterman Blay

Núcleo de Estudos da Mulher e Relações Sociais de Gênero (Center for the Study of Women and Gender)

Eva Alterman Blay (1937) is one of the first intellectuals to bring the gender issues into university. She faced, in the 1960s and 1970s, not only the military regime's censorship, but also prejudice, because other academics believed that it was a "minor issue." She created the Center for the Study of Women and Gender of the University of São Paulo (Nemge). She became a senator and presided the State Council for the Condition of Women of São Paulo.

The 1960s. Left-wing political factions were mobilizing themselves against the oppressive regime. Young academics and revolutionaries were breathing Marxist ideas. Eva Blay, who had just graduated in Social Sciences, chose a theme for her master's thesis: the female worker. "People laughed at me. Studying women's condition was perceived as something irrelevant and apolitical." When she went into the factories, Eva realized that it was handled as an "unimportant" issue indeed: women did not have any rights. "In a nail factory, I found a newborn baby inside a shoe box. The mother had no place to leave the baby." From Eva Blay's thesis stemmed her first book: "I have no place to live — Study of the Worker's Villages in São Paulo." Her fight, solitary at first, grew as the feminist movement in the country developed. She participated in the creation of the Feminine Movement for Amnesty.

The 1980s. As the country was going through the transition to democracy, Eva supported the creation of specific public policies for women. She presided the State Council for the Condition of Women of São Paulo, when she helped implementing a day-care program — there was only one in the city — and creating the first Police Precinct dedicated to assisting women. She called the government's attention to controversial issues such as equal pay and a system to stimulate for the candidacy of women for political office. She continued her career as a professor at the University of São Paulo, where she founded, in 1985, the Center for the Study of Women and Gender (Nemge). She became a senator in 1992; her term ended in 1995. As a professor, and scientific director of Nemge, she still does her utmost to fight for women's rights.

During the last three decades, the Brazilian feminist movement — which Eva Blay helped creating and fortifying — has organized over 3000 groups, which act on different areas in the country: non-governmental organizations, political parties, labor unions, universities, autonomous groups.

Brazil

Genoveva Ximenes Alves

Saint Paul's High School
Maryknoll Sisters

A history and cultural history professor at St. Paul's High School in Timor-Leste, Genoveva Alves is a peace trainer and founding partner in the transformation of St. Paul's into a school for peace. She trains, oversees, and assists the students in a peace program that teaches skills in dialogue, negotiation, and mediation. Prior to that, Genoveva worked in the forest with the East Timor resistance movement to fight the decades-long occupation by the Indonesian government. She played an integral role in the Timor Women's Organization (OMT) in support of the liberation movement.

After nine years in the East Timor forest working for the clandestine resistance movement, Genoveva Alves and her husband became active members of Aileu district community and worked in the education system. In 1999, after the Indonesian government and military left East Timor, Genoveva was visible in community activities such as organizing the Timor Women's Organization (OMT), volunteering and subsequently being contracted as a government secondary school teacher and conducting civic education and human rights trainings. She had played a key role in the OMT at the district level and then organized its support for the reconstruction movement. All schools in Aileu had been burned and looted during the Indonesian occupation. When the Ministry of Education under joint United Nations governance and local East Timor self-governance opened schools across the country, there were no desks, chairs, chalkboards, or textbooks. The District Education Officer, in cooperation with the Catholic parish, decided to open one secondary school, St. Paul's High School. Genoveva and others taught there first as volunteers in trying conditions.

In the past four years, Genoveva has become School Treasurer and the senior professor on the faculty. As a faculty member and secretary for the OMT, she has participated in trainings in leadership, facilitation, peace, reconciliation, conflict resolution, gender issues, human rights, and civic education, using the opportunities well to increase her knowledge and skills as a community organizer and leader. In 2002, she was chosen to sit on the community reconciliation panel for Aileu District, as the mandate of the Truth, Reception, and Reconciliation Commission was carried out. Thus, she heard the truth telling, the victims' claims, the accuseds' responses and admissions, and participated in the mediations of the panel.

On independence (1999), Timor-Leste schools were poorly resourced when the Ministry of Education re-opened them. Nevertheless, teachers like Genoveva Alves rallied to restore the education system and to adapt it to serve peace and conflict resolution purposes as well.

Nasreen Awan

Anjuman Falah-e-Niswan Chichawatni

Nasreen Awan (born 1961) got herself an education in her home district of Sangarh, a poverty-stricken part of Pakistan's Sindh province, against the most daunting odds. Then, she determinedly carved out a career for herself as social activist in a region where women were considered the property of their men, and not allowed to step out of their homes without male permission. Today, as head of an NGO and a district political functionary, she is an inspiration for hundreds of women trying to make a better life for themselves in a belligerently patriarchal society.

In the village in Sindh's Sanghar district where Nasreen Awan was born, the nearest road was three kilometers away, the nearest market seven kilometers away, and the only school lacked furniture and a roof. Determined daughter of an unlettered mother, Nasreen studied at the village primary school and then combined long walks with bus journeys to reach the secondary school in the nearest town, from which she matriculated. Nasreen was admitted to a college, but her father fell in with local custom and married the 16-year-old girl to his nephew. Nasreen's husband's family was opposed to her studying further. But, with her husband's support, she managed to graduate while living in Karachi with her elder sister and her brother-in-law.

Her next goal was to help others gain access to the opportunities she had made for herself. Her chance came in 1983, when she went to Chichawanti, her husband's family's small hometown in district Sahiwal of Punjab province. Noting the absence of decent schools, she set up a private school, and established skills development and vocational training centers for poor women by selling her own land and soliciting donations from the community. She allied herself with a local NGO, Anjuman Falah-e-Niswan Chichawatni, which worked in literacy, health, and poverty alleviation. Nasreen was elected the NGO's president in 1990. With its support, she established 13 vocational training institutes and an equal number of nonformal schools in villages around Sahiwal.

Nasreen set up a scheme to provide educational vocational training to women at their doorstep, which has so far served about 2250 women. Eventually, she set up a free legal aid cell and a shelter home for poor women. Nasreen finally entered politics' fold: in 2001, she was elected member of the Sahiwal district council. It was a fight well won.

A severe shortage of schools exclusively for girls is one of the main reasons for the very low level of literacy in Pakistan's Sindh province. Social taboos do not permit coeducational schools. In Punjab, the situation is a bit better, but not much.

Pakistan

Quratulain Bakhteari

Institute for Development Studies and Practices (IDSP)

Quratulain Bakhteari (born 1949) presides over a unique learning space in Pakistan's Balochistan province. Her brainchild, the Institute for Development Studies and Practices (IDSP), channels the energies of scores of young people, mainly from this poor and deprived region, by training them to be social activists and catalysts for change in their communities. The IDSP is the outcome of Quratulain's vast experience in development work, and her conviction that new ways must be found to integrate theory and practice in order to bring meaningful change.

After two decades of community-based development work, Quratulain Bakhteari was convinced that young people on short-term contracts in development projects were getting a raw deal — a different approach was needed to involve them in a meaningful and sustained way. Thus was her brainchild, the Institute for Development Studies and Practices, born in Pakistan's Balochistan province. Quratulain wrote the concept in 1997. It was tested in 1998 through a pilot involving five people working with her in women's education. The IDSP was established in 1999 to create a cadre of young people as grassroots development thinkers, planners, and practitioners. It now runs innovative certificate and diploma courses in community development, applies research, and initiates public projects.

Today, 400 youth are engaged in grassroots development work. Any young person who can read, write, and has an idea to put to the test can enrol in IDSP courses. In the 1970s, Quratulain became involved with the Orangi pilot project in Karachi, and began helping the residents of this poor township tackle urgent sanitation and sewage problems. But her community enterprise precipitated a family conflict, forcing her to choose between her work and life as a married woman with children. She chose the former, leaving home in 1983 and plunging into community-based development work. In 1992 she was reunited with her family.

Quratulain's work with pit latrines became the bedrock for government policy in developing low-cost sanitation in low-income areas. In 1988, she moved to Quetta to work on a water and sanitation project; later, as representative of an international agency, she helped the government of Balochistan set up about 1800 primary schools for girls in the province's backwaters.

Covering nearly 220,000 square miles, Balochistan, Pakistan's largest province, has less than seven percent of its population. Life quality indicators are abysmal: less than five percent have tapped drinking water, while the female literacy rate is under 15 percent.

"The East Timorese have to start from zero. They have to build their freedom into reality. They must take it one step at a time. Within time, progress will come about."

Paola Battagliola

Salesian Sisters

Sister Paola Battagliola (born 1952) is a dedicated missionary from Italy. She moved to East Timor in 1988 and set up two orphanages and a vocational training school for young girls in remote villages of Los Palos. Ever since, she has helped hundreds of East Timorese children attain better education and shelter in a volatile environment until the 1999 catastrophe. She now resides in Jakarta, as a Superior of a Salesian Sisters' School for East Timorese future young sisters.

When Sister Paola began her work as a missionary, she was assigned as the superior of three sisters. "We first arrived in Bakao city in the eastern part of East Timor, before moving to another remote area." They immediately set out for a remote mountain village named Venilale, located in the interior of the island. They had nothing but one suitcase each, containing their few belongings. "We worked very hard to adapt to the local culture and norms." Within ten years, two orphanages, a vocational training school for young women, two boarding facilities for highschool age orphan girls, two clinics, various youth groups, educational and health outreach programs for distant villages, and a center for street children were established. Today, there are a total of nine communities under the Salesian Sisters, both in Jakarta and Dili. "We took care of orphans; children abandoned by families and educated them in our orphanage. We wanted them to feel loved and appreciated. We also guided their spiritual knowledge." The two orphanages located in Venilale and Laga, in Los Palos district accommodate more than 240 children. The Sisters also opened health clinics near the orphanages to serve poor families. In the near future, the Salesian Sister wishes to open a new orphanage on Sumba Island, East Nusa Tenggara.

For the future, Sister Paola feels a huge amount of enthusiasm. "There is always hope along the way. We never give up our efforts. We have to work together. There should be coordination between church, organizations, networks and all people in harmony. We need to find our common ground. I like to dream. My dream is mainly for young people. I dream for them to get on their feet, help them prepare, help them find work or happiness in life. Help them clear their paths. Help them as a member of God's kingdom."

East Timor, a country of less than a million people, is struggling its way to democratic governance. The country survived the traumatic separation from Indonesia and is recovering with very slow, yet intensive, progress. Human rights violations have started to be revealed and the healing has begun.

Italy

Marta Benavides

Rural Cooperative of Planta Nueva
Lenca Civil Association
Highlander Center for Popular Education

Marta Benavides is a spiritual leader who has led many initiatives towards peace in El Salvador. Marta has faced great dangers and lost many friends to violence. She currently lives in Sonsonate, one of the most violent cities in El Salvador, and in Santa Ana where she cares for her elderly parents. In both places, she works with local people, manifesting peace through the creation of opportunities that nurture life, including training for livelihoods, cultural activities, education for sustainability and planting butterfly gardens.

Marta began working with marginalized communities as a student. Since then, her work has evolved into conflict transformation. Marta understands that one cannot force change: "You have to work with all the problems, because things do not change from one day to the next. Instead, we have to intentionally move from one stage to another according to our dreams. It is not about fighting and surviving. It is about living and being."

Due to assassinations and exile, Marta is one of the few remaining from her original group. During the war in El Salvador, Marta used "accompaniment" to enable her to work inside El Salvador. One time, she was accompanied by only one person when they were captured by the military. "The thing that most helped me through that was that I looked at the soldiers, and I realized that they were just young men. I realized they probably had been forced into the military, that they had no options in life, that they might be the only bread-winner in their families. And I no longer saw them with fear. I knew it would be hard for me — this was a very intense moment in my life — but, when I questioned myself, I knew that I would choose to do the same again."

Marta says that her love for El Salvador keeps her going. "Sometimes I wish I could stop because it is so difficult to see your country bleeding. There have been moments when I thought I could work within the government, or take a position of authority, but nobody is doing what I am doing. People have to see that transformation is possible. It will take a long time, and there is no glory in it, but it has to be done." Marta draws strength from her creativity. The butterfly gardens represent her love of life and El Salvador.

From 1980–1992, El Salvador was crippled by a civil war. During the 1980s, the military dictatorship received USD 6 billion in military aid from the USA. Peace agreements, signed in 1992, ended the armed conflict, but have not addressed the causes of the war or healed the society.

El Salvador

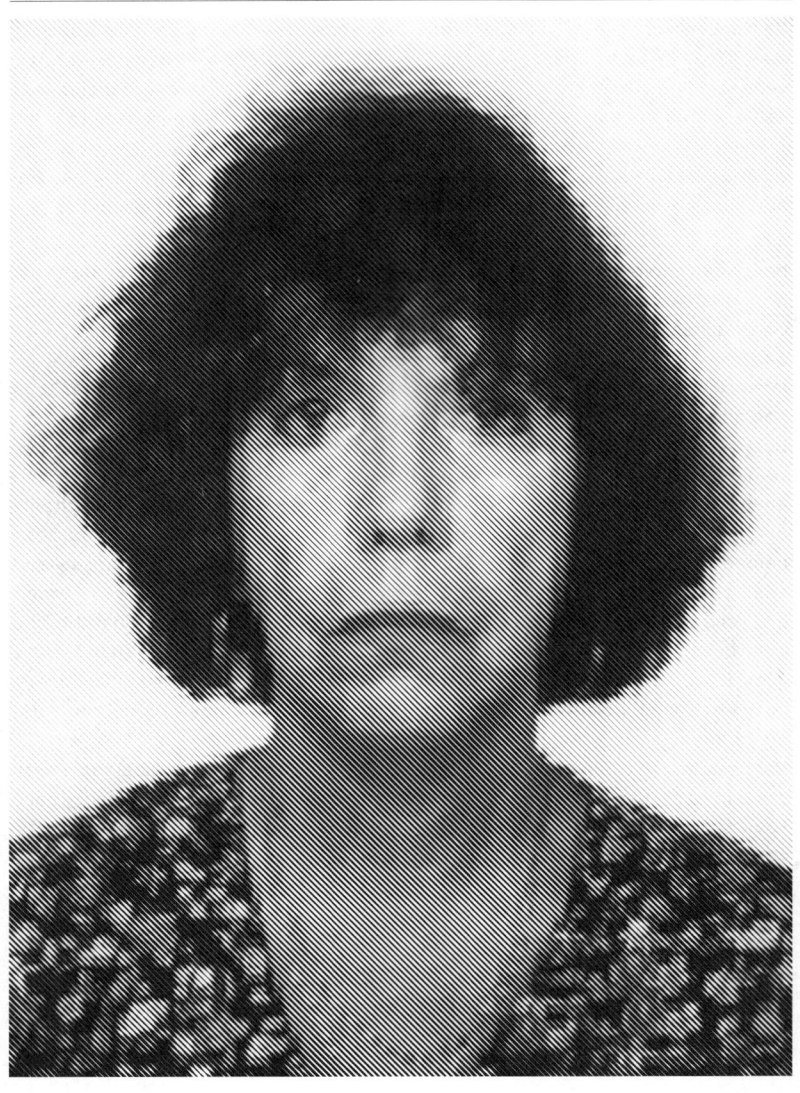

Elza Berquó

Centro Brasileiro de Análise e Planejamento (Brazilian Center for Planning and Analysis)

In 1969, Elza Berquó (1931) had to interrupt a brilliant career as a university professor because of the military regime. She was invited to work abroad, but she did not leave Brazil. The reason that made her stay is her belief in scientific knowledge as an important instrument against social injustice. Author of major researches on exclusion and population inequality, she provides the means for social movements and governmental entities to act.

Demographer, PhD in Biostatistics (Columbia University, New York), Elza Berquó was returning from a trip when she heard, on the radio, her name on a list of professors whose licenses had been revoked by the military dictatorship. "I was a professor at the School of Public Health in the University of São Paulo, and I was forced to retire. It was a tragedy, it was my life." On that same year, 1969, Elza and other well-known and persecuted academics founded the Brazilian Center for Planning and Analysis (Cebrap), a non-profitable organization, which aims to analyze the social reality of Brazil. They started to research and publish, and also to disturb the oppressive regime. When they published the book "São Paulo, Growth and Poverty" — showing the extraordinarily severe social inequality of the greatest Brazilian metropolis — a bomb was thrown into Cebrap. They did not give up.

Elza Berquó coordinates hundreds of researches about family structure, fecundity, population aging, reproductive health and sexual rights that were published in Brazil and abroad. She published the book "Young People on the Track of Public Policies" and coordinated the video "Breaking the Silence: Demolishing Racism in Schools." Aside from Cebrap, in 1982, on the country's transition to democracy, Elza founded the Nucleus of Population Studies of the University of Campinas (Nepo/Unicamp), where she currently coordinates the Reproductive Health and Sexuality Program. In 12 years, the Program has educated countless professionals from the entire country. In 1991, Elza also helped drawing up the Citizenship and Reproduction Committee (CCR), a place for debates and seminars. During that same year, she created, in partnership with the Mac Arthur Foundation, the first program for Afro-Brazilian researchers in Brazil.

Elza Berquó plays an important role as a member of official Brazilian dele-gations on many UN conferences: International Conference on Population and Development (Cairo, 1994); World Conference on Women (Beijing, 1995); and the Cairo + 5 International Conference (New York, 1999).

Elise Marie Biorn-Hansen Boulding

International Peace Research Association
Women's International League for Peace and Freedom (WILPF)
US Institute of Peace

For more than 50 years, Elise Boulding has helped to create networks of peace. Her work is founded in her Quaker faith and a spirituality that is grounded in listening and sharing. She has a special gift for envisioning a peaceful future and teaching others how to use envisioning to create peace. Elise cofounded the International Peace Research Association with her husband and served as its secretary general. Since its beginning, the organization has held 17 conferences in 16 countries. Elise is also former president of the Women's International League for Peace and Freedom (WILPF).

Norway was Elise's "safe place". Although she had grown up in the United States since the age of three, her bilingual parents spoke often of the beauty and peace of their home country. She was a college student when Norway was invaded during World War II, and was deeply affected. Elise's safe place was gone. Her profound understanding that peace was not a place, but a process, led her to join the Quaker faith, which is committed to dealing with violence by "reaching that of God in every human being".

Her years of organization and scholarship (she was chair of the sociology department at Dartmouth College) were also spent mothering five children. Her holistic approach to peace is grounded in everyday experiences. The conflict resolution skills she observed in her children's backyard sand play were the same ones required for international treaty negotiation at its best: listening, dialoguing, and sharing.

Central to Elise's uniqueness is her feeling and description of the "we-ness" of a world society and citizenship on planet earth. She brought the study of peace to academic stature through her development of courses at Dartmouth, and is recognized for her ability to write about nonviolence as both a philosophy and a practice. Through their organization, the International Peace Research Association, Elise and her husband have connected scholars and activists around the world in a quest for nonviolent conflict resolution. Elise served on the Board of Advisers of the Quaker UN Office and worked with Unesco's department of social science. A prolific author, she has written numerous books and helped launch newsletters for organizations such as Women Strike Peace. She was appointed by president Carter to the US Commission on Proposals for a National Academy of Peace and Conflict (now the US Institute of Peace) and was a 1990 Nobel Peace Prize nominee.

Elise began her work for peace during the 1950s in a political atmosphere that was suspicious and sometimes outright hostile toward such ideas. Because of her work, the study of peace is now a recognized field, with more understanding of the need for training in conflict resolution and mediation.

United States of America

"My motto is: 'If My people will humble themselves and pray and seek My face and turn from their wicked ways, then I will hear them and will forgive their sin and heal their land'."

Béatrice Félicité Bobo

Street children benefit from Béatrice Bobo's care, stop taking drugs and are freed from sex slavery, before returning to their homes. Since 1997, this 39-year-old widow has been raising three children, a niece and sheltering street children in her house, where she founded an evangelical mission. She does all her work at an individual level through counseling and intercession, door-to-door visits, audiovisual media and public speaking. She also reaches out and evangelizes to the political authorities in the Central Africa Republic.

Béatrice Félicité Bobo, a successful businesswoman, was defrauded of her business and no hope was left of recovering it. One day she met street children and heard God speaking to her, "Tell them about Jesus." She later discovered that in the capital, Bangui, an estimated 300,000 street children, some only five years old, lead a hand-to-mouth existence and some are caught in drugs and crime. She meets and listens to them, teaching them the ways of God. More than 400 street children have been reunited with their families or have found surrogate parents. She develops revenue-generating initiatives to help the children meet their needs. She sensitizes local churches to the children's plight and some come to her aid. Often, there are donations for the street children, but few to meet the constant basic needs for food, clothing and medicine, and none for her accumulated bills. Since her country is torn apart by war, corruption and ethnic conflict, she unites women from every status, regularly holding conferences and rallies to pray and work for national reconciliation and peace. Béatrice has had audiences with the prime minister and other government officials, who expressed solidarity with her and declared a period of prayer and fasting for the entire nation. Her vision of a peaceful future centers on all people heartedly returning to God.

The Central African Republic is ravaged by politico-military crisis and coup attempts. There is ineffective governance and rampant corruption. Children are most affected by the corruption and war.

"We will succeed in building a strong base for transforming the politics of power when together we weave a vision that in practice offers a way of life so alive it is impossible to resist."

Betty Burkes

Women's International League for Peace and Freedom (WILPF)
Hague Appeal for Peace
Cambridge Peace Commission

Betty Burkes (born 1943) is a lifelong educator and activist, working for a world where all human beings are celebrated for their brilliance and beauty, where people recognize their interconnectedness, where the earth is respected, and justice prevails. She has taught these principles in her Montessori preschool, brought them to the Women's International League for Peace and Freedom (as president, US section, and longtime board member), and used them in peace education in Albania, Cambodia, Niger, and Peru with the Hague Appeal for Peace and the UN Department of Disarmament Affairs.

Betty Burkes was born in Malvern, Ohio, in 1943. She is African-American, descended from enslaved people, and raised by working-class parents and loving grandmothers. After graduating from Ohio State University she taught in Ethiopia as a peace corps volunteer. Later, she founded a Montessori preschool on Cape Cod, serving as its director for 12 years, and offering young children an enriching learning environment where peacemaking and social justice mingled with the affirmation of childhood.

She has been involved with the Women's International League for Peace and Freedom (WILPF) as a branch member, as president (US section), and as a national board member (1989 to 2002), and is a member of the Cambridge Peace Commission. She served as pedagogical coordinator for the Hague Appeal for Peace in partnership with the UN Department of Disarmament Affairs in Albania, Cambodia, Niger, and Peru (2002 to 2005). The original mission of local organizations involved in this project was to disarm their communities. This emphasis shifted to the creation of programs that strengthen communities so that people can deal with problems differently, especially teaching young people alternative ways to handle conflicts so they no longer need knives and guns to protect themselves. Betty worked with local people to uncover their peacemaking traditions and to create programs and curricula, organizing to bring these traditions to the surface and to honor them.

Betty is a gifted writer, an inspiring speaker, and a loving collaborator. She has been honored with awards for antiracism and peacemaking, including the Fanny Lou Hamer Award and the NAACP Community Service Award, and was featured on the cover of Hope magazine (June 2004).

All her life, Betty Burkes has experienced the racism endemic in the United States. As an African-American woman she has constantly had to deal with both the racism and sexism of the wider society, specifically in the predominantly white organizations and communities where she has lived and worked.

United States of America

Urvashi Butalia

Zubaan Books
Kali for Women

Urvashi Butalia (born 1952) is the face and voice of feminist literature and publishing in India. In 1984, she set up Kali for Women, India's first feminist publishing house, from a little office in a garage and with almost no funds. Two decades later, Kali has succeeded in bringing to the fore the marginalized voices of Indian women.

Having worked with Oxford University Press, New Delhi, Urvashi Butalia thought extensively about setting up an exclusively feminist publishing house. In 1984, when she returned from London, she set up Kali for Women, India's first feminist publishing press, with the publisher and writer Ritu Menon. "Taking the Hindu goddess of power, Kali, as inspiration, I decided to dedicate my work to creating and carving spaces where women's voices could be heard, and where their wisdom and courage could be given the respect they deserved." Urvashi and Ritu had to quit their jobs to set up Kali, terribly short of cash, as a garage operation. Kali's arrival was greeted with some expectations and some skepticism. Distribution and marketing were a headache for a publisher as diminutive as Kali, but the women devised alternative logistics. In 2003, Kali for Women diversified into two sister imprints, with Urvashi setting up Zubaan Books (zubaan means tongue), which publishes books for young adults, a field that is fallow in India.

Urvashi is also an activist and a writer. Perhaps her best-known work is "The Other Side of Silence: Voices from the Partition of India", which has changed the historical perspective by focusing on those at the margins. She has also been part of groups working for conflict prevention and violence amelioration. As chairperson of the Aman Trust, she has worked in Kashmir and Northeast India, examining particularly the impact of conflict on the lives of women.

Urvashi has devoted more than two decades to the production and dissemination of knowledge to an undervoiced community. She has helped develop a space for, and corpus of, women's voices in the mainstream consciousness. She says: "The experience of working with women has been one I have never regretted, not for a day, not for a moment."

While a great deal was happening in the women's movement in India, it found little reflection in what was published. Mainstream publishers just did not consider women's writing seriously enough. The little that was published usually came from the west. But matters are changing swiftly.

India

Zaida Cabral

Danish International Development Agency (Danida)
ActionAid

Zaida Cabral, born in 1951 in Maputo (Mozambique), is an educationalist. She is currently an education advisor for the Danish NGO Danida in the Mozambiquan capital Maputo. She has a master's degree in education and has served as a researcher and as national director of primary education at the ministry of education. She was also a member of parliament. Her focus is on empowering women and the girl-child. She is one of the most prominent educationalists in Mozambique.

"Most women are really fighters for a better life," says Zaida Cabral about her observations of women for the past 20 years. But it could as well be her own life she is talking about. Born in a poor Muslim family in Mozambique, she could only complete four years of primary education. It was not until she was 19 years old that she was able to further her education — up to a master's degree in education which she gained at the age of 44. In between she struggled every step of the way and was supported by the people she worked with. "I think am a fighter," she says with a smile.

Becoming an educationalist was not her choice of career at all. But in post-colonial Mozambique, which had an illiteracy rate of 93 percent, the government opened doors for all to go to school and teachers were in high demand. Six months into her studies, she enjoyed it very much. Her first position after graduating was as a researcher for the Institute for Development of Education in Maputo. There she laid the foundation for a bilingual approach in primary education — which was after much resistance implemented 20 years later. In 1993, she moved to the ministry of education, and two years later she became a member of parliament for five years. Since 1995 she has worked as a consultant for international organizations and NGOs. Zaida is deeply involved in helping to develop a comprehensive education program for her country. She works at community level with schools and health centers. At national and regional level she lobbies tirelessly for access to education particularly for girls and the rural poor. "If you have women more educated, if they can make the choice between three or eight children, if they have opportunities, they will look at their lives differently," she says.

In 1979, when the colonialists, Portugal, pulled out of Mozambique, they left the country with few skilled workers and professionals. About 93 percent of the population was illiterate. In 2000, the literacy rate was 43 percent.

Reina Isabel Cálix

National Union of Peasants
Federation of Urban and Rural Women of Olancho

Resourceful since her childhood. A rural teacher since the age of 15. At age 33, she went into the field of adult education and started to take part of community social groups for the peasant causes. She went into the fight for the agrarian reform. She came close to two massacres, in 1972 and 1975. She survived and, in the following year, she began to organize groups of women. She is still a teacher. Nowadays, she teaches other apprentice teachers who, like herself, dream of creating a lullaby for world peace with their own words. That is Reina Isabel Cálix, a Honduran.

Since she was a child, she worked hard. Reina Isabel Cálix sold sweets prepared by her own hands under the watchful eye of her mother, a master in the art of making sweets. She was in the second grade but had never owned a pair of shoes. "I wore my first pair of shoes when I was 12." She is Honduran. She was born in 1939 in the poor neighborhood of Juticalpa, the main city of the province of Olancho.

When she finished the sixth grade, she asked her mother to help her to apply for a post in the rural area as an apprentice teacher. She got it. It was in 1954 and she earned 40 lempiras (US$ 2.5) a month. She moved on to other schools an — for ten years — taught pupils from first to third grade. Her path changed when she was 25 years old and the Radio-phonic Schools opened a different path. She was able to teach adults how to read and write. She also was taught: In the 1960s she participated in the fight for the agrarian reform, joining marches and occupying land. In 1972, the six peasant massacre happened very close to her. In 1975, the army broke up a march of 5000 people. The Honduran army occupied the headquarters of the National Union of Peasants, the Santa Clara Center. People were killed. Others were detained and then murdered. Reina was a witness. She survived. Eight months passed. When the army left the Santa Clara Center, only the walls and roof remained. No one wanted to go back. The women took the first step, settling themselves in the Center and beginning to organize them.

For 18 years now, Reina Isabel Cálix has taught apprentice teachers, 400 of them. 17,000 children from 90 villages, in 12 municipalities in Olancho, have received pre-school education thanks to them. 50 schools for adults, one itinerant sewing workshop, a course for qualifying bakers and one for horticulture are now available. Today, Reina is 67 years old and she keeps going.

Inequities in Honduras have trapped more than 70% of its rural population in poverty. Children in the countryside have less education than children in the cities. Women still have a weak political base and, in the workplace, they work in poorly remunerated jobs.

Honduras

Carmen Rosa Campos Mendoza

Women's Association for the Promotion of Sustainable Development in Chulucanas (Amprodesdch)
Committee against Poverty in Chulucanas

Carmen Rosa Campos Mendoza (33) uses dialogue and consensus to improve the lives of those around her. She works with the Federation of Shanty Towns, the Women's Association for the Promotion of Sustainable Development and for the Committee against Poverty in Chulucanas, Peru. Carmen has fought hardship, abuse and indifference, but has never lost her tenderness. She believes that "changing a country is the responsibility of many, and women are part of that process."

An outstanding ability for organizing, generating dialogue and overcoming misunderstandings: these are the tools which Carmen Rosa Campos Mendoza (33) uses to strengthen regional organizations and to transform the world around her. She is a mother of four boys and one girl, who dedicates herself to improving the lives of those around her.

Carmen went to the impoverished rural district of Morropón, Peru, and was inspired since an early age by her father's untiring work for the community. When he was unfairly arrested based on terrorism charges, Carmen fought for six years for his release, at a time when she suffered domestic abuse.

She developed her leadership skills gradually, starting off in college and Church groups. At age 22, she became president of the mothers' group in her shanty town, Luis de la Puente Uceda, an impoverished area. There, she put in place a system of job rotation so that everyone had a chance to be the director, a method which she now uses wherever she goes. She taught women that they can do more than stay home and helped them learn about health, human rights, the environment and the use of water. She then went on to build organizations such as the Federation of Shanty Towns and the Women's Association (Amprodesdch). She is also one of the promoters of the Committee against Poverty in Chulucanas. In her work, Carmen tries to empower women and people of disadvantaged backgrounds. She pushes for public policy changes and presents local authorities with solutions to combat poverty and discrimination, drawing some of her motivation from Gandhi, "who sought peace by using non-violent means." Carmen dreams of becoming a member of Congress and helping Peru develop a greater self-awareness. "We must have a firmer grasp on reality, so that we can bring about real changes. We must all take responsibility and women must help to fight inequalities."

"Mortality among mothers is very high in Piura. One of the causes is the inaccessibility of medical centers. The other is the high staff turnover in hospitals."

Peru

Blanca Campoverde

Fundación Niñez y Vida
Tierra de Hombres Ecuador

This year, she will complete 50 years of life. Thirty of them were spent educating the children of underprivileged classes. Blanca Campoverde, early orphan and adolescent mother, came from a poor family. Now she is one of the most important figures in the education sector in her country. She directs the Fundación Niñez y Vida (Childhood and Life Foundation), an organization that takes care of the education and health of children and youth.

She spent her childhood in Loja, a small city in Ecuador. At age 17, she became a mother. As a teacher, and already mother of two children, she moved to Quito, the capital. She began her work in a pioneer day care center, supported by Swiss personnel, in a poor neighborhood. Today she directs the center. She takes care of severely malnourished children, in need of affection. With the parents, she has succeeded in reducing the levels of alcoholism, drug addiction and domestic violence. "Blanca is a very special person, with a great intelligence. She is a self-taught person that people even ask in what university she has studied," says Florence de Goumoëns, the Swiss educator, who has known Blanca for more than 20 years.

When Blanca Campoverde arrived at the day care center, many years ago, she found the classrooms empty. She visited the houses in the neighborhood to convince the fathers and mothers about the need to educate their children. They were distrustful. The Swiss had blond hair and blue eyes. "Are you sure they do not want to steal the children and take them away?" they asked. But, with the presence of Blanca, a native with a kind face, they relaxed. The day care center became full: boys and girls, toys, colors, educational materials, fruit, music — until nothing else could fit. The educators, fathers and mothers built a bigger center, and then they built another one for young people. The girls and the boys know how to make bread, play music, create handicrafts, and they walk throughout the neighborhood, content, showing everyone the lettuce that they harvested after learning a difficult word: "hidroponía" (hydroponics is a technique for growing plants without soil). Blanca says: "Treating children with love is the only way to guarantee that, tomorrow, we will have human beings who are capable of contributing to peace."

Toctiuco is a poor neighborhood of Quito. Its population is the fruit of the wave of migrants that came in the 1970s. Oil production attracted peasants looking for employment. Today, the inhabitants of Toctiuco number approximately 25,000 settlers — both property owners and renters.

Ecuador

Tatyana Chabrova

Bolalar va Kattalar (Children and Adults)

Tatyana Chabrova (born 1955) is an educator and director of the NGO Bolalar va Kattalar (Children and Adults) which she founded in 1998 to explore, understand, and link the interests of both adults and children. Tatyana is a pioneer in developing new teaching methodologies and including social, governance, and rights issues in education. She has published over 30 books on children's education and has developed and delivered many methodology courses for teachers and educational experts. She is also the creator of a newspaper written by children called "Our Rights."

For the past 25 years, Tatyana Chabrova has been involved in educational, cultural, and social initiatives with children and adults. She began her teachers' training in Uzbekistan, and in 1988, she left for Moscow and Nizhny Novgorod to further her studies in that field. In the same year she won the prestigious Republican Contest of Educational Games in Developing Children's Creative Ability. Tatyana is the creator of new teaching methods for which she has received recognition from Mrs. Putin, wife of the Russian President, who sent her a letter in which she wrote, "I am excited about your books as these can serve to develop important ties between Uzbekistan and Russia."

Tatyana initiated a theater project in which children and adults act together. The actors create performances devoted to exploring social problems — Aids, drug abuse, and children's rights. Because of her efforts in this regard, Nane Annan, Kofi Annan's wife, wrote to her: "You do wonderful work for Aids awareness and drug prevention in Uzbekistan." Tatyana also set up a free art school for talented children, and organized children's art exhibitions in Uzbekistan, the Netherlands, USA, and Israel. In 1999, she and her children's group participated in the International Conference, Aral Sea — A Children's View, in Karakalpakstan. Since 1998, she has worked as the director of the NGO, Bolalar va Kattalar (Children and Adults) that she founded. The children in her organization created a newspaper called "Our Rights" for which they interview, draw, write articles, and take photos. She also published a book titled "A Constitution for Children" in which students learn about the Uzbek Constitution and practice writing and implementing a constitution. Tatyana says, "My books are my children and I always give all my heart to my children. If my work helps people, I am happy."

As a new state, Uzbekistan is undergoing significant social and economic transformation. The new priorities for this young state are democratic reform, developing a legal culture, and economic growth. There is also a need to transform teaching methodologies and to include awareness of social issues.

Uzbekistan

"Influencing age-old tradition requires one's patience and perseverance. You must be humble, use tact and respect their beliefs."

Violet Chavula

Church of Central Africa Presbyterian (Ccap)

Violet Chavula is the women's coordinator with the Church of Central Africa Presbyterian (Ccap), in charge of Blantyre presbytery. After living in London for several years, she moved to a remote village in Malawi. She is engaged in advocacy for the rights of girls and women and the protection of orphans.

The four girls could not grasp their predicament. Soon after their mother died after delivering a fifth daughter, their father deserted them. They faced another tragedy when the little baby fell sick and died shortly after.

An 80-year-old woman in their village, saddened by their tragedy, adopted the girls. They moved into the woman's little hut surviving on her meager resources.

Victoria Chavula was stunned by this woman's compassion and dismayed by the younger community's apathy. She mobilized the youth to renovate the woman's hut and the community's support for the woman and the girls.

But soon, Violet faced another disturbing issue. The old woman had no plans for the girls' education, but rather for them to mature and get married. She relentlessly implored the woman and eventually convinced her to send the girls to school. Stirred by this event, Violet began to advocate for girls' education within the community and started a program to care for orphans in the village and its environs.

Sixteen years on, Violet's commitment to this cause has not waned. "Fighting attitudes is no simple game," she whispers behind her modest smile.

In parts of Malawi, girls' enrolment in primary school is low. Girls repeat classes and drop out more than boys do. Women form the majority of the country's illiterate. Girls make up 39 percent of secondary school students and only 28 percent at the tertiary level.

Lucie Cheng

College of Journalism and Communications at Shixin University

Lucie Cheng is publisher of both Li Newspaper and Pots, dean of the College of Journalism and Communications at Shixin University, president of Bibliography Literature Publishing Inc, and professor at the University of California, Los Angeles. She served Chinese workers in Chinatown in the USA before she returned to Taiwan to inherit the Li Newspaper from her father. She opened the Social Development Research Institute at Shixin University and has promoted a series of alternative multimedia courses. She has been active in social and women's movements for 30 years.

Lucie Cheng was born in Hong Kong in 1939. She is one of the daughters of Cheng Shewo, a famous journalist and writer. She received her education in Beijing, Hong Kong, and Taiwan. In 1958, she went to the USA and obtained the master's degree in literature and journalism. Later, she received the doctorate degree of social science from the University of Hawaii.

For the past 30 years, she has incorporated the science of learning into social movements and education. Cheng served Chinese workers in Chinatown in the USA in her early life. As a scholar, she insists that research should be combined with community work. As such, she pays attention to long-neglected minority groups like the Chinese living in the USA, especially Chinese women. Her research on Chinese women in the USA in 1979 led to many academics taking up the study of overseas Chinese women.

In 1990, Cheng returned to Taiwan and inherited the Li Newspaper from her father, and the challenge to maintain the newspaper's principle of caring for vulnerable groups. She also took over the College of Journalism and Communications (later part of Shixin University) to train journalists for Taiwan. She opened the Social Development Research Institute at Shixin University and has promoted a series of alternative multimedia courses on cross-discipline and cross-religion. Cheng's recent research has focused on pornography in Taiwan and she has been working with other scholars and sex workers for the latter's rights. She has also drawn attention to sex industry policies and to the contribution of sex workers to the economy.

Though the ban on night activities was lifted in Taiwan in the 1980s, Taiwanese tend to be conservative. The Taiwan officials attract tourists using the porn industry but condemn it in public and arrest unlicensed prostitutes regularly.

China, Taiwan

Jana Civikova

Aspekt

Founded by Jana Civikova in 1993, the feminist organization Aspekt was the first to introduce feminist issues in Slovakia. Starting as a cultural journal, its spectrum widened into publishing, a feminist library, lectures, and workshops. Jana now concentrates on a feminist anthology and on Equal, an educational cooperation program on gender roles, stereotypes, and gender sensitive pedagogy. Workshops for teachers are being prepared and Aspekt is starting a three-year pilot project in a primary school.

Having left her original profession, she feels like an expert in everything and nothing. Jana Civikova (42) has not made use of her doctorate in literature for the last 12 years. The founder of the feminist organization Aspekt sits on a wooden conference table thinking how the mission of introducing feminism in Slovakia changed her life, wondering how a forerunner like Aspekt could be counted as a fringe group. During her student days, Jana Civikova was introduced to the famous book "Der kleine Unterschied und seine grossen Folgen" (The Little Difference and the Consequences) by Alice Schwarzer, and it took her quite a while to realize that everything that she had felt and all that had made her angry in the world was feminist. And ironically, that was after she got married. Living with her husband and her daughter (15), two dogs, tortoises, a chameleon, and Australian lizards in a 64-square meter apartment on the outskirts of the Slovakian capital Bratislava convinced Jana that irony helps her family survive in an environment so contrary to their moral ideals. Aspekt basically consists of only two women, Jana and her business partner. Jana Civikova stresses the importance of their partnership: "If one of us died, the other one would not be able to keep Aspekt alive." Sadly, there is no successor. And yet it is understandable, she says. What younger woman would like to take the responsibility, to fight and struggle like Jana and her partner have done for so many years? She does not complain. She is just worried about the fact that they are misunderstood. "We are treated like lunatics but we are not — it is all about surviving." When Jana and her partner are working like crazy these days it shows how extremely suitable the combination of a former Communist Pioneer and a Catholic is: "It makes a perfect workaholic team."

Up to the 1990s, feminism was absent in Slovakia. There were no media written from a feminist perspective, by women for women. Issues such as patriarchy, violence against women, reproductive rights were not discussed in any medium.

Slovakia

Stella Cornelius

Conflict Resolution Network (CRN)
United Nations Association of Australia (UNAA)
Australian Center for Peace and Conflict Studies, University of Queensland

Born in 1919, Australian Stella Cornelius has devoted a lifetime to peace, conflict resolution, and social justice issues. Her unique contribution to global peace has been to make access to conflict resolution training widely available. These skills are now used in workplaces, universities, schools, community organizations, and by individuals. For her lifelong community and peace work, Stella was awarded the Order of the British Empire (1979), Order of Australia (1987), and an honorary Doctor of Letters (1999). She is acknowledged as a Peace Messenger of the United Nations.

Stella Cornelius (86), the founder of "conflict resolution," runs her own home in Sydney, enjoys cooking fine food, drives a car, uses a computer and is thankful her memory "is reasonably good." On a typical day, her alarm goes off at 5:50 a.m. and she devotes her first hour to exercise: "For almost every day of my life, I have done workouts — breathing, arm exercises and such to make sure that physically I am as fit as possible." For Stella, the physical and the material, the intellectual and the emotional are only different ways to describe one entity and one personality. What is good in theory has to be good in practice. Unlike many of her generation, Stella enjoys the blessings of modern technology: "Every morning as I log on, the world comes rolling in at my feet." From her suburban home in Chatswood, she reaches out to people across the world with her message of peaceful conflict resolution: "The life of the elderly has not been better in any previous generation. Besides the internet, telephone hook-ups to international conferences are a great boon." Stella keeps abreast with the happenings in the world and is an avid reader of philosophy, history, literature, and fiction. It is not chocolates that she craves for, but "I suffer from psycho greed. I want to be involved in everything." She enjoys lunch with friends by the water and often has working luncheons at her home. For Stella, "work and play have deliciously mixed into a savory soup." For someone who has led such an exciting life, when asked would she like to write her autobiography, she quipped, "No, I am far too busy living up my life to write about it." So as the day draws to a close, it is back to the computer for Stella, connecting her to the conflict resolution world, replying to the many emails demanding her attention.

Stella Cornelius used her extensive management skills to set up the Conflict Resolution Network. Its purpose is to research, develop, teach, and implement the theory and practice of conflict resolution. Her model of conflict resolution is now used at global, national, local, and individual levels.

Australia

Jean Corrneck

Mother of Peace Community

Jean Corrneck has spent most of her working life as a social worker and nurse. She specialized in psychiatry nursing. After retirement she dedicated her life towards creating a sanctuary of love and care for Zimbabwe's orphaned and vulnerable children. She established the Mother of Peace Community which takes care of 170 children, from infants to school-going children. The children receive health care, social support, and are brought up in Zimbabwean culture and tradition. The orphanage also benefits members of the adjacent rural community through its farming and building activities.

Jean Corrneck attended mission schools in the Midlands and Masvingo provinces for her primary and high-school education. Thereafter she trained in general nursing and midwifery and took care of orphans in her own home. She later obtained a certificate in psychiatric nursing and a degree in social science in the UK. She returned to Zimbabwe in 1980. She worked in psychiatric clinics, conducted research and worked in government administration before retiring from the civil service in 1993. Jean recalls how the surroundings looked like before the children's orphanage was built. It was a remote area with no basic amenities. "There was not even a passable road or bridge to the proposed site of the orphanage. It was unimaginable to think that a building would be constructed there," she says adding, "There was no water supply close by, no ablution block or shops to buy food." Nonetheless, a road was constructed and piping was laid to take water to the site. The first house was completed after several months. Almost immediately on completion, the department of social welfare brought five children to the orphanage. Jean quickly realized that she needed to employ some local women as caregivers for the children. Meanwhile more children were being brought to the orphanage. Her vision was to find a way to make the land productive for agriculture. Other challenges for Jean were to improve both the nutrition of the children and their basic health care. A lot of farming activities dominate the 255-hectare land and the food is used to feed the children. The orphanage also rears cattle, chickens, rabbits, ducks and turkeys, all for the upkeep of the children.

Zimbabwe is currently experiencing unprecedented poverty, hunger and diseases forcing many Zimbabweans to flee the country in search of a better life. The spread of HIV/Aids is an added burden to the fragile economy and has given rise to millions of HIV/Aids orphans.

Zimbabwe

Neera Desai

Research Centre for Women's Studies (RCWS)
India Centre for Human Rights and Law (ICHRL)
Sparrow

Working with the Srimathi Nathibai Damodar Thackersey Women's University (SNDTWU), Neera Desai (born 1925) established two initiatives — the Research Center for Women's Studies (RCWS) and the Rural Development Program (RDP) — that endure to this day. She is also one of the pioneers of the feminist movement. Over the years, she has been associated with a number of research and women's organizations, and is a trenchant critic of the right-wing Narendra Modi government in Gujarat.

Neera Desai, doctor of sociology, was born into a highly educated and liberal family. Her education at some of the best institutions in the country exposed her to various intellectual currents, especially leftist political trends, which were prevalent then. In 1954, Neera joined the SNDTWU, establishing several new initiatives there, two of which were particularly significant — the RCWS and the RDP — as integral to the university's grassroots activities. At the time, the feeling in the academy was that, since the Indian constitution guaranteed gender equality, and there were no visible barriers for women's entry into higher education, having an exclusive women's university was "unnecessary". The SNDTWU groped for a new identity and rationale for its existence, and readily accepted Neera's suggestions. Nonetheless, she had to struggle to get the seriousness of feminist concerns accepted.

Neera has also contributed to the critical examination of policies that tended to marginalize women in the development process. Considered one of the pioneers of the feminist movement in the country, she has been a member of policymaking bodies, and was part of the Task Force on Education and Communication for Women in Self-Employment (1987 to 1988).

Over the years, Neera has also been associated with various research, and women's, organizations. She founded the Indian Sociological Association in 1951, and the Indian Association of Women's Studies in 1981. She is, furthermore, a trenchant critic of the right-wing government in Gujarat, and supports investigations into human rights' violations by the incumbent Narendra Modi government.

In the years following independence, the feeling in academia was that the Indian constitution guaranteed enough in terms of gender equality and that there was no need for separate research into women's issues. But both the education system and the policymaking bodies needed an overhaul.

India

Shanta Devi

Ankur–Society for Alternatives in Education

Shanta Devi's work with nonformal education is driven by her conviction that education is essential to a person's understanding of the world. She worked alone, and then with the Ankur — Society for Alternatives in Education, trying to reach out, particularly to women, children, and youth. Beside having supported human rights issues, Shanta campaigns for slum dwellers' rights, supporting HIV+ persons, sexual minorities, and fighting for nuclear disarmament. At 75, she is revered as "Shanta toofani" (thunderous).

Shanta Devi (born 1929) grew up watching-and was deeply disturbed by-the prejudice of her upper-caste Brahmin family against other castes. When she was 33, her husband died, leaving her to fend for herself and seven children. What followed was a period of abject poverty and ceaseless toil. Through her concern for her children's education and efforts to educate other children, Shanta was taken by the need to complete her own studies. Joining an adult education center for women, she completed her high school. Bitten by the bug, Shanta began teaching children informally after she completed her education in 1960. Her move to Delhi in 1977 pointed her in a new direction: she came in touch with Ankur, an NGO that provides nonformal education to economically deprived children, and joined it two years later. Beside her work with the Ankur nonformal education centers, Shanta spent extra time every evening at nonformal education centers for women, children, and youth. When her children grew up enough to be autonomous, Shanta began working full-time. She fought for the rights of slum dwellers, laborers, factory workers, rickshaw-pullers, autorickshaw drivers, street-children, hawkers and vendors, fish workers, blind children, and many more.

Over the years, Shanta has been involved, in every capacity imaginable, a wide range of issues — the Mathura Rape Case, the Roop Kanwar Sati (widow self-immolation), the Bhopal gas leak tragedy, the 1984 riots, housing-rights issues, child labor, domestic workers, jhuggi-jhonpri (slum cluster) issues, discrimination against HIV+ people, the Narmada Bachao Andolan, gay-lesbian rights, the antinuclear bomb campaign, and unemployment.

At 75, she is still active in protests, demonstrations, seminars, conventions, and workshops. There is enough reason why she is known as the "dharna (protest) lady" and "Shanta toofani".

In India, where almost a third of the population live below the poverty line and literacy hovers at the halfway mark (less than 40 percent for women), formal education is a luxury. Nonformal education that is molded to needs and circumstances has a better chance of reaching most people.

India

Mara Régia di Perna

Mara Régia di Perna (1952) is one of the pioneers of radio communication produced for women of popular social classes. She is the creator of many programs that educate, mobilize and entertain. One of them is "Natureza Viva" (Live Nature), which reaches the immensity of the Legal Amazon and foments a network of solidarity and services among female listeners.

Mara Régia has a passion for radio that began when she was six years old. Her grandmother used to ask for total silence when it was time for the radio soap opera. In exchange, she offered them cookies. Mara loved not only the cookies, but also the enchantment of the radio voices. "I am completely fascinated by this form of language; it goes straight to the heart."

As an adult, she used her fascination for radio as a tool for educating, mobilizing and entertaining millions of women in the city and in the forest. "I communicate services. I apprehend, I bring and I multiply information that influences and changes lives." On her shows, there are valuable tips regarding female health: how to prevent sexually transmitted diseases/Aids, uterus and breast cancers; precautions regarding childbirth, menopause and osteoporosis. She talks about sexual and domestic violence, child education, sexuality and environment. She stimulates women's self-esteem and favors the creation of income sources. "In order to be independent, you need to make your own money."

Her voice reaches places where radio is the predominant mean of communication, and proof of that is the fact that batteries are considered a primary necessity. In the heart of the Amazon, the female coconut breakers (women who gather coconuts and extract essences that are used to produce soaps, oils, etc.), cassava planters, laundresses, artisans and rural women in general tune in to listen to what Mara has to say. The program is highly interactive: she teaches, learns and shares. Women read recipes for medicinal herbs; they warn each other about the traffic conditions on the roads and about the navigation conditions in the rivers. They share their intimacies. They multiply methods of reaching goals. They are people who sometimes speak Portuguese incorrectly, but they think correctly.

The radio shows directed by Mara Régia are heard in all nine states of the Legal Amazon. It has a population of over 19 million inhabitants, in an area of over five million square kilometers. The region receives the least assistance from the government.

Brazil

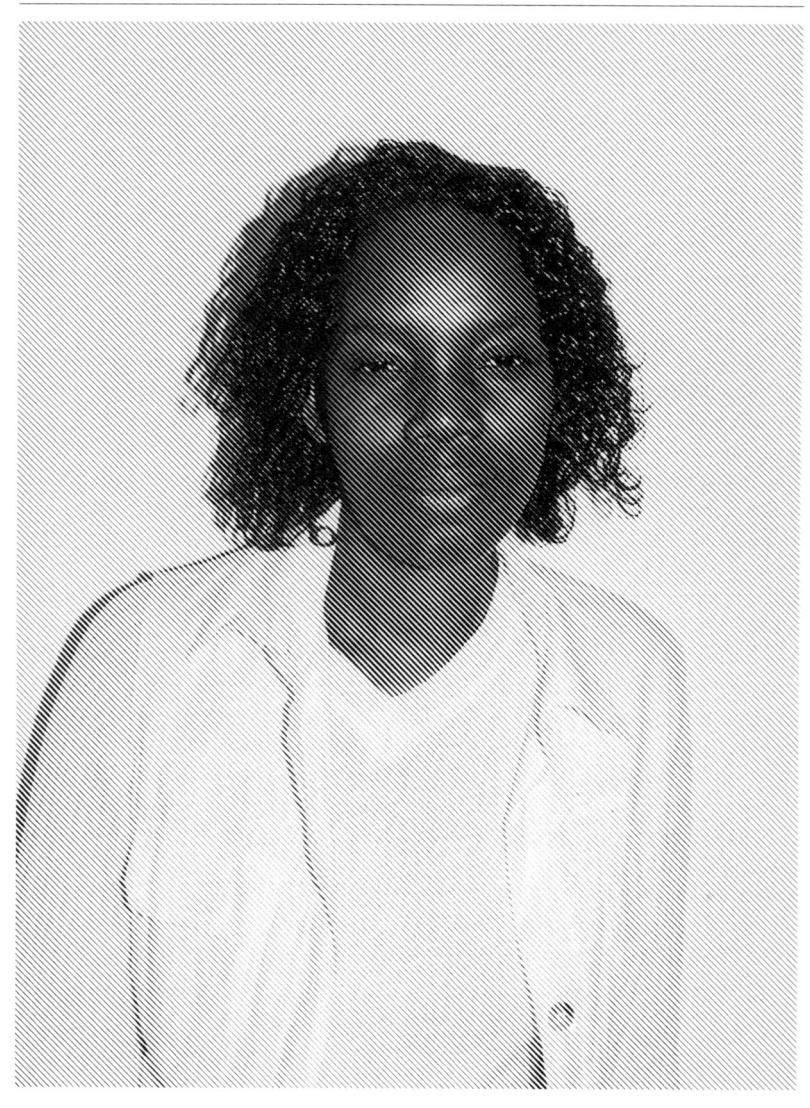

Jenet B Dlamini

Disabled Action Group (DAG)

Jenet Dlamini was born in Kwazulu Natal in South Africa in 1967. Due to her mother's ill health, she had to drop out of school and seek employment. At 23 she had a baby girl who was diagnosed with physical and psychological disabilities. This began Jenet's journey of discovery into the difficulties of raising a child with disabilities. In 1998 she joined a local group of mothers with disabled children, which merged in 2001 with other small groups to form a regional advocacy body, the Disabled Action Group (DAG). Jenet manages the local daily care center.

For those who live with children with disabilities, the road is very steep. Jenet Dlamini knows this very well from first-hand experience. "Life was difficult when I had to bring my daughter up. It feels like a burden, a challenging one, especially for the poor," she says. Out of the tough experience she had with bringing up her daughter, she founded the Thendanani Local Parents Center. This was a support group for people affected with disabilities. In 2001 this group was integrated in to a regional body called DAG. She was appointed center manager. The DAG center helps children living with disabilities and those who are affected by a disability and want to learn more about it. There is a day center that provides a hazard-free environment for the disabled. The center also provides wheel chairs and furniture for the disabled. The children are empowered to look for work opportunities in the commercial world.

Kwazulu Natal is one of the poorest provinces in South Africa. In the summer, diarrheal diseases are widespread, while in the winter people suffer from lung diseases. Factional fights are commonplace and HIV/Aids rates are the highest in the country. Hence disabilities, particularly among children, are not a priority.

South Africa

Douangdeuane Bounyavong

Douangdeuane Bounyavong (born 1947) is dedicated to the promotion of literacy and cultural experience through books in a country with a very limited reading tradition, due to lack of education and resources. She founded and is now directing and writing for a small independent publishing house, which focuses on titles for children and women, securing the necessary funding through successful networking abroad. She has established many libraries in rural regions and is working to improve the working conditions and quality of teachers.

Douangdeuane looks very intellectual with her delicate features and alert eyes behind gold-rimmed glasses. She goes around wearing a sinh, the traditional Laotian silk skirt. As an expert in Lao textiles she has written two volumes on the subject. But her best-known book is her family's story entitled, "When Mother was in Prison". Douang comes from a distinguished background. Her grandfather was a prominent poet and scholar, her deceased husband was one of Laos' foremost authors. She went to a teacher's college in Vientiane, studied in France and was later head of a high school. "I grew up with the love of books and find it sad that most children in my country know nothing of that wealth", she muses. "They learn to read in school, but afterwards they forget it. "In fact it is hard to encounter a reader in Laos.

So, in her small private publishing company, Douang concentrates on publishing high quality books for children, often illustrated by one of her two daughters who work in her enterprise. In order to make the books widely accessible, she has founded libraries all over the country and she gives story-telling seminars to teachers, "You must introduce the children to the beauty of the imaginary world to make them want to read about it," she says. At the same time, she researches women's and children's welfare and publishes her suggestions on how to improve these. She raises the finances for her activities by efficient lobbying with NGOs in many different countries. And she never gives up. "Many of my visions I will never be able to realize. But if one dream fails, another one comes to life."

After the long war, there are no worthwhile newspapers in Laos and books are prohibitively expensive. The country is swamped with trashy television shows from Thailand. Making good books accessible to the people of Laos is a means of strengthening their cultural identity.

Ingrid Eide

Against Nuclear Weapons
No to Nuclear Weapons

Ingrid Eide is a member of the Board of the United Nations Association, Norway. She co-founded the Peace Research Institute in Oslo in 1959, one of the first centers of peace research in the world. She has served a member of parliament and Deputy Minister of Education. She was an active member of the Executive Board of the United Nations Educational, Scientific and Cultural Organization (Unesco) and an early supporter of its Culture of Peace program. Ingrid is the former head of the Division of Women in Development of the United Nations Development Program (UNDP).

Ingrid Eide grew up in a suburb outside of Oslo during World War II. Both her parents were teachers, and were involved in the Resistance. Ingrid remembers lying awake at nights worrying about her mother and father being arrested and taken away. At the time, the Nazis were using her local school as a military camp, so she was unable to attend class. Mostly, her parents taught her at home, but sometimes she would go with her father, and sit in the back of his classroom.

One of her earliest memories is traveling through town with her father to the school where he worked. Next to her on the tram was a German soldier. "I looked at him and thought, maybe he has a little girl at home, just like me. It seems as if we could not be that different," she muses. As the war progressed Ingrid was sent away to spend a year with relatives on the west coast, as her parents felt she would be safer there. "My time in this small village was invaluable to my later work," she recollects. "I learned how a community works, how everyone has to contribute and work together." Ingrid's father was arrested and sent to a prison camp in Kirkenes, in the north of Norway. "When he came home he weighed 45 kilos," she remembers.

After the war was over, the awful truth emerged. Pictures of dead bodies in Auschwitz, destruction, the horror of war. Ingrid Eide was happy about the peace, but at the same time determined that this must never happen again. The seeds of a long political career for peace had been sown.

The Norwegian No to Nuclear Weapons aims to reduce nuclear arms, and impose an international ban on such arms. It also opposes the use of nuclear power. One of the main goals is to influence Norway in supporting the UN and other international organizations with their anti-nuclear campaigns.

Norway

"If we reach out to others with peace in our hearts, we exemplify what has to be done for the happiness of humankind."

Betty Faye

Red Cross Mbour; Association des Femmes Teinturières (Women Dyer Association); Association "Aimer et Respecter les Aînés" (Association "Love and Respect for the Elders")

Betty Faye was born in 1936 in Fatick, Senegal, into a large extended family. Thus, she learned early on that solidarity and respect are major assets for peace. When she was 20, she took up teaching and came to realize this profession inspired in her a strong desire to share the hope of a better future. She also created associations to support women and children and assumed responsibility for the local chapter of the Red Cross over which she still presides.

Betty Faye often went home late when her professional obligations kept her at work. Once, exhausted by a long day, she took a horse-drawn cab to go home without knowing that the half-starved horse had slaved away since morning pulling a variety of loads in the sweltering heat and under the blows of a whip. The horse fell and Betty was thrown onto the rocky road. But help was soon at hand; neighbors, family members, carters, men and women, young and old escorted her to the medical center which she left late in the evening with her arm in a cast and a sling. The crowd had grown larger in the meantime and decided to accompany her. It was quite a sight to see her sitting like a queen on the cart, moved to tears by this procession; moved also by the multitude of voices united in a hymn that said: "Praise to you Betty, you who live for the well-being of others." She stood up, supported by one of her sisters. She smiled, said a few words of thanks and encouragement to the crowd and told them: "This broken arm is the will of God. But as of tomorrow the struggle continues for our dignity, for our happiness, in harmony and peace."
Betty's commitment to peace is deep. She took possession of the word "peace" and made this word her reason for living, the light that guides her action and is the primary objective of her everyday struggle for human dignity. When I asked her about the meaning this word has for her, she answered with a serenity that revealed nothing of the illness that has kept her away from her country and her family for a long time: "Without peace our future will fall apart."

Education is the best way to inspire humans with the ideal of respect for others — regardless of origin, race, or religion. All conflicts are born of non-respect for other people and their rights. In other words, the condition for peace is mutual respect and generosity.

Senegal

भाई भी घर का काम कराये

तभी तो बहना पढ़ने जाये

Mohini Giri

Guild of Service
War Widows Association
Rail Chetna Yatra

Mohini Giri (born 1938) is a pioneer in empowering the marginalized, especially marginalized women, widows, Dalits, tribals, and the destitute. She began grassroots work when social work, or welfare activity, was considered little more than patronizing charity. The new dimension she gave to social work in India is now recognized as developmental work, where the marginalized are seen as architects of their own destiny, not as beneficiaries of "handouts".

When she was very young, Mohini Giri lived with her mother at the Shivananda Ashram (the divine life society) in Rishikesh. Swami Shivananda, a good surgeon, operated on thousands of patients who flocked to him. Mohini, at only nine years old, was his nurse. It is likely that the first seeds of social work were planted in her mind then. She married into a family of freedom-fighters, who encouraged her, around the time of the subcontinent-defining India-Pakistan war in 1971, to involve herself with social work. Mohini started taking care of wounded soldiers at the military hospitals, an experience that moved her powerfully. "They made me promise that I would take care of the families they left behind," she says. "The War Widows Association was established that year (1971) with those promises ringing in my ears."

Mohini also founded the Guild of Service, and runs homes and counseling centers for the rehabilitation and empowerment of destitute women and children at Vrindavan, Godhra, Srinagar, Sawai Madhopur, and Mathura. She has also been very active in the political empowerment of women. The aim of the Rail Chetna Yatra, another creative effort of Mohini's, is to raise public awareness about the demand for a 33 percent reservation for women in parliament. It was also due to her efforts that the first Mahila Parivarik Lok Adalat (a people's court for women) was organized to enable women in remote areas to access rapid justice.

It was Mohini who instigated the empowerment of the marginalized, beginning her grassroots work when social work, or welfare activity, was seen as charity. The dimension she has given to social work in India is now recognized as developmental work, where the marginalized are understood as architects of their own destiny, not as beneficiaries of largesse.

Mohini's work involves a whole range of issues: widows who were, and continue to be, among the most marginalized women in India; a 33 percent reservation for women in parliament; rapid-action people's courts for women in rural areas; and redefining "charity" as developmental work.

India

"Your work will wait for you to show natural phenomena and rainbows to your child, but these will not wait until you finish your work."

Mubarak Gurbanova

Medet
Civic Dignity

Mubarak Gurbanova (born 1963) is the head of the NGO Medet. She provides educational and job training opportunities to refugees, orphans, the young and the economically deprived. In four years, she has organized 100 seminars for 4000 people. She trains school teachers in the use of the new educational pedagogy on critical comprehension. As part of the Civic Dignity team she contributes to building a civil society in Turkmenistan, by providing training in civic education.

As a student, Mubarak Gurbanova was interested in the English language and dreamed of learning more about the English speaking world. However, the educational system during the Soviet era did not provide teaching on those countries. After high school she entered the Teacher Training Institute, Foreign Language faculty.

In 1991, when Turkmenistan gained independence and the Turkmen gates opened to the world, Mubarak's dream of teaching became a reality. In 1995, she began to participate in language and professional development activities and in community development training lessons of the Counterpart Consortium in Turkmenistan.

In 2001 Mubarak became a leader of Medet, an educational NGO, and began to work with the wider community including Afghan refugees. In 2002, Mubarak was at work when Jamile, an Afghan refugee, came to ask for help in finding a job. Mubarak said that if Jamile could encourage refugee children, especially girls, to take part in the organization, she would be glad to arrange language courses and civic education seminars for them. Jamile began to cry and said: "We came to Turkmenistan ten years ago, my husband left me with three sons and married another woman. As my sons did not speak Turkmen or Russian, they could not attend the local schools to receive an education. You are the first person who is happy to help me. I have lost everything: my country, parents, and husband. You are offering me an opportunity to change my life. Thank you."

Mubarak began to work with 150 families from the Afghan refugee community, believing that Afghans had to communicate more effectively with one another, be tolerant of opposing opinions and accept people from different cultures. Her dedication and belief that love is stronger than hate gives her the energy to continue to work with children and adults.

After the fall of the Soviet Union, Turkmenistan became independent. Although it remained an authoritarian state, some space was opened to introduce new elements in schools and methods of teaching, including civic education. The current state of the educational system in Turkmenistan is still poor.

Turkmenistan

Heide Göttner-Abendroth

International Academy Hagia

Dr Heide Göttner-Abendroth (born 1941) taught philosophy for ten years at the University of Munich and is the founder of modern matriarchal studies. Her 30 years of research in the field and her books focus on egalitarian and peaceful societies. They have been the basis for further studies in many countries. In 1986, she established the International Academy Hagia, which is primarily attended and supported by women. In 2003, she directed the First World Congress in Matriarchal Studies in Luxembourg, and in 2005, the Second World Congress with the title "Societies of Peace" in the US.

Heide Göttner-Abendroth is a philosopher and researcher on matriarchal societies and cultures. Born and raised in the former East Germany, her interest in how societies function developed early, and she always challenged social patterns. In 1973, she earned her doctorate in philosophy and theory of science at the University of Munich and taught there for ten years. Her research on structures that existed prior to patriarchy and patriarchal philosophy turned her world view and historical understanding upside down. In 1976, protesting against women's discrimination at the University, she joined the women's movement and became a pioneer of women's studies in Germany. She became known as a discerning critic of patriarchy and a researcher in matriarchal societies and cultures, and was the founding mother of modern matriarchal studies. Her research work spans more than 30 years. In her widely read books she fought prejudice against matriarchal forms of society. In her major work "Das Matriarchat" she shows that these societies are not dominated by women, but are based on the principle of balance between genders and generations and between humankind and the natural world. Guided by the value of motherliness, women organized egalitarian societies with intelligent conventions for the prevention of violence and the maintenance of peace. They are based on communication and finding consent and not on domination. From these insights, she gained her vision for a truly humane life for the future of humankind.
In 1986, she founded the independent International Academy Hagia for Modern Matriarchal Studies in Germany. In 2003, she guided the First World Congress on Matriarchal Studies in Luxembourg and was invited to direct the Second World Congress on Matriarchal Studies in Austin, Texas, in 2005. In so doing, she continues to contribute to a peaceful world.

Matriarchal studies have been subjected to attacks from scientific, psychological, and Christian communities, from the political right and left, from men and women. It has been perceived as a threat by the different patriarchal schools of thought and institutions, by both men and women alike.

Germany

"You only realize how far
you have come when
you lie in bed at night and
rethink the journey. I
just cannot recall whether
it was a village wag who
quipped: from small acorns
to mighty oaks."

Marion Hancock

Foundation for Peace Studies

In 1980, as a new mother listening to the news, Marion Hancock thought: "I should be doing something about this." "This" was nuclear disarmament and she went on to play a significant role in making New Zealand nuclear free. As director of the Foundation for Peace Studies, Aotearoa/New Zealand, her work broadened into peace work at an interpersonal level. It includes peace education in schools, violence prevention, and media work. Acutely aware of the increase in global violence, Marion is passionate about children growing to live peacefully together and realize their full potential.

The first magic moment took place in 1990 during Marion Hancock's involvement with the Votes for Peace campaign. This focused on persuading the political parties in New Zealand to adopt a nuclear-free policy. Years after New Zealand effectively became nuclear-free under a Labour government, Marion was still working with Votes for Peace. An election was looming and the National Party was saying it was going to reverse the policy. One evening, Marion received a phone call from a friend asking if she had seen the five o'clock news. National had changed its mind and adopted the nuclear-free New Zealand policy! It was what Marion had been working on for all that time and it came completely out of the blue. Fifteen years later, she still remembers that moment, and the elation she felt, as clear as day.

The second moment took place in 2004 when the Peace Foundation helped a Kenyan organization working on peace education in schools. In January, the director of the Kenyan organization sent an email out into the blue talking about their work, and their lack of equipment and funding. Could anybody please help? Marion received it at a time when she was not particularly busy and so she started communicating with him. Before long, her office floor was blanketed in computers, printers and all sorts of things to be sent out. When everything had arrived in Kenya, Marion received such a wonderful email from the director saying it was like all his Christmases had come at once: "Marion, I am so happy — kabisa (absolutely). Just need to sit for a day and take stock of all this." Such a clear indication, says Marion, of how easy it is for people in Western countries, relatively rich countries by comparison, to do what seems a little thing but to make such a huge difference for an organization in Africa.

Disarmament was the door through which Marion entered the peace movement. After helping achieve nuclear-free status for New Zealand, her work with the Peace Foundation evolved to focus on peace at an interpersonal level through peace education that strives to foster respect and empathy.

New Zealand

Bahia Hariri

Lebanese Parliament
Hariri Foundation
Arab Network for NGOs (ANNGOs)

Bahia Hariri (born 1952) is one of only three women of 128 Lebanese Ministers of Parliament. Her high profile as head of the Commission for Education and Culture (CEC) in Lebanon placed her at the forefront of fighting for the preservation of Lebanese cultural heritage. In recognition of her work on cultural issues, Bahia Hariri held many international posts, such as the Unesco Goodwill Ambassador in 2000, membership of the committee of the Parliamentary Network on the World Bank (PNoWB) and Head of the Women's Committee in the Arab Parliamentarian Union (HWCAPU).

During the Lebanese Civil War (1975—1991), Lebanon suffered from widespread destruction of its infrastructure. The War created numerous social problems, including the deterioration of living conditions, educational levels and health standards. The task of reconstructing the physical infrastructure of Lebanon is as daunting as the tasks of developing Lebanon's human resources through education, improving health care and eliminating poverty and gender inequality. Through her work as a Member of Parliament (MP) and Director of the Hariri Foundation, which has helped over 30,000 Lebanese youth around the world to further their education, Bahia Hariri has dedicated herself to the social reconstruction of Lebanon through emphasis on the development of human resources, particularly the Lebanese youth.

In Parliament she acts as head of the Educational Committee, she is instrumental in developing and instigating Lebanon's education policy and she undertook a number of pilot projects in different fields of study. Bahia proposed different learning models that eventually became very successful and were implemented in Lebanese schools. Utilizing her position as MP and Head of the Women's Committee in the Arab Parliamentarian Union (HWCAPU), she has committed herself to fighting to empower women who have suffered the consequences of gender inequality and a patriarchal society, both at national and regional levels, to develop job skills for the underemployed and unemployed and to increase the living standards of women and families. During all her memorable contributions and work in Lebanon, which began in 1979, Bahia has always strongly believed in developing partnerships between civil organizations and government in order to pursue human development projects in Lebanon. She has personally supervised many human development projects in her hometown, Sidon, and throughout Lebanon.

Bahia Hariri is a Member of the Lebanese Parliament. She also works diligently in Lebanon's non-governmental sector as Director of the Hariri Foundation, which provides educational opportunities for Lebanese youth around the world, and she heads the Women's Committee in the Arab Parliamentarian Union (HWCAPU).

Lebanon

Najwa Hassan

General Women's Union (GWU)
Union of Arab Writers (UAW)
Arab Union for Deaf Care Institutions

Najwa Kassab Hassan (born 1943) is former Syrian Minister of Culture and Professor of Sociology at Damascus University. She began her activities at Damascus University, advocating the importance of civil society institutions and the provision of social services for the less-privileged members of society, particularly the disabled and residents of under-developed rural areas. She devoted her life and research to supporting the rights of women and people with special needs.

Born in Damascus, Najwa Hassan was raised in a culturally influential family in Syria, whose diverse political and cultural currents helped to shape her profound views on issues about women's rights and gender equality. Her first PhD thesis is titled "The Concept of Man in Islamic Philosophy". For over 20 years she was an active member in the Syrian Parliament, benefiting from this position to defend the rights of the disabled and to give them access to public facilities. Along with her parliamentarian duties, she was also involved in the activities of the General Women's Union (GWU), the most important NGO in Syria working for women's issues. Her second PhD thesis, "Social Change in Syria", reflected her interest and is an outstandingly comprehensive study. Dr Najwa Hassan has covered all aspects of social change in Syria over a period of 30 years.

Despite the fact that hundreds of governmental positions have gone to women in Syria from the early 1970s till now, the number of women occupying these posts is still far less than the target of the Syrian government. Dr Najwa Hassan has supported the rights of women.

Syrian Arab Republic

"Our dream is simple: that children can read and write. That is all I can do for them."

Hermawati

SD Tunas Nelayan

Hermawati (born 1956) is a volunteer teacher in the tiny island Pulau Burung off South Kalimantan, Indonesia. This 49-year-old mother of three children has been providing free schooling for the island's poor children for 15 years, despite lacking proper education herself, using her own meager financial resources to build a modest school building and purchase learning materials. Her efforts have encouraged more parents to send their children to school.

Like many poor Indonesians, Hermawati had only a few years of formal schooling. In fact, she only completed elementary education. But she believes that experience belongs to the past, when schools were available only in big cities and poor parents were not aware of the importance of education. Now, things should be different. Hermawati was appalled that Pulau Burung Island, where she lived, did not have a school. The children had to take a boatride to get to school on the mainland. In most cases, the children were not allowed to get any education at all because their parents, who were mostly poor fishermen, were either reluctant or could not afford to send their kids to school. "It is very sad to see that many children here could not go to school, they could not read or write. We are living in the modern age, progressing forward, but the people here seem to go backwards," Hermawati was quoted by Kompas, a national newspaper.

So, in the early 1990s, relying on her own limited academic skills and her own funds, Hermawati started a free school for children on the island. In 1993, she managed to build an 18 square meter school building in her backyard using her family savings. Her lone crusade to combat illiteracy received little support. The government considered her curriculum inadequate and refrained from giving it formal recognition. Local residents were at first reluctant to send their kids to Hermawati's school because they could not afford to buy books. She almost closed it down in 2001 due to a severe lack of books and equipment. But providence was on her side. In 2004, an article about her work published in Kompas caught people's attention. Several people now help her as part-time tutors. Books and school equipment have been donated. More than 40 children now attend her school which, however, remains unaccredited by the government.

Pulau Burung is an island off South Kalimantan where poor fisherman's families live. Given the cost of admission, books and transportation, most parents are reluctant or unable to send their children to school. Therefore free schooling for the island's poor children is very important.

Indonesia

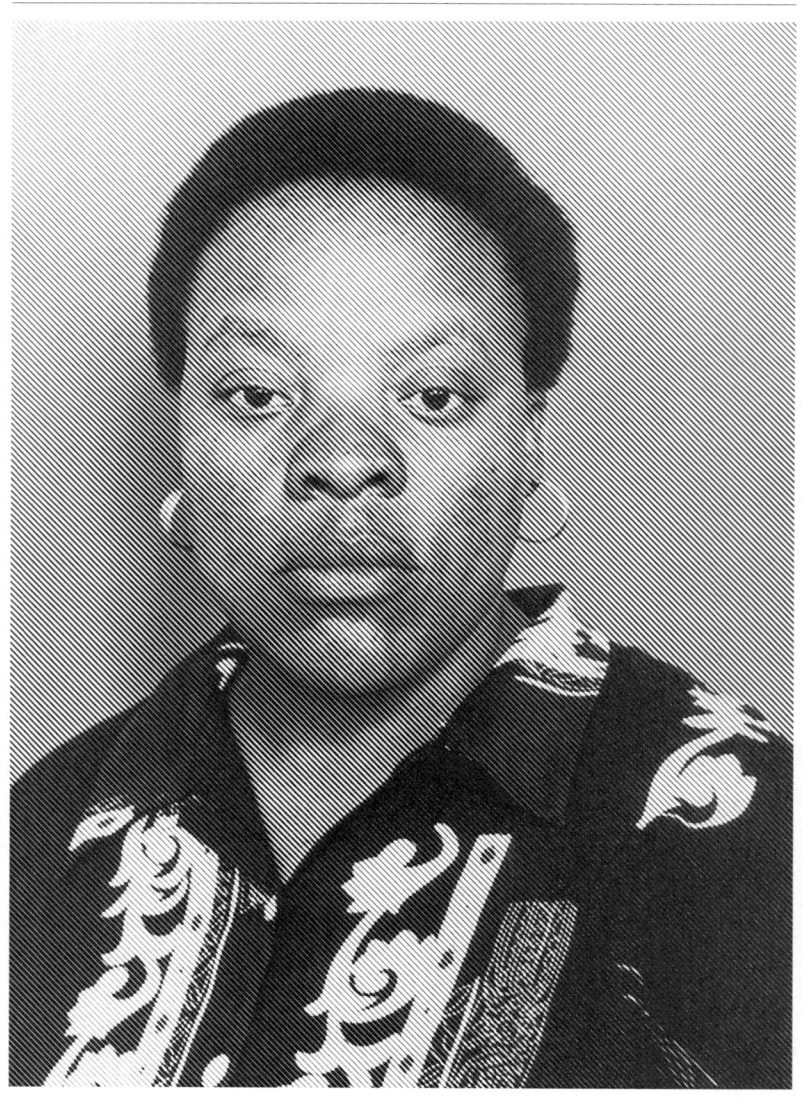

Busisiwe Virginia Hlomuka

Ezakheni Children's Center

Busisiwe Hlomuka (1965–2005) was born in KwaZulu Natal, South Africa. She fled from her home with her disabled child because her family and neighbors did not accept the child. Two years after she fled, around 1996, people in her new community started to bring their disabled children to Busisiwe for her to take care of them. That was the beginning of Ezakheni Children's Center for disabled children. Within a year the number had increased considerably because of HIV/Aids orphans.

"God blessed me with my child who has given me the ability to feed all the other children that are brought to me by the community. God can do miracles for you when you trust that He is the only salvation. I trust in God and each day I become stronger and stronger for all these children," said Busisiwe. She had started the center in a small shack with five children. After two years, the local council gave her a four-roomed brick house to accommodate 28 children. Neighbors were reluctant to help Busisiwe because some of the children were HIV positive: "People were scared of HIV/Aids."

With her First Aid skills, day-care and disability management skills, Busisiwe had to learn fast to deal with children with disabilities and at the same time pass on the knowledge to her assistants who had no formal training. With the help of KwaZulu Natal Department of Social Services, and some individuals in the community and the youth, Busisiwe got financial and social assistance. People donated clothes, food and toys for the children.

In 2001 Busisiwe received an award as the National Community Builder of the Year. The award brought heightened recognition of Busisiwe's work. Her work attracted researchers who highlighted the issue of HIV/Aids in KwaZulu Natal and its impact on children. Lately, the center has received increased assistance from different people and the staff has also increased. The department of health recently provided financial support to the center. However, she has always be concerned about the unskilled caregivers who work at the center and receive a low income. "The committed caregivers are either illiterate or semi-literate," said Busisiwe. Despite the problems, the center has gained recognition as a home for children living with disabilities and HIV/Aids. Busisiwe Hlomuka died in April 2005.

In parts of KwaZulu Natal superstitions exist about children living with disabilities: that they are a curse and should not live. The region is one of the poorest provinces in South Africa. It is rural and has inadequate infrastructure. HIV/Aids and other diseases affect its dense population.

South Africa

Lin Ching Hsia

Department of Applied Psychology, Fu-Jen Catholic University

After studying overseas, Hsia Lin Ching brought new ideas to Taiwan, a country which had suffered from severe political suppression. Today, she works with sex workers and on community adult education, as well as on capacity building and social awareness among young people. She is professor in the Department of Applied Psychology, Fu-Jen Catholic University, and director of Lu Di Community University, Taipei Province.

Born to a civil service family in Taiwan's nationalist government in the 50s, Hsia Lin Ching became influenced by leftist ideologies while studying in the US, where she also earned her master's and doctoral degrees in educational psychology and counseling. Back in Taiwan in 1977, she developed a career in education and joined the labor movement, focusing on women workers' rights. In the 1990s, she also supported the equal rights' movement of the sex workers, and the community adult education movement in Taiwan.

As an educational worker, Hsia has been trying to connect her professional practices with community action. She is a pioneer in developing "action research" in Taiwan. In a session in one of the community universities, she managed to get the over 150 students coming from different walks of life to talk about their life experiences and reflect upon them. Then she made use of these experiences to conduct a deep reflection by connecting them to the social context of Taiwan.

As an educational practitioner and researcher, Hsia has also intervened in education policies in Taiwan, such as the reform of the university entrance policy. She works with high-school teachers, treating them as educators and collaborative researchers to inquire into their dilemmas embedded in the educational practices and their interaction with educational reform. A professor of applied psychology in Fu-Jen Catholic University, Hsia also serves as the director of the Lu Di Community University in Taipei Province, and is consultant for the University Entrance Examination Center.

In Taiwan, political suppression was very severe in the 1950s under the Nationalist Party's rule. The return of many young scholars like Hsia Lin Ching after studying overseas and their bringing new ideas and energy to Taiwan was one of the important factors that has led to social transformation.

China, Taiwan

Devaki Jain

Singamma Sreenivasan Foundation

Devaki Jain (born 1933) is a pioneer in the field of women's studies in India and an institution-builder who combines vision with practical wisdom. She is also a grassroots worker, despite a heavy schedule of national and international commitments. Apart from her academic work, Devaki has been involved in marketing products generated by rural women and training these women to market medicinal herbal plants.

Graduating as an economist, Devaki Jain focused on development. She soon found herself studying the role of women in development, which became the bedrock of her career. Devaki displayed a remarkable capacity to network between diverse groups of people. This talent bore fruit when, in 1980, she founded the Institute of Social Studies Trust (ISST) to initiate and coordinate research and analyses on women's issues. At the ISST, which she headed until 1995, Devaki initiated pioneering research projects on new initiatives for women's development. The organization facilitated the birth of Mahila Haat, a market-window for women producers, supported a proposal to set up a women's publishing house and the development of many organizations for self-employed women.

The unflagging Devaki has also been a family counselor. Recently, she has been focusing her energies on training rural women to cultivate and market medicinal plants. In the past few years, she has devoted herself to building up the Singamma Sreenivasan Foundation in Karnataka, where she lives. The Foundation began by exploring alternative agricultural strategies that benefit women, but now works on a wider canvas of women-related issues.

Devaki was one of two women awarded the Bradford Morse Memorial Award at the World Conference in Beijing in 1995 "for outstanding achievements through professional and voluntary activities in promoting the advancement of women and gender equality for 20 years". She is actively involved with government forums and civil society initiatives on equity, development, self-government, and population; she has promoted women's studies through research and analyses; and she has encouraged appropriate policy interventions. Devaki has been an advocate of change through her writings in the media, speeches, and publications.

The concept of women's studies appeared as a serious discipline in India around the 1970s. While the subject took off with the University Grants Commission (UGC) developing a funding pattern for women's studies centers at Indian universities, women's organizations pursued it outside the UGC.

Haifa Jamal Al-Lail

Effat College in Jeddah (ECiJ)
Jeddah Chambers of Commerce (JCC)

Dr Haifa Jamal Al-Lail, Dean of Effat College in Jeddah, has been involved in education reform in Saudi Arabia since 1991, focusing on women's issues and cultural dialogue. Beside academia, Dr Haifa has worked with diverse organizations, such as the Jeddah Chambers of Commerce and the World Economic Forum. Internationally, she has worked tirelessly to voice the concerns of young women, especially combating stereotypes about Muslim women. Nationally, she has overseen the promotion of educational opportunities for young women.

As one of seven children raised in a single-mother home, Dr Haifa has drawn a great deal of inspiration from her widowed mother who insisted that all of her children — both male and female — graduate from university. Dr Haifa fulfilled her mother's wishes, and with her continued support and encouragement became the first Saudi national to complete a Doctorate in Public Policy, at the University of Southern California, Los Angeles. She is motivated in "knowing how much she herself would have fought for the idea that the misconceptions about Islam must be dispelled, and that women can play a positive role in doing so". The energy and commitment Dr Haifa draws from her mother, late daughter, who passed away in a road accident, and those close to her, finds its expression in the strategies and persistence she shows in pursuing her goals of achieving peace and harmony amongst peoples. Her commitment to peace came as a result of "seeing the tragedy of wars and violence in so many places — despite the lessons from history." This vision led her to speak at small gatherings at both local and regional levels. Her work has now progressed to an international level, where she participates in international forums and arenas, promoting dialogue and peace. Despite her international stature, she maintains that, "Small is beautiful. This is my strategy in achieving my goals in life." She believes that individuals have the most to gain from incremental, gradual improvement in their lives. She implements this notion by helping women within the education system in Saudi Arabia. With her encouragement, a large number of young women have pursued post-graduate studies at George Washington University and George Mason University. Often Dr Haifa would assist them in different ways, ranging from preparing applications to financial support.

As Dean of Effat College, Dr Haifa oversees the development of a liberal arts education, accentuating critical thinking amongst its female student population. She is directly involved in the direction and development of women's higher education in Saudi Arabia.

Saudi Arabia

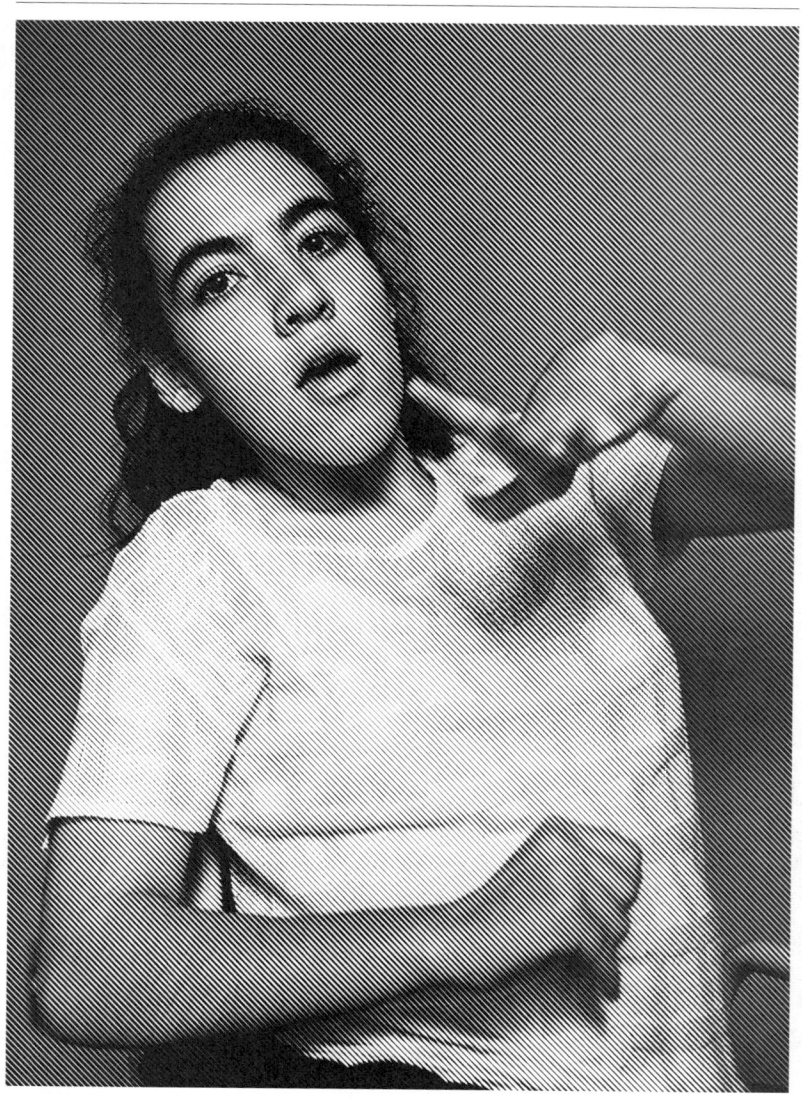

Sandra Jiménez Loza

Sandra Jiménez Loza (18) was born three months prematurely. The doctors said that she would not survive for more than 48 hours. She fought for her life in an intensive care unit for 15 days. Today, she hopes to become a film director and General Secretary of the UN. She was in a hurry to come into this world — just as she is in a hurry, today, to achieve her most important goal: to make humanity see the differences among people as richness.

"My family has always integrated me into all activities. They accepted me as I am, without any obstacles. Sometimes people do not know how to treat me. They do not know that, after all, I am just a person like anyone else, who needs a little more help to do some things. All of us need a little help and people to support us."

There is an enormous restlessness in this young girl. She is in a big hurry to do everything and is lucky, having survived a premature birth, due to lack of oxygen. As a result of those circumstances, Sandra Jiménez Loza has cerebral palsy, a paralysis that does not allow her to move her 18-year-old body in an independent manner. She has had medical treatment and physiotherapy since she was four months old. She uses a wheel chair. "I came into this world to change it," she assures us. "Ambitious? Of course!" she says laughing. "Since I was a little child, I liked to ask about things and that is the reason why I need to investigate and read, to talk and write about the things I know. I need to say, for example, that, in 2003, a single country spent more on arms than the entire Latin American foreign debt."

Sandra Jiménez Loza created the First Parliament for the Children and Youth of Mexico City, as a place to begin practicing democracy at an early age. She has participated in debates on the rights of disabled people and in the Women's and Children's Commission of the Legislative Assembly, to help pass the Law for the Protection of the Rights of Girls, Boys and Young People. She is the spokesperson on the rights of children in the Human Rights Commission of Unicef. "I want to be the General Secretary of the United Nations," she says emphatically. Sandra's ambition has no limits.

The situation of girls and boys in Mexico is deteriorating. The official figures show that child labor and sexual exploitation are growing. In the last few years, there have been national and international initiatives to include these children into programs that will change their lives.

Mexico

"My goal in life is to advocate a non-violent community where boys and girls have equal rights and access to education. I endeavor to change the conservative culture of Paktia through education."

Halima Khazan

Born in the eastern province of Paktia in 1953, Halima Khazan was the only woman in the province to finish high school. Then, she attended the Women's Teacher Training Institute in Kabul and soon after the completion of her teaching diploma she was appointed as a teacher, a career she has pursued for the past three decades. Halima has also arranged home schooling in order to encourage girls' education. She obtained assistance from the International Security Assistance Force (ISAF) to provide transport for girls who live in the remote villages of Gardez City, the capital of Paktia.

As the first high school graduate in the province Paktia, Halima Khazan was keenly aware of the disadvantaged status of women from her region. While forced to stay at home during the Taliban regime, she continued to provide home schooling for children. Motivated by the progress that some women in other provinces have achieved, she dedicated herself to changing people's attitude toward female education. She was an active participant in the local women's groups. Her vision of the future entails a non-violent community where boys and girls have equal rights. She is working hard to change the conservative culture of Paktia through persistent effort and education. Halima Khazan has been instrumental in encouraging girls to continue their education, and thanks to her efforts the only girls' high school in the province continues to receive more girls who are highly influenced by her exemplum. Halima Khazan has also helped to establish several adult literacy and tailoring courses for women. Furthermore, she writes regularly in the only local monthly magazine "Paktia Ghag" (Voice of Paktia) and she edits the women's page.

Hailing from Paktia, one of the most conservative provinces in Afghanistan, and being the first female high school graduate in the province, Halima Khazan has been dedicated to educating girls and empowering unfortunate women to become independent.

Afghanistan

Rajni Kumar

Springdales School

Rajni Kumar (born 1923) came to India with her Indian fiancé to join the freedom struggle, and made the country her home. In 1950, she set up a school for girls displaced by the partition. This work led her to conceptualize an institution that would link the process of education with life itself, and Springdales School was born in 1955. Her many innovative school programs — incorporating peace and human rights education in the curriculum, literacy projects, the "adopt a gran" project, and many others — have altered India's outlook on education.

At 16, Rajni Kumar (born Nancie Joyce Margaret Jones to British parents) became an activist in the antifascist resistance movement in England. She also joined the India League and the India Relief Committee for the sufferers of the 1942 Bengal famine. In 1946, with her costudent and fiancé Yudhister Kumar, she moved to India to participate in the freedom movement. Once there, she changed her name, married Yudhister in 1948, and made India her home. From 1950 to 1955, Rajni set up and ran a Hindu middle school for the girls of families displaced by partition.

By 1955, brimming over with ideas on education, she wanted to set up an institution that would interweave the process of education and life. She established Springdales School in her own home, with 24 children on the roster. Among the many innovative and path-breaking initiatives she introduced were peace and human rights education integrated within the curriculum, partnering with deprived children in state-run schools under the "twinning program", an Africa Club to support the antiapartheid movement, programs for women in urban slums, and the "adopt a gran" project with HelpAge India. She retired in 1988 at the age of 65, but continues to be active as chairperson of the Springdales Education Society. She is also voluntary coordinator of the Delhi Schools Literacy Project under the National Literacy Mission, motivating students and teachers in more than 60 schools to become involved in the eradication of illiteracy.

Rajni's vision for the future is to find ways to make educational systems more humane, equitable, and relevant to the changing world scenario, using technology to link schools and youth globally, and to incorporate education for peace, communal harmony, and international understanding into the curriculum of all schools.

The education system in India is focused on the child's academic development. In 1955, when Springdales School was set up, community service activities were not part of the school routine, and peace and human rights education was not part of the curriculum. It still is not in many schools.

India

"Solidarity and peace must be worked for from a base level, with openness and simplicity, looking with sincerity for the common good."

María Inmaculada Lacarra Cabrerizo

Mother Emilia School of Maiquetía
San Judas Tadeu School of Faith and Joy

The beginning of her pedagogical work in Venezuela was in the San Judas Tadeu School of Faith and Joy, in Caracas, in a community marked by violence and insecurity. Immersed in popular education since 1976, she initiated, in 1993, the project Education for Peace, the aim of which was to involve the educational community in the resolution of conflicts. Since 1999, she has directed the Mother Emilia School of Maiquetía, in the State of Vargas, where she is the driving force behind the initiative Constructing Peace with Solidarity. Her name is María Inmaculada Lacarra.

María Inmaculada Lacarra, born in Agreda-Soria, Spain, was a late arrival in the Lacarra-Cabrerizo family. She has only one sister. As a small child, she experienced the effects of the Civil War. In spite of that, her childhood seems to have remained undamaged: "I was surrounded by great affection and love from my family, a poor, working family, but, as I remember, we never lacked anything."

She adopted the religious life at age 15. In 1972, she came to Venezuela and lived in Cerro La Cruz, in the House of San Judas Tadeo, in Caracas. In 1993, as the director of the Educational Unit there, she initiated and promoted the project Education for Peace, as a response to the increasing violence in the community. This initiative envisages an open school, where the entire educational community participates. It would involve workshops, action in the streets and celebration of festivities in the most conflictive zones. A constant effort to promote unity between the families and the teaching team would be included. Violence is a reality that cannot be ignored. With her vision of an integrated society, this reality may change. The ones who build peace may prevail.

With an ability to handle conflicts that seems to be natural, María Inmaculada Lacarra believes that the building of peace must be based on the strength and local resources of the school and the community. "The project is a milestone that shows where we are going, a sample of what we are able to reach together, when we are in agreement. The greatest service I can give my people is to help them find the value we are missing the most: peace. Because it will not come through magic, we have to build it."

In 1993, the violence that exploded in Cerro de la Cruz, in Venezuela, was uncontrollable. Three teachers were victims of attacks, while the regular and frequent confrontations of armed groups in the zone continued. Today, a hope shows the promise of transforming violence into peace.

Venezuela

"I do not have a romantic image of peace. Peace is a way of managing conflicts through dialogue, through the mediation of reasoning."

Marta Lamas Encabo

Grupo de Información en Reproducción Elegida (GIRE)

Every Friday, Marta Lamas Encabo eats with her chosen family: 12 women that come to her house. Her consanguineous mother, father and brother are dead. Choice is an important word in her life. She has established in Mexico the pro choice organization, the Group of Information on Chosen Reproduction (Gire). She writes, acts, thinks and debates.

Marta Lamas Encabo likes cats and books. She sleeps with both, the cats in her bed, the books beside her. She was born in Mexico City. She grew up in a family originating from Argentina, surrounded by material comfort and personal freedom. "When I saw the contrast between Mexico and other places, it made me angry. I became politically radical when I was very young; I linked myself to the left and later on, to feminism." Singing gives her the most pleasure in life, but she decided, because of her social conscience, to dedicate herself to feminist politics.

She is recognized as one of the most prominent figures in the fight for women's rights in Mexico. She has been a staunch defender of women for three decades. Her most recent work has been focused towards the right to abortion. She believes that each person should have control over her own reproduction, and she believes that this is a basic freedom and a fundamental human right for women. "We must try to change the law, build organizations and give information about a crucial matter like abortion. The other line that is very interesting for me to pursue is the intellectual work, the publishing. For that reason, I publish a magazine called 'Feminist Debate.'"

Marta founded the Institute of Leadership Simone de Beauvoir, to train leaders for the women's movement and for the feminist movement. She also founded Semillas A.C., an institution that searches for and supports projects for all sorts of women. She is a constant presence in the mass media, writing items concerning women's lives. She is mentioned on the mass media on an average of ten times per month. She defines public opinion.

In a Catholic country like Mexico, fighting for abortion or for sexual and reproductive rights entails criticism and attacks from conservative organizations. In these cases, although it is legally established, the laicity of the Mexican State is weak.

Yevgeniya Leontyeva

Taurida National University Simferopol
Network of Cultural Exchange and Interethnic Trust

Yevgeniya Leontyeva has a profound knowledge of the unique ways that different ethnic, political, and social groups articulate their thoughts and she has developed the ability to communicate them from one language to another. A linguistic expert, she puts her skills to work in education, research, and interpretation/translation. In multi-ethnic and multi-linguistic Ukraine, she has assisted minority groups to make their voices heard and their positions understood, thus, helping to overcome prejudice and misinterpretation that lead to conflict.

Communication is a crucial part of the prevention and resolution of conflicts. Yevgeniya Leontyeva, born 1975 in Simferopol, has put her linguistic and interpreting skills to use in promoting understanding among different ethnic and linguistic groups in Ukraine. After finishing high school in 1993, she enrolled in the Faculty of Foreign Languages of the Simferopol State University and graduated in 1998. Yevgeniya immediately embarked on three areas of linguistics: education, scientific research, and translation/interpretation. An interpreter and translator in multi-ethnic Ukraine, Yevgeniya often worked under difficult and tense conditions caused by prejudice and misinterpretation. To overcome these difficulties, she uses a wide array of interlingual and intercultural communication skills that promote perception and mutual understanding among people of different languages and cultures. Using her interpretation skills, Yevgeniya Leontyeva has helped give a voice to the minorities in the country — the Crimean Tatars, Bulgarians, and Jews. She has helped them make their position known and to gain acceptance for their views among the majority of the population in the country and among the international community. She has also worked as an interpreter and translator during high level meetings of leaders of European states like France, Germany, England, and Finland. She assisted in the translation of official, business, and educational documents and made regular reports during scientific sessions. Her rich experience enables her to share her skills with her students and inspire them to direct their talents in many spheres.

In the last ten years, Ukrainian linguists have faced difficult challenges in their work as educators, researchers, interpreters, and translators. They had to work in a tense multi-ethnic atmosphere, with inadequate financial and material resources.

Ukraine

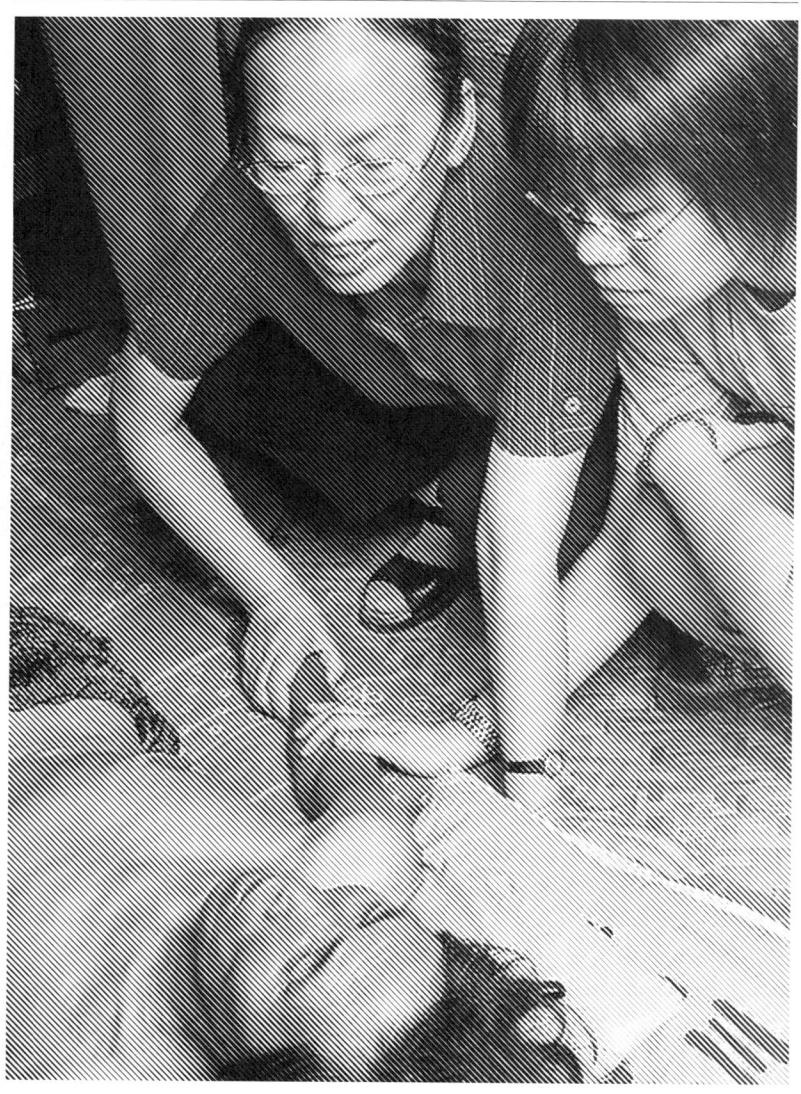

Jun Liang

Henan Community Education Research Center

One of the founders of the Women's Academy and Women's Museum in Henan Province, Liang Jun (60) is currently working with women's groups that provide training in women's development. In 1998 she established the Henan Community Education Research Center, which is dedicated to the construction of grassroots community organizations. The center also focuses on research into women's cooperation and development, peasant literature and art, and mutual aid among abused women in rural and urban areas.

In 1985 Liang Jun became a teacher at the Henan Women's Cadre School. The experience in research and training that she acquired here was put to good use in her extensive travels in subsequent years when she worked as a trainer in women's development. Contact with people from different communities taught her a great deal. She went on to found a women's academy in Henan Province, as well as the first women's museum in China, for which she also collected oral histories. Despite many difficulties, she continued to work for the development of grassroots organizations. In 1998 Liang Jun set up the Henan Community Education Research Center. Inspired by a "Gender and Participatory Development" seminar held by the Oxford Committee for Famine Relief (Oxfam), she started to assist grassroots peasant women to self-organize. She helped Wang Xia, a peasant woman from the Dengfeng mountain area of Henan, to establish a peasants' cultural group, named Rosy Clouds Culture and Art Performance Group, which popularized new ideas and new concepts using various cultural and artistic methods. She organized the Dengfeng Women's Traditional Arts & Crafts Cooperation Group and groups of abused women from urban and rural areas. She also looked at integrated methods for communities to intervene in domestic violence situations. In recent years she has worked with HIV carriers to establish the Red Ribbon Association whose motto is "self-rescue, self-help, mutual-help, help-others." She believes that it is peasant women who have given her wisdom and strength. It is they who promote the harmony and development of human beings and of society.

Mainstream society tends to discriminate and exclude women, especially peasant women and HIV-infected people. Culture can be a powerful tool for making people aware of their own power and strength.

China

Moema Libera Viezzer

Rede Mulher (Women's Education Network)
Latin-American and Caribbean Network of Popular Education
between Women (Repem)

Moema Viezzer (1939) is a weaver of networks, but not networks made of cotton. The networks she weaves have as raw material the transformation of relations. Change is the most important word in her dictionary. Mother of two daughters, she works for more balanced relations between women and men, between human beings and nature, between wealth and poverty. Today, she is an assessor of education for sustainability in Itaipu, one of the greatest hydroelectric power plants of the world.

The sad Brazil of 1973, gagged by military dictators, worked to persecute intelligence. Mainly, those involved with the resistance and with actions of transformation. In the Northeast of the country, young Moema Viezzer used to coordinate community health and educational projects. It was enough for her to appear in the dangerous list of the SNI (a Brazilian CIA). Her friends advised her to go into exile. Leaving Brazil was providential for a woman who was curious to discover new ways of thinking. In Mexico, she woke up to feminism and never again closed her eyes to it. When she met Bolivian Domitila Barrios de Chungura, Moema had the idea to write a book: "Se me deixam falar" (Let me speak). In it, Domitila narrates the awful life conditions and the oppressive system of the Bolivian mines. The book became a classic. Making contact with the feminists, Moema realized something: "Democracy, development and peace are not possible without woman's participation. We can not have an equal planet with unequal gender relations." With these thoughts, she came back to Brazil, in 1980, to found Rede Mulher (Women's Education Network), an NGO that became a Latin-American reference in education and qualification of women. Moema is also one of the founders of the Latin-American and Caribbean Network of Popular Education between Women (Repem). As she worked, she experimented and she articulated, Moema noticed the importance of the environment not only for humanity, but particularly for women. "A female eye overlooking social-environmental subjects is fundamental."
Today, Moema qualifies environmental educators and multiplies her own knowledge with men and women that work the land, water and with recycled materials. Moema Viezzer directs for emotional and organizational capacity to the construction of a planetary citizenship.

Moema Viezzer is involved in the conception of important documents regarding environmental culture. Among them, the Treaty of Environmental Education for Sustainable Societies and Global Responsibility. The Treaty is a basic instrument for the actions of environmental educators.

Brazil

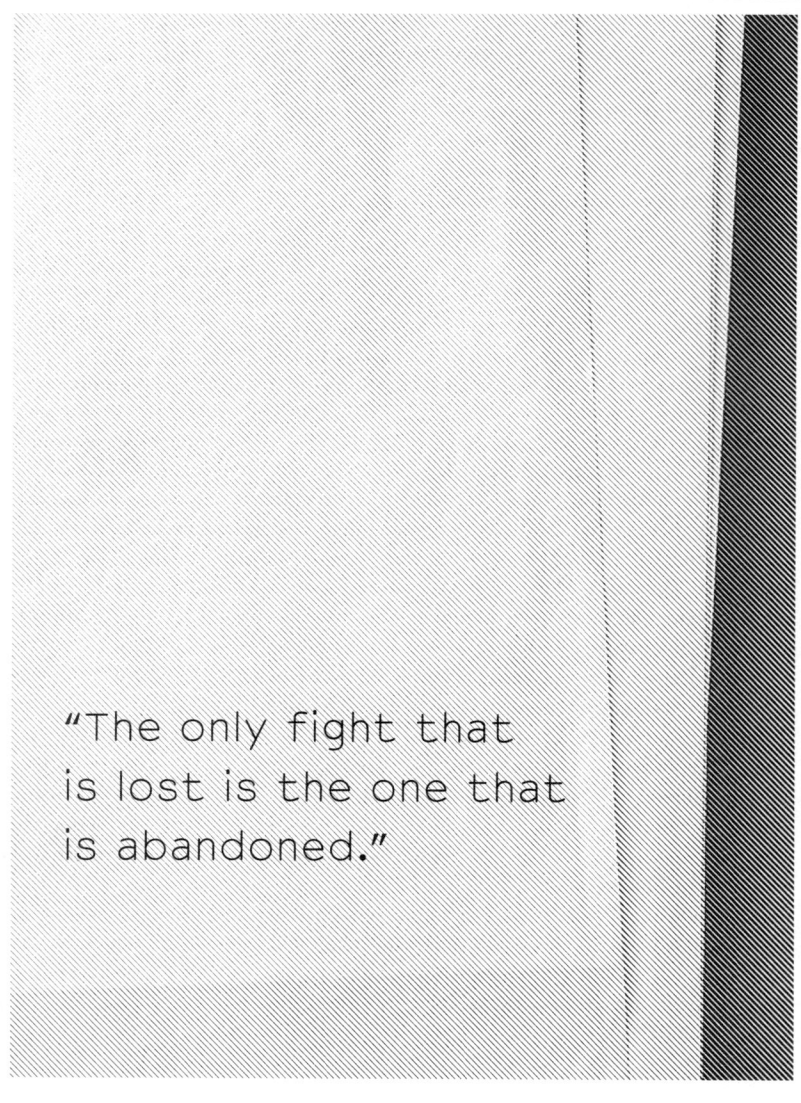

"The only fight that
is lost is the one that
is abandoned."

Sara Lovera López

Comunicación e Información de la Mujer (Cimac)

Sara Lovera is a journalist, a feminist, and she is Mexican. Raised by single women, she has a Mazahua grandmother (Mazahua is one of the many indigenous peoples in Mexico). "These women are independent; they never work as house servants. They are businesswomen. My grandmother told me that my freedom depends on having my own money and being wise. She did not know how to read or write, but she was wise. She and my mother insisted that I go to school. I never had the opportunity to become anything but an independent woman."

Sara Lovera (1968) started her professional career in Mexico, the country where she was born, at age 19. She is a journalist. "You think about what you can do to bring about justice. Later, you are going to have to decide what really matters, and what really matters is taking a position and revealing the facts. This is the reason for journalism." Over the decades, she has demonstrated this point. From 1968 to 1998, she worked as a reporter for several Mexican newspapers, "El Día", "El Nacional", "Uno más Uno", and "La Jornada." Since 1971, she has been a member of a variety of women's groups. She has lectured at a number of foreign and national universities. She has written essays, proposals and texts for publications of all types on one same subject: the condition of Mexican women — working women, rural women, native women, professional women, housewives, young women, sexual workers, lesbians, journalists, vulnerable women, politicians, homeless girls, mothers. She once read a saying on a wall. It has become her motto: "The only fight that is lost is the one that is abandoned." She does not abandon the fight.

In 1988, Sara, along with a group of journalists, founded the organization Communication and Information of Women (Cimac), a news agency dedicated to reporting on the situation of women. From this base, Sara has denounced the atrocities that the Mexican patriarchate has carried out against women. "A good journalist does not need to be a militant to report the truth. Women in Mexico continue to be pressured, tormented and discriminated against. There are humiliation circles built around women. It does not matter where the barriers are or what they want to do. We must report it." Sara is a militant, a journalist, and she really reports the truth!

The patriarchal system is organized to perpetuate injustices against women. It is based on authoritarianism where men have the power and the control over decisions — and even over the body of the women. Feminicide, marginalization and exploitation are constants against which feminism must fight.

———

Mexico

Liliana Lozanova Valcheva

National Trade Union in Education and Science (NTUES)
Women in Science
International Federation of Inventors' Association

Liliana Valcheva is a scientist and social activist for women's rights, advocating more involvement of women in the public sphere, including education and science to ensure that they are devoted to improving the quality of life and supporting a peaceful society. In 1987, shortly before the collapse of communism, Liliana was part of a group of women who began working to establish a women's movement in Bulgaria. She has also been active in human rights and working for peace outside of her country. During the wars in former Yugoslavia, she organized anti-war activities.

Liliana believes that Bulgaria's most important resource is its citizens. This belief has supported her during many years of efforts on a wide range of issues to improve the opportunities for human development in Bulgaria. She works to ensure that Bulgarian law supports equality for men and women and people from different ethnic backgrounds. She also supports education and research through advocating students' rights and better financing for Bulgarian universities and scientific institutions. As a leader within the Bulgarian non-governmental community, she works at international level to promote a more peaceful society. She is the founder and honorary president of the Bulgarian Association of Women in Science which has consultative status in the United Nations Economic and Social Council, and she participates in activities to establish a peace building commission for the Balkans.

A university professor, Liliana educates students on the social issues facing Bulgaria and its region, and the need for people from different backgrounds to work together. She gives priority to investment in scientific developments and new technologies that benefit people, eliminating hunger and poverty, and to environmental issues, such as air, water, and soil quality, and to ensuring that environmental resources are respected at the global level. Liliana has also been a lead activist in advocating the diversion of resources from military weapons to the development of technologies that will benefit agriculture.

She strongly advocates wider participation of women in the public sphere. She has also worked in the interests of women through the creation of three family planning centers that provide consultations, education, and assistance to students and young people. She has motivated women to take a more active role in institutions responsible for decision making in Bulgarian society.

Since the collapse of the Soviet Union, Bulgaria has been undergoing a transition to democracy. The peaceful nature of this transition has enabled civil society, women's rights, and peace organizations and movements to develop.

Bulgaria

"I have tried to use my own example to educate and inspire children and their parents. The force of knowledge is great and I hope to change the extent of poverty in my home village through knowledge."

Xinlan Ma

Weizhou Hui Women's Primary School

Ma Xinlan started her career as a teacher in 1971. Since 1985 she has been the headmistress of Weizhou Hui Women's Primary School. She and five other teachers established the school, a significant step in a region that has been slow to offer education to women, particularly those of national minorities.

Ma Xinlan was born in 1952 into a Muslim family in Weizhou, Tongxin County, Ningxia Autonomous Region. According to the local conditions and customs, it was difficult for girls to go to school. But the appearance of a young woman teacher changed Ma's destiny. Ma not only went to school as she wished, but also decided to become a teacher. In 1965 she completed her primary school education. At the time, only four girls in the township had finished primary school. Ma was accepted by Tongxin County Middle School with high scores. However, because the villages in the poor mountainous area where she lived were affected by the Cultural Revolution, she had to leave the school for the poor yellow earth at home. Fortunately, her strong wish to teach resulted in her getting a job as a village teacher in 1971, when positions were available in the county. She was 19 that year.

In 1985, under the auspices of local religious individuals and the education department, the Weizhou Hui Women's Primary School, which had been disbanded 30 years earlier, was re-established. Ma, who had 14 years of teaching experience, was assigned to be the headmistress of the school, an important step in a region known for its bad educational standards for minority women. The percentage of Muslim girls who attended school was less than 20, and those who quit after the third or fourth grade was 80 percent. For many years Ma advised and persuaded them to stay and her efforts paid off, with the percentages going up (98 percent, and 95 percent remaining in school). Girls were given vocational training as well. For Ma this is a labour of love.

In the Muslim minority region of Ningxi, apart from the geographical remoteness and the lack of educational resources, the native popular custom was that girls older than nine could not show their faces in public, come in contact with strangers or go to schools with boys.

China

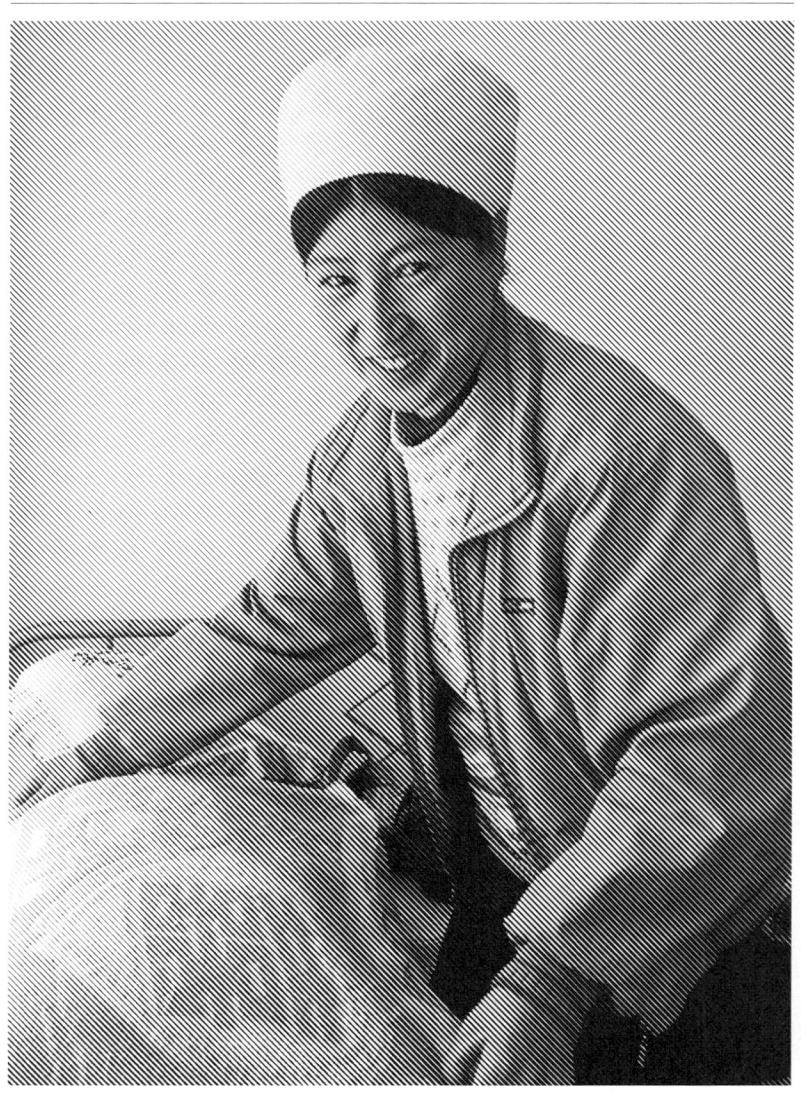

Zhiying Ma

Ma Zhiying lives in the remote Sabao Village, Zhengqi Town, Haiyuan County, Ningxia Muslim Autonomous Region. Here she has supported girls in difficult circumstances to complete their studies, with a scanty income of her own. Ma has contributed a great deal to the education of girls from China's western poverty regions.

Ma Zhiying is an ordinary Muslim woman, living in Sabao Village, a place "most unsuitable for human living" according to the World Food Program of the United Nations. Poverty and backwardness make education difficult, especially for women. Although Ma Zhiying finished senior high school with a good academic performance, she could not pursue further studies because her family was too poor. Ma worked as a cleaner in a market under the Commerce and Industrial Bureau with a monthly salary of 200 yuan. This meager sum, however, is the base of her altruism.

One day in 1997, Ma headed to work as usual. As she was passing by the Haiyuan No. 2 Secondary School, she saw a girl wandering up and down in front of the gate. Ma found out that the girl had been admitted to the school, but had to quit due to financial difficulties. She brought her back to her home. Another day in 1999, Ma Zhiying saw several girls standing around a kerosene stove cooking in a little alleyway. It turned out that their school did not provide a dormitory, so they had to rent as cheap a place as they could find, and often there was no room to cook. Ma brought them to her home. From then on, Ma's family began to reserve their three best rooms as free accommodation for peasant girls. Altogether 73 students have benefited from this. So far, Ma has spent 120,000 yuan on this work by trimming the family expenses.

In the past few years, over 30 of these girls have been accepted by universities. Whenever this happens, Ma becomes very excited, saying, "When a girl is accepted, I feel as if I were going to have my own university life." Ma got sacked from her job in 2002, but she did not give up her altruism.

Haiyuan county, in Ningxia Muslim Autonomous Region, is a place known to be "most unsuitable for human living" according to the World Food Program of the UN. Poverty and discrimination make education difficult. Wealthy children can afford a secondary education, for the others, primary education is the most they can get.

China

Ana Maria Machado

Academia Brasileira de Letras

Ana Maria Machado (1941) was born in a time when female presence in literature was still insignificant. Today, her work is eternalized in the Brazilian Academy of Literature, of which she is a part. She is the first writer of children's books to get into the Academy, and she always demonstrates the importance of this institution for the battle on prejudice against children that are many times seen as a second class public. She published more than 100 books.

Ana Maria Machado dedicates her mornings to writing fiction in a daily exercise of visiting a space in the subconscious. "It is necessary to be very humble and docile," she says. But make no mistake: Ana Maria's sweetness in writing does not stop her from being a warrior.

Her presence in juvenile literature began when she was exiled, after leaving Brazil threatened by the military dictatorship. When she returned, she worked as a journalist, fought against the censorship of the media and was the first woman to be the head of a news department. She directed the news department of the Jornal do Brasil radio station until 1980, period when democratic government was re-established. From then on, she dedicated herself exclusively to book writing, area in which she left important marks: she was the leader of the campaign for changing the cataloguing criteria in the National Library, demanding that female authors should also have the historical context of their work registered.

Ana Maria Machado lives in the district of Leblon, in Rio de Janeiro, where she was born. She believes that literature is an attempt to coordinate chaos, to look for some sense in the existence that lies beyond the barriers. Among her many activities, there is one that has occupied Ana Maria for more than 20 years: the qualification of teachers in Latin American. Organizer of seminars on this subject for Unesco, she gives lectures, conferences and promotes courses for educators. In her opinion, peace depends on this capacity of sharing cultures, ethnicities and religions, in other words, of being tolerant with those who are different. She believes that, in this aspect, Brazil has a great contribution to give, since this is a country where cultural and religious tolerance is admirable. "But all transformations are connected to justice," she affirms.

During her 33 year old career, Ana Maria Machado spread her work throughout 17 countries, with 14 million copies sold all over the world. In the year 2000, she was given the Hans Christian Andersen Prize for her work in juvenile literature.

Brazil

"I am involved in preparing the granddaughter of today to be the woman of tomorrow."

Hiri Maguiraga

Coordination des Associations et ONG Feminines du Mali (CAFO) locale, Nioro du Sahel

Hiri Maguiraga was born in Nioro du Sahel, a town in the Kayes region, in 1949. She is a teacher and a strong fighter for women's causes. She holds a diploma from the former Pedagogic Institute for General Teaching (IPEG). She is divorced and the mother of six children, a situation she does not regret at all and which she attributes to an act of God. And she says: "We cannot aspire to having a stable world until everyone has the right to education and women's education becomes a priority."

Madame Hiri Maguiraga is an educational adviser responsible for girls' schooling and the development of women. She is excited by the idea of promoting the development of women and preparing the granddaughter of today to be the woman of tomorrow. Her work encompasses information, education, communication (IEC), meetings, general assemblies, mounting projects, financial research, and the formation and development of partnerships. The struggle that pre-occupies Hiri Maguiraga goes back to the advent of democracy in Mali. This has favored the development of women's associations in the area of Nioro du Sahel that had only two associations in 1991, but has 33 today. This development had rapid consequences in the area since the majority of the rural women notice today that some of their rights are now recognized, especially in local level decisions. Thanks to the actions of Hiri Maguiraga and her colleagues, women do participate in the community management. This is a big advancement in a long cycle of ambient feudalism in relations between men and women. Now, the women have an equal chance of employment, work, professional remuneration, and the right to instruction. Under the direction of Hiri Maguiraga and her colleagues in the women's movement, women's associations also make a strong stand against forced marriages. They support civil marriage and the abandonment of the harmful practice of female circumcision.

Hiri Maguiraga works to improve access and attendance rates for girls at school. It is important to her to keep these girls in school, to avoid losing them to the early marriages that are the lot of many granddaughters in rural areas.

Regina Makunga

Zamani Pre-School

Regina Makunga was born in 1950. She grew up within the rural villages of Transkei. She loves children and has dedicated herself to nurturing and caring for them. Although she attained only primary level of education, her work in the community is outstanding. She is married.

When in 1994 the person previously in charge of Zamani Pre-School was appointed to parliament, the future of this community project looked bleak. No one was willing to take over only to have the project fail. Then Regina Makunga (Mam'u Makunga) volunteered to assist until a suitable and qualified person was available. The rest as they say, is history.

Zamani Pre-School is aimed at providing a refuge for non-school-going children and to assist them in their early childhood development. Mam'u Makunga and her staff provide a child-friendly environment, giving the children an opportunity to broaden their mind whilst instilling a sense of pride in their people's culture and heritage. The children interact and benefit from story telling. With limited financial resources, the staff depend more on their vast knowledge of traditional stories to pass on rather than on books.

Mam'u Makunga is a custodian of her people's culture and tradition.

She started to work toward a rejuvenation of the African culture long before it was fashionable. Her commitment and dedication to the preservation of her people's culture is profound. She tells stories and teaches the young about their culture and people.

Her community has started to realize what a great heritage they have and more people have started to embrace the spirit of African Renaissance.

Umtata, a small town in the Eastern Cape, is influenced by colonial and apartheid legacies. The historical times of destruction, "Nongqawuse" (kill the cattle, burn the crops), are still recalled. Most mineworkers were coerced to work, and people would rather not live on the land productively.

South Africa

Elizabeth "Betita" Martinez

War Times — Tiempo de Guerras
Institute for Multi-Racial Justice
Bay Area Veterans of the Civil Rights Movement

Elizabeth "Betita" Martinez has influenced the thinking and the actions of generations of scholars and community activists. She provides intellectual understanding, leadership and direction to struggles against racism, sexism, antiimmigrant bias, and in support of social justice and peace. Betita is a master connector, bringing communities and individuals together and insisting that we recognize the profound connection between all humanity.

It was a night in Cuba that will live forever in the recesses of Betita's memory. In August 1967, she had traveled from Havana to an island south of mainland Cuba called the Isle of Youth. Prior to the revolution this island was the site where Fidel Castro had been imprisoned for attempting to overthrow the Batista regime. The island had never been developed economically, until the idea emerged during the revolution to develop it as a giant youth project. In 1967 some 60 camps were set up for young people to plant, cultivate and harvest crops, and raise cattle. Betita spent two weeks there with about 400 young women between the ages of 14 and 20. They were daughters of urban working-class people who had historically been very marginal in prerevolutionary Cuba.

One night the director of the camp called the young women together in a huge courtyard to tell them about regulations that were to govern their activities at the camp. During the presentation she stated that one of the young women, Cusa, was being expelled from the camp for some unspecified reason. Cusa had asked for a second chance. In response to her request, the director threw the question open to the other young women. They all shouted "Yes!" Then they started playing music and singing the Internationale. The young women formed circles, holding hands and dancing and singing. Suddenly, as if by some invisible signal, they all rushed forward, forming a giant circle. They then rushed back, expanding the circle, then forward again. They did this repeatedly. Betita was overwhelmed by the poignancy of the young women expressing their solidarity with Cusa, the revolution and the spirit of unity. The moment called forth something deep within her to live up to that level of commitment to peace, justice and equality for the rest of her life.

Coming of age during World War II had a profound impact on Elizabeth Martinez. Overwhelmed by the killing and destruction of war, she recalls vividly that this period marked the beginning of her commitment to world peace, working within the USA against imperialism and for humanity.

United States of America

Dilorom Mukhsinova

Town Council

Dilorom Mukhsinova (born 1952) has been a school teacher since 1973. She is devoted to peace, freedom, and tolerance and the development of mutual understanding between people despite different views and social backgrounds. This is especially important in this region, the center of a major conflict zone in Central Asia with the danger of extremist tendencies increasing among youth and the local population. Dilorom's teaching supports tolerance and respect for the diverse cultures of the world and is a significant contribution to peace and harmony in her community.

Dilorom Mukhsinova is an outstanding teacher, who is encouraging cultural understanding and tolerance in an area that is prone to ethnic conflict. There are many obstacles and hindrances in the teaching profession in Uzbekistan, including a lack of current professional literature and opportunities for the professional development of teachers. Despite these challenges, Dilorom uses modern teaching methods that engage her students and involve them in social and public activities. Her students are taught social responsibility and are encouraged to take their lives in their hands by doing their best to improve the life around them. She educates her students to increase their consciousness of the world and engage in critical thought.

Dilorom has been successful in broadening the curriculum of study available to her students. She has initiated new courses in local and world cultures. She tries to inspire her students with a sense of curiosity and respect for both Uzbek and foreign cultures and teaches them that each culture and nation has its own traditions that have developed over hundreds of years. This serves as a premise for a spirit of peace, tolerance, and respect for both human beings within and outside their own culture and country. The result is that — in a country with relatively little Western and global exposure — students are being given an education that supports them in broadening their minds and thinking globally, while still being proud of their own culture and traditions.

Ferghana is a complex historical, social, and political region. It is at the center of a major conflict zone in Central Asia, with a growing influence of Islamic traditions and trends among youth. There is danger of extremist and fundamentalist tendencies increasing among the local population.

Uzbekistan

Rose Marie Muraro

Rose Marie Muraro (born 1930) was one of the pioneers in Brazil's feminist movement. All of her work is connected to the defense of human rights and women's rights, a militancy that she began in the 1940s together with progressive segments of the Catholic church. All together, Muraro published 26 books, always with the purpose of "giving women the power of speech."

When she started her militancy in the Catholic Action, in 1946, with Bishop Hélder Câmara, sexuality was still a taboo in Brazilian society. The task of beginning the debates on this subject was given to Rose Marie Muraro. In the 1980s, her book on the sexuality of the Brazilian woman was on the best-seller list for six months. In 1971, when she promoted the visit to Brazil of Betty Friedman, a North American feminist, Rose Marie Muraro contributed greatly to increasing feminism's popularity. Four years later, she was one of the founders of the Brazilian Women's Center. In 1985, she joined the National Council of Woman's Rights, an inedited experience in Brazil. During the Brazilian military regime, she had her work prohibited as it was classified by the censor as pornographic. She paid a high price for being a pioneer in the feminist battle, and, for many years, she was discriminated by Brazilian society for her ideas. This stigma still follows her, even though her contribution to the feminist cause has been recognized during the past 20 years, the period after the end of the military dictatorship. Her great passion, during 74 years of life, was the defense of human rights and of equality between men and women. Nowadays, she still believes that it is impossible to attain peace while there is still inequality.

Mother of five children, grandmother of 12 grandchildren and one great-grandchild, Muraro needs, now, help from her family to survive, because she has faced many health problems in the past three years. In spite of her enormous level of myopia that makes her technically blind, reading and writing is part of her daily work routine in her modest apartment in the district of Copacabana, Rio de Janeiro, the city where she was born.

Since the creation, in 1985, of the National Council of Woman's Rights, the attention towards public policies regarding women has been growing in the Brazilian State. Today, there is a Special Secretariat for Women Policies.

Dilshad Murtaza

K2 Development Organization

Denied the chance to complete her own education, Dilshad Murtaza has made it her mission to ensure that poor children in the northern areas of Pakistan are able to access educational opportunities. Dilshad, who has been involved in voluntary work for over two decades, set up the K2 Development Organization five years ago. Its aim is to help poor children and women, especially widows: 22 women have so far been provided with vocational training, and 108 poor children have become literate.

Married early, Dilshad Murtaza, a native of Hunza in Pakistan's northern areas, only managed to study until class seven. But the break in her schooling left her with a yearning for a proper education. Some years later, she managed to complete class eight, stopped from going further by the incessant challenges of family life. But Dilshad redirected her energies to the cause of education in a different way: she decided to run a vocational and literacy center in Gilgit — the administrative center of Pakistan's mountainous and poverty-stricken northern areas — for very poor children. Apart from free schooling, she also provides books and other materials. So far, she has educated 108 children up to class five. Her five-year-old organization, the K2 Development Organization, is named after the famous peak that towers over this arid expanse.

Dilshad has been involved in voluntary work in this region, one of the poorest in Pakistan, for over two decades. She launched K2 after the death of her husband, and after all her children had grown up, when she could give the organization enough time. She is, however, far from financially secure, struggling with impending penury both in her personal life and in her efforts to keep her organization going. Furthermore, her family have not been supportive of her voluntary work.

Dilshad also focuses on the plight of poor widows, most of whom cannot support their families after the death of their husbands, lacking simple education or vocational training. Dilshad's free training has so far helped 22 such women. Inspired by her pioneering role, other women have taken the initiative, setting up small local-level organizations such as the Sahara Development Organization, and the Mountage Development and Welfare Organization in other parts of Gilgit.

Gilgit is the administrative center of Pakistan's mountainous and poverty-stricken northern areas, its only claim to fame being the world's toughest mountain, K2, which towers over the expanse. But its poverty is endemic, and the position of its women dismal.

Sayed Naqi

Sayed Bibi Naqi was born in 1928 in Kabul, Afghanistan and has a BA in Literature. Having worked as a teacher, headmistress and principal in many schools in Kabul since the 1950s, she has a long experience in education. Now she is retired. As a tribute to her efforts, Bibi Naqi was promoted by His Majesty crown prince Ahmad Shah, the elder son of former King Mohammad Zahir, to head of education in Kabul. Thanks to her, many orphan girls and boys were able to attend schools with her encouragement and subsistence. She has received several medals and certificates of honor.

When Bibi Naqi went to school in Afghanistan in the 1950s, girls' education and going to school was a sinful act. However, Bibi Naqi completed her early schooling, on condition that she wore a veil. Her father could not afford to pay for her education. She had to work in the afternoon to support herself. Despite all these challenges, she studied and obtained a BA degree in Literature. At every step, she was encouraged by her parents and relatives to continue.

Bibi Naqi is working hard towards a peaceful future by building up a society void of violence and discrimination. She believes that Afghanistan is on the path to democracy and is heading towards a hopeful future, although there is still a long way to go. She has faced many challenges in her life, the toughest of which is discrimination against women's education and work.

Traditional customs did not make it easy for women to go to school in the 1950s. Striving for women's education is still needed.

Beggzadi Mahmuda Nasir

Central Women's University

When Beggzadi Mahmuda Nasir began her work on women's education in 1950, women in Bangladeshi society had nil space in public life. Coming from a liberal and educated family, Beggzadi had an advantage. Since she believes that education is essential to women's status, the deplorable condition of women's education disturbed her. Pursuing a dream with remarkable single-mindedness, Beggzadi set up the Central Women's College in 1956 and the Central Women's University in 1993.

Beggzadi Mahmuda Nasir was born in 1929 in undivided Bengal into a highly educated and liberal family, giving Beggzadi opportunities that few women of her time could count on. Studying at both Calcutta and Dhaka universities, she started her career in 1951 as a lecturer in English at Kumudini College, Tangail, Bangladesh. But teaching alone left her discontented: she firmly believed that the status of women in society would change only through the education of large numbers of women. In 1956, she founded the Central Women's College (CWC) in Dhaka. While friends and family were very supportive, funds barely trickled in. And then there were the bureaucratic barriers to cross. The college, however, flourished. In 1993, she founded the Central Women's University, the country's first women's university, in the campus of the CWC. From 1956 to 1992, she was the principal of the CWC, continuing as vice-chancellor of the university from 1993 to 1999. She is today chairperson of the institution's board of trustees.

Beggzadi was also the first woman member of the Syndicate of Dhaka University. She has received several state awards, was decorated by the Women's Federation for World Peace (Bangladesh) in 2001, and is a life fellow of the prestigious Bangla Academy. Beggzadi has spent 55 years working to promote education for women. With the odds — traditional and patriarchal-stacked against her, she convinced people that education is the route to women's liberation, and the primary condition for world peace.

Even today, female literacy in Bangladesh hovers around 28 percent. In the mid-1900s, the situation was much worse. There was no perceived need then for them to study, let alone pursue higher studies. With few exceptions, women were not active in the public domain.

Bangladesh

María Luisa Navarro Garrido

Sisters of the Sacred Heart
Community Center for Popular Promotion

Born in a house full of women, abounded with affections. Her mother wrote stories for a local newspaper and her father illustrated them. María Luisa Navarro Garrido knew about the existence of suffering, but did not experience it herself during her childhood. Since she was 20 years old, she was a nun. She has worked to promote public education in the most problematic villages of Venezuela. Her two passions: being religious and living from the heart.

"I am a woman who had two births, I was born and re-born," explains María Luisa Navarro Garrido. The first one was by the decision of her parents, in Madrid, Spain, in 1942. Her second birth was the result of her personal decision to live among the Venezuelan people. "Onto my Spanish roots the Venezuelan sap was engraved. That generated in me a great sympathy for this multicultural society and a special love for Bolivar's people and for the people of Don Quixote." The experience of living in an artisan's home made her sensitive to the daily things of life: "I specially loved the plants, I took care of them and I watered them and talked to them. Later, I discovered that I had an intense environmental consciousness that influenced a lot of the decisions I made in my life."

Educated in the School of the Sacred Heart, in Madrid, she chose the two major projects of her life: to be a nun and to live from the heart. She knew about the hard life of the peasants in the South of Spain. "I admired the courage of the women and my love for nature grew. I discovered my capacity to confront situations and I pledged my life to the struggles of the people."

In 1974, María Luisa Navarro Garrido arrived in the Paría peninsula, in the East of Venezuela. She was then 30 years old. Since then, she has carried on her work as a fighter for social causes, choosing to privilege those who are in most disadvantages in society and also striving for equal rights for women. "My achievements are collective achievements. They belong not to me but to the groups I work with. In Paría, I continued to discover more about the Venezuelan women, admiring their spirit of resistance and their courage. I felt pain for the injustice and inequality they suffered. I feel pain today for the disadvantages of the poor."

In the 1970s, the communities of the State of Sucre, in Venezuela, were characterized by very high poverty levels and poor provision of public education and health. This region has been traditionally excluded from benefiting from the wealth created by the oil development.

Venezuela

Loreta Navarro-Castro

Center for Peace Education (CPE)
Miriam College

Loreta Navarro-Castro (born 1948) is one of the pioneers of peace education research in the Philippines and founded the Center for Peace Education, based at Miriam College in Manila. As president of the college from 1987 to 1997, she took the lead in introducing peace-focused courses into the school curriculum and declared the school a Zone of Peace. Since 1997, the CPE has engaged with kindred institutions and has touched the lives of thousands of teachers and young people through its training programs in conflict resolution, peer-mediation and the promotion of a culture of peace.

In the early 1970s, before the dark days of Martial Law in the Philippines, Loreta Navarro-Castro, a young history teacher, would join protest rallies and marches against the regime of then President Ferdinand Marcos in Manila's tension-filled streets. She would join the marches but could not bring herself to mouth the angry chants, thinking: "Is this the message that we want to give? Will this kind of language change Marcos' heart and get us the results we want?"

Years later, her school, Maryknoll College, sent her to a conference on peace, economic equity, social justice and ecological balance in the United States. The ideas resonated with her right away. Shortly after the People Power Revolution of 1986 that toppled the dictator, Loreta was appointed president of Maryknoll College. During her 10-year term, she mainstreamed peace-focused courses into the school's curriculum, and convened a Peace Core Group. In 1991, the school declared itself a Zone of Peace, pledging to promote caring relationships, cooperation, nonviolent conflict resolution, and a simple lifestyle. Ending her term as president in 1997, she founded the Center for Peace Education at Miriam College (the new name for Maryknoll College) to continue her peace advocacy. Thousands of teachers and young people have benefited from its training programs and Loreta has learned that peace education is not just content, but also a process where "the medium is the message". She says: "Working for peace makes personal demands on us. We have to live it in our own lives, so that people will see us as credible agents. Otherwise the peace message will fail."

Although the Philippines has struggled with armed conflict for many generations, the advent of peace education in the country has come too slowly. Often marginalized because of its protracted outcome, peace education has found a home at the Center for Peace Education, based in Miriam College.

Philippines

Naw Zipporrah Sein

Karen Women's Organization (KWO)

Naw Zipporrah Sein was born in 1955 at Saw Kar Der Village, Kler Lweh Htoo District, Karen State, Burma. She was home educated by her mother before she went to school in the conflict zone in Karen State (Kaw Thoo Lie) where she completed her teacher education. For safety reasons, she sought refuge in Thailand in 1995 where she instilled and promoted education for Karen women in refugee camps. In 1998, Sein moved on to work for the Central Committee of the Karen Women's Organization (KWO) as coordinator and executive secretary, a position she still holds.

Naw Zipporrah Sein was born after the Karen people formed an army to fight Rangoon for their right to self-governance and sovereignty. Her family was part of the Karen revolutionary struggle, which meant they often had to move to flee persecution from the Burmese army. In 1995, Sein had to flee Burma and took refuge in Thailand. Although she and her compatriots were not given refugee status, she used her knowledge to promote education for Karen women, setting up a training system and advising Karen teacher groups. In 1995, Sein worked for the Karen Women's Organization as coordinator and executive secretary, but quit after two years to return to her full-time job as a teacher.

At KWO, Sein worked in seven refugee camps along the Thai-Burmese border and in internally displaced areas inside Karen State, helping women deal with family problems, sexual violence and drug abuse, and caring for orphans and unaccompanied children. Sein established a leadership school for young women that offered training courses to develop women's skills as professionals. She also set up a program for adult education, a safe house, a literary program, a nursery school, special needs education, a toy sharing program and a fundraising program. In 2003, Sein trained the staff of KWO to collect information from rape victims of the Burmese army. The information was compiled in a report called "Shattering Silence" which was launched at the 60th general assembly of the UN High Commission on Human Rights in Geneva in 2004. Sein has also worked on other initiatives to bring peace, freedom and equality for ethnic groups including an effort at national reconciliation in 2002.

The ethnic Karen people have been fighting for their right to self-governance and sovereignty. Many Karen people affected by persecution have fled to Thailand, where about 120,000 Karen refuge-seekers live in camps along the Thai-Burma border and hundreds of thousands work as migrant laborers.

Burma

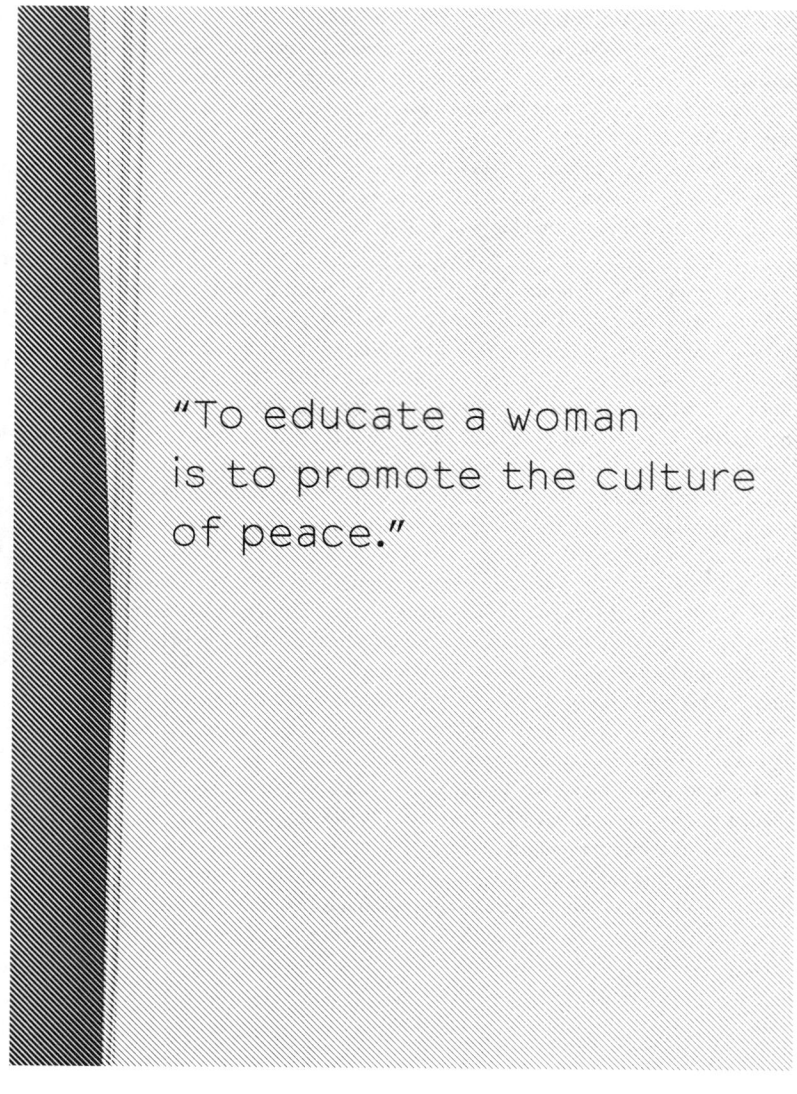

"To educate a woman
is to promote the culture
of peace."

Lea Ngaïdana

Association of Central African Women for the Fight Against Illiteracy (Afcla)

Lea Ngaïdana (45) founded the Association of Central African Women for the Fight Against Illiteracy (Afcla) in 2000. The association promotes literacy for women at all levels as the basis for fighting injustice, discrimination, violence, politico-military crisis and establishing long-lasting peace. Using communication, advocacy and negotiation, she helps women organize into working groups.

Lea Ngaïdana is the founder and chairlady of the Afcla. Since 2000 the association has promoted women to become partners. 80 percent of them are illiterate. She says the development of a country is achieved through better support for all women. This has not been the case in the Central African Republic where many women suffer daily violence.

Lea studied in Bangui where she obtained a technical and professional diploma, then joined the public service in 1984. She trained to become a literacy officer, and in 2002 she became the head of the literacy service. She has been awarded several distinctions for her contribution.

She uses information, eucation and communication, advocacy and negotiation to fight for the emancipation of rural women. Women of diverse backgrounds are organized into specific working groups, such as businesswomen, gardeners, food processors, farmers. However, her work is hampered by various problems including inadequate transport to the women's groups, often by public means. She also spends much time away from her family.

Lea raises financial support from international organizations. She successfully secured funds from the World Food Programme (WFP) and the Food and Agriculture Organisation (FAO) in 2004 to run literacy courses and start income-generating projects.

Lea was among a small group of women who presented peace proposals to the former president of the Central African Republic. In her capacity as assistant general secretary of the council of NGO's she also participated to preparatory seminars for the National Dialogue.

Lea has participated in meetings in support of peace organized by the UN agencies, the government and the civil societies, testifying her courageous involvement and devotion to the national cause and her conviction that development is possible only through lasting peace.

In landlocked Central African Republic, women have suffered successive politico-military crisis since 1996, in addition to various forms of violence and destructive traditions.

Central African Republic

Zeinab Nour

Zeinab Nour (born 1928) is a schoolteacher from El Gedaref State, Eastern Sudan. She was the first girl from the region to attend the Omdurman Institute for Teachers in 1939 and became a teacher in Eastern Sudan in 1941. For 47 years she has been supporting girls' education and women's empowerment. Her efforts are concentrated on combating the long-established social customs that have considered girls' education unnecessary and confined women's social role to marriage and procreation. Zeinab's work is coordinated with the Ministry of Education and other educational bodies.

Zeinab has always believed in and supported girls' right to education. She also has long-term experience in teaching, mainly in the remote suburbs of the Sudanese towns, where the education of girls was a breakthrough vision. The conditions of work in these areas were very difficult. In her words Zeinab recounts, "I was appointed as the Head of a School in El Khatmia, one of the suburbs of Kassala (a town several hours' journey from El Gadaref). On the way I had to cross a river running right through Kassala and dividing it into two. In autumn the river overflows and there was no means of transportation except being carried by people on special carriers. The school was at that time located in a wild, unpopulated area, with predatory animals. There was no electricity nor were there any other essential services in the area."
Zeinab, as the Head of the School, had to live on the school's premises. She brought along two of her cousins to stay with her, both of whom were influenced by her diligent character and later became teachers. Her dedication to girls' education and to the enhancement of their lives has sometimes put her own life and her children's lives at risk. In 1967 Zeinab received a promotion to join a school in a village called Kassab in El Gedaref. By that time, she was married and had four children, whom she had to take with her to work. The trip to and from work was hazardous and the only means of transportation was a market lorry. On one extremely rainy day, Zeinab and her kids boarded the lorry but just half an hour after the lorry had driven off, it broke down. It was windy and cold, and the kids were poorly; two had fever and felt sick. Luckily another truck passed by and took Zeinab and her kids to the nearest village. So, Zeinab's dedication to girls' education came from her commitment to bringing a real change to women's life in the Sudan.

Girls have benefited from Zeinab's painstaking work towards girls' education. Thanks to her unrelenting efforts, many girls have graduated from university and have become financially able to support themselves and their families. This is a step towards the development and welfare of the Sudan.

Nualnoy Timkoon

Ban Kru Noy Child Care Center

Nualnoy Timkoon, better known as "Kru Noy" (Teacher Noy) was born in 1944, one of 13 children, in Meenburi, Bangkok. The family lived in abject poverty, and early in life, Noy had to earn a living taking on any available job. Her experience of poverty inspired her to help vulnerable and marginalized children in urban areas, an advocacy she took up in 1980. "Ban Kru Noy" (Kru Noy's Home) was registered as a childcare center with the Department of Social Welfare in 1987. Kru Noy worked by herself for ten years before funders and organizations offered to help in various ways.

Nualnoy Timkoon, or Kru Noy, lived with her husband in an orchard area in the Ratburana neighborhood of Bangkok, a mega city that draws people needing jobs from everywhere. 13 years ago, Ratburana was a hub for all kinds of menial labor where a large number of migrant workers and their families built their homes on private land until they were evicted. In 1980, while staying home due to frail health, Kru Noy began helping marginalized children. Semi-paralyzed and unable to walk properly, she was attended by an eight-year old boy when her husband went to work. The migrant children in the neighborhood roamed the fruit orchards and randomly picked produce without asking permission, and the owners used sticks or slingshots to chase them away. But in her orchard, Kru Noy waved them to come closer. Soon she opened her house as a refuge where she fed the children and taught them how to read and write. Word of her kindness spread, bringing in more children who sought her help and her expenses grew. Undeterred by a lack of resources, she borrowed money to support her initiative. She was determined to help all children attain the same opportunity to become good citizens.

Ten years later, when word of her work had spread, material support began pouring in to Ban Kru Noy Child Care Center. She mounted a campaign to pressure state schools to accept vulnerable children and thus give them equal educational opportunities with or without evidence to prove they were born in Thai territory. In 1991, the government began allowing children without birth certificates to enroll in state schools. Many of the children she supported have graduated from university and have returned to help her at the Center. Kru Noy's work knows no end. She has very little private life, as she devotes herself entirely to increasing the opportunities for children who are neglected by society.

Ban Kru Noy Child Care Center provides a physical and spiritual refuge for the children of poor migrants who live in the teeming slums of Bangkok. Without intervention like Kru Noy's, such marginalized and vulnerable children would not have the opportunity to go to school and the option to improve their lives.

Thailand

Nun Pratin Kwan-On

Thai Nun Institute

Nun Pratin Kwan-On was born in 1944 in Bang-Jaan, Muang District, Pechaburi Province, and has been President of the Thai Nun Institute since 1996. She became a nun when she was 19 years old and studied Dharma, obtaining her Master's degree in India in 1976. She founded the Thai Nun Institute to help nuns in Thailand get an education and improve their status. She also established the Dharmajarinividhaya School in 1990 for young women, offering basic education, rights protection and advancement for young women in Thailand who lack the opportunity to improve their lives.

When she was young, Pratin Kwan-On's life was no different from that of other village girls. She went to primary school, after which she sewed for a living until she had health problems. When her father asked her to become a nun, she agreed, and in 1963, she entered a monastery in Wat Sanampram, Pechaburi Province, and studied Dharma. "As a nun I got to know chastity, learn the history of Buddhism, and learn about Dharma doctrine as a phenomenon," she says. "Before, I never knew that to be born, grow old, suffer and die are normal things." She finished her Dharma and Pali studies, achieving grade six, in 1970. In 1972, she went to India to study because there is no school for nuns in Thailand. Nun Pratin obtained her Bachelor's degree in Pali Arjariya and her Master's degree in history in India in 1976. While studying in India, she realized that one problem of Thai nuns is the lack of opportunity to study and she made it her goal to set up a school for nuns when she returned to Thailand. But firstly in 1977, Nun Pratin established the Thai Nun Institute in Pak-Tor district, Rachaburi province. Today, the Thai Nun Institute has 26 branches around the country and more than 10,000 members. Secondly in 1990, she founded the Dharmajarinividhaya School for young women who are interested in the study of Buddhism. The school also offers general subjects.

The Thai Nun Institute also established the Mahaprachabordee College in Nakornrachasima province in 1999 and offers Bachelor's degrees in general subjects and the study of Buddhism. It cooperates with the Institute of Thai Women Facilitation of the Mahamakut Rachavidhayalai University. Nun Pratin has spent more than 33 years initiating projects to improve the status of nuns in Thailand.

There are more than 10,000 nuns in Thailand, but they are not recognized by the Religion Department. The Thai Nun Institute has proposed the enactment of the Thai Nun Act, but the Department has refused to endorse it because the Buddhist Act makes no reference to nuns.

Thailand

Nikiwe Nyamakazi

Ithemba Youth Group

Nikiwe Nyamakazi (47) is a strong religious woman, who is raising her two children on her own. She is a member of the local Methodist Church. Nikiwe did her schooling in the townships around Port Elizabeth. She completed her education at Kamvelihle Adult School in Port Elizabeth and went on to work for the department of welfare as a youth caregiver. Nikiwe has dedicated her entire life to the upliftment of her people. She resigned from work to offer her time and house for the benefit of her people. She fights for the dignity and rights of the poor, sick and disenfranchized.

In the 1980s Nikiwe saw the need to open a pre-school for the underprivileged. This introduced her to the challenges that the people in her community have to face. Nikiwe became involved in her community from an early age. She understands the tremendous problems the youth has to face and has realized that to assist them requires a huge commitment from her and others who have a role to play.

Nikiwe also started a hospice to care for those dying of Aids, whose families could not afford to take care of them. She also regularly makes house visits to patients that are cared for by family members. She provides regular counseling and debriefing sessions to those affected and infected by the disease.

Her programs do not have a sponsor but depend on generous donations from members of the community and occasional assistance from the local business sector. The community has taken pride in, and ownership of, these programs and facilities. There is little security provided and programs rely on the vigilance of the community for surety. Nikiwe relies on the generosity of local undertakers and business to bury patients whose families cannot afford to bury them.

Port Elizabeth is a coastal city in Eastern Province, one of South Africa's poorest provinces, with record numbers of unemployment. The townships of Port Elizabeth are crowded, under-resourced, have huge unemployment rates and serious substance abuse problems.

South Africa

Silvia Vera Ocampo

Museo Argentino de Artistas Plásticas (Argentine Museum of Women Artists)
Association of Friends of the Museum

In her work, Silvia Ocampo has captured, with vitality and sensitivity, the social problems of her time. After graduating as a professor of Fine Arts, she joined the art studio of master Demetrio Urruchúa and took charge of it when, in 1955, the master was captured. She gave birth to the Del Plata Group. As a painter and designer, Silvia felt excluded "for being a woman." In reaction to that, she made a study of the situation faced by professional women and wrote two essays on the matter. She also founded a virtual museum of women artists.

Her mother gave birth to her in La Rioja, a province in the countryside of Argentina. But it was the capital city of Buenos Aires that gave birth to her as an artist and a woman aware of herself and her surroundings. She is Silvia Ocampo, a painter, feminist and social fighter.

Soon after her graduation from the National School of Fine Arts, she joined the art studio of master Demetrio Urruchúa, a painter with a social conscience who was convinced that the militancy of an artist must be reflected in his or her work. And Silvia, who had always been a non-conformist, absorbed that message. She took charge of the master's studio when, in 1955, he was captured as part of the repression Peron's government exercised against the people they considered as their ideological enemies. Along with other young male and female artists, Silvia Ocampo gave birth to the Del Plata Group, which arose from the studio of Urruchúa, and continued until its dissolution in 1964. This would be a time of integrated learning.

She has witnessed many things: the time of her master's detention; the cultural revolution of 1968; the vindication of the feminists; the repression carried out by the military dictatorship (1976-1983); the war between her country and Great Britain for the Falkland Islands in 1982; and the corruption of the "democratic governments." She has always been on the side of justice and peace. She has written about her feminism in two essays: "Equilibrium between the sexes — An analysis of the feminine matter" (1980) and "Male and Female Roles, Conditioning or Biology?" (1987). In 1997, she created the virtual Museo Argentino de Artistas Plásticas (Argentine Museum of Women Artists) on the internet, and now she is trying to make it real, through the creation of the Association of Friends of the Museum.

Throughout history, almost always, men have signed the works of art. Although today there are numerous female artists, few are valued for their work. The situation is not different in Argentina.

Argentina

Sophie Patty

Sophie Patty (born 1928) came to Jayapura in 1962 to spread Christianity. She travelled throughout the inland areas where she learned about the problems of the people and met many children who had been abandoned by their families. She cared for these children and with very limited resources, provided shelter and education for them. She later became involved in peace negotiations to resolve conflicts arising in the villages. Hundreds of men and women in Papua owe their lives to Sophie.

Sophie Patty, of Moluccan origin, first came to Papua as a member of a church mission to spread Christianity. "I remember those days. We had to report to the High Commander of West Irian in Jakarta in order to go to Papua," she recalls. The political conditions in Papua were very critical. The government issued a security alert in the island. Sophie was working with Dewan Gereja Indonesia (Indonesian Church Council) and was Council Secretary for Oikumene Christian Council from 1956 to 1962. Sophie travelled all over the island to understand the culture. She recounts, "I travelled to the remote inland, mountain and various districts. Because we had no money, I travelled by boat to visit other districts. On one trip, I travelled to Biak by boat, then to Manokwari and inland. We had to walk through the forest and it took three days just to reach the next village. We had no food at all."
In the 1970s, Sophie began to realize her dream to work with children and improve their education. "We worked with many kinds of children. We took in street children and taught them how to read and write after nine pm. We also introduced them to other materials according to their age and psychological development." Those who take refuge in her shelter are children whose parents have separated, are lost, dead or live in another district and therefore need a place to stay. Some children were abandoned at her doorstep. Sophie yearns for the day the children can help build a better Papua. "I dream that they will become highly responsible leaders. I am already 76 years old, but look at me: I am still able to work. I will continue helping the children, so that later they can help others."

In the 1960s, the Indonesian Government declared Papua a Military Operation Zone, raising tensions between ethnic groups and the military. Papua is almost untouched by development, but vested political and economic interests out to dominate its resources have turned it into a conflict area.

Indonesia

Jacqueline Pitanguy

Cidadania, Estudo, Pesquisa, Informação e Ação (Citizenship, Studies, Information, Action)

In the 1970s, Jacqueline Pitanguy (1945) was important in the creation and consolidation of a feminist flag, which contributed to the resistance to the military dictatorship. In the end of the 1980s, the sociologist and political scientist participated actively in the process of re-democratization of Brazil, defending women's benefits. Today, in charge of the Forum of the Civil Society of the Americas, founded by her, she became a respected leadership in the area of human rights, in the entire continent.

Jacqueline Pitanguy studied Sociology and Political Sciences in the United States, Europe and Chile, in a circuit which, since the beginning, guaranteed her a view of the international dimension of fight for democracy and for human rights. In her return to Brazil in the 1970s, she went to work in a research about the conditions of the job market and found out the size of the inequality between men and women. This discovery motivated her to integrate the group of founders of the new feminist movement in the country. From this time, she believes that the most important thing was the construction of a feminist flag that contributed to the resistance to the military dictatorship in all Latin America. "This was a mark in the history of Latin-American women."

When she completed ten years of feminist and left-wing militancy, Jacqueline took on the presidency of the National Council of Women's Rights, remaining there for four years. Created in 1985, when the advance of Brazil in the re-democratization process forced the Presidency to once again be occupied by a civilian, the Council was a pioneer initiative. It reunited state and civil society in the definition of public policies to attend women.

Today, Jacqueline Pitanguy's work goes beyond her duties as director of Cepia (Citizenship, Study, Research, Information and Action), a non-governmental organization created by her in 1990. Founder of the Forum of the Civil Society of the Americas, she is articulated in a network of organizations that acts in the area of human rights in the Continent. She woke up to the importance of uniting forces in Latin America when she lived in Chile during the democratic government of Salvador Allende. Since then, she has been building a "global view of the defense of human rights and of women's rights."

The National Council of Women's Rights was a model multiplied in many countries of Latin America. Until this day, it is responsible for the implementation of public policies regarding gender in Brazil.

Brazil

Marjorie Prentice Saunders

United Church

When she was a child, she chose a great road: God. Under his guidance, she carried out marriages, funerals, baptisms, qualifying courses for women, and workshops for educating immigrants. Marjorie Prentice Saunders was the first Jamaican woman to be a Minister of the Presbyterian Church. Revolutionary in her perspective, she was never afraid of breaking traditions. She gave a lifetime of service to education and social work through community mobilization.

Marjorie Prentice Saunders was born in 1913 in Galina, St. Mary, Jamaica. One hour after her birth, her parents took her by horse on a three-mile-long trip to attend the opening of the Synod of the Presbyterian Church. Since then, she has been near the Lord Jesus Christ. She was a privileged girl, she grew up surrounded by the love of seven siblings, and her family had the opportunity to guide the education of every one of them. She was always on the platform, next to her father. By his hand, she understood that education was like magic: it needed to be shared. She was a pioneer in the creation of preparatory schools for boys and girls. She helped to understand the importance of early childhood education. Under her leadership, the community programs grew until including regional and international collaboration.
She was commissioned by the United Church in Jamaica and Cayman Islands to carry out the Christian and social work among 4000 immigrants that lived in Sheffield, England. She helped to break the cultural barriers through study groups and she wrote the manual on "Living in Britain." She has been that, an indefatigable Minister of the Church. She registered the rights of women in the church and in society.

In Jamaica, there were numerous racial, gender and religious barriers that did not allow the majority of the population to get an education. Only the privileged ones had access to education. There was no consciousness of the importance of early childhood education.

Jamaica

Odonchimeg Puntsag

Liberal Women's Brain Pool (Leos)

Odonchimeg Puntsag (1961), a labor economist, has worked with different organizations, including the Liberal Women's Brain Pool (Leos). In 1999 she set up the Information and Education Center, which is principally a mobile library dedicated to bringing news and information to the more remote areas of Mongolia; whole communities are able to access a huge range of materials that were otherwise unavailable to them. The Center also runs training sessions on orientation and self-education, assisting readers in selecting books and themes that are relevant to their own situation.

Odonchimeg has seen vast changes in Mongolia since the decline of communism, not least of which is the growing divide between rich and poor. She feels there are many reasons for the growing poverty, for example that "people too readily accept becoming poor. Becoming poor in terms of livelihood and poor in terms of intellectual capacity are intertwined processes". The nomadic, isolated lifestyle of Mongolians makes access to news and information difficult, time-consuming and costly.

Odonchimeg hit upon the idea of a mobile library to reduce these constraints. She worked the principle to suit the Mongolian geography, life style and mentality, and invented an effective means of delivering a large and well-chosen selection of books to rural households. To promote the libraries and their effective use, workshops are run to help the readers choose subjects relevant to them, and understand the dynamics of the mobile library and book ordering process. The purpose of the libraries is to increase awareness of the current social, political and economic climate in Mongolia, and to assist people in understanding how to adapt and survive in a free market economy and a "democratic" society.

Odonchimeg has also helped establish a local home for orphans and street children. She says the orphanage "gives the children the chance to experience a few years of life in a familial context, before they leave at 16 or 17." The children are taught to plant and harvest vegetables, as well as to prepare and cook them. Sheep are also raised, providing a source of milk, wool and meat. The older children are encouraged to take responsibility for and train the younger ones. "Street children and orphans are a "time bomb"; they are our — adults' — fault and we bear the responsibility to correct the situation," she says.

The effects of the collapse of communism in 1989 are still being felt in Mongolia on various levels: social, political and economic. One of the major issues is that of growing poverty, which has led to, among other things, homelessness, alienation and familial disintegration.

Dilafrose Qazi

SSM College of Engineering — Baramulla, Kashmir

Dilafrose Qazi (born 1962) battles lack of security and harsh weather conditions in the violence-scarred state of Jammu and Kashmir to help the women and children, many of whom have been deprived of a proper education by the 16-year armed separatist struggle. Starting small with classes in cutting and tailoring for girls and housewives, Dilafrose now runs an engineering college and several primary schools and vocational training centers.

Dilafrose Qazi was born in Baramulla in the Kashmir Valley. It was a poorly literate family — no one had, in fact, been to school. Dilafrose's father made leather garments, and her mother wove pashmina shawls. With her mother determined to educate her two sons and two daughters, Dilafrose studied at a free government school, and then finished her masters in education as well as a law degree from Kashmir University. Unable, however, to land a government job, she started a small venture in rented premises in 1988: classes for girls and housewives in cutting, stitching, cooking, and shorthand. That was also the year she was married. Her venture picked up, but the beginning of the armed separatist struggle in the Kashmir Valley a year later put paid to its further growth. Everything — violence, state security, militants — worked against women and girls attending schools and colleges. Since Dilafrose had no other source of income, she had to shell out ransom to keep her classes going, and her husband was kidnapped for a while.

In 1994, Dilafrose procured land in the backward Baramulla district, inhabited mainly by the Shia community, to help them get an education. That small institution is now a hefty engineering college. Dilafrose also started a free primary school in 1996 in the village Divar Parihaspora in Baramulla district. In 1998, she opened another school in the village Sumbal in Dangarpora. In 2001, Dilafrose started a free primary school at Kunan Poshpora in the Kupwara district, a militant haven and military overkill zone. She organized self-help groups for the traumatized women, giving each a highbred cow and helping them run a dairy farm.

The armed separatist struggle in Kashmir, which began in 1989, made it extremely difficult for women and girls to go to schools and colleges, not just because of the gratuitous violence, but because militants from some hardline separatist groups forbade it.

India

Lalita Ramdas

Pak-India Forum for Peace and Democracy (PIFPD)

Lalita Ramdas (born 1940) stepped out of a conventional, hierarchical environment to become a voice in support of alternative education, gender sensitivity, secularism, peace, and nuclear disarmament. In the early 1980s, she put in place pathbreaking initiatives for development education in a number of elite schools. Living in a small village in India's west coast, she is involved in the life of the local community while pursuing citizens' peace initiatives with Pakistan and contributing to the global adult education movement.

One day she is sitting with teachers at a village school talking about the election violence and how teachers can try to counter this. The following day, she catches a train to travel several hundred miles to join up with volunteers in Ayodhya, where Hindu nationalists demolished a mosque in 1992, to give support to the town's Muslim minority. Lalita Ramdas, daughter and wife of high-ranking naval officers, turned from a quiet conformist to passionately handling a range of causes. She has worked for years as a simple community-level nonformal educator in Delhi's slums, participated in street theater to raise awareness on dowry, rape, and other gender issues, interacted with education policymakers, and founded Ankur (1980 to 1982), a society for alternatives in education. In 1984, in the aftermath of the anti-Sikh pogrom, Lalita testified against the government before a commission of inquiry.

Placed in a position of leadership when her husband came to head the Indian navy, Lalita worked to transform a traditionalist naval wives' association into a forum which took up issues such as gender justice and human rights. After her husband's retirement, the couple ensconced themselves in a village in Maharashtra, where they set up a local trust that worked in health and education.

Lalita contested and was elected president of the International Council for Adult Education in December 1994, when her village lacked phone, fax, and email. She also carried on her work as a peace activist, visiting Pakistan as a member of the Pak-India Forum. Soon after India's nuclear explosion at Pokhran, Lalita and her husband publicly opposed the government's decision, despite threats from a number of right-wing groups. They also spoke up fearlessly against the killings in Gujarat in 2002.

Adult education in India is a disputable terminology, lending itself to bipolar, often subjective, interpretations: either signature-based "literacy" or education as empowerment, depending on which state wants the highest statistics.

India

Betty Reardon

Peace Education Center at Teachers College (Columbia University)
Hague Appeal for Peace Global Campaign for Peace Education

Betty A. Reardon (born 1929) is acknowledged worldwide as a founder of peace education. For over 40 years she has developed curricula, taught courses, led teacher-training workshops, and given countless talks to grassroots meetings, university symposia, and international conferences. She founded the Peace Education Center at Teachers College (Columbia University) and has been centrally involved in organizing internationally for peace education. Now retired from Teachers College, she continues to travel widely and to teach about peace education in many settings.

Betty Reardon was brought up in Rye, near New York City. Recalling important influences on her life, she writes: "My mother was a feminist but did not know it and an outspoken antiracist when it was not the norm in the community. I had some wonderful teachers, one of whom taught the realities of racial injustice and 'internationalism' — taking us to sessions at Flushing Meadow where the UN General Assembly met before world headquarters were built." Betty became a teacher, and in 1963, she started full-time in peace education with the Institute of World Order. She was concerned with critical inquiry into war as a system. This was a difficult time to undertake such work in the USA as many people supported the Vietnam War. Betty was subject to "official observation" as were most peace movement people.

For over 40 years Betty has developed curricula for peace education, taught courses, led teacher-training workshops, and given countless talks to grassroots meetings, university symposia, and international conferences. She founded the Peace Education Center at Teachers College (Columbia University) and used this institutional niche to organize the International Institute on Peace Education. Betty was centrally involved in the Hague Appeal for Peace Global Campaign for Peace Education. She has been a visiting professor at universities across the USA and abroad, served as a consultant to several UN agencies and education organizations, and published widely on peace, human rights education, and women's issues. She is acknowledged worldwide as a pioneer and founder of peace education, and received the Unesco Honorable Mention Award in 2001. Betty has inspired many people to take peace work and education as their life's endeavor.

Recently, support for peace education and conflict resolution has gained ground in the USA, especially in elementary schools and communities. But at the national level ignorance of other peoples, mainstream media, and pressure to be "patriotic" all mobilize popular support for war and violence.

United States of America

"Nietzsche was right
when he said that history
is life. History is a
civilizing influence."

Irma Leticia Silva Rodríguez de Oyuela

National Autonomous University of Honduras
Center-American Chamber of the Book
International Institute for the Conservation of Monuments

Honduras, Tegucigalpa, 1935. A middle-class girl is born. Both her parents are schoolteachers, as were her grandmother and her great-grandmother. As time goes by, she will become a lawyer. But time turns things around and Leticia de Oyuela becomes a historian, which means that, in her own way, she also becomes a teacher.

"The greatest richness I have enjoyed has been my childhood," says Leticia Silva Rodríguez de Oyuela, with a smile, sitting in her wheelchair. However, reading her biography, you will think that the greatest richness has been her own life.

All the women in her family have been teachers. "I learned to read when I was four years old. At age nine, I knew almost all the classics." They lived in Tegucigalpa, the capital city of Honduras. In 1932, her mother married a teacher like herself, and one year later Leticia was born. At age 12, she applied for the teacher training school, but she was rejected because of her age. She entered the Central Institute for Boys, in the annex for girls. Later on, she studied Law and married a fellow classmate. He was appointed as consul in Spain. In Europe, she studied History and Aesthetics. When she returned, she directed the Extension Department of the National University where she formed small art schools and developed a strong publishing house.

In 1972, she was running the New Continent Publishing House and her Art Gallery, Leo. She took the work of several Honduran writers to international fairs and exposed them to the public. Grouped around the publishing house, there was a library, a center for antiques and plastic arts. She took 14 art exhibitions abroad. This hectic activity was suddenly cut short. She had a stroke and a heart attack. Her body was weakened, but her brain was not. She wrote history. She focused on characters that were considered secondary, which were mainly women.

In an environment where women were normally relegated to a secondary role, Leticia managed to command respect as an intellectual. By explaining the role of women and the forgotten people in Honduran history, she increased national consciousness of the situation. And without consciousness peace is not possible.

Honduran women have little access to education. Around the time of the 1950s, there were only two female doctors of law. They could not practice law since they did not have the right to vote.

Maria José Rosado Nunes

Católicas pelo Direito de Decidir (CDD)

Maria José Rosado Nunes (1945) was the first Brazilian nun to publicly criticize the sexist attitudes of the Catholic church's progressive wing. In the beginning of the 1980s, she contested left-wing religious authorities who "used to fight against poverty and for social justice, but not against the prohibition of women's right to become priests and not for women's sexual and reproductive rights." After leaving the church, she founded in Brazil an organization called Católicas pelo Direito de Decidir (Catholics for the Right to Decide).

Prostitutes of Barra do Mendes, a city in the hinterland of Bahia, used to live on Palha Street. To go from her house to the school, where she would give classes, the newly arrived nun Maria José Rosado Nunes had two options: walk down that street or go all the way around the church square. The decision was pretty obvious: take the longer way. Sister Zeca, as she was known, made a decision upon which she has based her life and that made her, years later, leave the church: saying no to any kind of discrimination against women. Zeca made friends among the women of Palha Street.

Two years later, she moved to the countryside of Acre, in the North of Brazil. As a member of Pastoral of the Land, the church's progressive wing, she used to go inside the forest to meet and bring together the rubber plant workers. Two more years went by. Zeca, graduated in arts, decided to go back to school. She moved to São Paulo, where she got a master's degree in sociology. Invited by feminists to participate in lectures, Zeca has openly opposed to the Catholic church's attitude towards women. She has faced fierce bishops and religious extremists.

In 1985, Zeca went to Europe to study for a post-doctoral degree from the School of High Studies of Paris, in France. When she came back to Brazil, five years later, she had left the church. Here, Zeca kept fighting and also continued her academic career. Nowadays, she is a professor of sociology of religion and gender at the Pontific Catholic University of São Paulo. In 1984, she founded the organization Catholics for the Right to Decide (CDD), which defends women's rights, especially when it comes to their reproduction and contraceptive choices.

Católicas pelo Direito de Decidir (CDD) was created in Latin America in 1987. Founded in Brazil in 1994, it has carried out an important work with health professionals from public hospitals that practice abortion on rape victims. "For being Catholics, many of them refused to have it done."

Brazil

Heleieth Saffioti

Heleieth Saffioti (1934) is a sociologist. She wrote dozens of books about the inequalities between men and women, emphasizing gender violence. She conquered every title in the academic career and has hundreds of articles published in Brazil and abroad. As a controversial and essential presence in feminist studies, Heleieth uses her teachings and her words as tools for building a better world.

"I was born in a place that had no electricity, where people lived and worked under the sunlight and the oil lamp. My father was a bricklayer and my mother a dressmaker. When I was ten years old, I used to embroider baby clothes." Little Heleieth loved studying and made curiosity her guiding star to learn what school had to offer. Another of this girl's characteristics that remained in the woman was her rebelliousness. "Being poor, my destiny was to be a dressmaker, and as a woman, to be a housewife. I changed both those destinies." Her strategy is to clearly say what she wants. That is how she got rid of a priest's attempt to catechize her: "If you, Sir, think that — with this authoritarian preaching — you are going to make me start believing in God, you are very wrong." This is Heleieth Saffioti, unafraid to speak her mind. "On the second day of my marriage, I explained to my husband that I would make all the decisions concerning my life."

As someone who learns, she is not reluctant to teach. "I teach at home, on the street and in the subway." She teaches at university and when she writes books. One of them is a best-seller with 12 successive editions: "O Poder do Macho" (Macho's Power). In the book "Gender, Patriarchate, Violence" (2004) she demonstrates all of her argumentative power with incisive writing, making the historical reasons for male domination very clear. For decades, her books, articles and lectures have been a theoretical source for feminist activism. When practice grows cloudy, her knowledge clarifies. At the same time that she teaches future masters in one of the most famous universities in Brazil, she gives lectures to women of little schooling. "In this life, what I most enjoy is people."

The production of feminist knowledge, which is rigorous and systematic, is a conquest for all women, educated or not. Less than a century ago, library book shelves lacked books on feminist subjects. Researchers had to dribble numerous obstacles in order to begin the construction of this knowledge.

Schuma Schumaher

Rede de Desenvolvimento Humano (REDEH)

Schuma Schumaher (born 1952) found feminism in the late 1970s, and it was like she had found the answers to the questions she had since her childhood. She lived in a small rural city in the state of São Paulo named Santa Fé do Sul, dedicated to the cultivation of coffee and cotton. Even though she worked in plantations since she was six years old, her biggest dream was to study.

With education and culture Schuma Schumaher, who already had a degree in pedagogy, was able to comprehend the ways of feminist militancy, which started in São Paulo City in the 1970s. During this period, she was part of the foundation of the Brazilian Women's Center and also of the first SOS Woman in Brazil, which helped women victims of violence. This group's effort was the first step in the creation of Police Precincts Specialized in Aiding Women Victims of Violence. After that, she moved on to work in the National Council of Woman's Rights, created by Brazil's first civil president after 20 years of military dictatorship. Schuma moved to Brasilia, the national capital, and her involvement with politics became more intense. In 1987, she was working actively in what was known as the Lipstick Lobby — a women's movement that fought for the inclusion of female rights in the new Brazilian Constitution.

Schuma Schumahers passion for movies and her work in the cultural scenario led her to Rio de Janeiro, where she moved to in 1988. In 1991, she started working at the Rede de Desenvolvimento Humano (Network for Human Development), a non-governmental organization she coordinated. She developed the project named "Woman — 500 years behind the curtains" — an extensive research on women's contribution to Brazilian history. With this project, a dictionary with the names of 500 women was produced. She believes that peace depends on the capacity of each person to live in society in a less violent manner. Ergo, feminism is a way of affirming women's rights, anti-racist and anti-homophobic.

Internationally, Schuma Schumaher attended two important UN conferences in the 1990s: ECO-92 (Rio de Janeiro), where she was directing the participation of REDEH in the Female Planet, and the Women's World Conference (1995, Beijing).

The battle on violence against women happens in Brazil throughout the actions of the Ministry of Justice, also throughout the actions of the Police Precincts Specialized in Aiding Women Victims of Violence. There are more than 200 of these specialized police precincts all over Brazil.

Brazil

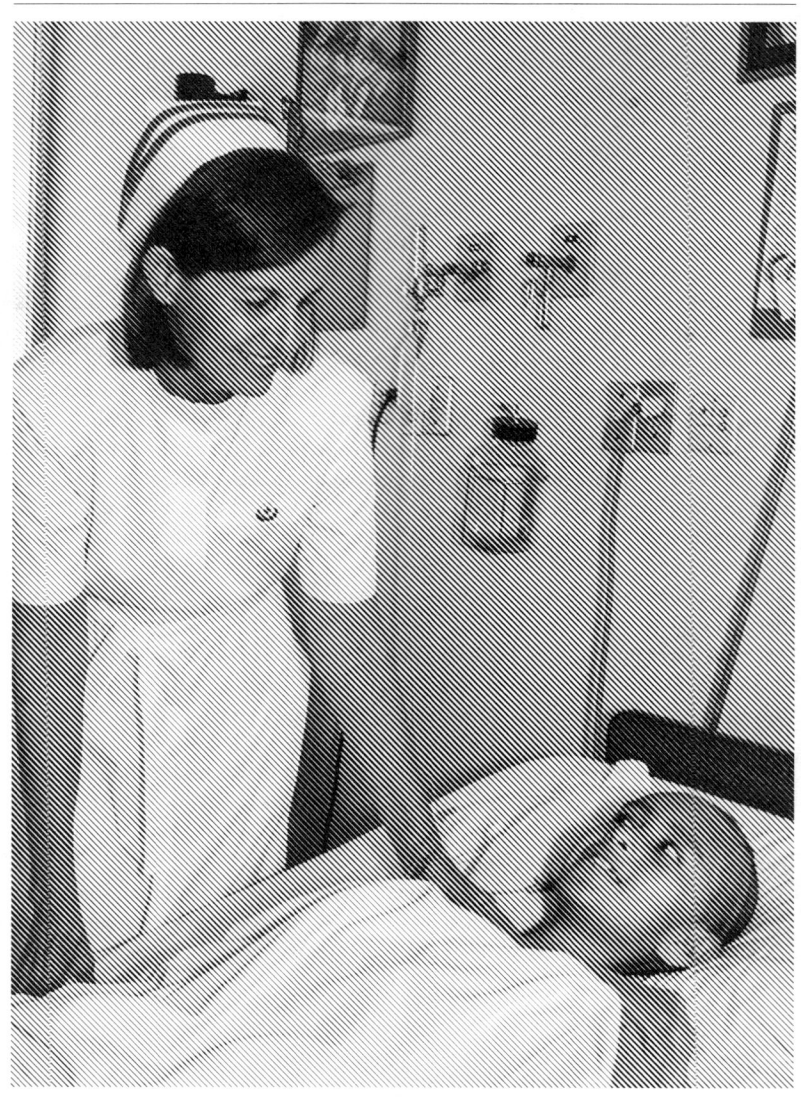

Maria del Pilar Sertvije de Mariscal

Mexican Red Cross

Maria del Pilar Sertvije de Mariscal has a large, united family. It even has its own "constitution." It has a tradition of voluntary social work, even though the focus has changed throughout the generations. She is the daughter of a wealthy businessman and, therefore, she has the option of dedicating her life to her passions: voluntary social work and nursing.

Maria was born in Mexico City, in 1946. She is the second child in a family of six daughters and two sons. Mexico is a country of great inequalities. She was taught by her father to be responsible and to support people with fewer resources. From her mother, she received firm values and a Christian education. "As a little girl, I was very much inspired by the life of the saints, and, in my imaginative play, I used to take on the role of a religious woman devoted to the service of others."

Since 1999, Maria del Pilar Sertvije de Mariscal has been the president of the Mexican Red Cross and is a member of different philanthropic organizations, such as the Merced Foundation and the Mexican Centre for Philanthropy. She is very interested in the improvement of the quality of vocational training for nurses. "The role of nurses must be dignified. In our country they are so poorly paid that no one wants to be a nurse. I have a great vocation for this work and the great luck of being able to dedicate myself to something I am fond of." Maria has been dedicated to voluntary service for 36 years. "I have tried to be where my work is most needed. I have many responsibilities and I am convinced that we have to serve the country." This inspirational woman, mother of four children, gains great satisfaction from her work.

The voluntary sector in Mexico is tending to decrease. In times of economic crisis, people are more worried about their own material security. Consumerism, egoism, and social apathy are growing. Donations are meagre and philanthropic institutions poorly supported.

Natalia Shabunz

Civil Dignity
Counterpart Consortium

Natalia Shabunz lives and works under Turkmenistan's authoritarian regime as a well-known educator, writer, and public and human rights activist. She started her work in Turkmenistan when civil society activism first began to take shape in the nation, but maintains that even today the democratic culture of the Turkmen population needs to be strengthened even more. Fighting some very difficult conditions, Natalia has often been persecuted by local authorities for her work in education and public activity.

Natalia Shabunz has been active in the public sector and the civil movement in Turkmenistan since 1993 — in schools, youth centers, and NGOs. Since 1999, she has been a trainer for the organization Counterpart Consortium, and is also a leader of the youth-centered NGO Civil Dignity. Natalia's books on civil society, democracy, and human rights are well-known throughout the Central Asian countries and the Confederation of Independent States (CIS). Her writing has helped challenge and alter national and international understanding of the political and human rights situation in Turkmenistan, and the general world outlook for people living under authoritarian regimes. Natalia has held hundreds of training programs and seminars for thousands of participants — NGO leaders, journalists, and women across the country and abroad. She has also participated in both regional and international conferences on education, rights, and NGO development, reporting and sharing her experiences with colleagues all over the world. During the years NGOs were suppressed by authorities, Natalia has been active in the struggle to support many NGOs in Turkmenistan and has helped their leaders do their jobs in these difficult political situations. Natalia has often been persecuted by local authorities herself, and she explains how she was "always under the watchful eye of Turkmen security services." She has been arrested several times, and is often "advised" to stop activities by the authorities. But even in these difficult conditions Natalia continues to do her job and unconditionally believes in the values of democratic change and human rights. Apart from supporting teachers and NGO leaders, her main focus is on youth and women, through whom she has had undeniable influence on Turkmenistan's civil society initiatives, and the people's struggle for rights.

Turkmenistan has been under a dictatorial authoritarian regime since 1991. NGOs are suppressed both officially and otherwise, and the rights of women and their equality are a serious issue, as are the problems among children and youth.

Turkmenistan

Nafisa Shargawi

Women Workers Union (WWU)
Sudanese Women General Union (SWGU)

Nafisa Mustafa Shargawi (50) was born in Port Sudan. She graduated from the Faculty of Arts, Cairo University — Khartoum Branch, and obtained a diploma in Information Systems. Now she is preparing for her MA in Islamic Studies. Nafisa is also the first woman journalist and writer in the Eastern State in the Sudan, regularly writes in the local and regional newspapers on women's and children's rights and is also a short story writer. Now she is the General Manager of the Information and Culture Ministry, Sudan.

Nafisa is also a journalist and TV presenter. Every day she faces many challenges in her work, immersed in her indefatigable efforts to unfold the truth and address crucial issues in the Sudan. One day she was covering a reportage in Port-Sudan Hospital with a photographer. She obtained permission from the hospital's general manager to visit the major operations theatre. She was shocked when she saw the place: there was no sterilizing system, the surgical tools were very old and there was no clean running water. The photographer took photographs to show the catastrophic condition of the hospital. While she was interviewing a group of patients, Nafisa was physically harassed by some hospital workers to obstruct her interviews. Fortunately, the hospital guard stopped them and saved her life. When the reportage was screened on Port-Sudan TV, the administration of the hospital punished all the people who had assisted Nafisa during her visit, and some of them were even fired. Nafisa's job was also at risk, as her coverage of the scene in the hospital put many officials in the hot seat and made them pressurize for her release from her job with Sudanese TV.
Nafisa wrote a lot of books, most of which openly address the social and cultural barriers to women's social and economical participation. She touched upon very sensitive issues that are not publicly open for discussion in Sudanese society and is working hard for a society where women can live peacefully and dignifiedly.

Nafisa's intellectual writing has a great impact upon society in the Sudan. She writes regularly in the local and regional papers, and she is a talented storywriter. She mainly addresses issues such as peace building, social justice, health care and education development.

Sudan

Komal Srivastava

Bharat Gyan Vigyan Samiti (BGVS)

Komal Srivastava (born 1960) set up the Rajasthan chapter of the Bharat Gyan Vigyan Samiti (India Knowledge and Science Center, BGVS) in 1992. Since then, she has convinced the state government of the need for a people-centered, democratic approach to literacy, and set up Samata, a women's forum for equality, education, and peace, which was very important for developing women's leadership within BGVS. Komal's single-minded commitment to social equality and her persuasive and principled leadership have changed Rajasthan.

Komal Srivastava is a knowledge maven: the Rajasthan chapter of BGVS has become one of its most active chapters. When Komal was cementing the unit, Ajmer district had been declared entirely literate, and the Rajasthan bureaucracy was set to implement a top-down approach in the rest of the state. Komal campaigned for a people-centered, democratic approach, turning the BGVS into the literacy campaign's main training agency. Today, Rajasthan's literacy rate has increased by 22.45 percent (the national average is 13.17 percent). Equally crucial is Komal's inculcation of a gender-sensitive approach in the hitherto male-dominated organization. She set up Samata, which grew into a women's network that set up 15,000 self-help groups, and covers 10,000 villages and more than 500,000 women.

Promoting literacy and education among those who have little access to it because they are socially excluded and impoverished is Komal's passion. She has been able to spotlight BGVS activities on Dalits, women, and other disadvantaged groups in Rajasthan, moving beyond rhetoric, and mentoring many innovations that have broken new ground in ensuring equality and participation. An unusual feature of BGVS work under Komal's leadership is the voluntary nature of its membership and activism. Unlike most NGOs, it does not depend on funding or a corpus of paid employees, but has been able to establish a volunteer base of nearly 3000 people in Rajasthan alone.

Komal's single-minded commitment to social equality, her ability to mobilize voluntary actions, and her persuasive and principled leadership have, in many ways, altered Rajasthan.

Even after the successful national literacy campaign, Rajasthan's average—up from 38.55 to 61.03 percent — is marginally below the national average of 65.38 percent. Literacy and education efforts are not people-centric or democratic — but further improvements will be unsustainable until they are.

India

Olena Suslova

Women's Information Consultative Center (WICC)

Olena Suslova, born in 1958, is an instructor, researcher, and editor. She is co-author of the Empowering Education Program (EEP) and has trained such diverse groups as youth, Romany teachers, Burmese refugees in Thailand, and Indonesian peace workers. Starting in 1996 with the EEP, based upon nonviolence, tolerance, and gender sensitivity, she developed it in her region and later on in ten other countries with help from the NGO she founded — the Women's Information Consultative Center (WICC).

During the early 1990s, as a member of the Ukrainian opposition, Olena Suslova joined a demonstration to demand the release of an oppositional deputy imprisoned on false charges. Crowds of demonstrators moved towards the prison, but halfway they met big military trucks coming towards them. It was evident that the trucks could stop the people by force. While Suslova's husband organized the crowds, she went to face the trucks. Her sister who followed her with Suslova's daughter (9) at a short distance yelled: "Think of your daughter, you fool!" "I thought: 'I could die now. I do not want to die in front of my daughter, I cannot leave her and my husband, but I also cannot go away,'" Suslova recalls. "It was a strong feeling! And I made my stand. I faced the truck drivers and I stayed there." Big wheels slowed down and finally stopped. "This moment I consider the starting point of Empowering Education, because I then realized the meaning of empowerment — it makes you feel strong without arms, without police, without trucks. You are strong owing to your confidence, peaceful aims, solidarity," Olena explains. Whenever she is exhausted, tired, or feels weak, she recalls that situation, remembering another world is possible if one aspires for a better future by peaceful methods.

Empowering Education, radical in its goals and soft in its appearance, helps people analyze their own life, avoid manipulation, deal with conflict, be sensitive to others and move ahead towards another world. The Orange Revolution in Ukraine confirmed that people have the knowledge, are capable of, and, finally, could gain peace by peaceful methods. Millions of Ukrainians stood up for their choice and made it clear. "I know many Empowering Education graduates who participated in this peaceful resistance and it was our contribution to its success," Suslova says.

The authoritarian educational system was preserved in many parts of the Ukraine after its independence in 1991, although in other parts democratic initiatives were started and new topics for the curricula chosen. More than ten years after transition, there is still a pressing need for educational reform in many countries of the former Soviet Union.

Ukraine

Piang Tahsim Albar

Amanat Foundation
Aksyon Para sa Kapayapaan at Katarungan (Akkapka)

In 1974, Piang Albar (born 1950), a Muslim community extension worker of Notre Dame of Jolo College in Sulu, was arrested on suspicion of being a member of the Moro National Liberation Front (MNLF). After a brief period of detention, she was put in the custody of the Carmelite nuns in Zamboanga City, where the idea of inter-faith dialogue as a way of resolving conflict germinated. With a core of Tausug women volunteers, Piang established the Amanat Foundation in 1985, to provide basic education to adult learners, women in particular.

Advocating education as a basic requisite to peace and development, Piang Albar and some Tausug women professionals organized the Amanat Foundation. Amanat has livelihood programs and a savings and loan cooperative, with particular focus on women. With initial support from the Asia Foundation and the United States Agency for International Development (USAID), Amanat expanded its services to municipalities in Sulu and Tawi-Tawi.

But in a bid for self-reliance, Piang decided to stop seeking funding assistance from donor agencies. She says that the Foundation's initial efforts to recruit women to attend literacy programs were met with indifference. The women were willing to join adult classes, but were restrained by their husbands or male family members, who said that attending school at their age would not make any difference anymore. So Piang worked to convince the men to allow the women to participate in the literacy program by inviting them to observe the activities of the learners and understand the goals and programs of the Foundation. The men — most of whom were unschooled — became learners themselves, joined the learners' cooperative, attended seminars and trainings. When Piang sought the support of religious and local leaders for the campaign to eradicate illiteracy, they did not oppose the idea of educating women. They found a basis for this in the Koran and the ahadith (sayings) of the Prophet of Islam: 'The search for knowledge is obligatory to Muslim men and women' who must 'seek knowledge from the cradle to the grave'. Hence, Piang asserts, "Discouraging women from seeking knowledge is not Islamic but the culture of the community or tribe." She says that the teachings of Islam actually encouraged her to pursue the goals and objectives of the Amanat Foundation.

In the past, the Muslims of Southern Philippines fiercely resisted Western education believing that it would lead to their conversion to Christianity. Women, especially, were not sent to school. Thus, Sulu's literacy rate of about 40 percent remains the lowest in the Philippines.

Gladira Auxiliadora Talavera García

Axunica
The We Bet on Life Foundation

She took care of her eight siblings and was not able to go to school. She was mistreated by her mother and also by the man she loved. She is Nicaraguan. Her legal name is: Gladira Auxiliadora Talavera García (52). People simply call her "Chilo." Women recognize in her a common past of poverty and — more than that — a present of organization of acts against disrespect and marginalization. "Chilo" listens, reflects, finds solutions, smiles and never backs down. Never.

Gladira Auxiliadora Talavera García — "Chilo" — is a Nicaraguan woman. Mistreated in her childhood, she worked as a domestic worker since she was a little girl. Later on, she became a seamstress. Then, a factory worker. In that moment, she began to realize she was not the only one. She understood that her companions also worked without any rest, suffered from hunger, were beaten by their men. "Instead of crying alone, let us organize ourselves," she said. They went on strike. They were fired, but "we took a machine with us, and we made them pay each one of us every dime." She smiles.

In 1979, the Sandinist Populist Revolution triumphed. The National Literacy Crusade taught thousands of people to read and write. "Chilo" was one of them. "I went to the first day of school full of enthusiasm. It was in 1980. I still treasure the diplomas. And the very best thing of all was learning how to write my own name!"

She has lived for nearly 30 years in Pancasán, in the province of Granada. During that period, she has been setting up collective projects and organizing participations in social actions. She has created permanent centers where hundreds of women can meet and participate in activities. One of her mottos is: "The differences we respect. The inequalities we fight." She is the director of two non-governmental organizations: Axunica, in Spain, and The We Bet on Life Foundation, in Nicaragua. "Working collectively is something that came as a blessing into my life. As did these two words: solidarity and peace. These two things coexist side by side. If there is solidarity, there is peace."

Just as in almost all of Nicaragua, in the province of Granada, the prevailing sexism makes women suffer all kinds of humiliation. There are not many places where women can find support and capacitating courses to learn how to respect themselves and, consequently, teach others to be respected.

Nicaragua

Zenaida Tan Lim

Sarang Bangun Foundation (SBF)

Zenaida "Zeny" Tan Lim set up the Sarang Bangun Foundation (SBF) in the early 1990s for the rehabilitation of widows and orphans, victims of the conflict between the Moro National Liberation Front (MNLF) and the Philippine government. With a groundswell of funds from donor agencies, Zeny was able to establish with SBF livelihood and skills training programs, an orphan care center in Sulu (with assistance from the Islamic Development Bank in Jeddah, Saudi Arabia), and the Sarang Bangun Learning Center in Zamboanga City, making quality elementary education accessible to the Muslim community.

Zenaida Tan Lim comes from a family with a history of public service. Her father was a well-loved governor of Sulu, her mother's clan is associated with the development of Jolo. Zeny's sister, the late Desdemonda Tan, was part of the Moro struggle for liberation as the wife of Nur Misuari, founder and chairman of the Moro National Liberation Front. Zeny herself was drawn to the task of rehabilitating the widows and orphans of the armed conflict between the MNLF and the Philippine government. Due to the conflict, a generation of Moros lost the chance of a better education. Thus, Zeny believes that education must be part of the continuing Moro struggle, and the idea of self-determination must include initiatives for a better future for the people. Zeny founded the Sarang Bangun Foundation (SBF) and the Sarang Bangun Learning Center in response to this need.

After over a decade, SBK has established a network of assistance and common efforts to provide Moro communities with education, livelihood and orphan care. In Sulu, the Consuelo Foundation, Save the Children Japan, Notre Dame Foundation and Unicef have partnered with SBF to provide vital assistance to women and children. The Sarang Bangun Learning Center in Zamboanga City has grown into a potent force in building a community of responsible Muslims. In 2003, the center's grade six pupils ranked third in the Metrobank-MTAP-Department of Education Mathematics Challenge, a close runner-up to the established Ateneo de Zamboanga University. Zeny says that SBF has done much to identify, understand and address the problems of the Moro communities, their aspirations and their prospects for a better life, guided by their faith, history, and culture.

The long history of conflict in Southern Philippines that ravaged its Muslim provinces, has left thousands of widows and orphans bereft of education, health and livelihood. Civil society initiatives have responded to some of these needs.

Sabriye Tenberken

Braille Without Borders (BWB)
Tibet Disabled Persons' Federation

Sabriye Tenberken, a German who became blind at the age of 12, established the first school for blind Tibetan children in Lhasa in 1998. She had to overcome numerous obstacles, including official indifference, active hostility, and irregular financial assistance, but today her Rehabilitation and Training Center for the Blind is transforming the lives of a growing number of blind Tibetan youngsters. The achievements of its students are beginning to change traditional Tibetan beliefs that blindness is a punishment for their sins in previous lives.

The arithmetic problem is written on the board: 9730 divided by 78. We are in the third grade class room of a boarding school in a small Tibetan town. Four of the center's students — three girls and a boy — recently have transferred to the school, and Sabriye wants to find out how they are doing. The teacher fires the math question, and all four of the center's children raise their hands. The teacher calls on Nyima. She jumps up and rattles off the answer. "All four children are doing very well," Sabriye whispers to me. "Recently there was no electricity one night, and our children were the only ones able to do their homework in the dark!"

After class, as we prepare to leave, Gyenzen, a tall 18-year-old boy, suddenly starts crying. "What's the matter?" Sabriye asks, sitting down beside him. Gyenzen is too upset to speak. Putting her arm around him, Sabriye slowly calms him. Finally, Gyenzen reveals that some boys threw stones at him but he does not know who they are, since he cannot see. Sabriye hugs him. "You are smarter than they are," she says. "They are probably jealous of you. Tell them that if they want to fight, they should come near you and fight with their hands!" Gyenzen nods and a smile brightens his tear streaked face. Sabriye sighs. "Blind people need a thick skin," she says. "It is wrong to overprotect them — and impossible anyway. It is important to give them courage and techniques to survive such things."

Until mid-1998, there was not a single school for blind children in Tibet. Then, Sabriye Tenberken started a school in Lhasa with six blind Tibetan youngsters. Despite enormous hardships — financially, emotionally, and medically — Sabriye kept the school going. Today, the Center for the Rehabilitation of the Blind is well established and known throughout Tibet and other parts of China as a model institution for blind children.

Traditional Tibetans believe that blindness is a punishment for sins committed in a previous life, that blind people are possessed by the devil, that they are cursed and dangerous. Blind children are often locked up at home or forced to beg in Lhasa and other Tibetan towns.

Germany

Tetyana Tkachenko

Women for the Future

Tetyana Tkachenko (born 1945) lived and worked as an English teacher in Kiev, 35 km from Chernobyl, when the nuclear catastrophe took place. It opened her eyes and changed her life. Working in the contaminated area for five years she developed a new child-centered holistic education for peace, democracy, and ecology. Her goal was to save the children and to work for a better world. Since 1991, she has been working in Ternopil, Ukraine, and is linked to an international network of peace education. In 1997, she founded the NGO Women for the Future.

"My life was cut into two parts on 26 April 1986 — before and after," Tetyana Tkachenko often says. It was the day the nuclear power station in Chernobyl exploded. Tetyana lived in the Kiev region, 35 km away, with her husband and daughter (5), where she also worked as a teacher. "We had no support, no help, our government did not even tell us the whole truth about the catastrophe," she recalls. "And one day, I woke up a different person: my eyes were open, my ears could hear… . I began to think and ask questions." Since the teachers had to keep their students in school all day after lessons because of the nuclear pollution outside, Tetyana worked out a concept called "to touch the child." "It was not easy at first, so we decided to work out our own democratic rules: togetherness, friendliness, fairness, happiness, empathy, and self-esteem which, in the long run, resulted in 'we-ness.'"

Tetyana and her students were not aware then that these principles were the actual principles of peace pedagogy and that their experiments were their first steps to self-esteem and civic courage. She worked in the contaminated Kiev region for five more years before her family was allowed to move to Ternopil in western Ukraine. These years were the beginning of her dedication to a new holistic peace education that was further developed when she was invited to international seminars and conferences in Europe and the US from 1991 onwards. She has written a lot of teaching material in English, integrating concepts to support self-esteem of the child and youth, peace at heart, respect of human rights, responsibility for the community and for the environment, culture of peace and understanding, conflict resolution, critical thinking, and active learning. In 1997, she initiated the NGO, Women for the Future in Ternopil which has spread to other cities since.

The authoritarian educational system was preserved in many parts of the Ukraine after its independence in 1991. In other parts democratic initiatives were started and new topics for the curricula chosen. The peaceful orange revolution gave schools even more chances for openness, peace, and democracy. In general, there still is a strong need for educational reform.

María Tila Uribe

Center of Labor Studies and Research (Cestra)

"My urge to rebel and to teach were born when I asked myself why Colombian history ignored women." Tila Uribe began teaching basic literacy at the beginning of the 1960s. Accused of subversion, she remained in prison for four years. After her liberation, she took her teaching experience to Nicaragua, invited by the Sandinista government. In 1985, she founded, in Bogota, the Centre of Labor Studies and Research (Cestra). It promotes the education of trade union members and rural workers focusing particularly on the elderly.

"The first thing I did in my life was to found a newspaper in my school," remembers Tila Uribe, a Colombian woman, born in 1931. At that time, when women were just educated for marriage, she constantly asked herself: "Why are women excluded from our history?" In the beginning of the 1960s, while she was rearing her children, she joined the groups organized by Camilo Torres to teach literacy skills to the people from the poorest neighborhoods in Bogota. Accused of subversion, due to her work teaching in the mountains of Antioquia, she spent four years in prison, in the place where her husband and her oldest son were also imprisoned. After they were liberated, the married couple published the book "From the inside" — a narrative about their experiences in prison. In 1990, the book was translated into French. With this book, the details of the struggle of the Colombian people became known in Europe. As a result, she was invited by the Sandinista government to bring the benefits of her teaching experience to the revolution.

"When we finished writing the "Mathematics for adults" teaching cards, I handed them over to the caricaturists, to the illustrators. I called the main character of the scheme Rosita, but the artists changed the name and called her Tila. Years later, I found out that in the North of Nicaragua, a lot of women were christened with my name."

She published the book "The hidden years: dreams and rebellions of the twenties" — which today is a reference at Colombian Universities. At the same time, she took on the post of Head of the History department at the National School for Female Leaders of Trade Unions. In 1985, she founded, in Bogota, the Centre of Labor Studies and Research (Cestra). It promotes the education of trade union members and rural workers focusing particularly on the elderly.

The violent Colombian history of the 20th century has relegated large sectors of the rural and urban population to illiteracy. As a group subordinated to male power, women have, nevertheless, been at the vanguard of the fight for independence and liberation for the Colombian people.

Colombia

Dao Thi Bich Van

Department of Education and Training Hanoi

With 16 years of teaching and service as the president of the school's labor union and ten years of participation in trade union activities, humanitarian programs and the struggle for women's promotion, Dao Thi Bich Van has made many contributions to education and to improving the plight of impoverished teachers and students in Vietnam.

The work of Dao Thi Bich Van requires patience, devotion and profound love. She organizes initiatives to improve the lives of disadvantaged people, especially teachers, the handicapped, and street children. Dao traveled to the countryside, where she saw the unhappy lot of teachers and students in remote regions and pledged to improve their lives. She established and managed humanitarian programs at the Department of Education and Training Hanoi and the Department's trade union, using all possible resources to guarantee their success. In the past ten years, she has mobilized teachers to donate to humanitarian programs and participate in humanitarian and social activities, raising billions of Dong annually, totaling more than USD three million. For street children, she marshaled vocational training teachers in Hanoi to give free classes in reading, writing and vocational training. She lobbied the Swiss organization Terre des Hommes to finance the building and equipment, and called on the Italian Motherless Association to donate USD 30,000 to upgrade the classrooms.

Using advanced teaching methodology with the slogan, "Discipline — Mercy — Responsibility", Dao's humanitarian work and scientific research have attracted hundreds of teachers in Hanoi. She organized a teachers' campaign, granting scholarships to poor but talented and hardworking students, and worked with the kind-hearted fund of Lao Dong (Labor), the longest-running newspaper of the Vietnam General Confederation of Labor, which has been published since 1946, to help teachers buy bicycles for transportation. At the trade union, she organizes sessions on gender for the teaching profession. Dao Thi Bich Van has helped improve the lot of teachers, especially those without long-term contracts, who work in distant and poor districts, receiving only the minimum wage without health or social insurance coverage.

Many poor rural teachers, women and children in the suburban area of Hanoi benefited from campaigns to raise donations and from education led by Dao Thi Bich Van.

Virginia "Gina" Vargas Valente

The Flora Tristán Center of the Peruvian Woman
Marcosur Feminist Articulation of Women
World Social Forum

She wanted to do things that no one had done before. She is an activist who thinks with pragmatism. She believes that life gave her an opportunity. Her independent life gave her the drive to strive for more. She felt that women had to change themselves, before they could change other things. Virginia "Gina" Vargas, the feminist, will soon be 60 years old and the Flora Tristán Center, one of her most important organizational efforts, is 25 years old.

Virginia "Gina" Vargas is an activist who reflects with pragmatism. She married and moved to Chile. She speaks with admiration about Salvador Allende, and she feels pain because of his violent death. Her father, whose memory she honors, always helped her without questioning. Her life as a feminist began by accident. She was working at the National Institute of Culture and was told to organize a course about the situation of women. She contacted specialists in Peru and other countries. She reflected, read, questioned. This course changed her life. The Flora Tristán Center was born at Gina's house. They discussed whether it should be an investigation center or a center for the confluence of women.

In 1982, when they organized a march in support of abortion, they began as 50, but were only 20 at the end. The repression was atrocious. Gina could not understand the lack of solidarity, especially from her second partner. "Then, I understood that it was not everyone else's problem. It was my own, in my daily life."

Peru was living a violent time. The feminists challenged it by organizing marches for peace. They felt that the situation of inequality against women was a permanent violation of peace. In 1997, along with a group of women, Gina formed Women for Democracy, and along with other organizations they confronted the dictatorship of Alberto Fujimori. Gina participated in the international arena. She joined the Marcosur Feminist Articulation of Women and the World Social Forum. "Our country is a kind of open wound. To change so many historical injustices, not only those related to gender, feminists need to accept an open dialogue with other movements."

Peru grows economically but that does not reflect in an improvement in the quality of life of the population. To change a country with so many historical injustices, not only those related to gender, feminists need to accept an open dialogue with other movements.

Peru

Venerable Dhammananda

Venerable Dhammananda Dr Chatsuman Kabilsingh (born 1945) is the leader of the Songdhammakalyani Temple in Nakhonpathom, the first temple for Buddhist nuns. She was ordained a "samaneri" (female novice) in February 2001 in Sri Lanka and given the name Dhammananda. In February 2003, she was ordained a "Bhikkhuni" (female Buddhist monk) in Sri Lanka according to the Theravada tradition. She works in education, runs women's training programs, gives dhamma talks on Buddhist teaching, and writes a regular newspaper column.

Before she became a female Buddhist monk, Venerable Dhammananda studied philosophy in India and completed her Master's degree at the McMaster University in Canada. She then obtained a PhD in Buddhism at Magadh University in India. She was 54 years old, married with three sons, and a professor of religion and philosophy in Bangkok's prestigious Thammasat University when she thought about being ordained as a Bhuddist monk. Venerable Dhammananda went to Sri Lanka to study and in one year, she had renounced her worldly life, including her marriage, and made the choice to be ordained.

Originally Buddhism allowed the ordination of women but after 700 years, the tradition was stopped. Now Venerable Dhammananda is working to revive that tradition that will allow women to walk the path opened by the Buddha, but she first has to convince Thai Buddhists that women have the right to be ordained. The Thai government and council of elder monks have not accepted her ordination despite her excellent academic credentials. As a professor at Thammasat University for 27 years, she established an international Buddhist women's movement. She has been the editor of Yasodhara, an international Buddhist magazine for women, for over 20 years and has written and translated more than 60 books. Some of her books have been translated into English. "My work is mostly about Buddhist teaching and how it is applied to people's lives. I believe that enlightenment is a quality of the mind, and the mind has no gender. It transcends the male and the female. When we reach that state, there is no gender anymore. I believe it is very important to have a good Buddhist education because people can be strengthened by the true Buddhist knowledge and by the true spirit of Buddhism, which allows them to overcome their limits and their hindrances."

"Thai Sanghas" (governing councils of Buddhist monks) are different from other Sanghas in that they are closely linked with the government and each Thai Sangha must be sanctioned by government. Venerable Dhammananda is working to revive the tradition that will allow women to walk the Buddist path.

Thailand

"Life is the best test for any theory. Critical times can help you go further."

Cleopatra Vnorovschi

Cleopatra Vnorovschi (1911–2005) has been a model of resistance to repression of the freedom of thought for many generations of students. As a professor of philosophy at the main universities of Moldova and a prolific writer, she gave people the support and courage needed to survive under harsh conditions of life and lack of freedom of expression and thought. After her retirement, she continued to teach and give interviews to the mass media, encouraging people in the difficult post-Soviet period in the Republic of Moldova.

Cleopatra Vnorovschi was born into an educated family in Ukraine and moved to Moldova with her family when she was seven years old. She studied in Chisinau and was one of the best students in her secondary school. From 1932 to 1936, she studied philology and philosophy in Iasi (now part of Romania) and later in Bucharest. She graduated from the University magna cum laude. Back in Chisinau, she was one of the best teachers at the girls lyceum. She was preparing her Ph.D. and admitted to the University of Paris, when World War II broke out and her family was evacuated to Uzbekistan. From a house full of books, Cleopatra and her family found themselves in a train of fear. Nobody knew where they were going or for how long. "We brought some books and crochet hooks. We crocheted many white napkins in a train full of misery and lice. People were smiling at us, but we still have those white napkins. Look at them — they have the forms of stars and flowers — some of the most beautiful things that God created on the earth. Those forms convince you to survive, to move away, to feel that there always will be something to help you see a better future." Cleopatra Vnorovschi had to learn how to survive in a very difficult situation, and she has taught others by her example how to manage difficult situations, how to survive hard times, and how to move forward.

After the war, her family came back to Moldova, and Cleopatra Vnorovschi began to teach again. She continued to teach students to appreciate freedom and to think freely despite the difficulties this caused her during the Soviet period. She was forced to teach only Marxist-Leninist philosophy, but she always managed to offer information about other philosophies and authors, for which she was dismissed from universities many times. Despite this, she never ceased to speak and write about freedom of thought.

The Communist regime prohibited freedom of thought and expression in Moldova. After the disintegration of the Soviet Union, Moldova became an independent Republic, free, but very poor and with a very weak civil society not used to thinking for itself.

Republic of Moldova

Rafaela Vos Obeso

The Meira Delmar Center of Documentation of the Woman,
University of the Atlantic

A sea in summer. That is a good image of the work Rafaela Vos Obeso has created during the last 28 years. She has organized her country women, drop by drop, so they have become at last like a human sea, warm, calm, but also strong and brave when the time to fight for their rights comes. She is a sociologist, historian, writer, brilliant professor at the University of Barranquilla. Rafaela is an eminent intellectual, and more than that, a humanitarian. A woman. A horizon.

We met her one afternoon in the hallways of the University of the Atlantic, in Barranquilla, Colombia, a dark-skinned woman with a beauty mark on her lip, in the right side of her face. Her body is robust and her look very intense. She is like the image of her people, a ray of light bathed by the waters of the beautiful Caribbean sea. She does not go unnoticed. She is a sociologist and a historian. She has a Masters in political sciences and another in history. Her name is Rafaela Vos Obeso. Like the horizon, you look at her and she guides you.

"Challenges are important for the transformation of humanity," she thinks, says and believes. Her life has been a challenge during every moment. She made the decision to educate and transform herself first, so that she would later be able to help and transform others. She has made her life into a project of enabling permanent interaction between social groups from all backgrounds. To see her is to believe in her. She emanates a strength that is conviction. "Re-education is a life option." She wants to re-educate us for peace. An intimate peace. A true peace. Her work as an activist has lasted for 28 years of untiring fight. "Our language does not use arms in a bid for power." Her weapons have been words. Words full of reconciliation, wisdom and hope.

As the afternoon comes to an end, Rafaela Vos Obeso goes into her office, but her work does not end at night. Her light is never extinguished.

Women in Barranquilla, Colombia, are expected to conform to traditional roles, where the inequality between men and women becomes very evident. Sexism is the prevailing culture. Raising the flag of human rights for women is going against the established social order.

Colombia

Guilan Wang

Kindergarten of Huangling County, Yan'an City, Shaanxi Province

Wang Guilan, who was born in 1949, has been inspired by the grand idea of serving the poorest. Over the past 30 years she has taught rural children how to read and write, and also how to be independent and responsible citizens. For Wang, rural education is the "cultural revolution" she wants to bring about. She is currently running a state kindergarten in Huangling County, Yan'an City.

Wang Guilan graduated in 1968 at the age of 19 from Beijing Normal College. Inspired by the idea of serving the poorest of the poor, Wang voluntarily went to the remote yellow-earth region of Shaanxi Province, along with 28,000 passionate educated youths. Thirty years later, when most had chosen to return to the city after the Cultural Revolution was over, she found herself still there. Wang feels a justifiable sense of achievement: "the villagers trust me a lot, and let me completely fulfill myself in the lecture room. In this village school, I teach language, mathematics, music and physical education. I teach the children everything I have learned. This makes me fulfill the values of life."

In 1974 Wang married a local mathematics teacher and they had two sons. Later she had several opportunities to go back to Beijing to teach, but she renounced them all, though not without some struggle with herself. However, she does not regret her decision because the yellow earth brings her true love and a community spirit of give-and-take: "In the process of developing my career, I have met sincere rural people who treat me like family. I cannot forget that whenever I do home visits or arrange parents' meetings, I am completely impressed by their generosity and hospitality."

Her contribution to rural literacy has won her the respect of her local community. In 1992 she was appointed schoolmistress of a local primary school. She is currently the general secretary of a local kindergarten.

During the Cultural Revolution (1966–1976), 15 million educated youths voluntarily or involuntarily went to the countryside throughout China. After 1978 most people returned to the cities, although a few, like Wang Guilan, did not join the trend.

China

Jianhua Wang

Xin Zhi Women's Vocational School

Wang Jianhua is one of the most influential people in private education in China. Since quitting her government job in 1989, she has invested every penny of her own and her family's to establish the Xin Zhi Women's Vocational School, which caters especially for young women from villages and rural areas. In the past 15 years the school has helped thousands of young women to find jobs, enabling them to pursue their dreams.

In Zhejiang Province, Wang Jianhua, an ordinary woman, has received public attention for her extraordinary achievements in education. In the late 1980s many young women were unable to get an education after junior high school because of a scarcity of resources. "Financial difficulties" was the usual excuse for parents to stop paying tuition fees for their daughters, and to ask them to work instead.

This cruel reality of young women's lives deeply saddened Wang Jianhua and motivated her to resign from her secure government job in order to start fund-raising for a school for young women. Wang believes that the best way to help women is to help them learn skills that can earn them a living, and, at the same time, to encourage them to be independent and to serve society. She rented premises, hired teachers, and recruited students while raising her baby daughter. The number of students at the school has gone up from 70 to almost 3000. And from a tiny roofless classroom, the school has become a campus of 30,000 square meters. Some 10,000 students have graduated from her school, and she has realized her goal of "supporting a family through a graduate."

Wang Jianhua resigned her secure government job in 1989 and set off on a rough but hopeful journey. Her mission was to provide vocational education for women in spite of huge pressure from the public. The Xin Zhi Women's Vocational School and two others are running with low tuition fees for poor families from rural areas.

China

Liwen Wang

Chinese People's Political Consultative Conference (Cppcc) of Leshan City

Wang Liwen is the deputy chair of the Chinese People's Political Consultative Conference (Cppcc) of Leshan City and an enthusiastic social worker. She is a defender of the rights of women and children, as well as an advocate for the development of ethnic minority areas. Though suffering from long hours of work and poor health, she has never stopped working.

Wang Liwen is a member and the deputy chair of the Cppcc of Leshan City. Since 1990, Wang has been deputy mayor of Leshan City of Sichuan Province of China, member of the Working Committee for Women and Children, and president of the Red Cross of Leshan City. She founded a kindergarten in 1993. Despite her ill health at the time, she impressed many people with her efforts at raising funds for the kindergarten. In 1996, she pioneered setting up a private-funded residence for the elderly. These projects for the elderly and children may be small in scale but they required enormous effort and their effects have been far-reaching. Wang seeks no compensation for her hard work. Over the years, she has also worked for the well-being of women peasants. Having founded the Leshan Women Housework School, she then worked with women peasants, impressing upon them the importance of good preparation and client identification to avoid scams and frauds while finding a job. To purchase teaching facilities, she has made frequent trips to rally the support of relevant departments of the government. Whenever a woman student finds a placement, she keeps in touch with her to offer support if needed. As the Cppcc holds its meeting in Beijing once a year, she also takes this opportunity to visit students who are working there.

Leshan Cty has been expanding rapidly with economic growth. Newly developed areas in the northern part attract people from the inner city. The increase in population puts pressure on the infrastructure and public services, thus creating serious problems for the Leshan government.

China

Marilyn Waring

Massey University

Marilyn Waring is a renowned New Zealand feminist, economic theorist, and academic. She criticised the UN's System of National Accounts for ignoring the environment, subsistence production, and women's productive and reproductive work and played an integral role in making New Zealand nuclear-free.

"With the privilege of education comes the obligation to teach. I had a chance to engage in particular institutional power dynamics very young. It is important to pass on all those skills and strategies, in whatever way. So that can be: in the foothills in Nepal; teaching African parliamentarians how to have transparent accountable budgets; working with communities to establish their own well-being indicators; supervising post-graduate students; fighting for a nuclear-free Pacific. I mean you take the commitment with you wherever you go.

One of the wonderful things in growing up when I grew up — this was before email and any of those kinds of things — was that there was a really wide women's feminist network. When I was in the New Zealand Parliament, on my desk I would have works by women from all over the world, voices of women that started to be articulated out of independence movements. They have no idea what their voice is doing for you at that moment. But it is putting the steel up your back that makes it possible for you to do the next impossible thing. And I guess that was the most important thing I ever did for anybody.

A really nice thing is becoming a kind of Dear Dorothy Dix. I mean younger women will call from places of unspeakable psychological and emotional battery, and they know they do not have to explain a thing to you, they know that you will believe everything. And, in fact, you know that it is probably worse than what they are actually saying because to stay sane and to actually survive you cannot really ever admit how bad it really is."

Waring made history during her political career when she withdrew her support from her party over the issue of a nuclear-free New Zealand, precipitating a snap election in 1984. Her action caused the fall of the National Government and subsequent election of a Labour Government, and led to New Zealand becoming the first country to ban nuclear ships from its harbours.

Cora Weiss

Hague Appeal for Peace
Global Campaign for Peace

Sakena Yacoobi

International Rescue Committee (IRC)

"To have a peaceful population," says Cora Weiss, "we must teach peace." This belief is the cornerstone of Cora's life's work. As president of the Hague Appeal for Peace, she is leading a campaign dedicated to the abolition of war. She brings her skills as a convener and an educator into diverse venues — from the classroom to the boardroom. She began her work in the early 1960s, when she cofounded Women Strike for Peace, which helped to bring about the end of nuclear testing in the atmosphere. In 1969, she led in organizing the largest protest against the Vietnam war.

It took Cora and her small staff three years to plan for the First Hague Peace Conference in The Netherlands. The result of her work was the largest civil gathering of international peace activists in history, with nearly 10,000 people from more than 100 countries in attendance. The May 1999 conference gave participants opportunities in 400 panels and workshops to discuss mechanisms for abolishing war and creating a culture of peace. The document adopted by the conference, the Hague Agenda for Peace and Justice for the 21st Century, was also unanimously adopted by the general assembly of the United Nations.

The conference launched a number of organizations, including Cora's Global Campaign for Peace, where she currently serves as president. The goal of the campaign is to build public awareness and political support for the introduction of peace education into all spheres of formal and informal education in schools throughout the world and to promote the education of all teachers to teach for peace.

Cora has demonstrated her knowledge of peacekeeping practices in the West Bank and Gaza Strip and in Santo Domingo. She is a vocal detractor of Nato expansion and participated in a citizen's mission on Nato expansion in London, Brussels, and Moscow in 1997. She was an active delegate to the World Council of Churches' Third World Conference on Women in Nairobi, Kenya, in 1995, and the NGO Women's Forum, Fourth World Conference on Women in Beijing, China, in 1995. She worked to create peace tents, places for women to speak and convene, at both conferences. Cora is president of the International Peace Bureau and the first recipient of the William Sloane Coffin Award for Peace and Justice offered by the Yale Divinity School.

An eloquent speaker, Cora uses her skills as an educator and her sense of humor to teach and inspire audiences of all ages in countries around the world. She is skilled at bringing people together; Cora has had a regular weekly radio program with women and is a widely published writer.

United States of America

Yuet Lin Yim

Ziteng ("Chinese wisteria")

Born in Herat, Afghanistan, Sakena Yacoobi obtained a BSc in Biological Sciences from the University of the Pacific, USA in the 1970s, and a Masters in Public Health from Loma Linda University, California. In the 1980s, she worked as a health consultant in California and Michigan and taught psychology, mathematics and biology at D'Etre University in Grosse Pointe, Michigan. From 1992-95, Sakena worked for the International Rescue Committee (IRC) in Pakistan. Thanks to Yacoobi the number of Afghan refugee girls enrolled in IRC-supported schools increased from 3000 to 15,000.

Professor Sakena Yacoobi developed a strong passion for learning from her childhood. Her desire for learning was boosted by her parents' enthusiasm to give her a good quality education. She was determined to study at the university and utilize her academic knowledge to help the women in her country. Although she was offered a place to study at the University of Kabul's Engineering and Medical Faculties, Yacoobi was unable to attend the faculty because there was no women's dormitory in Kabul. This obstacle seemed to place higher education just out of her reach. However, she remained resolute about achieving her goal. After the end of the Afghan-Soviet war, funding for education programs for Afghan girls and women began to dissipate. But she refused to accept these unfortunate circumstances and founded the Afghan Institute of Learning to continue the urgently needed health and education programs for Afghan women and girls that she had started through her work with the International Rescue Committee (IRC). Her vision of peace is to see more women involved in the leadership of the country as well as to educate as many women as she can.

Professor Sakena Yacoobi's major aim is to train as many women as she can in different disciplines, such as education, health, leadership development, empowerment of women and capacity building. This aim, she believes, will benefit the community with the skills of half of its members.

Yim Yuet Lin joined the workforce in Hong Kong with only a few years of basic school education. In the late 70s, Yim started to be involved in the labor movement. She saw how workers were exploited and she herself faced unjust treatment from her employer. In 1996, Yim and three other friends founded Ziteng (Chinese wisteria), a sex workers' concern group, which aims to provide support to sex workers.

Born to a poor migrant family from the Mainland, Yim Yuet Lin became a full-time factory worker when she was in her early teens. It was a time when there was a large demand on cheap labor and labor legislation was not yet in place. Having witnessed how her fellow factory workers were being exploited and fallen victim herself to unjust treatment by her employer, Yim became an active member of the labor movement. In 1989, she helped found the Hong Kong Women Workers' Association to address in particular women workers' predicaments and to protect their labor rights. In 1996, Yim and three other friends established Ziteng, a concern group that aims to provide direct services to sex workers and to eliminate discrimination and social exclusion. They believe sex work is work.

One of the main objectives of Ziteng is to foster the capacity of sex workers to organize themselves to define and defend their cause. In recent years, some sex workers have participated in rallies and activities complaining of police abuses and calling for the decriminalization of sex work. They appear in press conferences and for two consecutive years marched to the government house and police headquarters to file their complaints. They also go to conferences and exchanges to share their experiences. In 2003, over 30 sex workers took part in a photography project, an exhibition of photographs taken by sex workers themselves. This is the first of its kind in the Territory and has been very well received. Despite financial and human resources constraints, Ziteng under Yim's leadership has been able to explore new possibilities and continues its services to sex workers in Hong Kong and the Mainland. Among others, they have been able to forge links among sex workers in the region.

The late 1970s was a time when Hong Kong enjoyed an economic boom. There was an abundant supply of cheap labor and the political environment was comparatively stable. But grassroots workers were still very much exploited, as related legislation was far from satisfactory.

China, Hong Kong SAR

Fan Ying Yu

China Times Culture and Education Foundation

Yu Fan Ying, born in 1944, has been engaged in the movement for democracy, environmental protection, and reconciliation of ethnic groups in Taiwan for 40 years. As executive director of the China Times Culture and Education Foundation, she has promoted sustainable development. During the 2004 presidential election, there were serious rifts in society due to political opposition, and Yu organized "Action Alliance for Ethnic Equality" to alleviate social tensions.

Yu Fung Ying was born in Chongqing City, Sichuan Province, China. She received her bachelor's degree in business from Japan, and her master's degrees in sciences and business management from Stanford University. Yu is now the chief executive of the China Times Culture and Education Foundation that owns and operates newspapers, magazines, book publishing, websites, television stations and related databases, as well as three non-profit foundations. Yu also serves as a director for many private organizations and is head of the Water and Land Resources Working Group, National Council for Sustainable Development, Taiwan. She has been engaged in the movement of democracy, environmental protection, and reconciliation of ethnic groups in Taiwan for 40 years. As a member of the family owning one of the most important newspapers in Taiwan, the China Times, Yu provided protection for the liberalists and those who participated in the anti-Nationalist-Party movement when Taiwan was still under martial law.

After the lifting of the martial law in the early 1980s, Yu was very involved in the protection of rivers in Taiwan. She has helped to organize many seminars and public hearings on sustainable development. In 2004, when the presidential election triggered a deep division among social groups because of the differences in political affiliation, intellectuals who cared for the political ecology in Taiwan like Yu started to doubt whether ethnic conflicts could be solved by political means. They turned to the civil society to seek power, and together they organized an alliance for ethnic equality and demanded that politicians stop dividing people. They also asked the government to take care of the problems faced by brides and their children coming from the Mainland, and to guarantee that there is no action or speech that violates ethnic equality in the education system.

In Taiwan, political suppression was very severe in the 1950s under the Nationalist Party's rule. But social movements have always been strong and they have gained from the return of many scholars from abroad.

China, Taiwan

Guimei Zhang

Minzhu Middle School
Hua Ping Children's Home

Zhang Guimei is a teacher working in a destitute ethnic minority region. Regardless of the difficulties and sorrow of losing her husband and being ill herself, she has brought up and educated 54 orphans. Her students have not quit school and neither have they suffered from poverty.

Zhang Guimeng, born 1957 in Mudanjiang City, Helongjiang Province, works in Minzhu Middle School, Hua Ping County, Yunnan Provice, in a multi-ethnic mountainous area. In her 29 years of work, she has been awarded numerous honors; the one she cherishes most is the common title: a people's teacher.

When she was 38, Zhang's husband died of stomach cancer. Zhang herself had a tumor, which needed two operations within the year. Despite illness and pain, Zhang continued her work for the welfare of children. She has donated most of the money she earns or gets for medical treatment to poor children, orphans and schools in a rehabilitation village; as a result her savings are less than 3000 yuan.

As a teacher, Zhang loves the children like they were her own. She says, "Love is the key for heart-to-heart communication between teachers and students." Since all her students come from cultural minority groups and their level is lower than average, she has to work harder for longer hours to design teaching methods that can arouse their motivation to learn. Her efforts are well rewarded with their good results in public examinations.

In 1999, a Chinese American organization, "Mothers' Club", wanted to build an orphanage in Lijiang area, Yunnan Province. Hearing about Zhang, they decided to have the orphanage built in Hua Ping County, insisting that Zhang be the director. Since March 2001, Zhang has taken this second job, voluntarily becoming the "mother" of 54 children. Everyday, after teaching in Minzhu Middle School, she travels from the west side to the east side to her children in the Hua Ping Children's Home. Now Zhang faces a third operation for her tumor, and pain tortures her every day. But she chooses to work harder. She says, "My life is in my teaching."

Ethnic minorities face a difficult situation with lack of educational and other facilities. There are also many orphans who need help.

China

Hua Zhang

Zhang Hua was born in 1978 and has been a primary school teacher in a small remote village in west China from the age of 17. Many village folk have moved to urban areas, and Zhang teaches the children left behind in the village. The number of pupils has decreased in the past ten years to a mere six today.

Many a villager living in the remote mountains in west China has left home and moved to the town as young people flock to big cities for jobs with the increasing pace of urbanization in China. Zhang Hua also intended to find a job in the city after graduating from secondary school in 1995. But her teacher, who was going to retire soon, insisted that she stay behind to teach the children in the hills, as no other teacher was willing to take the job in this poor area. Zhang has stayed for ten years since then and turned from an ingenue to a mature young woman of 27. The number of pupils in the primary school has decreased from a few dozen to only six today.

Zhang is the last and only teacher and she teaches language, math, science, music, arts and sports. The pupils gather in a cave dwelling for lessons. When one class is having its lesson, the other pupils turn their backs to the blackboard to study on their own. Zhang receives a monthly salary of about 100 yuan but she often doesn't get paid on time with delays sometimes extending to more than a year. Yet she ignores the suggestion from her father and others to stop teaching when she fails to receive salary. "It is no fault of the children; I cannot ruin their study," she says.

A relative of Zhang found her a job in the city some years ago so that she could leave the poor mountain village. She had packed up her belongings but on the next day, after a long night of consideration, she went back to school again. "I will not find a job outside until the last pupil leaves the school," says Zhang.

More and more villagers have left their homes and lands in the remote villages to find jobs or to live in places close to the cities during the modernization and urbanization in China. But the children left behind in hill areas still have the desire, and should have the right, to receive education.

China

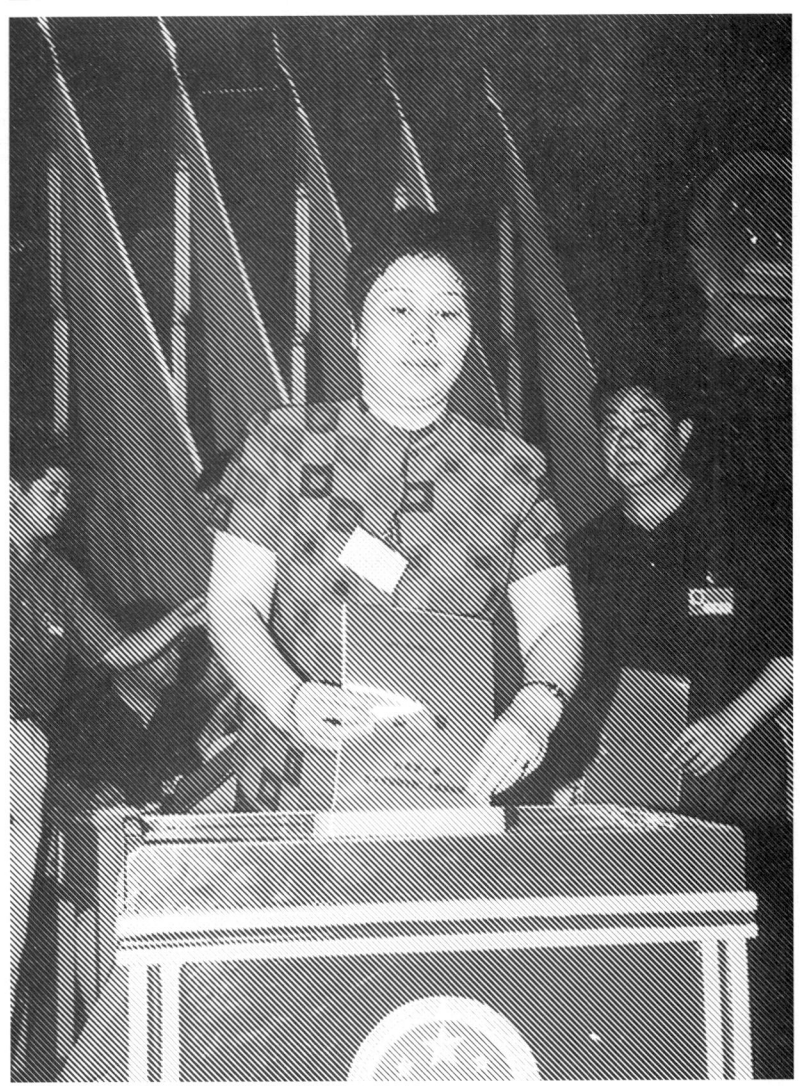

Xiaoxia Zhu

Working Committee on Women and Children
Communist Party of China (CPC), Xihua County Committee

Zhu Xiaoxia has introduced scientific marital and family planning ideas into her work for women and children, and has tried to convince families that happiness does not only lie in having male children. She has appealed to the community to pay attention to the vulnerable sectors of the population and has called on local civil servants to help poor schoolchildren and Aids orphans by initiating various programs for them.

Zhu Xiaoxia is a civil servant on the Working Committee on Women and Children of Xihua County, Zhoukou, Henan Province in China. She has been doing grassroots work in poor areas for a long time. Zhu was appointed deputy head of Huaiyang County in Henan Province in 1997, and was responsible for family planning and sanitation. Her investigations revealed deep discrimination against girls and a prevalent belief that family well-being lay in having sons. She decided to set up a council to promote new thinking about marriage and birth in Huaiyang County, and made efforts to propagandize the importance of late marriage, late birth, birth health, and gender equality. In 2001 the county was rated one of the nationwide models in implementing new norms for marriage and birth.

In June 2003 Zhu became head of the Organization Department and Standing Committee Member of the Communist Party of China (CPC), Xihua County Committee, in the hinterland of the usually flooded area of the Yellow River, where there are two provincially designated villages with a high incidence of Aids patients. Zhu has spent time learning about the situation of Aids orphans here and has worked with local civil servants to help poor schoolchildren and Aids orphans by initiating activities such as the Spring Buds Program and Aids Orphan Care Program. She has popularized knowledge about family planning and reproductive care and the importance of science and technology. She has also guided households in improving the quality of life by having fewer births. For example, she mobilized villagers to help collectively in the farm work of households without sons. Under her leadership the new ideas concerning marriage and birth spread quickly to 509 villages in over 20 townships in Huaiyang County.

Huaiyang County in Henan Province is a large agricultural county with a population of 1.2 million. It is historically and culturally rich but economically weak. Xihua County lies in the hinterland of the usually flooded area of the Yellow River. There are two villages with a high incidence of Aids.

China

Women's Efforts on Behalf of Environmental Justice and Ecological Security

Doris Wastl-Walter

Environmental problems and health threats are a special concern for women because in most cultures women are responsible for the survival, healthy nutrition, and well-being of the family. This is because worldwide, there are gendered environmental rights and responsibilities as well as a gendered division of labor. And as the following chapter shows, many women assert that there is no peace as long as there are no justice and security. Women argue for environmental justice and quality as well as the equal right of women to resource tenure. While struggling for their concerns, women have developed new forms of political activism and attempted to change traditional relations of power, in which women are generally marginalized. The activities of women working for a healthy and secure environment are focused on five main issues:

Consciousness raising and education

Several peacewomen are especially focused on education about environmental protection and ecology security, raising awareness of global risks and sustainability, and promoting non-violent modes of thought and ways of engaging with nature. Among our nominees, Vandana Shiva, Felícitas Estela Linares Meneses, and Olga Doronina, in particular, work in this way. In nearly all other projects, awareness raising and education are an intended side effect of the main purpose(s).

Environmental and health protection

Many women throughout the world are engaged in the combat against environmental degradation and health threats caused by huge infrastructure investments, such as dams, nuclear power plants, and gas pipelines. Many of them work as well on prevention, for example, attempts to heal the damage already caused. In the context of "1000 Peacewomen" these actions go from projects to supporting populations after the Super-GAUs of Bhopal and Chernobyl to more structural criticism offered by our Irina Grushevaya, Alla Yaroshinskaya, Solange Fernex, Suliana Siwatibau, Nabeela Al-Mulla, Gabriela Ngirmang, Helen John, Rebecca Johnson, and Rosalie Bertell. Although their common goal is to protect people from health threats, they have different special foci: While some are clearly antinuclear and try to make public the dangers and damage that have already occurred, others work against nuclear colonization of their living context on a global level. In other projects women like Leelakumari Amma, Bhinand Chotirosseranee, and Dawan Chantarahassadee raise apparently local or regional issues like waste water treatment, chemical disposal, and pesticide spraying, yet ultimately these are also global issues of ecological security.

Preservation of biodiversity

As women often work in subsistence agriculture and are responsible for the nourishing of their families, they become acutely aware of environmental degradation and its consequences. So women fight for biosecurity, for environmental conservation, for the protection of pristine forests, marshlands, soils, and ground water. In the following pages you will find the examples of Ivanka Nikolova Lecheva, Xiaoxi Li, and Julia Morton-Marr.

Resource tenure and accessibility

Asymmetrical entitlements to resources are an important environmental issue nearly everywhere, which means in practice that women often have little or no power over or access to resources like land and water. Women's de facto or de jure exclusion from property rights in most cultures and their lack of control over the material base — cattle, for instance — of their daily survival, are constant potential sources of conflict. Some women, like Maude Barlow and Samia Ibrahim, are fighting against this uneven and unjust distribution of means and facilities.

Sustainable development

The basic aim of all the nominated peacewomen is a healthy, secure, just, and non-violent living environment and they strive in various ways for that. But some are especially focused on a lasting and nature-oriented economic development that would also preserve natural resources, help women to generate an income and to be less endangered when doing their work. Sabine Lichtenfels, Grace Aboh, Zakia Arshad, and Nguyen Thanh Hien link environment and survival by initiating projects and inventing procedures to attain a sustainable development. Each of these nominees stands for thousands of other women living in similar circumstances and devoting their lives and work to protecting the environment, securing resources, and guaranteeing peace. They often start from very practical local experiences and move to highly political global issues like nuclear colonization.

Especially today, the impact of globalization and major economic and political changes on localities is inevitable, and there is virtually no place on earth where the consequences of human activities on the environment are not to be felt. We hope that the activism of these (and other) peacewomen and the shared knowledge brought to light through "1000 Women for the Peace Nobel Prize" lead to changing attitudes and increasing autonomy and political involvement on both local and global levels.

Doris Wastl-Walter is a professor of human geography and director of the Interdisciplinary Center for Women's and Gender Studies at the University of Bern in Switzerland.

"Our greatest assets are people and our natural resources, which need to be valued more if they are to become competitive."

Grace Aboh

Association for the Development of the Women of Sédji

A national of Benin, Madame Grace Aboh (62) has a lot of expertise in the socio-cultural reintegration of inmates of detention centers which has brought her international fame. This led to her being asked, at an international level, to form and organize women in the African subregions of the west where different countries have benefited from her know-how in the areas of the promotion of women, the improvement of the environment, living conditions for women and children, and, finally, financial capacities of women.

Grace Aboh looks for ways that will enable Benin people to ensure their economic independence through decent work. She trains women and young girls in activities likely to increase their income and improve their living conditions of their families. She initiated an ambitious program of recycling non-biodegradable plastic bags. Madame Dotou understood from the outset that if nothing is done, this refuse will have a serious effect on general life. It was for this reason she thought of recycling it. So, she has bags, clothes, and table mats made from the plastic bags that are thrown away on the streets and in public garbage disposals. Without recycling, Grace Aboh realized, plastic bags eventually will become a problem for communities.

Living in an evironment where the support of women is still needed badly, this courageous woman has led a lot of initiatives. Grace Aboh was born in Porto Novo in 1943. She did her primary and secondary studies from 1951 to 1963 and, in 1964, got an elementary Certificate of Educational Aptitude. In 1980, she created the first women's theatrical group "Qui dit Mieux." In 1994, the year of her retirement, she decided, with some friends, to establish the Association for the Development of the Women of Sédji. In 1995, the association quickly started training at a center for girls in Kouty to learn soap manufacturing, the preparation of gari (granulated cassava flour), palm oil, and groundnut oil. Grace Aboh is very interested in environmental issues and her association today is active in planting thousands of trees. She has been awarded several prizes: the Prize of Excellence in the Craft Industry, the National Lottery Prize for Excellence and, finally, the UN Prize for the Eradication of Poverty and Protection of the Environment.

Those who know her say she is unique in her field in that she never runs out of ideas. On a national level, Grace Aboh works in towns, communities, and areas to help with the reintegration of former women inmates in the country's prisons.

Benin

Nabeela Al-Mulla

Ministry of Foreign Affairs of Kuwait
Kuwait Mission to the United Nations (UN)
Board of Trustees of the American University in Kuwait (AUK)

Nabeela Abdulla Al-Mulla, born in Kuwait, is currently the Ambassador Extraordinary and Plenipotentiary and the Permanent Representative of the State of Kuwait to the United Nations (UN). She obtained her BA in Political Sciences in 1968 and an MA in International Relations four years later, both with distinction, from the American University of Beirut (AUB). She studied at a missionary boarding school (Beirut Evangelical School for Girls) and graduated from the AUB at the age of 20. She was Chairwoman of the Board of the International Atomic Energy Agency (IAEA) between 2002 and 2003.

The emphasis of the family on education and culture is a heritage of Nabeela Abdulla Al-Mulla's grandparents and father, who are renowned for their contribution to the political, social and cultural development in Kuwaiti society. She is currently the Ambassador Extraordinary and Plenipotentiary and the Permanent Representative of the State of Kuwait to the UN, a capacity that she worked on for several years in countries like South Africa, Namibia, Mauritius, Botswana and Zimbabwe, Austria, Hungary, Slovakia and Slovenia on non-residency basis. Nabeela Al-Mulla occupies several other international positions, representing Kuwait in a number of international bodies. She is Resident Representative of Kuwait to the UN Office in Vienna, the UN Industrial Development Organization (Unido), the International Atomic Energy Agency (IAEA), and she represented Kuwait at the Organization of the Petroleum Exporting Countries (Opec) Ministerial Meetings in 2002.

The choice to enlist in public life was a challenge to Nabeela Al-Mulla, given the prevalent lack of opportunity for women to advance and earn equal pay. She participated in Regular and Special Sessions of the General Assembly of the United Nations and represented the State of Kuwait in various Committee Panels and Conferences, such as talks on Arms Control and Regional Security in the Middle East and on Kuwait Prisoners of War (POWs) and detainees.

The high post of ambassadorship that Nabeela Al-Mulla occupies is a landmark for women in Foreign Affairs both in Kuwait and other countries in the region, given the fact that currently out of 191 member states' representatives, only nine women head the missions of their countries to the UN.

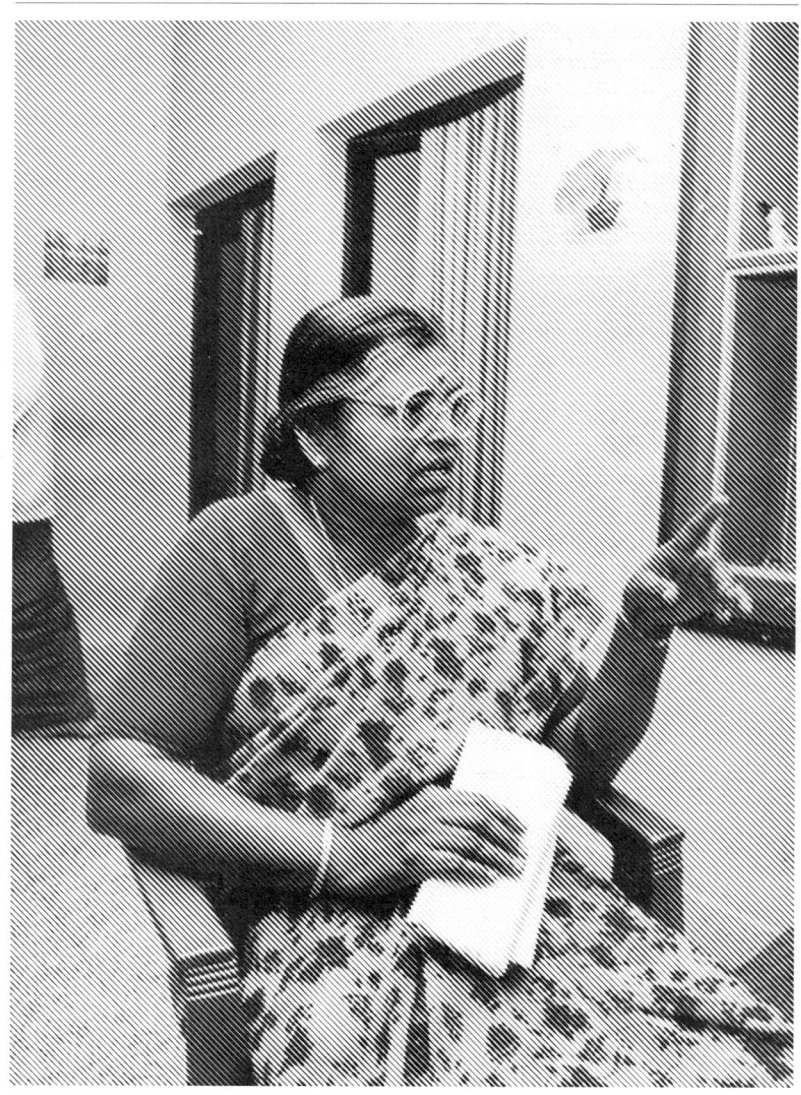

Leelakumari Amma

Government of Kerala

Leelakumari Amma (born 1948) won a one-woman campaign against the pesticide lobby, government departments, and her village's powerful plantation owners. Upon realizing that the spraying of the pesticide Endosulfan (classified as "highly toxic" by the US Environmental Protection Agency) was endangering her son's health, she won a court order banning the aerial spraying of pesticides on her village. Her struggle has set off wide-ranging discussions on pesticide impact on health, with countries such as Cambodia banning the use of Endosulfan.

After Leelakumari Amma moved to the Pullur-Periya panchayat in 1993, she and her family started developing health problems. She realized that these problems invariably peaked when the state-owned Plantation Corporation of Kerala (PEK) sprayed pesticides on the cashew plantation around her village. After speaking to other villagers, she understood that the problem was extremely widespread: Leelakumari decided to do something, and fast. But finding no support within her village, she resolved to wage a one-woman campaign against the pesticide spraying. Failing to persuade the authorities, she approached the courts, managing to get a stay. The plantation management, however, pressurized and intimidated her, forcing her to withdraw her case: she had, after all, to sustain her son's treatment, pay litigation costs, and struggle against aggravation from both family and society to pull out. But Leelakumari chose to redouble her efforts, contacting environmental groups and technical analysts. They found that the PEK had been using Endosulfan. Since 1978, the spraying of Endosulfan had resulted in high incidences of cancer, reproductive problems, congenital problems like cerebral palsy, and nervous system disorders.
Leelakumari's steadfastness paid off: the next year, before the start of the spraying season, she received an order from the court banning the aerial spraying of pesticides on her village. Her struggle has set off wide-ranging discussions on the impact of pesticides on health, with other countries, such as Cambodia, banning outright the use of Endosulfan. It is a matter of considerable societal pride that the personal struggle of a mother to protect the health of her children, and of others around her, could lead to such far-reaching changes.

The Indian government has a nonproactive history when it comes to keeping a watch on substances deleterious to public health. The pesticide Endosulfan, which was being used in Leelakumari's village, is banned in the USA, with the Environmental Protection Agency classifying it as "highly toxic".

India

Zakia Arshad

South Asia Partnership (SAP)

Zakia Arshad (born 1953) has worked for more than 25 years with Pakistan's marginalized, especially poor women and children. Of special significance has been her work as a master-trainer and evaluator of smokeless chullah (environmentally friendly cooking stove) projects with an array of organizations. She helped the Family Planning Association of Pakistan win the United Nations Environment Program's Global 500 Award for its work with smokeless chullahs.

Zakia Arshad began working for women and children's empowerment in the late 1970s, when society's attitude toward grassroots women was resistant. Considered unfit for mainstream development, and denied opportunities for education and health, they were considered male property.

Zakia has been working with marginalized women and children for more than half a century. She worked for 17 years with the Family Planning Association of Pakistan (Frap), and since the mid-1990s has been involved with the South Asia Partnership (SAP). She has been master-trainer with the Frap, SOS Villages Pakistan, the World Wide Fund for Nature (Pakistan), and other small organizations. Zakia encouraged the Frap to start smokeless chullah projects in Pakistan, and has been involved in training, through monitoring to evaluation. She organized 25 training events, in which 500 women in the four provinces participated, on the theme "health and safety measures for household women-benefits of the smokeless chullah".

Zakia has also carried out investigations for project design and implementation strategies on area development, NGOs, gender and development, and institutional-strengthening programs, as part of her work with the South Asia Partnership-Pakistan's (SAP-PK) year-long training Resource Development Program. As an advocacy coordinator with SAP-PK, Zakia's experience of working with different government departments has helped, including her involvement with the Ministry of Women's Development and Social Welfare, with whom she shared the findings of studies conducted by SAP-PK on gender discrimination against girls in six poverty-stricken districts of the Punjab. Zakia's spadework led to the ministry setting up a nationwide nutritional support program for girls. SAP-PK implemented the program, in which Zakia worked for three years, in six districts.

The environmentally friendly smokeless chullah protects women's health. Built of mud, it burns wood and dung, saving 35 percent of traditional fuel. It does not blacken utensils and kitchen walls. The technology has been adopted by rural women across Pakistan's four provinces.

Pakistan

Maude Barlow

The Council of Canadians
International Forum on Globalization
Blue Planet Project

Maude Barlow is the national chairperson of the Council of Canadians, Canada's largest citizen's advocacy organization with more than 100,000 members, and the founder of the Blue Planet Project, which works to stop commodification of the world's water. With more than 35 years of advocacy, grassroots organizing, and social activism, Maude is perhaps Canada's best-known voice of dissent against injustice. She is the recipient of numerous educational awards and has received honorary doctorates from four Canadian universities for her social justice work.

Maude is the middle of three daughters and grew up in a leafy, middle-class neighborhood of Ottawa, Canada. Hers was an idyllic childhood with parents she adored; her mother was a full-time homemaker and her father was a criminal justice advocate. It was her father who inspired Maude's early interest in social activism. He came from a poor Maritime family and put himself through university, earning an MA in social work. He had been witness to wartime atrocities and upon returning home was determined to change things for the better. He became an advocate for the reform of Canada's prison system. "I have to make sense of that (wartime experience) by building something so that my kids do not have to go through that," he said. His zeal for reform left an indelible mark on Maude. Like her father, she became a social crusader taking on all the major social issues of her generation.

Yet, her early adulthood echoed that of her mother. In the 1970s, Maude was a middle-class housewife. Eventually she got caught up in the women's movement, the revolutionary social current of her time. "This was a fabulous time to be in on the ground floor of what was just the most exciting movement of its time," she said. She ran the Office of Equal Opportunity at the city of Ottawa. At the age of 36, she catapulted onto the national scene consulting on women's issues for prime minister Pierre Trudeau. She was defeated in her first run for elected office for the Liberal Party, sending her on a new trajectory for her life. From then on, Maude worked to effect change from outside the system.

When world leaders embrace economic globalization, the rights and interests of individuals can erode. Often, those pushing for globalization have unlimited resources. Opposing such forces has taken a personal toll on Maude, who exerts high-level energy while maintaining a grueling travel schedule.

Canada

Rosalie Bertell

International Institute of Concern for Public Health (IICPH)
International Perspectives in Public Health
Grey Nuns of the Sacred Heart

Rosalie Bertell has worked for more than 50 years to expose the effects of radiation on the citizens of the world. A member of the Grey Nuns of the Sacred Heart, this "antinuclear nun" is an internationally recognized expert in the field of radiation. A doctorate in biometry gave her the academic background and her faith gave her the spiritual strength for her life's work — to fight against the earth's environmental contamination. She is founder and president of the International Institute of Concern for Public Health and editor-in-chief of International Perspectives in Public Health.

A public meeting in Buffalo in which county officials wanted to build a nuclear plant next to farms producing baby food became a watershed for Rosalie. When she saw that the only chairs on the stage were for five men advocating for the plant, she was the first person to march to the microphone, whereupon she demanded that the five nuclear experts give up their seats. The men were replaced with five women.

Rosalie is a formidable authority. When she testified before congress on the use of X-rays in shoe stores and annual medical X-rays in schools and at work, the practices were halted. She directed the International Medical Commission Bhopal which investigated the aftermath of the Bhopal disaster in India, organized the International Medical Commission Chernobyl to present testimony at the permanent people's tribunal, and helped the people of the Philippines with problems stemming from toxic waste left by the US military. She has worked with the Irish government to hold Britain responsible for the radioactive pollution of the Irish Sea, and is assisting the Gulf War Veterans and Iraqi citizens to deal with Gulf War syndrome. She is the author of "Handbook for Estimating the Health Effects of Ionizing Radiation" and the popular nonfiction book "No Immediate Danger: Prognosis for a Radioactive Earth", which has been translated into five languages.

No corporation or government is so powerful as to evade Rosalie Bertell's scrutiny. Her eyes, she says, have been opened to the reality of power. "War and money make the world go around. When you have money, you have to be prepared to go to war to protect it."

United States of America

Bhinand Chotirosseranee

Kanchanaburi Conservation Club
National Economic and Social Advisory Council (Nesac)

Bhinand Chotirosseranee is a founding member and current chair of the Kanchanaburi Conservation Club that has advocated for the environment for over two decades. Recently, she was elected one of 99 members of the National Economic and Social Advisory Council (Nesac), an independent regulatory body provided for in the 1997 Constitution. Nesac gives recommendations to government on the planning and implementation of public policies concerning the economy and society. Her work has been characterised by her adherence to non-violence in the face of threats to her security and that of her family.

Bhinand Chotirosseranee's involvement in environmental causes began 20 years ago when the Thai government initiated a plan to build a large hydroelectric dam in the Toong Yai Naresuan Wildlife Sanctuary, consequently declared a Unesco-"World Heritage", in Kanchanaburi, her home province. Realizing that the Nam Chone Dam was to be built on an active fault, she mobilized the Kanchanaburi Women's Group and local and international activists to campaign against the project until it was scrapped. The campaign prompted Bhinand to form the Kanchanaburi Conservation Club to lead the fight for the environment.

Her commitment and courage are second to none. After the coup d'etat in 1991, a huge blast occurred in the warehouses of the Port Authority in Bangkok, where toxic chemicals were kept, resulting in a number of casualties and fallout from the chemicals. The government hastily shipped the remaining chemicals to dumps in Kanchanaburi, where they leaked into the underground water and spread to the environment. Bhinand was the loudest protestor and for this she received death threats. But the campaign bore fruit when the military yielded to her demand to abide by the scientific rules of chemical disposal.

What made Bhinand known internationally was the protest she led against the gas pipeline from Burma to Thailand, which would have stretched through 200 kilometers of one of the most pristine forests in Thailand. Besides being an environmental risk, it would earn the Burmese military junta its largest foreign revenue ever, drawing outcries from anti-junta and human rights groups. The Kanchanaburi Conservation Club led a two-month blockade in the forest by several hundred protesters to prevent its construction, forcing government to hold public hearings. Although the people lost, the hearings paved the way for the passage of a new law on public hearings.

Bhinand Chotirosseranee has created an awareness of the importance of nature, and has nurtured sustainable co-existence between human beings and nature.

Thailand

Bat-Sereedene Byamba

Bat-Sereedene Byamba is a professor of medicine and a leading manager-innovator of the Mongolian health care system. Director of the largest medical institution in Ulanbataar and named Best Manager 2002, she is credited with reforming the system in the transition from socialism to market economy.

Bat-Sereedene Byamba was born in 1955 in the remote western part of Mongolia. No one could have guessed that a girl from this isolated periphery would one day become a professor of medicine and a leading manager-innovator of the Mongolian health care system. The P. N. Shastin Clinic Hospital with its 600-strong medical and service personnel is well known for its work, and Bat-Sereedene has been singled out as the "mother" of the largest health care institution in Mongolia. Appointed director in 1999, she initiated a process of reform and modernization that helped the hospital make the transition to a market economy. Specialists in medicine and health care are agreed that the leadership of Bat-Sereedene provides an excellent example in health care management in the post-socialist environment. The World Health Organization has also acknowledged the Shastin hospital as a promising model for the renovation of Mongolia's health care sector. Prof. J. Khairulla, a well-known neurosurgeon, says: "I taught medicine to Bat-Sereedene and now I am really proud of her. She made a discovery; she discovered the way medical institutions could work and how health workers could receive a wage appropriate to their work. She succeeded in reforming the whole philosophy pursued both during the 80 years of socialist rule and in the 15 years after the democratic revolution."

In 1999, the State-owned hospital was in complete disarray, its building occupied by renting organizations, its medical personnel prone to alcoholism, and its debt amounting to 47 million tugriks (its annual budget was 100 million tugriks). Nobody expected the new director to be able to deal with this situation. But Bat-Sereedene's reforms have yielded excellent results. The Shastin hospital now pays its staff better than four years ago and has recently invested 120 million tugriks in a computerization project.

The collapse of socialism in Mongolia nearly ruined the health care system and thousands of patients preferred to travel abroad for medical treatment rather than apply to national health care institutions. This situation could not last and a new system had to be put in place.

Mongolia

Dawan Chantarahassadee

Klong Dan Local Conservation Group

Dawan Chantarahassadee graduated from the Faculty of Political Science, Ramkamhaeng University, and is hailed as "an academic among commoners of Klong Dan". After working in a private firm, she returned to her birthplace and with her husband opened a restaurant in the community where she traces her ancestry back three generations. The turning point in her life was in 1999 when she became involved in the campaign against the corrupt Klong Dan Waste Water Treatment Project in Samut Prakarn (Klong Dan), East of Bangkok.

Dawan learned about the huge project in her community from a billboard. Upon reading the description she asked, "Is this right that all wastewater from other factories in Samut Prakarn shall be diverted to my community where no factory exists?" The Waste Water Treatment Project in Samut Prakarn was initiated in 1996 to handle the wastewater discharged by factories in Samut Prakarn, a growing industrial zone. But Dawan was concerned that the project would lead to the destruction of the environment and the coastal ecosystem including mangroves in Siam Bay, as well as ruining the livelihood of the local people, which is intricately dependent on the environment in the tributaries and the sea.

As Dawan studied the project, searching for information on its every aspect, analyzing all available documents, she found evidence of corruption involving influential people, including the local mafia. But that did not frighten this extraordinary woman. It prompted her to delve deeper into the project. Pushed by the Asian Development Bank (ADB), the project epitomized high-level corruption and a covert loan deal that, Dawan discovered, involved the Bank itself.

Dawan compares herself to a spider that stays in the middle of the web and weaves together everyone's efforts. She says that the key to the success of a campaign is support from other communities, local and international NGOs, academics, the media and the general public. Her perseverance was rewarded in 2004 when the government put a halt to the project and ordered an investigation into those involved in the scam, including former ministers, government officials and private businessmen. The people proposed that the project site be converted into a marine life research and nursery center even as they were monitoring the progress of the investigation of the corruption they exposed.

Evidence of rampant corruption in public projects has encouraged citizens to be vigilant and expose corruption where it occurs. Dawan Chantarahassadee exposed corruption in the huge Waste Water Treatment Project in Samut Prakarn, worth over US$ 500 million, forcing the government to order that it be temporarily halted.

Thailand

Olga Doronina

United Nations Environment Program National Committee for Russia

Olga Doronina, who was born in 1952, holds a PhD in biotechnology and was honored with the title "Inventor of the USSR." As an official of the Commission for the United Nations Environment Program and the State Committee on Science and Technology, she headed projects with various organizations. She is currently vice-president of the United Nations Environment Program National committee for Russia, where she focuses her activities on the issues of sustainable development, the environment, and global security. She is a reputed academician and a member of the Russian Academy of Science.

It happens that some stories have a profound effect on people's lives. The story that has always inspired Olga was the one told by her father who, while serving in northeastern USSR during World War II, was dispatched to deliver crucial intelligence information to military headquarters. In a severe snowstorm, his dog-sled team lost its way. Completely exhausted, both Olga's father and his dogs began to suffer from the cold and from hunger as the food supply dwindled. He divided what remained between the dogs and himself. Struck by the animals' heavy breathing, he decided to renounce his own share for their sake. He understood that everything depended on the team. In the end the mission was carried out successfully and the intelligence information delivered in time.

This story shaped Olga's conviction that in order to achieve a goal, not only is a strong personality necessary, but also common efforts and team work. Olga has worked for many years on issues of biotechnology and bio-security. An analysis of the tendencies in the modern world has convinced her of mankind's vulnerability in the face of environmental degradation and nuclear risks. In terms of scientific research, Olga was influenced by her teacher, the academician Nikita N. Moiseev, who introduced the concept of "the nuclear winter" and convinced the world of the monstrosity of using nuclear weapons.

Her scientific studies in the sphere of global security have led her to a deep conviction that only the firm resolve and enhanced will of the global community can stop the destructive processes of modern development. To raise the awareness of her compatriots on the issues of global risks and sustainability, Olga has written the book, "From Stockholm to Johannesburg," dedicated to 30 years of UN activities in the area of environmental pro-tection, health, and sustainable development.

Working with governmental bodies of the Russian Federation and cooperating with international institutions and organizations, Olga Doronina makes her contribution to global awareness by stressing the necessity of sustainable development and security in the face of the challenges of today's globalized world.

Russian Federation

Solange Fernex

Women's International League for Peace and Freedom (WILPF)
The Children of Chernobyl
European Green Party

Solange Fernex has been campaigning for the preservation of the environment, against nuclear power, and for equal rights for women for 40 years. Her activities as a member of the Green Party and of the European Parliament (1989—1994), of her town council (24 years), her involvement in several NGOs, her public presentations, numerous translations and books, her civic disobedience and her concrete actions promoting solidarity, have informed and inspired young people, helped others and encouraged them to shoulder their responsibilities, and served as a brilliant example to all.

February 1975: It is the beginning of the occupation of the Wyhl site, where a nuclear power plant is to be built on the German bank of the Rhine. After five months out in the rain, wind, and snow, Solange Fernex has just returned from Marckolsheim, where she had set up her tent in protest against the construction of a lead factory. But no time to rest: the German authorities begin the deforestation of the site. Solange recalls: "Our three boys unpacked the small tent and set it up in front of the bulldozer. The driver stopped, and the women of Wyhl climbed up on his vehicle. That was one of the magic moments, when you feel that everyone wants to take action and that all it needs is for one person to take the first step. Almost immediately, there was a multitude of tents on the site — they seemed to multiply in miraculous fashion like the proverbial loaves and fishes. In fact, it turned out that everyone had brought a tent in their car trunks. The people from the Wyhl region talked to the workers, the Alsatians were there out of solidarity and to show that the nuclear threat knows no boundaries." The victorious occupation of the site lasted until November 1975 (the forest in Wyhl was declared a nature reserve in 1995). It was followed by the occupation of Kaiseraugst in Switzerland, of Gerstheim, of Heiteren, of Fessenheim in the Rhine Plain. In February 1977, Solange, her son, and his friends went on an "unlimited hunger strike" in Fessenheim which lasted 23 days. During these days, thousands of white daisies were painted on the tarmac roads, as a symbol of non-violent resistance. And all the towns and villages in Alsace were renamed "Fessenheim." A victory of sorts was achieved after 17 days — a control commission was approved of which Solange became a member. In 1983, after the hunger strike for a nuclear freeze, Solange was hospitalized after 40 days.

Nuclear power currently provides about 17% of the world's electricity. Its use is controversial because of the unsolved problem of storing radioactive waste indefinitely. 75% of the electricity generated in France is generated with nuclear power. With 59 units, France has by far the most nuclear power plants in Europe. They are located throughout the country.

France

Irina Grushevaya

International Association for Humanitarian Cooperation (IAHC)

Irina Grushevaya (born 1948), a professor of German linguistics, has dedicated the past 16 years of her life to humanitarian causes. As president of the International Association of Humanitarian Cooperation, she works tirelessly to improve the lives of children (and adults) who are affected by the disaster of Chernobyl. She has enabled more than 150,000 children to be sent abroad for a holiday trip. Other focuses of her work are women's rights and security. She organizes exchanges between youth of the East and the West, and she is the center of a network of like-minded people.

The nuclear explosion at the Chernobyl power plant in 1986 turned Irina Grushevaya's whole life upside down. Since the regime had for years been concealing the real extent of the disaster, it was not until 1989, when her own children were showing signs of illness, that Irina, shocked by the deceit, took her family's and other people's destiny into her own hands. Irina, together with her husband, initiated the first civil non-governmental association — the Chernobyl Charity, which was intended to expose the massive cover-up around the Chernobyl disaster and to form self-assistance groups in the affected areas. Day by day, Irina persistently exposed the truth of Chernobyl to multitudes of people far and wide. She organized actions of protests and support groups, becoming a prime link between East and West.

In the course of 15 years of hard toil, Irina Grushevaya has created an extensive network of humanitarian cooperation, becoming an envoy of peace and a guardian of civil rights and the rights of children. In the course of all these hectic years, she has been initiating programs, projects, and organizing mass actions. Thanks to her commitment to the cause of truth, people worldwide are aware of the children of Chernobyl and the austere environment in which they live in Belarus. Despite repression, intimidation, and threats to her life, Irina extends her helping hand to victims of political and social persecution in her homeland — termed as the last dictatorship in Europe — who have become objects of human trafficking and violence. Though Irina calls her appeals to the public "hope in the land of hopelessness," she firmly stands for peaceful means as the only option in addressing a hopeless situation.

Irina's activities are exercised in the atmosphere of censorship, administrative restrictions, and defamation. The regime of Belarus does not support her work at all. On the contrary, it tries hard to block it wherever possible to the extent that she was even forced to live in exile (1997/98).

Belarus

Samia Ibrahim

Sudanese Environmental Conservation Society
El Hawdage Voluntary Association for Pastoralist Women

Samia Mohamad Ibrahim (47) was born in Gadarif State, Eastern Sudan. She obtained a first degree in Agriculture and Economics from Khartoum University and then an MSc in the same field from Oklahoma State University (USA). Samia works diligently for a healthy, natural environment, is a member of the Sudanese Environmental Conservation Association and also a member of El Hawdage Voluntary Association for Pastoralist Women. She works in liaison with all governmental and non-governmental environmental bodies.

Samia's work as an activist in environmental development, monitoring the con-ditions of forests and local cultivations, is vulnerable to many environmental hazards. One day she was called by the Minister of Agriculture to go on a field trip to the State forests. In her words Samia recollects, "Our visit was to cover the State forests from north to south. In the afternoon we entered a forest in the south part of Gedaref. We plowed ahead across that forest for hours and hours till we thought we had got lost there. Only at sunset could we find our way out. Then all of a sudden it rained heavily. The minister decided to shorten the trip and to go back home. The place was very dark and there were thunderstorms. We could not call our families from our cellular phones because the area was outside the network coverage. We worked against the clock, because we knew that if rain flooded a local canal, we would not be able to cross it. Luckily enough when we reached the canal, we sought help from a local man, who walked us across the canal before it got flooded. The water level almost reached our car windows. We had to stay there for two days with members of the local tribe in their tents. By midnight we got home. My husband was very worried about me. He told me that the area we visited is replete with land mines. It was a very interesting experience: full of risks but enjoyable."

Samia coordinates the work of different bodies concerned with the environment, such as city councils and voluntary organizations. The activities she organizes include distributing seed allocations to local farmers, supervizing the implantation of road trees, launching and overseeing cleaning campaigns and raising peoples' awareness of environmental development. Samia is currently working on a study about land utilization, which is one of the targets of a local environmental project.

Samia's work is mainly concerned with the protection and development of the environment and vegetation. She raises peoples' awareness of the importance of preserving and rationalizing the utilization of natural resources.

Sudan

Helen John

Campaign for Nuclear Disarmament (CND)
WoMenwith Hill (WwH)

The former nurse and midwife Helen John (born 1937) is vice president of the British peace organization 'Campaign for Nuclear Disarmament' (CND). For 25 years she has fought against nuclear weapons, and for 12 years against the largest US spy center in the world, at Menwith Hill, Yorkshire. Menwith Hill plays a big role in satellite-led US military strikes, as in Afghanistan or Iraq, and in the Star Wars plans of the Bush administration. It is also a major center of military, political and economic espionage. There, with civil disobedience, Helen John leads protest actions against the base.

Helen John simply does not accept that it is forbidden to enter the base. Together with her friend Anne Lee she kept cutting holes in the security fence of the US installation, which played a large role in the satellite-supported US military strikes against Afghanistan and Iraq. One day the two set off to complain to the US Commander about the lack of security at the base. "We went to the base and the workers there acted as if they did not see us. Helen kept saying 'Hello, have a good day,' but they still didn't see us. We came to the double glass door at the reception, but no one was there. The double steel doors opened and the office workers came out on a shift change. Helen politely held the door open and kept saying 'Good day!' When the last one had passed, we went in, into the top security area. A woman started screeching, 'Help! Security! Where is your identity card?' 'We don't need one,' we answered." "She called the Security Officer, who raced over immediately," Helen continues, "He called the British military police who are stationed at the base. He wanted to call a transport van to carry us off, but we said, 'No, no, we would rather walk, it is such a nice day!' And we were still dragging the fence behind us. He brought us to the main entrance, took the piece of fence and screamed 'Fuck off.' We jumped in my car, drove back to my house and I called the US Embassy. I said: 'Can you please help us? We were just in the top security area in Menwith Hill with a little present, and they yelled 'Fuck off!' at us. Now really, that is not polite!'"

Since 1993 with wit and nonviolent civil disobedience Helen John has been fighting in Britain against Menwith Hill, the largest US espionage center in the world. Political, military and economic information is collected there, and satellite photos for US military attacks are interpreted.

Rebecca Johnson

The Acronym Institute for Disarmament Diplomacy

For the last 22 years Rebecca Johnson, has been briefing diplomats on disarmament issues, keeping herself well informed and well placed to act as an indispensable link between grassroots activists, diplomats and politicians. Rebecca is vice chair of the Board of the Bulletin of Atomic Scientists, and a UK member of both the Monterey Non-proliferation Strategy Group and the Centre for Policy Studies, Moscow. She is Senior Adviser to the Hans Blix UN Disarmament Committee. Throughout the years Rebecca has worked cooperatively with women, and was a prisoner of conscience many times.

Rebecca Johnson, despite some health difficulties, always sets off on missions of peace promotion, consolidating negotiations for nuclear disarmament. Although she is no longer at risk of imprisonment, she still constitutes a key threat to US and British nuclear ambitions due to her relentless anti-nuclear campaigns. She diligently puts peace and welfare of humanity on the top of her life-long agenda, sharing information with other concerned individuals, regional and international bodies, in order to combat the nuclear strategies. She is acclaimed for her superior diplomatic skills, which she uses in the service of all humankind by pushing for the prevention of nuclear war and an end to the nuclear armament race.

Rebecca Johnson has been vigorously challenging diplomats on disarmament issues, acting as a crucial link between grassroots activists, diplomats and politicians.

United Kingdom

Xiaoxi Li

Li Xiaoxi is an associate professor at the Air Force Command College, Haidan District, Beijing. She was elected as the National People's Congress (NPC) representative of the district in December 1998. She has paid considerable attention to the construction and environment of Beijing and China as a whole, putting forward over 140 suggestions and motions, most of which concern the environment. She has saved the last piece of marshland in Beijing, and has striven for the well-being of both wild animals and humans.

For more than ten years, Li Xiaoxi (60) has worked for the environment. After arriving in Beijing in December 1998, she put forward over 140 suggestions and motions, including those received by the NPC and Beijing People's Congress through NPC representatives and Beijing People's Congress representatives. She tried to use her rights and obligations as an NPC representative to protect the environment.

In 2001, in order to protect the sole plain reed marsh in Beijing, Li went to Yangzhen reed pool marsh six times to conduct research. She publicized her opinions in the media and through Chinese People's Political Consultative Conference, objecting to the construction of a golf course and a large entertainment town around the marsh, but proposing to establish a marsh park. Her persistent efforts finally paid off: Beijing changed the regulation of its water systems, protecting trees on both sides of the penstocks. During her travels, wherever Li came across environmental pollution and wastage of natural resources, she spoke out against it and made feasible suggestions.

Li believes that animals have rights too and has done a survey of the illegal catching and killing of wildlife. She feels the law on wildlife protection needs modification. For human beings if there is clean air, clean water, good food and a good natural habitat, they need little else. This is a goal to which she is willing to devote her whole life.

In China's pursuit of economic growth, the environment is low on the priority list. There is little concern among the people and the bureaucracy is indifferent and irresponsible.

China

Sabine Lichtenfels

Tamera Peace Village

Sabine Lichtenfels is a peace activist in the Middle East and a co-founder of the model peace village Tamera in Portugal. Tamera, located on 330 acres of land in the south of Portugal, about 20 kilometers from the west coast, is a research settlement where the most important themes of a new, sustainable culture concept are developed. For the last 27 years Sabine has been working together with a sociologist on the "Healing Biotope 1 Tamera." The main focus of her political work is on training youth and on peace work in the Middle East.

"Find forms of living together that are no longer directed against life and love! Develop models for the peaceful co-existence of all beings! Develop pilot models for the answers to the burning questions of our time!" The theologian, peace activist, and author Sabine Lichtenfels has been following this imperative for 27 years. Her special focus is on the connection between outer networking and peace work, the creation of real alternatives and inner, human peace work.

Ten years ago she began the establishment of Tamera, the first healing biotope, in Portugal. Today, around 100 people are working here to create a self-sufficient solar energy settlement — a functioning life model as an example of a self-sufficient community for a nonviolent future civilization. Here, peace camps are held with participants from all parts of the world. A healing biotope is also being planned in the Middle East, and Palestinians and Israelis will be participating in this venture. "If we develop new life models in the areas of love, raising children, medicine, and ecology and succeed in creating systems of trust that are free of fear, then these models can be used in other places. They become contagious and have a healing effect. Still today, this idea empowers me."

Sabine Lichtenfels is especially committed to the younger generation, and she provides youth with orientation that protects them against resignation and feelings of powerlessness. To do this, she undertakes peace actions, pilgrimages and street retreats, political theater tours and study trips, for example to the Todas people of India, who have retained deep knowledge about how to care for nature. In the Mirja School of Peace in Tamera young people are trained as "peace workers" in preparation for carrying out missions in conflict areas, working with conflict resolution, and the establishment of future communities.

Worldwide, the politics of globalization has uprooted people from their natural anchor. The globalization of violence must now be followed by a globalization of peace.

Shu Ying Lin

Taipei Municipal Wen Shan Community College

Lin Shu Ying (54), originally a nurse, became a voluntary environmental worker for the Homemakers Union and Foundation in 1989, promoting recycling and the protection of the environment. In 1998 she joined the Wenshan Community College. In 2000, she promoted the protection of Ching-mei river through community education. Together with 17 community colleges, she formed the Alliance for the Protection of the Tamshui river.

In October 2000, the Xangsane typhoon hit Taipei; the Ching-mei river rose to alarming levels. Concerned people at the Wenshan Community College studied the area and the course of the river, and decided to call a meeting with the schools located along the course of the river to discuss its preservation. At the time Lin Shu Ying was the vice-director of the college. She had retired from her nursing position in 1985 at the age of 34. Her health care background helped her understand the relationship between environmental protection and health. In 1989, she joined the Homemakers Union and Foundation as a voluntary environmental worker. In 1998 community colleges started to flourish all over Taiwan. One of the first, Wenshan Community College, was established with the help of Homemakers Union and Foundation. Lin became closely linked to the community college, and one of its core personalities. "We wanted a more informal approach to the protection of rivers", Lin said. A series of activities were designed to attract schools, civic groups and local residents. Simultaneously, protection of rivers was included in the curriculum of regional history, becoming teaching material for education on local issues. All of the activities, speeches and exhibitions were designed to "draw the public closer to the river", said Lin. She talks about the history of water resource management in the Taipei basin: "Ching-mei river has played an important role since the reign of Emperor Qianlung, during the Qing dynasty. Starting from this river right beside us, our ultimate concern is the management of all water resources. Every year, I take students to the summit of Er-ge peak to look at the Fei-tsui reservoir and look into the problems of water usage. Once you understand the importance of the Wenshan district in managing water resources, you will know the importance of protecting rivers."

Taiwan's society and environment are paying a very high price for years of industrial development. Despite numerous recent civic movements, most of the people remain indifferent to issues of public concern. Policies, often carried out in the dark, make public participation even harder.

China, Taiwan

Felicitas Estela Linares Meneses

Instituto de Comunicación y Medio Ambiente (ICMA)

Felicitas Estela Linares Meneses is from Lima. She created the Communication and Environment Institute (ICMA), from which a huge innovative project for cross-cultural meetings and for the development of production units for the coastal and mountain region emanates. With them, she tries to contribute to national awareness of the need for a more integrated society.

Felicitas Estela Linares Meneses (65) is always doing new things. She has always done this. When she was four years old, she gathered things that could be reused from the rubbish dumps of Lima. After that, she became an organist, weaver, carpenter, and video maker. She is a mother and a friend who loves intensively. She experienced the war and the violence that devastated Peru during the 1980s. She was herself the center of many attacks. Her proposal: to work for national integration. "Our Andean and African roots allow us to project ourselves." She thinks that Peru must be remade, but not alone. She is the director of the Communication and Environment Institute (ICMA), from which she develops innovative, productive, and cross-cultural projects. "I have tried to imprint a new mentality on women." Her ideas gave birth to seven projects in different parts of the country. In El Carmen, in Chincha, in the administrative district of Ica, there is an exemplary work in La Casa de la Mujer (The House of Women), with a project called "Art with Dignity." In other regions, there are, for example, projects for empowering women, for the processing of milk products and for the marketing of agricultural and artisan products, among others.

It seems like Felicitas Estela Linares Meneses has no limits, nevertheless there is one: diabetes. She has a disciplined approach to her illness. "Every day, I control my level of glucose and follow my special diets, even if it seems rather complicated due to my continuous travels." She has a great fondness for crochet. "It is my therapy and my inheritance from my mother," and with the patience that only a weaver has, she transforms the bobbins of wool into beautiful blouses. As she weaves, memories flow connecting her to her history, to her dreams, to her new Peru.

Peru is a fragmented country. There must be more integration. Everyone must help with what they have, especially those who make the political decisions. The most expressive discrimination is the one against the indigenous people and those of African descent.

Peru

Julia Morton-Marr

International Holistic Tourism Education Center (Ihtec)
International School of Peace Gardens
Science for Peace

Julia Morton-Marr teaches children how to be citizens of the world. With an understanding that peace, justice, and the environment cannot be taught separately, Julia has developed curricula adopted in 3500 schools in 34 countries. In 1993, Julia founded the International Holistic Tourism Education Center and the International School of Peace Gardens. An array of topics — from conflict resolution and cultural understanding to geography and performing arts — are based on the three pillars of human sustainability: ecological integrity, social peace, and individual rights and responsibilities.

When disabilities resulting from a spinal fusion forced Julia out of teaching in a "four-walled" classroom in 1983, she continued her life's work in nontraditional ways. Growing up in South Africa and Sri Lanka, and teaching and learning in Canada, Australia, and the United Kingdom, Julia has a wide-angle view of the world. Her web-based education programs work in almost any environment, including public schools, prisons, and universities. In 1993, she joined with the children at St. Peter's Church in Erindale Mississaugo, Ontario, to celebrate the creation of the International School of Peace Gardens by planting its first peace tree. Children around the world have been planting trees ever since. Projects include a food security program in Ghana, conflict resolution peacetree plantings in Kenya, reforestation in Haiti, and establishing 2000 peace gardens in Hawaii.

Her projects encourage community service, the use of solar and wind energy, and learning in biologically diverse land laboratories. Her quiet work is nonpartisan, and her goals are to help people think for themselves. Her teaching inspires adults as well as children. Because of her advocacy, the Australian government initiated a walking trail and management plan to protect the water supply at the mouth of the River Murray. Julia launched the Marine Peace Parks project in Puerto Moreles, Quintana Ro, Mexico, and created the Creature Corridors at the First National Canada Trails Conference. She chaired the United Nations environment committee and serves on its advisory board, as well as serving on advisory boards for the Research Center for Global Governance in Brazil, the Voice of Women in Canada, and the Women's Peace Melody, which works with women and children in Burundi and Rwanda.

Julia has been called an "environmental Mother Teresa", because her work is primarily supported by personal funds. Countries that use her curricula include India, Israel, Iraq, Germany, and Russia.

Canada

Gabriela Ngirmang

Whatever view you hold of Gabriela Ngirmang as a peace activist (unheard of in Palau) or a Mirair (traditional title), a matriarch of Ikelau clan, she has made a lasting impression. Acclaimed as "valiant" in the Pacific Women's Conference in Guam (1989) for her successful defense of Palau's nuclear-free constitution, she features in a textbook for students of government as "a woman having political efficacy," vital for democracy. Gabriela believes politics is important not just for the powerful few but for everyone. Yet she never claims to be, or to have done, anything extraordinary.

In 1979, Palau's Constitutional Convention wrote the world's first nuclear-free constitution, voted upon by 92 percent of Palauan electorate. Gabriela attended one of the convention's proceedings in which a telegram from the US Ambassador came telling the convention to drop the "harmful substances" clause because it was inconsistent with the Compact of Free Association with the US. It was that day that Gabriela decided she had to rise up in defense of the nuclear-free constitution. Gabriela's traditional role as a matriarch in Ikelau clan obliged her to step in and protect Palau's land from being taken over by the US military as set forth in the compact. She felt it her responsibility to ensure future generations of Palauans would live in a nuclear-free land and waters. She says: "In Palau, women play a very important role in issues of policy. Women traditionally own and devise land. We control the clan money. We traditionally select our chiefs; women place and remove them. Having observed their upbringing closely, we are able to decide which men have the talent to represent our interests. From birth, Palauan women are responsible for the men. When men marry, the women arrange for the settlement, and when they die, women bury them. Women are caretakers of the environment." Gabriela feels a caretaker of the environment should not get paid because it is a duty to ensure the inherent right of future generations to live in a nuclear-free land and waters and to live in harmony with nature. What proved to be most difficult in her struggle was to gain unity among the Palauan people to resist the US military demands set forth in the compact. The economic benefits offered by the United States in the compact made Palauans forget their role as caretakers of the environment.

After World War II, Palau came under control of the US as part of the Trust Territory of the Pacific Islands. In 1994, Palau voted to become freely associated with the US while retaining their independence. This compact was a hotly debated issue as it allows the US broad powers (a.o. submarine testing). Palauans continue to defend their environmental heritage.

Palau

Nguyen Thanh Hien

Center for Studies and Applications of Microorganism Fertilizers

Dr Nguyen Thanh Hien (born 1940) studied nitrogen fixation biology in the Netherlands and the UK. After lecturing on genetics at Hanoi University for many years, she retired in 2000 to head the Center for Studies and Applications of Microorganism Fertilizers. She obtained a patent for the organic fertilizer BioGro, which helps preserve the environment and enriches the soil. With the Australian Center for International Agricultural Research (ACIAR), she introduced microorganism fertilizers in rice and vegetable production in Vietnam and Australia, benefiting millions of farmers.

Nguyen Thanh Hien says that her success is the product of her passion for science and her determination to succeed. She further attributes the success to her personality, ambition, and her desire to serve the community. Her dream is to develop a model of organic farming in Vietnam that will help farmers increase crop yields and incomes and preserve the environment. She has spared no efforts to realize that dream. The microorganism fertilizer she invented, BioGro, can replace 50 percent of chemical nitrogen fertilizers, help rehabilitate the soil, cut down production costs, and achieve high-yields.

Nguyen Than Hien has worked with foreign partners from the Netherlands, Sweden and Australia to introduce microorganism fertilizers in agricultural production. In collaboration with the French NGO Coopération Internationale pour le Développement et la Solidarité (Cidse), she built a model for growing organic vegetables in Yen Noi commune in Hanoi city, blazing a trail in non-chemical farming and proving to the world that it is possible to shift from chemical-based to organic farming. Hien set up the Center for Studies and Applications of Microorganism Fertilizers and traveled to every hamlet and village promoting its benefits and encouraging its use. The Center has transfered technology to farmers, and established a network of local agents covering Hanoi, Hai Duong, Ha Tay and Thanh Hoa provinces, and last year, these agents sold over 1000 tons of microorganism fertilizers. The feedback from farmers is that these fertilizers help cut down production costs, give higher crop yields and contribute to the preservation of the environment. Hien said she is confident that she will be able to form an organic farming industry in Vietnam which will improve farmers' lives and preserve the environment.

Since Hien's invention of BioGro was patented in 2000, she has worked to bring the product to farmers, women and enterprises. Besides growing organic vegetables, she has been helping the Bai Bang Paper Mill in a project to process the company's toxic wastes into organic fertilizers.

Viet Nam

Ivanka Nikolova Lecheva

Agricultural University Plovdiv
Balkans Ecoforum for Peace
Ecofarm

Ivanka Nikolova Lecheva is a leading expert in plant and environmental protection in Bulgaria. She is the only woman who is a dean of a faculty, and she works for equal rights for women in education. As a member of the Organizing Committee of the Balkans Ecoforum for Peace, Ivanka has participated in the development of a strategy for policy in the field of ecology. She promotes biodiversity and ecological farming and has carried out educational programs for children and young people on environmental protection and ecology.

As a member of the Organizing Committee of the Balkans Ecoforum for Peace, Ivanka Lecheva has participated in the development of a strategy for policy in the field of ecology, particularly in transboundary pollution of air, water, and soil. She was nominated as a representative of the association Women in Science in the Balkan Ecological Center. In 1995, within the project Women in Development, she helped prepare and present brochures in Bulgarian, English, Turkish, and Greek languages on ecology, children, and nature for a panel on women and science. The aim was to educate children on the protection of green systems in the cities: parks, gardens, flowers, trees. She also developed a special program aimed at ecological education of students and young people. Her desire is for children to live in harmony with nature. She has motivated young people from the Faculty of Plant Protection and Agroecology to establish a Young Ecologist Club within the NGO Green Balkans and she often gives lectures on the protection of biodiversity as a volunteer.

Ivanka believes that lifestyle is very important for young people and especially for women, since lifestyle particularly affects our food choices and consequently the safety of the food we eat. With a women's team, she has presented organic foods — produced at the Agricultural University at the Plovdiv Fair — at the College of Science and Technologies. As a member of Ecofarm, an association for ecological agriculture, she has participated regularly as a volunteer in workshops, training courses, and seminars, promoting organic farming, safe food, and environmental protection for a high quality of life.

As Bulgaria's political system changed, the challenge to ecologists has grown, especially in the area of education. Public awareness and action are needed on issues such as pollution (air, water, soil), biodiversity, food safety, and the role of women and children in environmental protection.

Bulgaria

Yuqin Niu

After 20 years, and despite financial difficulties and a lack of related expertise, Niu Yuqin has successfully completed the forestation of 73 square kilometers of land. In 1993 she was awarded the Dr Leo Prize by the UN's Food and Agriculture Organization, and later she was elected delegate to the 9th and 10th National People's Congress, the highest representative legislative body of the Chinese Government.

Walking in the dense forest, listening to the sounds of trees, Niu Yuqin hears them as greetings and "thank-you's." She planted these trees with her own hands. They are her achievement in life! With years of hard work, Yuqin turned 110,000 mu (73 square kilometers) of desert into a seemingly endless forest.

Every Sunday, she would come with her grandchildren to work in the woods. They would do some reading when they had rests. She feels proud and contented that her work of forestation can be carried on from generation to generation, turning all the deserts into oases.

It was especially difficult when Niu Yuqin and her husband first started to contract idle land for forestation and anti-desertification projects. There was no one to help; they had to rely solely on themselves to start everything up. At that time, life was especially harsh and difficult as her husband was afflicted with a bone tumor. They were poor and there was no way to get credit for extra expenses. Yuqin had to cope with enormous psychological pressure every day. But she survives. "My family name is Niu (ox). I was born in the Year of the Ox, surely I would be obstinate like an ox," she says. And it is this highly determined character that has taken her through these years, good and bad. She was elected delegate to the 9th and 10th National People's Congress, the highest representative legislative body of the Chinese Government. She is a representative of her home county, city, and province. She has gained respect from her fellow villagers. More importantly, she has succeeded in changing people's perspectives. Many people now take forestation seriously, and following in Yuqin's steps.

Aside from forestation, Yuqin also furnished the infrastructure of the village, such as school buildings and highways maintenance, contributing much to the development of culture and economy of the village.

Her work is highly appreciated by the government and environmental protection organizations. The sense of responsibility for environmental protection is getting higher and higher among her fellow villagers. The desert is now an oasis.

China

Lihong Shi

Global Environment Institute
Green Plateau Institute

Shi Lihong, an environmental activist, is responsible for the Global Environment Institute and is executive director of Wild China. She is very active in non-governmental environmental protection. One of the ways she contributes to the campaign for environmental protection is by making documentary films on the subject.

Shi Lihong started her environmental protection work because she was deeply impressed by the work of Liao Xiaoyi, the initiator of Global Village of Beijing, an environmental civil society protection organization. She had the opportunity to interview Liao in 1996 when she was a journalist with China Daily and that led to her becoming an environmental protection volunteer. Later she married a famous wildlife photographer and environmental activist.

In 1999 they quit their jobs and moved with their newborn baby to the habitat of Yunnan's black snub-nosed monkeys. Here in the northwest of Yunnan Province, together with local government, reserve area authorities and local people, they established a nongovernmental organization, Green Plateau Institute, to protect the natural environment. In 2003 Shi and her husband returned to Beijing and founded Wild China, an organization that produced documentary films on natural history and the environment. Shi turned her attention to the battle against dams across the Nujiang River (which translates as "Angry River"). In April 2004 she learned that Green Watershed, another environmental civil society organization in China, was organizing people along the Nujiang to visit the Manwan migrants. She decided to shoot the visit at her own expense and produced a 30-minute documentary film, "Voice of Nujiang". The film reflects the miserable situations of the migrants and the hard work environmental protection organizations had done to protect the river. It provided a sound base for the new anti-dam movements in China. Shi is currently filming the campaign to protect homes and oppose resettlement along the Jinshajiang River ("Golden Sand River").

In the 1990s the Chinese economy grew fast while the environment deteriorated quickly. Gross Domestic Product remained the dominant measure of progress, while people's organizations cautioned that rapid industrial and urban development could lead to heavy environmental costs.

Vandana Shiva

Research Foundation for Science, Technology and Ecology (RFSTE)

For three decades, Vandana Shiva (born 1952) has been promoting nonviolent ways of engaging with nature. Her Research Foundation for Science, Technology and Ecology (RFSTE), set up in 1982, is a pioneer in biodiversity conservation and protection of people's rights from threats to their livelihoods by centralized monoculture systems. Her focus on women's relationship to their natural resources, and her work on sustainability, people's rights, and the ethical implications of genetic engineering has fundamentally changed the practice and paradigms of agriculture and food production in India.

Vandana Shiva wears many hats — physicist, philosopher, ecofeminist, environmental activist, and writer. For over three decades, she has been promoting nonviolent modes of thought and ways of engaging with nature.

Vandana was born in Dehradun, the youngest child of parents involved with nature and conservation. Aspiring to be a scientist, she obtained her doctorate on quantum theory. But her primary area of work has centered on women's defense of nature, and on claiming their right to natural resources. In the 1970s, Vandana participated in the Chipko movement — a tree-hugging opposition to commercial logging, mostly by village women. It also sowed the seeds for her continuing work on the connection between environmental concerns and the rights of indigenous people to their resources.

In 1982, Vandana founded RFSTE in Dehradun, which works on biodiversity conservation and protecting people's rights from threats to their livelihoods and environment by centralized systems of monoculture in forestry, agriculture, and fisheries. In 1987, she set up Navadanya, which works to save native seeds, promote chemical-free agriculture, create awareness on the hazards of genetic engineering, and fight biopiracy. She is also a pioneer of the ecofeminist movement in India, stressing the interconnection between nature and women's oppression. Furthermore, Vandana has contributed in fundamental ways to changing the practice and paradigms of agriculture and food. Her books "The Violence of Green Revolution" and "Monocultures of the Mind" have become basic challenges to nonsustainable, reductionist green revolution agriculture. For more than 15 years, she has campaigned on the ethical and ecological impacts of the genetic engineering that propels the second green revolution.

Centralized systems of monoculture in forestry, agriculture, and fisheries pose a direct threat to people's right to their livelihoods and environment. Chemical agriculture, genetic engineering, and biopiracy all further the interests of the powerful, further marginalizing the disempowered.

India

Suliana Siwatibau

Fiji Council of Social Services (FCOSS)
Habitat for Humanity
Transparency International

Fiji biologist Suliana Siwatibau (63) works for peace and ecological justice. Her training in genetics helped in the struggle against nuclear colonialism in the Pacific. She co-founded the Against Testing on Moruroa (ATOM) Committee and co-wrote a church-sponsored primer on the dangers of radiation. She advocated for political equality and petitioned for a return to democracy after the military coup in May 1987. After 15 years of promoting alternative energy, resource management, and participatory community development regionally, she is developing a model of organic farming in Fiji.

"My involvement in public life began in the 1960s, before Fiji's independence in 1970. I was teaching at Adi Cakobau School (ACS) and was involved with the Young Women's Christian Association's Public Affairs Committee. My first foray into the public arena happened when a British Labor Government representative visited Fiji to find out what people's feelings and opinions were about independence. She asked for a meeting of women and we went along, a group of young Fijian women. We sat right at the back. A lot of older women, and women chiefs, were there. We listened to the British woman talk about countries which were independent and as soon as she had finished speaking, I jumped up to speak and others in our group followed. I said it was about time we were independent. I also talked about the different races in Fiji and said we should all be equal: we should have common roll for voting. Then another Fijian woman stood up and said we should abolish the Council of Chiefs. The next day, we featured in the papers and of course, there was a big furore. The Fijian chiefs were very upset. One of them rang the ACS Principal to complain, and the newspaper rang me up and asked if I had said that we should abolish the Council of Chiefs. I replied that a friend of mine had said that, but that I agreed with her. Of course that became another news story. One day, as I walked past the market, a whole group of Fijian men hurled abuses and threw some rotten tomatoes at me. I thought, "That's alright, there will be opposition." I expected it. It did not unnerve me. How do I explain the views I expressed? I had just come back from Auckland University where I had been active in the Student Christian Movement (SCM). The SCM was a very good training ground for analysis on issues of justice."

The contexts of Suliana Siwatibau's work have been nuclear colonialism in the Pacific, the overthrow of an elected government in Fiji through military coups in 1987 that forced voluntary exile on her and her family, and the search for development alternatives in the Pacific.

Fiji

Min Sun

Camellia — Humanistic Geography

Sun Min's concern has been to draw attention to those whose voices are silenced, particularly ethnic minority communities. She also works on tradition and ecological destruction, media and freedom of speech. As editor of Camellia — Humanistic Geography, she is able to raise these issues effectively.

Sun Min comes from a family of teachers. After graduating from university she worked on the socio-history, customs and oral histories of ethnic minorities in the Yunnan Province of China. As editor of Camellia — Humanistic Geography, Sun Min lent her voice to discussing the adverse effects of development, such as pollution, deforestation and loss of tradition, at a time when the mainstream discourse in China was about the market values. With her passion and keen sense of humanity, she was involved in the campaign for environmental protection. Her writing has mainly focused on the different modes of development, and the importance of not sacrificing one's cultural esteem for the sake of economic development.

In 1997 Sun Min conducted an investigation into the pollution problem of the Lake Dian basin and wrote a feature article "From a Lake of Life to a Lake of Death," which probed the rise of an urban city at the expense of a plateau lake. After the serious floods of October 1998, she interviewed the Bureau of Forestry at the middle and upper reaches of Yangtze River to look into the history of deforestation and its effects on local ecology. She then wrote a feature article entitled: "The Forbidden Forest." In 2004 she took part in the "Green Basin" project, which investigated the social impact of migration caused by big dams. In a series of investigations into the Lancang River, she noted that apart from poverty, the problems faced by migrants could not be solved by simply re-locating them. A lack of attention to detail can result in social turmoil.

In the second half of the 1990s economic development was given overwhelming importance in China, and its adverse effects such as pollution, deforestation and loss of tradition were ignored. The expansion of cities resulted in the spoiling of land and the pollution of rivers.

China

Guirong Tian

Xinxiang City Environmental Protection Volunteers Association

Tian Guirong set up a village-based environmental protection NGO. As a world-famous environmental protection volunteer, she has been awarded several times.

Tian Guirong (53) is an ordinary village woman from the northern part of China's Henan Province. She set up Xinxiang City Environmental Protection Volunteers Association — the first NGO of this kind in her native Henan Province and in the country as a whole. She also established the first environmental website in China, the http://www.greentian.org.

As a world-famous environmental protection volunteer, she was awarded the Ford Conservation and Environmental Grants. In addition, she has been honored as China's "Non-governmental Ambassador for Environmental Protection" by the United Nations Environment Program.

In 1998 Tian began an unusual self-financed project to collect used batteries. Traveling to Beijing after she had problems with her battery business she read an article, "Big Pollution by Small Batteries", and realized the serious negative impact of used batteries on nature. This led her to take up the project despite strong familial opposition. "Until my last breath, my struggle in environmental protection will never stop!" is her motto.

Guirong had spent some 90,000 yuan to collect 65 tons of used batteries, thus saving seven million square meters of land from pollution.

When Tian Guirong's collection of used batteries reached 65 tons, there were some misgivings about the efficacy of the exercise. Many people did not appreciate her efforts and even laughed at her. But the need for environmental protection is a very real one in China and she is committed to it.

China

Pinsong Wang

Born in 1924, Wang Pinsong is from Jinjiang Town, Shangri-la County, Yunnan Province. She contributes everything she has to help indigenous people and to unite people of different ethnic groups, including Naxi, Hmong, Lisu, Tibetan, Pumi, Bai, and Han, so that they can fight for their rights.

In 2004 the rights of indigenous people along the Jinsha River, including the right to live in that area, the right to preserve their living environment, and the right to development, were directly threatened by the expansion of corporations and modern development projects, particularly a hydropower project that was to be set up in the area. Wang Pinsong helped the indigenous people to fight for their rights. Her age did not allow her to be in the frontline but it did not deter her from participating actively in the struggle.

Wang Pinsong was raised under the "new-style" education in the late 1930s in China. She has never engaged in so-called "heroic" endeavors, nor is she known for her eloquence in articulating her aspirations. But she is a brave woman who is not afraid of power or authority; and no difficulties have ever stopped her from doing what she believes is right. She insists that "to gain a good life for every ethnic group" is a task of righteousness and will eventually be achieved. She forgives people who persecuted her and her husband, and actively builds solidarity with others. She is sensitive to generational differences and believes in working with the young. She is also a good mother and grandmother, despite facing many difficulties. For 70 years she has been engaged in agricultural labor in the community and she still works hard every day.

This is what makes her such an inspiring role model for people around her and ensures that she is much loved by the community.

Large corporations have planned to build dams everywhere around the Leaping Tiger Gorge area. This will result in displacing many communities and will damage the ecological environment. The people of Jinsha have mobilized to oppose this and to lobby the government for their rights.

China

Yongchen Wang

Green Earth Volunteers (GEV)

Wang Yongchen is a journalist at China's Central People's Radio Station and convener of Green Earth Volunteers (GEV). She realizes the strength of the media in environmental protection, using her professional expertise to promote environmental protection. A pioneer of radio programs on environmental concerns, such as "Classroom on Wednesday" and "Journalist Salon", she opens platforms for public education and debate, and aims to change and raise public awareness on the environment, the relationship between humans and nature, and social responsibility in the protection of nature.

Over the past 16 years, Wang Yongchen has actively participated in China's environmental protection movement as a journalist. It all began after she worked on stories covering the hunting of wild yaks in the Qinghai-Tibetan highland, and bird-loving primary school children in Jiangsu Province. She was deeply shocked at the way in which people were bringing about the destruction of nature, while impressed by the children's love and passion for it. This has served as the driving force for her dedication.

Wang understands the strength of the media in environmental protection and has been able to make full use of her expertise to promote environmental-protection education. She has produced many popular radio programs. Her program on nature and humans has been honored twice with the Asia-Pacific Broadcasting Union's "Grand Award." Together with Jin Jiaman, Wang founded GEV in 1996. The NGO focuses on environmental-protection education, with activities that include tree planting and bird watching. Wang has also initiated several public education and discussion platforms. The "Journalists' Salon" has become a place where experts, journalists, and environmental protection activists meet and discuss environmental subjects such as, among others, the Dujiangyan irrigation scheme in Sichuan Province, dam building in Lu Jiang, the hydropower project in Leaping Tiger Gorge in Lijiang, Yunnan Province, and the renovation of Yuan Ming Yuan in Beijing. Wang Yongchen is also a photographer and uses her skill to contribute to campaigns by holding exhibitions and discussions.

Over the past two decades, local government officials in China have focused on economic development while ignoring its adverse impact on the natural environment. Local governments turn a blind eye to both the importance of preserving the natural environment, and the potential risks to humans that these large-scale projects pose.

China

Wai King Wong

The founding member of Tai O Cultural Workshop

A Hong Kong native, Wong Wai King is a housewife living in Tai O, a small fishing village on western Lantau Island, the largest outlying island of Hong Kong. She began her community services for the elderly and people with different abilities in her home village in the early 1980s. From 1990 onward, she has actively engaged in safeguarding the ecological environment of Tai O, challenging government-corporation collusion and patriarchal ideologies. In 2001, she founded the Tai O Cultural Workshop, which keeps historical archives and objects from the small fishing village.

Very much alone in her decade-long struggle against government-corporation collusion and patriarchal ideologies, Wong Wai King has been daring in both words and actions in protecting the natural environment of her home village Tai O, a small fishing village on western Lantau Island, the largest outlaying island of Hong Kong. A long distance from the territory's efficient and modern transportation network, Tai O has been able to maintain its rich cultural heritage and natural environmental resources until the 90s before the government set eyes on Lantau Island's natural resources. Nonetheless, conservative patriarchal tradition has also taken sanctuary and stays strong and intact. Because of its remoteness, marginalized groups, including the elderly and people with other abilities, not only suffer from inadequate and inappropriate community care services, but also discrimination.

A housewife with only a few years of formal school education, Wai King began her social engagement in the 80s working with social workers in the community to provide care services to the elderly and people with different abilities. In the 90s, Wai King mobilized Tai O villagers and other Hong Kong people to voice their concerns on possible negative impact to the local culture and ecological environment when the government and corporations expressed interest in developing Tai O and Lantau Island as tourist attractions. In the face of resource constraints and opposition as well as hostility from men, Wai King upholds her beliefs and stays the course, not letting the government, property companies and fellow villagers destroy her beloved home village. In 2001, Wai King established the Tai O Cultural Workshop, which exhibits objects collected in the community that have historical and cultural value.

Hong Kong has urbanized rapidly in the past two decades. Land acquisition is an investment of high return. After 1997, reports of government-corporation collusion are common. Large-scale development eats into the biggest ecological area of Hong Kong, Lantau Island. And Tai O is the first to suffer.

China, Hong Kong SAR

Fengxiang Xu

Beijing Ling Mountain Ecology Research Institute
Beijing Ling Mountain Tibet Museum

Xu Fengxiang is a scholar in forest and highland ecology. For the past half century, she has been teaching, researching and taking on conservation work on forests, ecology and environmental protection. She has opened up the research realm in highland ecology and set up the Tibetan and Beijing ecology research institutes. She is now 74 years old, but continues to do field investigation and exploration in highland conservation.

Xu Fengxiang was born in south China. She is always "hiking along bumpy paths through forests and highlands." She is not only a nature lover, but has a tough and persistent character.

Exploring forests, especially in the highlands, has not been easy. She has worked extremely hard to discover precious biological resources, going three times to Motuo and Daguaiwan forests on the Yaluzhangbu River. During those expeditions she had to negotiate glaciers and mudslides. She took risks crossing single-plank bridges, and fell off her horse. In the forests she was attacked by blood-sucking insects, mites, and leeches, and once had more than 400 of them on her body. When she went into Motuo for the first time she was very sick, suffering from malaria and high fever and her bones were "nearly buried in the green mountains." After recovering and leaving the valley she said, full of spirit, "I survived and left Motuo: Even if I have only one breath left, I will not fall behind."

When she was over sixty she should have retired, but she has never stopped exploring the highlands, and is especially concerned with the conservation of vulnerable ecology. At 70 she climbed up to the Everest base camp for the second time to observe the ice and snow systems and their thawing. Through her persistence, many conservation areas have been set up. She is even called "the Goddess of the Forest" by the Tibetans.

In order to promote an alliance between Tibetans and the Han majority, and to let more people know about the beauty of the landscapes as well as Tibetans' honesty and kind-heartedness, the "Beijing Ling Mountain Tibet Museum" was set up, which not only provides information on the ecology of the plateau, but is also devoted to popularizing ecological science education for youngsters.

Ecological protection and improvement are limited to restricted areas in key cities, but ecological deterioration and destruction involve large-scale landscapes. Attention needs to be paid to all aspects of this serious problem.

China

"Success in controlling the desert needs the participation of people: only when there are more people taking part in this cause can there be less desert; and only the oasis can get the sand out."

Hailan Yang

Association of Women's Development and Promotion in Yinchuan

In 1997, unemployment pushed Yang Hailan into an unusual project: she established an ecological plantation in the desert to control the sand in Yongning County, Ningxia Province. In seven years she completed work on 520 mu (85.6 acres) of land. Now there are trees and forests on the once barren land, and it also grows edible crops, allowing for both an improvement in the ecological environment and local farming and husbandry.

The desert belt in Yongning County is located at the edge of the Tenger desert, where the ecological environment was very bad. For many years, both the central and local governments have invested a fair amount of money and labor to improve the situation. In 1997, the economic downturn in her company led to Yang Hailan being unemployed. She told her husband her idea of taking up projects to control the sand. However, her husband did not think this was a good idea. He was not sure whether she could make the project work for even the government had been unable to do so. The funds that would be required for such a project posed another problem.

Despite the disagreement of her husband, Yang invested all her savings and loans from her relatives in controlling the sand. Once her plantation in the desert began to develop steadily, she thought, "Why not call together all the women working in the countryside and organize them into a network for self-development?" That was when her ecological plantation in the desert came into being, and it has become a combination of making profit and protecting the environment. In 2002, together with some college professors, she carried out an experiment on breeding sheep "out of season", and successfully realized the dream of getting the beach sheep pregnant twice in a year. This success greatly stimulated the development of local husbandry. "More people means greater power. In the process of controlling the sand, we have benefit a lot, materially and spiritually. We gain much pleasure from the work. Only when there is more oasis can there be less desert, and can we lead a richer and more meaningful life." This is Yang Hailan's dream.

Yongning County is located at the edge of the Tenger desert, where the ecological environment is very bad. Both the central and local governments have been attempting to improve the situation for many years. Now there are large areas of artificial oasis, but also large unfinished projects.

China

Alla Yaroshinskaya

Soyuz Zhurnalistov Rossii (SZR)
Regionalny grazhdansky front (RGF)

Alla Yaroshinskaya was born in 1953. Holder of a PhD in Nuclear Security, her journalistic experience along with her work — in the parliament as a member of the Committee on Glasnost and Ecology (1989), in the Ministry of Mass Media, in the Presidential Council and the Committee on Women's Problems (1993–2000), and in cooperation with the UN on non-proliferation and women's rights issues — have been reflected in two dozen books of which she is author or co-author. Alla created the first private Ecological Fund in Russia. She is recipient of many international awards for her activism.

Alla Yaroshinskaya cannot lie. She cannot keep silent about the truth. Any attempt to intimidate her yields the opposite result: she becomes fearless. Communist authorities and the KGB listed Alla Yaroshinskaya as an 'unreliable' person when she was still a student. They threatened and intimidated her because of her human rights activities. The KGB kidnapped her and tried to break down her resistance, but in vain. She became co-founder of one of the first political clubs in the USSR, Za perestroiku (For Perestroika), and the NGO Regionalny grazhdansky front (The Regional Civil Front). She was persecuted both in the press and daily life; the authorities even tried to persuade her husband to divorce her. Even her son was discriminated against at school.

After the Chernobyl disaster in 1986, Alla went together with her husband to the contaminated areas. They discovered that the local people had been evacuated to areas that were no less dangerous and had to consume contaminated food and water in order to survive. She had to collect all the data for her research in secrecy since such activities were banned by the administration of the newspaper where she worked. For a long time she could not publish in any newspaper the terrible facts that she had collected. Therefore, she distributed them illegally to help the victims of Chernobyl. Alla was the first person to break the information blockade about Chernobyl in the Soviet parliament during the session broadcast on TV. Before the eyes of millions of citizens, she passed to Mikhail Gorbachev a videocassette on the terrible situation in which ordinary people lived and died in contaminated areas. Despite all the pressure and at the risk of her life, Alla made public top secret protocols of the Politburo on Chernobyl.

Alla Yaroshinskaya was persecuted by the Soviet authorities for her efforts to reveal the truth about Chernobyl. Living in Ukraine, she protested against the country's transformation into a 'communist reserve.' Under the growing pressure of the authorities, she was forced to emigrate to Russia.

Russian Federation

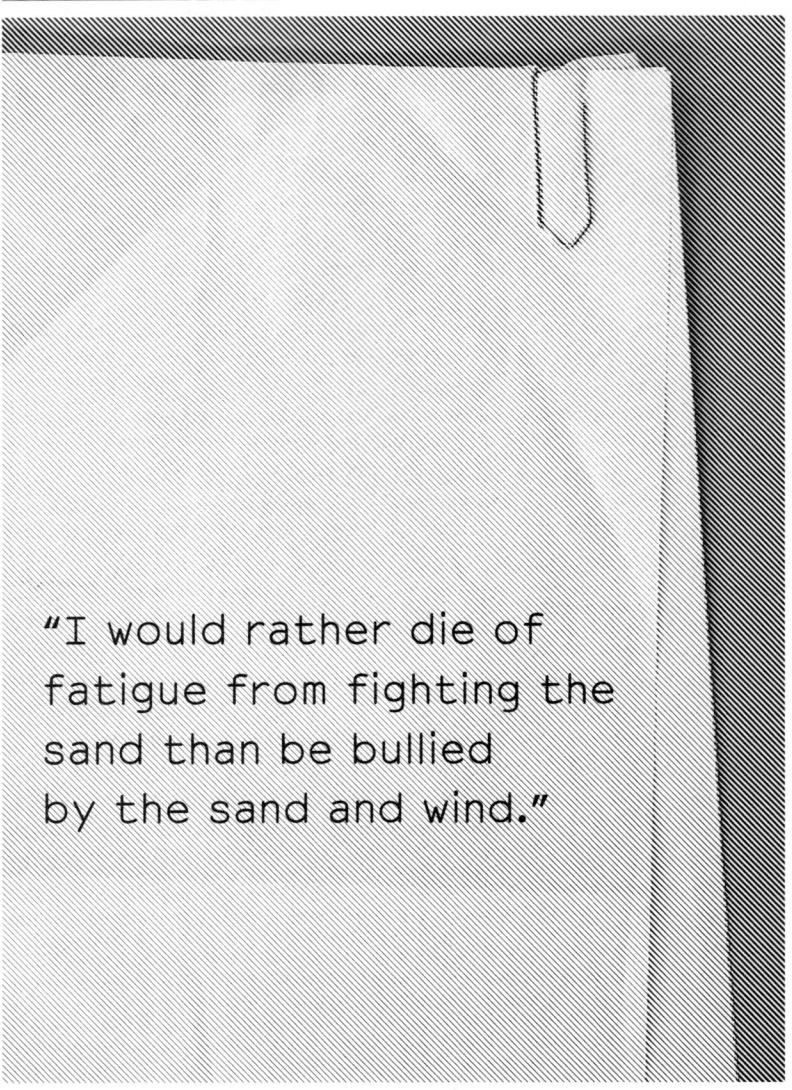

"I would rather die of fatigue from fighting the sand than be bullied by the sand and wind."

Yuzhen Yin

Yin Yuzhen has worked with an indomitable spirit for years, turning desert area into an oasis with more than 300,000 trees over nearly 10,000 acres. Seeking expert advice, with various other resources and by holding family symposiums, she created a scientific method for effective sand area restoration.

In 1985, Yin Yuzhen, a 20-year-old woman from Shannxi province, married and moved into the interior of Mu Us Desert in Inner Mongolia to an area named Jingbei Tang in Wushenqi. The adverse natural conditions were unimaginable and the sand was ubiquitous. All that they saw, touched, stepped on, at home or outside, was sand. The wind blew the grains into the nostrils, ears and mouth; when the storm stopped, the deadly silence was haunting; only Yin and her husband lived in that area.

The second day of her arrival, she made up her mind to fight the aridity to death and not be oppressed by the abominable conditions. In the second spring of her marriage, Yin began to dig irrigation ditches for water. But the storm blew away the ditches. In the winter she bundled the sunflower stems to prevent the wind from destroying them. The following spring she dug ditches, planting 5,000 willow trees. However, the grains again destroyed her efforts.

Learning from her failures she discovered scientific methods of planting trees and enabling them to survive. For over ten years, Yin Yuzhen has fought the tough weather conditions of the desert and has overcome the storms, the shifting sand and other difficulties such as the hard working conditions, inconvenient transportation and inadequate funds. She performed the miracle of preventing and controlling sand over a total area of 10,000 acres and discovered an advanced scientific method of sand prevention, which is effective for the local conditions.

Never discouraged by failure, she has not only improved her living conditions and changed her fate but also motivated many peasants and herdsmen to join her in afforesting the desert. She has made an immense contribution to the project of sand control and prevention in China.

The natural conditions in Mu Us desert are unimaginably adverse. The sand is ubiquitous; sand is what you see, touch, and step on — in or outside. The wind brings it into your nostrils, ears and mouth; when the storm stops there is a deadly silence because only Yin and her husband live in this desert.

China

Jianli Yun

Green Han River

Yun Jianli initiated the formation of Green Han River, an environmental protection organization, in 2002. She has put tremendous efforts into raising public awareness and concern in Hunan's Xiangfan City. As a result, the water quality of the Han River, which is the source of China's "South-North Water Transfer" (SNWT) project, has been improved.

Yun Jianli, once a high school teacher, retired in 1988 at the age of 55. At this turning point in her life, she decided to become a volunteer in environmental protection, which was a great surprise to her family and colleagues. In 2002 she initiated the formation of Green Han River, with virtually no resources whatsoever, and devoted herself wholeheartedly to environmental protection. "People who know me understand that it is because I care, while those who do not know me wonder what I am after," Jianli says.

When she first began her engagement with the green movement, people's awareness of environmental issues was minimal. Many people failed to understand her; others thought she was insane. Governmental officials thought she was too nosy, while factory owners were hostile.

Jianli visited villages, factories, and mountainous areas along the Han River to investigate the sources of pollution. She wrote over 100 reports and submitted more than ten motions to the government. As a result of the public education work of Jianli's green group, people's awareness of environment protection issues was much enhanced, efforts by environmental protection authorities were improved, and many small paper factories were closed down.

Jianli introduced environmental protection education to campuses, communities and villages, reaching over 60,000 people. The group has employed different approaches for different target communities, making their work more effective. The volunteer team in Xiangfan became larger and larger, with members' ages ranging from kindergarten age to over 80. People named her "Sister Yun of Environmental Protection," and children called her "Environmental Protection Granny."

Most people in Xiangfan City were unaware of the pollution in the Han River and of environmental issues. Xiangfan's economy was not sound either. When the Green Han River environmental protection group was first established, the situation was bleak and they faced many difficulties.

China

Luping Zhang

Beijing Human and Animal Environmental Protection
and Science Popularization Center

Zhang Luping started animal protection work in 1990. In 1997 she set up a science popularization center in Beijing and began to lobby for animal treatment and protection, as well as environmental protection for animals. In the course of her work, she has had to face considerable opposition, but has remained steadfast, despite continuing illness, and even at the cost of her property.

Zhang Luping was born in 1955 and joined the army in 1971. She also worked as a civil servant and editor of a press, in the real estate and food business, accumulating assets amounting to millions of yuan. In 1991, she had to have surgery for breast cancer, and it was then that she began her career with little animals. The animals gave her much love and happiness and she began to realize that there were large numbers of deserted animals in the major cities in China. She found it painful that people were so indifferent to this issue. She began to keep animals herself.

In the past ten years, she has given up chances of going abroad, of expanding her prosperous business, and a comfortable city life, all to pursue her passion. Even though the city regulations were not conducive to her work, she persisted and has brought hundreds of animals to live in positive surroundings. In 1997, Zhang set up the Beijing Human and Animal Environmental Protection and Science Popularization Center. This is the only non-profit making animal protection organization in China, which combines animal protection advocacy and animal rescue and treatment work.

Zhang's dedication eventually resulted in her work being taken seriously, both by society and the government. The Center has so far helped about 1,000 abused or abandoned small animals, and has a staff of over 20 persons. During the Sars period, the Center accepted over 150 abandoned animals. Zhang believes that it is necessary to mobilize the public to participate in animal rescue work. For her problems of animal abuse and abandonment are closely related to the problems of modern development with its increasing anthropocentrism and selfishness. She has taken the lead in mobilizing large numbers of volunteers to combine animal rescue and treatment work with advocacy work.

In contemporary urban China, as more people get affluent and take to having cats and dogs as pets, there is also a greater problem of animal abuse and abandonment. Especially during the Sars panic in 2003, large numbers of pets were abandoned. Today there is more animal protection awareness.

China

A Cultural
Conception of
Peace

Aminata Sow Fall

As I see it, the path of artistic creativity leads to peace. Indeed, peace springs from accepting others as physical, moral and spiritual entities, with their cultural specificities and their inalienable right to live in dignity and freedom.

Before writing a book, I know intuitively that it will imply encounters. Encounters with readers I know — the potential readership with whom I share a joint cultural heritage — and the many readers who extend to all imaginable geographic, linguistic, cultural, ethnic, religious or other horizons.

As a matter fact, I have for a long time been convinced that a work of art — especially a literary work — easily transcends borders, even when oppression and lawlessness set up shameful and useless barriers. I began traveling the world via books at a very young age, having first drunk deeply and well at the source of our oral literature and other traditional forms of cultural expression.

When reading foreign texts I was aware, of course, that I was exploring new domains with cultures, beliefs and civilizations that were very different from the ones I was familiar with. But I was also aware — although at the time I was unable to say why this was so — that something in the figures that peopled these texts "spoke to me" and invested my universe and myself.

I later discovered that this something is the crossroads generated and inhabited by the creative act. It is the very place in which our humanity resides; the place in which, over and above our differences, the borders that sometimes separate us, and the different situations in which we live, we share our condition. The human condition with what it contains — questions, doubts, metaphysical queries, sufferings and anguish — but also the quest for happiness and dreams of greatness and eternity. As a writer, I think that all humanity can get together in this place to dream of a world created in the image of our greatness, in peace and harmony.

Aminata Sow Fall, a Senegalese writer and educator, is the director of the Centre Africain d'Animation et d'Echanges Culturels and of the Khoudia publishing house in Dakar.

Almira Adiatullina

Soyuz zhenshchin-musulmanok Tatarstana (SZMT)
Zhenshchiny za dukhovnoye vozrozhdieniye (Women for Spiritual Revival)

Almira Adiatullina was born in 1938. In 1959 she enrolled at Kazan State University to study journalism. On graduating from the university, she worked as a journalist until her retirement in 1993. In 1995, Almira founded the NGO Zhenshchiny za dukhovnoye vozrozhdieniye (Women for Spiritual Revival), whose aim is to protect the freedom of religion in Russia and to defend the rights of Muslims. She is the leader of the Muslim women's movement in Tatarstan. Since 1997, she has been editor-in-chief of the Muslim women's newspaper 'Muslima.'

For the past half century, Almira Adiatullina has been living and working in Tatarstan. After having completed the Hadj in 1993, Almira devoted herself wholeheartedly to the revival of Islam in Tatarstan. In 1995, she founded the first Muslim women's organization Zhenshchiny za dukhovnoye vozrozhdieniye (Women for Spiritual Revival) with the aim of educating the younger generation in the spirit of religious values. Over the years, this organization has accomplished quite a lot. First and foremost are the annual contests for children in reciting the Koran, bringing together Muslim believers from all over Tatarstan and nearby regions. At this annual festival, children get the opportunity to show their mastery in reciting the Koran, while receiving additional knowledge on the moral foundations of their religion.

Almira has always been tireless in her social work. In 2002 and 2003, she and some other members of her organization actively fought to protect freedom of religion in Russia. Under Almira's leadership, a broad-scale PR campaign was successfully conducted on the protection of the rights of practicing Muslims in Russia. As a result of continuous court battles stemming from the lawsuits filed by Almira's organization against the Russian authorities, the prohibition of the Russian Ministry of the Interior Affairs on picturing Muslim women in their passports wearing a headscarf was abolished. This victory became the first successful attempt to enforce and defend religious rights of believers in post-Soviet Russia. Almira's cause was supported by world human rights organizations and the international media.

During the years of Soviet rule, strong atheism prevailed. Yet many people did not lose their faith in the Creator. Although today Muslims in Russia enjoy relative freedom in practicing their religion, Almira keeps on fighting against the still existing discrimination.

Russian Federation

Adiba Akhmedjanova

Sodruzhestvo
Association of Women Farmers

Adiba Akhmedjanova (born 1955) initiated the Women's Club of International Friendship called Sodruzhestvo (Cooperation) to bring women from different national origins together and promote mutual understanding. Uzbek women from villages can meet people from other countries and become familiar with the culture of different nations. She also founded an association for leadership development for girls and the Association of Women Farmers in the Tashkent Province. She provides women with assistance in the fields of human rights, legal advice and help in setting up small business enterprises.

Adiba Akhmedjanova dreamed of creating a place where women from different nations and cultures could meet and interact with the lives of Uzbek women in villages — a World Women's Club. She shared this dream with an employee who showed her an old neglected building which could be used for the club. The head of the Tashkent Region Administration supported the idea. But Adiba had no financial support. She and her team worked without any salary and even used their own money to create the club. They contacted the embassies of many countries in Uzbekistan and invited officials to its future location offering the space for exhibitions. Adiba said, "For rural women it would be a window to the world." At present, 16 countries are exhibited in the space. Rural women can experience different cultures and find new friends. Since the opening of the club, it has become a center of international meetings. Local women meet with foreign diplomats, artists, and writers and learn about different cultures, religions, and traditions. The club offers educational and cultural activities, and about 30 embassies and international organizations participate. "By getting to know each other, we improve our understanding, and this leads to peace, tolerance, and friendship," Adiba says.

In addition to creating international bonds, Adiba works hard to increase literacy among women and to improve their education. She assists women's NGOs and organizes seminars for rural women in the fields of human rights and legal education. To address unemployment in her region, Adiba has created special programs for women who want to start up their own small businesses. Thanks to Adiba, hundreds of women have found employment. She has built peace through the sharing of international cultures and traditions.

Old stereotypes in Uzbekistan are hard to overcome, including those about the place of women in society. There are still many obstacles to equality. Linking Uzbek women with women's movements on the world can help break their isolation and open up new vistas for women's participation in society.

Uzbekistan

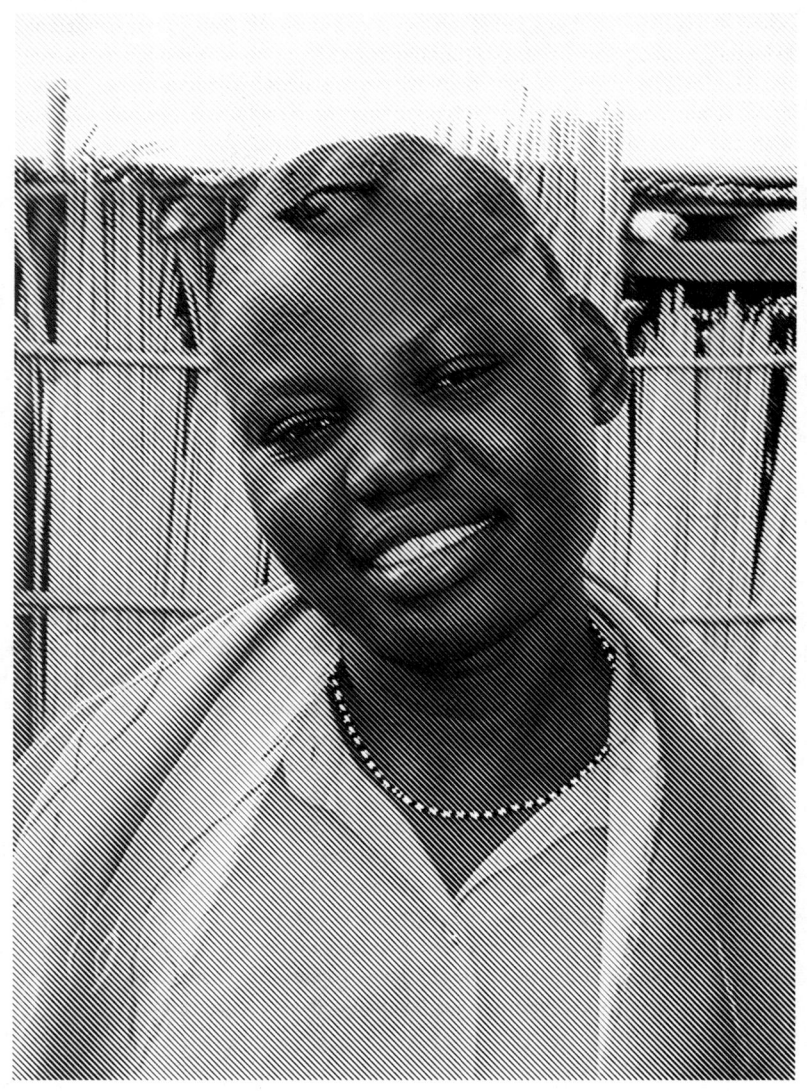

Anita Amiro

Kwoto Cultural Centre (KCC)

Anita Batris Amiro (32) is one of the pioneering Sudanese women who contributed to founding the Kwoto Cultural Center (KCC) in 1994. She is a singer, dancer and actress. Her works cover the entire Sudanese states, especially the capital Khartoum, where they are presented in international festivals and film competitions. Anita works hard to effectuate peace and love and to promote human rights in order to enhance the conditions of the displaced citizens of southern Sudan and the entire country.

Anita Batris Amiro has faced many challenges in her life. Her parents died when she was three months old. However, she surmounted her unfortunate social circumstances and successfully completed her high school education. Because she could not find financial support to pursue her university education she worked as a teacher in elementary schools from 1992 to 1993.

The Kwoto Cultural Center is dedicated to the betterment of people's lives through art works. The center promotes peace and reconciliation and fights epidemic diseases, such as HIV and Aids. Kwoto's quest for cultural pluralism represents the key initiative to the establishment of democracy in the Sudan. It strives for better understanding and tolerance of the cultural, ethnic and religious diversity in the Sudan, which has been the source of tension and violence in the country.

With the collaborative efforts of KCC members, Anita has helped to establish a cultural movement that supports Southern Sudanese people and allows them freedom of speech, which they were previously denied. The lack of democracy, tolerance, intercultural dialogue and respect for human rights in the Sudan has fueled the civil war that claimed the lives of approximately two million Sudanese and has displaced over four million people who had to leave their homes and live in large camps in very meager conditions. In this situation Anita thought that the best way of helping her people was by reaching them in their own environment. She held dancing and singing festivals in order to raise people's awareness of significant issues, such as peace promotion and fighting HIV/Aids. Anita encountered many difficulties in the course of her work, the greatest of which were her journeys to isolated areas, risking her life, due to the severely critical attitude of her shows towards the government's violation of human rights.

Cultural pluralism represents the key to the establishment of democracy in the Sudan. Through Anita's regular art performances, the displaced people in the outskirts of Khartoum are getting connected to their cultural roots and are learning to live together in harmony.

Sudan

Teresita Ang-See

Kaisa Para Sa Kaunlaran
Citizens' Action Against Crime (CAAC)
Movement for Restoration of Peace and Order (MRPO)

Chinese-Filipino Teresita "Tessy" Ang-See (born 1949), an academician, writer, and social activist, has helped free kidnap victims and sent their kidnappers to jail. She helped depose two corrupt presidents, assisted in leading children of war in Mindanao to the path of peace, and built a world-class museum showing the Chinese in Philippine life. In 1987, she co-founded Kaisa Para Sa Kaunlaran, to help Chinese-Filipinos integrate into mainstream Philippine society. Tessy works for peace and security, justice and development by harnessing the Chinese-Filipino community for nation building.

In a country divided by geography, economic disparity and ethnic prejudice, Chinese-Filipino historian and teacher Teresita Ang-See sees the need to build bridges of understanding between Filipinos and Tsinoys (Chinese Filipinos). Historically, in times of political turmoil, Chinese-Filipinos have chosen to be silent bystanders, resisting integration, and ready to pack up and leave in the face of unrest. This bothered Tessy, who has taught Chinese studies at leading universities and has written and coauthored more than 16 books on the Chinese in the Philippines.

In 1987, with young professionals and businessmen, she founded Kaisa Para Sa Kaunlaran, a movement working for the full integration of the Chinese-Filipino community. It publishes "Tulay" (Bridge), a fortnightly magazine on the Chinese in the Philippines, and maintains the Chin Ben See Memorial Library and the Kaisa Data Bank and Research Center. It also established the museum Bahay Tsinoy, the first repository of the historical and cultural legacy of the Chinese in all aspects of Philippine life.

Tessy is also a high-profile anti-crime advocate, who has pressured the government to act against criminality, especially the frequent kidnapping-for-ransom of ethnic Chinese. The killing in a shoot-out of a 15-year-old kidnap victim, whose bloodied body was dumped on the street side by side with her kidnappers for the media to feed on, made Tessy realize that more bridges were needed. With her own life and family at risk, she mobilized Kaisa to be the prime mover behind two anti-crime watchdogs that has saved kidnap victims and sent kidnappers to jail. "Peace," Tessy asserts, "is a condition where people can work effectively together, understand one another, regardless of race, creed, beliefs and tradition." In 1992, Tessy was chosen as one of The Outstanding Women in the Nation's Service.

For a long time, the Chinese in the Philippines were mired in a migrant mentality, refusing to be integrated and preferring to be bystanders in Philippine life. The distrust was mutual. Teresita Ang-See sees the need to build bridges of understanding between Filipinos and Tsinoys (Chinese Filipinos).

Zainah Anwar

Sisters in Islam (SIS)

With a group of women, Zainah Anwar wanted to find out if it was true that Islam discriminates against women. Turning to the Koran, they found that it advocates justice, equality, dignity and freedom. So they set up Sisters in Islam (SIS) which promotes women's rights within Islam. With the Legal Aid Center of the Malaysian Bar Council, the group opened a legal clinic which serves some 700 clients a year. It runs a legal advice column in a Malay daily to help women know their rights, and conducts monthly study sessions, public education programs and training on women's rights in Islam.

"We grew up with the idea that God is just, that Islam is a just religion," says Zainah Anwar, founding member and executive director of the NGO Sisters in Islam (SIS), based in Malaysia where Muslims make up the majority of the population. "Suddenly, as adults we were confronted with the realities of lived Islam, which was discriminatory against women, which was oppressive of women. It was hard for us, as believers and thinking individuals, to think that God would ever want to discriminate against one-half of the human race." That spurred Zainah Anwar and her friends to turn to the Koran to find out whether the scriptures were actually unjust towards women. There they discovered verses that talked about mercy and compassion and justice, and of men and women being each other's protecting friend and guardian.

For the women, discovering the Koran's insistence on enjoining what is just and on promoting the principles of justice, equality and dignity was a refreshing and liberating experience. "That was a turning point for us; it opened our eyes to the fact that this discrimination in the name of Islam was due to interpretation of the text rather than the text itself," she says, adding that it gave them the courage to share these views with the public. From that awakening, it was only a matter of time before SIS was formally registered in 1990. "We knew that we needed to claim the right and create the public space for a public discussion on Islamic issues," she says. "And also to educate Muslims and the public that when Islam is used as a sort of law and public policy to govern the private and public lives of citizens, then every citizen has the right to engage with Islam to define and talk about how it impacts on us as citizens of this country."

A battle is raging in Malaysia for the heart and soul of Islam, pitting conservative forces against those seeking a more enlightened interpretation of Islam.

Malaysia

Sarygul Bahadirova

National Committee of Women
Scientific Women
Writers' Union of Uzbekistan

Sarygul Bahadirova (born 1944) has devoted her life to the regeneration of the culture of Karakalpak people. Her main focus is the research and promotion on a global scale of the folk legacy of the Karakalpak people, who are currently confronted by an ecological disaster due to the drying up of the Aral Sea. Sarygul's mission is to preserve and pass on the people's spiritual legacy to new generations in order to encourage peace, international understanding, humanism, and kindness, key values of the centuries-old Karakalpak culture.

Sarygul Bahadirova is one of the founders of the study on the Karakalpak culture and on one of the region's most ancient art forms, the performance of "zhrau" (local folk music). She says, "A world without violence is the culture of a new century and is absolutely essential for the construction of a new democratic society."

One of the main tasks of Sarygul's research and practical work is the enrichment of world culture. In pursuit of these goals, she organized three international conferences with the participation of cultural scholars from Germany, Japan, Turkey, Cyprus, Azerbaijan, Kazakhstan, and Uzbekistan. These conferences were an opportunity for Sarygul to discuss Karakalpak culture with her foreign colleagues. She also published a related book. Each of these conferences turned out to be a genuine people's celebration of culture. During one conference devoted to the Karakalpak folk epos "Kyryk Kyz," Sarygul organized festivals on a Nukus racecourse, featuring demonstrations of Karakalpak folk traditions including horseback riding, traditional combat, pumpkin shooting, and many others. This forum undoubtedly helped to boost the spirits of the Karakalpak people, currently somewhat beaten down by the strictness of the totalitarian regime and the ecological crisis of the Aral Sea. In the Soviet era, the local folk epos was entirely repressed. The regeneration of the folk epos of the many disparate cultures of the former USSR, including the Kazakh, Bashkir, Tartar, and Nogay peoples, is of great importance. Organizing a world scientific forum devoted to the "Edige" epos, was Sarygul's contribution to the formation of a new important world culture. "It is important for me," she says, "that people achieve a mutual understanding and perception of each other's cultures."

Karakalpakstan is a small autonomous region of Uzbekistan. Its people have an ancient and distinctive history and culture, the study of which was banned during the Soviet period. In addition, the ecological tragedy of the Aral Sea has put the people on the brink of extinction.

Uzbekistan

Roselle Bailey

Ka ʻImi Na ʻauao O Hawaiʻi Nei

Roselle Bailey's life work is to teach and preserve Hawai'ian culture. She served as caretaker of one of the most significant sites to hula practitioners and helped to launch the Ka Ipu Kukui leadership training program at Maui Community College. Roselle also founded the halau Ka 'Imi Na 'auao o Hawai'i Nei, whose goal is both to maintain traditional Hawai'ian culture and traditions and to heal ethnic and cultural divisions among Hawai'ians and between people of all cultures.

"About ten years ago, a member of our hula group and dear friend Keani died. Roselle and I were among the hundreds of people at her funeral. It was such a sad and painful thing to lose a cherished friend. I was having a hard time of it. I found myself standing next to Roselle in the large crowd, felt her physical presence, her strength and her support. She saw how I was struggling, and said to me 'Carol, we have to do this for Keani.' With that, she squeezed my hand and started chanting. Roselle's simple sentence and her powerful chanting were a reminder of the beautiful friend I had lost, and that saying goodbye to her was the way that I could honor her." (Carol Pescaia)

"There was the time when we were on the Greek ship Lydia going from Beirut to Piraeus, Greece, via Port Said and Alexandria. Many Greeks were being deported from Egypt at the time. The decks of the 'Lydia' were burdened with Greek families and their belongings. It was in a sense bittersweet and like a large family party.

When they found out that I was Hawai'ian, they asked me to do the 'hula-hula'. After several dances, they did their dances for me to show their appreciation. Soon I found myself swept up into their circle trying to look good doing their dances. Such fun! To this day, whenever we hear Greek music, the images and warmth of the people aboard the Lydia are relived." (Roselle Bailey)

"A time past, breathed into life, is hula. It is the aloha (love), the 'eha (pain), the pono (hope), and the hu'eu (humor) of a people. It is the survival of that people. It is the heartbeat of Hawai'i. It is the soul of her people."

United States of America

Shana Chang

Alumni Association of Europe & America
China Artist Association

Apart from being an educator, Chang Shana is also engaged in the research and protection of Dunhuang cave art. As a professional scholar she has achieved great popularity because of her important creative designs and published works. She is committed to teaching, art, and the preservation of Dunhuang culture.

Born in Lyon, France, in 1931, Chang Shana began to study the art of mural painting in Dunhuang in 1945. Three years later she went to the USA for further studies. She was formerly head of the Central Academy of Arts and Design, and was among the first designers in industrial art. Currently she is the vice president of the China Artist Association.

In early 1943 her father, Chang Shuhong, took his family to Dunhuang and Chang, who was only 12, has been fascinated with the charm of Dunhuang art ever since. Influenced by her parents, little Chang developed an interest in painting. Her father encouraged her to study the French language and Western and Chinese art history. She also had to go to the Dunhuang caves every day to copy the cave paintings. In winter her father would also give her guidance in painting techniques. These activities laid a good foundation for her art. At the end of the 1950s Chang took part in the design, construction and decoration of "ten key buildings," including the Great Hall of the People and the National Art Museum in Beijing. In designing the ceiling of the dining hall of the Great Hall of the People, Chang adroitly applied the coffer pattern used in the Dunhuang mural paintings of the Tang Dynasty, demonstrating a combination of traditional and modern signs. This has become a classic example of Dunhuang art being integrated with modern architecture.

In 1982 Chang Shana took up the post of the Deputy Dean of the Central Academy of Arts and Design, and in 1983 she became the Dean, retiring in 1998. As a teacher she was known to be very strict. She was also very active in social work, with the sense of responsibility of an artist.

During her 50 years of teaching she has cultivated a new force in art design.

When Chang Shana returned to China in the 1950s, the demands made for the construction — in all aspects — of a new China, presented her with many new challenges, such as the task of integrating traditional Chinese culture and art into a modern era.

China

Paulina Chiziane

Núcleo das Associações Femeninas da Zambézia (Nafeza)
Red Cross Mozambique

Paulina Chiziane, born in 1955, grew up in Maputo, where she attended school. After publishing a number of stories in the Mozambican press, she wrote "Balada de Amor ao Vento" in 1989 and in 1996 "Ventos do Apócalipse". Her novel "Niketche: Uma Historia de Poligamia" (2002) was awarded the Jose Craveirinha Prize by the Association of Mozambican Writers. Paulina Chiziane worked for the Red Cross in Mozambique and as a technical adviser to different women's empowerment projects. Her writing reflects her encounters with women and the civil war that ravaged Mozambique.

Pauline Chiziane's first writings were diaries but unlike other girls she would write her dreams in the mornings in her dreams diary. When her friends discovered the beauty of her writing they asked her to support them writing love letters. This earned her the nickname "love secretary". As she grew older, politics in Mozambique changed with the crumbling of the fascist regime in Portugal; the independence movement grew and women started to focus on their rights.

Paulina Chiziane worked as a secretary in the ministry of health and later as an assistant in the laboratory of the ministry of agriculture. It was her employment with the Red Cross that made a mark in her life. She worked directly in dangerous areas supporting people in need. She started taking notes about everything that she saw, felt and even dreamt. Her encounters are reflected in her first book "Balada de Amor ao Vento" (Ballad of Love in the Wind), which is a story about a country woman who had to face patriarchal traditions in her search for her love and her own way in the world. This is the first book by a Mozambican woman after independence and the first book written by an African woman from the Portuguese-speaking countries. The book was a success, particularly because it was an African woman talking about women's condition in Africa, and it had support from women. The book was a critique on men but it helped bridge the barrier between men and women.

The civil war in Mozambique, the African myths and traditions, the women she trains on gender and her work to promote women's access to basic services and to development in Africa give Paulina Chiziane material for new books. Her books reflect women who fight to be heard, who fight for their rights, who fight to be free.

The civil war in Mozambique that started in 1977 and ended in the early 1990s is reflected in many works of art, literature, theatre, music or paintings. Paulina Chiziane highlights the importance of women's role by emphasizing their disadvantaged status in society.

Mozambique

Paula Clermont Péan

Pyepoudre Cultural Center

Actress, theater director, writer, professor of literature and theater, Paula Clermont Péan is the director of the Pyepoudre Cultural Center. It is a center for animation, training courses and public readings, founded by Paula, in Puerto Príncipe, in 1989. She was educated in France and in the United States. After returning to her home country, Haiti, she dedicated her work towards the promotion of popular culture and to the building of a network for the association of young people, affiliated to the Worldwide Federation of the Associations, Centers and Clubs of Unesco.

Some people think that culture is a luxury, especially if it is in one of the poorest countries in the world. However, Paula Clermont Péan, a Haitian, persists each day in her continuous effort to bring culture into people's lives. "This work makes people look at themselves, question themselves and see themselves as social actors in their society. It cultivates their curiosity. These dynamics create awareness, people realize their need to share their visions of the world, a world in which it is worth building peace."

In 1985, back in her home country after 16 years of absence, she changed her idea of creating an Art School and decided to wait until people came to her with their ideas of what they wanted. In its place, in 1989, she founded the Pyepoudre Cultural Center (the Dusty Feet Cultural Center): "With this center, I wanted to go to young people instead of asking them to come to me. I wanted to go to meet the young people wherever they were, in rural or urban spaces, in the suburbs or in the city."

In Haiti, the state has no political policies for young people and culture. Most of the population cannot pay for cultural activities. In the prevailing political climate, participation in those activities sometimes involves putting one's freedom and personal security at risk.

Haiti

Isabel Crook

Beijing Foreign Languages University

Isabel Crook worked in 1940 ∕ 41 in the Chinese rural reconstruction movement promoting cooperatives. Later she and her husband were requested by the new Chinese state cadres from the Foreign Ministry to stay and teach. After teaching for over 30 years, Isabel joined the International Committee for the Promotion of Industrial Cooperatives (ICCIC), an NGO that aims to further the development of cooperative economies in the present historical period to enable them to serve China's socialist modernization.

Isabel Crook, a Canadian anthropologist, has spent most of her life in China. During the Cultural Revolution, her husband was locked up in solitary confinement in Qincheng prison, while Isabel was locked up in the university campus. But she has no resentment — they were fully exonerated and were able to come through the experience strengthened rather than embittered. "I have many rich memories, and the bitterness has drifted away. Some people are not so fortunate so it is not so easy for them to forget the bitterness, and the sad memories are a burden to them. Those people that can remember the happier things lead a much better and healthier life," says Isabel. She was let out in 1972, her husband in 1973. They resumed their teaching at Beijing Foreign Languages University. Isabel has been writing a book on her early rural research, and has also kept up her political activism. She loves a poem by Bertolt Brecht: "The house was built with the stones that were there, the picture was painted with the colors that were there, the revolution was made by the rebels that were there." "It is such a realistic poem about the revolution," she says. "The revolution was made not by angels, but by ordinary people who wanted a just society. Of course they also made mistakes. That's an unavoidable part of the learning process."

The Chinese revolution has a complex history and was an inspiration for many people. During the Cultural Revolution, anyone with contacts abroad could be regarded as a spy. In 1973 Premier Zhou formally apologized on behalf of the Chinese Communist Party to foreigners who had suffered.

China

Maria Stella de Azevedo Santos

Maria Stella de Azevedo Santos (1925) is a spiritual leader in the Ilê Axé Opô Afonjá 'terreiro' — place where the rituals and cults are carried out — of Candomblé, in the city of Salvador. For the last 30 years, Mother Stella has occupied the position of Ialorixá, which is a priestess, the maximum female authority of the Candomblé. Through her religiosity, she works in her community and irradiates her pride of the Afro-Brazilian culture all over the country.

She learned with her grandmother the secret and the force of the Orixás that are the Gods of the Candomblé. Her grandmother learned with her mother. Maria Stella's great grandmother came to Brazil when she was nine years old. African, she came as a slave and never forgot the Ioruba's (people from the Southwest of Nigeria that had a strong social and cultural influence on the Northeast of Brazil) religion. At age 14, Stella began her initiation in the Candomblé. She worked and studied simultaneously. She graduated in nursing. In 1976, with 50 years of age, she was chosen as Ialorixá of the Terreiro Ilê Axé Opô Afonjá. She became 'Mother Stella of Oxóssi' (the Orixá that represents the figure of a hunter). Mother Stella is a woman who is also tuned into the problems imposed to Afro-Brazilians. In spite of how powerful the culture is, they are systematically discriminated and deprived of their rights and opportunities.

Today, the country is learning how to live with its religious diversity. Mother Stella has contributed to this effect. "People no longer have to hide their devotion to the Orixás." She stimulated the creation of an elementary school inside of the 'terreiro.' Maintained by the city hall of Salvador, the school teaches the Iorubá language and the respect to differences. Mother Stella also coordinates projects of income generation, through the industrial arts of the universe of the Orixás. She maintains a museum where the visitor makes contact with the cosmogony of the Candomblé.

80 years old, Maria Stella de Azevedo Santos is the testimony of a life dedicated to one love: the Candomblé. She is also a testimony of lucidity, in teaching us that the freedom for the practice of afro-descendent religions is the affirmation of Afro-Brazilian culture.

The Candomblé is a religion of African origin. It has a complex structure, in which the Orixás are gods. Each Orixá has its own function, color and instrument. All individuals possess all the Orixás, but one of them is always preponderant.

Brazil

Ruth de Souza

Daughter of a laundress and of a peasant, Ruth de Souza (1928) was born in Rio and was the first Afro-Brazilian woman to become an actress. In 1945, she founded the Afro-Brazilian Experimental Theater. She was the first Afro-Brazilian in the dramatic arts to play the role of Desdemona, a William Shakespeare character. Along with her colleagues, she was prohibited from entering a reception, an episode of prejudice that, in 1951, gave rise to the first Brazilian law against racism.

In love with movies since her youth, Ruth de Souza heard, whenever she expressed her desire to become an actress, this answer: "You cannot be an actress because you are an Afro-Brazilian." With a 60-year-old career, Ruth is living proof of the victory of tenacity against prejudice. "Racism was not much different from what it is today."

Confronting it, however, seemed absolutely natural to her. "I was always much respected," she affirms, "but Afro-Brazilian women are still invisible." Making way in the dramatic arts required her to confront the beauty standards of her time, which did not include Afro-Brazilians. "I am sure that my acting career helped change the perception that Brazilian society had of Afro-Brazilians," she says. Being the first Afro-Brazilian to go up on the stage of the Municipal Theater is one of the marks of Ruth's career. Her dedication to the theater had as a result a scholarship to study dramatic arts in the United States. Pioneer in Brazilian cinema, her debut was in 1947. Ruth starred in 22 movies, once as the main role, and she was nominated for the award of best supporting actress in the Venetian Film Festival, along with Katherine Hepburn and Lili Palmer. Ruth's professional trajectory is linked to the beginning of Brazilian television, where she began working in 1952.

Dedicated to her career, Ruth did not get married and she did not have children. But she did not make of this a way to escape of feminine standards. "It simply did not happen." She lives alone and believes that solitude helps bring her peace of mind and concentration. Among the various public recognitions of her work, Ruth highlights the badge of Official of the Rio Branco Order, with which the Brazilian government recognized her enormous contribution to the theatrical arts.

After 60 years of hard work and 70 characters in the theater, in TV and movies, Ruth de Souza was main character twice. She always played the supporting actress. The first Brazilian soap opera, with Afro-Brazilians playing main roles, went on the air only in 2004.

Hilda Dias dos Santos – "Mãe Hilda Jitolu"

Hilda Dias dos Santos (1923) is known, throughout Brazil, as "Mother Hilda." Ialorixá (maximum authority in the Candomblé religion) of the terreiro (place where the rituals of Candomblé are carried out) Ilê Axé Jitolu. She carries out the synergy between religiosity and social work. Owner of a refined consciousness of Brazilian racism: "Racism is still present, but today, Caucasians respect Afro-Brazilians." Part of this respect is the result of the work that she has been developing during 50 years.

The terreiro Ilê Axé Jitolu was founded by the pastry maker Hilda Dias dos Santos, in 1952. The terreiro — place where the rituals of Candomblé, religion originated from Africa, are carried out — was born in a straw shack. Located at the hill of the Curuzu, in the district of Liberdade, which is the most Afro-Brazilian of all the districts of Salvador, Bahia, the Ilê Axé and its Ialorixá have become a national reference.

At age 82, Mother Hilda tells the story of how she embraced the religion of the Orixás, the gods of Candomblé: "As a child, I was always passing out. The doctors were not able to solve the problem. I went into the Candomblé and the crises stopped." She married, had six children. She sold a lot of food at the doors of factories and boat terminals. One day, she felt prepared to turn her house into a terreiro for the practice of Candomblé. Mother Hilda opened up a school for the children of the Curuzu. She qualified boys and girls for the religion and for life. Through religious and recreational activities, she stimulated the strengthening of the self-esteem of the Afro-Brazilian youth. It was in a room of the Ilê Axé Jitolu that, in 1974, the Ilê Aiyê, a group formed solely by Afro-Brazilians, was born exalting afro beauty.

Mother Hilda continues her work of educational extension for the construction of citizenship. Besides elementary school, there are percussion, dance and professionalizing courses. There is a team working on the Notebooks of Education that are about Afro-Brazilian cultural themes. Now, she wishes for the community of the Curuzu to become a 'cultural corridor,' a space that irradiates the Afro-Brazilian culture from Bahia. Mother Hilda says that "the next step is an existence, a life, with quality and peace."

The carnival group Ilê Aiyê was created in 1974 and it does much more than entertain. It is a group of Afro-Brazilian culture and dance. It is directed by Vovô, biological and spiritual son of Mother Hilda. It displays an unmistakable expression of anti-racism.

Brazil

Marilou Diaz-Abaya

Mothers for Peace
Activists for Peace

Marilou Diaz-Abaya (born 1955), the most awarded Filipino woman filmmaker, says that movies should not only entertain but should compel the audience to re-examine their own beliefs and value systems as they grapple with the truths magnified onscreen. Despite the limitations on free expression imposed by martial law and the commercial demands of movie-making, she has, since 1980, managed to make films that tackle controversial issues like domestic violence, migration, child labor, the justice system, marine destruction, nationalism, and lately, the Muslim conflict in Southern Philippines.

Marilou Diaz-Abaya's film opus, "Bagong Buwan" (New Moon) sheds light on a difficult subject and could help Christian Filipinos finally understand the roots of the long-running Muslim conflict in the south. By showing how war continues to displace lives that could be their own, and how war perpetuates itself on succeeding generations, Marilou says she hopes that the movie could become "an instrument of peace instead of being an end in itself." Months of research, interaction with Muslim communities and filmmaking inside a war zone converted Marilou, a Christian, into an active peace advocate. She commutes regularly between Manila, where she teaches film, and the Muslim south, where she works with Mothers for Peace, a group that champions the role of women as peacemakers.

To keep herself grounded on the issue and to contribute insights on how Christians and Muslims can work together, she has become a frequent speaker and resource person in various peace fora in Mindanao. She also organized Activists for Peace, which invites performers, visual artists and academicians to exchange messages of peace and dialogues of culture. She later became involved with the Silsilah Peace Institute that trains workers in the skills of peacemaking and in interfaith dialogue. In the past 25 years, Marilou Diaz-Abaya has made 21 movies, "two-thirds of them flops," she says. She has used her extensive experience in public affairs television to help local communities to develop their own alternative media and sources of entertainment and information. "We must work to make media a balancing factor," she says. "It is important to equalize access to information because those who control the media practically control all civilization."

Filipino movies have mainly entertained their audiences without challenging them to re-examine their own beliefs and value systems as they grapple with the truths magnified onscreen. Marilou Diaz-Abaya has resisted that trend by tackling controversial social issues in her films.

Xiuyu Dong

Chinese Cultural Forum

Dong Xiuyu helped to set up Dushu Magazine, one of the most prominent and outspoken journals for intellectuals in China. As a publisher of serious works, and with nearly two decades of experience, Dong helped to turn the Joint Publishers company back from the verge of bankruptcy to profit-making. She also managed to produce quality books and magazines. After retirement, she set up the Chinese Cultural Forum which is a venue for scholars from within and outside China to interact and exchange experiences.

Dong Xiuyu retired after two decades of work with the Joint Publishers, but she continues to be active in cultural work. She established the Chinese Cultural Forum with a focus on educational reform, cultural change and institutional innovation. Dong Xiuyu has devoted much of her working life to facilitating cooperation in publishing between mainland China, Hong Kong and Taiwan, cutting across political differences, and striving for exchanges among intellectuals from these regions. This is her contribution to working for peace in this area of tension.

From 1956 to 1979, Dong Xiuyu worked in the People's Press as proofreader, as vice-director in the press department and editor in the editing office of the Party's history. In 1979, she took part in setting up Dushu Magazine and was vice-director in the editing department. She was responsible for commissioning and interviewing, as well as for works in literature, history, philosophy and economics. Dushu Magazine continues to be published today, and Dong Xiuyu set up several new imprints and series.

In 1987, she was sent to Hong Kong where she turned Joint Publishers' heavy deficit into profit, and made the imprint a name to be reckoned with. In 1993, Dong Xiuyu went back to Beijing and helped save the Beijing Joint Publishers from bankruptcy, leading the company to an increase in profit by more than 30 times. Joint Publishers then got its own buildings, opened new bookstores and set up three new magazines. In 1998, Dong Xiuyu suffered a major setback when she developed breast cancer. However, no sooner had she had surgery that she hurried back to her desk, and continued to work while receiving radioactive treatment.

Publishing in China since the reform policy of 1978 has focused on profit, and reform of the cumbersome structure has been difficult. In a world increasingly dominated by profit, it is also difficult to remain independent, keep up good intellectual work and deal with moral and ethical issues.

China

Madeeha Gauhar

Ajoka Theatre

If alternative theater is today a vibrant form of political expression in Pakistan, a large share of the credit goes to Ajoka Theatre and its founder, Madeeha Gauhar, a theater director and human rights activist. Led by Gauhar for over 20 years, Ajoka has been, and continues to be, an integral part of the struggle for a secular, democratic, humane, just, and egalitarian Pakistan.

At a time when Zia-ul-Haq's regime had blocked all avenues for political expression in Pakistan, Madeeha Gauhar decided to start an alternative theater group, Ajoka Theatre, which was born in 1983. The group began modestly operating out of the homes of its members, using money raised from personal contributions and donations by activist supporters and audiences. Soon, it built up a reputation for taking up bold and topical themes, including the eroding rights of women, the plight of bonded labor, minorities facing an assault on their rights, and religious intolerance, which had been given official patronage. With censorship in force, Madeeha and her band lived with the fear of arrest, and worse. Madeeha had to quit as lecturer at a girl's college because her theater activism was intolerable to the regime. She was also briefly jailed for demonstrating, along with other women activists, against a proposed discriminatory Law of Evidence.

Ajoka has become one of Pakistan's foremost theater groups. The group has over 40 original plays and adaptations to its credit, uses prosceniums to street theater, and regularly holds theater training workshops for community groups and cultural activists all over Pakistan. Although political conditions have changed since Madeeha started her work, discrimination and intolerance have hardly faded into history. She is using theater to promote peace between Pakistan and India: Ajoka has participated in cultural exchanges between the two countries. In March 2004, Ajoka Theatre organized the first-ever India-Pakistan Women's Theater Festival in its homebase, Lahore. Ajoka still has to deal with attempts to censor its productions, and its director has been harassed by orthodox groups that have filed cases against her for defaming Pakistan and/or Islam.

Although sociocultural and political conditions have changed since Gauhar started her work in alternative theater, discrimination and intolerance have not disappeared. Ajoka's mandate is still of the essence.

Jhamak Ghimire

Jhamak Ghimire (born 1980), a differently abled young woman who does not have a single academic qualification, has enriched Nepal's literary world by writing hundreds of poems, songs, stories and essays. Her books have won major literary awards, and she is a regular columnist for Kantipur, a leading Nepali daily. Jhamak is an inspiration to thousands of able and differently abled people in Nepal who are familiar with her remarkable story.

Jhamak Ghimire cannot speak, move, sit easily or use her hands. Yet, this formidably intelligent girl from a poor family in a remote Nepal village has managed to get her voice heard all over the country. What Jhamak suffers from is unclear — some doctors say cerebral palsy — but she can only see, hear and partially move her legs, which she uses to communicate with a deeply impressed readership. Entirely self-taught, she learnt to read and write by mimicking her younger sisters and brothers.

It began when she was seven years old: she heard the Ramayana (Indian epic) being recited by her father. When, one day, she saw her father pressuring her younger sister to study, it aroused her curiosity and enthusiasm. She began to practice writing the alphabet with her feet, and learnt the Devanagari script within a week. Although all she knows of the world is what she reads, sees from the window of her room, and learns from her limited social interactions, it has generated a wealth of material. Jhamak's talents first came to light in 1994 when a journalist, who lives near her in Dhanakuta, wrote about her in a local weekly newspaper. Other newspapers and magazines began raving about her work and personality. Then, various organizations and readers helped her publish her books, so far five in number, with another three in the pipeline.

Jhamak has won literary awards such as the Kabitaram Bal Sahitya Prativa Puraskar and the Aswikrit Bichar Sahitya Puraskar. In her weekly column in Kantipur, she focuses on children's and women's issues, and sociocultural and political vices and achievements. The most amazing quality in Jhamak is her ability to rise above her physical situation with almost supernatural levels of courage and determination. That is why she is such an inspiration to thousands of Nepalis and a leading national personality.

There are an estimated 2.5 million disabled people in Nepal, but few government plans and programs target them, and state resources allocated for them are paltry. Only lately has the government provided them with separate identity cards that can help them access various facilities.

Nepal

Limota Goroso Giwa

International Women's Communication Center (IWCC)

Hajiya Limota Goroso Giwa, born in Ilorin, in Kwara state of Nigeria, was raised by fishing grandparents. Her father, an imam (leader for Muslim prayers), died when she was 11. She studied human rights at the University of Columbia and obtained her masters in social planning. A senior advocate on women's rights and coordinator of women and fishery projects in riverine communities in Nigeria, she occupies several humanitarian posts, among them coordinator of the Pan-African and West African Women. In addition, Goroso Giwa addresses issues around the trafficking of Kwara women to Saudi Arabia.

For more than 20 years, Limota Goroso Gewa has held workshops, visited communities, counseled, mobilized women and girls to promote women's rights, justice, and fairness. Being a native of Kwara, a Muslim state where most of the men do not want women to go to school, Goroso had the incredible idea of creating an NGO, the International Women's Communication Center (IWCC), focusing on girls and married women who have not had the chance to go to school, as well as orphans and street children. Events between 1999 and 2000 between Muslims and Christians caused enormous damage: many houses were burnt and many lives were lost. Goroso fought to re-establish peace between Muslims and Christians, bridging the gulf between these two large religious communities. She initiated and presided over the Committee for Peace between Muslims and Christians of Ilorin. It is thanks to her efforts that the youth and religious groups today live in peace. Initially, her mediation was rejected as she was taken for a woman who tried to substitute herself in a man's role in a sensitive conflict. Religion aside, it is difficult for many to understand why the daughter of an imam strove for peace between Muslims and Christians.

Nigeria consists of approximately 50% Muslims (north), 40% Christians (south), and 10% of other faiths. The country had been ruled by a military dictatorship until 1999, when the first president in two decades was elected democratically. Since 1999, eight states have adopted Sharia (Muslim) law which consequently led to conflicts between Christians and Muslims.

Nigeria

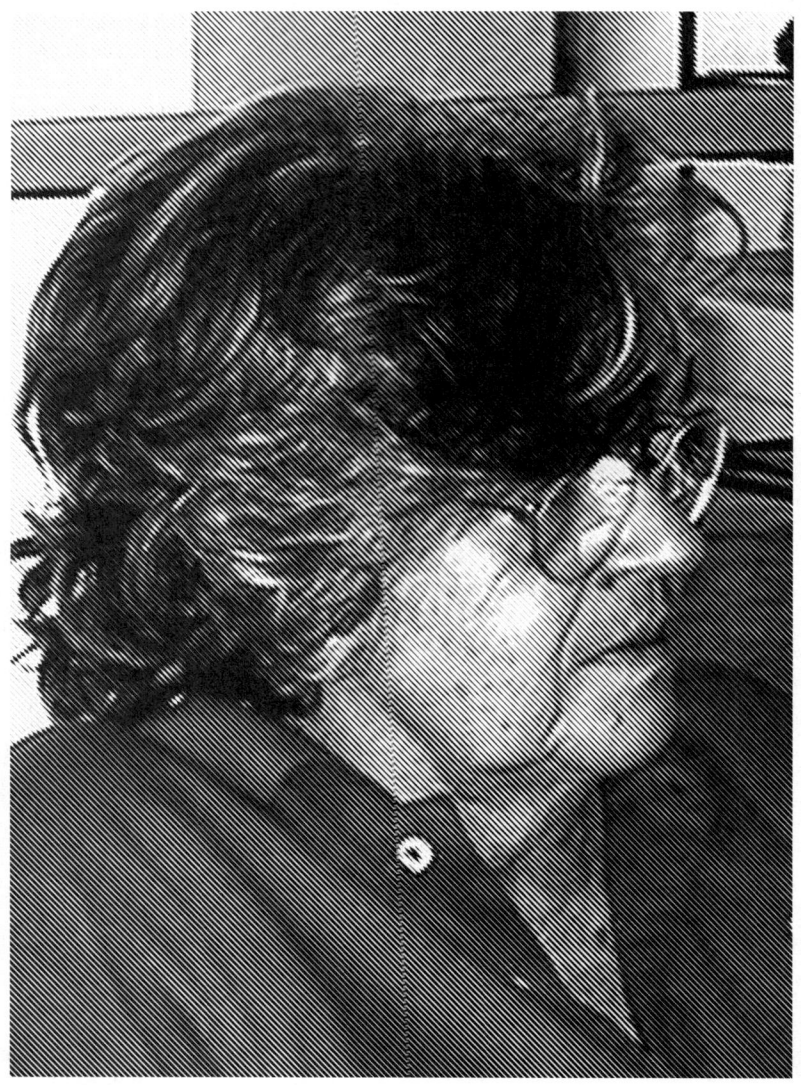

NièdE Guidon

Fundação Museu do Homem Americano (Museum of the American Man Foundation)

Nième Guidon (1933) is the most famous Brazilian archeologist. Thanks to her ideas and organizational skills, the National Park of the Serra da Capivara was founded in the state of Piauí, located in Brazil's distant countryside. Inside the Park, there is one of the largest and most important collections of cave paintings made by the American man. Nième is a visionary, finding possibilities beyond the circumstances. The archaeologist and her teamwork have sown the seeds of development and culture in extremely poor villages surrounding the National Park.

In archeology, centuries mean nothing, millennia really matter. Human presence on Earth is absolutely previous to writing and documentation. Some of the proofs of human existence before the invention of writing are cave paintings. Nième Guidon looked for and found a treasure in the caves of the poorest Brazilian state, Piauí. "One hundred thousand years ago, there were human societies living here." The paintings were hidden by the forest and mistreated due to the irregular occupation of the sites. Nième organized an archeological mission, supported by the French government, to begin the excavations.

In 1986, she created the Fundação Museu do Homem Americano (Museum of the American Man Foundation), a non-governmental organization in charge of a center for research and teaching of archeology, also responsible for the National Park of the Serra da Capivara. As a consequence of Nième's effort, the Park was added to Unesco's List of Humanity's Heritage. However, this Heritage is constantly being threatened by hunters and by Brazilian society's carelessness, when it comes to the preservation of cultural heritage. The archeologist and her team of 190 people received several death threats. In 2001, a forest ranger was killed by a hunter.

Nième Guidon is sure that the best guards for the Park are the communities living around it. To accomplish such task, development and education are essential. The museum maintains an art school for kids and teenagers, and it supports tourism and handcraft pottery. This scientist's current challenge is to build, in a city near the Park, an international airport, which could bring the state three million tourists per year. Tourism will economically develop the Piauí in an unforeseen manner, creating thousands of jobs. What is more, it will guarantee the protection of the Park's fauna, flora and cave paintings.

Created in 1979, the National Park of the Serra da Capivara has a perimeter of 214 kilometers. Besides its fauna and flora, it has 400 archeological sites — and 260 of them have cave paintings. Those paintings are the oldest ones in all of America.

Brazil

Cecile Guidote Alvarez

Philippine Educational Theater Association (Peta)
Movement for a Free Philippines
International Alliance of Concerned Artists for Human Rights and Peace (ACAHRP)

Cecile Guidote Alvarez (born 1943) founded the Philippine Educational Theater Association (Peta), a pioneering theater group that honed creative artists and audiences through children's, college, and community theater. For 38 years, Peta has depicted social issues through original Filipino plays, using the language of the masses and alternative theater spaces. Today, as executive director of the National Commission for Culture and the Arts, Cecile has been described as a "cultural caregiver".

Cecile Guidote Alvarez has served the Filipino public for years through the arts as a theater artist, producer, director and founder of cultural movements. As a 16-year-old talent of the Paulinian Players Guild, she was tapped to join the Ateneo Summer Graduate School Theater, where she was exposed to a theater workshop with disabled children at the National Orthopedic Hospital. Seeing the children emerge from hopelessness to confidence, Cecile discovered the power of the arts to transform the marginalized youth into creative individuals. At 18, Cecile directed the award-winning TV series, "Teenagers", which tackled problems of the youth. From this early exposure to theater arts, Cecile envisioned a theater not just for entertainment, but also as a significant social venue that could articulate the aspirations of the Filipino people. From 1964 to 1967, she pursued graduate studies at the State University of New York and the Trinity University in Texas. She returned to the country in 1967 with her graduate thesis entitled "Prospectus for a National Theater" which envisioned a Philippine national theater movement. This became the basis for the Philippine Educational Theater Association (Peta) that Cecile founded and directed in 1967. For 38 years, Peta has honed creative artists who made successful careers in the Philippine theater and movie industry. The pioneering theater movement has regional chapters involving children's theater, college theater, community theater and traditional arts. Currently, as executive director of the National Commission for Culture and Arts, Cecile continues her lifetime commitment of "cultural care giving" by providing free arts training to street children, the disabled and indigenous youth. Cecile attests that "the arts are a peaceful and powerful means of transmitting values."

Before the 1960s, theater in the Philippines was the domain of the elite. Filipinos were culturally dominated by the US, and generally unaware of Asian and non-Western theater. State funding for theatre arts was nil and theater arts education did not feature in the school curriculum.

Philippines

Ratna Indraswari Ibrahim

Bakti Nurani
Entropic Foundation
Yayasan Pajoeng

Ratna Indraswari Ibrahim (born 1960) lives in East Java, Indonesia. At the age of 13, she was stricken with polio and other orthopedic diseases that permanently hindered the functions of her arms and legs. Her family encouraged her never to lose hope in spite of her disabilities. She writes short stories about discrimination against women that are published regularly in Indonesian newspapers. Ratna is also involved in local campaigns to improve accessibility for people living with disabilities and to save the urban forest in her hometown, Malang.

Ratna Indraswari Ibrahim opens her door to everyone who wants to discuss women's rights, the environment and culture. "It is not easy for me to go out, so I offer my house as the gathering place," she explains. Stricken with polio and other orthopedic diseases at the age of 13, Ratna's arms and legs are permanently damaged. Her mother encouraged Ratna to become a writer and taught her to be independent in spite of her disability. Aware that most women in society are unfairly treated from childhood, disadvantaged by the unequal distribution of work in the family, she uses discrimination against women as the main theme of her short stories published by national newspapers.

Ratna has strong opinions about cultural perceptions and the state's policy on accessibility for people with disabilities. She observes that people with disabilities are denied the opportunity to participate in public life because they are considered a curse to their family and community. Women and children with disabilities, especially from poor and uneducated communities, often experience harassment and sexual violence. She urges government to issue policies in providing adequate physical and social infrastructure for the disabled.

Ratna began her campaign for the rights of the disabled in 1977 when she founded Bakti Nurani, an NGO that appeals to international organizations to provide wheelchairs for poor children with disabilities and meets with the local parliament on the issue of accessibility in public places. Ratna is also involved in environmental work through the Entropic Foundation that she helped initiate. In 1998, she set up Yayasan Pajoeng to work on cultural issues. With activists, artists and students who regularly meet at her house, she set up the "Forum Pelangi" (Rainbow Forum) to discuss women's rights, the environment and culture.

The Indonesian government has allocated almost no resources to integrate the disabled into society. In 1995, government statistics estimated that about six million of Indonesia's 220 million population live with disabilities. Discrimination against the disabled is common in many communities.

Indonesia

Salma Jayyusi

The Project for the Translation of Arabic (Prota)

Born in 1927, Salma Khadra Jayyusi is a gifted poet, with a critically distinguished vision. Her contribution to shaping the Arab cultural landscape and its multi-disciplinary interface with the world spanned over 50 years and crossed geographical and linguistic boundaries. A Palestinian, she was one of the early innovators in the contemporary Arab literary movement that emerged after the occupation (Nakba) of Palestine in 1948, focusing on the tumult of Arab critical debates on literature and its interaction with society.

Salma Jayyusi's scholarly venture took her on a long journey in life. On a visit to the US in 1980, she realized that the influence of Arab culture on Americans was far less than she had expected. Motivated by the belief that mutual understanding between nations can only be based on the promotion of reciprocal knowledge between cultures, and determined to bring the heritage of Arab and Islamic culture to a wider audience, she was inspired to found The Project for the Translation of Arabic (Prota). For two and a half decades, she dedicated herself to making that visionary project a success.

Two significant dimensions of this endeavor stood out: Salma Jayyusi was constantly concerned with popularizing the superb achievements of profound literary figures in Arabic scholarship as well as the voices of writers who would easily have been overlooked, particularly young women poets and writers. Secondly, the project, like all visionary works, underwent a process of development and innovation, expanding beyond the boundaries of regional literature, especially with the addition of East/West Nexus to Prota in 1992. This is also a project for the dissemination of Arabic literature and Arab/Islamic culture and history. In this, Jayyusi's vision and accomplishments were to produce not only a frame for deeper knowledge and broad-mindedness between the Arab and the Anglophone world, but also within the Arab world itself. Jayyusi's work demanded courage and willingness to stand alone and surmount the obstacles that encounter those women who are keen on venturing into the public domain. She worked hard to persuade people from cross-sectional scholarly settings to share visions towards the development of the project. Salma's journey has assisted in building a cultural bridge between a multitude of voices and positions, while managing to communicate them to the world at large.

Jayyusi's efforts — as a scholar, translator, anthologist, analyst and disseminator of Arabic literature, both classic and contemporary — were aimed at exposing a Western audience to the heritage of Arab culture at a time when only few people were working on these issues due to various obstacles in the Arab world.

Occupied Palestinian Territory

Sheema Kermani

Tehrik-e-Niswan
Pakistan India Forum for Peace and Democracy
Pakistan Peace Coalition

Sheema Kermani's efforts to revive dance in a conservative society have created a cultural revolution in Pakistan. Her dauntless efforts to integrate, mainstream, and mobilize classical dance, theater, television, and drama as forms of alternative communication have been liberating, particularly for women. In an environment of animosity and suspicion, dance/drama is a medium widely accepted by all segments of society and helps to foster peace and friendship in the region.

Sheema Kermani was born in 1951 into a middle-class educated family in Rawalpindi, Pakistan. She studied fine arts, film, and art appreciation and trained herself in classical music and Indian dance. Kermani's concern with issues of justice, peace, and women's rights persuaded her to set up the Tehrik-e-Niswan, a cultural action group to create awareness about the subordinate status of women in society and the antiwomen laws. Using dance, drama, and music, Tehrik-e-Niswan and Kermani took up relevant social issues to create public awareness and to bring to light the antiwomen nature of society. Her activities forced the state to introduce an amendment to the Performing Act Ordinance by which all dance performances by women were banned. This ban is still operational and artists have to obtain a no-objection certificate, which states, "dances, obscenity and nudity not allowed." However, she defies these bans and continues to perform and also teach classical dance.

She has also lectured and written extensively on the history, significance, beauty, and importance of fine arts. Having traveled widely across the globe she has to her credit many ballets, most prominent among them The Song of Mohenjodaro, and Indus and Europe. In a country where dance is a taboo, her performances have succeeded in initiating dialogues and discussions toward progressive change in cultural norms, unfair practices, and social values. Sheema has thus been an integral part of the feminist movement of resistance in Pakistan. Through her efforts to integrate women's rights, cultural heritage, and creative expression she has reached out to the young and old, men and women. Kermani's relentless criticism of the antiwomen policies and laws of the state introduced during martial law in the 1980s and still in force in the country has led to far greater awareness among people.

When Sheema Kermani started her work in the early 1980s, the atmosphere was antiwomen and oppressive. Thirty years later, although the situation seems improved, the South Asia region is in severe danger of resurgent patriarchy, religious fundamentalism, and increasing violence against women.

Pakistan

Zarina Khan

Zarina Khan Productions

Zarina Khan (born 1954), philosopher, poet, actor, theater and movie director is a true world citizen. In 1993, as war raged in Sarajevo, Zarina set up a workshop there. This gave rise to "The Dictionary of Life," a play that toured Europe, and has been renewed in new contexts in Beirut, the Balkans, and strife-ridden suburbs, wherever one struggles for human dignity. Author of several books on human rights, architect of many projects on children's rights, Zarina's articles on "a new way of teaching peace" have been published in many languages.

Zarina Khan was still a little girl when she understood what was important, even vital to her. In school one day, she pocketed a piece of chalk without permission. Her teacher followed her closely to see what she would do with it. Zarina drew a circle on the ground and stood in the middle, then invited other children into it to act out roles she had imagined. When asked what she was doing, she replied that she was playing. The word she used was right: Zarina was creating a play, a space to share emotions with others. "It is called theater."

She studied human rights, specifically children's rights, and philosophy, which she still teaches. She put on her first play at the age of nine, just as she began writing poetry as soon as she had mastered the alphabet. She has persistently pursued both vocations. Her experience in philosophy, theater, and film led her to devise a method in writing workshops and theatrical practice, adapted to all levels from primary school to university.

Over the past several years, Zarina has elaborated workshop productions throughout the world, thus encouraging cultural exchanges and understanding. In 1993, she set up the Theater and Liberty in War operation, implementing a writer's workshop in Sarajevo's war zone. This project gave rise to "The Dictionary of Life," a play which toured throughout Europe, enlightening audiences about the civic responsibility we all must bear. In 1995, Zarina was invited by Unesco to join a committee on the Culture of Peace. In 1996, she finished her feature film "Ados Amor" which she made with a group of teens living in a culturally and economically deprived environment. This film has been selected for festivals around the world, and is often showed during conferences against racism. Her documentary "Essabar or the Shelter of Being" was awarded First Prize at the Festival for Mental Health in France.

Sarajevo, October 1993: a city in agony, death on every corner and in every face, people struggling to survive in terrifying conditions. This was the context for Zarina Khan's workshop, a space in which people could re-cover their dignity and stand up to face the world. Her mission is to build bridges.

France

Kongdeuane Nettavong

National Library of Laos

Kongdeuane Nettavong was born in 1947 in Muang Chiang Kwang, northern Laos. After finishing secondary school in 1970, she went to Laval University in Quebec, Canada for her Bachelor's Degree in Geography, then to France in 1973 for her Master's degree in Archives. She has pursued a literacy program for the Laotians by setting up libraries, publishing books in Lao and encouraging people to read. She has been Director of the National Library of Laos since 1989.

Normally, Lao officials retire at the age of 55. But not Kongdeuane. Even after she retired, the government asked her to continue working as director of the National Library of Laos. Apart from her routine work in the office, Kongdeuane has created many projects to improve the literacy of the people of Laos, such as the "Literacy Cultivation Project" built on three strategies: encouraging people to read books, encouraging the publication of Lao textbooks, and setting up school libraries, people's libraries, libraries for the masses and Knowledge Development Centers in villages, districts, and at provincial levels. She also introduced the idea of book bags and book boxes to collect book donations for schools in remote areas that do not have libraries. Kongdeuane delivers the donated books herself through the Caravan Puppet Theater, which she heads, using puppet theater to encourage children to read. She usually supervises the construction of the libraries herself, designs and produces the puppets with her team and performs and provides the voices for puppet shows.

Another project is the Preservation of Lao Palm Leaf Manuscripts Program. Her team goes around the country surveying palm-leaf manuscripts in the temples and training villagers to restore decaying manuscripts and keep them in a safe place, thus preserving the cultural heritage and wisdom of the Lao nation. Kongdeuane also initiated the Archives of Traditional Laotian Music Project, which has recorded in VCD format the music of the minority ethnic groups in Laos and encourages the training of the new generation in traditional music. A music lover who plays the khan, she has taken the initiative to transcribe khan music and sounds and compare these with international notes.

For 60 years, under French rule, Laotians lost their cultural identity. After their liberation from France, the Lao people worked to restore their languages, culture and identity.

Lao People's Democratic Republic

"No human being
or living creature
deserves to be
killed or eliminated.
His destiny cannot
be solved here,
on earth."

Lina Kostenko

Lina Kostenko is one of the greatest national contemporary poets in Ukraine. She (74) now works as a member and inspirer of expeditions to Chernobyl. She is an expert in ethnology, folk culture, and sociology. Together with a group of volunteers, she works to preserve the culture and history of Chernobyl. The volunteers meet with people who refused to leave their homes and provide assistance or just listen to their history. As a poet, she feels responsibility for every word she produces. For her, the main criterion is truth.

Lina Kostenko was born in 1930 in the region of Kiev. She was a teenager when World War II broke out and she witnessed the occupation of her homeland by German troops. Those events found reflection in poems; she began to write them at the age of 14. After the war, she graduated from the Moscow Institute for Literature. After her studies, she returned to Ukraine and wrote and published a series of poetry books (1957, 1958, and 1961). The beginning of her creative activity coincided with the zenith of the authoritarian regime of the Soviet Union. Those who were dedicated to higher arts could not have their own vision of life and could not express themselves, but had to adapt their poems to the demands of socialist realism. However, in the 1960s, she expressed the desires and aspirations of the post-war generation of Ukrainian writers. Among them were Vasyl Simonenko, Mykola Vinhranosky, and Ivan Drach. Their project was to re-vitalize Ukrainian literature and to make space for a national literature, independent from the influence of political dogma and the current communist regime. Together with other independent authors she signed various petitions in defense of political prisoners, supporting people punished for their freedom of opinions. She was never indifferent to the miseries and sorrows of other people, something that is revealed in her poems and actions. She is a talented woman who enjoys life and, in spite of her age, is very energetic and active. By meeting people and staying close to nature, she perceives other people's pain as her own. That is why the famous poet has chosen to go to Chernobyl, one of the most painful areas in Ukraine, to save the culture and the trust of people with the power of humanism.

Under the Soviet regime, freedom of literary and cultural expression was repressed in Ukraine. Today, the culture of the Chernobyl region, devastated by the radioactive nuclear disaster, risks being lost.

Ukraine

Ching Chee Lee

Retired pastor

Born in Hong Kong in 1932, Pastor Lee Ching Chee has devoted herself to the duties of the church and education. She has rewritten the history of the ministry, which was once monopolized by male pastors. A female leader in the church, Pastor Lee was officially ordained pastor in the 1960s when the church was very conservative. Pastor Lee has paved the way for female ministry, and has proved that both sexes should enjoy an equal opportunity to serve in the ministry. She has been noted for her peaceful and cooperative approach.

Pastor Lee Ching Chee is the first female pastor in the history of ministry in Hong Kong, which was once monopolized by men. She was ordained pastor in the 1960s when the church was very conservative, and paved the road for female ministry in the church. Subsequently, the church began to recognize the status of women and the principle of sexual equality in leadership. In the 1980s and 1990s, different denominations of the church started to change their tradition of ministry and female pastors were ordained. Pastor Lee played both the role of a pastor in the church and an educator in school. Refusing to be confined by narrow-minded ideas and old-fashioned education methods, she abolished religious education examinations, and abandoned the use of outdated textbooks and directive teaching methods. Instead, she organized discussion-oriented curricula for religious education, and added the sharing of experience from teachers in morning prayers in addition to religious messages. She taught religious education in a different manner, sharing with students their changes brought by religion so that the knowledge and learning they acquired would be relevant to reality and their life. Between 1977 and 1981, Pastor Lee worked in England as secretary for mission education in the Council for World Mission. She visited many countries including many that were unstable politically, and where people were socially and economically impoverished. She was once in Northeast India when there was curfew after midnight. She visited Belfast in Northern Ireland in times of fierce guerrilla warfare. She listened to complaints from discontented workers in mines 2,600 feet below ground level in Wales. Despite the difficulties she was successful in her mission of enhancing understanding and establishing cooperation between the Council for World Mission and Third World churches.

Even today, no woman can be ordained in the Catholic Church of Hong Kong while only a few female pastors have been ordained in the Christian Church. Women have been isolated from the ministry and traditional theology, which is dominated by men who do not know how to respect and manage differences.

China, Hong Kong SAR

Fenglan Liu

Liu Fenglan, an ordinary woman from Baishihang Village, Zhaoyuan City, Shangdong Province, has spent virtually her entire life in the service of others, offering and giving help whenever she can. She shares her gains and experiences without reserve because her dream is to live in a world that is full of love, and where life is peaceful and serene.

Liu Fenglan cannot remain unconcerned when she sees others in difficulty. Her childhood experiences inspired her intense interest in learning, especially for national policies, laws and regulations. Ever since she was in the first grade of middle school, she used to write letters and petitions on behalf of others. Even today many people visit her to enquire about legal problems, or ask for her views, as she is publicly regarded as the one who has the best understanding of laws, the best ideas, and is the most warmhearted. Therefore, the folks affectionately call her "the Ph.D. lady". The farmland of Baishihang Village has not been redistributed since 1982, and this has led to uneven land distribution. In addition, taxes are exorbitant and levies unreasonable. Liu made all kinds of efforts to familiarize people with laws and the latest national policies.

On November 24, 2004, Liu was elected member of the village committee on the eighth election of the village committee. By standing for election, she intended to make clear that no village officer has the position by inheritance. Every villager can try to be master of the village. Villagers' rights are not given, but gained through struggle. Benefits cannot be protected by relying on others, but by being active.

Land in Baishihang Village in Shandong Province has not been redistributed since 1982, which leads to severe disproportion; sometimes a family of seven or eight members possesses farmland for two persons, while a family of two persons have farmland for seven or eight persons.

China

"To learn from one another, to share the fruits of talents and gifts, as individuals and as peoples, brings about reciprocal enrichment. It is the way that will bring us to unity in the plurality."

Chiara Lubich

Focolare Movement

Chiara Lubich's work for peace started during World War II. In Trent, in an air-raid shelter, she read Jesus' last testament with her first companions: "That all may be one." That "all" became their horizon; that program for universal unity, became the reason for their lives. This project now involves more than two million people, giving life to a large-scale movement of spiritual and social renewal, multicultural and multifaith, the Focolare Movement, present in 182 nations.

Trent 1943. It was in the time of war that Chiara Lubich's work of peace and unity was born. Barely 20 years old, faced with the ruins that hate had brought about, she lived an experience of the essence of God: Love, an experience immediately shared by many. "The Gospel became the only book we read, the only light of our life," she wrote. She understood that "the commandment of mutual love contained the law for composing people and all things in a new order." Jesus' testament, "That all may be one," became the goal of their lives: to bring unity in every point of division. "Let us put everything in common: goods, houses, money. Life changed. Every day the number of people grew around us. Wherever we worked, in offices, schools, and businesses, a new climate was built. Hates and gripes were dispelled. Many families came together again in harmony and peace. We were convinced that the Gospel held the answer to every personal and social problem."
The small group became a movement of spiritual and social renewal, multicultural and multifaith, the Focolare Movement, characterized by dialogue, present in 182 nations. More than two million people are involved. Chiara Lubich reads in the profound changes of this time, the beginning of a new world, of a united world. To bring this about many projects came to life, like 26 little publishing houses, 33 small towns of witness in various phases of development, the project for an Economy of Communion, the Movement for Unity in Politics, 1000 social projects and 14,000 adoptions at a distance. Where does the strength to take this work ahead come from? Chiara Lubich responds: "It is a gift of the Spirit, a charisma. I am only an instrument in God's hands to bring about his project."

In the current age of change, in the face of terrorism, increased conflicts on interpersonal, societal, political levels, a growing gap between rich and poor, Chiara Lubich's work shows, as in a "worldwide laboratory," a world of peace, united in diversity, that opens up new roads towards this goal.

Italy

Nadja Mehmedbasic

Nadja Mehmedbasic completed her law studies in Sarajevo. Since 1965, she has worked as a journalist, first for radio and then for television where she was responsible for the production of documentary films. Many of her documentaries promoting peace and tolerance have received international prizes and awards. During the war (1992—1995), she remained in besieged Sarajevo and worked to bring people closer together. After the war, she has continued to document the tragedy of the war and the needs of women survivors.

During the war, Nadja remained in besieged Sarajevo with her family. From the first day, she demonstrated her willingness to work against war and to promote peace and tolerance. In her television job, she worked on programs ranging from information to public commentaries and news advisories. At that time, her basic message was that "a person is never and will never be stronger with weapons only." Her work on documentaries became the space in which Nadja fought against the war and campaigned for tolerance, peace, and love, hoping for happier childhoods for future generations. Those were the topics she explored during this harsh time while Sarajevo was under siege. "Bez Rat Hasem" (May peace be with you) is a story about Jews in Bosnia who, right before the outbreak of the war, celebrated the 500th anniversary of their arrival in their new homeland. Because of previous cruel experiences, this war left them with thousands of extremely difficult questions and dilemmas. Based on the diary of one Jew from Sarajevo, Nadja produced the documentary film "They Missed Our Heart," a true war love story that promotes the value of collective life, understanding, and tolerance among peoples, no matter to which nation or faith they belong.
One of Nadja's most important projects during the war was publishing "Friend," a paper sponsored by the Red Cross of Sarajevo. Nadja participated in defining the paper's concept, so that it would not only have a humanitarian character, but also once again bring people, who were torn apart by war, closer together. Ever since the paper's release, many famous authors, poets, journalists, and all those who know the meaning of true friendship, have participated and worked closely together to find the right words.

After the declaration of independence on 6 April 1992, Bosnia and Herzegovina was attacked by Serb forces who did not want to secede from Yugoslavia. Bosnian people were murdered, imprisoned, or expelled from almost 70 percent of the territory. Sarajevo was likewise under siege during the Balkan war.

Bosnia and Herzegovina

Zezé Motta

Centro Brasileiro de Informação e Documentação do Artista Negro
(Center of Information and Documentation of the Afro-Brazilian Artist)

Zezé Motta (1944) had always been involved with art: since her childhood, in a private school, until becoming a professional in a theater course, in which she was discovered for the production of a musical. Her mother is a dressmaker and her father a musician. Actress, singer and director of a non-governmental organization that supports young Afro-Brazilians in the tough task of becoming actors, Zezé has helped to value the Afro-Brazilian woman through memorable characters.

In her teenage years, when she used to help her mother with her sewing, Zezé Motta spent the days listening to the radio. It was her father who noticed that on the third time that she heard a song she was able to sing it perfectly. "He discovered my vocation to be a singer," she says. Zezé started her acting career in a musical. She was chosen after a closing ceremony of a theater course, which she paid for with the salary she earned working as an employee of a Pharmaceutical laboratory.

Zezé concluded Elementary School in an experimental school founded by progressist sectors of the Catholic Church inside a poor community in Rio. She started to make contact with the theater. And with the racism, that was also manifested very early. From a neighbor she heard: "Do you have to study theater to play the role of a maid?" The question, which seemed inappropriate to someone who had great career plans, reappeared in her life when Zezé started to receive invitations to work on TV. The only role available was as maid.

Protagonist of the slave Chica da Silva in a movie named after this character, Zezé divides life between before and after this character that projected her allover Brazil and overseas. The question of where Afro-Brazilians belonged in Brazilian society led Zezé to the Afro-Brazilian movement and to the foundation of a NGO: Center of Information and Documentation of the Afro-Brazilian Artist (Cidan). In the militancy for more space for the Afro-Brazilians in the movies, theater and television, she noticed that there was a lack of opportunities, which was a consequence of the lack of qualification of young actors. "I noticed that it was necessary to stop complaining about prejudice and start doing something about it," she says.

Zezé Motta played important Afro-Brazilian characters such as the slaves Chica da Silva and Dandara (of the movie 'Quilombo'). In her work of qualifying actors, she has provided around 400 young and poor Afro-Brazilians with an artistic and cultural qualification.

Brazil

Kishwar Naheed

Hawwa Crafts Cooperatives (HCC)

For over four decades, Kishwar Naheed has been a fearless and independent voice in support of the arts and culture in Pakistan, in an environment that has, at times, been extremely hostile. In her current role as coordinator of Hawwa Crafts Cooperatives, this gifted feminist writer, poet, and activist has been responsible for reviving dying crafts in remote areas of Pakistan, and for helping about 2000 craftswomen make better lives for themselves.

Kishwar Naheed was born into a middle-class family that educated its sons well but only taught its daughters to read and write before arranging marriages for them. Kishwar insisted on higher education, did her masters, and wrote poetry. She married a man of her own choice, was disowned by her family, and became a civil servant, a career which she pursued for 38 years. Sent on leave for five years when the country was under martial law, she went to court to protest her suspension, and was reinstated. She was briefly arrested in February 1983, along with other women activists, for protesting against the proposed Law of Evidence that was discriminatory to women. Kishwar used her leave to promote home-based entrepreneurship among rural women and revive dying crafts in Pakistan's remote areas, becoming involved with Hawwa Crafts Cooperatives, which has, over the past 20 years, trained and upgraded the skills of 2000 craftswomen.

As a writer, too, Kishwar was in trouble under martial law. Two of her books were banned, and she was also briefly arrested on charges of spreading pornography. Frequently under surveillance, she had to send her two sons, aged 16 and 18, out of Pakistan, for fear that the martial law regime or the fundamentalist forces might use them to intimidate her. In 1998, Kishwar, then working as director general of culture, resigned from the service when the minister of culture objected to a classical dance festival in the country.

This pioneer in feminist and resistance literature has produced nine volumes of poetry, eight books on women's issues, eight books of translations of contemporary resistance and international literature, and 12 books for children. She has also written weekly columns for newspapers. Kishwar, who lives in Islamabad, also works as consultant with Action Aid and the Asian Development Bank.

Religious fundamentalists in Pakistan often rail against classical dance performances and other cultural activities, interpreting them as contrary to Islamic culture and values. But a strong movement is building up against such obscurantism.

Pakistan

Holly Near

Redwood Records

For more than 30 years, Holly Near has used her music to inspire social change. She has sung on picket lines, in prisons, and at Carnegie Hall. She has worked with the United Farm Workers, Central and Latin American solidarity groups, labor unions, women's groups, antiracist organizations, gay and lesbian rights organizations, disability rights educators, and environmental groups. She was one of the first artists to use her political beliefs to form her own record company, and her independence has cost her access to the mass media. Instead, she inspires change community by community.

It was happening again. Holly Near had begun her concert protesting the Vietnam War, when authorities declared a bomb threat and ordered audience members and musicians to clear the room. Holly stayed. The "threats" had happened so often that she knew them for what they were: a right-wing tactic to stop war protests. Over the years, the scene would be repeated in different ways and in different places. In El Salvador, Holly was part of a music festival devoted to opposing death squads. When soldiers pointed machine guns at the artists and told them that they could not perform, Holly stayed. And she sang.

Born in rural California, Holly has been singing since she was a small child. In the late 1960s she was drawn into the antiwar movement and began to use her voice to inspire social change. She started working professionally in 1971, and her first international work was with the Free The Army group, entertaining and supporting active soldiers who resisted war and racism. When Holly tried to get a record contract in the early 1970s, she was encouraged to change her lyrics. Rather than do so, she became one of the first artists to use her political beliefs to start her own record company. Holly used her company, Redwood Records, to produce other cultural artists. She coordinated the first Sweet Honey in the Rock tour in California and recorded their first album on her label. She also brought many international artists to the USA who sang in support of solidarity, including Inti Illimani, the acclaimed Chilean ensemble.

Holly's songs are anthems of hope and critical thinking, calling on the audience to rise up to their best selves. She was one of the first artists to include an American Sign Language interpreter at her concerts, and her inclusion transformed hundreds of people into advocates for disability rights and services.

Most of the progressive music we hear today, including women's music, has been directly inspired and influenced by Holly Near. The whole phenomen of the "cultural worker" can be directly linked to her pioneering endeavors.

United States of America

"My films are deeply concerned with this life in which I also live. I can deeply sense how terrible it is for a collective to be without memory. I record the human condition of life in turbulence."

Ying Ning

Ning Ying is a well-known film director born in Beijing. She has so far made five feature films and numerous documentaries. The "Beijing Trilogy" is well known for depicting disappearing traditional ways of life, the difficulty of coping with the new changes, and the anxieties of the new generation. Ning has also depicted urgent social issues and imbalanced development in China, such as HIV/Aids, trafficking of women, and street children.

Ning Ying is a well-known film director. She was born in the 1950s to parents who were Beijing intellectuals. At the age of 22 she joined the Beijing Film Academy where her classmates were some of the "fifth generation" of Chinese film makers. She later studied in Italy at the Centro Sperimentale di Cinematografia, becoming assistant director on Bertolucci's 1987 film, "The Last Emperor."

Ning Ying returning to China the following year, and has since made five feature films and numerous documentaries. She says, "I first set out to explore Beijing in 1992 with 'For Fun,' a comedy about disappearing traditional ways of life. In 1995, with the black-humored 'On the Beat,' I focused on the emerging new reality and the difficulty of coping with it. In 'I Love Beijing,' the magnitude of changes shaping our lives and the anxieties of the new generation are represented in a rhapsody form, through the eyes of a young, restless taxi driver."

Ning Ying has a deep concern for the underprivileged in the lower strata of society. She records urban social transformations of the 1990s and the way the lives of ordinary folk are squeezed, rewritten and exploited by such transformations. She is also actively involved in documentaries covering the Third World. She depicts urgent social issues, imbalanced development in China, HIV/Aids, the trafficking of women, and street children. In 2001 Ning Ying made a documentary called "Railroad of Hope," which relates a journey of over 3000 kilometers that she made with hundreds of agricultural workers, during which she interviewed peasants who were taking up jobs away from their homes in anticipation of a better future. "Railroad of Hope" was awarded the Grand Prix du Cinema du Réel in Paris in 2002. The award citation calls the film "outstanding for the power of its images, its full and deeply penetrating vision."

Changes in the 1990s led to further social division and marginalization in society. Mainstream media presents the changes either as success stories for the competent or accounts of inevitable sacrifice that are making China strong. Yet some media workers and filmmakers are concerned for the marginalized.

China

Lydia Nyati-Ramahobo

Lydia Nyati-Ramahobo (48) was born in Botswana. She obtained her Masters' and PhD degrees in Applied Linguistics at the University of Pennsylvania. She is associate professor and dean at the Faculty of Education at the University of Botswana. She is co-founder of the Kamanakao Association, a pressure group for the linguistic and cultural rights of the Wayeyi tribe. She is also founder of Reteng, a multicultural coalition of Botswana people. Through her efforts, the government of Botswana set up a committee to review all laws that discriminate against non-Tswanas.

Though the Wayeyi tribe are the majority in Botswana, theirs is a minority language. Many Wayeyi are afraid to disclose that they are Wayeyi, derogatorily referred to as "makoba" (stupid people). Lydia Ramahobo herself is a member of the Wayeyi. Unfortunately the Botswana government has supported the oppression of the Wayeyi, both during the colonial era and at the present time.

Lydia is working in the area of human rights, specifically dealing with linguistic and cultural rights of non-Tswanas. The constitution of Botswana, the Chieftainship Act, and the Tribal Territories Act only recognize the Setswana-speaking tribes at the exclusion of 26 others. As a result, only the Setswana language and culture occupy the public space.

Non-Tswanas have no rights to land, and can be dislocated without compensation. Their children learn in Setswana and English. Their traditional chiefs are neither recognized nor admitted to the House of Chiefs, which is part of the legislative branch of the government. The Wayeyi's struggle for freedom in 1936, 1946—48 and 1962 failed to liberate them from subjugation. Through Lydia's efforts, the government of Botswana set up a committee to review all laws that discriminate against non-Tswanas. As a result, the Wayeyi cultural festival started in 2000, and in 2002, the Kalanga started their Domboshaba cultural festival.

Due to social and cultural discrimination, non-Tswanas lack basic social services. The majority live in rural areas, are poverty stricken, ravaged by disease, largely illiterate and jobless. Their languages and cultures are endangered as they assimilate into Tswanadom.

Tenzin Palmo

Dongyu Gatsal Ling Nunnery (DGLN)

Tenzin Palmo was born in 1943 as Diane Perry and was raised in London. At the age of 18, while still in the UK, she became a Buddhist. Two years later, she set off to India to pursue her spiritual path. In 1964, Tenzin became one of the early Westerners to be ordained as a Tibetan Buddhist nun. She studied under her guru, His Eminence the Eighth Kamtrul Rinpoche, for six years. Tenzin spent the following twelve years undertaking more intensive practice in smaller monasteries in the Himalayas, remaining in retreat during the long winter months when it snows for half of the year.

Seeking isolation and better conditions for intense Buddhist spirituality, Tenzin Palmo retreated to a cave near a monastery in the Himalayas. In 1988, she left the cave and went to stay in Italy where she exchanged knowledge with Buddhist and Christian nuns and monks. Before Tenzin's guru Kamtrul Rinpoche passed away in 1980, he had on several occasions requested her to start a Buddhist nunnery. In 1992, the lamas of her monastery repeated this request and Tenzin accepted.

She now lives at the Himachal Pradesh, India, where she has succeeded in temporarily establishing the Dongyu Gatsal Ling Nunnery (DGLN), initially accommodating 25 nuns. Every year Tenzin travels for three months to give teachings and to raise funds for the nunnery. Tenzin is dedicated to helping anguished women who have much devotion to Buddhism but little help and encouragement. She says, "Our Dongyu Gatsal Ling Nunnery is an attempt to redress this century's long neglect." Recounting some of the painstaking efforts that women take to pursue their spiritual path, Tenzin narrates, "Ani Zangmo was a nun in Lahaul at the Tayul Gonpa where I lived. One day she asked if she could borrow my copy of the 'Life of Milarepa', a famous yogi saint of our tradition. Of course, I was happy to lend it to her, but a few days later she returned it with tears in her eyes. She could read the words but could not comprehend the meaning." Tenzin relates another story of women committed to pursuing Buddhist spiritual life and ordinance. She says, "Zangmo, from a prosperous Lahauli family, had been betrothed to a young man. She protested that she only wanted to be a nun, but her family was more interested in creating a good connection with another family. The night before her marriage, Zangmo cut off her beautiful long hair, her 'crowning glory', so that all plans for the wedding would be cancelled."

Women from Tibet and the Himalayan border regions, following the Drukpa Kargyu lineage of Buddhism, have been denied equal opportunity for spiritual advancement. Tenzin Palmo works towards reviving the tradition of female yogis, so that they can develop their intellectual and spiritual potential.

Valeria Porokhova

Rossiyskaya akadiemiya estiestviennykh nauk (Raen)

Valeria Porokhova (born 1940) graduated from Moscow State Pedagogical Institute of Foreign Languages and worked as a lecturer for 18 years. She now works at the Russian Academy of Natural Sciences. Valeria has made a successful translation of the Koran into Russian. The edition, published in 1995, was the first to be available in Russia, Central Asia and the Caucasus.

In January 2005, in Astana, the capital of Kazakhstan, the audience in the huge City Hall — that has gathered to discuss the issues of inter-religious dialog — gets up to welcome an elegant lady: Valeria Porokhova, the author of the Russian translation and commentaries to the Holy Koran.

Back in 1985, married to a Syrian Muslim, Valeria moved to Damascus, where she embraced Islam and embarked on a ten-year project of translating the Holy Koran. When the translation was completed, in 1995, she sent it to the Al-Azhar Islamic Research Academy in Cairo, Egypt. It went through a most meticulous scrutinization process and was eventually approved for publication. Since then, hundreds of thousands of copies have been distributed throughout the former Soviet Union, particularly in the republics of Central Asia and the Caucasus. This is particularly significant since the Muslims there had no access to a Russian translation and commentary to the Koran in Soviet times and, as a rule, they neither speak nor read Arabic.

Upon her return to Russia in 1997, Valeria began to hold public conferences on the Koran and on Islam in general. In her frequent appearances on TV and radio programs, she emphasizes the non-violent nature of Islam and aims at creating a better understanding of this religion among the non-Muslim population of the former Soviet Union. After more than 70 years of Communist rule, people generally have little understanding of religious matters. Valeria is convinced that religious feelings are not only sacred for every believer, but are also a very powerful factor in uniting people. They can help to bring people together. Her activism to educate people about religion — Islam, in this case — can therefore be seen as an effective and valuable tool to empower people and to unmask the distorted usage of religion by many political regimes.

Valeria is actively involved in interreligious dialog. She advocates the non-violent nature of Islam and aims at creating a better understanding of Islam in Russia — where religious discrimination against Muslims, based upon deep-rooted stereotypes, still exists.

Russian Federation

Xin Qi

Qi Xin is 68 years old. Since the 1980s she has been leading, providing guidance, organizing and planning, and participating in most of the archaeological excavations in the Beijing area. Her research unfolds the historic process of cultural integration among the Han and the few ethnic groups from Northern China.

Qi Xin has been working in the Beijing Cultural Relics Establishment since she graduated from Beijing University in 1961. Through archaeological excavations, data processing, and multi-disciplinary integrative research, Qi Xin discovered that cultural integration and exchange between the Hu and Han ethnic groups occurred in three areas — West Liao River and Yongding River basins, North Shanxi Province, and north of the Yellow River. Qin's archaeological findings prove that Beijing culture carries both central China culture and minority culture of ethnic groups from the northern China grasslands.

China experienced a boom in the real estate industry recently and Qi Xin has called for cultural relics surveys to be carried out before any construction project can begin; she believes that Beijing is full of underground treasures. She and her colleagues actively undertake cultural relics excavation projects often rescuing and protecting cultural relics found in construction sites. However, more often they have to do excavations passively. As member of Standing Committee, Beijing Municipal People's Congress and the support of representatives, Qi Xin saw the endorsement of the regulations that stipulate that surveys for cultural relics must be made before construction projects are to begin.

In Beijing today, the cultural relics department surveys and excavates before the construction of highways, gas pipelines, etc.

The Han culture prevails in China but archaeological finds show that Beijing was a center of cultural merging of ethnic minority culture from the North and Han culture from Central China. Qi Xin has done much research of this kind over the past 44 years that recognizes ethnic minority living and culture.

China

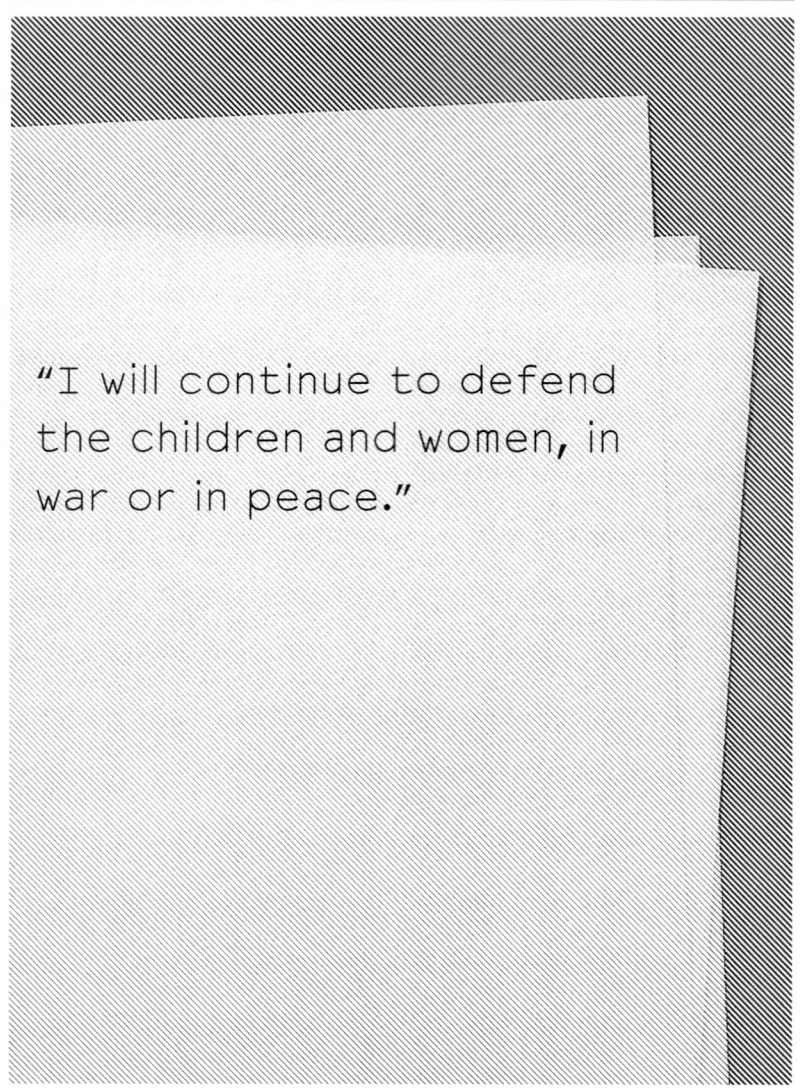

"I will continue to defend the children and women, in war or in peace."

Brigitta Renyaan

Gerakan Perempuan Peduli (GPP)
Putri Bunda Hati Kudus — Order of the Sacred Heart of Princess Mary

Sister Brigitta Renyaan was born in Langur, Maluku, in 1953. After finishing teacher's college, she took her vows as a nun of the order of the Sacred Heart of Princess Mary and devoted herself to guiding the youth. With the outbreak of violence in Maluku, she focused her efforts on women and established the Forum for Women's Welfare Gerakan Perempuan Peduli (GPP) in 1999, and she worked in Soya, Ambon, at a camp for internally displaced persons. Working with refugees, Brigitta has met people at their most vulnerable. She is acknowledged as a counselor, teacher and mediator.

On December 26, 1999, Sister Brigitta Renyaan invited Moslem and Christian orphans to an inter-faith gathering in Silo to mark both Christmas and the breaking of the Moslem fasting month. The religious tensions in Ambon were heating up, the Silo church and An' Nur mosque had been burned down and the gathering angered some Christians who surrounded the building demanding that the event be cancelled. Sr Brigitta faced the crowd and said, "Go ahead, if you want to bomb us! Let us all die!" Her challenge dispersed the crowd. For Malukkans, Sr Brigitta's name evokes peace. After graduating from the Fajar Langgur Teacher's College in 1973, she entered the monastery and taught elementary school for over 15 years at the Xaverius Catholic School in Ambon where she welcomed non-Christian students, setting the tone for the school.

The children at Xaverius are taught the spirit of tolerance from a young age. On one occasion in the fasting month, when the Christian children were told that their Moslem schoolmates were fasting, they too wanted to fast. "I am not a teacher of religion but a general teacher who tries to support children's development and creativity according to their respective religious values," says Sr Brigitta. In 1999, she co-founded Gerakan Peduli Perempuan (GPP) to address the effects of the Maluku conflict on women. Through GPP, Sr Brigitta and her friends have lobbied for an end to the violence in Ambon, counseled displaced children, provided aid — including inter-faith spiritual guidance — to survivors of the religious strife. Sr Brigitta is happy to see peace in Ambon, but she warns that the work of reconciliation and stabilization is not done.

The economic and political tensions among the different cultures in Maluku were worsened with the entry of the Indonesian military. Hundreds of peace-building efforts have been initiated in the islands by local churches, mosques and local, regional and international organizations.

Indonesia

Mallika Vikram Sarabhai

Darpana Academy of Performing Arts

Dancer, choreographer, actor, and writer Mallika Sarabhai (born 1953) has been using art as a medium to fight injustice for the past 22 years. From working with children to working on making space for women's issues in the media, Mallika has helped expand the role of art in social change. At present, she is engaged in a legal battle with the Gujarat government on the "planned genocide" of Muslims in 2002, an action that has caused the government to lash out at her with all its resources.

Mallika is known across the world as a dancer, choreographer, director of experimental theater, actor, writer, editor, and publisher, and many other things besides. And through the status she enjoys across the world as a performer, Mallika has dedicated her entire life to fighting injustice. For the past 22 years, her writing columns and articles, performances, which include touring the remotest Indian villages as well as across the world, her work in urban slums and villages, and with children in schools have set the tone. Most recently, Mallika stood up to fight a legal battle with the Gujarat government about the "planned genocide" of Muslims in 2002, following the Godhra train conflagration. She has been threatened, pilloried, and accused of misrepresenting facts by the Gujarat government, but she has remained steadfast in her convictions.

Through her work with the Darpana Academy of Performing Arts, of which she is director, and Darpana's social wing, Darpana for Development, Mallika has reached distant audiences. She also initiated Jaagruti, a project that involves schoolchildren in environmental issues, in which all levels of Ahmedabad's school system participate. In addition, she has initiated several other projects: on ethics, capacity-building of tribal women, and initiating discussions on women's issues in the media.

Mallika believes that the performing arts can play a vital role in reaching out to people, especially those who are deprived of social and educational privileges. Her work is multilayered; some of it is at the grassroots, some of it among the urban underprivileged, some of it among the urban middle class, and some of it among the urban elite.

In the charged atmosphere of the late 1970s and the early 1980s, socially relevant art and the women's movement had begun to show society the way forward. A number of issues that did not find expression otherwise found a voice through theater and dance.

India

Mrinalini V. Sarabhai

Darpana Academy of Performing Arts

Mrinalini V Sarabhai (born 1918), renowned dancer and choreographer, is credited with the fusion of traditional "pure" dance forms with contemporary issues. She has addressed a range of issues like communal harmony, environmental issues, alcoholism, gambling, dowry, sexual harassment, female foeticide, Aids awareness, leprosy, corruption, family planning, and women's rights. She gave the Indian dance world a sense of direction: a shift from the traditional to the contemporary by forcefully addressing social issues.

Renowned and venerated dancer and choreographer Mrinalini Sarabhai single-handedly took classical Indian dance beyond the shores of India, giving Bharatanatyam (a classical dance form of southern India) a cachet of respect throughout the world. More crucially, she is responsible for the "fusion" of this traditionally purist art form with burning contemporary issues. Deeply interested in dance and theater as a child, Mrinalini braved social opposition to take up Bharatanatyam. As an adult, she began to use dance as a tool for social change, leading to her founding the Darpana Academy of Performing Arts in 1948.

Mrinalini has received numerous awards, recognitions, and honors. She has come a long way from the time when her concept of the arts was regarded as unviable, even alien, and support and funds for her performances were wanting. Even now, her relentlessness has led to opposition: her involvement in a peace meeting on the Gujarat genocide, for example, led to the stoning of the Darpana Academy.

The simplicity of Mrinalini's expression helps everyone, regardless of caste, class, religion, or region, understand the true complexity of the cardinal issues.

When Mrinalini was young, women from "good families" were discouraged from dancing. Nor were the classical dance forms geared toward contemporary concerns. Departure from tradition was considered a dilution of the art's "purity". Mrinalini single-handedly charged that citadel.

India

Tripurari Sharma

Alarippu
National School of Drama

Tripurari Sharma (born 1956) initially chose theater as a means of expression to shrug off middle-class conventions and to seek an identity. It did not take her long to realize that it was more than that: it was an intimate way of revealing and connecting with the lives of women audiences and sharing their perspective with the world. Evolving a play through collective interaction has helped bring theater out of closed spaces, and into the lives of Indian women.

Tripurari Sharma has been at the forefront of theater-based activism in India. She graduated in English literature from Miranda House College, Delhi University, in 1976, and the National School of Drama in 1979. Those were years after the draconian emergency, when dissent had been ruthlessly suppressed. Tripurari saw theater as a means to share and talk about the lives of women. Her travels across the country, performing plays, conducting workshops, and working in close conjunction with the local people helped concretize her approach — to evolve plays collectively. Her attitude to the issues of peace, women's rights, human rights, and the right to information have helped break the traditional barrier between high art and grassroots communication. Her work with traditional theater — and her attempt to carve space for contemporary issues in it — is remarkable.

In 1983, Tripurari set up Alarippu, an organizational platform for her work and for the people associated with it. Alarippu and Tripurari have also been associated with the Mazdoor Kisan Shakti Sangathan (laborers' and farmers' power collective), and its campaign on the right to information, from the very beginning. They toured villages in Rajasthan, devising and performing plays, the impact of which was tremendous in terms of consciousness-raising, and pressuring the government to enact the Right to Information Act.

Beside the severe financial constraints with which she worked, she also found that her group was resistant to her method of collectively evolving a play. Moreover, there was no space where women could show their work. While it was not easy to keep the process going, and growing, Tripurari's conviction won the day.

Many women in India do not have an available platform to creatively express themselves. In the mid to late 1970s, socially relevant theater and the women's movement began to herald the way forward. A number of previously locked issues found expression and acceptance through theater.

India

"I found a gold mine in the hearts of the Japanese people."

Yukika Sohma

Association for Aid and Relief
Japan — The Republic of Korea Women's Friendship Association
Ozaki Memorial Foundation

Yukika Sohma, known for her power to mobilize the moral and spiritual strength of the citizens of Japan, founded the country's first nongovernment relief organization to aid refugees. The daughter of Yukio Ozaki, the father of Japanese parliamentary democracy, Yukika called upon each citizen of Japan to give one yen to help Indochinese refugees in the late 1970s, thus beginning her life's work. Today called the Association for Aid and Relief, her organization was largely responsible for the Japanese government's decision to sign the international treaty to ban landmines.

The Japanese are cold and uncaring. That was the reputation they had gained in the late 1970s, but growing up, Yukika Sohma watched her parents model a behavior that was anything but cold. Her father, who served in the Japanese Parliament for 63 years (a world record for parliamentary service), spent a lifetime opposing war. As mayor of Tokyo, he presented Washington D.C. with its cherry trees, as a gesture of gratitude to President Roosevelt, who had initiated the peace talks that ended the Russo-Japanese War. But at a time when refugees were pouring out of Cambodia, Yukika knew that her country was doing nothing to help.

With faith that Japanese needed only to be asked to show that they had big hearts, she asked. "If every Japanese gives one yen we will have 120 million yen, over one million US dollars," she said. Money and checks poured in, and in less than four months she had reached her target. And so was born Japan's first private refugee relief organization, the Association to Aid Indochinese Refugees. Yukika continued to ask, and the Japanese continued to give. When she found that Cambodian refugees needed housing, she launched a second appeal with the theme: "Don't you want a second house-in Cambodia?" When a period of intense cold hit Southeast Asia, she asked for 1000 tons of clothing. She broadened the scope of the organization, changing its name in 1984 to Association for Aid and Relief. She ignited a spirit of altruism that resulted in worldwide efforts, particularly in Africa. Her organization built libraries, dug wells, and initiated campaigns to buy blankets and send milk and water. In 1991, the fall of the Soviet Union created a new flow of refugees, and she mobilized volunteers to work in Croatia, Serbia-Montenegro, Bosnia-Herzegovina, and Macedonia to give medical aid, mental care, artificial limbs, and wheelchairs.

When Yukika first asked people to help those in need, the spirit of altruism in her country needed awakening. "The concept of social welfare and voluntary service is relatively new in a society where the welfare of each family member is the responsibility of the head of the family," she explains.

"The economic promotion of women is one of the fundamental ways of giving women a sense of dignity."

Cissé Hadja Mariama Sow

Union des Femmes Oulémas de Guinée (UFOG)
West Africa Network for Peacebuilding (WANEP)

Cissé Hadja Mariama Sow was born in Guinea and is a national of that country today. She is president of the Union of Oulémas Women of Guinea (UFOG) and has had a brilliant political and professional career. Madame Sow was born into a large Peuhl family in the region of Labé in Guinea. She is married and is the mother of eight children.

Cissé Hadja Mariama Sow has worked for women's causes for more than 50 years and has never given up work despite her advanced age since, according to her, there are always challenges and it is necessary to confront them. She favors the training and education of women so that they learn to defend their rights as wives and mothers. Therefore, she encourages mobilizing and creating awareness among women through women's associations in Guinean civil society. The success of her work can be measured by how she propelled Guinean women into an African women's movement. The fight of Guinean women under the first president after Guinea's independence (1958 — 1984) was so well conducted that she served as a reference for women of other African, especially French-speaking, countries.

The president of the Union of the Oulémas Women of Guinea (UFOG) and of the Coordination Office of the Associations of the Muslim Women of Guinea, she tirelessly works for religious participation and for the creation of an interreligious space. She campaigns for the unification and consolidation of peace in the region of the River Mano. Her association's goal is to promote this Muslim religion in the country while fighting against religious fanaticism.

Cissé Hadja Mariama Sow has campaigned a great deal in youth organizations, particularly in the Youth for a Democratic African Gathering (RDA) and in the Organisation of Guinea Workers' Unions. She was elected as general secretary of the Union of Revolutionary Women of Guinea. In 1972, she was elected representative to the National Assembly where she remained for 12 years. She was the first president of the Association of Women of West Africa (AFAO) reflecting on the concept of western Africa under the aegis of Economic Community of West African States (ECOWAS).

Cissé Hadja Mariama Sow was at the forefront of the women's movement in her country and worked tirelessly so that Guinean women became aware that their rights are equal to those of men.

Susan Sygall

Mobility International USA (Miusa)
National Clearinghouse on Disability and Exchanges
Disabled Women's Coalition

Susan Sygall is an internationally recognized expert in leadership programs and international educational exchange for persons with disabilities, with a particular emphasis on women. From her wheelchair, Susan inspires people to achieve more than they — and society — thought possible. She has changed the lives of countless women, often in the most isolated parts of the world. She cofounded Disabled Women's Coalition, the Berkeley Outreach Recreation Program, and Mobility International USA, where she serves as executive director.

Susan was studying at the University of Queensland in Brisbane, Australia, on a Rotary International scholarship, when two thoughts occurred to her: first, that the international exchange was a life-changing event, and second that people with disabilities were usually not part of such programs. She knew that she had the power to change things. While completing her master's degree in therapeutic recreation at the University of Oregon, she cofounded Mobility International USA (Miusa). Miusa first hosted an international work camp to build an accessible trail system and camp outside Eugene, Oregon. Today, 24 years later, the organization has worked with 80 countries and has provided exchange programs for more than 2000 people with disabilities. Miusa has hosted exchange programs with Japan, Mexico, Costa Rica, England, Uzbekistan, Vietnam, and others.

When Susan tackles a project, boundaries disappear. Her spirit of adventure has taken her backpacking through Europe and Israel, hitchhiking through New Zealand, and riding local buses through Mexico, Guatemala, Indonesia, and Thailand. The special focus of her passion is women with disabilities; she cofounded The Disabled Women's Coalition and spearheaded the 1995 International Symposium on Women with Disabilities in Beijing, the 1997 Women's Institute on Leadership and Disability, and the 1998 International Symposium on Microcredit for Women with Disabilities. Everyone benefits when people with disabilities are empowered. The beneficiaries of Susan's work include government officials, teachers, youth, families, and policy makers.

As a woman with a disability, Susan's challenge has been to confront preconceived notions of what people, especially women, can do. She works with organizations such as the American Friends Service Committee to include people with disabilities when rebuilding war-torn places like Afghanistan and Iraq.

United States of America

Pauline Tangiora

Maori Women's Welfare League
World Forum for Fisher Peoples (WFFP)
Indigenous Initiative for Peace

Pauline Tangiora is a Maori elder from the Rongomaiwahine Tribe on the East Coast of the North Island of Aotearoa. She is the former president and currently vice president of WILPF Aotearoa, the former representative for the World Council for Indigenous Peoples, and a member of the Earth Council. She has represented Aotearoa at many international fora. She says, "My idea of government is that you run a country not with a party stick but with what you really have to offer. People come together with all their skills from whatever background and work for the benefit of the whole community."

"How can you have a just war? War is not just. In 2003, I visited a hospital in Iraq. I saw a young mother with her baby, and two or three children. I put my hand out to her to hold the baby. She gave me the baby; it was very tiny, two weeks old. She told me that, in the first Gulf war, she had been in the south when the Americans dropped their uranium-tipped weapons, and now 11 years on, all her children had been born with leukemia. The two beside her had cancer, the last baby they said would die. Now, there is the extremity of what humanity does to humanity.

But I also know joyful things. At the World Forum of Fisher Peoples in Thailand, we were asked to meet Thai fisher folk on the Malaysian border. They were to be moved out because of government plans to put in a gas or oil plant in the area. I was asked to speak. I told them I understood why they felt bound to their land. When I finished they were so happy: they said that was how they felt, but nobody cared. This was their land, their working life, their spiritual life, their interaction, and connection with people over the border: how could they take up their soul from out of the earth and transplant it somewhere else? So it gave them hope that other people saw it. So what you do in life can give hope.

Prison is a terrible place to go, but it is also a place of hope. This is my 40th year of visiting in a prison. It does not matter if someone in your family has done something, you cannot throw them away. Better they come out knowing you cared enough to visit or write to them every week. A long time ago, I sent a card to a man in prison. Years later, one officer said to me, 'You know this guy, that card you sent him 20 years ago he carries round in a plastic bag in his pocket, and sometimes you see him sit outside and read it.'"

Pauline Tangiora is a New Zealand Maori elder who works in many capacities with her Maori community and with the wider public nationally and internationally. She is heavily involved in advocacy for indigenous people's rights and for peace in the world.

New Zealand

Tran Thu Ha

Hanoi National Conservatory of Music

Born in 1949 to a family with a musical tradition, Tran Thu Ha is not only a famous and talented pianist but also a teacher and administrator. She holds a doctorate in music and has been conferred the titles, "People's Teacher" and "Labor Hero". As Rector of the Hanoi National Conservatory of Music, she has trained several generations of outstanding teachers and pianists and opened up opportunities for cultural exchanges between Vietnam and many countries in the world.

Asked to describe her accomplishments in music, Tran Thu Ha enumerates: gestation, scientific research, teaching and performing. Ever since she was a piano student, Tran Thu Ha has performed all over her country. She has played as a soloist with different symphony orchestras such as the European Orchestra and the Vietnam National Symphony Orchestra, and has worked as a recording artist for programs produced by Voice of Vietnam and Vietnam Television, as well as for classical music tapes and CDs.

Tran Thu Ha was a leading professor of piano when she was named Rector of the Hanoi National Conservatory of Music in 1996. When she took on this position, the facilities at the Conservatory were very poor. It had only a few pianos, so that many students had to share one piano, and teaching materials such as music books, discs, and tapes were rare. Under her able leadership, students began receiving international awards, the Hanoi Philharmonic Orchestra was revived, the Conservatory received applications from students in the region, and visiting professors have come from other countries. And, with international financial assistance, it was able to buy expensive musical instruments. Today, the Hanoi Conservatory is listed as one of the great conservatories in the world, a "model" for regional conservatories. If culture is one of the key fields to open exchange and integration among countries, "People's Teacher" Tran Thu Ha has contributed much to the promotion of cultural exchange and the strengthening of Vietnam's friendship with many countries. Her success can be traced back to her family's deep musical tradition. She is the daughter of "People's Artist" Thai Thi Lien, one of the founders of the Hanoi National Conservatory of Music, and the older sister of "People's Artist" Dang Thai Son, a talented pianist who graduated from the Conservatory.

With Vietnam's economic difficulties, the public paid little attention to the arts. But when Tran Thu Ha was chosen to head the Hanoi National Conservatory of Music, she put Vietnam on the international map as a center for music education.

Adrienne van Melle-Hermans

Vrouwen voor Vrede (Women for Peace)

Adrienne van Melle-Hermans has been tirelessly battling the polarization of her native country for many years. She fights racism, fosters cooperation between religions, and spreads understanding between women of many cultures at many different levels. She has represented Women for Peace at conferences, workshops, and across all media. Adrienne also works extensively at grassroots level, setting up meetings and discussions in homes and community centers, reaching out to those women herself. Although illness curtails some of her activities, her fight goes on.

Adrienne van Melle-Hermans is not sure whether what she does is measurable. She thinks her mission — to raise women's consciousness and change the way that people think — cannot be counted in terms of facts, figures, or statistics. The fruits of her labor are sometimes very, very real. She recalls the time when she, along with the Women for Peace group she helped to set up, was campaigning to set up the institution which eventually became the United Nations International Criminal Tribunal for the Former Yugoslavia in The Hague. The women began a petition and placed an advertisement in the national Dutch newspaper "De Volkskrant." It attracted thousands of signatures, and many, many contributions of money from people throughout the Netherlands. The women took the petition and their plea for a tribunal to the Netherlands parliament building to present it to the Minister of Foreign Affairs. The women told stories of atrocities suffered during the conflict in the Balkans: terrible tales of rape camps and mass killings. Their stories affected this otherwise rather cynical politician so much, that he broke down. "He was there and I was next to him and he started to cry," recalls Adrienne. In fact, Adrienne remembers being astonished at just how generous her fellow country people had been. She says that there was so much money left after the appeal that, in 1994, the group was able to set up a therapy center to help ease the trauma of women and children who had been victims of the Balkan conflict. That therapy center is still running, and is still receiving money from the Dutch government, several hundred euros a month. And if that is not a concrete, measurable result, then what is?

The Balkans are a classic example of ethnic groups who had happily lived side-by-side for years suddenly turning on each other. On a lesser scale, the Netherlands, a country which has always been praised for its tolerance, is now experiencing its own period of ethnic hatred.

Netherlands

Paddy Walker

Pan-Pacific and South East Asia Women's Association (PPSEAWA)

Paddy Walker (87) has been driven all her life by a passion to achieve lasting peace in the world around her. She founded Pacifica (1974) to help Pacific Islander immigrants adjust to life in New Zealand. It was her initiative to develop the PPSEAWA Peace Gardens that have been established in Malaysia, Singapore, Samoa, and the Cook Islands; Fiji's Peace Garden is now being developed. Paddy works tirelessly with youths. Her vision is to generate new ideas about peace.

Paddy Walker's mixed Cook Islander and New Zealander cultural background equipped her with the compassion and knowledge to spend a lifetime building peace and understanding between peoples of different backgrounds and cultures. To help Pacific Islanders make the transition between life in their island communities and life in New Zealand, Paddy founded Pacifica; she was its first president. This organization was supported by the government and became an important and powerful force to bridge the gap between Pacific and New Zealand cultures.

Paddy's ideal world of peace and harmony is reflected in tranquil garden settings. Thus, she was inspired to develop Peace Gardens in PPSEAWA member countries. These have been established in Malaysia, Singapore, Samoa, and Cook Islands; Fiji is developing its Peace Garden now. The gardens represent peace and cooperation between PPSEAWA member countries and provide a tranquil place for visitors to enjoy. They symbolize peace, harmony and understanding in a world too often torn by war and strife.

Paddy actively promotes ideas of peace to adults and young people in the Pacific. This includes a children's program of reading, storytelling and drama as well as learning peace songs Paddy has composed. In her role as Peace Ambassador for PPSEAWA she has developed and promoted a "Design for Young Peace" program for schools in the South Pacific. She has worked on this through addressing school students in Samoa, Fiji, and in her home country of Cook Islands. Paddy's vision and passion remain to generate new ideas about peace — so that young people learn to become bridge builders for a "world fit for children."

In the 1960s, many Pacific Islanders migrated to New Zealand to find work and improve their living standards. The transition from island community life to western city life was difficult for many families. Paddy Walker's Pacifica organization helped them to adjust to their changed lifestyle.

Cook Islands

Rurui Shi

China Buddhist Association
Qintai Home for the Aged

Born in 1967, Shi Rurui is founder of the Buddhist School for Nuns at Pushou Temple, Mount Wutai. She has a strong interest in Buddhist education and the Buddhist religion and has helped repair the Jixiang Primary School so that poor children have a decent environment to study in. Her other projects include improvement of infrastructure in mountainous areas, and providing financial support to people with different abilities. She has helped with the construction of the Qintai Home for the Aged.

A native of Shanxi Province, China, Shi Rurui became a Buddhist nun in 1981 after graduating from Taiyuan Teachers' College. Education has always been close to her heart and she has worked for the education and capacity building of Buddhist nuns. She strongly believes that women have an equal responsibility for building a world in which people live in harmony with each other and with nature. In 1992 Shi Rurui, a disciple of the late Monk Tongyuan, called for donations from the public to build the Buddhist School for Nuns from the ruins of the historic Pushou Temple of Mount Wutai, one of the Holy Mountains of China's Buddhist religion. The school, as part of the now renovated Pushou Temple, has received hundreds of nuns from various parts of the country.

Shi Rurui does not hesitate to strive for what seems impossible. As a nun with little resources, she has helped mobilize nearly one million Yuan to support all kinds of social projects. Among others, the Jixiang kindergarten and primary school in Shanxi's Taiyuan municipality and Wutai county were rebuilt with public donations collected by her, and she personally helped sponsor the educational expenses of three poor children.

Apart from this, Shi Rurui has helped mobilize funding for the construction of a bridge in a village in Northeast Shanxi, thus significantly improving the transportation situation that local villagers have faced for many years.

The problem of the elderly is yet another issue Shi Rurui has taken up by providing financial support to single elderly people in the old revolutionary district west of Mount Taiheng in Shanxi Province. She is now working on the construction of the Qintai Home for the Aged, an establishment that provides care and services to the marginalized single elderly communities. The project has received strong support form local government.

Daisaku Ikeda, a Japanese writer and peace activist, describes this era as one that is "selfish and irresponsible" with the two main issues of the world being war and peace. Affluence in material life and spiritual deprivation is the disease of all societies. It is just such deprivation that Shi Rurui addresses in her work with the poor and Buddhism.

China

Xia Wang

Happy Peasants Cultural Society

Wang Xia, a peasant woman, uses art performance as a means to promote the Party and state policies that defend the rights of peasants. She works to enrich the material and spiritual life of peasants, and foster harmonious village development. The "Happy Peasant Cultural Society," which she set up in 2005, offers many programs and contributes much to the village's cultural development.

Born in 1969, Wang Xia is a peasant woman from Dengfeng City in Henan's central mountain district. She uses literature and art to encourage villagers' participation and to popularize messages from the Party and the state that are beneficial to peasants.

In June 2000, with an initial sponsorship of 2000 yuan as startup capital, she set up the Rainbow Arts Performing Team and directed the jingle, "Family Planning is Good." In 2001, "Mountain Flower," a play based on real-life cases of unequal land distribution and abuse of peasant women, became a great success. It was performed more than 100 times. Wang's works, including "Mountain Flower," "Red Leaves," "The Hope of the Village," and "Calculations of a Young Couple," were turned into a TV series. Among them, "Mountain Flower" is her signature work, the most influential masterpiece.

Wang registered the Happy Peasants Cultural Society in January 2005, with different units, including the promotional unit (the former art performing team), the elderly unit, the health unit (providing health support for women), and the anti-family-violence unit. These touch upon various aspects of village life and as the activities increase there is higher participation. Wang Xia has worked for a long time to mobilize peasants, and through her work she has established the importance of using literature and art to create public awareness.

Since the late 1980s, peasants have been largely marginalized, and the conditions of their lives have not merited much attention. Community life too has fragmented so there are fewer collective activities.

China

Lihua Xie

China's Women's Federation
China Women's Daily
Rural Women Know All magazine

Xie Lihua was born in 1951 in Chanyi County, Shandong Province. She served in the military in 1969. In 1985 she became editor and reporter for China Women's Daily, and eight years later she took over as deputy editor-in-chief. She also founded China's first magazine for rural women. Over the years she has encouraged rural women to write for the magazine and participate in the work of putting it together. She also conducts courses for literacy, micro finance and reproductive health.

In 1993 Xie Lihua founded China's first magazine for rural women, Rural Women Know All. At the same time she developed a series of programs serving rural women that included literacy courses, micro financing and reproductive health. In the twelve years since she founded the magazine, she has encouraged rural women to participate in various aspects of its production. They have been trained to become correspondents, making the magazine one that is truly for rural women and by rural women. They are also centrally involved in the development and implementation of community projects. Because the purpose of Xie's work is to serve rural women, she relates to them as if they were family. No matter what questions or problems they bring up, Xie responds with compassion and patience, and does her best to help them reach a solution. Therefore, rural women do not see Xie as a "city person," but as a family member. Xie may have wavered at times during the past ten years, but she has persisted. "In my adulthood, I have become one of Beijing's residents, but the moment I set foot on the soil of my hometown, hear the rich village sounds and taste the local food, I truly feel that my roots are still deep in the earth of the village." Her work has the support of many people, including Wu Qing, daughter of the famous writer Bing Xin and a delegate to the National People's Congress.

At a time when the issue of women's rights is gaining more and more attention, rural women remain marginalized. Although half of the nation's 800 million peasants are women, this huge community is rarely considered or discussed by the city elite.

China

玫瑰盛開　楊祖珺十五年來時路

楊祖珺／著

Tsu Chuen Yang

Yang Tsu Chuen, assistant professor of Communication in Chinese Culture University, with a Ph.D. in Communication from University of Massachusetts Amherst, has been involved in social movements in Taiwan such as "Sing our own songs" (1977—80), "The Lin Cheng Chieh street swirl" (1986), "Homeward Bound Freely and Fearlessly" of the mainlanders in Taiwan and the overseas Taiwanese dissidents (1987—89), and "The National Committee on Judicial Reforms" (1987—88). She became a political personality in the opposition movement in the 1980s, and published various magazines and books.

In the 1970s, studying in Tanchiang University, Yang Tsu Chuen took part in the folk song movement for cultural reflection. On graduation, she participated in cultural movements, social service, and the opposition movement. She organized the New Voice Integrated Arts Troupe, toured factories, campuses and villages to sing socially conscious songs in dialects and indigenous languages.

Unfortunately, the Nationalist government regarded her as involved in a conspiracy to reveal social evils joining students and workers movements. After that, she gradually became a political personality in the camps of the opposition. In the 1980s, she published "Progress Weekly", translated "The Green Protest", M. Parenti's "Democracy for the Few", joined the movement on the streets, participated in the founding of the Democratic Progressive Party and in election campaigns. During this period, she served as founding member of the DPP and member of its first central committee. She also served as the board chair of Wan Ching Association, initiator and editor of "Spring Wind Monthly", "Progress Weekly", and "Strait Review".

Yang continues to participate in the social movement as an academic scholar. Her writings include "The Roses are Blooming" (1992), "With Love, Dreams, and Hopes" (1993), "The Great Love of Women" (1994), and "Taiwanese Betrayed" (2005).

Taiwan's frustrations in foreign relations in the 1970s caused the young generation to awake, and search for their identity asking "Who am I?" In the social transition, there arose a campus folk song movement by young people in "singing our own songs".

China, Taiwan

Daiyun Yue

Modern Literature and Comparative Literature of Beijing University

Yue Daiyun established the new discipline of comparative literature and comparative culture in the early 1980s when China introduced the household responsibility economic reform. As the world becomes more unstable and the global situation is getting more tense, Yue Daiyun advocates the Chinese philosophy of "cooperation and harmony" as a critique of the increasing unfairness and injustices of globalization, and to protest against unilateralism, wars and violence in the world.

Since adolescence, Professor Yue Daiyun (70) has been a liberal, has cared for grassroots communities and has participated actively in the struggle for social reforms. In the early 1950s she joined the Chinese Language Department at Beijing University as a teacher, being a distinguished young scholar and a founding member and organizer of the Chinese International Youth Peace Alliance. For 23 years she was called a "rightist," and was subjected to various kinds of social injustice and discrimination. Yet, she kept her optimism and proactive spirit, continuing to study foreign languages and show concern for society even while working as a cleaner.

In the early 1980s, Yue Daiyun established the new discipline of comparative literature and comparative culture in Beijing University. Her efforts have led to comparative studies becoming the most vigorous and critical academic discipline in the China of the 1980s. It has been recognized by the State Council as one of the four principle strands of Chinese literature studies. As a result of her endeavors, comparative studies has changed the conservative and closed academic environment. More importantly, the Eurocentric comparative studies scene has been shaken, and a Chinese perspective has now been incorporated. Yue is especially concerned about globalization of economy and technology, and ways in which literature can promote diversification of culture, and communication and understanding of different cultures. She opposes cultural hegemony and annexation.

As the world becomes more unstable and tense, Yue advocates the Chinese philosophy of "cooperation and harmony" as a critique of increasing injustices of globalization, and to protest against unilateralism, wars and violence.

Professor Yue Daiyun established the new discipline of comparative literature and comparative culture in the early 1980s when China introduced the household responsibility economic reform. As conservatism prevailed in those days, Yue has had to face tremendous resistance and pressure.

China

Ling Zhao

Peasants' Children — China Rural Development and Promotion Association, Beijing Normal University

Zhao Ling was born in 1980 and is now president of the Peasants' Children — China Rural Development and Promotion Association in Beijing Normal University. For many years she has been concerned about the education of migrant workers' children. She organizes educational activities for these children, and conducts surveys of college students aimed at supporting peasants. Her actions inspire many college students to be concerned about agriculture, rural areas and peasants, as well as the conditions of migrant workers from the countryside. Such activities have now spread throughout the country.

Like many children born in the 1980s, Zhao Ling spent her childhood and adolescence with few worries about things like food or clothes, and knowing nothing about crops. She was an only child, and spent her time learning and studying.

Zhao's life began to change after she joined college. She participated in the "inquiry on the oral history of the changes in rural society of southern Jiangsu Privince" project in Nanquan County, Wuxi City, Jiangsu Province. When peasants, poverty, and suffering entered her worldview, her innocence came to an end. Ever since then she has looked for every chance to participate in activities that relate to realities on the ground. In 2001, as an exchange student, she went to Beijing Normal University, where she got to know a students' society called Peasants' Children — China Rural Development and Promotion Association, and to take part in their activities. This made her "experience the genuine homecoming of her own life."

In the countryside she started to love the smell of the soil, as well as the unpretentious feelings of the peasants. She found rural life much more humane and natural than city life. While studying she used her spare time to act as a voluntary teacher in the self-funded school for children of transient migrant workers, and participated in surveys conducted by her college that focused on the situation of peasants in the country.

Zhao and her comrades are clear that their lives will be close to the earth, and that their attention will always be turned to disadvantaged groups.

The generation of urban children born in the 1980s is facing a society in which the craze is for money and commodities. People's lives are increasingly oriented towards the developed Western countries. Most youngsters no longer talk about social responsibility or historical responsibility.

China

Xiaoying Zheng

China's Central Opera Theater

Zheng Xiaoying rebuilt the Central Opera Theater's orchestra from ruin after the Cultural Revolution. She initiated the Music-Loving Women's Orchestra, set up the Xiamen Philharmonic Orchestra and has contributed valuably to promoting the popularization of classical music in China.

Zheng Xiaoying (75) is China's first female opera and symphony orchestra conductor and the first Chinese orchestra conductor to take the international opera stage. She rebuilt the Central Opera Theater's orchestra after China's Cultural Revolution. She has often been invited to give performances on important occasions in the country, and has conducted more than 20 Chinese and foreign operas. Articles on her and her achievements often appear in the media. Zheng has traveled abroad over 30 times to conduct operas or to give lectures. She is the first Chinese conductor that has been invited to conduct well-known operas overseas.

Her achievements on the international stage have changed preconceptions or prejudices about Chinese or oriental women. Since 1978 she has used various means to popularize Chinese and Western classical music. Her direct audience is over 300,000. Come wind or rain, she always reaches the theater one hour before a performance and gives a 20-minute lecture on music knowledge and the theme of the opera music to be performed.

Performance is blended with lectures, and this is known as the Zheng Xiaoying Mode. Over a period of six years in the late 1980s, Zheng led the volunteer group Music-Loving Women's Orchestra to present over 200 performances in schools and factories, which were well received by the public. At the United Nations Fourth World Conference on Women in 1995, she conducted the group's performance of Beethoven's Ode to Joy before tens of thousands of women representatives from all over the world. In 1998, Zheng founded China's first philharmonic orchestra, which is non-government run, the Xiamen Philharmonic Orchestra. It has become the city's pride.

Zheng has made a great contribution to enhancing people's cultural life and the development of orchestras in China.

The Cultural Revolution disrupted music education in China. Superficial music was popular in the post-Cultural Revolution period. Zheng rebuilt the Central Opera Theater's orchestra from ruin, and volunteered to introduce world classical music in various ways in 1978.

China

Guangren Zhou

Zhou Guangren Piano Art Center

Zhou Guangren, one of the most distinguished Chinese women of the 20th century, is a famous pianist, educationist, and music/social activist. She has made a tremendous contribution to the popularization of piano education by promoting piano grade examinations and conducting international competitions in China. She has also systematically introduced Chinese piano works to the world.

Zhou Guangren is professor for life at the China Central Music College. She is the first person in China to have won prizes in international piano competitions. Keen on popularizing the piano, she has founded two amateur youth piano schools. She has promoted piano grade examinations, conducted international competitions in China, and systematically introduced Chinese piano works to the world. She is an excellent disseminator of piano culture and her continuous efforts to promote the piano have left a mark in almost all major cities in China.

In 1980 she was invited to tour the USA and she lectured in 29 universities and staged over 30 performances in as many cities. She is the first person to systematically introduce Chinese piano music and history to the world. Since 1981 she has also served as an adjudicator in over 20 international piano competitions.

In 1982, when she was moving a piano for a concert, she broke three fingers. Although she managed to have the use of her fingers restored after an operation, playing the piano became very painful. In order to play again, she suffered the pain and agony of continuous practice. She also went into teaching piano to teenagers in order to continue her zeal for music.

Zhou Guangren is devoted to the cause of the piano not only for her own sake, but also, ultimately, for the nation as a whole.

Zhou Guangren learnt to play the piano 60 years ago when China was still under the rule of Japanese imperialism. In 1949, when the new People's Republic of China was formed, she started her career as a pianist. In those times playing the piano was considered a luxury and it was not well appreciated.

China

Politics
and Governance

Peter Maurer

–
Q

Wherever global politics are debated today, the multitude of views on how best to promote and secure peace and security is a vivid reminder of the expression that there is no issue more divisive in politics than peace: Should the international community sanction the aggressors or negotiate with them, deal with immediate threats or address the root causes of conflict first, insist on human rights at all times or compromise in order to spare lives in the short term? In responding to such questions, public policies are articulated, instruments and institutions created, norms and laws are decided upon and mechanisms devised. While politics for peace are articulated, some of the challenges unfold:

The struggle for a more integrated approach to peace, security, development, human rights and humanitarian action, while important deficiencies in the international community's response to complex emergencies, from Darfur to the Great Lakes region, from Central Asia to Central America are obvious.

The challenge of establishing multi-track and multi-stakeholder peace processes.

The need to keep humanitarian action distinct from political- and security-driven interventions, as we see the weakness of overarching political logics pay its tribute, resulting in an insufficient distinction between humanitarian and political endeavors and in the questioning of humanitarianism's impartiality.

The importance of gender mainstreaming in peace-building, as we are reminded almost daily that men's wars are not women's wars, and men's peace is not women's peace.

The need to find a better understanding of the role, function and possible cooperation between regional and global actors.

The need to support key areas of post-conflict peace-building more substantively, in particular security sector reform, disarmament, demobilization and reintegration of combatants, as well as the rule of law.

The question of how best to operationalize private-public partnerships and to put them to better use for economic development, peace and human rights.

While the list is growing, so are dilemmas of public policy:

The dilemma of finding an adequate balance between strengthening the state and strengthening civil society.

The dilemmas of rights-based versus needs-based, of conditional versus transformational approaches.

The dilemma of prevention: While preventive approaches are increasingly seen as necessary and useful, they remain difficult to resource and too often lack sustained political support.

The dilemma of regional- or group-specific approaches versus global efforts: How can the international community support specific efforts without undercutting global standards?

The ability to respond creatively to some of the challenges is crucial for the UN and for the strengthening of multilateral approaches to peace-building and peace-making. The international community, as well as the UN system at large, will have a unique opportunity in September 2005 to agree on some important reforms. Broader conceptual agreement on post-conflict peace-building, the responsibility to protect, the use of force, on terrorism and non-proliferation are important foundations for institutional reform such as the creation of a peace-building commission and of a human rights council.

While the international community is busy improving its governance of peace, the main challenges remain at the national level, where agreement on laws and institutions is often difficult. In many countries, though, political consensus emerges that the creation and expansion of a democratic space for politics, transparent law-making and respect for the rule of law, as well as equal and fair access to justice are crucial factors in effective peace-building.

More importantly, bridging the cultural gap between the political worlds of men and women — the transformation of the political space in a gender perspective — is essential. Experience over the past decade has shown that women have specific needs during conflict as they are particularly exposed to the increasingly deliberate targeting of civilians, refugees and internally displaced people and to sexual violence by men, soldiers and even peace-keepers. In this context accountability, zero-tolerance policies and new priorities to prevent and address areas of concern are necessary. Past experiences even more though have shown that women have developed an impressive resistance to violence and violations of fundamental rights and have become formidable agents for peace-building and -making. Those efforts need targeted support and encouragement on a national and inter-governmental level. When men's wars are not women's wars, specific problems must be addressed — when men's peace is not women's peace, women's efforts need more space to develop their full potential.

Peter Maurer, Dr Phil., Ambassador and Permanent Representative of Switzerland to the United Nations in New York. He studied history and international law and has been a member of the Swiss Foreign Service for almost 20 years. In this article, he expresses his personal views and does not engage the Department of Foreign Affairs.

—

Q

Tiba Al Maoli

Omani Parliament
Omani Women's Association

Born in 1963 in Muscat, Oman, Tiba Mohammad Rashed Al Maoli obtained a BA in Arabic and Literature from Beirut University in 1992. She is the first Omani woman to be nominated for the Omani Legislative Council, and has helped to found a women's association that works to educate women in the Seeb area, just outside Muscat. Tiba is known for her commitment to the betterment of her community by advocating justice and equality. But on 13th July 2005 Tiba Al Maoli was sentenced to 18 months' imprisonment by a Lower Court in Muscat in connection with her criticisms of the government.

Tiba Al Maoli is a communications specialist and journalist and has published short stories and poems both in the Omani and Arab press. She began working as an intermediate schoolteacher in 1983, before becoming a broadcaster and program producer in 1986. In 1996 she became a member of the board of directors of the Muscat Association for Childcare and Mentally Disabled Children. In the same year, she was appointed as the Chief Executive Officer (CEO) of the Omani Women's Association.

Since 1994, she has been a member of the Oman Legislative Council for two terms, a position that facilitated her advocacy for free elections. She participated with other members of the Legislative Council in drafting two significant laws in Oman: Silk Alqadi Law and Al Ahwal Al Shakhseyya Law. She has worked to develop cultural, economic and artistic programs and has lectured extensively on gender, politics and pedagogy.

People in the Arab Gulf area, including the Sultanate of Oman, are encountering many societal challenges. They have to work hard for a better future for the new generations, particularly with regard to women's rights. Tiba Al Maoli is an example for this.

Oman

Moza Al-Malki

World Federation for Mental Health (WFMH)
Moza Al-Malki Center for Training and Rehabilitation (MMCTR)

Moza Abdullah Mohammad Al-Malki was born in 1957 in Doha, Qatar. She obtained a BA in Psychology from Beirut University in 1978, an MA from LaVern University, USA, in 1986, a PhD in Clinical Psychology from the University of Abertay, Scotland, in 2000, and she has been an Assistant Professor in the Department of Psychology, Qatar University since 1987. She is the director of the Moza Al-Malki Center for Training and Rehabilitation (MMCTR), and she is also affiliated with the World Federation for Mental Health (WFMH). Moza Al-Malki has several published research papers and books.

In addition to her mother tongue, Arabic, Moza Al-Malki speaks French and English fluently. Moza Al-Malki pursued a teaching career in the Ministry of Education in Qatar from 1974 to 1982. In 1986 she became the Headmistress of the Model Primary School, and in 1992 she was appointed as Head of Programs and Activities in the Qatari Red Crescent Society. Since 1990, she has lectured and run seminars at state-run schools and has written extensively in the Qatari and Gulf press. In 1995, Moza Al-Malki was appointed as the Gulf region's Vice-President of the World Federation for Mental Health (WFMH). In this position she has worked in a variety of voluntary capacities including the Psychiatric Department at the Al Rumailah Hospital. She is an active member of many regional and international committees and she has received many awards for her significant work.

Every day, more official jobs are secured by women in Qatar, thanks to the efforts of women like Princess Moza Al-Malki. Women assume positions of authority, including ministries in the Qatari government, headship of universities and municipal council membership.

Qatar

Zuleika Alembert

Zuleika Alembert (1922) started her political militancy fighting against the dictatorship of Getúlio Vargas during the Estado Novo (1937—1945), the New State — second phase of Vargas' first government. She was elected constituent deputy for the state of São Paulo, affiliated to the Communist Party of Brazil. She fought for the formulation of a specific public policy for women. She was one of the founders of the State Council for the Female Condition in São Paulo. Since 1992, she supports ecofeminism.

At age 83, living alone in Rio, Zuleika Alembert is a woman that exhales physical strength and, above all, an impressive intellectual knowledge when it comes to defending the union between the preservation of the environment and gender equality. As a congresswoman, she defended the Christmas bonus that led to the 13th salary benefit. As a militant of the Communist Party in the 1940s, she began supporting the incorporation of gender matters to the Marxist battle. For many years, she considered herself a "Marxist that used to study women's problems." In 1980, she accepted a feminist identity inside the party and, three years later, when she left the party, she dedicated herself exclusively to the cause.

Her militancy as a communist began when she was a congresswoman in the 1940s. She lost the right to fulfill her term of office when the Communist Party was classified as illegal. Between 1951 and 1954, she was the general-secretary of the Communist Youth. Ten years later, the military coup persecuted her and so she carried on her mission illegally. Exiled, she militated against the Vietnam War, helped other Brazilians that had been exiled and was one of the creators of the Committee of Brazilian Women Living Abroad — to help refugees that arrived in Paris, running from the military coup that brought down Salvador Allende from the presidency of Chile.

Author of eight books, she has just published a collection of articles called 'Women in History — The History of Women.' Zuleika sustains that, in the search for gender equality, democracy is a fundamental aspect. "As long as, in Brazilian politics, only 10% of the elective positions are occupied by women, we will not be able to say that democracy is a reality."

The joining of the political, economical and environmental aspects with equality of gender is a reality in many countries, including Brazil. During ECO-92, women were put in charge of the task of promoting, in Rio, Female Planet, a pioneer initiative in uniting both fields.

Brazil

Dametken Alenova

Birlik

Dametken Alenova is the leader of the NGO Birlik ("unity"), which promotes democratization and the development of civil society in Kazakhstan. Despite her own persecution by state authorities, Dametken has fought to help the poor and struggled against governmental corruption. Her work has no doubt improved the situation in the country.

Born in Russia in 1948, Dametken Alenova has been a professor of biotechnology since 1983, publishing over 60 scientific works. She has been credited with several inventions. She entered into business during the Perestroika period, when teachers' work was devalued and research no longer funded, subsequently founding her first NGO to help small businesses and entering politics. She has written numerous articles about governmental corruption and has run for public office.

Despite the fact that she and her family have been persecuted by state authorities, she has persistently worked for democratization. Her struggle against corruption via mass media publications has had considerable public resonance. As a result of her work corruption has become less pervasive. The tax and customs legal framework has been revised. Small business taxation has become less subjective. Public leaders have raised their profiles in dealing with social issues.

Birlik fights poverty and economic and social injustice and seeks to consolidate NGOs in pursuit of their common goal: to establish a civil society in Kazakhstan.

The authorities of Kazakhstan persecute those who stand in opposition to them. A member of the opposition can be placed under constant surveillance by the government. Corruption of local officials is the main obstacle faced by small business owners.

Kazakhstan

Hanan Ashrawi

Miftah Palestinian Liberation Committee (MPLC)
Women for Peace and Justice in Palestine (WPJP)
National Reform Committee (NRC)

Hanan Ashrawi was born in 1946 in Nablus in an Anglican Christian family; her father had settled the family in Ramallah after the 1948 war. She completed her BA in English Literature at the American University in Beirut (AUB) and her PhD in Medieval Literature at the University of Virginia in 1971. From 1974—1995 she was a professor of English literature at Birzeit University (BZU), where she established BZU's legal aid committee and became Dean of the Faculty of Arts (1986—1990). Hanan Ashrawi is a member of the Palestinian Legislative Council and a human rights activist.

Hanan Ashrawi has played an efficient role in representing the Palestinians in the peace negotiations from the late 1980s onwards, when the Palestinian Liberation Organization (PLO) members were debarred from the talks. She was part of the advisory council and spokeswoman for the Palestinian delegation at the Madrid peace talks in 1991, though she voiced reservations about some of the Palestinian leadership's standpoints. Hanan wanted to resign from the participating Palestinian delegation during the Oslo Accords in 1993, but she was urged to continue the talks with the Palestinian negotiating team. However, her discontent with the negotiations finally made her withdraw from the team at the end of 1993. She formed the Miftah movement, a pro-democracy NGO, of which she remains the Secretary General.

Between 1996 and 1998, Hanan Ashrawi was the Palestinian Authority Minister for Higher Education, before leaving to vote against the Palestinian Authority Cabinet (PAC) in 1998, despite being offered the tourism portfolio. Appointed as spokeswomen of the Arab League in 2001, with special emphasis on the Palestinian issues, she was a signatory to the 2002 statement in al-Quds, that appealed for an end to the suicide bombings.

Hanan Ashrawi lives with her family — she was married to a photographer in 1975 and has two daughters and one grandchild — in her home opposite the "Muqaata" (the Presidential Residence) compound in Ramallah. She is the author of several poems, short stories, articles and books on Palestinian culture and politics and became a symbol of Palestinian national identity after appearing on American ABC-TV's Night Line in 1988. Thanks to her political savvy and eloquence that debunked the "negative stereotypes of Palestinians", Hanan Ashrawi became a familiar face in the international media.

Palestinians have always needed subtle, skilful individuals to represent them internationally, particularly in the media. Dr Hanan Ashrawi has managed to debunk the negative stereotypes about Palestinian representation and to show the world the true face of the Palestinian negotiator.

Occupied Palestinian Territory

"We are all warriors in our own small orbits and these efforts will lead us toward a society free of religious obstacles, bring freedom from hunger, and end all kinds of discrimination."

Shirin Banu

Prip Trust

Shirin Banu (born 1951) has blended very effectively her experience in politics and with the women's movement in her work on the empowerment of grassroots-level women leaders. She has motivated women leaders of the Union Parishad (grassroots legislative unit) to coalesce into an elected women's forum that can collectively bargain to assert their rights and powers. She has also worked to create local women's groups to unite women in rural Bangladesh against fundamentalism.

Shirin Banu comes from a liberal, politically active background. Both her parents were active members of the communist party. Her mother was the first female whip of the parliamentary party and the first general secretary of the Mahila Awami League. It obviously led to Shirin being politically active from her student days.

One of the country's best-known freedom-fighters, Shirin was perturbed that women were denied the opportunity to fight on the frontlines. Therefore, she disguised herself as a man and joined the war, living daily with the fear of being unmasked. Postwar reality was a big disappointment. Bangladesh's secular constitution was replaced by an Islamic one and the people did not, Shirin says, "get freedom of religion, freedom from hunger, or freedom from discrimination."

Shirin's work with the women's development program of the Bangladesh Academy for Rural Development set the course for her life's work. The spirit of the women in rural Bangladesh stirred her, leaving a lasting impression. Around 1998, she joined the Prip Trust. She now works with women leaders in rural Bangladesh, her most remarkable achievement being the setting up of a forum of elected women in the Union Parishad (Bangladesh's smallest legislative unit), who would work together to assert their inalienable rights and power.

Predictably, Shirin faced raucous opposition from fundamentalist groups. But she knew that if the community stood together and raised its voice, it would stymie the fundamentalists. It was to this end that she created several local women's organizations. "We are all warriors in our own small orbits and these small efforts will lead us toward a society free of religious obstacles, bring freedom from hunger, and end all kinds of discrimination," she says.

Women's groups in Bangladesh are fighting for women's right to direct election to parliament, which has the ruling party nominating women to it. In 1998, the government passed a bill that gave village women the right to contest in direct elections at the local-government level.

Bangladesh

Togo Mariam Baro

Jigisèmè
Association des Municipalités du Mali (AMM)

Born in Gapes, an area of the Mopti region, in 1958, Togo Mariam Baro climbed the local ladder to get to the post of magistrate and mayor of the community of Gapes. She came to this position because of her activities as president of the association Jigisèmè, a popular women's organisation in Gapes. Jigisèmè means to rediscover hope. She is also second communication secretary of the Association of Municipalities of Mali (AMM).

After her basic studies at the school of Bankass (1965–1976), Madame Togo Mariam Baro went to Bamako for secondary school studies at the Sankoré High School (1976–1978), then to the professional school Course Pigiers (1978–1980). In November 1995, she did a course on dyeing, ointments, and soap making in Diallassagou. In March 1997, the courageous Mariam Baro participated in a seminar on the charter, the Mali constitution and the electoral law organized by the Commission on Promoting Women in Bankass. In August 1999, she took part in a workshop on the better management of resources of the Diankoumera forest in Bamako, held by Aves and the Food and Agricultural Organisation. In 2000, Madam Mayor held a special forum on the question of community organized by Fenu and Packob. These forums presented an opportunity to better equip herself to manage the Gapes community. The positive efforts of this management were noted by Malians. This lady, who is moving in a wheelchair, never failed in her duties as local women's association president or as community Mayor. As if that was not enough, during the past five years she has taken part in about 30 seminars and workshops. The organizers of these different fora wanted to take advantage of Mariam's experience to encourage other mayors to do the same in the management of their respective communities. During all her professional life, Mariam Baro worked on a supportive approach to the development process, the promotion of women, and the fight against illegal trade in children.

Togo Mariam Baro is active in the association Jigisèmè and has spent five years in community management as the mayor of Gapes. She is very self-disciplined and always arrives on time in the general assemblies and other meetings.

Jurema Batista

Asamblea Legislativa de Río de Janeiro

Jurema Batista (1947) carried out three mandates as town councilor (Labor Party). Her electoral base is in Morro do Andaraí, Rio, where she was raised. She is a Brazilian Literature professor, and her first activity was teaching needy children. She is a member of the slum movement, the Afro-Brazilian movement, the women's movement, and she is currently a state representative and president of the Commission for the Fight against Discrimination and Prejudice based on Race, Color, Ethnicity, Religion and Nationality.

In tiny maid's rooms at the back of their houses, that is where middle-class families keep everything they do not want anymore, including old books and magazines. These leftovers nourished little Jurema's interest in reading. She used to sleep with her mom at the house where she worked and would only go back to the slum in Andaraí on the weekends. It was then that she encountered the first of her passions: Brazilian literature — which led her to university where she got a degree in Arts.

The experience of living in the house where her mother worked and in the slum at Andaraí gave Jurema the consciousness of the difference between the rich and the poor. "I grew up with these two separate views of the world, and this is the source of my will to fight for change," she says. This feeling grew stronger in the 1980s, when a worker was assassinated during a police invasion in the slum. After this episode, Jurema founded the first association of residents of a poor community. She sued the police officer and he was convicted for murder.

During the trial, she became aware of the racism problem in Brazil. She quickly moved on to the Afro-Brazilian movement. She also found out that there was an even more excluded category: women. In 1985, she founded the Nizinga Collective of Afro-Brazilian Women. Jurema Batista run for town councilor in 1992 and was elected with 5000 votes, which were in large part from the people of Andaraí, where she still lives. She moved from the slum to the neighborhood, but she did not go very far from her origins. She has three daughters and one granddaughter. Jurema is proud of having given her girls the opportunity to go to university. "It was a personal victory."

Jurema Batista was able to conclude her studies at university, in a country where 17 percent of the Afro-Brazilian population is illiterate. Her oldest daughter already has a degree in law, the second one studies journalism and the youngest is attending university to receive a degree in history.

Brazil

Nino Burjanadze

Parliament of Georgia

Nino Burjanadze is the Speaker of the Parliament of Georgia. A well-known scholar, lawyer, and human rights protector, she was the first woman in Georgia to become a speaker of parliament. For many years before that, she led human rights and law commissions at the national and international level. Nino Burjanadze is famous as a leader and an example of peaceful conflict resolution during the Rose Revolution in 2003, the most important moment in developing and modernizing Georgia.

Nino Burjanadze believes that she has to use her capabilities to contribute to building a better future for Georgia, to resolve the problems Georgia is now facing, and to create the maximum of possibilities for the realization of the Georgian people's and each person's potential. She wants to contribute to building a strong and united Georgian state, with the true values of justice and rule of law.

She remembers the significant moment when she participated in her country's greatest change in recent history. "One of the most remarkable and unforgettable episodes of my life, perhaps, will be the memory of our entry into the building of Parliament during the Rose Revolution, where the representatives of the government party were declaring themselves winners of the rigged elections of 2 November 2003 and preparing for the plenary session. It was a crossroads between the old and the new. It was the end of the past, of the economically weak and disintegrated Georgia and the starting point for building a strong, united, and European country. The drive, motivation, unanimity, and determination of thousands of people participating in the meeting was really astonishing and amazing."

After the Rose Revolution Nino assumed the presidency until new elections could be held. In 2004, she was elected as a Speaker of the Parliament. She has always worked for democratic reforms and for Georgia becoming a part of the European Union. She considers serving people a privilege that one should deserve. "Parliament should always be a representative body; we must always keep in mind and understand that we represent tens of thousands of people, who have trusted in us," Nino Burjanadze says.

Georgia is a multi-ethnic state that has suffered from ethnic tensions and conflicts. After the collapse of the Soviet Union, Georgia was an unstable country with a bureaucratic government. In 2003, the peaceful Rose Revolution paved the way for building a democratic society.

Tatiana Chertoritskaya

Sotsyal-Democratichiesky Kongress Zhenshchin (Sdkz)
Institute of Social Sciences
Russian Union of Writers

Tatiana Chertoritskaya was born 1948. She holds a PhD in philology and is both a well-known scientist and a specialist in the traditions of the Old Believers (a schismatic group of the Russian Orthodox Church). She is deputy of the Russian State Duma, and has worked in various federal bodies. In 2002 she founded and headed the women's NGO Sotsyal-Democratichiesky Kongress Zhenshchin (Sdkz) ("Women's Social-Democratic Congress"), which now has 55 regional offices. Tatiana focuses her efforts on fighting for gender equality, peace, and building civil society.

In 1974 Tatiana set off on her first scientific expedition to the Altai Mountains in order to study remote rural communities that were still observing the traditions of the breakaway Orthodox group, the Old Believers. She saw astonishing poverty and destitution in the mountain villages, where communist authorities, in their fight against religion, had even confiscated the ancient icons and prayer books that had been treasured by the inhabitants for ages. Yet the people had remained kind-hearted and hospitable. She remembers the words of one of the local elders: "If you don't lose yourself, you'll find everything." These words remain engraved in Tatiana's memory. She has always tried not to lose herself.

In October and November 1993, for the first time in her life, Tatiana saw fierce clashes and blood in the streets of Moscow, when the Russian parliament was taken by force by presidential troops. Tatiana was deeply convinced that only peaceful measures should have been used to resolve the conflict. It also became clear to her then that she too, as a woman, publicist, lecturer and historian, should join the ranks of peace advocates.

In 1994 Tatiana, herself a deputy of the State Duma of the Russian Federation, learnt from a radio news report about the invasion of Russian troops in Chechnya. The women deputies were unanimous in their opposition, but there were too few of them in positions of power. It was then that Tatiana asked: "Why are resolutions in favor of peace, so very obvious for every mother, not adopted by the majority power-wielding men? How can a balance of forces be achieved?"

Since then Tatiana has been actively fighting to stop the bloodshed in Chechnya, realizing the crucial role to be played by women in finding peaceful solutions to armed conflicts.

Heading the women's NGO Sdkz, which now includes a network of 55 regional offices, Tatiana steers projects aimed at promoting women's rights, peace-keeping, improving living standards, and achieving an open dialogue between the authorities and society.

Russian Federation

Luci Teresinha Choinacki

Câmara dos Deputados (Chamber of Deputies)

For being a peasant, poor, and not having a diploma, Luci Teresinha Choinacki (born 1954) faced all kinds of prejudice when she was elected State Representative, in 1986, for the state of Santa Catarina. Four years later, she got to Brasilia. As a Federal Representative on her third mandate, Luci fights for women's rights and for the land reform. She was able to obtain retirement rights and the right to maternity leave for the female peasants.

Women from all over Brazil, wearing straw hats and slippers, entered the Representative Council in Brasilia. Luci Teresinha Choinacki, the Federal Representative, whose white skin is marked by the sun from her childhood years working the land, remembers the unforeseen moment, in 1992. The peasants pressured the government to approve their right to retirement. "For the first time, rural women entered the plenary assembly, to demand their rights."

First born in a family of small agriculturists of Polish descent, Luci was born in Descanso, a city in the countryside of Santa Catarina, and had to drop out of school when she was 12. Her mother was sick and her father went bankrupt, so they were not able to take care of their other six children. She got married when she was 17. Soon, the first of her four children was born. Her political militancy only began years later in the progressive movements of the Catholic church. Luci was also involved in the Movement of Female Peasants, which gained strength in the beginning of the 1980s. As a coordinator, she used to travel to cities mobilizing peasants. "We were building our fighting banner: stimulation of syndicalism, documentation, retirement, maternity salary and political participation." She helped to structure the Partido dos Trabalhadores (Labor Party), in which she became an executive secretary. In 1986, she was elected State Representative. "I had no knowledge of the power mechanism, but I had within me the fight of the poor and of the oppressed women." In 1990, she was elected Federal Representative. From then on, the peasants had a representative in Brasilia and they were able to achieve the right to maternity salary and retirement. Re-elected for the third time in 2002, Luci Teresinha Choinacki took on another battle: to conquest the right to retirement pay for housewives over 60.

According to the report about the Feminization of Poverty, elaborated by Luci Teresinha Choinacki, in 2004, the government is lacking structural policies that provide women with their autonomy and economical emancipation (day care for children, professionalizing courses, land reform).

Benedita da Silva

Partido dos Trabalhadores (PT)

Benedita da Silva (1942) began her political career in the 1980s with the foundation and presidency of the Association of Women from Chapéu Mangueira, a slum in Rio, where she was born and lived for 57 years. She was elected town councilor once and federal deputy twice. She was the first woman to be elected for the senate (1994) and the first woman to govern the state of Rio. She occupied the Ministry of Social Assistance for one year.

Daughter of a laundress and of a peasant, raised with 14 siblings, Benedita da Silva was the only one in her family to obtain a university degree. Her mother was a midwife in the community, and she was the inspiration for Benedita's work as nursing assistant. She was able to conclude a course on social service in 1982, the same year she was elected for her first political term as a town councilor.

Her trajectory is marked by sexual abuse, which she suffered in her childhood; by the loss of a son, who died of starvation; and by the desire to have a different life. Several times, Benedita had to collect left-over food from the trash to feed her family. Until she began her political mobilization, she was always a quiet woman. "Just like many other thousands of Afro-Brazilian women who live oppressed by poverty and by the lack of an active voice in society." Her community work privileged Afro-Brazilian women who did not have the right to vote in community meetings. Benedita founded and became president of the Association of Women from Chapéu Mangueira, an organization that established a pioneer dialogue between women from the slum and middle-class feminist institutions.

Benedita's mother ironed clothes for a living and was hired by the Kubitschek family when Juscelino Kubitschek was running for president in the 1950s. Benedita was a girl who delivered the clothes to the house of the Kubitschek family. Elected for her first term as a federal deputy in 1986, she occupied the Deputies' Chamber along with Marcia Kubitschek, daughter of Juscelino. Married, mother of two and grandmother of four, her political career is marked by the defense of women's and Afro-Brazilian's causes. Today she dedicates herself fulltime to the Benedita da Silva Foundation that assists the poor and Afro-Brazilians.

Benedita da Silva is responsible for bills such as the one that recognizes Afro-Brazilian leader Zumbi de Palmares as a national hero and also the one that guarantees labor rights for domestic workers, a field of work occupied mostly by Afro-Brazilians.

Brazil

Maria de Jesus Haller

Movimento Popular de Libertação de Angola (Mpla)
Union of Angolan Writers

The first woman ambassador from Angola, Maria de Jesus Haller, was born in 1923 to a 12-year-old Angolan mother. Her father, the Portuguese owner of the plantation, sent her to Portugal at the age of three. Twelve years later a short-lived but decisive reunion with her mother provided the incentive for her political commitment. She became a teacher, then a journalist fighting racism and discrimination. Her years of activism in the Angolan liberation movement earned her the post of ambassador to Sweden, soon after her country's independence.

Angolan political activist Maria de Jesus Haller is a slight and soft-mannered woman. But when she speaks, everybody listens. In fact, in 1974 whilst attending a United Nations conference in Hungary she interrupted the conference and asked the permission to have the floor. She was then the representative of the Mpla, the Popular Movement for the Liberation of Angola, dedicated to freeing Angola from Portuguese domination. At the time, however, liberation movements such as the Mpla were admitted to United Nations conferences only as observers and could not take an active role in debates. Maria de Jesus Haller changed that. "That was my moment of glory," she says, "all the press was on me. Angola had never been mentioned as much as it was that day."

Today, after two decades of conflict, Angola is finally at peace. The brutal colonial past, however, is not easily forgotten. "The tragedy with colonialism is the question of dignity. We were told we were good for nothing. We longed for dignity, not only bread to feed ourselves."

Maria de Jesus was separated from her mother at the age of three and sent to Portugal for schooling. She returned many years later, an adolescent imbued with European prejudice. "My mother spoke to me in her native tongue and I said I did not speak that dog's language. It is so stupid that one says things one does not feel inside, only repeating what others have said. Then my mother told me that my father had taught me many things, but he had left out the most essential part, which is, this land is ours." And Maria's lifelong commitment began: to tell the world, "this land is ours".

At the age of 80, with five decades of political activism behind her, Maria de Jesus Haller still believes that hope for a better future lies with the people. "What Africa has is the courage of its people, it is extraordinary," she says.

When Maria de Jesus Haller was born, Angola was under Portuguese dominion, and slaves worked the land of the European owners. Angola's independence in 1975 soon gave way to a bloody civil war that lasted two decades.

Angola

Luiza Erundina de Souza

Congresso Nacional

Luiza Erundina de Souza (1934) is one of the female symbols of Brazil's recent political history. She started with the fights of popular classes, became town councilor, mayor, representative and senator. She was one of the founders of the Partido dos Trabalhadores (PT), the Labor Party, which she left in 1996. Her honesty in dealing with public affairs is recognized as an example, even by her opponents.

In 1988, she was running for the position of mayor of the largest city in South America. São Paulo went to sleep as a conservative town and woke up with its first female mayor. Besides being a woman, she belonged to the PT, a left-wing party, and was born in the Northeast, one of the poorest regions of Brazil. The mayor was not inexperienced. She had already been elected town councilor and she had knowledge of the political strength of mobilization and popular participation.

She and her other nine siblings lived, during their childhood, with a dry climate and the drama of rural exodus. As an adult, she arrived in São Paulo and found the people form the Northeast piled up in slums. She graduated to be a social worker, and she did what she knew best: organizing people. As mayor, Luiza Erundina's biggest concern was directed at the most vulnerable population. Not only did she open health centers in the abandoned regions of the city, she also opened a space for discussing health assistance. She not only built schools and day cares, but she also discussed education. Her administration had women playing key roles. Luiza believes that "women have two challenges: to conquer power and to exercise it in a better manner than men do." This powerful woman knows that "power does not belong to the one who exercises it, but to the one that delegates it." She is convinced that democracy lives essentially in the power that emanates from the people.

After conquering city hall (1988–1992), she kept on winning elections. Today, Luiza Erundina de Souza is a Representative for the State of São Paulo, and she continues constructing the dream of a more supportive and fair country. "A dream that is so grand that I cannot dream it alone."

São Paulo is an enormous Latin-American metropolis. Its 11 million inhabitants live with tremendous inequalities of income, goods and services. The richest city in Brazil collects 'islands of excellence' and 'complexes of misery.' It presents more problems than solutions.

Brazil

Sheila Didi

Aruna Asaf Ali Memorial Trust (AAAMT)

Since her childhood, Sheila Didi (born 1928) has been a passionate supporter of causes: first, it was the cause of independence in Kenya, where she grew up; at university, she embraced students' and peace movements; in India, where she has lived for the past 50 years, Sheila has been a driving force in the trade union movement in the northern Indian state of Punjab. She has also fought injustice against women in many forms—at the workplace, as targets of communalism and armed conflict, and as victims of domestic violence.

As a schoolgirl born in Nairobi, Sheila Didi witnessed two independence movements. She participated in rallies in Kenya against apartheid and for independence. At university, in Cardiff, South Wales, where she studied economics, and while training to be a barrister at Lincoln's Inn, she was equally active. When, in 1956, Sheila came to live in India and married a trade union leader, her life changed, but her commitment and involvement in rights movements did not. She worked with her husband to mobilize women workers in the textile industry for better wages and service conditions. Her struggles bore fruit in Ludhiana. Sheila also worked among urban and rural women to make them aware of their rights, mobilizing them through the Punjab Istri Sabha, a branch of the National Federation of Women.

In 1965, Sheila's husband became the general secretary of the Trade Union Congress of Punjab. In 1966, she shifted to Chandigarh, and began to practice as an advocate in the Punjab and Haryana high court. She had three children, all under the age of ten. But Sheila found time to organize a women's movement in the slums of Chandigarh under the guidance of the general secretary of the Punjab Istri Sabha. She became closely involved with the Punjab Istri Sabha Relief Trust, which helped widows and children affected by the now-defunct separatist struggle. As militancy abated, the movement's goals changed to equality, peace, eradication of poverty, democracy, secularism, and social justice.

Sheila is involved with the Aruna Asaf Ali Memorial Trust (AAAMT), which coordinates schemes for the socioeconomic uplift of women, runs schools for street-children, a counseling center for marital and other problems, and conducts workshops for the poor.

The decade-long separatist militancy in Punjab took its toll of everyone, but particularly women and children. Since the struggle's abatement, the goals of the progressives have changed to more generic development.

India

"Never bill for your personal time, and strive to accomplish all you started."

Valentyna Dovzhenko

All-Ukrainian Charity Foundation of Hope and Good Will
Union of Ukrainian Women
Women for the Future

Valentyna Dovzhenko (57) is actively engaged in public service work at national and international levels. Through governmental and non-governmental organizations, she focuses on developing strategies to resolve issues related to protecting the rights of women and children (UN Convention on the Rights of the Child), high risk groups (e.g. HIV/Aids), poverty alleviation, violence and gender discrimination (UN Convention on the Elimination of All Forms of Discrimination against Women), and nonviolent conflict resolution.

Valentyna Dovzhenko works for the rights of women, families, and children in Ukraine and is involved in promoting nonviolent conflict resolution. She has worked in armed conflict areas in Peru and Columbia and participated in negotiations with terrorists during the hostage crisis in the Dubrovka Theatre Center in Moscow. She brought attention to the global and long-term impact of the Chernobyl accident, urging UN member countries to assist Ukraine in implementing a specialized program for the medical rehabilitation and social re-adjustment of children affected by the disaster. Thanks to Valentyna's active involvement on the document's final draft, a provision has been included substantiating the need to protect children from natural and anthropogenic (such as Chernobyl) disasters, as well as the necessity of paying special attention to the needs of children in countries with a transition economy.

She has succeeded in involving the international community in solving the local problems that affect children and women. Valentyna headed the Ukrainian delegation to the 27th Special Session on Children of the UN General Assembly in New York, in May 2002. In her presentation she had the audience focus on a proposal concerning the reduction of global expenses on arms by ten percent in order to steer that volume of funds towards developmental efforts. She never gives up on the idea that the most complicated problems may have simple solutions; the only hard — though not impossible — thing, is just to find them.

Ukraine's 2002 parliamentary elections showed a further dip in the already low number of women in Parliament (only five percent). Among the top levels of ministry and civil service, only two percent are female. Involving women in national policy, planning, and implementation of development programs remains a challenge.

Ukraine

Elena Ershova

Konsortsyum zhenskikh nepravitielstvennykh assotsyatsyi (Consortium of Women's Non-governmental Associations)

Elena Ershova, holder of a Master's degree in International Relations and a PhD in History, has for over 20 years been a researcher with the Institute for US and Canada Studies in Moscow. Today she is an active campaigner for peace and women's rights. Closely cooperating with both governmental structures and NGOs, she promotes gender equality and peace. Elena has been working with the US Agency of International Development in the field of gender and development. She has participated in numerous conferences and has published widely on gender issues and on the peace movement.

The experience of studying the antiwar movement in the USA and of engaging in contact with pacifists has had a huge impact on Elena's life. When she left the Institute for US and Canada Studies in 1993, she decided to work freelance and to establish an independent women's organization. She became one of the founders of a movement that advocated for true and genuine equality of opportunity. Soon thereafter, the movement turned into an independent force in Russia with Konsortsyum zhenskikh nepravitielstvennykh assotsyatsyi (Consortium of Women's Non-governmental Associations), Elena's main creation, as one of its major components. Elena's experience has helped her secure grants from the US Agency of International Development (Usaid) to implement her projects. When Elena created the Consortium, she was already a mature woman with established views and solid knowledge. The Consortium eventually turned into a network association with federal status and at present comprises 166 organizations from over 50 regions in the country. All of them are grass-roots initiatives created by women. The Consortium's mode of operation is based on horizontal, rather than vertical, relationships among the organization's members, and functions as a network of equal partners. The Consortium conducts a dialogue with the government on the most acute social problems. Elena views this cooperation with the authorities as a great opportunity to change the rules of the game in society and help overcome multiple barriers in the way of democratization in Russia, including the still remaining practice of discrimination against women. Elena believes that without equal rights for women, it is impossible to change the existing world of violence and social inequality, and make it more humane.

The Consortium, one of whose founders was Elena Ershova, is now a network association with federal status and comprises 166 women's grass-roots organizations that actively promote gender equality and peace, while maintaining a dialog with the Russian government.

Russian Federation

Nilda Estigarribia

Comisión Nacional de Derechos Humanos (Conadeh)

Nilda Estigarribia grew up fighting against the abuses committed by the Paraguayan military dictatorship led by General Alfredo Stroessner (1954—1989). She was part of the only organization for the defense of human rights to exist during that period. She was under observation by the military forces. Several times, she escaped becoming a victim of repression. She was constantly banging on the doors of police stations and jail cells to find and assist torture victims. The Dictatorship ended — but her activism did not. There are still many tasks pending.

Nilda Estigarribia discovered militancy as an adolescent in the Youth Club of a censured political party, during the toughest period of the Paraguayan military dictatorship (1954—1989). She knew then that the fight for social causes and human rights would always be a priority for her.

She was born in the countryside, part of a large middle-class family. She got a medical degree in 1966. As a student, she did her residency in public hospitals, where she was greatly affected by the people she encountered, who were in enormous need. In the meantime, she continued her militancy in the Club Avalón — most of whose members were sympathizers of the Authentic Radical Liberal Party (Plra) or other opponents of the dictatorial government of Alfredo Stroessner. At that time, every meeting ended up being suppressed — and with a number of people being imprisoned and tortured. That was the end for several members of Nilda's club: "I saw how my companions went to jail." She and other female fellows were saved from being captured. "I was in charge of giving direct assistance to the imprisoned, tortured and ill."

The dictatorial regime ended. Nilda kept on being active in the Authentic Radical Liberal Party, and was elected as a member of Parliament for the period of 1993—1998. She presided over the committees for Health and Human Rights and approved policies for social benefit. Nowadays, she is a member of the Comisión Nacional de Derechos Humanos, the Paraguayan National Commission for Human Rights (Conadeh).

With the end of the dictatorship in 1989, the Paraguayan population hoped for a future ruled by justice. But inequalities remained. The poor population continues to suffer under the regime of 'democratic' governments. The intervention of human rights organizations is still urgently necessary.

Maria Domingas Fernandes

Fokupers

Activist, leader, civil servant, and founder of the women's organization, Fokupers, Maria Fernandes began her life's work for human rights and justice for East Timor in high school. She was instrumental in mobilizing the population to vote during the UN-sponsored referendum for independence in 1999 and organized the first National Women's Congress in 2000 that produced a National Platform for Action. She currently serves as the director of the Office for the Promotion of Equality and directly advises the Prime Minister on all issues relating to gender equality.

Maria Fernandes was one of the main women leaders organizing resistance activities against Indonesian occupation of Timor-Leste, after the invasion in 1975. When her child died, as did hundreds of other children, of a suspected overdose administered in the Indonesian campaign to kill off the Timorese people, Maria and her husband sent information to international organizations to highlight the abuses and try to prevent further deaths. When her husband was imprisoned by the Indonesian administration, Maria had to raise and provide for her children alone, but she continued to support the resistance movement against the Indonesian occupation, and more particularly against the abuses women were suffering. She helped set up the Popular Organization of Timorese Women (OPMT) and worked as a civil servant in the Department of Industry and Commerce, a dual role that involved many risks to her personal safety. In 1994, she was arrested by Indonesian soldiers and threatened and intimidated over her resistance activities. In 1997, Maria founded Fokupers and during the UN-sponsored referendum for independence in 1999, was involved in mobilizing the population to vote. As a result, her family had to flee to the hills to escape the systematic campaign of violence by Indonesian and militia forces. But Maria continued to organize assistance for those who were sick and was among the first people to return to Dili to confront the devastation left by the Indonesian campaign. Maria organized the first National Women's Congress in 2000 that produced a National Platform for Action. She stood in the first national elections in 2002 but, despite not winning a seat, she was made Director of the Office for the Promotion of Equality and directly advises the Prime Minister on all gender equality issues.

Indonesia invaded East Timor in 1975 and began a systematic campaign of settler occupation and decimation of the Timorese as a people (more than 200,000 were killed). In 1999, despite more violence, the Timorese voted for independence in a UN-overseen referendum, and achieved it in May 2002.

Timor-Leste

Mrinal Gore

Swadhar
Keshav Gore Smarak Trust (KGST)

Influenced by Mahatma Gandhi's Quit India exhortation as a youngster, Mrinal Gore (born 1928) chucked in a promising career in medicine to devote herself to organizing the poor and the disenfranchised. For more than half a century, she has been involved with a series of organizations and leading protests both on the streets and in the corridors of power, focusing on women's rights, civil rights, communal harmony, and trade union activities.

As a young woman, Mrinal Gore gave up a career in medicine and became a full-timer with the Rashtriya Seva Dal (a wing of the congress party), organizing housewives for sociopolitical work, and later joined the socialist party. In 1950, Mrinal became secretary of the Goregaon Mahila Mandal, working for the uplift of women in the Bombay suburb; the following year, the organization established a family planning center. In 1961, when she was elected to the Bombay Municipal Corporation, Mrinal began the long, arduous struggle to get waterlines and an adequate water quota for the city's thronging poor and lower-middle-class inhabitants. Success took many dry years to arrive. In 1972, Mrinal was elected to the Maharashtra legislative assembly on a socialist party ticket.

Mrinal was instrumental in setting up the Anti-Price Rise Committee in 1972, which had mobilized the largest ever turnout of women since the independence movement. Mrinal, who vehemently protested the then prime minister Indira Gandhi's imposition of the draconian emergency in 1975, was elected to parliament in 1977.

In 1983, Mrinal established Swadhar, a support center for women victims of domestic violence, and the Committee for Action Against Atrocities on Women. The Shramjeevi Mahila Sangh was also established under her leadership, set up expressly for women employees who were not taking part in the activities of the general union. In 1985, when she was elected to the Maharashtra legislative assembly, she continued taking up issues concerning women and other oppressed sections of society. Her most notable legislative action was introducing a bill to prevent sex determination tests that often led to female foeticide. Through a resolution in 1986, the government finally banned these tests.

In post-independence India, the Indian National Congress had the mandate to govern until the first general elections. The socialist party, acidic in its criticism of Nehruvian policies, focused on the rights and political parti-cipation of women, Dalits, workers, and religious minorities.

India

Helena Greco

Movimento Feminino Pela Anistía (Women's Movement for Amnesty)
Grupo Tortura Nunca Mais (Group Torture Never More)

Helena Greco (1916) was one of the founders and also the director of the Women's Movement for Amnesty (MFPA) in Minas Gerais State. This movement helped to bury the Brazilian military dictatorship that began in 1964. Later on, she was elected town councilor of Belo Horizonte City and joined the Group Torture Never More, whose main goal is to denounce and eradicate all forms of torture practiced by the police.

She was 60 years old when, for the first time, she faced the truculence of the police and was sprayed with lachrymatory gases. It happened at a protest against the arrest of students that were contrary to the military dictatorship. From then on, she did not stop. Right after that, she founded and directed the Women's Amnesty Movement, in Minas Gerais State. It was the end of the 1970s, and Helena was fighting for the return of the exiled and for democratic freedom. She suffered threats, risked herself. "They threw a bomb at my house. Luckily, the bomb hit the fence and fell on the sidewalk. It made a big hole."

With a degree in pharmacy and mother of three children, she quickly understood that political participation was the key to defeat dictatorship and to build a real democracy. She stood side by side with those who had no land, no home and no rights. She was opposed to infantile labor and joined feminism. She helped to implant the city's first shelter home for women living in violent situations. In 1982, at age 67, she was elected town councilor representing the Partido dos Trabalhadores (Labor Party), of which she was one of the founders. She did such a great job that she was re-elected. She participated actively in the Group Torture Never More and denounced doctors that were conniving with tortures inflicted by the organs of repression. She also created the First Permanent Human Rights Committee to exist in a municipal chamber.

Today, she is 89 years old and says that "the most important thing is to be ready to do what needs to be done." She is right: much needs to be conquered in order for Brazilians to truly — and not only theoretically — be citizens.

In Brazil, human rights are systematically disrespected. Despite of civil society's undeniable victories for the construction of democracy, "the right to have rights is not still for everyone."

Brazil

Cristina Guseth

Freedom House

Cristina Guseth has been working for human rights and the empowerment of civil society in Romania since 1991. From 1991 to 1997, she worked with the Soros Foundation in Romania in its pioneering work to develop a free press in the country. She helped establish the BBC Radio and TV Journalism School, the only vocational broadcast school in Romania. Cristina Guseth is the director of Freedom House, Romania. In 2004, Freedom House joined the Coalition for a Clean Parliament to inform Romanian citizens and improve accountability of their representatives in Parliament.

Cristina Guseth's family experienced the lack of personal freedom and civic liberties under the communist regime in Romania. Since the political change in 1989, she has taken the opportunity to work in the human rights field, promoting and sustaining democratic values. She has been working to empower Romanian citizens, to raise their awareness about their civic and political rights, and to encourage them to stand up for those rights.

As the director of Freedom House, Cristina Guseth recently received an award for the most important contribution to democracy building, dismantling the communist structures, and the rebirth of hope in Romania. It was awarded by the Timisoara Society, the first significant organization representing Romanian civil society. The Romanian Revolution of 1989 started in Timisoara, and marked the fall of the communist regime — one of the most oppressive dictatorships in southeastern Europe. It marked the turning of Romanian society to democratic and European values. The award was given to Freedom House for being part of the Coalition for a Clean Parliament, a project that started in March 2004, an election year in Romania. The purpose of the Coalition project was to prevent election and re-election of candidates with a record of corruption.

From 1991 to 1997, Cristina Guseth worked for the Soros Foundation for an Open Society and was responsible for many programs and projects in media, public relations, public administration, and civil society education. One of the most important was the establishment of the BBC Radio and TV Journalism School, the only vocational broadcast school in Romania.

Under the totalitarian regime of Ceausescu, there was no freedom of expression or information in Romania. Since the fall of this regime in 1989, civil society and a free press have been developing, but according to Transparency International's yearly reports, Romania has a high level of corruption, especially in the political sphere.

Romania

Ha Thi Kiet

Vietnam Women's Union

In Xuan Quang, a remote village in Tuyen Quang steeped in old customs and male chauvinism, no one thought that Ha Thi Khiet, born in 1950 to the Tay ethnic minority group, would become a high government official known nationally and internationally. She was born to a large, poor family. Growing up with gender bias, Ha Thi Kiet saw that the only way to improve her life was to secure an education. Her activities in public policy, law and development have benefited thousands of people, especially poor women in remote areas, who now have equal opportunity to participate in society.

Ethnic people in Chiem Hoa, a remote district, talk about the "Madame Khiet Bridge". Its real name is Chiem Hoa Bridge, across the Lo River, but since it was built in 1997, the bridge has had a special meaning because it has saved many lives; there had been many accidents each year on the swift-flowing river. Before the bridge was built, local people in Chiem Hoa and other remote regions had few opportunities to study, improve their knowledge, exchange goods and do business because transport was inconvenient. When Ha Thi Khiet became General Secretary of the Tuyen Quang Province Party Committee, the highest leader in the province, she had the bridge built. Since then, the lives of the local people have improved because they no longer have to use boats or ferries to get across.

When Ha Thi Khiet went to Hanoi to take on positions as Deputy in Vietnam's National Assembly, Member of the Party Central Committee of Vietnam, President of the Vietnam Women's Union, and Chair of the National Committee for the Advancement of Women in Vietnam (NCFAW), the local people showed their gratitude and respect by naming the bridge "Madame Khiet Bridge".

In remote and mountainous areas of Vietnam, women suffer serious gender inequality and rarely get the chance to go to school. Meanwhile, at national level, women are overcoming political, economic and social obstacles to advancement in all aspects of their lives.

Viet Nam

Asha Hagi Elmi Amin

Save the Somali Women and Children (Sswc)

Born in 1962 in the Galgaduud region of Somalia, Asha Hagi Elmi had more opportunities than many of her fellow countrywomen. Since the formation of Save the Somali Women and Children (Sswc), Asha Elmi has distinguished herself as a peace activist. She has invested her education and skills to advocate for women's participation in decision-making and to empower women from all walks of life. Asha Elmi has been an important liaison with the Somali peace process teams.

Asha Elmi firmly believes that women's contributions will advance peace and political processes and ensure Somalia's development as a stable, democratic and competitive state. For more than a decade she has devoted herself to advocating for Somali women to exercise their rights in peace negotiation and political decision-making. She has worked incessantly in pursuing viable peace for her country, engendering the peace process and promoting women's rights and living conditions in Somalia. In 1986 she completed an economics degree at the Somalia National University (SNU), and by 1991 she had obtained a master's degree in management and organisational development and another master's in business administration from the United States International University (Usiu) in Nairobi, Kenya. As a student, her leadership skills were visible. She was elected chairperson of the SNU Student Association. As a post-graduate student, she accepted a position in the Somali government's ministry of finance but served only for a short period. Her commitment to peace and gender issues compelled her to move to the non-governmental organizations sector.

In 1992, Asha Elmi, together with a core group of women intellectuals comprising a cross-section of the community, made a commitment that eventually became Save the Somali Women and Children. Ashas vision for Somalia flickered and then flourished despite the constant unaccommodating and indeed hostile conditions. She not only believed that women could contribute to the peace process but that they would be essential to developing a sustainable peace agreement for their country's future. In its early stages Sswc's advocacy program was a cause of annoyance to the warlords.

Somali society is fiercely patriarchal. The gender disparity in the traditional clan system has a negative impact on women's rights, development opportunities, and relations with foreign partners. Female genital mutilation, polygamy and the unequal treatment of women are institutionalized practices.

Somalia

"My idea is to transform
Russia into a new country
of freedom and social
justice, in which human life
is the primary concern
and the supreme value."

Irina Hakamada

Nash Vybor

Irina Hakamada, who was born in 1955, holds a PhD in economics. A well-known politician, in 1997 she headed the Governmental Committee on Small Business Support. Elected to the State Duma, she has been its deputy chairperson since 2000. Irina participated in the work of the UN General Assembly Session in 2002. She is co-chairperson of the Russian Public Council on Education Development and head of the charitable fund "Vale Hospice International." She is now a leader of a new democratic party, Nash Vybor, and focuses her activities on promoting the ideals of civil society in Russia.

In 2004 Irina Hakamada ran for the presidency. This was a time when, after the defeat of all the liberal forces of the country in the parliamentary elections of the previous year, many people were anticipating the decline of democratic values in Russia.

Irina addressed the people with the clear message that they should not be afraid. She recognized it was necessary to admit that Russian democratic politicians had made mistakes, but at the same time stressed that people should not become disillusioned. She called for promoting the ideals of civil society and democracy. She endorsed the creation of a new democratic party capable of opposing the autocratic tendencies in the country. The party was based on a grassroots movement with a special phone center where citizens could express their views on Russian society's most urgent and serious problems. The project was called "Modern Power for Modern People." An analysis of the information obtained provided input for the Nash Vybor ("Our Choice") party program, which aimed at formulating a model for Russia's future development.

The project proved that all the old myths about Russian society being conservative, non-progressive, and Byzantine did not correspond to reality. The new generation of Russians wants to live in a free society with opportunities for personal and professional development. That is why Irina's platform to transform Russia into a modern democratic society is based not on trying to change the people, but rather on changing the power wielded by the authorities ever-ready to resort to propaganda.

Irina declares that she wants Russia to become a country where all citizens can live with dignity, where they will not to be afraid of being persecuted by the authorities for their beliefs, where they will enjoy equal opportunities, and where human life will be the primary concern.

In the present-day Russian Federation autocratic tendencies are becoming more and more pronounced. Irina Hakamada is trying to revive the democratic forces in the country and to unite the efforts of all those who believe in the values of civil society.

Russian Federation

Soknan Han Jung

United Nations Development Program (UNDP)

Born in Seoul, Korea, Soknan Han Jung holds a B.A. in economics and an M.B.A. from New York University, Stern Graduate School of Business. She is married to an architect and has two children. As a United Nations (UN) development specialist, she has created innovative interventions that are recognized as best practices and are being replicated the world over. A unique aspect of her work is the stress on team effort, broad-based partnerships, and participatory dialogue. Under her leadership, the UN has a valuable advisor for Romania in its drive to join the European Union.

Soknan Han Jung arrived in the US in 1972 with the deep desire to help develop the values of real democracy. This was the main reason she felt the need to join the United Nations system in 1985, seeing the UN as the right environment where she could dedicate her entire life to peoples' peace and prosperity. During her long career as a development practitioner, Soknan Han Jung has dedicated her efforts to fighting poverty and HIV/Aids, promoting human rights and gender equality, and building sustainable capacities for democratic governance and economic development in developing countries. Since her assignment as UN Resident Representative in Romania, she has persistently led the multi-agency support to the national response to HIV/Aids. As chairperson of the UN Theme Group on Health and HIV/Aids, she has promoted high-level policy dialogue and advocacy on women's empowerment, established a broad-based coalition of stakeholders and public-private partnerships for decentralized development, and enabled interventions in support of vulnerable groups. Under her supervision, the UN has become a valued and trusted advisor on key development issues for Romania in its drive to become a member of the European Union. One unique feature of her work is the emphasis on team effort, broad-based partnerships and participatory dialogue around key development issues. Her capacity to mobilize energies and reach out to stakeholders is recognized and admired by partners from government, civil society, and the donor community, earning her in 2003 the honor of being among the "Persons of the Year" in Romania, under the foreign diplomats category.

The UN work in Romania and other eastern European countries is still in the area of democratic governance and decentralized development, sustained economic growth, and fight against poverty and diseases like HIV/Aids. These countries aspire to become members of the European Union.

Romania

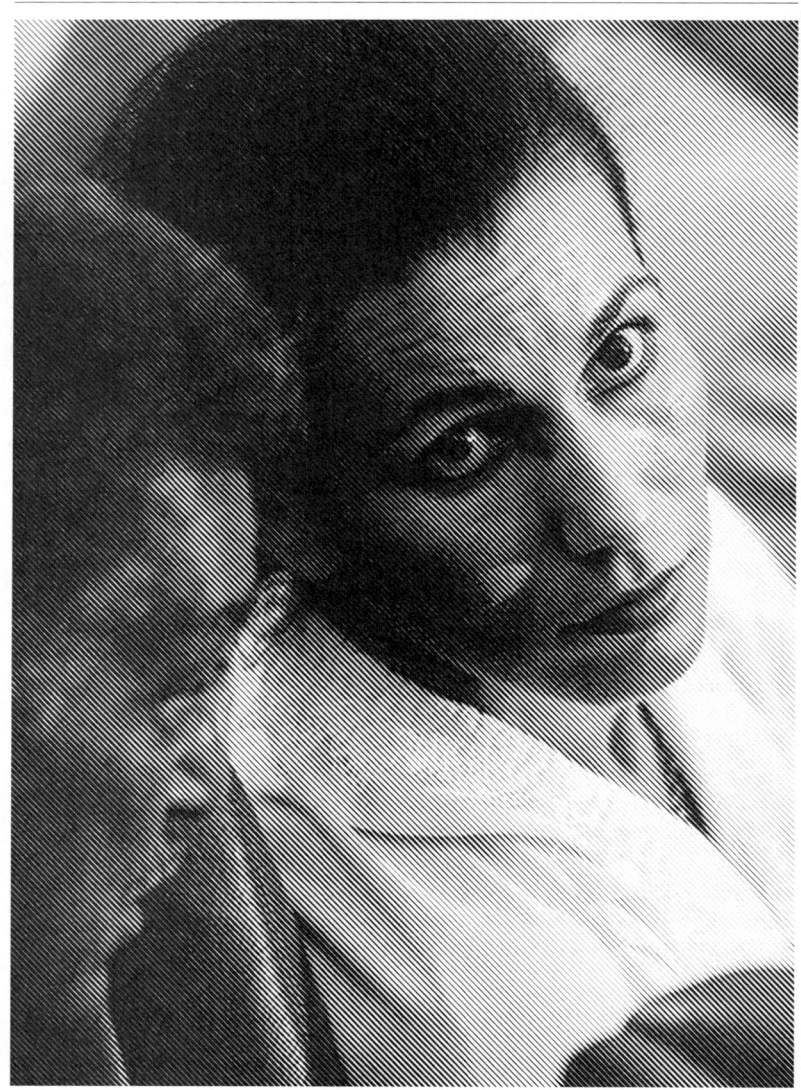

Louisa Hanoun

Algerian Workers Party
Algerian Parliament (AP)
The Algerian Association for Human Rights

Louisa Hanoun has been the leader of the Algerian Workers Party since 1990. She is a human rights activist and key member of the opposition in Algeria and has argued in favor of a peaceful solution to the Algerian civil war through roundtable dialogue between warring factions and the government. In 2004 Louisa Hanoun was nominated by the Party as presidential candidate. She has endured arrest and imprisonment, yet has remained faithful to her political stands and humanist principles.

For Louisa Hanoun peace is a centripetal force, the very foundation of life on which all other human ambitions are built. She expresses her perspective of peace in her war-torn country, Algeria, saying, "Peace is my highest priority and a prerequisite on top of my electoral agenda for the presidency office. Peace has been our aim since 1992. We have emphasized this aim continuously. We want to restore confidence and hope to Algerians, curb violence and put an end to the guerrilla war that is being fueled under the cloak of terrorism and religious fundamentalism. We want to end this vicious hollow circle, so as to alleviate the suffering of the people after seven years of violence. This manifesto of peace will sound salutary enough to gentle people everywhere, but the true impact of these words can only be fully felt by citizens of a country in which no family has been untouched by violence. Each orphan, each widow, each gang victim is longing for an end to this bloodshed."

Louisa Hanoun has campaigned tirelessly for human rights, demanding that a new constitution be drafted, stipulating the irreversible adoption of democracy. Although she ran for president, she appears to be quite free of personal ambition, driven more by her sense of responsibility than the usual aspirations of a politician's ego. Having said she would support any candidate who has the same perspective on peace, she identifies the insidious process of privatization as a real cause of poverty that fuels violence: "My aim is to rescue the country from the present cycle of terror, and to see peace and true democracy prevailing in Algeria."

In 2004 Louisa Hanoun stood as a presidential candidate, the first woman from North Africa and the Middle East to have run for such a high office, a breakthrough within the region with regard to the status of women. She worked towards a peaceful solution to the Algerian civil war and to promote the rights of women.

Algeria

Belela Herrera

The United Nations High Committee for Refugees
Vice Minister for Foreign Affairs of Uruguay

Her life changed with the Chilean state coup against Salvador Allende, in 1973. At that time, Belela Herrera, born in Uruguay and mother of five children, lived in Chile. The country had to respect a curfew and go through disappearances and daily arrests that were kept quiet. Her house became a refuge for Chileans and people of other nationalities who were persecuted by the military. She saved several people's lives, putting her own life at risk during her work for the United Nations High Committee for Refugees. Today, Belela is 77 years old and Vice Minister for Foreign Affairs of Uruguay.

"I studied in a German school. We sang the Nazi anthem with our arms stretched out. I took my arm down saying that I am Uruguayan," remembers Belela Herrera (77). She was only ten, then, and belonged to what was called the Uruguayan elite. "Later on, I realized that that was an evil thing and I denied all that it stood for." In spite of her history of protest, at age 21, she married the son of the Minister of Foreign Affairs and they had five children. In 1969, her husband was elected as Business Attaché of the Uruguayan Embassy in Chile. "That was the year of the Presidential elections." Salvador Allende won and with him came the installation of a Socialist government in South America. The state coup of September 11th, 1973 intervened; Belela divorced and lost her diplomatic immunity. "At that time, there were 10,000 foreign citizens in Chile. Most of them had been persecuted in their own countries." It was necessary to negotiate for their guarantees as well as for the safety of the Chileans, all of them persecuted by the military dictatorship of Augusto Pinochet. "I could not breathe at home because of all the people there, the ones we had to hide and the others who came to help."

Even though she lacked a university degree, she joined the United Nations High Committee for Refugees and managed to get political asylum for people from Chile, Brazil, Mexico, Argentina, Uruguay, Peru, Spain, El Salvador, Haiti, South Africa, Nicaragua, Panama and Bolivia.

Belela Herrera, the current Vice Minister for Foreign Affairs of the government of President Tabaré Vásquez, opened the doors of many countries for numerous persecuted families, but her own country, Uruguay, closed its doors to her until 2004. "When they were opened for me, it was like those big iron doors from the past, with two policemen on each side, the doors that I entered looking for prisoners."

From the 1970s to the 1980s, Brazil, Uruguay, Argentina, Chile, Bolivia and Paraguay lived under military dictatorships. That was a period of forced disappearances and clandestine assassinations of civilians and militants from left-wing groups. Such a period was the end for half a million people.

Uruguay

Laurice Hlass

United Nations Relief and Works Agency (UNRWA)
World Committee on Tourism Ethics (WCTE)
Queen Alia Foundation for the Deaf and Dumb (QAFDD)

Born in Jaffa, Palestine, Laurice Hlass was forced to flee her country in 1948 when Israeli forces occupied her hometown, massacring some of her family members. Raised in a financially poor family, she struggled to obtain a scholarship to pursue her education in the US. In 1969, she became the first female Jordanian diplomat to work as Deputy Jordanian Representative in the UN. For so long, Her Excellency Laurice Hlass has worked within various organizations towards protecting the rights of refugees, women and children.

For over 20 years, Laurice Hlass has supported and promoted activities that raised awareness of gender and peace issues, human rights and refugee living standards. The latter aspect of her work is a particularly important facet of her commitment to peace, as she herself was exiled from her country and her hometown Jaffa after the 1948 war and the occupation of Palestine. The pain of exile was aggravated by the loss of many family members who were murdered — some in front of her — by Israeli soldiers. While receiving an education and earning a respectable and lofty position in the Jordanian government and society, she had been involved in a number of governmental and non-governmental initiatives aimed at addressing the plight of refugees.

Most difficult however has been her work with refugee and rural communities in Jordan. Conditions in many of the villages, districts and camps were very poor and often insecure. The work she was engaged in was often very physically demanding and emotionally draining, involving many sleepless nights in order to complete her projects or assist a family in need. Her commitment to refugee and rural communities has never waned in over 20 years of commitment to bettering their conditions. In doing so, she has inspired many women in these communities to further their education and improve their social situation. Whether through vocational or skills training, or simply small personal discussions, Laurice Hlass has touched the lives of so many young Jordanians and others throughout the world. In Morocco for example, where she worked in small communities on issues of community development, many mothers named their daughters after her in recognition of her contribution to improving their lives.

Laurice Hlass has worked with small and rural communities throughout Jordan and the Palestinian refugee camps. As president of the Young Women's Christian Association (YWCA) and member of the Mizan Law Group for Human Rights, she helped to empower women and advocate Human Rights conventions.

Jordan

Chuen Juei "Josephine" Ho

Gender/Sexuality Rights Association of Taiwan

What Ho Chuen Juei "Josephine" (54) has done is to challenge bigotry and prejudice with her academic work and her social participation and activist writing. In challenging traditional social hierarchies and self-righteous morality, Ho hopes to work toward equality, peace and justice. Although she has suffered attacks and legal prosecution because of her efforts, she has never lost her persistence in her human rights ideals.

The turbulent social movements in Taiwan since the lifting of the marital laws in 1987 provided Ho Chuen Juei "Josephine" with optimal opportunities to stand with many workers who became jobless overnight because of the newly spreading phenomenon of capital flow. In addition to the workers' movement, Ho is best known for her work in gender and sexuality rights movements. In the early 1990s, Ho and other feminist scholars were instrumental in raising social concern for issues such as sexual harassment and domestic violence. Ho also attended to subjects in different social positions, including lesbians, sexually active youths, sex workers, transgender women, and other sexual minorities. Ho is considered the most outspoken activist in these areas in Taiwan.

To further promote a diverse and inclusive social space for discussions of marginal topics, Ho established the Centre for the Study of Sexualities at National Central University. Academic activities such as holding annual conference on gender and sexuality research have been held since 1996; a total of 19 books have been published. In addition, Ho was a founding member and a long-term supporter of the Gender/Sexuality Rights Association of Taiwan which has just won the 2004 Felipa Award from the International Gay and Lesbian Human Rights Commission for its outstanding contribution.

16 years of continuous selfless work toward de-stigmatization has proven Ho to be a devoted activist and scholar.

Ho works in a social context highly inhospitable toward emergent non-normative genders and sexualities. Although Taiwan has opened up new values and new practices, gender/sexuality-related issues are still controversial, as they threaten to challenge deep-rooted prejudices and securities.

China, Taiwan

Ana Theresia Hontiveros-Baraquel

Coalition for Peace
Philippine Panel in Peace Negotiations with the National Democratic Front (NDFP)

Ana Theresia "Risa" Hontiveros-Baraquel's (born 1966) activism has evolved with the struggles of the progressive movement. Her journey has brought her to various arenas of engagement where she has played different roles — from a student leader working the parliament of the streets during the martial law period, to peace advocate establishing "zones of peace", to peace talks panelist negotiating with leaders of the armed left, and now a legislator engaging the state from within. She believes that lasting peace can only be achieved through social, economic and political reform.

It is said that crisis usually brings out the best in people. This is particularly true in the case of Risa Hontiveros-Baraquel, whose activism grew during the Marcos dictatorship in the Philippines. The country was in deep social and political turmoil and Risa rose to become a notable figure in the anti-dictatorship movement as a student leader and founding member of the Student Christian Alliance. Risa considers herself a child of various streams of thought, inspired by the ideas of Gandhi and Paolo Freire, active non-violence and Latin American liberation theology. Seeing life through such lenses, Risa is certain that fundamental changes are needed in Philippine society. But she is firm in her belief that this should be achieved not through armed struggle, but through peaceful means.

Even as a child Risa was revolted by physical violence, thus her progressive but pacifist stance as an activist. Helping grassroots communities establish zones of peace in villages across the archipelago, she underscores the atrocities that both state and non-state actors inflict on others that in turn result in cycles of violence. Risa advocates a more holistic approach to peace, which has made her explore various formal and informal venues for intervention. Married to a police officer and the mother of four children, Risa is secretary general of the Coalition for Peace and recently, she assumed the post of representative of the Akbayan Citizen's Action Party in the Philippine Congress. Through the peace movement and the commitment of peace workers like Risa, peace advocacy in the Philippines has gradually attained the urgency and attention it deserves.

The costs of the continuing armed conflict in the Philippines have given rise to citizens' groups pushing for thoroughgoing political, economic and social reforms and urging both the government and the armed rebel forces to come to the peace table and negotiate an end to the violence.

Philippines

Swanee Hunt

Women and Public Policy Program (Harvard University)

Swanee Hunt is helping to shape policies that affect women worldwide. As ambassador in Vienna, she launched the Vital Voices Democracy Initiative and Conference, which united 320 international women leaders in business, law, and politics. The conference inspired Vital Voices of Northern Ireland, the Americas, the Baltics, Nordics, Russia, and others. Today, Vital Voices is a global partnership supporting women's progress in building democracies, strong economies, and peace. Swanee Hunt has used her influence to connect with policymakers and dignitaries around the world.

When Swanee Hunt introduced the Vital Voices Conference in Vienna in 1997, she shared experiences growing up as the daughter of a wealthy Texas businessman. When she was in her 20s, she toured one of her family's new hotels. "The managers had named each of seven suites for leaders from that city's history. I noticed the names were all of men. 'Where are the women?' I asked. 'Women? We didn't find any women leaders in the city's history. There weren't any.' I was told. Somehow, I did not believe that. So I hired my own researcher and she discovered that while the men 150 years ago were building slaughterhouses and punching holes in the ground, the women had founded hospitals, started schools, and set up the post office. You see, it matters who writes the history books."

Born with a family fortune and educated with a B.A. in philosophy, two masters in psychology and religion, and a doctorate in theology, Swanee has lived a life of privilege. Nonetheless, she has spent her life advocating for the disenfranchised. As ambassador in Vienna, she extended her influence to the neighboring Balkan states, hosting negotiations and symposia in pursuit of peace. She organized projects yielding books for Sarajevo's destroyed National Library, trees for the parks denuded during the siege, and six tons of musical instruments for ravaged Bosnian schools. She worked with Bosnian women and religious leaders as they united across former war lines, and recounted her experiences in her book, "This Was Not Our War: Bosnian Women Reclaiming the Peace".

Following her ambassadorship, she began her current role as director of the Women and Public Policy Program at Harvard's John F. Kennedy School of Government. At the school, Swanee created Women Waging Peace, a revolutionary program to connect women leaders in conflict areas to one another and to policymakers worldwide.

Because of multilayered barriers that prevent women from reaching the negotiating table, their numbers there are minimal. There is no major economic investment in women's peace initiatives.

United States of America

Duong Thu Huong

Duong Thu Huong (born 1947) calls herself an exile in her own country. A veteran of the Vietnam War and the war with China, she was disillusioned with the regime and became a vocal advocate of human rights and democratic reforms. She published short stories and novels about hunger and malnutrition in Vietnam, but her books were banned and she was expelled from the Communist Party. In 1991, she was imprisoned for seven months without trial. Duong Thu Huong lives and writes in Hanoi under permanent surveillance and is not allowed to travel abroad.

Duong Thu Huong was only 20 years old during the Vietnam War when she became the leader of a youth brigade of 40 "singing soldiers" sent to the frontline in Quang Binh, where most of the bombings were taking place. For eight years, she lived with soldiers in small underground tunnels, singing and writing lyrics for the encouragement of the troops. Duong Thu Huong was one of three members of her group who survived the war. In 1975, she worked as a screenwriter in Hanoi. Four years later, she became the first female film correspondent during the war against China. It was this war that disillusioned her forever.

Back in Hanoi in 1980, she published novels and short stories about hunger and malnutrition in Vietnam, which found a large readership. But her work was banned from publication in 1982. Duong Thu Huong never wanted to become a writer. "It happened inadvertently. It happened because of the pain, I felt,". she says. She finds herself in a continuing "war against the authorities and against a dictatorial regime". Her bestseller "Paradise of the Blind" scandalized the Communist Party, which banned her books and expelled her from the party, but she continued to criticize the socialist system. On April 14, 1991, the secret police surrounded her mother's house in the center of Hanoi. Duong Thu Huong was arrested and imprisoned in solitary confinement. She was accused of collaborating with foreign countries and "revealing state secrets" and held for seven months and seven days without trial. But they could not break her courage. Once out of prison, she continued to criticize the leadership, blaming them for corruption and loss of democracy in Vietnam. She continues to write and remains hopeful that one day, the Vietnamese people will live better lives. "There is still a long way to go, but I remain hopeful, for without hope, it's hard to live this life," she says.

With "Doi Moi" (Opening Up) the Vietnam government opened the market, the right to private property was restored and the country was opened to foreign investors. But the Communist Party continues to deny freedom of speech and utilize the secret police against its critics.

Viet Nam

"Dr Hutchinson is a woman of strength, courage, and resilience and inspires the same in her students and peers. As her students, we would like her silent efforts to be recognized and made visible."

Sharon Hutchinson

University of Wisconsin (Madison)
Civilian Protection Monitoring Team

For the past 25 years, Sharon Hutchinson has initiated grassroots efforts and focused international attention on human rights abuses in war-torn Sudan. An anthropologist at the University of Wisconsin (Madison) and a human rights consultant, her research has taken her to the frontlines. As one of the monitors on the Civilian Protection Monitoring Team, she has helped investigate and document attacks against civilians by the Sudan Army, the Sudan People's Liberation Army, and government-allied militias. Her book "Nuer Dilemmas" is a core textbook in many American and European universities.

Sharon began her research in southern Sudan in the late 1970s and early 1980s during the tempestuous years preceding the civil war. When she returned to Nuerland in the 1990s, she found the people physically and emotionally exhausted. When oil was discovered in southern Sudan and the killing intensified, Sharon felt that she must play a role in mediating dialogue between the Sudan People's Liberation Army, the Government of Sudan, and the US State Department, to bring about a ceasefire in the country's long civil war. Her passion continues to be to ensure that the voices of the southern Sudanese reach US and international human rights communities. It is a responsibility that she has carried with humility and devotion. She helped organize grassroots peace activities and guided aid work through NGOs such as Amnesty International and Save the Children, and conducted extensive undercover work documenting civilian human rights abuses for Human Rights Watch and Amnesty International. She is working on constructing three elementary schools in the Western Upper Nile and is in the process of developing curriculum materials.

Educated, passionate, and fluent in Arabic, French, Spanish, and Nuer, Sharon represents a threat to those who profit from subjugation of the southern Sudanese. She has been threatened with assassination many times, but nothing has stopped her efforts to expose the country's human rights' abuses.

United States of America

Fatima Ibrahim

Sudanese Women's Union (SWU); Women's International Democratic Federation (WIDF); Committee Against Violation of Women's, Youth and Students Human Rights (CAVWYSHR)

Fatima Ahmed Ibrahim (72), born in Khartoum, is a Cambridge University graduate. She worked as a schoolteacher, but later resigned to work voluntarily full-time in the Sudanese Women's Union, over which she presided in 1956. Her main work focuses on gender equality in decision-making, social justice and human rights. Fatima became the first Sudanese woman member of parliament through the democratic election in the Sudan in 1965 and won the United Nations Award for Outstanding Achievements in the Field of Human Rights in 1993.

When Fatima obtained a Cambridge University Certificate, she dreamt of studying at the University of Khartoum, Sudan. But her father could not afford her higher education expenses. So, she decided to work as a schoolteacher and married a famous political activist and trade unionist in Sudan, who later won an International Peace Medal for his remarkable political achievements. In 1971, due to the country's anarchic political conditions, he was executed and she was jailed, leaving behind a one-year-old child for her family to look after. While in prison, she was denied food and medicine, and her medical condition seriously deteriorated. Thanks to Amnesty International, Fatima is alive and is now the president of the Women's International Democratic Federation (WIDF).

While still in high school, she launched a newsletter addressing political and social issues, such as women's rights and British Colonialism. She also wrote on the same subjects in public newspapers and organized the first women-initiated strike in the Sudan, which was provoked by the policies of the British administrations in girls' schools. It followed the dropping of science subjects from the curriculum under the pretext that Sudanese girls are less-qualified to study science. The strike organizers were expelled from the schools, only to be allowed later to resit the Cambridge University International Exam.

In 1952 Fatima sought to transform WIDF into a political party in order to protect the social and political rights of women, especially with regard to being elected as members of parliament. The islamic parties, who considered that women's participation in political life and the equality of men and women contradict the Sharia Law, had unfortunately lobbied against her proposal. Fatima studied the elements of Islamic jurisprudence thoroughly and provided counter-evidence to this claim.

Fatima Ibrahim's main work focuses on gender equality in decision-making, social justice and human rights. Her working agenda was also set up to fight racial discrimination and child exploitation. She strives to support women's participation in political life and civil society building.

Sudan

Tiina Ilsen

Organization for Security and Cooperation in Europe (Osce)
Office for Democratic Institutions and Human Rights (Odihr)

Tiina Ilsen has worked with the gender unit of the Osce Office for Democratic Institutions and Human Rights (Odihr) since September 1999, focusing on the promotion of women's rights. She also created the Women's NGOs Coalition in Georgia, an organization dedicated to promoting gender equality. She works on programs in legal literacy, vocational training, leadership development, and political participation. She has played a key role in shaping the Osce policy, philosophy, and program portfolio for women's rights.

Tiina Ilsen has played a major role in analyzing the current situation of women in Georgia and has created the Women's NGOs Coalition to unite all women's non-governmental organizations in the country. The head of Odihr's gender unit (based in Warsaw), Tiina has worked tirelessly to empower women in Georgia's new democracy.

In June 2000, she initiated a meeting of the women heads of NGOs working on women's issues. The meeting, entitled Women Leaders: Creating a Coalition of NGO Leaders in Georgia, was organized by Odihr expert trainers to develop awareness of gender issues, in addition to establishing a coalition and developing the skills to manage it effectively. Tiina was the driving force behind the creation of the coalition, established in response to the expressed desire of women leaders in Georgia to join together in their work to promote gender equality in civil society. Members completed additional training between 2000 and 2003 and established an action plan around six working groups to promote women in politics, education, health care, economics, conflict resolution and peace building, and the media.

The launch of the coalition has enhanced women's initiatives, promoted the idea of gender equality, and improved and unified the achievement of their goals. The organization provides women with a forum in which to tackle problems together, supporting one another as they work to achieve their goals. The coalition also has positioned women to take an active role in shaping society, particularly during the Rose Revolution in Georgia.

The situation in Georgia is unstable because of conflicts in two areas: Abkhazia and South Ossetia. The participation of more women peace makers in decision-making positions will help resolve conflicts in these areas.

Georgia

Tolekan Ismailova

Civil Society Against Corruption

A public activist since 1977, Tolekan Ismailova carries out her activities at three levels: grassroots, national, and international. She works with local communities, NGOs, and political parties and cooperates with international organizations, such as the United Nations and Human Rights Watch. As the executive president of the NGO Civil Society Against Corruption, she is a leader of the democratic movement in Kyrgyzstan. She is involved in the field of social justice and human rights protection.

Tolekan Ismailova works in the field of social justice and human rights protection. Since 1977, she has been a leader of the democratic movement in Kyrgyzstan. She has been at the forefront of the struggle against corruption in her country and the establishment of the NGO Civil Society against Corruption. Tolekan uncovered many cases of corruption in the official structures of Kyrgyzstan that led to the dismissal of corrupt officials. She stood at the head of many human rights and anti-poverty initiatives in her country. She promotes the development of democratic values and contributes to the improvement of the political and economic situation in Kyrgyzstan. She also advocates for public involvement in solving the social and political problems of the country. Tolekan participates in many spheres of public life: in social and democratic education, in the political and economic arenas, and in the defense of human rights. She provides support to regional and district NGOs and to political parties through training seminars, educational courses, and monitoring of elections. Tolekan is a very honest and industrious person. As a recognized leader, she extends great devotion and energy to each individual she serves and with her high level of self-awareness, she provides a real example and model to other women. She works not for money or any awards or prizes, but for the improvement of the current situation in Kyrgyzstan and the enhancement of the quality of life of the people.

Since the collapse of the Soviet Union in 1990, Kyrgyzstan is still struggling to fully transform itself into an effective democratic country. Corruption is a major problem and a main cause of the people's poverty and low standard of living. After a sudden revolution and President Akayev's resignation in the spring of 2005, the political situation remains uncertain.

Kyrgyzstan

Izabela Jaruga-Nowacka

Izabela Jaruga-Nowacka went into politics in 1991, shortly after Poland's political system had transformed from communism to democracy. An ethnographer specializing in Mongolian culture, she quit her scientific career and was a co-founder of the Union of Labor (she left the party in April 2004). She was Poland's first Government Plenipotentiary for Equal Status of Men and Women. Fifteen years after the beginning of her political career she became Deputy Prime Minister. She is known for her uncompromised fight for human rights, especially those of women and sexual minorities.

"Patriarchy! We give you five years at the most. Until the 100th anniversary of International Women's Day in 2010!" Izabela Jaruga-Nowacka, Deputy Prime Minister, was shouting from a moving platform during the International Women's Day demonstration in Warsaw. This demonstration is organized regularly by an informal coalition of Polish women's organizations. Izabela Jaruga-Nowacka was present this year, the year before, and the year before that — in fact, every year since the early 1990s. She was there when she won a seat in parliament (first in 1993, then in 2001), when she became Poland's first Government Plenipotentiary for Equal Status of Men and Women in 2001 and finally as Deputy Prime Minister in 2004. From a truck she was talking to thousands of women, men, and children. She thanked "the real men of all sexual orientations who are not afraid to fight for equal gender rights." Then, with her bodyguard trying to be invisible, she walked with the rest of the demonstrators. On the way, as usual, they met a right-wing counter demonstration with slogans aimed at her personally. Izabela is well known for her uncompromised stance on women's rights. She stands for: the right to abortion (which in Poland is allowed only when a woman's life is in danger), equal gender representation in the workplace, family, and politics, and for registering homosexual partnerships. Bishop Tadeusz Pieronek called her "feminist cement which will not alter even if treated with acid." That statement did not make her back off. "I think Poland will soon be equal. We have equality in our Constitution and I feel it is my duty to fight for women's rights," she says.

In 1989, the political system in Poland began to change from communism to democracy. Later, it appeared that this was a democracy of men, rejecting or ignoring the human rights of women. Few women are involved in politics. Women from the grassroots to the government level are working to change this.

Poland

Yu-Jin Jeong

National Campaign for Eradication of Crimes by US Troops
Safe Korea
East Asia–US–Puerto Rico Women's Network Against Militarism

Yu-Jin Jeong grew up during the politically oppressive 1960s to 1980s when South Korea was under US-backed military dictatorships. She was active in promoting democratic reform of South Korea's higher education curriculum. This student movement was part of a larger anti-imperialist movement that opposed the legacy of South Korea's dictatorship. Because of her student activism, Yu-Jin was arrested and sentenced to prison for about a year. In 2000, she began research in Okinawa on the impact of US militarism and Okinawan women's nonviolent organizing work for demilitarization and peace.

Yu-Jin's work is related to US militarism in South Korea: sexual violence against women, military prostitution, ecological and human devastation caused by military training and bombing practice, car accidents, violent fights with civilians, and petty crimes such as burglary and theft. Yu-Jin's primary goal is to protect and promote the rights of civilians, especially women and children, whose lives are further exploited, impoverished, and marginalized by militarism. She has worked on these issues with the National Campaign for Eradication of Crimes by US Troops.

Yu-Jin's work is unique in that it makes connections between imperialism, militarism, sexism, and classism that are specific to South Korea. The male-dominant, anti-imperialist nationalist movement in South Korea disregards the human rights of women and children. Because of Korea's patriarchal values, the women in military prostitution are easily dismissed and regarded as "dirty, lowly women" even by the politically progressive activists. Yu-Jin's method is participatory-she listens and supports the work of other organizations that are negatively impacted by militarism. Her method also involves empowering people by giving visibility and voice to those who are victims and survivors of military violence. Yu-Jin's activities are rooted in her understanding of solidarity-for her it represents "one's ability to feel the suffering of others who are different from you," nation/race/class/gender-wise.

Yu-Jin's work has influenced and inspired younger generations of feminist activists throughout South Korea. These younger women are promoting and carrying out public peace education, peace performances, and other nonviolent, creative actions in order to promote a culture of peace. The younger activists influenced by Yu-Jin are now leading the conscientious objector movement in South Korea.

South Korea's national security law has been used during three decades of US-backed military dictatorships to oppress political dissent. People who opposed the presence of the US military in South Korea were imprisoned as Communists in the name of national security even through the 1990s.

Republic of Korea

Zanaa Jurmed

Convention on the Elimination of All Forms
of Discrimination against Women (Cedaw)

Zanaa Jurmed, born 1950, an eminent political leader and civil society advocate, was a key activist of the pro-democracy movement and her name is synonymous with its success in the 1990s. She is a spokesperson on women's and human rights issues in the country and abroad. Her commitment to democratic ideals and her peacemaking skills won her the first headship of the capital city organisation of the Mongolian Democratic Party. Since 1992 Zanaa has played a leadership role in many NGOs.

Zanaa Jurmed surprised her colleagues at the Foreign Language University, when she joined the Mongolian Democratic Union and began to provide venues for meetings for young people in the pro-democracy movement. Thousands of demonstrators in the cold March days of 1990 were surprised to see an elegant woman serving hot drinks and offering face masks to the hunger-strikers occupying the central square of the capital. Her demands for the resignation of the Politburo, for a multiparty system and pluralistic society, often led to clashes with the army. Her father once asked her, "What will happen to you if the army is ordered to crack down on protestors?" She said, "I would rather die than live under such a regime!"

Zanaa has been in the forefront of building a modern civil society in Mongolia for the past 15 years; her distinguished leadership recently won her the Order of the Polar Star by decree of the president. In the first democratic election in 1992, Zanaa won a seat in the Capital City Khural of citizen's Representatives. Standing for democratic forces at that crucial moment in the history of the nation, she used the people's mandate for starting reforms that have had a positive impact on today's Mongolia.

Over time, Zanaa's focus shifted from politics to the social sphere. Since 1992 Zanaa has initiated and founded a number of women and human rights NGOs now operating nationwide. After the Jakarta Regional Conference on Gender Equality in 1996, Zanaa established the National Watch Network Center of the Convention on the Elimination of All Forms of Discrimination against Women (Cedaw), widely recognized as the intellectual stronghold of women's NGOs in Mongolia.

Zanaa was national coordinator of the International Civil Society Forum — 2003 held in Ulaanbaatar, a major turning point in the globalizing of her individual experience and in Mongolian civil society.

Mongolia is undergoing a difficult transition to a civil society. The country needs leaders committed to the democratic cause and grassroot structures representing the public. In this respect, non-governmental organizations led by well-known personalities such as Zanaa Jurmed become a driving force.

Wahu Kaara

Kenya Debt Relief Network (Kendren)
African Social Forum
Kenya Social Forum

Wahu Kaara, a 53-year-old widow, describes herself as a global social justice activist. The former history and Kiswahili teacher says she has been radical from an early age, having been involved in promoting social justice and economic democracy for 30 years. Her political activities define her radical nature. Despite the repression from the government and the hard times she experienced when her husband was forced into exile, the mother of four relentlessly worked locally and is today involved internationally in the African Social Forum and the Kenya Debt Relief Network.

"I never wanted my students to be stereotypes," the passionate Wahu says. "Every human being is important and has a role in life." Her role in life was defined by politics. She learnt about communism, the ideals of justice and equity during her university studies in the 1970s. The political consciousness she gained in those days has been her greatest strength. Wahu began work as a teacher and later as a principal in a rural school. After she had had her daughter and three sons, she began to pay attention to government repression through political community theatre. In 1986, her husband was forced into political exile and went to neighboring Tanzania. He left her behind with their four children, all below the age of ten. She sustained her family only through great sacrifice. In the 1990s the democratization process began in Kenya and Wahu became actively involved in founding organizations. Her first experience in mobilizing people was at the Freedom Corner, in Nairobi's Uhuru Park, where political activists joined mothers of political prisoners in demanding for the release of their detained sons. She says political consciousness, especially for women, is critical in the fight for human rights and economic justice. "Women are responsible for sustaining life but often their ideas are not accepted in decision making." Wahu laments that this is the universal situation for women. Courageous and outspoken, she is familiar with the ideas of economists such as George Soros and is today involved in the Kendren. This has given Wahu an international platform. She is also active in the African Social Forum whose ideas she has taken down to the grass roots. Wahu confidently says, "African women are not dying for Africa anymore, they want to live for Africa."

In the early 1990s, the democratization process began in Kenya, following international pressure to introduce multiparty politics. Previously, one party, Kanu, ruled Kenya. Among the first expressions for democratic change was a protest to release political prisoners at Nairobi's Uhuru Park in 1992.

"To love and protect people. To follow the dictates of my conscience and always fight for the rights of people, their honor and dignity."

Nina Karpachova

Ukrainian Parliament Commission for Human Rights
Hope — Center for the Protection of Children's and Women's Rights
World Congress of Ukrainian Lawyers

Nina Karpachova was elected Ukrainian Parliament Commissioner for Human Rights in 1998. Her top priorities include safeguarding individual's rights to a fair trial, freedom of speech, the rights of orphans, the disabled, people affected by HIV/Aids, victims of Chernobyl, and persons deprived of liberty. She advocates for the rights of migrant workers and has taken action against trafficking in women. From early on, she boldly denounced torture and defended the right to peaceful assembly. She has been instrumental in bringing Ukraine to sign international rights conventions.

The appearance of a long awaited human rights protection institution — the Commissioner for Human Rights — and the election of Nina Karpachova to this office had a noticeable impact on the moral and psychological climate in Ukraine. Now, ordinary people feel protected, no longer alone in a struggle for their rights. They have regained faith and hope and have someone to turn to with their grief and complaints against indifferent officials.

Almost every other appeal to the Commissioner is a cry from the heart, a plea for help: "You are our last hope." People believe in her, and an avalanche of appeals has descended on Nina's office. Throughout the years, over 500,000 people — Ukrainians, foreigners, and refugees — have had recourse to the Commissioner's office. People write to thank her. One person she helped wrote: "My mother and I sincerely appreciate your consideration of our grief. If the world is inhabited by people like you, it is worthwhile living and bringing up children and grandchildren, knowing that the law will stand up for the poor as well."

In a survey probing how employees from the Ministry of Internal Affairs complied with the constitutional rights and freedoms of citizens, the Commissioner revealed that in most regions, the police did not comply with the law and used physical violence against its citizens and subjected them to inhumane and degrading treatment. Frequently, individuals under investigation endured torture. In many cells there was inadequate access to fresh air and daylight. The Commissioner brought these problems to the attention of the State's leadership, but also to the national and international public. Because the Commissioner constantly monitors how individuals, temporarily deprived of liberty, are given their rights, treatment by the police changed considerably.

Although Ukraine achieved independence in 1991 with the dissolution of the USSR, democracy remained elusive and human rights abuses were rampant. In 2004, a peaceful mass protest, the so-called Orange Revolution, swept into power a reformist slate, bringing new hope for the protection of human rights.

Ukraine

"We cannot have a
solid democracy unless
there is a good flow
of information reaching
the people."

Mariama Keïta

Coordination des Organisations Non Gouvernementale et Associations
Féminines Nigériennes (Congafen)
Association for Democracy, Liberty and Development

The communication professional Mariama Keïta was born in Niamey, capital of Niger, in 1946. She is a well-known personality in the annals of the African press. She has been a member of the Superior Communication Council of Niger and received national recognition for a long and brilliant career in her country.

Madame Mariama Keïta is the leader of the Association for Democracy, Liberty and Development where she has worked since the creation of good governance in a democratic Niger. She is also president of the Commission on Information, Communication and Training. She was general manager of Radio Niger. Mariama Keïta is the first journalist of Niger to be awarded a degree from Maisons Laffitte France. She has around 15 certificates of professional training as well as a license in English from the Faculty of Letters at the University of Abdou Moumouni in Niamey. From 1992 to 1993, she was in charge of broadening and executing a project for creating awareness among the people on issues of the constitution, legislative and presidential elections, thus preparing them for the first democratic elections in Niger. From 1993 to 1994, she ran a project to form the Association of Democracy, Liberty and Development to reinforce the institutional capacities of NGOs for a democratic culture. This is just to name a few of her projects. Being part of the Nigerian intelligentsia, Mariama is active in the media, businesses, non-governmental organizations, and associations. She also served as a trainer for the National Center of Improvement managing courses on business communication, and as the president (1994—1997) of the Coordination of Niger Women's NGOs and Associations. This structure, known as Congafen, is the first collective of NGOs and women's association dealing with grouping and coordinating the activities of these NGO in a transparent, democratic way.

After the 1999 coup, a council was established to oversee the drafting of a constitution for a republic with a semi-presidential system. In votes that international observers found to be free and fair, the new constitution was approved. The 2004 presidential election was the first one with a democratically elected incumbent and a test to Niger's young democracy.

Yu Jane Ku

Taiwan Human Rights Association
Media Watch and Education Foundation

Ku Yu Jane, born in 1965, is the executive secretary of the Taiwan Human Rights Association and the director of the Media Watch and Education Foundation. She fights for the rights of illegal immigrants, mental patients and indigenous people in Taiwan. She believes that human rights work is a kind of collective project that needs mutual understanding and learning among people.

As a human rights activist, Ku Yu Jane fights for the rights of marginal groups and tries to eliminate prejudice and discrimination against them. For example, she participated actively in the indigenous people's movement and published an article called "The Land Crisis of Taiwan Indigenous People: a preliminary study of the political and economic structure of the Equal Rights' Association in the mountainous region", which evaluates the land problems faced by the indigenous people living in the mountains. This article aroused much attention in the public. In 2003, together with lawyers and social workers who care for the prevention of domestic violence, Ku published a book called, "The One Hurting Me is the One Closest to Me" (Shang Zhou Press, 2003) to raise awareness of the seriousness of domestic violence in Taiwan. Touching stories from six typical categories of people related to domestic violence, including foreign brides, Chinese Mainland brides, indigenous women, the abusers, drug addicts' family members, and children witnessing marriage violence, formed the substance of this book.

Ku believes that human rights work is a kind of collective project that needs mutual understanding among people, and she plans to popularize human rights education in schools and communities. She is also keen to work on international human rights issues for she believes that human rights issues are transnational. Ku is also concerned about the media and advocates monitoring and critiquing programs for their biases.

In Taiwan, as the society becomes more tense due to political divisions and the economic downturn of the last decade, issues like migrant workers' rights and discrimination against brides coming from Mainland China and other South-East Asian countries become more acute.

China, Taiwan

Barbara Lee

House International Relations Committee
Congressional Progressive Caucus
Congressional Black Caucus (CBC)

Barbara Lee, democratic California congresswoman, gained international attention as the only member of congress to vote against the post-9/11 resolution giving president Bush unbridled power to use military force against anyone suspected of having committed the acts, or intending to do so in the future. She is a leader in promoting policies that foster international peace, security, and human rights, and is at the forefront in promoting legislation to stop the spread of HIV/Aids and promote treatment. She consistently advocates for the most vulnerable, especially women and children.

The bumper stickers reflect deep respect and gratitude: "Barbara Lee Speaks For Me". Lee was the only member of congress to speak on September 14, 2001, and to vote against the president's decision to use military force to retaliate for the September 11 attack. "September 11 changed the world," she told her colleagues. "Our deepest fears now haunt us. Yet I am convinced that military action will not prevent further acts of international terrorism against the United States." Barbara's lone vote is consistent with her years of service in the US congress and in the California state legislature, where her actions reflect a brave and deep commitment to humanistic values. She has been a leader in promoting policies that foster international peace, security, and human rights, sponsoring legislation against the doctrine of preemptive war, cosponsoring legislation to create a cabinet-level department of peace, and leading congress' bipartisan effort to end the genocide in Darfur, Sudan. Barbara has been a leader in protecting free speech by opposing media consolidation. She has introduced legislation to make communities safer by providing after-school programs in public housing and to protect tenants from arbitrary evictions. Barbara has led the fight against predatory lending by banks and to create the Global Fund to Fight HIV/Aids, and has sponsored legislation to protect Aids orphans. She is one of most active legislators trying to end homelessness.
Barbara was born in El Paso, Texas. She entered college as a single-mother, first graduated from Mills College, then received her master of social work from UC Berkeley. She served in the California state assembly from 1990 to 1996, in the California state senate from 1996 to 1998, and served as chief of staff in the office of her predecessor, congressman Ron Dellums.

Congresswoman Barbara Lee could have voted with the rest of congress. It would have been easy to go with the rest and vote for war after the September 11 attacks. But she courageously stuck to her own beliefs and convictions. The lone vote for peace belonged to Barbara Lee.

United States of America

Jun Li

Yongfeng Neighborhood Committee

Li Jun is secretary of the Party Committee and director of the Yongfeng Neighborhood Committee, Shenyang City, Liaoning Province. Her longstanding and selfless community work has brought substantial changes to this urban neighborhood. Not only have her efforts helped to improve the electricity and water supply, but community relationships have also been regenerated. Even though she fell critically ill due to such hard work, she did not stop.

Before she took early retirement and committed herself to the community development work, Li Jun had worked for four decades and had been promoted from an ordinary salesperson to a leadership position. In March 1999 she retired from the leadership of the regional technical coordination office, and chose to serve the local community by taking up the responsibility of "premier of the alley." However, the reality of the situation put her under severe strain. Yongfeng community is an old urban residential area with many things in a shambolic state. The area was inhabited by elderly people and laborers. As newly elected director of the neighborhood committee, she immediately became the undeserved target of the residents' anger. But she was determined to gain their understanding and support and she persevered and succeeded in solving community problems.

For instance, a malfunctioning heating system had affected 477 households and residents had protested time and again. This came to Li's notice and she and a group of cadres and party members of the community visited all households in the area to motivate them to help. Her enthusiasm, sincerity and patience eventually touched their hearts. In less than a month, she had collected 300,000 yuan for improving the heating system. The money was handed over, work began immediately and the project was completed. Among her many other projects, Li has called for donations for a community resident with a malignant tumor, arranged funerals for poor families, sought reemployment opportunities for unemployed workers, and organized activities for a relief program for tsunami victims in South Asia. No matter how serious or small the problem is, she is eager to help, and this has made her neighborhood a better place to live in.

Yongfeng community was an area of shacks where dwellers were either laborers or poor, elderly people. The area lacked many facilities, and had many problems that no one was willing to address. Li Jun was determined to serve the community and be the leader of the dwellers.

China

Xuebo Li

The People's Government of Chifeng City

Since taking up her position as vice mayor of Chifeng City, Inner Mongolia, Li Xuebo has developed a strong gender consciousness. She strives to find ways of helping poor women who live on poor land to increase their income. She encourages the women to be independent and self-supporting, and have self-respect. Her work has helped improved their living conditions and has enhanced their status.

Li Xuebo is Han Chinese and does not belong to any political party. She graduated from the Liaoning Institute of Finance, and has since served as an officer and deputy director in the Statistics Bureau, deputy director of the Rural Enterprises Bureau, and vice-chairperson of the Political Consultative Committee in Chifeng city.

Chifeng is an underdeveloped area in southeast Inner Mongolia Autonomous Region where the Han people constitute the majority of the population and the Mongolian people self-govern themselves. There are 12 counties among which ten are considered "poor." The population of the city is 4.6 million, with 512,000 living below the poverty line. Among these, 342,000 are women and children. As vice major of Chifeng City since October 2001, Li Xuebo has been working hard to alleviate poverty and to improve the quality of infertile land.

Also director of the Women and Children Working Committee of Chifeng, Li is whole-heartedly committed to women's work. She has established new working mechanisms aimed at alleviating poverty, including small-scale credit, exporting labor, soliciting relief funds for victims of natural disasters, establishing "hand-in-hand" groups, helping girl students go back to school, and so on. These mechanisms have effectively helped improve their living conditions and their status in the family and society. She regrets neglecting her own family's needs because of her busy work schedule. Her physical health is deteriorating because her life has been so busy and tiring. What motivates her most is creating an environment in which both women and men can develop equally. When faced with difficulties and pressure, she thinks of the women who desperately need her help. She evaluates the performance of various departments according to their achievements in the development of issues relating to women and children.

Chifeng City is one of the 18 areas in China where poverty is widespread. The natural environment is demanding and living standards are low. People are conservative and those living in pastoral areas are even more reluctant to accept new ideas and influences; it is difficult to change them.

China

Hilda Lini

Vanuatu National Council of Women
Tuvanuatu Komiuniti
Pacific Concerns Resource Centre (PCRC)

Hilda Lini coordinated the Executive Committee of the Women's Wing of the Vanuatu Liberation Movement from 1977 until the country's independence in 1980. She was awarded the Independence Medal for Victorious Contribution to Vanuatu Independence and was the only woman member of Parliament from 1987 to 1998, holding several portfolios. She was a founding member of the Vanuatu National Council of Women and in 1996 co-founded the Tuvanuatu Komiuniti, a network of indigenous leaders throughout Vanuatu communities who wish to preserve Vanuatu's indigenous system of peaceful co-existence.

A mother of two children and a chief in Raga women's chiefly society on Pentecost Island, Vanuatu, Hilda Lini has held a number of key positions in her own country and the Pacific region. She was in the Cabinet in the Vanuatu Peoples' Provisional Government (1977—1978), a founding member of the Vanuatu National Council of Women and the only woman member of parliament (1987—1998). There, the indigenous leaders of Turaga and Vanuatu approached her to assist in mobilizing them to preserve indigenous values of collective ownership, peace, and human security that they felt were fast eroding. They felt alienated from national decisions affecting their people. A chief herself, Hilda understood the issues they raised and in 1996 co-founded the Tuvanuatu Komiuniti, a network of indigenous leaders throughout Vanuatu who wish to preserve their indigenous system of peaceful co-existence, based on collective ownership, shared responsibility, and community account-ability.

Hilda maintained that her country's acceptance of Western development strategies overlooked fundamental indigenous values. Therefore, she opposed Vanuatu's acceptance of the World Bank/International Monetary Fund model of structural adjustment programs. In the early 1990s, as a result of her challenges to the status quo, she was banned from entering French Pacific territories. In 1993, under the pro-French Prime Minister, she lost her portfolio as Minister of Health because of her anti-nuclear stance, at a time when France was still conducting nuclear tests in its Pacific colonies. In 2000, Hilda became director of the Pacific Concerns Resource Center (PCRC), the international secretariat of the Nuclear Free and Independent Pacific Movement. She resigned from PCRC in 2004 and is now doing work in her home island, Pentecost.

Vanuatu is unique in that it was colonized by two European powers. After its independence in 1980, its leaders faced management of Anglophone and Francophone systems of administration and social services. They chose non-alignment in international politics and practised Melanesian socialism.

Gladys Marín Millié

Chilean Communist Party

Gladys Marín's 'footprint' remains. It is in the people of her country and in the world that admired her leadership, just as they admired the fighting spirit that sustained her, in the struggle against the tyranny that devastated Chile from 1973 to 1990. It was the same spirit that gave her the strength to overcome the pain of exile, of knowing that her husband had disappeared, of being far away from her two sons. She believed that, "the ideals of justice, peace and solidarity, the ideals of communism, are going to destroy the awful myths propagated against the left-wing movement."

"Gladys' life happened along with the life of Chile. There are no events in these decades that do not involve 'mutual footprints.'" This text was written by composer and singer Silvio Rodríguez in the preface to the Cuban edition of 'Life is Today', his autobiography, published in 2003. He is referring to Gladys Marín.
She was born in 1941, in Curepto, a region of Chile. At age 11, she went alone to Santiago to study at the Normal School. "In 1958, I joined the Communist Youth, where I found my ideals of social justice, peace and solidarity." She was elected a Member of Parliament in 1965. Her second mandate was interrupted, in 1973, by the military coup led by General Augusto Pinochet, which brought down the government of the United Popular Party of President Salvador Allende. Escaping from hell, separated from her children and husband, she was obliged to go into exile in Europe. "In 1976, when I was in Costa Rica working for the Chilean resistance, I knew that my husband was captured by the forces of repression. He never, ever reappeared." In 1978, Gladys returned clandestinely to Chile as part of Return Operation. "I had Spanish papers and a Spanish accent and I was wearing braces and false hips and breasts to make me look fatter." After the return of democracy, in 1994, she was elected General Secretary of the Communist Party, and, in 1999, she was the first woman to be a candidate for the presidency of Chile. She was also the first person to take action against Augusto Pinochet and help achieve his eventual detention in London.
In 2003, Gladys Marín was diagnosed as having a brain tumor. She still had the strength to "say goodbye to my people and my compañeros." In March 2005, a crowd that was even joined by the country's president, Ricardo Lagos, said a moving goodbye to her on the streets of Santiago.

The international persecution of the communist organizations was taken to such extremes by the Chilean military dictatorship that it resulted in the disappearance of many people and in the exile of the survivors. The search for equality and human rights signaled the return of democracy.

———
Chile

Nela Martínez Espinosa

Women's Continental Front for Peace and Against Intervention

A world fighter for peace, against military dictatorships and imperialism. She turned her indignation into a campaign for the human rights of both men and women. From different departure points, she contributed to the thoughts and actions behind the construction of citizenship for women. In 1940, Nela Martínez Espinosa led the occupation of the Presidential Palace where she was chosen, by the people, to manage the country for three days. After a popular election, she was elected the first female member of the Parliament of Ecuador.

"Is an Andean culture possible? I think that it is necessary. It is vital to dream of it. The autonomy that was lost — 500 years ago — must be found again and rebuilt as the birthright of the sons and daughters of this unique and intangible place, which, nevertheless, is threatened by the insane superiority complex of the white race," states Nela Martínez Espinosa. She achieved a brilliant leadership role in the Ecuadorian left-wing movement, participating in the foundation and consolidation of the first trade unions and indigenous organizations. Along with her contemporaries, she created the first women's organizations: the Ecuadorian Feminine Alliance, in 1937; and the Union of Revolutionary Women from Ecuador, in 1952, within which she founded and directed the first magazine for the women of the country. In the 1940s, she led the occupation of the Presidential Palace, where people chose her to manage the country for three days. After that, in a popular election, she was elected as the first female member of the Parliament of Ecuador.

As an anti-fascist fighter, she participated in the foundation of the World Peace Council (1949), in Paris, and in the fight against the nuclear bomb. She founded and directed the International Democratic Women's Federation, supported the achievements of Manuela Sáenz Aizpuru, Colonel of the Liberating Army, in the fight for Independence and worked intensely for the defense of human rights, in committees of solidarity with the populations who were invaded or attacked by dictatorships. She generously opened her own home to refugees of different countries. Nela Martínez Espinosa died late 2004 after she was selected to be among the 1000 Women for the Nobel Peace Prize 2005.

In Ecuador, the resistance to women's political action is also related to the patriarchal nature of society. Since the beginning of the 20th century, female workers, peasants, teachers and intellectuals began to participate in popular movements and trade unions.

Ecuador

Fiame Mataafa

Samoa Young Women's Christian Association (YWCA)
National Council of Women
Inailau Women's Leadership Network (IWLN)

For over 30 years, Fiame Mataafa has worked on, and been a role model for, promoting and advocating socio-economic and political equality for women and girls in Samoa, through her NGO involvements and her role as politician and Minister of Education. The mentoring of young women leaders is a specific focus, as is a community education program focusing on literacy and business skills training for people with special needs, a first of its kind for Samoa. She effectively bridges and mediates modern and customary faaSamoa (Samoan way of life) ways for herself and for Samoan women and girls.

"To me the faaSamoa (Samoan way of life) embodies principles of inclusion, contribution or service (tautua), fairness and justice. Everyone has a right to family resources and a duty to contribute to the family good. I learned these values in our daily life. People roll their eyes when Samoans talk about the complementarity of male and female in the faaSamoa: they can only see women as being marginalized. But my parents gave respect and support to each other in all their endeavours. Together they kept an eye out for everyone: people from all walks of life would come and share their concerns with my parents, old or young, from town or village. Their satisfaction and meaning in life came from doing this well. As a result, our family is poor in the monetary sense, but that is not what matters.

I did not realize how much this sense of responsibility, duty and continuity, integral to my father's chiefly title, was part of me until my father died suddenly. Then I appreciated the fullest meaning of my father's place, and my place as his daughter within the extended family and within the developing nation of Samoa. My father held three major matai (chiefly) titles but they did not pass automatically to me. My family decided we would fight for what were my right and my place. I learned first hand the importance of focus and commitment to a cause. My family was totally committed, helping build the power base of people support and knowledge. We should never underestimate the amount of knowledge and history and precedence in an oral culture. Our appeals were held before a court of males. The questioning was grueling but I won the second time. That action brought home to me the power of formalized, agreed to, and written down ideals to support the rights of the people to a fair and just deal. These are the strategies I use in my ministerial role and in my other activities."

The participation of women and girls in formalised leadership and decision-making forums is a key issue in Samoa today. Males usually win the matai (chief) titles holding power over the extended family system and customary land tenure and only matai can stand for parliament.

"Many people who have come through 30 years of struggle have found themselves isolated, disowned at the most personal level. The post revolutionary period has no time for enlightened criticism!"

Bernadette McAliskey

Irish Republican Socialist Party (IRSP)

Bernadette Devlin McAliskey (born 1947) was a student at Queen's University, Belfast, when the civil rights movement in Northern Ireland took to the streets in 1968. Bernadette became its radical icon and she was elected to the House of Commons in 1969. Having lost that seat in 1974, she campaigned for the Irish Republican Army (IRA) hunger strikers in 1980/81. In recent years, she has opposed the Good Friday Agreement of April 1998 on the grounds that it cemented British rule and Irish partition.

"So, people now want much more than they would happily have settled for. If, instead of beating our heads on 5th October 1968, the government had given us housing and votes, we would probably all have gone home and left it at that," says Bernadette Devlin McAliskey. After the murderous ambush on herself and her husband by loyalist killers in 1981, Bernadette understandably does not welcome strangers to her home in the town of Coalisland. It was most surprising to see how much she had aged and how careless she had become about her appearance. Was this the older version of the girl in the miniskirt who had slapped a British Home Secretary in the House of Commons? Yet, her sharp and unforgettable analysis of the conflict in Northern Ireland is punctuated by a wry humor and her eyes sparkle like they must have done all that time ago.

Bernadette still is a formidable foe of all those who have settled comfortably into the status quo. She lamented the British obsession with security legislation and policy at the time and speaks about a government that only understood the language of force. "And people like myself are left bankrupt and are consistently arguing, as we do, that there is some other way." She has, therefore, never fully answered the question about her attitude to violence — she would probably say it is the wrong question. And so, she has, over the years, mixed with curious people, always searching for political soul mates but rarely finding them. She was always stronger in her analysis of the past and present than in her expectancies for the future. Because, whereas her own motivation has, over time, clearly become ideological and favorably disposed to the radical left, the guiding forces in Northern Ireland have remained tribal. Today, Bernadette has become a marginal, slightly bitter voice, but powerful nonetheless whenever she chooses to speak up.

Bernadette McAliskey was much more than a poster girl — but she was that as well. She represented the face of intelligent resistance against systematic discrimination and the abuse of State power in Northern Ireland since 1968. Her voice is, therefore, unique and lonely at the same time.

United Kingdom

Cynthia McKinney

US Congress
Committee on Armed Services
Committee on the Budget

Cynthia McKinney is an outspoken leader for peace, human rights, and justice. As a result of questioning her congressional colleagues about the lack of full investigation after September 11 attacks, a retaliatory campaign successfully unseated her for one term, but in 2004 she was easily reelected. In her first term, she got legislation passed to extend health benefits for Vietnam War veteran victims of Agent Orange and sponsored legislation to end the use of depleted-uranium weapons. As a ranking member of the Human Rights Subcommittee, she prompted the UN to investigate the Rwanda genocide.

Cynthia McKinney was born in Atlanta, the daughter of former Georgia state representative Bill McKinney, one of Atlanta's first black law enforcement officers. She received a bachelor of arts in international relations from the University of Southern California and an master of arts in law and diplomacy from the Fletcher School of Law and Diplomacy; she is working toward a PhD at the University of California, Berkeley.

When Cynthia, then a member of the Georgia house of representatives, spoke on the floor against the US bombing of Baghdad in 1991, her colleagues were so offended they walked out on her. By contrast, women civic leaders were so inspired they asked her to run for congress. Her successful bid allowed her to continue her fight against US military policy.

Cynthia used her ten years in congress to support her Georgian constituents and a larger, worldwide public. She hosted the first delegation of Afro-Latinos from Central and South America and worked with the World Bank and the US state department to recognize Afro-Latinos. She stood with Aboriginals against Australian mining companies and with the U'wa people of Columbia in their fight to save their land from oil rigs. For the farmers of Georgia, she brought hundreds of millions of dollars in the form of an Enterprise Community grant. Cynthia worked with the chair of the Veterans Affairs Committee to strengthen the budget for homeless veterans and to protect the Atlanta Regional Veterans Affairs Hospital. Many overlooked veterans received medals because of her work. When she was defeated in 2002, Cynthia had begun to look into the treatment of women members of the armed Services.

It is often not politically expedient to speak out against war in a country whose manufacturers export more weapons than any other country in the world.

United States of America

Marta Lucía Micher Camarena

The Mirabal Sisters Human Rights Center
Feminist Millennium and Democratic Revolution Party

They thought of calling her Lourdes, but they named her Lucía. Marta Lucía: "Malú." She could have been an opera singer, but she became a politician. Decisions, denials, experiences have made the girl that studied piano and song into a defender of women's rights. A defender of herself.

In Guanajuato (state of Mexico; known for its cultural, political and religious conservatism), a young person can still be sent to jail for drawing graffiti. "Malú" began her struggle with the fight for laic education and for the defense of human rights for women. The fight for sexual rights was the most confrontational.

"I studied music in an official school. My family was in the well-off middle class. But I had classmates who lacked everything, even the instruments to practice on. At home, we had two pianos and my classmates had none. Many of them were virtuous, yet they had to rent their instruments. When I was 17 years old, I did an entrance exam for La Scala in Milan. I went to Italy and during one of the examinations I lost my voice. I thought, 'Well, this is not for me.' I stayed. I studied art history and got to know the student strikes. I went back in 1973, questioning my view of reality. I began to study at the National Autonomous University of Mexico." She joined a reflection group coordinated by Jesuits. Life turned upside down. She chose to identify herself with the poor and, from that moment on, she lived as one of them. She also chose the countryside instead of the city and started projects in support of nursery school education, women's rights and human rights. She has worked for feminism, for 20 years. She taught the current president of Mexico, Vicente Fox, to speak in a non-sexist language.

Today, Marta Lucía Micher Camarena is a federal member of Parliament for the Democratic Revolution Party.

The state of Guanajuato is known in Mexico for its conservatism. It is attached to the principles of the Catholic Church. It is a bastion of right-wing politics. It is a tough territory to fight for laic freedom and for women's sexual and reproductive rights.

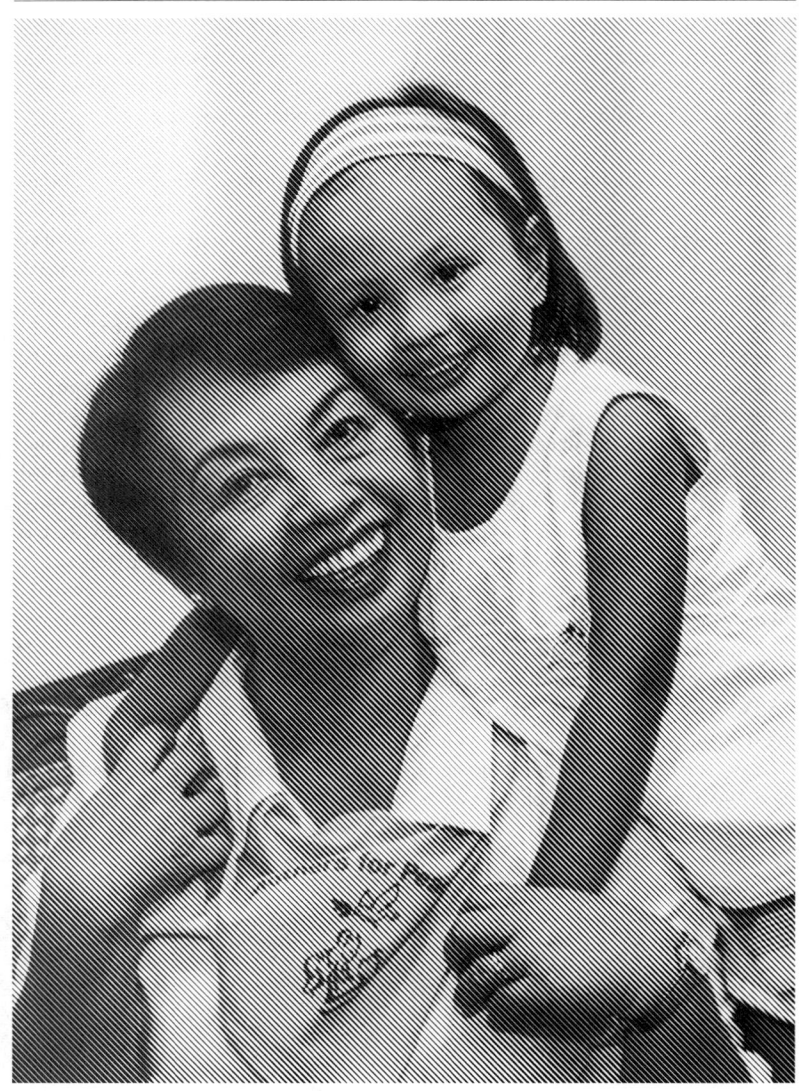

Irene Morada Santiago

Mindanao Commission on Women
Mothers for Peace Movement
Institute for Women's Leadership

For 30 years, Irene Morada Santiago has been at the forefront of efforts to improve the status of women in the Philippines and the world. Starting as a grassroots organizer of minority Muslim women in southern Philippines, she has worked on issues of poverty, peace and conflict, politics and governance, empowering women so they are taken seriously and are placed in major decision-making positions. She was the executive director of the highly successful NGO Forum on Women 1995 in China, which will be remembered for its impact on the issues that confronted women at the end of the 20th century.

Irene Morada Santiago remembers the day two drunken soldiers broke into the seminar hall and opened fire with their M-16 rifles. In front of her, 20 women and 23 children cowered for safety, terrified. It was in the mid-1970s, at the height of the secessionist rebellion waged by the Moro National Liberation Front against the Philippine government. It was against this political landscape that Irene, a graduate of Columbia University Graduate School of Journalism, founded the Kahayag Foundation. The Davao City-based NGO brought her to dangerous places in Mindanao, organizing poor Muslim women. The experience with the soldiers left Irene a changed person. "Yes, I was scared," she admits, "but I realized that I could be scared and still be brave. I was able to make those soldiers go away. So now being scared doesn't stop me from doing anything."

Irene's education, training, experience, determination, courage and boundless energy has brought her to the forefront of national and international work for women, founding or cofounding many organizations and networks along the way. In 1988, she was appointed Chief of the Asia/Pacific Section of the United Nations Development Fund for Women (Unifem), based in New York. Irene focused on innovative ways to connect grassroots level needs of women to the macropolicy environment. Upon her return to Mindanao after more than a decade of international work, Irene engaged in peace advocacy. In 2001, she became a member of the government peace panel, negotiating a peace agreement with the Moro Islamic Liberation Front. She formed the Mindanao Commission on Women, an NGO composed of Muslim, Christian and Lumad (indigenous) women to advocate for a gender perspective in the peace discourse. Currently, Irene Morada Santiago is chair and CEO of the Mindanao Commission on Women and convenor of the Mothers for Peace Movement.

In Muslim Mindanao and the Asia/Pacific area, patriarchy is deeply embedded in the political, economic and cultural structures, and the participation of women in politics and governance is severely restricted.

Philippines

Mu Sochua

Sam Rainsy Party

Mu Sochua (born 1954) is deputy head of the steering committee of the opposition Sam Rainsy Party in Cambodia. A former minister of Women's and Veterans' Affairs, Mu spearheaded the drafting of the law on domestic violence and trafficking. A catalyst for policy reform and institution building for the advancement of women and children's rights, she advises international organizations promoting women's rights. She authored the Prevention of Domestic Violence law (pending parliament approval) and advocates for a quota system to ensure the participation of women in politics.

Mu Sochua left Cambodia at the age of 18, when the war in Vietnam spilled over into her country, to reside in Paris and then America. Nine years later, she returned to her homeland. "I never stopped thinking about going home," she says. Wearing the traditional Cambodian dress, she stands out in whatever position she holds — government minister, Cabinet spokesperson, human rights activist or member of the opposition party. In 1995, Mu Sochua chaired the Coalition of Cambodian Women for Beijing. She raised funds for 115 grassroots women to attend the Fourth World Conference on Women in Beijing where she launched a project called "Women Weaving the World Together". She also helped raise funds to bring Cambodian women together to launch the first 100 meters of the 1000 meters of the Cambodian Women's Peace Ribbon to Beijing 1995.

In 2004, Mu brokered a deal with Thailand allowing trafficked Cambodian women to go home rather than be thrown in jail as illegal immigrants. She also crafted a similar arrangement with Vietnam. As a member of the opposition party Sam Rainsy, Mu continues to promote the advancement of women. A program that she started recently, helps women to be economically independent in order to resist traffickers. Under the program, women borrow about USD 100 dollars to buy a cart that they use to sell their products to tourists. The message of the program is clear: "Give women a chance".

About 45 percent of Cambodian people live below the poverty line and the numbers are increasing. Some 85 percent of young women and girls leave their villages to find work. It was reported that there are over 80,000 sex workers in Cambodia; a large number of them are under 16 years of age.

"We should examine and modify our policies to make them suitable for the country's development and international integration."

Nguyen Thi Hoai Thu

Commission on Social Affairs of Vietnam's National Assembly

Nguyen Thi Hoai Thu (born 1943) has served as a deputy in Vietnam's National Assembly for six consecutive terms, from 1976 to the present. As a member of the Assembly's Standing Committee and chairperson of the Commission on Social Affairs, she monitors the implementation of laws at grassroots level and carries the petitions of the people on burning issues to the National Assembly, which is responsible for drawing up suitable policies for practical life.

The members of Vietnam's National Assembly are familiar with Nguyen Thi Hoai Thu, who speaks in a soft voice about burning societal issues. As chair of the National Assembly's Commission on Social Affairs, she presents the people's problems with convincing analyses of reality and root causes, so that the members of the National Assembly understand the problems clearly, and draw up the appropriate policies. In this way, she has made a great contribution to dealing with the government's limitations and improving policies to protect laborers and secure the welfare of ordinary people. Nguyen Thi Hoai Thu was working for the Youth's Union when she was nominated to stand for election as a deputy in the National Assembly. In the Commission on Social Affairs, she supervises the implementation of policies on health, health care, and the prevention of social problems such as drugs, prostitution, and HIV/Aids. Nguyen Thi Hoai Thu also works on policies for labor, employment, wages, insurance, disabled people, orphaned children, migration, population, family, gender, religion, hunger eradication, and poverty alleviation. The government has modified and supplemented its policies as a result of her interventions and influence. Her presentations at the National Assembly, in public forums and in national and international conferences and seminars have raised awareness and changed behavior in society and promoted change and development in a constructive and peaceful manner. Having experienced the Vietnam War, she understands the costs of armed conflict and holds that nothing is more precious than peace, which is why she tries her best to listen to the people and serve their needs. In this way, Nguyen Thi Hoai Thu helps create peace, stability and development for the people of Vietnam and the world.

Thousands of marginalized people — the poor, the elderly, HIV/Aids affected people, etc. — need someone who supervises and monitors the implementation of laws at grassroots level and brings their issues and petitions to the National Assembly for consideration in the development of government policies.

Viet Nam

"I think it's like a dark, dark cloud and a period of great anxiety. If we lose, it's horrible, and if we win, it's horrible. Those of us in this movement want every soldier saved and home."

Grace Paley

War Resisters League
Greenwich Village Peace Center
Women's International League for Peace and Freedom

Grace Paley (born 1922) is Poet Laureate of the state of Vermont. Her politics are fundamental to her art, and a large part of her past 50 years has been spent in political action — from weekly silent vigils to marches and street rallies. In the past 30 years Grace has played a crucial role in promoting learning about the struggle of Muslims, Christians, and Jews in Palestine and Israel. Her peace work is inclusive of environmentalist and feminist thinking, and through it Grace continues to act locally, think globally, and inspire people all over the world.

Grace Paley's writing, teaching, and speaking engender fierce attachment: Grace has fans like a film star. She is unusual in the worlds of literature and politics, partly because she is so passionately active in both, and partly because she engenders great warmth and affection from her colleagues in both. It is no exaggeration to say that she is revered as a political activist and thinker in much the same way she is revered as a writer of stories and poems.

In the past 30 years, Grace's writing has grown to articulate her politics; she is devoted to making connections among issues, and shows the intricate webs linking such constellations as famine, literacy, and the global dominance of biotechnology in agribusiness.

She is now over 80, working mostly in New York and Vermont, and yet she still travels frequently to other states and other countries: as a member of the Greenwich Village Peace Center, the War Resisters League, and the Women's International League for Peace and Freedom, as well as the Women's Pentagon Action and several Jewish peace organizations. During the Vietnam war, Grace was a delegate to the World Peace Conference and a member of peace missions to Hanoi. She visited with Soviet dissidents, and travelled to Chile, Nicaragua, and El Salvador, learning about liberation and peace movements there, and then teaching about what she had learned when she returned to the USA.

Grace has often focused on the relationships between peace, work, and the health of women and children, arguing against forced sterilization, nuclear proliferation, and bioengineering of food and seeds, and in favor of abortion rights, access to contraception, and small farms and rural communities. She also discusses the dangers of fundamentalism — in any religion.

1922 was the year Gandhi was sentenced to six years in prison for civil disobedience, the first Irish government free of England was formed, President Harding ordered US troops home from the Rhineland, and Grace was born in New York City to Ukrainian Jews who had fled pogroms.

United States of America

Maria Lorenza Palm-Dalupan

When the Filipino people ousted the dictator Marcos in a non-violent revolution, Maria "Binky" Lorenza Palm-Dalupan (born 1952) heeded the call to help rebuild democracy. She served two presidents as Executive Director of the Peace Commission, the National Unification Commission (NUC) and the Office of the Presidential Adviser on the Peace Process (OPAPP). Her office developed peace policy, supported peace negotiations, coordinated reforms to address causes of armed conflicts and partnered with stakeholders in and out of government in an effort to build a culture of peace in the country.

Like many Filipinos during the martial law period (1972—1986), Binky wanted nothing to do with the government. So she immersed herself in academic work (anthropology) and later pursued higher studies in the US. Coming home in 1985 to join the pro-democracy campaign, she stayed on to serve in the new government that needed all the help it could get. For ten years, Binky ran the government peace office on behalf of several Presidential Peace Advisers. With a committed staff, she helped formulate, organize and manage government peace policies and programs responding to such factors as the dynamics between civilian and military sectors in government, changing levels, character and impact of the armed conflicts, strengthened interaction with civil society peace advocates and the growth of community-based peace initiatives.

Binky nurtured the shift in official policy to a broader vision of peace as more than the absence of an armed conflict. The peace process is seen as a non-violent social transformation, working quietly, setting the foundation and infrastructure for all stakeholders in the peace process. When she left government in 1996, her office was overseeing the government's comprehensive peace program, "Six Paths to Peace", a package of reforms linked together by three underlying principles: societal transformation towards justice, equity, humanity and pluralism; people's participation; and non-violence. Recognizing that government is a source of and party to the armed conflicts, Binky sees the necessity and value of working for peace from within government. "To achieve sustainable peace, government must be transformed into an instrument of social justice and an enabler of peace. That is the potential and the continuing challenge of peace workers in government."

After the People Power Revolution that ended 14 years of martial law in the Philippines in 1986, the structure of the Marcos dictatorship had to be dismantled, democracy had to be restored and warring factions in Philippine society had to be reconciled if peace was to be restored.

Ruth Sando Perry

Peace Now
Perry Center

Ruth Sando Perry (born 1939) was a lecturer at the University of Liberia before settling in Monrovia where she worked in a bank and created the NGO Peace Now. As the first female Head of State and Chairperson, Council of State of the Liberia National Transitional Government, Ruth Sando Perry presided over the disarmament of the warring parties in Liberia, repatriated and resettled refugees and displaced people, and conducted internationally acclaimed free and fair democratic elections.

The month of August 1997 was a historic moment when, for the first time, a woman was elected unanimously over two male contestants as leader of an African government by the authorities of the Economic Community of West African States (ECOWAS). Ruth Sando Perry had a very difficult mandate to execute, but she succeed where many failed and established the first peace framework in seven years and guided the country to democratic elections. She is gifted with the traditional capacity to direct and, with a great degree of patience, wisdom and faith in God, she faced the trials imposed by conflict resolution. Her efforts brought about the installation of a peaceful environment: she insisted on disarmament and the repatriation of refugees. As head of state, she worked also on the problem of child soldiers. On this last issue she contextualized where exactly in Liberia large numbers of children were being used as soldiers.

Her coming to political power gave rise to great hope throughout the country. Ruth Sando Perry encouraged many groups of women to participate actively in politics. Today, she continues to educate people of developing countries with the intention of increasing awareness on the problems of peace, gender, and security. Madam Ruth Sando Perry is the second Balfour African President-in-Residence at Boston University's African Presidential Archives and Research Center.

The instability in Liberia had started in 1989 with the Nimba rebellion which quickly transformed itself into a destructive war that lasted seven years, caused the death of 200,000 people, made 2.5 million homeless, and 250,000 others took refuge in neighboring countries.

Liberia

Fanny Sonia Pollarolo Villa

Consejo Nacional para el Control de Estupefacientes (Conace)

Fanny Pollarolo's role in Chile's political, cultural and social arena is momentous and irreplaceable. As a Member of Parliament, she has had a fundamental role in the legal defense of sexual minorities. She has been a driving force in the decriminalization of sodomy and was the creator of the Aids law, which was passed to fix the responsibility of the State in that matter. Her work has been crucial for bringing together different sectors whose common aim is to build a democracy respectful of the rights of a diverse society.

Linares, a city in the south of Santiago, the capital of Chile, is an important farming and livestock center. Fanny Pollarolo was born there in 1935. Her community work began as a doctor and Psychiatry professor. After the state coup of 1973, she went into exile in Argentina, where she remained until 1975. "During the period of repression, I went back to the country to work for the Vicariate for Solidarity, and the Foundation for Social Aid, directed by the Christian Church." In 1977, she set up the Medical Psychiatric Program for the victims of repression, which she directed until 1986. "There, I was able to learn about the effects caused by torture, exile and other severe violations of human rights." Until the end of the military dictatorship in 1990, she was in the front of the fight for the return of democracy. As a member of parliament for the socialist party, her work between 1994 and 2002 "focused on the situation of children, adolescents lacking schooling, homosexual communities, people with HIV, and the defense of women's right to sexual and reproductive health, without discrimination, coercion or violence."

"From a young age, we women are treated as if we have no ability to make decisions about ourselves." That was her statement during a convention to mobilize people against the banning of the pill for preventing pregnancy. "The shortage of information and the systematic neglect of women's sexual rights affect mostly adolescents of poor backgrounds, who are the mothers of almost 40,000 of the children born in Chile every year."

Today, Fanny works on the National Council for the Control of Narcotics (Conace), where she is dedicated to the rehabilitation of children living on the streets. Her leadership continues to put the quality and feeling of the women's work at the service of the population.

The military dictatorship that governed Chile, between 1973 and 1990, entailed the systematic violation of the political and individual rights of the people. It involved severe damage to the labor, family and sexual health situations. It had a particular impact on women and children.

Chile

Sahana Pradhan

Women's Security Pressure Group (WSPG)

Sahana Pradhan (born 1927) is one of Nepal's veteran politicians and social activists. She is a politburo member of the Nepal Communist Party (United Marxist-Leninist), and president of the Women's Security Pressure Group, which lobbies for women's sociopolitical rights nationally. Sahana is a symbol of the struggle for women's education and political rights in Nepal.

Sahana Pradhan's childhood was shaped and disrupted by the experience of living through World War II in Burma — it gave her the rare opportunity to go to school. But when she returned to Nepal in the middle of the war, social conservatism and lack of opportunities made it extremely hard to continue with her education. But Sahana became one of the first women in Nepal to finish secondary school within the country. She and her elder sister came into contact with young Nepali revolutionary fighters, one of them their own younger brother, who started to teach them at home. Their parents, who initially opposed this, later consented, principally because Sahana and her sister rebelled. Both sisters appeared for matriculation privately and passed.

Sahana came into contact with the Communist Party of Nepal when she married its founder and joined the party. However, once she had two children to look after, she began to teach at the university, resuming her political career when her children were older, and contributing to the 1990 movement for democracy. She was coordinator of the Bam Morcha (Joint Forum of Communist Parties), one of the groups leading the movement.

Today, she is a politburo member of the Nepal Communist Party, and president of the Women's Security Pressure Group, which lobbies for women's sociopolitical rights nationally. It is Sahana's struggle that has made it possible for women to vote and to stand for election.

Due to the reservation of five percent seats for women in the lower house of parliament, and three seats in the upper house, women in Nepal have become ministers and vice-speakers. Around 40,000 women representatives have been elected and nominated to village and district development committees.

Ester Rahal

General National Council of Southern Kordofan State (GNCSKS)
Sudanese Parliament

Ester Kuku Rahal (45), originally from the Nuba Mountain region in Sudan, did not receive formal early education. The dominant cultural traditions in her family did not consider girls' education important. However, after she had married and become a mother of four children she went to evening school. Ester began to participate in many discussions on peace and became a member of the GNCSKS. She is involved in the activities of many NGOs, flagging up demanding issues, such as peace and social development and became the first woman to represent Nuba Mountain's women in the Sudanese Parliament.

Ester is very much respected and applauded by the younger generations in Sudan. They call her "Mama Ester" as a gesture of reverence and admiration. She exhibits a very courageous charisma, as she is very vocal and challenging when she addresses issues relating to peoples' essential needs and livelihood. Ester learnt how to read and write, and most significantly she now speaks English fluently. That is why she is always invited to represent the Nuba Mountain's women, locally and internationally, in South Africa, Nairobi, Kampala and Geneva. Ester's interpersonal skills are awesome, and she always catches the attention of her audience with her friendly impromptu talks. She is extremely dedicated to probing demanding issues raised in her local community vis-à-vis the enhancement of the dwindling conditions of women's lives, which touch a large number of local people.

Esther's long-life mission is to promote peace in the Nuba Mountains region in the Sudan. She is the first woman to represent the Nuba Mountains, locally and internationally, in many world gatherings in places such as South Africa, Kenya, Kampala and Geneva.

Sudan

Bihodjal Rahimova

Unifem

Bihojal Rahimova (born 1941) is a national adviser of the Unifem Project "Rights for the Land and Economic Safety of Rural Women" in Tajikistan. Owing to her efforts there have been significant changes in land reform legislation as well as in the state program on equal rights and possibilities for men and women. She pays special attention to the issues of access to land and credit for rural women. She brings to this task long experience as an important political figure in the Soviet Union and a profound concern for the rights of women.

Bihodjal Rahimova was born in the village of Yova in Khojand province. Her dream was to become an engineer. A hard-working woman, she is capable of working 24 hours, day and night, without complaint. Her adherence to principles and trustworthiness in relation to any kind of work won her the respect of thousands of people not just in Tajikistan, but in the other republics of the former USSR as well. She personifies the image of an emancipated Tajik woman: creative, educated, independent minded, active, driven, and energetic. Her mission is in politics. There are few individuals in Tajikistan and Central Asia who are like Bihodjal. She is the first and only woman in Central Asia to occupy a very high post in the former Soviet Union — Deputy Chairman of the Council of Ministers of the USSR. Her main commitment is giving help to the people in need. Those who elected her know that she always keeps her word and fulfills her promises.

The hardest period of her life, just as for many Tajik people, was the period of civil war in 1992–1994, when the fate of Tajikistan was being decided, when people were being openly killed, and when all human values were ignored. There was a real threat to her life and family, and they had to move from Dushanbe to Khojand. She had to re-examine everything: her life, family, position, and the people around her. She made the decision to stand with the people who want peace and prosperity for Tajikistan.

The day of reconciliation came and now peace and order in Tajikistan are getting better and better. Life is becoming more stable, despite the economic difficulties. Bihodjal has the qualities of a real leader, she is rebellious and shrewd, but with an enormous thirst for justice and a sincere desire to fulfill her work. She is a fine politician and a good role model for all people, especially the young.

The war in Tajikistan left an indelible mark in people's memories. Women and children suffered. Poverty and unemployment, especially in rural areas, put women in great difficulties. Many lost their husbands during the war and were left alone to support their families.

Maria Reinat-Pumarejo

Institute for Latino Empowerment (ILE)
People's Institute for Survival and Beyond
East Asia–US–Puerto Rico Women's Network against Militarism

Maria Reinat-Pumarejo has played a key role in ending the use by the USA of the island of Vieques, Puerto Rico, as a military base. Her world view of peace and justice has energized and empowered working-class women to uproot racism and sexism. In 1992, her struggle against racism prompted her to cofound the Institute for Latino Empowerment (ILE). In 1995, in collaboration with the People's Institute for Survival and Beyond, ILE extended its efforts to include white people and other people of color in its mission, resulting in the Undoing Racism Organizing Collective in the Northeast.

Born into a working-class family, Maria was adopted into a family of similar background when her parents separated. She began working at age 14. Maria obtained a bachelor of arts in social sciences with a concentration in history from the University of Puerto Rico and worked as a computer consultant. Poverty and the political situation prompted her to immigrate to the USA. A young, single mother, she was determined both to support her family and to get an education. She worked three jobs, and obtained a master of arts in education and counseling psychology from the University of Massachusetts.

Maria began her work in social and political transformation in 1988 at Casa Latina, a nonprofit project in Northampton, Massachusetts, one of only three Latino organizations led by a woman in the area at that time. She cofounded ILE in 1992, and in 1997 returned to Puerto Rico. There, she focused her energy — often employing civil disobedience — to bring about the demilitarization of the island of Vieques by the USA, which had used the area for the past 60 years for bombing exercises. The occupation has resulted in at least one death and caused cancer and massive environmental degradation. The campaign resulted in an announcement by president Bush that the US navy would leave Vieques, an important step in the establishment of self-determination for all of Puerto Rico and a victory for others worldwide who are campaigning to rid their lands of US military bases and installations.

When Maria began her work in the USA, there were few organizations engaged in transforming the poverty and neglect of Puerto Ricans. Latin activists were often harassed, arrested, or even killed by police officers.

Puerto Rico

Dorothy Rupert

Women's International League for Peace and Freedom (WILPF)
Women's Action for New Directions (Wand)

Dorothy Rupert (born 1926) served 35 years as a public high school teacher and counselor, 14 more years in the Colorado House and Senate, and decades in the peace and women's rights/human rights movements. She has consistently supported education, relentlessly and courageously tackled difficult legislative issues, and traveled the globe for peace. Dorothy embodies commitment, passion, vitality, caring, sincerity, never-give-up determination, and joy. As she nears 80, these traits shine more brightly than ever.

"We discovered that a powerful way of truly seeing another person is to look into each other's face and with no words say 'I am glad you are here. You have every right to be here.'" Dorothy Rupert shares this memory from the UN Conference on Women in Beijing in 1995. It is an image that says much about this woman whose life is all about really seeing and honoring others. After a visit in Africa where she had met a 16-year-old victim of female genital mutilation, Dorothy determined to learn the truth about mutilation in her home state of Colorado and do everything possible to stop it. She wrote and passed legislation making it a felony. Having seen buttons in Beijing that read: Thursdays in Black: Demanding a World without Rape and Violence, Dorothy organized a button campaign back home, modeled after Women in Black, the Palestinian and Israeli women who stand together outside the Knesset to advocate nonviolence. She distributed over 10,000 buttons. And in Beijing Dorothy heard the stories of 35,000 women from all over the world, and within months after returning home she gave 50 talks and wrote editorials on their behalf. By the time she traveled to Beijing, Dorothy had served 35 years as a high school teacher and counselor, 14 years in the Colorado legislature, and decades in the peace and women's rights/human rights movements. She earned the reputation of one who would fight for those who had no voice. More than 40 plaques on her capitol office walls testify to Dorothy's effectiveness and the appreciation of many diverse groups for her work.

Dorothy's life and work cannot be summed up in a word or two, but there are a few words that come to mind, her own words: "My dream is for all of the world's little girls to have access to a progressive education where their learning opens doors to whole new possibilities for them to live their dreams."

There is a systematic effort underway in the USA to dismantle social programs. President Bush is promoting privatization of social security, and his judicial appointments threaten to roll back abortion rights, environmental regulations, affirmative action, civil liberties, and civil rights.

United States of America

Lataben Sachde

Kutch Mahila Vikas Sangathan (KMVS)

For 15 years, Lataben Sachde (born 1963) has been working with elected women, and studying their perspective on good governance. The change her leadership has brought about is evident in the way that women leaders execute their positional power in their respective villages. i.e., responsibly. An estimated 500 "leaders" have stepped out of their restrictive social mores, challenging the patriarchal setup. Lataben and her team are the quiet force that has initiated a powerful grassroots movement of women claiming their public spaces.

Lataben Sachde had to struggle with her in-laws to work with the Kutch Mahila Vikas Sangathan (KMVS). She also had to overcome her own lack of exposure and specific educational skills within the organization. Fifteen years later, Lataben is one of the leaders of the organization. Her work with KMVS is centered on the political empowerment of rural women. She inspires by personal example, and has built the capacities of women in governance and political leadership at the village level. Lataben's focus is on nurturing political leadership within the village and the community.

Lataben hails from the Kutch district, which gives her an edge in understanding the social dynamics of the region. For over a decade and a half, she has been interacting with women who have been elected, and understanding their perspective on what comprises good governance. She also interacts with the government machinery to understand its perspective, so as to strategize and make an entry point into the system.

The change brought about by Lataben's leadership is evident in the governance behavior of the women leaders in their respective villages. An estimated 500 leaders have been able to step out of their restrictive social mores, challenging the existing patriarchal setup.

Lataben's capacity to manage her familial responsibilities and her responsibilities at work has finally won her the respect of her in-laws. They now understand and support her work in the field. She and her team are the quiet force that has initiated a powerful grassroots movement of women claiming their public spaces.

Women in the Kutch area of Gujarat are among the most disempowered in India. In this situation, if elected women representatives move out of the shadow of the men who put them in power, and work toward realizing the import of their positions, the social benefits will be enormous.

India

"I fight for women's economic advancement."

Moussomakan Sakiliba

Gnélény

Moussoumakan Sakiliba (born 1951) has associated herself with activities that promote women. With Gnélény she and her co-activists organize themselves around the activities of development, focusing on the primary sector and the transformation of agricultural products.

Moussoumakan Sakiliba quickly understood that community life is carried by development. This is why she chose this area to work with other women of her country. She is the administrative secretary of the women's association of Bafoulabé called Gnélény. The women in the association focus on the primary sector and the transformation of agricultural products. With this, they give themselves the potential for know-how and and self-improvement. More than that: the members of Gnélény are not afraid to go beyond the economical fight. Thus, the association is interested, more and more, in the electoral processes and encourages its activists to participate in the decision-making process of the community. Each woman is encouraged to choose freely the party that best represents her hopes.

Moussoumakan is known in her environment for her determination to confront difficulties tenaciously. These are: the poor perception of women's struggle in society; the weak purchasing power of women-headed households; the domination of women called to subject themselves to their husband's authority; the growing volume of domestic work; the absence of support for women's causes; the absence or insufficiency of financial sources for local development; the high rate of illiteracy among woman or the ignorance about relevant texts on the rights of the woman.

She is president of the body co-ordinating women's non-governmental organizations and associations, which is a part of Coordination of Associations and Women's NGOs (CAFO), in the area of Bafoulabé. Moussoumakan does not like to talk about herself. She prefers to leave to others judgement of her actions.

According to Moussoumakan Sakiliba, the work of the association movement consists of helping women to get together to discuss and decide on solutions to their many problems. An association of women should also defend the moral interests of its members.

Bouthaina Shaaban

Damascus University (DU)

Bouthaina Shaaban is a professor of English literature at Damascus University (DU), a writer and the Syrian Minister of Expatriate Affaires. Before assuming her current ministerial job, she was director of the Foreign Media Department at the Ministry of Foreign Affairs in Syria. She has a PhD and an MA in English Literature from the University of Warwick, UK, in addition to a BA in English Literature from DU.

Inspired by her strong-willed mother, Bouthaina Shaaban has been dedicated to lifting the social injustices that have befallen women in the Arab world. Her subsequent involvement in politics and foreign affairs, as Syrian president Hafez al-Asad's interpreter during peace negotiations, set her on a different career path. Over the past ten years, Bouthaina Shaaban has set a shining example for women who are looking forward to working close to the decision-makers in her country.

Bouthaina commenced her study in the UK at a time when the social conditions in Syria had prevented many women from traveling abroad by themselves and from building up a better career. When she started her job at the Ministry of Foreign Affairs it was generally inappropriate for women to work in politics. However she surmounted all these social challenges and eventually obtained her degree and returned home so that her country could benefit from her experience. She joined the Syrian Ministry of Foreign Affairs as an advisor in 1988. Since then, Bouthaina Shabaan has efficiently represented Syria as a notorious spokeswoman at international level. She is also a talented author. So far she has published four books and has written chapters in many others.

Inspired by her mother, Bouthaina Shaaban completed her PhD in the UK when social conditions in Syria had prevented many women from traveling abroad. When she started her job at the Ministry of Foreign Affairs it was generally inappropriate for women to work in politics.

Nafisa Shah

Pakistan government

Only two of Pakistan's 101 district mayors are women, and Nafisa Shah (born 1968) is one of them. A distinguished woman administrator in an almost exclusively male domain, Nafisa has set new standards for integrity in her conflict-torn and crime-ridden district. She leads from the front in dealing with injustices against women and the poor, and has made her district a model of community-supported development.

Nafisa Shah was in the midst of a thesis on honor and violence at Oxford University when she made her entry into politics. In 2001, she had traveled from Oxford to her hometown in Upper Sindh to carry out field research when her politically active family drafted her into an electoral battle. The 37-year-old, put up as a candidate in a local election, ended up as district mayor of Khairpur in Upper Sindh — one of two women in Pakistan to hold such a post. Nafisa's task was to maintain law and order, and run the district government. Khairpur, with 1.7 million people spread over 16,000 square kilometers of semiarid land, has an annual homicide rate of more than 300. Poverty levels are higher than the national average, and literacy is as low as 13 percent among rural women.

Few people expected Nafisa to last the course, but she is setting an example of personal honesty and integrity in an environment where both have long been discarded. In a district where justice is traded in government offices, Nafisa tries to deliver real justice. She has doggedly pursued murder cases to their conclusion, despite police impediments and has stood up to land-grabbers, encouraging the formation of hundreds of community organizations working on low-cost development projects through government grants.

Nafisa started out as a journalist. Reporting for the liberal, progressive magazine, Newsline, she wrote on violence against women, immigrants, refugees, and poor and underrepresented communities. The first detailed expose on "honor killings" in Upper Sindh was hers, for which she won the All Pakistan Newspaper Society Award in 1995. She was also given a United Nations Environment Programme youth award for reporting on environmental degradation, and the Bagby scholarship to Oxford University, where she researched honor killings. Now, as part of her job, she deals with them all the time.

District governments are a recent phenomenon in Pakistan, introduced in 2000 by General Pervez Musharraf's plans for structural reform. Education, health, finance, land tax, agriculture, community development, and information technology now fall under the district administrator.

Pakistan

Marina Silva

Ministério do Meio Ambiente (Ministry of the Environment)

Maria Osmarina Marina Silva de Lima (1958), known nationally as Marina Silva, is the State Minister of the Environment, in the government of Lula da Silva. Before, she was a community leader, a town councilor, a federal deputy and senator, always as a part of PT (Labor Party). She has four children, and she is an emblem of the defense of the Amazon forest and of the people that live there. She is a firm defender of sustainable development.

She defines herself as a woman moved by faith and by determination: "Faith so as not to be discouraged by the impossible. Determination is to face the difficulties of what is possible." Marina Silva was born in the heart of a rubber plantation in the countryside of Acre, one of the states of the Legal Amazon. She and her family worked removing latex from rubber trees, extractive activity by excellence and one depreciated by tradition. Her future would be like the one of thousands of girls born under adverse economic conditions and whose dreams are crushed in a quotidian of struggle. That would have been her future, but Marina comprehended the invaluable importance of political organization.

Marina Silva stood out beside Chico Mendes, in the firm defense of a Sustainable Amazon, which means the defense of an economic action that guarantees quality of life for the people and the preservation of natural resources. Chico Mendes was assassinated in 1988 by farmers. Marina kept on listening to the heart of the people from the forest.

With her undeniable charisma, she obtained the Ministry of the Environment with the support of environmentalists, community leaders, groups and associations of Amazonian women. In Brazil, the defense of the environment is a crusade. By tradition, there are two forces which are constantly colliding. One of them, predatory, aiming to become wealthier and walking over everything: people, animals, forests. The other one acts in benefit of the workers' lives and of the biodiversity. Marina is for the protection of everything that lives; a woman that esteems values. According to her, the real Gross Internal Product of a nation is its human values: "Maybe it is a soft internal product." Soft and powerful like the Amazon — like Marina Silva.

A history of beating the odds. Only at age 14, Marina Silva learned the four mathematical operations and how to tell time. At age 47, she directs a Ministry of the State. All of this done without ever betraying the forest and its inhabitants.

Brazil

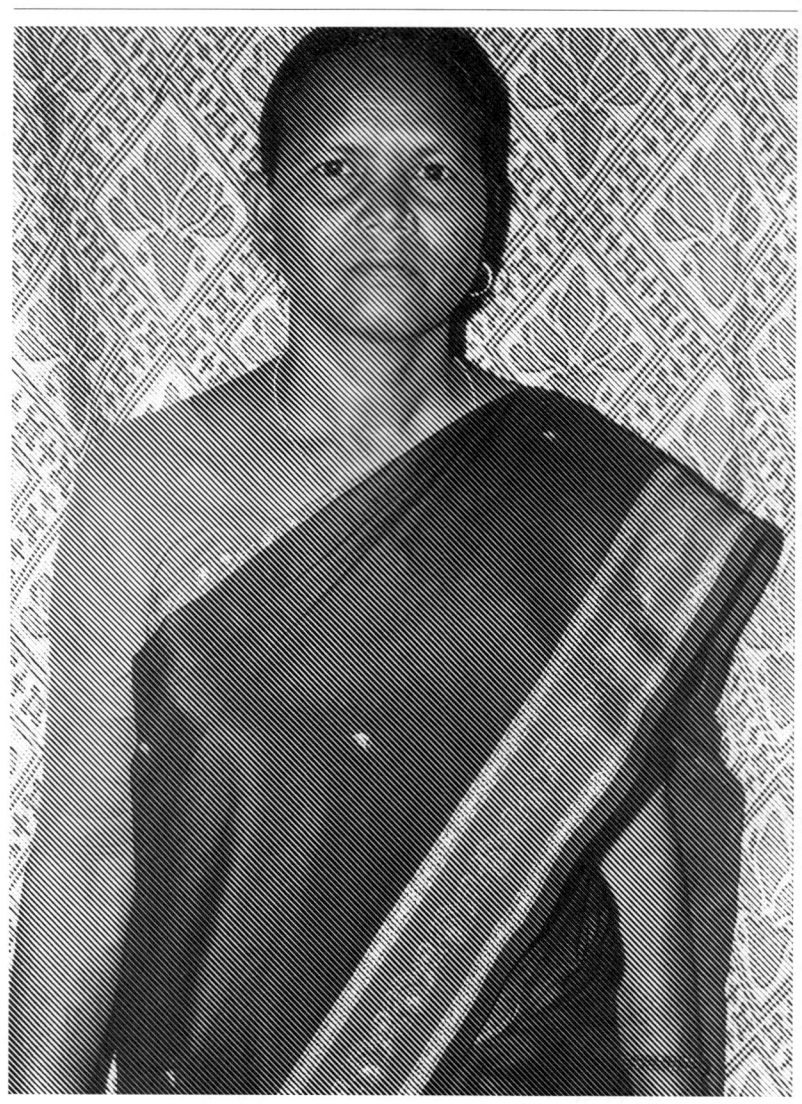

Sonia

Mahila Samakhya

Sonia (born 1968) — village head (sarpanch) of Ninhi Charhi — comes from a poor family of Kol adivasi (tribal people) agricultural workers. For over 16 years, she has motivated other women in her village to educate themselves. Sonia also won the panchayat (body of elected representatives of a village) elections despite efforts by the locally powerful to beat her down. Her five years as chief have changed the face of her village beyond recognition, bringing to it education, water, electricity, healthcare, sewage disposal, and a local newspaper that she publishes in the local language.

Sonia is a strong young woman. From a poor family of Kol adivasi agricultural workers, she joined the Mahila Samakhya Education Center 16 years ago, and has motivated other women in her village to educate themselves. After she became village head, she arranged for the primary school — until then used as a cattleshed and hay barn — to be spruced up so that children could study in it.

She also freed adivasi lands. With little more than her firm resolve, perseverance, and ability to rally people to her fight against powerful adversaries like local politicians and the police authorities, she organized an agitation on the issue of agricultural laborers' rights, which led to increased payments for the workers. Her five years as sarpanch have seen the face of the village altered beyond recognition. Besides handpumps for clean water, she also got drainpipes built for sewage disposal. Sonia has also brought in electricity connections and proper roads. She keeps track of government schemes for social welfare, and has ensured that 60 of the village elderly receive an old age pension under a government scheme.

The most remarkable thing about this petite, soft-spoken woman is her boundless energy. Apart from handling her responsibilities as village chief, Sonia also publishes a newspaper, Khabar Lahariya, in the local Bundeli language. The newspaper aims to disseminate national and international news. Sonia's strength and courage are mesmeric, but quiet. Rudeness and imprecision are not options.

Women village heads have proved more often than not to be more effective than men: they are driven by conscience, responsibility, and an innate honesty, and they are slowly changing the face of rural India.

India

Heloneida Studart

Asamblea Legislativa de Río de Janeiro

Heloneida Studart (1932) is on her fourth mandate as state representative. She was elected for the first time in 1978, with 60,000 votes, and has always fought for the country's democratization. In 1975, she founded the Brazilian Woman Center. She worked side by side with feminists fighting for amnesty and participated on the creation of the State Council for Female Rights. She has been making her mandates a space for the defense of human rights.

Thanks to her father, a revolutionary abolitionist (one who fought for the abolition of slavery), the young Heloneida did not cut off her relationship with her family when she was 18 and moved from her hometown, Fortaleza, to Rio. She grew up listening to her aunt saying that "women do not have the right to want anything." No women from her family had ever worked when she decided to move to Rio willing to publish her first romance novel and to pursue a career as a writer. As the granddaughter of Baron Studart and the only girl in a family of three brothers, Heloneida rejected the traditional education she received in the Northeast.

Heloneida Studart's first job in Rio was to run a traveling library that took books, movies and lectures to working-class neighborhoods. This experience led her closer to left-wing political groups and stimulated her to found the Union of Cultural Entities, of which she was president until 1969, when she was arrested by the military dictatorship, installed in Brazil in 1964. During the 1970s, she worked as the editor of 'Manchete magazine.' In 1989, she joined the Partido dos Trabalhadores (Labor Party). As a journalist, she also participated in the International Woman's Congress that took place in Mexico, in 1975. "All the women had a common complaint: male oppression," she remembers. When she returned to Brazil, Heloneida Studart helped to found the Brazilian Woman Center. She is a romance novel writer and has 12 published books, such as the essay 'Mulher Objeto de Cama e Mesa' (Woman: object of bed and table). Heloneida is also a well-known playwright. 'Homem não entra' (Men not allowed) was her play, and it was on for five years, defending ideals of progress and female promotion. "Nowadays, feminist ideals are totally disseminated."

Brazilian feminists played a decisive role in the fight for political amnesty, demanding the return of their relatives who were exiled during the military dictatorship. The campaign, which began on 1978, allowed all those that had been persecuted by the military regime to return to Brazil.

Brazil

Yanxia Su

Heilongjiang Sumeng Forestry Development Co. Ltd.

Su Yanxia was born in 1970 and started her career in farming and forestry from selling grape seedlings after she had failed her college entrance examination in China's Northeastern Heilongjiang Province. In the past ten years she has saved and helped propagate many endangered tree species. Elected as a delegate to the National People's Congress, the highest legislative body, she has used her status as a people's representative to draw government attention to agriculture and the problems of farmers, as well as to get more peasant representatives into decision-making positions.

Su Yanxia, a rural woman from China's Northeastern Heilongjiang Province, founded the Heilongjiang Sumeng Forestry Development Co. Ltd. in 1994. Yanxia worked hard to develop her business. She taught herself through self-study and worked as an apprentice to 18 professionals. She has technical links with eight research groups and has undertaken 36 experimental projects. She has contributed to production and research aspects of ecological projects involving special species of vegetables, flowers, fruits, and high-quality crops. She was also responsible for an exemplary case of reforming low-yielding land, and made a breakthrough by breeding a tree species, the yew, that is under first-class state protection. Her company now holds over 33 million yuan of fixed assets and has extensive land.

There are five specialized plots for crops, vegetables, orchids, flowers and water plants. There are 20 greenhouses for the breeding of over 1200 species of yew and dragon spruce seedlings. Over the past decade Yanxia has offered technical services to over 500 orchid farmers, received over 6000 visitors, and answered some 21,000 written enquiries. She has also sent out technical information and free seedlings worth about 150,000 yuan. In 1998 she was elected as a delegate to the ninth National People's Congress, the highest-level legislative body. Since then she has been calling for equal citizen status for China's farmers. She advocates the formation of professional associations and economic cooperation organizations, and enthusiastically promotes the journal, Farmer Cooperative Law.

In the 1980s there was a brain drain from the countryside, with many young people going to urban areas, thereby denying many villages the opportunity to develop and prosper. Young people like Su Yanxia, who chose to work in the countryside, are rare.

China

Pura Sumangil

Concerned Citizens of Abra for Good Government (CCAGG)
Transparency and Accountability Network (Tr-Ac Net)
Cordillera Women's Network for Peace and Development

Pura Sumangil was born in 1941 in Nueva Ecija province. She came to Abra in 1970 to be ordained an Auxiliary by the local Bishop and she never left. In her 35 years in Abra, she has been a teacher, counselor, community organizer and civic leader, all of which come under her work for peace and good governance. In 1986, she cofounded the Concerned Citizens of Abra for Good Government (CCAGG), a NGO working for economic emancipation, monitoring government, empowerment and building citizenship. In 1997, she received the Aurora Aragon Quezon Peace Award.

Pura Sumangil believes that people can always find common ground to settle their differences and that peace and good governance are the solution to the problems of Abra, her adopted province, and the entire country. She also believes that disputes at grassroots level can be resolved by involving the people through feedback and dialogue. After the snap elections in 1986, Pura, then a volunteer at the National Movement for Free Elections (NAMFREL) worked with other like-minded citizens to form the CCAGG. Local governments did not welcome the idea of private citizens monitoring their performance and Pura received death threats, but the group persisted in exposing graft and corrupt practices through citizen vigilance.

Working with the Tingguian tribe in the late 1980s, Pura became involved in the reconstruction of war-torn communities in the uplands. She was a co-convener of the National Unification Commission, now Office of the Presidential Adviser on the Peace Process (OPAPP), where she was consulted on the causes of community unrest in Abra and the Cordillera Autonomous Region. She assisted rebel returnees in Abra and the Cordillera, linking them up with government agencies, funding agencies and NGOs for their development projects and for scholarship programs for their children. Pura works with regional, national and international organizations such as United Nations Development Program (UNDP), Transparency International, the National Peace Council, Cordillera Peace Forum, Commission on Audit, National Movement for Free Elections (NAMFREL) and local government units of Abra that advocate peace and good governance. She has presented papers in international conferences in The Hague, Bangkok and New York, and is also a member of Abra's Council of Elders, which facilitates peace talks between warring politicians.

The province of Abra is dusty, destitute, underdeveloped and conflict-ridden. The Concerned Citizens of Abra for Good Government (CCAGG) believes that the key to liberation from underdevelopment and political instability lies in monitoring the performance of elected officials and other government officials.

Philippines

Barbro Sundback

Ålands fredsinstitut (Åland Islands Peace Institute)
Emmaus Åland (Peace Association-Emmaus)
Finnish Music Information Center (Fimic)

Barbro Sundback has believed in politics and peace for all of her working life, and she has seen politics and democracy as the only possible way to achieve justice and peace. A founding member of several peace groups on the Åland Islands she has also represented Åland internationally, and is not only a well-respected and popular member of Parliament, but also its speaker. She is chairperson of the Board of the Åland Islands Peace Institute, founded in 1992 by the Åland Islands Peace Association. She is also a member of the Peace Association-Emmaus.

Barbro Sundback (born 1945) has been a member of parliament since 1979. She has also been deeply involved in peace education and peacebuilding activities. She is chairperson of the Board of the Åland Islands Peace Institute, founded in 1992 by the Åland Islands Peace Association. The institute does both practical and theoretical work on security policy, minority groups, and issues relating to the Baltic Sea region. Barbro is also a member of the Peace Association-Emmaus which carries out actions to help prevent and resolve conflicts, including demonstrations and campaigns.

Barbro says: "Getting involved in peace work was a long process for me. Politics came first. Then, I found the threat of a nuclear holocaust so frightening and so hopeless. I got involved in the peace marches through Europe in the 1980s and met so many different people who wanted to act for peace instead of shrugging their shoulders and doing nothing. I did not want to become cynical. It is healthier to have hope. With time I have come to think that the most important thing is the process of working together. The main obstacle to peace is the conception that war is somehow inevitable. That concept is built into the patriarchal structures of our society, and the people who uphold it are probably the ones who are themselves ready to use violence to achieve their goals. If you believe violence is a solution, it becomes one."

With the threat of a nuclear holocaust during the cold war, many people became involved in peace activities and joined together to establish institutions for peace education and conflict resolution. Today, there is as great a need as ever for such institutes and activities.

Finland

"It is imperative there should be kindness towards truths other than ours."

Maria Szyszkowska

Internationale Gesellschaft "System der Philosophie"
Société Européenne de Culture
Don Quixote Club

Maria Szyszkowska, is a senator, professor, philosopher, lecturer, and writer. She lives according to Kant's philosophy that law should guarantee freedom for everyone. She has proposed the first bill in Poland on registered partnerships for homosexual couples and a bill on euthanasia. In her busy life she has written twenty-five books on philosophy, politics, and law. She has edited over thirty. Tolerance and empathy are the most important values she tries to implement in society. She is always in hurry, always swimming against the current.

January 2004: a senate debate in Poland on a proposed bill on registered partnerships for homosexual couples. The author of the bill, Maria Szyszkowska, persuades other senators: "This is an act of justice to the most numerous minority in Poland. Law is the only way to change social consciousness." You easily could feel the tension in the air. There were more media representatives, radio microphones, and TV cameras than usual. "It is an attack on the family! Aids will spread after the bill will be accepted," shouted one of the right-wing senators. The bill is the result of a more than one-year long cooperation with Polish Lesbian Gay Bisexual Transsexual (LGBT) organizations. According to the bill, homosexual couples shall have the civil and economic rights of married couples. That day, the senate agreed to further work on the bill.

Improving law is one of the ways Maria Szyszkowska has chosen to promote tolerance. Apart from that, she writes books and lectures throughout Poland. Usually, she wakes up at 6 a.m. in the morning. As on Friday, 26 March 2004. She sorts out her notes and at 8 a.m. she gives instructions to her assistant for the next week. At 10:30 she takes part in the Senate Commission on Culture and Mass Media. Then she goes to her office and meets a leftist politician. She calls a taxi to bring her a vegetarian dish. Then she visits a prison, talks to a prisoner. "I have some ideas about changing the situation of prisoners but I have to learn more," she says. At 6 p.m., she attends a meeting of the Société Européene de la Culture. From there, she comes back home to meet a journalist. She has an hour for him and hurries to the Polish news channel TVN 24 to take part in a discussion on euthanasia. She goes to bed at 1 a.m. The next day she takes part in a five-hour demonstration against the war in Iraq. She is the only parliamentarian there.

In 1989, the political system in Poland began to change from communism to democracy. This has made possible the expression of a wide variety of views in politics. Still, in a country dominated by Roman Catholic views, it is not easy to bring up controversial subjects such as rights for homosexuals.

Rozlana Taukina

Institute for War and Peace Problems
Central Asia Independent Mass Media Association
Reporters without Borders

Rozlana Taukina is a journalist and human rights activist working in the tough climate of economic collapse and political crisis in a Kazakhstan recently freed after decades of authoritarian rule. A well-known face in the national news media and correspondent for Reporters without Borders, Rozlana has dedicated her career — at much personal risk — to defending the mass media and individual journalists threatened with censure and repression.

Rozlana Taukina is a fighter who has spearheaded efforts within her country to bring about democratic reform and freedom in this challenging period of transition after the collapse of authoritarian rule. In 1991, she began organizing protests speaking out against repression and courageously defending the rights of the Kazakh people to free information and honest and free elections. If the authorities had not shut it down in 1997, the independent television and radio company she started would have been the most popular and distinguished in Kazakhstan. Rozlana has fought for the release of individual journalists imprisoned by the authorities and organized public condemnation when the Kazakh police killed the daughter of a woman journalist.

Rozlana has written extensively on policy questions and the problems of bringing democracy to Kazakhstan. A gifted public speaker, she also organizes seminars and round tables on democracy and gives her considerable energy and leadership to several organizations fighting for freedom and democracy in Kazakhstan. These include the Forum of Democratic Forces, the Institute for War and Peace Problems, the foundation Journalists in Danger, and the Central Asia Independent Mass Media Association. She is also the Kazakhstan correspondent for Reporters without Borders.

There is a saying in Almaty that if Rozlana were connected to a power station, she could generate enough energy to light the streets for one month. Her charismatic leadership style, her gift for managing creative people, and her broad global vision led her to be nominated as a candidate to the local Parliament. Rozlana says that she is happy to carry out her social and public activity for the sake of the future of her children. She really cannot imagine her life without work, without fighting for the welfare and prosperity of her people, especially children.

Kazakhstan is dealing with the economic collapse, political crisis, and cultural backlash of a country recently freed of authoritarian rule. There is still government repression of key freedoms, including the freedom of free speech and expression.

Kazakhstan

Irina Unzhakova

Status Women's Federation of Eastern Kazakhstan

Since 1999, Irina Unzhakova has lobbied and worked to support women in the political and socio-economic sphere. As president of the Status Women's Federation of Eastern Kazakhstan and regional coordinator of a national advocacy program, she has lobbied for bills on self-government, the environment, election reforms, the communal system and has influenced the opening of the mass media. A well-known leader of the women's movement in Kazakhstan, she has fought for women's participation and influence at local and national levels. She has also designed and carried out advocacy campaigns.

Born 1964 in the small Siberian town of Ust-Kut in Eastern Kazakhstan, Irina Unzhakova lost her mother at the age of ten and grew up quickly, playing both nurse and mother to a younger brother. As a student, Irina became involved in student activities, and during the years of the Communist Party's authoritarian policy (around 1986), she openly made public speeches against national policy.

After 1997, Irina worked as a journalist and news editor for a TV station, as well as press secretary for the head of the local administration of the city of Ust-Kamenogor. But her desire to serve was overpowering and — leaving her career in government — she went to work in the non-governmental sector.

Since 1999, Irina and her team have worked for and expanded the influence of women at local and national levels. Through extensive educational activities among the women of Eastern Kazakhstan and through regular informative meetings and seminars both in the cities and districts around the region, she explains to women the patriarchal character and injustice of traditional models of behavior in men and women and the possibilities of overcoming them. She talks about women and success and about being women on their way to self-recognition and self-realization. Irina is also involved in monitoring governmental and judicial bodies, deputy elections, lobbying of truce envoys, and the development of budget transparency. In 2002, the "Different and Equal" weekly initiative started under her guidance. Step by step, her team at the Status Women's Federation of Eastern Kazakhstan is changing attitudes towards women in politics and society.

Kazakhstan is a dynamically developing country, but the status of women in the country is still low, and women politicians are not taken seriously. The Status Women's Federation works to change attitudes towards women politicians and to increase women's participation in society and political life.

Kazakhstan

Chea Vannath

Center for Social Development (CSD)

Chea Vannath (born 1948) is president of the Center for Social Development (CSD), which promotes school curricula on transparency, monitors the courts and parliament and organizes public debates on the Khmer Rouge tribunal, corruption and other issues. After the Khmer Rouge seized power in 1975, Chea was forced to work in labor camps before escaping to Thailand and on to the US. After living as a refugee in America for more than ten years, she returned to Cambodia in 1992 to participate in rebuilding her country.

Chea Vannath trudged muddy, mine-infested roads to flee to safety in 1980. The Vietnamese troops had just regained power from the Khmer Rouge and the life of her husband, a former major in the Cambodian army, was in jeopardy. So, they escaped to Thailand, from where they went to America. She worked in the US government's refugee programs and obtained her Master's degree in public administration at Portland State University. The UN-sponsored general election in 1992 brought her back to her homeland as a translator for the United Nations Transitional Authority in Cambodia (Untac). Post-election Cambodia saw international aid pouring into the country, raising concerns about corruption in a country where 36 percent of the population live below the poverty line and the monthly income of government officials ranges from USD 20 to 40.

Chea decided to be involved in the monitoring of international aid through the Center for Social Development (CSD), which she now heads. Established in 1995, CSD coordinates the Coalition for Transparency Cambodia (CTC) that aims to eradicate corruption in the country. It was the driving force in the drafting of an anti-corruption law pending in parliament. Its monthly public fora, which tackle sensitive issues, provide a venue for public debate. Its monthly bulletin monitors and exposes the performance of key players in socio-economic and political spheres. Its "Parliamentary Watch" and "Court Watch" projects ensure the transparency and accountability of the legislature and the judiciary. The CSD's human rights and anti-corruption activities have put it in the line of fire and its leader at grave risk. Yet, Chea is not discouraged. She says she can stand up to anybody. "What I am trying to do is beyond me. I do not do it for myself," she declares, adding that it is important that people are able to express their opinions.

After the UN-sponsored general elections in Cambodia, huge amounts of international aid poured into the country. The inflow of billions of dollars into the public sector raised concerns about corruption in a country where government officials earn between USD 20 and USD 40 a month.

Shuxia Wang

Lijiazhuang Women's Association and Fruit growers' Association
Peasant Women magazine

Wang Shuxia was deprived of the right to go to university because she was too short. Refusing to be cowed down, she pursued her dreams, and in 1997 became a volunteer distributor of Peasant Women, a magazine to promote new thoughts and ideas in rural China. In August 2004, she founded a local women's association for the protection of women's rights and led the setting-up of cooperative groups for fruit-planting peasants to help them cooperate and coordinate for their rights.

Born December 1961, Wang Shuxia is from Fenyang, Shanxi Province. She was deprived of the right to go to university for an absurd reason beyond her comprehension, but did not give up the pursuit of her dreams. In 1995, she heard about a magazine called Peasant Women. She helped to disseminate the ideas in this publication. Some years later, in 2003, she met Dr Wen Tiejun and, attracted by his theories of peasant cooperation, she decided to dedicate herself to this, starting with her home village. A year later, in 2004, she founded a local women's association whose members include many men, and whose members have gone up from 26 to 140. In the same year she helped to establish cooperative groups of fruit-planting peasants. Although cooperation is not a familiar concept among peasants, Wang believes it is the only way to develop. She does not deny that it is fraught with difficulties, but is convinced that success follows hardship. Wang has been an inspiration to many around her, including her female friends and her husband. She believes strongly that women hold up half the sky and she wants all her women friends to proclaim this. She has sacrificed a great deal for her public activities but she always says: "I have no regrets!"

The rights of rural women are always ignored, while individually peasants are unable to confront market risks. With the deterioration of public services in China, peasants have low morale and low self-esteem. Voluntary cooperation among peasants is a new experiment to help them improve their status.

China

Lo Sai "Rose" Wu

Hong Kong Christian Institute (Hkci)
Civil Human Rights Front (Chrf)

Rose Wu Lo Sai (54) works in the field of community development. She has brought civil and community concerns to the church since the 80s. An educator, feminist and Christian social activist, Rose is founder and leader of several NGOs that work for gender equity, social justice, political and civil rights and against poverty. She was convener of the Civil Human Rights Front in 2002—04, an alliance of NGOs instrumental in organizing the rally on 1 July 2003 when over 500,000 people took to the streets to protest against government bureaucracy and the controversial draft National Security Bill.

Rose speaks softly, listens attentively and speaks her mind. Reflective, uncompromising, critical of the mainstream church, Rose has a doctor of ministry degree from Boston, and identifies herself as a feminist and Christian social activist. Rose has played strategic roles in the women, social, civil and political fronts in Hong Kong since the 80s. She is emphatic that different social and political movements are and should work as an organic and integrated whole. She served as the first female executive committee member of the Hong Kong Alliance in Support of Patriotic Democratic Movements in China, an alliance set up shortly after China's Tiananmen pro-democracy movement in 1989. She took on the post of general secretary of the Hong Kong Women Christian Council (Hkwcc) from 1993 to 1998. It was the period when equal opportunities for women were vigorously fought for. A faithful Christian, Rose has always — despite criticism from the church and others — been supportive of sex workers and sexual minorities. Her book, "A Dissenting Church" (2003), positions her in a prophetic church to confront society's injustices. Rose upholds the principles of diversity, openness, good governance, social justice, respect for basic human rights and love. Before and after the 1997 handover, Rose initiated and promoted cooperation among civic groups. The July First Linkage and the Civil Human Rights Front (Chrf) were set up in this regard. They have not only acted as platforms for consultation and dialogue among groups with different opinions, but also as a space where people could work together for a shared goal. The Chrf was critical of the Hong Kong government's controversial draft National Security Bill in 2002. The alliance, with Rose as convener from 2002 to 2004, was instrumental in organizing the pro-democracy rallies in 2003 and 2004.

The late 80s in Hong Kong were a time when elites and entrepreneurs domi-nated. Grassroots groups had no rights and no voice in governance. Women were marginalized. Another major challenge was the political, economic and social instability and disruption of people's livelihoods.

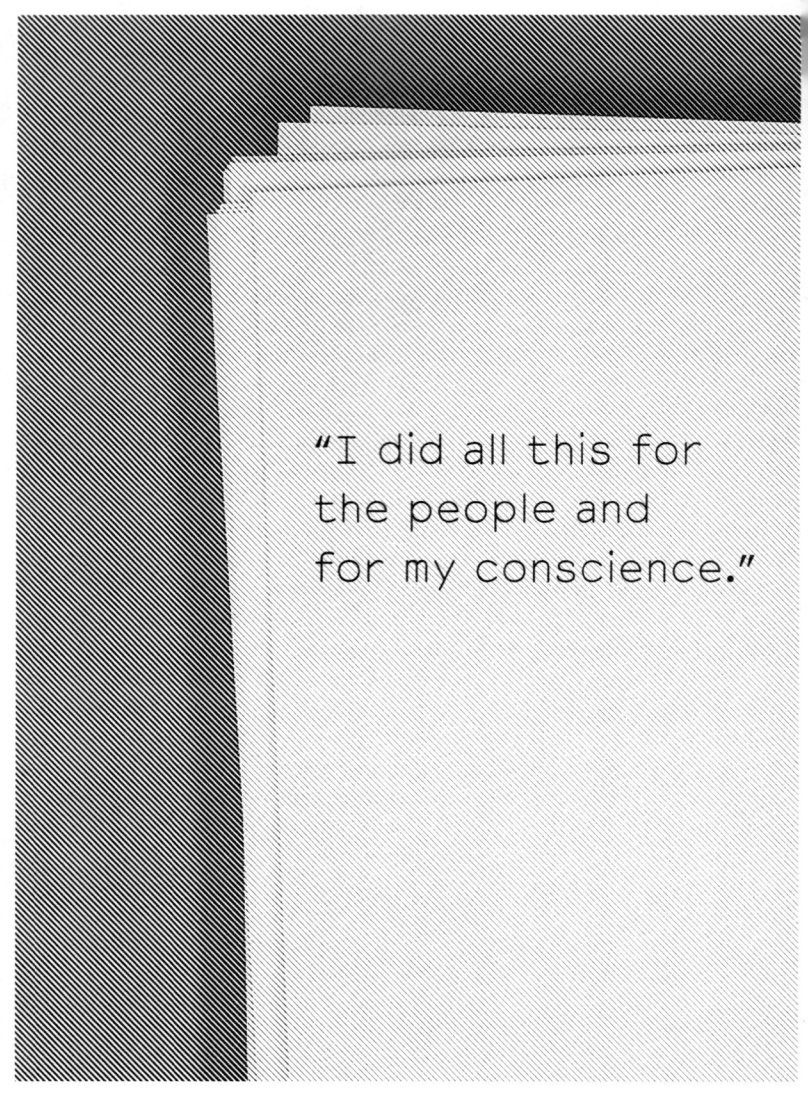

"I did all this for the people and for my conscience."

Jingrong Xiao

Village party secretary, Inner Mongolia

Xiao Jingrong has been secretary of the Party Committee of Qidafen Village, Qiaotou Town, Ongniud Banner, Chifeng in Inner Mongolia, since 1974. She has faced a great deal of hardship in her thirty years of political leadership, particularly in her struggle to lift the village out of poverty.

Qidafen Village was well-known in the region for being a place where people lived on infertile land, took charity grain sent by the state, and survived on subsidies and loans. That was the situation Xiao Jingrong faced when she first took up her position. Could she work miracles in such a poor village?

Xiao soon found a solution for the village. She began by building up strong and energetic leadership cadres. The next step was to solve the problem of water supply, which was the fundamental cause of poverty and an obstacle to the development of agriculture.

The poor village where Xiao lives is in a typical drought area. One has to drill down 80-100 meters into the ground before a well can supply water, and it costs 50,000 yuan per well. It was a difficult task, yet the first deep well was constructed in 1975 and it irrigated more than 300 mu (50 acres) of land and led to an increase in production of 200,000 kilograms of grain that year. Two other such wells were constructed in 1978 and 1979 and the irrigation area increased to 1000 mu (165 acres) by 1982, which represented one mu of irrigated land per capita. The gross production of grain increased dramatically from 250,000 kilograms to 1 million kilograms.

Xiao Jingrong and her cadres have helped improve both the hygiene of the village and the quality of its people. Xiao's duties include dealing with policy but also addressing things such as neighborhood quarrels, divorce, etc.

Qidafen Village was like many villages: poor, badly resourced, and infertile, with its people living on state charity. Bringing about a change here was not easy, the more so for a woman.

China

Tuul Yondon

Elected member, Baganuur District Khural
Liberal Women's Brain Pool (Leos)

Born in 1957, Tuul Yondon followed in her father's footsteps and, having graduated, chose a career with the army. In 1989 her husband, an army man too, joined the pro-democracy movement in which Tuul was also involved. Her first achievement was setting up the local section of the Liberal Women's Brain Pool (Leos). She worked on implementing many local projects for women. Tuul was elected to the Baganuur District Khural as a citizens' representative and was nominated to represent Mongolian women at the 1995 Women's Conference in Beijing.

Tuul Yondon joined the pro-democracy movement early, at a time when many in the country were still cautious about its fate. While still a student, she decided to follow the family tradition of military service and worked with the border troops. She married Bayar, an officer, and spent 20 years in the remote regions of Mongolia. During this time, Tuul learned much that stood her in good stead later when she helped people survive and succeed in the harsh times of transition. In an attempt to help poor families in local areas, Tuul implemented ten training and support projects that improved things for them in Baganuur.

Her political career began with volunteering for NGOs. She organized the first local branch of Leos, which now has 200 active members. Tuul says: "The transition to democracy and market economy revealed all the great faults of the socialist system. An uncertain political situation, a failed national economy, faulty State mechanisms and widespread unemployment left women and children without any social care. We, women, felt we had to fight for our lives. Fortunately, NGOs have also become active in this."

Tuul works on large and small projects. In 1997 she secured a small grant to save the lives of 25 dystrophic children suffering from malnutrition. She monitors processes in Baganuur and raises awareness of the possible consequences of any major developments. Baganuur is the site of a large prison and Tuul's protest helped to reverse the government decision to build a second one there. Tuul now calls for the public attention to the problem of increasing uranium pollution of the environment in conditions of open pit coal mining in Baganuur. Thanks to her efforts to increase women's political activity, 25 percent of the seats in the Baganuur district Khural of representatives belong to women as do half the administrative positions.

Democratization in Mongolia involves social activists across the country who understand that guaranteeing the constitutional rights of citizens needs a solid economic base and strengthening of economically weak communities. Social workers like Tuul help to train people in the market economy.

Mongolia

"To contribute to issues that are to the benefit of the community and society at large, I think this is worthwhile even if it is at the expense of personal interests."

Guixin Yu

Women's Federation of Qianxi County, Hebei Province

After she was transferred to the Women's Federation of Qianxi County, Yu Guixin was able to build up a much deeper understanding on women's issues. She and her fellow workers in the Women's Federation attend courses on related legislation, and organize legal and gender training for women in the villages. She also set up a domestic violence complaints center, and provides forensic medical services, with the overall goal of promoting the protection of women's rights.

Yu Guixin was born to a peasant family in China's Hebei Province in 1962. At the age of 20 she was admitted to the Yutian Normal School and following her graduation became a teacher. In 1988 she was transferred to the Qianxi Women's Federation. It was here that she started to work for the betterment of the lot of women. An innovative person, she is currently chairperson of the Qianxi Women's Federation. In rural areas, people — women's federation officials included — often lack legal knowledge and have a low level of awareness of gender equity. Guixin took the lead, using of her spare time to study law and become a qualified legal practitioner. Many of her fellow workers were inspired and followed suit. Meanwhile, she worked on popularizing legal education at a county level, and made innovative attempts to promote policies and rights protection.

In Qianxi, Guixin worked on establishing a violence-free family community and setting up a Family Violence Complaints Center. A clinic that provides forensic medical services has also been opened. Since many women are ignorant of their legitimate legal rights and interests when they get divorced, Guixin offers "pre-divorce" courses to women in the county. A network is formed by the provincial women's federation, the county legal service center, and the village right-protection team to promote better cooperation among the various levels of concerned organizations. This network ensures that related problems are In an innovative manner, Guixin has initiated the procedure of direct election in the election of women representatives to local, regional and national legislative bodies, enhancing women's participation in local democracy and governance. This has helped promote grassroots women's political participation, and the protection of women's rights in rural China.

In the rural areas of China people are often lacking in knowledge about their legal rights and gender equity. Legal education is needed at this level but there is a shortage of individuals and organizations that are qualified to deliver it.

China

"This is the first step of reform. We shall learn democracy by practicing democracy. Only when there is democracy in the Chinese Communist Party can China have democracy in the country as a whole."

Jinming Zhang

Zhang Jinming, now director of the Chinese Communist Party's Organization Department of Ya'an City, Sichuan Province, implemented direct elections at local government level in 1998. It was the first year that this was piloted at a grassroots level. In August 2002 she piloted direct elections for the Party Congress representatives at a city and county level. She has been relentlessly promoting the democratization process in China.

Zhang Jinming is one of the pioneers in China's local democratization process. The problems resulting from corruption and malpractices of local government officials have been the driving force behind her relentless efforts in promoting local democratization over the past years. In 1998 Jiming, then secretary of the Communist Party in Suining City, implemented direct elections at local government level. The legitimacy of such electoral practice at a grassroots level has been a very sensitive issue. Although it is well received by the local community, as well as local and foreign academics and researchers, Jinming has been under enormous pressure from her supervisors. "On legal grounds, what matters is whether we uphold legal principles and core values. The rules and regulations can and will change over time. In this sense, direct elections, in which power goes to the people, are in line with what is laid down in our constitution. We can even say that direct elections are more in line with our constitution than what we had before," Jinming says.

In 2002 Jinming, appointed standing committee member of the Party Committee and Director of Organizational work of Ya'an City, started to pilot direct elections of Party Congress representatives at a city and county level. Again, the pilots were proven to be successful. "This is only the first step of reform. We shall learn democracy by practicing democracy. Only when there is democracy in the Chinese Communist Party can China have democracy in the country as a whole," Zhang says.

When Zhang Jinming started her service in the government, she witnessed serious cases of corruption and abuse by government officials. Jinming believes that change can only take place if government officials are elected by and accountable to the people.

"Being a woman does not necessarily mean that you are gender conscious. We should challenge existing rules of the game, including existing mechanisms that cause and perpetuate gender inequality."

Youyun Zhang

Zhang Youyun was born in 1940. She worked at the Ministry of Foreign Affairs and was involved in the negotiations with Britain for Hong Kong's future. In 1990 she joined Ministry of Labor. In 1994 she became a member of the International Labor Organization (ILO) and was also appointed Special Adviser on Women Workers' Questions and Director of the Bureau for Gender Equality.

Zhang Youyun was born into a patriotic military family in the former Republic of China. She studied first at Beijing Foreign Studies University, majoring in English, and then in Britain at the University of Bath. In 1974, she began her career as an interpreter in the Ministry of Foreign Affairs. From 1990 to 1994, Zhang Youyun held the position of Deputy Director of the Foreign Affairs Department of the Ministry of Labor, before being promoted to Director. In 1994 she joined the ILO, where she was designated Special Adviser on Women Workers' Questions, and became Director of the Bureau for Gender Equality. Together with her colleagues, she committed herself to changing the organizational concept of the ILO and to bringing the gender problem center-stage in the strategic goals of the organization.

Zhang Youyun worked hard to form and implement the strategy and action plan for mainstreaming the gender problem within the ILO. She also established a gender network within the organization, which functioned as a catalyst for promoting equality between men and women in the labor force.

Under her leadership the ILO developed various channels of training which helped improve the staff's capability in highlighting the gender problem and the sex ratio within the ILO, thus changing the ILO into an organization that respects gender equality, both in human resource development and personnel policies. Zhang represented the ILO Director-General and headed the ILO delegation to the 23rd UN Special Session on Women 2000: Gender equality, development and peace for the twenty-first century. She also represents the ILO on the UN Interagency Committee on Women and Gender Equality and the UN Commission on the Status of Women.

When Zhang Youyun joined the ILO, gender issues and her department were not treated seriously within the organization. The department lacked staff, finance, and experience or precedents that could be used as reference points; it also did not get much support from top-level staff.

China

"I have no regrets and I will fight again against such injustice in the future."

Yinxiu Zhu

Zhu Yinxiu, a brave peasant laborer, appealed against the township government's ill-treatment of her family — arbitrary fines, detentions and searches, and infliction of personal injuries. The incident was exposed in the media and the arbitrary levies on peasants were corrected to a large extent.

Zhu Yinxiu's brother-in-law, Chen Jiabao, returned to his home in Anfu, Jiangxi Province, during the outbreak of Severe Acute Respiratory Syndrome (Sars) in China. His family reported his return to the local township government because he had to be quarantined by law. Officials imposed a fine of 1000 yuan without reason and began to take the family's cattle and a motorcycle without giving a receipt or indicating the cash value of these items. When Zhu tried to take photos as evidence, the cadres quickly called more personnel from the township government and police station. Threatening to take away Chen Jiabao under the terms of existing regulations, they then tried to rob Zhu of her camera. The family and the cadres came to blows and police arrested Chen Jiabao and Chen Jialai, Zhu's husband. The cadres were unable to find the camera but they took Chen Jialai's agricultural vehicle and Zhu's motorcycle. Zhu and her husband were ordered to surrender the camera and hand in a behavior review; Chen Jialai was beaten up; the family had to pay 2300 yuan to recover the agricultural vehicle.

Zhu decided to protest publicly against this abuse, despite discouragement from friends and relatives. She asked the media for help, and China Youth Daily published a full-page story. The Anfu city government immediately put out two urgent circulars stating that migrant workers returning home should not be subject to any arbitrary observation fees, check-up fees, isolation fees, deposits, or guarantee money by any township or village government, and that any fees and personal articles that had been collected must be returned at once. The practice of collecting arbitrary charges were corrected to a large extent and the economic burden on local peasants was alleviated. The cadres involved in the incident were transferred to other townships.

Zhu fought a winning battle for justice.

Many low-level government units misuse their power and oppress the people despite the rule of law. Instead of submitting to humiliation and abuse to avoid trouble — like most other people do — Zhu fought back and finally won.

China

Shehla Zia

Aurat Foundation

Shehla Zia (1947 to 2005) was a trained lawyer specializing in criminal and constitutional law who devoted her energies to securing women's legal rights in Pakistan for 35 years, both as a practicing lawyer and in her role as a joint director of Aurat Foundation, a leading NGO working for women's empowerment. Shehla was also director of the foundation's legislative watch program, which monitors women's participation in the legislative process.

Women's legal rights were Shehla Zia's focus from the start of her career. One of Pakistan's pioneering women lawyers, Shehla received her bachelors in law from Punjab University in the late 1960s. For the next 11 years, she worked as a law associate specializing in women's legal rights. She then became a partner with a prominent law firm run by women, AGHS Law Associates, where she worked for five years. In 1986, Shehla joined Aurat Foundation as joint director, and director of its legislative watch program. Here, she focused on issues including legal and constitutional rights issues of Pakistani women, women's political education, their participation in the legislative system, gender sensitization for NGOs and federal government officials, and governance issues. Shehla collaborated with other organizations, and contributed to national and international policy debates. She worked in 2001 as a consultant on the review of the women and children's program of the AGHS legal aid cell. She also prepared labor law booklets for factory women, and provided inputs on women's development for the Eighth National Five-Year Plan. She researched a report on women's participation in political and public life in Pakistan in 1999, as part of a larger project undertaken by International Women's Rights Action Watch-Asia Pacific to monitor whether governments had fulfilled their women's equality obligations. Shehla researched women's legal position in Pakistan, and the legal and policy framework within which NGOs operate. She contributed to her country's report to the World Conference for Women in Beijing in 1995 on the issue of power and decision-making and also contributed to a report by a national commission of inquiry on women on political participation, violence against women, and development rights.

Women's legal and constitutional rights issues, their political education, participation in the legislative system, gender sensitization of NGOs, and governance issues have become matters of radical concern in Pakistan.

Pakistan

"We worked magic together"

The Coordinators of the Project

When I was young and full of dreams and hopes, I wanted to break away from the narrow confines of a small town (Maceió Alagoas) and be an airplane pilot, to be as free as I thought. When that was not possible, I became a flight attendant. To fly, for me, was to get to know the world, listen to other voices, other human experiences, to know freedom, to meet different people. Now that I am 80 years old and with the 1000 Peacewomen project, one part of this dream has been achieved. I have been a militant since 1945 fighting for peace, freedom, justice, respect for the worth of women; for work, education, culture and leisure for everyone; for solidarity between men and women of all races and all colors. I am still fighting for these until now. When the Swiss women gathered women from many countries in Bern and invited me to be the coordinator for Brazil, a huge net was drawn in my head, made by so many hands and so many desires to share knowledge, friendship and the possibility of contributing, all together, to a safer, more equal and happier world. The project has helped us to know ourselves, to honor women everywhere, to see with different eyes the struggle of each woman, to understand the meaning of their work, to trust even more in our strength, and make the women's voice stronger and more beautiful in our defense of humanity, which is our reason for being.

Clara Charf, Coordinator for Brazil

I was cynical at first but the optimism of the Swiss women was contagious, and the camaraderie that was developed among the coordinators made it difficult not to be swept into the idea of leveling the playing field and getting the world to recognize and acknowledge the vital work women do for peace. And finding these women has been such an enriching experience that, whether or not the Nobel Committee buys into the idea of awarding these 1000 women the Nobel Peace Prize in 2005, we have already won. The amazing lives we have uncovered and documented, the friendships we have made, and the worldwide network that has been built through this project are priceless gifts that have enriched our lives, our work, and our world.

Paulynn Sicam,
Philippines, Co-Coordinator for Southeast Asia

When Rebecca first introduced the project to me, I immediately agreed to become the coordinator for Southern Africa. At home, I had already started a small documentation on the women who had fought side by side with men to gain freedom from colonialists in Malawi, because only the men were recognized and honored. I therefore appreciated the Swiss initiative, which swallowed my small vision. As coordinator, this was a big challenge for me especially since I was already involved in other programs and initiatives nationally and in my region. The first thing I did was to fall in love with the project, owned it, and dedicated myself to it. I worked with women's organizations and networks, embassies, churches, religious organizations, media and village chiefs. At first, the response was lukewarm. But as I pressed on, the networks understood the objectives of the initiative and they began to help it succeed. There were hitches along the way, the work involved driving long distances, but knowing that I was working for the benefit of our nominees and eventually for society as a whole gave me satisfaction and made me more determined to see the initiative through. Moreover, our gatherings in Bern and Zurich, where we shared ideas that contributed to achieving our goal, taught me that as a group, you can achieve a lot, even what you think is impossible. Determination is the key.

Vera Chirwa, Malawi,
Co-Coordinator for Southern Africa

When invited to join the 1000 Peacewomen initiative, I did not hesitate even for a moment to embrace the idea and everyone who was part of this initiative. Two years down the line and after successfully completing the enormous and challenging task of selecting 158 Peacewomen from South Asia, I feel stronger, more energetic, more pro-life and pro-peace, and more hopeful. The over two-year journey of this initiative was itself a journey of peace and for peace. This journey has been part of the destination. We got connected and reconnected to a large number of people working for just peace. Journalists, writers, photographers, editors, filmmakers whom we invited to work have all felt privileged and enriched by getting to know strong, fearless, creative women working for just peace. This connecting and networking has strengthened our resolve. The coming together of small lamps of peace work spread around the world has made us realize how big we can be if we join hands. We can now prove what we knew intuitively: it is women's peace work that has ensured the survival of our fragile universe. We know this initiative has strengthened the global movement for just peace.

Kamla Bhasin,
India, Coordinator for South Asia

—

To me, as coordinator of the Balkan region, where a terrible war took place ten years ago, the project has extraordinary importance. Working in this project, I have had the opportunity to meet a number of incredible peace activists and thereby extend our women's network. Our network , "Fokus", which linked 36 women NGOs from all over Bosnia and Herzegovina, has now grown to 66 women's organizations from the entire region of Southeastern Europe, creating a solid starting point for the re-establishment of permanent peace in this very troubled part of the world. With the project, women — such as the courageous and fearless women of Serbia — have become visible. They raise their voices against the existing system, often risking their own lives by doing so. The support of the women's network assures them that they are not alone anymore, and that their voices are heard not only in the Balkans, but everywhere in the world.

Fadila Memisevic,
Bosnia Herzegovina, Coordinator for the Balkan region

The idea of the project was unique and fascinating. When I read about it, how it was started and its noble aim, I immediately wanted to participate in it. I have had the opportunity to meet wonderful women from all over the world, to learn about the work of women from different regions and cultures. At first it was not easy, especially in my region, where the word "peace" has a very sensitive meaning. But after we had explained our understanding of peace, that it means the work done to ensure human security in different aspects of life, the idea was accepted. The moments that will always be with me are our coordinators' meetings, where we worked as a family. Although we came from different countries, we spoke the same language — peace.

Aida Abu Ras,
Jordan, Coordinator for the Middle East

What really matters is to have food, to have a place to sleep, a way of making a living and to live in peace. And the most important thing is to achieve it together; women and men in the same struggle. This is the synthesis of a life philosophy I learned from Dora Paiva da Silva, a nominee from Uruguay. Since I had the privilege of joining this project — a privilege for which I am grateful from the bottom of my heart — I have learned so much about life. If for any reason I should forget, I shall be reminded by another nominee, the one who writes with capital letters in each message: COUNT ON ME FOR WHATEVER YOU

NEED or, CAN I GIVE YOU A HAND WITH ANYTHING? or, PLEASE JUST TELL ME HOW I CAN HELP YOU. Those last words come from Sandra Jiménez, an 18-year old Mexican in a wheel chair. It would be shameful to forget.

Nora Franco,
El Salvador, Coordinator for Latin America and the Caribbean

African women have played an important role for centuries, keeping the community together, mediating and solving many problems. However, only after the African countries were given their independence did it become apparent how important the role of the women really is. African women have proved that their talents go far beyond farming and creating a family. By managing conflict situations with sensitivity, the African woman has earned social respect. The project allowed us to appreciate the work of many women. This is why I feel fortunate to participate in this work of justice, as I call it. To me, it means finally making the work of strong women accessible to a wider public. Even though I expected to face financial, logistic, communication or political difficulties — some of which were almost unsolvable — 39 women from West Africa have been nominated. Apart from the work itself, the sense of human warmth, solidarity and trust among the coordinators from the different countries made participating in this project an incredible experience as we learned to understand and accept each other's emotions (the tears in my eyes, the joy I feel). I call this cultural diversity and understanding "the rainbow".

Fatoumata Maiga,
Mali, Coordinator for Western Africa

Without support from sisters, brothers, friends and all the network groups, especially in the Mekong region, it would not have been possible to succeed in this work. The lives and works of the 1000 Peacewomen encourage us to continue peace-building efforts in every corner of the world.

Kratae Supawadee,
Thailand, Coordinator for the Mekong region

Coming from a country where we had more than two-and-a-half decades of war, destruction, lack of law enforcement, all kinds of discrimination and violations of human rights, especially women's rights, it was a great honor and pleasure for me to be part of this project. Finding new friends and meeting other women was very important to me. Hearing about their experiences, hopes and difficulties in other parts of the world has empowered me and given me courage. It has also encouraged the women in Afghanistan who survived, watching their houses being destroyed, loved ones killed and their children die from hunger and lack of medicine. This has encouraged me to continue the struggle against all kinds of discrimination and all forms of injustice in society. The teamwork was always joyful and I learned a lot of lessons from being part of this project. Together, we can bring positive changes, peace with social justice and equality in this world.

Sima Samar,
Afghanistan, Coordinator for Afghanistan

It has been a blessing and an enormous privilege to have been involved in the coordination of this project. The last two years of my life have been the richest and most challenging I have known. I turned 30 on the plane journey over to the first coordinators' workshop in Bern, and arrived a virtual teen next to the extraordinary and accomplished women who came for the meeting. And yet I was always treated as an equal, with warmth and respect. Somehow I felt like I had come home. We came from vastly different contexts and had many personal differences but we worked magic together. And we worked very hard — through the inevitable tears as well as laughter. These last two years, I have learned the subtle power of inspiration and charisma to bring about change in people's lives.

Nicci Simmonds,
New Zealand, Co-Coordinator for Oceania

My Mother, ordinary and extraordinary, has been the image of peacewoman for me. Bringing up her children in straitened circumstances in an era of political flux, Mother imbued her children with a sense of responsibility, teaching them the values of her favorite idiom: not to yield to the seductions of wealth and fame, not to waver under the pressures of poverty and humbleness, not to succumb to the threats of power and force. It is my deep appreciation and love for her that teaches me the importance of empathy, and it is this empathy that guides me to the joys and sorrows, the hopes and aspirations that lie at the heart of the stories of the 1000 Peacewomen, and more. I see Mother in their images, defying the powerful, the greedy, the mean, and dedicated to making the world a better one for the children. Their stories must be told, for generations to come, to listen to, and take pride in.

Kin Chi Lau,
Hong Kong, Coordinator for China and Mongolia

This is one of the most inspiring projects I have been involved in. I teach about war, militarism, and women in my university courses, where we learn many truths about the world, US government and corporations, and lives of women who daily face wars, oppression, and other severe difficulties many people in the United States never know and think about. Both my students and I are often overwhelmed by the dire conditions facing the world, especially the women and children in it. Through this project, I learned that thousands of women in the world are out there, struggling against great odds, under threat, to make it a better place for us all. Sharing this reality inspired us to see possibilities, to keep working for change, and to connect our struggles to those of others around the world. Personally, the friendship and real sisterhood we have developed during the past few years will stay with me forever. I have loved this work!

Margo Okazawa-Rey,
USA, Coordinator for North America, Japan and the Koreas

When I was invited to be a coordinator for my region, I felt honored and proud. I met women from the most diverse countries — from different cultures, religions, experiences and life styles — but we had a common aim: to show to the world the important role of women in building and keeping peace. The project became an important part of my life. I worked for three years with the best women and learned from them. When I started to collect nomination forms and read about the Peacewomen, their life and work, I realized how little I have done in my life and how many possibilities there are to do more. I also learned from my colleagues, the coordinators, and always felt their support and solidarity. I am proud to be in the company of the best women in the world.

Marina Pikulina,
Usbekistan, Coordinator for Central Asia and Eastern Europe

—
R

On an unforgettable summer day in June 2003 in Khartoum, I got a phone call from Switzerland inviting me to join the 1000 Peacewomen project. It was like breathing fresh air after struggling in deep waters. At the time, the peace talks in my country were failing, and we were feeling ignored and forgotten. Working with the project has given me hope, energy and reassurance that we have a better future to work for. For one, it has shown me that we are not alone in suffering from conflict and insecurity, but more than that, it has proven beyond doubt that there is a way if we can come together, learn from each other, have trust in ourselves and celebrate our strengths. The project has impacted on me in a way I did not anticipate when I joined. In plain and simple words, it added value to my activism and feminism. I feel proud to have been a part of such a wonderful group. I rejoice in that and cherish all the moments of hope, frustration, hard work and love we have shared.

Asha Elkarib,
Sudan, Coordinator for the Horn of Africa

As I watched the 21 women (from the 27 women nominated from the Philippines) gathered at our public event announcing the 1000 Peacewomen on 29 June 2005, I felt the wisdom and the rightness of the project. There was a special joy among the nominees in not just being one woman alone receiving an award. Most of these women shun the spotlight anyway. I think they were glad to be among sisters working for peace, when at times one may have felt alone in her journey. And here they were — a big bunch of women happily celebrating together! This is what I love about the project: that we celebrate women, and that we are many. It is a blessing to be working with the wonderful regional coordinators, the Association, secretariat and friends, that we gather together, make decisions together, talk and walk and dance and sing. Surely, this way, we are making peace.

Karen Tanada,
Philippines, Co-Coordinator for Southeast Asia

Being part of this project has been a great experience and a huge source of revelation and inspiration. On a continent ravaged by conflict, genocide, poverty and illiteracy, I have met and shared the experiences of women who are determined to effect change, and bring about peace, reconciliation, development, hope and human dignity. The traditionally "weaker sex" not only in Africa, but all over the world, is relentlessly fighting back against the evils faced by their societies. Most of the Peacewomen are of humble background, but their determination makes their image larger than life. The 1000 Peacewomen epitomize the highly laudable efforts of millions of other women towards a more peaceful world. This initiative deserves unflinching support from all people of goodwill to ensure that the visibility and recognition of the Peacewomen's work is perpetuated. I feel proud to have crossed paths with these Mothers of Peace.

Cecile Mukarubuga,
Kenya, Coordinator for Great Lakes Region, East and Central Africa

I am one of two project managers in the head office in Bern and additionally, the coordinator for Western Europe responsible for 60 women from 19 different countries. Combining both tasks was not always easy, but I managed. This project is an amazing example of peace practice based on respect, truth and unprejudiced interest. Peace is a common goal and we work for it by agreeing on common principles, but our difficulty — and joy — was in adjusting these to our specific regional contexts. Every decision we made during our coordinators' meetings in Switzerland was an intercultural voyage around the world as we became familiar with diverse regional conditions. We discussed, worked hard, laughed, cried and danced in an atmosphere where age, origin and language were no barriers. It was a space to change or balance our perspectives. What touches me most is that our vision of peace is shared by thousands of people in the world — among them our nominated women. This gives me strength, encouragement and joy.

Maren Haartje,
Switzerland, Coordinator for Western Europe

It is a blessing to be part of this project and work with some of the most amazing women from around the world. I found this project to be particularly important because of the equal space given to women in the Pacific. We now are not only inspired by the stories of women everywhere but also of women close to us who we can relate with. I have enjoyed every moment spent on this project as we made decisions, talked about what was happening around the world, listened to stories, met with the other coordinators (some of who should be nominated themselves!), met with nominees, sang, talked, danced, laughed, cried — and all the stressful moments as well, like meeting deadlines. Each contribution towards peace is important and the Pacific region would not have been able to do what it needed to do for this project without the help of ECREA, the Bern office, our donors, advisors, photographers, editors, writers, the many supporters of the project, nominators, and of course the nominees — thank you!

Sandy Fong,
Fiji, Co-Coordinator for Oceania

I strongly believe that one can gauge the political health of a country by the way it engages with its citizens, especially its minority citizens: religious and ethnic groups, and women. I put women into the category of "minorities" not because their numerical standing is less than men, but because in many countries of the world they continue not to receive the political, economic and personal rights that are accorded to men. Watch, then, how a country treats its women and you learn much of the values that that society adheres to. From my work on this project — in which I have not only recorded the work of the women who fall into my regions, but have discussed with other coordinators the work women do across the world, often in very dire circumstances — I have become even more convinced that those who speak of relative values do so only when it serves as a philosophy for oppression. The women's narratives in these pages are testimony that although there are ethnic, cultural, linguistic and religious differences between peoples, there are absolute values. From the hundreds of mechanisms for building and sustaining a rational and humane world presented in this book, there emerges what I hope can be formulated into a universal idea of peace.

Anita Mir,
United Kingdom, Coordinator for UK and Ireland,
the Maghreb region, Iran and Iraq

The project had an immeasurable positive impact on me. Just being part of an international initiative built up my confidence even more. I felt empowered by the opportunity to access confidential information on women's work, sharing ideas and sentiments with other coordinators from all over the world, respecting our professional callings and each other. I was humbled by the commitment of women to peacekeeping in small and big ways for all peoples, irrespective of gender and age, despite all the obstacles and the violence in the world. Generally, the process left me paralyzed because I had a lot of assumptions about the so-called "global village" (South Africa included) and its commitment to women's emancipation. I thought this initiative would get enormous support from all quarters. But the Nobel Peace Prize is directly associated with the elite, the rich and the famous, which excludes many peace-builders and this shall continue for a very long time to come. This is very sad because it reflects the society's narrow interpretation of peace and peace-building. And for this reason, I hope that this project can be revived ten years from now.

Nomvuyo Skota Dayile,
South Africa, Co-Coordinator for Southern Africa

Dealing with conflicts, conciliation and reconciliation are of great importance to me and are part of my life. As the assistant to the project I am happy to be able to fully support this initiative which is making visible the worldwide effort and work of women for peace. It is a great opportunity to be able to contribute to building hope and encouragement.

Regula Küng,
Switzerland, Project Assistant, head office

So many women are able to accomplish the impossible, but hardly ever are their efforts recognized. I am therefore happy to be part of this thrilling and important project. Thanks to international public relations work, we are able to highlight what women achieve everyday. Their work is now made visible, and not only within their sphere of activity. It is important that we did this and that we continue to do so. Everyday. For all of us.

Barbara Mangold,
Switzerland, PR Assistant to the project

Lessons to Be Learnt – Purpose and Relevance of the Scientific Project

Susanne Stalder and Doris Wastl-Walter

S

"1000 Women for the Nobel Peace Prize 2005" also includes a scientific dimension. The project gives us a unique opportunity to learn from the initiatives and experiences of these Peacewomen and to enrich the existing international knowledge base not only for the study of peace and conflict, but also, for example, economics, development studies, media studies, geography, political science and international relations, and education. This is a significant opportunity to learn from precious experience with peace initiatives in many contexts. We will be able to contribute to these multiple efforts by generating knowledge and making lessons learnt available to the scientific community as well as to activists and politicians in diverse contexts worldwide. The basic assumption of the whole project, as well as of the scientific project, is not that women are biologically more peaceful or less aggressive than men, but rather that they are, through their socialization and special roles in society, especially concerned by issues of violence, insecurity, and poverty and therefore act explicitly on their special needs using their specific social and cultural capital. The relevance and impact of the women's peace-building efforts will become evident through this project, and it will be shown that these efforts touch an important range of levels and issues.

First of all, we want our research to strengthen the nominated peace women's initiatives. We hope that this international academic interest and acknowledgement will encourage the projects on various levels, strengthening them politically and making their situation more visible and secure. From a different perspective, we also want to initiate, facilitate, and monitor an international exchange of ideas, experiences, and strategies, through which the individual Peacewomen themselves can benefit from each other's knowledge and bring new input into their work. These networks should be extended and become international. The knowledge that our group will be able to articulate and make transferable should be returned to the nominees' working contexts and support their projects.

Second, the various academic disciplines should be enriched by the analysis, interpretation, and publication of research based on this data set, including the concrete experience and knowledge of these Peacewomen and the multiple roles of women in conflict resolution and peace building. Research on peace and conflict lacks comprehensive studies of women's various contributions to peace. Their experience and knowledge should be made accessible to generate new insights and theories for reconsidering solutions to conflicts in both war and non-war situations.

Third, the knowledge accumulated and generated by the academic group should have an impact on local, regional, national, and international policies and thus foster future political endeavors for peace and social change.

At the political level, new processes and initiatives should be promoted to improve living conditions in order to achieve a socially just and secure society. At the time of writing this text, primary research on the nomination forms, biographies, and project descriptions is still ongoing. The first results will be available when this book comes out. They will be published on the website: www.1000peacewomen.org.

Scientific potential and challenges of the project

What is extraordinary about "1000 Peacewomen" is its unique data set. There are about 2000 nominations of women working for peace throughout the world, which includes the 1000 women selected and documented in this book as well as about 1000 others suggested for the nomination. In addition, biographies are included in this documentation and there is information on homepages and in project descriptions that we can gather. This very rich data set gives us insight into countless women's initiatives in various contexts. Yet the richness of the material is also quite challenging, as these approximately 2000 nomination forms have been filled in by numerous people from different backgrounds in different languages and with different levels of detail. Since the nominations have come from a third person and not the nominee herself, the precision of the information also varies. However, such a large number of case studies allows for statistically significant results from the analysis of the living and working conditions of the women. Our first attempt will be to obtain a quantitative, statistical overview of selected criteria. For the first run, we will categorize the data according to the personal situations of the women nominated, such as their family background and situation; educational, professional, and geographical backgrounds; their motivation for and the goal(s) of their peace project(s); methods and strategies of their work; their alliances and networks, and finally their achievements. Using these criteria, we hope to learn more about the context in which the women have developed and carry out their activities.

The next step will be an analysis of the range of activities of the women nominated. The book at hand shows just how diverse their concerns and activities are. Each of the activities of the women touches on several issues, and many women organize diverse projects simultaneously to deal with problems on various levels. To understand this interconnectedness and the specific reasoning flowing from it is our next research goal.

The third step is to select some women for in-depth research on special issues. Some research has already started, for example, on projects against structural violence, and on leadership, economic, and environmental issues. The methods used at this stage of the research are mainly qualitative — ethnographic methods such as participant observation, in-depth interviews,

—

S

and focus groups. Another potential direction for research on the given data set lies in the geographical distribution of the women nominated: each of 155 countries is represented by from one to over ninety nominees, and this data also reflects the living conditions and the political situation in those countries.

Thus later we will be able to bring the initial results into their geographical as well as political and economic context to understand prevailing relevant local situations. In this way, we will finally be able to interpret the commonalities and differences of the various initiatives.

In summary, the overview of the global variations and their implications comes from the manifold empirical data set, not from an abstract theoretical approach, and will be analyzed and interpreted in the light of recent general, but also especially feminist peace and security studies.

The research network

An initial analysis of the data as described cannot exploit the full potential of the experiences and the know-how of the nominees. To capture these possibilities, researchers from many disciplines and cultural backgrounds are required, researchers who will investigate questions and issues of pertinence relevant to their own research and discipline. Personal knowledge of the various situations and familiarity with the specific living situations and contexts of the Peacewomen will allow a deeper understanding for their concerns and needs. In addition, each discipline has its own paradigms, theories, and methods for approaching research questions and therefore produces different results. To come to a more profound and comprehensive understanding of the initiatives in order to extract the lessons to be learnt, many such contributions are needed. Therefore our group hopes to encourage more researchers from all over the world and various disciplines to join the research network, one of the three mainstays of "1000 Peacewomen" besides the collective nomination and the documentation to be found in this book. Establishing an international network of gender-focused peace researchers will allow for broadening the scientific scope and insights gained. With their common focus, they may be able to overcome geographical and disciplinary boundaries and contribute to an improved and empirically based understanding of the peace work of countless women that up to now has remained essentially invisible. By going public with these results, it is hoped that the network will be able to go beyond the boundaries of academia and make an impact on governments, public policies, and civil society.

In this book are the portraits and biographies of the 1000 women nominated collectively for the Nobel Peace Prize 2005. The documentation aims to make these women and their achievements visible and acknowledged worldwide.

Going further, the research network aims at the academic evaluation of the nominees' work in order to learn from their experience, which will be recognized and analyzed. The research results will be published widely as lessons learnt. The research network has been called into life to study the issues, strategies, working methods, motivation, visions, and networks of women in the most varied conflict situations, as well as the living conditions and circumstances in which these women became activists. Consequently, these women will be validated as actresses for and experts on peace in academic discourse.

The basic research concept has not been to define peace in Switzerland from a western, European perspective, but, following Galtung (1996), to start with a broad approach that would be filled with content — bottom-up — by the multitudinous individual projects. The guidelines for the nominations were discussed initially several times by the board and the group of academics and finally at the coordinators' meeting in order to adapt them to various contexts worldwide. So the methodological approach was in line with "grounded theory" (see Glaser, Strauss 1967), which starts with empirical case studies and builds theory grounded on them. Our group considers women working for peace as experts and wants to start from their knowledge and experience. This theoretical and methodical approach distinguishes itself from most other studies on peace and conflict. Consequently, we intend to broaden academic concepts in international relations with the results of our project. Our group is storing and working on the data and will pass the research results on to governments, civil society, and international organizations in order to develop new peace strategies. In this way the preservation of this thousand-fold peace work and its international impact will be guaranteed after the closure of the project.

References: Galtung, Johan (1996): Peace by Peaceful Means. Oslo: PRIO; London, Thousand Oaks CA: Sage Publications / Glaser, Barney G., Strauss, Anselm L. (1967): The Discovery of Grounded Theory. Strategies for Qualitative Research. / Aldine de Gruyter, New York.

Susanne Stalder, a geographer and PhD student in business ethics in St. Gallen, is project manager for the study "Peacewomen Worldwide", which is conducting a primary analysis of data from the 1000 women for the Nobel Peace Prize 2005 project.

Doris Wastl-Walter is a professor of human geography and director of the Interdisciplinary Center for Women's and Gender Studies at the University of Bern in Switzerland.

—

S

The World in Loving Hands!

1000 Peacewomen Across the Globe

Monika Stocker

T

The wars of the 20th century convulsed our planet: world wars, colonial wars, wars of liberation, wars for oil, water and natural resources; wars about boundaries; wars for racial or religious supremacy; wars and the violence they wreak on women.

The 21st century was also born in pain: terrorism and the insecurity it generates has shaken the world, as did the demented idea that one can fight terrorism with more violence and the curtailment of civic and human rights. Terrorism and the response to it have frightened people, isolated groups and drawn sharp boundaries among human beings. They have made people evil.

In spite of the terrors of the 20th century and the upheavals of the 21st, there are thousands of women who have kept a fast hold on life, who fight and nurture, educate and enable, who stand tall and react wherever basic rights are violated. This knowledge gives us hope for the present and the future. 1000 Peacewoman across the globe.

Our project is coming to an end, but the message lives on. We have documented the life stories of a thousand women and presented them to the Nobel Committee and to the world. Now, our book will bring these biographies to thousands of men and women, to young people and children. The 1000 women have become visible; their lives have been recorded and acknowledged. 1000 Peacewoman across the globe.

In December 2005, the small board of the Swiss Association and its office will be expanded or replaced by internationally active women. A transition period lasting until mid-2006 will allow for the creation of an organization based on new international networks. 1000 Peacewoman across the globe.

We have opened 1000 books. The one you hold in your hands is the key to further developments — it contains names, addresses, regional networks, information and coordination possibilities which are the keystone of the 1000 Peacewoman across the globe.

Over a three-year period, twenty coordinators from all regions of the world built up the project, set up electronic and traditional networks for simple, rapid and effective communication. The network they have created offers a unique opportunity for research and development, for development cooperation policy efforts, for theme-oriented cooperation among those who are committed to build a better world. Whatever shape the new organization will take, the network will subsist — via e-mail, databank and Internet, and via practical initiatives.

Our work goes on. What a wealth of opportunities has been opened to us: there will be regional networks with global coordination, the voices of the coordinators will continue to be heard, researchers will study the lives and work of the Peacewoman and publish the results of their work, international organizations will work with us and fight by our side.

Through this book, the free emancipated voice of the 1000 Peacewoman across the globe will be heard loud and clear. The women are experts on security affairs — a World Security Council in fact, with recognized and experienced global leaders able at any time to convoke a world forum on human security, with specialists on violence-related issues who can propose creative and workable solutions. We have formed a UN with a specifically feminine viewpoint. Battling and embracing — the world in loving hands!

The resources are there. The experience is there. There is a wealth of striving and living, of resistance and hope. Let us use these 1000 Peacewoman across the globe for the good of humanity.

Monika Stocker, a peace activist , is the vice-president of the Association 1000 Women for the Nobel Peace Prize 2005 and a member of the City Council of the city of Zurich.

—

T

Our Heartfelt
Thanks

Eva Mezger and Rosmarie Zapfl

U

In the name of the 1000 women, the board of the Association, the office and the coordinators worldwide, we would like to thank all those who supported the project by their honorary activities, their ideas and their financial assistance. Our project was a success because many people in many countries wanted women's peace work to be made visible and given due acknowledgement.

Let us mention first the precious volunteer work by women and men who helped organize meetings and other events, wrote letters, translated texts, blazed the trail for contacts with financial backers and helped us in countless ways. We trust that their commitment to the project and the knowledge that their action was an investment in hope is a fitting compensation for their generosity. Further thanks goes to the coordinators and the countless women who worked with them, calling for nominations in the different countries. Their support was invaluable; the linking of the different networks created new ones and strengthened or revived old ones.

Our special thanks goes to Swiss Foreign Minister Micheline Calmy-Rey, who supported our initiative from the start and provided us with resources and valuable advice to get started. We would also like to thank the Swiss Agency for Development and Cooperation (SDC) and the Swiss embassies all over the world, who were very helpful in advising and supporting the coordinators and the project.

Many people contributed generously because they believed in our vision to honor the often quiet and unnoticed work that women do for peace. Over 400 individuals, associations, women's organizations worldwide, charities, and office and practitioners' groups bought "peace shares" which we launched to ensure basic project funding. Many institutions and individuals took over a sponsorship over 5000 Swiss francs. Many more donated according to their means, which helped the project a lot. And without the help of the many journalists, photographers, translators and editors, who have been working at high speed and for little money, this book would not have been made.

We would also like to express our gratitude to all the sponsors and donors in Switzerland and other countries, whose generous contributions helped us organize the coordinators' meetings; the nominations of the Peacewoman; the writing, translating and editing of their biographies; the production of this book; the preparation of the exhibition and the Internet platform; the organization of more than forty press conferences all over the world when we announced the names of the 1000 women collectively nominated for this year's Nobel Peace Prize; and the academic research on the work of the 1000 Peacewomen.

U

The project attracted scores of sponsors and donors large and small. Among them, we would like to mention the following who sponsored over 10,000 Swiss francs or comparable amounts in countries of the global South:

Arbeitsgemeinschaft der Hilfswerke, Alliance Sud, Bern, Switzerland
atelier Oï – SA, Architecture et Design, La Neuveville, Switzerland
Berghof-Stiftung für Konfliktforschung GmbH, Berlin, Germany
Berti Wicke Stiftung, Zurich, Switzerland
Brigitta Züst, Luzern, Switzerland
Christkatholische Kirchen und Kirchgemeinden der Schweiz, Switzerland
Consejería en Proyectos – Project Counselling Service (PCS)
CUT, São Paulo, Brazil
Deutsche Gesellschaft für Technische
Zusammenarbeit GmbH, Eschborn, Germany
Diakonia, Sundbyberg, Sweden
Eidgenössisches Departement für auswärtige Angelegenheiten EDA,
Bern, Switzerland
ewz, Zurich, Switzerland
Evangelisch-reformierte Kirchen und Kirchgemeinden
der Schweiz, Switzerland
Exekutivfrauen Schweiz, Zurich, Switzerland
filia.die frauenstiftung, Hamburg, Germany
Ford Foundation, Brazil
Frauen für den Frieden Schweiz und Regionalgruppen, Switzerland
Global Fund for Women, San Francisco, USA
Hamasil Stiftung, Zurich, Switzerland
Hotel Bern, Bern, Switzerland
Institut für Auslandsbeziehungen e. V. (ifa) – Projekt Zivile
KEYSTONE Switzerland
Konfliktbearbeitung (zivik), Berlin, Germany
Jubiläumsstiftung der Zurich Versicherungs-Gruppe, Zurich, Switzerland
Migros-Genossenschafts-Bund, Zurich, Switzerland
Natura, São Paulo, Brazil
NZAid, Wellington, New Zealand
Oxfam Australia, Fitzroy, Australia
Paul-Schiller-Stiftung, Lachen, Switzerland
Petrobras, Rio de Janeiro, Brazil
Public Politics for Women Secretary, Brasília, Brazil
Raiffeisen-Jubiläumsstiftung, St. Gallen, Switzerland
Römisch-katholische Kirchen und Kirchgemeinden der Schweiz,
Switzerland

—

Eva Mezger is a member of the board of the Association 1000 Women for the Nobel Peace Prize 2005. She is a TV presenter and journalist.

Rosmarie Zapfl is a member of the board of the Association 1000 Women for the Nobel Peace Prize 2005. She is a member of the National Council (Swiss Parliament) and of the Council of Europe

—
U

Abboud Samer, PhD in Political Economy, Canada, 119, 335, 531, 611, 614, 741, 747, 940 **Abdul-Hadi Faiha,** writer and research consultant, Occupied Palestinian Territory, 26, 96, 151, 338, 486, 490, 533, 708, 742, 876, 912, 913, 916, 980 **Absatarov Emil,** journalist, Kyrgyzstan, 687 **Akayev Vakhit,** Russian Federation, 21 **Akibayashi Kozue,** independent writer, Japan, 247 **Al-Zekri Mohammad,** PhD and freelance author, Bahrain, 5, 340, 489, 817 **Alfonso Valdés Yanet,** Cuba, 195, 408, 780 **Alioth Martin,** freelance journalist, Ireland, 963 **Allain Fatima Pir T.,** Women's Feature Service, Philippines, 794 **Alvarenga Luis,** Colombia, 40, 41 **Amuhire Anita Dancilla,** Rwanda, 99 **Arcana Judith,** independent writer, United States of America, 969 **Ardón Ana María Ardón,** Guatemala, 558 **Ardón Quezada Ana María,** Guatemala, 188, 293, 329, 331, 578 **Arnold Patricia,** independent journalist, Italy, 114, 498, 540 **Astemirova Zara,** teacher, Russian Federation, 131, 619

Bai Liang, China, 253, 548, 892, 998 **Balci Mehmet,** Geneva Call, Switzerland, 519 **Balkan Mirit,** freelance writer, Israel, 31, 105, 250, 284, 342, 551, 552, 584 **Banks Bobbie Wrenn,** Women's Alternatives for New Directions (Wand), United States of America, 84, 977 **Bapu Marie,** 349 **Batchuluun,** P. N. Shastin Clinic Hospital, Mongolia, 823 **Bauerdick Rolf,** independent journalist, Germany, 62 **Baumann-von Arx Gabriella,** Switzerland, 652 **Bazyleva Tamara,** Russian Federation, 825 **Belevich Albina,** Club of International Friendship, Uzbekistan, 855 **Bengelstorff Anja,** freelance journalist, Germany, 14, 85, 160, 213, 229, 387, 428, 661, 673, 720, 952 **Bhandari Neena,** foreign correspondent, Australia, 264, 278, 600 **Bhasin Kamla,** South Asia" Network of Gender Activists and Trainers – Sangat, India, 588 **Bhatiasevi Aphaluck,** Thailand, 314, 463, 475, 477, 598 **Biasini Gina,** Venezuela, 523, 751 **Bishop Elaine,** student, Dem. Republic of the Congo, 118 **Bisonga Jean-Eudes,** swisspeace, Fast Project, Dem. Republic of the Congo, 34 **Bo Liang,** China, 527, 831 **Braendle-Rothlisberger Erica,** SER Foundation, 110 **Brown Nina,** Irati Wanti, Australia, 305 **Bush Melanie E. L.,** City University of New York (Cuny), United States of America, 763

Caffarella K., International Women's Development Agency (Iwda), Australia, 286 **Camargo Díaz Miladys,** Venezuela, 317, 769 **Campos Cecile,** Dagbladet, Norway, 735 **Cardoza Melissa,** Mexico, 258, 269, 292, 370, 534, 537, 599, 748, 752, 756, 789, 965 **Chan Shun Hin,** China, Taiwan, 288, 325, 562, 745, 993 **Chelyshev Vitaliy,** "The Journalist" magazine, Russian Federation, 850 **Cheng Kon Kon,** China, Taiwan, 303, 642, 833 **Chirwa Daring,** Nations Publications, Malawi, 623, 624, 625, 666, 725 **Chu Caixia,** China, 365, 478, 759

Absatarov Emil, Kyrgyzstan, 687 **Adams Eddie,** Keystone/AP, 25 **Albers Karin,** Germany, 4, 54, 337, 566 **Bacon Elinor,** 887 **Brunner Assunta,** Switzerland, 36, 104, 222, 521 **Cahambing Mylene,** 386 Chase Jon, Harvard News Office, United States of America, 943 **Chhachhi Sheba,** India, 51, 190 **della Valle Alessandro,** Keystone, Switzerland, 92, 563 **Ernst Fred,** Keystone/AP, 920 **Fong Sandy,** Fiji, 225, 710, 930 **Frey Magdalena,** Austria, 155 **Friholt Ola,** Sweden, 61 **Gerlock Ed,** Philippines, 45, 224, 290, 341, 515, 970 **Gill Gauri,** India, 11, 68, 173, 183, 226, 279, 280, 281, 300, 315, 319, 392, 396, 420, 452, 454, 467, 528, 650, 685, 692, 719, 731, 978 **Gillieron Laurent,** Keystone, 494 **Gostoli Renzo,** Keystone/AP, 923 **Greco Franco,** Keystone, 492 **Gupta Neelam,** India, 24, 46, 176, 347, 348, 500, 589, 637, 682, 737, 792, 896, 926 **Hoshiko Eugene,** Keystone/AP, 211 **Jabbar Sonia,** India, 354, 535, 730, 931 **Johnson Giff,** 357 **Keystone,** AP/APTN, 643 **Kronenberg P.,** 797 **Logghe Yves,** Keystone/AP, 333 **Lutz Christian,** Keystone/AP, 114 **Makaiba Generosa,** 796, 966 **Mangold Barbara,** Switzerland, 342, 490, 540, 584, 591, 916 **McGuinness Fiona,** United States of America, 180, 269, 292, 370, 534, 537, 599, 748, 784, 789, 809, 965 **Meissner Ursula,** Germany, 203 **Neuhaus Gabriela,** Switzerland, 147, 338, 437, 458, 551 **Norwood John,** United States of America, 672 **Ochiai Yuriko,** Japan, 171 **Peres Eraldo,** Keystone/AP, 982 **Pitarakis Lefteris,** Keystone/AP, 607 **Ragg Judith,** Fiji, 30, 66, 76, 124, 153, 210, 248, 278, 286, 287, 305, 461, 600, 644, 728, 842, 959 **Rajakaruna Anoma,** 13, 52, 141, 187, 189, 209, 487 **Richardson Wesley,** 976 **Salmon Tatiana,** 294 **Senna Abdelhak,** Keystone/EPA/AFP, 938 **Shoba,** Italy, 498 **Stephan Christiane,** Germany, 145, 167, 605 **Tivane Sergio,** Mozambique, 862 **Wansi Katherine,** 986 **Welti Doerte,** Switzerland, 228, 339 **Wernli Katharina,** Switzerland, 546 **Wipple John,** United States of America, 977 **Zobel de Ayala Jaime,** 794

Editors

Judith Anderson, USA **Altantuya Batdorj,** Mongolia **Urvashi Butalia,** India **Meera Butalia,** India **Chan Wai Fong,** China **Chan Shun Hing,** China **Chung Hsiu Mei,** China **Mahmoud El-Kastawy,** UK **Gary Fliszar,** Switzerland **Arlene Griffin,** Fiji **Han Xiaoning,** China **Juhi Jain,** India **Marilee Karl,** Italy **Wacango Kimani,** Uganda **Loh Yuen Ching,** China **Leonardo Muller,** Brazil **Vicky Quinlan,** Italy **Paulynn Sicam,** Philippines **Vera Vieira,** Brazil **Luana Yoko Vieira Komatsu,** Brazil **Women's Feature Service,** India **Noa Zanolli Davenport,** USA

Translation

Ana Paula Borges, Brazil Julia Droeber, UK Anna Gyorgy, Germany Frédérique Ingignoli, Switzerland Deb Johnson, Honduras Helen Littlewood, New Zealand Liliana Malant, Spain Morven McLean, Switzerland Vanessa Mock, Netherlands Bonodji Nako, Chad Eduardo Perini Rodrigo, Brazil Jeannette Regan, Switzerland Zosia Rozankowska, France Julia Slater, Switzerland Mary Staehelin, Switzerland Heidi Uetz, Switzerland Dörte Welti, Switzerland Marie-Louise Zimmermann, Switzerland

Project management

by 1000 Women for the Nobel Peace Prize 2005, Switzerland, Rebecca Vermot, Maren Haartje

Project coordination

by KONTRAST, Switzerland, Ursi Schachenmann

Text editing

by KONTRAST, Switzerland, Anne Blonstein, Ursula Eichenberger, Marion Elmer, Ingrid Essig, Bill Gilonis, Teresa Go, Nadine Olonetzky, Tricia Schmid, Christian Schmidt, Karina Wisniewska

Picture editing

by KONTRAST, Switzerland, Koni Nordmann

Index by keyword

Access to health care

628
670
699
735
757
798
803
883
927
933
936

Latin America, Caribbean
258
293
318
447
525
526
534
554
556
564
565
581
779
785
863
922
925
929

North America
304

South Asia
13
168
320

750
792
870
871
894
895
896
931
981

Southeastern Asia
36
45
186
874
986

Caste system; class discrimination

Africa
889

Eastern Asia
955

Latin America, Caribbean
440

South Asia
235
312
731
931

Child labor

Africa
429

Europe
512

Latin America, Caribbean
440

South Asia
346

Child prostitution	Child soldiers	Child trafficking	Children's rights
North America	Africa	Africa	Africa
568	1	358	18
	123	680	123
			181
		Eastern Asia	429
		216	437
			665
		North America	697
		568	717
			729
		South Asia	733
		241	744
			762
			773
			776

Central Asia, Middle East
3
724
742
810
912

Eastern Asia
171
256
379
702
909

Europe
35
58
69
512
591
628
634
660
663

		Corruption	Death penalty

687
696
797
927

Latin America, Caribbean
195
569
599
601
615
629
723
748
760
780
972

North America
568
977

Oceania
210
641

South Asia
97
129
307
355
378
679
692
731
750
926

Southeastern Asia
598
774
778
893

Corruption

Africa
516

Central Asia, Middle East
485
915
948

Europe
572
933

Latin America, Caribbean
502

Southeastern Asia
314
507
521
608
824
944
986
991

Death penalty

Central Asia, Middle East
505

Democratization

Africa
808
836
946

Central Asia, Middle East
539
593
920
948
990

South Asia
320
399
452
877

Eastern Asia
532
561
951
995
997

Southeastern Asia
45
968
970

Europe
544
670
936
937
949
988

Latin America, Caribbean
510
556
581
914
925
932
939
984

Oceania
30
287
579

Destruction of the environment

Africa
816
828

Eastern Asia
368
840
845
846

Europe
826
937

Latin America, Caribbean
553
612

North America
821

Oceania
278
305
461
600
740
836

South Asia
315
589
841

Development

Africa
102
194
334
387
403
419
428
438
449
470
620
828
918
974

Central Asia, Middle East
119
343
423
738
741

Eastern Asia
367
368
478
480
806
823
833
845
846
849
888
897

Europe
61
669

Drug Trafficking	Education
South Asia	
547	

Education

Africa
759
781
805
807
813
814
833
846
848
852
861
869
904
905
907
908
910
911

322
363
416
438
717
729
736
762
776

Central Asia, Middle East
82
488
609
708
724
738
742
764
790
810
859
876
912
980

Europe
125
146
239
634
638
663
684
686
693
713
739
753
797
798
803
838
880

Eastern Asia
83
367
414
436
478
482
483
585
642
654
745
754

Latin America, Caribbean
236

265
273
282
292
298
306
364
370
408
453
506
509
511
525
530
700
709
715
721
722
723
751
752
755
756
769
777
780
785
786
787
788
789
795
801
804
863
865
873
885

Empowerment towards independence								Environment			
Africa	**North America**	**Oceania**	**South Asia**	**Central Asia, Middle East**	**Eastern Asia**	**Europe**	**Southeastern Asia**	**Africa**	**Central Asia, Middle East**	**Eastern Asia**	
166	55	287	209	82	253	12	132	127	817	303	383
198	296	294	281	119	308	540	214	816		397	510
345	324	959	307	335	390	638	225			473	714
422	327		347	342	482	797	359			642	732
441	899		351	388			410			831	755
446			360	394			463			833	769
460			420	398			484			839	834
492			424	405			576			840	914
697			457	489			710			843	976
773			459	855			930			844	982
791			730				934			845	
971			896							847	
										848	
										849	
										851	
										852	
										853	

Environment (continued):

North America
25, 820, 821, 835, 887, 969, 977

Oceania
842

South Asia
218, 299, 320, 353, 430, 464, 818, 819

Europe
330, 825, 826, 827, 830, 832, 838, 850

Latin America, Caribbean
257, 310

Southeastern Asia
122, 142, 175, 193, 316

Fair wages	Female genital mutilation	Forced marriages	Forced prostitution
Eastern Asia	Africa	Europe	Eastern Asia
436	166	174	240
450	229		244
	563	Latin America, Caribbean	604
Latin America, Caribbean		169	
418			Europe
			167
South Asia			199
443			201
			228
			237
			South Asia
			241

— W Index by keyword

Identity

Africa
597
889

Southeastern Asia
677

Central Asia, Middle East
859

Europe
15
295
854

Latin America, Caribbean
230
246
257
261
263
266
269
275
277
283
285
292
306
318
329
331
332
466
537
834
863
865
866
867
873
885

Internally displaced persons; refugees

Africa
160
322
432
456

Central Asia, Middle East
151
538
577
593

Eastern Asia
897

Europe
15
21
32
33
108
112
115
144
145
161
163
270
384
433
522
546
619
663
884

Latin America, Caribbean
426

North America
20

South Asia
93
528
683

Southeastern Asia
128
137
142
143
242
659
677
701
771
893

	Microcredit	Migrants	Militarization
Southeastern Asia 94 122 778	Eastern Asia 366 906	Central Asia, Middle East 335	Central Asia, Middle East 552
	Latin America Caribbean 364	Eastern Asia 465 909 999	Eastern Asia 43 247 950
	South Asia 351	Europe 270 384 522 524	Europe 573 825 829
		Latin America, Caribbean 28	Latin America, Caribbean 553 564 581 612 976
		Oceania 903	North America 956 964 969
		Southeastern Asia 313 341 361 520	South Asia 52 75 189
			Southeastern Asia 290 515

W Index by keyword

Orphans of war

Africa
18
89
437
456

Eastern Asia
950

South Asia
75

Patriarchal discrimination

Africa
425
495
935
971
979

Europe
739

Oceania
286

South Asia
173
190
227
402
631
681
917

Southeastern Asia
255
802

Peace education

Africa
2
9
14
17
22
34
49
85
98
102
107
110
118
120
123
140
160
192
221
428
717
736
772
862

Central Asia, Middle East
151
162
584
747
876
916

Eastern Asia
43
80
100
103

Europe
6
8
10
15
27
32
56
58
60
61
63
65
71
81
106
114
115
131
134
135
146
149
157
158
289
542
543
583
735
793
798
832
878
902
987

Latin America, Caribbean
23
28

Political rights

_____

W Index by keyword

W Index by keyword

Sustainable development		Teenage pregnancy	Trafficking in organs

Sustainable development

Africa
88
127
421
791

Central Asia, Middle East
338
339
342
489
912
940

Eastern Asia
397
481
689
812
831
844
847

Europe
330
825
937

Latin America, Caribbean
982

North America
471
820

Oceania
842

South Asia
406
459

Southeastern Asia
36

Teenage pregnancy

Africa
456
673

Latin America, Caribbean
633
972

Trafficking in organs

Europe
575

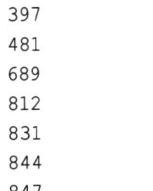

Women's rights

Africa
9
16
22
34
49
88
102
156
166
181
191
192
194
208
213
221
232
245
336
349
358
375
387
401
403
417
421
425
428
469
470
492
501
508
513
559
649
675
720
772

862
872
918
938
979

Central Asia, Middle East
4
139
223
251
339
388
393
394
398
427
490
496
531
582
584
611
626
643
742
790
855
913
940
947
975
980
990

Eastern Asia
100
103
215
240

247
254
276
301
390
391
411
450
478
480
481
527
906
996
998

Europe
12
27
56
61
174
249
302
333
455
519
540
546
583
622
636
669
727
827
850
890
891
921
927

928
949
953

Latin America, Caribbean
40
188
195
236
263
269
292
293
298
331
344
370
373
381
382
383
389
418
453
502
523
547
566
571
578
594
601
616
630
656
674
709
721
752
756

Imprint

© 2005 Scalo

Concept and Production: KONTRAST Zurich, Switzerland
www.kontrast.ch

Bookconcept and design: Alberto Vieceli, Tania Prill, Zurich, Switzerland
with Kristina Milkovic, Piero Glina
www.prill-vieceli.cc

Databases: Marco Liniger, Bern, Switzerland

Production: Robert Züblin, Zurich, Switzerland
www.proofbooks.ch

Lithography: Egli.Kunz & Partner Polygrafie AG
Glattbrugg, Switzerland, www.ekp.ch

Printing and binding: C.H. Beck, Nördlingen, Germany
www.becksche.de

Scalo head office: Scalo Verlag AG
Schifflände 32, CH-8001 Zurich, PO Box 73
CH-8024 Zurich, Switzerland
tel: +41 44 261 0910, fax: +41 44 261 9262
publishers@scalo.com, www.scalo.com

Distributed in North America by Prestel,
New York; in Europe, Africa and Asia by Thames
and Hudson, London; in Germany, Austria
and Switzerland by Scalo.
ISBN 3-03939-039-2